LANGUAGE AND NATURE

John Huehnergard (photo by Christopher Rose)

LANGUAGE AND NATURE

PAPERS PRESENTED TO JOHN HUEHNERGARD ON THE OCCASION OF HIS 60TH BIRTHDAY

edited by

REBECCA HASSELBACH

and

NAʿAMA PAT-EL

STUDIES IN ANCIENT ORIENTAL CIVILIZATION • NUMBER 67
THE ORIENTAL INSTITUTE OF THE UNIVERSITY OF CHICAGO
CHICAGO • ILLINOIS

Library of Congress Control Number: 2011933159
ISBN-10: 1-885923-91-0
ISBN-13: 978-1-885923-91-2
ISSN: 0081-7554

The Oriental Institute, Chicago

Published 2012. Printed in the United States of America.

STUDIES IN ANCIENT ORIENTAL CIVILIZATION • NUMBER 67
THE ORIENTAL INSTITUTE OF THE UNIVERSITY OF CHICAGO

Series Editors
Leslie Schramer
and
Thomas G. Urban
with
Rebecca Cain *and* Zuhal Kuru

Series Editors' Acknowledgments
Jessen O'Brien and Tate Paulette assisted in the production of this volume.

Cover prepared by Kristy Shuey of 2nd Street Design Lab, Austin, Texas
Selection of Ethiopic, Ugaritic, Akkadian, Hebrew, and Old South Arabian texts.
We thank the Semitic Museum, Harvard University, Wayne T. Pitard, and John Huehnergard for their use.

Printed by McNaughton & Gunn, Saline, Michigan

The paper used in this publication meets the minimum requirements of American National Standard for Information Services — Permanence of Paper for Printed Library Materials, ANSI Z39.48-1984.

Table of Contents

Contributors and Affiliations

Eran Cohen, Department of Linguistics, The Hebrew University of Jerusalem

Lutz Edzard, Department of Culture Studies and Oriental Languages, University of Oslo

Steven E. Fassberg, Department of Hebrew Language, The Hebrew University of Jerusalem

Daniel E. Fleming, Department of Hebrew and Judaic Studies, New York University

W. Randall Garr, Department of Religious Studies, University of California, Santa Barbara

Gideon Goldenberg, Department of Linguistics, The Hebrew University of Jerusalem

Edward L. Greenstein, Department of Bible, Bar Ilan University

Charles G. Häberl, the Center for Middle Eastern Studies, Rutgers University

Jo Ann Hackett, Department of Middle Eastern Studies, The University of Texas at Austin

Rebecca Hasselbach, Department of Near Eastern Languages and Civilizations, University of Chicago

Wolfhart Heinrichs, Department of Near Eastern Languages and Civilizations, Harvard University

Jeremy M. Hutton, Department of Hebrew and Semitic Studies, University of Wisconsin–Madison

Shlomo Izre'el, Department of Hebrew Culture, Section of Semitic Linguistics, Tel Aviv University

Geoffrey Khan, Hebrew and Semitic Studies, University of Cambridge

Leonid Kogan, Institute of Oriental and Classical Studies, Russian State University for the Humanities

Paul Korchin, Religion Program, University of Alaska Fairbanks

Dennis Pardee, Department of Near Eastern Languages and Civilizations, University of Chicago

Naʿama Pat-El, Department of Middle Eastern Studies, The University of Texas at Austin

Gary A. Rendsburg, Department of Jewish Studies, Rutgers University

Aaron D. Rubin, Classics and Ancient Mediterranean Studies, Penn State University

Prods Oktor Skjærvø, Department of Near Eastern Languages and Civilizations, Harvard University

Richard C. Steiner, Bernard Revel Graduate School, Yeshiva University

David Testen

Ofra Tirosh-Becker, Department of Hebrew Language, The Hebrew University of Jerusalem

Josef Tropper, Theologische Fakultät, Humboldt-Universität, Berlin

Wilfred van Soldt, Institute for Area Studies, Leiden University

Richard K. Walton, Author and Videographer

X Bonnie Woods, Artist and Designer

Andrzej Zaborski, Afroasiatic Linguistics, Jagellonian University, Krakow

Tamar Zewi, Department of Hebrew Language, Haifa University

Preface

This volume includes thirty contributions — twenty-nine papers and one artistic contribution — by John's colleagues, former students, and friends, on a variety of topics, representing John's versatility and many interests:

Eran Cohen reviews and discusses the functional value of Akkadian *iprus* in conditional clauses in epistolary and legal texts. Cohen points to the syntactic environment and the genre as conditioning factors.

Lutz Edzard discusses the Akkadian injunctive *šumma*, used in oath formulae, where it expresses positive statement when it is followed by a negation particle. Edzard examines whether this pattern should be considered an elliptical conditional.

Steven E. Fassberg deals with verbal *t*-forms that do not exhibit the expected metathesis in Hebrew and Aramaic of the Dead Sea Scrolls. Fassberg suggests an explanation on the basis of diachronic evidence as well as comparative evidence from other Aramaic dialects.

Daniel F. Fleming asks who were the ʿApiru people mentioned in Egyptian texts in the Late Bronze Age and what was their social standing as is reflected in the Amarna letters.

Randall Garr studies one class of denominal *hiphil* verbs and asks why these verbs are assigned to the causative stem despite their non-causative semantic content.

Gideon Goldenberg discusses the concept of vocalic length and the status of *yā, waw,* and *ʾalif* in Arabic grammatical tradition and in the medieval Hebrew tradition that was its product.

Ed Greenstein suggests that the roots of biblical wisdom can be located in second-millennium Canaanite literature by identifying wisdom sayings and themes in the Ugaritic corpus. This is a part of the author's ongoing research into this genre.

Charles Häberl looks into predicates of verbless sentences in Semitic and particularly in Neo-Mandaic, which exhibits syntactic subtleties not found in the classical Semitic languages.

Jo Ann Hackett takes another look at Ugaritic *yaqtul* and argues for the existence of a preterite *yaqtul,* contra several recent studies.

Rebecca Hasselbach tackles the evasive origin of the Semitic verbal endings *-u* and *-a* and explains their development in the various branches.

Wolfhart Heinrichs's contribution is a study of a passage from Ibn Khaldūn's Muqaddima on the pronunciation of Arabic *qāf*. This study shows that Ibn Khaldūn held innovative views of language and its evolution.

Jeremy Hutton sheds more light on tG forms in Biblical Hebrew, through an analysis of the anomalous form *təpôṣôtîkem*. This study further uses comparative evidence to suggest a better understanding of this, and similar forms.

Shlomo Izre'el offers a revised and improved version of his important study of the language of the Amarna letters, so far available only as an unpublished manuscript.

Geoffrey Khan discusses the functional differences between the preterite and the perfect in NENA. Khan suggests that one of the functions of the perfect is marking a speaker's attitude toward the event.

Leonid Kogan offers a comparative etymological study of botanical terminology in Akkadian.

Paul Korchin argues that occurrences of the cohortative in Biblical Hebrew that do not conform to the normative volitive function, the so-called pseudo-cohortatives, represent instances of a "centrifugal" directive affix expressing motion away from the speaker/main event.

Dennis Pardee provides a detailed description and explanation of his understanding of the Hebrew verbal system as primarily expressing aspect, tense only secondarily.

Naʿama Pat-El continues the discussion of the origin of the Hebrew relative particle *šeC-* from a syntactic perspective. She argues that, based on its syntactic distributions, the origin of the particle from the relative particle *ʾăšer* as proposed by John Huehnergard is more likely than a recent suggestion that the two particles are unrelated.

Gary A. Rendsburg argues in favor of Late Biblical Hebrew features in the book of Haggai against Young, Rezetko, and Ehrensvärd, who denied the presence of such features in the text. Rendsburg argues that Late Biblical Hebrew features are found in various layers of grammar and style throughout the book.

Aaron D. Rubin provides Semitic etymologies of two Modern South Arabian words, *lxm* 'shark,' and Mehri *nəxāli* 'under.'

Prods Oktor Skjærvø elucidates a passage from the Pahlavi *Rivāyat* and discusses the Pahlavi verb **āwās* 'to dry.'

Richard C. Steiner discusses a universal that governs the evolution of phonological rules and applies it to the reconstruction of Proto-Semitic. He proposes a new vowel syncope rule for Proto-Semitic construct forms that accounts for many alternations and biforms throughout the Semitic languages, and for phonological enigmas such as Hebrew *šte*^{y} 'two of (fem.),' *mălăk̲ăt̲* 'queen of,' *lĕb̲ăn* 'white of,' Aramaic *tarte*^{y} 'two of (fem.),' Arabic (*i*)*smu* 'name of,' Mehri *bərt* 'daughter of,' and Akkadian *ašti* 'wife of (gen.).'

David Testen argues that the traditionally reconstructed case system is a secondary development and that the original system should be reconstructed with a contrast of nominative *-*u*- and a genitive with two allomorphs, *-*i*- and *-*ay*-.

Ofra Tirosh-Becker discusses the language of a Judeo-Arabic translation of portions of the books of Prophets and argues that the language is characterized by a mixture of conservative and colloquial linguistic elements.

Josef Tropper argues that Akkadian poetry, as well as Northwest Semitic poetry, are based on certain metric principles, based on stressed and unstressed syllables.

Wilfred van Soldt lists and discusses personal names ending in -*āyu* from Amarna. This contribution is a continuation of his recent work studying the orthography of personal names in this language.

Richard K. Walton, a naturalist with a special interest in Concord, Massachusetts, contributes a paper about the jumping spiders (Araneae: Salticidae) of the region. His short paper is accompanied by a series of videos showing these spiders in their natural habitats.

Andrzej Zaborski, in the sole Afroasiatic contribution, suggests that Berber and Cushitic preserve archaic features that have been lost for the most part in the Semitic languages. One such example, which is discussed at length, is the verbal suffixes of the prefix conjugation.

Tamar Zewi offers a comparative study that purports to show that prepositional phrases function as subjects in a variety of Semitic languages. Zewi provides a constructive discussion and suggests a number of explanations to this phenomenon.

We started working on this volume in early 2009 without John's knowledge and with the help of his wife and our teacher, Jo Ann Hackett. We wish to thank all the contributors to this Festschrift for their participation and for their help and patience. Special thanks go to Jo Ann Hackett, who was always ready to answer our questions and offer invaluable advice. Finally, we wish to thank the Oriental Institute and Thomas Urban, Leslie Schramer, and Rebecca Cain for their help with the publication.

Rebecca Hasselbach
Naʿama Pat-El

John as a Teacher and Mentor

Being one of John's students has been a great honor and, at the same time, a bit of a challenge. It is hard not to become too exuberant when describing our time at Harvard–NELC, and we know that many of his students feel the same.

Given the size of the field in Semitic linguistics, John does not admit many students, and we all remember the moment when, sitting in his office as a prospective student, he advised us to seriously consider a minor field in addition to Semitic philology to enhance our later prospects, "just in case." Most of us did not take his advice, not because we did not appreciate it, but because it was hard enough to live up to his expectations in Semitic linguistics, let alone take on another field of study. John himself regularly audits classes in other departments, showing us that education does not have an end point.

As for his life outside academia, John is a very private man. We all read his papers and knew his opinions about everything Semitic, but most of us knew little of how he spends his free time and what are his hobbies and non-linguistic interests. It took quite a bit of inquiry to discover that he is a passionate bird watcher and naturalist and even co-authored articles on nature. Visiting his Carlisle home for his annual BBQ for students, we learned of his passion for Darwin (both man and dog) and his love for art and photography. Only after he went through knee surgery did we know of his habit to run marathons. How he finds time for all this is still a mystery.

As a teacher and mentor, he treated us all equally with professional respect. He might not have discussed many issues concerning his life outside academia, but once we raised a linguistic issue, a wealth of information would pour out uninterrupted: the history of the debate, major breakthroughs, empirical data, and references. If he did not remember something, out came a 3-by-5-inch index card from his front pocket, on which he would quickly scribble the request with a fancy pen to attend to it later. Many of us still seek his advice and opinion even as we hold our own teaching positions.

His enthusiasm to share his knowledge does not set him apart from other great teachers; what does, however, is his willingness to share his own ideas and even unpublished research without limit. On many occasions, once learning of a student's interest in a certain topic, he would hand over his notes and data he had collected for years. He never limited his gift, never asked not to use it and never demanded to be mentioned in the paper: on the contrary. (We secretly refer to it as "John's Freedom of Information Act.") This character trait shows his unequaled prioritization of scholarship and dissemination of knowledge over personal fame. The obvious result is seen in the many papers he co-authored with his students.

Indeed, John treats his students as peers and expects them to be mature scholars while in graduate school. His famous "Turbo-Hebrew" class is a classic example. In this class students are requested to research the text and its linguistic pitfalls before coming to class, not merely read it and sit sheepishly in the room while he untangles the difficulties for them. This attitude and his subtle pressure on all his students to conform to the highest academic levels produced and instilled confidence in us.

His teaching does not end with supplying us with knowledge and understanding our limits; one of the major things he exemplifies is respect, toward both peers and adversaries. He takes everyone seriously, no matter how wrong he thinks the person's ideas might be. He does not speak ill of those with whom he disagrees, and he teaches his students to learn from everything and everyone. His criticism of others is always professional, deferential, and gracious, and he asks his students to behave similarly, in person as well as publicly.

While each of us carries many personal anecdotes about John and our time as his students, we all share reverence for him as a mentor and advisor, and we see him as a paragon of excellence in scholarship and intellect.

Rebecca Hasselbach
Naʿama Pat-El

Students of John Huehnergard

1996	Edwina M. Wright†	Studies in Semitic Historical Semantics: Words for "Man" and "Woman"
1996	Joshua T. Fox	Noun Patterns in the Semitic Languages
1997	Paul V. Mankowski	Akkadian and Trans-Akkadian Loanwords in Biblical Hebrew
1998	Eugen J. Pentiuc	Studies in Emar Lexicon
1999	Allan C. Emery	Weapons of the Israelite Monarchy: A Catalogue with Its Linguistic and Cross-cultural Implications
2001	Paul D. Korchin	Markedness and Semitic Morphology
2001	Chulhyun Bae	Comparative Studies of King Darius's Bisitun Inscription
2004	Rebecca Hasselbach	A Historical and Comparative Study of Sargonic Akkadian
2004	Aaron D. Rubin	Studies in Semitic Grammaticalization
2005	Mark Arnold	Categorization of the Hitpa'el of Classical Hebrew
2005	David Elias	Tigre of Habab: Short Grammar and Texts from the Rigbat People
2006	Charles G. Häberl	The Neo-Mandaic Dialect of Khorramshahr
2008	Naʿama Pat-El	Studies in the Historical Syntax of Aramaic
2009	Elitzur Bar-Asher	A Theory of Argument Realization and Its Application to Features of the Semitic Languages
2012	Ahmad Al-Jallad	Ancient Levantine Arabic: A Reconstruction based on the Earliest Sources and the Modern Dialects

The Research of John Huehnergard

For over thirty years, John Huehnergard has rigorously advanced the study of Semitic philology through his work on the languages of the ancient Near East and the Semitic language family as a whole. John's research is truly exceptional in its breadth and depth and has become an important milestone in the field of comparative semitics. His work ranges from studies of sounds, morphemes, syntax, and etymologies of words in individual Semitic languages; descriptions and grammars of languages such as Akkadian and Ugaritic; and editions of ancient texts — to important reconstructions of Proto-Semitic features and even descriptions of the Swamp Milkweed Leaf Beetle found in Carlisle, Massachusetts. The courses he taught throughout his career likewise reflect the breadth of his scholarship. These include classes in all levels of Akkadian and Hebrew, various dialects of Aramaic, Ethiopian Semitic in its various ancient and modern forms, Old South Arabian, Ugaritic, classes in Semitic linguistics, and even Middle Egyptian. John's work is an inspiration for every scholar in the field and his rigorous application of linguistic methodology a guideline for his students and future scholars.

John's interest in Semitic languages began when he went to college at Wilfried Laurier University (Waterloo, Ontario), where he studied religion and culture. One summer, he took a class in Hebrew, and this class got him hooked on ancient Semitic languages. He graduated from college in 1974 and, after an influential conversation with M. Coogan, who at this time taught at St. Thomas, decided to go to Harvard to work on Semitic languages. At Harvard, he studied with T. O. Lambdin, F. M. Cross, and W. L. Moran. After John discovered Akkadian, Moran became his primary mentor. Even before graduating from Harvard with distinction in 1979, John became an assistant professor at Columbia University (1978–1983), where he taught Akkadian, Ugaritic, and Mesopotamian and Egyptian history in the departments of Middle Eastern Languages and Cultures and History. In 1983, he was appointed associate professor at Harvard University, where he worked until 2009 as professor of Semitic Philology. In 2009, he moved to Austin, where he is now teaching in the Department of Middle Eastern Studies at the University of Texas.

It is impossible to give recognition to all the various projects John has worked on so far and his achievements in a short introduction to his scholarship. The following is merely an attempt to focus on some of his major interests, being aware that this short description cannot give full credit to a scholar like John.

Most of John's early work, including his dissertation, and a significant number of his later studies are on Semitic languages that are part of ancient Near Eastern cuneiform culture. His first book *Ugaritic Vocabulary in Syllabic Transcription*, published in 1987 (revised edition 2008), is a compilation of Ugaritic words that are attested in Akkadian texts written at Ugarit. The study serves to enhance our understanding of Ugaritic — a language usually written in a consonantal alphabet with only few vowel indications. By analyzing syllabically written material, John made major improvements to our understanding of Ugaritic phonology and, as a direct consequence, its morphology. Another ancient Near Eastern language John has worked on assiduously is Akkadian, including its various dialects. His main interest lies in the reconstruction and understanding of developments of certain linguistic features. His work on Akkadian includes numerous articles on Akkadian phonology, morphology, and syntax, such as "Asseverative **la-* and Hypothetical **lū/law* in Semitic" (1983), which goes beyond Akkadian and is still a major work on the reconstruction of asseverative particles across Semitic; the seminal "On Verbless Clauses in Akkadian" (1986), which establishes and explains certain word order phenomena involving predicate and subject in Akkadian verbless clauses that lead to important distinctions of this clause type also in Proto Semitic; "Stative, Predicative, Pseudo-verb" (1987), an article that deals with the status of the Akkadian stative as either verbless clause or (partially) verbalized, an issue that is very much debated among Semitic scholars; the important dialect study on *The Akkadian of Ugarit* (1989), a monograph that investigates all Akkadian texts from Ugarit regarding orthography, phonology, morphology, and syntax; and "Akkadian ḫ and West Semitic *ḥ" (2003), which suggests the existence of a thirtieth Proto Semitic consonant — the traditional reconstruction assumes twenty-nine consonantal phonemes for Proto Semitic. This reconstruction also argues for a voiced-voiceless-emphatic triad in the gutturals. John's work on Akkadian culminates in the *Grammar of Akkadian* (1997; 3rd edition, 2011), a teaching and reference grammar of Akkadian that is now used as the standard introduction to Akkadian in universities around the world.

Besides Akkadian and Ugaritic, John has worked on many other Semitic languages, specifically Northwest Semitic languages such as Hebrew and Aramaic. Some of his studies on these languages include "The Feminine Plural Jussive in Old Aramaic" (1987), which, based on epigraphic data, establishes that Aramaic originally had a feminine plural ending on verbs *-na* like Hebrew and Arabic. This discovery, in turn, allows us to reconstruct this ending as a feminine plural marker for Proto Semitic. His article "Historical Phonology and the Hebrew Piel" (1992) provides a detailed discussion of the various forms of the D-stem in Semitic and its different vocalizations in the perfect, which again leads to a revised reconstruction of this stem in early Semitic. The article "Hebrew Verbs I-*w/y* and a Proto-Semitic Semitic Sound Rule" (2005) equally goes beyond Hebrew and attempts to explain assimilations of the semi-vowels /w/ and /y/ in Semitic languages that probably go back as far as Proto Semitic.

As these few examples of John's research show, his studies, although they often start out with a phonological or morphological problem in a single Semitic language, go beyond the scope of the language in question and have important implications for the reconstruction of Proto Semitic. Throughout his research, John has made major progress in the reconstruction of Proto Semitic that has radically changed our understanding of the language family. His article on "Afro-Asiatic" (2008) summarizes his work up to this point and represents a brief description of Proto Semitic as far as we can reconstruct it today.

Another major interest of John is Semitic sub-grouping. In his research, he has greatly improved our understanding of how the individual Semitic languages are related to one another by establishing innovative features that mark different sub-branches of Semitic and by making a strict distinction between true innovations and archaic retentions. The currently widely used Semitic family tree is much more firmly established thanks to John's meticulous work. His work on sub-grouping includes studies on various sub-branches and individual languages of Semitic, such as "Remarks on the Classification of the Northwest Semitic Languages" (1991), where John argues for an independent and new branch of Northwest Semitic that is represented by the inscription found at Deir Alla (Jordan) — this inscription has long defied classification as either Canaanite or Aramaic — and "What Is Aramaic?" (1998), an article in which John provides the first detailed overview of which features can actually be reconstructed to Proto Aramaic and serve as identifying characteristics of this language. In addition, John has written various articles on Semitic sub-grouping in general, including "Features of Central Semitic" (2005) and the "Phyla and Waves: Models of Classification" (2011). Many of the features that determine sub-grouping in Semitic are also found in John's more descriptive works on Semitic languages, such as "Languages: Introductory Survey" (1992), "Semitic Languages" (1995), and "Introduction" to *Beyond Babel* (2002). These surveys of Semitic languages and their main features are major reference works for scholars from all fields who wish to familiarize themselves with the basics of Semitic languages and Semitic linguistics.

In all of his research, John strictly adheres to the principles and methodologies of historical and comparative linguistics. Combined with his eye for detail, this methodological rigor is what truly marks his work. In years of teaching, he has imparted his diligent methodology and enthusiasm for Semitic languages to generations of students who follow in his footsteps and have become leading scholars in the field of Semitic linguistics.

John is truly an exceptional and remarkable scholar, and it is a great honor to present this volume to him.

Rebecca Hasselbach
Naʿama Pat-El

Publications of John Huehnergard

1979 The Akkadian Dialects of Carchemish and Ugarit. Ph.D. dissertation, Harvard University.

1981 "Akkadian Evidence for Case-vowels on Ugaritic Bound Forms." *Journal of Cuneiform Studies* 33: 199–205.

1982 "El-Amarna Letter 252." With Baruch Halpern. *Orientalia* 51: 227–30.

Review of R. Caplice, *Introduction to Akkadian*. With Daniel C. Snell. *Bibliotheca Orientalis* 39: 122–31.

1983 "Asseverative **la-* and Hypothetical **lū/law* in Semitic." *Journal of the American Oriental Society* 103: 569–93.

"Five Tablets from the Vicinity of Emar." *Revue d'Assyriologie* 77: 11–43.

1984 "On Breaking Teeth." With Jo Ann Hackett. *Harvard Theological Review* 77: 259–75.

1985 "Biblical Notes on Some New Akkadian Texts from Emar (Syria)." *The Catholic Biblical Quarterly* 47: 428–34.

"A Dt Stem in Ugaritic?" *Ugarit-Forschungen* 17: 402.

1986 "On Verbless Clauses in Akkadian." *Zeitschrift für Assyriologie* 76: 218–49.

"RS 15.86 (PRU 3, 51f.)." *Ugarit-Forschungen* 18: 169–71.

"RS 19.55 (PRU 4, 293b)." *Ugarit-Forschungen* 18: 453.

Review of A. Abou-Assaf, P. Bordreuil, and A. R. Millard, *La statue de Tell Fekherye*. *Bulletin of the American Schools of Oriental Research* 261: 91–95.

Review of F. E. Greenspahn, *Hapax Legomena in Biblical Hebrew*. *Bulletin of the American Schools of Oriental Research* 264: 88–90.

"Note brève (**šanā'iš)." *Revue d'Assyriologie* 80: 191.

"Texts and Fragments (an Ur III Tablet in the Collection of the Museum of World Cultures, UNC Wilmington)." *Journal of Cuneiform Studies* 38: 245.

1987 *Ugaritic Vocabulary in Syllabic Transcription*. Harvard Semitic Studies 32. Atlanta: Scholars.

"Stative, Predicative, Pseudo-Verb." *Journal of Near Eastern Studies* 46: 215–32.

"The Feminine Plural Jussive in Old Aramaic." *Zeitschrift der deutschen morgenländischen Gesellschaft* 137: 266–77.

"Northwest Semitic Vocabulary in Akkadian Texts." Review of D. Sivan *Grammatical Analysis and Glossary*. *Journal of the American Oriental Society* 107: 713–25.

"Three Notes on Akkadian Morphology." In *Working with No Data: Semitic and Egyptian Studies Presented to Thomas O. Lambdin*, edited by D. Golomb, pp. 181–94. Winona Lake: Eisenbrauns.

"Thomas O. Lambdin." In *Working with No Data: Semitic and Egyptian Studies Presented to Thomas O. Lambdin*, edited by D. Golomb, pp. ix–xii.

Review of W. R. Garr, *Dialect Geography of Syria-Palestine, 1000–586 B.C.E.* *Journal of Biblical Literature* 106: 529–33.

1988 "The Early Hebrew Prefix-conjugations." *Hebrew Studies* 29: 19–23.

"The Museum of World Cultures Elamite Brick." *Discoveries* (Newsletter of the Museum of World Cultures, UNC Wilmington): February 1988.

Articles "Ctesiphon," "Cuneiform," and "Elamite." In *The Encyclopedia of Asian History*, edited by A. T. Embree. New York: Scribner's.

1989 *The Akkadian of Ugarit*. Harvard Semitic Studies 34. Atlanta: Scholars.

1990 *Lingering over Words: Studies in Ancient Near Eastern Literature in Honor of William L. Moran*. Co-editor with I. Tzvi Abush and Piotr Steinkeller. Harvard Semitic Studies 37. Atlanta: Scholars.

1991 “Remarks on the Classification of the Northwest Semitic Languages.” In *The Balaam Text from Deir Alla Re-evaluated* (Proceedings of the International Symposium held at Leiden 21–24 August 1989), edited by J. Hoftijzer and G. van der Kooij, pp. 282–93. Leiden: Brill.

“More on KI.*erṣetu* at Emar.” *Nouvelles Assyriologiques Brèves et Utilitaires* 2/58: 39.

“Further South Semitic Cognates to the Akkadian Lexicon.” In *Semitic Studies in Honor of Wolf Leslau on the Occasion of his Eighty-fifth Birthday November 14th, 1991*, edited by A. S. Kaye, vol. 1, pp. 690–713. Wiesbaden: Harrassowitz.

1992 “Languages: Introductory Survey.” In *Anchor Bible Dictionary*, edited by D. N. Freedman, vol. 4, pp. 155–70. New York: Doubleday.

“Hurrian” In *Anchor Bible Dictionary*, edited by D. N. Freedman, vol. 4, pp. 216–17.

“Historical Phonology and the Hebrew Piel.” In *Linguistics and Biblical Hebrew*, edited by W. R. Bodine, pp. 209–29. Winona Lake: Eisenbrauns.

“The Twentieth North American Conference on Afroasiatic Linguistics.” *Languages of the World and Linguistic News Lines* 5/3: 59–60.

1993 “The Development of the Third Person Suffixes in Phoenician.” *Maarav* 7: 183–94.

“The Twentieth North American Conference on Afroasiatic Linguistics.” *Orientalia* 62: 11–13.

“Meskene (Imar/Emar), A. Philologisch.” In *Reallexicon der Assyriologie*, edited by D. O. Edzard, vol. 8, p. 83. New York: de Gruyter.

1994 Review of J. Levi, *Die Inkonguenz im biblischen Hebräisch*. *Hebrew Studies* 35: 174–81.

1995 “*sām*: The Semitic Languages. An Overview.” With Andrew Rippin and Wolfhart Heinrichs. In *Encyclopedia of Islam*, vol. 8, pp. 1007–11. Leiden: Brill.

“Semitic Languages.” In *Civilizations of the Ancient Near East*, edited by J. M. Sasson, vol. 4, pp. 2117–34. New York: Scribners.

“OBCT Hamrin Basin no.21.” *N.A.B.U.* 4/106: 92–93.

“No šukunu at Ras Shamra.” *N.A.B.U.* 4/107: 93.

“Introduction,” “Dialects of Aramaic,” “Orthography and Phonology,” “Glossary,” “Bibliography,” and revisions to main text in T. O. Lambdin, *An Introduction to the Aramaic of Targum Onqelos*. Cambridge: Department of Near Eastern Languages and Civilizations.

1996 “A Byblos Letter, Probably from Kāmid el-Lōz.” *Zeitschrift der Assyriologie* 86: 97–113. Reprinted in *Kāmid el-Lōz*, vol. 20: *Die Keilschriftbriefe und der Horizont von el-Amarna*, edited by Rolf Hackmann, pp. 87–102. Bonn: Rudolf Habelt.

“New Directions in the Study of Semitic Languages.” In *The Study of the Ancient Near East in the Twenty-first Century: The William Foxwell Albright Centennial Conference*, edited by J. Cooper and G. M. Schwartz, pp. 251–72. Winona Lake: Eisenbrauns.

1997 *A Grammar of Akkadian*. Harvard Semitic Studies 45. Atlanta: Scholars.

Key to A Grammar of Akkadian. Harvard Semitic Studies 46. Atlanta: Scholars.

“Akkadian.” In *The Oxford Encyclopedia of Archaeology in the Near East*, edited by E. M. Meyers, vol. 1, pp. 44–49. New York: Oxford.

“Emar Texts.” In *The Oxford Encyclopedia of Archaeology in the Near East*, edited by E. M. Meyers, vol. 2, pp. 239–40.

“Akkadian Grammar.” Review article of W. von Soden with W. Mayer, *Grundriss der akkadischen Grammatik* (third edition). *Orientalia* 66: 434–44.

“The Form *i-na-a-ku-um-mi* in KBo 1 5 iii 59.” *N.A.B.U.* 4/139: 129–30.

1998 *A Grammar of Akkadian*. Second, revised printing. Harvard Semitic Studies 45. Atlanta: Scholars.

“Notes on *Ras Shamra-Ougarit* VII.” Review article of P. Bordreuil, ed., *Une bibliothèque au sud de la ville: les texts de la 34e campagne (1973)*. *Syria* 74: 213–20.

“What is Aramaic?” *Aram* 7: 265–86.

“A Grammar of Amarna Canaanite.” Review article of A. F. Rainey, *Canaanite in the Amarna Letters*, 4 volumes. *Bulletin of the American Schools of Oriental Research* 310: 59–77.

1999 "Ugaritic Words in Syllabic Texts." In *Handbook of Ugaritic Studies*, edited by W. G. E. Watson and N. Wyatt, pp. 134–39. Leiden: Brill.

"The Akkadian Letters." In *Handbook of Ugaritic Studies*, edited by W. G. E. Watson and N. Wyatt, pp. 375–89.

"On the Etymology and Meaning of Hebrew *nābîʾ*." *Eretz Israel* 26: 88*–93*.

"A Cuneiform Lexical Text from Ashkelon with a Canaanite Column." With Wilfred H. van Soldt. *Israel Exploration Journal* 49: 184–92. Reprinted in *Ashkelon 1: Introduction and Overview*, edited by L. E. Stager, J. D. Schloen, and D. M. Master, pp. 327–32. Winona Lake: Eisenbrauns.

2000 "Old South Arabian Inscriptions in the Harvard Semitic Museum." In *The Archaeology of Jordan and Beyond: Essays in Honor of James A. Sauer*, edited by L. E. Stager, J. A. Greene, and M. D. Coogan, pp. 196–206. Winona Lake: Eisenbrauns.

Key to A Grammar of Akkadian, second, revised printing. Harvard Semitic Studies 46. Winona Lake: Eisenbrauns.

A Grammar of Akkadian. Third, revised printing. Harvard Semitic Studies 45. Winona Lake: Eisenbrauns.

"Proto-Semitic Language and Culture." In *The American Heritage Dictionary of the English Language*, pp. 2056–59. Fourth edition. Boston: Houghton Mifflin.

"Appendix II: Semitic Roots." Ibid., 2062–68.

"A šà bala-a Tablet." With Tonia M. Sharlach. *Journal of Cuneiform Studies* 52: 123–25.

2001 Review of G. Beckman, *Texts from the Vicinity of Emar in the Collection of Jonathan Rosen*. *Orientalia* 70: 133–36.

Review of Robert Hetzron, ed., *The Semitic Languages*. *Journal of the American Oriental Society* 121: 148–49.

Historiography in the Cuneiform World: Proceedings of the XLVe Rencontre Assyriologique International, co-editor with Tzvi Abusch, Paul-Alain Beaulieu, Peter Machinist, and Piotr Steinkeller. Bethseda: CDL Press.

Preface, in Chulhyun Bae, *The Targum of Genesis*. Seoul: Hannim.

2002 "*izuzzum* and *itūlum*." In *Riches Hidden in Secret Places: Ancient Near Eastern Studies in Memory of Thorkild Jacobson*, edited by Tzvi Abush, pp. 161–85. Winona Lake: Eisenbrauns.

"Bibliography of Thorkild Jacobson." With Tzvi Abush. In *Riches Hidden in Secret Places: Ancient Near Eastern Studies in Memory of Thorkild Jacobsen*, edited by Tzvi Abush, pp. ix–xvii.

"Introduction." In *Beyond Babel: A Handbook for Biblical Hebrew and Related Languages*, edited by J. Kaltner and S. L. McKenzie, pp. 1–18. Atlanta: Society of Biblical Literature.

"Comparative Semitic Linguistics." In *Semitic Linguistics: The State of the Art at the Turn of the Twenty-first Century*, edited by Shlomo Izre'el, pp. 119–50. Winona Lake: Eisenbrauns.

"The Hebrew and Aramaic Languages." With Jo Ann Hackett. In *The Biblical World*, edited by J. Barton, vol. 2, pp. 3–24. London: Routledge.

Review of T. Muraoka and B. Porten, *Grammar of Imperial Aramaic*. *Journal of the American Oriental Society* 122: 604–07.

Review of Mireille Hadas-Lebel, *Histoire de la langue Hébraïque: des origines à l'époque de la Mishna*. 4th ed. *Journal of the American Oriental Society* 122: 651–52.

2003 *Leaves from an Epigraphist's Notebook*. By Frank M. Cross; co-editor with Jo Ann Hackett. Harvard Semitic Studies 51. Winona Lake: Eisenbrauns.

Amarna Studies. By W. L. Moran; co-editor with Shlomo Izre'el. Harvard Semitic Studies 54. Winona Lake: Eisenbrauns.

Revision of Robert Hetzron, "Semitic Languages." In *Oxford International Encyclopedia of Linguistics*, edited by W. J. Frawley, vol. 4, pp. 29–33. Second edition. Oxford: Oxford University Press.

"Akkadian *ḫ* and West Semitic **ḥ*." In *Studia Semitica*, edited by L. Kogan, pp. 102–19. Moscow: Russian State University for the Humanities.

"The Alphabet on a Late Babylonian Cuneiform School Tablet." With Frank M. Cross. *Orientalia* 72: 223–28.

Review of Françoise Briquel-Chatonnet, ed., *Mosaïque de langues, mosaïque culturelle: le bilinguisme dans le Proche-Orient ancien*. *Journal of Near Eastern Studies* 62: 294–98.

2004 “Afro-Asiatic.” In *The Cambridge Encyclopedia of the World’s Ancient Languages*, edited by R. D. Woodard, pp. 138–59. Cambridge: Cambridge University Press.

“Akkadian and Eblaite.” With Christopher Woods. In *The Cambridge Encyclopedia of the World’s Ancient Languages*, edited by R. D. Woodard, pp. 218–87.

Translation of “Ancient South Arabian.” By N. Nebes and P. Stein. In *The Cambridge Encyclopedia of the World’s Ancient Languages*, edited by R. D. Woodard, pp. 454–87.

“Hammurabi.” In *Berkshire Encyclopedia of World History*, edited by W. H. McNeill, vol. 3, pp. 882–84. Great Barrington: Berkshire.

“YOS 2/AbB 9 no. 40, 20–21: Distributive Possession in an OB Letter.” *N.A.B.U.* 4/87: 88.

2005 *A Grammar of Akkadian*. Second edition. Harvard Semitic Studies 45. Winona Lake: Eisenbrauns.

Key to A Grammar of Akkadian. Second edition. Harvard Semitic Studies 46. Winona Lake: Eisenbrauns.

“Features of Central Semitic.” In *Biblical and Oriental Essays in Memory of William L. Moran*, edited by A. Gianto, pp. 155–203. Rome: Pontificio Istituto Biblico.

“William L. Moran.” With Tzvi Abusch. *Archiv für Orientforschung* 50: 511–12.

“Reflexes of **qatl* Forms in Gəʿəz.” In *Semitic Studies in Honour of Edward Ullendorff*, edited by G. Khan, pp. 26–36. Leiden: Brill.

“Johann Heinrich Hottinger.” In *Elementale Quadrilingue*, edited by J. F. Coakley, pp. 1–4. Oxford: Jericho Press.

2006 “On the Etymology of the Hebrew Relative *šɛ-*.” In *Biblical Hebrew in Its Northwest Semitic Setting: Typological and Historical Perspectives*, edited by S. E. Fassberg and A. Hurvitz, pp. 103–25. Winona Lake: Eisenbrauns.

“Proto-Semitic and Proto-Akkadian.” In *The Akkadian Language in Its Semitic Context: Studies in the Akkadian of the Third and Second Millennium B.C.*, edited by G. Deutscher and N. J. C. Kouwenberg, pp. 1–18. Leiden: NINO.

“Hebrew Verbs I-*w/y* and a Proto-Semitic Sound Rule.” In *Memoriae Igor M. Diakonoff (Babel und Bibel 2)*, edited by L. Kogan, N. Koslova, S. Loesov, S. Tishchenko, pp. 459–74. Winona Lake: Eisenbrauns.

“Biodiversity Corner: Swamp Milkweed Leaf Beetle.” In *Carlisle (MA) Mosquito* (July 21, 2006): 14.

Henry David Thoreau: Speaking for Nature. With Richard K. Walton. DVD. Concord: Three Rivers Productions.

2007 “*qātîl* and *qətîl* Nouns in Biblical Hebrew.” In *Shaʿarei Lashon: Studies in Hebrew, Aramaic, and Jewish Languages Presented to Moshe Bar-Asher*, edited by A. Maman, S. E. Fassberg, and Y. Breuer, vol. 1, pp. *3–*45. Jerusalem: Bialik Institute.

“Northwest Semitic Languages.” With Rebecca Hasselbach. In *Encyclopedia of Arabic Language and Linguistics*, edited by K. Versteegh, vol. 3, pp. 408–22. Leiden: Brill.

“Some Aspects of the Cleft in Semitic Languages.” With Naʿama Pat-El. In *Studies in Semitic and General Linguistics in Honor of Gideon Goldenberg*, edited by T. Bar and E. Cohen, pp. 325–42. Münster: Ugarit.

“Bible-Translations: Ancient Translations: Ethiopic.” In *Encyclopedia Judaica*, edited by F. Skolnik, vol. 3, pp. 601–02. Second edition. Jerusalem: Macmillan.

“Michael Patrick O’Connor.” With Jo Ann Hackett. *SBL Forum* (June 27, 2007):
http://sbl-site.org/Article.aspx?ArticleId=693

“Comments on Yushu Gong, ‘Graph-typology of Ancient Chinese and Sumerian Writing Systems — A Comparative Perspective.’” In *Oriental Studies (Peking): Special Issue: Collection of Papers on Ancient Civilizations of Western Asia, Asia Minor and North Africa*, pp. 109–15.

2008 *Ugaritic Vocabulary in Syllabic Transcription*. Revised edition. Harvard Semitic Studies 32. Winona Lake: Eisenbrauns.

“Additions and Corrections” to *Ugaritic Vocabulary in Syllabic Transcription*, published online:
https://www.eisenbrauns.com/ECOM/_2IA0LS3H8.HTM
http://utexas.academia.edu/JohnHuehnergard/Papers/170732/2008_Ugaritic_Vocabulary_in_Syllabic_Transcription_Additions_and_Corrections

“*Qiṭṭa*: Arabic Cats.” In *Classical Arabic Humanities in Their Own Terms: Festschrift for Wolfhart Heinrichs on His 65th Birthday Presented by His Students and Colleagues*, edited by B. Gruendler, pp. 407–18. Leiden: Brill.

"Languages of the Ancient Near East." In *The New Interpreter's Dictionary of the Bible*, edited by K. D. Sakenfeld, vol. 3, pp. 576–80. Nashville: Abingdon.

"On Revising and Updating BDB." With Jo Ann Hackett. In *Foundations for Syriac Lexicography* III: *Colloquia of the International Syriac Language Project*, edited by J. Dyk and W. T. van Peursen, pp. 227–34. Piscataway: Gorgias.

A Grammar of Akkadian. Second edition, second, revised printing. Harvard Semitic Studies 45. Winona Lake: Eisenbrauns.

"Edwina Maria (Wyn) Wright." In *SBL Forum* (January 10, 2008): http://www.sbl-site.org/publications/article.aspx?articleId=745

"Afro-Asiatic." In *The Ancient Languages of Syria-Palestine and Arabia*, edited by R. D. Woodard, pp. 225–46. Cambridge: Cambridge University Press.

"Akkadian and Eblaite." With Christopher Woods. In *The Ancient Languages of Mesopotamia, Egypt and Aksum*, edited by R. D. Woodard, pp. 83–152. Cambridge: Cambridge University Press.

Translation of "Ancient South Arabian." By N. Nebes and P. Stein. In *The Ancient Languages of Syria-Palestine and Arabia*, edited by R. D. Woodard, pp. 145–78. Cambridge: Cambridge University Press.

2009 "A Proper View of Arabic, Semitic, and More: A Response to George Mendenhall." With Gary A. Rendsburg and Aaron D. Rubin. *Journal of the American Oriental Society* 128: 533–41.

"Silver from the Souk: Semitic Loanwords in English." In *The Bible and Our World: Ancient Lessons for Today*. DVD. Washington, D.C.: Biblical Archaeological Society.

Key to A Grammar of Akkadian. Second edition, second, revised printing. Harvard Semitic Studies 46. Winona Lake: Eisenbrauns.

2010 "Hammurabi." In *Berkshire Encyclopedia of World History*, edited by William H. McNeill, vol. 3, pp. 1185–86. Second edition. Great Barrington: Berkshire.

Reader, exercises and texts. In *A Basic Introduction to Biblical Hebrew*, by Jo Ann Hackett. Peabody: Hendrickson.

2011 *A Grammar of Akkadian*. Third edition. Harvard Semitic Studies 45. Winona Lake: Eisenbrauns.

"Proto-Semitic Language and Culture." In *The American Heritage Dictionary of the English Language*, pp. 2066–69. Fifth edition. Boston/New York: Houghton Mifflin Harcourt.

"Guide to Appendix II." Ibid., pp. 2070–71.

"Appendix II: Semitic Roots." Ibid., pp. 2072–78.

"Phyla and Waves: Models of Classification." With Aaron D. Rubin. In *Semitic Languages: An International Handbook*, edited by Stefan Weninger in collaboration with Geoffrey Khan, Michael P. Streck, and Janet Watson, pp. 259–78. Handbücher zur Sprach- und Kommunikationswissenschaft. Berlin: de Gruyter Mouton.

"Commentary: Don't Close Book on Humanities." With Jo Ann Hackett. In *Austin American-Statesman*, Sunday, May 15. Section D, pages 1, 8. Online: "Two Texas Professors on Why Academic Research Matters": http://www.statesman.com/opinion/insight/two-texas-professors-on-why-academic-research-matters-1475412.html. Also in *Houston Chronicle*, Monday, May 16.

Review of *Akten des 7. internationalen Semitohamitistenkongresses, Berlin 2004,* edited by Rainer Voigt. *Journal of the American Oriental Society* 131: 709.

2012 "Third Person Possessive Suffixes as Definite Articles in Semitic." With Naʿama Pat-El. *Journal of Historical Linguistics* 2(1): 25–51.

In Press *An Introduction to Ugaritic*. Peabody: Hendrickson.

"The Etymology of Hebrew and Aramaic *ykl* 'to be able.'" With Saul M. Olyan. *Journal of Semitic Studies.*

"Canaanite Shift." In *Encyclopedia of Hebrew Language and Linguistics*, edited by G. Khan. Leiden: Brill.

"Hebrew Loanwords in English." Ibid.

"Philippi's Law." Ibid.

"Relative Particle (Morphology and Historical Background)." Ibid.

"Segholates (Historical Background)." Ibid.

"Hebrew as a Semitic Language." Ibid.

"The Biblical Prohibition against Tattooing." With Harold Liebowitz. *Vetus Testamentum.*

A Brief Note on the Festschrift Illustrations

During 1983 I met John Huehnergard and Jo Ann Hackett when I had an exhibition of paintings in Los Angeles at Occidental College; Jo Ann was teaching there, John was teaching at Columbia, and I was living in Boston. We kept in touch, and eventually all of us ended up in Boston-Cambridge. Ever since, despite later geographical changes, we have remained close. Art has always been a common denominator for us, so I feel especially honored to be included as illustrator in this important scholarly work.

I am neither a scholar of Near Eastern languages and cultures, nor any scholar at all. Rather, I am a visual artist who also likes language. Through the illustrations I hope to somehow portray dimensions of John Huehnergard that might not otherwise come across in the articles, namely, his vast interests in the wider humanities and natural sciences, and his fine sense of humor.

Initially, my grand idea was to come up with a series of small, witty, and fresh cuneiform signs, a leitmotif similar to the graphic "spots" in the New Yorker. But given my grand limitations with the language, I found it excessively difficult to be witty in Neo-Assyrian. In any case, the inevitable flaws in these illustrations might provide their own comic relief, and if they bring a smile to a few faces, then perhaps I've succeeded. And if cuneiform, specifically, and language in general can be looked at in a slightly different way as a result of these drawings, then that is even better. At the very least, the illustrations are designed to provide additional visual flow and rhythm to the book, whether or not one can read cuneiform.

As an outsider to the field of Semitic languages, I have relied on Neo-Assyrian signs here rather than an earlier form of cuneiform or other later written language simply because, for me, they were the easiest to make, and with them my connection with John is most clear.

Also, as an outsider, I thought my best recourse was to return to some original cuneiform, which I found in abundance at the Pergamon Museum in Berlin. Secondarily, I purchased a battered edition of René Labat's *Manuel d'épigraphie Akkadienne* (1959) and a second edition of Huehnergard's *A Grammar of Akkadian* (2005). Kathryn Slansky and Jo Ann Hackett spurred me on with their initial enthusiasm and encouragement, and Slansky along with Eckart Frahm took a look at the final drawings. The insightful article by Benjamin Studevent-Hickmann "The Ninety-degree Rotation of the Cuneiform Script" (2007) helped me with my new personal interest in the curious transformation of the signs over time, from vertical to horizontal. Parts of Rebecca Hasselbach's *Sargonic Akkadian* (2005) served as overview for a time period I found most interesting in the history of writing.

Regarding technical matters, there was much trial and error. In the end, I avoided Photoshop in hopes of more closely simulating the physicality of a scribe writing cuneiform, to catch some tactile sense of the actual handwork. I fashioned homemade tools carved out of plastic cork and used the tools as ink stamps to arrive at a stylized, standard typography. Then, manually, I drew into the images further with pen and ink for graphic uniformity. I used a small mirror to decide on the bilateral compositions.

Among the many cuneiform artifacts at the Pergamon Museum, my favorites are perhaps the stamps and cylinder seals because they announce a change in the writing technology. With them, images and signs can be reproduced countless times, as small precursors of movable type and the printing press. The scribe's time is potentially freed up, economically and manually, and there can be more aesthetic focus on other aspects of the communication. When cuneiform becomes added to representational images, the long cycles of repeating marks and bands created by those marvelous tools, the cylinder seals, can begin to provide an almost cinematic, seamless view into the culture.

On the stamps and cylinder seals, the scribes carve the cuneiform signs in reverse to create a legible sign when it is stamped or rolled out as a print on clay. That is, the scribe is making a legible sign from its mirror image. Or, conversely, a mirror image of the sign occurs in the print when the "correct" version of the sign is carved into the printing implement. In either case, there is a close connection between the "correct" sign and the "backwards" sign. To an artist who likes language, this is intriguing.

I decided to use bilateral shapes in the illustrations because I have been exploring bilateral shapes visually and conceptually in my paintings for many years. By using those shapes in the context of cuneiform, I tried, among other things, to put myself inside the mind of a scribe whose goal is to create the sign in reverse on a stamp or cylinder seal. Interestingly, for many of the less complex cuneiform signs I have used in this Festschrift, they are the same in their reversed mirror image as they are in their "correct" form.

A jump in technology, such as the cylinder-printing rollers for making seals, can often lead to a change in accessibility to a language, as well as an aesthetic and mental jump in how one sees and how one understands what one sees. Did this change in technology contribute to a ninety-degree change in orientation of the signs? If the cylinders were also worn as beads on a necklace, or stored on sticks and mounted horizontally, thus perhaps familiarizing the viewer with seeing them horizontally rather than vertically, could this have also hastened the change in orientation? Did writing the signs backwards have an effect on how a scribe could see and think? A contemporary artist can only speculate.

In some cases the stylized signs for each chapter of the Festschrift relate to the specific article. I also wanted to include signs for flora and fauna of the geographic region, so I have done that as often as possible. (For example, *ettûtu*, for spider, manages both connections preceding Richard Walton's article.) And then sometimes I include a sign simply because I find it beautiful and direct, and a good visual fit for the article, regardless of the sign's meaning. My apologies to anyone who tries to find any other connection between those signs and the subsequent articles.

In conclusion, ever since my daughter Dorian was a child, John Huehnergard and Jo Ann Hackett have been her great and kind mentors. Eight years ago, Dorian named her only son "John," in honor of John Huehnergard. My young grandson John has a lot to live up to.

Any scholarly tribute to John Huehnergard must simultaneously include a tribute to Jo Ann Hackett for the long and deep collaboration between those two souls, without which John's work might have faltered. I am pleased to be part of this Festschrift tribute, and to have also learned a great deal in the process. May we all continue to solve language mysteries.

X Bonnie Woods
Berlin, 2012

****

Biography of X Bonnie Woods

X Bonnie Woods is an artist and designer based in Boston and Berlin. She is intrigued by the connections between image and language and has also worked in maps and in Braille. In addition to having exhibited her paintings and photos widely in the United States and Europe, she worked as a documentary photographer at Ground Zero during September–October 2001, and in post-Katrina New Orleans. Woods would like to thank Kathryn Slanski for her help and encouragement in this project, although Doctor Slanski is not to be held responsible for artistic license taken by Woods, who has used Neo-Assyrian cuneiform as a departure point for these illustrations.

Functional Values of *iprus* Forms in Old Babylonian *šumma* Protases

Eran Cohen, The Hebrew University

Background and General Objectives

John Huehnergard is nowadays known chiefly as a comparative Semiticist. However, in the earlier phases of his career, he had spent both time and effort making his mark on various issues of Akkadian linguistics and was persistent enough to confidently oppose, when necessary, authoritative figures.[1] This paper is intended as a tribute to this part of his work and to his perseverance.

The paper deals with several important and interesting linguistic points that came up while investigating the conditional structures of Old Babylonian. The project started with the epistolary corpus and was further expanded to include the law collections and the omens.[2] In this paper, I would like to concentrate on the verbal form IPRUS and its functional values in *šumma* protases in both Mesopotamian letters and laws, and to attempt to explain the differences.

Since the functional value of a form is derived from its opposition to other forms, I will occasionally discuss the functional values of other forms in the same paradigm with IPRUS. The text corpus used includes the Mesopotamian law collections and the letter corpus from Mesopotamia proper.

A note is due: the described research is complex, involving numerous details. Naturally, in a paper of this scope, not every point can be properly elaborated.

The Laws: General Observations

Trying to determine a temporal functional value (of course, it does not have to be temporal) of these IPRUS forms depends on choosing some arbitrary reference point — for instance, the point in which the law is composed, or the point in which a legal decision is made. This is essentially the strategy taken in most cases so far. Instead, it seems more useful to postpone these decisions and try first to examine the laws for what they are.

[1] One prominent case was writing his 1986 and 1987 papers (originally meant to be one paper) in response to Kraus 1984b, all papers dealing with non-verbal clauses and the stative.

[2] This paper emanates from a manuscript of a book analyzing and describing the conditional structures in Mesopotamian Old Babylonian, which is planned to be published with Eisenbrauns in the series Languages of the Ancient Near East.

The conditional structures in the laws exhibit, right away, various characteristics that are very different from the ordinary conditional[3] structures found in the letters:

1. They are impersonally constructed, containing third person only. The first and second persons occur only in direct speech.[4]
2. Unlike the letters, which are dictated by, as well as addressed to, a specific, concrete person, the laws do not necessarily emanate from a particular speaker, nor are they directed at a specific addressee, but rather at anyone, anytime.
3. Contrary to the dialogic environment in the letters, they lack characteristics of *hic et nunc* 'here and now,' showing no concrete reference to a specific time or location.
4. They are devoid of forms that denote speaker-oriented modality, such as directives (signaled by precative forms), except in rare occurrences of direct speech (where there is a speaker, albeit not a specific speaker but rather a prototype).
5. They do not have a textual context specific to each (as opposed to the conditional structures in the letter corpus). This makes them all refer to the same, unchanging background, whatever it may be.[5]
6. Going deeper, the substantives in their first occurrence in a law represent a prototype — a man, a woman, a slave. This has no explicit expression in Akkadian, since noun determination (which often covers generic noun marking as well) is not consistently marked. In their second occurrence in the laws, substantives are characterized just enough to be distinguished from a seemingly identical substantive (exx. 1 and 2):

ex. 1. *ša elīšu kišpū nadû* 'the one who is blamed with witchcraft'

ex. 2. *ša elīšu kišpī iddû* 'the one who blamed him of witchcraft' (CH §2)

But they hardly become any more specific than that: even when a substantive is followed by the pronoun *šū* (e.g., *awīlum šū*), it still refers to the same non-specific, prototypical man mentioned beforehand. Note that in the letters we generally find the opposite — namely, specific, definite, real referents.

These points are all characteristic of **generic conditionals**. They are described by Snitzer-Reilly (1986) as timeless, impersonal dependencies where every occurrence mentioned in the protasis has its consistent consequence(s) in the apodosis. In those cases it is common to have a paraphrase of 'if' by 'when(ever),' for instance, in Classical Arabic *ʾin* 'if,' *ʾiδā* 'if, when,' and *kullamā* 'whenever' are interchangeable (Peled 1992, p. 25, ex. 33). Podlesskaya (2001, p. 1000) refers to the similarities of this type of conditionals (which she terms "habitual") with temporal clauses and relative clauses (see further below).

These characteristics have serious repercussions on the cardinal time reference in the laws. Consequently, one issue to be re-evaluated presently in view of these observations is tense in the laws. Another is the syntactic form of the laws.

Different Strategies

Conditional structures in Old Babylonian are subdivided into several patterns — *šumma* structures (*GAG* §161; Huehnergard 2005, §17.3b), paratactic structures (*GAG* §160 "ohne einleitende Partikel" — IPARRAS or IPRUS as

[3] **Ordinary conditionals** are structures containing two domains of events or state of affairs, both found somewhere on the **epistemic scale** — that is, they constitute a **modal expression** whereby neither side can be confirmed or denied at the time of utterance, and the likelihood of one domain (the apodosis) to take place depends directly on the realization of the other domain (the protasis). This precludes many other uses of the conditional structure (concession, inference, circumstance, etc.).

[4] *ana abim murabbīšu ū ummim murabbītišu ul abī atta ul ummī atti iqtabi* 'If he says to the father raising him or to the mother raising him "you are not my father, you are not my mother"' (CH §192). Note that 'he' who says is no one in particular (it may in principle apply to a female just as well).

[5] As is explained below, this is true for *primary* laws, which state a case for the first time. Secondary laws — namely, ones that continue, or are dependent on, a preceding law — are of course referential to it. Any attempt to find such context in the CH prologue is problematic, since there is actually a shift between two extremely different genres, royal inscriptions and legal codes, which happen to cohabit the same text.

well as LIPRUS in the protasis; Huehnergard 2005, §17.3a "unmarked conditions"). Further elaboration of the paratactic patterns is found in Cohen 2005, pp. 144–60 (precative protasis) and 161–79 ("indicative" protasis). In Cohen 2006b, pp. 559–61, there is a short survey of other conditional patterns.

The variety of patterns turns out to be an important tool of inquiry into the collective nature of conditional groups. Further examination of the laws, especially the laws of Eshnunna (LE) and the edicts,[6] reveals several strategies at work. The group of strategies used to formulate the laws is *not* identical to the one used for conditional structures in the letter corpus; there is some overlap, but some strategies are unique to each genre. Consequently, the overall effect is not quite the same. For instance, one strategy used only in the letters to signal condition is the one introduced by modal particles. Whenever *midde* or *pīqat* (otherwise 'maybe, perhaps') is followed by one IPARRAS form or more (as protasis) and one or more PURUS or LIPRUS forms (as apodosis), it forms with them a conditional pattern. This pattern is more or less equivalent to the other patterns in the letters, in producing a modal expression in which two states of affairs are interdependent on each other:

ex. 3. ***pīqat*** *kaspam* ***irrišūka lā tanaddiššu***[7] 'If they ask you for silver, do not give it' (AbB 1, 139:9′–10′)

This is a regular conditional pattern in epistolary Old Babylonian (see Cohen 2006b, p. 561).

Note, however, that this pattern is not found in the laws. We do find, in common with the epistolary conditional structure, *šumma* structures and two different paratactic patterns. We also find two strategies in the laws that are frequent in the letters, but have no affinity whatsoever with conditional structures — the *ša* strategy and the *ūm* strategy.[8] Table 1.1 shows the entire group of strategies:[9]

Table 1.1. Syntactic strategies that express laws

	conditional type	protasis	(forms)	connective	apodosis (forms)
A	**conditional particle**	*šumma*	***iprus*** ***iptaras*** *iparras* *paris*	—	***iparras*** predicative noun NVC CS
B	"relative"	*ša*	*iparrasu*		*iparras*
C	"temporal"	*ūm*	*iparrasu*		*iparras*
D	**paratactic**		*iparras*	(*-ma*)	*iparras*
E	**precative**		*liprus*		NVC, *šumma* CS

CS = conditional structure, NVC = non-verbal clause

The *ša* strategy in the laws, or rather the *adjective clause* strategy (pattern B in the table), seems to be both common and crucial for understanding the nature of the laws:

ex. 4. *awīlum* ***ša*** *ina bītim ša muškēnim ina bītim ina muṣlālim* ***iṣṣabbatu*** *10 šiqil kaspam išaqqal* ***ša*** *ina mūšim ina bītim* ***iṣṣabbatu*** *imât ul iballuṭ* 'A man **who is caught** in the house of a commoner inside the house at midday shall pay 10 sheqels (of) silver; **he who is caught** inside the house at night shall die, he will not live.' (LE §13)

In the Edict of Ammīṣadūqa (EA), a royal extension to the laws, structures with *ša* freely alternate with *šumma* structures, both in the same function, expressing laws:

[6] Possibly due to normalization of their language, the laws of Ḫammurabi seem to be quite unified and show far less diversity than the laws of Eshnunna, which turns out to be a disadvantage in these circumstances.

[7] The form LĀ TAPARRAS is a respectable member of the PRECATIVE group, serving as the negative counterpart of PURUS.

[8] *šumma* [...] *riksātim u kirram ana abīša u ummiša iškun-ma īḫussi aššat* ***ūm ina sūn awīlim iṣṣabbatu*** *imât ul iballuṭ* 'If [...] he arranges a contract and a nuptial feast and marries her, she is a wife. T**he day she is caught in the lap of a man**, she shall die, not live' (LE §28). *ūm* introduces a new clause, while the *time* the woman is caught is immaterial. It is the case of adultery itself to which the corrective measure applies.

[9] The fields show the forms that figure in each functional slot.

ex. 5. ***ša*** *še'am kaspam ū bīšam ana šīmim ...* ***iddinu****-ma kanīkam* ***ušēzibu*** *...* 'He **who lends** barley, silver or property as price ... and **draws up** a document ...' (EA §9[10])

Compare with the better-known formulation:

ex. 6. [***šum***]***ma*** *awīlum še'am ū kaspam ana ḫubullim* ***idd***[***in***] *u ṭuppam* ***ušēzib*** *...* '[I]**f** a man **gi**[**v**]**es** as interest-bearing loan barley or silver, and draws **up** a document ...' (EA §7)

In the letters, these two strategies are not even similar: *šumma* patterns signal ordinary conditions, whereas *ša* structures never do. **The two strategies coincide only in laws.**

In the letters, what few legal formulations we find are very instructive:

ex. 7. ***awīlum balṭum gimil gāmilišu utār*** *šumma balṭāku gimillaka utār* '**A healthy man returns his benefactor's favor.** If I live/am healthy, I will return your favor.' (AbB 3, 33:24–26)

ex. 8. ***ša lā izzazzu mim<ma> ulileqqe*** [*sic*] *... 7 mana aklam išdudūnim ulazzaz-ma* [*sic*] *mannum litēršu* '**He who does not serve does not take anything.** ... They provided me with seven minas of food; if I do not serve, who would pay it back?' (AbB 11, 27:12–17)

The legal protasis is basically given the form of an adjective,[11] either simple (*balṭum* 'alive, well') or complex (*ša lā izzazzu* 'he who does not serve'). This is done in the letters in order to distinguish between two markedly different expressions — a generic formulation of a rule of conduct, on the one hand (the law), as opposed to an epistemic interdependency, a modal expression that expresses likelihood (the ordinary condition), on the other.

Note that the law in both cases (exx. 7 and 8) is evoked for a currently relevant reason stated immediately thereafter. The law itself is formulated as a **general truth**, while its desired application is firmly anchored in the here and now of the speaker. In both examples this part is incidentally an **ordinary conditional**, which cannot stand for a law in the epistolary genre.

Athanasiadou and Dirven (1996) primarily differentiate between two types of conditional — **course-of-event conditionals** and **hypothetical conditionals**. While the hypothetical conditionals refer to a single occurrence, the former represent relations between recurring events. These events belong to a world of *reality*, characterized by an interchange between *if* and *whenever*, which does not alter their reality status. The events are characterized as "generally occurring events" rather than *hic et nunc* occurring events, namely, events that take place in a specific time and location.

The hypothetical issue is in principle *absent* from the laws — whereas in ordinary conditionals in the letters, the conditional structures express obvious uncertainty, conforming with the idea of "maybe." This is evident from the *ša* clause formulation as well, especially when compared, inside the letters, to *šumma* conditionals. This strategy seems to be representative of the strategies expressing a law. Uncertainty is not a factor in these laws, but it is a central facet of the conditionality type found in the letters. The table ennumerates the differences between the two types:

Table 1.2. Differences between generic and hypothetical conditionals

Parameter	*Generic Conditionals*	*Hypothetical Conditionals*
modality	realis	irrealis
introductory particles	if/whenever/(he) who	if/maybe
hic et nunc ('here and now')	none or very little	specific time and location
specificity of occurrence	generally recurring	single occurrence
co-text	none	almost always

[10] In the edicts there is a greater variety, and IPRUSU is found in addition to IPARRASU, without any appreciable difference.

[11] In the letters as well as in the laws; compare ***lā zīzu*** 'without inheritance' in LE §16.

Types of Genres

I have spent some time characterizing the language of the laws. The epistolary language has not received a similar specialized description. It seems, however, to be dialogic in nature when compared with the characterization of the dialogue in the epic (Cohen 2006a, pp. 36–38). The point of this is the profound difference between these two Old Babylonian genres (letters and laws) despite many external linguistic similarities between them.[12]

In the literature, the differences between the genres are sometimes disregarded; in *GAG* §161 hardly any such distinction is mentioned (except under h, discussing single verbal forms in the law), and letters are not mentioned as a separate genre, although many of the examples in *GAG* are taken from them.

Streck (1999, pp. 112–13) refers to the function of IPTARAS in a chain (i.e., IPRUS-MA ... IPTARAS) in *šumma* clauses of the Ḫammurabi letter sub-corpus, but adduces examples *from the laws*. Streck in this case presupposes identity between the two genres. The only reason to adduce from another corpus is that the chain he wants to illustrate is simply not attested inside *šumma* protases in the letters (unlike the laws, where it is normal).

On the other hand, as early as Maloney 1982, we find two distinct chapters — "Verbal Usage in *šumma*-Clauses" (chapter 3) and "Verbal Usage in the CH and LE" (supplement). The description is dedicated to the form IPTARAS, whose functional value is different across the two genres, and the distinction is hence inevitable. This has become the norm with Metzler 2002 (chapter 2 devoted to laws and omens with notable differences) and in Loesov 2004, where the two genres, letters and laws, are referred to separately.

Protatic *iprus* Forms in the Letters

The epistolary language has, on the whole, received less attention than the laws, and IPRUS forms have drawn far less interest than IPTARAS. In the letter itself, being dialogic in nature (see Cohen 2006a, pp. 36–38), one might have expected the verbal forms to demonstrate *temporal* functions rather than, for example, *aspectual* ones (as one finds in the epic narrative, ibid., pp. 54–63). Since, however, one often observes a peculiar behavior within conditional clauses,[13] the issue calls for confirmation.

The form IPRUS in epistolary *šumma* protases is discussed separately in Maloney 1982, pp. 219–30 and 251–54. Maloney (ibid., pp. 229–30) cannot decide between past and present-future and resorts to saying that the form signals that the condition is real. This of course is true also when IPARRAS is in the protasis. Leong (1994, pp. 118–22) mentions, for the functional value of IPRUS, two kinds of anteriority — one of the present and one of the future. It is Loesov (2004, pp. 141–44) who provides the ultimate solution:

> The non-negated Preterite in *šumma*-clauses denotes facts *anterior to the coding time*, while the *negated Preterite can have both past and future reference.* (ibid., p. 141, my emphasis)

The past value of IPRUS forms within epistolary *šumma* clauses, as observed by Loesov, is best seen when the context and the protasis are co-referential, and the same lexemes as well as participants are found. Such protases are termed **verificational protasis**. It is often attested in the Ḫammurabi letters sub-corpus,[14] but not exclusively:

ex. 9. *ina* GN *ṭātum* ***ibbašī****-ma* (*ib-ba-ši-ma*) *awīlû ša ṭātam ilqû u šībū ša awâtim īdû ibaššû* (*i-ba-aš-šu-ú*) (...) [(20)] *warkatam purus-ma šumma ṭātum* ***i***[***b***]***baš***[***i***] *kaspam u mimma ša ina ṭâtim i*[*lq*]*û kunkam-ma* ... [*š*]*ūb*[*i*]*l*[*a*]*m* ... '"In GN **bribery took place** and the people who took bribe and witnesses who know this matter exist" ... look into the matter and if **bribery too[k p]lace**, seal the silver and whatever one to[ok] as bribery and s[en]d me ...' (AbB 2, 11:7–13, 20–24)

---

[12] Ungnad 1903–1905 undoubtedly served as basic for the description of both laws and the epistolary language. The languages are very similar morphologically and (morpho-)syntactically, but above this level there are considerable dissimilarities.

[13] For instance, the difference that exists in Biblical Hebrew among *ʾim yiqṭol*, *ʾim* (*yeš/ʾeʸn*) *qōṭel*, and *ʾim qāṭal* does not seem to be temporal.

[14] For a list of these letters, see Streck 1999, p. 103 n. 13.

In this example a crime is reported, told (lines 7–13) as a past event. In the royal letter, the purpose of the conditional construction is verifying the report. Whether the directives in the apodosis are to be carried out depends on the results of the verification. This co-referentiality between the reportative context and the verificational protasis compels us to recognize the past value of IPRUS in the protasis.

The form LĀ IPRUS has two distinct values in epistolary *šumma* protases: it is the negative form of both IPRUS and IPTARAS. Loesov (2004, p. 141) observes that LĀ IPRUS can have both past and future reference. LĀ IPRUS forms are often regarded as the negative allomorph of IPTARAS (e.g., Streck 1999, pp. 107–08), but there are examples that show that these forms negate the form IPRUS as well. The following letter demonstrates this value of LĀ IPRUS:

ex. 10. **a.** PN_1 *ša ḫumāšim kīam ulammidanni umma šū-ma* [(7)] *eqel bīt abīya ša ištu ūmī mādūtim ṣabtānu* PN_2 *sukkukum mār* PN_3 *ibquranni-ma* PN_4 *ālum u šībūtum izzizū warkat eqlim šuāti* ***iprusū-ma*** *kīma* PN_3 *abi sukkukim eqlam šuāti lā iṣbatu eqlum šū ṣibitni-ma* ***ubirrūnim-ma*** *ṭuppam* ***iddinūnim*** *u ina ṭuppim ša iddinūnim* PN_3 *abi sukkukim [ana] šībūtim* ***šaṭer*** *inanna sukkukim mār* PN_3 *eqlī ibtaqranni* [(20)] *u šê inaṣṣar kīam ulammidanni* 'The wrestler PN_1 informed me thus: "My family's field, which we possess for a long time, PN_2 the deaf, son of PN_3, claimed (it) and PN_4, the town and witnesses served, they investigated the matter of this field and established that PN_3, father of PN_2 the deaf, did not possess the field (and that) this field was our possession and they gave me a document and in the document which they gave me, PN_3, father of the deaf, is registered [as] witness. Now the deaf, son of PN_3, has claimed my field and (additionally) he holds my barley." Thus he informed me.' (AbB 4, 40:5–21)

b. *šumma kīma* PN_1 *ša ḫumāšim iqbû warkat awâtim ša eqlim šuāti* PN_4 *ālum u šībūtum* ***iprusū-ma*** *eqlam ana* PN_1*-ma* ***ubirrū*** *u ina ṭuppim* PN_3 *abi sukkukim ana šībūtim* ***šaṭer*** [(28)] *eqlam u šeʾam ana* PN_1*-ma terrā* 'If, as the wrestler PN_1 said, PN_4, the town and witnesses (themselves) investigated the matter of the field and established the field (as belonging) to PN_1, and (additionally) in the document PN_3 the father of the deaf was registered as witness, return the field and barley to PN_1.' (AbB 4, 40:22–28)

c. *šumma warkat eqlim šuāti* ***lā ipparis*** PN_4 *eqlam šuāti* ***lā ubīr****-ma ana* PN_1 ***lā iddin*** *kakkum ša ilim ana eqlim lirid-ma attunu ālum u šībūtum awâtim ša eqlim šuāti maḫar ilim birrā-ma eqlam ana dūrišu idnā* 'If the matter of the field was not investigated, PN_4 did not establish this field and did not give (it) to PN_1, may the divine emblem descend to the field and you, town and witnesses, establish the matter of this field in front of God and assign the field its permanent status.' (AbB 4, 40:29–36)

The letter has three parts: **a.** the complaint (lines 7–20), referring to *past occurrences*; **b.** a verificational clause, referring, like any affirmative IPRUS form in the protasis, *to the past* (lines 22–27) and its apodotic directives (line 28); and **c.** the *alternative* (lines 29–36). This last part is the **negative** of the verificational clause; this means that LĀ IPRUS forms are here **negating** IPRUS **and not** IPTARAS **forms**, all having **past value**.

On the other hand, the existence of another homonymous (but functionally different) LĀ IPRUS form in the protasis is beyond any doubt:

ex. 11. *aššum ipir* PN *nadānim lū ašpurakkum ammīnim lā taddin ipir* PN *a[n]a ma[t]ī tanaddi[n]* ***idin*** *šumma* ***lā [t]addin*** *a[š]apparam-ma ipir [š]attiša ina bītika tanaddin* 'I *did* write to you about giving PN's ration, why did you not give (it)? When do you intend to give PN's ration? **Give** (it)! If [you] **will not have given** it,[15] I will write and you will (have to) give the yearly ration out of your house.' (AbB 2, 129:4–19)

This example has maximum resumption — both general and immediate context, protasis and apodosis, all show the same lexeme, *nadānum*, always referring to the same event. The event has not yet taken place by the time of the utterance (this is evident from the imperative *idin* in the same utterance). This resembles the various IPTARAS forms: PN is expected to have his ration by a certain point in the future, and that as a result of the addressee

[15] Standard English requires "if you have not given," which neutralizes present and future perfect. The situation in Old Babylonian is similar, but in this case we know it means the future perfect.

giving it to him at a moment prior to that point in the future. In fact, in *šumma* protases IPTARAS forms signal "non-past perfect."

In all these occurrences, the dialogue rules: there is a fixed reference point — to wit, the point of utterance, the "speaker's now" — a specific speaker, and a designated addressee, and each conditional structure has its own particular context.

Two additional issues need to be mentioned as summary — first, mentioned above, is that in the epistolary protasis there are hardly any chains of verbal forms interconnected via the particle *-ma*. Second, unlike the chain, where the difference between IPRUS and IPTARAS is hardly temporal, and unlike the single-clause protases in the laws where there may be no difference at all between the two forms, in the epistolary *šumma* protasis, they have a clearly distinct functional value — whereas IPRUS signals *past*, IPTARAS signals *non-past perfect*, usually actualized as future perfect and only rarely as present perfect.

Protatic *iprus* Forms in the Laws

Having looked already into the textual nature of the laws and discussed the epistolary protasis and the temporal value of IPRUS, we now proceed to the long-debated functional value of IPRUS in the laws. Here the form has been claimed to signal the following functional values:

1. **preterite** (the additions to *GAG* §161, following Hirsch 1969)
2. **present** (*GAG* §161c)
3. **future anterior** (Streck 1999, p. 113)
4. **anterior to the recipient point of view** (Metzler 2002, p. 875)
5. forming the **"narrative"** part of the law (Loesov 2004, pp. 148–50)
6. depicting **background activities** as opposed to IPTARAS forms (Maloney 1982, p. 278) — however, both IPRUS and IPTARAS together are essentially viewed as **aoristic**:

> it is probably best to consider the preterites and perfects in the legal sections of the CH as well as the LE **as essentially aoristic** (in the etymological sense). They serve to express **punctual events**, as opposed to the present-future, **but their tense reference is really indeterminate**. The **law** codes themselves **provide no strong contextual indicators to help** us in this area, and so we shall leave the question aside here. (Maloney 1982, p. 263, my emphasis)

Such variety implies that this work is not finished yet; it seems to me that it is possible to settle a few problems and point out several sources for the difficulties encountered. I chose to place Maloney's description at the end because he reached results very similar to the ones obtained here from a different angle and method.

The following is a representative example of a protasis — a PARIS form serving as circumstantial and a list of actions:

ex. 12. *šumma kalbum šegī-ma bābtum ana bēlišu* ***ušēdī****-ma kalabšu* ***lā iṣṣur****-ma awīlam* ***iššuk****-ma uštamīt* 'If a dog is raving and the ward authorities **notify** its owner but (the owner) **does not guard** his dog and **it bites** a man and kills him ...' (LE §56)

Note that the example is not interpreted as if IPRUS forms imply present tense, or any tense at all, for that matter.[16] Rather, IPRUS in a chain seems to represent an **unmarked event** (Maloney's "aorist," that is, non-specific, or general, tense). Example 12 has three such events: notifying, not-preventing, and biting. The discussion of how this form is to be translated is not as important as understanding what it does — IPRUS represents a **non-specific**

[16] It is rendered with the English present tense: "Sentences in the present tense sometimes refer to a state which **holds at all times** or at every time in the existence of the referent of the subject. Such sentences are called **universal** (or **gnomic**) sentences" (Declerck 2006, p. 130, my emphasis).

act that has a consistent association with a certain mode of action (in the apodosis). It therefore has **no real time of its own** and is analogous to saying the following:

> Under California Civil Code Section 3342, the owner of the dog who **bites** another person, is liable regardless of the former viciousness of the dog or the owner's knowledge of such viciousness. (Gibson 2009, my emphasis)

Note that *bit* instead of *bites* would mean a specific case. This is a generally valid statement. So are the Old Babylonian laws. The English present tense is suitable for rendering it because it is a general rather than specific present, whereas the English preterite is rather specific.

To corroborate these conclusions, we need to compare cases of IPRUS with the functions of IPARRAS, since functional values can only be arrived at via opposing forms that interchange in the same functional slot, in our case the protasis. The main values of IPARRAS forms in a *main* protasis[17] are the following:

Expressing a circumstantial:

ex. 13. *šumma aššat awīlim ša ina bīt awīlim wašbat ana waṣêm pānīša ištakam-ma sikiltam* ***isakkil*** *bīssa* ***usappaḫ*** *mussa* ***ušamṭa*** *ukannūšī-ma* 'If a man's wife who is living in a man's house decides to leave (while) **she acquires** property **illegally, squanders** her own house, (and) **belittles** her husband, she will be convicted and ...' (CH §141)

Conveying will or intention:

ex. 14. *šumma ina atḫī ištēn zittašu ana kaspim* ***inaddin*** *u aḫūšu šâmam ḫašeḫ* ... 'If in a partnership, one **wants to sell** his share and his partner is willing to buy ...' (LE §38)

Communicating a potential:

ex. 15. *šumma igārum* ***iqâm****-ma bābtum ana bēl igārim ušēdī-ma igāršu lā u<dan>nin igārum imqut-ma mār awīlim uštamīt* ... 'If a wall **is about to collapse**, and the ward authorities notify the wall's owner but he does not reinforce his wall, and wall collapses and causes the death of a member of the *awīlum* class ...' (LE §58)

The common denominator for all these functions is their duration, all basically **describing a state**. So, confronted in one group with PARIS forms (see *šegi* 'is raving,' ex. 12), IPRUS covers **punctual actions**. Such opposition lies in the aspectual spectrum and is comparable to the functions in narrative (Cohen 2006a, pp. 54–63), and it accordingly may be termed "events" versus "descriptions," despite the fact that these events do not necessarily take place and are in fact still considered non-specific (the agent is always a prototype).

There are of course exceptions. In some cases, brought up by Hirsch (1969, pp. 123–25; which eventually set off a partial correction in *GAG*), IPRUS forms are not generic; Hirsch phrases it differently, saying that they cannot be translated as present, and consequently (but wrongly) draws the conclusions that all IPRUS forms should be counted as denoting the past. Examples 16 and 17 are some of his evidence:

ex. 16. *šumma awīlum nadītam īḫuz-ma amtam ana mutiša iddin-ma mārī ittalad warkānum amtum šī itti bēltiša uštatamḫir aššum mārī* ***uldu*** *bēlessa ana kaspim ul inaddišši* ... 'If a man marries a *nadītum* and she gives a maid to her husband and she bears children, thereafter the maid considers herself on equal status as her mistress, (but) because she **bore** children, her mistress may not sell her ...' (CH §146)

ex. 17. *šumma mārī* ***lā ulid*** *bēlessa ana kaspim inaddišši* 'If she **did not bear** children, her mistress may sell her' (CH §147)

---

[17] See further below, discussion of **secondary protases**.

The first occurrence of the lexeme 'to bear a child' is in the form *ittalad*. This form describes a general case (a maid giving birth) and is hence not referential to any preceding context, not being anchored anywhere — our standard generic occurrence (for the laws). In contrast, the same lexeme, first in the causal clause (*aššum ... uldu* in ex. 16) and then in the second protasis (ex. 17, *šumma ... lā ulid*), *is* referential and *does* have a context. The adverbial clause in example 16 has its own main clause (*ul inaddišši*) for context, while the secondary *šumma* clause in example 17 has the primary law in example 16 for context. Both occurrences must be rendered by a **preterite** because they are referential to the first mention of the lexeme, referring to one and the same action. The form *uldu* and *lā ulid* are referential to *ittalad*. Here we do have tense, albeit a relative one.

Hirsch (1969, pp. 123–25) was on to something: he put his finger on cases where this special property of the laws, the generic quality, is absent. Hirsch (ibid., pp. 120–23) adduces other examples, of IPARRAS, which do not conform with the values we suggested above, but rather denote the **present**. The common denominator of all his examples is the fact that they all come from **secondary protases**. These protases are different from primary protases in that they are referential to some external reality, and therefore relative tense is found in them as well as other types of referentiality. For instance, we know perfectly well to whom *lā ulid* in example 17 refers.

Protatic *iprus* Forms: Conclusions

The form IPRUS in the theoretical framework of this research is shown to have several functions in the protasis depending on the genre and syntactic environment. When negated, it has to do, in the letters, with two different forms, both IPRUS and IPTARAS. There it has *temporal* oppositions with the other forms that figure in the same slot — past when affirmative, either past or (future) perfect when negative. This is made possible by the fact that these *šumma* protases always have a real context and are often *referential* to events outside the protasis.

To extract the function of IPRUS in the laws, one first had to study the laws textually and then work within the restrictions of the genre: there the oppositions seem to be *aspectual*, and IPRUS denotes an event that is essentially tenseless and is not actually referential to anything external to the protasis. A generic expression has universal validity, way beyond the time it was formulated, or used. Therefore, these questions, provided that one accepts the generic nature of these structures, are irrelevant. It does not really matter *when* the law was written, nor *who* wrote it, nor *when* the offense took place. What matters is the type of offense, the corresponding corrective act, and the interdependency between them, all of which are signaled by the various structures that together form the paradigm of the Old Babylonian laws.

Table 1.3 summarizes these conclusions and includes, in addition, a mention of secondary protases:

Table 1.3. Comparative view of *iprus* forms in *šumma* protases

Forms	*Values*		
šumma protasis	letters (non-chained clauses)	laws	
		(chained clauses)	secondary protasis
IPRUS~ LĀ IPRUS$_1$	**past**	**event**	**relative past**
IPTARAS~ LĀ IPRUS$_2$	(non-past) perfect	chain-final event	
IPARRAS	**non-past**	**description**	**relative present**

In such protases, being *referential* to external events, one finds, again, tense. Since the reference point is not the point of the utterance, such tense is considered relative tense.

Abbreviations

AbB 1	Fritz Rudolf Kraus. *Briefe aus dem British Museum (CT 43 und 44).* Altbabylonische Briefe in Umschrift und Übersetzung 1. Leiden: Brill, 1964.
AbB 2	R. Frankena. *Briefe aus dem British Museum: LIH und CT 2–33.* Altbabylonische Briefe in Umschrift und Übersetzung 2. Leiden: Brill, 1966.
AbB 3	R. Frankena. *Briefe aus der Leidener Sammlung (TLB IV).* Altbabylonische Briefe in Umschrift und Übersetzung 3. Leiden: Brill, 1968.
AbB 4	Fritz Rudolf Kraus. *Briefe aus dem Archive des Šamaš-ḫāzir in Paris und Oxford (TCL 7 und OECT 3).* Altbabylonische Briefe in Umschrift und Übersetzung 4. Leiden: Brill, 1968.
AbB 11	Marten Stol. *Letters from Collections in Philadelphia, Chicago, and Berkeley.* Altbabylonische Briefe in Umschrift und Übersetzung 11. Leiden: Brill, 1986.
CH	Codex Ḫammurabi (cited by §)
EA	Edict of Ammīṣadūqa (Kraus 1984a, pp. 169–83)
GAG	Wolfram von Soden. *Grundriss der akkadischen Grammatik.* 3rd edition. Analecta Orientalia 33/47. Rome: Pontificium Institutum Biblicum, 1995.
GN	geographical name
LE	Reuven Yaron. *The Laws of Eshnunna.* 2nd edition. Jerusalem: Magnes Press, 1988.
PN	proper noun

Bibliography

Athanasiadou, Angeliki, and René Dirven

1996 — "Typology of If-Clauses." In *Cognitive Linguistics in the Redwoods: The Expansion of a New Paradigm in Linguistics*, edited by Eugene H. Casad, pp. 609–54. Cognitive Linguistics Research 6. Berlin: Mouton de Gruyter.

Cohen, Eran

2005 — *The Modal System of Old Babylonian.* Harvard Semitic Studies 56. Winona Lake: Eisenbrauns.

2006a — "The Tense-aspect System of the Old Babylonian Epic." *Zeitschrift für Assyriologie* 96: 31–68.

2006b — "Syntactic Marginalia in Old Babylonian," a review of *Letters in the Louvre*, by K. R. Veenhof. *Journal of the American Oriental Society* 126/4: 551–65.

Declerck, Renaat

2006 — *The Grammar of the English Tense System: A Comprehensive Analysis.* Berlin: Mouton de Gruyter.

Gibson, R. Sebastian

2009 — "Dog Bite Law in California: Can a Dog Bite a Lawyer in California and Get Away with It?" Accessed February 21, 2009, http://www.hg.org/article.asp?id=6036

Hirsch, H.

1969 — "Zur Frage der t-Formen in den keilschriftlichen Gesetzestexten." In lišān mitḫurti*: Festschrift Wolfram Freiherr von Soden zum 19.4.1968 gewidmet von Schülern und Mitarbeitern*, edited by Wolfgang Röllig, pp. 119–31. Alter Orient und Altes Testament 1. Kevelaer: Butzon & Bercker; Neukirchen-Vluyn: Neukirchener Verlag.

Huehnergard, John

1986 — "On Verbless Clauses in Akkadian." *Zeitschrift für Assyriologie* 76: 218–49.

1987 — "'Stative,' Predicative Form, Pseudo-verb." *Journal of Near Eastern Studies* 46/3: 215–32.

2005 — *A Grammar of Akkadian.* 2nd edition. Harvard Semitic Studies 45. Atlanta: Scholars Press.

Kraus, Fritz Rudolf

1984a — *Königliche Verfügungen in altbabylonischer Zeit.* Studia et documenta ad iura Orientis antiqui pertinentia 11. Leiden: Brill.

1984b *Nominalsätze in altbabylonischen Briefen und der Stativ.* Mededelingen der Koninglijke Nederlandse Akademie van Wetenschappen, Afd. Letterkunde, Nieuwe Reeks, deel 47/2. Amsterdam: Royal Netherlands Academy.

Leong, Tien Fock

1994 Tense, Mood and Aspect in Old Babylonian. Ph.D. dissertation, University of California–Los Angeles.

Loesov, Sergey

2004 "T-perfect in Old Babylonian: The Debate and a Thesis." *Babel und Bibel* 1: 83–182.

2005 "Additions and Corrections to 'T-perfect in Old Babylonian.'" *Babel und Bibel* 2: 713–17.

Maloney, John Frederick

1982 The T-perfect in the Akkadian of Old Babylonian Letters, with a Supplement on Verbal Usage in the Code of Hammurapi and the Laws of Ešnunna. Ph.D. dissertation, Harvard University.

Metzler, Kai Alexander

2002 *Tempora in altbabylonischen literarischen Texten.* Alter Orient und Altes Testament 279. Münster: Ugarit-Verlag.

Peled, Yishai

1992 *Conditional Structures in Classical Arabic.* Studies in Arabic Language and Literature 2. Wiesbaden: Otto Harrassowitz.

Podlesskaya, Vera

2001 "Conditional Constructions." In *Language Typology and Language Universals: An International Handbook*, edited by Martin Haspelmath, Ekkehard König, Wulf Oesterreicher, and Wolfgang Raible, vol. 2, pp. 998–1010. Berlin: de Gruyter.

Snitzer-Reilly, Judith

1986 "The Acquisition of Temporals and Conditionals." In *On Conditionals*, edited by Elizabeth C. Traugott, Alice ter Meulen, Judith Snitzer-Reilly, and Charles A. Ferguson, pp. 309–31. Cambridge: Cambridge University Press.

Streck, M. P.

1999 "Das 'Perfekt' *iptaras* im Altbabylonischen der Hammurapi-Briefe." In *Tempus und Aspekt in den semitischen Sprachen: Jenaer Kolloquium zur semitischen Sprachwissenschaft*, edited by Norbert Nebes, pp. 101–26. Jenaer Beiträge zum Vorderen Orient 1. Wiesbaden: Harrassowitz.

Ungnad, Arthur

1903–1905 "Zur Syntax der Gesetze Hammurabis." *Zeitschrift für Assyriologie und vervandte Gebiete* [I] 17 (1903): 353–78, [II] 18 (1904–1905): 1–67.

2

The Hypotaxis-Parataxis Dichotomy and Elliptic Conditional Clauses in Semitic

*Lutz Edzard, University of Oslo**

In a seminal paper of 1983, "Asseverative **la* and Hypothetical **lu/law* in Semitic," John Huehnergard traced the etymology of asseverative and conditional particles in Semitic in their syntactic context. Inspired by Huehnergard's paper, I address a modal-deontic feature in Akkadian treaty texts and other documents, namely, the injunctive *šumma* (*lā*) clauses (oath clauses/*Schwursätze*). Two issues arise in this context: (1) Do the resulting syntactical structures synchronically have to be considered as hypotactic or paratactic and (2) is it appropriate in this context to label the *šumma* (*lā*) clauses "elliptic conditional clauses"?

Introduction

Among the formal features in Akkadian treaty texts, one finds the individual clauses or "paragraphs" of the treaty introduced by the conditional marker *šumma* (*lā*). Normally, this conditional marker introduces the protasis of a conditional sentence, as in legal texts like the Codex Hammurabi. However, the particle *šumma* is also widely attested in oath sentences (see von Soden 1995, p. 293 [= §185g–i] and Huehnergard 2005, pp. 437f. [= §36.3]), in which the "Boolean" value of the sentence is seemingly inverted. Thus, *šumma* introduces negative statements ("may not") and *šumma lā* positive statements ("may"). Here are three examples of such inverted positive statements:

ex. 1. *šumma aḫī Purattim gulgullātim lā umalli*

'I will fill the banks of the Euphrates with skulls' =
"if I won't fill the banks of the Euphrates with skulls, <<negative consequence>>"

ex. 2. *šumma ... lā umalli u lā uṣṣiṣ*

'I shall ... certainly fill and ... bend' =
"if I won't fill and bend, <<negative consequence>>"

ex. 3. *šumma ... lā attalk-ak-kim-ma u ṣibût-ki lā ētepuš*

'I will certainly come to you and carry out your wish' =
"if I (will) have not come to you and carried out your wish, <<negative consequence>>"

* This is an elaborated version of a similar paper (L. Edzard 2010), which draws on some of the same sources. Thanks to Michael P. Streck for comments on this earlier version. Responsibility remains with the author alone.

As we see further below, the inherent logic in such clauses as examples 1 to 3, at least from a diachronic perspective, probably is that an apodosis *à la* "may I die" or "may I be cursed" has to be mentally supplied after the respective protases. In other words, in a diachronic analysis, the oath clauses may be analyzed as elliptic conditional sentences.[1] In a synchronic analysis, however, *šumma* and *šumma lā* may have to be analyzed as asseverative particles that can be rendered by "certainly not" and "certainly," respectively.

In the following, an attempt is made to present the synchronic analysis in a comparative Semitic and typological perspective. First, I show that injunctive forms and protases can appear in comparable syntactical distribution. In a second step, I assemble data on elliptic (or "defective") conditional clauses (protases) in general, independently of the issue of injunctions.

Conditional Clauses and Hyperbolic Imperatives

The connection between conditional clauses and/or hyperbolic imperatives, to allude to the title of a paper by Lawler (1975), has not escaped the attention of theoretical linguistics. In this context, it is important to note that conditional structures are not necessarily hypotactic, but may be paratactic as well (see also Haiman 1983).[2] Lawler's (1975, p. 371) examples involving the conjunctions *and* and *or* are as follow:

ex. 4. a *Open the window and I'll kill you.*

b *Open the window and I'll kiss you.*

c *Open the window or I'll kill you.*

d *?Open the window or I'll kiss you.*

Obviously, example 4a could be paraphrased as "if you open the window, I'll kill you," 4b as "if you open the window, I'll kiss you" (assuming that being kissed is desirable), and 4c as "if you don't open the window, I'll kill you." Only example 4d is semantically ill formed (unless being kissed is undesirable).

German, among many other languages, allows for similar constructions. König (1986, p. 234) offers the following example, which likewise can be paraphrased by a conditional structure:

ex. 5. *Störe ihn nicht, dann wird er dich auch nicht stören.*

'If you don't disturb him, he won't disturb you either.'

Turning to Semitic, injunctives in the protasis of a conditional structure are also attested in Akkadian. Consider the following example, in which the protasis consists of two precative verb phrases, *līter limṭī-ma* (see Huehnergard 2005, p. 146):

ex. 6. *kaspum līter limṭī-ma ul atâr-ma ul araggam*

'let the silver increase, let it decrease, and I will not contest again' =
"whether the silver increases or decreases, I will not contest again"

Diehl (2004, pp. 100–03 and 331–35) adduces relevant examples from Biblical Hebrew, in which the injunctive forms (mostly imperatives) function as protases:[3]

ex. 7 *zō(ʾ)ṯ ʿăśū wi-ḥyū* (Gen 42:18) 'do this, and live'[4] =

"if you do this, you will live"

---

[1] Tietz (1963, pp. 87–90) problematizes the term "ellipsis" in this context and operates with the alternative term "brachylogy," as it is not clear a priori whether the optative use of certain particles preceded the conditional use, and as "elliptic" structures were not necessarily conceived as such by native Semitic speakers.

[2] Diem (2002) makes the same point for complement clauses (e.g., *ʾan yafʿala*).

[3] See also GKC 325 (= §110f) and Bergsträsser 1929, p. 50 (= §10k).

[4] The immediate translations of biblical verses (between '...') are based on the JPS 1917 edition (see http://www.mechon-mamre.org), unless indicated otherwise, with modern English verb forms and pronouns being used.

The second member of such constructions need not be an imperative. One encounters also examples with a consecutive perfect in the second position (the "apodosis," if one so pleases):

ex. 8. *harʾē-nū nā(ʾ) ʾeṯ-məḇō(ʾ) hā-ʿīr wə-ʿāśīnū ʿimmə-ḵā ḥāseḏ* (Judg 1:24)

'show us, we pray you, the entrance into the city, and we will deal kindly with you' =
"if you show us the entrance into the city, we will be kind to you"

This phenomenon has also caught the attention of the native Arab grammarians, who commented on structures such as

ex. 9. *uṭlub tağid* 'search [and] you will/shall find' =

"if you search, you will find"[5]

which, according to the native Arab(ic) grammarians, had an underlying representation *ʾin taṭlub tağid*. According to Sībawayhi, al-Ḫalīl claimed regarding injunctive forms in a protasis position *ʾanna hāḏihī l-ʾawāʾila kulla-hā fī-hā maʿnā ʾin* "that all these first parts [of the sentence] have the inherent meaning 'if'" (Sībawayhi 1881–1889, ch. 253, p. 399).[6]

The examples in this section illustrate the ambivalent position of such sentences between paratactic and hypotactic structures: while the surface structure is clearly paratactic, the "underlying" logical form ("deep structure") is hypotactic. This is at least the standard position in the ("Eurocentric") literature that a priori associates a hypotactic structure with a conditional sentence. Whether this is really the case in Semitic, that is, whether paratactic structures cannot be equally supposed to be underlying, remains to be seen.[7]

Conditional Clauses without an Apodosis

"Defective" or elliptic conditional clauses (protases) are attested sporadically, irrespectively of whether they convey an injunctive sense. Reckendorf (1921, pp. 515f. = §264.4), among others, devotes some space to the phenomenon of conditional clauses without an apodosis. Here is an example:

ex. 10. *fa-ʾin ʾabat muhāğiratu qurayšin*

'and if the emigrants from Qurayš are unwilling [, then what?]'

A frequent explanation offered by the grammars of Arabic is that the apodosis is clear anyway in such cases and hence does not have to be spelled out. Pragmatically, such examples are not rare in oral registers of languages. In German, for instance, it is perfectly normal to utter examples as

ex. 11. *Ja, wenn du meinst.*

'Well, if you think so [, do it. (But I have warned you.)]'

Relevant examples also appear in the context of disjunctive conditional clauses (see Brockelmann 1913, p. 653 [= §439]):

ex. 12. *ʾin tamamta ʿalā mā kāna bayn-ī wa-bayna-ka wa-ʾil-lā nāğaztu-ka*

'if you fulfill our agreements [, it is good]; if not, I shall draw into battle against you'

---

[5] For a thorough discussion of such implied conditionals, see Reckendorf 1921, pp. 491f., and Peled 1987.

[6] For the topic of conditional clauses in general in the native Arab(ic) tradition, see Dévényi 1988 and 2007, as well as Versteegh 1991. See also Trumpp 1881.

[7] James Dickins (pers. comm.) points out that the intonational structure of seemingly paratactic structures (as in implied conditionals) often is indeed hypotactic, e.g., in the New York bumper sticker running "you touch-a my car I break-a your face." While "car" will be pronounced with ascending tone, "face" will be pronounced with descending tone.

Renate Jacobi (1967), Bernhard Lewin (1970), and Helmut Gätje (1976), among others, have analyzed the type of conditional clauses in which the apodosis does not express a direct consequence of the protasis, but rather reflects a logical break or split ("Bedingungssätze mit [logischer] Verschiebung" in the German grammatical nomenclature). One could also argue that the apodosis proper is missing and that the extant apodosis is really the beginning of a new syntactic period. The best-known example in this context emanates from the Joseph story as related in *sūra* 12:

ex. 13. *ʾin yasriq fa-qad saraqa ʾaḫun la-hū min qablu* (Qurʾan 12:77)

'if he has stolen [, it is not noteworthy, because] already one of his brothers has stolen earlier' (see Brockelmann 1913, p. 645 [= §430])

The further analysis of this type of "defective" conditional clause with a logical break, however, is not the subject of this paper.

Elliptic Conditional Clauses as Polite Injunctions and Oath Clauses

Based on the previous observations and, notably, Huehnergard 1983, there is solid evidence that (a) injunctives and protases have a comparable distribution, that (b) elliptic conditional clauses are typologically nothing unusual, and that (c) conditional markers are — at least in the Semitic scenario — etymologically related to certain injunctive markers. As a result, we are prepared to analyze the two most relevant types of elliptic clauses in our context. In terms of deontic modality, conditional clauses without an apodosis can constitute a formal and polite order or rather injunction. Alternatively, the elliptic conditional clauses can constitute assertory or promissory oath clauses, depending on the use of tense and/or aspect (see below). Let us turn first to the polite order or injunction type. Conditional clauses as polite injunctives (both with the real particle *ʾin* and the irreal particle *law*) are widely attested in Arabic (as they are in many other languages).[8] An example involving the particle *ʾin* is the following:

ex. 14. *fa-ʾin raʾā l-ʾamīru ʾan yaʾmura bi-ʾiṯbāti-hā la-hū*

'if the Emir wishes to order that they [2500 dirham that are the subject of this episode] be ascribed to him' = "may the Emir be so kind as to order that they be ascribed to him"

Regarding the latter example, Diem (2002, p. 136) provides a slightly different interpretation: "Wenn also der Emir befehlen möchte, sie [2500 Dirham] ihm gutzuschreiben, (dann möge er es tun!)." Examples involving the Arabic particle *law*, on which I have been focusing so far, include the following:

ex. 15. *law ʾarsalta ʾilā ṭabībin*

'if you could have sent for a doctor' (see Brockelmann 1913, p. 658 [= §443])

ex. 16. *law kāna yanfaʿu l-ʾinẓāru*

'if only the postponement would be useful' (see Reckendorf 1898, p. 709 [= §233])

ex. 17. *law raǧaʿnā*

'if we returned' = "let us return" (see Reckendorf 1921, p. 516)

ex. 18. *law ʾan-nī ʾaʿrifu-hū*

'if I only knew him'

ex. 19. *law saʾalta-hū ʾan yuqīma ʿinda-nā*

'had you only asked him to stay with us'

---

[8] See also Ullmann 1998, pp. 36f. and 53ff.

ex. 20. *ʾinna ʾabā bakrin rağulun raqīqun lā yusmiʿu n-nāsa fa-law ʾamarta ʿumara*

'ʾAbū Bakr is a weak man whose voice would be difficult for the people to hear, so I wish you ordered ʿUmar [to conduct the prayer]' (see Peled 1992, p. 53).

Comparable examples involving the conditional marker *ʾim* (which is etymologically related with both Akkadian *šumma* and Arabic *ʾin*)[9] are also found in Biblical Hebrew:

ex. 21. *ʾim tittēn ʿērāḇōn ʿaḏ šolḥe-ḵā* (Gen 38:17)

'will you give me a pledge, till thou send it' (see Brockelmann 1913, p. 658 [= §445])

The same observations hold for the conditional marker *lū*:

ex. 22. *lū yišmāʾēl yiḥye lə-p̄āne-ḵā* (Gen 17:18)

'oh that Ishmael might live before You!' (see Brockelmann 1956, p. 6 [= §8b])

In Gəʿəz, one also finds relevant examples involving the particles *sōba* and *ʾəm*:

ex. 23. *sōba mōtna*

'had we only died' (see Brockelmann 1913, p. 658 [= §443])

ex. 24. *ʾəm nassāḥku*

'if (only) I had repented!' (see Lipiński 2001, p. 547)

Huehnergard (1983, p. 570), based on Wagner (1953, p. 19 [= §24]), also adduces a relevant example from the Modern South Arabian language Jibbali (or "Śḥeri"):

ex. 25. *bu-lú yəkīn ʿáśri*

'would that he were my husband'

Comparable Akkadian examples involving the particle *lū* exhibit a wider semantic range (see Huehnergard 1983, p. 572, and 2005, p. 326). I do not consider here concessive clauses (e.g., *kussī-šu lū iḫḫaser* 'even though his saddle was broken') and alternatives in a string of clauses (e.g., *šumma awīlum lū kaspam lū ḫurāṣam lū wardam lū amtam ... ū lū mimma šumšu ... ištām* 'if a man has purchased (be it) silver, (be it) gold, (be it) a male slave, (be it) a female slave ... or anything at all ...' = Codex Hammurabi §7), which are not directly germane to the discussion at hand. Relevant examples, however, are as follow:

1. Optative

ex. 26. *lū ašpur-aš-šum*

'would that I had written him' = "I should have written him" / "had I only written him"

ex. 27. *lū awīlat*

'would that you were a man' = "(may you) be a man" (see von Soden 1995, p. 292 [= §185b], and Huehnergard 1983, pp. 572–74)

2. Attainable wishes and injunctions:

ex. 28. *sîn ... lū rābiṣ lemutti-šu*

'may Sîn be the bringer of evil against him'

[9] As is well known, comparable phonological correspondence (š / h / ʾ) is also attested in the Semitic personal pronouns and causative prefixes (see, e.g., D. O. Edzard 1984 and Lipiński 2001, pp. 547f.). Contra Voigt (1995), I do not believe that it is meaningful to reconstruct a proto-form in this context.

ex. 29. *lū šalmāta lū balṭāta*

'(may you) be well and healthy'

3. Asseverative particle in oaths (before preterite and durative):

ex. 30. *lū išām*

'indeed he [will have] purchased'

ex. 31. *lū anaddi-kum*

'I will certainly give you'

Let us turn now to the other type of elliptic conditional clauses, namely the so-called oath clauses. There is a clear semantic connection between the oath clauses in Classical Arabic and *šumma* (*lā*) clauses in Akkadian contractual documents (and elsewhere). In both cases, one can reasonably argue that grammaticalization has taken place. The "missing" apodosis is no longer felt as such. Grammaticalized *ʾin* / *ʾil-lā* oath clauses are widespread in Classical Arabic. Here are some relevant examples:

ex. 32. *ʾanšudu llāha ʿabdan ʿalima ʾanna l-ī tawbatan ʾil-lā ʾaḫbara-nī*

'I implore — by God — a man, who knows my repentence, to tell me' (see Brockelmann 1913, p. 657 [= §443])

ex. 33. *bi-ḥayāt-ī ʾil-lā ʾanšadta-nī l-bayta*

'by my life, you must recite this verse for me'

ex. 34. *našadtu-ka llāha ʾin rimta hāḏā l-makāna ʾabadan*

'I implore you to never leave this place'

ex. 35. *ʾaqsamtu ʿalay-kum ʾin baraḥtum*

'I implore you not to go away' (see Nöldeke 1897, p. 114)

ex. 36. *ʾaqsamtu ʿalay-ka ʾil-lā ḫaṭabta Lubnā li-bni-ka Qays*

'I implore you to marry Lubnā with your son Qays'

Wright (1967, vol. 2, pp. 339f. [= §186, Rem. c]) and W. Fischer (2006, pp. 205f. [= §456]), among others, devote some space to this kind of logically inverted oath clauses. The idea is that the negative consequence (apodosis) of the protasis (e.g., *ʾil-lā ḫaṭabta Lubnā li-bni-ka Qays* in the last example) is not mentioned, but nevertheless implied. Therefore, a translation *à la* "I implore you ..." is warranted in such cases.

Comparable examples are found in both Akkadian (ex. 37) and Hebrew (ex. 38) (see Brockelmann 1913, p. 658 [= §445]), and, according to Lipiński (2001, p. 549), even in Tamazight Berber (ex. 39):[10]

ex. 37. *šumma lā iqbi-an-ni*

'if he didn't tell me [that], [may I die]' = "he must tell me"

ex. 38. *ʾim lō(ʾ) neḥzaq mē-hem*

'if we shall not be stronger than they, [may I die]' = "we must be stronger than them"

ex. 39. *uḷḷah mš žriḫ*

'by God, if I have thrown [it], [may I die]'

[10] Examples 37–39 are excerpted from Lipiński 2001, p. 549.

A number of Hebrew oath clauses compiled by Brockelmann (1913, pp. 658f. [= §445], and 1956, pp. 161f. [= §170]) illustrate the phenomenon of logical conversion after the particle *ʾim* even better:

ex. 40. *tәhī nā ʾālā bēnōṯē-nū ... ʾim taʿăśē ʿimmā-nū rāʿā* (Gen 26:28–29)

'let there now be an oath between us ... that you will do us no hurt'

ex. 41. *wә-ḥē nap̄še-ḵā ʾim ʾeʿśe ʾeṯ-had-dāḇār haz-ze* (2 Sam 11:11)

'and as your soul lives, I will not do this thing' (see GKC 472 = §149c)

ex. 42. *hinә-nī nišbaʿtī bi-šm-ī hag-gāḏōl ʾāmar YHWH ʾim yihye ʿōḏ šәmī niqrā(ʾ) bә-p̄ī kol ʾīš yәhūḏā ʾōmēr ḥay ʾăḏōn-āy YHWH bә-ḵol ʾereṣ miṣrāyim* (Jer 44:26)

'I hereby swear by my great name, says YHWH — my name shall no more be invoked in the mouth of every Judahite in the land of Egypt who says "(by) the Lord YHWH's life"' (see Waltke and O'Connor 1990, p. 679 = §40.2.2b)

Again, the (negative) apodoses to the protases *ʾim taʿăśē ʿimmā-nū rāʿā*, *ʾim ʾeʿśe ʾeṯ-had-dāḇār haz-ze*, and *ʾim yihye ʿōḏ šәmī niqrā(ʾ) bә-p̄ī kol ʾīš yәhūḏā* ..., are omitted in these examples, thus yielding the inverted logical meaning.

Let it also be mentioned that concessive *kī ʾim* clauses may have their origin in such elliptic constructions, as claimed by Brockelmann (1913, p. 659 [= §445c], and 1956, p. 162 [= §170c]).[11] An example is the following:

ex. 43. *ḥē p̄arʿō(h) ʾim-tēṣәʾū miz-ze kī ʾim bә-ḇō(ʾ) ʾăḥī-ḵem haq-qāṭan hēnnā* (Gen 42:15)

'as Pharaoh lives, you shall not go forth hence, except your youngest brother come hither'

šumma (*lā*) Clauses in Akkadian Treaties

As was stated initially, the phenomenon of (seemingly) elliptic conditional clauses is already attested in Akkadian and analyzed as such in Wolfram von Soden's *Grundriss* (1995, p. 293 [= §185g–i]) and John Huehnergard's *Grammar* (2005, p. 438 [= §36.3]). Clauses in contracts and treaties beginning with *šumma* 'if' can be translated by "may you not," and clauses beginning with *šumma lā* can be translated by "may you." (This is not to say that *all* contractual clauses have to start out in this way.) Formally, one could argue that the apodosis is introduced later in the treaty, when the dire consequences are listed, which apply in the case that the contracting parties do not follow up on the individual clauses. Streck (1998), however, argues against this view.

The Vassal Treaties of Esarhaddon with various Iranian notables are an important case in point (see Wiseman 1958 for the *editio princeps* as well as Reiner 1969, pp. 534–41; Borger 1961/1964; 1983, pp. 160–76; Watanabe 1987; and Parpola and Watanabe 1988 for further editions and translations). Streck (1998, pp. 187–90) has analyzed the syntactic function of the *šumma* (*lā*) clauses in this context. Referring to previous works, *inter alia* by Watanabe (1987, pp. 28ff.) and Parpola and Watanabe (1988), he comes to the conclusion that genuine conditional clauses in this textual genre have either a perfect predicate (e.g., §7, lines 83–84: *šumma* [...] *ana šīmti ittalak* 'if [...] he has died ...') or a stative (verbal adjective) predicate (e.g., §12, lines 138–39: *šumma* [...] *ṣabāti-šunu duāki-šunu maṣâkunu* ... 'if you can arrest (and) kill them ...'). Grammaticalized *šumma* (*lā*) clauses (a term not used by Streck), however, are always characterized by a predicate in the imperfect (durative), typically in the subjunctive ("affirmative") (e.g., §4, line 55: *šumma attunu tunakkarā-šu-ni* '(by God), you will not be hostile to him') and have to be considered syntactically independent in a synchronic perspective.[12] While it is true that promissory oaths are usually expressed by a predicate in the durative (imperfect), the perfect can also occur in such structures, as in example

[11] On the issue of concessive clauses in this context, see also Huehnergard 1983, p. 574.

[12] See Streck 1998, p. 190: "Daher [...] sind sind die Stipulationen [i.e., the individual paragraphs of the treaty, LE] und die Flüche nicht als Protasen und Apodosen eines Konditionalgefüges, sondern als syntaktisch selbständig und die Stipulationen als Schwüre aufzufassen." Already Brockelmann (1913, p. 641 [= §425]) made the point that the verbs in Akkadian protases lacked the final vowels typical of verbs in subordinate clauses. See also D. O. Edzard 1973 on the question of "moods" in Akkadian in relation to the concept of "subordination."

3 cited above: *šumma ... lā attalk-ak-kim-ma u ṣibût-ki lā ētepuš* 'I will certainly come to you and carry out your wish' (see von Soden 1995, p. 293 [= §185g]).

In the large volume *Ancient Near Eastern Texts Relating to the Old Testament*, Erica Reiner (1969) concedes this grammatical point ("oath clauses") but chooses nevertheless to translate the individual paragraphs with conditional clauses introduced by "if (not)," as do Borger (1983) and Watanabe (1987) in their German translations, but not Wiseman and Parpola/Watanabe in their editions of 1958 and 1988, respectively. In order to illustrate this central issue, the translations of Reiner (1969), followed by Borger (1983), and Wiseman (1958), followed by Parpola and Watanabe (1988), are reproduced in the following excerpts of the treaty (following the transcription in Watanabe 1987, pp. 146, 156, and 162). Here is the first set of provisions in the treaty, which is embedded in paragraph 4:[13]

ex. 44. Vassal Treaties of Esarhaddon, example of several grammaticalized injunctive protases

49 *<šumma attunu> ina eqli ina berti āli*[14]
50 *lā tanaṣṣarā-šū-ni ina muḫḫi-šu lā tamaḫḫaṣā-ni*
51 *lā tamuttā-ni ina ketti ša libbī-kunu*
52 *issē-šu lā tadabbubā-ni milku danqu*
53 *ša gammurti libbī-kunu lā tamallikā-šu-ni*
54 *ḫarrānu danqu ina šēpē-šu lā tašakkanā-ni*
55 *šumma attunu tunakkarā-šu-ni issu libbi aḫḫī-šu*
56 *rabûti ṣaḫ(e)rūti ina kūmu-šu ina kussî Aššur*
57 *tušeššabā-ni šumma abutu ša Aššur-aḫu-iddina šar māt Aššur*
58 *tennânī tušannâ-ni šumma Aššur-bāni-apli marʾa rabiʾu*
59 *ša bēt ridūti ša Aššur-aḫu-iddina šar māt Aššur (bēl-kunu)*
60 *(ukallimū-ka-nūni) ḫanûmma lā tadaggalā-ni*
61 *šarruttu bēluttu ša māt Aššur ina muḫḫi-kunu lā u[pp]ašu-nī*

49 You will
50 protect him in the country and in town; you will fight,
51 and (even) will die, for him. You will speak
52 with him in the truth of your heart, you will give
53 him sound advice loyally.
54 You will set a fair path at his feet.
55 (You swear) that you will not be hostile to him nor will you
56 seat one of his brothers, older or younger, on the throne of Assyria
57 in stead of him. That the word of Esarhaddon, king of Assyria,
58 you will neither change nor alter. That you will
59 serve only Ashurbanipal, the crown-prince,
60 whom Esarhaddon, king of Assyria, your lord (hereby commends),
61 that he will exercise the kingship and dominion over you

(Vassal Treaties of Esarhaddon, §4, Wiseman 1958, pp. 32, 34)

[13] The paragraph numbering is, of course, a modern editorial convention. Still, as in this example, a paragraph may comprise several provisions. Otherwise, both the transcription and the translations are oriented at the line structure in the original tablets (often they cannot be made to be totally overlapping).

[14] *<šumma attunu>* probably has to be supplemented here in the initial lacuna; see Watanabe 1987, pp. 61, 146.

If you do not serve him in the open country and in the city, do not fight and even die on his behalf, do not always speak the full truth to him, do not always advise him well in full loyalty, do not smooth his way in every respect; if you remove him, and seat in his stead one of his brothers, younger or older on the throne of Assyria, if you change or let anyone change the decree of Esarhaddon, king of Assyria, if you will not be subject to this crown prince designate Ashurbanipal, son of Esarhaddon, king of Assyria, your lord, so that he cannot exercise kingship and lordship over you.

(Vassal Treaties of Esarhaddon, §4, Reiner 1969, p. 545)

After a while, the list of clauses is interrupted by paragraph 25, which restates the "ground rules" of the treaty in the form of an anacoluth (part of §25). As we see below, this circumstance lends support to the idea of analyzing both the stipulations and the curses of the treaty as (synchronically) independent syntactic units:

ex. 45. Vassal Treaties of Esarhaddon, example of an intervening anacoluth

283 *adê annûte ša Aššur-aḫu-iddina šar māt Aššur*

284 *ina muḫḫi Aššur-bāni-apli marʾi šarri rabiʾi ša bēt ridūti*

285 *u aḫḫē-šu marʾē ummī-šu ša Aššur-bāni-apli marʾi šarri rabiʾi*

286 *ša bēt ridūti udanninū-ni issē-kunu*

287 *iškunū-ni tāmītu utammû-ka-nūni*

283 As for these treaty-provisions which Esarhaddon, king of Assyria,

284 has firmly made with you concerning Ashurbanipal,

285 the crown-prince (and) his brothers, son(s) by the same mother

286 as Ashurbanipal, the crown-prince,

287 he has made you take an oath

(Vassal Treaties of Esarhaddon, §25, Wiseman 1958, p. 50)

This treaty which Esarhaddon, king of Assyria, has established with you in a binding fashion, under oath, on behalf of the crown prince designate Ashurbanipal and his brothers, sons by the mother of the crown prince designate Ashurbanipal.

(Vassal Treaties of Esarhaddon, §25, Reiner 1969, p. 537)

Finally, paragraphs 35 and 36 of the treaty stipulate that the tablet on which the treaty is written may not be altered in any way, let alone be destroyed. It is only in paragraphs 37 to 106 that the series of dire sanctions set in, should the treaty not be followed. Here are paragraphs 37, 38, and 38A:

ex. 46. Vassal Treaties of Esarhaddon, example of several apodoses (curse formulae)

414 *Aššur šar ilānī mušīm [šīmāti] šīmat lemutti*

415 *lā ṭābti liš[īm-k]unu šabût* (older editions: *abutu*) *šēbūtu*

416 *kišid littū[ti a]ji iqīš-kunu*

417 *Mullissu ḫīrtu narāmta-šu amāt pî-šu*

418 *lilammin-ma aji iṣbata abbūt-kun*

419 *Sîn nannar šamê u erṣetim saḫaršubbû*

420 *liḫallip-kunu ina pān(ē) ilānī u šarri e<r>ēb-kunu aji iqbi*

421 *kīma sirrē-me ṣabīti ina ṣērim rupdā*

414 '(if you do,) [may Ashur, king of the] gods who decrees the fates,
415 [decree for you] evil and not good. May he never grant
416 you fatherhood and attainment of old age.
417 [May Ninlil], his beloved wife [evilly interpret the] utterance
418 of his mouth evil, may she not intercede for you.
419 [May Sin], the brightness of heaven and earth, clothe you with
420 [a lep]rosy; [may he forbid you entering into the presence of the gods]
421 [or king (saying): 'Roam the desert] like the wild-ass (and the ga-zelle'

(Vassal Treaties of Esarhaddon, §§37, 38, and 38A, Wiseman 1958, p. 60)

May Ashur, king of the gods, who determines the fates, decree for you an evil, unpropitious fate, and not grant you fatherhood, old age, ... ripe old age. May Ninlil, his beloved wife, induce him to pronounce evil for you and may she not intercede for you. May Anu, king of the gods, rain upon all your houses disease, exhaustion, *diʾu*-disease, sleeplessness, worries, ill health. May Sin, the luminary of heaven and earth, clothe you in leprosy and (thus) not permit you to enter the presence of god and king; roam the open country as a wild ass or gazelle!

(Vassal Treaties of Esarhaddon, §§37, 38, and 38A, Reiner 1969, p. 538)

Interestingly, the structure of the treaty allows for both a diachronic and a synchronic analysis of the *šumma* (*lā*) clauses. From a bird's perspective, the large apodosis in the form of dire sanctions stipulates a diachronic analysis. Thus, *šumma* (*lā*) can be literally translated as "if (not)," as done by Reiner (1969), Borger (1983), and Watanabe (1987). Read in isolation, and especially in view of the intervening anacoluths (e.g., §25 cited above), a synchronic analysis is warranted, which parses the (historically) conditional *šumma* (*lā*) clauses as grammaticalized oath sentences, in line with Parpola and Watanabe's (1988) and Streck's (1998) analyses. Such sentences can be rendered simply by an injunctive form, which reverses the "Boolean" value of the clause — that is, a sentence starting with *šumma* will be translated as "You will (certainly) not ...," and a sentence starting with *šumma lā* will be translated as "You will (certainly) ...." As we have seen, Wiseman (1958) already exploited this option in his translation, which works out nicely, especially in view of the intervening anacoluths in the treaty body.[15] Needless to say, the curses then have also to be understood as independent syntactic units, not as apodoses.

Conclusion

Given the comparative Semitic scenario regarding the particles *lū*/*law* and **l*(*v*), on the one hand, and typological observations on "elliptic" conditional clauses, on the other hand, the functioning of the Akkadian *šumma* (*lā*) oath clauses appears to be perfectly natural and understandable. The explanation of such syntactic constructions was further corroborated by recourse to the evidence of comparable constructions in Classical Arabic with *ʾin*/*ʾil-lā* and *law*/*law lā*, as well as in Biblical Hebrew with *ʾim*/*ʾim lō*(*ʾ*) and occasionally *lū*. The issue of whether the constructions in question diachronically are truly "elliptic" (a notion that is problematic in the first place) must remain open. Especially in view of the comparable distribution of independent or paratactic injunctive clauses, on the one hand, and genuine conditional clauses, on the other hand, it is equally possible that these constructions are just traces of originally independent optative clauses. In that perspective, the concept of grammaticalization would not really be pertinent here.[16]

---

[15] Streck (1998, p. 190 n. 46) also adduces the case of the intervening precative form *lipluḫū* 'let them revere' in §34, line 396, which supports the syntactic independence of the stipulations and the curses.

[16] Rubin (2005) does not include optative/conditional particles in his overview of grammaticalization phenomena in Semitic.

Abbreviation

GKC — Wilhelm Gesenius, Emil Kautzsch, and Arthur E. Cowley. *Gesenius' Hebrew Grammar*. Edited by E. Kautzsch, translated by A. E. Cowley. 2nd English edition. Oxford: Clarendon Press, 1910.

Bibliography

Bergsträsser, Gotthelf

1918–1929 *Hebräische Grammatik.* Leipzig: J. C. Hinrichs.

Borger, Rykle

1961/1964 "Zu den Asarhaddon-Verträgen aus Nimrud." *Zeitschrift für Assyriologie* 54 (1961): 173–96; 56 (1964): 261.

1983 "Assyrische Staatsverträge." In *Texte aus der Umwelt des Alten Testaments*, edited by Rykle Borger and Otto Kaiser, pp. 155–77. Gütersloh: Gerd Mohn.

Borger, Rykle, and Otto Kaiser

1983 *Texte aus der Umwelt des Alten Testaments* I/2. Gütersloh: Gerd Mohn.

Brockelmann, Carl

1913 *Grundriss der vergleichenden Grammatik der semitischen Sprachen*, Volume 2: *Syntax*. Berlin: Reuther and Reichard.

1956 *Hebräische Syntax.* Neukirchen: Verlag der Buchhandlung des Erziehungsvereins Neukirchen Kreis Moers.

Dévényi, Kinga

1988 "The Treatment of Conditional Sentences by the Mediaeval Arabic Grammarians: Stability and Change in the History of Arabic Grammar." *The Arabist: Budapest Studies in Arabic* 1: 11–42.

2007 "Jazaʾ." In *Encyclopedia of Arabic Language and Linguistics*, Volume 2, edited by Kees Versteegh, pp. 477–81. Leiden: Brill.

Diakonoff, Igor

1965 *Semitokhamitskie jazyki: Opyt klassifikatsii (Semito-Hamitic Languages: Essays in Classification).* Moscow: Nauka.

Diehl, Johannes F.

2004 *Die Fortführung des Imperativs im Biblischen Hebräisch.* Münster: Ugarit-Verlag.

Diem, Werner

2002 "Nichtsubordinatives modales *ʾan yafʿala*: Ein Beitrag zur Syntax der nachklassischen arabischen Schriftsprache." In *"Sprich doch mit deinen Knechten aramäisch, wir verstehen es!" 60 Beiträge zur Semitistik: Festschrift für Otto Jastrow zum 60. Geburtstag*, edited by Otto Jastrow, Werner Arnold, and Hartmut Bobzin, pp. 113–45. Wiesbaden: Harrassowitz.

Edzard, Dietz Otto

1973 "Die Modi beim älteren akkadischen Verbum." *Orientalia* 42: 121–41.

1984 "'Ursemitisch' **hūʾa, *šīʾa?*" *Studia Orientalia* 55/10: 249–56.

Edzard, Lutz

2010 "Injunctive Protases and the Grammaticalisation of Elliptic Conditional Clauses in Semitic." In *Verbal Festivity in Arabic and other Semitic Languages* (Proceedings of the Workshop at the Universitätsclub Bonn on January 16, 2009), edited by Lutz Edzard and Stephan Guth, pp. 74–93. Wiesbaden: Harrassowitz.

Fischer, August

1948 "Grammatisch schwierige Schwur- und Beschwörungsformeln des Klassischen Arabisch." *Der Islam* 28: 1–105.

Fischer, Wolfdietrich

2006 *Grammatik des Klassischen Arabisch.* 4th edition. Wiesbaden: Harrassowitz.

Gätje, Helmut

1976 "Zur Struktur gestörter Konditionalgefüge im Arabischen." *Oriens* 25–26: 148–86.

Haiman, John

1983 "Paratactic If-clauses." *Journal of Pragmatics* 7: 263–81.

1986 "Constraints on the Form and Meaning of the Protasis." In *On Conditionals*, edited by Elizabeth C. Traugott, Alice ter Meulen, Judith Snitzer-Reilly, and Charles A. Ferguson, pp. 215–27. Cambridge: Cambridge University Press.

Huehnergard, John

1983 "Asseverative **la* and Hypothetical **lu/law* in Semitic." *Journal of the American Oriental Society* 103/3: 569–93.

2005 *A Grammar of Akkadian.* 2nd edition. Winona Lake: Eisenbrauns.

Jacobi, Renate

1967 "Bedingungssätze mit Verschiebung." *Zeitschrift der Deutschen Morgenländischen Gesellschaft* 117: 78–86.

König, Ekkehard

1986 "Conditionals, Concessive Conditionals and Concessives." In *On Conditionals*, edited by Elizabeth C. Traugott, Alice ter Meulen, Judith Snitzer-Reilly, and Charles A. Ferguson, pp. 229–246. Cambridge: Cambridge University Press.

Larcher, Pierre

2009 "Les systèmes conditionnels en *ʾin* de l'arabe classique." *Bulletin d'études orientales* 58: 205–32.

Lawler, John M.

1975 "Elliptical Conditionals and/or Hyperbolic Imperatives: Some Remarks on the Inherent Inadequacy of Derivations." In *Papers from the Eleventh Regional Meeting of the Chicago Linguistic Society*, edited by Robin E. Grossman, L. James San, and Timothy J. Vance, pp. 371–82. Chicago: Chicago Linguistic Society.

Lewin, Bernhard

1970 "Non-conditional 'If' Clauses in Arabic." *Zeitschrift der Deutschen Morgenländischen Gesellschaft* 120: 264–70.

Lipiński, Edward

2001 *Semitic Languages: Outline of a Comparative Grammar.* 2nd edition. Orientalia Lovaniensia analecta 80. Leuven: Peeters.

Nöldeke, Theodor

1897 *Zur Grammatik des classischen Arabisch.* Vienna: C. Gerold. Reprinted Darmstadt: Wissenschaftliche Buchgesellschaft, 1963.

Nötscher, Friedrich

1953 "Zum emphatischen Lamed." *Vetus Testamentum* 3: 372–80.

Parpola, Simo, and Kazuo Watanabe

1988 *Neo-Assyrian Treaties and Loyalty Oaths.* State Archives of Assyria 2. Helsinki: Helsinki University Press.

Peled, Yishai

1987 "Conditional Sentences without a Conditional Particle in Classical Arabic Prose." *Zeitschrift für Arabische Linguistik* 16: 31–43.

1992 *Conditional Structures in Classical Arabic.* Wiesbaden: Harrassowitz.

Pritchard, James B.

1969 *Ancient Near Eastern Texts Relating to the Old Testament.* 3rd edition. Princeton: Princeton University Press.

Reckendorf, Hermann

1898 *Die syntaktischen Verhältnisse des Arabischen.* Leiden: Brill.

1921 *Arabische Syntax.* Heidelberg: Carl Winter.

Reiner, Erica

1969 "Akkadian Treaties from Syria and Assyria." In *Ancient Near Eastern Texts Relating to the Old Testament*, edited by James B. Pritchard, pp. 531–41. Princeton: Princeton University Press.

Rubin, Aaron D.

2005 *Studies in Semitic Grammaticalization.* Winona Lake: Eisenbrauns.

Sībawayhi, ʾAbū Bišr ʿAmr ibn ʿUṯmān

1881–89 *Kitāb Sībawayhi: Traité de grammaire arabe.* 2 volumes. Edited by Hartwig Derenbourg. Paris: Imprimerie Nationale. Reprinted Hildesheim: G. Olms, 1970.

Streck, Michael P.
1998 "Die Flüche im Sukzessionsvertrag Asarhaddons." *Zeitschrift für Altorientalische und Biblische Rechtsgeschichte* 4: 165–91.

Testen, David
1993 "The East Semitic Precative Paradigm." *Journal of Semitic Studies* 38/1: 1–13.

Tietz, Renate
1963 Bedingungssatz und Bedingungsausdruck im Koran. Ph.D. dissertation. Tübingen.

Traugott, Elizabeth C.; Alice ter Meulen; Judith Snitzer-Reilly; and Charles A. Ferguson
1986 *On Conditionals.* Cambridge: Cambridge University Press.

Trumpp, Ernst
1881 *Der Bedingungssatz im Arabischen.* Sitzungsberichte der Königlich Bayerischen Akademie der Wissenschaften zu München, Philosophisch-philologische Klasse 2/4. Munich: Bayerischen Akademie der Wissenschaften.

Ullmann, Manfred
1998 *Sätze mit lau.* Beiträge zur Lexikographie des klassischen Arabisch 14. Munich: Bayerischen Akademie der Wissenschaften.

Versteegh, Kees
1991 "Two Conceptions of Irreality in Arabic Grammar: Ibn Hišām and Ibn Ḥāǧib on the Particle *Law.*" *Bulletin d'Études Orientales* 43: 77–89.

Voigt, Rainer M.
1995 "Akkadisch *šumma* 'wenn' und die Konditionalpartikeln des Westsemitischen." In *Vom Alten Orient zum Alten Testament: Festschrift für Wolfram Freiherrn von Soden zum 85. Geburtstag am 19. Juni 1993*, edited by Manfried Dietrich and Oswald Loretz, pp. 517–28. Alter Orient und Altes Testament 240. Kevelaer: Butzon and Bercker.

von Soden, Wolfram
1995 *Grundriss der akkadischen Grammatik.* 3rd edition. Analecta orientalia 33. Rome: Pontificium Institutum Biblicum.

Wagner, Ewald
1953 *Syntax der Mehri-Sprache: Unter Berücksichtigung auch der anderen neusüdarabischen Sprachen.* Berlin: Akademie-Verlag.

Waltke, Bruce, and Michael O'Connor
1990 *An Introduction to Biblical Hebrew Syntax.* Winona Lake: Eisenbrauns.

Watanabe, Kazuo
1987 *Die adê-Vereidigung anläßlich der Thronfolgeregelung Asarhaddons.* Baghdader Mitteilungen, Beiheft 3. Berlin: Gebr. Mann.

Wiseman, Donald J.
1958 *The Vassal-treaties of Esarhaddon.* London: The British School of Archeology in Iraq.

Wright, William
1967 *A Grammar of the Arabic Language.* 3rd edition. 2 volumes. Translated from the German of Caspari, rev. W. Robertson Smith and M. J. de Goeje. Cambridge: Cambridge University Press.

3

t-Stem Verbs without Metathesis in Aramaic and Hebrew Documents from the Judean Desert

Steven E. Fassberg, The Hebrew University of Jerusalem

1. Introduction

The publication over the past sixty years of Aramaic and Hebrew documents from the Judean Desert has dramatically transformed our understanding of the linguistic landscape in Palestine before and after the beginning of the Common Era. The Aramaic manuscripts have demonstrated the heterogeneity and dialectal variation of the language during the Middle Aramaic period; the Hebrew documents have done the same for the Hebrew of the late Second Temple period and for Tannaitic Hebrew. The linguistic impact of the finds from the Judean Desert — the Dead Sea Scrolls, Ben Sira, the Bar Kosiba letters, and legal documents — cannot be overestimated.

One salient feature of the Aramaic and Hebrew documents that has surfaced since the publication of the first documents in the 1950s is the extent of *t*-stem verbs without the expected metathesis of the derivational *t* and an initial sibilant radical. In addition, there are now examples from the Judean Desert of the lack of partial assimilation of derivational *t* to a neighboring *z*, as well as the total assimilation of *z* to derivational *t*. Qimron (1976, pp. 189–81; 1986, pp. 55–56) has collected the relevant Hebrew material, Folmer (2003) the Aramaic, and Mor (2009, pp. 95–96) has added some additional observations. The Hebrew forms, according to Qimron, reflect spoken speech. Folmer, on the other hand, hesitates to draw a definitive conclusion from the Aramaic data, noting that the non-metathesized forms might be due to speech, substandardness, or hypercorrection.

Before the discovery of the Judean Desert documents, a few non-metathesized forms were known from Nabatean and Palmyrene; there were also isolated examples of the lack of partial assimilation of *t* to a neighboring *z*, as well as of the total assimilation of *z* to *t*. The new examples from the Judean Desert corroborate the existence and extent of the phenomenon. The relationship of the non-metathesized forms to earlier and later forms in Aramaic and Hebrew, however, has not yet been fully explained. The purpose of this paper is to examine the origin and development of the non-metathesized *t*-stem verbs in Middle Aramaic and in the Hebrew of the Dead Sea Scrolls in the light of the diachronic development of both languages. The wider perspective of comparative Semitics will also be taken into consideration.

2. Evidence from Middle Aramaic, and from Second Temple and Tannaitic Hebrew

2.1. Aramaic

The *t*-stems with I-sibilant roots in the Aramaic Dead Sea Scrolls correspond to what is common in earlier and later Aramaic, namely, metathesis of *t* and an I-sibilant radical (Fitzmyer 2004, p. 280; Sokoloff 1974, pp. 181–82).

See, for example, אשתני 'it changed' (1QGenAp II 11), אשתבשון 'they were confused' (1QGenAp V 16). One also finds metathesis and partial assimilation of *t* to *z*, for example, אזדהרו 'be careful!' (1QTQohath ar I i 4).

The situation differs, however, in Jewish Aramaic documents from after the destruction of the First Temple (68 C.E.) until the end of the Second Revolt (135 C.E.), where only non-metathesized forms are attested. Examples from the legal documents include אתזבן 'it was sold' (5/6Hev 7:16,54 [P. Yadin 7]) and יתשוי 'it will be placed' (Ketef Jericho 3:5 [DJD 38]). In three other verbs, which are also from legal documents, there is no metathesis, if one analyzes the forms as אִתְפְּעֵל (tG), and not אִתַּפְעַל (tC):[1] מתזנן 'they are provided for' (5/6Hev 10:14,15 [P. Yadin 10] and Mur 21:11) and מתזנה 'she is provided for' (Mur 21:15). Another possible example with derivational *t*, תשבתא/יי (5/6Hev 10 [P. Yadin 10]), is apparently an error for תשתבא/יי 'you will be taken captive.' The Bar-Kosiba letters reveal more non-metathesized forms: התשכו (= התשכחו) 'they were found' (P. Yadin 54:6), יתשכח 'he will be found' (P. Yadin 54:10), התשדר 'send!' (P. Yadin 53:4). An additional example, whose reading is not certain, is תדהרון 'you should be careful' (P. Yadin 50:6); the orthography seems to reflect the total assimilation of the initial radical *z* to the derivational *t* > *d*.[2]

In Nabatean, on the other hand, one finds both metathesized and non-metathesized I-sibilant verbs. The forms without metathesis, which, some have argued, reflect the Arabic V stem تَفَعَّلَ,[3] are יתשנא 'he will change' (CIS II 350:4)[4] and יתזבן 'he will be sold' (CIS II, 208:4). Nabatean forms with metathesis are ויזתבן 'he will be sold' (but without partial assimilation; Jaussen and Savignac 1909, p. 151, 5:5) and ישתכח 'he will be found' (Hammond, Johnson, and Jones 1986, 78:3).

Palmyrene, like Nabatean, has both metathesized and non-metathesized I-sibilant verbs. There is one unequivocal non-metathesized example: מתזבנא 'she is sold' (CIS II, 132). Context demands that two additional forms from the famous tariff of Palmyra be taken as *t*-stems with assimilated derivational *t*: יזבן 'he will be sold' (CIS II, 3913 ii 56), מזבן 'he is sold' (CIS II, 3913 ii 136). Metathesis is attested in Palmyrene in משתדן 'they are thrown away' (CIS II, 3913 ii 108) and אשתח (= אשתכח) 'it was found' (Inv 10 127:3).

In Hatran the evidence with sibilants is limited to three examples, all of which exhibit metathesis (Beyer 1998, p. 138): אצטבו 'they agreed' (H336b:2; 343:2) and משתמשין 'they are served' (H408:7). There is total regressive assimilation of derivational *t* to the first radical in two other examples without sibilants (Beyer 1998, p. 128): לקטיל (< לתקטל) 'he will be killed' (H336b:10; 343:7) and לרגים (<לתקטל) 'he will be stoned' (H343:9).

A transcription of Aramaic in the New Testament also shows an example of an assimilated derivational *t* (Morag 1972): ἐφφαθά (=אִתְפְּתַח) 'be opened!' (Mark 7:34).

2.2. Hebrew

Metathesis is the rule with triliteral verbs in the Hebrew Dead Sea Scrolls in both biblical and non-biblical texts (Qimron 1976, p. 180; 1986, p. 55). The majority of quadriliteral verbs show metathesis,[5] though non-metathesis is attested in תתזעזע 'she will be shaken' (1QH XIV 27) and יתשגשגו 'they will grow tall' (1QH XVI 9). There are a few other curious examples that would appear to reflect a certain confusion on the part of scribes (Qimron 1986, pp. 55–56). In ת'ד(ז)עזע 'she will be shaken' (1QH XV 9; cf. 1QS VIII 8 יזדעזעו), the scribe has clearly erased a *zayin* after the *daleth* and added another *zayin* after the *taw*; the form before the erasure and addition of supralinear *zayin* is a non-metathesized form with partial assimilation (תדזעזע), whereas the form after erasure and with the supralinear addition turns the verb into the classical form with metathesis (תזדעזע). In התשעתשעו (1QIsa[a] 29:9) the incorrectly placed second *taw* above the line suggests scribal uncertainty (Kutscher 1974, p. 346).

Qimron (1976, p. 102) wonders if the orthographies of two more examples originate in a tension between what the scribe may have said or heard and what he knows to be the classical form: יזד עזרע (= יזדעזע?) (1QS X1 4); תשת שע (= תשתעשע) (1QH[a] XVII 8). Another possible form shows up in a document from after the destruction

---

[1] See §3.2 below.

[2] For expected תזדהרון. See Folmer 2003, p. 234 n. 6, for a discussion of the form, and n. 26 below.

[3] For bibliography, see Folmer 2003, p. 238, who shows convincingly that the phenomenon need not be attributed to Arabic. See also Morgenstern 1999, p. 139.

[4] In the same inscription, there are two examples of non-I-sibilant verbs: יתבקר 'it will be examined' (CIS II, 350:3) and יתרהן 'it will be pawned' (CIS II, 350:4). The root רהן is clearly a loan from Arabic.

[5] Qimron (1986, p. 55) mentions ten examples.

of the Second Temple: ומתשדר 'and sends/strives?' (Mur 49:3).[6] This verb is typically Aramaic, yet the occurrence of]ש במקום in the same extremely fragmentary text makes it impossible to decide if ומתשדר is an Aramaism in a Hebrew text or]ש במקום is a Hebraism in an Aramaic text.

The late medieval, artificial hybrid of Hebrew and Aramaic known as Late Samaritan Hebrew (Florentin 2005, pp. 203–07, 230–34) also evidences many examples of *t* preceding a sibilant (יתסגי 'it will increase') and *t* following a sibilant (משתמע 'it is heard').

3. Comparative and Diachronic Evidence

3.1. Comparative Semitic

t-stems are generally thought to have been formed in Proto-Semitic with a prefixed derivational *t*,[7] but when the first verbal radical was a sibilant, the *t* metathesized with the sibilant.[8] According to Greenberg (1950, pp. 175–88), this was part of a general Semitic phonological restriction on dentals followed by sibilants.[9] It is widely held that the infixing of *t* in sibilant environments was later generalized to other radicals in certain daughter languages (Wright 1890, p. 208; Bergsträsser 1928, p. 13; Fleisch 1961–79, vol. 2, pp. 287–88 [§129ee]). *t* is prefixed in Aramaic tG/tD/tC and Hebrew tD, except when the verb is I-sibilant. *t* is infixed in Akkadian Gt/Dt/Št, and apparently also Eblaite.[10] There are other languages in which *t* occurs prefixed in some stems but infixed in others: Arabic Gt/St but tD, Ugaritic Gt/Št but tD, Gəʾəz tG/tD but St. Our jubilarian believes that the regular infixing of *t* in the Akkadian verbal system is a shared East Semitic innovation (Huehnergard 2006, pp. 14–15).

The description given above is schematic. A closer look at the different Northwest Semitic languages (Garr 1985, pp. 119–20) reveals variant forms. In Phoenician and Punic, where tD forms seem to be the norm,[11] Gt (or Dt?) forms are attested in the dialect of Old Byblian: תהתפך 'may it be overturned' (*KAI* 1:2), תחתסף 'may it be torn away' (*KAI* 1:2). There is one transliterated example in Punic of a *t*-stem verb with a sibilant: *ysthyalm* 'I ask them on my behalf' (Poenulus 931). In the Moabite Mesha stela, one finds the infixed *t*-stem forms ואלתחם 'and I fought' (*KAI* 181:11) and בהלתחמה 'when he fought' (*KAI* 181:19). The language of the Deir Alla combinations seems to show prefixed *t*-stems: אתיחדו 'they gathered together' (*KAI* 312 1:5), ליתעץ 'he will not seek advice' (*KAI* 312 B:9), ליתמלך 'he will not take counsel' (*KAI* 312: B:9).

3.2. Evidence from Other Aramaic Periods

The long history of Aramaic provides an interesting diachronic view of *t*-stems. The limited corpus of Old Aramaic inscriptions exhibits both Gt (or Dt?) and tG (or tD?) forms. One finds יגתזר 'it will be cut off' (*KAI* 309:23;

---

[6] For a discussion of this form and the possibility that it is an Aramaism, see Mor 2009, p. 96. Folmer (2003, p. 239) would include שהתשלחו (Ḥev 51:2) as an example of a tD form, though the form is usually taken as a G imperfect following the relative *šɛ-* (=שתשלחו). On the writing of *heh* following the relative *šɛ-*, see Fassberg 1996.

[7] This derivational *t* marks reflexivity, reciprocity, or passivity in the daughter languages (Brockelmann 1908, pp. 529–35 [§257]; Lieberman 1986, p. 613; Lipiński 2001, pp. 404–11 [§§41.20–32]). On the question of whether the Proto-Semitic derivational prefix was *ta or *t, see Diem 1982; Garr 1993, pp. 192–93; Kienast 2001, p. 217 [§189.5–6].

[8] E.g., Brockelmann 1908, p. 268 [§98]. In what is a minority view, Lipiński (2001, p. 40507 [§41.21–25]) believes that *t* was originally infixed in Semitic languages and that what appears to be metathesis involving sibilants in fact reflects the original Proto-Semitic situation. Joüon and Muraoka (2009, pp. 67–68 [§17b]) do not rule out this possibility (contra Joüon 1923, p. 50 [§17b]). Kienast (2001, p. 217 [§189.5]) reconstructs a prefixed *ta-*, which was metathesized in Akkadian, the Arabic VIII form, all *t*-causative stems, but in Hebrew only in sibilant-initial roots. Lieberman (1986, p. 615) is of the opinon that the St stem is what drove analogies leading to the infixing of the *t*. For a complex reconstruction of the derivational prefix and its position, see Diem 1982.

[9] See Malone 1971 on the dating of the metathesis.

[10] The meager evidence from Amorite (one geographical name and one proper name) seems to point to Gt. See Huffmon 1965, pp. 81, 94.

[11] They are poorly attested (Friedrich, Röllig, and Amadasi Guzzo 1999, p. 94 [§149]).

Tell Fekherye), בה]לתחמה 'when] he fought' (*KAI* 310; Tel Dan), יתשמע 'it will be heard' (*KAI* 222 A1:29; Sefire),[12] and ישתחט 'it will be slaughtered' (*KAI* 222:A1:32; Sefire).[13]

Official Aramaic overwhelmingly shows tG and tD forms and the metathesis of *t* and sibilants (Muraoka and Porten 2003, pp. 25–26), for example, אשתאר 'it remained' (TAD B3.12:6), as well as the shift *t* > *d*, for example, אזדהרו 'be careful!' (TAD A4.1:5; Muraoka and Porten 2003, p. 17). There are, nonetheless, variant forms. The *qəre* of the I-*z* verb הזמנתון (< ? הזדמנתון) 'you agreed together' (Dan 2:9) reflects a form with an assimilated *t*,[14] either *hizzᵉmintūn* or *hizzammintūn* (Rosenthal 2006, p. 46). Moreover, a lack of metathesis with sibilants in tG stems is commonly argued for II-w/y verbs in Official Aramaic (and in subsequent periods — Brockelmann 1908, p. 616 [§280]; Bauer and Leander 1927, p. 145 [§46n]), for example, יִתְּשָׂם 'he will be placed' (Ezra 4:21), יִתְּזִין 'he will be nourished' (Dan 4:9).[15]

Late Aramaic sources are of particular interest for understanding the forms attested in Middle Aramaic. In addition to the classical Aramaic *t*-stem forms found in both eastern (Jewish Babylonian, Mandaic) and western (Jewish Palestinian, Christian Palestinian, Samaritan) dialects, one finds clear proof of regressive assimilation of *t*, which is reflected in the orthography א(י)קטל (< אתקטל ; Yalon 1931; Epstein 1960, p. 50; Ben-Ḥayyim 1981, pp. 207–08; Morgenstern 2007, pp. 272–74). In Syriac (Duval 1881, p. 105; Nöldeke 1904, p. 20), *t* assimilates in pronunciation before *t* and *ṭ*, but not in orthography, for example, ܐܶܬ݁ܛܰܫܺܝ *eṭṭašše* 'it was concealed'; *t* also assimilates in pronunciation before *d* with an unreduced vowel, for example, ܢܶܬ݁ܕ݁ܰܟ݂ܪܳܟ݂ *neddaxrāx* 'he remembers you'; when *d* is realized with a reduced vowel, it assimilates progressively to the derivational *t*, for example, ܐܶܬ݂ܕ݁ܟ݂ܰܪ *ettəxar*. The assimilation of *t* resulted in gemination of the contiguous consonant, which is still attested in the traditional pronunciation of Eastern Syriac (Duval 1881, p. 109; Nöldeke 1904, p. 13), the oral tradition of Samaritan Aramaic (*iffāta* = אִתְפְּתַח 'it opened up' [Ben-Ḥayyim 1967, p. 235 line 109]), and the Yemenite oral tradition of Jewish Babylonian Aramaic, even with gutturals (איענש = אִתְעֲנֵשׁ *ʾiᶜᶜənes̆* 'he was punished' [Morag 1988, p. 140]).[16]

In the Late Aramaic period, the total assimilation of *t* and subsequent gemination were not limited to *t*-stem forms with initial non-sibilant. There are also examples with sibilants in all dialects (Nöldeke 1875, p. 214; Ben-Ḥayyim 1981, pp. 207–08), save Syriac, in which forms may have existed in speech but were not represented in writing. See, for example, Jewish Palestinian אשכח (= אשתכח) 'he was found' (Ben-Ḥayyim 1981, p. 208), Christian Palestinian ܝܨܠܒ *yiṣṣeləb* 'he will be hanged' (Bar-Asher 1977, p. 472 n. 365), Samaritan מסכי (= מסתכי) *missāki* 'looking forward' (Ben-Ḥayyim 1967, p. 92 line 51), Jewish Babylonian איצריך (= אצטריך) 'was required' (Friedman 1995, p. 42), and Mandaic נישפיך (= נשתפך) 'it will be poured' (Nöldeke 1875, p. 214). The phenomenon was probably much more widespread than indicated by the orthography (Bar-Asher 1977, p. 225 n. 287).[17]

Neo-Aramaic witnesses a significant reduction in verbal stems, particularly in *t*-stems. Analogical and phonological processes are responsible for the merger and loss of stems:[18] the assimilation of the derivational *t* and the subsequent simplification of gemination undoubtedly played a role in the reduction of verbal stems. In Northeastern Neo-Aramaic, the *t*-stems have merged into other stems and disappeared completely (Nöldeke 1868, p. 207). Neo-Mandaic has preserved only a few examples of *t*-stems. For example, from the dialect of Ahwaz, Macuch (1965, pp. lxi, 247, 267–68; 1989, pp. 40, 64–65) cites tG *egṭel* (= אִתְקְטֵל) 'he was killed,' tD *ekammar* (= אִתְכַּמַּר) 'he returned,' and a tC *etaqliḇat* 'she turned around' (Macuch 1993, pp. 76–77). The few verbs that Häberl (2009, pp. 221–23) notes from the dialect of Khorramshahr include, for example, tG *epseq* (= אִתְפְּסֵק) 'he became extinct,' tD *kammar* 'he returned,' tC *etaqlaḇ* 'he turned around.' Examples with metathesis known from both Ahwaz and

---

[12] Ben-Ḥayyim (1971, p. 249) interprets this as a reflexive-passive *t*-stem of a C verb because of the lack of metathesis.

[13] Rosenthal (1969, p. 660 n. 10), followed by Garr (1985, p. 119), suggests another example of infixed *t* in ירתשה [ל]ה אשם 'May a name not be acquired by [h]im!' (KAI 222 A3:24–25), though the passage is usually taken as ירת שר[ש]ה 'May his sci[on] inherit no name!'

[14] It is also possible that *t* had already shifted to *d* and only then assimilated. See §4 below.

[15] Ben-Ḥayyim (1971, p. 249), however, has persuasively interpreted the lack of metathesis in II-w/y verbs as reflecting an original reflexive-passive *t*-stem of C: *yithaśām > *yittaśām > *yittəśām*. He bases this on two factors: (1) there is no metathesis of *t* and the sibilant, and (2) the G active/Ct passive relationship in Aramaic parallels the relationship of II-w/y verbs in Hebrew G/Cp (hufᶜal) stems.

[16] The oral tradition follows the written tradition. *t* is realized only when it is preserved in the consonantal text, e.g., אתנטילת *ʾitnəṭelaṯ* 'she was taken' (Morag 1988, p. 140).

[17] In his discussion of the Christian Palestinian Aramaic material, Bar-Asher (1988, p. 52) has suggested that scribes sometimes wrote the historical *t* in order to distinguish the *t*-stem forms (tG/tD אפעל /eppeᶜel/, /eppaᶜᶜal/ with assimilated *t*) from two other homographs: G אפעל /efᶜal/ with prosthetic *aleph* and C אפעל /ʾafᶜel/.

[18] See, e.g., the system of stems in Koy Sanjaq as described by Mutzafi (2004, pp. 75–77).

Khorramshahr are Gt *eṣṭəḇā* 'he was baptized' (Häberl 2009, p. 221; Macuch 1993, p. 429), and from only Ahwaz Dt *eštallem* 'he was welcome' (Macuch 1993, p. 439; Häberl 2009, pp. 221–22 n. 182).

In the dialects of Western Neo-Aramaic (Maʿlula, Baxʿa, and Jubbʿadin), the only native Aramaic verbs derived from *t*-stems that have survived are the G verbs *ičxel* (< tG אִתְּכַל; √תכל) 'he trusted' and *ičneḥ* (< tG/tC אִתְּנַח; √ נוח) 'he rested,' as well as with metathesis *išṭaʿ* (< Dt אִשְׁתַּעִי) 'he played'; non-native *t*-stem verbs are borrowings from Arabic (Spitaler 1938, pp. 41–43). Central Neo-Aramaic, as represented by Ṭuroyo and Mlaḥsô, preserves the older tG, tD, and tC stems after the assimilation of the derivational *t* and the loss of gemination (Ritter 1990, pp. 55–56; Jastrow 1997, p. 360):

tG Late Aramaic *meṯpəʿel* > **meppəʿel* > *mıfʿīl*

tD Late Aramaic *meṯpaʿʿal* > **meppāʿal* > *mīfāʿıl*

tC Late Aramaic *mettafʿal* > *mītafʿıl*

An inherited I-sibilant verb that still shows metathesis is *maštāʿe* (< Dt אִשְׁתַּעִי) 'he plays' (Jastrow 1985, p. 87 [§85]). In other I-sibilant verbs, however, there is no metathesis since the derivational *t* has been lost at a previous stage of the language, for example, tG *mísəm* 'he is placed' (< tG/tC מִתְּשָׂם; Jastrow 1985, p. 80 [§78]).

3.3. Evidence from Other Hebrew Sources

Although Biblical and Tannaitic Hebrew regularly exhibit metathesis of the derivational *t* and an I-sibilant radical, there is, nonetheless, one example in which it does not occur: וְהִתְשׁוֹטַטְנָה 'run to and fro!' (Jer 49:3).[19] Moreover, there seem to be possible traces of additional variant stems in Biblical Hebrew, some more certain than others: tG, tGp, tD, tDp, and tC. The following verbs have been suggested by different scholars (see, e.g., Joüon and Muraoka 2009, p. 147 [§53g–h]):

tG הִתְפָּקְדוּ 'they were mustered' (Judg 20:15); הִתְרָחַצְתִּי 'I washed myself' (Job 9:30; Dan 2005)

tDp הֻכַּבֵּס 'it was washed out' (Lev 13:55), הֻטַּמָּאָה 'she was defiled' (Deut 24:4), הֻדַּשְּׁנָה 'it got fat' (Isa 34:6)

tGp הָתְפָּקְדוּ 'they were mustered' (1 Kgs 20:27)

tC תִּתָּבָר 'you shall be pure' (2 Sam 22:27; √ברר); יִתָּכֵן 'it will be established?' (Ezek 33:17; √כון), וַתֵּתַצַּב 'and she stationed herself' (Exod 2:4; √יצב); תְּתַחֲרֶה 'you shall contend with' (Jer 12:5 √תחרי; Blau 1957)

Variant infixed *t*-stem forms have also been proposed for the verbs השתין 'urinate' (שין 'urine' attested as a *kətiv* in שיניהם 'their urine' [2 Kgs 18:27; Isa 36:12]) and even for התל 'mock' from הלל (Lipiński 2001, p. 406 [§41.23]). Moreover, scholars (e.g., Bergsträsser 1929, p. 100 [§18i]) have viewed some place names as relics of old infixed *t*-stem forms: אֶשְׁתָּאוֹל (Josh 15:33), אֶלְתְּקֵא (Josh 19:44), אֶשְׁתְּמוֹעַ (Josh 21:4).

Some of the assimilations of derivational *t* attested in Aramaic dialects are paralleled in Biblical and Tannaitic Hebrew. *t* assimilates regularly before other dentals (e.g., מְדַבֵּר 'speaking' 2 Sam 14:13, הִטָּהֲרוּ 'purify yourselves!' Gen 35:2), and sporadically before other consonants, including sibilants (Gesenius, Kautzsch, and Cowley 1910, p. 149 [§54]),[20] for example, תִּכּוֹנָנִי 'you will be established' (Isa 54:14),[21] תִּכַּסֶּה 'it will be covered' (Prov 26:26), תִּשּׁוֹמֵם 'you will destroy yourself' (Ecc 7:16), הִזַּכּוּ 'make yourselves clean!' (Isa 1:16). Although some of the examples have

[19] Since the Middle Ages, many have attributed the lack of metathesis of the sibilant and *t* to the avoidance of three consecutive dentals (Joüon and Muraoka 2009, p. 146 n. 3 [§53e]).

[20] Baden (2010) believes that the consonantal biblical text contains many more examples than those commonly cited in grammars. He is inclined to interpret many N-vocalized verbs as tD with assimilated *t*. Ben-Ḥayyim (2000, pp. 117–18) points out that in the Samaritan reading tradition of the Pentateuch, there are verbs realized as tD with assimilated *t* whose consonantal frame reflects N. He adds that the tD realization was in fact more common in the Samaritan vernacular than in the Pentateuchal reading tradition. See also Florentin 1992.

[21] 1QIsa^{a} reads תתכונני. See Kutscher 1974, pp. 345–46.

been viewed as scribal errors (Joüon and Muraoka 2009, p. 147 n. 1 [§53e]), the existence of the phenomenon in Tannaitic Hebrew manuscripts (Bar-Asher 1983, pp. 145–47), for example, ואפלל (< ואתפלל) 'I will pray,' points to a genuine linguistic feature. The Masoretic pointings וְנִוַּסְרוּ 'and they will submit themselves to chastisement' (Ezek 23:48) and וְנִכַּפֵּר 'and it will be expiated' (Deut 21:8) also reflect the assimilation of the derivational *t*; these are Tannaitic pointings of the *nitpaʿʿal* stem, which have been imposed here on the *nifʿal* forms of the consonantal biblical text.[22]

4. Proposed Explanation of the Phenomenon in the Judean Desert Forms

In the light of the different *t*-stem forms attested in Northwest Semitic in general, and in Aramaic in particular, the non-metathesized forms found in the Aramaic documents from the Judean Desert should be viewed as authentic, vernacular *t*-stem forms, which existed side-by-side with more classical metathesized forms, and whose roots probably go back to an earlier period of Aramaic. The non-metathesized forms are not direct reflexes of Proto-Semitic forms since early Semitic did not allow the sequence of dental and sibilant.[23]

The Aramaic data can be explained by two analogies:

1. *qaṭṭel* : *hitqaṭṭel* : : *zabben* : X ; X = *hitzabben*

2. *ṭallem* : *hiṭṭallem* : : *qaṭṭel* : X; X = *hiqqaṭṭel*

Analogy 1, the generation of a *t*-stem from its related non-*t*-stem verb and its extension to verbs I-sibilant, is possibly attested already in Old Aramaic יתשמע (**yitšəmaʿ?*) and appears several times in Middle Aramaic in the Judean Desert material (e.g., התשדר *hiṯšaddar*, יתשכח *yiṯšəḵaḥ*), and in Nabatean[24] and Palmyrene. Analogy 2, the assimilation of *t* to following dentals and its extension to non-dentals, shows up in Middle Aramaic in Hatran לקטיל *liqqəṭel* and לרגים *lirrəgem*; it is widely distributed over Late Aramaic dialects. This second analogy could have led to forms with a geminated sibilant such as *hizzabben*, which are spotted first in Official Aramaic הזמנתון *hizzəmintūn/hizzammintūn*, show up in Middle Aramaic in Palmyrene יזבן *yizzabben* and מזבן *mizzabben*, and are documented in all Late Aramaic dialects except for Syriac, where in all likelihood the orthography masks the phenomenon.

It is also possible to view the origin of *hizzabben* and similar forms with geminated sibilants as arising not from analogy 2, but directly from *hitzabben* (the result of analogy 1), as suggested by Cantineau (1935, p. 92), Rosenthal (1936, pp. 56–57), and Bar-Asher (1988, p. 50 n. 95) for each of the dialects they described.[25] A dissenting voice is that of Ben-Ḥayyim (1981), who argues that the examples in Late Aramaic stem from the metathesized classical forms, that is, *hizdabben* > *hizzabben*.[26] Ben-Ḥayyim notes that, although progressive assimilation is not as common as regressive assimilation, dentals are attested assimilating progressively to sibilants.[27]

As for Hebrew, even though there are variant *t*-stem forms in Biblical Hebrew, as in Aramaic and other Northwest Semitic languages, the limited distribution of non-metathesized forms has led scholars (Gzella 2007, p. 102; Mor 2009, p. 96) to see Aramaic influence in the Judean Desert documents. This assessment is further strengthened when one notes that the only (certain) non-metathesized forms in Hebrew are attested with *t*-stem forms of the quadriliterals זעזע and שגשג, both of which may possibly have been asociated by speakers with common Aramaic roots: זעזע with Aramaic זוע,[28] and שגשג[29] with Aramaic שגא/שגי.[30]

---

[22] Bar-Asher 1992, p. 125.

[23] This restriction no longer operated in later stages of the languages. See, e.g., the Greek loan into Syriac ܕܬܣܐ 'first thread of a web' (Sokoloff 2009, pp. 716, 872), or the Persian loan into Late Biblical Hebrew פַּתְשֶׁגֶן 'copy' (Est 3:14; 4:8; 8:13).

[24] Cantineau (1930, p. 73) prefers this explanation to the possibility of Arabic influence.

[25] Schulthess (1924, p. 22) attributed examples of geminated sibilants in Christian Palestinian Aramaic to Arabic influence.

[26] If the reading תדהרון in P. Yadin 50:6 is correct and not merely a scribal error, then this form could have developed from תזדהרון with regressive assimilation. See §2.1 above.

[27] See, e.g., in Arabic V, VI, and VIII *t*-stems (Wright, Smith, and de Goeje 1896, pp. 64–65; Fleisch 1961–79, vol. 1, pp. 96–97 [§15]). Brockelmann (1908, p. 157 [§56]) points out that the original form of the VIII stem in Arabic was tG and not Gt, and thus the assimilations with sibilants that took place reflected, in fact, the more frequent regressive assimilation.

[28] Cf. from the same semantic field the Hebrew roots נוע, חרד, רגז, רעד.

[29] Brown, Driver, and Briggs (1906, p. 691) take it from סוג/שׂ; Koehler, Baumgartner, and Stamm (1994–2000, p. 13066) consider it a biform of שׂגי/א.

[30] The Hebrew root that belongs to this semantic field is רבב.

CONCLUSION

The non-metathesized *t*-stems in Aramaic attested in documents from the Judean Desert (as well as from other Middle Aramaic sources — Nabatean, Palmyrene, and the New Testament) reflect vernacular forms that may have arisen early in Aramaic and Northwest Semitic on the analogy of *t*-stem forms with I-non-sibilant radicals. In addition, the widely distributed Late Aramaic evidence of assimilated derivational *t* next to non-sibilants and sibilants suggests that existence of the phenomenon in the preceding Middle Aramaic period was more widespread than the conservative orthography reveals.

The few examples of non-metathesized *t*-stems in Hebrew documents from the Judean Desert are most likely the result of Aramaic influence at this period.

Abbreviations

C — causative stem (e.g., Hebrew הִפְעִיל)

CIS — *Corpus Inscriptionum Semiticarum.* Paris: Academie des inscriptions et belles-lettres, 1881–

D — stem with doubled medial consonant (e.g., Hebrew פִּעֵל)

DJD 38 — James Charlesworth et al. *Miscellaneous Texts from the Judaean Desert.* Discoveries in the Judaean Desert 38. Oxford: Clarendon, 2000

G — ground stem (e.g., Hebrew פָּעַל)

Inv — *Inventaire des inscriptions de Palmyre.* Beirut: Imprimerie catholique, 1930–

KAI — Herbert Donner and Wolfgang Röllig. *Kanaanäische und aramäische Inschriften.* Volume 1. 5th edition. Wiesbaden: Harrassowitz, 2002

N — stem with prefixed *n*- (e.g., Hebrew נִפְעַל)

p — internal passive

S — stem with prefixed *s*- (e.g., Arabic سَفْعَلَ)

Š — stem with prefixed *š*- (e.g., Akkadian *šuprusum*)

t — stem with affixed *t*

TAD — Bezalel Porten and Ada Yardeni. *Textbook of Aramaic Documents from Ancient Egypt, Newly Copied, Edited and Transliterated into Hebrew and English.* 4 volumes. Jerusalem: Department of the History of the Jewish People, Hebrew University, 1986–1999

Bibliography

Baden, Joel S.

2010 — "Hithpael and Niphal in Biblical Hebrew: Semantic and Morphological Overlap." *Vetus Testamentum* 60: 33–44.

Bar-Asher, Moshe

1977 — *Palestinian Syriac Studies: Source-texts, Traditions and Grammatical Problems.* Jerusalem: n.p. [In Hebrew]

1983 — "A Preliminary Study of Mishnaic Hebrew as Reflected in Codex Vatican 32 of Sifre-Bemidbar." *Teʿuda* 3: 139–65. [In Hebrew]

1988 — "Le syro-palestinien: études grammaticales." *Journal asiatique* 276: 27–59.

1992 — "The Conjugations of Mishnaic Hebrew (A Morphological Study)." *Language Studies* 5–6 (Israel Yeivin Festschrift): 123–51. [In Hebrew]

Bauer, Hans, and Pontus Leander

1927 — *Grammatik des Biblisch-Aramäischen.* Halle: Max Niemeyer.

Ben-Ḥayyim, Ze'ev

1967 *The Literary and Oral Tradition of Hebrew and Aramaic amongst the Samaritans*, Volume 3, Part 2: *The Recitation of Prayers and Hymns*. Jerusalem: Academy of the Hebrew Language. [In Hebrew]

1971 "Comments on the Inscriptions of Sfire." *Lĕšonénu* 35: 243–53. [In Hebrew]

1981 "Word Studies III." *Tarbiẕ* 50: 192–208. [In Hebrew]

2000 *A Grammar of Samaritan Hebrew Based on the Recitation of the Law in Comparison with the Tiberian and Other Jewish Traditions*. Jerusalem: Magnes; Winona Lake: Eisenbrauns.

Bergsträsser, G.

1929 *Hebräische Grammatik*. 2 volumes. Leipzig: J. C. Hinrichs.

Beyer, Klaus

1998 *Die aramäischen Inschriften aus Assur, Hatra und dem übrigen Ostmesopotamien: (datiert 44 v. Chr. bis 238 n. Chr.)*. Göttingen: Vandenhoeck and Ruprecht.

Blau, Josua

1957 "Über die t-form des Hifʿil im Bibelhebräisch." *Vetus Testamentum* 7: 385–88.

Brockelmann, Carl

1908 *Grundriss der vergleichenden Grammatik der semitischen sprachen*, Volume 1: *Laut- und Formenlehre*. Berlin: Reuther and Reichard.

Brown, Francis; S. R. Driver; and Charles A. Briggs

1906 *A Hebrew and English Lexicon of the Old Testament*. Reprint 1959. Oxford: Clarendon Press.

Cantineau, Jean

1930–1932 *Le nabatéen*. 2 volumes. Paris: Ernest Leroux.

1935 *Grammaire du palmyrénien épigraphique*. Cairo: Imprimerie de l'institut francais d'archéologie orientale.

Dan, Barak

2005 "הִתְרָחַצְתִּי (Job 9:30): Another Vestige of the Light *hitpaʿel* Conjugation in Biblical Hebrew." *Lĕšonénu* 67: 143–45. [In Hebrew]

Diem, Werner

1982 "Die Entwicklung des Derivationsmorphems der *t*-Stämme im Semitischen." *Zeitschrift der Deutschen Morgenländischen Gesellschaft* 132: 29–84.

Duval, Rubens

1881 *Traité de grammaire syriaque*. Paris: F. Vieweg.

Epstein, J. N.

1960 *A Grammar of Babylonian Aramaic*. Jerusalem: Magnes; Tel Aviv: Dvir. [In Hebrew]

Fassberg, Steven E.

1996 "The Orthography of the Relative Pronoun -שה in the Second Temple and Mishnaic Periods." *Scripta Classica Israelica* 15: 240–50.

Fitzmyer, Joseph A.

2004 *The Genesis Apocryphon of Qumran Cave 1 (1Q20): A Commentary*. 3rd edition. Biblica et Orientalia 18/B. Rome: Pontifical Biblical Institute.

Fleisch, Henri

1961–1979 *Traité de philologie arabe*. 2 volumes. [1] Beirut: Imprimerie catholique; [2] Beirut: Dar al-Mashreq.

Florentin, Moshe

1992 "The Disappearance of the Internal Passive and the Status of נפעל and נתפעל in the Samaritan Tradition and Mishnaic Hebrew." *Lĕšonénu* 56: 201–11. [In Hebrew]

2005 *Late Samaritan Hebrew: A Linguistic Analysis of Its Different Types*. Studies in Semitic Languages and Linguistics 43. Leiden: Brill.

Folmer, Margaretha L.

2003 "Metathesis in Jewish Aramaic: A So-called 'Pan-Semitic Feature' Reconsidered." In *Hamlet on a Hill: Semitic and Greek Studies Presented to Professor T. Muraoka on the Occasion of His Sixty-fifth Birthday*, edited by M. F. J. Baasten and W. Th. van Peursen, pp. 232–43. Orientalia Lovaniensia Analecta 118. Leuven: Peeters.

Friedman, Shamma

1995 "An Ancient Scroll Fragment (B. Ḥullin 101a–105a) and the Rediscovery of the Babylonian Branch of Tannaitic Hebrew." *Jewish Quarterly Review* 96: 9–50.

Friedrich, Johannes; Wolfgang Röllig; and Maria Giulia Amadasi Guzzo

1999 *Phönizische-Punische Grammatik.* 3rd edition. Analecta Orientalia 55. Rome: Pontifical Biblical Institute.

Garr, W. Randall

1985 *Dialect Geography of Syria-Palestine, 1000–586 B.C.* Philadelphia: University of Pennsylvania Press.

1993 "The *Niphal* Derviational Prefix." *Orientalia* 62: 142–62.

Gesenius, Wilhelm; Emil Kautzsch; and Arthur E. Cowley

1910 *Gesenius' Hebrew Grammar.* Edited by E. Kautzsch, translated by A. E. Cowley. 2nd English edition. Oxford: Clarendon Press.

Greenberg, Joseph H.

1950 "Patterning of Root Morphemes in Semitic." *Word* 6: 162–81.

Gzella, Holger

2007 "Elemente systemischen Sprachkontaktes in den hebräischen Bar-Kosiba-Briefen." In *... der seine Lust hat am Wort des Herrn! Festschrift für Ernst Jenni zum 80. Geburtstag*, edited by Jürg Luchsinger, Peter Mathys, and Markus Saur, pp. 93–107. Alter Orient und Altes Testament 336. Münster: Ugarit-Verlag.

Häberl, Charles G.

2009 *The Neo-Mandaic Dialect of Khorramshahr.* Semitica Viva 45. Wiesbaden: Harrassowitz.

Hammond, Philip C.; David J. Johnson; and Richard N. Jones

1986 "A Religio-legal Nabataean Inscription from the Atargatis/Al-ʿUzza Temple at Petra." *Bulletin of the American Schools of Oriental Research* 276: 77–80.

Huehnergard, John

2006 "Proto-Semitic and Proto-Akkadian." In *The Akkadian Language in Its Semitic Context: Studies in the Akkadian of the Third and Second Millennium B.C.*, edited by Guy Deutscher and N. J. C. Kouwenberg, pp. 1–18. Leiden: Nederlands Instituut voor het Nabije Oosten.

Huffmon, Herbert B.

1965 *Amorite Personal Names in the Mari Texts: A Structural and Lexical Study.* Baltimore: Johns Hopkins University Press.

Jastrow, Otto

1985 *Laut- und Formenlehre des neuaramäischen Dialekts von Mīdin im Ṭūr ʿAbdīn.* 3rd edition. Wiesbaden: Harrassowitz.

1997 "The Neo-Aramaic Languages." In *The Semitic Languages*, edited by Robert Hetzron, pp. 334–77. London: Routledge.

Jaussen, Antonin, and R. Savignac

1909 *Mission archéologique en Arabie (mars–mai 1907): de Jérusalem au Hedjaz Médain-saleh.* Paris: E. Leroux.

Joüon, Paul

1923 *Grammaire de l'hébreu biblique.* Rome: Pontifical Biblical Institute.

Joüon, Paul, and Takamitsu Muraoka

2009 *A Grammar of Biblical Hebrew.* Second reprint of the 2nd edition, with corrections. Subsidia Biblica 27. Rome: Gregorian and Biblical Press.

Kienast, Burkhart

2001 *Historische semitische Sprachwissenschaft.* Wiesbaden: Harrassowitz.

Koehler, Ludwig; Walter Baumgartner; and Johann Jakob Stamm

1994–2000 *The Hebrew and Aramaic Lexicon of the Old Testament.* Translated and edited under the supervision of M. E. J. Richardson. 6 volumes. Leiden: Brill.

Kutscher, Edward Yechezkel

1974 *The Language and Linguistic Background of the Isaiah Scroll (1QIsa[a]).* Leiden: Brill.

Lieberman, Stephen J.

1986 "The Afro-Asiatic Background of the Semitic N-stem: Towards the Origin of the Stem-afformatives of the Semitic and Afro-Asiatic Verb." *Bibliotheca Orientalis* 43: 577–628.

Lipiński, Edward

2001 *Semitic Languages: Outline of a Comparative Grammar*. 2nd edition. Orientalia Lovaniensia Analecta 80. Leuven: Peeters.

Macuch, Rudolf

1965 *Handbook of Classical and Modern Mandaic*. Berlin: Walter de Gruyter.

1989 *Neumandäische Chrestomathie mit grammatischer Skizze, kommentierter Übersetzung und Glossar*. Porta Linguarum Orientalium, n.s., 18. Wiesbaden: Harrassowitz.

1993 *Neumandäische Texte im Dialekt von Ahwāz*. Semitica Viva 12. Wiesbaden: Harrassowitz.

Malone, Joseph L.

1971 "Systematic Metathesis in Mandaic." *Language* 47: 394–415.

Mor, Uri

2009 The Grammar of the Epigraphic Hebrew Documents from Judaea between the First and the Second Revolts. Ph.D. dissertation. Ben-Gurion University of the Negev. [In Hebrew]

Morag, Shelomo

1972 "Ἐφφαθά (Mark 7:34): Certainly Hebrew, Not Aramaic?" *Journal of Semitic Studies* 17: 198–202.

1988 *Babylonian Aramaic: The Yemenite Tradition. Historical Aspects and Transmission, Phonology, the Verbal System*. Jerusalem: Ben Zvi Institute. [In Hebrew]

Morgenstern, Matthew

1999 "The History of the Aramaic Dialects in the Light of Discoveries from the Judaean Desert: The Case of Nabataean." *Eretz-Israel* 26 (Frank Moore Cross Volume): *134–*142.

2007 "On Some Non-standard Spellings in the Aramaic Magic Bowls and Their Linguistic Significance." *Journal of Semitic Studies* 52: 245–77.

Muraoka, Takamitsu, and Bezalel Porten

2003 *A Grammar of Egyptian Aramaic*. 2nd revised edition. Handbuch der Orientalistik 32. Leiden: Brill.

Mutzafi, Hezy

2004 *The Jewish Neo-Aramaic Dialect of Koy Sanjaq*. Semitic Viva 32. Wiesbaden: Harrassowitz.

Nöldeke, Theodor

1868 *Grammatik der neusyrischen Sprache am Urmia-See und in Kurdistan*. Leipzig: T. O. Weigel.

1875 *Mandäische Grammatik*. Halle: Buchhandlung des Waisenhauses.

1904 *Compendious Syriac Grammar*. Translated by James A. Crichton. London: Williams & Norgate.

Qimron, Elisha

1976 A Grammar of the Hebrew Language of the Dead Sea Scrolls. Ph.D. dissertation. Hebrew University of Jerusalem. [In Hebrew]

1986 *Hebrew of the Dead Sea Scrolls*. Harvard Semitic Studies 29. Atlanta: Scholars Press.

Ritter, Hellmut Ritter

1990 *Ṭūrōyo: Die Volkssprache der syrischen Christen des Ṭūr ʿAbdîn*, Volume C: *Grammatik*. Stuttgart: Franz Steiner.

Rosenthal, Franz

1936 *Die Sprache der palmyrenischen Inschriften und ihre Stellung innerhalb des Aramäischen*. Mitteilungen der Vorderasiatisch-aegyptischen Gesellschaft 41. Leipzig: J. C. Hinrichs.

1969 "Canaanite and Aramaic Inscriptions." In *Ancient Near Eastern Texts Relating to the Old Testament*, edited by James B. Pritchard, pp. 653–62. 3rd edition with supplement. Princeton: Princeton University Press.

2006 *Grammar of Biblical Aramaic*. 7th edition. Porta Linguarum Orientalium, n.s., 5. Wiesbaden: Harrassowitz.

Schulthess, Friedrich

1924 *Grammatik des Christlich-Palästinischen Aramäisch*. Tübingen: J. C. B. Mohr.

Sokoloff, Michael

1974 *The Targum to Job from Qumran Cave XI*. Ramat-Gan: Bar-Ilan University.

2009 *A Syriac Lexicon: A Translation from the Latin; Correction, Expansion, and Update of C. Brockelmann's Lexicon Syriacum*. Winona Lake: Eisenbrauns; Pistcataway: Gorgias Press.

Spitaler, Anton

1938 *Grammatik des neuaramäischen Dialekts von Maᶜlūla (Antilibanon).* Deutsche morgenländische Gesellschaft 26. Leipzig: F. A. Brockhaus.

Sznycer, Maurice

1967 *Les passages "puniques" en transcription latine dans le "Poenulus" de Plaute.* Paris: Librairie C. Klincksieck.

Wright, William

1890 *Lectures on the Comparative Grammar of the Semitic Languages.* Cambridge: Cambridge University Press.

Wright, William; W. Robertson Smith; and M. J. de Goeje

1896 *A Grammar of the Arabic Language.* 3rd edition. 2 volumes. Cambridge: Cambridge University Press.

Yalon, Henoch

1931 "Assimilation of תי"ו in Hebrew and Aramaic." *Tarbiz* 3: 99–106. [In Hebrew]

4

People without Town: The ʿ*apiru* in the Amarna Evidence

*Daniel E. Fleming, New York University**

Egyptian texts for the Late Bronze Age name two classes of people in the southern Levant that are neither regional labels nor specific polities: the *shosu* and the ʿ*apiru*. The former are associated more narrowly with the southeastern steppes that border the Arabian Desert, while the latter are a class encountered more widely across Canaan, Syria, and farther north. By the geography alone, it is not surprising that the *shosu* are linked to pastoralism and nomadic life, though Egyptian texts do occasionally mention the existence of towns in "*shosu*-land" (Routledge 2004, pp. 77–78). The ʿ*apiru* are more widespread and more difficult. They cannot be defined by cities and kingdoms in the standard fashion; indeed, they are regarded as the antithesis of these in some statements, and the category somehow identifies a non-standard relationship to settlements and their polities. Many of the Amarna letters, especially those sent to the Egyptian court by their vassals in Canaan, mention the ʿ*apiru*, often with the assumption that they stand outside the web of loyalty to the empire.[1] These texts date to the mid-fourteenth century, and the image of outsiders to the Egyptian system has offered a tantalizing background to the emergence of Israel, even if there is no relation to the word 'Hebrew' (ʿ*ibrî*).[2] The numerous Amarna references to the ʿ*apiru* have greatly influenced definitions of the type as renegade outsiders.[3] Dever (2003, pp. 179, 181) calls them "landless" and among the impoverished and socially marginalized, the "social bandits."[4] Liverani (1979)

* As with so many before and after my time as a student, John Huehnergard played a crucial role in my training and in my sense of what it meant to be a good teacher to scholars in training. His devotion to this task was phenomenal; with John, we knew that we mattered, and this gave us the best of motivations to work for him in return. In the time since my graduation in 1990, John's work and his mind have been a persistent point of reference in my own study of the Near East. I have realized with time that our reasons for pursuing the form and meaning of words diverge somewhat. Where John attends above all to the language itself, which he understands far better than I, I am preoccupied more with the societies that produced and used these words. I offer this article to John with the greatest appreciation, recognizing that it is just this sort of social study of a difficult word of uncertain nominal form. The paper is drawn from one chapter in my forthcoming book, *The Legacy of Israel in Judah's Bible*.

[1] Nadav Na'aman (2005, p. 277) cautions that in contrast to Egypt's wars against the *shosu*, Egyptian scribes rarely treat the ʿ*apiru* as enemies. The writers of the Amarna letters thus reflected their own use of the term, with their own attempt to get the Egyptians to consider such people a danger.

[2] On this well-worn problem, with bibliography and a new proposal, see my "Mari's ʿ*iBrum* and the Bible's ʿ*ibrî*: An Alternative Origin for 'Hebrew,'" forthcoming in *Catholic Bible Quarterly*. The biblical word "Hebrew" does not derive from the old West Semitic term ʿ*apiru*, though it may come from the same root and be indirectly related. George Mendenhall (1962) first proposed that Israel began as ʿ*apiru* who rejected the dominance of their Egyptian-affiliated city rulers. The hypothesis has been much criticized, even as it opened the door to more durable interpretations that did not depend on bringing the Israelites in as outsiders by migration.

[3] It is now generally agreed that the term represents a category rather than a proper noun, but this was once considered possible for some examples, at least (e.g., Pohl 1957, p. 159; de Vaux 1968, pp. 226–27). Ivanov (1974, pp. 39–40) offers an early (Marxist) argument that this is truly a social and not an ethnic group. Note that three Amarna letters use the KI-determinative for localities (EA 215: 15; 289: 24; 298: 27), but this seems to reflect the scribes' attempt to treat these as comparable to political entities (see Astour 1999, p. 33).

[4] Dever aligns himself not far from Mendenhall, emphasizing the lowland urban origin of the new highland population and accepting a peasant revolt in some form, which he would call "agrarian reform" (p. 189). Norman Gottwald (1979, pp. 401, 404) considered them outlaws to the established order.

argued that to become an ʿ*apiru* meant to abandon the king and become a rebel.[5] More neutrally, they may be seen as refugees or migrants, populations that could represent a threat to the longstanding locals.[6]

Above all, the problem with the standard interpretation of the ʿ*apiru* is the conclusion that they were not fully integrated into the society of town dwellers. In the Amarna letters, the ʿ*apiru* generally appear as powerful groups with effective political leadership on a scale that could be seen to threaten every city-based vassal in the Egyptian Levant. Peoples identified as ʿ*apiru* defeated or won the support of major towns and would have incorporated large populations that were indistinguishable from those of the kingdoms they overwhelmed. The ʿ*apiru* peoples were never identified by a city center, however, and some of Egypt's vassals regarded them as intrinsically resistant to Egyptian authority. In the end, they have something in common with the Hana of Zimri-Lim and the Binu Simʾal in the early second-millennium Mari archives, where the Hana/Simʾal are a population named by its mobile potential and yet carrying the identity of a whole city-based kingdom. Both the Binu Simʾal and their Binu Yamina counterparts in the Mari evidence represent modes of political and social identity not defined by towns, somehow like the ʿ*apiru*, a similarity to which I return below.[7]

Amarna's ʿ*apiru* Powers

The ʿ*apiru* category appears in over fifty of the 350-plus letters found at el-Amarna in Egypt. Among Egypt's Asian vassals, ʿ*apiru* people were a constant presence and concern. In fact, however, a majority of these texts refer not to unnamed bands of ne'er-do-wells but to particular political threats associated with two impressive leaders. To the north, the land of Amurru, a highland polity never defined by a city center, was led by Abdi-Aširta, the scourge of Rib-Hadda, the ruler of Byblos who lived with the persistent terror of being overrun by this powerful inland neighbor. Rib-Hadda repeatedly identifies Abdi-Aširta with the ʿ*apiru* in his missives to the Egyptian king, and he spits out the term as a pejorative epithet that proves at least an inclination to escape pharaoh's authority. Farther south, also in the highlands, Labʾayu governed a people also linked strongly to the ʿ*apiru*. Brendon Benz (2012) proposes that Labʾayu's domain included the city of Shechem but was not defined by this or any single center.[8]

In large part because the Amarna letters reflect such concern about conflict with Abdi-Aširta and Labʾayu, the majority of references to the ʿ*apiru* treat them as a military opponent — not from the Egyptians' own point of view, but from the view of individual city-based rulers in the Levant. Rib-Hadda of Byblos and others speak of "the war of the ʿ*apiru*" (EA 68, 71, 75, 185, 243, 313, 366), and there is repeated nervousness about who may "join" the ʿ*apiru*, not as individuals enlisting in banditry but as whole populations who could switch allegiance in favor of Abdi-Aširta or Labʾayu, if not others.[9] Such populations are often identified by their towns, either generically (EA 74, 116, 117, 144, 189) or with specific names, as Ṣumur (EA 76), Byblos (Gubla, EA 104), and Hazor (EA 148). Whole 'lands' (*mātu*) are sometimes at stake (EA 77, 79, 85, 88, 272, 273, 290), and Rib-Hadda, never one to hold back for fear of overplaying his hand, once declares that *all* the lands of the pharaoh, as far as Egypt, may become part of Abdi-Aširta's ʿ*apiru* (EA 88). Other letters describe more than just conflict and concern; actual ʿ*apiru* successes are characterized by incorporation of towns and lands (EA 83, 85, 90, 118, 286, 288).

[5] See the objection in Astour 1999, p. 32.

[6] Ahlstöm (1986, p. 12) compares them to the resident aliens described by the Hebrew term *gēr*. Na'aman (1986) defines them first of all as "migrants" and then discusses at length how the term took on a derogatory aspect in the Amarna letters. Buccellati (1977) likewise accepts the notion of displaced persons but distinguishes the *munnabtūtu* as "politically displaced" from the ʿ*apirū* as "socially uprooted." See also I. M. Diakonoff 1982, p. 96: "They were persons who, fleeing from their communities because of impoverishment, had lost their civil rights and roamed about the neighboring countries, settling in the difficult accessible maquis and living by robbery, hired labour or as hired warriors."

[7] On the social landscape of the Mari archives, see most recently Durand 2004 and Fleming 2004. For the key identification of Zimri-Lim and his ruling family as Simʾalite, see Charpin and Durand 1986. On Zimri-Lim's political life as a Simʾalite, see the recent work of Miglio (2010).

[8] In Benz's interpretation, Shechem itself originally designated a larger region, from which the city took its name.

[9] For ease of reference, I cite the letters simply by number. The locations of the specific mentions are easily found in the classic translations of Moran (1992), with a still useful edition of the Akkadian in Knudtzon 1964.

This majority of Amarna references has generally been explained as derived from the primary identity of the *ʿapiru* as a class of people who have lost all affiliation by the settled "towns" and "lands" that define ordered society under Egypt's empire and its vassal domains. Whether or not this can be maintained on some other basis, the mass of Amarna usage does not serve this interpretation. Most often, the *ʿapiru* are linked to major political powers in the Levantine highlands that seem to challenge the stable configuration of city-based dominions under Egyptian rule. Occasionally, these *ʿapiru* are distinguished from the individuals who lead them, so that they represent a separate social force, capable of acting in support of or against other groups or leaders. Abdi-Aširta's army is said to be strong "through the *ʿapiru*," who will enable him to take over two cities if he can assemble them for the purpose (EA 71; cf. 76, 85, 91). Later in his career, Rib-Hadda writes that Aziru, the son of Abdi-Aširta, has assembled the *ʿapiru* and addressed them with plans to assault Byblos (EA 132). The *ʿapiru* are viewed as a body that can gather to make decisions in distinction from an individual leader even while they may be in service to such a leader.

In this respect, the *ʿapiru* of Abdi-Aširta and his son resemble the Hana of King Zimri-Lim at Mari, who counts on these kinsmen as his primary base of power and yet has to negotiate their support in any given undertaking. Also like the *ʿapiru*, the term *hana* defines a social category, in this case the people who live outside of settlements with flocks on the move. In the peculiar Mari usage, Zimri-Lim's entire Simʾalite people is identified by this mobile pastoralist element, even though many of the Simʾalites are settled in towns.[10] The Mari Hana do not explain the particular meaning of the word *ʿapiru*, but the parallel adds to the impression that the *ʿapiru* cannot easily be understood as marginal to the social and political landscape to which they contribute. In both cases, a category that derives from notions of mobility and separation from towns is linked to the core constituency of kings who have a base of power outside of any one city center, yet who still rule from urban capitals.

One of the rare letters from Labʾayu himself offers a closer view of the *ʿapiru* that should not be pejorative. In EA 254, Labʾayu responds to pharaoh's request that this leader hand over his son for a visit to Egypt, an invitation that forced submission to the suzerain. Labʾayu insists that he would give anything the king requests, including his own wife if so ordered. Unfortunately, his son has been frustratingly out of contact. Moran translates the excuse, "I did not know that my son was consorting with the Apiru. I herewith hand him over to Addaya." Without the assumption that the *ʿapiru* category is necessarily negative in this case, the key lines may be rendered differently: "I did not know that my son was going around with the *ʿapiru*, and I hereby entrust him to Addaya."[11] For Labʾayu, if his son is not currently with him, he is naturally with the *ʿapiru*, who are understood to live or move at a distance from their king, rather like the Hana of Zimri-Lim. As addressed by Labʾayu, the *ʿapiru* are a coherent population with an established relationship to him, yet whose movements cannot be managed by the ruler they acknowledge.

Such independence may reflect a life in more remote areas, especially in highlands and inland regions that were less accessible to Egyptian power. The realms of Abdi-Aširta and Labʾayu appear to have been more difficult for Egypt to control than the city-centered polities of the lowlands, and we also find one rare positive reference to the *ʿapiru* in a letter from Biryawaza of Damascus, also inland. In proclaiming his loyalty and availability, Biryawaza lists his military resources: "Indeed I myself, along with my troops and my chariots, along with my kin, along with my *ʿapiru*, and along with my *sutû*, am at the service of the archer-troops, wherever my lord the king may command" (EA 195: 24–32).

In this account, the ruler at Damascus seems to define his own people by the different categories of their relationship to him, none of which needs to be considered outside the normal social order. By their combination, the opening troops and chariots appear to reflect Damascus itself, so that the other three groups all stand at a physical distance and must be associated with Biryawaza by commitments appropriate to their ways of life. First, his kin, or "brothers," would represent a following that is constituted as his own clan or tribe, a bond not dependent on residence in the same town or settlement. The Sutû are widely known as nomads.[12] In the Mari evidence, where large groups are defined by connections that bridge settlement and steppe, farming and flocks, in what are often called "tribal" peoples, the Sutû are a much smaller group, never identified with settled life and

[10] I elaborate my interpretation of the Hana category in *Democracy's Ancient Ancestors* (Fleming 2004, pp. 47–50, 85–92, and 148–50), with a revision of my general understanding of the Hana in Zimri-Lim's kingdom in Fleming 2009.

[11] The verb translated by Moran as "consorting" is in the Gtn iterative stem of the verb *alāku* ('to go'), which I render by its common meaning as "go around."

[12] The one extended study is still that of Heltzer (1981).

distinct from the well-attested Binu Simʾal and Binu Yamina populations.[13] In the Damascus letter as well, these may be nomads, entirely separate from towns. This leaves the *ʿapiru*, who are neither direct kin nor true nomads. However we define them, the *ʿapiru* are equally committed to Biryawaza as his own, with no greater sense of social or political distance. Another Amarna letter (EA 318), perhaps from somewhere in Syria, follows the term *ʿapiru* with the *habbātu*, perhaps even as a gloss on the common writing SA.GAZ: "Save me from powerful enemies, from the hand of the *ʿapiru*, the *habbātu*, and the Sutû — so save me, O great king, my lord!" The word *habbātu* in this use may be derived from a verb of movement, crossing from one domain to another, rather than "to rob," so that we cannot identify the *ʿapiru* here with "bandits."[14] We are left with the same combination of *ʿapiru* and Sutû.

If we understand the *ʿapiru* as runaways, detached from the social bonds of settled society and gathered in bands of renegades on the fringes of regular civilization, one answer would be to consider such military support as grounded purely in financial and practical motives. When associated with Abdi-Aširta, Labʾayu, and Biryawaza, the *ʿapiru* may be understood as mercenaries.[15] Support for such an interpretation could then be found in EA 246, a letter to pharaoh from Biridiya, ruler of Megiddo, who complains of payments to the *ʿapiru* in what might be taken as a scheme to buy military muscle. Biridiya concludes, "My lord the king should know: the two sons of Labʾayu have indeed given their silver to the *ʿapiru* and to the Sutû ...," evidently in connection with war against Megiddo. Before we conclude that this describes an obvious mercenary arrangement, we must keep in mind that the Amarna evidence does not generally characterize the *ʿapiru* as professional soldiers for hire, and this is not the only way to account for such exchange. In a Mari letter published under the tantalizing title "Vie nomade," Hammi-ištamar, leader of the Yaminite Uprapû people, scoffs at the attempts of his counterpart to guarantee the support of his fighters by paying them silver:

> You put your trust elsewhere, thinking, "I have given silver to my tribe." What is this silver of yours that you gave? All of your silver that you gave — I know about it. Yesterday, all your tribe assembled at Hen, and the one who loves you was saying, "Write to him so he will go," while the one who rejects ("hates") you was saying, "He should not bother coming." Now if I did not make a habit of turning up in person, they would never manage to act as one.[16]

Yasmah-Addu offers silver to his own *liʾmum* or 'tribe,' the term that defines his Yarihû people as a whole. This has nothing to do with the employment of foreigners and instead involves a leader's strategy for persuading his own people to join him in a dangerous military undertaking. Biridiya's opponents may well be the people of Labʾayu and sons, classified by *ʿapiru* and Sutû groups, as in the list of Biryawaza's fighters at Damascus. In the Amarna correspondence, the *ʿapiru* represent the category more feared and loathed than the Sutû, and it is their name that embodies potential rebellion in the mind of Rib-Hadda at Byblos. It seems that in Amurru of the north, at least, the *ʿapiru* were most central to defining the political role of populations not identified by their settled abode.

---

[13] To my knowledge, there is no systematic treatment of the Sutû in the Mari evidence; for sporadic references, see Fleming 2004, pp. 99, 209; others can be found by browsing the published volumes of Mari letters.

[14] See *CAD* s.v. *ḫabātu* A v. (1) to rob, take away by force; (2) to commit a robbery; *ḫabātu* D v. (1) to move across, make an incursion, a razzia into enemy territory. Both verbs are common in the Old Babylonian period (early second millennium), with continued use in Babylonian dialects, as discussed in the dictionary articles. Na'aman (1994, pp. 398–99) calls these "outlaw refugees." Von Soden (1984) observed that the term SA.GAZ (for *habbātu*, the related noun) is usually read as "bandit," including in his own *AHw*, from the verb "to rob," but that there is a homonym meaning "to wander." The two verbs may have the same foundational meaning, so that the *ʿapiru* cannot be interpreted as outside the law based on this comparison. Bottéro (1972) likewise emphasizes the importance of the SA.GAZ connection: if this truly means "bandit," then it would provide a firm starting point for a negative meaning — except that the root may not be universally pejorative. The basis for seeing the *ʿapiru* as unstable and dangerous really comes from Amarna.

[15] Ahlström (1986, p. 12) considers the lists of *ʿapiru* fighters in texts from Alalakh to be mercenaries (AT 180–84). Grabbe (2007, p. 48) mentions together the notions of mercenaries and thieves in connection with EA 68, 185, and 186. Bottéro (1972, p. 25) mentions the basis for considering them a military force; they are found in enlistment accounts already at Mari; this is also the entire purpose of their listing in the mid-second-millennium text published by Mirjo Salvini (1996). Military enlistment does not mean "mercenary" service, as is discussed further below. In fact, it is not entirely clear that the category of "mercenary" is appropriate to any military service in this pre-imperial period.

[16] The text is A.1146, in Marello 1992.

ʿapiru in Stable Relationships

In all of the evidence for the *ʿapiru*, which has been gathered above all by Bottéro, it is clear that they are not defined by cities and settlements, even if they may inhabit these.[17] In this respect, we must keep in mind the ubiquitous Hana of the Mari archives, whom Zimri-Lim rules as his core Simʾalite population, towns and all, even though the word means something like "tent dweller," the antithesis of settled life. Zimri-Lim's own people were identified by a way of life in which many of them did not participate. While the *ʿapiru* may be difficult to lay one's hands on, as with Labʾayu's son in EA 254, the purely nomadic existence seems to be claimed already by the Sutû category. The explanation for such groups may remain elusive as well, but perhaps we do best to begin by looking back at the early phenomenon.

Several texts from the early second millennium, before the term *ʿapiru* became a fixed type, attest a verb that appears to be cognate with the noun, without being simply denominative.[18] Whatever the original meaning of the root, in common usage, the verb always has to do with departure from one's home to take up residence in a different place, especially a different political entity. Repeatedly, the verb accompanies a claim of legitimate absence and assumes a recognized standing, not just in the new location but in the home left behind.

In one Mari letter, the governor of Qaṭṭunan, the northernmost district of the kingdom, writes to the king to anticipate the possibility that men who came through Qaṭṭunan will file a false complaint. They may charge the governor with holding two diplomats in custody, when these prisoners are nothing of the sort: "One Numhean was resident in Saggaratum and moved away to Kurdâ; and one man is in the service of (a man named) Sagaran."[19] In this mix, Saggaratum is the city center of another district in Zimri-Lim's Mari-based kingdom; Numhâ is the name of a people identified specially with the city center of Kurdâ, so that this man 'moved away' (verb *habārum/ʿapārum*) from a town where he was a relative foreigner back into the kingdom defined by his own Numhâ people. Although he is moving into something that looks like home terrain, it is still a departure from Zimri-Lim's authority. This is far from departure toward status as an outcast. So far as one could still question whether the verb is in fact cognate with the noun, the Mari texts include references to the *ʿapiru* status itself that involve the same movement from one political domain to another. One letter from Terru, sometime ruler of Urkesh, defines the status by departure (verb *waṣûm*): "I make constant blessing on [my lord's] behalf. Now, I have had to abandon the comfort of my house, and so I have left to live as an outsider at (the town of) Shinah. My lord must not be neglectful regarding this."[20] Terru's town has forced him out of power, and he has fled to a neighboring polity.

The question, then, is how such displaced people came to be identified by large groups. The notion of their gathering in "bands" does not explain the scale and integration of the Amarna evidence and is not required by the *ʿapiru* evidence as a whole. In evidence slightly later than that of Mari, the so-called *habiru*-prism of Tunip-Teššup, from roughly the late seventeenth century, counts by name three groups of *ʿapiru* fighters joined under three leaders, in a total of 438 men available to the ruler of this upper Tigris kingdom (Salvini 1996). Neither the men nor their leaders receive any further title, and they are counted simply as *ʿapiru*, a category evidently sufficient to record their commitment to Tunip-Teššup. It would seem that this mass of men lives within Tunip-Teššup's domain but will not fight with town and village units, which are based on long-term solidarity and serve together. Wherever and however they live, they are joined for military service under a separate census category, and this is what unites them for classificatory purposes. In actual combat, such groups would probably have moved and camped and fought together, as they were organized under this heading.[21]

---

[17] The most systematic work on the cuneiform evidence has been that of Jean Bottéro, first in *Le problème des Ḫabiru* (1954) and updated in *RlA* 4 (1972), and then in *Nomads and Sedentary Peoples* (1981). See also Greenberg 1955. Other reviews of the evidence have largely been based on the primary evidence gathered by Bottéro.

[18] For listed examples, see the two long treatments by Bottéro, with Mari examples gathered in my "Mari's *ʿiBrum*." The verb is written in cuneiform with HA/IH, etc., and the labial B/P may be read either way. By comparison with the *ʿayin* preserved at Ugarit and in Egyptian, the first consonant is surely this one, and the middle radical remains to be interpreted (see Borger 1958). Whichever consonant is to be found in the early second-millennium texts, the verb is almost certainly cognate with the noun.

[19] 1 ^{lú}*Nu-ma-ha-yu ù i-na Sa-ga-ra-tim*^{ki} *wa-ši-ib ù a-na Kur-da* [32] *ih-bu-ra-am ù* 1 LÚ *wa-ar-ki Sa-ga-ra-an i-la-ak* (ARM 27, 116: 31–32).

[20] "I have left to live as an outsider" is *a-na ha-pí-ru-tim at-ta-ṣí* (see ARM 28, 46: 2′–8′); the translation depends on the meaning of the term under discussion, of course.

[21] Many of the earlier *ʿapiru* references, from the early second millennium, have to do with soldiers; see Bottéro 1954 for the texts.

If the identification of *ʿapiru* groups in later texts does reflect a social reality with real links to this terminology and experience, then it is possible that they initially consisted particularly of men who were gathered to fight as units and then maintained such communities over longer periods, beyond their commitments to the kings who identified them this way. Although the Tunip-Teššup text shows a kind of *ʿapiru* census, even if as a catch-all, it may be that by declining to assimilate into other defined communities, they committed themselves to leaders without accepting the framework of census by settlements, like Mari's Hana people, who also fought by independent agreement. Such independence from accounting by royal census would have been anathema to imperial rulers like the Egyptian pharaohs, even as large polities such as those of Abdi-Aširta with Amurru and of Labʾayu in the southern highlands could be founded on such an alternative social order.

Most simply, it appears that the *ʿapiru* of the later second millennium, including the usage associated with the Amarna letters, represents a social approximation of the Hana in the Mari letters. At Mari, that term may refer to Zimri-Lim's Binu Simʾal people but is ultimately a social category defining those not identified by town of residence. The *ʿapiru* are rooted in a terminology as old as the Hana, though with a slightly different meaning. If the word *hana* derives from the root /*ḥny*/ 'to camp,' then the category focuses on the mode of residence, which depends on movable tents rather than fixed houses.[22] In contrast, the verb *ʿab/pāru* has to do with movement, leaving one residence to take up another. Only the word *hana* envisions life with movement as a habit, whereas the *ʿapiru* category is rooted in the notion of a single disruption. They share, however, the picture of people who continue to be identified by the fact that they cannot be related to a town of current and permanent residence. The question is who such people can be when they represent a large social class, and here again, Mari offers a useful point of reference, because this archive gives us an unusually detailed view of the world away from settlements.

In the social landscape offered by the Mari archives, there are no appreciable numbers of migrant bandits or gangs of dislocated people who live outside of urban boundaries. Equally, there is no special concern to define "resident aliens," a class of permanent outsiders who may reside in a town long-term and yet who are always foreign.[23] Where groups of significant scale are considered as peoples identified by names, these are of the sort commonly called "tribal": the Binu Simʾal and the Binu Yamina, the Numhâ, the Yamutbal, and others. The question is what such groups may be when identified as a class by those who have no interest in their particular associations. By the time of the Amarna letters, the answer may be *ʿapiru*. The earliest treatment of *ʿapiru* as massed groups appears to have been for military enlistment, when such people lived in the domain served and yet could not be said to originate there. We know neither the backgrounds of these people nor their current affiliations — only that the government did not know how to count them by towns. In the Amarna correspondence, however, the *ʿapiru* are coherent, connected, and the primary political base for the kingdoms of Amurru and Labʾayu, as seen from outside. If we set aside the assumption that the backcountry of the southern Levant was populated by disaffiliated bands with no durable identity, and we consider the Mari landscape as a comparison, it is more likely that the population not defined by towns would have maintained identities that could transcend settled space. Such identities would look like those of the Binu Simʾal and the Binu Yamina at Mari, where they are called "tribal." One Mari text identifies a fighting force of *ʿapiru* as explicitly belonging to one such group, the Yamutbal, serving under a Yamutbal leader who has offered to help Mari capture a recalcitrant city.[24] These are not people who are displaced from their proper places in a social system; they are merely classed as a group traveling from what one might consider a fixed home base, or without one — yet identified adequately as Yamutbal on the move.[25]

---

[22] For this proposed etymology, which suits the actual usage of the noun, see Durand 1992, pp. 113–14; cf. Fleming 2004, p. 47.

[23] This is what is envisioned for the biblical *gēr*, a category that is compared to the *ʿapiru* by Ahlstöm (1986, p. 12). In the Bible, this class is of interest for the individual legal standing of its members, not because any large communities of *gērîm* are recognized and feared or courted.

[24] 30 $^{\text{lú.meš}}$*Ya-mu-ut-ba-la-yu ha-bi-ru i-na qa-ti-šu i-la-ku* 'Thirty Yamutbalite *ʿapiru* are under his command' (A.2939: 13–14, in Charpin 1993, p. 188; cf. Bottéro 1954, no. 19; Pohl 1957, p. 159).

[25] Although his sense of the ancient social landscape reflected earlier conceptions, Michael Astour (1999, p. 36) offered an interpretation of the *ʿapiru* that anticipates mine and likewise works especially from the Amarna evidence. He observes that "the perfectly sane view of the Ḫapiru as seminomadic tribal intruders of the tilled land, for all its textual and historical support, was all but drummed out in the nineteen twenties and thirties." The idea of the *ʿapiru* as "aliens, i.e. immigrants, fugitives, refugees, people of most diverse geographical or ethnic origin, who had nothing in common with each other but their homelessness, who were kept apart from the indigenous population by special discriminatory laws" was a retrojection of post–World War I European experience onto the past by the likes of Benno Landsberger and Julius Lewy (Astour 1999, pp. 36–37). Likewise, Michael Rowton followed Landsberger in denying the *ʿapiru* any tribal identity, even though there was no basis to know they lacked such organization: "If the Ḫapiru 'bands' were externally similar to tribal units, the right thing is to admit that they were indeed tribal units. ... History shows that wherever one finds independent armed bands, these were always ethnically homogeneous"

The *ʿapiru* of Amarna would not be "tribes" in any direct sense, especially as viewed from inside. Rather, they would include so-called tribal peoples as viewed from outside by the rulers of towns not invested in this social framework, undifferentiated from others without town-based identity. This would explain why the Egyptians did not fight against the *ʿapiru* or consider them enemies; the *ʿapiru* who fought for Egypt were simply people from such tribe-like groups — not nomads, not necessarily herdsmen, but listed this way as the most convenient way to take their census for military purposes. Viewed this way, the *ʿapiru* need not be detached from the social order, and we need not even assume that they had cut ties to settled homes and kin. They were identified as without a fixed town of residence, like Mari's Hana, but this may often have reflected an integrated society of farmers and herdsmen.

The *ʿapiru* in the Landscape of the Late Bronze Age Southern Levant

The political landscape of the southern Levant during the Late Bronze Age remains something of a conundrum, worth further study.[26] Despite the fact that archaeologists and historians alike know about the *ʿapiru* and attempt to account for them, their supposed character as displaced persons places them outside the normal classifications of study based solely on excavation and survey. In search of identities for the inhabitants of any setting — urban, rural, or hinterland — the primary occupants are rarely considered not to belong. Instead, one speaks of townspeople and villagers, farmers and herdsmen, agricultural and pastoralist ways of life, degrees of craft specialization in urban situations, and so on. Where are the *ʿapiru* in the excavated and surveyed landscape of the Late Bronze Age southern Levant?

Certain basic facts are available. In the early to mid-second millennium, the Middle Bronze Age IIB marked a high point in local life, as measured by large populations in numerous sites. This thriving period overlapped with the so-called Hyksos rule in the Egyptian north, when links between Egypt and Asia were vigorous (Frankel et al. 2001, p. 129; cf. Broshi and Gophna 1986). The end of the Middle Bronze Age came with Egyptian invasion of the Levant as one expression of a major political transition, and many of the great walled cities suffered destruction or damage. Egypt ruled the Mediterranean Levant as "Canaan" through the Late Bronze Age, from the later sixteenth century through the early part of the twelfth. Viewed from the Egyptian side, the earlier phases of conquest and consolidation were followed by the establishment of military strongholds and administrative centers in a system that resulted in the relatively stable rule of the more southern lands, at least, through the Amarna period and the fourteenth century (Weinstein 1981).[27] The Egyptians faced more difficulty with the local regimes in the thirteenth century and responded with more intrusive policies, reflected in further construction.

There is considerable discussion over how Egyptian rule was expressed in actual local conditions as encountered in archaeological research. Gonen (1984, p. 63) tracks the numbers of settlements across southern Palestine throughout the Late Bronze Age. The numbers for the Middle Bronze II are roughly matched by the thirteenth century, with gradual recovery after the vast drop-off in the sixteenth century.[28] Many more of the later sites are small, and where the Middle Bronze towns survived, it was often on a much smaller scale. The result would have been a vastly smaller population, concentrated near the coast and in the lowlands.[29] Although there is some

(ibid., p. 40). This is a remarkably independent and insightful line of reasoning, in response to the basic nature of the evidence. Note that Rowton (1976, p. 14) considered the *ʿapiru* to reflect the "continuous seepage from the tribe" that occurs when "nomadic" tribes are in close contact with sedentary populations — a reconstruction that displays his understanding of Near Eastern society as ultimately polarized between sedentary and nomad as fully separate groups.

[26] This is the general problem investigated by Brendon Benz (2012 and n. 8, above).

[27] Higginbotham (2000, p. 1) emphasizes the significant rebound of the region after the initial wave of Egyptian destructions in the sixteenth century.

[28] For the Bronze Age, these are Middle Bronze II (54), sixteenth century (24), fifteenth century (28), fourteenth century (48), thirteenth century (56). These numbers are only based on excavated sites; survey evidence sharpens the pattern (Gonen 1984, p. 66, table 2). Frankel et al. (2001, pp. 128–30) observe a similar pattern for the Upper Galilee, which they compare with the Benjamin region, where the reduction is even sharper.

[29] Herzog (2003, p. 93) bases this conclusion on the work of Bunimovitz (1989, p. 152), who estimated a change from 137,000 to 27,600 between Middle Bronze II and Late Bronze I, with the early impact of the Egyptian takeover.

question about the possible reuse of the great Middle Bronze ramparts at some sites, Late Bronze towns seem to have been generally unfortified. Reinforced palaces formed the central strongholds of these sites, reflecting their modest scale (Herzog 2003, pp. 89–92; cf. Gonen 1984, pp. 69–70). Bunimovitz (1995, p. 323) considers that while in the Middle Bronze, the concentration of large sites in the southern coastal plain suggests a unified polity — which he does not name — the Late Bronze Age shows little such political integration. This is the landscape of "semi-autonomous states" visible in the Amarna correspondence. Despite Gonen's count of small settlements, Bunimovitz emphasizes the essentially urban nature of the Late Bronze population (1995, p. 324).[30] For him, there was no true circle of "peasants" dependent on the urban centers that would provide the basis for a "revolt" in Mendenhall's terms. Instead, the conflict at the end of the Late Bronze Age must have been between sedentary and non-sedentary groups.

In general, this leaves us with a countryside occupied by few fixed settlements, without large populations of farming villages dependent on urban centers. People either live in towns or not, and if they do not, the first conclusion is that they are pastoralists. Yet the *shosu* herdsmen known to Egypt are identified with lands to the south and east of the highlands that came to be occupied by Israel and that are visible in the Amarna correspondence. Given the frequent association of the *ʿapiru* with the regions outside of town centers, in highland strongholds like Amurru to the north and the region surrounding Shechem to the south, we may wonder whether these peoples could also be involved with what Anne Porter calls "broad range" herding, beyond the limits of daily travel from towns.[31] Mari shows us that such groups developed forms of social organization that allowed them to maintain bonds across space, with group members resident both in settlements and in herding camps, thus distributing labor according to need. The actual names of groups not defined by town centers seem to have been beyond the interest of the vassals who reported to Egypt. Mari's insight into this world is rare in the ancient Near East, a reflection of the unusual identity and circumstances of Zimri-Lim.

If something like this scenario is conceivable, then the southern Levant in the thirteenth century would have been occupied by a mosaic of political forms with diverse characters. Some would have been constituted by central towns with limited scope, as commonly imagined. Especially in the highlands and farther inland, however, society may not have been divided between socially separate urbanites and country pastoralists. The peoples of the steppe may have been linked by social bonds that formed the basis for polities incorporating urban populations as well. A model may be the kingdom of Labʾayu in the Amarna evidence, where town centers like Shechem did not define his people, and his son could conveniently be found far from town with the *ʿapiru* when his Egyptian overlords called.

Abbreviations

ARM 27	Maurice Birot. *Correspondance des gouverneurs de Qaṭṭunân*. Archives royales de Mari 27. Paris: Editions Recherches sur les Civilisations, 1993
ARM 28	Jean-Robert Kupper. *Lettres royales du temps de Zimri-Lim*. Archives royales de Mari 28. Paris: Editions Recherches sur les Civilisations, 1998
EA	Moran 1992

[30] Killebrew (2005, p. 97) contrasts the continuity between Middle and Late Bronze material culture patterns in Canaan with the breakdown into distinct regional material cultures in the early Iron Age.

[31] Porter 2012, chapter 1.

Bibliography

Ahlstöm, Gösta W.

1986 *Who Were the Israelites?* Winona Lake: Eisenbrauns.

Astour, Michael C.

1999 "The Hapiru in the Amarna Texts: Basic Points of Controversy." *Ugarit-Forschungen* 31: 31–50.

Benz, Brendon C.

2012 The Varieties of Sociopolitical Experience in the Amarna Age Levant and the Rise of Early Israel. Ph.D. dissertation. New York University. [Projected date]

Borger, Riekele

1958 "Das Problem der *ʿapiru* ('Ḫabiru')." *Zeitschrift des Deutschen Palästina-Vereins* 74: 121–32.

Bottéro, Jean

1954 *Le problème des Ḫabiru à la 4ᵉ Rencontre Assyriologique Internationale.* Paris: Imprimerie Nationale.

1972 "Ḫabiru." *Reallexikon der Assyriologie* 4: 14–27.

1981 "Les Ḫabiru, les nomades et les sédentaires." In *Nomads and Sedentary Peoples: 30th International Congress of Human Sciences in Asia and North Africa*, edited by J. Silva Castillo, pp. 89–107. Mexico City: Collegio de Mexico.

Broshi, Magen, and Ram Gophna

1986 "Middle Bronze Age II Palestine: Its Settlements and Population." *Bulletin of the American Schools of Oriental Research* 261: 73–90.

Buccellati, Giorgio

1977 "ʿApirū and Munnabtūtu — The Stateless of the First Cosmopolitan Age." *Journal of Near Eastern Studies* 36: 145–47.

Bunimovitz, Shlomo

1989 The Land of Israel in the Late Bronze Age: A Case Study of Socio-cultural Change in a Complex Society. Ph.D. dissertation. Tel Aviv University. [In Hebrew]

1995 "On the Edge of Empires — Late Bronze Age (1500–1200 B.C.E.)." In *The Archaeology of Society in the Holy Land*, edited by Thomas E. Levy, pp. 320–31. New York: Facts on File.

Charpin, Dominique

1993 "Un souverain éphémère en Ida-Maraṣ: Išme-Addu d'Ašnakkum." *MARI* 7: 185–87.

Charpin, Dominique, and Jean-Marie Durand

1986 "'Fils de Sim'al': les origines tribales des rois de Mari." *Revue d'Assyriologie* 80/2: 141–83.

de Vaux, Roland

1968 "Le problème des Ḫapiru après quinze années." *Journal of Near Eastern Studies* 27: 221–28.

Dever, William G.

2003 *Who Were the Early Israelites and Where Did They Come From?* Grand Rapids: Eerdmans.

Diakonoff, I. M.

1982 "The Structure of Near Eastern Society before the Middle of the 2nd Millennium B.C." *Oikumene* 3: 7–100.

Durand, Jean-Marie

1992 "Unité et diversités au Proche-Orient à l'époque amorrite." In *La circulation des biens, des personnes et des idées dans le Proche-Orient ancien* (actes de la 38ᵉ Rencontre Assyriologique Internationale, Paris, 8–10 juillet 1991), edited by Dominique Charpin and Francis Joannès, pp. 97–128. Compte Rendu Rencontre Assyriologique Internationale 38. Paris: Éditions Recherche sur les civilisations.

2004 "Peuplement et sociétés à l'époque amorrite (I): Les clans Bensim'alites." *Amurru* 3: 111–97.

Fleming, Daniel E.

2004 *Democracy's Ancient Ancestors: Mari and Early Collective Governance.* Cambridge: Cambridge University Press.

2009 "Kingship of City and Tribe Conjoined: Zimri-Lim at Mari." In *Nomads, Tribes, and the State in the Ancient Near East: Cross-disciplinary Perspectives*, edited by Jeffrey Szuchman, pp. 227–40. Oriental Institute Seminars 5. Chicago: The Oriental Institute.

Frankel, Rafael; Nimrod Getzov; Mordechai Aviam; and Avi Degani

2001 *Settlement Dynamics and Regional Diversity in Ancient Upper Galilee: Archaeological Survey of Upper Galilee.* Jerusalem: Israel Antiquities Authority.

Gonen, Rivka

1984 "Urban Canaan in the Late Bronze Period." *Bulletin of the American Schools of Oriental Research* 253: 61–73.

Gottwald, Norman K.

1979 *The Tribes of Yahweh: A Sociology of the Religion of Liberated Israel, 1250–1050 B.C.E.* Maryknoll: Orbis Books.

Grabbe, Lester L.

2007 *Ancient Israel: What Do We Know and How Do We Know It?* London: T. and T. Clark.

Greenberg, Moshe

1955 *The Ḫab/piru*. American Oriental Series 39. New Haven: American Oriental Society.

Heltzer, Michael

1981 *The Suteans*. Series maior 13. Naples: Istituto Universitario Orientale.

Herzog, Ze'ev

2003 "The Canaanite City between Ideology and Archaeological Reality." In *Saxa Loquentur: Studien zur Archäologie Palästinas/Israels: Festschrift für Volkmar Fritz zum 65. Geburtstag*, edited by Cornelis G. den Hertog, Ulrich Hübner, and Stefan Münger, pp. 85–96. Alter Orient und Altes Testament 302 Münster: Ugarit Verlag.

Higginbotham, Carolyn R.

2000 *Egyptianization and Elite Emulation in Ramesside Palestine: Governance and Accommodation on the Imperial Periphery*. Culture and History of the Ancient Near East 2. Leiden: Brill.

Ivanov, V. V.

1974 "Ḫabiru in Cuneiform Hittite and Luwian Texts." In *Internationale Tagung der Keilschriftforscher der sozialistischen Länder, Budapest, 23–25 April 1974*, edited by G. Komoroczy, pp. 39–40. Budapest: Eötvös Loránd Tudományegyetem, Ókori Történeti Tanszék.

Killebrew, Ann E.

2005 *Biblical Peoples and Ethnicity: An Archaeological Study of Egyptians, Canaanites, Philistines, and Early Israel 1300–1100 B.C.E.* Archaeology and Biblical Studies 9. Atlanta: Society of Biblical Literature.

Knudtzon, J. A.

1964 *Die el-Amarna-Tafeln*. Aalen: Otto Zeiler (from 1915 edition).

Liverani, Mario

1979 "Farsi Habiru." *Vicino Oriente* 1–2: 65–77.

Marello, Pierre

1992 "Vie nomade." In *Recueil d'études en l'honneur de Michel Fleury*, edited by Jean-Marie Durand, pp. 115–25. Florilegium Maniarum. Mémoires de NABU 1. Paris: SEPOA.

Mendenhall, George

1962 "The Hebrew Conquest of Palestine." *Biblical Archaeologist* 25/3: 66–87.

Miglio, Adam E.

2010 Solidarity and Political Authority during the Reign of Zimrī-Līm (c. 1775–1762 B.C.). Ph.D. dissertation, University of Chicago.

Moran, William L.

1992 *The Amarna Letters*. Baltimore: Johns Hopkins University Press.

Na'aman, Nadav

1986 "Ḫabiru and Hebrews: The Transfer of a Social Term to the Literary Sphere." *Journal of Near Eastern Studies* 45: 271–86.

1994 "The Canaanites and Their Land." *Ugarit-Forschungen* 26: 397–418.

2005 "The Town of Ibirta and the Relations of the ʿ*apiru* and the Shasu." In *Ancient Israel and Its Neighbors: Interaction and Counteraction Canaan in the Second Millennium B.C.E.*, pp. 275–79. Winona Lake: Eisenbrauns.

Pohl, Alfred
1957 "Einige Gedanken zur Habiru-Frage." *Wiener Zeitschrift für die Kunde des Morgenlandes* 54: 157–60.

Porter, Anne
2012 *Mobile Pastoralism and the Formation of Near Eastern Civilizations: Weaving Together Society*. Cambridge: Cambridge University Press.

Routledge, Bruce E.
2004 *Moab in the Iron Age: Hegemony, Polity, Archaeology*. Philadelphia: University of Pennsylvania Press.

Rowton, Michael
1976 "Dimorphic Structure and the Problem of the *'apirû-'ibrîm*." *Journal of Near Eastern Studies* 35: 13–20.

Salvini, Mirjo
1996 *The Ḫabiru Prism of King Tunip-Teššup of Tikunani*. Documenta Asiana 3. Rome: Istituti editoriali e poligrafici internazionali.

von Soden, Wolfram
1984 Review of *Ḫabiru-Hebräer: Eine sozio-linguistische Studie über die Herkunft des Gentiliziums 'ibrî vom Appellativum ḫabiru*, by Oswald Loretz. *Ugarit-Forschungen* 16: 364–68.

Weinstein, James M.
1981 "The Egyptian Empire in Palestine: A Reassessment." *Bulletin of the American Schools of Oriental Research* 241: 1–28.

5

Denominal, Lexicalized *hiphil* Verbs

W. Randall Garr, University of California, Santa Barbara

1. Introduction

The *hiphil* is widely recognized as a stem that "serves mainly as the **causative** of the *qal*" (Blau 2010, §4.3.5.7.1 [emphasis original]; see also Bergsträsser 1929, §§19a–a*; and Tropper 1990, pp. 16–17; cf. Speiser 1936, pp. 23–24 = 1967, pp. 404–05).

> **וּבָאָה** הַשֶּׁמֶשׁ The sun will set. (Mi 3:6)
>
> **וְהֵבֵאתִי** הַשֶּׁמֶשׁ I will make the sun set. (Am 8:9)

> וְחַטֹּאתֶיךָ לֹא **אֶזְכֹּר הַזְכִּירֵנִי** Your sins I remember no more. Help me remember! (Is 43:25–26 [after NJPS])

> וְהַחוֹסֶה בִי יִנְחַל־אֶרֶץ Whoever takes refuge in me will possess the land. (Is 57:13)
>
> אַתָּה **תַּנְחִיל** אֶת־הָעָם הַזֶּה אֶת־הָאָרֶץ You will lead this people to possess the land. (Jo 1:6)

It has a distinct and definable profile. The *hiphil* "has a clearly derivational status: it is completely predictable in form, and largely predictable in function; it is fully productive in that it can be derived from all kinds of verbs, both intransitive and transitive" (Kouwenberg 1997, p. 250, on the Akkadian Š stem). It usually adds an external agent to the underlying nonderived verb (ibid., p. 243).

A number of *hiphil* verbs, however, do not conform to this model. Bergsträsser labels this group "isolated" (1929, §19b; see also Waltke and O'Connor 1990, §27.4). Joüon prefers "pseudo-*hifil*" (Joüon and Muraoka 2006, §54f). In either case, these verbs have *hiphil* morphology but are often non-productive and largely unpredictable in semantic content. Such verbs are assigned to the *hiphil* stem on a lexical basis. Two common verbs in this category are הִכָּה 'hit, strike' (נכ"ה) and הִשְׁלִיךְ 'throw'; their attestation lies entirely or predominantly in the *hiphil* and associated passive. The majority of these verbs, though, originate from nonverbal roots. That origin may be prepositional, as in הִגִּיד 'inform, tell' < נֶגֶד 'facing, opposite' (Waltke and O'Connor 1990, §27.4b). The origin may be adjectival, as in הִלְבִּין 'turn white' (Jo 1:7; Is 1:18; Ps 51:9; see also Dn 11:35) < לָבָן 'white' or הִצְנִיעַ 'act modestly' (Mi 6:8) < צָנוּעַ 'modest' (Prov 11:2). Frequently, that origin is nominal: for example, הֶאֱבִיר 'soar' (Job 39:26) < אֵבֶר 'wing,' הִמְטִיר 'rain' < מָטָר 'rain,' and הֵעִיד 'testify' < עֵד 'witness.' Yet whether the *hiphil* be de-prepositional, de-adjectival, or denominal,[1] its morphological assignment is uniformly lexical. Such verbs are called LEXICALIZED.[2]

---

[1] Cf. the widespread archaic alternative "denominative."

[2] Cf. "LEXICAL causative," which is also unproductive but expresses a cause-effect relationship in a *non*derived stem: e.g., הָרַג 'kill' (as opposed to הֵמִית 'put to death').

Practically all lexicalized *hiphils* are non-productive, morphologically causative, and semantically non-causative (Premper 1987, p. 119; in conjunction with Bybee 1985, p. 18).

This study focuses on the denominal subset of lexicalized *hiphils* (see Gerber 1896, pp. 36–50 for an overambitious yet incomplete discussion). It is a delimited group whose members are identifiable and relatively uncontroversial, and it constitutes the largest class within lexicalized *hiphils* (~35 percent). It has not been determined, however, why this semantically non-causative group bears causative grammatical coding (see, in this context, Steiner 1997, p. 161). In general terms, grammarians attribute the causative form to the effecting nature of these *hiphil* verbs (Gesenius 1910, §53g; and Joüon and Muraoka 2006, §54d; for a compatible notion, see Porges 1875, pp. 297–98). But they also recognize that this feature does not explain every denominal, lexicalized *hiphil* or, for that matter, non-denominal, lexicalized *hiphils*. An explanation should be available, though (cf. Jenni 2000, p. 87 = 2005, p. 101). Functionalists, for example, believe that the relationship between form and meaning is "non-arbitrary" (see Bybee, Perkins, and Pagliuca 1994, p. 40). They claim that "certain formally identifiable morphemes in the languages of the world have certain semantic properties and are drawn from certain areas of semantic space" (ibid., p. 37; see also Kemmer 1993, pp. 8, 222; and, somewhat differently, Næss 2007, p. 4). This credo suggests, in fact, that all *hiphil* verbs — causative and non-causative — share "certain semantic properties."

2. The Causative *hiphil*

The morphological and semantic templates for denominal, lexicalized *hiphils* lie in the sphere of causativity. For as the consensus holds, the *hiphil* is a prototypical causative structure. It has two identifiable parts. Its root or basic verb expresses effect, result, or consequence. Its derivational morphology — a combination of prefixed **ha-* and infixed *-ī-* — expresses cause or antecedence. Together, they form a single clause comprising two discrete sub-events: "X (the subject) caused that Y (the second subject) be or do something" (Waltke and O'Connor 1990, §27.1e; see also Joüon and Muraoka 2006, §54d). Stated differently, an "entity (person, thing, abstract force) either brings about ... or, at the very least, fails to prevent" the situation expressed by the non-causative verb (Comrie 1985, p. 330; see also Lewis 1973, p. 563; or Tropper 1990, p. 3).

2.1. Causer

By definition, all causative structures commence with a CAUSER. The causer is the newly introduced actor that initiates, controls, or is responsible for — "causes" — the subsequent situation (see Speiser 1936, p. 29 = 1967, p. 412). The causer is usually an agent, whether human (Jo 1:6; Is 43:26) or divine (Am 8:9). Sometimes, however, it is neither.

מִנְחַת זִכָּרוֹן **מַזְכֶּרֶת** עָוֺן (It is) a meal offering of recollection, recalling wrongdoing. (Num 5:15)

הַגֶּשֶׁם וְהַשֶּׁלֶג ... הִרְוָה אֶת־הָאָרֶץ **וְהוֹלִידָהּ וְהִצְמִיחָהּ** The rain and the snow ..., having watered the earth, will get it to bear and sprout ... (Is 55:10)

וּבוּז־מִשְׁפָּחוֹת **יְחִתֵּנִי** The scorn of clans made me terrified. (Job 31:34); see also

וְהָעֹרְבִים **מְבִיאִים** לוֹ לֶחֶם וּבָשָׂר The ravens brought him bread and meat. (1 Kgs 17:6)

In all cases, though, the causer is the force that initiates and propels the dependent situation. It is a force that proceeds from the causer and usually moves outward.

2.2. Impingement

The manner by which the causer effects the dependent situation is never expressed in the *hiphil* (Jenni 1992, p. 84 = 1997, p. 169). It may be conveyed by physical contact and manipulation (1 Kgs 17:6; see also Is 55:10). It may be an act of assistance (Is 43:25) or leadership (Jo 1:6). It may be an abstract and overwhelming power (Am 8:9), or it may be perceived as an undeflectable stimulus (Job 31:34). Regardless, it is dynamic and impinging.

2.3. Causee

The force of the causer impinges upon a referentially discrete CAUSEE. The causee may be a coparticipant — whether cooperating or not — in the effected situation (Jo 1:6; Job 31:34), in which case the causee is an instrument through which the causer effects the ultimate causative goal. Alternatively, the causee may lack agentive force and, controlled by the causer, become a dynamic patient (Am 8:6). The force of the causer affects the causee, making a transition between antecedent/cause and consequence/effect.

2.4. Resultant Change of Status

The transition marks the onset of the dependent situation expressed by the embedded non-causative verb. While this situation may be transitive (Jo 1:6), intransitive (Am 8:9), or ambitransitive (see Is 43:26), it consistently registers a change that would not have occurred without instigation by the causer — at least in the mind of the speaker or writer. The type of change is broad: for example, location (1 Kgs 17:6), position (Am 8:9), experience (Job 31:34), cognition (Is 43:26), or even regeneration (see Is 55:10). The type naturally depends on the situation expressed by the non-causative verb. Still, this change marks the goal and endpoint of causative force initiated by the causer. Causative input effects perceptible change.

3. Denominal, Lexicalized *hiphil* Verbs

The semantic profile of this group seems very different from that of the causative *hiphil*. It is not derived from a simpler, non-causative verb. It does not add a new, external agent to a basic proposition and thereby rearrange any underlying participants. Though morphologically transparent and bipartite, it does not express two discrete sub-events in a cause–effect relationship. Rather, it expresses a single unmediated event.

3.1. Directed, Initiating Force

Whereas the activity of the causative *hiphil* is largely initiated by an agentive causer, this causative role fades in denominal, lexicalized *hiphils*. An agent may initiate a process and produce the underlying nominal: for example, הִצְהִיר 'make oil' (Job 24:11) and, perhaps, הֶעֱצִיב 'idolize' (Jer 44:19). An agent may provide or contribute a nominal: for example, הִנְעִיל 'give shoes' (2 Chr 28:15) and הִקְרִיב 'offer (sacrifice)' (for the latter, see Gerber 1896, pp. 44–46). An agent may impose a nominal through directive order: for example, וַיַּהַס in Num 13:30: "Caleb hushed the people" (cf. Tawil 2009, p. 87a). The agent need not be part of a causer–causee relationship.

The grammatical subject of denominal, lexicalized *hiphils* may also have a variety of referents. In the examples above, it is a human agent who instigates, controls, and effects. The same is true for הִזְעִיק 'let out a cry' (Job 35:9); see also the divine agent of הִמְטִיר 'rain.' In other examples, the agent behaves in a focused and deliberate manner or, at least, is perceived as such: for example, הִזִּיר 'undertake and perform Nazirite practice; abstain' (Num 6:2.3.5.6.12), הֵעִיד 'testify,' and arguably הִפְרִיא 'act like an ass' (Hos 13:15; see 8:9) (see Waltke and O'Connor 1990, §27.4a; and, perhaps, Kienast 2001, §188.1d, for the behavioral component). Alternatively, the subject may be a semantic patient — undergoing and without control (Talmy 1976, p. 89; in conjunction with Mithun 1991, p. 527). On occasion, that patient is human, as in הֵצַר 'be in labor' (Jer 48:41, 49:22). It may be faunal, as in הִתְאִים 'have twins' (Sg 4:2, 6:6). Or it may be inanimate, especially a meteorological phenomenon, as in הִשְׁלִיג 'snow' (Ps 68:15).

These denominal, lexicalized *hiphils* share several features with their canonical counterpart. First, the activity expressed by the verb originates in the subject. Whether it is agentive or patientive, the subject is the sole party responsible for — "causes" — the activity. Second, the subject radiates energy or force. It usually initiates the activity as if by intervention. Or, the source may be internal and arise spontaneously by natural cause. It need not have an external source. Third, the energy or force is channeled along a particular path (Matisoff, cited in Li 1993, p. 355). In a minority of cases, that energy stays within the subject. For the most part, however, it is directed outward. It proceeds away from the subject in transitive, intransitive, and ambitransitive clauses.

3.2. Motion

In the canonical *hiphil*, the causer embodies an instigative force that affects the causee and motivates the situation expressed by the non-causative base. This energy has a source, affects a referentially discrete intermediary, and usually rests at a goal; since these stages cannot be rearranged, the propelling force in the causative *hiphil* proceeds in only one direction. It emanates from the causer, proceeds along a path, and reaches an endpoint.

This unidirectional force has several manifestations in the denominal, lexicalized *hiphil*. It may be an audible outburst, as in הִזְעִיק 'let out a cry.' It may have an inchoative reading, as in de-adjectival *hiphil*s (e.g., Bergsträsser 1929, §19d) and, perhaps, הֶאֱלִיף 'increase a thousandfold' (Ps 144:13). The force may transfer its nominal along a path and attain its goal, as in וַיַּנְעִלוּם 'they gave them shoes' (2 Chr 28:15) (see Nyberg 1920, p. 251). Or the force may be physical movement directed at its underlying nominal: הֵימִין 'go right' (Gen 13:9; 2 Sam 14:19; Ez 21:21) and הִשְׂמְאִיל 'go left' (Gen 13:9; 2 Sam 14:19; Is 30:21; Ez 21:21) (Porges 1875, p. 298; and Brockelmann 1908, §257Ghη [p. 528]); see also הִצִּיעַ 'bed down' (יצ"ע) (Is 58:5; Ps 139:8; see also Is 14:11; Est 4:3). Unidirectional force can be interpreted concretely.

3.3. Instrument

As in the canonical *hiphil*, the manner by which the subject conveys its animating force is not expressed. In the examples given in §2.2, the manner must be inferred. Most have a common element. Whether physical contact, manipulation, assistance, or leadership, that common element is the (human) body. Among non-denominal, lexicalized *hiphil*s, for instance, הִכָּה 'hit, strike' involves a large part of the upper body. הִשְׁלִיךְ 'throw' involves the hands and arms. The force of the *hiphil* is commonly conveyed through the body or a body part.

Among denominal, lexicalized *hiphil*s, the underlying nominal may name an instrument. The instrument may be the gear or device that accomplishes an activity: for example, הִקְצִיעַ 'scrape' (Lev 14:41); see also מַחְצְצִרִים/מַחְצְרִים 'playing the trumpet' (1 Chr 15:24; 2 Chr 5:12, 7:6, 13:14, 29:28 [*ktiv*]). הָפֵחַ 'trapped' (Is 42:22 [passive]) may belong here too, though its nominal also represents the goal of the activity. In each case, the underlying instrument is an alienable entity. In other cases, though, it is an inalienable body part: for example, הֶאֱבִיר 'soar' and הֶאֱזִין 'listen up, pay attention to'; see also הִלְשִׁין 'badmouth' (Prov 30:10). In these latter *hiphil*s, the subject uses the appropriate body part to activate or accomplish a physical, cognitive, or communicative activity.

3.4. Resultant Change of Status

Whether a *hiphil* be causative or not, the outcome is the same: a state or status that is perceptibly different from what obtained before. In denominal, lexicalized *hiphil*s, that difference is often obvious. For example, when the *hiphil* effects the underlying nominal, that nominal — which did not exist beforehand — is completely new. The instigative force may be external, as in הִגְשִׁים 'make rain' (Jer 14:22), הִקְהִיל 'assemble' (lit. 'make ___ into a קָהָל'), and probably הֶחֱרִים 'destroy' (lit. 'make ___ a חֵרֶם'). Alternatively, the force may develop internally: for example, הֵנֵץ 'blossom' (Sg 6:11, 7:13; see also Eccl 12:5) and הִשְׁרִישׁ 'take root' (Ps 80:10 [subj. 'vine']). The resultant change may be an altered physical state: for example, מוּפָז '(gold) plated' (פז"ז) (1 Kgs 10:18 [passive]). It may be location, as in הֵימִין 'go right,' or even ownership, as in הִנְעִיל 'give shoes.'

One last *hiphil* category, in fact, denotes ownership: הִפְרִיס 'have hoofs,' הִקְרִין 'have horns' (Ps 69:32), and, perhaps, מַשְׁכִּים 'ballsy' (אש"ך?) (Jer 5:8) (Nyberg 1920, p. 272; see also Bauer and Leander 1922, §38z″). In this instance, the change — formation, development, and growth — has already occurred. The goal is therefore attained and persists as a state of existence.

4. The *hiphil*

This discussion of the *hiphil* aims to correlate a "formally identifiable morpheme" with "certain semantic properties ... drawn from certain areas of semantic space" (see §1). The morpheme is clear. But the semantic properties remain unidentified, in part, because causativity has been interpreted narrowly. Once that concept is broadened and its constituents isolated, though, a new semantic picture of the *hiphil* emerges.

Causativity has a schematic structure. On one analysis, that structure is bipartite, having an antecedent cause and a consequent effect; energy, as it were, moves from source to goal (Radden 1985, p. 187). On another analysis, the structure is tripartite: anteriority, a discrete transition, and consequence (Talmy 1985, p. 330). Again, the situation progresses in one direction only.

But not all causatives are alike.

> הַגֶּשֶׁם וְהַשֶּׁלֶג ... **וְהוֹלִידָהּ** The rain and the snow ... will get [the earth] to bear ... (Is 55:10)

> תֶּרַח **הוֹלִיד** אֶת־אַבְרָם אֶת־נָחוֹר וְאֶת־הָרָן וְהָרָן **הוֹלִיד** אֶת־לוֹט Terah fathered Abram, Nahor, and Haran; and Haran fathered Lot. (Gen 11:27)

> וְעַתָּה יְהוָה אֱלֹהֵי יִשְׂרָאֵל **הוֹרִישׁ** אֶת־הָאֱמֹרִי מִפְּנֵי עַמּוֹ יִשְׂרָאֵל וְאַתָּה תִּירָשֶׁנּוּ הֲלֹא אֵת אֲשֶׁר **יוֹרִישְׁךָ** כְּמוֹשׁ אֱלֹהֶיךָ אוֹתוֹ תִירָשׁ וְאֵת כָּל־אֲשֶׁר **הוֹרִישׁ** יְהוָה אֱלֹהֵינוּ מִפָּנֵינוּ אוֹתוֹ נִירָשׁ Now Yahweh, Israel's God, has driven the Amorites away from his people Israel. And you'd possess [their territory]? Don't you possess what Chemosh your god gives you to possess? (Shouldn't) we possess all that Yahweh our God has driven from us (and has given us to possess)? (Judg 11:23–24)

> לֹא־תִרְאֶה אֶת־חֲמוֹר אָחִיךָ אוֹ שׁוֹרוֹ נֹפְלִים בַּדֶּרֶךְ וְהִתְעַלַּמְתָּ מֵהֶם **הָקֵם תָּקִים** עִמּוֹ You mustn't observe your fellow's ass or ox fallen on the road and ignore it. You must get it up with his help. (Dt 22:4)

> **וַהֲקֵמֹתָ** אֶת־הַמִּשְׁכָּן Then you will erect the tabernacle. (Ex 26:30; see also 40:2.18; Num 7:1, 9:15, 10:21)

As these texts illustrate, some causative *hiphil* verbs express two distinct sub-events that stand in a cause–effect relationship; they are instigated by a causer and involve an intermediary (second subject) executing the effect (INDIRECT CAUSATIVE) (e.g., Kittilä 2002, p. 261). Frequently, however, causatives express single events. Absent an intermediary, the causer not only instigates but is also directly responsible for the activity as well as any dependent change (DIRECT CAUSATIVE) (ibid., p. 259). In the indirect causative, the cause-effect relationship involves a causer, causee, and effected situation reflecting a change of status. In the direct causative, the cause–effect relationship is condensed; it has an agent and a patient. The direct causative resembles a simple transitive clause registering immediate affect or effect.

Denominal, lexicalized *hiphil*s substantially follow the pattern of the direct causative. Whether transitive, intransitive, or ambitransitive, they too signify immediate affect or effect. Moreover, they have a number of semantic properties in common with direct causatives and, ultimately, prototypical indirect causatives. First, they are each initiated by a causative force that is represented grammatically as the subject. Its specific nature varies: for example, external or internal, applied or spontaneous, controlled or uncontrolled. It nevertheless instigates, propels, and is responsible for — "causes" — the subsequent situation. It is dynamic and goal-oriented. Second, this force is conveyed along a path. That path may be an overt causee, an underlying instrument, an appropriate body part, or a natural direction. The path is the channel through which the force attains or effects its goal. Third, the channeled force produces a change. Usually the change is perceptible and clear. Occasionally, it is inferred from the result. In either case, the force reaches its endpoint.

Inasmuch as the semantic properties common to *hiphil* verbs rely on linguistic abstractions of force dynamics (Talmy 1986), they also resolve another semantic issue troubling the study of the *hiphil*. The *hiphil* projects different degrees of transitivity.

וַאדֹנָי **הִשְׁמִיעַ** אֶת־מַחֲנֵה אֲרָם קוֹל רֶכֶב קוֹל סוּס קוֹל חַיִל גָּדוֹל The Lord caused the Aramean camp to hear chariots, horses — a great army. (2 Kgs 7:6)

וְהַמֶּלֶךְ אָסָא **הִשְׁמִיעַ** אֶת־כָּל־יְהוּדָה Then King Asa called all Judah. (1 Kgs 15:22)

וְלֹא־**תַשְׁמִיעוּ** אֶת־קוֹלְכֶם You mustn't let your voice be heard. (Jo 6:10)

וְהִשְׁמִיעוּ They will sound out. (Ez 27:30)

A "causative" *hiphil* may be ditransitive, monotransitive, or intransitive. Transitivity, then, is not an intrinsic feature of the *hiphil*. It is an epiphenomenon that depends on a linguistic interpretation of force dynamics as well as the number and roles of participants in an expressed activity (cf. Kienast 2001, §188.2).

Bibliography

Bauer, Hans, and Pontus Leander

1922 *Historische Grammatik der hebräischen Sprache des Alten Testamentes*. Halle: Niemeyer.

Bergsträsser, G.

1929 *Hebräische Grammatik*, Part 2: *Verbum*. Leipzig: Hinrichs.

Blau, Joshua

2010 *Phonology and Morphology of Biblical Hebrew: An Introduction*. Linguistic Studies in Ancient West Semitic 2. Winona Lake: Eisenbrauns.

Brockelmann, Carl

1908 *Grundriss der vergleichenden Grammatik der semitischen Sprachen*, Volume 1: *Laut- und Formenlehre*. Berlin: Reuther and Reichard.

Bybee, Joan L.

1985 *Morphology: A Study of the Relation Between Meaning and Form*. Typological Studies in Language 9. Amsterdam: Benjamins.

Bybee, Joan; Revere Perkins; and William Pagliuca

1994 *The Evolution of Grammar: Tense, Aspect, and Modality in the Languages of the World*. Chicago: University of Chicago Press.

Comrie, Bernard

1985 "Causative Verb Formation and Other Verb-deriving Morphology." In *Language Typology and Syntactic Description*, Volume 3: *Grammatical Categories and the Lexicon*, edited by Timothy Shopen, pp. 309–48. Cambridge: Cambridge University Press.

Gerber, Wenzel J.

1896 *Die hebräischen Verba denominativa insbesondere im theologischen Sprachgebrauch des Alten Testamentes. Eine lexikographische Studie*. Leipzig: Hinrichs.

Gesenius, Wilhelm

1910 *Gesenius' Hebrew Grammar*. Edited by E. Kautzsch and A. E. Cowley. 2nd English edition. Oxford: Oxford University Press.

Jenni, Ernst

1992 "Kausativ und Funktionsverbgefüge: Sprachliche Bemerkungen zur Bitte: «Führe uns nicht in Versuchung»." In *Das universale Gebet: Studien zur Unservater. Jan Milič Lochman gewidmet zum 70. Geburtstag*, pp. 77–88. Theologische Zeitschrift 48/1. Basel: Reinhardt.

1997 *Studien zur Sprachwelt des Alten Testaments*. Edited by Beat Huwyler and Klaus Seybold. Stuttgart: Kohlhammer.

2000 "Aktionarten und Stammformen im Althebräischen: Das Pi'el in verbesserter Sicht." *Zeitschrift für Althebraistik* 13: 67–90.

2005 *Studien zur Sprachwelt des Alten Testaments*, Volume 2. Edited by Jürg Luchsinger, Hans-Peter Mathys, and Markus Saur. Stuttgart: Kohlhammer.

Joüon, Paul, and T. Muraoka

2006 *A Grammar of Biblical Hebrew*. 3rd edition. Subsidia Biblica 27. Rome: Pontificio Istituto Biblico.

Kemmer, Suzanne

1993 *The Middle Voice*. Typological Studies in Language 23. Amsterdam: Benjamins.

Kienast, Burkhart

2001 *Historische Semitische Sprachwissenschaft*. Wiesbaden: Harrassowitz.

Kittilä, Seppo

2002 *Transitivity: Towards a Comprehensive Typology*. Yleisen kielitieteen julkaisuja/Publications in General Linguistics 5. Turku: University of Turku.

Kouwenberg, N. J. C.

1997 *Gemination in the Akkadian Verb*. Studia Semitica Neerlandica 32. Assen: Van Gorcum.

Lewis, David

1973 "Causation." *Journal of Philosophy* 70: 556–67.

Li, Fengxiang

1993 "An Examination of Causative Morphology from a Cross-linguistic and Diachronic Perspective." In *Papers from the 27th Regional Meeting of the Chicago Linguistic Society 1991*, Part 1: *The General Session*, edited by Lise M. Dobrin, Lynn Nichols, and Rosa M. Rodríguez, pp. 344–59. Chicago Linguistic Society 27:1. Chicago: Chicago Linguistic Society.

Mithun, Marianne

1991 "Active/Agentive Case Marking and its Motivations." *Language* 67: 510–46.

Næss, Åshild

2007 *Prototypical Transitivity*. Typological Studies in Language 72. Amsterdam: Benjamins.

Nyberg, H. S.

1920 "Wortbildung mit Präfixen in den semitischen Sprachen." *Le monde oriental* 14: 177–288.

Porges, Nathan

1875 "Ueber die Verbalstammbildung in den semitischen Sprachen." *Sitzungsberichte der philosophisch-historischen Classe der kaiserlichen Akademie der Wissenschaft* 79: 281–354.

Premper, Waldfried

1987 "Kausativierung im Arabischen (Ein Beitrag zur sprachlichen Dimension der Partizipation)." *Arbeiten des Kölner Universalien - Projekts (akup)* 66: 1–131.

Radden, Günter

1985 "Spatial Metaphors Underlying Prepositions of Causality." In *The Ubiquity of Metaphor: Metaphor in Language and Thought*, edited by Wolf Paprotté and René Dirven, pp. 177–207. Current Issues in Linguistic Theory 29. Amsterdam: Benjamins.

Speiser, E. A.

1936 "Studies in Semitic Formatives." *Journal of the American Oriental Society* 56: 22–46.

1967 *Oriental and Biblical Studies: Collected Writings of E. A. Speiser.* Edited and with an introduction by Jacob J. Finkelstein and Moshe Greenberg. Philadelphia: University of Pennsylvania Press.

Steiner, Richard C.

1997 "Ancient Hebrew." In *The Semitic Languages*, edited by Robert Hetzron, pp. 145–73. London: Routledge.

Talmy, Leonard

1976 "Semantic Causative Types." In *The Grammar of Causative Constructions*, edited by Masayoshi Shibatani, pp. 43–116. Syntax and Semantics 6. New York: Academic Press.

1985 "Force Dynamics in Language and Thought." In *Papers from the Parasession on Causatives and Agentivity at the Twenty-first Regional Meeting, Chicago Linguistic Society, April 25–27, 1985*, Part 2, edited by William H. Eilfort, Paul D. Kroeber, and Karen L. Peterson, pp. 293–337. Chicago Linguistic Society 21:2. Chicago: Chicago Linguistic Society.

1986 "Force Dynamics as a Generalization over 'Causative.'" In *Languages and Linguistics: The Interdependence of Theory, Data, and Application*, edited by Deborah Tannen and James E. Alatis, pp. 67–85. Georgetown University Round Table on Languages and Linguistics 1985. Washington, D.C.: Georgetown University Press.

Tawil, Hayim ben Yosef

2009 *An Akkadian Lexical Companion for Biblical Hebrew: Etymological-semantic and Idiomatic Equivalents with Supplement on Biblical Aramaic.* Jersey City: Ktav.

Tropper, Josef

1990 *Der ugaritische Kausativstamm und die Kausativbildungen des Semitischen: Eine morphologisch-semantische Untersuchung zum Š-Stamm und zu den umstrittenen nichtsibilantischen Kausativstämmen des Ugaritischen.* Abhandlungen zur Literatur Alt-Syrien-Palästinas 2. Münster: Ugarit-Verlag.

Waltke, Bruce K., and M. O'Connor

1990 *An Introduction to Biblical Hebrew Syntax.* Winona Lake: Eisenbrauns.

6

The Treatment of Vowel Length in Arabic Grammar and Its Adaptation to Hebrew

Gideon Goldenberg, The Hebrew University of Jerusalem

The phonological value of vowel length was one of the questions that medieval Arab grammarians treated with thoughtful attention and great insight. Their work on this as on other matters does still excite interest not only as a chapter in the history of linguistic thought, but also as an important achievement in itself, which would challenge any present-day linguistic theory. Some doubts and inconsistencies concerning the phonological interpretation of long vowels in Arabic (and in cognate languages) are still found in scholarly discussions on the subject among linguists of our day as among their medieval predecessors.

The ideas that medieval Arab philologists had on long vowels will better be presented as conceived from three different points of view: (a) structural analysis, (b) theoretical speculation, and (c) phonetic description.

I. Structural Analysis of Long Vowels

Structurally long vowels were clearly understood as being necessarily a realization of vowel + weak consonant (VC). In the classical terminology, 'consonants' (σύμφωνα), in contrast to 'sonants' (φωνήεντα), are literally defined by not sounding on their own (καθ' ἑαυτὰ φωνὴν οὐκ ἔχει), needing some other element "with" which they would gain sonority. In this literal sense, 'consonant' will not be inapposite in the present context. In Arabic grammar, consonants (*ḥurūf*, here literally referring to the letters of the alphabet) are considered the basic sound units. Vowels (*ḥarakāt*, lit. 'movements') are indispensable, but they are additions (*zawāʔid*) added to link between the letters in order to make speech realizable[1] as if consonants were the bricks and vowels the mortar. Without a vowel, a consonant would not be pronounceable.[2] It is therefore the consonant that is said to be "vowelled" (*mutaḥarrik*, lit. 'movent') when it supports a following vowel; the arresting consonant ('coda') of a syllable, necessarily "unvocalized," is said to be *sākin* 'quiescent' or 'motionless.'

[1] The clearest expression of this conception is attributed to al-Xalīl: *wa-zaʕama l-Xalīlu ʔanna l-fatḥata wa-l-kasrata wa-l-ḍammata zawāʔidu, wa-hunna yalḥaqna l-ḥarfa li-yūṣala ʔ ilà l-takallumi bihī. wa-l-bināʔu huwa l-sākinu llaḏī lā ziyādata fīhi* "al-Xalīl claimed that the *fatḥah* and the *kasrah* and the *ḍammah* [i.e., 'the three vowels'] are augments, and they are affixed to the letter in order that its pronounceability is achieved; the building element is the unvowelled which has no addition" (Sībawayh II 315:2–4).

[2] Arab linguists asked the question what one could do if one wished for some reason to pronounce a consonant in isolation. About al-Xalīl it was told that when he wanted to pronounce a single consonant in order to discover its point of articulation, he would open his mouth with a *ʔalif* and then get to produce the consonant, like *ab*, *at*, *aḥ*, *aʕ*, *aġ* (al-Xalīl *Kitāb al-ʕayn* 52:12–13), certainly a device for attempting to pronounce consonants unvowelled, as bare as possible. Ibn Ǧinnī asked the same question, and answered it similarly: if the consonant is *sākin*, i.e., with no vowel following, one needs to add a prothetic vowel. For pronouncing *b*, *ṣ*, or *q*, one must say *ib*, *iṣ*, *iq*, respectively. And if you wish to say, e.g., that the word *Bakr* begins with a *b*, you say that it begins with *bah*, and *ṣilah* begins with *ṣih* (Ibn Ǧinnī *Xaṣāʔiṣ* I 27:14–28:5).

In our terms we might say that a syllable must be either CV̆ or CV̆C, no clusters being normally tolerated. When the arresting quiescent consonant of a closed syllable is "weak," represented by one of the 'weak letters' (*ḥurūf al-līn, ḥurūf al-ʕillah*), the sequence of homorganic VC will yield a smooth long vowel: *uw* → *ū*, *iy* → *ī*, *a*א → *ā*,[3] so that the "weak letters" are at the same time 'letters of prolongation' (*ḥurūf al-madd*). These letters, *ʔalif*, *wāw*, and *yāʔ*, which correspond to the three vowels *a*, *u*, and *i*, respectively, are the most common of all letters susceptible to being *zawāʔid* (v. Sībawayh II 349:11–16). They are said to be *ʔummahāt al-zawāʔid* (Sībawayh II 350:2–3, 351u, 352:1, 354:1; cf. Ibn Ğanāḥ *Kitāb al-Lumaʕ* 34:9). *Wāw* and *yāʔ* represent, in the first place, semi-vowels, or glides (*w*, *y*), and /*uw*/ or /*iy*/, the same as /*aw*/ or /*ay*/, do not differ structurally from any other VC sequence. The *ʔalif*, however, does not represent anything else but the zero consonant arresting a syllable whose center is the vowel *a*, and the presence of *ʔalif* is only manifested through the length of the vowel.

W, *y*, and *ʔalif* are, then, regarded as three phonemes; *w* and *y* are sometimes, and *ʔalif* is always, found to be "weak" following a homorganic vowel together with which they form long vowels. The change of a long vowel means in Arabic grammar a change of a short vowel with the corresponding conditioned 'change' or 'substitution' (*qalb* or *ʔibdāl*) of the arresting weak consonant. In a word like *ḏū* 'possessor of,' which is *ḏā* in the accusative and *ḏī* in the genitive, the Arab grammarian would recognize /*ḏuw*/, /*ḏiy*/, and /*ḏa*א/ with the final weak "unvowelled" *w* changing to *y* after *i* and to *ʔalif* after *a*.[4] All three are equally regarded as "unvowelled" consonants.[5] Even long vowels resulting from the contraction of V+weak C+V would be presented as VC with the C becoming *sākin* 'motionless' 'unvowelled,' for example *uwu* > *uw*, pronounced [*ū*].[6]

The common shortening of a long vowel in a closed syllable would consequently be described as falling out or elision (*suqūṭ* or *ḥaḏf*) of the arresting weak quiescent: the actual realizations of, for example, *ḏuw* + *l-ʕimāmah* 'turbaned (person), sarıklı,'[7] as *ḏul-ʕimāmah*, or of *ḏa*א + *l-ʕimāmah* as *ḏal-ʕimāmah* or of *ḏiy* + *l-ʕimāmah* as *ḏil-ʕimāmah*, would be presented, like any other vowel reduction, as cases of elision of the weak consonant to avoid, the same as required with any other sequence of consonants, the 'meeting of two quiescents' (*iltiqāʔu l-sākinayni*, also *iğtimāʕu l-sākinayni*, or *al-ğamʕu bayna sākinayni*), that is, to avoid the nascence of a cluster.[8]

The meeting of two unvowelled consonants is generally permitted only in pause (v. infra), where pausal increase of sonority is said to enable syllabic realization of consonants. Long vowels, however (and diphthongs), are allowed to occur before geminate consonants in connected speech (*fī l-darağ*) as well.[9] This would mean, in terms of Arabic grammar, the "meeting of two quiescents," the first of which is "a weak consonant" as in *da***אb***batun* [*dābbatun*] 'animal, beast,' *yaẓlimu***wn***niy* [*yaẓlimūnnī*] 'they (pl.) oppress me, they do me wrong,' *yaẓlima***אn***niy* [*yaẓlimānnī*] 'they (du.) oppress me,' *taẓlimi***yn***niy* [*taẓlimīnnī*] 'you (sg.f.) oppress me' (or forms like *duwa***yb***batun* 'little animal.'[10] Such exceptional violation of the basic rule is explained by abstract features of the sequence in question: Sībawayh would say that the weak consonant, though (in this position) unvocalizable, is here regarded as quasi-syllabic, as if it were vocalized, or in the status of 'vowelled' (*bi-manzilati mutaḥarrikin*).[11] Ibn Yaʕīš tries to be more precise when formulating the same idea, saying that in the weak consonant (qua "letter of prolongation"), it is the length that here takes the position of a vowel.[12]

---

[3] The Hebrew letter א represents here for convenience the Arabic weak *ʔalif* (ا). It marks a phonological segment functionally present though phonetically void; v. infra.

[4] In forms derived from roots with medial *w*, like *dār* (√*dwr*) or *rīḥ* (√*rwḥ*), the *w* is said to be *mayyitah sākinah* 'dead and quiescent' (al-Zamaxšarī *Mufaṣṣal* 182:14) or *ḍaʕīfah mayyitah li-sukūnihā* 'feeble and dead because of its being unvowelled' (Ibn Yaʕīš *Šarḥ al-Mufaṣṣal* X 88:2), and therefore easily replaceable by another weak quiescent.

[5] ... *ʔanna hāḏihi l-ʔaḥrufa llāʔī yaḥduṯna li-ʔišbāʕi l-ḥarakāti lā yakunna ʔillā sawākina li-ʔannahunna maddātun, wa-l-maddātu lā yataḥarrakna ʔabadan* "... that these letters that occur for satiating the vowels (v. infra) are inevitably 'vowelless' because they are lengthening, and the lengthening (letters) will never be 'vowelled'" (Ibn Ğinnī *Sirr ṣināʕat al-ʔiʕrāb* 31:16–17).

[6] *Wa-***fuʕul***un ʔin kāna min al-wāwi sukkinat ʕaynuhū l-iğtimāʕi l-ḍammatayni wa-l-wāwi fa-yuqālu* ***nūr****un wa-***ʕūn***un* "and [the pattern] *fuʕul*, i.e., **CuCuC**, if it is from [root with] *wāw*, i.e., **CuwuC**, its medial radical will become vowelless, i.e., **CuwuC** > **CuwC**, because of the combination of the two *u*-vowels with the **w**, and it will be said [***nuwur***^{un} > ***nuwr***^{un}] ***nūr***^{un}, [ʕ***uwun***^{un} > ʕ***uwn***^{un}] ***ʕūn***^{un}" (al-Zamaxšarī *Mufaṣṣal* 181:19). The words referred to here are *nūr*, that is, one of the plural forms of *nār* 'fire,' and *ʕūn*, plural form of *ʕawān* 'middle-aged' or the like, both being of the *fuʕul* pattern.

[7] For the use of this phrase for doctor of religious law, one of the *ʕulamāʔ*, cf. Dozy II 169a:23–29.

[8] See al-ʔAzharī *Tahḏīb al-luġah* I 52:2–4; cf. Sībawayh II 276–77; al-Zamaxšarī *Mufaṣṣal* 167–68; Ibn Yaʕīš *Šarḥ al-Mufaṣṣal* IX 120–21.

[9] Such gemination would generally result from the reduction of short vowels between identical consonants, as in *ḍāllīna* for **ḍālilīna*, or *ʔinna l-māl‿laka* for *ʔinna l-māla laka*.

[10] See, e.g., Sībawayh II 407; al-Zamaxšarī *Mufaṣṣal* 167 (§663); Ibn Yaʕīš *Šarḥ al-Mufaṣṣal* IX 121–22; Fleisch *Traité* I 163–65.

[11] *li-ʔanna ḥarfa l-maddi bi-manzilati mutaḥarrikin fī l-ʔidġām* (Sībawayh II 407:15.17).

[12] As an explanation of the first condition allowing such a sequence (viz., that the first of the two meeting quiescents must be a weak consonant), Ibn Yaʕīš states *ʔanna l-madda llaḏī fī ḥurūfi*

If the weak *ʔalif* before geminates can be said to be *bi-manzilati mutaḥarrikin*, still it cannot become a "vowelled" consonant in reality unless it is "strengthened" into a glottal stop,[13] as happened actually in that form of speech that would have *daʔabbatun* for *daאbbatun* [*dābbatun*], *ḍaʔallīna* for *ḍaאllīna* [*ḍāllīna*], or *ibyaʔaḍḍa* for *ibyaאḍḍa* [*ibyāḍḍa*], and so on.[14] The variation [*ā*]/[*aʔ*] in representing an original /*a*א/ is not in itself restricted to this environment, but is rather reported to have been existing in doublets such as [*bāzun*]/[*baʔzun*], [*al-ʕālamu*]/[*al-ʕaʔlamu*].[15]

Ibn Ǧinnī explained that the *a*-coloring of the weak quiescent *ʔalif* — 'as if it were vowelled,' *bi-manzilati mutaḥarrikin* — is induced by the preceding adjacent *fatḥah* (Ibn Ǧinnī *Xaṣāʔiṣ* III 147), but the addition of an actual vowel that should resolve the cluster created by the meeting of the two vowelless consonants necessarily requires the "strengthening" of the weak consonant *ʔalif* into a glottal stop (*hamzah*), its closest related sound, which is able to carry a vowel. In any case, *ā* (/*a*א/) > *aʔa* as in *ḍaʔallīna*, *ibyaʔaḍḍa*, or *iḥmaʔarra* can mean for the Arab grammarian nothing but *aʔ* (< *ā*, /*a*א/) + *a*. The interpretation of -*aʔa*- in such forms as a division of the long *ā* into two short *a*-vowels separated by a *hamzah*, as made by H. Fleisch,[16] is alien to Arab grammatical theory. Ibn Ǧinnī, as quoted above, explained that it was the *ʔalif* that was changed into a *hamzah* when the addition of a following vowel was necessary.

The structural analysis of long vowels in the Arabic grammatical tradition can now be summed up: (i) the formation of a long vowel as such belongs to the level of actualization; (ii) its underlying structure involves the sequence of V + homorganic weak C: /uw/, /iy/, or /aא/; and (iii) the first constituent in such a sequence is a vowel (by definition short) and the second one a consonant, weak, quiescent (unvowelled), and non-syllabic. Ultra-long vowels in pausal position or in otherwise closed syllables are treated in the terms of the basic theory and optionally resolved accordingly.

In Arab grammatical theory, the fact that the *ʔalif* is "abstract" and incapable of carrying a vowel (i.e., being the onset of a syllable) is no reason to deny its status as a *ḥarf* in the phonological sense of the term, that is, consonant. Indeed, if 'consonant' is conceived according to the original meaning of σύμφωνον in Western terminology, defined as a segment of speech not sounding on its own, then *ʔalif* might even be considered *the* prototypical consonant. The status of *ʔalif* in Arabic grammar was the subject of a controversy among Western Arabists in the mid-nineteenth century. G. A. Wallin followed the Arab grammatical tradition in regarding *ʔalif* as the weak quiescent silent segment, whereas H. L. Fleischer expressed his disinclination to recognize "thát abstract *ʔalif*" as a consonant, since "jeder Consonant muss eine Sylbe einleiten können" (apud Wallin *Laute des Arabischen* I 1–4 and note).

The theoretical structural nature of the Arab traditional doctrine is reflected in the following story about the renowned Baghdadi grammarian al-Zaǧǧāǧ (844–923), who explained the intolerability of two successive weak quiescents in word-inner position and the compulsory elision of one of them. To a man who prolonged the sound of the *ā* in his speech, claiming that he was combining the two *ʔalif*s, al-Zaǧǧāǧ said, "even if you had protracted (the sound) all day long, it would have been only one single *ʔalif*."[17] Measuring the physical length of vowels belongs in Arabic culture to another realm of learning.

---

l-maddi yaqūmu maqāma l-ḥarakati "that the length which is in the letters of prolongation takes the position of a vowel" (Ibn Yaʕīš *Šarḥ al-Mufaṣṣal* IX 122:4–5. He goes on, explaining the second condition of the same (viz., that it must be *fi l-ʔidġām*, where the second quiescent and the consonant that follows should be identical to form a geminate), saying that *al-sākin ʔiḏā kāna mudġaman yağrī mağrà l-mutaḥarriki li-ʔanna l-lisāna yartafiʕu bihimā dufʕatan wāḥidatan* "the quiescent [that follows the long vowel] when it is assimilated [with the following consonant] is similar to a vowelled consonant because the tongue is raised in both of them in one stroke" (Ibn Yaʕīš *Šarḥ al-Mufaṣṣal* IX 122:5–6). I am not certain that I understand this argument.

[13] *al-ʔalifu ʔiḏā taḥarrakat inqalabat hamzatan* (Ibn Ǧinnī *Sirr ṣināʕat al-ʔiʕrāb* 37:4; Ibn Ǧinnī *Xaṣāʔiṣ* III 147:12); *li-ʔanna l-ʔalifa ḥarfun ḍaʕīfun wāsiʕu l-muxraği lā yaḥtamilu l-ḥarakata, fa-ʔiḏa ḍṭurrū ʔilà taḥrīkihī qalabūhu ʔilà ʔaqrabi l-ḥurūfi ʔilayhi wa-huwa l-hamzah* (Ibn Yaʕīš *Šarḥ al-Mufaṣṣal* IX 129:11–130:2 = ibid., X 12:14–15).

[14] See Ibn Ǧinnī *Xaṣāʔiṣ* III 147–48; al-Zamaxšarī *Mufaṣṣal* 168:15–17 (§665), 172:16–17 (§683); Ibn al-ʔAnbārī *Ġarīb ʔiʕrāb al-Qurʔān* 41; Ibn Yaʕīš *Šarḥ al-Mufaṣṣal* IX 129–30, X 12–13; Fleischer *Kleinere Schriften* I 48; Nöldeke *Zur Grammatik* 8 with Spitaler's Anhang ibid., pp. 126–27; Fleisch *Traité* I 164–65.

[15] See, e.g., Ibn Ǧinnī *Xaṣāʔiṣ* III 147:7–12; al-Zamaxšarī *Mufaṣṣal* 172:17 (§683); Ibn Yaʕīš *Šarḥ al-Mufaṣṣal* X 13.

[16] "Une manière d'éviter ce genre de syllabe ultra-longue a été de diviser la voyelle longue en deux brèves, séparées par un *hamza*. De *(i)fʕālla* naissait *(i)fʕaʔalla: iḥmārra > iḥmaʔarra*"; Fleisch *Traité* II 333 (§ 133 f); cf. ibid., I 165 (§34 i), I 167 (§34 n), II 453 (§ 148 a).

[17] *Fa-qāla lahū ʔabū ʔisḥāq: law madadtahā ʔilà l-ʕaṣri la-mā kānat ʔillā ʔalifan wāḥidah* (Ibn Ǧinnī *Xaṣāʔiṣ* II 493:7–8).

Vowel length is thus conceived not as a supra-segmental feature, nor segmental in the sense that it is attributed to particular segments; it is not described as a "quality" applicable to vowels (Beeston *Arabic Today* 16), and certainly not as VV. In the modern treatment of Arabic phonology, the clearest description of long vowels was made by H. Blanc, who analyzed them as /VC/ compound phonemes that are not set apart from other combinations of VC by any essential difference (Blanc *North Palestinian* 42–44).[18] This brings us back to the Arab grammatical tradition. Vowel length in this sense also plays an important role in morphology and thus belongs to the core of language structure (cf. Goldenberg *Principles* 37–42 [18–23]).

Whereas consonant gemination is essentially /C_1C_1/, that is, C + an identical segment of the same class, structurally equivalent to any CC, a long vowel conceived as /VC/ is not V + an additional V and will not be represented properly if the same device, such as /:/, is used for both.

It will be noticed that in Arabic grammatical tradition there is no reference to a "long vowel" as a phonological unit, neither is there any reference to the notion of "syllable."

II. Theoretical Speculations

While the structural analysis as here described was clear and consistent and rather commonly accepted throughout the history of Arabic grammar, medieval scholars were troubled by some relevant questions as to the relation between the vowels and the corresponding weak consonants with regard to their articulation and origin and the nature of their contact within the long vowels. There was the question of how to understand a long vowel both as one inseparable phonetic unit and at the same time as "vowel-plus," and there was the unanswered question of how one could regard the most fully vocalic of all sounds (the long vowel) as being brought to its vocalic perfection by means of an "unvowelled" consonant. Without shaking the basic structural analysis, some Arab grammatical thinkers tried in many ways to answer those questions.

(a) First it was recognized that *a* and *ʔalif*, *u* and *wāw*, *i* and *yāʔ* come from the same place of articulation, or from the same phonetic origin, *yaʕnī ʔanna al-fatḥata tuzādu ʕalà l-ḥarfi wa-muxrağuhā min muxraği l-ʔalifi, wa-kaḏālika l-kasratu min muxraği l-yāʔi wa-l-ḍammatu min muxraği l-wāw* "it means that the *fatḥah* is added to the letter and its origination is from the place of origination of the *ʔalif*, and likewise the *kasrah* is from the place of origination of the *yāʔ*, and the *ḍammah* — from the place of origination of the *wāw*" (al-Sīrāfī ad Sībawayh II 315).

(b) The question then was whether the vowel came from the homorganic consonant or the consonant from the vowel. The idea that the consonant (*ḥarf*) was the origin and that vowels came, or were extracted, from the corresponding consonants had actually commanded general assent. Al-Xalīl, for example, after his statement that the unvowelled *ḥarf* is the building element (v. n. 1), says that the vowels "are from" the weak consonants: *al-fatḥatu min al-ʔalifi wa-l-kasratu min al-yāʔi wa-l-ḍammatu min al-wāw* (apud Sībawayh II 315:4). More explicitly it is said that the *ʔalif*, the *yāʔ*, and the *wāw* — *hiya l-ḥurūfu l-maʔxūḏatu minhā l-ḥarakāt* "they are the letters from which the vowels 'are taken'" (al-Sīrāfī ad Sībawayh II 135), or *al-ḥurūfu l-mutawallidatu ʕanhā l-ḥarakāt* "the letters from which the vowels 'are born'" (al-Zağğāğī *ʔĪḍāḥ* 124:5). This opinion is repeatedly expressed in many writings.

The opposite idea is mentioned as held by some of the grammarians: *wa-qad qāla baʕḍuhum: al-ʔalifu min al-fatḥati wa-l-yāʔu min al-kasrati wa-l-wāwu min al-ḍammah* "some of them say: the *ʔalif* is from the *fatḥa* and the *yāʔ* from the *kasrah* and the *wāw* from the *ḍammah*" (al-Zağğāğī *ʔĪḍāḥ* 123; cf. al-Sīrāfī ad Sībawayh II 315).[19]

(c) In the phonetic tractate of Ibn Sīnā, a "sounding" *ʔalif*, *wāw*, or *yāʔ* and its corresponding vowel are said to be "sisters": *al-ʔalifu l-muṣawwitatu wa-ʔuxtu-hā l-fatḥah ... al-wāwu l-muṣawwitatu wa-ʔuxtu-hā l-ḍammah ... al-yāʔu l-muṣawwitatu wa-ʔuxtu-hā l-kasrah ...* "the *ʔalif* when it marks a long vowel and its sister the *fatḥah* ... the *wāw* when it marks a long vowel and its sister the *ḍammah* ... the *yāʔ* when it marks a long vowel and its sister the *kasrah* ..."

---

[18] VC as an optional type of a long vowel analysis is not unknown in twentieth-century theoretical phonology (Goldenberg *Principles* 54 [35]).

[19] In other words, perhaps less clearly, it was said about the *ʔalif*, the *yāʔ*, and the *wāw*, *ʔanna hāḏihi l-ḥurūfa murakkabatun min al-ḥarakāti ʕalà qawli baʕḍi l-naḥwiyyīn* "that these letters are made of the vowels, according to some of the grammarians" (Ibn al-ʔAnbārī *ʔAsrār al-ʕArabiyyah* 322–23).

(Ibn Sīnā *Ḥudūṯ al-ḥurūf* 43).[20] In another version of Ibn Sīnā's book, a different terminology is used: instead of *al-ʔalif al-muṣawwitah* and its 'sister' *al-fatḥah* and so on, it speaks (with regard to the *muṣawwitāt*) about *al-ʔalif al-kubrà* and *al-ʔalif al-ṣuġrà*, that is, 'the larger *ʔalif*' and 'the lesser *ʔalif*,' and the same with the the *wāw* and the *yāʔ*, *wa-kullu ṣuġrà fa-hiya wāqiʕatun fī ʔaṣġari l-ʔazminah, wa-kullu kubrà fa-fī ʔiḍʕāfihā* "and every 'lesser' is of the shortest duration, and every 'larger' in twice as long" (Ibn Sīnā *Ḥudūṯ al-ḥurūf* 19:14–19).

The meaning of *ʔalif*, *wāw*, and *yāʔ* in this treatise is different from the pure structural sense they have in the grammatical tradition. All letters are mainly classified as either *muṣawwitah* 'sounding,' which are *ʔalif*, *wāw*, and *yāʔ*, or *ṣāmitah* 'mute,' which are all the others.[21] The "vocalic" letters are thus regarded as being sonant when they mark long vowels, not considered isolated from the corresponding short vowels (or vowel signs) but compared to them.

(d) Reminiscent of that approach is the old tradition mentioned by Ibn Ǧinnī, telling that some people of old (*mutaqqadimū l-qawm*), or grammarians of old (*mutaqqadimū l-naḥwiyyīn*), used to call the vowel a little *ḥarf*: *yusammūna l-fatḥata l-ʔalifa l-ṣaġīrata, wa-l-kasrata l-yāʔa l-ṣaġīrata, wa-l-ḍammata l-wāwa l-ṣaġīrah* "they would call the *fatḥah* a little *ʔalif*, the *kasrah* a little *yāʔ* and the *ḍammah* a little *wāw*" (Ibn Ǧinnī *Sirr ṣināʕat al-ʔiʕrāb* 19:11–12; idem *Xaṣāʔiṣ* II 315:7–8). Though this story is integrated in the phonological issues raised by Ibn Ǧinnī, historically it stands for itself and might even be related originally to the graphical relation between vowel-signs and the "letters of prolongation."

(e) The vowel is sometimes said to be **part** of the *ḥarf* "from which" it comes. In discussing substitutions of vowels and weak letters, Sībawayh mentions several times the indispensability of those letters or their parts in all such cases (Sībawayh II 349:12, 357:16–17; especially al-Sīrāfī ad Sībawayh II 315), as generally said in the commentary about the three weak letters that *al-kalām lā yaxlū minhunna ʔaw baʕḍihinna* "speech would not dispense with them or with their parts" (Sībawayh II 315). Occasionally the grammarian was kind enough to add after *minhā ʔaw min baʕḍihā — wa-baʕḍuhā ḥarakātuhā* "and their parts are their vowels" (Sībawayh II 165:3). The idea of the vowels being part of the weak letters was emphasized by Ibn Ǧinnī: *iʕlam ʔanna l-ḥarakāti ʔabʕāḍu ḥurūfi l-maddi wa-l-līn ... fa-l-fatḥatu baʕḍu l-ʔalifi wa-l-kasratu baʕḍu l-yāʔi wa-l-ḍammatu baʕḍu l-wāw* "know that the vowels are parts of the weak letters of prolongation ... the *fatḥah* is part of the *ʔalif*, the *kasrah* is part of the *yāʔ* and the *ḍammah* part of the *wāw*" (Ibn Ǧinnī *Sirr ṣināʕat al-ʔiʕrāb* 19:8–11; ibid., 20:10.14). Sometimes, various conceptions, not always compatible, are considered in the same context.

(f) A vowel has also been conceived as a deficient (or defective, incomplete, or imperfect) form of the homorganic *ḥarf*. This theory is attributed to the Greek logicians (*ʔaṣḥāb al-manṭiq min al-Yūnāniyyīn*), who regarded the nominative *-u* and generally the *ḍamm* and its "brothers" (i.e., the vowels close to it) as *wāw nāqiṣah* 'incomplete *wāw*,' the *kasr* 'and its brothers' *yāʔ nāqiṣah*, and the *fatḥ* 'and its brothers' *ʔalif nāqiṣah*" (al-Xwarizmī *Mafātīḥ al-ʕUlūm* 46).

(g) The various ideas about the relation of the vowels to the corresponding weak letters are connected with one another, but they often lack consistency. In Ibn Ǧinnī's writing vowels are said to be parts (*ʔabʕāḍ* or *ʔağzāʔ*)[22] of the *ḥurūf*, their beginnings (*ʔawāʔil*)[23] or their little (*ṣaġīrah*)[4] or incomplete (*nāqiṣah*)[25] counterparts; the *ḥurūf* being "saturated" (or "satiated") or completed vowels (*ḥarakāt mušbaʕah*[26] or *mutakammilah*[27]). It could be said that the *ḥurūf* are born (*mutawallidah*)[28] or growing (*mutanaššiʔah*)[29] from the vowels, but to explain that the vowels are parts of the *ḥurūf* and at the same time to say that the *ḥurūf* follow the vowels that precede them (*tatbaʕu l-ḥarakāti llatī qablahā*)[30] is rather loose.

Also the vowels are said to be called *ḥarakāt* 'movements' because a vowel moves (*tuqliqu*)[31] the *ḥarf* with which it is combined (i.e., which it "vocalizes") and drags it (*taǧtaḏibuhū*)[32] toward the *ḥarf* of which it is a part.

---

[20] A similar comment in the text of Sībawayh II 165:2–3 is of uncertain authenticity; cf. Sībawayhi in the edition by ʕAbd al-Salām Muḥ. Hārūn III (Cairo 1971), 544:11.

[21] *ʔimmā* ***muṣawwitah****, wahiya llatī tusammà fī l-ʕArabiyyah ḥurūf al-madd wa-l-līn, wa-ʔimmā* ***ṣāmitah****, wahiya mā siwāhā* (e.g., al-ʔĪǧī *Mawāqif* II 20–21); see further Versteegh *Greek Elements* 21; and Morag 1979.

[22] For *ʔabʕāḍ*, v. supra (g); *ʔağzāʔ* in Ibn Ǧinnī *Sirr ṣināʕat al-ʔiʕrāb* 27:1.

[23] Ibn Ǧinnī *Sirr ṣināʕat al-ʔiʕrāb* 20:14, 27:1.

[24] See supra (d).

[25] Ibn Ǧinnī *Sirr ṣināʕat al-ʔiʕrāb* 30:12.

[26] Ibn Ǧinnī *Sirr ṣināʕat al-ʔiʕrāb* 27:1–4; cf. ibid., 20:15, 34:12. The same is also said in terms of lengthening (*ʔiḏā maṭalta* 'if you lengthen,' e.g., Ibn Ǧinnī *Xaṣāʔiṣ* II 315:9) or completing (*ʔiḏā tammamtahā* 'if you complete it,' e.g., Ibn Ǧinnī *Sirr ṣināʕat al-ʔiʕrāb* 34:12).

[27] Ibn Ǧinnī *Sirr ṣināʕat al-ʔiʕrāb* 30:15.

[28] Ibn Ǧinnī *Sirr ṣināʕat al-ʔiʕrāb* 27:4–5.

[29] Ibn Ǧinnī *Sirr ṣināʕat al-ʔiʕrāb* 26:11.

[30] Ibn Ǧinnī *Sirr ṣināʕat al-ʔiʕrāb* 30:10.

[31] Ibn Ǧinnī *Sirr ṣināʕat al-ʔiʕrāb* 30:12.

III. Phonetic Actualization

The reference made above (§II (c)) to Ibn Sīnā was mainly intended to mention his view that a short vowel and its long counterpart are "sisters," but in what follows, the alternative version of his *ʔAsbāb ḥudūṯ al-ḥurūf* is shown to have stated that a short vowel is of minimal duration and that a long vowel is twice as long. The latter statement is typical of *tağwīd* instructions and differs from the grammatical explanations. In the orthoepic literature, all details of correct recitation of the holy text are meticulously discussed and the necessary rules formulated. Whereas for the grammarian it was important to stress that a long *ā*, regardless of its actual duration, involves one single *ʔalif* and no more,[33] the orthoepist was interested in the exact duration of sounds, often trying to define it in absolute terms, and would refer to the "letter of prolongation" (i.e., long vowel) as VV, the "satiation" (or "saturation") of a vowel interpreted in this context as doubling the vowel: *iʕlam ʔanna l-ʔalifa murakkabun min fatḥatayni wa-l-wāwu murakkabun min ḍammatayni wa-l-yāʔu murakkabun min kasratayni, fa-ʔiḏā ʔašbaʕta l-fatḥata yatawalladu minhā ʔalifun wa-ʔiḏā ʔašbaʕta l-ḍammata yatawalladu minhā l-wāwu wa-ʔiḏā ʔašbaʕta l-kasrata yatawalladu minhā l-yāʔ* "know that the *ʔalif* is composed of two *fatḥas*, the *wāw* is composed of two *ḍammas* and the *yāʔ* is composed of two *kasras*, and if you 'satiate' the *fatḥah* a *ʔalif* is born from it and if you 'satiate' the *ḍammah* a *wāw* is born from it and if you 'satiate' the *kasrah* a *yāʔ* is born from it" (al-Qārī *Minaḥ* 50:34–36).

Generally we are reminded that, as already mentioned above, the violation of some strict phonological rules is permitted in pausal position: *al-waqfu yağūzu fīhi ltiqāʔu l-sākinayn* "in a pause, the meeting of two quiescents is permitted" (ibid., 50:18), but in the orthoepic literature, special attention was paid to special lengthening, which has traditionally been preserved in certain positions in the recitation of the Qurʔān. The term *madd* in its specific sense refers mainly to such extra lengthening, which makes an important chapter of *tağwīd*.[34] Unlike grammatical length, which is analyzed as VC (with a weak C), in this sense, *al-madd laysa ḥarfan wa-lā ḥarakatan bal ziyādatun ʕalà kammiyyati ḥarfi l-madd* "the *madd* is not a 'letter' nor a vowel but an addition to the quantity of the 'letter of prolongation'" (al-Qārī *Minaḥ* 49:21), that is, addition to duration marked by the "letter of prolongation." It was said to imitate the prolongation of syllables witnessed in the *qirāʔah* of the Prophet (ibid., 50:2–3).

According to some writings, the actual duration of such extra-long vowels (*miqdār al-maddāt*) was measured in units, the basic unit being the *ʔalif*,[35] as to how many times one could pronounce, or write, the word *ʔalif* in the time that the extra-long vowel takes. The duration of the *madd* could also be measured by folding the fingers and so on (al-Qārī *Minaḥ* 49:13–19; Bakalla *Vowel Length* 200–01).

Such *madd*, and the orthoepic teachings as a whole, differ radically from the grammatical analysis of the language. Only in the context of practical performance was it said that *ʔalif* is the combination of two *fatḥahs*.

From the examination of the relevant literature, it becomes clear that in Arabic grammar throughout its history [V̄] = /V̆C/, where the C is *w* or *y* or א. Theoretical speculations reflected the effort to bridge the gap between the abstract notion of a weak quiescent consonant that embodies length as a segment and the realization of the /V̆C/ as one long V. Phonetic description of V̄ as V̆ + V̆ is only found in the orthoepic literature, in the practical teaching of recitation of the Qurʔān, as part of defining the actual quantity of normal vowel duration, where the excessive *madd* is not required.

IV. Long Vowels in Hebrew Grammar

Medieval Arabic-written Hebrew grammar was in a sense a direct product of the development of Arabic linguistics, at the time when literary and scientific activities of the Jews in general, mainly in Islamic Spain, were given an unusual impetus by the vitality shown in Arabic letters and scholarly work.

---

32 Ibn Ğinnī *Sirr ṣināʕat al-ʔiʕrāb* 30:13.

33 See supra §I and n. 17.

34 Cf. the special chapter on such *madd* in Bravmann *Materialen* 76–81; Gade *Tajwīd*; Nelson *Tajwīd*.

35 *Al-ʔalif allaḏī huwa l-madd al-ʔaṣlī* (al-Qārī *Minaḥ* 49:21).

The most important of all Jewish linguists of the time was the tenth-century Hebrew scholar Yəhūdā b. David Ḥayyūǧ. His adaptation of Arab grammatical doctrines laid the foundation to all further development in the field. Among other things, Ḥayyūǧ introduced into Hebrew grammar the idea that a long vowel was the actualization of V + weak quiescent C, namely, [ā] = /aא/, [ū] = /uw/, and [ī] = /iy/.[36]

In Hebrew, however, greater abstraction was needed because of the more complicated vowel system and the less consistent morphology and orthography. Ḥayyūǧ soon discovered that in many cases he could not easily establish in each case which of the three weak quiescent consonants was there in the first place and what was the direction of substitution. He stated that he would give up that problem and be satisfied with establishing the presence of a weak consonant without specifying whether it was *ʔalif* or *wāw* or *yāʔ*. In discussing the *verba mediae infirmae*, Ḥayyūǧ states without former planning, *wa-laysa ġaraḍī fī taʔlīfi hāḏihi l-ʔafʕāli l-layyinati l-ʕayni tamyīza ḏawāti l-wāwi min ḏawāti l-yāʔi ʔiḏ lā yamtāzu ḏālika fī ǧullihā li-btidāli ʔaḥadihimā min al-ʔāxari fi l-taṣrīfi wa-ḥtiyāzihā mawḍiʕahā fi l-tafʕīl; lākin ġaraḍī taʕrīfu mawḍiʕi l-sākini l-layyini wa-l-tanbīhu ʕalà ʔannahū ʕaynu l-fiʕli wāwan kāna ḏālika l-sākinu ʔaw yāʔ* "it is not my intention in compiling these verbs with a weak medial radical to distinguish those that have *wāw* from those that have *yāʔ*, since that is not distinct in most of them because of the substitution of one of the two for the other in the derivation and the replacement of (one another) in the formation; but my intention is to apprise of the place of the weak quiescent and to give notice that it is the medial radical whether that quiescent is a *wāw* or a *yāʔ*" (Ḥayyūǧ *Ḥurūf al-līn* 87:15–88:1).

Ḥayyūǧ came to use the general term *al-sākin al-layyin* 'the weak quiescent' for what some twentieth-century linguists would regard as an archiphoneme. This *sākin layyin* might change forms or be assimilated in a following consonant, represented through length or elided. The term still covers, in Ḥayyūǧ's terminology, the three weak consonants when, unvowelled, they follow the homorganic vowel.

A further stage in the development of the theory of long vowels in Hebrew grammar was probably reached by Šmūʔēl ha-Nāgīd (ʔAbū ʔIbrāhīm ʔIsmāʕīl ibn Naġrella, 993–1056), Ḥayyūǧ's disciple, poet, scholar, statesman, and general, who regarded "the weak quiescent" as a zero phoneme, and no longer as a neutralizing position of *ʔalif*, *wāw*, and *yāʔ*. "The weak quiescent" as such can still also be a radical, and long vowels should seemingly in this view be interpreted as /a0/, /u0/, /i0/, /e0/, and so on. References to quotations from writings of Šmūʔēl ha-Nāgīd and a discussion of their meaning are fully given in Goldenberg *Weak Quiescent* 289–90).

Prosodically lengthened vowels are considered in Ḥayyūǧ's theory equivalent to VC the same as those incorporating a weak radical. Ḥayyūǧ explained it very clearly: *laysa fī* ***lḗḵ, šḗḇ, rḗḏ*** *sākinun mutawassiṭun min ʔaṣli l-luġati wa-ʔinnamā huwa maddun bi-l-laḥni llaḏī tuqraʔu bihī, fa-ʔiḏā zāla l-laḥnu zāla ḏālika l-maddu, wa-l-dalīlu ʕalà ḏālika min* ***'lĕ̄ḵ****-ləḵā́ mē-ʔarṣəḵā́', 'wə-****lĕ̄ḵ****-ləḵā́ ʔɛl-ʔɛrɛṣ hammōriyyā́',* ***'lĕ̄ḵ****-nā́ ʔɛl-haṣṣṓn', 'qūm ʕălē Ḇēʸṯ-ʔēl wə-****šĕ̄ḇ****-šā́m' allatī laysa fīhā laḥnun wa-lā sākin* "there is not in **lḗḵ, šḗḇ, rḗḏ** a medial quiescent inherent in the word; it is because of the accent with which it is read that [the vowel] is long, and when the accent goes away that length goes away, and the proof of it is from ***'lĕ̄ḵ****-ləḵā́ mē-ʔarṣəḵā́'* [Gen 12:1], *'wə-****lĕ̄ḵ****-ləḵā́ ʔɛl-ʔɛrɛṣ hammōriyyā́'* [Gen 22:2], ***'lĕ̄ḵ****-nā́ ʔɛl-haṣṣṓn'* [Gen 27:9], *'qūm ʕălē Ḇēʸṯ-ʔēl wə-****šĕ̄ḇ****-šā́m'* [Gen 35:1], where there is no accent and no quiescent" (Ḥayyūǧ *Ḥurūf al-līn* 72:10–15). To make sure that the positional length of *ḗ* in *lḗḵ* and so on is still regarded as involving a weak quiescent, we may quote Ḥayyūǧ's explicit statement mentioning *al-sākin al-mutawassiṭ fī lḗḵ, šḗḇ, rḗḏ* "the medial quiescent in *lḗḵ, šḗḇ, rḗḏ*" (ibid., 72:17–18).[37]

The medieval Arabic-Hebrew view of vowel length as a weak quiescent segment, without recognizing in fact long vowel phonemes, and without direct reference to syllables, makes an integral part of consistent morphological analysis of Arabic and other Semitic languages (e.g., Goldenberg *Principles* 38–43 [19–24]; idem *Morphological Analysis* 178–88 and elsewhere; cf. for the Akkadian Izre'el *Segmental length*). Closely examined, the traditional analysis seems arguably capable of challenging any other phonological theory old or new.[38]

---

[36] For a more detailed study of vowel length, weak radicals, and the meaning of "weak quiescent" in medieval Hebrew grammar, cf. Goldenberg *Weak Quiescent*, where the translated Hebrew terminology with its pitfalls is also discussed.

[37] In discussing vowel duration in Biblical Hebrew, some confusion is sometimes caused by involving orthoepic instructions for degrees of stress-related duration irrespective of vocalic structure.

[38] A comprehensive survey and thorough critical examination of modern phonological theories with regard to vowel length, done with rare clarity, will be found in Odden *Vowel Length*.

Abbreviations

C	consonant
f.	feminine
pl.	plural
sg.	singular
V	vowel

Bibliography

al-ʔAzharī *Tahḏīb al-luġah* — ʔAbū Manṣūr Muḥammad b. ʔAḥmad al-ʔAzharī (895–980). *Tahḏīb al-luġah*, Volume 1. Edited by ʕAbd al-Salām Muḥammad Hārūn. Cairo: Al-Muʔassasah al-Miṣriyyah al-ʕāmmah li-l-taʔlīf wa-l-ʔanbāʔ wa-l-našr, Al-dār al-Miṣriyyah li-l-taʔlīf wa-l-tarǧamah, 1964.

Bakalla *Vowel Length* — Muḥammad Ḥasan Bakalla. "The Contribution of the Arabs and Muslims to the Study of Vowel Length." The 50th Anniversary of Phonetic Society of Japan and The Proceedings of the World Congress of Phoneticians. *The Study of Sounds* 18 (1978): 197–202.

Beeston *Arabic Today* — Alfred Felix Landon Beeston. *The Arabic Language Today*. London: Hutchinson, 1970.

Blanc *North Palestinian* — Haim Blanc. *Studies in North Palestinian Arabic: Linguistic Inquiries among the Druzes of Western Galilee and Mt. Carmel.* Oriental Notes and Studies 4. Jerusalem: Israel Oriental Society, 1953.

Bravmann *Materialen* — Meir Max Bravmann. *Materialen und Untersuchungen zu den phonetischen Lehren der Araber.* Inaugural-Dissertation Breslau. Göttingen: Dietrichsche Universitäts-Buchdruckerei, 1934.

Dozy — Reinhart Pieter Anne Dozy. *Supplément aux dictionnaires arabes.* 2nd edition. 2 volumes. Leiden: Brill, 1927.

Fleisch *Traité* I — Henri Fleisch. *Traité de philologie arabe*, Volume 1: *Préliminaires, phonétique, morphologie nominale.* Institut de lettres orientales de Beyrouth, Recherches 16. Beirut: Imprimerie catholique, 1961.

Fleisch *Traité* II — Henri Fleisch. *Traité de philologie arabe*, Volume 2: *Pronoms, morphologie verbale, particules.* Faculté des Lettres et des sciences humaines de l'Université Saint-Joseph, Beyrouth, Recherches, Nouvelle Série: A. Langue arabe et pensée islamique 11. Beirut: Dar el-Machreq, 1929.

Fleischer *Kleinere Schriften* — Heinrich Leberecht Fleischer. *Kleinere Schriften.* 3 volumes. Leipzig: Hirzel, 1885–1888.

Gade *Tajwīd* — Anna M. Gade. "Recitation of the Qurʾān (chapter on 'The System of *tajwīd*')." *Encyclopaedia of the Qurʾān*. Edited by Jane Dammen McAuliffe, Volume 4. Leiden: Brill, 2004.

Goldenberg *Morphological Analysis* — Gideon Goldenberg. "Word-structure, Morphological Analysis, the Semitic Languages and Beyond." In *Proceedings of the 10th Meeting of Hamito-Semitic (Afroasiatic) Linguistics* (Florence 18–20 April 2001), edited by Pelio Fronzaroli and Paolo Marrassini, pp. 169–93. Quaderni di Semitistica 25. Florence: Department of Linguistics–University of Florence, 2005.

Goldenberg *Principles*	Gideon Goldenberg. "Principles of Semitic Word-structure." In *Semitic and Cushitic Studies*, edited by Gideon Goldenberg and Shlomo Raz, pp. 29–64. Wiesbaden: Harrassowitz, 1994. Reprinted in *Studies in Semitic Linguistics: Selected Writings*, by Gideon Goldenberg, pp. 10–45. Jerusalem: Magnes Press, 1998.
Goldenberg *Weak Quiescent*	Gideon Goldenberg. "The Weak Quiescent and the Hebrew Root." *Lĕšonénu* 44/4 (1980): 281–92. [In Hebrew]
Ḥayyūǧ *Hurūf al-līn*	Yəhūdā (ʔAbū Zakariyyā Yaḥyà) b. David al-Fāsī Ḥayyūǧ (10th century). "Kitāb al-ʔafʕāl d̲awāt ḥurūf al-līn." In *The Weak and Geminate Verbs in Hebrew by Abû Zakkariyyâ Yaḥyâ ibn Dâwud of Fez known as Ḥayyûǧ*, pp. 1–219. Arabic text for first time by Morris Jastrow. Leiden: Brill, 1897.
Ibn al-ʔAnbārī *ʔAsrār al-ʕArabiyyah*	ʔAbu l-Barakāt ʕAbd al-Raḥmān b. Muḥammad Ibn al-ʔAnbārī (1119–1181). *ʔAsrār al-ʕArabiyyah*. Edited by Muḥammad Bahǧat al-Bayṭār. Damascus: Al-Maǧmaʕ al-ʕilmī al-ʕArabī, 1957.
Ibn al-ʔAnbārī *Ġarīb ʔiʕrāb al-Qurʔān*	ʔAbu l-Barakāt ʕAbd al-Raḥmān b. Muḥammad Ibn al-ʔAnbārī. *Al-Bayān fī ġarīb ʔiʕrāb al-Qurʔān* I. Edited by Ṭāhā ʕAbd al-Ḥamīd Ṭāhā. Cairo: Wizārat al-t̲aqāfah, Dār al-kātib al-ʕArabī li-l-ṭibāʕah wa-l-našr, 1969.
Ibn Ǧanāḥ *Lumaʕ*	Jonah ʔAbu l-Walīd Marwān Ibn Ǧanāḥ (11th century). *Kitāb al-Lumaʕ: Le livre des Parterres fleuris*. Paris: F. Vieweg, 1886. [In Judeo-Arabic]
Ibn Ǧinnī *Sirr ṣināʕat al-ʔiʕrāb*	ʔAbu l-Fatḥ ʕUt̲mān Ibn Ǧinnī (915–1002). *Sirr ṣināʕat al-ʔiʕrāb* I. Edited by Muṣṭafà al-Saqā, Muḥammad al-Zafzāf, Ibrāhīm Muṣṭafà, and ʕAbdallāh ʔAmīn. Wizārat al-maʕārif al-ʕumūmiyyah — ʔIdārat al-t̲aqāfah al-ʕāmmah — ʔIdārat ʔiḥyāʔ al-turāt̲ al-Qadīm. Cairo: Muṣṭafà al-Bābī, 1954.
Ibn Ǧinnī *Xaṣāʔiṣ*	ʔAbu l-Fatḥ ʕUt̲mān Ibn Ǧinnī (915–1002). *Al-Xaṣāʔiṣ*. Edited by Muḥammad ʕAlī al-Naǧǧār. 3 volumes. Cairo: Dār al-kutub al-Miṣriyyah, 1952–1956.
Ibn Sīnā *Ḥudūt̲ al-ḥurūf*	ʔAbū ʕAlī al-Ḥusayn b. ʕAbdallāh Ibn Sīnā (980–1037). "ʔAsbāb Ḥudūt̲ al-ḥurūf." In *Фонетический трактат Авиценны*: Текст, перевод, исследование. Владимир Григорьевич Ахвледиани, Тбилиси: Мецниереба, 1966.
Ibn Yaʕīš *Šarḥ al-Mufaṣṣal*	Muwaffaq al-Dīn ʔAbu l-Baqāʔ Yaʕīš b. ʕAlī Ibn Yaʕīš. (1158–1245) *Šarḥ al-Mufaṣṣal* [li-l-Zamaxšarī]. 10 parts. Cairo: al-Munīriyyah, 1928–1931.
al-ʔĪǧī *Mawāqif*	ʕAḍud al-Dīn ʔAbu l-Faḍl ʕAbd al-Raḥmān b. Rukn al-Dīn ʔAḥmad b. ʕAbd al-Ġaffār b. ʔAḥmad al-ʔĪǧī (1281–1355). *Kitāb al-Mawāqif*. 3 volumes. Beirut: Dār al-Ǧīl, 1997.
Izre'el *Segmental Length*	Shlomo Izre'el. "Segmental Length: A View from Akkadian." In *Studies in Semitic and General Linguistics in Honor of Gideon Goldenberg*, edited by Tali Bar and Eran Cohen, pp. 13–28. Alter Orient und Altes Testament 334. Münster: Ugarit-Verlag, 2007.
Morag *Muṣawwitāt*	Shelomo Morag. "Some Notes on *muṣawwitāt* in Medieval Hebrew and Arabic Literature." *The Journal of the Ancient Near Eastern Society of Columbia University* 11 (1979): 85–90.
Nelson *Tajwīd*	Kristina Nelson. "Tajwīd." In *Encyclopedia of Arabic Language and Linguistics*, edited by Kees Versteegh, Volume 4. Leiden: Brill, 2009.
Nöldeke *Grammatik*	Theodor Nöldeke. *Zur Grammatik des Classischen Arabisch*. Originally published 1897. Im Anhang: *Die handschriftlichen Ergänzungen in dem Handexemplar Theodor Nöldekes*, edited with additions by Anton Spitaler. Darmstadt: Wissenschaftliche Buchgesellschaft, 1963.
Odden *Vowel Length*	David Odden. "The Representation of Vowel Length." http://www. ling.ohio-state.edu/~odden/Vowel%20Length.pdf. To be published in *The Blackwell Companion to Phonology*, edited by Marc van Oostendorp, Colin J. Ewen, Elizabeth Hume, and Keren Rice. Forthcoming.

al-Qārī *Minaḥ*	ʕAlī b. Sulṭān al-Qārī (d. 1605). *Kitāb al-Minaḥ al-fikriyyah ʕalà matn al-Ğazariyyah (wa-bi-hāmišihī Šarḥ Zakariyyā al-ʔAnṣārī ʕalà Muqaddimat al-Ğazariyyah).* Cairo: Maṭbaʕat al-Maymaniyyah, 1890/1891.
Sībawayh	ʔAbū Bišr ʕAmr b. ʕUṯmān Sībawayh. *Kitāb Sībawayhi.* 2 volumes. Būlāq: Al-Maṭbaʕah l-kubrà l-ʔamīriyyah, 1898–1900.
al-Sīrāfī	ʔAbū Saʕīd al-Ḥasan b. ʕAbdallāh b. al-Marzubān al-Sīrāfī (903–979). *Šarḥ Kitāb Sībawayh.* Printed in the margins of Sībawayh.
Versteegh *Greek Elements*	Cornelis Henricus Maria (Kees) Versteegh. *Greek Elements in Arabic Linguistic Thinking.* Studies in Semitic Languages and Linguistics 7. Leiden: Brill, 1977.
Wallin *Laute des Arabischen*	Georg August Wallin. "Ueber die Laute des Arabischen und ihre Bezeichnung." I. *Zeitschrift der Deutschen Morgenländischen Gesellschaft* 9 (1855): 1–69; II. *Zeitschrift der Deutschen Morgenländischen Gesellschaft* 12 (1858): 599–665.
al-Xalīl *Kitāb al-ʕayn*	ʔAbū ʕAbd-al-Raḥmān al-Xalīl (718–776). *Kitāb al-ʕayn.* Edited by ʕAbdallāh Darwīš. Baghdad: Maṭbaʕat al-ʔĀnī, 1967.
al-Xwarizmī *Mafātīḥ al-ʕUlūm*	ʔAbū ʕAbdallāh Muḥammad b. ʔAḥmad b. Yūsuf al-Kātib al-Xwarizmī (10th century). *Mafātīḥ al-ʕUlūm — Liber Mafâtîh al-olûm explicans vocabula technica scientiarum.* Edited by Gerlof van Vloten. Leiden: Brill, 1895.
al-Zağğāğī *ʔĪḍāḥ*	ʔAbu l-Qāsim ʕAbd-al-Raḥmān b. ʔIsḥāq al-Zağğāğī (d. 949). *Al-ʔĪḍāḥ fī ʕilal al-naḥw.* Edited by Māzin al-Mubārak. Cairo: Maktabat Dār al-ʕUrūbah, 1959.
al-Zamaxšarī *Mufaṣṣal*	ʔAbu l-Qāsim Maḥmūd b. ʕUmar al-Zamaxšarī (1075–1144). *Kitāb al-Mufaṣṣal fi l-naḥw: Al-Mufaṣṣal, Opus de re grammatica Arabicum.* Edited by J. P. Broch. Christianiae: Mallingii, 1879.

7

Wisdom in Ugaritic

Edward L. Greenstein, Bar-Ilan University

The study of the so-called wisdom literature of the Hebrew Bible has flourished spectacularly in the past half century. Wisdom is typically conceived as an international literary category (much broader and vaguer than a genre), the Hebrew exponents of which manifest a worldly, non-parochial character. For that reason, wisdom books like Proverbs, Job, and Qohelet pay little if any attention to specifically biblical concerns like the covenant, its laws, and its rituals, and the historical traditions of Israel (see, e.g., Murphy 1992, pp. 921–22).[1] The international character of biblical wisdom is often underscored by reference to the impact of foreign literatures upon it. Conventionally, it is the influence of Egyptian, Mesopotamian, and Hellenistic literature that is cited. Accordingly, the article on "Wisdom in the O[ld] T[estament]" in the standard *Anchor Bible Dictionary* (Murphy 1992) includes sections on Egypt, Mesopotamia, and Hellenistic literature in its chapter on "Extra-biblical Wisdom" (ibid., pp. 928–30). In a similar vein, the volume *Wisdom in Ancient Israel* (Day, Gordon, and Williamson 1995) has chapters on Egyptian, Babylonian, and Aramaic wisdom (the proverbs of Aḥīqar) in the part entitled "The Ancient Near Eastern Setting [of Israelite Wisdom]" (ibid., pp. 17–52).[2] The fact that an Egyptian text, the Instructions of Amenemope (see, e.g., Emerton 2001), and certain Mesopotamian texts — such as *Ludlul bēl nēmeqi* ("Let Me Praise the Lord of Wisdom," sometimes called "the Babylonian Job") and the Dialogue between a Master and His Servant (sometimes called "the Dialogue of Pessimism") — would seem to have had a direct influence on works of biblical wisdom (viz., Proverbs, Job, and Qohelet, respectively; for the last see, e.g., Greenstein 2007) bolsters the significance of the somewhat remote neighbors of Israel, Mesopotamia, and Egypt on the development of biblical wisdom (cf., e.g., Perdue 2008, p. 49).

Evidence of a far more local breeding ground for biblical wisdom — the Syro-Canaanite cultures of the mid- to late second millennium B.C.E. — has been sporadically acknowledged but widely neglected. As late as 1999, a scholar of biblical wisdom could assert, "with the probable exception of *Ahikar* [*sic*], we know nothing of the wisdom literature which may have been produced in the nations close to Israel, and which may have served as a conduit for Egyptian and Mesopotamian material" (Weeks 1999, p. 8). And yet, not only have various scholars called attention to the likely sources of biblical wisdom in earlier Canaanite culture (e.g., Albright 1955; Thompson 1974, pp. 54–57; and see below), but also several works of Sumero-Akkadian wisdom have been found at Ras Shamra-Ugarit and brought to light (see esp. Nougayrol 1968, pp. 265–300; Khanjian 1974; Arnaud 2007, pp. 139–93).[3]

---

[1] It should be noted that Murphy is citing features of wisdom indicated by von Rad (1972) and criticizing them for their lack of nuance. The present essay is drawn from a larger study that the author is conducting together with Dr. Yoram Cohen of Tel Aviv University on the Syro-Canaanite roots of Israelite wisdom. Our research has been supported by a grant from the Israel Science Foundation (no. 621/08), and we have been brilliantly assisted by Ms. Sivan Kedar and Ms. Shirly Natan-Yulzary. This article is essentially my own work, in which I have been assisted in particular by Ms. Natan-Yulzary. Texts in Ugaritic are cited according to their *CAT* (KTU) number (Dietrich, Loretz, and Sanmartín 1995).

[2] The same three literatures are classified in Walton 1989, pp. 169–97. Clifford (1999, pp. 9–17) surveys precursors of Proverbs in Egypt, Mesopotamia, and Syro-Palestine, but of the last category, he cites only Aḥīqar. On the other hand, Clifford (1975) has shown awareness of Canaanite language and motifs in Proverbs. For a comparison of Proverbs 9 to a scene in the Kirta epic, see Lichtenstein 1968.

[3] For a bibliographic survey of this literature, see Mack-Fisher 1990a. Although Ugarit is located north of what was regarded as Canaan proper in the second millennium B.C.E., its striking and extensive affinities to Canaanite language, literature, and culture place it squarely within the cultural orbit of Canaan; see, e.g., Pitard 2002, pp. 253–55; cf. Golden 2004; Yon 2006, pp. 1, 7.

In addition to a short set of proverbial sayings (Nougayrol 1955, pp. 311–24; Lambert 1960, p. 116; Khanjian 1974, pp. 140–43; Kämmerer 1998, pp. 174–75; Arnaud 2007, pp. 139–40),[4] there are three major works of wisdom among the Akkadian texts from Ugarit. One is a relatively lengthy instructional or advice piece in dialogue form with versions known at Emar and Boghazkoy as well — the Wisdom of Šūpē-awēli (Nougayrol 1968, pp. 273–90; Khanjian 1974, pp. 148–76; Dietrich 1991, pp. 33–68; Kämmerer 1998, pp. 176–207; Arnaud 2007, pp. 148–79);[5] the father-son exchange is reminiscent of the classical Mesopotamian work, the Instructions of Šuruppak (cf., e.g., Nougayrol 1968, pp. 275–76; Seminara 2000, pp. 527–28; Alster 2005, pp. 41–42). This Akkadian work from Ugarit displays a number of parallels in theme and formulation to the biblical books of Proverbs and Qohelet (see, e.g., Smith 1975; Hurowitz 2007). A second major Akkadian text from Ugarit is a concise version of the Babylonian classic *Ludlul bēl nēmeqi* — a pious sufferer's complaint and his restoration by Marduk (Nougayrol 1968, pp. 265–73; Khanjian 1974, pp. 191–206; Dietrich 1993, pp. 62–67; Kämmerer 1998, pp. 160–63; Arnaud 2007, pp. 110–14).[6] This text, like its apparent Mesopotamian prototype, displays numerous affinities to the book of Job (see, e.g., Khanjian 1975; Ben Basat 2008). The third Akkadian composition from Ugarit that can be classified as wisdom is a Mesopotamian classic, known in Sumerian (Alster 2005, pp. 288–311; cf. Klein 2000), and found at Emar as well (Arnaud 1987, pp. 359–65) — the Ballad of the Early Rulers or "A Life without Joy" (Nougayrol 1968, pp. 291–300; Dietrich 1992; Kämmerer 1998, pp. 208–13; Alster 2005: 312–19; Arnaud 2007, pp. 142–48). Its sober reflection on the ephemeral existence of even the greatest of men recalls the fatalistic outlook of Qohelet (cf., e.g., Lambert 1995; Gianto 1998; Klein 2000, pp. 214–15).

Despite the clear existence in second-millennium B.C.E. Syro-Palestine of literary works similar in type and content to biblical wisdom, some biblicists adhere to the old notion that wisdom literature must be a late development in the formation of the Hebrew Bible (e.g., Toy 1916, pp. xx–xxxi; Scott 1965, pp. xxxv–xxxix). It is assumed that such a development — cosmopolitan in character — could only have taken place through the influence of foreign wisdom in the mid-first millennium B.C.E. (cf., e.g., Westermann 1995, p. 5).[7] Works of wisdom among the Syro-Canaanite scribes of the mid- to late second millennium B.C.E. could well have passed from their largely Mesopotamian sources — or, in some cases, like the poem of the pious sufferer (the Ras Shamra *Ludlul* text), sources of inspiration — to the Canaanite cultural-literary heritage (cf. Gray 1970; Wiseman 1977, pp. 86–87; Mattingly 1990, p. 325; Perdue 2008, p. 39). Scribes who were trained in the Mesopotamian cuneiform tradition and who produced the Akkadian wisdom texts at Ugarit wrote — and transmitted texts — in the local Ugaritic language as well (see, e.g., Saadé 1988; van Soldt 1995a; Márquez Rowe 2008; cf., e.g., Horwitz 1979; Mack-Fisher 1990b, p. 115; Hawley 2008, esp. pp. 60–61).[8] The wisdom literary traditions — both written and oral (see, e.g., Carr 2005, pp. 27–29 and passim) — represented in the Akkadian texts from Ugarit could well have been conveyed through some form of Canaanite intermediation to the early Hebrew scribes. Throughout the land of Canaan, scribes were educated in the Akkadian tradition (e.g., Demsky 1990; Horowitz and Oshima 2006), a situation that enabled the easy transmission of culture; and the transparent continuities between Ugaritic literature of the late second millennium B.C.E. and Hebrew and Phoenician literature of the first millennium B.C.E. (e.g., Cassuto 1971; Greenfield 1971; Greenfield 1987; Greenstein 1996) make it necessary to assume an unbroken literary chain of tradition from Canaanite to later biblical literature.[9] The fact that the unique Ugaritic alphabet was adapted and utilized

[4] The text is a Hurrian bilingual; for the Hurrian text, see E. Laroche in Nougayrol 1955, pp. 313–24. Another important study of this bilingual text is Dijkstra 1993. This text is passed over in the survey of Syrian precursors to Proverbs by Fox (2000, p. 23).

[5] For additional and very helpful analyses of this text, see also Seminara 2000; Hurowitz 2007. For the Emar text, see Arnaud 1987, pp. 377–82. For an analysis of the Hittite version, see Keydana 1991.

[6] On the relationship of the Ras Shamra *Ludlul* to Job, see Craigie 1985; Ben Basat 2008. Dietrich (1993, pp. 62–63) and Arnaud (2007, p. 110) categorize the Ras Shamra version of *Ludlul* as a hymn. Although there is certainly a component of praise for Marduk in this piece, as there is in *Ludlul* ('Let me praise!'), even in the section of praise, the erstwhile suffering of the speaker is strongly evoked.

[7] Westermann, like Pfeiffer (1948, pp. 653–59), discriminates between secular wisdom, which he attributes to an earlier popular provenience, and religious proverbial wisdom, which he attributes to later foreign influence. Pfeiffer ascribes the emergence of religious wisdom to Deuteronomistic theology. The presence of "religious" wisdom along with "secular" wisdom at ancient Ugarit undermines the assumptions of such opinions; see further below.

[8] For the significance of the scribal invention of the alphabetic cuneiform writing system for writing Ugaritic — and occasionally other languages — see Sanders 2009, pp. 54–58. Of course, the Akkadian written at Ugarit, while generally similar to other forms of "peripheral Akkadian" in the Middle Babylonian period, also exhibits unique local features; see Huehnergard 1989; von Soldt 1991; von Soldt 1995b. And, as is well known, scribes at Ugarit writing Akkadian frequently inserted Ugaritic glosses in their texts; see Sivan 1984; Huehnergard 1987.

[9] The arguments of Morrow 2008 and Rainey 2008 to the effect that the Canaanite sources were drawn upon by Hebrew writers

within Canaan, as far south as Beth Shemesh, in the late second millennium B.C.E. (see, e.g., Sanders 2006, and the references there), means that the earliest Hebrew scribes, who emerged in that same period, could even have read Ugaritic unmediated (Greenstein 1996, pp. 26–31). But we need not assume that much in order to allow that Syro-Canaanite wisdom literature in Akkadian flowed into the stream of the biblical tradition.

Even without acknowledging that particular influence, several scholars have speculated that Israelite wisdom drew on Canaanite and/or Ugaritic precursors (e.g., Blank 1962, p. 855b; Rofé 2009, p. 521). However, there is, and has for many decades been, evidence of Canaanite wisdom, in addition to the relatively recently discovered trove of Akkadian wisdom from Ras Shamra. Canaanite documents without any direct dependence on Mesopotamian sources attest a local tradition of wisdom. Proverbs and gnomic sayings are embedded in several text types in the ancient Near East — both belles lettres and such mundane fare as letters (e.g., Beckman 1986; Hallo 1990; Hallo 2004, p. xi).[10] And just as proverbs and wisdom-like observations are incorporated within the Mari correspondence (Marzal 1976; Sasson 1995; Durand 2006), so are they employed to make a rhetorical point in several Canaanite letters from the El Amarna correspondence (e.g., Albright 1943; Marcus 1973; Hess 1993; Bodi 2006; and esp. Cochavi-Rainey 1997). These Amarna proverbs, which display the distinctive Canaano-Akkadian that characterizes virtually all the letters from Canaan found at El Amarna (see esp. Marcus 1973 and Hess 1993), represent the most quintessential wisdom genre.[11] In addition to the best-known proverbs from this corpus — about the ants who bite back (Hess 1993) and the unplowed field (Marcus 1973) — there is the analogy of the cooped-up king to a caged bird (EA 74: 45–46 etc.; Moran 1992, pp. 143); the saying of the townspeople "A deed that has not been done since time immemorial has been done to us" (EA 122: 40–44; trans. Moran 1992, p. 201);[12] and the proverb-like metaphor "a brick may move fro[m u]nder [its] par[tner]; still I will not move from [un]der the feet [of the k]in[g], my lord" (EA 266: 18–25 etc.; trans. Moran 1992, p. 314). Proverbs belong to the scribal curriculum (e.g., van Soldt 1995a, pp. 182–83; Byrne 2007, p. 20a), and it may be surmised that the scribes of second millennium Syro-Palestine so assimilated sapiential literature that they could make use of it at will no matter what type of text they were writing.

Back in the early 1940s, Albright (1943, p. 7) pointed to the most salient of the Amarna proverbs as the best evidence of wisdom among the Canaanites. At that time, no wisdom literature was known or discerned among the texts from Ugarit. Since then, as we have seen above, works of wisdom have come to light at Ras Shamra; but because they are primarily in Akkadian, it has often been claimed that there is no native wisdom — no wisdom in Ugaritic (e.g., Sparks 2005, pp. 75–76; Márquez Rowe 2008, pp. 95–96; cf., e.g., Murphy 1981, p. 27a; Crenshaw 1985, pp. 370–71). The chapter "Wisdom" in the multi-volume anthology *Ras Shamra Parallels*, while acknowledging that "wisdom literature is present in Ugarit" (Khanjian 1975, p. 373), deals only with the Akkadian texts. The first full-length study of all the Akkadian wisdom texts from Ugarit (Khanjian 1974) devotes barely two pages to a handful of Ugaritic passages reminiscent of wisdom. On the basis of three examples, only two of which are properly interpreted[13] and only one of which might, in my judgment, be regarded as sapiential,[14] it is concluded

---

for the first time in the mid-first millennium B.C.E. do not come to terms with the massive evidence of literary and linguistic continuity between Ugaritic and biblical literature, beginning with the very earliest stages of Hebrew literature. See my arguments case by case in Greenstein 1996.

[10] This is not the place for an extended discussion of the definitions of proverb and proverbial expression. For an exemplary treatment, see Fontaine 1982, for whom a "traditional saying" is characterized by its brevity, its occurrence in a fixed form, its elevated style, and its lack of grammatical continuity with the surrounding discourse (ibid., p. 73). For my purposes I adopt the definition of a proverb by the folklorist Hasan-Rokem (1990, p. 108): "A proverb is a short text summarizing an idea formulated in such a way that it implies collective experience and wisdom, and is applicable to numerous situations." A proverbial expression, in my usage, sounds like a wisdom observation but is less pithy than a proverb (cf. Bodi 2006, pp. 40–41).

[11] For the Canaano-Akkadian language, see especially Rainey 1996 and Izre'el 1998.

[12] Compare biblical expressions in Gen 20:9; Qoh 1:10–11; Dan 9:12.

[13] The phrase *wum tšmḫ mab* (*CAT* 2.16.10–11) can hardly mean "May my mother derive pleasure from my father" (Khanjian 1974, p. 208). For discussion of the various perspectives — and despite that a similar mistranslation — see Cunchillos 1989, pp. 299–300 (n. 18). For one thing, the reading *mab* is uncertain; the *b* may be a *d* (Dietrich, Loretz, and Sanmartín 1995, p. 167). For another, the preposition *m* in Ugaritic does not mean "from." For yet another, if *mab* were a prepositional phrase, one would expect to find the genitive suffix *-iya* (written *y*). The parsing and translation of Pardee (2002, p. 89; cf. Bordreuil and Pardee 2009, p. 236) — "so may my mother cause *Maʾʾabû* (PN) to rejoice" — violate no Ugaritic norms and are therefore to be preferred.

[14] The analogy found in two Ugaritic narrative poems (Baal and Kirta) comparing someone's longing to the attachment of a cow to her calf strongly resembles a motif known from the Sumerian lamentation literature and is more appropriately classified with that genre rather than with wisdom; see, e.g., Greenstein 2001a, p. 97. The rhetorical pattern *k...k...km...* of the Baal passage does resemble a rhetorical pattern found in Prov 25:20: כ...כ...כן... (Story 1945, p. 322) — but only the pattern is common to the two passages. Khanjian (1974, p. 207) regards the following Ugaritic

that wisdom might not be "limited to the Akkadian texts alone and that there was wisdom in Ugarit which was expressed in the local dialect" (ibid., p. 207). Of course, one cannot gainsay the fact that "there is no wisdom poetry in Ugaritic comparable to Job, Proverbs, or Ecclesiastes" (Pardee 2000, p. 62a). Nevertheless, in what follows I intend to show that there are several proverbial expressions embedded in the Ugaritic texts from Ras Shamra and that the two epic texts in Ugaritic (Aqhat and Kirta) are suffused with wisdom themes. Without aspiring to be comprehensive, I believe that the extent and quality of the Ugaritic examples demonstrate that wisdom was integral to Canaanite culture.

An Akkadian letter from Carchemish to an official at Ugarit explicitly cites a saying (*teltu*(*m*)) of the Hittites: "A certain man has been imprisoned for five years; and when they said, 'Tomorrow they will release you,' he choked (or strangled himself)" (Nougayrol 1968, pp. 108–10; Khanjian 1974, pp. 145–47). However one understands the irony — just as he was to go free, he choked, either from joy at the news or by accident — or whether he killed himself in his misery just before he received the news that he was about to be freed, the purpose of the citation would seem to be to make the point that timing is everything; delaying an action may achieve a result opposite from the intention. Unfortunately, there do not appear to be any proverbial sayings in any of the Ugaritic letters from Ras Shamra.[15]

The following sentence from a Ugaritic letter may, however, have a sapiential background: *wyd ilm p kmtm ʿz mid* 'There is plague [lit., the hand of a god] here, for death is very strong' (*CAT* 2.10.11–13; cf. Pardee 2002, p. 108 with n. 152).[16] Although the strongest biblical parallel is, as Avishur (2007, pp. 157–59) maintains, 1 Sam 5:11b — "For there was a panic of plague/death (מות) throughout the town; the hand of God was very heavy there" — the theme of the power of death and the language in which it is formulated (*mt ʿz*) recall the simile in Song 8:6a: 'For love is as strong as death' (כי עזה כמות אהבה). Zakovitch (1992, pp. 133–34) quite trenchantly points out the didactic character of the entire unit (vv. 6–8), which, in a manner entirely peculiar among the love poems of the Song of Songs, comments on love philosophically, in the abstract (cf. Klein 1997, p. 64). Almost every line of this unit has a parallel in the book of Proverbs, leading Zakovitch to conclude, very plausibly, that the section has been influenced by that wisdom text. If that is the case, then there is a good likelihood that the simile "love is as strong as death," with its gnomic character, lies behind the scribe's formulation in the Ugaritic letter.

Be that as it may, a passage in the Baal cycle shows clear affinities to a didactic passage in Proverbs (cf., e.g., Schoors 1972, p. 20). Let us begin by looking at Proverbs 6:16–19:

> These six things YHWH hates (שנא),
> And seven are abominations to him:
> Haughty eyes, a lying tongue, and hands that spill innocent blood;
> A heart that devises evil schemes,
> Feet that run quickly to (do) evil;
> A deceitful witness giving false testimony;
> And one who spreads contention (מדנים) among brothers.

---

couplet as a wisdom saying (*CAT* 1.23.56): *bm nšq whr / bḥbq wḥ*[*m*] *ḥmt* "By kissing there is impregnation, by embracing there is conception" (cf. Pardee 1997, p. 281 with n. 57). I do not regard this worldly observation as proverbial, however, because it does not stand out from its context (see n. 10 above) but is an integral part of the narrative sequence.

[15] Wiseman (1977, p. 89) points to a possible example in a juridical text (RS 17.376 + 377; Nougayrol 1970, p. 26, lines 20–21), but the passage is too broken to establish its gnomic character. Dijkstra (1999, p. 152) interprets and classifies *CAT* 2.2 as a wisdom exercise. This analysis does not seem likely. First, the fragment appears to be part of a larger document, possibly a letter (see Herdner 1963, text 59, pl. 46, fig. 113; cf. Dietrich, Loretz, and Sanmartín 1995, p. 161) — although no letter formula is preserved, it does feature some "I"–"you" discourse. Second, Dijkstra's interpretation involves several restorations and several moot readings of signs, especially at the beginnings and ends of lines; moreover, he treats the fragment as though it were an almost complete tablet, so that the end of one line continues almost directly in the following line — which appears to be an erroneous assumption. (I am indebted to West Semitic Research for their assistance in clarifying the readings in this text. I expect to publish my transliteration of this text on another occasion.) And even if Dijkstra's reading and translation of the fragment are correct, the result is incoherent — according to him, in the first part, the addressee is advised to seek well-being, and in the second part, he is assured that Baal will grant him the children he has asked for. In both parts, it should be mentioned, the verb for asking (*šʾl* and *ʾrš*, respectively) is mostly restored.

[16] For *yd ilm* in the sense of 'plague' or the like, see Pardee 1987, p. 67.

On account of its striking similarities in theme, literary structure, and language, the following Ugaritic passage (*CAT* 1.4.3.17–21) would appear either to serve as a distant source of the unit in Proverbs or to reflect a shared literary template:

> *dm ṯn dbḥm šna bʿl / ṯlṯ rkb ʿrpt*
> *dbḥ bṯt wdbḥ*[17] *dnt / wdbḥ tdmm amht*
>
> For two feasts Baal hates, / three the Rider of the Clouds:
> A feast of shame and a feast of contention,
> And a feast of the lewdness of maids.[18]

The two passages begin almost identically: there are X number of things that the high god hates (*šna*/שנא). Both passages open with a couplet structured by a graded numerical sequence in parallelism (two-three, six-seven). In both passages the objects of hatred are itemized (three and seven, respectively). And one of the hated items is 'contention' (*dnt*/מדנים). I maintain that the affinities in content and form between the two passages suggest that the Ugaritic passage has been borrowed from a sapiential source. Such a conclusion may be supported by the fact that, as Smith and Pitard (2009, p. 477) observe, the unit does not easily "fit[...] into the context of the speech in which it occurs." Note, too, that Baal has apparently been speaking in the first person and that, with this unit, he shifts, speaking of himself in the third person. Such shifts can indicate the embedding of a proverbial saying (see n. 10 above). The parallel passage in Proverbs 6 would also seem to be autonomous — it is "the only numerical saying in the book outside of chap[ter] 30" (Clifford 1999, p. 77), where we find a string of them.

The Aqhat epic is often held up as a unique example of Ugaritic wisdom by virtue of its protagonist, the righteous judge Danel (Dāna-ʾilu),[19] who is almost certainly to be identified with the figure Danel (דנאל) mentioned twice in Ezekiel 14 (vv. 14, 20) and once in a north Canaanite context (Ezek 28:3), where he is characterized as a paragon of wisdom (see, e.g., Story 1945, p. 326; Day 1980; Day 1995, pp. 57–59; cf., e.g., Mack-Fisher 1990b, p. 109; Marquéz Rowe 2008, p. 97). Below I discuss additional wisdom motifs and themes in this epic; but here I would call attention to an apparently sapiential remark made by Aqhat in his refusal of the goddess Anath's offer of immortality (*CAT* 1.17.6.35–38):

> *mt uḫryt mh yqḥ / mh yqḥ mt aṯryt*
> *spsg ysk [l]riš / ḥrṣ lẓr qdqdy*
> *[ank?] mt kl amt / wan mtm amt*
>
> A mortal — what future can he attain? / What hereafter can a mortal attain?
> Glaze will be poured on (my) head, / Plaster on my crown.
> [I] will die the death of everyman; / I will die like a mortal.[20]

Many if not most specialists have come to understand the reference to glaze/plaster on the head as a figure for old age (cf. Hos 7:9; Ginsberg 1945b, p. 21 n. 56) — the hair turning white (see, e.g., Spronk 1986, p. 152 n. 3; Pardee 1997, p. 347 n. 46; de Moor 2003, pp. 144 nn. 197–98; contrast Margalit 1983; Margalit 1989, pp. 307–10).[21] The "philosophical" — wisdom — character of Aqhat's reply to the goddess has been keenly discerned by Margalit (1989, p. 307). Aqhat's realism, "eschew[ing] comforting illusions," is an outlook shared by the Ugaritic Baal cycle, by Job in his dialogues, "and by ancient Near Eastern 'Wisdom' literature generally" (cf. Khanjian 1974, p. 119).

---

[17] The repetition of *wdbḥ* on the tablet is uncontroversially understood as dittography.

[18] The philological options for interpreting these lines are laid out in, e.g., van Zijl (1972, pp. 88–94), Caquot, Sznycer, and Herdner (1974, p. 201), and Smith and Pitard (2009, pp. 475–79). Obviously I derive *dnt* (**dīnatu*) from *dw/yn*; cf. Hebrew מדון 'contention' and Akkadian *dittu* (underlyingly /diintu/) 'lawsuit' (the Arabic verb *dāna* 'to be base,' another plausible etymon, is not otherwise known in Ugaritic); and *tdmm* (read perhaps *tdmt* = **taḏimmatu*; cf. Smith and Pitard 2009, pp. 461, 477) from **ḏmm* = Hebrew זמם and cf. זמה 'perversity' and Arabic *ḏamma* 'to find blameworthy.' The interpretation of *dbḥ dnt* as 'feast of contention' finds support in the Hebrew wisdom expression זבחי ריב 'feasts of strife' (Prov 17:1). Fox (2009, pp. 623–24) elaborates the ways in which a "feast" or, in his understanding, a "sacrifice" can be contentious.

[19] The hero's name, meaning "El judges," as well as the matching name of his wife, Dānatiya (*dnty*), signify Danel's judicial role; Ginsberg 1945a, p. 4 n. 6; cf. O'Connor 2006, pp. 280–82.

[20] Or "I will die, yes, die" (parsing as an infinitive absolute with enclitic *mem* rather than as a noun with the adverbial suffix *-am*).

[21] For the difficulties of determining the precise meaning of Ugaritic *spsg* and *ḥrṣ*, see the detailed discussion in Wright 2001, pp. 148–52. Wright himself does not offer a compelling alternative (see p. 111).

It is expressed in a quasi-syllogistic fashion: all humans die, I am human, ergo I will die (Margalit 1989, p. 307).[22] The generality of the observation, together with the figurative expression, establishes the proverbial character of Aqhat's discourse.

Further support for the gnomic quality of Aqhat's reply can be garnered from his ensuing pronouncement (lines 39–41): *qštm* [   ] *mhrm / ht tṣdn tinṯ* [*bh*?] 'Bows are [the implements of?] soldiers! Do females go hunting [with one]?' This essentializing remark, which infuriates the goddess to the point of murder, constitutes yet another general observation. Anath explicitly recognizes Aqhat's impudence as a juvenile attempt at wisdom, referring to the youth sarcastically as *ʿmq nšm* 'the wisest of people' (*CAT* 1.17.6.45; cf. Natan-Yulzary 2007, p. 170).[23]

Anath responds further to Aqhat threatingly, warning that she will meet him on the 'path of defiance' (*ntb pšʿ*), on 'the path of pride' (*ntb gan*) (*CAT* 1.17.6.43–44). These locutions conform to a metaphoric pattern, wherein a person's good and bad conduct is analogized to a road or path. Instances of this pattern in Hebrew wisdom are abundant. Psalm 1, a "wisdom song" (Weiser 1962, p. 103), is a parade example. With the language of the Aqhat passage under discussion in mind, compare Proverbs 12:28:

> בְּאֹרַח-צְדָקָה חַיִּים וְדֶרֶךְ נְתִיבָה אַל-מָוֶת׃
> On the road of righteousness is life,
> And the course of its path (נתיבה) is not-dying.

One might infer that the metaphor is a wisdom cliché.

The epic of Kirta, on the wisdom themes of which I shall expatiate below, would also seem to incorporate pronouncements of wisdom. When Kirta appears to be dying, his younger son Ilḥaʾu poses a theological paradox: *ap ab ik mtm tmtn* 'O father, how can you die like a mortal?' (*CAT* 1.16.1.3–4; cf. 17–18).[24] The king, observes Ilḥaʾu, is called a 'son of El' (*bn il*; ibid., line 20). If so, how can kings die, when gods do not — *uilm tmtn* 'Do gods, after all, die?' (ibid., line 22).[25] This piece of philosophical reasoning, expressed in almost catechistic terms, may not be gnomic in its formulation, but it is, in the manner of many proverbs, concise and marked by assonance (*ʾū ʾilūma tamūtūna*). Moreover, the paradox is a distinctive form of wisdom (see, e.g., Thompson 1974, pp. 68–72 and passim), characteristic of both Qohelet and its Mesopotamian counterpart, the Dialogue between a Master and His Servant (Fox 1987; Greenstein 2007).[26]

Toward the end of what remains of the Kirta epic, the monarch's elder son, Yaṣṣib, accuses his (formerly) ill father of malfeasance and demands that he cede the throne to him. Prominent among the accusations are the following lines (*CAT* 1.16.6.44–50):[27]

> *šqlt bġlt ydk / ltdn dn almnt / ltṯpṭ ṯpṭ qṣr npš*
> *ltdy ṯšm ʿl dl / lpnk ltšlḥm ytm / bʿd kslk almnt*
>
> You've let your hand fall to vice.[28]
> You don't pursue the widow's case,
> You don't take up the wretched's claim.
> You don't expel the poor's oppressor.[29]
> You don't feed the orphan who faces you,
> Nor the widow who stands at your back.

---

[22] For a brief discussion of syllogistic-type argument in ancient Near Eastern literature (including the Hebrew Bible), see Greenstein 2002, pp. 452–53; see now also Herzog 2009.

[23] The term for "wise" is derived etymologically from *ʿmq* 'deep' as in Akkadian *emqu* and occasionally Hebrew עמק; see further Greenstein 2003, pp. 261–63. Some (e.g., del Olmo Lete and Sanmartín 1996, p. 80) render *ʿmq* as 'strong,' referring to Akkadian *emūqu* 'strength.' However, the Akkadian word occurs only as a noun, neither as a verb nor an adjective, and I am not convinced that there is any cognate in Ugaritic.

[24] The parallel passage has *k* 'like.' For the problem of interpreting *ik* 'how' in the first passage, see Pardee 1973, p. 231. For Kirta's illness and evident mortality as a sign of his humanity, see, e.g., Knoppers 1994, p. 579; cf. Kleven 1988, p. 40.

[25] Parker (1989, pp. 180, 213) interprets the question ambiguously (perhaps the gods do actually die) as an expression of theological skepticism. Wyatt (1996, pp. 296–99) insists that Kirta be understood mythologically as a son of El.

[26] The essence of this paragraph is drawn from Greenstein 2001b, p. 6.

[27] The reading and translation follow Greenstein 1997, p. 41.

[28] Cf. Hebrew עול(ת)ה (Ginsberg 1946: 49) and cf. Ps. 125:3, where we find the locution לא שלח יד בעולתה 'did not extend a hand to vice.'

[29] Cf. Hebrew שסה and Amos 5:11 (Ginsberg 1946, p. 49).

Although the passage does not in and of itself belong to a wisdom genre, it bears a strong resemblance to Job 22:6–9,[30] where Eliphaz accuses Job of similar deeds of injustice:

> כִּי-תַחְבֹּל אַחֶיךָ חִנָּם וּבִגְדֵי עֲרוּמִּים תַּפְשִׁיט:
> לֹא-מַיִם עָיֵף תַּשְׁקֶה וּמֵרָעֵב תִּמְנַע-לָחֶם:...
> אַלְמָנוֹת שִׁלַּחְתָּ רֵיקָם וּזְרֹעוֹת יְתֹמִים יְדֻכָּא:

> For you seize a pledge from your brothers without cause,
> By stripping the clothes off the naked.
> You give no water to the weary, / and withhold food from the hungry.
> Widows you send away empty-handed,
> And the arms of the fatherless you push away.[31]

The Kirta passage also resembles Psalm 82:2–4, where the old gods are similarly charged with failure to promote justice:[32]

> עַד-מָתַי תִּשְׁפְּטוּ-עָוֶל וּפְנֵי רְשָׁעִים תִּשְׂאוּ-סֶלָה:
> שִׁפְטוּ-דַל וְיָתוֹם עָנִי וָרָשׁ הַצְדִּיקוּ:
> פַּלְּטוּ-דַל וְאֶבְיוֹן מִיַּד רְשָׁעִים הַצִּילוּ:

> How long will you take the side of the corrupt,
> Showing favor to the wicked? (Selah!)
> Take the side of the poor and the fatherless,
> Render justice to the needy and indigent!
> Rescue the poor and the desperate,
> Save (them) from the hand of the wicked!

Aside from the recurrent motif of giving succor to the widow, the orphan, and the needy, one finds in both the Ugaritic and biblical passages the word *ġlt*-עולה 'vice, corruption' as well as the cognate terms for 'widow,' 'orphan,' and 'taking up a ca(u)se' (*ṯpṭ*-שפט). The usage of the materials in Job 22, as well as the general inclusion of justice and caring for the weak as a theme in the ancient Near Eastern wisdom texts (for Mesopotamia, see, e.g., Lambert 1960, pp. 100–02, lines 56–65; for Egypt, see, e.g., Lichtheim 1976, pp. 141–42), provide a basis for surmising that the theme of doing justice and caring for the powerless in Kirta, as in Job and Psalms, has a wisdom source (see, e.g., Fensham 1962; Weinfeld 1985, pp. 129–30). As mentioned above, it is the Ugaritic Danel's devotion to justice that leads to his reputation as a sage.

For a final example of a wisdom-related passage in Ugaritic, we turn again to the Baal cycle and to part of Baal's cryptic message to Anath inviting her to come and hear a further message (*CAT* 1.3.3.20–28):

> *dm rgm iṯ ly wargmk / hwt waṯnyk*
> *rgm ʿṣ wlḫšt abn / tant šmm ʿm arṣ / thmt ʿmn kbkbm*
> *abn brq dltdʿ šmm / rgm ltdʿ nšm / wltbn hmlt arṣ*

> For I have a word[33] that I would tell you, / a message I would relate —
> A word of tree and a whisper of stone,
> A converse[34] of heaven with earth, / of the sea with the stars.
> I understand lightning the heavens know not,
> A thing[35] people know not, / the masses of the earth do not understand.

---

[30] Cf., e.g., Pope 1965, p. 150.

[31] Reading תְּדַכֵּא with the ancient translations (see Dhorme 1967, p. 329). I follow Tur-Sinai and Ginsberg in understanding Eliphaz to be parodying the charges that Job believes God is holding against him — exaggerating the accusations to show the absurdity of Job's claim; see Greenstein 2009, pp. 347–48.

[32] For the overall interpretation of the psalm, see Parker 1995.

[33] Ugaritic *rgm* is apparently used here in the sense of 'message' (derived metonymically from 'voice'), but on account of Baal's being a storm god who thunders, there is, as in Akkadian *rigmu* and Hebrew קול, a punning connotation of 'thunder' as well.

[34] See, e.g., Smith and Pitard 2009, p. 227.

[35] Here *rgm* 'voice, word' is generally understood to denote the derived sense of 'thing' or 'matter' (cf. Hebrew דבר and Akkadian *āwatu*; for the vocalization of the latter, see Greenstein 1984, p. 37), but in parallelism with *brq* 'lightning' it might actually denote 'thunder' (see n. 33) and produce a true pun.

Baal's claim to special, esoteric knowledge — in itself a sign of wisdom (cf. Wyatt 1996, pp. 257–58) — recalls the rhetoric of the Lord from the whirlwind in Job, for example, Job 38:33–35:

הֲיָדַעְתָּ חֻקּוֹת שָׁמָיִם אִם-תָּשִׂים מִשְׁטָרוֹ בָאָרֶץ:
הֲתָרִים לָעָב קוֹלֶךָ וְשִׁפְעַת-מַיִם תְּכַסֶּךָּ:
הַתְשַׁלַּח בְּרָקִים וְיֵלֵכוּ וְיֹאמְרוּ לְךָ הִנֵּנוּ:

Do you know the regularities of the heavens?
Have you imposed their regimen on earth?[36]
Can you raise your voice toward a cloud,
And be answered by a downpour?[37]
Can you send lightning bolts on their way,
As they say to you, "Yes, sir!"[38]

Just as YHWH is pointing to his exclusive knowledge — including his control of lightning — so, it would seem, is Baal. My comparison to Job is not meant to suggest a literary dependency, only a common background in a wisdom mindset. Baal's rhetoric, as well as his claim to esoteric knowledge, are not proverbial, but they are sapiential in character.

As said above, literary works in Ugaritic are replete with wisdom motifs and themes. Wisdom notions may inform a narrative even if it is not of a marked didactic character, just as proverbs may add rhetorical power to a letter that is not sapiential in its thrust.[39] The Aqhat epic features the positive figure of Danel the righteous judge (see above) as well as the negative example of Aqhat the impudent youth (see above and cf. Prov 14:3; 16:18; 29:23; Qoh 7:8–9). Wisdom can be discerned in several other aspects of the Aqhat text.

Most striking among these is the fourfold presentation of the so-called duties of the son — the services that a son is meant to perform for his father during his life and after his death (*CAT* 17.1.25–33; 42–48 [plus missing lines]; 17.2.1–8 [plus missing lines]; 14–23).[40] The duties involve diverse services, such as repairing the father's roof and supporting him when he is drunk, on the one hand, and making funerary offerings after he is dead, on the other.[41] The repetitive enumeration of the duties in a fixed form, outside the action sequence of the narrative (cf. Margalit 1989, p. 280; Wright 2001, p. 69), gives the impression of a set piece, imported into the present context; its pronounced ethical character, focused on filial piety, bespeaks a wisdom association (van Selms 1954, p. 101; Healey 1979, p. 356; Avishur 2007, pp. 142–44) — in which case the pericope may comprise a wisdom saying and belong to the preceding discussion.

Healey (1979, p. 356), following Eissfeldt (1966), compares the pericope to some biblical ethical instructions. Compare, for example, the Ugaritic duty *ṭbq lḥt niṣh / grš d ʿšy lnh* "who suppresses the slander of his [viz., his father's] maligners,[42] who dispels the one who acts against him," with Proverb 22:10: "Dispel (גרש) the scoffer and

[36] Read משטרן with plural possessive suffix, referring to חקות; so, e.g., Kahana 1928, p. 209.

[37] In parallelism with the following verse, in which the meteorological phenomenon is said to speak in response, read תענך "it (the downpour) answers you" for תכסך; so Kahana (1928, p. 210) on the basis of context and the Greek; cf. Dhorme 1967, p. 591.

[38] Lit., "here we are"; for הנה + pronominal suffix as an expression of compliance, see, e.g., Gen. 22:1, 7, 11; cf. Akk. *anna/u* 'yes' and post-biblical הן.

[39] Well-known studies highlighting wisdom themes in biblical narratives are Talmon 1963; von Rad 1966; and Whybray 1968; see also McKenzie 1967. The critical remarks of Crenshaw (1995) do not undermine the basic arguments of these and similar studies. My approach is closer to Whybray's than to von Rad's. While von Rad understands the Joseph story as a didactic tale, Whybray discerns wisdom themes and motifs within the David narratives, which are not in and of themselves didactic.

[40] For the literary effect of the fourfold repetition, see Greenstein 2000, pp. 144–45; cf. Wright 2001, p. 69.

[41] The precise interpretation of several lines is debated. For philological analyses, see, e.g., Lewis 1989, pp. 53–71; Boda 1993; Wright 2001, pp. 48–69; Avishur 2007, pp. 130–47. Wright maintains that all the activities take place while the father is alive (cf. Schmidt 1994, pp. 59–62), but many scholars see the cultic acts described connected to mortuary offerings (for a list up till 1994, see Schmidt 1994, p. 59 n. 69). I understand the reference to setting up a stela and cult object (*ztr*), raising the father's spirit (*qṭr* // *ḏmr*), and the consumption of offerings in the temple to reflect most simply the activities of ancestral worship. Concerning *ḏmr*, lit. 'strength, force,' see Lewis (1989, p. 63), who, like others who preceded him, compares זמרת in Exodus 15:2. However, I parse the second clause of the pertinent couplet differently than does Lewis. I would render the couplet thus: "Who raises his spirit from the earth, / the force of his (burial-)place (or: shrine) from the dust." Compare the syntactic structure of the preceding couplet (with gapping of the verb): "Who sets up a stela of his divine-ancestor, / in the sanctuary the cult-symbol of his kinsman."

[42] See, e.g., Lewis 1989, p. 66; Boda 1993, p. 17.

contention goes away; and dishonorable accusations will cease." Even more to the point in the context of Aqhat is this advice from a sapiential psalm (Ps 127:4–5; cf., e.g., Gerstenberger 2001, pp. 346–47):

> Like arrows in the hand of a warrior, / thus are the sons of (one's) youth.
> Happy is the man who has filled his quiver with them;
> They will not be discomfited when they contend with (his) adversaries at the city-gate.

The first couplet is formulated as a proverb, and the second elaborates it (Weiser 1962, p. 766).

Wisdom literature in the Hebrew Bible is often characterized by stark contrasts between the righteous, who are wise, and the wicked, who are foolish or even roguish (see, e.g., Otzen 1974; Kugel 2003, pp. 143–48, 240–41). The *dramatis personae* in the Aqhat epic are aligned in a similar fashion, as we meet with two gendered pairs, in each of which one member represents the wise and the other the fool or the rogue. The two male protagonists, Danel and Aqhat, have been characterized above. The father is portrayed as a righteous judge, and his efforts both to obtain a son (a six-day ritual of entreating the deity during which he never leaves the sacred precincts [*CAT* 1.17.1]) and to locate him or his remains (having deduced from the flight of the vultures overhead that his son's carcass may be the source of the attraction [*CAT* 1.19.1–3; cf. Greenstein 2000, p. 143]) evince a deliberate and persevering character (cf. Sun 2008, p. 118). His son, Aqhat, manifests foolishness ("youthful intemperance," as Landy 1981, p. 10, puts it) in a number of ways: he speaks arrogantly to the goddess Anath; not only does he reject her demand for his bow, but he also insults her as a goddess, accusing her of falsehood — and he insults her as a female to boot (see above).

We find a similar contrast between the two leading female characters, Anath and Pughat — Danel's daughter and Aqhat's sister (see Walls 1992, pp. 206–10). Anath is, like Aqhat, impetuous — after plotting Aqhat's murder in her rage, she seems to regret her impulsive behavior and weeps (*CAT* 1.18.4.39; cf. Sun 2008, p. 101). Pughat, on the other hand, who is explicitly characterized as wise — "the one who knows the path of the stars" (*CAT* 1.19.2.2–3, 7; ibid., 4.38) — exhibits the same deliberation and perseverance that her father does. She tracks down and apparently, by means of a clever subterfuge, slays the henchman who killed Aqhat (*CAT* 1.19.4).

Pughat's triumph is facilitated by a double gender reversal that recapitulates the gender issues that exacerbate the conflict of wills between Anath and Aqhat (cf. Hillers 1973; Landy 1981, pp. 11–13). Pughat, whose name not incidentally means 'girl' (*pġt*; cf., e.g., O'Connor 2006, p. 278), dresses like a warrior in order to slay her brother's assassin but disguises her masculine garb with a female costume, in order to gain entry to the soldiers' camp. She blurs gender boundaries while her brother Aqhat had insisted on maintaining them. He rejected Anath's proposition to turn him immortal, whereby he would transgress the boundary between human and god, and he denied Anath's assertion of male prerogatives — to hunt and therefore need a bow (cf. Sun 2008, p. 96).

The transgression of borders leads to disorder, if not chaos, and herein lies the irony — and perhaps the subversiveness — of the tale. The creation and maintenance of order are a premiere feature of ancient Near Eastern and biblical wisdom (e.g., Crenshaw 1995, pp. 344–54, 494–98; Perdue 2008, pp. 109–10). The father god of the Ugaritic pantheon, El (ʾIlu), is apparently the creator god at Ugarit — the establisher and maintainer of order — and it is he alone among the gods who is expressly called 'wise' (*ḥkm*; e.g., CTA 1.4.5.3–5; see, e.g., Handy 1994, pp. 79–92; Greenstein 2003, pp. 260–62 with references). In Ugaritic metaphysics, as in that of Egypt and the Bible, wisdom and order are interconnected. In Aqhat, it is the foolish eponymous hero of the tale who presses for order and his transgressive sister Pughat who proves to be wise. The conclusion of the story is missing, but it seems almost certain that in the end, the sensible (Danel and Pughat) succeed, whereas the petulant (Aqhat and Anath) fail.

The epic of Kirta is not a didactic tale, but it is one whose leading protagonist is a sort of righteous sufferer — a stock figure of ancient wisdom — and whose plot turns on a number of wisdom themes.[43] The figure of the pious sufferer, well developed in Mesopotamia (see Mattingly 1990) and best known from the book of Job, was, as mentioned above, represented at Ugarit by a local Akkadian version of the Babylonian classic "Let Me Praise the Lord of Wisdom." Aspects of King Kirta of the Ugaritic epic can be, and have been, compared to the story of Job (e.g., O'Connor 1989; Parker 1989, pp. 146–47), and Kirta, too, has been classified as a "righteous sufferer" (e.g., de Moor 1986, p. 14). Both Kirta and Job suffer through no fault of their own. Job learns of the ruin of his estate and the death of his servants through an uninterrupted sequence of messenger reports, blow after blow (Job 1); and

[43] The following discussion has been drawn from Greenstein 2001b, pp. 8–13.

the death of Kirta's children is reported by the narrator in a single stream of narration (*CAT* 1.14.1).[44] Both Job (ch. 42) and Kirta (*CAT* 1.15.3) are restored, receiving new children in place of those who died. Although Kirta is not explicitly described as righteous, as Job is (Job 1), Kirta, like Job (1:8; 2:3; 42:7–8), is called 'the servant' (*ʿbd*-עבד) of the deity. Moreover, he is, like Job (29:12–17), one who defended the powerless as part of his public service (see above). On the other hand, Kirta's suffering is not drawn out like Job's, nor does Kirta brood philosophically over the possible causes of his afflictions, as Job does.

However, Kirta follows the dictates of wisdom when he follows El's instructions to the letter. Obedience is the beginning of wisdom (cf. Prov 1:7 etc.). Although there is one thing Kirta does that is not part of El's directions (see below), there is nothing in the hundred lines of instructions that El directs him to do that he does not perform (cf., e.g., Parker 1977, esp. p. 174). Ideally, a monarch in the Syro-Canaanite-biblical milieu was meant to govern through wisdom (see, e.g., Isa 11:2; Prov 8:15–16; cf., e.g., Weinfeld 1972, pp. 244–47, 254–57; Launderville 2003, esp. pp. 298–300). Thus the biblical king Solomon, in a scene reminiscent of Kirta's request for children (see Seow 1984), turns down wealth and honor and asks for wisdom (1 Kgs 3:3, 9).[45]

Kirta, too, would have done well to have asked for wisdom because his second affliction (after his loss of family) might have been prevented had he applied the wisdom befitting a king. Kirta was stricken with illness, as was Job. The apparent cause was Kirta's failure to fulfill a vow he made to the goddess Asherah (ʾAṯiratu) during his seven-day march to Udum, where he was to obtain his princess bride (*CAT* 1.15.3.25–30; see Greenstein 1997, pp. 26–27). Kirta's one departure from El's instructions was to stop at the shrine of El's consort Asherah midway on the journey and to make a vow in exchange for her support (*CAT* 1.14.4.19–43).[46] When Kirta's eight children were all born, a process that must have taken years, the happy father had not yet paid his vow — but, as the narrator takes pains to remind us, Asherah remembered the vow (cf. Loewenstamm 1992, pp. 196–97). Kirta's deviation from El's directions and his failure to pay the vow, in particular, proved nearly fatal for the king.

The importance of fulfilling a vow to a god is a commonplace of ancient Near Eastern wisdom. Qohelet (5:3–5) has this to say about it:

> When you vow a vow to God, do not delay in paying it.
> For He has no desire in fools — what you have vowed, pay!
> Better it is not to have vowed than to vow and then not pay.
> Do not allow your mouth to cause your flesh to sin.
> And do not say before the angel — it [viz., what I said] was a mistake.
> Why should God get angry over your speech [lit., voice] and ruin the work of your hands?

Similar advice is found in Proverbs 20:25, Ben Sira 18:22–23, the Torah (Num 30:3; Deut 23:22–24),[47] and ancient Near Eastern literature in general (see Parker 1979; 1989, pp. 172–74). The importance of fulfilling a vow informs the episode in which Absalom goes to Hebron under the pretense that he must pay a vow (2 Sam 15:7);[48] and it takes on grand — and grotesque — proportions in the story of Jephthah (Judg 11; see esp. Marcus 1986). This piece of wisdom also finds a place in the Akkadian wisdom written at Ugarit (Arnaud 2007, p. 139: 1–2; cf. Khanjian 1974, pp. 140–43):

---

[44] A large number of specialists interpret the passage in question to refer to the death of Kirta's seven wives. This is not the place to discuss the issue at any length; see Greenstein 2006, p. 93 n. 91 for some linguistic points. I would only reiterate here that from the perspective of narrative structure and theme, it only makes sense if Kirta lost his children and not a series of wives. In order to produce the eight children he sired according to the opening of the epic (*CAT* 1.14.1.7–9), he had need of only one wife. Once blessed by El, he will sire another eight children, all by the same wife. When El asks Kirta what he is lacking that leads him to weep, he indicates a lack of children (*bnm*; *CAT* 1.14.2.4–5), not wives, and it is children that El promises him: the princess bride he obtains will bear him a male heir (*CAT* 1.14.3.48–49). Finally, the number of children that Kirta's new wife produces for him is eight (*CAT* 1.15.2.23–25 and col. 3 there) — the same as the number of children Kirta had had at the start. The tale revolves around children, not wives. Accordingly, I refer the reader to my translation of the passage at issue (Greenstein 1997, p. 12).

[45] For parallels elsewhere in the ancient Near East, see Weinfeld 1972, pp. 247–54.

[46] For the possible motivation of Kirta's curious gesture, see Greenstein 2000, pp. 150–51.

[47] For the origins of the Deuteronomy passage in wisdom, see Weinfeld 1972, pp. 270–72.

[48] Whybray (1968, p. 70) identifies a wisdom element in this aspect of the story.

šukun kaspa ša mamīti itti ilī teleq[q]i
mamīta pilaḫemma pagarka šullim

Deposit the silver of a vow — you will get it (back) from the gods.
Respect a vow — thus take good care of yourself!

Kirta, therefore, forgoes wisdom by failing to pay his vow after receiving the blessings he had sought.

But Kirta also — like Job — never seems to have learned the actual cause of his catastrophic illness. Support for this supposition may be gathered from a scene from the period of his debilitation in which Kirta instructs his youngest daughter, Thitmanit (Octavia), to offer a vow for the sake of his healing (*CAT* 1.16.1.48): *ndr šqrb ksp / bmgnk wḫrṣ lkl* 'Make a vow and offer up silver, / by your donation — gold for all!' (see Greenstein 1998, p. 114 for the reading and translation). It seems improbable that Kirta would have his beloved daughter make a vow on his behalf had he remembered that he himself had a vow to fulfill. As the proverb goes, "Like a dog who returns to his vomit is a fool who repeats his blunder" (Prov 26:11). We ought to assume that the king has entirely forgotten his vow to Asherah and that he is ironically commissioning another vow, unaware that all his troubles stem from his failure to pay the former vow.

As indicated above, Kirta commits another error, more subtle than that concerning the vow, but no less serious. Traditional wisdom teaches that a person should punctiliously follow and not at all deviate from divine instructions. The biblical teacher par excellence, Moses, advises as follows: "You are to be careful to do as YHWH your God has commanded you; do not turn from it to the right or the left" (Deut 5:28). This Deuteronomistic formulation has its source in wisdom, as verses like the following from Proverbs 4:27 suggest: "Do not bend right or left, / Turn your foot from evil."[49] Moreover, the same literature teaches that one should neither add to nor subtract from divine instructions (Weinfeld 1972, pp. 261–65), as the sage Qohelet reiterates (3:14).[50] King Kirta, in making the vow to Asherah, broke with accepted wisdom in adding to the directions he received from El and made an apparently unnecessary vow (see above). His forgetting to pay the vow nearly cost him his life; and it was the disability he suffered as a result of his neglect that prompted his elder son Yaṣṣib to challenge him for the throne. And so did the king who was desperate for an heir set off a series of events that ended with his cursing his presumptuous son (*CAT* 1.16.6.54–58).

A wise king was meant to understand that "a person's heart (i.e., mind) designs his path, but the Lord fixes his steps" (Prov 16:9); "many are the designs in a man's heart, but it is the Lord's counsel that is upheld" (Prov 19:21). That one should be chary of one's own instincts and try to follow the ways of the gods is a theme one finds in several biblical narratives (see, e.g., von Rad 1966, p. 297, concerning Joseph and his brothers, and Whybray 1968, pp. 62–66, concerning David). Kirta's older son Yaṣṣib would have done well to have learned this lesson. Instead he obeyed the promptings of his own heart in demanding that his father relinquish the throne to him (*CAT* 1.16.6.25–54). The wisdom that one should rely on the determinations of the deities instead of on oneself is expressed in the Ballad of the Early Rulers, an Akkadian wisdom text found at Ugarit (Arnaud 2007, pp 142–43, lines 1–2, 12′):

itti (d)Ea uṣṣurāma uṣṣurātu / [i]na ṭem ilīma us<su>qā usqētu
awīlūtu ša[kān]i ša ramanīša lā īdū

Ordinances are ordained by (the god) Ea.
Lots are allotted by order of the gods.
Humankind does not know how to po[siti]on itself.[51]

Human limitations in knowing what is right is a biblical theme as well (see, e.g., Prov 20:24; Qoh 6:12; cf. Khanjian 1975, p. 383).

Yaṣṣib's behavior, however, ignores other wisdom lessons as well. For one thing, he should know that it is imprudent to anger a king. Compare Proverb 20:2: "The dread rage of a king is like the growl of a lion — whosoever provokes his anger jeopardizes his life" (cf. Prov 19:12). For another thing, it is unseemly to disrespect one's

[49] Additional examples from Deuteronomy and the Deuteronomistic literature are Deut 2:27; 17:11, 20; 28:14; Josh 1:7; 23:6; 1 Sam 6:12; 2 Kgs 22:2; Weinfeld 1972, p. 339.

[50] See also Deut 4:2; 13:1.

[51] For a different restoration and slightly different understanding of this line, see Khanjian 1974, pp. 184, 187.

parents. As Proverbs 30:17 delicately puts it, "The eye that scorns a father, and shows contempt for a mother's discipline — ravens of the wadi will pluck it out, and young vultures will eat it."[52] For a more banal image, see Proverbs 20:20. In any event, like father like son: both Kirta and Yaṣṣib violate the principle of wisdom: "Do not be wise in your own eyes" (Prov 3:7). They both pursued schemes of their own imagination and brought misfortune upon themselves.

These characters of Ugaritic narrative present a model lesson of what happens when wisdom is ignored. And yet, a prominent theme of ancient Near Eastern wisdom is that one can never really ascertain what the gods have in mind (Lambert 1960, p. 40, lines 36–38):

> Who can learn the mind of the gods in the heavens?
> The counsel of the underworld gods, who can understand?
> Where have people learned the ways of the gods?[53]

It is perhaps as a response to this frustration that the son in the Akkadian Wisdom of Šūpē-awēli answers the didacticism of his father by comparing humanity to a variety of wild animals (Arnaud 2007, p. 153, lines 131′–135′) — "we are offspring of the wild donkey" (trans. Foster 2005, p. 419).

The vagaries of the human condition and of our relationship to the gods are a subject that, as we have seen, preoccupied the storytellers of Ugarit as well. Although no Ugaritic wisdom works per se have yet been found at Ras Shamra, the number of Ugaritic passages that evince wisdom themes and forms, and the wisdom issues that pervade Ugaritic narrative, should suffice to make it clear that wisdom was native as well as imported and that the full-blown wisdom texts we find in the Hebrew Bible may well be the heirs of an old Canaanite legacy.

Abbreviations

CAT	Dietrich, Loretz, and Sanmartín 1995
EA	J. A. Knudtzon. *Die El-Amarna-Tafeln mit Einleitung und Erläuterungen.* 2 volumes. Vorderasiatische Bibliothek. Leipzig: J. C. Hinrichs, 1915
PN	personal name
RS	signature of texts found at Ras Shamra

Bibliography

Albright, William F.

1943 "An Archaic Hebrew Proverb in an Amarna Letter from Central Palestine." *Bulletin of the American Schools of Oriental Research* 89: 29–32.

1955 "Some Canaanite-Phoenician Sources of Hebrew Wisdom." In *Wisdom in Israel and in the Ancient Near East Presented to Professor Harold Henry Rowley by the Society for Old Testament Study in Association with the Editorial Board of Vetus Testamentum, in Celebration of His Sixty-fifth Birthday, 24 March 1955*, edited by Martin Noth and David Winton Thomas, pp. 1–15. Supplements to Vetus Testamentum 3. Leiden: Brill.

Alster, Bendt

2005 *Wisdom of Ancient Sumer.* Bethesda: CDL Press.

[52] In Egyptian art the Canaanite god Ḥoron is depicted as a vulture (Rütterswörden 1995, p. 807). In Kirta's curse of Yaṣṣib, his impertinent son, he invokes the god Ḥoron to crack open his son's head (*CAT* 1.16.6.54–57). Perhaps this Canaanite tradition lies behind the imagery in Prov 30:17.

[53] Literally in the singular: *alakti ili.*

Arnaud, Daniel

1987 *Recherches au pays d'Aštata. Emar VI/4.* Paris: Editions Recherche sur les Civilisations.

2007 *Corpus des textes de bibliothèque de Ras Shamra-Ougarit (1936–2000). Aula Orientalis* Supplement 23. Barcelona: Editorial Ausa.

Avishur, Yitzhak

2007 *Comparative Studies in Biblical and Ugaritic Languages and Literatures.* Tel Aviv–Jaffa: Archaeological Center Publication.

Beckman, Gary

1986 "Proverbs and Proverbial Allusions in Hittite." *Journal of Near Eastern Studies* 45: 19–30.

Ben Basat, Kobi

2008 Job in Ugarit? A New Way of Looking at the Text RS 25.460. M.A. thesis, Tel Aviv University. [In Hebrew]

Blank, Sheldon H.

1962 "Wisdom." In *The Interpreter's Dictionary of the Bible: An Illustrated Encyclopedia Identifying and Explaining all Proper Names and Significant Terms and Subjects in the Holy Scriptures, Including the Aprocrypha, with Attention to Archaeological Discoveries and Researches into the Life and Faith of Ancient Times*, edited by George A. Buttrick, pp. 852b–861a. New York: Abingdon Press.

Boda, Mark J.

1993 "Ideal Sonship in Ugarit." *Ugarit-Forschungen* 25: 9–24.

Bodi, Daniel

2006 "Une locution proverbiale à Mari, El-Amarna et dans la Bible." *Journal asiatique* 294: 39–52.

Bordreuil, Pierre, and Dennis Pardee

2009 *A Manual of Ugaritic.* Linguistic Studies in Ancient West Semitic 3. Winona Lake: Eisenbrauns.

Byrne, Ryan

2007 "The Refuge of Scribalism in Iron I Palestine." *Bulletin of the American Schools of Oriental Research* 345: 1–31.

Caquot, André; Maurice Sznycer; and Andrée Herdner

1974 *Textes ougaritiques*, Volume 1: *Mythes et legends.* Paris: Cerf.

Carr, David M.

2005 *Writing on the Tablet of the Heart: Origins of Scripture and Literature.* New York: Oxford University Press.

Cassuto, Umberto M. D.

1971 "The Relationship between Ugaritic Literature and the Bible." In *The Goddess Anat*, translated by Israel Abrahams, pp. 18–52. Jerusalem: Magnes.

Clifford, Richard J.

1975 "Proverbs IX: A Suggested Ugaritic Parallel." *Vetus Testamentum* 25: 298–306.

1999 *Proverbs: A Commentary.* Old Testament Library. Louisville: Westminster John Knox Press.

Cochavi-Rainey, Zipora

1997 "Selected Similes, Descriptions, and Figures of Speech from the El-Amarna Letters and Their Biblical Parallels." *Lešonénu* 60: 165–79. [In Hebrew]

Craigie, Peter C.

1985 "Job and Ugaritic Studies." In *Studies in the Book of Job*, edited by Walter E. Aufrecht, pp. 28–35. Waterloo: Wilfrid Laurier University Press.

Crenshaw, James L.

1985 "The Wisdom Literature." In *The Hebrew Bible and Its Modern Interpreters*, edited by Douglas A. Knight and Gene M. Tucker, pp. 369–407. Philadelphia: Scholars Press.

1995 *Urgent Advice and Probing Questions: Collected Writings on Old Testament Wisdom.* Macon: Mercer University Press.

Cunchillos, Jesús-Luis

1989 "Correspondance." In *Textes ougaritiques*, Volume 2: *Textes religieux et rituels,* edited by André Caquot, Jean-Michel de Tarragon, and Jesús-Luis Cunchillos, pp. 239–421. Littératures anciennes du Proche-Orient 14. Paris: Éditions du Cerf.

Day, John

1980 "The Daniel of Ugarit and Ezekiel and the Hero of the Book of Daniel." *Vetus Testamentum* 30: 174–84.

1995 "Foreign Semitic Influence on the Wisdom of Israel and Its Appropriation in the Book of Proverbs." In *Wisdom in Ancient Israel: Essays in Honor of J. A. Emerton*, edited by John Day, Robert P. Gordon, and H. G. M. Williamson, pp. 55–70. Cambridge: Cambridge University Press.

Day, John; Robert P. Gordon; and H. G. M. Williamson

1995 *Wisdom in Ancient Israel: Essays in Honor of J. A. Emerton*. Cambridge: Cambridge University Press.

del Olmo Lete, G., and Joaquín Sanmartín

1996 *Diccionario de la lengua ugarítica*. 2 volumes. Aula orientalis. Supplementa 7-8. Barcelona: Editorial AUSA.

de Moor, Johannes C.

1986 "The Crisis of Polytheism in Late Bronze Ugarit." In *Crises and Perspectives: Studies in Ancient Near Eastern Polytheism, Biblical Theology, Palestinian Archaeology, and Intertestamental Literature: Papers read at the Joint British-Dutch Old Testament Conference, held at Cambridge, U.K., 1985*, edited by A. S. van der Woude, pp. 1–20. Oudtestamentische Studiën 24. Leiden: Brill.

2003 "Theodicy in the Texts of Ugarit." In *Theodicy in the World of the Bible*, edited by Antti Laato and Johannes C. de Moor, pp. 108–50. Leiden: Brill.

Demsky, Aaron

1990 "The Education of Canaanite Scribes in the Mesopotamian Cuneiform Tradition." In *Bar-Ilan Studies in Assyriology Dedicated to Pinchas Artzi*, edited by Jacob Klein and Aaron Skaist, pp. 157–70. Ramat Gan: Bar-Ilan University Press.

Dhorme, Edouard

1967 *A Commentary on the Book of Job*. Translated by Harold Knight. London: Thomas Nelson.

Dietrich, Manfried

1991 "Der Dialog zwischen Šūpē-amēli und seinem 'Vater': Die Tradition babylonischer Weisheitssprüche im Westen." *Ugarit-Forschungen* 23: 33–68.

1992 "'Ein Leben ohne Freude...': Studie über eine Weisheitskomposition aus den Gelehrtenbibliotheken von Emar und Ugarit." *Ugarit-Forschungen* 24: 9–29.

1993 "Babylonian Literary Texts from Western Libraries." In *Verse in Ancient Near Eastern Prose*, edited by Johannes C. de Moor and Wilfred G. E. Watson, pp. 41–67. Alter Orient und Altes Testament 42. Kevelaer: Butzon and Bercker.

Dietrich, Manfried; Oswald Loretz; and Joaquín Sanmartín

1995 *The Cuneiform Alphabetic Texts from Ugarit, Ras Ibn Hani and Other Places* (KTU: 2nd enlarged edition). Münster: Ugarit-Verlag.

Dijkstra, Meindert

1993 "The Akkado-Hurrian Bilingual Wisdom-text RS 15.010 Reconsidered." *Ugarit-Forschungen* 25: 163–71.

1999 "Ugaritic Prose." In *Handbook of Ugaritic Studies*, edited by W. G. E. Watson and Nicolas Wyatt, pp. 140–64. Handbuch der Orientalistik 39. Leiden: Brill.

Durand, Jean-Marie

2006 "Dictons et proverbes à l'époque amorrite." *Journal asiatique* 294: 3–38.

Eissfeldt, Otto

1966 "Sohnespflichten im Alten Orient." *Syria* 43: 39–47.

Emerton, J. A.

2001 "The Teaching of Amenemope and Proverbs XXII 17–XXIV 22: Further Reflections on a Long-standing Problem." *Vetus Testamentum* 51/4: 431–65.

Fensham, F. Charles

1962 "Widow, Orphan, and the Poor in Ancient Near Eastern Legal and Wisdom Literature." *Journal of Near Eastern Studies* 21/2: 129–39.

Fontaine, Carole R.

1982 *Traditional Sayings in the Old Testament: A Contextual Study*. Bible and Literature Series 5. Sheffield: Almond Press.

Foster, Benjamin R.

2005 *Before the Muses: An Anthology of Akkadian Literature*. 3rd edition. Bethesda: CDL Press.

Fox, Michael V.
1987 *Qoheleth and His Contradictions.* Journal for the Study of the Old Testament. Supplement Series 71. Sheffield: Almond Press.
2000 *Proverbs 1–9.* Anchor Bible 18A. New York: Doubleday.
2009 *Proverbs 10–31.* Anchor Yale Bible 18B. New Haven: Yale University Press.

Gerstenberger, Erhard S.
2001 *Psalms,* Part 2, *and Lamentations.* Forms of the Old Testament Literature 15. Grand Rapids: Eerdmans.

Gianto, Augustus
1998 "Human Destiny in Emar and Qohelet." In *Qohelet in the Context of Wisdom,* edited by Antoon Schoors, pp. 473–79. Bibliotheca Ephemeridum theologicarum Lovaniensium 136. Leuven: Leuven University Press/ Uitgeverij Peeters.

Ginsberg, H. L.
1945a "The North-Canaanite Myth of Anath and Aqhat." *Bulletin of the Schools of Oriental Research* 97: 3–10.
1945b "The North-Canaanite Myth of Anath and Aqhat, II." *Bulletin of the Schools of Oriental Research* 98: 15–23.
1946 *The Legend of King Keret: A Canaanite Epic of the Bronze Age.* American Schools of Oriental Research. Supplementary Studies 2–3. New Haven: American Schools of Oriental Research.

Golden, Jonathan M.
2004 *Ancient Canaan and Israel: An Introduction.* Oxford: Oxford University Press.

Gray, John
1970 "The Book of Job in the Context of Near Eastern Literature." *Zeitschrift für die alttestamentliche Wissenschaft* 82: 251–69.

Greenfield, Jonas C.
1971 "Scripture and Inscription: The Literary and Rhetorical Element in Some Early Phoenician Inscriptions." In *Near Eastern Studies in Honor of William Foxwell Albright,* edited by Hans Goedicke, pp. 253–68. Baltimore: Johns Hopkins University Press.
1987 "The Hebrew Bible and Canaanite Literature." In *The Literary Guide to the Bible,* edited by Robert Alter and Frank Kermode, pp. 545–60. Cambridge: Belknap Press.

Greenstein, Edward L.
1984 "The Phonology of Akkadian Syllable Structure." *Afroasiatic Linguistics* 9: 1–71.
1996 "The Canaanite Literary Heritage in Ancient Hebrew Writing." *Michmanim* 10: 19–38. [In Hebrew]
1997 "Kirta." In *Ugaritic Narrative Poetry,* edited by Simon B. Parker, pp. 9–48. Society of Biblical Literature, Writings from the Ancient World 9. Atlanta: Scholars Press.
1998 "New Readings in the Kirta Epic." In *Past Links: Studies in the Languages and Cultures of the Ancient Near East,* edited by Shlomo Izre'el, Itamar Singer, and Ran Zadok, pp. 105–23. Israel Oriental Studies 18. Winona Lake: Eisenbrauns.
2000 "The Role of the Reader in Ugaritic Narrative." In *"A Wise and Discerning Mind": Essays in Honor of Burke Long,* edited by Saul M. Olyan and Robert C. Culley, pp. 139–51. Brown Judaic Studies 325. Providence: Brown Judaic Studies.
2001a "The Lament over the Destruction of City and Temple in Early Israelite Literature." In *Homage to Shmuel [Aḥituv]: Studies in the World of the Bible,* edited by Zipora Talshir, Shamir Yona, and Daniel Sivan, pp. 88–97. Beersheva: Ben-Gurion University of the Negev Press. [In Hebrew]
2001b "The Ugaritic Epic of Kirta in a Wisdom Perspective." In *Studies in Judaica,* edited by Yair Hoffman, pp. 1–13. Te'uda 16–17. Tel Aviv: Tel Aviv University. [In Hebrew]
2002 "Some Developments in the Study of Language and Some Implications for Interpreting Ancient Texts and Cultures." In *Semitic Linguistics: The State of the Art at the Turn of the Twenty-first Century,* edited by Shlomo Izre'el, pp. 441–79. Israel Oriental Studies 20. Winona Lake: Eisenbrauns.
2003 "The Poem on Wisdom in Job 28 in Its Conceptual and Literary Contexts." In *Job 28: Cognition in Context,* edited by Ellen van Wolde, pp. 253–80. Biblical Interpretation Series 64. Leiden: Brill.
2006 "Forms and Functions of the Finite Verb in Ugaritic Narrative Verse." In *Biblical Hebrew in Its Northwest Semitic Setting: Typological and Historical Perspectives,* edited by Steven E. Fassberg and Avi Hurvitz, pp. 75–102. Winona Lake: Eisenbrauns.
2007 "Sages with a Sense of Humor: The Babylonian Dialogue between a Master and His Servant and the Book of Qohelet." In *Wisdom Literature in Mesopotamia and Israel,* edited by Richard J. Clifford, pp. 55–65. Symposium Series 36. Atlanta: Society of Biblical Literature.

2009 "The Problem of Evil in the Book of Job." In *Mishneh todah: Studies in Deuteronomy and Its Cultural Environment in Honor of Jeffrey H. Tigay*, edited by Nili S. Fox, David A. Glatt-Gilad, and Michael J. Williams, pp. 333–62. Winona Lake: Eisenbrauns.

Hallo, William W.

1990 "Proverbs Quoted in Epic." In *Lingering over Words: Studies in Ancient Near Eastern Literature in Honor of William L. Moran*, edited by Tzvi Abusch, John Huehnergard, and Piotr Steinkeller, pp. 203–17. Harvard Semitic Studies 37. Atlanta: Scholars Press.

2004 "Foreword." In *A Culture of Desert Survival: Bedouin Proverbs from Sinai and the Negev*, by Clinton Bailey, pp. ix–xvi. New Haven: Yale University Press.

Handy, Lowell K.

1994 *Among the Host of Heaven: The Syro-Palestinian Pantheon as Bureaucracy*. Winona Lake: Eisenbrauns.

Hasan-Rokem, Galit

1990 "And God Created the Proverb ...: Inter-generic and Inter-textual Aspects of Biblical Paremiology — Or the Longest Way to the Shortest Text." In *Text and Tradition: The Hebrew Bible and Folklore*, edited by Susan Niditch, pp. 107–20. Society of Biblical Literature Semeia Studies. Atlanta: Scholars Press.

Hawley, Robert

2008 "On the Alphabetic Scribal Curriculum at Ugarit." In *Proceedings of the 51st Recontre Assyriologique Internationale held at the Oriental Institute of the University of Chicago, July 18-22, 2005*, edited by Robert D. Biggs, Jennie Myers, and Martha T. Roth, pp. 57–67. Studies in Ancient Oriental Civilization 62. Chicago: The Oriental Institute.

Healey, John F.

1979 "The *Pietas* of an Ideal Son in Ugarit." *Ugarit-Foruschungen* 11: 353–56.

Herdner, Andreé

1963 *Corpus des tablettes en cunéiformes alphabétiques découvertes à Ras Shamra-Ugarit de 1929 à 1939*. 2 volumes. Mission de Ras Shamra 10. Paris: Imprimerie Natonale/Librairie orientaliste Paul Geuthner.

Herzog, Eliezra

2009 "The Triple Rhetorical Argument — An Expression of Syllogism in the Bible." *Beit Mikra* 54: 62–82. [In Hebrew]

Hess, Richard S.

1993 "Smitten Ants Bite Back: Rhetorical Forms in the Amarna Correspondence from Shechem." In *Verse in Ancient Near Eastern Prose*, edited by Johannes C. de Moor and Wilfred G. E. Watson, pp. 95–111. Alter Orient und Altes Testament 42. Kevelaer: Butzon and Bercker.

Hillers, Delbert R.

1973 "The Bow of Aqhat: The Meaning of a Mythological Theme." In *Orient and Occident: Essays Presented to Cyrus H. Gordon on the Occasion of His Sixty-fifth Birthday*, edited by Harry A. Hoffner, Jr., pp. 71–80. Alter Orient und Altes Testament 22. Kevelaer: Butzon and Bercker.

Horowitz, Wayne, and Takayoshi Oshima

2006 *Cuneiform in Canaan: Cuneiform Sources from the Land of Israel in Ancient Times*. Jerusalem: Israel Exploration Society/Hebrew University of Jerusalem.

Horwitz, William J.

1979 "The Ugaritic Scribe." *Ugarit-Forschungen* 11: 389–94.

Huehnergard, John

1987 *Ugaritic Vocabulary in Syllabic Transcription*. Harvard Semitic Studies 32. Atlanta: Scholars Press.

1989 *The Akkadian of Ugarit*. Harvard Semitic Monographs. Atlanta: Scholars Press.

Hurowitz, Victor A.

2007 "The Wisdom of Šūpê-amēlī — A Deathbed Debate between a Father and Son." In *Wisdom Literature in Mesopotamia and Israel*, edited by Richard J. Clifford, pp. 37–51. Symposium Series 36. Atlanta: Society of Biblical Literature.

Izre'el, Shlomo

1998 *Canaano-Akkadian*. Languages of the World 82. Munich: Lincom Europa.

Kahana, Avraham

1928 *The Book of Job*. Torah, Nevi'im u-Ketuvim with a Scientific Commentary. Tel Aviv: Meqorot. [In Hebrew]

Kämmerer, Thomas R.

1928 šimâ milka: *Induktion und Reception der mittelbabylonischen Dichtung von Ugarit, Emār und Tell el-ʿAmārna.* Alter Orient und Altes Testament 251. Münster: Ugarit-Verlag.

Keydana, Götz

1991 "Anhang: Die hethitische Version." *Ugarit-Forschungen* 23: 68–74.

Khanjian, John

1974 Wisdom in Ugarit and in the Ancient Near East with Particular Emphasis on Old Testament Wisdom Literature. Ph.D. dissertation, Claremont Graduate School.

1975 "Wisdom." In *Ras Shamra Parallels* II, edited by Loren R. Fisher, pp. 371–400. Analecta orientalia 50. Rome: Pontifical Biblical Institute.

Klein, Jacob

1997 *ʿolam hattenakh: megillot* [The Five Scrolls]. Tel Aviv: Davidson-Itti. [In Hebrew]

2000 "'The Ballad about Early Rulers' in Eastern and Western Traditions." In *Languages and Cultures in Contact: At the Crossroads of Civilizations in the Syro-Mesopotamian Realm; Proceedings of the 42th [sic] RAI*, edited by Karel van Lerberghe and Gabriela Voet, pp. 203–16. Orientalia Lovaniensia analecta 96. Leuven: Peeters.

Kleven, Terence

1988 "Kingship in Ugarit (*KTU* 1.16 I 1–23)." In *Ascribe to the Lord: Biblical and Other Studies in Memory of Peter C. Craigie*, edited by Lyle Eslinger and Glen Taylor, pp. 29–53. Journal for the Study of the Old Testament Supplement 67. Sheffield: JSOT Press.

Knoppers, Gary N.

1994 "Dissonance and Disaster in the Legend of Kirta." *Journal of the American Oriental Society* 114: 572–82.

Kugel, James L.

2003 *The God of Old: Inside the Lost World of the Bible.* New York: Free Press.

Lambert, W. G.

1960 *Babylonian Wisdom Literature.* Oxford: Clarendon Press.

1995 "Some New Babylonian Wisdom Literature." In *Wisdom in Ancient Israel: Essays in Honor of J. A. Emerton*, edited by John Day, Robert P. Gordon, and H. G. M. Williamson, pp. 30–42. Cambridge: Cambridge University Press.

Launderville, Dale

2003 *Piety and Politics: The Dynamics of Royal Authority in Homeric Greece, Biblical Israel, and Old Babylonian Mesopotamia.* Grand Rapids: Eerdmans.

Landy, Francis

1981 *The Tale of Aqhat.* London: Menard.

Lewis, Theodore J.

1989 *Cults of the Dead in Ancient Israel and Ugarit.* Harvard Semitic Monographs 39. Atlanta: Scholars Press.

Lichtenstein, Murray H.

1968 "The Banquet Motif in Keret and in Proverbs 9." *Journal of the Ancient Near Eastern Society of Columbia University* 1: 19–31.

Lichtheim, Miriam

1976 *Ancient Egyptian Literature. A Book of Readings*, Volume 2: *The New Kingdom.* Berkeley: University of California Press.

Loewenstamm, Samuel E.

1992 "On the Theology of the Keret-epic." In *From Babylon to Canaan: Studies in the Bible and Its Oriental Background*, pp. 185–200, by Samuel E. Loewenstamm. Jerusalem: Magnes Press.

Mack-Fisher, Loren R.

1990a "A Survey and Reading Guide to the Didactic Literature of Ugarit: Prolegomenon to a Study on the Sage." In *The Sage in Israel and the Ancient Near East*, edited by John G. Gammie and Leo G. Perdue, pp. 67–80. Winona Lake: Eisenbrauns.

1990b "The Scribe (and Sage) in the Royal Court at Ugarit." In *The Sage in Israel and the Ancient Near East*, edited by John G. Gammie and Leo G. Perdue, pp. 109–15. Winona Lake: Eisenbrauns.

Marcus, David

1973 "A Famous Analogy of Rib-Haddi." *The Journal of the Ancient Near Eastern Society of Columbia University* 5: 281–86.

1986 *Jephthah and His Vow*. Lubbock: Texas Tech Press.

Margalit, Baruch

1983 "The 'Neolithic Connexion' of the Ugaritic Poem of Aqht." *Paléorient* 9: 93–98.

1989 *The Ugaritic Poem of AQHT: Text, Translation, Commentary*. Beihefte zur Zeitschrift für die alttestamentliche Wissenschaft 182. Berlin: Walter de Gruyter.

Márquez Rowe, Ignacio

2008 "Scribes, Sages, and Seers in Ugarit." In *Scribes, Sages, and Seers: The Sage in the Eastern Mediterranean World*, edited by Leo G. Perdue, pp. 95–108. Göttingen: Vandenhoeck and Ruprecht.

Marzal, Angel

1976 *Gleanings from the Wisdom of Mari*. Studia Pohl 11. Rome: Pontifical Biblical Institute.

Mattingly, Gerald L.

1990 "The Pious Sufferer: Mesopotamia's Traditional Theodicy and Job's Counselors." In *Scripture in Context*, Volume 3: *The Bible in the Light of Cuneiform Literature*, edited by William W. Hallo, Bruce W. Jones, and Gerald L. Mattingly, pp. 305–48. Ancient Near Eastern Texts and Studies 8. Lewiston: Edwin Mellen.

McKenzie, John L.

1967 "Reflections on Wisdom." *Journal of Biblical Literature* 86: 1–9.

Moran, William L.

1992 *The Amarna Letters*. Baltimore: Johns Hopkins University Press.

Morrow, William S.

2008 "Resistance and Hybridity in Late Bronze Age Canaan." *Revue Biblique* 115: 321–39.

Murphy, Roland E.

1981 "Hebrew Wisdom." *Journal of the American Oriental Society* 101: 21–34.

1992 "Wisdom in the OT." In *Anchor Bible Dictionary*, Volume 6, edited by David N. Freedman, pp. 920–31. New York: Doubleday.

Natan-Yulzary, Shirly

2007 "Characterization and Text Texture in Ancient West-Semitic Literature from Ugarit." *Shnaton – An Annual for Biblical and Ancient Near Eastern Studies* 17: 161–97. [In Hebrew]

Nougayrol, Jean

1955 *Textes accadiens et hourrites des archives est, oust, et centrales*. Le palais royal d'Ugarit 3. Mission de Ras Shamra 6. Paris: Imprimerie Nationale/Librairie C. Klincksieck.

1968 "Textes suméro-accadiens des archives et bibliothèques privées d'Ugarit." In *Ugaritica* V, by Jean Nougayrol, Emmanuel Laroche, Charles Virolleaud, and Claude Schaeffer, pp. 1–446. Mission de Ras Shamra 16. Paris: Librairie Orientaliste Paul Geuthner.

1970 *Textes en cunéiformes babyloniens des archives du grand palais et du palais sud d'Ugarit*. Le palais royal d'Ugarit VI. Mission de Ras Shamra 12. Paris: Imprimerie nationale-Librairie C. Klincksieck.

O'Connor, Daniel J.

1989 "The Keret Legend and the Prologue-Epilogue of Job." *Irish Theological Quarterly* 55: 1–6.

O'Connor, M.

2006 "The Human Characters' Names in the Ugaritic Poems: Onomastic Eccentricity in Bronze-age West Semitic and the Name Daniel in Particular." In *Biblical Hebrew in Its Northwest Semitic Setting: Typological and Historical Perspectives*, edited by Steven E. Fassberg and Avi Hurvitz, pp. 269–83. Winona Lake: Eisenbrauns.

Otzen, Benedikt

1974 "Old Testament Wisdom Literature and Dualistic Thinking in Late Judaism." In *Congress Volume, Edinburgh 1974*, pp. 146–57. Supplements to Vetus Testamentum 28. Leiden: Brill.

Pardee, Dennis

1973 "A Note on the Root *'tq* in CTA 16 I 2,5 (UT 125. KRT II)." *Ugarit-Forschungen* 5: 229–34.

1987 "As Strong as Death." In *Love and Death in the Ancient Near East: Essays in Honor of Marvin H. Pope*, edited by John H. Marks and Robert M. Good, pp. 65–69. Guilford: Four Quarters Publishing.

1997 "Canonical Compositions (West Semitic)." In *The Context of Scripture*, Volume 1: *Canonical Compositions from the Biblical World*, edited by William W. Hallo and K. Lawson Younger, Jr., pp. 241–356. Leiden: Brill.

2000 "Ugaritic Studies at the End of the Twentieth Century." *Bulletin of the Schools of Oriental Research* 320: 49–86.

2002 "Ugaritic Letters." In *The Context of Scripture*, Volume 3: *Archival Documents from the Biblical World*, edited by William W. Hallo and K. Lawson Younger, Jr., pp. 87–116. Leiden: Brill.

Parker, Simon B.

1977 "The Historical Composition of the *Krt* and the Cult of El." *Zeitschrift für die alttestamentliche Wissenschaft* 89/2: 161–75.

1979 "The Vow in Ugaritic and Israelite Narrative Literature." *Ugarit-Forschungen* 11: 693–700.

1989 *The Pre-Biblical Narrative Tradition: Essays on the Ugaritic Poems* Keret *and* Aqhat. Society of Biblical Literature Resources for Biblical Study 24. Atlanta: Scholars Press.

1995 "The Beginning of the Reign of God: Psalm 82 as Myth and Liturgy." *Revue biblique* 102: 532–59.

Perdue, Leo G.

2008 *The Sword and the Stylus: An Introduction to Wisdom in the Age of Empires*. Grand Rapids: Eerdmans.

Pfeiffer, Robert H.

1948 *Introduction to the Old Testament*. New York: Harper and Row.

Pitard, Wayne T.

2002 "Voices from the Dust: The Tablets from Ugarit and the Bible." In *Mesopotamia and the Bible: Comparative Explorations*, edited by Mark W. Chavalas and K. Lawson Younger, Jr., pp. 251–75. Grand Rapids: Baker Academic.

Pope, Marvin H.

1965 *Job*. Anchor Bible 15. Garden City: Doubleday.

von Rad, Gerhard

1966 "The Joseph Narrative and Ancient Wisdom." In *The Problem of the Hexateuch and Other Essays*. Translated by E. W. Trueman Dicken, pp. 292–300. London: Oliver and Boyd.

1972 *Wisdom in Israel*. Translated by James D. Martin. New York: Abingdon Press.

Rainey, Anson F.

1996 *Canaanite in the Amarna Tablets: A Linguistic Analysis of the Mixed Dialect Used by the Scribes from Canaan*. 4 volumes. Leiden: Brill.

2008 "The Northwest Semitic Literary Repertoire and Its Acquaintance by Judean Writers." *Maarav* 15: 193–205.

Rofé, Alexander

2009 *Introduction to the Literature of the Hebrew Bible*. Jerusalem Biblical Studies 9. Jerusalem: Simor.

Rütterswörden, U.

1995 "Horon." In *Dictionary of Deities and Demons in the Bible*, edited by Karel van der Toorn, Bob Becking, and Pieter W. van der Horst, pp. 805–08. Leiden: Brill.

Saadé, Gabriel

1988 "La vie intellectuelle et l'enseignement à Ougarit." In *Ascribe to the Lord: Biblical and Other Studies in Memory of Peter C. Craigie*, edited by Lyle Eslinger and Glen Taylor, pp. 69–90. Journal for the Study of the Old Testament Supplement 67. Sheffield: Sheffield Academic Press.

Sanders, Seth

2006 "Alphabetic Cuneiform Texts." In *Cuneiform in Canaan: Cuneiform Sources from the Land of Israel in Ancient Times*, by Wayne Horowitz and Takayoshi Oshima, pp. 157–66. Jerusalem: Israel Exploration Society/ Hebrew University of Jerusalem.

2009 *The Invention of Hebrew*. Chicago: University of Illinois Press.

Sasson, Jack M.

1995 "Water beneath Straw: A Prophetic Phrase in the Mari Archives." In *Solving Riddles and Untying Knots: Biblical, Epigraphic, and Semitic Studies in Honor of Jonas C. Greenfield*, edited by Ziony Zevit, Seymour Gitin, and Michael Sokoloff, pp. 599–608. Winona Lake: Eisenbrauns.

Schmidt, Brian B.
1994 *Israel's Beneficient Dead: Ancestor Cult and Necromancy in Ancient Israelite Religion and Tradition.* Forschungen zum Alten Testament 11. Tübingen: Mohr Siebeck.

Schoors, Anton
1972 "Literary Phrases." In *Ras Shamra Parallels: The Texts from Ugarit and the Hebrew Bible* I, edited by Loren R. Fisher, pp. 1–70. Analecta orientalia 49. Rome: Pontifical Biblical Institute.

Scott, R. B. Y.
1965 *Proverbs: Ecclesiastes.* Anchor Bible 18. Garden City: Doubleday.

Selms, A. van
1954 *Marriage and Family Life in Ugaritic Literature.* London: Luzac.

Seminara, Stefano
2000 "Le Istruzioni di Šūpê-amēlī: Vecchio e nuovo a confronto nella 'sapienza' siriana del Tardo Bronzo." *Ugarit-Forschungen* 32: 487–529.

Seow, Choon-Leong
1984 "The Syro-Palestinian Context of Solomon's Dream." *Harvard Theological Review* 77/2: 141–52.

Sivan, Daniel
1984 *Grammatical Analysis and Glossary of the Northwest Semitic Vocables in Akkadian Texts of the 15th–13th Centuries B.C. from Canaan and Syria.* Alter Orient und Altes Testament 214. Kevelaer: Butzon and Bercker.

Smith, Duane E.
1975 "Wisdom Genres in RS 22.439." In *Ras Shamra Parallels*, Volume 2, edited by Loren R. Fisher, pp. 215–47. Analecta Orientalia 50. Rome: Pontifical Biblical Institute.

Smith, Mark S., and Wayne Pitard
2009 *The Ugaritic Baal Cycle*, Volume 2: *Introduction with Text, Translation and Commentary of KTU/CAT 1.3–1.4.* Supplements to *Vetus Testamentum* 114. Leiden: Brill.

van Soldt, W. H.
1991 *Studies in the Akkadian of Ugarit Dating and Grammar.* Alter Orient und Altes Testament 40. Kevelaer: Butzon and Bercker / Neukirchen-Vluyn: Neukirchener Verlag.
1995a "Babylonian Lexical, Religious, and Literary Texts and Scribal Education at Ugarit and Its Implications for the Alphabetic Literary Texts." In *Ugarit: Ein ostmediterranes Kulturzentrum im alten Orient: Ergebnisse und Perspektiven der Forschung*, Volume 1: *Ugarit und seine altorientalische Umwelt*, edited by Manfried Dietrich and Oswald Loretz, pp. 171–212. Münster: Ugarit-Verlag.
1995b "The Akkadian of Ugarit: Lexicographical Aspects." *Studi epigrafici e linguistici* 12: 205–15.

Sparks, Kenton L.
2005 *Ancient Texts for the Study of the Hebrew Bible: A Guide to the Background Literature.* Peabody: Hendrickson.

Spronk, Klaas
1986 *Beatific Afterlife in Ancient Israel and in the Ancient Near East.* Alter Orient und Altes Testament 219. Kevelaer: Butzon and Bercker.

Story, Cullen I. K.
1945 "The Book of Proverbs and Northwest Semitic Literature." *Journal of Biblical Literature* 64: 319–37.

Sun, Chloe
2008 *The Ethics of Violence in the Story of Aqhat.* Piscataway: Gorgias.

Talmon, Shemaryahu
1963 "'Wisdom' in the Scroll of Esther." *Vetus Testamentum* 13: 419–55.

Thompson, John M.
1974 *The Form and Function of Proverbs in Ancient Israel.* The Hague: Mouton.

Toy, Crawford H.
1916 *A Critical and Exegetical Commentary on the Book of Proverbs.* International Critical Commentary. New York: Charles Scribner's Sons.

Walls, Neal H.
1992 *The Goddess Anat in Ugaritic Myth.* Society of Biblical Literature Dissertation 135. Atlanta: Scholars Press.

Walton, John H.

1989 *Ancient Israelite Literature in Its Cultural Environment*. Grand Rapids: Zondervan.

Weeks, Stuart

1999 *Early Israelite Wisdom*. Oxford: Oxford University Press.

Weinfeld, Moshe

1972 *Deuteronomy and the Deuteronomic School*. Oxford: Clarendon Press.

1985 *Justice and Righteousness in Israel and the Nations: Equality and Freedom in Ancient Israel in Light of Social Justice in the Ancient Near East*. Jerusalem: Magnes. [In Hebrew]

Weiser, Artur

1962 *The Psalms: A Commentary*. Translated by Herbert Hartwell. Old Testament Library. Philadelphia: Westminster.

Westermann, Claus

1995 *Roots of Wisdom: The Oldest Proverbs of Israel and Other Peoples*. Translated by J. Daryl Charles. Louisville: Westminster John Knox Press.

Whybray, R. Norman

1968 "Wisdom in the Succession Narrative." In *The Succession Narrative: A Study of II Samuel 9-20, [and] I Kings 1 and 2*, pp. 56–95. London: SCM Press.

Wiseman, D. J.

1977 "Israel's Literary Neighbors in the 13th Century B.C." *Journal of Northwest Semitic Languages* 5: 77–91.

Wright, David P.

2001 *Ritual in Narrative: The Dynamics of Feasting, Mourning, and Retaliation Rites in the Ugaritic Tale of Aqhat*. Winona Lake: Eisenbrauns.

Wyatt, N.

1996 *Myths of Power: A Study of Royal Myth and Ideology in Ugaritic and Biblical Tradition*. Ugaritisch-biblische Literatur 13. Münster: Ugarit-Verlag.

Yon, Marguerite

2006 *The City of Ugarit at Tell Ras Shamra*. Winona Lake: Eisenbrauns.

Zakovitch, Yair

1992 *The Song of Songs: Introduction and Commentary*. Jerusalem: Magnes. [In Hebrew]

Zijl. Peter J. van

1972 *Baal: A Study of Texts in Connexion with Baal in the Ugaritic Epics*. Alter Orient und Altes Testament 10. Kevelaer: Butzon and Bercker.

8

Predicate Nominals and Related Constructions in Neo-Mandaic

*Charles G. Häberl, Rutgers University**

This paper is a small contribution to the much larger project of developing a metalinguistic framework for discussing the Semitic languages that is viable both individually and cross-linguistically. My own interest in this project owes much to John Huehnergard's influence, whose scholarship — bridging as it does areas as diverse as linguistic typology, the diachronic and synchronic description of the Semitic languages, interconnections among these languages extending even into the greater Afroasiatic language phylum, and the broader question of language contact — represents some of the last century's most profound contributions to the subject.

1. Introduction

The term "predicate nominal" describes a variety of phrases in which the semantic content of the predication is provided not by a verb but by a noun. It belongs to a wider category of related constructions that employ a noun or some other complement such as an adjective or a prepositional phrase to indicate equation, attribution (predicate adjectives), location (predicate locatives), existence (existential constructions), and possession (possessive clauses), among other types of predication.[1] All of these constructions are characterized by the lack of a "semantically rich" verb, one that contributes to the meaning of the clause by supplying the major semantic content of the predication. In languages such as Russian, Hungarian, Turkish, and most classical Semitic languages, it is possible to dispense with the verb altogether in the simple present.

Generally, the verb employed in such constructions will be either a copular verb or some kind of "grammatical verb," namely, one that is inflected to express predication but contributes little if anything to the meaning of the predicate. While predicate nominals and related constructions are interesting for several reasons, they merit particularly close attention due to the fact that they serve as a basic grammatical template that adapts to serve many other functions in discourse (Payne 1997, p. 113).

Classical Mandaic, a Semitic language belonging to the eastern subgroup of Aramaic dialects, preserves the full panoply of constructions found in these languages.[2] Its modern reflex, Neo-Mandaic, not only preserves the original strategies for dealing with predication, but also has innovated a much fuller repertoire for dealing with predication than any of the related Aramaic dialects. Through these strategies, which are the subject of this contribution, speakers of Neo-Mandaic are able to make fine distinctions in the syntax of the nominal sentence,

* I am much obliged to the volume editors, Rebecca Hasselbach and Naʿama Pat-El, for their careful attention to earlier drafts of this contribution and the many helpful suggestions that they have made for its improvement. Abbreviations are explained at the end of the text; copular verbs are glossed with the word "be."

[1] For predication in Semitic, see Goldenberg 1998 and 2005. For a cross-linguistic perspective on predicate nominals, see Payne 1997, p. 111.

[2] Nöldeke (1875, §273) noted that Mandaic nominal sentences retain their Semitic character to a much greater extent than Syriac or any of the later Semitic languages.

including distinctions not found in these other languages or even in its immediate linguistic ancestor. In order to introduce the syntax of the predicate nominal and related constructions in its proper context, it serves to first survey these languages and their treatment of analogous constructions.

1.2. Presentation of the Data

The majority of the data cited herein have been collected from standard sources on the various languages, such as religious texts and reference grammars. The one major exception is the data from the Neo-Mandaic dialect formerly spoken in Khorramshahr, Iran, which were collected during the course of my own doctoral research, conducted under Huehnergard's supervision.[3] The fact that these data are not available elsewhere is in some ways both a blessing and a curse; on the one hand, they offer crucial information and a new perspective on one of the most important surviving Aramaic dialects, but on the other hand, the usefulness of these data is mitigated by the fact that they, having been freshly collected, have yet to be analyzed and presented in their proper context. This article is a modest attempt to provide a context for a portion of these new data and highlight their relevance to scholars of Aramaic and linguists in general.

A potential obstacle to the comparison of the data is posed by the widely varying standards applied to the description of individual Middle Eastern languages. Even an issue as basic as transcription is problematic, due to the fact that each language is generally transcribed according to a different scheme, which makes comparison difficult. Furthermore, while Huehnergard inculcated in his students and colleagues a respect for transcription and the use of a uniform system for precisely this purpose, transcription continues to be unpopular among the great bulk of scholars who work exclusively within individual languages, as they generally prefer to cite examples from these languages in their original scripts.[4]

Comparatively little effort has been made to develop a metalinguistic framework for discussing these languages that is viable both individually and cross-linguistically. Most descriptions of these languages employ idiosyncratic mixed systems based partially upon the grammar of classical European languages like Greek and Latin (using obscure metalinguistic terms such as "subjunctive" or "accusative," which are freighted with cultural baggage and not entirely appropriate for the object languages) and partially upon these languages' own grammatical traditions (using terms such as *iḍāfa* or *eẓāfe*, which are borrowed directly from the object languages and therefore more appropriate, but completely opaque to all scholars not versed in these languages). Such mixed systems present clear obstacles to the comparison of the grammatical structures of these languages.

Most of the metalinguistic conventions currently employed by linguistic typologists, such as interlinear morphosyntactic glosses, have yet to be applied extensively to the languages of the Middle East and have been ignored by Semitists in particular. Because these conventions have proven to be extremely useful for facilitating the description of different languages and the comparison of their structural diversity, I have attempted to apply them to each language. Examples drawn from the languages surveyed are given a line-by-line analysis with interlinear glosses, utilizing a slightly modified version of the Leipzig Rules followed by a free translation.[5] I have opted to use the Leipzig Rules because they reflect current notational conventions in glossing morphosyntax and because they have the most currency among documentary linguists. According to these conventions, each of the following examples is left aligned, vertically, word for word, with the gloss beneath it. Segmentable elements are separated by a dash, both in the example and in the gloss. When a single element in the example corresponds to several English elements (words or morphemes), each element in the gloss is separated by a period.

[3] The fruit of this research was eventually published as Häberl 2009.

[4] The transcription scheme adopted here for Hebrew and Syriac is that of the Society for Biblical Literature, as indicated in their *Handbook of Style*, §§5.1–9; for Classical Arabic, that of the Deutsche Morgenländische Gesellschaft adopted in 1936 by the International Convention of Orientalist Scholars; for Classical Mandaic, that adopted by Drower and Macuch 1963; and for Neo-Mandaic, the scheme that I developed for Häberl 2009.

[5] For a more thorough description of the Leipzig Glossing Rules, see Lehmann 1983 and more recently Croft 2003, pp. xix–xxv.

2. Biblical Hebrew

Roughly contemporaneous with Old Aramaic and Phoenician, and preceded only by Akkadian, Eblaite, and Ugaritic, Biblical Hebrew is one of the earliest attested Semitic languages and is the best documented and most thoroughly studied of the ancient Semitic languages. Furthermore, as a member of the Northwest Semitic subfamily, it is more closely related to Aramaic (and therefore Mandaic) than most other attested Semitic languages. Finally, there is no evidence for contact between Biblical Hebrew and Mandaic, as they are separated from each other by a considerable geographic distance and a span of several centuries.[6] For these reasons, it provides an excellent point of departure for this survey.

2.1. Predication in Biblical Hebrew

In Biblical Hebrew, a personal or demonstrative pronoun may be used to express predication in verbless clauses, as in example 1, but its appearance is not obligatory, as indicated in example 2:

ex. 1.	*YHWH*	*hûʾ*	*hā-ʾĕlōh-îm*	*ʾên*	*ʿôḏ*	*mil-ləḇadd-ô*
	PN	3SG.M	DEF-god-PL	EXT.NEG	else	beside-3SG.M

The LORD is God; there is none else beside him. (Deut 4:35)

ex. 2.	*YHWH*	*haṣ-ṣaddîq*	*wa-ʾănî*	*wə-ʿamm-î*	*hā-rəšāʿ-îm*
	PN	DEF-righteous	and-1SG	and-people-1SG	DEF-wicked.PL-PL

The LORD is the righteous one, and I and my people are the wicked. (Exod 9:27)

This copula pronoun can intervene between the subject and the predicate, as in example 1 above, or follow the predicate:

ex. 3.	*zôḇ-ô*	*ṭāmēʾ*	*hûʾ*
	discharge-3SG.M	unclean	3SG.M

His discharge is unclean. (Lev 15:2)[7]

As noted above, such basic nominal sentences are restricted to the simple present.[8] Predicate nominals in all other tenses, moods, and aspects are indicated by a copular verb, √*h-y-h*:

ex. 4.	*wə-ʾēlleh*	*hāy-û*	*bənê*	*ʾohŏlîḇāmâ*
	and-these	be.PFV-3PL	son-PL	PN

And these were the sons of Oholibamah ... (Gen 36:14)

[6] Mandaean traditions of a Palestinian origin aside, the Mandaic language is clearly related to the Eastern Aramaic dialects of Mesopotamia rather than the Western Aramaic dialects of the Levant; see Nöldeke 1875, p. xxv.

[7] It should be noted that the identity of this pronoun and the function that it performs within the Biblical Hebrew nominal sentence has been the subject of much discussion; see, for example, Dyk and Talstra 1999, pp. 173–75.

[8] For the expression of tense in nominal sentences in Biblical Hebrew, see Zewi 1994.

2.2. Existential Predication in Biblical Hebrew

Existential predication is expressed by the particles *yēš* 'there is/are' and *ʾên* 'there isn't/aren't,' as in example 1 above and in examples 5 and 6 below.[9] Generally the tense, aspect, and mood of the clause must be determined from context, although they may be expressed with the copular verb √*h-y-h* in the place of the existential particle.

ex. 5. *wə-gam yēš gōʾēl, qārôḇ mimmenn-î*
and-also EXT kinsman close from-1SG
... and there is also a kinsman who is closer than me. (Ruth 3:12)

ex. 6. *ʾên leḥem wə-ʾên mayim*
EXT.NEG bread and-EXT.NEG water
There is no bread and there is no water. (Num 21:5)

ex. 7. *way-yə-hi ʾîš ʾeḥāḏ miṣ-ṣorʿāh*
CONS-3SG.M-be.IPFV man one from-PN
There was a man from Zorah ... (Judg 13:2)

These same particles are also used to express predicate locatives:

ex. 8. *lû yēš-ḥereḇ bə-yāḏ-î*
if EXT-sword in-hand-1SG
If only there were a sword in my hand ... (Num 22:29)

ex. 9. *ʾên-yôsēf b-ab-bôr*
EXT.NEG-PN in-DEF-pit
Joseph was not in the pit. (Gen 37:29)

2.3. Possessive Clauses in Biblical Hebrew

Biblical Hebrew employs the predicate locative construction to express the notion of possession. In fact, the equivalent construction found in languages such as English, in which a special verb "to have" is used to express possession, is not necessarily the most common cross-linguistically.[10] In the case of Biblical Hebrew, possession is expressed using a variety of prepositions, the most common of which is the preposition *l-* 'to, for.' The preposition may optionally be preceded by the existential particles *yēš* and *ʾên*, as in the following examples. Note again that the tense of the possessive clause must often be determined from context, although the copular verb √*h-y-h* may be used to express possessive clauses in tenses other than the simple present.

ex. 10. *wə-l-ô šətê nāš-îm*
and-to-3SG.M two wife.PL-PL
... and he had two wives... (1 Sam 1:2)

ex. 11. *yēš l-î rāḇ*
EXT to-1SG much
I have plenty. (Gen 33:9)

[9] In addition to serving to indicate existential predication, these two particles can also serve in a variety of different functions when modified with a possessive suffix. The inflected forms of *yēš* appear almost exclusively after *ʾim* 'if' where they serve in precisely the same function as the independent pronoun (e.g., Gen 24:49). The more common inflected forms of *ʾên* frequently negate sentences with participial predicates (e.g., Exod 5:10) or, more rarely, adjectival and adverbial predicates (e.g., Ps 73:5).

[10] This is the position of Payne (1997, p. 126); a dissenting view is offered by Stassen (2009, pp. 64–69).

ex. 12.	*ʾên*	*l-āh*	*wālāḏ*
	EXT.NEG	to-3SG.F	child

She had no child. (Gen 11:30)

ex. 13.	*lōʾ-yi-hyeh*	*lə-ḵā*	*ʾĕlōh-îm*	*ʾăḥēr-îm*	*ʿal-pānā-y*
	NEG-3SG.M-be.IPFV	to-2SG.M	god-PL	other-PL	upon-face.PL-1SG

You will have no other gods before me. (Exod 20:2)

3. Classical Arabic

Arabic, the language of the Qurʾan and of the classical literature of Islam, is the most widespread of the Semitic languages and, through its standardized version and daughter languages, the most widely spoken as well. From the time of Islamic conquest of the Near East until the present date, the Mandaeans have lived alongside speakers of Arabic, resulting in a prolonged contact situation that has profoundly influenced the modern Mandaic language. The traces of this contact are apparent in the lexicon of Neo-Mandaic and from its phonology, but surprisingly absent from its syntax.

3.1. Predication in Classical Arabic

In Classical Arabic, a "linking" pronoun much like that attested in Biblical Hebrew is employed to express predication, but its appearance is much more regular than in Biblical Hebrew. It serves primarily to eliminate ambiguity, expressing predication only when both the subject and the predicate of the clause are definite, as in example 14, and following the subject as a rule. Classical Arabic dispenses with this pronoun as superfluous whenever the subject of the clause is definite and its predicate is indefinite, as in example 15. As in Biblical Hebrew, clauses in tenses other than the simple present must employ a copular verb, √*k-w-n*, which typically stands at the head of the clause before its subject; see example 16 below.[11]

ex. 14.	*aḷḷāh-u*	*huwa*	*l-ḥayy-u*	*l-qayyūm-u*
	God-NOM	3SG.M	DEF-living-NOM	DEF-self.subsisting-NOM

God is the living, the self-subsisting.

ex. 15.	*as-sulṭān-u*	*marīḍ-u-n*
	DEF-sultan-NOM	sick-NOM-INDF

The sultan is sick.

ex. 16.	*kāna*	*huwa*	*wa-ʾaxū-hu*	*muʿallim-īna*	*bi-ṭ-ṭāʾif-i*
	be.PFV	3SG.M	and-brother.NOM-3SG.M	teacher-PL.OBL	in-DEF-Taʾif-GEN

He and his brother were teachers in al-Taʾif.

Note that the predicate follows the subject and takes the oblique case, as if it were the object of a transitive verb. Nominal sentences may also be introduced by the "topicalizing" particle *ʾinna*, in which case the subject of the clause follows the particle appearing in the accusative case, and its predicate follows the subject appearing in the nominative case, as in example 17. The copula pronoun may follow the subject of the nominal sentence, as in example 18, but its appearance is not obligatory:

[11] Unless otherwise specified, the following examples are taken from Wright 1996. Note that this copula pronoun can be omitted under certain circumstances; ibid., ii §128–29.

ex. 17.

ʾinna	*ḷḷāh-a*	*ṯāliṯ-u*	*ṯalāṯat-i-n*
TOP	God-ACC	third-NOM	three-GEN-INDF

Verily God is one of three.

ex. 18.

ʾinna	*l-ʾāxir-at-a*	*hiya*	*dār-u*	*l-qarār-i*
TOP	DEF-last-SG.F-ACC	3SG.F	abode-NOM	DEF-steadfastness-GEN

Verily the world to come is the everlasting abode.

3.2. Existential Predication in Classical Arabic

The predicate locative construction is formed with the use of the preposition, but without any additional particle, such as an existential particle or the copula pronoun. If the subject of the clause is indefinite, then the predicate must precede it, as in example 19; if the subject is definite, on the other hand, the predicate may follow or precede it without any change in meaning, as in example 20.

ex. 19.

fi-d-dār-i	*mraʾat-u-n*
in-DEF-house-GEN	woman-NOM-INDF

There is a woman in the house.

ex. 20.

zayd-u-n	*fi-l-masjid-i*	or	*fi-l-masjid-i*	*zayd-u-n*
PN-NOM-INDF	in-DEF-mosque-GEN		in-DEF-mosque-GEN	PN-NOM-INDF

Zayd is in the mosque.

These constructions are negated with the particle *laysa*, which is inflected as if it were a verb in the perfective, but renders the imperfective, as in example 21. In many respects, *laysa* behaves like an existential particle similar to Biblical Hebrew *ʾên*. It may be governed by the copular verb in the perfect tense to express the negative imperfect of that verb, as in example 22. Note that the object of *laysa* is often (but not exclusively) marked with the preposition *bi-* rather than the accusative.

ex. 21.

laysa	*ʿuḏr-u-n*	*fī*	*tark-i*	*t-taʿallum-i*
EXT.NEG	excuse-NOM-INDF	in	neglect-GEN	DEF-learning-GEN

There is no excuse for neglecting the acquisition of knowledge.

ex. 22.

kāna	*n-nabīy-u*	*laysa*	*bi-ṭ-ṭawīl-i*	*wa-lā*	*bi-l-qaṣīr-i*
be.PFV	DEF-prophet-NOM	EXT.NEG	OBJ-DEF-tall-GEN	and-NEG	OBJ-DEF-short-GEN

The Prophet was neither of high nor low stature.

In the Qurʾan, the indeclinable particle *lāta* appears once in its place:

ex. 23.

wa-lāta	*ḥīn-a*	*manāṣ-i-n*
and-EXT.NEG	time-ACC	avoidance-GEN-INDF

... and there wasn't time to escape (*Ṣād* 38:3)

Likewise, the indeclinable particle *ʾin* behaves in a similar manner, appearing (like *laysa* and *lāta*) in initial position:

ex. 24.

ʾin	*kull-u*	*man*	*fī*	*s-samāwāt-i*	*wa-l-arḍ-i*
EXT.NEG	all-NOM	who	in	DEF-heaven.PL-GEN	and-DEF-earth-GEN

There is no one in heaven and earth

ʾillā	*ʾātī*	*r-raḥmān-i*	*ʿabd-an*
except	come.PTC	DEF-merciful-GEN	servant-ACC-INDF

except he who comes to the Merciful only as a servant. (*Maryam* 19:93)

3.3. Possessive Clauses in Classical Arabic

As in Biblical Hebrew, possessive clauses are expressed using a predicate locative construction:

ex. 25.	*kāna*	*tājir-u-n*	*wa-kāna*	*la-hu*	*ban-ūna*	*ṯalāṯ-at-u-n*
	be.PFV	merchant-NOM-INDF	and-be.PFV	to-3SG.M	son.PL-PL.NOM	three-SG.F-NOM-INDF

There was a merchant and he had three sons.

4. Classical Syriac

Classical Syriac is an Aramaic dialect roughly contemporaneous with and closely related to Classical Mandaic. Initially the dialect of the city of Edessa (*Urhāy*), it was eventually adopted by all Aramaic-speaking Christians throughout the Middle East as their primary language of worship and scholarship.

4.1. Predication in Classical Syriac

As in Biblical Hebrew and Classical Arabic, predicate nominals are often marked by the personal pronoun in Classical Syriac. This personal pronoun may agree fully with the subject in person and number, as in example 26, or appear in the third person and agree only in number. When this pronoun marks the predicate, it often assumes an enclitic form. This enclitic pronoun is most often attached to the head noun of the predicate, as in example 28, and may even intervene between the noun and any adjective modifying it, as in example 29. Note that the predicate may appear before the subject of the clause, so long as it is marked by the enclitic pronoun.[12]

ex. 26.	*ḥənan*	*(ḥ)nan*	*bənay*	*ʾaḇrāhām*
	1PL	1PL	son.PL	PN

We are the sons of Abraham. (Aphr. 331:5)

ex. 27.	*ḥənan*	*ennon*	*bənay*	*ʾaḇrāhām*
	1PL	3PL.M	son.PL	PN

We are the sons of Abraham. (Aphr. 331:15)

ex. 28.	*raḇ-(h)ū*	*ḥeṭṭāh-eh*
	great-3SG.M	sin-3SG.M

His sin is great. (Aphr. 45:10)

ex. 29.	*ḥezwā-(h)w*	*daggālā*
	vision-3SG.M	false

It is an apparition. (Matt 14:26)

As Nöldeke (2001, §313) notes, there is a wide variety of ways to express the nominal sentence in Classical Syriac, demonstrated by the following possible variations on the two sentences examples 26 and 27 from the *Homilies of Aphraates* cited above:

ex. 30.	*ḥənan*	*bənay*	*ʾaḇrāhām*	*(ḥ)nan*
	1PL	son.PL	PN	1PL

We are the sons of Abraham. (Nöldeke 2001, §313)

[12] The examples that follow are collected from Nöldeke 2001 and from Joosten 1992. The authoritative study on nominal sentences in Syriac remains Goldenberg 1983. The texts employed by Nöldeke 2001 and cited here include Wright 1869 ("Aphr.") and Assemanus 1748 ("Mart."). All examples from the Bible are quoted according to the Peshitta version.

ex. 31. *bənay* *ʾaḇrāhām* *(ḥ)nan*
son.PL PN 1PL
We are the sons of Abraham. (Nöldeke 2001, §313)

These types of predicate nominals (i.e., those in which predication is marked by the linking pronoun) are negated with the negative particle *lā* followed by the perfect of the copular verb √*h-w-y*, which invariably stands at the head of the clause, as often do Biblical Hebrew *ʾên* and Classical Arabic *laysa*. Despite the fact that this copular verb is fully inflected, it does not express past tense or perfectivity, but merely the negation of the predicate nominal, much like these other particles:[13]

ex. 32. *lā* *həwā* *ḡaḇrā* *ʾalāhā*
NEG be.PFV man God
God is not a man. (Num 23:19)

ex. 33. *lā* *həwī-ṯ* *gaḇrā* *ḏə-mell-ē*
NEG be.PFV-1SG man of-word-PL
I am not a man of words. (Exod 4:10)

Furthermore, while predicate nominals are normally marked in this manner, with some exceptions (see Nöldeke 2001, §310), predicate adjective constructions are generally marked by the absolute state, and not by the enclitic pronoun.

ex. 34. *sərāq-ē* *ḇə-gabb-aw(hy)* *neḡr-ē* *ḇə-ḥaṣṣ-eh* *wa-zʿōr-īn* *l-eh*
comb-PL on-side-PL.3SG.M lash-PL on-back-3SG.M and-small-PL to-3SG.M
Lacerating combs (were) in his sides, lashes (were) on his back, and (they were) trifling to him (Moes. II, 56 v. 124)

ex. 35. *təḵīl* *ʿal* *ʾalāhā*
trusting upon God
He is confident in God. (Matt 27:43)

4.2. Existential Predication in Classical Syriac

Much like Biblical Hebrew, existential predication is expressed with an existential particle, in this case *ʾīṯ* 'there is/are' and its negative *lā ʾīṯ* / *layt* 'there is/are not,' both of which can also serve as copulas in the simple present when inflected with the pronominal suffixes, as in examples 38 and 39.

ex. 36. *kaḏ* *ʾīṯ* *l-āḵ*
when EXT to-2SG.M
When it is there for you = when you have it. (Prov 3:28)

ex. 37. *ʾen* *layt* *kē(ʾ)n-ē*
if EXT.NEG just-PL
If there are no just persons .... (Aphr. 458:9)

ex. 38. *gaww-āh* *ʾīṯ-eh* *ʾōrēšlem*
inside-3SG.F EXT-3SG.F PN
Jerusalem is inside her. (Aphr. 98:9)

[13] See Joosten 1992, p. 586. Joosten's analysis of *lā hwā* and related constructions was recently rephrased and clarified by Pat-El 2006, pp. 335–36.

ex. 39. *ḥənan* *ʾīṯayn* *bənay* *ʾaḇrāhām*
1PL EXT-1PL son.PL PN
We are the sons of Abraham. (Nöldeke 2001, §313)

ex. 40. *(ʾ)naḥnan* *lā-ʾīṯayn* *ḥarrāš-ē*
1PL NEG-EXT-1PL magician-PL
We are not magicians. (Mart. I, 182, 3)

4.3. Possessive Clauses in Classical Syriac

Example 36 above demonstrates that the existential particle can also be used to express possession in the simple present by means of a predicate locative, as in Biblical Hebrew. To express this and other kinds of predication in all other tenses, an enclitic form of the copular verb √*h-w-y* is employed, in a manner analogous to the copular verb in Biblical Hebrew and Classical Arabic.

ex. 41. *ʾalāhā* *ḇə-hōn* *ʾīṯ-aw(hy)-(h)wā*
God in-3PL.M EXT-3SG.M-be.PFV
God was in them. (Aphr. 70:6)

ex. 42. *qərāš-ē* *ḏə-ḏahḇā* *ʾīṯ-(h)wa-w* *lə-hōn*
earring-PL of-gold EXT-be.PFV-3PL to-3PL
They had golden earrings. (Judg 8:24)

ex. 43. *w-layt-(h)waw* *mayyā*
and-EXT.NEG-be.PFV-3PL water
There was no water. (Exod 17:1)

5. Classical Mandaic

Having surveyed the evidence from some of the languages related to Neo-Mandaic, we may now turn to its direct ancestor, Classical Mandaic. Classical Mandaic is known exclusively from the Mandaean religious texts, chief among which is the *Ginza Rba*, the “Great Treasure.” This book is divided into two volumes. The first volume, the *Right Ginza*, which is the larger of the two, is an eclectic assortment of legends, prophecies, prayers, hymns, historical anecdotes, and no fewer than seven differing accounts of the creation of the world. The second volume, the *Left Ginza*, is concerned exclusively with death and the fate of the soul in the afterlife.

5.1. Predication in Classical Mandaic

In Classical Mandaic, predication may be expressed simply by juxtaposing the subject of the clause with its predicate as in all of the languages treated above, or by linking the two by means of a personal pronoun as in the Semitic languages introduced above (in the case of Classical Mandaic, these pronouns are **hu** ‘he,’ **h‘** ‘she,’ or **hinun** ‘they’). This pronoun always follows the subject of the clause as in Classical Arabic, rather than following the head noun of the predicate as in Classical Syriac. Less frequently, the existential particle (variously written **‘t**, **‘it**, or **ait-**) is used in conjunction with this pronoun, resulting in a shift of word order as the subject follows the predicate of the clause:[14]

---

[14] The following examples are taken from Macuch 1965, p. 442.

ex. 44. **dmut-ai-hun dmauat-ata 'pik-ata**
form-PL-3PL.M form.PL-PL perverted-PL
Their appearance is (of) perverted shapes. (Petermann 2007, 139:9f.)

ex. 45. **ana hu hiia, ana hu šrara**
1SG 3SG.M Life 1SG 3SG.M Truth
I am the Life, I am the Truth. (Petermann 2007, 207:15)

ex. 46. **'it 'laita šumia hu u-'it titaita arqa h'**
EXT upper heaven 3SG.M and-EXT lower earth 3SG.F
Heaven is the upper part, and Earth is the lower part. (Petermann 2007, 201:12)

As in Biblical Hebrew and Classical Syriac, this existential particle can also take personal suffixes, in which case it behaves more explicitly as a copula:

ex. 47. **ait-ak mn iuma qadmia**
EXT-2SG.M from day first
You were from the first day (Petermann 2007, 7)

ex. 48. **kḏ ana luat-ik l-ait-an**
when 1SG with-2SG.F NEG-EXT-1SG
When I am not with you. (Petermann 2007, 156:15)

5.2. Possessive Clauses in Classical Mandaic

Likewise, in conjunction with an enclitic preposition and a personal suffix, the existential particle can express possession. In this capacity it is occasionally followed by the relative pronoun **ḏ**-:

ex. 49. **'t-b-ak haila**
EXT-in-2SG.M power
There is power in you = you have power (Petermann 2007, 173:16).

ex. 50. **'t-l-h̲ ḏ-gubr-ia u-'nš-ia**
EXT-for-3SG.M REL-man.PL-PL and-women-PL
There are men and women for him = he has men and women. (Petermann 2007, 280:14)

There is no enclitic form of the copular verb √*h-w-y* such as that found in Classical Syriac, demonstrated in examples 41–43. Therefore, the tense of the clause must be derived from context (Macuch 1965, p. 440), as demonstrated in example 47 above and the following example:

ex. 51. **u-anpiš-u-ia l-ziua-i ḏ-'t-l-ia**
and-extended.PFV-3PL.M-3SG.M OBJ-radiance-1SG REL-EXT-for-1SG
and they extended my radiance over what I had (Petermann 2007, 91:17)

6. Neo-Mandaic

Neo-Mandaic shares with the other languages surveyed the possibility to dispense entirely with the copula in the simple present. Otherwise, predication may be expressed in one of three now-familiar ways:

- with an enclitic pronominal copula, which is suffixed directly to the predicate;

- with an independent copula, *ekt-*, which also follows the predicate and is invariably modified by a pronominal suffix that agrees in number and gender with the subject; and
- with a copular verb, *həwā* ~ *həwi* (*hāwi*) 'to be.'

Note that both the enclitic copula and the independent copula follow the predicate, as in Middle Persian but unlike the other Semitic languages surveyed above, including Classical Mandaic. Predictably, as both are limited to the simple present, the copular verb *həwā* ~ *həwi* (*hāwi*) 'to be' must be used to express more complex distinctions in tense, aspect, or mood.

6.1. The Enclitic Pronominal Copula

The enclitic pronominal copula takes the following forms, seen here on the adjective *šəbir* 'good':

Person	*Singular*	*Gloss*	*Plural*	*Gloss*
3rd	*šəbir-yē*	s/he is good	*šəbir-non*	they are good
2nd	*šəbir-yāt*	you are good	—	—
1st	*šəbir-nā*	I am good	—	—

Note that the enclitic pronominal copula does not distinguish between masculine and feminine gender in the third person, and that there are no enclitic forms for the plural second and first persons.[15]

The enclitic pronominal copula is most commonly used with predicate adjectives, predicate locatives, and interrogatives. Note that it attaches to the final element of the predicate, as demonstrated in example 53, and not merely the head noun of the predicate, as in the Classical Syriac examples given above.

ex. 52. *šəbir-nā*
good-1SG
I am good.

ex. 53. *ahni* *barra* *əm-welā̱t-non*
3PL outside from-city-3PL
They are outside the city.

ex. 54. *qazġān-d-e* *elli-yē?*
cauldron-of-1SG where-3SG
Where is my cooking pot?

Clauses containing the enclitic pronominal copula are negated with the negative morpheme *lu* 'non-,' which appears before the predicate:

ex. 55. *lu* *ṣonʿa-yē*
non- good-3SG
It is not good.

When an interrogative pronoun or question word anticipates the predicate of a sentence or the object of a verb rather than its subject, it may be followed by the enclitic pronominal copula:

ex. 56. *mo-yyē* *hab̲t-ell-i?*
what-3SG give.PFV-2SG-OBJ-3SG.M
What did you give him?

---

[15] The independent copula is employed in their place; see below.

ex. 57.	*mu*	*ha̱bt-ell-i*
	what	give.PFV-2SG-OBJ-3SG.M
	What did you give him?	

ex. 58.	*mu*	*zipān-i*	*min*	*mojur-nā*
	what	liar-INDF	from	what.kind-1SG
	What a liar he is, in comparison to me!			

Whenever the enclitic pronominal copula is attached to a noun modified by a pronominal suffix ending in a vowel, an epenthetic *-h-* intervenes between it and the copula:

ex. 59.	*mojur*	*bā̱b-ah-yē*
	what.kind	father-3SG.F-3SG
	What's her father like?	

Although the process by which it arose is not entirely clear, this enclitic pronominal copula is likely derived from the independent personal pronouns. Interestingly, this enclitic form always follows the predicate of the nominal sentence, as in Syriac and Persian, rather than its subject, as in Classical Mandaic. Homologous enclitic forms of pronominal origin are also attested in Central Aramaic dialects such as Turoyo and the Northeastern Neo-Aramaic dialect of Halabja (Fox 1994, p. 158), but not in other Northeastern Neo-Aramaic dialects, which use a different set of enclitic forms whose origins are subject to debate. According to Khan (1999, pp, 103–04), these enclitic forms may be derived from an irregular or suppletive part of the copular verb √*h-w-y* rather than the personal pronouns as in Central Aramaic and Neo-Mandaic.

6.2. The Independent Copula and Its Development

No homologous or analogous form to the Neo-Mandaic independent copula, *ek̲t-*, is attested in the other surviving Eastern Neo-Aramaic dialects. The origins of this copula, which does not appear independently of its pronominal suffixes, have thus far not effectively been identified. Rudolf Macuch (1965, p. 379) derives it from the demonstrative pronoun **ʿka** *ekkā* 'there,' which expresses the predication of existential clauses in Neo-Mandaic:

> I can only explain the *t* of these forms by the progressive assimilation of sonority of the encl. *d* (cf. §106b): **ekde* > **ekte* > **eχte* (§20 **k**). This enclitic, used otherwise only with substantives, proves a substantival use of **ʿt**, **ʿka**, so that the forms could be interpreted as "my being" etc.[16]

Macuch's explanation is not satisfactory, if only for the reason that **ʿka** does not take pronominal suffixes in either Classical or Neo-Mandaic, and it fails to explain how this demonstrative pronoun came to assume the functions of the Classical Mandaic existential particle **ʿt**. There is, in fact, no reason to assume that the modern independent copula is anything other than the reflex of the classical existential particle. The unusual form of this reflex can be explained by a feature of Mandaic phonology. In Neo-Mandaic, all word-internal syllables must have an onset, and lax vowels are generally not tolerated in open accented syllables. Consequently, whenever a vowel is added to a closed accented syllable containing a lax vowel, the coda of the accented syllable is geminated to provide the following syllable with an onset. The geminated consonant thus straddles the syllable boundary, such as examples 60 and 61. If the second syllable is deleted (for example, in the bound form preceding a noun or adjective with which it is in construct), or the accent shifts from the first syllable, the gemination will be lost.

	Unbound	*IPA*	*Bound*	*Gloss*
ex. 60.	*zammā*	[ˈzæm.mɔ]	*zam*	blood (Classical Mandaic **zma** or **ʿzma**)
ex. 61.	*bellā*	[ˈbɛl.lɔ]	*bel*	husband (Classical Mandaic **bla**)[17]

[16] Macuch's identification of the two particles with one another is endorsed by Müller-Kessler 2003, pp. 642–43.

[17] As the Classical Mandaic forms suggest, the geminated consonant is not etymological; cf. Syriac *dəmā* 'blood,' cs. *dem*, and Syriac *baʕlā* 'husband,' cs. *bəʕel*.

The reverse, namely the gemination of a consonant that was not formerly geminated, occurs whenever an inflectional morpheme (e.g., a pronominal suffix) is added to a closed accented syllable containing a lax vowel. The coda of the closed accented syllable is geminated, leaving the syllable structure intact, as below, example 62 becomes example 63.

ex. 62.	*həzon*	[hə.ˈzon]	they saw
ex. 63.	*həzonna*	[hə.ˈzon.na]	they saw her

With one exception, all Neo-Mandaic consonants can be geminated in this manner. The sole exception is the voiceless interdental fricative /θ/. Whenever /θ/ closes an accented syllable to which a vowel is added, the outcome is the cluster [χt] rather than the expected [θθ]. This sound change is most evident from the paradigm of the verb *meṯ* ~ *moṯ* (*māyeṯ*) 'to die'; compare examples 64 and 65 with example 66. It is also apparent from the modern form of the abstract ending *-oḵtā* (Classical Mandaic **-uta**), as in example 67. Additionally, it is attested in a rare variant of the word for cow, example 68.

ex. 64.	*meṯ*	[mɛθ]	he is dead
ex. 65.	*mieṯ*	[mĭɛ̆θ]	I will die
ex. 66.	*meḵtat*	[ˈmɛχ.tat]	she is dead
ex. 67.	*goṭloḵtā*	[gʌt.ˈlʌχ.tɔ]	massacre
ex. 68.	*tureḵtā*	[tu.ˈrɛχ.tɔ]	cow[18]

Examples of the sequence [θθ] *do* occur in Neo-Mandaic. Such examples either are etymological or result from the assimilation of certain consonants (such as dentals and, in an earlier stage of the language, nasals) to a following interdental fricative /θ/, such as ex. 69 from Classical Mandaic **'nta** (cf. Syriac <ʾN̲TTʾ> *attəṯā* 'woman') and ex. 70 from the verb *ḥaddeṯ* ~ *ḥaddeṯ* (*əmḥaddeṯ*) 'to speak.'

ex. 69.	*eṯṯā*	[ˈɛθ.θɔ]	woman
ex. 70.	*qəmḥaṯṯen*	[qm.ˈħaθ.θɛn]	they speak

This same sound change is responsible for the unusual form of the allomorphs of the modern reflex of the existential particle **'t** after the addition of the pronominal suffixes; instead of the expected reflex *eṯ [ɛθ], it regularly takes the form *eḵt-* [ɛχt], for example, example 71.

ex. 71.	*eḵtaḵ*	[ˈɛχ.taχ]	you (m.sg.) are

The erstwhile existential particle is negated with the negative morpheme *lá-* 'not,' the vowel of which becomes elided. The set of pronominal suffixes used is the same that serves as possessive and object suffixes on the noun and verb, respectively:

Copula	Gloss	*lá-* + Copula	Gloss
eḵt-i	he is	*l-eḵt-i*	he is not
eḵt-a	she is	*l-eḵt-a*	she is not
eḵt-aḵ	you (m.sg.) are	*l-eḵt-aḵ*	you (m.sg.) are not
eḵt-eḵ	you (f.sg.) are	*l-eḵt-eḵ*	you (f.sg.) are not
eḵt-ē	I am	*l-eḵt-ē*	I am not
eḵt-u	they are	*l-eḵt-u*	they are not
eḵt-əḵon	you (pl.) are	*l-eḵt-əḵon*	you (pl.) are not
eḵt-an	we are	*l-eḵt-an*	we are not

[18] This form is derived from Classical Mandaic **turita**; cf. DC 46 **turikta**. The more usual form of this word is *turtā* [ˈtuɹ.tɔ]; Drower and Macuch 1963, s.v. **tura**.

The independent copula generally follows the predicate, or interrogative pronoun in interrogative clauses. The relationship among the constituents of the clause may be either strictly equative ("He is a Mandaean") or merely ascriptive ("He is sick"). While the independent copula may be used to express both, the enclitic pronominal copula can only be used for the latter. The strictly equative sense of the clause must be expressed by either the independent copula in the simple present or the copular verb *həwā* ~ *həwi* (*hāwi*) in other tenses.[19]

ex. 72. *kəfen* *l-ek̠t-ē*
hungry NEG-COP-1SG
I am not hungry.

ex. 73. *man* *ek̠t-ak̠*
who COP-2SG.M
Who are you?

ex. 74. *an* *qanāyā* *ek̠t-ē*
1SG smith COP-1SG
I am a smith.

6.3. The Neo-Mandaic Copular Verb *həwā* ~ *həwi* (*hāwi*)

Cognate to the copular verbs √*h-y-h* and √*h-w-y* introduced in §2.1 and §4.1 above, and formally analogous to the copular verbs √*k-w-n* introduced in §3.1, the Neo-Mandaic copular verb *həwā* ~ *həwi* (*hāwi*) 'to be' is the only form of the copula that can be inflected for tense, aspect, or mood. The perfective form is generally used for past-tense clauses; it is inflected by means of suffixes indicating the gender and number of the subject and is negated with the negative morpheme *lá-*:

Copula	*Gloss*	*lá- + Copula*	*Gloss*
həwā	he was	*lá-hwā*	he was not
həw-at	she was	*lá-hw-at*	she was not
həw-et	you (sg.) were	*lá-hw-et*	you were not
həwi-t	I was	*lá-hwi-t*	I was not
həw-on	they were	*lá-hw-on*	they were not
həwi-ton	you (pl.) were	*lá-hwi-ton*	you (pl.) were not
həwi-ni	we were	*lá-hwi-ni*	we were not

The imperfective form of the verb is used for clauses in the future tense or the subjunctive mood; the base of this form of the verb is the active participle (hence the term "participial present tense," which was employed in Macuch 1965, §204), which is inflected with a separate set of suffixes, and (when describing factual statements and positive beliefs) the indicative mood marker *qə-*. It is also negated with the enclitic prefix *lá-*:

Copula	*Gloss*	*lá- + Copula*	*Gloss*
qə-hāwi	he will be	*lá-q-hāwi*	he will not be
qə-hāwy-ā	she will be	*lá-q-hāwy-ā*	she will not be
qə-hāw-et	you will be	*lá-q-hāw-et*	you will not be
qə-hawi-nā	I will be	*lá-q-hawi-nā*	I will not be
qə-hāw-en	they will be	*lá-q-hāw-en*	they will not be
qə-haw-etton	you will be	*lá-q-haw-etton*	you will not be
qə-haw-enni	we will be	*lá-q-haw-enni*	we will not be

[19] Compare the distribution of the Spanish copulas *ser* and *estar*, e.g., *Ofelia está enferma* 'Ofelia is sick,' *Ofelia es enferma* 'Ofelia is a sick woman,' and *Ofelia es profesora* 'Ofelia is a teacher,' but never ***Ofelia está profesora* (examples from Payne 1997, p. 120).

Unlike the enclitic pronoun and the independent copula, the syntax of the verb *həwā* ~ *həwi* (*hāwi*) follows that of other transitive verbs, that is, the subject of the clause precedes it, and its complement generally follows it. While the copular verb *həwā* ~ *həwi* (*hāwi*) is necessary to introduce action in the past tense, it may be followed by the enclitic pronoun or independent copula in subsequent clauses, once the tense and aspect have been established.[20]

ex. 75. *ya yeki həwā marizi*
a someone be.PFV ill
There once was a man who was ill.

ex. 76. *həwā ya yeki pahli-d-i yəhem-yē ṣāt-i*
be.PFV a someone beside-of-3SG.M seated-3SG.M hear.PFV-3SG.M
There was someone, sitting beside him, who heard him.

6.4. Possessive Clauses in Neo-Mandaic

As in the other Semitic languages surveyed above, as well as non-Semitic languages such as Middle Persian and Russian, Neo-Mandaic uses a predicate locative construction to express the notion of possession. In Neo-Mandaic, the subject of the clause, namely the possessed, is indicated by the proclitic preposition *l-* 'to, for.' When the subject is expressed by means of a pronoun, both may be attached to the independent form of the copula:[21]

Copula + l-	*Gloss*	*lá- + Copula + l-*	*Gloss*
eh-l-i	he has	*l-eh-l-i*	he doesn't have
eh-l-a	she has	*l-eh-l-a*	she doesn't have
eh-l-ak̲	you (m.sg.) have	*l-eh-l-ak̲*	you (m.sg.) don't have
eh-l-ek̲	you (f.sg.) have	*l-eh-l-ek̲*	you (f.sg.) don't have
eh-l-ē	I have	*l-eh-l-ē*	I don't have
eh-l-u	they have	*l-eh-l-u*	they don't have
eh-l-ək̲on	you (pl.) have	*l-eh-l-ək̲on*	you (pl.) don't have
eh-l-an	we have	*l-eh-l-an*	we don't have

When used to express possession in a declarative sense, the copula always stands at the head, in contrast with other predicate nominal constructions, in which the predicate precedes the copula.

ex. 77. *eh-l-i rāzā d-Šāmeš*
COP-for-3SG.M secret of-PN
He has Šāmeš's secret.

ex. 78. *eh-l-ē pās-i*
COP-for-1SG pass-INDF
I have a pass.

In interrogative clauses, by contrast, the preposition is attached to the interrogative pronoun or question word, and the whole prepositional phrase is modified by the copula (in the simple present tense, the enclitic pronominal form of the copula is employed). As demonstrated in example 56, the interrogative pronoun serves as the predicate of the clause.

---

[20] Predictably, due to its absence in the classical stage of the language, Neo-Mandaic preserves no reflex of the enclitic form of this verb, which distinguishes it from the other surviving Eastern Neo-Aramaic dialects (Fox 1994, p. 158).

[21] The preposition **b-**, which was used alongside **l-** in the classical dialect as demonstrated in example 49 above, has become obsolescent in the modern language.

ex. 79. *ahni* *el-man-non*
3PL for-who-3PL
Whose are these?

Note the unexpected allomorph of the copula before the proclitic *l-* 'to, for.' Macuch (1965, p. 65) derives *ehl-* from Classical Mandaic **'t-l-** and adduces several examples of Neo-Mandaic words in which Classical Mandaic /t/ has become /h/, but does not isolate the specific environment in which this sound change occurs.

This sound change appears to be the result of the lenition of /θ/ before a syllable beginning with a consonantal segment. As a result, the voiceless interdental fricative /θ/ becomes /h/ or even disappears entirely. Evidence for such a sound change is not lacking in the contemporary sister dialects of Aramaic, as place names containing the Aramaic element *bēṯ-* 'house of' attest.[22] In the Aramaic of the Babylonian Talmud, /θ/ often drops out word-finally in the words *bê* 'house,' and *šabbā* 'week,' and the feminine singular of participles and verbs in the perfect. Furthermore, this sound change is not unattested in Classical Mandaic. Macuch (1965, p. 203) identifies five examples of the deletion of /θ/ in compounds formed with the word **baita** 'house,' including **bimanda** (= **bit manda** 'house of knowledge'), the sacred space in which many Mandaean rituals take place.

This sound change does not appear to be productive in Neo-Mandaic, although it has left numerous traces in the paradigm of the verb. When the third feminine singular *G*-stem perfective form of the root √*'-m-r* takes a pronominal object with *l-*, the /θ/ is weakened to an /h/, which then disappears, causing the following /l/ to become geminated:

ex. 80. *mārelli* [mɔ.ˈrɛl.li] she told him[23]

Likewise, the reflexive morpheme *t-* has been deleted from all verbs in the so-called reflexive stems save one, *eṣṭəḇā* ~ *eṣṭəḇi* (*meṣṭəḇi*) 'to be baptized,' in which it has undergone metathesis with the following sibilant and is therefore no longer followed by a stop, fricative, or sonorant. The loss of the reflexive morpheme was already well underway in the classical dialect (Macuch 1965, pp. 266–67). While it is difficult to isolate the precise environment in which this sound change occurred, especially considering that it is no longer productive and seems not to have affected all of the various dialects represented by the corpus of the Talmud or the Classical Mandaic literature, the major difference between *ehl-* and these other examples is that the accent continued to reside upon the syllable in which /θ/ became lenited; as I note above, Mandaic phonology does not permit lax vowels in open accented syllables, thus necessitating the retention of some glottal friction to maintain a closed syllable, even as oral contact was lost.

As expected, the verb *həwā* ~ *həwi* (*hāwi*) 'to be' is employed in the place of the simple present copula in all other tenses.

ex. 81. *bieṯ* *mand-i* *həwā-l-u*
house knowledge-INDF be.PFV-OBJ-3PL
They had a 'House of Knowledge.'

6.5. Existential Clauses in Neo-Mandaic

The survival of the old Classical Mandaic existential particle in the form of the Neo-Mandaic independent copula raises an interesting question: Why has its independent form, Classical Mandaic **'t**, not survived? This particle is no longer used to express existential predication, for which the particle *ekkā* (Classical Mandaic **'ka** 'there') is now exclusively used.[24]

---

[22] Michael Morony (2005, p. 177) cites Greek *Begarmeon* and Arabic *Bajarma* for Syriac *Beth Garme*, Arabic *Baʿarbaya* for Syriac *Beth ʿArbhaye*, Arabic *Bazabda* for Syriac *Beth Zabhde*, Arabic *Bahudhra* for Syriac *Beth Nuhadhra*, Arabic *Barusma* for Syriac *Beth Rushme*, Arabic *Baniqya* for Syriac *Beth Neqya*, Arabic *Badaqla* for Syriac *Beth Deqla*, Arabic *Badaraya* for Syriac *Beth Daraye*, and Arabic *Bakusaya* for Syriac *Beth Kusaye* as examples of this phenomenon.

[23] Although this form is problematic for several reasons, perhaps the most striking feature is the deletion of the /t/ of the personal morpheme *-at* from the expected form ***amraṯli* (< *amraṯ* + *li*)

[24] Müller-Kessler (2003, p. 642) derives this particle from the existential particle 't and the deictic element *k'*.

ex. 82. *ekkā* *Hēyi,* *ekkā* *Mār-ē,* *ekkā* *Mandā* *d-Hēyi*
EXT life EXT lord-1SG EXT knowledge of-life
Life exists, God exists, Knowledge-of-Life exists!

ex. 83. *mend-i* *l-ekkā*
thing-INDF NEG-EXT
There isn't anything.

In this case, the old Classical Mandaic existential particle still survives in a restricted role (that of the copula, which was formerly only one function of the existential particle), whereas the derived form *ekkā* has assumed its basic role (of existential predication).

6.6. The Neo-Mandaic Copula as an Auxiliary

One of the most characteristic properties of the copula, cross-linguistically, is its propensity to serve as an auxiliary (Payne 1997, p. 117). In the case of the Neo-Mandaic copula, its most frequent use as an auxiliary is in the passive voice of the verb, which is often rendered by means of the passive participle with the copula in an analytic construction.[25] The paradigm of the construction is illustrated below with the verb *gəṭal* ~ *gəṭol* (*gāṭel*) 'to kill':

Person	Present (Short)	Present (Long)	Perfective	Imperfective
3rd m.sg.	*gəṭel-yē*	*gəṭel ek̠t-i*	*gəṭel həwā*	*gəṭel qə-hāwi*
3rd f.sg.	*gəṭil-i*	*gəṭilā ek̠t-a*	*gəṭilā həw-at*	*gəṭilā qə-hāwy-ā*
2nd m.sg.	*gəṭel-yāt*	*gəṭel ek̠t-ak̠*	*gəṭel həw-et*	*gəṭel qə-hāw-et*
2nd f.sg.	*gəṭel-yāt*	*gəṭilā ek̠t-ek̠*	*gəṭilā həw-et*	*gəṭilā qə-hāw-et*
1st sg.	*gəṭel-nā*	*gəṭel ek̠t-ē*	*gəṭel həw-it*	*gəṭel qə-hawi-nā*
3rd pl.	—	*gəṭilen ek̠t-u*	*gəṭilen həw-on*	*gəṭilen qə-hāw-en*
2nd pl.	—	*gəṭilen ek̠t-ək̠on*	*gəṭilen həwi-ton*	*gəṭilen qə-haw-etton*
1st pl.	—	*gəṭilen ek̠t-an*	*gəṭilen həwi-ni*	*gəṭilen qə-haw-enni*

Note that this analytic passive construction is formally no different from the predicate adjective constructions cited above, such as examples 52 and 72. As the enclitic and independent forms of the copula are used for all statements in the simple present tense, the imperfective is reserved for statements in the progressive present or the future tenses. Likewise, the subjunctive of *həwā* ~ *həwi* (*hāwi*) 'to be,' which is regularly derived from the imperfective after the removal of the indicative marker and pretonic reduction, is used to indicate modality (suggestions, wishes, and hopes):

ex. 95. *yəhim-en* *ek̠t-an*
seated-PL COP-1SG
We are seated.

ex. 96. *yəhim-en* *qə-haw-enni*
seated-PL IND-be.PTC-1SG
We are being / will be seated.

ex. 97. *yəhim-en* *haw-én*
seated-PL be.PTC-1SG
Let us be seated.

This construction is already well represented in Classical Mandaic (see Macuch 1965, pp. 433–34).

[25] The passive voice is not exclusively expressed by this analytic construction; in fact, the impersonal 3rd pl. is more common when rendering the passive, at least in the speech of my chief informant, although the reverse appears to be true in the Neo-Mandaic texts from Ahvaz collected by Rudolf Macuch.

7. Conclusions

The syntax of the various forms of the copula and of predicate nominal and related constructions in Mandaic is consistent with that of other Semitic languages. Despite the prolonged contact situation between Mandaic and other languages such as Arabic and the Iranian languages, all forms of the copula and the various constructions expressing predication are quite clearly reflexes of those found in Classical Mandaic and earlier stages of the language. The proof of this is the use of an independent form of the copula in affirmative statements, which is attested in Biblical Hebrew and Classical Syriac, but not Classical Arabic. Furthermore, this independent form of the copula is derived from an existential particle, like Biblical Hebrew and Classical Syriac. Therefore, it is reasonable to assume that the treatment of predicate nominals and other related constructions described above is the natural result of internal developments within Mandaic (and more broadly Semitic) rather than that of contact influence.

Nevertheless, there are some important distinctions between the syntax of these constructions in Mandaic and in the related Semitic languages. Some form of the copula is necessary to express possession, much like Classical Syriac, but unlike Biblical Hebrew and Classical Arabic, which allow for the notion of possession to be expressed by a nominal sentence. Unlike Classical Syriac, however, there is no enclitic form of the copular verb — a feature that distinguishes Neo-Mandaic from all other surviving Aramaic dialects. Also, a distinction between ascriptive and equative clauses has arisen in Neo-Mandaic, the former being expressed by either the independent or the enclitic forms of the copula, and the latter being represented exclusively by the independent form of the copula. Finally, the particle *ekkā* has replaced the Classical Mandaic existential particle, which now serves exclusively as the independent copula.

Abbreviations

ACC	accusative	M/m.	masculine
COP	copula	NEG	negative
cs.	construct state	NOM	nominative
DC	Drower Collection of Mandaean manuscripts in the Bodleian Library, Oxford	OBJ	object
		OBL	oblique
DEF	definiteness	PL/pl.	plural
EXT	existential particle	PN	proper noun
F/f.	feminine	PRES	present
GEN	genitive	PST	past
PTC	participle	NEG	negation
IND	indicative	SG/sg.	singular
INDF	indefiniteness	SUBJ	subjunctive
IPFV	imperfective	TOP	topicalizer

Bibliography

Assemanus, Stefano Evodio

1748 *Acta Sanctorum Martyrum Orientalium et Occidentalium*. Rome: Joseph Collini.

Croft, William

2003 *Typology and Universals*. Cambridge Textbooks in Linguistics. Cambridge: Cambridge University Press.

Drower, Ethel S., and Rudolf Macuch

1963 *A Mandaic Dictionary*. Oxford: Clarendon Press.

Dyk, Janet W., and Eep Talstra

1999 "Paradigmatic and Syntagmatic Features in Identifying Subject and Predicate in Nominal Clauses." In *The Verbless Clause in Biblical Hebrew: Linguistic Approaches*, edited by Cynthia L. Miller, pp. 133–86. Winona Lake: Eisenbrauns.

Fox, Samuel

1994 "The Relationships of the Eastern Neo-Aramaic Dialects." *Journal of the American Oriental Society* 114/2: 154–62.

Goldenberg, Gideon

1983 "On Syriac Sentence Structure." In *Aramaeans, Aramaic, and the Aramaic Literary Tradition*, edited by Michael Sokoloff, pp. 97–140. Ramat Gan: Bar Ilan University Press.

1998 "On Verbal Structure and the Hebrew Verb." In *Studies in Semitic Linguistics: Selected Writings*, edited by Gideon Goldenberg, pp. 148–96. Jerusalem: Magnes Press.

2005 "Pronouns, Copulas, and a Syntactical Revolution in Neo-Semitic." In *Studi Afroasiatici: XI incontro italiano di linguistica camitosemitica,* edited by Alessandro Mengozzi, pp. 243–57. Milano: Franco Angeli.

Häberl, Charles G.

2009 *The Neo-Mandaic Dialect of Khorramshahr*. Wiesbaden: Harrassowitz.

Joosten, Jan

1992 "The Negation of the Non-verbal Clause in Syriac." *Journal of the American Oriental Society* 112/4: 584–88.

Khan, Geoffrey

1999 *A Grammar of Neo-Aramaic: The Dialect of the Jews of Arbel*. Handbuch der Orientalistik 47. Leiden: Brill.

Lehmann, Christian

1983 "Directions for Interlinear Morphemic Translations." *Folia Linguistica* 16: 193–224.

Macuch, Rudolf

1965 *Handbook of Classical and Modern Mandaic*. Berlin: de Gruyter.

Morony, Michael G.

2005 *Iraq after the Muslim Conquest*. 2nd edition. Piscataway: Gorgias Press.

Müller-Kessler, Christa

2003 "Aramaic *'k', lyk'* and Iraqi Arabic *'aku, maku*: The Mesopotamian Particles of Existence." *Journal of the American Oriental Society* 123/3: 641–46.

Nöldeke, Theodor

1875 *Mandäische Grammatik*. Halle: Weisenhaus.

2001 *Compendious Syriac Grammar*. Reprint of the 1904 edition. Winona Lake: Eisenbrauns.

Pat-El, Naʿama

2006 "Syntactic Aspects of Negation in Syriac." *Journal of Semitic Studies* 51/2: 329–48.

Payne, Thomas E.

1997 *Describing Morphosyntax: A Guide for Field Linguists*. Cambridge: Cambridge University Press.

Petermann, J. Heinrich

2007 *The Great Treasure*. Piscataway: Gorgias Press.

Stassen, Leon

2009 *Predicative Possession*. New York: Oxford University Press.

Wright, William

1869 *Homilies of Aphraates, The Persian Sage*. London: Williams and Norgate.

1996 *A Grammar of the Arabic Language Translated from the German of Caspari and Edited with Numerous Additions and Corrections*. New impression reprint of the 3rd edition. Beirut: Librarie du Liban.

Zewi, Tamar

1994 "The Nominal Sentence in Biblical Hebrew." In *Semitic and Cushitic Studies*, edited by Gideon Goldenberg and Shlomo Raz, pp. 145–67. Wiesbaden: Harrassowitz.

9

Yaqtul and a Ugaritic Incantation Text

*Jo Ann Hackett, University of Texas at Austin**

Ever since Edward Greenstein's 2006 article "Forms and Functions of the Finite Verb in Ugaritic Narrative Verse," the once largely accepted occurrence of a *yaqtul* preterite in Ugaritic has been a matter of discussion.[1] Until this time, most Ugaritiologists had simply assumed that Ugaritic, like so many other languages, included a *yaqtul* preterite in its repertoire (although their explanations of the form often differed) and found it useful to have such a verb when a doublet contained both a prefix-conjugation verb and a suffix-conjugation verb, for instance.

One would a priori look for a *yaqtul* preterite in Ugaritic, given that it exists, often in some restricted context, in Amarna Canaanite, Akkadian, Arabic, Aramaic, Ethiopic, Hebrew, and Moabite, although not, apparently, Phoenician; the *yaqtul* preterite, then, is by definition a proto-Semitic feature, and so one would not be surprised to find it in Ugaritic. Cyrus Gordon (1998), Eddy Verreet (1988), and Daniel Sivan (1997) all attest to a preterite *yaqtul*, although with various degrees of certainty. Josef Tropper's more recent 2000 *Ugaritische Grammatik* (§73.25) also describes a "Kurzform" of the prefix conjugation that serves as both preterite and jussive. Actually, he says the PKKi, our preterite *yaqtul*, represents the perfective aspect that is usually in the past. John Huehnergard in his "Ugaritic Outline" (2009, unpublished manuscript) also assumes a *yaqtul* preterite. Both these scholars note a few exceptions to an otherwise well-attested form.

More recently still, however, Dennis Pardee and Pierre Bordreuil (2004) claimed that the inconsistent use of the short form of III-*y* verbs leads us to a lack of certainty about the existence of the *yaqtul* preterite, and in their translations, they do not use it. (Here, I am assuming that the grammatical statement is Pardee's work since he is the grammarian of the two.) The book is now in English (Bordreuil and Pardee 2009), and the section about the absence of *yaqtul* preterites is even stronger (p. 49):

> Greenstein's arguments (2006) have convinced us that the level of uncertainty is too high to continue taking /YQTL/ forms of III-y roots in poetry that are written without the third radical as /YQTLØ/ perfectives; in his view, the /YQTLØ/ perfective/preterite was no longer operative in poetic narrative, and the two principal forms were /QTLa/ and /YQTL/ — according to his hypothesis, the /YQTLu/ and /YQTLØ/ forms would have lost distinctive functions, and both would have been used as "historical futures."[2]

In this paper, I first review some of the evidence that should decide whether the Ugaritic verbal system includes a *yaqtul* preterite; second, I give examples of such a form; and third, I show in an incantation text how the small change from *yaqtulu* to *yaqtul* in one place can make more sense of the text. The example is truly minor, but when my students and I studied the text in a Ugaritic seminar in 2009, it seemed clear to me that avoiding the *yaqtul* preterite had forced Pardee and Bordreuil to suggest a less likely interpretation of the beginning of the text than I will suggest.

---

* This paper is dedicated to John Huehnergard, who has read and commented on everything I've ever written, including this paper (although he didn't realize he was editing an article for his own festschrift).

[1] Greenstein has in fact been making similar claims since at least 1988; see his 1988 article and his long 1998 review of Daniel Sivan's Ugaritic grammar. But his 2006 article (revised from a paper read in the Israel Academy for Advanced Studies in 2002) is thorough and is dedicated specifically to the question at hand.

[2] See Pardee in the present volume, n. 5.

Greenstein uses as his sample the three large epics from Ugarit: Aqhat, Baal, and Kirta. In doing so, he is dealing with most of the poetry we have from Ugarit, and so it is a perfectly fine corpus for deciding whether there is a possibility of finding *yaqtul* preterites. His description of the evidence he uses to prove his point is somewhat different from the kinds of evidence that I would allow myself, however. He says (2006, p. 81),

> The claim [that there is a *yaqtul* preterite in Ugaritic] is based on two phenomena: (a) that III-*y* verbs often appear with the final *y* apocopated — which is interpreted to mean that the form is *yaqtul* rather than *yaqtulu*; and (b) that several YQTL forms append the suffix -*n* — which is interpreted to mean that the form is *yaqtulu* rather than *yaqtul*. An examination of the full evidence, however, can lead to a very different interpretation.

And as Greenstein points out, Ugaritic prose seems to use *yaqtulu* for future/durative verbs and *qatala* for past tense. In fact, one of Greenstein's arguments is that since we know Ugaritic regularly used *qatala* for its past tense, there was no reason for it to have a *yaqtul* preterite. In other words, a language should not have two past-tense verbs operating at the same time. In poetry, however, archaisms occur, as we all know, and the argument suggesting that poetic texts cannot show evidence of two forms with the same or similar functions carries little weight, it seems to me. The Hebrew Bible alone provides evidence against such an assumption.

I would present the evidence for a *yaqtul* preterite in a different order from Greenstein's: I would look for, first, singular and 1cp III-*aleph* verbs that end in *ʾi*, indicating that there is either a long *ī*-vowel or no vowel at all after the *aleph*; second, any plural or dual verbs without the -*n* ending that accompanies their long forms; and third, the short forms of III-*y* verbs.

First, III-*aleph* verbs. Such a singular verb or a 1cp verb in the prefix conjugation with a syllable-ending *ʾi* would be a *yaqtul* verb. Even once such verbs are found, they have to be verbs that are not jussive because no one doubts the fact of a *yaqtul* jussive in Ugaritic; it is the preterite use of the same form that is in question. But Greenstein finds not a single instance of a non-jussive singular III-*aleph* verb with a syllable-ending *ʾi* in his corpus. He does recognize the form *ispi* in *CAT* 1.5.i.5, but notes that Pardee (Pardee 2003, p. 265) translates 'I am devoured' as though the verb were indicative, and Smith (1997, p. 41) translates as volitive, 'Let me devour' (which is probably correct). I have to agree that there is practically no example of the *yaqtul* form with singular III-*aleph* verbs in the Ugaritic poetry we have, even if we accept a liberal interpretation of one or two forms.

When I examined III-*aleph* verbs,[3] I came up with only two certain examples, one from Greenstein's corpus and one outside it.

Example 1. *CAT* 1.14.II.26–31

In the Kirta story, *CAT* 1.14.ii.26–31 says:

> *wyrd / krt . lggt . ʿdb / akl . lqryt / ḥṭt . lbt . ḫbr / yip . lḥm . dḫmš / mgd ʹ [.] ṯdṯ. yrḫm / ʿdn [.] ngb . wyṣi / ṣbu . ṣbi . ngb / wyṣi . ʿdn . mʿ.*

The lines are directed at Kirta, which is made clear by the reference to 'your army' *ṣbuk* in line 35, so it makes sense to translate the passage as volitive and the *yaqtul* forms as jussive.

> wa-yarid Kirta li-gaggāti ʿadbu / ʾakla li-qaryīti / ḥittata li-Bêti Ḫubūri / yaʾpi laḥma dā-ḫamši / magīda ṯadīṯi yaraḫīma / ʿadānu nagubu wa-yaṣiʾ / ṣabaʾu ṣabaʾi nagubu / wa-yaṣiʾ ʿadānu maʿʿu
>
> Now, let Kirta come down from the roof, [let him] prepare food for the city, wheat for Bêt Ḫubūr; let him bake bread for five months, provisions for six. Let the equipped host go forth, the great equipped host, let the strong host go forth. (Note that my vocalization makes *ʿdb* in line 27 an infinitive, substituting for a volitive form.)

[3] I used Josef Tropper's list of III-*aleph* verbs in order to look up the ones that might be considered *yaqtuls*: Tropper 2000, pp. 619–24.

CAT 1.14.iv.8–12 is very similar, but this time the passage is in the third person, and not directed at Kirta, and so a volitive form is not really called for. It can easily all be read in the past tense, getting rid of the infinitive and translating a suffix conjugation there, suggesting that we translate the whole little section in the past tense. The passage is the same, except for the w at the beginning, but now we can read,

> yarid/yarada Kirta li-gaggāti ʿadaba / ʾakla li-qaryīti / ḥittata li-Bêti Ḫubūri / yaʾpi laḥma dā-ḫamši / magīda ṯadīṯi yaraḫīma, and so forth.
>
> Kirta came down from the roof, prepared food for the city, wheat Bêt Ḫubūr; he baked bread for five months, provisions for six (and so on).

It is not impossible to read the whole thing in the narrative present, as Greenstein has (1997, pp. 18–19), dealing with the infinitive again or, as he would have it, simply translating a suffix conjugation as a variant rather than as a past tense, and doing the same with the short forms *yip* and *yṣi*, but my reading gives a reason for the short form both times, without equating *yip* and *yipy* or *yṣi* and *yṣy*, and uses what appears to be a suffix conjugation more reasonably as a past-tense verb. H. L. Ginsberg, I should add, in his old but wonderful "Legend of King Keret" (1946), also translates these verbs in the second occurrence of the passage as past tense and then switches to narrative present in the next line, when we begin having *yaqtulu* verbs, and it still makes perfect sense. In fact, you can actually go all the way back to line 50 of the tablet before and find the following verbs, all of which can be taken as either *yaqtul* preterites or suffix conjugations: *yḫṭ, yrtḥṣ, yadm, yrḥs, ʿrb, lqh* (bis), *yṣq,ʿly, rkb, nša, dbḥ, šrd, yrd, ʿdb, yip, yṣi* (reconstructed), *yṣi*. And, by the way, Ginsberg does go this far back with his past-tense translation.

Example 2. *CAT* 1.96:3

Greenstein mentions this very confusing text, and it also happens to be the text about which I wrote my Ugaritic paper when I was a graduate student. It contains another good example, I think. When I was a graduate student, it definitely concerned the goddess Anat, and now it seems to be leaning toward the Evil Eye, since the first word is clearly ʿ-n-n and not ʿ-n-t. Whether ʿ-n-n is 'eye' (that is, the Evil Eye) plus enclitic *-n* or simply a mistake for Anat,[4] there is clearly a III-*aleph* non-jussive *yaqtul* in the text, along with what may be another non-jussive *yaqtul*, if tp can really be taken to be a *yaqtul* verb from the root p-h-*y* that has somehow assimilated the *h*.

> Lines 1–4
>
> *ʿnn/ʿnt! . hlkt . wšnwt / tp . aḫh . wnʿm . aḫh / kysmsm . tspi . širh / l . blḥrb . tšt . dmh . lbl . ks.*
>
> ... ʿênu-nv/ʿAnatu halakat wa-šanuwat[5] / tippê[6] ʾaḫāha wa-nuʿmu ʾaḫīha / ka-yasimsimi[7] tissapiʾ šiʾrahu / libal ḥarbi tištê damahu libal kôsi ...
>
> The Evil Eye/Anat moved/walked along and flashed. It/She saw the fairness of its/her brother, and that the pleasantness of its/her brother was lovely. It/She ate his flesh without a knife; it/she drank his blood without a cup ...

Even though this is a strange text,[8] and we have little idea what it means, it is probable that two suffix-conjugation verbs are followed by what should be three *yaqtul* verbs, the first possibly a short-form III-*y* verb, the next a Niphal III-*aleph* verb that ends in *ʾi*, and again a short-form III-*y* verb. It would seem to be obvious to translate at least the eating and drinking passage in the past tense.

---

[4] See Lewis 1996.

[5] From Arabic *snw/y* 'shine, glisten, flash'?

[6] A difficult verb, to be sure. Here, I have assumed the verb is a *yaqtul* form, derived from the III-weak root p-h-y, and that the h has assimilated to the p. I.e., *tiphay > *tiphê > tippê.

[7] Vocalized according to Arabic *wasīm*.

[8] Greenstein (1998, p. 410) calls the text a scribal exercise that begins with a probable error and has a syllabic sequence on the flip-side. He feels for these reasons that the text's verbs are not reliable examples of Ugaritic usage. Still, it is there, and the verbs are written correctly for a past-tense account (assuming that use of *yaqtul*).

Example 3. *CAT* 1.2.IV.2

A third example is in *CAT* 1.2.iv.2: it has the form *aṣ̌ṣi hm*. There is no context, unfortunately, but both Greenstein (1997, p. 102) and Bordreuil and Pardee (2009, p. 159) bother to translate it. They both translate future, however: 'I will send them out' and 'I will force them to leave,' even though the verb clearly ends in *ʾi*. In Greenstein's translation (1997), and in the Bordreuil-Pardee *Manual* (2004, 2009), many passages are translated as narrative present, no matter what the verbs involved. Without context, none of us can use this example as evidence, but with a final *ʾi*, I think the assumption of future tense is misguided.

Greenstein's second line of evidence concerns the *-n* attached to the end of some verbs, but he himself proves that *-n* can be added to practically any verb, so its presence tells us really nothing. Its absence, on the other hand, where it is expected, as in dual and plural verbs, is important. In other words, I would turn Greenstein's second criterion on its head and say that any prefix-conjugation form that ends in *-n* in the long form is a possible *yaqtul* preterite when it occurs without the *-n* ending. It is also possibly a jussive and in some cases a subjunctive, so those categories would then need to be ruled out before we could feel sure that we had a *yaqtul* preterite.

Example 4. *CAT* 1.15.III.17–18

In the Kirta epic, in *CAT* 1.15.iii.17–18, after El declares that he will make Kirta's youngest daughter the first-born (*ṣgrthn . abkrn*) and ends his speech, the gods who have gathered leave.

> *tbrk . ilm . tity / tity . ilm . lahlhm / dr il . lmšknthm*

We know that we are speaking of plural gods, and the verbs are written without the final *-n*. They really should be plural past tense:

> *tibarrikū ʾilūma taʾtiyū / taʾtiyū ʾilūma li-ʾahalīhumu / dôru ʾili li-miškanātihumu.*
>
> 'The gods blessed, (then) left; the gods left for their tents; the circle of El for their dwellings.'

It is consistent and exactly what we would expect of such verbs. In fact, the rest of that part of the story reads perfectly well as past tense: "She conceived and bore him a son," and so on. Note also that one of the verbs in this passage is a plural of the III-*y* verb ʾ-t-*y* in what seems to me to be a clearly *yaqtul* plural form, and there is no reason to suggest that it is jussive, but rather simply past-tense indicative.

Finally, we turn to III-*y* verbs in general. Greenstein presents a long and involved discussion of III-*y* singular verbs, finally arriving at the conclusion that the triphthong *-iyu* can contract (although obviously not always), so that *yabnû*, for instance, can be the same as *yabniyu*. His argument here is a little vaguer than I am making it. He actually says (2006, pp. 84–85), "Ugaritic exhibits a general tendency to curtail or contract final syllables containing the glide *y*," and he points us to two articles by Sivan for further proof (1982; 1984). Both Tropper (2000, p. 195) and Huehnergard (2008, pp. 288–92), however, do not allow for triphthongs in *-iyV* to contract, and they have evidence to support their position: words such as *apy* /ʾāpiyu/ 'baker' and *hy* /hiya/ 'she.' While several other triphthongs contract, this one does not. This would mean that all short forms from III-*y* verbs with an *i* stem vowel, that is, *yaqtil*-forms (as most III-*y* verbs are) — *yabniyu, yaʿniyu*, and so on — would represent truly jussive/preterite forms and not simply variants of the longer forms.

Consequently, I looked at several III-*y* verbs of the form *yaqtil-*, a form that in the indicative would give us *-iyu* in the 1cs, 2ms, 3ms, 3fs, and 1cp, and a final *-n* in the 2fs, 2mp, 2fp, 3mp, or 3fp (and the dual forms). The verbs in the first list, found without final *-y*, and those in the second list, found without final *-n*, are signs of a verb type other than the *yaqtulu* long form. Although not all of these "short" III-*y* verbs actually occur in extant texts, many do;[9] I checked the list of G-forms that are missing *-y* or *-n*, as the case may be. I also looked at all the occurrences of the verb ʿ-n-*y* that Greenstein reports, which is a large set. My conclusion was, briefly, that the

---

[9] Again, Tropper's list (2000, pp. 653–71) is invaluable.

short forms were either volitive or preterite, as Huehnergard's and Tropper's analyses suggested would be the case.[10] I use only two here.

Example 5. *CAT* 1.19.IV

In the Aqhat epic, in *CAT* 1.19.iv, Danel has gone around cursing certain cities (and his going is expressed with *ymǵ*, so he 'arrived' at those cities, rather than the narrative present translation 'comes' in Parker 1997b, p. 75[11]), after which we read (lines 8–11),

> *dnil . bth . ym{.}ǵyn . yšt/ql . dnil . lhklh . ʿrb . b/<bth b>kyt . bhklh . mšspdt . bḥẓrh / pẓǵm . ǵr*

In this passage, Danel arrives home (or "when" he arrives home), the professional weepers have come, or perhaps had already come — ʾarabā, suffix conjugation, past tense. Next, lines 11–13,

> *ybk . laqht / ǵzr . ydmʿ . lkdd . dnil / mt . rpi ...*

Danel wept — *yabki*, past tense — for Aqhat. This goes on for days and months and years, and again *yabki . laq/ht* and so on. Then, in the seventh year, the text says, *yʿn [dnil mt] rpi*, Danel spoke — *yaʿni* (line 18). I see no reason for translating this passage as narrative present when the verbs as they stand tell the story quite nicely.

Example 6. *CAT* 1.4.VI.16

In another, simple example, in the Baal epic, in *CAT* 1.4.vi.16, Kothar-wa-Ḫasis builds Baal's house this way: *tbnn*. This can only be *tabni* with enclitic *-n*, or possibly the final *-n* as an object suffix, even though the suffix is not necessary in this sentence.

I also dealt with all of the ʿ-n-*y* examples in Greenstein's article, the ones from Aqhat, Baal, and Kirta, and I think his numbers actually point to a different conclusion from the one he presented. Briefly, he points out that this verb is almost always used in a formula, sometimes followed by the prefix-conjugation *y/tšu* 'he/she lifted up [his/her voice],' but most often it is not found with that verb. In the thirty-eight clear forms he finds, only four use the long form *yʿny*, whereas thirty-four use the short form *yʿn*. Furthermore, three of the four long forms occur with *Kirta ṯʿ* 'Noble Kirta' as subject; in fact, Kirta never occurs as the subject of the short form. The fourth occurrence is also in the Kirta story, and once (or maybe twice) *ǵazru ʾilḥaʾu* is the subject. It seems to me that the burden of proof lies with the person who needs to explain the long form in its very limited use: the long form suggests the narrative present, and the narrator may have had some reason to use that meaning in these few places; or the answer could be metrical, as Greenstein suggests. But the weight of the evidence falls with the short form. It can in every occasion be translated easily as past tense, even in those few cases where *y/tšu* follows, since the prefix conjugation could simply be a circumstantial addition.[12]

Example 7. RS 92.2014

Finally, I turn to the incantation text that made me want to restore past-tense *yaqtul* to Ugaritic: RS 92.2014 (text 18 in Bordreuil and Pardee 2004 and 2009), which they call "An Incantation against Snakes and Scorpions." After all these examples, I have to admit that the small change that started me on this path is something of an anti-climax, but here are the first five lines:

> (1) *dy . l . ydʿ . yṣḥk . u zb* (2) *w . ank . aṣḥk . amrmrn* (3) *ʿṣ . qdš . w . ʿlk . l .* (4) *tʿl . bṯn . w . tḥtk*
> (5) *l . tqnn. ʿqrb.*

[10] In a couple of cases, such as *CAT* 1.5.vi.16 and 1.12.i.35, I had to allow for a change of tense between one "paragraph" or even one doublet and the next, but even there, I would rather stick to the general rule about verb forms than to ignore all the others in order to make the difficult ones work more easily.

[11] Of which article I was the editor, so I formally present my mea culpa here.

[12] See GKC 120c and note 2 for examples in Hebrew, plus the information that the syntax is "frequent in Arabic and in Syriac."

> Bordreuil and Pardee translate: "When the unknown one calls you and begins foaming, I, for my part, will call you. I will shake pieces of sacred wood, so that the serpent does not come up against you, so that the scorpion does not stand up under you."

The problem, of course, is with the first line, and the one point I want to make about the text is that it makes more sense if the first line describes something that has already happened. Bordreuil and Pardee translated by adding "When" at the beginning of the text — "When the unknown one calls you and begins foaming ..." — so that it reads as though the unknown one is the one who begins foaming. But the one who is unknown is the person who has cursed our victim (Pardee says the same in 2000, p. 830), so I am not certain why he or she is foaming. I have translated as if *yṣḥk* is a *yaqtul* past tense, with a 2ms object suffix: "One who is unknown has called you, and moreover 'it' has foamed/frothed."[13] The last part of the line is difficult, to say the least, but I think it refers to a result of snake-bite — a foaming wound, frothing at the mouth, something like that — and it is something that has already happened. (I am interpreting *zb* as a suffix-conjugation verb.) The attacker has "called" the victim — called his name, perhaps, within a curse that has brought a snake to bite him — and moreover, foaming has happened (literally, 'it has foamed,' and "it" could perhaps be our victim's wound[14]). The healer then says in the next line that he will now call the victim (or call his name), but this time within a healing ritual, and he goes on to perform the ritual.[15]

If the text had actually begun "when" or "whenever," I would have no problem with Bordreuil and Pardee's interpretation of the verb for calling, although I still think the foaming word is a problem — but in fact the text does not start that way. The text as it is makes better sense when we assume that (the text's author believes) the sorcerer has already cursed the victim and the victim has been bitten by a snake or scorpion, so that already he is frothing at the mouth or his wound is foaming. It is not unusual for an incantation text to begin this way, with a decscription of what has (already) happened to bring the victim to the healer, before we read that the healer then performs the ritual.

While it is not impossible to read most Ugaritic finite verbs as narrative present, as Greenstein and Bordreuil and Pardee have demonstrated, I have tried to show that there is still a distinction being made in Ugaritic between *yaqtul* and *yaqtulu*, and I much prefer the nuanced distinctions in time that using *yaqtul* preterites allows.

Abbreviations

CAT	Dietrich, Loretz, and Sanmartín 1995
GKC	Gesenius, Kautzsch, and Cowley 1910
RS	signature of texts found at Ras Shamra

Bibliography

Bordreuil, Pierre, and Dennis Pardee

2004 *Manuel d'ougaritique*. 2 volumes. Paris: Paul Geuthner.

2009 *A Manual of Ugaritic*. Linguistic Studies in Ancient West Semitic 3. Winona Lake: Eisenbrauns.

[13] I think the verb for "knowing" is probably another *yaqtul*, this time plural *yadiyū*: one whom they do not know, the "they" being impersonal.

[14] Naʿama Pat-El has pointed to Lev 15:25, where the woman's blood 'flows' abundantly. In this case also, the 'foaming' or 'frothing' does not happen to a person, but to the afflicted one's 'wound.'

[15] The second part of the text is more general and tries to deny any potency to the words of the evil people who have cursed our victim.

Dietrich, Manfried; Oswald Loretz; and Joaquín Sanmartín

1995 *The Cuneiform Alphabetic Texts from Ugarit, Ras Ibn Hani and Other Places* (KTU: 2nd enlarged edition). Münster: Ugarit-Verlag.

Gesenius, Wilhelm; Emil Kautzsch; and Arthur E. Cowley

1910 *Gesenius' Hebrew Grammar*. Edited by E. Kautzsch, translated by A. E. Cowley. 2nd English edition. Oxford: Clarendon Press.

Ginsberg, Harold L.

1946 *The Legend of King Keret: A Canaanite Epic of the Bronze Age*. American Schools of Oriental Research. Supplementary Studies 2–3. New Haven: American Schools of Oriental Research.

Gordon, Cyrus

1998 *Ugaritic Textbook*. Revised reprint. Analecta Orientalia 38. Rome: Pontifical Biblical Institute.

Greenstein, Edward L.

1988 "On the Prefixed Preterite in Biblical Hebrew." *Hebrew Studies* 29: 7–17.

1997 "Kirta." In *Ugaritic Narrative Poetry*, edited by Simon B. Parker, pp. 9–48. Writings from the Ancient World 9. Atlanta: Scholars Press.

1998 "On a New Grammar of Ugaritic." Review of *A Grammar of the Ugaritic Language*, by Daniel Sivan (Brill: Leiden, 1997). *Israel Oriental Studies* 18: 397–420.

2006 "Forms and Functions of the Finite Verb in Ugaritic Narrative Verse." In *Biblical Hebrew in Its Northwest Semitic Setting: Typological and Historical Perspectives*, edited by Steven E. Fassberg and Avi Hurvitz, pp. 75–102. Jerusalem: Hebrew University Magnes Press; Winona Lake: Eisenbrauns.

Huehnergard, John

2008 *Ugaritic Vocabulary in Syllabic Transcription*. Revised edition. Harvard Semitic Studies 32. Winona Lake: Eisenbrauns.

2009 "Ugaritic Outline." Unpublished manuscript.

Lewis, Theodore

1996 "The Disappearance of the Goddess Anat." *Biblical Archaeologist* 59: 115–21.

Pardee, Dennis

2003 "Ugaritic Myths." In *The Context of Scripture*, Volume 1, edited by William W. Hallo and K. Lawson Younger, Jr., pp. 241–83. Leiden: Brill.

Parker, Simon B.

1997a *Ugaritic Narrative Poetry*. Writings from the Ancient World 9. Atlanta: Scholars Press.

1997b "Aqhat." In *Ugaritic Narrative Poetry*, edited by Simon B. Parker, pp. 49–80. Writings from the Ancient World 9. Atlanta: Scholars Press.

Sivan, Daniel

1982 "Final Triphthongs and Final *yu/a/i - wu/a/i* Diphthongs in Ugaritic Nominal Forms." *Ugarit-Forschungen* 14: 209–18.

1984 "Diphthongs and Triphthongs in Verbal Forms of Verba Tertiae Infirmae in Ugaritic." *Ugarit-Forschungen* 16: 279–93.

1997 *A Grammar of the Ugaritic Language*. Translated by Anson Rainey. Handbuch der Orientalistik 28. Leiden: Brill.

Smith, Mark S.

1997 "The Baal Cycle." In *Ugaritic Narrative Poetry*, edited by Simon B. Parker, pp. 81–180. Writings from the Ancient World 9. Atlanta: Scholars Press.

Tropper, Josef

2000 *Ugaritische Grammatik*. Alter Orient und Altes Testament 273. Münster: Ugarit-Verlag.

Verreet, Eddy

1988 *Modi ugaritici: Eine morpho-syntaktische Abhandlung das Modalsystem im Ugaritischen*. Orientalia Lovaniensia Analecta 27. Leuven: Peeters.

10

The Verbal Endings -*u* and -*a*: A Note on Their Functional Derivation

Rebecca Hasselbach, University of Chicago

1. Introduction[1]

As is well known, Semitic languages make use of various vocalic markers to express subordination and modal notions on the verb. These markers include -*u*, used to indicate subordination in East Semitic and the indicative imperfect in Central Semitic; -*a*, which marks mood in Central Semitic but seems to occur as subordinate marker in East Semitic; and -*Ø*, which expresses mood (jussive) and perfect tense/aspect in all major Semitic sub-branches. It has been suggested by various scholars that the endings -*u* and -*a* are derived from original case markers,[2] the ending -*u* presumably originates in the nominative -*u*, while -*a* is considered to reflect the accusative.[3]

Despite the fact that the derivation of verbal affixes from nominal markers is cross-linguistically well attested, internal Semitic problems have been cited against a common derivation of the East and Central Semitic morphemes. These arguments are primarily based on the functional differences of the endings -*u* and -*a* — specifically the ending -*a* does not seem to have any functional relationship in the two branches. Brockelmann (1908, p. 554) went so far as to state that given that both the forms and functions of modal endings differ significantly in the individual languages, it is impossible to discern a coherent system of modal forms for Proto Semitic. It is the purpose of this paper to investigate the potential functional relationship of the forms in -*a* in the various Semitic sub-branches and to evaluate the proposed nominal derivation of the verbal endings -*u* and -*a*.

1.1. The Nominal Derivation of Finite Verbal Forms in Semitic

The notion that the verbal markers -*u* and -*a* are derived from the nominal system can in part be connected to the assumption that verbal forms in Semitic generally originate in verbless clauses. The fact that at least the East Semitic predicative verbal adjective/stative — the West Semitic suffix conjugation/perfect — is derived from a nominal clause has been recognized early on in the study of the Semitic verbal system.[4] In early discussions,

[1] Abbreviations used in this paper include the following: ABS = absolute state; ACC = accusative; ACT = active; c = communis; COH = cohortative; CSTR = construct state; DEF = definite; DIR = directive morpheme; DUR = durative; EA = El Amarna; ENER = energic; f = feminine; GEN = genitive; IMP = imperative; IMPF = imperfect; INDIC = indicative; INFIN = infinitive; m = masculine; NOM = nominative; p = plural; PERF = perfect; pl = plural; PN = personal name; PRED = predicate; PRET = preterite; PTC = participle; REL = relative pronoun; s = singular; SING = singular; SUBJ = subjunctive; VENT = ventive; VOC = vocative.

[2] See, e.g., Kuryłowicz 1949, p. 53; Voigt 1997, p. 219; Voigt 1999, p. 13; Lipiński 2001, p. 359.

[3] Voigt, for example, suggested that the non-nasalized noun in the accusative (-*a*) corresponds to the West Semitic perfect (*qatala*) and to the prefix conjugation (*yaqtula*), the nasalized noun in the nominative (-*um*) corresponds to the relativized prefix conjugation in -*u* (*yaqtulu*) in East Semitic and the indicative imperfect in Central Semitic, while the nasalized accusative (-*am*) corresponds to the ventive (Voigt 1997, p. 220; 1999, p. 13).

[4] For a summary of the early discussion, see, e.g., Fleisch 1975, p. 8. For the assumption that Semitic verbs are ultimately derived from verbless clauses, see also Kuryłowicz 1949, p. 51; Hodge 1974, p.22; Goldenberg 1983, p. 113.

it has likewise been suggested that the prefix conjugation might go back to a nominal clause based on a verbal noun or verbal adjective. Wright, for example, states, "Verbal forms in Semitic are really nominal forms, mostly in combination with pronouns. Each person of the verb is, so to say, a sentence, consisting of a noun and a pronoun, which has gradually been contracted and shriveled up into a single word" (1890, p. 164). The development of a verbal form from an original nominal clause involving a verbal adjective and independent personal pronouns is known not only from the Akkadian predicative adjective/stative but also from other Semitic languages, such as Syriac. In Syriac, adjectives and particularly participles serving as predicates appear in the so-called status absolutus, or unmarked state, and are as a rule accompanied by a shortened form of the independent pronoun in the second and first persons that indicates the subject. In combination with the participle, the shortened form of the pronoun is commonly suffixed to the participle (Nöldeke 1904, pp. 45, 247):

zakkāy-Ø (ʾ)*nā*
innocent.ABS I
'I am innocent'

qāṭl-aṯ
kill.PTC.ACT.ms-2ms
'you (ms) kill'

In fact, almost every non-verbal predication requires a personal pronoun indicating the subject in Syriac. This construction and the obligatory use of an independent pronoun make a nominal clause in Syriac, as noted by Goldenberg (1983, p. 112), rather verb-like since the predicate in these cases is "actually conjugated." It has been repeatedly observed that this construction in Syriac resembles the predicative adjective/stative of Akkadian.[5] In several modern Aramaic dialects, the participle plus personal pronoun replaced the original imperfect and developed into a finite verbal form. In Urmia, for example, only the imperative is still productive as a derivative of the original imperfect, while other verbal forms were replaced by newly developed forms.[6] The grammaticalization of original verbless clauses into finite verbal forms is thus not uncommon in Semitic.

The observable developments in both Akkadian and Aramaic strengthen the claim that Semitic verbal forms are generally derived from verbless clauses. The fact that verbal forms are derived from nominal clauses can also be observed beyond Semitic. Hodge argues that historically all verb forms in Egyptian are derived from nominal constructions. In fact, he claims, "One of the implications of the history of the Egyptian language is that verbs are not primes in the linguistic order of things."[7] Instead, according to Hodge, verbs are semantic-formal combinations that are the result of language internal developments. Given these general tendencies, it is very likely that we are indeed dealing with grammaticalized verbless clauses involving a verbal adjective/verbal noun and a pronoun in the case of all major Semitic verbal conjugations. Another argument in favor of an adnominal derivation of the Semitic prefix conjugation is the fact that the pronominal elements of the first and second persons are still clearly identifiable as being derived from the attested independent pronouns.[8]

Since verbal forms are derived from original verbless clauses through the grammaticalization of a nominal and pronominal element, it seems likely that the modal endings, which phonologically resemble Semitic case markers, are likewise derived from the nominal system. The question remains how these endings, specifically *-u* and *-a*, can be derived on a functional level. In order to answer this question, I will first briefly review the main attestations and suggested reconstructions of these two verbal markers and subsequently propose a functional derivation. Since the evidence for the two endings is well known, examples have been kept to a minimum.

---

[5] See, e.g., Gai 1984, p. 72. A similar situation is found in Eastern Aramaic dialects contemporary to Syriac such as Mandaic and the Aramaic of the Babylonian Talmud.

[6] Hodge 1975, p. 2. For the grammaticalization of nominal clauses into finite verbs, see also Rubin 2005, pp. 27–28. A similar development occurred in Tigrinya (Rubin 2005, p. 31).

[7] Hodge 1974, p. 22. See also Hodge 1975, p. 2.

[8] For a recent study of the derivation of the prefixes of the prefix conjugation from independent pronouns, see Hasselbach 2004.

2. The Ending *-u*: Distribution and Function

The verbal ending *-u* is attested in Akkadian, Ugaritic, early Canaanite — represented by the evidence from letters dating to the fourteenth century B.C. found at Tell El-Amarna in Egypt — and Classical Arabic.[9]

2.1. The Ending *-u* in Akkadian

In Akkadian, *-u* is used to mark verbs in any kind of subordinate clause. It can be formed of all tenses, meaning it does not modify tense but is syntactically conditioned.[10]

Subordinate marker in relative clause:

šarrāq-am	*ṣeḫr-am*	*ša*	*ina*	*eql-ī-ni*	*ni-ṣbat-u*	*ni-dūk*
thief-ACC	young-ACC	REL	in	field-GEN-1cp.GEN	1cs-seize.PRET-SUBJ	1cs-kill.PRET

'we killed the young thief whom we had seized in our field'

Subordinate marker in temporal clause:

inūma	*âm*	*ta-šām-u*	*ta-llik-am*
when	grain.ACC	2ms-buy.PRET-SUBJ	2ms-come.PRET-VENT

'when you had bought the grain, you came here'

mār-um	*šū*	*warki*	*abū-šu*	*i-mūt-u*	*i-rgum*
son-NOM	that	after	father.NOM-3ms.GEN	3ms-die.PRET-SUBJ	3ms-sue.PRET

'that son brought suit after his father had died'

Although it is commonly referred to as "subjunctive," the Akkadian form has no functional parallel with the "subjunctive" modal form known from Indo-European languages. As von Soden states, the Akkadian form is "eine Art Genitivendung des Verbum finitum."[11] Instead of the traditionally used term "subjunctive," it has become more common in recent years to refer to this form as "subordinating marker/form."[12]

In addition to its use in subordinate clauses, *-u* is used in main clauses after *šumma* 'when' in both promissory (involving a present-tense verb) and assertory (with a preterite verb) oaths:[13]

Assertory:

umma	*šunū-ma*	*kirûm*	*pānûm*	*burr-u*	*ina*	*il-im*	*te-lqû*
say	they.mp-and	orchard.NOM	previous.NOM	confirmed-NOM	in	god-GEN	2ms-take.PRET.SUBJ

'the previous orchard was confirmed; you (ms) took (it) under (an oath to) a god'

---

[9] For the hypothesis that the ending *-u* as marker of the imperfect expressing present/future is also preserved in a few Ethiopian languages — mainly languages of the Gurage cluster (Muher, Gogot, Soddo); see Leslau 1967. Leslau himself admits, however, that there might be a different derivation of the imperfects in *-u* in these languages. The evidence from Ethiopic has thus not been included in the present investigation.

[10] Huehnergard 1998, pp. 183–85; Kienast 1960, p. 154. For the examples given, see Huehnergard 1998, pp. 185, 284.

[11] Von Soden 1995, p. 135.

[12] See, e.g., Huehnergard 1998, p. 183.

[13] Von Soden 1995, p. 136; Hecker 1968, p. 133; Kienast 1960, p. 155. For the examples, see Huehnergard 1998, p. 437. Von Soden did not provide an explanation why the subordinate marker is used in oaths, stating, "Wie sich dieser für einen Modus relativus sehr eigenartige Sprachgebrauch erklärt, ist noch unbekannt" (1995, p. 136).

Promissory:

ina	*maḫar*	*awīl-ē*	*annût-im*	*kiam*	*i-qbû*	*umma*	*šunū-ma*	*nīš*	*šarr-im*
in	before	men-GEN	these-GEN	thus	3m-say.PRET.pl	say	they.mp-and	life.CSTR	king-GEN

ana	*dayyān-ī*	*ni-llak-ū-ma*
to	judges-GEN	1cp-go.DUR-SUBJ-and

'before these men they said as follows: by the life of the king, we will go to the judges'

2.2. The Ending -*u* in Ugaritic

In Ugaritic, *yaqtulu* is directly attested in the singular in roots III-ʾ that are written with <ʾU> and by the addition of final -*n* in the second feminine singular and the second and third person plural.[14] It is used as imperfect indicative, expressing present and, less frequently, future events. In addition it is frequently used in circumstantial clauses:[15]

For present:

mh	*t-arš-n*	*btlt*	*ʿnt*
what	2fs-wish.IMPF-INDIC	virgin	PN

'what do you wish, virgin Anat?'

For future:

zbl	*ʿ ršm*	*y-šu*
sick	bed	3-take.IMPF.INDIC

'the sick one will take his bed'

For circumstantial with past reference:

y-ṯb	*l*	*kḥṯ*	*aliyn*	*bʿl*	*pʿn-h*	*l*	*t-mǵy-n*	*hdm*
3m-sit.PRET	to	throne	mighty	Baal	feet-3ms.GEN	not	3-reach.IMPF-INDIC.DUAL	footstool

'he sat down on the throne of mighty Baal, his feet not reaching the footstool'

The form *yaqtulu* is also used in temporal and relative clauses, where its use resembles Akkadian -*u*.[16]

In relative clause:

il	*mṣrm*	*dt*	*t-ǵr-n*	*npš*	*špš*
gods.CSTR	Egypt	REL.mp	3p-protect.IMPF-INDIC.PL	life.CSTR	sun

'the gods of Egypt who protect the life of the sun'

In temporal clause:

w	*k*	*l*	*y-ḫru*	*w*	*l*	*y-ṯtn*	*s_3s_3w*
and	when	not	3-defecate.INDIC.SING	and	not	3-urinate	horse

'and when the horse does not defecate and does not urinate'

Lastly, *yaqtulu* can appear in both the protasis and apodosis of a conditional clause:[17]

---

[14] Tropper 2000, p. 458.

[15] Tropper 2000, pp. 458, 684–88.

[16] Tropper 2000, p. 686.

[17] Tropper 2000, p. 686.

In both protasis and apodosis:

hm	*t-ʿp-n*	*ʿl*	*qbr*	*bny*	*t-šḫṭ-n-nn*
if	3-fly.IMPF-INDIC.PL	over	grave.CSTR	son-1cs.GEN	3-wake.IMPF-INDIC.PL-3ms.ACC

b	*šnt-h*
in	sleep-3ms.GEN

'if they fly over the grave of my son they wake him from his sleep'

2.3. The Ending *-u* in Early Canaanite

In early Canaanite, *yaqtulu* is used as imperfect indicative. It is the standard form to express present and future. It can further stand for continuous or repeated action in the past and for circumstantial events. As circumstantial, most attestations have past reference:[18]

For the present:

anumma	*anākū-ma*	*e-rriš-u //*	*ʾaḫriš-u*	*ina*	^{URU}*šunama*
now	I-PRED	1cs-cultivate-INDIC.SING	(gloss)	in	Shunem

'now it is I who is cultivating in Shunem'

For the future:

i-naṣṣar-ū-šu	*adi*	*yi-mluk-u*	*šarr-um*
1cs-guard-INDIC.SING-3ms.ACC	until	3ms-take.counsel-INDIC	king-NOM

'I will guard him until the king takes counsel'

For circumstantial with past reference:

šanītam	*šar*	^{KUR}*mitanni*	*aṣi*	*adi*	^{URU}*ṣumura*
second	king.CSTR	Mitanni	go.out.3ms	up.to	Ṣumur

u	*yu-baʾʾû*	*alāka*	*adi*	^{URU}*gubla*
and	3ms-seek.INDIC	go.INFIN	up.to	Byblos

'Furthermore, the king of Mitanni came out as far as Ṣumur and was seeking to come to Byblos'

2.4. The Ending *-u* in Classical Arabic

In Classical Arabic, *yaqtulu* is used in the same environments as in Ugaritic. Its main use is for verbal actions referring to the present or future:[19]

For present:

ʾa-ʿlam-u	*mā*	*lā*	*ta-ʿlam-ū-na*
1cs-know.IMPF-INDIC.SING	what	not	2-know.IMPF-mp-INDIC

'I know what you do not know'

---

[18] Rainey 1996, vol. 2, pp. 7, 228–30, 234. For the examples, see ibid. I have not indicated the verbal base as PERF, IMPF, etc. in the examples from early Canaanite since the system used by the scribes differs significantly from normative Semitic usage.

[19] Fischer 1987, p. 93.

For future:

ta-jid-u	*kull-u*	*nafs-in*	*mā*	*ʿamil-at*
3f-find.IMPF-INDIC.SING	every-NOM.CSTR	soul-GEN	what	do.PERF-3fs

'every soul will find what it has done'

It is further frequently used for circumstantial events and for repeated actions with present and past reference:[20]

For circumstantial:

ʾa-rā-ka	*ta-bkī*
1cs-see.IMPF-2ms.ACC	2ms-cry.IMPF

'I see you crying'

For repeated action:

ʾa-ʿfu	*ʿan^{i}*	*l-jāhil-i*	*wa-ʾu-ʿṭī*	*s-sāʾil-a*
1cs-forgive.IMPF	PREP	DEF-ignorant-GEN	and-1cs-give.IMPF	DEF-ask.PTC.ACT.ms-ACC

'I (habitually) forgive the ignorant one and give to the asking one'

As such it denotes imperfect(ive) tense/aspect. In addition, *yaqtulu* appears in subordinate clauses such as relative clauses:[21]

ʾal-qawm-u	*llaḏīna*	*yu-ʾmin-ū-na*
DEF-people-NOM	REL.mp	3-believe.IMPF-mp-INDIC

'the people who believe'

In very few instances, *yaqtulu* can appear in the apodosis of a conditional clause when it follows another verb in the jussive and is connected by either *wa-* or *fa-*. In this case, the verb can also appear in the jussive or in the subjunctive.[22]

2.5. Summary of the Evidence for *-u*

Akkadian, Ugaritic, and Classical Arabic share only one environment in which *yaqtulu* is used, namely, certain types of subordinate clauses including relative clauses. Otherwise, the function of this verbal form does not overlap in East and West Semitic. In East Semitic, it is a subordinate marker for all types of subordinate clauses, and it is used in oaths. In West Semitic, *yaqtulu* primarily marks aspect, more specifically imperfective aspect, including present and future tense. It also appears in most types of subordinate clauses. For limitations on the use of *-u* in subordinate clauses in Classical Arabic, see §3.1 below. Lastly, in rare instances, the ending *-u* can occur in conditional clauses in Classical Arabic and Ugaritic.

2.6. The Ending *-u*: Functional Reconstruction

The etymological relationship of *yaqtulu* in East and Central Semitic is widely accepted.[23] The more difficult issue is the functional relation of *yaqtulu* in these two branches of Semitic. The main question regarding the ending *-u* is whether it originally reflected indicative or subordinating function. Most scholars consider the use of **yaqtulu* in subordinate function original while its use as imperfect indicative is thought to be secondary. The

[20] Fischer 1987, pp. 93–94.

[21] Fischer 1987, p. 194.

[22] Wright 1898, vol. 2, p. 40.

[23] See, e.g., Kienast 1960, p. 154.

subordinate function of this verbal form is further often connected to relative clauses. Kuryłowicz, for example, who suggested that *yaqtulu* might be of nominal origin, thought that it was originally only used after relative pronouns, as in *ša ikšudu*, which he considers to have had the meaning 'le vainqueur de' before its verbalization.[24] In his opinion, *yaqtulu* thus functions like the nominative.[25] A similar original restriction of *yaqtulu* to relative clauses has been suggested by Kienast with regard to Akkadian. Kienast assumes that relative clauses originally were dependent on a noun in the construct, as in *bīt īpušu* 'the house he built,' since, according to him, it is not possible to reconstruct a single form of the relative pronoun for Proto Semitic.[26] When a relative clause is dependent on a noun in the construct, it is solely the form of the verb that marks relativizing function since the construct itself does not express this function. With the development of relative pronouns, the old relative form, according to Kienast, lost its restricted use and was extended to other subordinate clauses in Akkadian, while in West Semitic, it was expanded beyond the subordinate clause.[27] The same basic assumption that *yaqtulu* originates in subordinate clauses, although without the limitation on relative clauses, is found in Hamori's study of the Semitic verbal system, where he claims that the transition from subordinate to imperfect indicative happened through circumstantial constructions involving the imperfect that had a close parallel in relative clauses.[28] This means that a sentence like "a man came in speaking (IMPF)" has a very similar meaning to "a man came in who spoke (SUBJ)," where the first is expressed by an imperfect and the second by a subordinate marker. The semantic similarity of these two constructions, according to Hamori, led to the extension of the use of *yaqtulu* from subordinate clauses to circumstantial constructions and subsequently to a generalization of *yaqtulu* as general imperfect indicative.

The development suggested by Hamori from relative clause > circumstantial > imperfect indicative is, in my opinion, very convincing. He has proven with relative certainty that the subordinating function of *-u*, as suggested by various scholars before him, is more original than its use as imperfect indicative. The subordinating function should thus be reconstructed as the primary function of *-u*.

3. The Ending *-a*: Distribution and Function

A verbal ending *-a* is, just like *-u*, attested in Central Semitic languages, more specifically in Classical Arabic, Ugaritic, early Canaanite, and Hebrew. In addition, a form *iprusa* occurs in a few texts in a sub-corpus of Old Akkadian.

3.1. The Function of *-a* in Classical Arabic

The subjunctive of Classical Arabic primarily occurs in subordinate clauses. As such it expresses an act that is dependent on that mentioned in the previous clause.[29] It occurs after the particles *ʾan* 'that' and *ʾallā* 'that not,' after which it expresses intention, wish, expectation, command, or prohibition.

For a wish:

ʾarad-tu	*wa-ʾaḥbab-tu*	*ʾan*	*ʾu-bayyin-a*
wish.PERF-1cs	and-desire.PERF-1cs	that	1cs-make.clear-SUBJ

la-hum	*ṭarīq-a*	*t-taʿallum-i*
to-3mp.GEN	way-ACC	DEF-learning-GEN

'I wished and desired to make clear to them the path of learning'

---

[24] Kuryłowicz 1949, p. 53.

[25] Kuryłowicz 1949, p. 54.

[26] For the assumption that it is possible to reconstruct a full paradigm of relative pronouns for Proto Semitic, see, for example, Huehnergard 2006, p. 118, and Hasselbach 2007, pp. 20, 24.

[27] Kienast 1960, pp. 155–58.

[28] Hamori 1973. A connection of *yaqtulu* with subordinate clauses has also been suggested by Lipiński, although he further claims that *-u* reflects an original ergative case (2001, p. 359). Voigt likewise assumes that the West Semitic imperfect goes back to a relative construction that corresponds to the Akkadian subjunctive (1997, p. 218).

[29] Wright 1898, vol. 2, pp. 24–26.

For a command:

ʾamar-tu-ka *bi-ʾan* *ta-fʿal-a* *kaḏā*
command.PERF-1cs-2ms.ACC in-that 2ms-do-SUBJ thus
'I commanded you to do thus/such a thing'

The omission of *ʾan* before the subjunctive is very rare.

It further occurs after a number of particles meaning 'that, in order that,' including *kay*, *li-*, *liʾan*, and *ḥattā*. These particles introduce purpose clauses and indicate the intention of the agent:[30]

tub *li-ya-ġfir-a* *la-ka* *llāh-u*
repent.IMP.ms so.that-3ms-forgive-SUBJ to-2ms god-NOM
'repent, so that god may forgive you'

The subjunctive originally only occured after *ʾan* and *ḥattā* when these particles express intent or consequence/result, otherwise the perfect or imperfect are used. In post-Classical Arabic, the use of the subjunctive has been extended so that it occurs regularly after these two particles.[31]

It is further used after *fa-* when the particle "introduces a clause that expresses the result or effect of a preceding clause":[32]

ʾiġfir *l-ī* *yā* *rabb-i* *fa-ʾa-dḫul-a* *l-jannat-a*
forgive.IMP.ms to-1cs VOC lord-1cs that-1cs-enter-SUBJ DEF-garden-ACC
'forgive me, o my lord, so that I may enter Paradise'

The preceding clause in this case has to contain an imperative or another modal form expressing a wish. In this use, *fa-* is equivalent to *ḥattā* with the meaning 'in order that, so that.'

The subjunctive can further follow *ʾaw* when it is used with the meaning 'unless (that),' that is, when it is semantically equivalent to *ʾillā ʾan*. It also occurs after the particle *ʾiḏan* 'in that case' when it begins a clause that expresses result or effect.[33]

la-ʾa-qtul-anna *l-kāfir-i* *ʾaw* *yu-slim-a*
truly-1cs-kill-ENER DEF-unbeliever-GEN unless 3ms-surrender-SUBJ
'I will certainly kill the unbeliever, unless he becomes a Muslim'

ʾiḏan *lā* *ʾu-hīn-a-ka*
well.then not 1cs-insult-SUBJ-2ms.ACC
'well then, I will not insult you'

In all these usages, the subjunctive has future sense.[34]

Furthermore, the subjunctive is used for negating the future after the particle *lan* (*< *lā ʾan*):[35]

lan *ya-zūr-a-ka* *ʾabadan*
not 3ms-visit-SUBJ-2ms.ACC ever
'he will never visit you'

The appearance of the subjunctive after this negative particle clearly seems to be motivated by the fact that it contains *ʾan*.

30 Wright 1898, vol. 2, p. 28.
31 Fischer 1987, p. 97.
32 Wright 1898, vol. 2, p. 30.
33 Wright 1898, vol. 2, p. 33.
34 Wright 1898, vol. 2, p. 22.
35 Fischer 1987, p. 97.

Lastly, there are instances in which the subjunctive can be used in conditional clauses: when a verb in the jussive in either the protasis or apodosis is followed by another verb that is connected by either *fa-* or *wa-*, the second verb can occur in the subjunctive, although this use is rare. In this environment, the jussive and indicative can occur as well.[36]

To summarize, the subjunctive in Classical Arabic expresses wish, command, and purpose, although only in subordinate clauses.[37]

3.2. The Use of *-a* in Ugaritic

Ugaritic likewise has a form of the prefix conjugation ending in *-a*. This ending can so far only be traced in the 1cs and 3ms in roots III-ʾ in volitive function, that is, when it functions like the jussive.[38]

uba
'I shall enter'

i-qra	*ilm*	*nʿ[mm]*
1cs-call.COH	gods	pleasant

'I shall call the pleasant gods'

Attestations for other persons are doubtful. In volitive function, the seemingly same notion can usually also be expressed by the jussive instead of *yaqtula*.[39]

3.3. The Use of *-a* in Early Canaanite

Early Canaanite *yaqtula*, also called "subjunctive" or "volitive," is used for all persons, although the forms known so far comprise only singular and 1cp forms. It is used to express wish, request, and demand, in addition to purpose clauses. The latter occurs when the clause is dependent on another injunctive clause.[40]

For wish, request, and demand:

kīnanna	*yu-ḫammiṭ-a*
thus	3ms-hasten-SUBJ

'thus may he hasten'

ul	*yu-paḫḫir-a*
not	3ms-assemble-SUBJ

'let him not assemble'

[36] Wright 1898, vol. 2, p.40.

[37] See also Blau 1971, p. 142; Kienast 1960, pp. 155, 164; Lipiński 2001, p. 360.

[38] Tropper 2000, pp. 455–56.

[39] Tropper 2000, pp. 456.

[40] Rainey 1996, vol. 2, pp. 255–57. According to Moran, the form *yaqtula* occurs seventy-four times in the six letters from Byblos. Of these occurrences, thirty-six seem to be direct volitive and thirteen indirect volitive, meaning they occur after another injunctive form such as the imperative (Moran 1960, p. 11). Moran states that there is a clear contrast in use between *yaqtulu* and *yaqtula* in the Byblos letters, which, according to him, proves that *yaqtula* does not represent the Akkadian ventive (ibid., pp. 6–8, 11). For an interpretation of most of these *yaqtula* forms as volitive, see also Blau 1971, pp. 135–36. Another argument against the interpretation of these forms as ventive is that the ventive is no modal form but a directional morpheme, while many of the occurrences of *yaqtula* in early Canaanite are clearly modal. For the interpretation of the ventive as non-modal see Edzard 1973, p. 127. Despite following Moran's ground-breaking analysis from 1960 in principle, Rainey concludes, "It is abundantly clear that the EA texts have not given us any conclusive evidence for the existence of a Canaanite *yaqtula* pattern" (Rainey 1996, vol. 2, p. 262). At the same time, Rainey argues in favor of a Northwest Semitic *yaqtula* pattern based on comparative evidence from Arabic (subjunctive), Hebrew (cohortative), and a Ugaritic example (ibid.).

For purpose clause:

a-qbi	*ana kâta*	*lā*	*i-leʾʾu*	*u-ššar-šu*	*ul*	*yi-šma*	*Abdi-Aširta*
1cs-say.PRET	to you.ACC	not	1cs-be.able	1cs-send-3ms.ACC	not	3ms-hear.SUBJ	PN

'I said to you: I am not able to send him lest Abdi-Aširta hear …'

The indirect volitive that denotes purpose or intended result occurs in paratactic sentence structures and contrasts with *yaqtulu* that states a simple fact.[41] An important observation made by Moran is that the use of *yaqtula* in purpose clauses is governed by what he calls "modal congruence." Modal congruence means that when the first clause states a fact in the perfect or indicative, the purpose clause is likewise in the indicative. When the first clause, however, has an imperative, jussive, or *yaqtula* form expressing wish, the purpose clause verb is either in the jussive or in the volitive, meaning it conforms to the injunctive form of the first clause.[42]

Lastly, *yaqtula* can appear in both the protasis and apodosis of conditional clauses:[43]

In protasis:

inūma	*a-mūt-a*	*mīnu*	*yi-naṣṣar-ū-ši*
if	1cs-die-SUBJ	who	3m-protect-pl-3fs.ACC

'if I die, who will protect it?'

In apodosis:

šumma	*i-rām*	*šarr-u*	*bēl-ī*	*abad*	*kitt-ī-šu*	*u*
if	3ms-love	king-NOM	lord-1cs	servant.CSTR	faith-GEN-3ms.GEN	and

uššir-a	*3 awīl-ē*	*u*	*i-bluṭ-a*	*u*	*i-naṣṣir-a*	*āl-am*	*ana*	*šarr-i*
send.IMP-SUBJ	3 men-ACC	and	1cs-live-SUBJ	and	1cs-guard-SUBJ	city-ACC	for	king-GEN

'If the king, my lord, cares for his faithful servant, send the three men that I may survive and that I may protect the city for the king'

The form *yaqtula* can thus be used in the same environments as the jussive in early Canaanite. Rainey states that the examples from the El-Amarna correspondence seem to suggest that *yaqtula* was used in almost complete parallelism with the jussive.[44]

3.4. The Use of the Cohortative in Hebrew

The cohortative in Hebrew occurs primarily in the first person with only a few exceptions. The basic meaning of the cohortative is, as stated by Gesenius and Kautzsch (1910, p. 130), as follows: "The *cohortative* expresses the direction of the will to an action and thus denotes especially self-encouragement (in the 1st plur. an exhortation to others at the same time), a resolution or a wish." Waltke and O'Connor (1990, p. 573) state that the Hebrew cohortative has two main functions: (1) as "direct volitive" expressing a wish, request, or command, and (2) as "indirect volitive" in clauses of purpose or intended result.[45] This functional distinction of the cohortative is syntactically conditioned by whether it occurs in independent or dependent clauses. In independent clauses, the cohortative expresses will. When it follows an imperative or jussive after *waw*, it expresses intention or intended consequence, that is, purpose.

---

[41] Blau 1971, p. 136.

[42] Moran 1960, pp. 8–10. Moran claims that this modal congruence is rigorously observed in early Canaanite (ibid.). He also claims that the same modal congruence is attested in Classical Arabic when *yaqtula* is used after *fa-* and the latter stands after an imperative, negative command, wish, jussive, or particle of exhortation or reproach. Moran states that "one seems to discern an older rule of modal congruence," meaning that *yaqtula* was originally a modal form corresponding to such forms as the jussive and imperative (Moran 1960, p. 12).

[43] Rainey 1996, vol. 2, p. 260.

[44] Rainey 1996, vol. 2, p. 263.

[45] For this type of distinction, see also Blau 1971, p. 133, where he calls the indirect use "volitive."

For wish/will:

ʾē-ləḵ-ā	*wə-ʾe-rʾ-ennû*
1cs-go.IMPF-COH	and-1cs-see.IMPF-3ms.ACC

'I will go and see him' (Gen 45:28)

nē-ləḵ-ā	*dōṯāyn-ā*
1cp-go.IMPF-COH	Dotan-DIR

'let's go to Dotan' (Gen 37:17)

For purpose:

wə-hāḇîʾ-ā	*l-î*	*wə-ʾō-ḵēl-ā*
and-bring.IMP.ms-3fs.ACC	to-1cs	and-1cs-eat.IMPF-COH

'and bring it to me so that I may eat' (Gen 27:4)

In these cases the purpose clause is governed by the same rule of modal congruence as mentioned in the case of early Canaanite.[46]

The cohortative can further appear in conditional clauses, in both the protasis and apodosis.[47]

In protasis:

ʾīm	*ʾ*^{a}*-ḏabbər-ā*	*lō(ʾ)*	*yē-ḥāśēḵ*	*kəʾēḇ-î*
if	1cs-speak.IMPF-COH	not	3ms-be.relieved.IMPF	pain-1cs.GEN

'if I speak, my pain is not relieved' (Job 16:6)

In apodosis:

mî—yi-ttən-ēnî	*šāmîr*	*šayiṯ*	*b-am-milḥāmā*	*ʾe-pśəʿ-ā*	*b-āh*
who—3ms-give.IMPF-1cs.ACC	briars	thorns	in-DEF-war	1cs-march-COH	in-3fs

'if only there were briars and thorns confronting me, I would march against them in battle'
lit., 'whoever would give me briars and thorns ...' (Isa 27:4)

In the rare occurrences when *-a* is found on a third-person verb, it expresses wish in independent clauses:[48]

hā-ʾōmərîm	*yə-mahēr*	*yā-ḥîš-ā*
DEF-say.PTC.ACT.mp	3ms-make.haste.IMPF	3ms-speed.IMPF-COH

maʿ^{a}*śē-hû*	*ləmaʿan*	*ni-rʾe*
deed-3ms.GEN	so.that	1cp-see.IMPF

'who say: let him make haste, let him speed his work that we may see' (Isa 5:19)

The Hebrew cohortative is thus functionally close to early Canaanite *yaqtula* as analyzed by Moran. In fact, Moran claims that almost two-thirds of *yaqtula* forms in the Byblos letters conform exactly to the use of the cohortative in Biblical Hebrew.[49]

---

[46] Moran 1960, p. 11.

[47] Gesenius and Kautzsch 1910, p. 320; Waltke and O'Connor 1990, pp. 574–75. According to Blau, the use of the cohortative in *ʾim*-clauses in Biblical Hebrew is rare and only a marginal phenomenon (Blau 1971, p. 134).

[48] Gesenius and Kautzsch 1910, p. 130; Moran 1960, p. 11.

[49] Moran 1960, pp. 1–6. See also Blau 1971, p. 135.

3.5. Derivation of the Hebrew Cohortative

The etymological and functional connection between early Canaanite *yaqtula* and the Hebrew cohortative has been recognized ever since Moran's groundbreaking study of the forms.[50] The use of *yaqtula* in Ugaritic likewise fits the functional range of the corresponding forms in Canaanite, so that we can say that Northwest Semitic languages exhibit a uniform functional range of this verbal form. The more problematic question is how the Northwest Semitic forms relate to the subjunctive attested in Classical Arabic. In the scholarly literature, we find two main derivations for the Hebrew cohortative, both of which connect it to verbal forms attested in Classical Arabic. The first suggested derivation is from the energic ending *-an*, a reconstruction that has found wide support among Semitic scholars.[51] Closely related to this derivation is the assumption that the Hebrew cohortative ultimately goes back to the ventive, since the ventive and energic are commonly assumed to be etymologically related.[52] The second proposed reconstruction connects the Hebrew cohortative to the Classical Arabic subjunctive ending *-a*.[53] Although there are still proponents of the first derivation today, Moran's paper on early Canaanite *yaqtula* contains important arguments against a derivation from the energic. Moran showed convincingly that early Canaanite *yaqtula* corresponds to a significant degree to the Hebrew cohortative in terms of function. Early Canaanite, however, has a separate energic form *yaqtulanna*. Thus, if any Classical Arabic form can correspond to the Hebrew cohortative, it is the subjunctive, not the energic.[54]

If the Classical Arabic subjunctive is related to Canaanite *yaqtula*, the question remains how to explain the functional differences between the two. Blau argued that it seems unlikely that the volitive developed from the subjunctive and that it is more likely that the volitive sense is the original one. Parallels for a development from volitive to subjunctive are, according to Blau, known from other languages. The use of *yaqtula* for the subjunctive presumably "developed from clauses in whose paratactic original form *yaqtula* was used to express volition."[55] Moran likewise explains the restricted use in Classical Arabic by an earlier paratactic stage. This earlier use can presumably still be noticed in the use of the subjunctive after *fa-*, *wa-*, and *ʾaw*, in clauses that have no introductory conjunctions, and in the rare use of the subjunctive in the protasis and apodosis of conditional clauses. All these usages, according to Moran, allow for the independent use of *yaqtula* found in the Amarna letters.[56] Although, as I argue in §4 below, I do not follow Moran's and Blau's directionality of the proposed semantic change, their arguments point to an important connection between the Classical Arabic and Northwest Semitic *yaqtula* forms. There are, as they show, a few usages of *yaqtula* that overlap in Canaanite and Classical Arabic. These include its use in purpose clauses and its use in conditional clauses, which argues in favor of a derivational relationship of the two types of *yaqtula*.

Before trying to connect the remainder of the functions, it is helpful to ask how we can categorize the Central Semitic *yaqtula* forms functionally and from a cross-linguistic perspective.

Modal forms have often been described — based on an Indo-European model primarily established on the basis of languages such as Classical Greek and Latin — in terms of realis ~ irrealis, which can also be expressed as indicative ~ subjunctive.[57] There are, of course, well-known inherent problems in transferring both the terminology and definition of grammatical forms and concepts from one language/language family to another. I nevertheless start with a general description of indicative ~ subjunctive based on the Indo-European understanding of the terms and, I hope, show that they, in this particular case, can indeed be applied to the Semitic evidence.

The subjunctive as described in typological literature has several main functions and syntactic characteristics. It is primarily found in subordinate clauses, that is, it is the typical mood used for subordination.[58] This

[50] Before the discovery of *yaqtula* in early Canaanite, it had been suggested that the Hebrew cohortative was derived from locative *-h* or from a demonstrative. For a discussion of the history of the derivation of the Hebrew cohortative, see Israel 2007, p. 115.

[51] For a discussion, see Israel 2007, p. 117.

[52] This derivation has, for example, been suggested by Voigt (1997, p. 220; 1999, p. 13). See also Lipiński 2001, p. 361, and Israel 2007, pp. 123, 134. The latter assumes that there are two main hypotheses for the derivation of the cohortative: first from the energic and second from the ventive (ibid.). Since the energic and ventive most likely go back to the same original morpheme, the "two" hypotheses cited by Israel are considered a single one in this paper.

[53] For a discussion of the two derivations, see also Blau 1971, p. 135.

[54] Moran (1960, p. 17) states that the existence of early Canaanite *yaqtula* establishes the origin of the Hebrew cohortative from *yaqtula*, not *yaqtulan*. See also Blau 1971, p. 135.

[55] Blau 1971, p. 143.

[56] Moran 1960, p. 12.

[57] Palmer 2001, p. 3.

[58] Palmer 2001, p. 5.

close connection has led to the statement by some linguists that one of the functions of the subjunctive is "simply that of being subordinate."[59] The use in subordinate clauses can even be extended to clauses that have no inherent notion of irrealis. The functions of the subjunctive in subordinate clauses can be quite varied, typically more varied than in main clauses. Some of its main functions in subordinate clauses include future reference and the expression of wishes, fears, commands, and requests. It is further often used to indicate what is reported, as in German "er sagte er wäre krank," that is, it is used after verbs of speaking and so on.[60] The subjunctive is common in temporal clauses to refer to hypothetical future events. More importantly, it is used in conditional clauses in several languages, including Classical Greek and Latin. It is also often attested in purpose clauses. Indo-European languages that make such use of the subjunctive include Classical Greek, Latin, Spanish, and Italian.[61] When no notion of purpose is present in these languages, they use the indicative instead.

In main clauses, the subjunctive is used for wishes referring to the future, as, for example, attested in Latin, Italian, and Portuguese.[62] The subjunctive is further used instead of an imperative or jussive to express a polite command in Italian and Spanish and as a notional jussive for the first person in Classical Greek and Spanish ("let us sail").[63]

Almost all the functions of the subjunctive attested in Indo-European languages have correspondences in Semitic. In Semitic, the subjunctive of Arabic is primarily found in subordinate clauses, reflecting its common association with subordination cross-linguistically. In subordinate clauses, it can appear for purpose clauses, which is attested in Classical Arabic, Hebrew, and early Canaanite, and for content clauses after verbs of speaking, commanding, wishing, and believing, which is the typical construction of these clauses in Classical Arabic, where content clauses are introduced by the particle *ʾan* followed by a verb in the subjunctive. In main clauses, it primarily expresses wish or corresponds to the jussive, which is the situation we find in Ugaritic, early Canaanite, and Hebrew. The subjunctive can appear in conditional clauses, which we find, although not as a common construction, in all the Semitic languages under discussion. Lastly, the subjunctive, especially in subordinate clauses, tends to have future reference, which is, again, exactly what we find in Classical Arabic. It is therefore, in my opinion, justified to functionally identify Central Semitic *yaqtula* with what is commonly called the "subjunctive" in typological literature. This identification also allows us to explain the restriction of the morpheme to subordinate clauses in Classical Arabic and its seemingly unusual occurrences in conditional clauses. How the syntactic limitations in Classical Arabic might have arisen will further be discussed in §4 below.[64]

3.6. The Use of *-a* in Old Akkadian

It has been a matter of dispute whether Old Akkadian possesses a form that corresponds morphologically to Central Semitic *yaqtula*. In a sub-corpus of Old Akkadian texts from the Diyala region of Iraq, a form *iprusa* appears a few times in subordinate clauses. Kienast argued that these *iprusa* forms reflect ventives without mimation.[65] This interpretation faces the problem that the ventive is not otherwise attested without mimation in Old Akkadian. Other scholars have thus argued that the *iprusa* forms are not related to the ventive but rather represent a subordinating morpheme that reflects either a different Akkadian dialect or an Amorite substrate.[66]

---

[59] Jespersen as quoted in Palmer 2001, p. 108.

[60] Palmer 2001, pp. 111–13.

[61] Palmer 2001, pp. 125–28.

[62] Palmer 2001, p. 132.

[63] Palmer 2001, pp. 138–40.

[64] In other language families, especially Native American families and those of Papua New Guinea, the terms "realis" and "irrealis" have been adopted to describe basically the same contrast as the one expressed by "indicative" and "subjunctive" in Indo-European. The basic functions of the realis/irrealis markers are the same as in Indo-European, that is, the irrealis can express future events, commands, exhortations, warnings, etc. (Palmer 2001, pp. 145–48). There is thus not always a clear functional distinction between the two sets of terms. The function in main clauses, however, can differ. The use of the subjunctive in main clauses does not commonly include the notions of denial and futurity or its use in questions. These notions are, however, associated with the irrealis (Palmer 2001, pp. 186–88). The subjunctive further has a stronger association with subordinate clauses than the irrealis. Lastly, realis/irrealis systems are often binary, while indicative/subjunctive systems often also include a jussive and imperative (ibid., pp. 186–88). The Semitic evidence is thus closer to the Indo-European concept of indicative/subjunctive than to realis/irrealis.

[65] Kienast 1960, p. 152 n. 2; 2001, p. 272.

[66] Edzard 1973, p. 127; Hasselbach 2005, p. 204. Edzard leaves the question of the origin of the *iprusa* forms open, while others, such as Israel, assume that these forms are from Amorite (Israel 2007, p. 131).

In order to understand the use of *iprusa* in Old Akkadian, it is helpful to look at the attestations of the morpheme. There are only five attestations of *iprusa* known to me:

1 PN, 1 PN, 1 PN. ... ŠU.NIGÍN 10 LAL 2 AB+ÁŠ-*bu-ut mu-tu-tu* É *a-na* DINGIR-*a-zu* ***iš-du-da***

'1 PN. ... Total of 8 witnesses that Mututu measured the house for Ilum-asû.' (OAIC 1)

PN, PN ... AB+ÁŠ 1 (PI) ŠE *gi-nu-nu a-na dar-e-tum* ***i-ti-na*** GEMÉ *ib-bu-bu*

'PN ... witnesses that Ginunu gave one PI of barley to Darʾetum, slave girl of Ibbubu.' (OAIC 3)

PN, PN ... AB+ÁŠ *en-ma ma-nu-nu a-na gi-nu-nu in* É *ši* ***uš-da-a-bi-la*** *a-na si-tim* ŠÁM-*me lu-uš-ku-ul-kum*

'PN ... witnesses that Manunu thus (said) to Ginunu: In the house which I considered, let me weigh out the rest (lit. for/to) of the price for you.' (OAIC 10)

3 QA ZÍD.GU 1 QA ŠU.I 1 QA KUG.BABBAR-*sa* 1 QA ANŠE.LIBIR.SAL *šu a-na šu-ni-tum* ***a-ti-na***

'(Of the) 3 QA of GU-flour, 1 QA: the barber; 1 QA: Kaspūša; 1 QA: the mare. That is what I gave to Šunîtum.' (OAIC 21)

10 ŠE.GUR ŠE.ḪAR.A[N] *na-bí-um ik-sur* 10 (GUR) *na-bí-um a-na e-na-na* EDIN *i-dím* ŠE.ḪAR.AN *è-ni-um šu na-bí-um in i-te-su* ***ik-su$_4$-ra*** 10 (GUR) *in* É-*ti la-ni* SAL.LÚ.TÚG 5 (GUR) *in* É-*ti* TÚG.DU$_8$ 5 GUR [...] *-lum*

'10 GUR of ḪAR.AN-barley Nabium bound/joined(?). 10 GUR Nabium gave(!) to Enana, the potter. (Of) the ḪAR.AN-barley of Enium which Nabium bound/joined(?) with his hand, 10 GUR are in the house of Lani the woman-fuller, 5 GUR are in the house of the upholsterer, 5 GUR ...' (OAIC 36:1–14)

All these occurrences appear in relative clauses, which can be either syndetic or asyndetic. The occurrences in OAIC 1, 3, and 21 clearly reflect verbs in subordinate function, twice dependent on a noun in the construct, and once dependent on the relative pronoun *šu*. OAIC 36 also clearly reflects a verb in subordinate function in a past-tense context dependent on a relative pronoun. The only occurrence that might be interpreted as reflecting a different, perhaps volitive, function is found in OAIC 10, where *iprusa* is followed by a precative and might be translated as "in the house that I shall consider, let me weigh out ..." — although it is difficult to prove such an interpretation, and thus I prefer the simple interpretation as subordinate form.

The interpretation of the ending *-a* in these texts as ventive without mimation is unlikely in my opinion because the same verbs, markedly *šadādum* and *nadānum*, are not used with the ventive in the same corpus when they are not in a subordinate clause; see, for example, *iš-du-ud* 'he measures' (OAIC 2:4; 8:21) and *i-ti-in* 'he gave' (OAIC 4:5). In the case of the semantically problematic verb *ik-su$_4$-ra*, the same verb occurs without *-a* in a main clause in the same text.

The fact that we are dealing with an allomorph of *-u* and not the ventive is further confirmed by texts of similar structure found in the same sub-corpus that use *-u* instead of *-a*, such as the following:

e-nu na-bí-um šu-ut gi-šum íl-gi-am-ma ***it-ba-lu*** *na-bí-um* KÁ [d]*Tišpak it-ma*

'(In respect to) the utensils of Nabium which Gišum took and carried away, Nabium swore in the gate of Tišpak.' (OAIC 7:21–26)

In this clause, we find the same dependency of a verb in the subordinate clause to a relative pronoun, although in this case the 3ms verb is marked by *-u* with another preceding subordinated verb that is marked by the ventive (*íl-gi-am-ma*), which clearly has mimation.

Given these facts, it seems very likely to me that we are indeed dealing with a subordinate marker and not with a shortened form of the ventive in these occurrences. The primary function of *iprusa* in Old Akkadian seems to be to mark a verb as subordinate, that is, it is functionally parallel to normative Akkadian *-u*, as also attested in the remainder of Old Akkadian texts from the Diyala region and beyond.

4. The Derivation of *-a* and *-u*

The question that remains is whether the Old Akkadian verbal ending *-a* and the Central Semitic ending *-a* can be connected etymologically. Most scholars who accept the existence of Old Akkadian *iprusa* are hesitant to claim a direct connection between the West and East Semitic morphemes because of their functional differences.[67] In East Semitic, *-a* is used as subordinate marker, while in West Semitic, it is a modal form, which, as argued above, can best be described as subjunctive from a cross-linguistic perspective. Blau suggested, based on Jacobsen, that *iprusa* in Old Akkadian presented the subject as "willing," in order to make a hypothetical connection with the Arabic subjunctive and Canaanite *yaqtula*.[68] Other scholars, such as Israel, assume that there is no relationship between the two morphemes.[69]

The solution to the functional problem, in my opinion, lies in the above-mentioned nominal derivation of verbal forms in Semitic. If the verbal forms themselves are derived from nominal clauses, it would be no surprise to find vestiges of the nominal morphology on these forms. Even without a derivational connection between nominal and verbal forms, it is a well-known phenomenon cross-linguistically that case markers can develop into non-case markers, especially into verbal affixes. In some instances, case itself can be marked on the verb. In others, the original case marker can be reinterpreted so that the original marking remains but signals a new function.[70] It has been observed that local expressions can develop into markers of tense and aspect. One example of such a development is found in Kala Lagua Ya, an Australian language, where almost the whole system of cases was transferred to the verbal system and developed into tense/aspect markers. The original ergative and accusative developed into completive, the dative/allative into incompletive, the comitative into habitual, the ablative into past tense expressing yesterday, and the locative into an immediate past marker.[71] Although this is not the situation we find in Semitic, it shows the potential connection between case and verbal markers.

Another common — and more relevant in our context — grammaticalization path is from case marker to clause subordinator, which is the most salient attested development. The development from case to subordinate marker is usually based on the principle of extension, meaning that the use of case markers is extended from (non-verbal) nouns to nominalized verbs such as the infinitive, gerundives, participles, and finally to subordinate clauses.[72] In many case languages, at least some type of subordinate clause is marked by historical case markers.[73]

The subordinate markers that arose from original case markers can further acquire new functions. As mentioned in §3.5 above, subordinate clauses tend to express modally marked meanings, which, in Indo-European terms, are commonly referred to as "subjunctive" or "irrealis." Because of this functional connection between clause subordination and certain modal functions, it may happen when a case marker has been grammaticalized into a clause subordinator, that it acquires modal meanings, specifically modal meanings associated with subjunctive moods.[74]

This means that we can trace a cross-linguistic grammaticalization path from case marker > subordinate marker > modal marker (= subjunctive-marker).

Considering the Semitic evidence, this development is extremely close to what we can observe in this language family. The nominative marker *-u*, as has been suggested before, grammaticalized into a subordinate marker, a development that corresponds to cross-linguistically common tendencies. In this function, it is attested in Akkadian. It then extended its function to main clauses on the basis of circumstantial constructions mentioned in §2.6 above, and it became the marker of the imperfective aspect in Central Semitic. The use of *yaqtulu* in certain subordinate clauses in all Central Semitic languages that preserve *yaqtulu* is a vestige of its original subordinating function. The use of *yaqtulu* in oaths in Akkadian might be connected to the tendency of subordinate clauses to

---

[67] This problem is independent of whether *yaqtula* in Old Akkadian is a substrate from another Semitic language such as Amorite.

[68] Blau 1971, pp. 143–44.

[69] Israel 2007, p. 132.

[70] Blake 2001, p. 180.

[71] Blake 2001, p. 180.

[72] In Semitic, nominalized verbs are, of course, marked with the same case markers as nouns in general, which might be interpreted as an initial step in an extension process as described here based on typological observations.

[73] Heine 2009, p. 468. In Tibeto-Burman Newari, the ergative/instrumental developed into a temporal clause subordinator that is suffixed to verbs (ibid.).

[74] Heine 2009, p. 469.

express modal notions and thus for the subordinate marking morpheme to be extended to modal functions since oaths are naturally related to wishes semantically and to conditional clauses syntactically.[75]

The situation concerning *yaqtula* is a bit more complex. Just like *-u*, the final *-a* in this form is the result of grammaticalization from an original case marker, the accusative. Also parallel to *-u*, it was first grammaticalized into a subordinate marker. This original function is attested in the examples from Old Akkadian cited above. Unlike *-u*, *-a* did not further grammaticalize into a tense/aspect marker but into a modal marker, as attested in Classical Arabic, early Canaanite, and Hebrew. The original connection of *-a* with subordination is still found in Classical Arabic, where *-a* primarily appears in subordinate clauses. In early Canaanite and Hebrew, its use was extended to main clauses, and it became a general marker of modality, specifically for the expression of wishes. This extension from subordinate to main clauses can explain the frequent functional overlap of *yaqtula* and the jussive in early Canaanite. This overlap is not original to the forms but the result of a secondary extension of the innovative modal form *yaqtula*.

The seemingly unbridgeable differences in the use of *yaqtula* in East and West Semitic are thus the result of a process of grammaticalization that was further advanced in West than in East Semitic — assuming that the Old Akkadian examples are not the result of substrate influence, in which case they would represent different stages of the grammaticalization process in the same sub-branch of Semitic.

To conclude, the verbal endings *-u* and *-a* are derived from original case markers. Both first grammaticalized into subordinate markers, corresponding to cross-linguistic tendencies — this initial grammaticalization process most likely occurred in Proto Semitic since we find verbal forms in *-u* and *-a* in all major branches of the language family. Subsequently, the two endings developed differently in individual sub-branches/languages of Semitic. The original association with subordination is still clearly noticeable for both endings. The rare usages of both endings in conditional clauses can be explained by their shared derivation and grammaticalization paths.

Abbreviation

OAIC — Ignace J. Gelb. *Old Akkadian Inscriptions in the Chicago Natural Museum: Texts of Legal and Business Interest.* Chicago: Chicago Natural History Museum, 1955.

Bibliography

Blakc, Barry J.
2001 *Case.* Cambridge: Cambridge University Press.

Blau, Joshua
1971 "Studies in Hebrew Verb Formation." *Hebrew Union College Annual* 42: 133–58.

Brockelmann, Carl
1908 *Grundriss der vergleichenden Grammatik der semitischen Sprachen,* Volume 1. Berlin: Reuther and Reichard.

[75] For a description of oaths in terms of wishful exclamations and their syntactic similarity to conditional clauses in Hebrew, see Waltke and O'Connor 1990, p. 679. For similar constructions in Akkadian, see Huehnergard 1998, p. 438. If this interpretation of *yaqtulu* in Akkadian oaths is correct, it implies that *-u*, similar to *-a* in West Semitic, developed certain restricted modal functions in East Semitic that are reflected in its use in oaths, despite its primary use as subordinate marker.

Edzard, Dietz O.

1973 "Die Modi beim älteren akkadischen Verbum." *Orientalia* 42: 121–41.

Fischer, Wolfdietrich

1987 *Grammatik des Klassischen Arabisch*. Porta linguarum orientalium 11. Wiesbaden: Harrassowitz.

Fleisch, Henri

1975 "Le verbe du sémitique commun les discussions a son sujet." *Semitica* 15: 5–18.

Gai, Amikam

1984 "Predicative State and Inflection of the Nominal Predicate in Akkadian and Syriac." *Afroasiatic Linguistics* 9: 72.

Gesenius, Wilhelm

1910 *Gesenius' Hebrew Grammar*. Edited by E. Kautzsch and A. E. Cowley. Second English edition. Oxford: Clarendon Press.

Goldenberg, Gideon

1983 "On Syriac Sentence Structure." In *Arameans, Aramaic and the Aramaic Literary Tradition*, edited by Michael Sokoloff, pp. 97–140. Ramat-Gan: Bar Ilan University Press.

Hamori, Andras

1973 "A Note on *Yaqtulu* in East and West Semitic." *Archiv Orientalni* 41: 319–24.

Hasselbach, Rebecca

2004 "The Markers of Person, Gender, and Number in the Prefixes of G-preformative Conjugations in Semitic." *Journal of the American Oriental Society* 124: 23–35.

2005 *Sargonic Akkadian: A Historical and Comparative Study of the Syllabic Texts*. Wiesbaden: Harrassowitz.

2007 "Demonstratives in Semitic." *Journal of the American Oriental Society* 127: 1–27.

Hecker, Karl

1968 *Grammatik der Kültepe-Texte*. Analecta orientalia 44. Rome: Pontificium Institutum Biblicum.

Heine, Bernd

2009 "Grammaticalization of Cases." In *The Oxford Handbook of Case*, edited by Andreĭ L'vovich Malchukov and Andrew Spencer, pp. 458–69. Oxford: Oxford University Press.

Hodge, Carleton T.

1974 "Verbum Mortuum est. Vivat Verbum!" *Language Sciences* 29: 22–23.

1975 "The Nominal Sentence in Semitic." *Afroasiatic Linguistics* 2/4: 1–7.

Huehnergard, John

1998 *A Grammar of Akkadian*. Harvard Semitic Studies 45. Atlanta: Scholars Press.

2006 "On the Etymology of the Hebrew Relative *šɛ-*." In *Biblical Hebrew in Its Northwest Semitic Setting: Typological and Historical Perspectives*, edited by Steven E. Fassberg and Avi Hurvitz, pp. 103–25. Winona Lake: Eisenbrauns.

Israel, F.

2007 "Il coortativo e le sue origine storiche." In *"Der seine Lust hat am Wort des Herrn!" Festschrift für Ernst Jenni zum 80. Geburtstag*, edited by Jürg Luchsinger, Hans-Peter Mathys, and Markus Saur, pp. 108–42. Münster: Ugarit.

Kienast, Burkhart

1960 "Das Punktualthema **japrus* und seine Modi." *Orientalia* 29: 151–67.

2001 *Historische semitische Sprachwissenschaft*. Wiesbaden: Harrassowitz.

Kuryłowicz, Jerzy

1949 "Le système verbal du Sémitique." *Bulletin de la Société de linguistique de Paris* 45: 47–56.

Leslau, Wolf

1967 "Hypothesis on a Proto-Semitic Marker of the Imperfect in Gurage." *Journal of Near Eastern Studies* 26: 121–25.

Lipiński, Edward

2001 *Semitic Languages: Outline of a Comparative Grammar*. Second edition. Orientalia Lovaniensia analecta 80. Leuven: Peeters.

Moran, W. L.
1960 "Early Canaanite *yaqtula*." *Orientalia* 29: 1–19.

Nöldeke, Theodor
1904 *Compendious Syriac Grammar*. Reprint 2001. Winona Lake: Eisenbrauns.

Palmer, Frank R.
2001 *Mood and Modality*. Second edition. Cambridge: Cambridge University Press.

Rainey, Anson F.
1996 *Canaanite in the Amarna Tablets*. 4 Volumes. Handbuch der Orientalistik 25. Leiden: Brill.

Rubin, Aaron D.
2005 *Studies in Semitic Grammaticalization*. Harvard Semitic Studies 57. Winona Lake: Eisenbrauns.

Tropper, Josef
2000 *Ugaritische Grammatik*. Alter Orient und Altes Testament 273. Münster: Ugarit-Verlag.

Voigt, Rainer
1997 "Zur Nominal- und Verbalnasalierung im Semitischen." *Zeitschrift für die Kunde des Morgenlandes* 87: 207–30.
1999 "Nominal (and Verbal) Nasalization and the Nominal Plural Morphemes in Semitohamitic." In *Afroasiatica Tergestina* (Papers from the 9th Italian Meeting of Afro-Asiatic [Hamito-Semitic] Linguistics Trieste, April 23–24, 1998), edited by Marcello Lamberti and Livia Tonelli, pp. 11–22. Padova: Unipress.

von Soden, Wolfram
1995 *Grundriss der akkadischen Grammatik*. 3rd edition. Analecta orientalia 33. Rome: Pontificium Institutum Biblicum.

Waltke, Bruce K., and Michael P. O'Connor
1990 *An Introduction to Biblical Hebrew Syntax*. Winona Lake: Eisenbrauns.

Wright, William
1890 *Lectures on the Comparative Grammar of the Semitic Languages*. Reprint 2002. Piscataway: Gorgias.
1898 *A Grammar of the Arabic Language*. Third edition. Reprint 1999. Cambridge: Cambridge University Press.

11

Ibn Khaldūn as a Historical Linguist with an Excursus on the Question of Ancient *gāf*

Wolfhart Heinrichs, Harvard University

When we examine the many selective translations of parts of Ibn Khaldūn's *Muqaddimah* that have been produced since the days of Silvestre de Sacy, we will mostly find his novel theories on history and society represented there.[1] And this is, of course, as it should be. But it is also in a sense regrettable, because the weighty last chapter of the *Muqaddimah*, chapter 6, stretching over more than the third volume in Rosenthal's translation, often does not receive the attention it deserves. In this chapter Ibn Khaldūn presents a grandiose picture of the *universitas litterarum islamicarum*, the system of Islamic disciplines and sciences.[2] This in itself may not make it interesting reading, since the genre dealing with the "division of sciences" was nothing new at the time of Ibn Khaldūn — it had been around since at least the fourth/tenth century. But Ibn Khaldūn does not, as he could have done, simply summarize what others have said in this respect.[3] On the contrary, not infrequently he adds a fresh and sometimes critical perspective to the topic at hand — a perspective that usually flows from the larger context of his developmental theory of culture and society. If I am not mistaken, the only work specifically devoted to chapter 6 of the *Muqaddimah* is the 1912 doctoral dissertation of Simon van den Bergh.[4] Very little attention has, however, been given to Ibn Khaldūn's ideas concerning language and linguistics — this despite the fact that some of these ideas are rather revolutionary. Kees Versteegh has included a section from the *Muqaddimah* plus commentary in his fascinating book on the Arabic linguistic tradition, but to my mind he did not pick the most interesting passage.[5]

In what follows, I would like to subject to a close reading a passage that deals with the language of the Bedouins at the time of Ibn Khaldūn. I should add that the chapter subjected here to close scrutiny and commentary and dealing specifically with Bedouin dialects by no means exhausts Ibn Khaldūn's treatment of linguistic themes. He has much more to say about the old *fuṣḥā*; he discusses the urban dialects and the influence of substratum and adstratum languages, and he has much to say about language instruction. One need only follow up the many references given in the index of Rosenthal's translation under "language, linguistics" to get an impression of the full breadth of his interest in language matters.

---

[1] See, e.g., Silvestre de Sacy 1826–27, vol. 1, pp. 370–411, vol. 2, pp. 279–336, vol. 3, pp. 342–46; Schimmel 1951; Bousquet 1961; 1965.

[2] Some of the anthologies do include excerpts from chapter 6; thus, e.g., Silvestre de Sacy 1829, pp. 167–86 [Arabic], 408–47, 472–76; Issawi 1950, pp. 149–79; Labica 1965, pp. 137–77; likewise the Arabic selection by Pérès (1947, pp. 60–70).

[3] See, e.g., Heinrichs 1995, pp. 119–39.

[4] Van den Berg 1912. With regard to language, the author deals only with Ibn Khaldūn's description of the four linguistic disciplines (*naḥw* "grammar," *lugha* "lexicography," *bayān* "rhetoric," and *adab* "philology" [in the old sense of "love for language and literature"]), not with the latter's own linguistic ideas.

[5] Versteegh 1997, pp. 153–65. Two earlier works on Ibn Khaldūn's attitude and approach to language, Arabic first and foremost, deserve mention here: Irving 1959, pp. 185–92; and Cooke 1984, pp. 27–36. Their focus is different, as neither deals with the unusual historical-linguistic perspective proposed by Ibn Khaldūn. The same is true for the more recent article by Ben-Ari (2009, pp. 219–30).

As a general framework for the treatment of this topic before Ibn Khaldūn, I may mention the following:

(1) There was no scholarly interest in dialects, except in the context of the poetics of *zajal*, the — originally Andalusian — dialect poetry.[6] It is only much later that Yūsuf al-Maghribī (d. 1019/1611) compiled a dictionary of Egyptian Arabic words, but even he is, at least explicitly, more interested in proving the true "Arabicness" of these words rather than taking them for what they are: words from a different register, or even a different variety, of the Arabic language.[7]

(2) The geographers at times make remarks about the linguistic situation of the region they are dealing with. Thus, al-Hamdānī (mid-fourth/tenth century) in his *Ṣifat Jazīrat al-ʿArab* describes the dialect geography in his native Yemen, but mainly in terms of good and bad Arabic and giving only general, impressionistic, details.[8] Similarly, al-Muqaddasī (d. after 381/991), in his *Aḥsan al-taqāsīm fī maʿrifat al-aqālīm*, often remarks on the linguistic peculiarities of the areas he describes.[9]

(3) If non-*fuṣḥā* Arabic is discussed at all, it is usually under the rubrics of *fasād* 'deterioration, corruption' and *laḥn* 'solecism' against the background of the pure *fuṣḥā* language. However, the works on *laḥn al-ʿāmma* (or: *laḥn al-ʿawāmm*) deal with solecisms of the semi-literate, not with the everyday speech of the person in the street.[10] Some of these mistakes may be used to infer dialect features, but it is not a rich source for this purpose.

Ibn Khaldūn, though certainly subscribing to the idea of the *fasād* of the pure Arabic language, does not simply reject the result of this *fasād* as worthless. In fact, he fights the prejudices of the well-educated elite with regard to the spoken language and attempts, quite successfully, to deal with it equitably and in historical perspective.

The passage I would like to look into deals with the language of the Bedouins at the time of Ibn Khaldūn. I shall follow Franz Rosenthal's translation (iii, 344–51),[11] with occasional suggestions for improvement.

The title of the section in question here is "Contemporary Arabic is an independent language different from the languages of the Muḍar and the Ḥimyar" (*fī anna lughata 'l-ʿarabi li-hādhā 'l-ʿahdi mustaqillatun mughāyiratun li-lughati Muḍara wa-Ḥimyar*). As Rosenthal remarks in a footnote, "Ibn Khaldūn is thinking here of Bedouin Arabic." This becomes, of course, clear from indications within the section, but it is already understood from the use of the term *ʿarab*, which, in the usage of Ibn Khaldūn as well as before and after him, predominantly refers to Bedouins (less frequently to urban speakers of Arabic, who are often not of pure Arab descent).[12] What he is saying, then, is that the Bedouin language of his day is a language separate from the language of the ancient Arabs, that is, the original *fuṣḥā* (why he uses *lughat Muḍar wa-Ḥimyar* for this is tentatively explained below). This is a distinctly novel idea, which implicitly removes the "corruption" label from this type of speech and endows it with the dignity of a legitimate language.

Ibn Khaldūn starts the section as follows: "We find that with regard to clear indication of what one wants to express and full expression of meaning, Arabic (as it is spoken today) follows the ways of the Muḍar language." In other words, with regard to the essential function(s) of language, contemporary Bedouin Arabic proceeds along the lines of the ancient *fuṣḥā*. By saying that, Ibn Khaldūn puts the two speech forms on an equal footing as languages. The name he uses for the ancient *fuṣḥā*, that is, *al-lisān al-muḍarī* (or: *lughat Muḍar*), is based on the idea that the Muḍar tribes (Muḍar b. Nizār b. Maʿadd b. ʿAdnān[13]) were farthest from any area where agriculture and

[6] The groundbreaking work is Ṣafī al-Dīn al-Ḥillī (d. ca. 749/1348): *al-Kitāb al-ʿĀṭil al-ḥālī wa-'l-murakhkhaṣ al-ghālī* (see Hoenerbach 1956). For linguistic peculiarities of *zajal*, see pp. 31–52 [Arabic], and Hoenerbach's list in his German analysis of the work, pp. 59–61.

[7] Yūsuf b. Zakariyyāʾ al-Maghribī: *Dafʿ al-iṣr ʿan kalām ahl Miṣr. Udaleniye bremeni bremeni s reči žiteley Egipta*, see ʿAwwād 1968; for the author's intentions, see folio 2a, lines 7–11: *fa-qaṣada 'l-faqīru Yūsufu 'l-Maghribiyyu — adkhalahū 'llāhu fī shafāʿati 'l-nabīyi 'l-ʿarabīyi — an yurattiba hādhā 'l-kitāba ʿalā abhaji 'l-tartīb / wa-yuhadhdhiba mā yaqaʿu min ʿawāmmi ahli Miṣra bi-an yurajjiʿahū ilā 'l-ṣawābi wa-hādhā huwa 'l-taʿrīb / mughtarifan mina 'l-Qāmūsi wa-'l-ʿUbāb / wa-mubayyinan limā ḥukima bi-khaṭāʾihī annahū ṣawāb.*

[8] See below, n. 29.

[9] See Miquel 1988, pp. 333–48.

[10] For an overview and evaluation of this literature, see ʿAbd al-Tawwāb 1967 and Maṭar 1966.

[11] To reduce the number of footnotes, I have inserted references to Rosenthal's translation in the text; I am quoting Rosenthal 1967. In the same way, I quote at times the French translations by Monteil 1967–1968 and Cheddadi 2002.

[12] See the important remarks in Mahdi 1964, pp. 199–200 n. 5; and the criticism of Rosenthal's equation *ʿarab* = "Arab" by Hodgson (1974, vol. 2, pp. 481–82 n. 13).

[13] ʿAdnān is the patriarch of the Northern Arabs, but Maʿadd, Nizār, and Muḍar are all used to designate the Bedouin population of Najd and adjacent areas.

animal husbandry could be found — that is, they were the most distant from Syria, Iraq (i, 266), and also Yemen; they were the true Bedouins, living hard lives, jealously guarding their pedigrees and their language.[14]

He continues, "The only loss is that of the vowels indicating the distinction between subject and object." This must be considered shorthand; obviously, Ibn Khaldūn must have been aware that the *iʿrāb* vowels also served other purposes. He may have been prompted to use this abbreviation by the sentence that follows: "Instead, one uses position within the sentence and syntactic combinations (*qarāʾin*) to indicate certain special meanings one wants to express." (Monteil [p. 1267]: "que l'on remplace par la position (respective des mots) dans les phrases et les combinaisons (*qarāʾin*) de syntaxe correspondant aux nuances de la pensée"; Cheddadi [p. 1106]: "Cela est remplacé par la position [des mots dans la phrase] et par les procédés [syntaxiques] qui indiquent certaines circonstances particulières que l'on veut exprimer.") This is a crucial sentence. Ibn Khaldūn shows an astonishing awareness of the fact that other linguistic phenomena may substitute for desinential inflection and make up for its lack; in other words, the lack is not a deficiency. But what exactly are these other phenomena? Rosenthal's translation may need some fine tuning here. The Arabic runs as follows: *fa-'ʿtāḍū minhā* [sc., *al-ḥarakāt*] *bi-'l-taqdīmi wa-'l-taʾkhīri wa-bi-qarāʾina tadullu ʿalā khuṣūṣiyyāti 'l-maqāṣidi*. The word pair *taqdīm wa-taʾkhīr* is a technical term in grammar and in rhetoric, indicating an unusual reversal of word order, usually for the purpose of emphasis.[15] But it seems clear that our author wants to use this term here in the vaguer sense of word order in general, so Rosenthal is certainly right when he interprets it as "position within the sentence." This, too, is a perspicacious insight on the part of Ibn Khaldūn. The change from the more synthetic *iʿrāb* Arabic to the more analytical *iʿrāb*-less Arabic entails a more rigid word order, a phenomenon that can be seen in the history of other languages as well and may even be universal[16] (compare the free Latin word order with the much more regulated word order in the Romance languages).[17] But what is the other element he mentions, the *qarāʾin*? Rosenthal's "syntactic combinations," which appear in Monteil's translation as *combinaisons de syntaxe*, and in Cheddadi's as *procédés [syntaxiques]*, is rather opaque and does not reflect the basic meaning of *qarīna*.[18] For a correct appraisal, we need to draw on the technical use of this term as it is found in grammatical discourse, a fact that has not yet attracted much attention. Ibn al-Ḥājib (d. 646/1249), in *al-Risāla al-kāfiya*, where he discusses the permissibility of the word order VOS, instead of the regular VSO, says in one passage, "If the nominal inflection is absent on the surface from both of them [i.e, subject and object, as in *ḍaraba ʿĪsā Mūsā*] and likewise the *qarīna* [is absent] ..., putting it [i.e., the subject] first is obligatory."[19] According to the commentator, Raḍī al-Dīn al-Astarābādhī (seventh/thirteenth century, exact dates unknown), the *qarīna* is a word or feature that disambiguates the syntactic functions of the ambiguous subject-object pair. It may be either a lexical or morphological item (*qarīna lafẓiyya*) or a semantic property (*qarīna maʿnawiyya*). Compare the following examples adduced by Raḍī al-Dīn:

ex. 1. *ḍaraba Mūsā ʿĪsā 'l-ẓarīfu* '(It was) ʿĪsā, the dandy, (who) beat Mūsā.' Here the apposition *al-ẓarīfu* shows that ʿĪsā is the subject; therefore, it is permissible to put the object, Mūsā, first.

ex. 2. *ḍarabat Mūsā ḥublā* '(It was) a pregnant woman (that) beat Mūsā.' Here the gender agreement shows that *ḥublā* is the subject, which makes this word order permissible.

ex. 3. *ḍaraba fatāhu Mūsā* '(It was) his slave (that) Mūsā beat.' If the intended meaning were "His slave beat Mūsā," the sentence would be ungrammatical; except for this very circumscribed situation, where the object precedes the subject, the anaphoric pronoun must not precede its antecedent.

---

[14] As Ibn Khaldūn explains elsewhere (i, 265–66), this would include tribes like Quraysh, Kināna, Thaqīf, Asad, Hudhayl, and Khuzāʿa, but exclude Ḥimyar, the Kahlān tribes (Lakhm, Judhām, Ghassān, Ṭayyiʾ, and Quḍāʿa), and Iyād. Muḍar's "brother," Rabīʿa, is not mentioned here either way, but elsewhere (iii, 343) they are listed alongside the Southern Arabs (Ḥimyar etc.); their "linguistic habits" are imperfect due to their proximity to the Persians.

[15] A highly sophisticated discussion of *taqdīm wa-taʾkhīr* may be found in Maḥmūd Muḥammad Shākir, ed., 1984, pp. 106–09.

[16] See the discussion in Harris and Campbell 1995, pp. 21ff., 233ff. I am grateful to John Huehnergard for drawing my attention to this reference.

[17] On the opposition "synthetic vs. analytic" as applied to *fuṣḥā* and Neo-Arabic, see the debate between Corriente and Blau: Federigo Corriente 1971, pp. 20–50; Joshua Blau 1972, pp. 29–38; F. Corriente 1973–74, pp. 154–63.

[18] Silvestre de Sacy (1829, p. 410) and de Slane (1868, p. 334) both render this term "certains accessoires," which is even vaguer.

[19] Mukarram (Makram?), ed., 2000, vol. 1, p. 184. See also al-Rifāʿī 1983, vol. 1, pp. 256–57, where Jāmī makes the important statement that the *qarīna* is something that disambiguates subject and object, but not as part of the original coining of the language (*lā bi-'l-waḍʿ*), as *iʿrāb* would be. Some criticism of this notion may be found in the gloss on Jāmī's commentary by ʿIṣām al-Dīn al-Isfarāʾīnī (1864, pp. 89–90).

ex. 4. *akala 'l-kummathrā Mūsā* '(It was) Mūsā (who) ate the pears.' Real-life probability determines subject and object.

ex. 5. *istakhlafa 'l-Murtaḍā 'l-Muṣṭafā* '(It was) al-Muṣṭafā [honorific of the Prophet] (who) appointed al-Murtaḍā [honorific of ʿAlī] his successor.' Chronology determines subject and object.

Examples 1–3 are examples of *qarāʾin lafẓiyya*, 4 and 5 of *qarāʾin maʿnawiyya*. If there is no *qarīna* to be detected, a sentence like *ḍaraba ʿĪsā Mūsā* can only mean 'ʿĪsā beat Mūsā.'

It seems very probable that Ibn Khaldūn had such instances of *qarīna* in mind when he characterized the syntactic means of Bedouin dialect. The peculiarity of these examples is, of course, that all subject and object nouns end in *alif maqṣūra* and, thus, show no overt inflection; by this fact they become an appropriate model for *iʿrāb*-less dialect Arabic.

In what follows Ibn Khaldūn presents a characterization of the old *fuṣḥā* (the Muḍar language, in his terminology), described in contrast to all other existing languages, including, it seems, the contemporary Bedouin Arabic. He does this in very abstract terms, which makes it rather difficult to discern to what he is alluding. He looks at the situation from the angle of *bayān* and *balāgha*, that is, clarity (in the sense of unambiguous expression) and optimal economy (this meaning of *balāgha* 'eloquence' becomes clear from subsequent indications of Ibn Khaldūn), and says that, in the old *fuṣḥā*, these qualities were more common and more deeply rooted. He proceeds to explicate this by stating first — and this seems to be a universal rule — that words per se indicate ideas per se (*al-alfāẓ bi-aʿyānihā dāllatun ʿalā 'l-maʿānī bi-aʿyānihā*). But this one-to-one relationship between words and ideas (or words and referents) is something like a series of dots of reality mapped onto language. The referents are surrounded by circumstances that specifically belong to them, and these, because they are attributes or characteristics of the referent, need to be taken into account, when it comes to the conveyance of what is intended to be said. Ibn Khaldūn says that this halo of circumstances is called *bisāṭ al-ḥāl*, which Rosenthal renders fairly literally as "the spread of the situation" and Monteil (p. 1267) as *l'exposé de l'état* [*des choses*] (but he mistranslates the sentence), while Cheddadi (p. 1107) omits the metaphor *bisāṭ* and says *les 'circonstances.'* The word *bisāṭ*, of course, also means 'carpet,' and I find the metaphorical interpretation quite appealing: the "carpet of the situation" — with all its threads and patterns and colors. *En passant* one might note that, by introducing the genitive construct *bisāṭ al-ḥāl* with the phrase *yusammā* 'it is called,' Ibn Khaldūn intimates that this is a technical term of sorts. One wonders in what context it was historically invented. Rosenthal provides quotation marks but no reference (nor do Monteil and Cheddadi). It is not listed in the large dictionary of technical terms by al-Tahānawī (d. after 1158/1745), the *Kashshāf iṣṭilāḥāt al-funūn*.

Now with regard to this "carpet of the situation" that surrounds each referent, there is a difference between the old *fuṣḥā* and all other languages in the way they express it linguistically. In the other languages, the circumstances are as a rule expressed by words that have been specifically coined for them. In the old *fuṣḥā*, however, they are expressed by certain conditions and peculiarities in the combinations and compositions of words, such as changed word order (*taqdīm wa-taʾkhīr*), ellipsis (*ḥadhf*), inflectional vowels (*ḥarakāt iʿrāb*), and at times also the use of non-independent particles (*al-ḥurūf ghayr al-mustaqillah*). These four linguistic phenomena probably do not constitute an exhaustive list, and they are rather inhomogeneous. What they have in common is the fact that they convey meaning without the help of full-fledged words.[20] This is also the reason that Arabic is terser and less prolix than other languages. Fortunately, Ibn Khaldūn adduces at least one example to make his point (iii, 345); it is an anecdote involving the early grammarian ʿĪsā b. ʿUmar (d. 149/766–67) and an anonymous colleague of his. The latter said to ʿĪsā, "I find duplications in Arabic speech. The (three) sentences, 'Zayd is standing' [*Zaydun qāʾimun*], 'Behold, Zayd is standing' [*inna Zaydan qāʾimun*], and 'Behold, Zayd is indeed standing' [*inna Zaydan la-qāʾimun*] all mean the same." ʿĪsā replied,

> (No! All three) mean something different. The first (sentence) gives information to a person who has no previous knowledge as to whether Zayd is standing (or not). The second (sentence) gives information to a person who has heard about it but is uncertain about it.[21] And the third (sentence) gives information to a

[20] See also Rosenthal 1967 III, p. 321, where the same idea is expressed, exemplified, in this passage, by *iʿrāb* vowels and patterns of nominalization.

[21] Both Rosenthal and Cheddadi (2002, p. 1107) have "denies" (*nie*); the Arabic has *taraddada fīh* 'is uncertain about it,' which Monteil (1967–1968, p. 1268) correctly renders "La seconde (i.e., *inna Zaydan qāʾimun*) rassure un hésitant."

person who knows it but persists in denying it. Thus, the meaning differs according to the different situations (one wants to express).

One might mention in passing that this story is a migrant anecdote. It is also told, though with some variation in the explicated meanings ("information," "answer to a question," "answer to a denial"), as a dialogue between the grammarian al-Mubarrad (d. 285–286/898–899) and the philosopher al-Kindī (d. after 252/865).[22] This situates it in the incipient battle between the grammarians and the logicians, and thus it gains poignancy by proving that the logician's disdain for the fuzziness of everyday language is ill founded. In our context, the story points out that the situational fine tuning of a sentence can be achieved by the absence or presence of "non-independent particles," in this case *inna* and *la-*. As the example suggests, by "non-independent particles" he means what the grammarians call *ḥurūf al-maʿānī*, 'function particles,' and not, as one might think at first blush, single-letter particles that are attached to the words they govern. In other words, its opposite, *al-ḥurūf al-mustaqilla*, would be "independent words" that have their own essential meaning and not just relational meanings as the particles do.

At this point in his description of the linguistic situation, he changes his emphasis somewhat by stressing the continuity between the old *fuṣḥā* and the contemporary Bedouin language. This gives him a chance to debunk the opinion of contemporary grammarians that eloquence had vanished from the (spoken) Arabic language, because the *iʿrāb* had vanished. He attributes it to their professional biases and blinders.

He then explains why so much attention was lavished on the old *fuṣḥā* and repeats the *communis opinio* that it became corrupted after the conquests due to contacts with non-Arabs. Interestingly, he says at this point that through these contacts it was transformed into another language: *wa-ṣārat malakatuhū* [i.e., *malakatu lisāni Muḍar*] *ʿalā ghayri 'l-ṣūrati 'llatī kānat awwalan fa-'nqalaba lughatan ukhrā*, which should likely be translated 'and the competence (*malakah*) to speak it [i.e., the Muḍarī language] turned into something else than what it had originally been and it became another language.' (Rosenthal [p. 346]: "(At that time) the (Arabic linguistic) habit took on a form different from the one it had had originally." Monteil [p. 1269]: "C'est alors que l'habitude linguistique prit une autre forme et que l'idiome de Muḍar devint une autre langue." Cheddadi [p. 1108]: "La langue mudarite perdit sa forme originelle et se transforma en une autre langue.") In other words, the natural competence of the native speakers turned into the insufficient competence of those who picked up the language for practical reasons. But since the sources of the religion were laid down in the old *fuṣḥā*, scholars started a rescue mission by establishing the laws that governed the language and turning the knowledge of Arabic (the old *fuṣḥā*) into a science (called *ʿilm al-naḥw wa-ṣināʿat al-ʿarabiyya*).[23]

But then Ibn Khaldūn offers an extraordinary thought. If one were to lavish on contemporary Bedouin Arabic the same attention that the old *fuṣḥā* has been accorded, and if one found out, by induction, the rules that govern it, one might find that the function of the *iʿrāb* vowels has been taken over by other things that have their own peculiar rules. They may even be rules that regulate the ends of words but in a manner different from the old *fuṣḥā*. Here Ibn Khaldūn is reiterating his initial thought that the old *fuṣḥā* and the contemporary Bedouin language are two different languages, each with its own separate methods of expressing relationships. But he adds the twist that the two languages have a different status, in the sense that the Bedouin language has not been turned into an object of intense grammatical scrutiny and codification as the old *fuṣḥā* had been. This also means that he is quite willing, which even today many laymen in Arab countries are not, to accord the term "language" to a speech form that has not (or has only marginally) been reduced to writing.

Ibn Khaldūn closes that paragraph with the short and enigmatic sentence *fa-laysati 'l-lughātu wa-malakātuhā majjānan*. Rosenthal (p. 347) translates this as 'Languages and (linguistic) habits are not matters of chance.' Monteil (p. 1270) says, 'Ni les langues, ni les habitudes linguistiques, ne sont "gratuites,"' while Cheddadi (p. 1108) has, 'Les langues et les habitus qui leur correspondent ne son pas le fruit du hasard.'[24] I would like to suggest 'arbitrary' for *majjānan*, not, of course, in the sense of the arbitrariness of the linguistic sign. What he wants to say is that, when rules fall away, other rules take their place; arbitrariness in the system cannot be tolerated, as it will be an obstacle to communication. And this arbitrariness has to be kept away from the *lughāt*, that is, the languages considered as systems, as well as from their *malakāt* 'habits' or, as I would prefer, 'competenc(i)e(s).' In the preceding chapter,

---

[22] Maḥmūd Muḥammad Shākir, ed., 1984, p. 315.

[23] It is also possible that Ibn Khaldūn's statement about the change in *malakah* refers to this stage: the natural competence of the native speaker is superseded by the "artificial" competence of those who learn the language according to rules from teachers and books.

Ibn Khaldūn had equated, rather than juxtaposed, *lughāt* and *malakāt* and compared the latter (or both) to a "craft" (*ṣināʿa*): "all languages are habits similar to crafts" (p. 342. The slight contradiction between the two statements may be resolved as follows: when speaking about "languages and their competenc(i)e(s) [i.e., competence in using them]," one differentiates between language as it exists outside of the individual speaker as an abstract system codified in a grammar, on the one hand, and language as it exists in the mental competence of the individual speaker, on the other; if you equate the two, *lughāt* and *malakāt*, you mean to point out that language as a system, actually and concretely, exists only in the mind of the one who can use it. In addition, the term *malakah* indicates that the ability to use a language has to be acquired; it is not there naturally. Ibn Khaldūn neatly and succinctly describes this process following the above quotation, and it is likewise implied in the parallel he draws between *lughāt/malakāt* and "crafts": by repeating acts that imitate acts of a competent speaker/craftsman, the *malakah* is gradually acquired. In short, translating *malakah* as 'competence' appears to be very appropriate, also in view of modern linguistic usage. Issawi uses "skill" in the same passage, which is a felicitous choice, though it lacks the technical character that "competence" has.[25]

The next paragraph is also surprising and somewhat mysterious (p. 347). Ibn Khaldūn says that the relationship between the contemporary Bedouin language and that of Muḍar (the old *fuṣḥā*) is the same as that between the Muḍar language and Ḥimyaritic. In other words, linguistic changes also took place in the transition from Ḥimyaritic to Muḍarī. "This fact," he says, "is attested by the transmitted material available to us (*yashhadu bi-dhālika 'l-anqālu 'l-mawjūdatu ladaynā*)"[26] (Monteil [p. 1270]: "comme le montrent les documents qui nous sont parvenus"; Cheddadi [p. 1109]: "comme l'attestent les matériaux qui nous sont parvenus.") And he asserts the ignorance of those who claim that Muḍarī and Ḥimyaritic are one and the same language. Notwithstanding the fact that it is difficult to make out what he had in mind with regard to Ḥimyaritic, it is quite clear that he is extending his diachronic historical view of language backward into the past, thus, I think, pointing out that the Arabic language has never ceased to develop and transform itself.

What could he have had in mind, when speaking of Ḥimyaritic? "Ḥimyarī" in medieval Arabic texts has at least three different referents:

(1) It might refer to the Sabaic language and script of the inscriptions left by the Ḥimyar, the last indigenous ruling people of Yemen, and by all their predecessors. The script remained known in Islamic times for a while. There are some early Islamic inscriptions in Sabaic script, but in Arabic language,[27] and al-Hamdānī in the tenth century was still able to read the Sabaic inscriptions for the names they contained, but could no longer understand them.[28]

(2) It might denote the language of the Ḥimyar themselves, who spoke a language different from the Sabaic they usually wrote in. This language continued to be used in Islamic times. We have some sentences and words transmitted in medieval Arabic texts; they have, to varying degrees, the appearance of an aberrant type of Arabic.[29] The medieval authors who mention this language usually declare it to be totally incomprehensible to an Arabic

---

[24] Similarly already Silvestre de Sacy (1829, p. 413), who has "... les langues et les facultés de les parler ne sont point produites par le hasard, ni dépourvues de motifs," which de Slane (1868, p. 337) repeats, omitting the last phrase.

[25] Issawi 1950, p. 149.

[26] Rosenthal's rendering of this intriguing sentence seems to agree with Monteil's (1967–68, p. 1270) "comme le montrent les documents qui nous sont parvenus," but diverges sharply from de Sacy's (1829, p. 413) "Nous en avons une preuve dans la formation étymologiques de quelques-uns des mots qui ont passé des Himyarites dans notre langage," followed by de Slane's (1868, p. 337) "Cela nous est attesté par les changements de signification que certains mot ont subis chez nous." Rosenthal and Monteil understand *naql* in the sense of "transmission, tradition," while de Slane falls back on the meaning "semantic shift" (*naql al-maʿnā*). De Sacy's interpretation may be based on the same idea, but is less clear; he seems to derive his interpretation from Ibn Khaldūn's remark that some lexicographers believe that the word *qayl* 'leader,' of Ḥimyaritic origin (and denoting something Ḥimyaritic!), is somehow derived from the Arabic *qawl* 'speaking,' which he denies on the grounds that they are two different languages. In view of this example, it is possible that the "transmitted material" refers to Ḥimyaritic words adduced and glossed in dictionaries, especially the *Shams al-ʿulūm* of Nashwān al-Ḥimyarī (see also Aḥmad 1916). But he does not cite Nashwān anywhere. In view of this fact, it seems more likely that the "transmitted material" refers to works like Kropp 1982, see also n. 32.

[27] Robin 1976, pp. 188–93; 1992, p. 134.

[28] See Löfgren 1965.

[29] On Ḥimyarī and Ḥimyarī-influenced Arabic, see the description of the linguistic situation in Müller, ed., 1968, pp. 134–36, translated and commented on by Rabin (1951, pp. 43–48). Rabin also adduces two snippets of Ḥimyarī attested in the sources, to which can now be added the material from the astronomical work *Kitāb al-Tabṣira fī ʿilm al-nujūm* of the Rasulid ruler al-Malik al-Ashraf Abū 'l-Fatḥ ʿUmar b. al-Malik al-Muẓaffar Yūsuf (r. 1295-97), discussed in Saliba 1985.

speaker. From the preserved fragments, one would not necessarily think so. This may mean either that the fragments have undergone Arabization at the hands of copyists, or that they are specimens of Ḥimyaritic-influenced Arabic. According to al-Hamdānī, genuine Ḥimyaritic shaded into the surrounding Arabic dialects to various degrees. It is quite possible that the original Ḥimyaritic was neither Arabic nor Old South Arabian.[30]

Since Sabaic as a language was no longer known to the medieval Arab authors, they assumed that the Old South Arabian inscriptions were composed in the Ḥimyaritic they knew, or knew about. This is also the reason that the "Old South Arabian" inscriptions forged by the Yemeni patriots al-Hamdānī and Nashwān al-Ḥimyarī (d. 573/1178) are written in some sort of Ḥimyaritic.[31]

(3) Genealogically, the Ḥimyar form part of the Southern Arabs who are personified as Qaḥṭān (Ḥimyar b. Sabaʾ b. Yashjub b. Yaʿrub b. Qaḥṭān). The Qaḥṭān were supposed to have spoken, in the legendary past, the first pure Arabic. According to Ibn Saʿīd (d. 685/1286), whose work was used by Ibn Khaldūn, "the Banū Qaḥṭān are known as [*al-ʿarab*] *al-ʿāriba*, the 'Pure Arabs,' because they made their speech into (true) Arabic (*aʿrabū*; may also mean: "introduced inflection into their speech") and composed good poems, as opposed to the Extinct Arabs (like ʿĀd and Thamūd etc.) whose language had been confused ([*al-ʿarab*] *al-mubalbala al-bāʾida*, referring to the Confusion of the Tongues)." Of Qaḥṭān's son, Yaʿrub, it is said that "he was the first to speak clear Arabic," and "the first among the Arabs to compose poetry in its various meters and genres." Ḥimyar himself, that is, the tribal patriarch, is said to have composed the first Arabic dirge, bewailing his father.[32] This idea of pure Arabic originating, against all evidence, among the early Southern Arabs, which finds its completion in the equally surprising idea that the Northern Arabs are *mustaʿriba*, "Arabized," has to be attributed to Yemeni *shuʿūbiyya* (esprit de corps): the undeniable title to glory of the Northern Arabs, the prophethood of Muḥammad, was "counterbalanced" with the glorious history and cultural achievements of the Southern Arabs, which necessarily included language and poetry.

Which of the meanings of "Ḥimyarī" did Ibn Khaldūn have in mind? If his historical remark about the shift from Ḥimyaritic to Muḍarī is to make any sense, he cannot be talking about the language of the Ḥimyarites, as understood by al-Hamdānī and Nashwān al-Ḥimyarī. It seems likely that his notion of "Ḥimyarī" is an aggregate of the legendary origin of pure Arabic among the Southern Arabs, including Ḥimyar, and the use of "Ḥimyar" as a name for the formerly ruling people of Yemen. We have to keep in mind that Ibn Khaldūn's family was of Southern Arab extraction, and he probably viewed the past glory of the Ḥimyarites with interest and pride. The "transmitted material available to us" most likely refers to legendary reports like those quoted from Ibn Saʿīd, often going back to Ibn Hishām's (d. 218/833) *Kitāb al-Tījān.*

Next (pp. 348–51), he has a lengthy disquisition on one of the characteristic features of the contemporary Bedouin language, to wit, the sound *g*, which is the Bedouin realization of the sound *q* in standard pronunciation. He says that all Bedouin speakers have it, while the urban speakers do not. This distinction is, of course, still valid today, though rather than "urban," one uses the more comprehensive term "sedentary." Ibn Khaldūn now makes the interesting point that, since it is shared by all the Bedouins, it must have belonged to the old *fuṣḥā*, the Muḍarī language. Even the Prophet, he says, may have had the *gāf* pronunciation. Ibn Khaldūn admits to not knowing how the split into *qāf* and *gāf* dialects came about. Since the urban speakers of Arabic[33] are also mostly descendants of the Muḍar, there is no good reason for the split. The problem is very clearly stated. His ingenious solution is that there is a certain variability in the pronunciation of the *qāf* from one kind of Arabic to the other.[34]

[30] The so-called Hymn of Qāniya, a second/third-century extended rock graffito in Sabaic script, representing a hymn to the goddess Shams, has been tentatively identified as Ḥimyaritic by its discoverer; see ʿAbdallāh 1988. However, Stein (2008) has argued that the three inscriptions (including the Hymn of Qāniya) that were considered to be sufficiently divergent from "normal" Sabaic to be candidates for being "Ḥimyaritic" were all in rhymed poetry, the divergences thus being attributable to that particular medium. He goes even further by putting "Ḥimyarī" texts in Arabic literature, and the modern Yemeni *k*-dialects (*gumuḵ* = *qumṯu*) in the same tradition.

[31] Rabin 1951, pp. 42, 48.

[32] Kropp 1982, pp. 81, 83, 87, 213, 215, 221.

[33] It should be noted here that Ibn Khaldūn considers urban Arabic, like Bedouin Arabic, a separate language, as well. See Rosenthal, trans., vol. 3, pp. 351–53.

[34] See Rosenthal, trans., vol. 3, pp. 349, lines 3ff.; 350, lines 23–25; 351, lines 1–3.

Excursus: The Plausibility of Bedouin *gāf* Being a Feature of the Ancient *fuṣḥā*

A short aside on this problem may not be amiss, if only to show that Ibn Khaldūn had the right idea, when he posited *gāf* for the old *fuṣḥā*. In fact, the *gāf* pronunciation is highly likely, as it offers a convincing explanation of the shift from *gīm* to *jīm*, which would otherwise be difficult to explain: once the *qāf* had become *gāf*, it pushed the original *gīm* forward to a dorso-prepalatal articulation.[35] That a *gāf* did arise and, subsequently, a *gāf*/*qāf* split did develop must have something to do with the switch from an ejective (Ethiopian-style) to a uvularized[36] (Arabic-style) pronunciation for the "emphatics." This assumption rests on the presupposition that the ejective pronunciation (glottalization) is proto-Semitic, while uvularization in Arabic is an innovation; though there is no total unanimity on this score, the direction of development suggested here seems to take better care of all the relevant phenomena. This then is the scenario: when the proto-Semitic (or, more cautiously: pre-Arabic) ejectives /tʾ/, /ṯʾ/, /sʾ/, /tˡʾ/, and /kʾ/ were shifted to uvularized "emphatics," the first four changed their secondary articulation from glottalized to uvularized without a problem, becoming /ṭ/, /ḏ̣/, /ṣ/, and /ḍˡ/ (the last one indicating the lateral pronunciation of *ḍād* as described by Sībawayh).[37] But the /kʾ/ was in the awkward position that, when uvularization set in, the primary articulation (velar) and the secondary articulation (uvularized) were very close to each other. A uvularized velar[38] would presumably be identical with a uvular /q/. Note that, with the indigenous grammarians, the first four phonemes, but not *qāf*, are *muṭbaqa*, 'emphatic,' because they consider the retraction of the back of the tongue characteristic for *iṭbāq*. After losing glottalization, /q/ could either stay voiceless or become voiced.[39] In this latter respect, it resembles some of its "emphatic" sisters: the reflex of earlier /tʾ/ may appear as both /ṭ/ and /ḍ/,[40] and that of /ṯʾ/ as both /ṯ̣/ and /ḏ̣/. The reason that these "emphatics" in Arabic vacillate between voiced and voiceless has to be sought in the fact that the "emphatics" form a third series alongside the voiced and voiceless series (t-d-ṭ, s-z-ṣ, etc.); their mark is "emphaticness," that is, uvularization, and their being voiced or voiceless is immaterial for the phonemic system.

---

[35] Cantineau (1960, p. 57) says, "En arabe ancien, le point d'articulation de la sonore *g* a été, d'une façon inconditionnée et pour des raisons qui nous échappent, reporté très en avant, dans la région prépalatale." Since he posits the *gāf* pronunciation for ancient Arabic (ibid., p. 67), it is somewhat surprising that he did not suggest the connection between the rise of *gāf* and the rise of *jīm*. However, Cantineau assumes a development g > j even before the q > g development set in, and so does Blanc (1969) in his painstaking study of the *qāf*/*gāf* split. The relative chronology of /g/ > /j/ and /q/ >/g/ still deserves further attention, but this footnote is not the place for it.

[36] I am using the term "uvular" and derivatives rather than "velar" or "pharyngeal," which can also be encountered in this context, because it seems to me the phonetically most appropriate term. Depending on the individual language or dialect, one should, however, not discount the possibility of a wider articulatory area for the production of "emphasis," including "velar" and "pharyngeal." What caused the switch from glottalization to uvularization is still moot and cannot be discussed here. For one suggested solution to the problem, see Zemánek 1996 (my thanks to John Huehnergard for drawing my attention to this booklet).

[37] On the unexpected voicing of /ḍ/ and /ḍˡ/, see below.

[38] Not listed in the IPA; there is no diacritic for "uvularization."

[39] Ejective sounds are per se voiceless, as the glottis is closed. Interestingly, T. M. Johnstone (1987, p. xiii) mentions that /ṣ/ (= /sʾ/) is "partially voiced"and /ḏ̣/ (= /ṯʾ/ ? [not clear]) is "partially voiceless" in the Modern South Arabian languages. This was not too clear to me, so when I met one of the few specialists on Modern South Arabian, Antoine Lonnet, at a conference in Paris in 2007, I asked him about the voiced ejectives, and he produced some, but not being a seasoned phonetician, I had trouble identifying what I heard; there seemed to be a creaky voice effect on the following vowel.

[40] The standard pronunciation would, of course, be /ṭ/. But Sībawayh describes it as /ḍ/, and the latter appears as /ṭ/ in some Northern Yemeni dialects; see Cantineau 1960, p. 32, and Behnstedt 1987, p. 5.

The attestations of voiceless and voiced realizations of the Arabic "emphatics" are as follows:

	Glottalized (ejective)	*Uvularized*
Dental	*tʾ*	*ṭ* (voiceless, standard pronunciation)
		ḍ (voiced, Sībawayh's description of *ṭ* as *majhūra*[41])
Interdental	*ṯʾ*	*ḏ̣* (voiced, standard pronunciation)
		ṯ̣ (voiceless, dialect of the Banī ʿAbādil in Northern Yemen[42])
Sibilant	*sʾ*	*ṣ* (voiceless, standard pronunciation)
		ẓ (voiced, Qurʾānic reading of Abū ʿAmr Ibn al-ʿAlāʾ[43]: ***aẓ-ẓirāṭ*** for *aṣ-ṣirāṭ* in *al-Fātiḥa*)
Lateral	t^{l}ʾ	$ḍ^{l}$ (voiced, Sībawayh's description, uvularized /l/ in Dathīna, Yemen)
		Uvular
Velar	*kʾ*	*q* (voiceless, standard pronunciation)
		G (voiced, Northern Arabia and other dialects, Persian pronunciation of <q>) In most Bedouin dialects, the latter is further shifted to *g*.

This would suggest that /kʾ/ after deglottalization became either /q/ (voiceless uvular) or /G/ (voiced uvular). The latter, attested in a few modern dialects,[44] mostly became regular /g/. This seems to have happened in the Central Arabian area, the center of camel nomadism and of the language of poetry. It is interesting to note that the grammarian Sībawayh also heard something like /g/ or /G/, since he classes the *qāf* with the *majhūra*, namely voiced, sounds. The /q/ pronunciation of the sedentary dialects may be a feature of early Arabic in the Fertile Crescent, which developed under the influence of Aramaic, though this is far from proven. Maxime Rodinson's attempt to make the case that the ancient pronunciation of *qāf* in Arabic was predominantly /q/ is based on transliterations of names into — mainly — Greek and Latin (inscriptions and otherwise);[45] most of his sources hail from outside the posited *gāf* area. Since most *qāf* dialects as well as standard Arabic also have *jīm*, in which case the push-chain *gāf* > *gīm* = *jīm* does not really work anymore, there is a problem here that has mostly been solved by assuming borrowing, either of *jīm* or of *qāf*. Since widespread bilingualism can be assumed among the *anbāṭ* (peasants, whether originally arabophone or aramaeophone) — see also cognate spelling of Arabic words with the Aramaic alphabets of the Fertile Crescent — the borrowing of *qāf* from Aramaic into Arabic seems natural. However, my point in the above list is that, when glottalization is superseded by uvularization, the resulting uvularized sound may unpredictably have resulted in a voiced or voiceless sound, and, at this point, the substrate (or adstrate) languages (like Aramaic) may have influenced the choice of the Arabic speakers.

41 As far as the much-debated pair *majhūra/mahmūsa* in Sībawayh's terminology is concerned, I follow Henri Fleisch (1958), who has (to my mind) proven that the terms correspond with "voiced"/"voiceless."

42 See Behnstedt in n. 38.

43 Thus Cantineau (1960, p. 46), who quotes Ibn Yaʿīsh's commentary on al-Zamakhsharī's grammar *al-Mufaṣṣa*; see Yaʿqūb 2001, vol. 5, p. 520. The context is phonemes and allophones in the Arabic language. Ibn Yaʿīsh goes into considerable detail, as follows: "And likewise the *ṣād* which is like *zāy* (i.e., voiced), just as they say *maẓdar* for *maṣdar* and *yaẓduqu* for *yaṣduqu* [assimilation of voiceless *ṣād* to the voiced *dāl*]. And *al-ṣirāṭ al-mustaqīm* (Surah 1, 6) has been read giving the *ṣād* a whiff of *zāy* (*bi-ishmāmi 'l-ṣāda 'z-zāya*). This is the reading of Ḥamza. Transmitted from Abū ʿAmr there are four readings of this: (1) "al-ṣirāṭ" with the [first consonant] between *ṣād* and *zāy* [i.e., /ẓ/}; ʿUryān b. Abī Shaybān transmitted this, saying: I heard Abū ʿAmr recite "al-ṣirāṭ" between *ṣād* and *zāy*, as if he imbued the *ṣād* with the voice (*ṣawt*) of *zāy*, so that it would agree with the *ṭāʾ* (of *ṣirāṭ*) in its being voiced (*fī l-jahr*) [following Sībawayh's description of *ṭāʾ*], because the *ṣād* is voiceless (*mahmūsa*), but *ṭāʾ* and *dāl* [referring back to *maẓdar*] are voiced [*majhūratān*], so there is incompatibility and disagreement between the two. So they imbued the *ṣād* with the voice of the *zāy* because it [the *ṣād*] is its [the *zāy*'s] sister in sibilance and place of articulation, and agreeing with the *ṭāʾ* and the *dāl* in being voiced. So the two sounds are close to each other and not very different." I have translated this passage, because it indicates that the existence of the /ẓ/ is a result of the aesthetics of Qurʾānic recitation; we cannot be sure that it was a regular sound in any dialect, nor can we reject this idea.

44 Cantineau 1960, p. 69. One might also adduce the Persian pronunciation /G/ of /q/ in Arabic loans (and some indigenous words, such as *qashang* 'elegant').

45 Rodinson 1970.

The close reading of Ibn Khaldūn's chapter has revealed, against the background of the linguistic tradition in which he stood, a number of novel positions in his views of language:

(1) He still subscribes to the "corruption" theory, that is, the "corruption" of the old *fuṣḥā*, the Muḍarī language; however, the result of the "corruption" is a new language and not corrupted Muḍarī.

(2) The means a language has to express specific relations may change over time; *iʿrāb* may be replaced by *qarāʾin* and so on.

(3) A dialect is a language without an explicit grammar.

(4) Language change occurred at least twice in the history of Arabic (Ḥimyaritic > Muḍarī > contemporary Bedouin language).

(5) Phenomena in existing language forms may be traced back to more ancient forms through comparative methods: the *gāf* seems to be attributable to the old *fuṣḥā*.

The common denominator for most of these views is Ibn Khaldūn's diachronic-historic approach, which tries to ignore, and sometimes combat, the numerous biases surrounding the Arabic language. The latter stem mainly from the view of Arabic as a language that is static and immutable. Kees Versteegh has pointed out that diachronic perspectives in language study arise from an awareness of chronologically distant varieties of the same language, such as Homeric versus Attic Greek, and/or from an interest in other languages than one's own. Arabic language scholars were lacking, he says, in both respects.[46] Ibn Khaldūn is the exception to this verdict. Whether he had a good knowledge of other languages is none too clear. He certainly knew some Berber, since he discusses the question of transliteration of Berber words into Arabic script (i, 65–68), and he glosses a number of Berber words throughout his work (see Rosenthal's index under "Berber"). More importantly, he speaks about the characteristics of (all) other languages in comparison with those of Arabic (see above); though, on what empirical evidence he does so is unclear. With Versteegh's other criterion we are on *terra firma*. The alleged immutability of Arabic is jettisoned, in two separate steps. First, he shows that the speech of the contemporary Bedouins is a language in its own right, not just corrupted Muḍarī. But he does not stop there. In a second move, he proposes that the Muḍarī language itself is the result of a historical development, this time from Ḥimyaritic. Despite the fact that he has very little evidence to offer for his contention, the idea is ingenious, since it makes the "immutable" *fuṣḥā* even more prone to change. He is, of course, aware of the fact that Muḍarī and contemporary Bedouin differ in their cultural status (language of revelation and all intellectual pursuits vs. everyday colloquial), but he makes the important observation that, if the Bedouin language had been subjected to the same scrutiny and language guardianship that the Muḍarī language had enjoyed, one would realize that it did indeed have all the trappings of a real language.

It is the seriously historical view of all cultural artifacts, including language, that allowed Ibn Khaldūn to see many phenomena with fresh eyes, unencumbered by many of the prejudices and foregone conclusions that dominated the existing discourse, based as it was on the idea of stable systems of language as well as knowledge. This freshness makes reading his insightful discussions so enjoyable.

[46] Versteegh 1997, pp. 105–06. In their — of necessity — synchronic study of the "immutable" Arabic language, they were, of course, eminently sophisticated and successful.

Bibliography

ʿAbd al-Tawwāb, Ramaḍān
1967 *Laḥn al-ʿāmma wa-'l-taṭawwur al-lughawī*. Cairo: Dār al-Maʿārif.

ʿAbdallāh, Yūsuf M.
1988 "Naqsh al-qaṣīda al-ḥimyariyya aw tarnīmat al-Shams." *Raydān* 5: 81–100 (Arabic section).

Aḥmad, ʿAẓīmuddīn
1916 *Die auf Südarabien bezüglichen Angaben Našwān's im Šams al-ʿulūm*. Leiden: Brill.

ʿAwwād, ʿAbd al-Salām Aḥmad, editor
1968 Yūsuf b. Zakariyyāʾ al-Maghribī. *Dafʿ al-iṣr ʿan kalām ahl Miṣr. Udaleniye bremeni s reči žiteley Egipta*. Facsimile edition. Moscow: Nauka.

Behnstedt, Peter
1987 *Die Dialekte der Gegend von Ṣaʿda (Nord-Jemen)*. Wiesbaden: Harrassowitz.

Ben-Ari, Shosh
2009 "Language, Civilisation and Globalisation in the 14th Century: Historical Periodicity and the Evolution of Language at [*sic*] Ibn Khaldūn." *Acta Orientalia Academiae Scientiarum Hungaricae* 62: 2.

Blanc, Haim
1969 "The Fronting of Semitic G and the *QĀL-GĀL* Dialect Split in Arabic." In *Proceedings of the International Conference on Semitic Studies, held in Jerusalem, 19–23 July 1965*, pp. 7–37. Jerusalem: Israel Academy of Sciences and Humanities.

Blau, Joshua
1972 "On the Problem of the Synthetic Character of Classical Arabic as against Judaeo-Arabic (Middle Arabic)." *Jewish Quarterly Review* 63: 29–38.

Bousquet, Georges-Henri
1961 *Les textes économiques de la Mouqaddima, 1375–1379, [par] Ibn Khaldoûn. Classés, traduits et annotés*. Paris: M. Rivière.
1965 *Les textes sociologiques et économiques de la Mouqaddima, 1375–1379, [par] Ibn Khaldoûn. Classés, traduits et annotés*. Paris: M. Rivière.

Cantineau, Jean
1960 *Cours de phonétique arabe*. Paris: C. Klincksieck.

Cheddadi, Abdesselam, translator
2002 *Ibn Khaldûn — Le Livre des Exemples. I. Autobiographie, Muqaddima: Texte traduit, présenté et annoté*. Bibliothèque de la Pléiade 490. Paris: Éditions Gallimard.

Cooke, Miriam
1984 "Ibn Khaldun and Language: From Linguistic Habit to Philological Craft." In *Ibn Khaldun and Islamic Ideology*, edited by Bruce B. Lawrence, pp. 27–35. International Studies in Sociology and Social Anthropology 40. Leiden: Brill.

Corriente, Federigo
1971 "On the Functional Yield of Some Synthetic Devices in Arabic and Semitic Morphology." *Jewish Quarterly Review* 62: 20–50.
1973–1974 "Again on the Functional Yield of Some Synthetic Devices in Arabic and Semitic Morphology." *Jewish Quarterly Review* 64/2: 154–63.

de Slane, Willliam McGuckin
1868 *Prolégomènes d'Ibn Khaldoun*. Paris: Imprimerie Impériale 1868 [= Notices et extraits des manuscrits de la Bibliothèque Impériale, Volume 21].

Fleisch, Henri
1958 "Mağhūra, mahmūsa, examen critique." *Mélanges de l'Université Saint Joseph* 35: 193–210.

Harris, Alice C., and Lyle Campbell
1995 *Historical Syntax in Cross-linguistic Perspective*. Cambridge: Cambridge University Press.

Heinrichs, Wolfhart

1995 "The Classification of the Sciences and the Consolidation of Philology in Classical Islam." In *Centres of Learning. Learning and Location in Pre-modern Europe and the Near East*, edited by Jan Willem Drijvers and Alasdair A. MacDonald, pp. 119–40. Leiden: Brill.

Hodgson, Marshall G. S.

1974 *The Venture of Islam. Conscience and History in a World Civilization.* 3 volumes. Chicago: University of Chicago Press.

Hoenerbach, Wilhelm, editor

1956 *Ṣafī al-Dīn al-Ḥillī (d. ca. 749/1348): al-Kitāb al-ʿĀṭil al-ḥālī wa-'l-murakhkhaṣ al-ghālī.* Wiesbaden: Franz Steiner.

Irving, Thomas B.

1959 "A Fourteenth-century View of Language." In *The World of Islam: Studies in Honour of Philip K. Hitti*, edited by James Kritzeck and R. Bayly Winder, pp. 185–92. London: Macmillan.

al-Isfarāʾīnī, ʿIṣām al-Dīn

1864 *Ḥāshiya ʿalā Sharḥ al-Jāmī li-'l-Kāfiya.* [Istanbul]: Maṭbaʿ Bōsnawī al-Ḥājj Muḥarram Afandī.

Issawi, Charles

1950 *An Arab Philosophy of History: Selections from the Prolegomena of Ibn Khaldun of Tunis (1332–1406).* London: John Murray.

Johnstone, Thomas M.

1987 *Mehri Lexicon and English-Mehri Word-list.* London: School of Oriental and African Studies.

Kropp, Manfred, editor and translator

1982 *Ibn Saʿīd al-Maghribī: Nashwat al-ṭarab fī taʾrīkh jāhiliyyat al-ʿarab; Die Geschichte der "reinen Araber" vom Stamme Qaḥṭān.* 2nd edition. Frankfurt am Main: Peter Lang.

Labica, Georges

1965 *Le rationalisme d'Ibn Khaldoun: Extraits de la Muqaddimah (Histoire, sociologie, politique, sciences, philosophie), choisis et classés avec avant-propos, notes et index.* Translated by Jamel-Eddine Bencheikh. Algiers: Centre pédagogique Maghribin.

Löfgren, Oscar

1965 "al-Hamdānī." In *Encyclopaedia of Islam*, Volume 3, edited by H. A. R. Gibb, pp. 124–25. Facsimile 1. Leiden: Brill.

Mahdi, Muhsin

1964 *Ibn Khaldûn's Philosophy of History: A Study in the Philosophic Foundation of the Science of Culture.* Chicago: University of Chicago Press.

Maṭar, ʿAbd al-ʿAzīz

1966 *Laḥn al-ʿāmma fī ḍawʾ al-dirāsāt al-lughawiyya al-ḥadītha.* Cairo: al-Dār al-Qawmiyya.

Miquel, André

1988 *La géographie humaine du monde musulman jusqu'au milieu du 11ᵉ siècle.* Civilisations et sociétés 7. Paris: École des hautes études en sciences sociales.

Monteil, Vincent, translator

1967–1968 *Ibn Khaldûn: Discours sur l'histoire universelle (al-Muqaddima), Traduction nouvelle, préface, notes et index.* 3 volumes. Beirut: Commission Libanaise pour la Traduction des Chefs-d'œuvre.

Mukarram, ʿAbd al-ʿĀl Sālim, editor

2000 *Ibn al-Ḥājib: al-Kāfiya fī 'l-naḥw, sharḥ Raḍī al-Dīn al-Astarābādhī.* 2 volumes. Cairo: ʿĀlam al-Kutub.

Müller, David Heinrich, editor

1968 *al-Hamdānī: Ṣifat Jazīrat al-ʿArab, Al-Hamdânî's Geographie der Arabischen Halbinsel.* Leiden: Brill.

Pérès, Henri

1947 *al-Muntakhab min "al-Muqaddimah" wa-"Kitāb al-ʿIbar" l-Ibn Khaldūn.* Algiers: Imprimerie officielle.

Rabin, Chaim

1951 *Ancient West Arabian.* London: Taylor's Foreign Press.

al-Rifāʿī, Usāma Ṭāhā, editor

1983 [1403] *Jāmī, al-Fawāʾid al-Ḍiyāʾiyya, sharḥ Kāfiyat Ibn al-Ḥājib.* 2 volumes. [Baghdad:] Wizārat al-awqāf wa-'l-shuʾūn al-dīniyya.

Robin, Christian

1976 "Résultats épigraphiques et archéologiques de deux brefs séjours en République Arabe de Yémen." *Semitica* 26: 167–93.

1992 "Les écritures de l'arabe avant l'Islam." In *L'Arabie antique de Karib'îl à Mahomet: nouvelles données sur l'histoire des Arabes grâce aux inscriptions*, edited by Christan Robin, pp. 127–37. Aix-en-Provence: Édisud 1992 [= *Revue du Monde Musulman et de la Méditerranée* 61 (1991–93)].

Rodinson, Maxime

1970 "Sur la prononciation ancienne du qāf arabe." In *Mélanges Marcel Cohen; études de Linguistique, Ethnographie et Sciences connexes offertes par ses amis et ses élèves à l'occasion de Son 80ème Anniversaire: Avec des Articles et études inédits de Marcel Cohen*, edited by David Cohen, pp. 298–319. Paris: Mouton.

Rosenthal, Franz, translator

1967 *Ibn Khaldûn: The Muqaddimah: An Introduction to History.* 3 volumes. 2nd edition. London: Routledge and Kegan Paul.

Saliba, George

1985 "A Medieval Note on the Himyaritic Dialect." *Journal of the American Oriental Society* 105/4: 715–17.

Schimmel, Annemarie

1951 *Ibn Chaldun: Ausgewählte Abschnitte aus der Muqaddimah.* Tübingen: J. C. B. Mohr.

Shākir, Maḥmūd Muḥammad, editor

1984 *ʿAbd al-Qāhir al-Jurjānī, Dalāʾil al-iʿjāz.* Cairo: Khānjī.

Silvestre de Sacy, Antoine Isaac

1826–1827 *Chrestomathie arabe, ou, Extraits de divers écrivains arabes, tant en prose qu'en vers, avec une traduction française et des notes, à l'usage des élèves de l'École royale et spéciale des langues orientales vivantes.* 3 volumes. 2nd edition. Paris: Imprimerie royale.

1829 *Anthologie grammaticale arabe: ou, Morceaux choisis de divers grammairiens et scholiastes arabes, avec un traduction française et des notes.* Paris: Imprimerie Royale.

Stein, Peter

2008 "The 'Himyaritic' Language in Pre-Islamic Yemen: A Critical Re-evaluation." *Semitica et Classica* 1: 203–12.

van den Bergh, Simon

1912 *Umriss der muḥammedanischen Wissenschaften nach Ibn Ḫaldūn.* Leiden: Brill. Originally doctoral dissertation Freiburg im Breisgau.

Versteegh, Kees

1997 *Landmarks in Linguistic Thought* III: *The Arabic Linguistic Tradition.* New York: Routledge.

Yaʿqūb, Imīl Badīʿ, editor

2001 *Ibn Yaʿīsh (d. 643/1245): Sharḥ al-Mufaṣṣal li-'l-Zamakhsharī.* Six volumes. Beirut: Dār al-Kutub al-ʿIlmiyya.

Zemánek, Petr

1996 *The Origins of Pharyngealization in Semitic.* Prague: Enigma Corporation.

12

A Morphosyntactic Explanation of *təpôṣôtîkem* (Jer 25:34)

*Jeremy M. Hutton, University of Wisconsin-Madison**

1. Introduction

The anomalous lexeme *təpôṣôtîkem* in Jeremiah 25:34 has been the subject of much speculation. The word's form is unclear morphologically, and this lack of clarity has resulted in a variety of bewildering translations. The verse provides some context, but the lexeme under investigation can be understood (or misunderstood) to comport with that context in a variety of ways. The complete verse reads,

(34aα) *hêlîlû hārōʿîm wəzaʿăqû wəhitpalləšû ʾaddîrê haṣṣō(ʾ)n*
(34aβ) *kî-mālǝʾû yəmêkem liṭbôaḥ*
(34b) *ûtəpôṣôtîkem ûnəpaltem kiklî ḥemdâ.*

Hebrew manuscripts have exhibited a variety of pointings, all of which have influenced subsequent interpretation to one degree or another (see Barthélemy 1986, pp. 658–59). As is perhaps to be expected in such cases of ambiguity among the Hebrew traditions, the ancient translations also differed in their treatment of the word *təpôṣôtîkem*. The Septuagint (LXX[OG]) (= 32:34) omits the word entirely, although it has been rendered by subsequent recensions as καὶ οἱ σκορπισμοὶ ὑμῶν ('and your dispersions'). The Peshiṭta reads *wttbrwn* ('and you will be shattered'), while the Targum translates ותתבדרון 'and you will be scattered.' McKane thus suggests that "both versions assume a verb, and only a verb will fit into the syntax of the verse," and assumes that the Peshiṭta likely rendered Hebrew נפץ and the Targum, Hebrew פוץ (McKane 1986, p. 652). However, in addition to the confusing morphology of the Hebrew word, one suspects that the graphic similarity in both the Aramaic block-script (ד vs. ר) and the Syriac Estrangela (ܕ vs. ܪ) further complicated the text-critical relationship between the Targum and Peshiṭta. Specifically, the orthographic difference between these two versions is limited to the omission of only one letter in the latter, a letter that is itself graphically similar to an immediately contiguous grapheme.

English translations, too, have handled verse 34b differently, depending on their analysis of *təpôṣôtîkem* and the concomitant understanding of the word's relation to verse 34a. Some understand *təpôṣôtîkem* to be a mispointed nominal form (emended to *təpôṣôtêkem*) following directly on the preceding noun (emphasis added here):

KJV: ... for the days *of your slaughter and of your dispersions* are accomplished; and ye shall fall like a pleasant vessel.

* It is a pleasure to have the opportunity to honor John Huehnergard in this publication. I thank here Rebecca Hasselbach and Naʿama Pat-El for their gracious invitation to contribute an essay commemorating Professor Huehnergard's work in the field of Semitic Philology — and particularly, his work in Hebrew verbal morphology. Additional thanks go to Aaron Rubin, who graciously read and commented on an earlier draft of this paper. As always, all mistakes remain the sole responsibility of the author.

ASV: ... for the days *of your slaughter and of your dispersions* are fully come, and ye shall fall like a goodly vessel.

RSV: ... for the days *of your slaughter and dispersion* have come, and you shall fall like choice rams.

Other translations understand the word as a verb, separating verse 34b from the preceding stich as an independent clause coordinated with the preceding one by a conjunction:

JPS: .... For the day of your slaughter draws near. *I will break you in pieces*, And you shall fall like a precious vessel.

NIV: .... For your time to be slaughtered has come;
you will fall and *be shattered* like fine pottery.

The NRSV attempts to split the difference, rendering *təpôṣôtîkem* as a noun, but separating it from the preceding clause with an m-dash:

NRSV: .... for the days of your slaughter have come — *and your dispersions*,
and you shall fall like a choice vessel.

Unfortunately, this tactic and its accompanying enigmatic lineation only serve to obfuscate an already difficult passage.

Grammarians have regularly analyzed *təpôṣôtîkem* as either the product of textual corruption or a conflation of the regularly formed verbs *tāpûṣû* (i.e., the 2.m.pl. *qal* imperfect √פוץ) and *hăpîṣôtî* (i.e., the 1.c.sg. *hipʿil* perfect √פוץ; e.g., GKC §91l). However, I will argue in this paper that the verb shows indications of being a morphosyntactically conditioned 1.c.sg. perfect of a tG-stem verbal form of √פוץ. Although uncommon in Biblical Hebrew, the tG-stem is found in a number of roots that seem to have been productive for at least some of the time of the Hebrew Bible's composition. Usually, these occurrences are found in texts deriving from Northern Israelite (i.e., Benjaminite and Ephraimite) contexts and exhibiting a set of linguistic features identifiable as markers of a specifically Northern (Israelian) Hebrew dialect (Yoo 1999, pp. 134–36). The word has undergone a regular developmental process, with cognate developments still found in the chronologically later but geographically overlapping dialect of Samaritan Hebrew.

2. Morphological Analysis: Previous Interpretations

It is quite common for grammarians to analyze *təpôṣôtîkem* as a nominal form with the 2.m.pl. possessive suffix attached. Such understandings usually reconstruct a *t*-preformative nominal form *təpôṣâ*[1] or *təpûṣâ*, in which *ō̂* and *ū* alternated somewhat irregularly.[2] While some seem to consider the form the result of normal development, Bauer and Leander parse the form as a noun, simultaneously correcting the suffix to *-êkem*, but recognize that it is most likely a (misanalyzed) corrupted verbal form ("wahrsch. aber eine entstellte Verbalform" [BL §28x]); see earlier Qimḥi 144 n. c; Olshausen 1861, 400 §213d). This interpretation led to the translations of KJV, ASV, and RSV (see above).

Some scholars have analyzed the form as a verb (e.g., Saadia; see Skoss 1942, pp. 209–10 and n. 19), many suggesting that it has undergone some form of corruption. Ibn Janaḥ and Judah ibn Balaam (both cited in Barthélemy 1986, p. 659; and Skoss 1942, p. 210 n. 19) and ibn Parḥon (1844, 52b s.v. פוץ) identify the form as a *hipʿil* perfect in which the *hê* has been replaced by *tāw* (see also Hitzig 1841, pp. 205–06; Graf 1862, pp. 336–37).[3] On this model,

[1] E.g., Vulgate, *et dissipationes vestrae* ('and your dispersions'); Rashi (cited in Barthélemy 1986, p. 659); Qimḥi 144 §37p(b); BDB 807a, s.v. תפוצה; Böttcher 1868, p. 33 n. 2; Mühlau and Volck 1883, p. 667, s.v. פוץ *Hithpal.*; Carroll 1986, p. 505; G. Fischer 2005, p. 731; cf. Gesenius 1817, p. 254.

[2] BL §74h′ with reference to §14q; Kuriakos 1973, p. 121; see also Barthélemy 1986, pp. 658–59, for further discussion of manuscript evidence.

[3] Ibn Janaḥ used this same explanation to describe *tirgaltî* in Hosea 11:3 (1875, p. 664).

the word comprises a *forma mixta* in which the verb *tăpîṣôtî* (i.e., the 1.c.sg. *hipʿil* perfect with an anomalous *t*-prefix) has been conflated with the regularly formed verb *tāpûṣû* (i.e., the 2.m.pl. *qal* imperfect; see, e.g., GKC §91l) or with the nominal form *təpûṣôt* (i.e., the f.pl. of *təpûṣâ*; Ḥayyuj, cited in Chomsky 1952, p. 194 n. 256, and Barthélemy 1986, p. 659; Graf 1862, pp. 336–37; Keil 1872, p. 288; L. Allen 2008, p. 282). Weiser suggested reading *wə-nippaṣtîkem*, translating "ich zerschmettere euch" (1952, p. 230 and n. 1; cf. Bright 1965, p. 159).

The preceding solutions posit the necessity of some sort of textual emendation to provide a clear reading of the word. There is, however, a solution that suggests a clear meaning of the verb without requiring emendation of the text. Gesenius recommended this plausible explanation in his *Thesaurus*, when he parsed the verb as a *tipʿel* (*TLHC* 2:1095; see also Gesenius 1817, p. 254). König (1881, pp. 471, 557), too, approached the verb as a causative *tipʿel*, comparing the form to *tirgaltî* (Hos 11:3) and *məturgām* (Ezra 4:7; see König 1881, p. 217; and Yoo 1999, p. 136 for this category). They add this form to the list given in the latest edition of Gesenius' grammar, which conspicuously omits the form currently under discussion (GKC §55h), despite its inclusion in the *Thesaurus* and the *Lehrgebäude*. This list includes (a) תתחרה (*tətaḥăre[h]*) and מתחרה (*mətaḥăre[h]*), respectively 'you contend with' and 'one contending with' (Jer 12:5; 22:15), (b) מתרגם (*məturgām*) 'translated, interpreted' (Ezra 4:7), and (c) תרגלתי (*tirgaltî*) for meaning, see Hutton and Marzouk 2012 (Hos 11:3).

3. Establishing the Parameters

For the most part, the following analysis concurs with Gesenius' interpretation of the verb's morphology, since several difficulties emerge in the attempts to explain these forms other than as legitimate verbal forms. The lexemes mentioned above (*tətaḥăre[h]*/*mətaḥăre[h]*, *məturgām*, and *tirgaltî*) are often analyzed as quadriliteral denominalizations (i.e., verbalizations) of *t*-preformative nouns, as is *təpôṣôtîkem*, as discussed earlier. This interpretation may, in fact, prove an adequate understanding of the second of these lexemes (*məturgām*), since it is treated the same way in other Semitic languages that seem to have received the word as an Akkadian loan, possibly via Aramaic, and thus as the quadriliteral root תרגם (see, e.g., BDB 1076a).[4] But explanation as a quadriliteral denominalization seems unlikely for the first (*tətaḥăre[h]*/*mətaḥăre[h]*) and third (*tirgaltî*). Although there was at some point a Hebrew noun תחרה (/taḥărâ/) related to Mishnaic Hebrew תחרות (*taḥărût*) and Aramaic תחרותא (*taḥărûtā*; Jastrow 1662), the earliest attestations of the noun in Sir 31:29; 40:5 (cited by Joüon 1:169 §59e; see also BDB 354a, s.v. חרה *hitpaʿel*) are both too textually inconclusive and too chronologically late to serve as decisive proof of the verb's identity as a denominalized form (cf. discussion in Hutton and Marzouk 2012). Similarly, we may regard as dubious the attempt by Tur-Sinai to link *tirgaltî* to Akkadian *tarkullu* 'mooring post' (1967, p. 431). Although the connection would have justified the various ancient versions' interpretation of the verb as some sort of "binding," both major dictionaries of Akkadian analyze the word as a Sumerian loan (*CAD* T, p. 236; cf. *AHw* 1330). If the word is no longer taken to be derived from Semitic *RGL* 'foot,' then it is pointless to try to justify the versions' disparate translations incorporating some sort of "binding," since all of them also depend precisely on the self-evidently podiatric connotations of the word to justify the "binding" nuance of the word (cf. Hutton and Marzouk 2012). The difficulties encountered in analyzing any of these verbs as denominalized lexemes suggest that an alternative explanation is warranted, at least in the cases of *tətaḥăre(h)*/*mətaḥăre(h)*, *tirgaltî*, and *təpôṣôtîkem*.

In the following analysis, the prefixed forms *tətaḥăre(h)* and *mətaḥăre(h)* (imperfect and participle, respectively) will not figure heavily into the discussion. Instead, the major point of concern here is the anomalous appearance of the *tV- prefix onto the perfects *tirgaltî* and *təpôṣôtîkem*, and particularly the latter. If these verbs' respective morphologies are in fact to be subsumed under the general rubric of Semitic t-stems, why do they not appear in Hebrew as ***hitrVgaltî* and ***hitpôṣôtîkem*, with the **hit-* prefix common to the *hitpaʿel*, the Hebrew

[4] Compare, for example, the Old Assyrian verb *ragāmu* (Gt) 'raise claims against each other' (*AHw* 942a; *CDA* 295a; *CAD* R, pp. 63b–64a) and the more common Assyrian and Babylonian nominal form *targumannu* 'interpreter, dragoman' (*AHw* 1329b; *CDA* 400a; *CAD* T, pp. 229a–30a). The same quadriliteral root appears as the Ethiopic Q-stem verb *targʷama* 'to translate.'

reflex of the Semitic tD-stem?[5] In this study, I demonstrate that the representatives of the putative "*tipʿel*" stem are most likely analyzed as morphosyntactically constrained forms demonstrating otherwise regularly developed morphology. If correct, this conclusion brings in its wake two corollaries. First, although those who parse the verb *təpôṣôtîkem* as a verbal *tipʿel* stem are essentially justified, the common description of the prefixed **tV-* as a causative marker akin to the *hV-* prefix of the *hipʿil* (e.g., Ibn Janaḥ [Barthélemy 1986, p. 659]; Parḥon 1844, 52b; Hitzig 1841, pp. 205–06; Graf 1862, pp. 336–37; see above) is incorrect. Second, it becomes probable that we should reconstruct a (semi-)productive tG-stem[6] in Northern (i.e., Israelian) Hebrew, as evidenced in the work of the northern prophets Jeremiah (12:5; 22:15; 25:34) and Hosea (11:3).

4. The Derivational Prefix in Semitic

Although an extended discussion of the presence of the tG/Gt-stem in Proto-Semitic and of the tG-stem in Hebrew is not possible here, a brief review of its development in Hebrew is warranted. Comparative evidence from the wider Semitic language family demonstrates conclusively that a tG-stem existed in Proto-Semitic (in which the derivational **t* was prefixed; Diem 1982; Lieberman 1986; Garr 1993; Testen 1999). The tG-stem (represented in some languages by its metathesized counterpart, the Gt-stem) was subsequently inherited by the major Semitic sub-families and appears productively in East Semitic,[7] as well as in the various sub-groupings of West Semitic, among which are (a) the Ethiopian languages,[8] (b) the non-Northwest branches of Central Semitic,[9] and (c) the Northwest branch of Central Semitic represented by Ugaritic,[10] Deir Alla,[11] the Aramaic dialects (along with the related Samʾalian),[12] and the Canaanite dialects.[13]

In an article dealing primarily with the Hebrew *nipʿal*, Garr (1993) has shown that in Proto-Semitic the derivational prefixes */n-/ and */t-/ were most likely attached immediately to the verbal base. When this verbal base was */-qtal/, as in the Proto-Semitic verbal adjective (which was appropriated as the suffix-conjugation in West

[5] Throughout this study, I distinguish between the tG- and Gt-stems and between the tD- and Dt-stems. This distinction does not derive from an original Proto-Semitic or Proto-Northwest Semitic distinction; both groups most likely began as tG and tD (Diem 1982; Lieberman 1986; Garr 1993; Testen 1999). The distinction emerged as various languages began to infix the derivational **t* instead of prefixing it; the stems diverged functionally as well in the different languages, but this divergence is an effect of the languages' respective developments and is not predicated on the morphological distinction between prefixed **t* and infixed **t*.

[6] By "(semi-)productive" I mean a grammatical form that, when analyzed synchronically, is used in new formulations and compositions (i.e., is *productive*) while at the same time, when viewed diachronically, is in the *process* of becoming *vestigial*. Because the tG-stem was used in a variety of forms and with at least five different verbal roots (see below, §8), it seems as though the stem was productive in northern Hebrew for at least part of the biblical period (until ca. 600 B.C.). However, the rarity of the stem as it may be traced in Biblical Hebrew, combined with the clear indications that the stem was not recognized by the Masoretes as independent of the *hitpaʿel*, suggests that the tG-stem was already becoming vestigial — if not entirely so — by the time of the closure of the Hebrew canon.

[7] E.g., Akkadian: Inf.: *pitrusum*; Dur.: *iptarras*; Perf.: *iptatras*; Pret.: *iptaras*; Imptv.: *pitras*; Part.: *muptarsum*; Vb. Adj.: *pitrus-* (Gelb 1952, p. 222; *GAG* 120–21 §92; Huehnergard 1997, pp. 390–93).

[8] E.g., Classical Ethiopic: Pref.: *yətqat(t)al*; Suff.: *taqat(a)la*; Imptv.: *taqatal*; Inf. *taqatəlo(t)* (Dillmann 1907, pp. 151–53 §80 [stem III, 1]; Lambdin 1978, p. 205 [Gt]; Tropper 2002, pp. 103–04, esp. §44.442 [stem T_1]).

[9] E.g., Classical Arabic: Pref.: *yaqtatilu*; Suff.: *(i)qtatala*; Imptv.: *(i) qtatil*; Vb. Noun: *(i)qtitālᵘⁿ* (i.e., the VIII-stem; W. Fischer 2002, p. 98 §162g, 240 para. 6). Fischer notes further, "Pre-classical Arabic had a *t*-prefix," i.e., as still demonstrated in the *ta*-prefix of the tD- (V) and tL- (VI) stems (ibid., p. 98 §162g n. 4, also p. 27 §47).

[10] Pref.: *yiqtatvl-*; Suff.: *ʾiqtatvl-*; Imptv.: *(ʾi)qtatvl-* (*UT* 1:81 §9.33; Segert 1984, p. 66 §54.32; Tropper 2000, pp. 518–32 §74.23; Sivan 2001, pp. 128–31).

[11] Pref.: *ytqtl*(?); Suff.: *ʾtqtl*(?) (see Hoftijzer and van der Kooij 1976, pp. 192, 228–29, 256–57, 292:I 7 [= line 5 in McCarter 1980; and Hackett 1984]; II 9 [2x]; V; but cf. Garr 1985, pp. 119–20; Hackett 1984, pp. 40, 64, 96, 97).

[12] Garr 1985, p. 119; Tropper 1993, p. 311; Huehnergard 1995, p. 274 n. 35. Dialects displaying the tG include Biblical Aramaic (Bauer and Leander 1927, p. 90 §28a; Rowley 1929, pp. 79–80; Rosenthal 1995, p. 46 §99), Palestinian Aramaic (Stevenson 1924, pp. 44–46 §16; Golomb 1985, pp. 133–35; Fassberg 1990, pp. 177–78 §134 [despite calling it a "Gt-stem"]), Syriac (Hutchinson 1855, pp. 58–59 §21; Nöldeke 1904, pp. 106–07 §162; Arayathinal 1957, pp. 282–87 §§111–14; Coakley 2002, pp. 68–70), and the dialects recorded in the inscriptions at Sefire (Sf I A 28, 29; Sf I B [9]; Sf I C [7]; Fitzmyer 1995, pp. 86, 87, 103, 195; cf. Dupont-Sommer 1958, pp. 214, 241; and Greenfield 1964, p. 308), Nerab 2.4 (Gibson 1975, p. 98), and Zinjirli (ancient Samʾal; *KAI* 214:30; Sarauw 1907, pp. 60–61; Dion 1974, pp. 166–70; Muraoka 1984, pp. 95–98 §§11–12). Dialects displaying the Gt include that recorded at Tell el-Fakheriyah (line 23; Abou-Assaf, Bordreuil, and Millard 1982, pp. 37, 46; cf. Kaufman 1982, p. 173; Muraoka 1984, p. 95 §10).

[13] E.g., Byblian Phoenician (Pref.: *yqttl*; Harris 1936, p. 43 §13.7; Friedrich and Röllig 1999, p. 94 §150; Krahmalkov 2001, p. 157) and Moabite (*KAI* 181:11, 15, 19, 32; Jackson 1989, pp. 111, 117, 121).

Semitic), the resultant form (**/n=qtal/) contained a word-initial triconsonantal cluster. Although such clusters were apparently unproblematic in pre-Proto-Semitic, they were not permissible in Proto-Semitic. Some daughter languages of Proto-Semitic inserted an anaptyctic */a/ between the derivational prefix and the base of the verbal adjective in order to alleviate this triconsonantal cluster, yielding **/n=qtal/ > */naqtal/ (cf. Akk. *naprus* and Heb. *niqtal*, each displaying further language-internal developments; contrast Arab. VII *infaʿala*, which did not insert an anaptyctic vowel).[14] The same innovation, Garr argues, occurred in the causative Š-stem perfect (**/š=qtal/ > */ša=qtal/ [> */ha=qtil/ in many daughter languages; cf. Heb. *hipʿil*]). According to Garr, however, a separate verbal base was used in the N-stem prefixed forms, in which the derivational morpheme becomes medial, since it follows the inflectional prefix. Cross-Semitic comparison demonstrates that the verbal base of the prefixed conjugation forms was not */-qtal/ but rather */-qatil/ (cf. Akk. *tapparis*, Arab. *tanqatil*, Heb. *tiqqātēl*). In contrast, the lack of inflectional pronoun prefixes in the infinitive and imperative forms — based as they were on the imperfect form — created yet another problem. The biconsonantal cluster, which was permissible in Proto-Semitic (hence, */n=qatil/), was not tolerated in most of the daughter languages. These daughter languages developed a prothetic syllable */ʾV-/ in order to alleviate the word-initial consonant cluster (cf. Eth. *ʾanqalqala*; Ug. *ʾištmʿ* [/ʾištamaʿ/ < **štamaʿ*] 'listen!' [m.sg.] [*KTU* 1.16 VI 42]; and the Canaanite toponyms *ʾeštāʾōl* [Josh 15:33; Judg 13:25], *ʾeštĕmōaʿ* [Josh 21:14], *ʾeltĕqōn* [Josh 15:59], *ʾeltĕqē* [Josh 19:44; 21:23]). Several languages show the lenition of the causative morpheme in the C-stem: phonemic */š/ (= IPA [s]) > /h/.[15] In these languages, the anaptyctic prefix of the N-stem infinitive also became aspirated as a result of the analogical extension of the /h-/ (< */š/) to all derived stems. For this reason, we find in these languages derived stems beginning with */hV-/, such as Heb. *nipʿal* imptv. *hiqqātēl*; compare the *hitpaʿel* perf. *hitqattēl*, and so on. Thus, Garr's solution deftly explains the variation of the derivational morpheme's presentation throughout the Hebrew *nipʿal* paradigm: *niqtal* ~ *yiqqātēl* ~ *hiqqātēl*.

We can reconstruct similar developmental processes for the t-stems of the Semitic languages. In pre-Proto-Semitic, the derivational **t* was prefixed directly to the verbal base, yielding */t=q(V)tVl/. Because of the complex developmental processes undergone by this form, each of its constituent elements will be handled separately in the following discussion. First I treat the morphology of the verbal base */q(V)tVl/, and then the morphology of the prefixed derivational **t*.

5. The Verbal Base of the tG-Stem in Semitic and in Hebrew

Although the presence of a tG-stem in Hebrew is still contested in some camps (e.g., Bean 1976, pp. 17–19), enough cross-Semitic and Hebrew-internal evidence exists to situate the (semi-)productive existence of the stem in some varieties of Biblical Hebrew on solid ground. One of the primary indicators of this productivity is the probable presence in Biblical Hebrew of a tG-stem in the roots of *RGL* (*tirgaltî* [Hos 11:3][16]), *PQD* (e.g., *hitpāqĕdû* [Judg 20:15, 17][17]), *ŠYN* (*maštîn* [1 Sam 25:22, 34; 1 Kgs 14:10; 16:11; 21:21; 9:8]),[18] *ḤRH* (*tətaḥăreh* and *mətaḥăreh* [Jer 12:5; 22:15]), and *PWṢ* (the verb currently under examination). Many of these roots exhibit abnormal morphologies in the preserved forms. Some require independent analysis (e.g., *RGL* [Hutton and Marzouk 2012] and *PWṢ*), some require corroboration from later Hebrew traditions (e.g., *PQD*, which appears in the tG-stem in Samaritan Hebrew [*itfāqādu*; Ben-Ḥayyim 2000, p. 119; Arnold 2005, pp. 8, 143 G1]),[19] and some require corroboration from cognates in other Semitic languages (e.g., *ŠYN*).

---

[14] This insertion of the anaptyctic vowel is unrelated to the "intrusive vowel" intervening between consonantal personal markers and the verbal base in the G-stem imperfects, as reconstructed by Hasselbach (2004).

[15] Leslau 1944; Bravmann 1969; Voigt 1994; 1995.

[16] Hutton and Marzouk 2012.

[17] BL 281 §38f; Bergsträsser 1929, 2.100 §18i; Yalon 1932, p. 217; Blau 1957, p. 386; Schottroff 1976, p. 468; Garr 1985, p. 120; Testen 1999, p. 5; Arnold 2005, p. 143 G1; Creason 2007, p. 40.

[18] BL 405 §56u″; *HALOT* 1479, s.v. שׁין; Krebernik 1991, 238 §3.1.7; *IBHS* 425 n. 1; cf. BDB 1010a, s.v. שׁין. The form, of course, is an original tG-stem, which has subsequently undergone the typical metathesis of the derivational **t* with the root-initial sibilant.

[19] Two prefixed-*t* stems are found in Samaritan Hebrew: one "with geminated second radical," corresponding to the Biblical Hebrew *hitpaʿel* = Proto-Semitic tD-stem, and one "with simple second radical," corresponding to the Proto-Semitic tG-stem and identified here as synonymous with the so-called Hebrew *tipʿel* (Ben-Ḥayyim 2001, p. 119 §2.1.5.1; cf. Macuch 1969, p. 292 §73, who apparently considers the latter an Aramaic morphological loan). For Hebrew in the post-biblical Jewish tradition, see Ornan 1990.

Cross-Semitic comparison is inconclusive as to the vowel pattern of the tG-stem verbal base(s). In Arabic, the base of the Gt- (VIII)-stem perfect was */-qatal/ (e.g., [*i*]*qtatal*; cf. Akk. perf. *iptatras*, pret. *iptaras*; Eth. impf. *yəqat*[*t*]*al*, perf. *taqat*[*a*]*la*, imptv. *taqatal*), although the other forms are formed on a */-qatil/ base (Arab. impf. *yiqtatilu*, imptv. [*i*]*qtatil*, part. *muqtatil*; cf. Eth. inf. *taqatəlot*[?]) or a */-qitāl/ base (verb. noun [*i*]*qtitāl*^{un}; for these forms, see charts in W. Fischer 2002, p. 240; and Bennett 1998, p. 104). Aramaic evidence would support a */-qatil/ base in the perfect (BiblAram. [*h*/ʾ]*itqətēl* < */hitqatil/ [e.g., *hitrəḥīṣû*,[20] Dan 3:28], cf. Syr. *ʾētqətēl* / *ʾētqətīl*), imperfect (BiblAram. *yitqətēl* [e.g., *yitʿăbēd*, Dan 3:29], cf. Syr. *nētqətēl* / *nētqətīl*), and participle (BiblAram. *mitqətēl* [e.g., *mityəhēb*, Ezra 4:20], cf. Syr. *mētqətēl* / *mētqətīl*). The verbal base of the infinitive, however, was most likely */-qatāl/ (BiblAram. *hitqətālâ* [e.g., *lə-hitqəṭālâ*, Dan 2:13]; cf. the Canaanite toponyms mentioned above with form *ʾeqtətōl*; for Aramaic forms, see Bauer and Leander 1927, pp. 106–09 §34). The evidence from Ugaritic is sparse, thanks to its general orthographic lack of vowels, combined with complications occasioned by the possibility of syncope of the theme vowel (e.g., Tropper 1990; 2000, pp. 518–19 §74.232.1, 528 §74.234.1; cf. Krebernik 1991, pp. 229–31 §2.1.3; Huehnergard 1987, pp. 320–21; Sivan 1984, pp. 172–73). Despite the surfeit of ambiguous evidence, it may be summarized here that Hebrew's closest relatives seem to exhibit a propensity toward verbal bases in the */-qatal/ or */-qatil/ categories, perhaps with passive and active semantic values, respectively.

Hebrew-internal evidence is equally ambiguous. Although the one Biblical Hebrew root demonstrating a relatively paradigmatic form, *PQD*, provides evidence of a *t*-prefixed verbal stem in which the middle radical lacked gemination, the root appears too infrequently to provide much evidence as to the vowels in the stem's paradigmatic verbal base. We can at most posit an original */-qatVl/ base, in which the thematic vowel has been reduced in each exemplar because of the addition of 3.m/c.pl. suffixes (cf. the prefix-form [*way-*]*yitpāqĕdû* [Judg 20:15] and the suffix-form *hitpāqĕdû* [Judg 20:15, 17]). In isolation, the verb *tirgaltî* also provides minimal information, since its perfect base can be derived from either */-qtVl/ or */-qVtVl/. Yet, comparing *hitpāqĕdû* and *tirgaltî* side by side may prove instructive. We may accept with some degree of certainty the vowel */a/ between R_1 and R_2 suggested by the former verb, on the basis of cross-Semitic comparison (although cf. §7, below, for an alternative explanation of *tirgaltî*'s development from */-qtal/). Evidence from the latter verbal exemplar limits the thematic vowel to */a/ or */i/ (> /a/ by Philippi's law; Lambdin 1985), again in conformity with the cross-Semitic data summarized above. Finally, we may find some Hebrew-internal corroboration for a tG-verbal base */-qatil/ — albeit derived from a later vocal tradition — in the single case of Babylonian pointing reading *hitnāśēʾ* (Ezek 17:14; for text, see Kahle 1913, p. 195; cited by Bergsträsser 1929, 2.100 §18i).

The verbal base of the tG-stem in Hebrew is thus quite difficult to determine with certainty. Nonetheless, enough evidence exists to suggest that we are dealing with a */-qatVl/ base, in which V = /a/ or /i/, and in which the middle radical is singleton (i.e., not geminate).

6. Prefixed Derivational **t* in Hebrew

Whereas Ethiopic alleviated the initial consonant cluster of the tG-stem through epenthetic insertion of a vowel *following* the derivational **t* (see Eth. perf. *taqat*[*a*]*la*, imptv. *taqatal*, and inf. *taqatəlo*[*t*]), most other West Semitic languages prefixed the epenthetic vowel to the verbal base in all forms. This prefixation of the tG- and tD-stems' epenthetic vowel *before* derivational **t* stands in contrast to the N-stem, where, as was seen above, many languages inserted the vowel after the derivational morpheme in the perfect. In the N-stem, consistency was maintained only in Arabic, where we find perfect *inqatala*, imperfect *yanqatilu*, infinitive *ʾinqitāl*^{un}, and so on. This consistency, however, was the norm in the tG-/Gt-stem of all Central Semitic languages and the tD-stem of the Northwest Semitic languages (though cf. the Arab. and Ug. tD-stem and the Arab. tL-stem). In the various reflexes of these stems, whenever the inflected verbal form was not naturally prefixed with a personal morphological marker (/yV-/, /tV-/, /ʾV-/, or /nV-/) or the participial morpheme (/mV-/), an epenthetic prefix (/ʾV-/) was inserted before the cluster comprised of -tR_1-/-R_1t-:

---

[20] The long /ī/ thematic vowel presumably developed here as a response to the open syllable formed by the suffixation of the 3.m.pl. morpheme. However, Bauer and Leander (1927, p. 108 §34h–j) derive the perfect verbal base originally from */-qatal/. Since none of the Biblical Aramaic 3.m.sg. perfects is formed from a strong root, it is quite difficult to validate this assertion, and */qatil/ is not precluded.

	Perf.	Imperf.	Imptv.	Inf.	Part.
Arab. Gt	***(i)qt***_atala_	***yaqt***_atilu_	***(i)qt***_atil_	***(i)qt***_itāl_^{un}	***muqt***_atil_^{un}
Arab. tD	*taqattala*	*yataqattalu*	*taqattal*	*taqattul*^{un}	*mutaqattil*^{un}
Ug. tD	***ʾiqt***_atVla_	***yiqt***_atVlu_	***ʾiqt***_atil_	***tVqt***_atVlu_	***muqt***_atVlu_
Ug. tD	*taqattVla*	*yiqtatVlu*	*taqattVI*	*tVqattVlu*	*muqattVlu?*
Aram. tG	****(h/ʾ)itq***_atil_	****yitq***_atil_	****(h/ʾ)itq***_VtVl_	****(h/ʾ)itq***_atālā_	****mitq***_atil_
Aram. tD	****(h/ʾ)itq***_attal_	****yitq***_attal_	****(h/ʾ)itq***_attal_	****(h/ʾ)itq***_atālā_	****mitq***_attil_
Syr. tG	***ʾetq***_ət_$^{\bar{\imath}}/_{\bar{e}}$_l_	***netq***_ət_$^{\bar{\imath}}/_{\bar{e}}$_l_	***ʾetq***_atl_	***metq***_ətālū_	***metq***_ət_$^{\bar{\imath}}/_{\bar{e}}$_l_
Syr. tD	***ʾetq***_attal_	***netq***_attal_	***ʾetq***_attal_	***metq***_attāl_	***metq***_attal_
Heb. tD	***hitq***_attēl_	***yitq***_attēl_	***hitq***_attēl_	***hitq***_attēl_	***mitq***_attēl_

The precise nature of the epenthetic syllable requires further analysis, because it is manifested differently in the various Central Semitic languages. In most languages, it displays a great deal of language-internal regularity, appearing throughout the paradigm regardless of morphosyntactic environment. For example, so far as the grammars are concerned, Biblical Hebrew and all forms of Aramaic maintain the syllable ubiquitously, even if the constituent consonant gradually shifted from /h/ to /ʾ/ in Aramaic. In Biblical Aramaic, this alternation between the prefix consonants in the tG *hitpeʿel* and *ʾitpeʿel* stems and between the tD *hitpaʿal* and *ʾitpaʿal* stems, which for the most part appears to be chronologically and dialectally conditioned, is purely formal and does not affect the semantic value of the word:

tG: *lə-hitqəṭālâ* ('to be killed,' Dan 2:9)

vs. *ʾetʿăqarû* ('they were plucked up,' Dan 7:8)

tD: *hitnaddābû* ('they offered freely,' Ezra 7:15)

vs. *ʾityāʿaṭû* ('they have consulted,' Dan 6:8)

In Biblical Hebrew, the prefix /ʾVt-/ occurs once on a t-stem form: in Psalm 76:6 we find *ʾeštôləlû* ('they are spoiled'). One might posit that this form shows Aramaic influence, a particularly compelling hypothesis in light of the many cases of the Aramaizing *ʾapʿel* causative stem found irregularly in Biblical Hebrew (e.g., the perf. *ʾegʾāltî* ['I have stained,' Isa 63:3], inf. abs. *ʾaškîm* ['persistently,' Jer 25:3], and possibly imptv. *ʾabrēk* ['kneel down!' Gen 41:43; see Böttcher 1868, p. 281 §1015; cf. Lambdin 1953, p. 146; Janssen 1956, p. 68; *HALOT* 10, s.v. אברך]). Regardless of the linguistic source of the odd form *ʾeštôləlû*, it is clear that the lexeme fits into the broader developmental context of Northwest Semitic.

In two reasonably well-attested Central Semitic languages, however, the morphosyntactic environment constrains the morphological realization of this epenthetic prefix. Like Hebrew and Aramaic, Ugaritic and Arabic normally affix this epenthetic prefix to otherwise unprefixed t-stem forms: the perfect, the imperative, and the infinitive (/verbal noun). For example, the imperative in Ugaritic is realized as *iqttl* (/ʾiqtatal/) when sentence-initial or independent. However, when the Ugaritic imperative is preceded by a conjunction, the operation of sandhi eliminates the epenthetic prefix of the isolated imperative form.[21] The two forms appear together in the sequence *ištmʿ wtqġ* (/ʾištamaʿ wa[t]taqaġ/ 'give heed and attune your ear,' 1.16.VI.29–30, 42; see Sivan 2001, p. 131;

[21] Lass (1984, p. 70) describes sandhi as "syntactically conditioned allomorphy, with rules operating on the termini of the peripheral morphemes of words of any internal structure," that is, variation in morphology conditioned by the syntactic environment and manifested at word boundaries; cf. the distinction made by Hock (1991, p. 246) between external sandhi (occurring at word boundaries) and internal sandhi (occurring word-internally with the addition or deletion of morphemes). Insofar as the Semitic languages rely heavily on inseparable prepositions and affixed personal morphemes to augment their nominal and verbal systems, it is difficult to make a hard distinction between Hock's "internal" and "external" sandhi. For studies of sandhi in Northwest Semitic languages, see Tsumura 1991; 1997 and sources cited there. For sandhi more generally, see W. Allen 1962; and Anderson 1986.

Krebernik 1991, p. 231 §2.1.4; cf. Tropper 2000, pp. 527–28 §74.233).[22] The verbal noun similarly exhibits a variety of forms (e.g., Huehnergard 1987, p. 321; Krebernik 1991, pp. 231–32 §2.1.5; Tropper 2000, pp. 530–31 §74.236; see also ibid., p. 573, §74.434 for the tD-stem).

Arabic also exhibits a variation in the morphology of such forms, similarly conditioned by morphosyntactic environment. When naturally resulting biconsonantal clusters were sentence-initial or isolated, Classical Arabic alleviated these clusters by prefixing an epenthetic vowel, marked with *alif al-waṣl*. This epenthetic syllable was ubiquitously represented in the orthography of non-classical Arabic[23] with an *alif* (hence {*ʾQTTL*} /ʾiqtatala/). However, in Classical Arabic this epenthetic syllable was pronounced only in certain environments, such as when in sentence-initial position (e.g., *ʾistamiʿ* 'Listen!'[24]). This epenthetic insertion was represented orthographically through the addition of the epenthetic vowel in those positions where the syllable was pronounced in Classical Arabic, with the concomitant insertion of the glottal-stop marker *hamza*. In most environments, however, the word-initial consonant cluster was alleviated in one of two ways, each of which was affected by sandhi and is marked orthographically through the addition of *waṣla*, the marker of elision, to the *alif*. If the consonant cluster was not already alleviated naturally by following a word ending in a vowel (e.g., *qāla stamiʿ* 'He said, "Listen!"'), a connecting vowel /i/ was added orthographically to the *preceding* word (e.g., *qālati stamiʿ* < **qālat stamiʿ* 'She said, "Listen!"').[25] Thus, it is evident that even though Classical Arabic does not exhibit the epenthetic insertion in most syntactic structures, non-classical Arabic partakes in the same epenthetic insertion of */ʾV-/ before a word-initial consonant cluster comprising -tR_1-/-R_1t- as do the other Central Semitic languages. Because of its retention of case vowels and other conservative morphological features, Classical Arabic had fewer environments than non-classical Arabic in which epenthesis was necessary.

With respect to the tG/Gt-stem, the significant difference between Arabic and the Northwest Semitic languages lies in the conditioning environment. As Garr notes, in Ugaritic specifically, "[t]he prothetic syllable … is sensitive to the derivational boundary separating the initial two consonants," in that its insertion occurs only when this boundary is present (1991, p. 153). We might generalize this principle to Northwest Semitic as a whole, citing the alleviation of the biconsonantal, mono-morphemic Proto-Semitic cluster */bn/ 'son' in Hebrew and Aramaic through the insertion of a medial anaptyctic vowel (PS */bn/ > Heb. *ben*, Aram. *bar*; Testen 1985). In contrast, Arabic usually alleviates an initial consonant cluster through sandhi or with the insertion of *alif al-waṣl*, regardless of whether the cluster spans a morphemic boundary (PS */bn/ > CArab. [*ʾi*]*bn*).

Classical Arabic seems to be the outlier among the Central Semitic languages in its non-operation of epenthetic insertion preceding the consonant cluster occasioned by the addition of derivational **t*. However, the evidence from Ugaritic indicates that the phenomenon obtained in Northwest Semitic as well, at least in limited environments or under sporadically operating constraints. Ugaritic is not the only Northwest Semitic language displaying evidence of this phenomenon. In fact, a third language — Hebrew — demonstrates the non-operation of epenthetic vowel insertion on a t-stem perfect in a well-defined morphosyntactic environment in later recorded dialects of the language (see below). An examination of a few derived-stem verbal forms in Mishnaic Hebrew leads to a fuller discussion of the environmentally constrained tG-stem perfect forms in Samaritan Hebrew.

In Mishnaic Hebrew, asserts Segal (1927, p. 58 §115), the *nipʿal* infinitive lost the consonant /h-/ of its epenthetic prefix when following an inseparable preposition (e.g., ליבטל /l-ibbaṭēl/ < */lə-hibbaṭēl/ < */l-hinbaṭil/; the *yôd* seems to mark the short /-i-/ epenthetic vowel). Typically, this apocope of /h-/ is presumed to occur as a function of the elision of intervocalic *hê*, known from elsewhere in Hebrew. However, Aaron Rubin and Naʿama Pat-El have independently drawn my attention (pers. comm.) to the fact that the form of the infinitive in Mishnaic Hebrew may have come about by anology with the imperfect; if this is the case, the apocope of */h/ discussed is no longer an issue. Rather, in light of the foregoing discussion, we may wonder whether some dialects of Hebrew allowed the *nipʿal* infinitive to remain without prefix when following an enclitic particle preposition or a vowel-final

[22] For additional cases of sandhi in Ugaritic, see Tsumura 1991; 1997, pp. 579–81; and Sivan 2001, pp. 32, 138.

[23] I have taken the terminology "non-classical Arabic" from W. Fischer 2002, p. 12 §19.

[24] All Arabic examples except *qālati stamiʿ* (below) were taken from Abboud and McCarus 1983, p. 58. I am grateful for the help of Safwat Marzouk in understanding the operation of *alif al-waṣl*.

[25] Philippi 1895, pp. 188–92; Lambert 1895, pp. 225–28; Hämeen-Antilla 1984, pp. 305–13; Garr 1991, pp. 147, 153; W. Fischer 2002, pp. 12–13 §§19–22; although, cf. Barth 1894, pp. 7–10.

word (i.e., *n=qatil > inqatil / -V# __, with sandhi then operating on the two consecutive vowels). More accurately stated, it may be that the development of the epenthetic prefix consonant was blocked in environments where sandhi operates. Indeed, a similar morphological phenomenon is not unknown in Biblical Hebrew, where we find in the Masoretic text the forms *ûbikkāšəlô* (< **û-bə-hikkāšəlô*, literally 'and in his being tripped,' Prov 24:17), *bēhārēg* (< **bə-hēhārēg*, 'in the killing of,' Ezek 26:15), and *bēʿāṭēp* (< **bə-hēʿāṭēp*, 'in the faintness of,' Lam 2:11; cf. Ps 61:3) and others.[26] Clearly, this was not the form that became generalized throughout Biblical Hebrew; nonetheless, its existence in Biblical Hebrew and Modern Hebrew is noteworthy.

Moreover, grammarians of Samaritan Hebrew regularly describe the "collapse" of the epenthetic syllable in the perfect of the *hitpaʿel* stem(s) (see above) when the verbal exemplar follows the conjunction *wa-*. In the Samaritan recitation tradition, we find forms "such as *wētqaddeštimma* והתקדשתם, *wētmakkertimma* והתמכרתם, *wētbårråk* והתברך, [and] *wētbårråku* והתברכו" (Ben-Ḥayyim 2001, p. 119 §2.1.5.1) as well as *ētāllak* and *ētāttanu* (Arnold 2005, p. 9; see also Macuch 1969, p. 291 §aα).[27] According to Ben-Ḥayyim,

> A feature to be noted especially is the length of the vowel *ē* in the syllable *wēt-* in the perfect, for as a rule *waw conjunctive* attaches itself directly to the vowel of a word beginning with an original guttural consonant, such as ועשרון : *wišron*, ואת : *wit*. Thus, **wit-* and not *wēt*, is to be expected. This would seem to indicate that what we have here is a different origin, as if it were **wahit* > **wa'it* ... > *wēt*, i.e., that the vowel *a* of the *waw conjunctive* was not elided here as in the other combinations. (2001, p. 119 §2.1.5.2)

Although it is currently impossible to describe fully the developmental changes that yielded the Samaritan Hebrew forms (Ben-Ḥayyim 2001, pp. 92–93 §1.5.3.4: the problem "requires further study"), it is clear that one of two processes is at work in this dialect of Hebrew: either (a) the */h/ of the *hitpaʿel* prefix has elided in environments involving the prefixation of the conjunction, or (b) the regular development of the t-stems' epenthetic syllable (*∅ > *ʾV- → *hV- / #__tq[V]tal*) was arrested or blocked entirely in those same environments, so that the epenthetic syllable never fully developed as it did in the remainder of the paradigm, but instead allowed the present pronunciation to obtain. Orthographically, the first option is preferable, since it would explain the presence of *hê* in the written forms. Phonologically, however, the second option is more consistent with the forms of the proposed Biblical Hebrew tG-stem we have been examining, as the following discussion will show. If this latter solution is the case, the presence of *hê* in the Samaritan Hebrew forms may be explained as a case of orthographic leveling: on this model, it was never pronounced.

7. Morphosyntactic Conditioning Environments of the So-called *tipʿel*

The first point of note upon reconsidering the forms *təpôṣôtîkem* and *tirgaltî* is that, although they are generally handled extra-contextually (see, e.g., GKC §§55h, 91l), they each appear in linguistic environments replicating the same conditions governing the elision or non-development of *hê* in the Mishnaic and Samaritan Hebrew examples described above. To be specific, the form *tirgaltî* appears immediately after the 1.c.sg. independent pronoun *ʾānōkî*. If we accept the general applicability of the morphosyntactic explanation proposed here, two avenues are then open to us to describe the lexeme *tirgaltî* more precisely. Each of the following solutions assumes that, when following words or proclitic morphemes ending naturally in vowels, the Hebrew tG-stem perfect did not need to insert an epenthetic vowel to alleviate its word-initial consonant cluster. Instead, it preferred to allow sandhi to take effect, which blocked the expected development of the epenthetic syllable. Thus, while development of an epenthetic syllable */hi-/ broadly obtained, juxtaposition with a preceding vowel-final word optionally prevented this development.

---

[26] Cf. GKC §51l; BDB 742, s.v. עטף III; BL 228 §25z; Joüon 1:150 §51b; also Rendsburg 1982; Tsumura 1997.

[27] Naʿama Pat-El has kindly brought to my attention the argument presented by Kutscher (1962, pp. 18–19) explaining the loss of /ʾ/ in the direct-object marker in some forms of Hebrew and Aramaic. The process is not entirely identical to the one presented here, since Kutscher does not relate this syncope to a vowel-final preceding word. Nonetheless, the problem deserves further study.

(Solution 1): Positing an original verbal base */-rgal/ (see above) allows us to reconstruct an analogical process whereby the proto-Masoretic reading tradition substituted a known vowel pattern on an unfamiliar derived stem's consonantal structure (תרגלתי). The form clearly comprised two elements: a derivational prefix ת, recognizable from the *hitpaʿel*, and the verbal root רגל. This composite derived form stood over against the expected development of the form ****hitrgaltî** (with its analogically anticipated orthographic realization **התרגלתי, not to mention its violation of rules of syllabification in Hebrew) and instead paralleled that of the *nipʿal* perfect. This analogue allowed the pre-Masoretic vocal tradition to insert the same vowels into the new form's consonantal structure, yielding **niR₁R₂aR₃-* → */tirgal-/.

(Solution 2): It is possible to obtain the same form *tirgaltî* by reconstructing the direct affixation of derivational **t* to the verbal base */-ragVl/. On this model, we postulate the form's morphological development in the following manner. We begin by positing the (optional?) blocking of the normal development of the epenthetic syllable when following a vowel-final word:

(1) **ʾanōkī t=ragVltī* > **ʾanōkī tragVltī*

This form was presumably stable throughout the era of spoken Biblical Hebrew, but with the reduction of unstressed short vowels in open, unaccented syllables, a morphologically unstable form developed:

(2) **ʾanōkī tragVltī* > ***ʾanōkī trəgVltī*

Not recognizing the effect of the juxtaposition, the pre-Masoretic tradition inserted an anaptyctic vowel of indeterminate quality between the derivational prefix and the verbal base, which quickly reduced to vocalic *šəwăʾ* and then became *ḥîreq* by the rule of *šəwăʾ*. Concomitantly, the thematic vowel either retained its original identity as */a/, or developed into /a/ through the operation of Philippi's law (**í > á / _CCV#*; hence, */-rəgíltī/ > /-rəgáltî/; Lambdin 1985):

(3) ***ʾanōkī trəgVltī* > **ʾanōkī tərəgVltī* > **ʾanōkī tirgVltī* > *ʾānōkî tirgaltî*

In either of these reconstructed scenarios — that is, analogical extension from the *nipʿal* or natural development — the morphogenesis of *tirgaltî* may plausibly be traced to its morphosyntactic environment, in which the form followed a vowel-final word and was thus eligible for sandhi.

Similarly to the case of *tirgaltî*, the verb *təpôṣôtîkem* is actually prefixed with the *waw conjunctive* and must be analyzed as *ûtəpôṣôtîkem*. Here, however, the two variant explanations of the form's development — that is, normal development and analogy — coalesce. Again, we begin by assuming that the form's expected development of the epenthetic prefix /hi-/ was blocked by the possibility of sandhi's operation on the vowel-final preceding word. In this case, the preceding word was the prefixed conjunction. The conjunction most likely began in Proto-Semitic as the labiovelar approximant glide [w], "with rounding at the lips and vocalic articulation in the velar area" (Hock 1991, p. 135). In Tiberian Hebrew, this morpheme is realized in two different ways. In most contexts, the consonant remained articulated as [w], which was followed by an anaptyctic vowel (*/wV-/) realized as vocalic *šəwăʾ* in Biblical Hebrew (*wə-*). However, in contexts preceding consonant clusters and (other) bilabials, the conjunction's consonantal articulation had been weakened (perhaps already in Proto-Semitic or Proto-West Semitic) so that only the high, back vocalic articulation was perceived, hence its final realization in Tiberian Biblical Hebrew as *û-* (cf. *ûšəmûʾēl* [1 Sam 2:18]):[28]

(1) PS **w t=pVṣ-* > PNWS **ū tpVṣ-*

Because the middle radical of the root פוץ was originally */w/, the resultant theme vowel must have been either /ō/ or /ū/. Both vowels are commonly represented in middle weak roots in the *nipʿal*; the alternation between the two is predicated on the personal inflection of the verb. In the 3rd person, we find the ō-vowel predominant, with the lengthening of the anaptyctic vowel alleviating the word-initial consonant cluster. For the most part, the vowel is unmarked by a *mater lectionis* (e.g., *nāmōg* [1 Sam 14:16; Nah 2:7]; *nāśōg* [2 Sam 1:22]; *nāsōg* [Ps 44:19];

[28] For the semivocalic nature of the labiovelar glide [w] and its various alternations and common developments, see, e.g., Hock 1991, pp. 17–18 §2.1.7 and esp. 135–36 §7.3.6; Chitoran and Nevins 2008, p. 1901 and bibliography cited there.

nādōš [Isa 25:10]; *nāpōṣâ* [Jer 10:21]; *nāpōṣû* [Gen 10:18; 2 Kgs 25:5; Jer 40:15; 52:8; Ezek 28:25; 29:13; 34:6, 12]; *nāmōgû* [Exod 15:15; Josh 2:9, 24; Jer 49:23]; *nāzōrû* [Isa 1:4; Ezek 14:5]; *nāsōgû* [Isa 42:17; Jer 38:22]; *nākōnû* [Ezek 16:7; Prov 19:29]; *nābōkû* [Joel 1:18]; *nāpōšû* [Nah 3:18]), with the sole exception of *nābôkâ* (Est 3:15), where the vowel is marked. In the 1.c.sg. and 2.m.pl., the anaptyctic vowel has been reduced to *šəwăʾ*, and the ū-vowel occurs in the 1.c.sg. forms (e.g., *nəsûgōtî* [Isa 50:5]; *nəpûgōtî* [Ps 38:9]). In the 2.m.pl., however, the forms containing ō continue to predominate: *nəpōṣôtem* (Ezek 11:17; cf. *nəpôṣōtem* [Ezek 20:34] and *nəpōṣōtem* [Ezek 20:41]); and *nəqōṭōtem* (Ezek 20:43; 36:31) over against a few anomalous forms (*nēʿōr* [Zech 2:17]; *nāmōṭṭû* [Ps 17:5]). It is tempting to assume that the consonantal structure תפוצותיכם has been mistakenly pointed with a medial /ô/, on analogy with the other 1.c.sg. forms adduced above containing the vowel /û/. However, the heavy suffix at the end of the word may have conditioned the quality of the vowel, in a manner similar to the role of the heavy suffix on the 2.m.pl. forms, which seems to have preserved the /ô/ vowel. Thus, we may suggest that the form is, if not the expected one, an explicable one nonetheless:

(2) PNWS **ū t=pVṣōtī=kVmV* > PHeb. **ūtpōṣōtīkim*

As in the case of *tirgaltî* described above, a morphologically unstable form developed — unless, that is, an anaptyctic vowel between the derivational prefix and the verbal base had not already developed on analogy with the same development in the *nipʿal*:

(3) PHeb. **ūtpōṣōtīkim* > **ūtəpōṣōtīkim* > TibHeb. *ûtəpôṣôtîkem*

Again, the morphosyntactic environment of this tG-stem perfect form has blocked the development of the epenthetic prefix /hi-/.

8. Conclusion

Two distinct conclusions have been reached here concerning the lexeme *ûtəpôṣôtîkem* in Jeremiah 25:34. The first pertains to the specific morphological development of the word and its semantic value, the second more broadly to the analysis of the purported *tipʿel* stems in general.

I have traced the lexeme's development from an original tG-stem form, which, when following a word permitting sandhi to alleviate its initial consonant cluster, was irregularly prevented from developing the expected epenthetic /hi-/ prefix characteristic of the t-stem perfects in Hebrew (the vast majority of which are currently pointed as tD-stem *hitpaʿel*s). Orthographically, the omission of a prefixed ה in the two verbs discussed in §7 above may be described in the words of O'Connor (1983, p. 441) as "*sandhi* writings or utterance-level parsings." Otherwise, the word has developed predictably, with the exception of the pointing of the medial vowel as a long-ō vowel rather than a long-ū. But here, too, the morphosyntactic presence of the heavy 2.m.pl. object suffix *-kem* may have influenced the theme vowel on analogy with the effects of the 2.m.pl. subject suffix in the *nipʿal* perfects of middle-weak roots. Given the difficulty of predicting the precise semantic value of tG- and tD-stems merely from their morphology (e.g., *IBHS* 424–29 §26.1), the word *ûtəpôṣôtîkem* may best be translated simply as "and I will scatter you," founded on the basic meaning of the root פוץ 'to scatter.'[29] This word, comprising verse 34bα, continues the idea from verse 34a and persists in envisioning the individuals under judgment as a flock of sheep. Although the Septuagint allows this image to endure in the remainder of verse 34, drawing the falling leaders in comparison to the choice animals falling in the slaughter ('and you will fall like the chosen rams' [καὶ πεσεῖσθε ὥσπερ οἱ κριοὶ οἱ ἐκλεκτοί]), the Masoretic text shifts the image to one of an earthenware vessel falling — either falling off something onto a lower surface, or simply falling over, perhaps. For the purposes of the present study, it

[29] Although the t-stem in Biblical Hebrew (usually realized as the *hitpaʿel*) is typically reflexive in usage, it is not limited to such semantic values (see, e.g., Grüneberg 2003, pp. 191–210). The case is presumably the same for the originally tG-stem, which demonstrates transitivity in some Ugaritic cases, for example (e.g., Smith 2006, p. 77). Unfortunately, a thorough cross-Semitic investigation of the various usages of the tG-stem is impossible here, for considerations of space; such a study would undoubtedly be a desideratum in Semitic studies (see already the recent linguistic studies of Streck [2003] and Arnold [2005]).

is unnecessary to hypothesize the developmental history of the variants, as is attempted by J. Gerald Janzen (1973, p. 14, 194 n. 17). Rather, in both cases the image is naturally one of the sickeningly wide distribution of constituent pieces (i.e., "scattering"). In the Masoretic text, the word *ûtəpôṣôtîkem* functions as a pivot between the two metaphors of verse 34. In verse 34abα, the best of the sheep are being chosen for the slaughter, and the flock is thus "scattered" — that is, dispersed or distributed — while in the context of verse 34bαβ, the word proleptically anticipates the fate of the polity's leadership, comparing them to a "vessel" that will fall (*ûnəpaltem*), shatter (implicitly), and have its sherds scattered (made explicit through the anticipatory use of the verb *ûtəpôṣôtîkem*). This scattering is all too well known to those who have dropped a favorite vase or carafe. Thus, despite its semantic coincidence with the image of the Masoretic text, reliance on the purported Syriac rendering of Hebrew נפץ to justify this image is unnecessarily circular, since the lexeme could be the result of graphic confusion combined with haplography, as suggested above (cf. Targ. *wttbdrwn* vs. Pesh. *wttbrwn*).

Alongside this exegetical possibility of *ûtəpôṣôtîkem* arises a set of principles guiding my interpretation of the putative *tipʿel* stem. As has been discovered in the preceding discussion, the morphology of the so-called *tipʿel* is in reality morphosyntactically — and optionally — conditioned by an environment in which the preceding word ends in a (long) vowel. Thus, the form is much more plausibly construed within the broader rubric of the Semitic tG-stem than as a development internal to Hebrew and derived from *t*-preformative nouns, as Barth suggested long ago (1889, pp. 278–81 §180a, esp. 279; 1894, pp. 19–21). There is, properly speaking, no *tipʿel* stem, although the original Hebrew tG-stem may occasionally take that form when environmentally constrained. Moreover, I have sought to show elsewhere that the Hebrew tG-stem is plausibly reconstructed as a productive stem in some varieties of Hebrew; the unrecognized exemplars of this stem were subsequently conflated with — and pointed as — the *hitpaʿel* (Hutton and Marzouk 2012; see previously Bergsträsser 1929, 2.100 §18i; Yalon 1932, p. 220; Speiser 1955, pp. 118–21; Dombrowski 1962, pp. 220–23; Boyle 1969; Siebesma 1991, pp. 167, 169; see also Ornan 1990; but cf. Bean 1976, pp. 9, 17–19; and *IBHS* 424 §26.1.1.a). In particular, this seems to be the case for the bundle of dialects commonly known as "Israelian Hebrew" (e.g., Rendsburg 2002, esp. pp. 17–26; Yoo 1999, esp. pp. 12–17), in which can be found plausibly reconstructed tG-stem forms of the verbal roots *RGL*[30], *PQD*,[31] *ŠYN*,[32] *ḤRH*, and *PWṢ*.[33] If this analysis is correct, the productive or semi-productive use of the tG-stem would potentially serve as an isogloss between Israelian (Northern) and Judahite (Southern) Hebrew dialects.

Abbreviations

AHw	Wolfram von Soden. *Akkadisches Handwörterbuch*. 3 volumes. Wiesbaden: Harrassowitz, 1965–1981.
Akk.	Akkadian
Arab.	Arabic
Aram.	Aramaic
BDB	Francis Brown, S. R. Driver, and Charles A. Briggs. *A Hebrew and English Lexicon of the Old Testament*. Reprint 1959. Oxford: Clarendon Press, 1907.
BiblAram.	Biblical Aramaic
BL	Hans Bauer and Pontus Leander. *Historische Grammatik der hebräischen Sprache des Alten Testaments*. Halle: Niemeyer, 1922.
c.	common
C	consonant
CAD	A. Leo Oppenheim et al. *The Assyrian Dictionary of the Oriental Institute of the University of Chicago*. Chicago: The Oriental Institute of the University of Chicago, 1956–2010.

[30] Hutton and Marzouk 2012.

[31] BL 281 §38f; Bergsträsser 1929, 2.100 §18i; Yalon 1932, p. 217; Blau 1957, p. 386; Schottroff 1976, p. 468; Garr 1985, p. 120; Testen 1999, p. 5; Arnold 2005, p. 143 G1; Creason 2007, p. 40.

[32] BL 405 §56u″; *HALOT* 1479, s.v. שׁין; Krebernik 1991, 238 §3.1.7; *IBHS* 425 n. 1; cf. BDB 1010a, s.v. שׁין.

[33] Cf. GKC 151 §54l.

CArab.	Classical Arabic
CDA	Jeremy Black, Andrew George, and Nicholas Postgate, editors. *A Concise Dictionary of Akkadian*. SANTAG 5. Wiesbaden: Harrassowitz, 1999.
Eth.	Ethiopic
f.	feminine
GAG	Wolfram von Soden. *Grundriss der akkadischen Grammatik*. 2nd edition. Analecta orientalia 33. Rome: Pontificium Institutum Biblicum, 1995.
GKC	Wilhelm Gesenius, *Gesenius' Hebrew Grammar.* Edited by Emil Kautsch. Translated by Arthur E. Cowley. 2nd edition. Oxford: Oxford University Press, 1910.
GVG	*Carl* Brockelmann. *Grundriss der vergleichenden Grammatik der semitischen Sprachen*. Hildesheim: Olms, 1966.
Heb.	Hebrew
HALOT	Ludwig Koehler, Walter Baumgartner, and Johann Jakob Stamm. *The Hebrew and Aramaic Lexicon of the Old Testament*. 2 volumes. Leiden: Brill, 2001.
IBHS	Bruce K. Waltke and Michael P. O'Connor. *An Introduction to Biblical Hebrew Syntax*. Winona Lake: Eisenbrauns, 1990.
impf.	imperfect
imptv.	imperative
inf.	infinitive
inf. abs.	infinitive absolute
Jastrow	Marcus Jastrow. *A Dictionary of the Targumim, the Talmud Babli and Yerushalmi, and the Midrashic Literature*. New York: Judaica Press, 1971.
Joüon	Paul Joüon. *A Grammar of Biblical Hebrew*. Translated and revised by T. Muraoka. 2 volumes. Subsidia biblica 14/1–2. Rome: Editrice Pontificium Institutum Biblicum, 1991.
KAI	Herbert Donner and Wolfgang Röllig. *Kanaanäische und aramäische Inschriften*, Volume 1. 5th edition. Wiesbaden: Harrassowitz, 2002.
KTU	Manfried Dietrich, Oswald Loretz, and Joaquín Sanmartin. *The Cuneiform Alphabetic Texts: From Ugarit, Ras Ibn Hani and Other Places*. Abhandlungen zur Literatur Alt-Syrien-Palästinas und Mesopotamiens 8. 2nd enlarged edition. Münster: Ugarit-Verlag, 1995.
LXX	Septuagint
m.	masculine
MT	Masoretic text
part.	participle
perf.	perfect
PHeb.	Proto-Hebrew
pl.	plural
PNWS	Proto-Northwest Semitic
pret.	preterite
Qimḥi	Chomsky 1952
sg.	singular
Syr.	Syriac
Suff.	suffix form
TibHeb.	Tiberian Hebrew
TLHC	Wilhelm Gesenius. *Thesaurus Philologicus Criticus Linguae Hebraeae et Chaldeae Veteris Testamenti*. Leipzig: Vogel, 1839.
Ug.	Ugaritic
UT	Cyrus H. Gordon. *Ugaritic Textbook*. 3 volumes. Analecta orientalia 38. Rome: Pontifical Biblical Institute, 1965. Revised reprint 1998.
V	vowel
Vb. Adj.	verbal adjective
Vb. Noun	verbal noun

Bibliography

Abboud, Peter F., and Ernest N. McCarus

1983 *Elementary Modern Standard Arabic*, Part 1. Cambridge: Cambridge University Press.

Abou-Assaf, Ali; Pierre Bordreuil; and Alan R. Millard

1982 *La statue de Tell Fekherye et son inscription bilingue assyro-araméenne*. Études Assyriologiques. Paris: Éditions Recherche sur les civilizations.

Allen, Leslie C.

2008 *Jeremiah: A Commentary*. Old Testament Library. Louisville: Westminster John Knox Press.

Allen, W. Sidney

1962 *Sandhi: The Theoretical, Phonetic, and Historical Bases of Word-Junction in Sanscrit*. Janua Linguarum 17. The Hague: Mouton.

Anderson, Henning, editor

1986 *Sandhi Phenomena in the Languages of Europe*. Trends in Linguistics Studies and Monographs 33. Berlin: Mouton de Gruyter.

Arayathinal, Thomas

2007 *Aramaic (Syriac) Grammar*, Volume 1. Gorgias Historical Grammars 2. Piscataway: Gorgias Press.

Arnold, Mark A.

2005 Categorization of the Hitpaᶜēl of Classical Hebrew. Ph.D. dissertation, Harvard University.

Barth, Jakob

1889 *Die Nominalbildung in den semitischen Sprachen*. Leipzig: J. C. Hinrichs.

1894 "Zur vergleichenden semitischen Grammatik." *Zeitschrift der Deutschen Morgenländischen Gesellschaft* 48: 1–21.

Barthélemy, Dominique

1986 *Critique textuelle de l'Ancien Testament*, Volume 2. Orbis biblicus et orientalis 50/2. Göttingen: Vandenhoeck and Ruprecht.

Bauer, Hans, and Pontus Leander

1927 *Grammatik des Biblisch-Aramäischen*. Halle: Niemeyer.

Bean, Albert Fredrick

1976 A Phenomenological Study of the Hithpa'el Verbal Stem in the Hebrew Old Testament. Ph.D. dissertation, Southern Baptist Theological Seminary.

Ben-Ḥayyim, Ze'ev

2001 *A Grammar of Samaritan Hebrew: Based on the Recitation of the Law in Comparison with the Tiberian and Other Jewish Traditions*. Revised edition. Winona Lake: Eisenbrauns.

Bennett, Patrick R.

1998 *Comparative Semitic Linguistics: A Manual*. Winona Lake: Eisenbrauns.

Bergsträsser, Gotthelf

1929 *Hebräische Grammatik*. 2 volumes. Leipzig: F. C. W. Vogel and Hinrichs.

Blau, Joshua

1957 "Über die t-Form des Hifᶜil im Bibelhebräisch." *Vetus Testamentum* 7: 385–88.

Böttcher, Friedrich

1868 *Ausführliches Lehrbuch der hebräischen Sprache*. Volume 2. Leipzig: J. A. Barth.

Boyle, Milton Lorimer

1969 Infix-T Forms in Biblical Hebrew. Ph.D. dissertation, Boston University.

Bravmann, Meïr M.

1969 "The Semitic Causative-Prefix *š/sa*." *Le Muséon* 82: 517–22.

Bright, John

1965 *Jeremiah: A New Translation with Introduction and Commentary*. Anchor Bible 21. Garden City: Doubleday.

Carroll, Robert P.
1986 *Jeremiah: A Commentary*. Old Testament Library. Philadelphia: Westminster Press.

Chitoran, Ioana, and Andrew Nevins
2008 "Introduction." *Lingua* 118: 1900–05.

Chomsky, William, editor
1952 *David Ḳimḥi's Hebrew Grammar (Mikhlol)*. New York: Bloch Publishing for Dropsie College for Hebrew and Cognate Learning.

Coakley, J. F., editor
2002 *Robinson's Paradigms and Exercises in Syriac Grammar*. 5th edition. Oxford: Oxford University Press.

Creason, Stuart
2007 "*PQD* Revisited." In *Studies in Semitic and Afroasiatic Linguistics Presented to Gene B. Gragg*, edited by Cynthia L. Miller, pp. 27–42. Studies in Ancient Oriental Civilization 60. Chicago: The Oriental Institute.

Diem, Werner
1982 "Die Entwicklung des Derivationsmorphems der t-Stämme im Semitischen." *Zeitschrift der Deutschen Morgenländischen Gesellschaft* 132: 29–84.

Dillmann, August
1907 *Ethiopic Grammar*. Second edition. Edited by Carl Bezold. Translated by James A. Crichton. London: Williams and Norgate. Reprint Ancient Language Resources, Eugene: Wipf and Stock, 2005.

Dion, Paul-Eugène
1974 *La langue de Ya'udi: Description et classement de l'ancien parler de Zencirli dans le cadre des langues sémitiques du nord-ouest*. Waterloo: Éditions SR.

Dombrowski, Bruno W. W.
1962 "Some Remarks on the Hebrew Hithpa'el and Inversative -t- in the Semitic Languages." *Journal of Near Eastern Studies* 21: 220–23.

Dupont-Sommer, André, with Jean Starcky
1958 "Les inscriptions araméennes de Sfiré (Stèles I et II)." In *Mémoires présentés pars divers savants à l'Académie des Inscriptions et Belles-Lettres* 15, pp. 197–351, pls. i–xxix. Paris: Imprimerie Nationale.

Fassberg, Steven E.
1990 *A Grammar of the Palestinian Targum Fragments from the Cairo Genizah*. Harvard Semitic Studies 38. Atlanta: Scholars Press.

Fischer, Georg
2005 *Jeremia 1–25*. Herders theologischer Kommentar zum Alten Testament. Freiburg: Herder.

Fischer, Wolfdietrich
2002 *A Grammar of Classical Arabic*. Third edition. Translated by Jonathan Rodgers. New Haven: Yale University Press.

Fitzmyer, Joseph A.
1995 *The Aramaic Inscriptions of Sefire*. Revised edition. Biblica et orientalia 19A. Rome: Editrice Pontificio Istituto Biblico.

Friedrich, Johannes, and Wolfgang Röllig
1999 *Phönizisch-Punische Grammatik*. Third edition. Analecta orientalia 55. Rome: Pontificium Institutum Biblicum.

Garr, W. Randall
1985 *Dialect Geography of Syria-Palestine, 1000–586 B.C.E.* Philadelphia: University of Pennsylvania Press.
1993 "The *Niphal* Derivational Prefix." *Orientalia* 62: 142–62.

Gelb, Ignace J.
1952 *Old Akkadian Writing and Grammar*. Materials for the Assyrian Dictionary 2. Chicago: University of Chicago Press.

Gesenius, Wilhelm
1817 *Ausführliches grammatisch-kritisches Lehrgebäude der hebräischen Sprache mit Vergleichung der verwandten Dialekte*. Leipzig: F. C. W. Vogel.

Gibson, John C. L.

1975 *Textbook of Syrian Semitic Inscriptions*, Volume 2: *Aramaic Inscriptions*. Oxford: Clarendon Press.

Golomb, David M.

1985 *A Grammar of Targum Neofiti*. Harvard Semitic Monographs 34. Chico: Scholars Press.

Graf, Karl Heinrich

1862 *Der Prophet Jeremia*. Leipzig: Weigel.

Greenfield, Jonas C.

1964 "Linguistic Matters in the Sfire Inscriptions." *Leshonenu: Journal for the Study of the Hebrew Language and Cognate Subjects* 27–28: 303–13. [In Hebrew]

Grüneberg, Keith N.

2003 *Abraham, Blessing and the Nations: A Philological and Exegetical Study of Genesis 12:3 in its Narrative Context*. Beihefte zur Zeitschrift für die alttestamentliche Wissenschaft 332. Berlin: Walter de Gruyter.

Hackett, Jo Ann

1984 *The Balaam Text from Deir ʿAllā*. Harvard Semitic Monographs 31. Chico: Scholars Press.

Hämeen-Antilla, Jaakko

1984 "The Prothetic Vowel (*waṣla*) in Classical Arabic." In *Studia Orientalia Memoriae Jussi Aro Dedicata*, pp. 305–13. Studia orientalia 55. Helsinki: Societas Orientalis Fennica.

Harris, Zellig S.

1936 *A Grammar of the Phoenician Language*. American Oriental Series 8. New Haven: American Oriental Society.

Hasselbach, Rebecca

2004 "The Markers of Person, Gender, and Number in the Prefixes of G-Preformative Conjugations in Semitic." *Journal of the American Oriental Society* 124: 23–35.

Hitzig, Ferdinand

1841 *Der Prophet Jeremia*. Leipzig: Weidmann.

Hock, Hans Heinrich

1991 *Principles of Historical Linguistics*. 2nd edition. Berlin: Mouton de Gruyter.

Hoftijzer, Jacob, and G. van der Kooij, editors

1976 *Aramaic Texts from Deir ʿAlla*. Documenta et Monumenta Orientis Antiqui 19. Leiden: E. J. Brill.

Huehnergard, John

1987 *Ugaritic Vocabulary in Syllabic Transcription*. Harvard Semitic Series 32. Atlanta: Scholars Press.

1995 "What Is Aramaic?" *Aram* 7: 261–82.

1997 *A Grammar of Akkadian*. Harvard Semitic Series 45. Atlanta: Scholars Press.

Hutchinson, Enoch, translator

1855 *Uhlemann's Syriac Grammar*. New York: Appleton.

Hutton, Jeremy M., and Safwat Marzouk

2012 "The Morphology of the tG-Stem in Hebrew and *Tirgaltî* in Hos 11:3." *Journal of Hebrew Scriptures* (anticipated 2012).

Ibn Janaḥ, Abu 'l-Walîd Marwân

1875 *The Book of Hebrew Roots*. Edited by Adolf Neubauer. Oxford: Clarendon Press.

Jackson, Kent P.

1989 "The Language of the Mesha Inscription." In *Studies in the Mesha Inscription and Moab*, edited by Andrew Dearman, pp. 96–130. Archaeology and Biblical Studies 2. Atlanta: Scholars Press.

Janssen, Jozef M. A.

1956 "Egyptological Remarks on *The Story of Joseph in Genesis*." *Jaarbericht van het Vooraziatisch-Egyptisch Genootschap: Ex Oriente Lux* 14 (1955–1956): 63–72.

Janzen, J. Gerald

1973 *Studies in the Text of Jeremiah*. Harvard Semitic Monographs 6. Cambridge: Harvard University Press.

Kahle, Paul

1913 *Masoreten des Ostens: Die ältesten punktierten Handschriften des Alten Testaments und der Targume.* Beiträge zur Wissenschaft vom Alten Testament 15. Leipzig: J. C. Hinrichs.

Kaufman, Stephen A.

1982 "Reflections on the Assyrian-Aramaic Bilingual from Tell Fakhariyeh." *Maarav* 3: 137–75.

Keil, Carl Friedrich

1872 *Biblischer Commentar über den Propheten Jeremia und die Klagelieder.* Biblischer Commentar über das Alte Testament III/2. Leipzig: Dörffling and Franke.

König, Friedrich Eduard

1881 *Historisches-kritisches Lehrgebäude der Hebräischen Sprache.* Volume 1. Leipzig: J. C. Hinrichs.

Krahmalkov, Charles R.

2001 *A Phoenician-Punic Grammar.* Handbuch der Orientalistik 54. Leiden: Brill.

Krebernik, Manfred

1991 "Gt- und tD-Stämme im Ugaritischen." In *Texte, Methode und Grammatik: Wolfgang Richter zum 65. Geburtstag*, edited by Walter Gross, Hubert Irsigler, and Theodor Seidl, pp. 227–70. St. Ottilien: EOS Verlag.

Kuriakos, Luke M.

1973 *Non-paradigmatic Forms of Weak Verbs in Masoretic Hebrew.* Quilon: Assisi Press.

Kutscher, Yehezkel

1962 "The Language of the Hebrew and Aramaic Letters of Bar Kochbah and Those of His Generation, Part 1: The Hebrew Letters." *Leshonenu: Journal for the Study of the Hebrew Language and Cognate Subjects* 26: 7–23. [In Hebrew]

Lambdin, Thomas O.

1953 "Egyptian Loan Words in the Old Testament." *Journal of the American Oriental Society* 73/3:145–55.

1978 *Introduction to Classical Ethiopic (Geʿez).* Harvard Semitic Series 24. Missoula: Scholars Press.

1985 "Philippi's Law Reconsidered." In *Biblical and Related Studies Presented to Samuel Iwry*, edited by Ann Kort and Scott Morschauser, pp. 135–45. Winona Lake: Eisenbrauns.

Lambert, Mayer

1895 "L'élif wesla." *Journal Asiatique* 9/5: 225–34.

Lass, Roger

1984 *Phonology: An Introduction to Basic Concepts.* Cambridge Textbooks in Linguistics. Cambridge: Cambridge University Press.

Leslau, Wolf

1944 "Le rapport entre *š* et *h* en semitique." In *Annuaire de l'Institut de Philologie et d'Histoire Orientales et Slaves* 7, pp. 265–72. New York: Éditions de l'Institut.

Lieberman, Stephen J.

1986 "The Afro-Asiatic Background of the Semitic N-stem: Towards the Origins of the Stem-afformatives of the Semitic and Afro-Asiatic Verb." *Bibliotheca Orientalis* 43: 577–628.

Macuch, Rudolf

1969 *Grammatik des samaritanischen Hebräisch.* Studia Samaritana 1. Berlin: de Gruyter.

McCarter, P. Kyle

1980 "The Balaam Texts from Deir ʿAllā: The First Combination." *Bulletin of the American Schools of Oriental Research* 222: 49–60.

McKane, William

1986 *A Critical and Exegetical Commentary on Jeremiah*, Volume 1: *Jeremiah I-XXV.* International Critical Commentary on the Holy Scriptures of the Old and New Testaments 21. Edinburgh: T. and T. Clark.

Mühlau, Ferdinand, and William Volck, editors

1883 *Wilhelm Gesenius' Hebräisches und Chaldäisches Handwörterbuch über das Alte Testament.* 9th edition. Leipzig: Vogel.

Muraoka, Takamitsu

1984 "The Tell-Fekherye Bilingual Inscription and Early Aramaic." *Abr-Naharain* 22 (1983–1984): 79–117.

Nöldeke, Theodor
1904 *Compendious Syriac Grammar*. Translated by James A. Crichton. London: Williams and Norgate. Reprint, Ancient Language Resources. Eugene: Wipf and Stock, 2003.

O'Connor, Michael P.
1983 "Writing Systems, Native Speaker Analyses, and the Earliest Stages of Northwest Semitic Orthography." In *The Word of the Lord Shall Go Forth: Essays in Honor of David Noel Freedman in Celebration of His Sixtieth Birthday*, edited by Carol L. Meyers and M. O'Connor, pp. 439–65. Winona Lake: Eisenbrauns.

Olshausen, Justus
1861 *Lehrbuch der Hebräischen Sprache*. Braunschweig: Vieweg and Sohn.

Ornan, Uzzi
1990 "Two Types of Hitpaʿel." In *Studies on Hebrew and Other Semitic Languages, Presented to Professor Chaim Rabin on the Occasion of His 75th Birthday*, edited by M. Goshen-Gottstein, S. Morag, and S. Kogut, pp. 1–3. Jerusalem: Academon. [Hebrew, with English summary on p. vii]

ibn Parḥon, Solomon ben Abraham
1844 *Maḥberet He-Aruch*. Edited by Solomon Gottlieb Stern. Pressburg: Schmid.

Philippi, F.
1895 "Das Alifu'l Waṣli." *Zeitschrift der Deutschen Morgenländischen Gesellschaft* 49: 187–92.

Rendsburg, Gary A.
1982 "*Laqṭîl* Infinitives: Yiph'il or Hiph'il?" *Orientalia* 51: 231–38.
2002 *Israelian Hebrew in the Book of Kings*. Bethesda: CDL Press.

Rosenthal, Franz
1995 *A Grammar of Biblical Aramaic*. Sixth revised edition. Porta Linguarum Orientalium, neue Serie, 5. Wiesbaden: Harrassowitz.

Rowley, Harold H.
1929 *The Aramaic of the Old Testament*. London: Oxford University Press.

Sarauw, Chr.
1907 "Zu den Inschriften von Sendschirli." *Zeitschrift für Assyriologie* 20: 59–67.

Schottroff, W.
1976 "dqp *pqd* heimsuchen." *Theologisches Handwörterbuch zum Alten Testament* 2: 466–86.

Segal, Moses H.
1927 *A Grammar of Mishnaic Hebrew*. Oxford: Clarendon Press. Reprint, Ancient Language Resources. Eugene: Wipf and Stock.

Segert, Stanislav
1984 *A Basic Grammar of the Ugaritic Language with Selected Texts and Glossary*. Berkeley: University of California Press.

Siebesma, P. A.
1991 *The Function of the Niph'al in Biblical Hebrew: In Relationship to Other Passive-reflexive Verbal Stems and to the pu'al and hoph'al in Particular*. Studia Semitica Neerlandica 28. Assen: Van Gorcum.

Sivan, Daniel
1984 *Grammatical Analysis and Glossary of the Northwest Semitic Vocables in Akkadian Texts of the 15th–13th c. B.C. from Canaan and Syria*. Kevelaer: Butzon and Bercker; Neukirchen-Vluyn: Neukirchener Verlag.
2001 *A Grammar of the Ugaritic Language*. Handbook of Oriental Studies 28. Leiden: Brill.

Skoss, Solomon L.
1942 "A Study of Inflection in Hebrew from Saadia Gaon's Grammatical Work 'Kutub al-Lughah.'" *Jewish Quarterly Review* 33: 171–212.

Smith, Mark S.
2006 *The Rituals and Myths of the Feast of the Goodly Gods of KTU/CAT 1.23: Royal Constructions of Opposition, Intersection, Integration, and Domination*. Resources for Biblical Study 51. Atlanta: Society of Biblical Literature.

Speiser, E. A.
1955 "The Durative Hithpa'el: A *tan*-Form." *Journal of the American Oriental Society* 75: 506–14.

Streck, Michael P.
2003 *Die akkadischen Verbalstämme mit* ta-*Infix*. Alter Orient und Altes Testament 303. Münster: Ugarit-Verlag.

Stevenson, William B.
1924 *Grammar of Palestinian Jewish Aramaic*. Oxford: Oxford University Press. Reprint, Ancient Language Resources. Eugene: Wipf and Stock, 1999.

Testen, David
1985 "The Significance of Aramaic *r* < **n*." *Journal of Near Eastern Studies* 44: 143–46.
1999 "Arabic Evidence for the Formation of the Verbal Noun of the Semitic Gt-Stem." *Journal of Semitic Studies* 44: 1–16.

Tropper, Josef
1990 "Zur Vokalisierung des ugaritischen Gt-Stammes." *Ugarit Forschungen* 22:371-73.
1993 *Die Inschriften von Zincirli*. Abhandlungen zur Literatur Alt-Syrien-Palästinas 6. Münster: Ugarit-Verlag.
2000 *Ugaritische Grammatik*. Alter Orient und Altes Testament 273. Münster: Ugarit-Verlag.
2002 *Altäthiopisch: Grammatik des Geʿez mit Übungstexten und Glossar*. Elementa Linguarum Orientis 2. Münster: Ugarit-Verlag.

Tsumura, David Toshio
1991 "Vowel *sandhi* in Ugaritic." In *Near Eastern Studies: Dedicated to H. I. H. Prince Takahito Mikasa on the Occasion of His Seventy-fifth Birthday*, pp. 427–35. Bulletin of the Middle Eastern Culture Center in Japan 5. Wiesbaden: Harrassowitz.
1997 "Vowel sandhi in Biblical Hebrew." *Zeitschrift für die Alttestamentliche Wissenschaft* 109: 575–88.

Tur-Sinai, N. H.
1967 *The Plain Meaning of the Bible*, Volume 3/2. Jerusalem: Kiryath Sepher. [In Hebrew]

Voigt, Rainer M.
1994 "Der Lautwandel s^1 > *h* in wurzellosen Morphemen des Alt- und Neusüdarabischen." In *Semitic and Cushitic Studies*, edited by G. Goldenberg and S. Raz, pp. 19–28. Wiesbaden: Harrassowitz.
1995 "Akkadisch *šumma* 'wenn' und die Konditionalpartikeln des Westsemitischen." In *Vom Alten Orient zum Alten Testament: Festschrift für Wolfram Freiherrn von Soden zum 85. Geburtstag am 19. Juni 1993*, edited by M. Dietrich and O. Loretz, pp. 517–28. Alter Orient und Altes Testament 240. Kevelaer: Butzon and Bercker; Neukirchen-Vluyn: Neukirchener Verlag.

Weiser, Arthur
1955 *Das Buch des Propheten Jeremia*, Volume 1: *Kapitel 1-25,13*. Alte Testament deutsch 20. Göttingen: Vandenhoeck and Ruprecht.

Yalon, Henoch
1932 "Hithpāʿelformen im Hebräischen." *Zeitschrift für die Alttestamentliche Wissenschaft* 50: 217–20.

Yoo, Yoon Jong
1999 Israelian Hebrew in the Book of Hosea. Ph.D. dissertation, Cornell University.

13

Canaano-Akkadian: Linguistics and Sociolinguistics

*Shlomo Izre'el, Tel Aviv University**

1. Introduction

1.1. The Amarna Letters and Their Language

The Amarna letters are named after the site in Egypt in which they were discovered. These letters were sent to the Egyptian pharaohs Amenophis III and (his son) Akhenaten around the middle of the fourteenth century B.C. Among the senders were the kings of Babylonia, Assyria, Hatti, and Mittani, as well as minor rulers of the Near East at that time. The letters were written in the cuneiform script, most of them in Akkadian or what was thought to be Akkadian by the scribes who wrote them (I elaborate on this issue below). During the second millennium B.C., Akkadian, or what is now termed Peripheral Akkadian, served as the lingua franca, that is, the diplomatic language, of the ancient Near East. Many of the letters were sent to the Egyptian pharaohs by the rulers

* This paper is in essence a revision of the first part of a paper delivered at the El-Amarna Centennial Symposium held in Chicago in February 1987. The written version of that paper was submitted for publication in the proceedings of that conference, which, however, have never been published. Machine-typed copies of that paper (now available on the Internet; see Izre'el 1987b) have been circulating and were occasionally referred to by some of my colleagues on various occasions (I am thankful that they have found this paper worthy of academic discussion). In the meantime, some advances in the study of both Canaano-Akkadian and the theoretical foundations upon which this paper was written have been made, as well as the publication of a new hypothesis by Eva von Dassow on the nature of the language as being Canaanite rather than a mixed Canaano-Akkadian dialectal continuum. Therefore, I felt it necessary to make the paper available to the public in a revised form to fit the accumulation of knowledge since its initial delivery. As the version published here is sizeable enough, space has not permitted me to include some discussions included in the previous versions (see below, n. 27). These discussions are still available for the reader online in an intermediary version, which includes some revisions made on the 1987 version (Izre'el 2007a). Acknowledgments: In its primary version, the lecture given at the Amarna centennial has benefitted from comments from the original audience. The ideas that formed the basis for that lecture have been presented on various occasions before different audiences, with yet accumulated gains I have received from the interaction with the audience. Robert Wilson, Anson F. Rainey, Gideon Goldenberg, Baruch Podolsky, and Naphtali Kinberg commented on some of the issues presented in this paper when preparing the original version. Tony Badran read an intermediary version some years ago. Ehsan Yarshater, Baruch Podolsky, and David Yerushalmi assisted me with issues concerning Loterā'i (see §1.5). Eva von Dassow and Jun Ikeda kindly sent me their papers before their publication. Uri Horesh assisted me in eliminating substratal influence from yet another intermediary, revised version, and Eitan Grossman has contributed significantly to make my ideas expressed therein more clear. Just before sending this last version for publication, I had the privilege to present my ideas before an audience at Tsukuba University, Japan, where, again, I benefitted from comments from the audience. Masamichi Yamada and Jared Miller addressed my queries about Akkadographs in Hittite. Jared Miller has further sent me some valuable comments on a previous draft of this version. Mark Weeden discussed with me logography in Hittite texts. Seth Sanders has commented elaborately on a draft of this revised version, offering many important insights. I thank all of you, colleagues and friends, for your kindness and willingness to help. I further thank the editors of this volume, Rebecca Hasselbach and Naʿama Pat-El, who kindly accepted to include this long article in this volume, and for some constructive comments. Both the editors and I believe that John will appreciate this contribution, as he was one of the first to hold the original paper in his hands and use it, to my satisfaction. (John: you can discard your copy of the 1987 paper now.) May it be a worthy tribute to my colleague and friend, from whose wisdom and scholarship I have benefitted so much during decades of friendship.

of Canaanite city-states, which were at that time under the sovereignty of Egypt. When we examine the letters in terms of their linguistic structure, we realize that most of them were not written in the common Peripheral Akkadian dialect, but rather in a mixed language: Akkadian almost entirely predominated in its lexical inventory, while Canaanite, the mother tongue of the scribes who wrote these letters, predominated in the domain of grammar. The latter influenced the syntax and the morphology of this mixed language and affected its phonology and semantics. Here and there a purely Canaanite word appears, written in the cuneiform syllabary, serving as a reading aid, typically used to translate or to clarify an Akkadian word or a (Sumerian) logogram. These are the famous glosses of the Amarna letters.

To highlight the characteristics of this mixed language and the differences between the language of the Canaanite letters and that of letters from other sites, let us take a look at two passages from the Amarna correspondence.

ex. 1. ^{m}*ḫa-ti-ip i-il-la-kà-am* ^{5} *ù ú-ub-bá-la-am a-ma-te*.MEŠ ^{6} LUGAL EN-*ia bá-nu-tam ù* DÙG.GA-*ta* ^{7} *ù ḫa-ad-ia-ku ma-gal ma-gal* ^{8} *ù* KUR-*ia ù* ŠEŠ.MEŠ-*ia* ^{9} LÚ.MEŠ.ÌR *ša* LUGAL EN-*ia* ^{10} *ù* LÚ.MEŠ.ÌR ^{m}*tù-u-tù* EN-*ia* ^{11} *ḫa-du*$_4$*-nim* ⸢*ma-gal*⸣ *ma-gal* ^{12} *i-nu-ma i-il-la-kà-am* ^{13} *ša-ar-ru ša* LUGAL EN-*ia* ^{14} UGU-*ia iš-tu a-ma-te*.MEŠ ^{15} EN-*ia* DINGIR-*ia* ⸢^{d}UTU$_x$(ERIM)-*ia*⸣ ^{16} *ù iš-tu a-ma-te*.⸢MEŠ⸣ ^{m}*tù-u-tù* ^{17} EN-*ia la a-pa-aṭ-ṭar*

'Ḫatip has come and brought the nice and good words of the king, my lord, and I am very very glad. My land and my brothers, the servants of the king, my lord, and the servants of Tutu, my lord, are very very glad when the breath of the king, my lord, comes to me. From the orders of my lord, my God, my Sun-God, and from the orders of Tutu, my lord, I shall not deviate.' (EA 164:4–17)

ex. 2. *a-nu-ma* ^{23} ⸢*iṣ*⸣*ṣú*$^{!}$*-ru ù a-nu-ma* ^{24} [*i*]*š-te-m*[*u*]UD.KAM-*ma* ^{25} *ù mu-ša a-wa-ti*$_7$.MEŠ *ša* ^{26} LUGAL EN-*ia ù yi-il*$_5$*-ma*$^{!}$[*-ad*] ^{27} LUGAL EN-*ia a-na* ÌR-*šu* ^{28} *nu-kúr-tu*$_4$ *iš-tu* ḪUR.SAG ^{29} *ana ia-ši ù ra-as̤-pa-ti*$_7$ \ *b*[*a-n*]*i-t*[*i*] ^{30} É 1-*en* URU *ma-an-ḫa-ti*$_7$ *šum-ši* ^{31} *ana šu-ši-ri a-na pa-ni* ^{32} ÉRIN.MEŠ *pí-ṭá-at* LUGAL EN-*ia*

'Here I guard and here I obey day and night the orders of the king, my lord. May the king, my lord, be informed about his servant: There is war from the mountain against me. So I built '*bani:ti*' one house, Manḫati by name, to prepare for the *pḏt*-troops of the king, my lord.' (EA 292:22–32)

The first passage is taken from a letter of Aziru, the ruler of the northern land of Amurru, and it is written in a language that shows close affinities with Akkadian. The second passage is taken from a letter of Ba'lushiptu, ruler of the city of Gezer in southern Canaan, written in the mixed language used by Canaanite scribes, which I have termed Canaano-Akkadian (Izre'el 1998a).

For the differences, note especially the use of the verbs. The two letters can be distinguished both in their verbal morphology and in their TAM (= Tense-Aspect-Mood) system. The letter from Amurru, EA 164, has the prefix *a-* for the 1SG (*apaṭṭar*, line 17) and *i-* for the 3rd person (e.g., *illakam*, lines 4, 12); it also has the ending *-u:ni*(*m*) for the 3PL (*ḫadu:ni*(*m*), line 11). It uses the ventive ending *-am* extensively (*illakam*) and the normal Akkadian imperfective ("present-future," "durative") and stative forms. The Gezer letter, on the other hand, has forms with initial *i* for the 1SG (*iṣṣuru*, line 23), while the 3SGM has a *y-* prefix, as in the Northwest Semitic (henceforth: NWS) languages (*yilmad*, line 26); there is extensive use of the NWS suffix conjugation with active meaning, both by means of attaching the suffix verbal person morphemes to Akkadian stems (as in *raṣpa:ti*, line 29), and by using pure Canaanite patterns (this feature is attested here only in the gloss for *raṣpa:ti*, viz., *bani:ti* 'I built'). Another important feature is the use of the Canaanite verbal modus morphemes, as in *iṣṣuru* and *ištemu* (lines 23 and 24, respectively), reflecting the indicative ending, or *yilmad*, reflecting the jussive -Ø suffix.

1.2. The State of the Art

The Amarna tablets have drawn much attention since their discovery in 1887, and considerable research effort has been invested in studying the linguistic characteristics of these letters. The last decade of the nineteenth century saw the decipherment and the publication of the texts. The first decade of the twentieth century witnessed Knudtzon's great achievement in the publication of his monumental edition of the texts (Knudtzon 1907 [= 1915, vol. 1]), still the standard edition in use today. There immediately followed studies by Böhl (1909), Ebeling (1910; also in Knudtzon 1915, pp. 1358–1583), and Dhorme (1913–1914), who gave us the first descriptions of the language of these texts and noted the mixed nature of Canaano-Akkadian, in which many of the letters from Canaan were written. After a few decades of neglect, the 1950s and 1960s gave us the studies by Albright (mainly 1942; 1943a, b; 1944) and especially by Moran, who described the syntactic features of the Amarna letters from Byblos and who was the first to see that the Canaanite modal system was an inherent feature of the language of these letters (Moran 1950a; see his collected Amarna studies, 2003). The 1980s was the age of morphological study, mainly by Rainey (1971; 1973; 1975; 1976; 1978b), and the beginnings of holistic and detailed studies of several subcorpora within the Canaanite domain, written at Tel Aviv University under Rainey's supervision (Nitzan 1973; Izre'el 1976, 1978; Finkel 1977; Rabiner 1981). These lines of research have become mainstream in the linguistic study of the Amarna letters. Scholars followed the path paved by Moran and Rainey with studies of the larger corpus or of specific subcorpora, either holistically or for specific linguistic domains, mainly morphology and morphosyntax (Youngblood 1961; Kossmann 1987–88; Smith 1998; Westhuizen 1992; 1993; 2005; Tropper 2005; Cochavi-Rainey and Rainey 2007; Korchin 2008). Syntax and discourse structure have also been given attention (Finley 1979; Hayes 1984; Gianto 1990; Rainey 1992; 1996, vol. 3 in passing and ch. 8; Westhuizen 1994; Zewi 1995; 1999; Israel 2006), as has phonology (Shehadeh 1968; 1987; Izre'el 1987a; 2003a; Sivan 1984). Apart from these studies, progress has been made in the study of the lexicon (mainly Ebeling in Knudtzon 1915; Rainey 1970; 1978a; Moran 1984; Sivan 1984; Izre'el 1998b; 2003b; Tawil 2009), as well as in the study of phraseology, idiomatics, style, and rhetoric (e.g., Böhl 1914; Jirku 1933; Gevirtz 1973; Liverani 1983; Hess 1989; 1990; 1993b; 1998; Mangano 1990; Izre'el 1995a; Rainey 2002, pp. 50–53). Rainey has continued his research in both the morphology and semantics of the verb and in other domains, a research effort that culminated in his four-volume book (Rainey 1996), a significant achievement that includes penetrating observations on the verbal system and on other domains (writing, nominals, adverbs, and particles). I myself have published a concise grammar of Canaano-Akkadian, which consists of a description of its phonology, morphology, and syntactic structure (Izre'el 1998a [2005]). This research effort has benefited much from Moran's comprehensive edition of the Amarna tablets in translation, which includes a detailed commentary with philological and linguistic notes (Moran 1987; 1992). Hess (1984; 1986; 1993a; 2003) has studied the proper names, including personal, divine, and geographical names.

Also, minute investigations of other subcorpora from the Amarna archives have been conducted (Adler 1976 on the Mitanni letters; Izre'el 1985; 1991a on the letters from Amurru; Cochavi-Rainey 1988; 1989; 1990a; 1990b; 1993; 1998; 2011 on the Egyptian letters; Cochavi-Rainey 2003 on the Alashia letters; for a very brief summary, see Rainey 2002, pp. 47–49).

In addition to the Amarna find, cuneiform tablets have been unearthed in the Canaanite territories (Horowitz, Oshima, and Sanders 2006). These tablets have enriched our linguistic data, having added some interesting linguistic insights on the accumulated knowledge of Canaano-Akkadian (e.g., Rainey 1976), but more significantly, they have taught us lessons about the sociolinguistic setting of Canaano-Akkadian. An interesting find in this respect is a small cylindrical letter found in Beth Shean (Horowitz 1996; Horowitz, Oshima, and Sanders 2006, pp. 48–49), written in Canaano-Akkadian. While cuneiform tablets for internal objectives had been known for quite some time, this latter find may suggest that Canaano-Akkadian was employed also for correspondence within the Canaanite territories and not only for correspondence between Canaanites and foreigners. Yet a more appealing alternative is that this small cylinder was actually used in scribal education (Rainey 2003, pp. 239–40). I return to this issue later (§1.5). Still a case in point — although attested in a text sent from out of the borders of Canaan — is EA 170, a letter sent to Aziru, the ruler of Amurru, by his brother and son, while Aziru was in Egypt. This letter seems to forward sensitive data to Aziru about the advance of the Hittites in the Amurru region, with a note about the relationship between Amurru and the Hittites, Egypt's enemies. This letter was written in (Peripheral) Akkadian. One might ask at this juncture why a confidential letter like this would be written in the lingua franca if not due to the lack of any written codes to forward a message to their king other than Akkadian. However, one may bear in mind that Hurrian had had the tradition of being written in the Akkadian cuneiform syllabary, so that the use of the Akkadian lingua franca in this letter might have been the medium used by the scribes of Amurru by rote. In fact, this very letter exhibits — apart from Hurrian interference — also the use of Hurrian glosses (Izre'el 1991a, vol. 1, pp. 371–73). In another place (Izre'el 1995b, pp. 105–07) I suggested that it was the scribe who served as the messenger, personally carrying this tablet to Egypt. If indeed so, this would make the case even more intriguing.

(For a detailed Amarna bibliography, see Heintz 1982; 1995; Heintz and Millot 1995; 1996; 2000; Heintz, Millot, and Mehmedi 2003; Heintz, Mehmedi, and Vita 2006.)

1.3. Attitudes toward Canaano-Akkadian and Its Linguistic Nature

Considerable progress has indeed been made. During the last few decades, scholars dealing with the language of the Canaanite Amarna letters have become more and more aware of its structural nature. This awareness is the result of the change in attitude toward the language: once considered a degraded form of Akkadian, it has now been recognized that it possesses an elaborate linguistic system of its own.

As late as the 1970s, the scribes of Canaan were regarded as writing in a barbarous language. The following is an exemplary remark by William L. Moran, the scholar who — more than anyone else — has contributed to our understanding of the structure of Canaano-Akkadian. In his entry on the Amarna tablets in the *Encyclopaedia Judaica* from 1971, he writes,

> The letters are ... written in Akkadian, the lingua franca of the Ancient Near East in the second millennium B.C.E. In general, the language belongs to the "peripheral Akkadian" found at Nuzi, Alalakh, Ugarit etc. Eloquent and moving as it may be at times, it lacks all elegance; it is awkward, often barbarous, betraying the scribes' ignorance not only of Akkadian but of their native speech.[1] This is especially true of the letters from Phoenicia and Palestine. (Moran 1971, p. 933)

Well, this is a good description as far as an "Akkadophile" is concerned. From the eyes of a potential member of the Babylonian Language Academy, had one existed, the language of the Canaanite scribes would indeed be regarded as barbarous Akkadian:

> It is no wonder that Assyriologists found the texts difficult and frustrating; they represent such a radical departure from the Akkadian norm that many were disposed to call them "barbaric." Today that charge can no longer be sustained, especially for the letters written from the land of Canaan, that is the Levant south of the Nahr el-Kebîr and ancient Kedesh on the Orontes. (Rainey 1996, vol. 2, p. 1)

Indeed, some twenty years later, in his introduction to his translations of the Amarna letters, Moran writes,

> In the southern tradition the transformation of the Babylonian language and the resulting deviations from normal usage were far more radical than in most forms of Hurro-Akkadian (i.e., the Peripheral Akkadian dialects used in the northern Levant and beyond, marked by Hurrian influence; S.I.). Indeed, so radical is the transformation that one may ask whether the language of this tradition, even when qualified as "extremely barbarized," should be called Babylonian at all. It is a pidgin in which the Babylonian component is mainly lexical, whereas the grammar is profoundly West-Semitized, most notably in the word order and, most important of all, in the verbal system. The language can only be described as an entirely new code, only vaguely intelligible (if at all) to the West Semite because of the lexicon, and to the Babylonian because of the grammar. (Moran 1992, pp. xxi–xxii)

It has thus become a consensus that the language exhibited by Amarna letters from Canaan is not to be regarded and analyzed as a corrupt form of Akkadian, but as a linguistic system bearing its own features. As such, it deserves due consideration and description other than looking at it and evaluating it through the filters of standard Akkadian. This "new code," to use Moran's terminology, served its purposes as a means of communication, being an offshoot of the Akkadian lingua franca of Western Peripheral Akkadian.

1.4. Theoretical Background

This change in attitude is the result of substantive progress in general linguistics and theoretical linguistics during the twentieth century. Theoretical linguistics has developed new ways of looking at languages and

---

[1] I find this comment quite perplexing. How can speakers be ignorant of their own native speech?

analyzing languages. Structuralism brought with it the call for distinguishing between synchronic and diachronic studies of language. This call highlighted the necessity of defining and describing the systemic relationships between linguistic components. It has also resulted in the recognition of the essential difference between *langue* and *parole*, or — much later — between *competence* and *performance* (see, e.g., Sampson 1980, pp. 45–46, 49–50). For our needs, it would be better to follow the Saussurian conception of these terms. Thus *langue* will be considered as the linguistic system of the community, *parole* as the speech production of an individual within the linguistic community (de Saussure 1955, p. 37).

Linguistics has developed an interest in various specific aspects of human language behavior of the community and of the individual. Subdisciplines of linguistics — sociolinguistics, dialectology, anthropological linguistics, cultural linguistics, and so on — have arisen in response to new questions and problems, such as those related to registers, diglossia, bilingualism, multilingualism, and other phenomena of language contact, to name but a few. Notably, variation has become an issue of importance in the study of both synchronic and diachronic aspects of a language, and the recognition that variation as an inherent feature of language is slowly gaining general acceptance. (A convenient, comprehensive overview of the state of the art in these areas will be found in Chambers, Trudgill, and Schilling-Estes 2002.)

With regard to the question of language contact, which interests us here, we have come to know contact-induced languages with features similar to those of Canaano-Akkadian, such as stem borrowing in Maltese (Aquilina 1965, pp. 201–07; Drewes 1994, pp. 89–91; cf. already Izre'el 1978, pp. 79–80 n. 262), Ma'a (or Inner Mbugu) (Goodman 1971; Thomason 1997b), Media Lengua (Muysken 1994; 1997), Michif (Bakker 1994; Bakker and Papen 1997), Copper Island Aleut (Menovshchikov 1968, pp. 404–05; Golovko 1994; Thomason 1997a), and Loterā'i (Yarshater 1977). We see below (§1.5) samples from some of these languages to show the similarities in structure between these languages and Canaano-Akkadian. Data from these and many other languages of contact may now greatly enhance our ability to understand the complicated phenomena that we are faced with when studying the language of the Canaanite Amarna letters. Indeed, a relatively recent collection of linguistic descriptions of mixed languages (Bakker and Mous 1994) includes also a brief description of Canaano-Akkadian (Kossmann 1994).[2] Therefore, along with the consensus of the nature of Canaano-Akkadian as a linguistic system that deserves study in its own right rather than a corrupt form of Akkadian, there is wide consensus of the nature of Canaano-Akkadian as a contact language, similar to many attested linguistic systems.

1.5. Terminology and Concepts

When scholars began to realize the nature of the structural profile of the language written by the Canaanite Amarna scribes, they looked for a convenient term to describe it. Terms are important, because a term is a linguistic sign, of which the *signifié* is a concept, and therefore reflects our view of the nature of this language. In the first version of this paper (Izre'el 1987b), I used the term *jargon* (cf. also Albright 1966, p. 4), referring more to the sociological aspect of the term than to its linguistic one. As a sociological term, a jargon is a type of language used by a professional or another specialized group. However, as a general term it can also be understood as a "confused unintelligible language," or as "a strange, outlandish, or barbarous language or dialect" (*Merriam-Webster* 1994–96; see also Crystal 2010, p. 451). While it had been used in the past to indicate a mixed language (Hall 1966, p. xiv), in more recent studies of language contact, this term has sometimes come to stand for an unstable pre-pidgin state of a language, extremely reduced in form and use (Mühlhäusler 1997, vol. 6, pp. 128–38; Matras 2009, p. 278). My faithful reader already knows, and will become even more aware later, that this is not a happy term for Canaano-Akkadian.

Moran has used the term *pidgin* (see citation above), a term used also by Ikeda (1992). It is also used indiscriminately by Rainey (e.g., 1996, vol. 2, pp. 17, 29), along with other terms (including *jargon*; see below), although he claims that the term *interlanguage* better fits this type of language than *pidgin* (1996, vol. 2, pp. 31–32, in a section entitled "The Late Bronze *Jargon* in Canaan"; my emphasis). For both Moran and Rainey, it seems, the term *pidgin* means a linguistic type consisting of features from different languages.

---

[2] Kossmann terms it *Amarna Akkadian*. I myself fancied once the term *Amarnaic* (1995a, p. 2418; also Ikeda 1992). Both terms imply that the interference took place in Egypt, which is obviously not the case.

A pidgin is a much-reduced language that arises on the lexical basis of a model language in a bilingual or a multilingual society, where no indigenous tongue serves as a common language. When such a language becomes a native language for a specific community, it is called a *creole*. As such, it expands so that it can serve for all needed communicative purposes like any other native tongue (Hymes 1971; Romaine 1988; Holm 1988–1989; Mühlhäusler 1997; Matras 2009, §10.2). Pidgins and creoles are, hence, products of language contact *par excellence*, so that — apart from the study of various contact phenomena and languages of contact — it is this specific branch of the linguistic science that may prove central to a deeper understanding of language-contact phenomena.

Clearly, Canaano-Akkadian was not a native tongue, and hence the use of the term *creole* for it would be inappropriate. But also the use of the term *pidgin* for this linguistic continuum hardly fits. Among other issues, one may note that "pidgins are not mixed languages in the sense most often intended. It appears that the most mixed area is the lexicon, where syncretisms of various types are common, and not syntax" (Mühlhäusler 1997, p. 5). This is certainly not the case of Canaano-Akkadian. I further believe that the emergence of Canaano-Akkadian was not similar to the emergence of the commonly attested pidgins, that is, it was not developed out of an urgent need for oral communication among parties or individuals, but was rather the result of a break in a long tradition of cuneiform writing in the Levant (Izre'el 1995a, p. 2418).

The term *interlanguage*, or rather, *institutionalized interlanguage*, has been suggested for Canaano-Akkadian by Gianto (1990, pp. 10–11; 2000). Interlanguage is "a system of rules said to develop, in the mind of someone learning a foreign language, which is intermediate between that of their native language and that of the one being learned" (Matthews 2007, p. 198). I doubt whether the circumstances of the emergence of Canaano-Akkadian would permit us to regard the outcome as an imperfectly learned language at a synchronic view, as required by the term "interlanguage." Was Akkadian education so impoverished that scribes could not learn enough as to make their way toward the goal of writing a sentence in Peripheral Akkadian? In fact, they could, at least for the rote opening formulae as well as in other contexts. As against Gianto's claim, the Canaanite cuneiform scribes were not denied access to the target language, as they were receiving letters written in Peripheral Akkadian throughout this whole period, and at times they accommodated their writing to conform to the language and style they were reading from the pharaoh's letters (see below, §3.2). Moreover, cuneiform education in second-millennium Canaan seems to have been rather widespread, although precise measures are still wanting. The find suggesting scholarly activity within the boundaries of mid-second-millennium Canaan includes, inter alia, lexical tablets of local origin, produced either in the place of their find or elsewhere in Canaan (Goren, Finkelstein, and Na'aman 2009). Thus the Gilgamesh fragment from Megiddo was probably originated in Gezer (op. cit.). Goren, Finkelstein, and Na'aman (2009, p. 771) suggest that the scribes attending the Gezer school studied classical literary texts of the Mesopotamian scribal tradition and distributed them to other Canaanite centers like the one in Megiddo. The existence of a school at Megiddo is further inferred by certain features in the letters sent from that site, notably the use of tripartite glosses, reminiscent of the three-column lexical tablets used for scribal education (Izre'el 2003b, p. 91). One other indication of scribal education at Megiddo is the use of the Akkadian 1SG affix of the suffix conjugation form *-a:ku*, as against standard Canaano-Akkadian *-a:ti* or *-ti* (Izre'el 2005, p. 4). The question of impoverished education may surface at this point, especially as there has not been any solid proof of scribal education in Canaano-Akkadian (Sanders 2009, p. 83). An *argumentum ex silentio* can hardly be sustained, for either claim. However, I still believe that — due to the break in direct contacts between Canaan and the northern Levant mentioned above — the curriculum of the Canaanite scribal schools did include training in letter writing in Canaano-Akkadian rather than in standard Akkadian or Peripheral Akkadian of any type known to us (e.g., Egyptian Akkadian or Syrian Akkadian). How this was done we can only guess, and the very term suggested by Gianto, "institutionalized interlanguage," claims precisely that. As is noted below, variation in the output language of different scribes does not necessarily entail impoverished education, and the rules of intertwining elements from Canaanite and Akkadian into the Canaano-Akkadian system may have well been variable in various scribal schools within the Canaanite region or just used variably by different scribes.

At this juncture, one will recall the small cylinder from Beth-Shean mentioned above (§1.2), which may well be an educational artifact. As against Horowitz's suggestion that this small cylinder served as an intelligence mail (1996, pp. 213–17), Rainey (2003, pp. 239–40) reminds us of the inscribed cylinder found at Amarna (EA 355) that exhibits a series of repeated identical signs. While the genre of this text is still under discussion (for the various suggestions, see Izre'el 1997, pp. 41–42), the very fact that it was found among scholarly tablets at the so-called records office at Amarna (op. cit., 3, 4–9) suggests precisely that: this item did serve as a scholarly artifact. One should especially recall the actual text inscribed on the Beth-Shean cylinder, which says, "To Lab'aya, my lord, speak. Message of Tagi: To the king, my lord: I have heard your message to me" (cf. Horowitz 1996, p. 210; Horowitz, Oshima, and Sanders 2006, pp. 48–49). As such, it does not seem to include a real, actual message on behalf of an alleged sender, but a standard text of letter writing.[3] In that it reminds us of three fragments from the scholarly corpus found at Amarna, EA 342, EA 343, and EA 344, which seem to be exercises in letter writing (Izre'el 1997, pp. 20–23). Notably, some features of at least one of these fragments, EA 343, may suggest that the scribe who inscribed this practice tablet was not Egyptian but Canaanite (op. cit., p. 22, comment to line 4). If indeed the Beth-Shean cylinder can be regarded as an exercise in letter writing, then it can serve as evidence for scribal education in the same language used for writing letters to Egypt, namely, Canaano-Akkadian.

Cases of fossilized, or stabilized, interlanguage are attested mainly among minority ethnolects (Matras 2009, pp. 58, 76), but imperfect second-language acquisition is one of the major constructs in the formation of many cases of contact-induced languages, notably pidgins (op. cit., pp. 77, 284). In such cases, "interlanguage" would be a term that refers to the historical emergence of that language, not a denotation of its synchronic status. When the term "interlanguage" is to be used as a denotation for a synchronic status of linguistic use, it should refer to a dynamic situation where learners are still in the process of learning the language and therefore the form of their interlanguage is due to change in time. This is not a happy term for the denotation of the languages of minority ethnolects or English in India, thus described and called "collective interlanguage" by Matras (2009, p. 76).

To my mind, the best term used so far for indicating the nature of Canaano-Akkadian is "mixed language." There is no consensus on what constitutes a mixed language. Still, in their essence, mixed languages are languages that show a mixture of linguistic features from different systems to the extent that their genetic affiliation cannot be ascribed to one of their sources (Matras 2009, p. 288, following Thomason and Kaufman 1988). While not attempting a definition of the term, Bakker and Mous still see similarities among the languages described in their collection *Mixed Languages* (1994). They do, however, propose the term "language intertwining" "for the process forming mixed language showing a combination of the grammatical system (phonology, morphology, syntax) of one language with the lexicon of another language" (Bakker and Mous 1994, pp. 4–5). As mentioned above (§1.4), Canaano-Akkadian is included among the languages listed therein. In fact, there are no two mixed languages described in the extant literature that are similar in their mixture of different components, and Canaano-Akkadian is not exceptional in this matter (*pace* Sanders 2009, pp. 88–89). A few examples may suffice to illustrate the point.

The African language Ma'a (or Inner Mbugu), spoken in Tanzania, consists of Bantu grammar and mixed Bantu and non-Bantu (largely Cushitic) lexicon (Goodman 1971; Mous 1994; Thomason 1997b). In the following example (taken from Mous 1994, pp. 175–76; 2003, p. 9; Matras 2009, p. 297), the Ma'a (Inner Mbugu) text (in the first line) is compared with Normal Mbugu (in the second line). The elements in Ma'a that would be different in Normal Mbugu are italicized, whereas all others are printed in underlined roman characters. Mostly, it will be content words that will be replaced by Non-Bantu elements.[4]

ex. 3.	hé-*ló*	mw-*agirú*	é-*sé*-we	kimwéri	*dilaó*	w-a	*yá*	*i-dí*	*l-á*	lusótó
	hé-na	m-zima	é-tang-we	kimwéri	m-fumwa	w-a	i-i	i-sanga	l-á	lusótó
	16-have	1-elder	1-call-PAST.PERF	Kimweri	king	1-CON	this	5-land	5-CON	Lushoto

'There was an elder called Kimweri, king of this land of Lushoto.'

Media Lengua is a language spoken in central Ecuador. Its basic structure is Qechua, whereas the vast majority of its lexical stems are taken over from Spanish. In the following example (taken from Muyskin 1997, p. 365), Spanish stems and their respective glosses are printed in italics, whereas Qechua morphemes are printed in underlined roman characters.

[3] The two broken lines would not include more than two or three words, which would not detract from this impression.

[4] Grammatical glosses: ABSolutive; ACCusative; BENefactive; CAUSative; CONnective; DATive; DEFinite article; EPENthetic segment; GENitive; H_N = nominal head (*ša*; see Izre'el 2005, 3.1.4); JUSsive; NEGative; OBLique case; PAST; PLural; NOMinative; PASSive; PERFect; POSSessive; PROGressive; PRESent; RELative; REPetitive; SG = singular; SUBJunctive; 1st person. The numbers in the gloss line indicate nominal classes; see Mous 2003, ch. 6, for details.

ex. 4. *Unu fabur*-ta *pidi*-nga-bu *bini*-xu-ni

one favor-ACC *ask*-NOM-BEN *come*-PROG-1

'I come to ask a favor.'

Michif is a North American language composed mainly of Cree (Native American) and French components. Michif exhibits, by and large, a split between the nominal domain, which is mostly of French origin, and the verbal one, which is mostly Cree. In the following example (taken from Bakker 1994, p. 28; cf. Matras 2009, p. 303), French elements and their respective glosses are printed in italics, whereas Cree elements are printed in underlined roman characters.

ex. 5. *un vieux* ana ayi *un vieux* opahikêt ê-nôhcihcikêt ...

an old this uh *an old* trapper trapped

êkwa ayi *un matin* êkwaniskât ahkosiw

and uh *one morning* woke-up be.sick

'An old trapper this uh an old trapper was trapping
and uh one morning he woke up sick.'

Mednyj Aleut, the Aleut dialect of the Copper Island in the far eastern part of Russia (near Alaska), exhibits a mixture between Russian and Aleut (Menovshchikov 1968, pp. 404–05; Golovko 1994; Thomason 1997a). Here again, the split is between the nominal and the verbal domains: nouns and their inflections are largely of Aleut origin, and finite verbs originate largely in Russian. In the example below (taken from Golovko 1994, p. 115), the Russian elements are italicized; the Aleut elements are printed in underlined roman characters.

ex. 6. *boochki*-x' *ni*-umnaa-*l* *poetomu* taanga-gan huzu-u hyuu-*l*

barrel-ABS.SG *NEG*-tight-*PAST* *so* water-REL all-POSS drip-*PAST*

'The barrel had a hole in it, so all the water went away.'

Our last example is taken from a language that is usually ignored in the discussions of contact languages in general and of mixed language in particular. This is the mixed language of Persian Jews known as Loterā'i, in which Hebrew and Aramaic lexemes are introduced into the grammatical frame of their Persian dialect. As summarized by Yarshater (1977, p. 1), Loterā'i serves to protect the privacy of conversation among members of the community in the presence of gentiles. Loterā'i is a mixed language. Pronouns, adjectives, and the majority of nouns and verbal bases, as well as some prepositions, are Semitic, whereas verbal endings, modal prefixes, suffix pronouns, most of the particles, and the sentence structure are Iranian.

In the following example (taken from Yarshater 1977, p. 2), Semitic elements are printed in italics, Iranian elements in underlined roman characters.

ex. 7a. *anni bāy* un b *ez* on xiābān, šon vā-*ez*-on

I want-1SG SUBJ-*go*-1SG street go REP-*go*-1SG

'I want to go out (lit. in the street); I shall go and return.'

ex. 7b. vaxti *ez(z)*-id-am[5] *derax*-e *nāšim gādul*-ie, be-š-*meštā*-n-ā

when *go*-PAST-1SG *with*-GEN *wife big*-DEF DAT-3SG-*say*-EPEN-PAST

anni tām mi-*āš*-un-am

I whole PRS-*do*-CAUS-1SG

'"When I went to the wife of the elder one," she said, "I shall put it right."'

---

[5] Both *-am* and *-on/-un* (colloquially) mark the 1SG.

The notion of mixed language has been subject to debate mainly due to the fact that languages taken as prototypical of language mixtures are not identical in the way their structural components reflect the originating languages of contact. Thus Matras (2009, pp. 303–04) wonders "whether it is at all possible to define a structural prototype for mixed languages, or whether the only feature that defines them as a unique sub-type of contact language is the history of their emergence coupled with an unusual — by comparison with cases of gradual borrowing — combination of sub-components." Matras then suggests that "[t]he mixed language prototype is thus not a lexicon-grammar split, but a split between finite verb inflection or the 'predication-anchoring language,' and the bulk of referential lexical vocabulary, or 'content-reference language.'" "This kind of split," writes Matras, "can be explained in terms of the language processing mechanism and especially the mechanism of selection and inhibition of wholesale components within the repertoire: the anchoring of the predication is the more intuitive, less conscious mental act" (2009, pp. 304–05). The concentration on the verbal domain in Canaano-Akkadian seems to fit this explication of the outcome of a community where two languages are at play, in our case — Canaanite speaking scribes learning and using Akkadian, or rather Canaano-Akkadian, as their language of written communication.

As we do not have direct access to the emergence of Canaano-Akkadian, any attempt to classify it according to any speculative non-linguistic setting must be viewed as precisely that: speculative. One should note at this juncture that there have also been some arguments raised against classifying types of linguistic mixture along historical grounds (Winford 2010, pp. 182–85).[6] On the other hand, Canaano-Akkadian certainly exhibits structural traits that show a similar split between its linguistic components described above, where the key feature is the verbal inflectional morphology that is purely Canaanite (but see below, §3, for an analysis of the complexities of the overall system). We have already seen above (ex. 2) one example of Canaano-Akkadian in an extract from a letter from Baʾlushiptu of Gezer to the pharaoh. In the following Canaano-Akkadian example, extracted from another letter from Gezer — this time from Yapaʾu — the originating languages of the different components are indicated as follows: the Akkadian components in italics, the Canaanite ones in underlined roman characters.[7]

ex. 8.	*mimma*	*ša*	*q*<u>a</u>*b*<u>a</u>-<u>ø</u>	*šarr-u*	*be:l-i-ya*	*ana*	*ya:ši*
	everything	H_N	*say.*<u>PAST</u>-<u>3SGM</u>	*king-NOM*	*lord-GEN-*$1SG_{GEN}$	*to*	$1SG_{OBL}$

<u>ø</u>-*išteme*-<u>ø</u>-*šu* *magal* *damqiš*
<u>1SG</u>-*hear.PRF*-<u>JUSS</u>-$3SGM_{ACC}$ *much* *beautifully*
'I have heard very well everything that the king, my lord, has said.'

šani:ta *innepša:*-<u>ti</u> *ki:ma* *ri:qi* ...
moreover *make.PASS*-<u>PAST</u>.<u>1SG</u> *like* *pot-GEN* ...
'Moreover: I have become like a pot ...' (EA 297:8–16)

As one can see, the vocabulary — lexical and function words alike — is largely of Akkadian origin, whereas the inflectional morphology of the verb is largely Canaanite. One should note that even the non-concatenative morphemes within the verbal forms can at times be Canaanite, whereas the roots are Akkadian. In our example, this is the case with the form *qaba* 'he said' (Izre'el 2005, pp. 28–29). Interestingly, the use of grammatical morphemes is not the same in the nominal and the verbal domains, as the nominal domain — very much like the cases of Michif and Mednyj Aleut — consists of morphemes of the same origin as the lexemes, in our case Akkadian. In many instances Canaano-Akkadian shows convergence in form of Akkadian and Canaanite components, notably in the pronominal and case systems, as well as in some stem — or pattern — formations. As regards pronouns and case markers, paradigmatic comparison suggests that the convergent forms are basically part of the Akkadian rather than the Canaanite component of the language. Thus, for example, the genitive 1SG pronominal suffix, which had been identical in Akkadian and Canaanite, must be compared to the 3rd-person forms with /š/, which are part of the Akkadian paradigm (for the Canaano-Akkadian paradigm as a whole, see Izre'el 2005, p. 20). As for

[6] Winford reshuffles the classification of contact languages in general and tries to do it on different terms altogether; see Winford 2007.

[7] For the grammatical glosses, see note 4 above.

the case system, although the forms and function of the case ending in the two languages are similar, the lack of the Canaanite plural ending *-ma* suggests that the nominal number-case indicators *-u:* and *-i:* should be regarded as Akkadian, and by implication the system as a whole. For the plural-masculine in their unbound forms, compare, for example, the commonly attested *šamu:*, *šame:* 'heaven' with the Canaanite gloss *šamu:ma* (EA 211:17; cf. Izre'el 2005, p. 16).[8]

All in all, I do not see any fundamental differences between the morphological structure of Canaano-Akkadian and those languages usually taken as prototypical to language mixing or ones that eluded the general linguistics literature such as Loterā'i (*pace* Sanders 2009, p. 89). In addition to the morphological split, one should note that the syntax of Canaano-Akkadian is also largely Canaanite (Izre'el 2005, §3), as is much of its grammatical semantics (with some inevitable lexical semantics as well; Izre'el 2005, §5; for the general issue of lexical semantics in contact languages, see, e.g., Lefebvre 2008).

One other point raised against using the concept of "mixed language" as a theoretical construct for the study of Canaano-Akkadian is that all mixed languages described in the literature essentially rise in the context of a spoken environment (von Dassow 2004, pp. 649–50 and n. 20). As we shall see below (§4), while Canaano-Akkadian was essentially employed in the written medium and was probably intended by and large to be used in written communication, the formation of Canaano-Akkadian cannot be understood unless it was spoken in some form at least at the time of its emergence. I should also add at this juncture that whether there was any direct contact at any time between Canaanites and Akkadian speakers is not something that I should consider in order to classify or define the nature of the resulting contact between the languages (*pace* Sanders 2009, pp. 88–90). One should recall at this point that whereas older cuneiform documents from Canaan show (Peripheral) Akkadian related to the Old Babylonian period, Canaano-Akkadian data seem to be attested in written documents from Ta'anach dating perhaps to the late fifteenth century (Rainey 1999; Horowitz, Oshima, and Sanders 2006). This points to the potentiality of further finds in the area to make the research into the origins of Canaano-Akkadian rely on more solid bases than the materials found hitherto, including also, I hope, some clues about the sociolinguistics of the emergence of the mixed language and the linguistic contacts between Canaanite speakers and Akkadian speakers at various points in the history of this region. At this stage of research and with the existing stock of written materials available to us, I would argue that the linguistic materials as reflected in the cuneiform find is enough to determine the structural similarity between known mixed languages and Canaano-Akkadian.

One other term that may well fit the nature of Canaano-Akkadian is "fused language." This term, which I prefer over "fused lect" (Auer 1999),[9] refers to a linguistic continuum that has resulted from the mixing of two linguistic systems and that has gone through a process of grammaticalization so that it has become characterized by "rule governed, nonvariable structural regularities" (Auer 1999, p. 310). In this meaning, "nonvariable" does not mean that linguistic variation does not exist, but that the use of elements borrowed from the two languages in contact is governed by rules and that the borrowed elements are not freely interchangeable. In other words, variation is not random, and the system shows stabilized form-function relationships. According to Auer,

> While L[anguage] M[ixing] by definition allows variation (...), the use of one "language" or the other for certain constituents is obligatory in F[used] L[ects]; it is part of their grammar, and speakers have no choice. (Auer 1999, p. 321)

While this definition of the term may seem to be too neat, it may fit well the nature of Canaano-Akkadian, as is perhaps the case with other mixed languages. However, the difference between the hitherto categorized

[8] Blau (1970, pp. 36–37) suggests that the Canaanite case system had already been in decline during the Amarna period, judging from pseudo-corrections and (rare) inconsistencies in the use of cases according to our expectations of the system based on comparative evidence. While this is not the place to discuss this contention, one could think of geographical or other variation in the employment of case system. Of course, if Blau's thesis is correct, it will give further support to the point raised here, i.e., that the case system is part of the Akkadian component of the system rather than a carry-over from Canaanite. For an overall survey of the Canaano-Akkadian case system, see Kossmann 1987–88. For some Canaanite substratal influence in the preservation of case endings in the construct state, see Rainey 1996, vol. 1, pp. 174–75.

[9] Auer refers to Matras 1996 for this term, and to Scotton 1988 for the term "fused variety." For more recent discussion of the notion of Fusion by Matras, see Matras 2005; Matras 2009, p. 363 (index). For the term "lect," see below, n. 14.

mixed languages and the so-called fused lects still needs further investigation (Auer 1999, pp. 321–32 and n. 20; cf. Matras 2009, p. 318 n. 8).

One might also suggest the term "hybrid language," which is usually not associated with any specific type of language contact (although it can sometimes be associated with code switching; cf. Auer 2005). Therefore, I could resort to this solution. However, the use of this term would not be transparent enough for the actual split between linguistic components in Canaano-Akkadian, which, as mentioned, does resemble, to the best of my judgment, other cases of mixed language hitherto described, without ignoring the differences.

Therefore, I see no real point at this stage of research in discarding the accepted term *mixed language* as the term that — as I have tried to argue above — fits best the nature of Canaano-Akkadian.

The aim of this paper is to pinpoint some key features of Canaano-Akkadian and its sociolinguistic setting, which may serve us well in deepening our understanding of this linguistic continuum in any future research. In what follows, I first discuss in some detail the perception of Canaano-Akkadian by the Canaanite scribes, suggesting that they thought of this mixed language as Akkadian (§2). I then proceed to ask whether we can share the ancient scribes' view of Canaano-Akkadian as Akkadian (§3). This is done by discussing variation as an inherent characteristic of Canaano-Akkadian, along with its implications for the nature of the language as a single linguistic system. I then delve into the issue of the underlying spoken reality of Canaano-Akkadian (§4). In the last, concluding section (§5), I again inquire into the identity of Canaano-Akkadian, now from the point of view of the two languages involved: Akkadian and Canaanite. The study concludes with a few remarks on synchrony and diachrony and on some prospects for possible inquiries concerning sociolinguistic aspects of the Canaanite Amarna letters and related texts (§6).

2. What Did the Canaanite Scribes Think of the Language They Were Writing?

The language written by the Canaanite scribes, like any other linguistic system, served as a means of communication. As far as we know now, Canaano-Akkadian was used for correspondence between Canaanite and Egyptian scribes (and officials?) of that time. The Canaanite scribes would write their letters in Canaano-Akkadian, but could understand the letters sent to their rulers on behalf of the Egyptian pharaoh perfectly well. These letters were written in Egyptian Akkadian, a closely related variety of the northwestern Akkadian lingua franca of that time (Cochavi-Rainey 1988; 1998; Edel 1994). The Egyptian scribes who received letters from Canaan could, for their part, understand the mixed language of these letters.

Yet there was a significant difference between the languages of these parties. The structure of Egyptian Akkadian was closely related to that of other Akkadian dialects; the linguistic varieties used by the Canaanite scribes had many structural traits similar or identical to contemporary NWS dialects. The structural gap between the languages used by the Canaanite scribes and Egyptian Akkadian was sometimes very large. I am not at all confident of the mutual intelligibility of these languages had an Egyptian scribe encountered his fellow Canaanite scribe in face-to-face interaction. I also suspect that previous training was needed for an Egyptian scribe to understand a Canaanite scribe, and vice versa, even in writing. From a sociolinguistic point of view, the language of the Egyptian scribes was superior to that of the Canaanite scribes. In other words, it served as a superstratum.

In spite of the marked difference between Egyptian (or other Peripheral) Akkadian and Canaano-Akkadian, I argue that the Canaanite scribes perceived their language of correspondence as (a dialect of) Akkadian. This perception can be shown in different ways, of which the most conspicuous manifestations are the following: the use of Akkadian opening formulae (§2.1); the perception of Canaanite glosses as foreign words and the occurrence of Akkadian glosses in the texts (§2.2); the use of genuine Akkadian verbal morphology within the letters (§2.3); the occurrence of Akkadian-like hyper-corrections (§2.4); the fact that the lexical basis of that language and the bulk of its nominal grammatical domain are almost purely Akkadian and thus give an overall Akkadian look to the language (§2.5). To these factors one may add the important psychological factor of their using the Akkadian script. Although the use of script cannot serve as a sole argument (cf. the use of cuneiform script for Hittite and Hurrian), in this case it may well support this claim, given all other arguments. An illuminating paragraph in this respect written by Weeden on the use of cuneiform in Hittite will be cited in §5 below.

2.1. Opening Formulae

The Canaanite scribes used letter-opening formulae and some other formulae that had been adopted from Mesopotamian chancellery practice. In these formulae, the scribes used, in most cases, genuine standard Akkadian expressions and standard Akkadian verbal forms. A typical example is the following:

ex. 9. *a-na* LUGAL-*ri* EN-*ia* ^{d}UTU-*ia* ^{2} *qí-bí-ma* ^{3} *um-ma* ^{m}*ri-ib*-^{d}IŠKUR ÌR-*ka-ma* ^{4} *a-na* GÌR.MEŠ EN-*ia* ^{d}UTU-*ia* ^{5} *7-šu 7-ta-an am-qú-ut*

'To the king, my lord, my Sun-God, say: Message of Ribhaddi, your servant:
I fall at the feet of my lord, my Sun-God, 7 times (and) 7 times.' (EA 104:1–5, Byblos)

The training of the Canaanite scribes had indeed been based on the usual practice of Mesopotamian scribal schools (cf. below, §4.0; further Knutson 1982 and especially Mynářová 2007; for opening formulae in general, see Salonen 1967). In Ugarit, scribes used Akkadian formulae in Akkadian letters, and the opening formulae of letters written in Ugaritic exhibit strong similarities to the Akkadian formulae, to the point that some are literal translations (Ahl 1973; Knutson 1982; Cunchillos 1999; Huehnergard 1999; Hawley 2003). Still, they did not use Akkadian words in these formulae but did translate them into Ugaritic. As we see below, there are some indications that the opening formula had also been pronounced (§4.1.5).

2.2. Glosses

The Canaanite scribes regarded the Canaanite glosses as foreign words. By "foreign" I mean not foreign to their native tongue, but foreign to the linguistic system they were writing in (cf. Gianto 1995, p. 73). These glosses — and not the so-called Akkadianisms (§3.0) — were, in most cases, marked by a *Glossenkeil* (cf. Artzi 1963). Most instructive is the gloss *na-aš-ša-a* in the following passage:

ex. 10. *li-il-ma-ad* LUGAL-*ru* EN-⸢*i*⸣*a* ^{12} *i-nu-ma* LÚ.SA.GAZ *š*⸢*a*⸣ ^{13} *yi-na-aš-ši* \ *na-aš-ša-a* ^{14} *i-na* KUR.KI.ḪÁ *na-da-an* ^{15} DINGIR-*lu*$_{4}$ *ša* LUGAL-*ri* EN-*ia* ⸢*a*⸣-*na i*⸢*a*⸣-*ši* ^{16} *ù i-du-uk-šu*

'May the king, my lord, be informed that the Apiru man who had become elevated '*naššaʔa*'
in the lands, the god of the king, my lord, gave to me and I killed him.' (EA 366:11–16, Gath)

The gloss *na-aš-ša-a* translates *yi-na-aš-ši*, a verbal form typical of Canaano-Akkadian. It has Canaanite markers for person (*y*-) and mood (-*ø*), and these are annexed to a stem taken from Akkadian, namely, *-inašši-* (<*i+našši*; Izre'el 2005, pp. 30–32; 2007a, §5.2). The roots were very similar in the three cognate languages, namely, Akkadian, Canaanite, and Canaano-Akkadian. The Canaano-Akkadian verbal form *yinašši* was glossed not because the scribe felt it necessary to interpret the lexical difference between the two forms, but to interpret the *grammatical* differences between them.

He thus used a verbal form stemming from the Canaanite, namely, *naššaʔa*, to interpret the form he used in the flow of his letter. It is the first form, *yinašši*, that he regarded as Akkadian.

The existence of Canaanite glosses is well understood if one takes into consideration the imperfect knowledge of Canaanite scribes of the language they were using. However, the Amarna letters further exhibit Akkadian glosses, and one wonders what the need of such glosses was if the language as a whole would not be interpreted by its users as an Akkadian system. One interesting case is the invention of an Akkadian-like noun that glosses a Sumerogram in a letter from Egypt to Milkilu, the ruler of Gezer, probably by one of his scribes (Izre'el 1995b, pp. 109–18):

ex. 11. MÍ.DÉ \ *ša-qí-tum*

'woman-cupbearer' (EA 369:8)

The equation between the Sumerogram DÉ and the Akkadian term *šāqû* is attested only in lexical lists (*AHw* 1181a; CAD Š/1, p. 24b) and seems to be evoked in this case only due to scribal education. As the feminine counterpart of the referent "cupbearer" seems to have not been known in Mesopotamia, the acute need for this linguistic innovation arose in the context of the demand of women cupbearers on behalf of the pharaoh from his vassal

Milkilu, and therefore the scribe had to generate this form. Why would he not write it down in his own mother tongue? The answer to this question seems to be clear: the linguistic system he wrote in was not Canaanite but one that he regarded to be Akkadian.

One other case in point is the occurrence of a Canaano-Akkadian gloss in a letter from Jerusalem:

ex. 12. [*ú*]-*ba-na la-a* GAZ \ *di*$_{12}$-[*k*]*a-t*[*i*]

'I was almost killed.' (EA 287:73)

This verb, translating the Sumerogram GAZ, consists of a stem originating in the Akkadian stative and the person morpheme, *a:ti*, in itself a hybrid form consisting of the Canaanite person suffix *ti* preceded by the vowel *a:*, which originates in the stative conjugation of Akkadian (Rainey 1996, vol. 2, p. 285). As in other cases of non-Canaanite glosses, the only way I can explain the occurrence of a Canaano-Akkadian gloss is the perception of the scribe that his language of correspondence in this letter is not Canaanite. As we see below (§4.1.5), there are indications that Akkadian glosses were actually pronounced.

2.3. Hyper-corrections

An example of hyper-correction is attested in the form *i-ru-da-am* found in a letter from Gezer. The context is as follows:

ex. 13. *tu-šu-ru-ba-ni* [19] *a-na* URU.DIDLI.KI-*ni-ia* [20] *u* ⌜*lu-ú*⌝ *i-ru-da-am* [21] LUGAL EN-*ia ki-ma ša* [22] A.A-*ia u t*[*á-p*]*á-ti-*[*ia*]

'May you[10] (re)admit me into my cities, so that I may serve the king, my lord, like my father and [my] co[llea]gues.' (EA 300:18–20)

The meaning of the Akkadian verb *ara:du* is 'to descend.' As a verb of motion, it may be used in standard Akkadian with the ventive ending. In Canaano-Akkadian, however, there exists a verb *ara:du*, which is a denominative from *ardu* 'servant,' thus denoting 'to serve.' Additional ventive endings in forms of this verb with the meaning 'to serve' are hence unwarranted. The verb *i:rudam* is found in a final clause that requires a (Canaanite) volitive form, since it follows another volitive verb (cf. Moran 1960 = 2003, #10).[11] Therefore, either the long or the short volitive is expected, since regarding their volitive force, *yqtlø* and *yqtla* are essentially the same (cf. Moran 1950a, p. 105 = 2003, pp. 97–98). The scribe of this letter chose the long volitive not haphazardly, but because he sought to make use of a "good" Akkadian form. However, he went too far. Knowing the (correct?!) spelling of the ventive ending in Akkadian, he added an *am* sign at the end. By adding the *-am* ending to this verb instead of the long volitive ending *-a* (i.e., with no *m*), the scribe felt he granted it a better Akkadian look (cf. Izre'el 1978, excursus C and p. 82 n. 278[b]).

Such hyper-corrections could not have occurred unless the scribes were unaware of the alleged Akkadian nature of the language they were using. Mimation is a feature of older dialects of Akkadian and might have preserved as a spelling anachronism, as is the case in core Akkadian texts or in some Peripheral Akkadian dialects (see, e.g., Izre'el 1991a, 1:§1.7). However, in this case we might think of this spelling not as an anachronism, but as an indication of the actual pronunciation of this ending, due to the lack of historical tradition of the pronunciation of this specific verb with mimation and, especially, due to the explicit use of a final *Vm* syllabic sign (as against a final *Cvm* one). Such spellings may have pointed to the actual pronunciation of forms preserving mimation also in core Akkadian dialects in some cases, as I have tried to show elsewhere (Izre'el 2000; for a suggestion that mimation in Akkadograms in Hittite texts was pronounced, see Weeden 2007, pp. 20–21; for Canaano-Akkadian cf. also, briefly, Izre'el 2005, p. 13). Another possible case of hyper-correction has been suggested in Izre'el 2005 (p. 12; cf. below, §4.1.3). Such cases stress the need for further investigation in order to search for similar phenomena.

---

[10] Moran (1992, p. 341) takes *tušu:rubani* as a 3SGF. Cf. Izre'el 1978, p. 80 n. 265.

[11] There has been some discussion regarding the nature of the "long" volitive; see Izre'el 1978, pp. 80–82; Rainey 1991–93; 1996, vol. 2, pp. 254–63; Tropper 1997; 1997/1998, p. 136; Huehnergard 1998, p. 71; Korchin 2008, §4.3.

2.4. The Lexicon

It is repeatedly noted above that the lexical basis of Canaano-Akkadian is almost purely drawn from Akkadian. This is not a minor trait of a language as regards the way its speakers perceive it. On the perceptual level, the lexicon is by far more prominent than the grammatical structure, and people tend to perceive the identity of their language according to its lexical basis, its vocabulary, even if it has a remarkably different syntax than does the standard variety of the language. This is so in many areas in the world where English is spoken, notably the language of African American on one hand and pidgin varieties on another. A Nigerian student once told me that "in Nigeria there is Pidgin English and Grammar English; in Pidgin English there is no grammar," he said, "but people understand."

I have argued that the Canaanite scribes perceived their language of correspondence as (a dialect of) Akkadian. Would it be justified also for us, as students of Canaano-Akkadian, to describe this complicated situation as a single linguistic system? In order to address this question, we should discuss with some detail the notion of variation in the Amarna letters.

3. Variation

Variation appears to be found everywhere throughout Canaano-Akkadian. Variation is not only geographical; it is also influenced by the tradition of each scribal school, sometimes by idiosyncrasies of a certain scribe. Moreover, variation may be found within one and the same text. It thus appears that variation is an inherent characteristic of the language employed by the Canaanite Amarna scribes. By this attribute, Canaano-Akkadian is not different from any other natural language, written or spoken.

Variation in the Amarna letters is based on structured changes between components of (Peripheral) Akkadian and of Canaano-Akkadian. The (Peripheral) Akkadian components that occur within a text written in Canaano-Akkadian have been termed "Akkadianisms" (Izre'el 1978, §7.2.1; 2005, p. 5; following, e.g., Rainey 1975, p. 420; 1996, vol. 2, p. 23). Akkadianisms are found in Canaano-Akkadian in letter-opening formulae and in a few other formulaic phrases. Of course, these are rote phrases and formulae learned at school for serving the traditional functions in letter openings. However, aside from these formulae, there are many other Akkadianisms used in the Amarna letters sent from Canaan. For example, one will note the standard Akkadian imperative, attested with great frequency, and especially precative forms of the verb, which are utterly foreign to NWS dialects. Such are also a plethora of other verbal forms. Note the following example:

ex. 14. *ù* ŠEŠ-*ia* TUR *iš-tu ia-ti* [17] *i-na-kar*$_5$*-mi* URU.*gub-la*.KI [18] *a-na na-da-ni* URU.KI-*li* [19] *a-na* DUMU.MEŠ ÌR-^{m}*a-ši-ir-ti*

'My brother, (who is) younger than me, became hostile towards Byblos, in order to hand the city to the sons of Abdi'ashirti.' (EA 137:16–19)

The form *i-na-kar*$_5$(*-mi*) 'he has become hostile' is the only finite verbal form in this letter of Ribhaddi, the ruler of Byblos,[12] that has an Akkadian structure. All other 3SGM forms have an initial *y-* marker for this person, for example, *yi-iš-mi* 'he heard' (line 7), *yi-mur* 'he saw' (line 20), *ia-an-aṣ-ni* 'he despised me' (line 23), and many others.[13]

Akkadianisms are used in the great majority of cases not as haphazard insertions, but in perfectly fitting contexts, and one can formulate rules for their occurrence. These rules can be either linguistic or discoursive.

[12] This letter was not sent from Byblos, but from Beirut (cf. lines 14–15). Yet its language does not resemble that of the other Amarna letters from Beirut (EA 141–43; probably also EA 97–98). Several similarities in style to the other Byblos letters perhaps indicate that a scribe from Byblos may have accompanied Ribhaddi in his journey. Further research may yield more solid conclusions.

[13] Knudtzon's *i*[*-tu-ur*] (line 9) should be corrected to *i*[*a-tu-ur*], to conform with the pattern attested in other forms of this verb in Amarna (Ebeling in Knudtzon 1915, p. 1530).

Before illustrating these rules, I wish to introduce the theoretical framework that I find most appropriate to deal with the complex linguistic continuum of the Canaanite Amarna letters.

3.1. Theoretical Framework

A Canaanite scribe was almost always writing on behalf of a local vassal ruler, who was always inferior in rank compared to the addressee, be it the pharaoh himself or one of the Egyptian officials. From a comparison of the language of each of the Canaanite scribes to the language of the Egyptian scribes, it seems preferable to consider that we are dealing with two distinct linguistic systems, for the most part. Admittedly, in certain instances, there are minor differences between the language of the Egyptian and Canaanite scribes. As such, they may be regarded as different variants of the same language. Nevertheless, in most of the subcorpora from Canaan, the two languages show deep and significant structural differences between them.

Canaanite scribes usually read Egyptian Akkadian in the letters they received from the pharaoh's scribes. Whether they had been taught also to write in the standard Peripheral Akkadian system is not a question that can be solved with our present knowledge (but cf. the remarks below, §4.0). What we do know is that the scribes of Canaan wrote in a different language and that the language they were using was an accepted linguistic system among the chancellery officials of Canaan.

Research in linguistic variation has shown that a speech community's language, that is, any natural language, forms a system of "orderly heterogeneity," which implies that variation is omnipresent and non-random, constrained by multiple linguistic and social factors (Montgomery 2007, p. 118, citing from Weinreich, Labov, and Herzog 1968, p. 100). Yet there are linguistic situations where variation is especially prominent and displays large, sometimes even extreme, divergences between lects.[14] Parallels to the linguistic situation attested in the Amarna correspondence can be found in similar contexts elsewhere. Variation in the context of two different linguistic structures will be found in diglossic situations as defined by Ferguson (1959), namely, the use of significantly different linguistic systems in various registers, notably in writing and speech, as in Arabic-speaking communities (see further Fishman 1967; Fasold 1984: ch. 2; Kaye 2001).

A continuum of variants used by scribes in various diglossic settings is probably not the case here (for a suggestion to thus treat the Arabic diglossia, see Hary 1996). In the Arabic-speaking communities, a single person would use both extremes and the continuum between those two extremes in various situations. He would speak his native dialect at home and write in Modern Standard Arabic, and when speaking in a formal situation, he would go along the continuum to various extents. As against this situation, Peripheral Akkadian and Canaano-Akkadian would not be used discretely by one and the same scribe. He would read a letter in Egyptian Akkadian and write in Canaano-Akkadian. The Canaanite scribe's diglossia would therefore manifest itself between his reading the letters he was receiving from Egypt and the ones he himself would write. However, when looking at the language of the scribal community of Canaan as a whole, a linguistic continuum is what we observe. The Amarna letters indeed form a continuum of lectal varieties.

Clear cases of continua within a linguistic community that are similar in some respects to the Amarna Canaanite situation may be found in several creole-speaking areas where there has been continued contact with the model language. In such communities, a plethora of lects forms a vast continuum of linguistic varieties. The creole basilect is found at one of its extreme points. The acrolect, that is, the model language, is found at the other extreme. This linguistic situation is generally termed a "postcreole continuum" (see, e.g., Holm 1988–89, vol. 1, pp. 9, 52–60; Mühlhäusler 1997, pp. 11–12, 211–21; Kaye and Tosco 2001, pp. 96–97).

Two approaches have been developed to handle such cases of variation. One tends to distinguish between two or more linguistic systems with a great deal of overlapping between the systems (e.g., Tsuzaki 1971; cf. also Winford 1985). The other approach regards this linguistic situation not as a static one, but rather as a dynamic

[14] The term "lect": (used in sociolinguistics or dialectology aside the term of "language variety") is used here to indicate a single linguistic system, whether of a single scribe or of a single text reflecting a unique linguistic system of its own, even from among a choice of texts written by one and the same scribe. The notion of lect was introduced by C.-J. N. Bailey, who used "lect" as a "non-committal term for any bundling together of linguistic phenomena" (Bailey 1973, p. 11).

system, in which both the community and the individual play different rôles within each situation. As such, this approach provides for one linguistic system in which variation follows specific and orderly rules. Such rules may be either obligatory or optional and are regulated by linguistic and by discoursive factors.

It is this latter method that has been preferred and adopted by dialectologists and sociolinguists, since variability has gained recognition as an inherent structural feature of language per se (Decamp 1971; Bailey 1973; Labov 1971; Petyt 1980, chs. 5 and 8; Chambers and Trudgill 1998, ch. 9; Chambers, Trudgill, and Schilling-Estes 2002 in various chapters; for yet another alternative, see Matras 2009, pp. 4–5).

Two main objections have been raised against postulating more than one system. One is in the domain of the community. Here it would require either attributing to each idiolect its own distinct system or postulating two or three systems within the community with many points of interference and overlapping between them, and a lot of variation within each. The second objection is relevant to the domain of the individual, that is, the idiolect. Here we would have to posit too many switches from system to system within a single discourse.

Both objections will prove valid for the linguistic description of the El-Amarna letters from Canaan, since there is variation not only between the different scribes, but also within the linguistic output of each scribe. Therefore, I would like to suggest the second approach for their study. I suggest that Canaano-Akkadian be treated as a single linguistic system consisting of lectal varieties stretching between the extreme of the clear cases of the mixed language of the Canaanite letters, and the opposite extreme of lects closer to standard Peripheral Akkadian as used by some Canaanite scribes. This methodology will not only help us in our endeavor to understand the essence and the spirit of this language as it was perceived by the scribes themselves, but also allow us to contextualize the variety of Akkadianisms properly, that is, within *Canaano-Akkadian*. It must be stressed: this language, with all its variants, did serve as an accepted — and most probably, learned — means of communication, so that it must have had a basic structural system that was relatively solid. As such, variation must be admitted into the description of this system.

This concept of a single system will also help us to account for Akkadianisms within a single letter, numerous as they may be, and to distinguish them from clear cases of slips into a different linguistic system, in our case Peripheral Akkadian, occurring in a haphazard manner and without apparent governing rules (cf. Izre'el 2007a, §5.3). Akkadianisms that regularly appear in the flow of the text should be described according to rules that govern them. If some of the Akkadianisms are to be proven haphazard or when an irregular code switching occurs, these may be considered as calques or insertions from a different linguistic system.

I believe that a great majority of Akkadianisms are structurally determined. That is, occurrences of forms that are closely related to or identical with the analogous forms of standard Akkadian can be determined and anticipated by rules. In the following sections, I deal with several types of variation, the rules that govern them, and the triggers for variant forms.

3.2. Intrasystemic Variation

Variation within the system is a feature of the *langue* (see above, §1.4). Its manifestations can be observed mainly as dialectal or idiolectal peculiarities. Intra-systemic variation usually manifests itself by differences among individual texts or groups of texts. There are, however, notable instances in which variations are found within one and the same text.

Apparent cases of switching toward the Akkadian superstratum also belong to this kind of variation. It is the task of the student of Canaano-Akkadian to find out whether these switches are structural, and if they are, to describe the circumstances under which they tend to appear in each case. These circumstances may be triggers that are either lexical or discoursive, obligatory or optional. In the following two sections, I illustrate some types of triggers for variation.

3.2.1. Lexical Triggers

An example of a lexical trigger that may induce an apparent deviation from the system is the surfacing of an Akkadian prefixed stative verbal form of *idû* 'to know,' a form with exceptional behavior also within the structure of standard Akkadian. Many of the Canaanite Amarna scribes (yet by no means all of them) would use the standard

Akkadian forms of this verb: *i-de* for the 1SG and the 3SGM, *ti-de* for the 2SGM, and so on (cf. Ebeling in Knudtzon 1915, pp. 1420–21; Rainey 1973, pp. 244–47; 1996, vol. 2, pp. 323–28). For example, in EA 100 (a letter from the city of Irqata), the scribe wrote,

ex. 15. *i-de lìb-bi* LUGAL EN

'May the heart of the king, the lord, know ...' (EA 100:8–9)

In this letter we also have *[t]i-de* 'you know' (line 23). All other 3SGM verbs in this letter have an initial *y-*:

yu-wa-ši-r[a 'he sent' (line 11); *yi-iq-bi* 'he said' (line 13);
yi-ìš-mi 'may he listen' (line 31); *ia-di-na* 'may he give.' (line 33)

This is, obviously, a lexical trigger that constrains verbal forms of *idû* from admitting the *y-* prefix of the 3SGM. In other words, the verb *idû* does not inflect according to the Canaano-Akkadian norm and thus might be regarded as an apparent exception to the system. However, the constraints that inhibit the affixation of *y-* to this verb are controlled by rules within the system. Therefore, the form *i:de*, although closely related to standard Akkadian norms, must be regarded as part of the linguistic system of Canaano-Akkadian.

3.2.2. Discoursive Triggers

Several southern Canaanite scribes, when representing the words of the pharaoh to their ruler and quoting them, or when referring to the pharaoh's words even without directly quoting them, use verbal forms closer to the Akkadian standard than in the rest of the letter. Examples:

ex. 16. *a-wa-at ul-te-bi-la* LUGAL

'The order that the king has sent' (EA 267:9–10; Milkilu of Gezer)

a-wa-at iq-ba(sic)*-bi* LUGAL

'The order that the king has said' (EA 275:9–10; Ya'zibhadda, of an unknown city in southern Canaan)

a-wa-at iš-tap-pár LUGAL

'The order that the king has sent' (EA 276:9–10; same ruler as EA 275 above)

a-wa-ti$_7$.MEŠ$^!$ *ša iš-pu-ur* LUGAL

'The orders that the king sent' (EA 292:18–19; Ba'lushiptu of Gezer)

mì-ma ša i-qa-ab-bi LUGAL

'Everything that the king has said' (EA 298:14–16; Yapaʾu of Gezer)

All other verbs in these texts, as well as the system itself, are Canaano-Akkadian. This discoursive trigger that brings about the use of an Akkadian form in an otherwise mixed environment is optional or lect dependent. Thus, another scribe of Yapa'u of Gezer writes in the same context as follows:

ex. 17. *mi-im-ma ša qa-ba* LUGAL

'Everything that the king said' (EA 297:8–9)

Here the scribe made use of a typical NWS suffix-conjugation pattern, namely, the active Canaanite stem *qatal* (see above, notes to ex. 8), instead of the Akkadian imperfective-*iparras* form (*iqabbi*) that his fellow scribe used.[15]

---

[15] Note the absence of the subjunctive, which is typical of these texts.

Note that we can formulate discoursive rules that operate on various lects in the same way, yet the output would not necessarily be the same. That is, whereas the rule may determine the conditions for the use of a form consisting of purely Akkadian material, the form itself may vary and be — in the examples given — one of the various forms cited.

When we deal with quotes from the pharaoh's letters, one may claim that quoting is an act of code switching that takes the scribe from Canaano-Akkadian to Egyptian Akkadian. However, in the citations above, this is not the case, and it is only *reference* to the pharaoh's orders that brought about the use of Akkadianized forms.

While this rule is optional, as we have seen, whenever the need for the same underlying meaning (*signifié*) shows up, a variant form may still surface. This occurs not only in actual quotes from the pharaoh's letters, but, interestingly, also in a pseudo-citation from the king's words:

ex. 18. *ù ki-i i-qa-bu* LUGAL *a-na mi-nim iš-tap-r*[*u*] [31] [m]*ri-ib-*[d]IŠKUR *ṭup-pa a-na ma-ḫar be-li-š*[*u*]

'Concerning (that) what the king has said: "Why does Ribhaddi keep sending a tablet to his lord?"' (EA 106:30–31; Byblos)[16]

Here one notes the surfacing of a form without the *y-* prefix of the 3SGM, namely, *ištapru* 'he keeps sending.' Note further the Akkadianized verb introducing the citation, *iqabbu*. In a similar environment in the very same letter, the surfacing form does carry this prefix:

ex. 19. *šá-ni-tam a-na mi-nim* [14] *yi-iš-tap-ru* [m]*ri-ib-*[d]IŠKUR *ki-na-an-na-ma* [15] *ṭup-pa a-na* É.GAL

'Furthermore: Why does Ribhaddi keep sending a tablet this way to the palace?' (EA 106:13–15)

Here the subject is Ribhaddi rather than the pharaoh, and therefore the surfacing form is the one typical of the mixed language.[17]

In some letters, the discoursive trigger may act upon the entire letter. In another letter from Byblos, EA 81, the form *iq-bi* 'he said' is attested without the *y-* (line 11). This lack of the Canaanite-originating prefix is probably triggered by the existence of the same form in the opening formula, common in Byblos, which is also attested at the beginning of this letter (although fragmentary):

ex. 20. [[m]*ri-ib-*[d]IŠKUR *iq-b*]*i a-na* EN-[*šu*]

'[Ribhaddi sa]y[s] to [his] lord' (EA 81:1)

In the opening address, this standard Akkadian form is of course the rule. In such cases, we might also posit a lexical trigger rather than discoursive. We might formulate a rule that inhibits the annexation of the *y-* prefix in 3SGM forms of *qabû*, as was the case with *idû* (§3.2.1). These questions need, however, much further research.

We have seen that the Canaano-Akkadian system integrates components that are closely related to the (Peripheral) Akkadian linguistic system. We have further seen that these components are governed by rules and therefore must be regarded not as haphazard borrowings into the Canaano-Akkadian system, but as integral to it. As mentioned, these items have been termed "Akkadianisms." The term "Akkadianisms" may thus be misleading, as it may suggest that the scribes themselves looked upon such forms as foreign to their linguistic system. However, it is my claim that both the occurrence of Akkadian glosses (§2.2) and this complex situation, where hybrid forms and (Peripheral) Akkadian forms occur within one system and are bound by rules, support the hypothesis that the Canaanite scribes indeed perceived their chancellery language as Akkadian.

Moreover, the rules governing variation in Canaano-Akkadian, both the lexical and the discoursive ones, are similar to rules governing variation in natural languages everywhere. I believe that the set of examples for such rules as the ones given above suffice to support the claim that Canaano-Akkadian could not have been an artificial invention of a certain scribal school or of a specific scribal community, as has been suggested by Rainey (1975, pp. 423–24; cf. also Izre'el 1978, p. 83, mentioned further in §5 below; Rainey 2002, p. 50; see further §5 for von Dassow's hypothesis). It must have been a product of a natural linguistic development, as attested in various

[16] Moran 1992, p. 179: "How can the king say: ..."

[17] *Pace* Moran (1992, p. 179 with n. 2), who suggests that this too is a quote from the pharaoh's letter.

linguistic communities elsewhere (see §1.4 and especially §1.5 above; further illustrative examples and discussion can be found, inter alia, in Gardner-Chloros 2009). By implication, this further supports an assumption of an underlying spoken reality for that language.

4. Canaano-Akkadian Had an Underlying Spoken Reality

Being a written language used for specific purposes, the language of the Amarna Canaanite scribes manifests conventional scribal formulaic phrases of various kinds, and some adopted learned spellings. These are also found elsewhere in the Akkadian correspondence, both in the core areas, namely, Mesopotamia proper, and in the periphery. This trait was one of the characteristics of scribal training in the Mesopotamian culture in all periods and all geographical areas (Lambert 1957–60; Oppenheim 1977, ch. 5; Knutson 1982; Mynářová 2007; Pearce 1995; cf. Artzi 1990; Izre'el 1997).

Indeed, the prominence of Canaano-Akkadian as a language whose manifestations are in a written medium may explain many of its linguistic traits. However, although it may explain the origin of some elements of this complicated linguistic structure, the emergence and structuring of the system are essentially the same as in spoken languages. Moreover, an underlying spoken reality for the language attested in the Amarna letters can be shown to have existed, albeit not as a native tongue or in use in everyday speech. By "underlying spoken reality" I mean that the texts written in Canaano-Akkadian did not serve as a visual code on its own, but represent a language that can be decoded phonemically rather than solely graphemically. An underlying spoken reality would be necessary first and foremost for the emergence of Canaano-Akkadian, at least in scribal communities. I further claim that Canaano-Akkadian continued to play a role not only as a written code, but also as a genuine linguistic system, which was necessary for maintaining the scribal curriculum at Canaanite cuneiform schools, when the scribes-to-be would have vocalized words in that language. I further claim that this language was — at least potentially — pronounced. In any case, it had a phonological system underlying the graphemic strings as they are attested in Canaano-Akkadian texts. On the other hand, with the data at hand at this stage, we are unable to tell whether Canaano-Akkadian might have actually served in the spoken medium not only by the scribes during their studies or as a potential living language while writing and reading these texts, but also elsewhere, as well as, perhaps, by wider circles of speakers, like high officials (cf., for now, Ikeda 2010, for Emar).

In what follows, I try to support this hypothesis with some data, first dealing with some phonological features and by adducing support for the thesis that Canaano-Akkadian was indeed pronounced (§4.1), then by dealing with morphological, morphophonological, and morphosyntactical features, from diachronic and synchronic points of view (§4.2).

4.1. Phonological Features Representing an Underlying Spoken Reality

In the domain of phonology, we have strong evidence for the spoken reality of the mixed language itself, which manifests occasionally in spelling.

4.1.1. $i \rightarrow$ E = $i \rightarrow e$[18] (Evidence from Amqi)

Let us first observe some consistent spellings attested in some of the letters from Amqi (the Lebanese Baqa; EA 173–80, 363), which are unusual elsewhere in the Amarna correspondence, yet are the norm in this group of letters. These letters were written by scribes of the same school, as they exhibit striking similarities, not only in contents, but also in form (cf. Knudtzon 1915, p. 1278 n. 1; cf. Goren, Finkelstein and Na'aman 2004, ch.8). In these

[18] In formulae, lowercase characters represent phonemic or phonetic values; uppercase characters stand for sign forms. An arrow indicates representation in writing for uppercase characters, a linguistic change for lowercase characters.

letters, we find only once the sign *i*: ⌜*i*⌝-*na* 'in' (EA 179:21).[19] This spelling is in complete accordance with the standard Akkadian norm. In all other instances where we would have expected *i* to appear, the sign *e* is used instead:

ex. 21. *e-ba-ša-nu* 'we are' (EA 174:8 etc.); *e-ba-aš-še* 'he is' (EA 179:15); *e-din* (most probably for *idin*) 'give!' (EA 179:23); *e-na-ṣa-ar* 'I guard' (EA 179:26; for 1SG forms with initial *i*, see Izre'el 2007a, §5.2; for *naṣa:ru*, ibid., §5.2.2.3.3); also *e-ša-te* 'fire' (EA 174:13); *ni-e-nu* 'we' (EA 174:8 etc.); *te-na-ṣa-ru* 'they (will) guard' (EA 180:8)

This constant spelling with *e* signs should be interpreted as reflecting a genuine pronunciation. The two following 1PL forms offer further support in favor of this conclusion:

ex. 22. *ni-e-ta-lí* 'we have come' (line 4); [*ni*]-*e-na-ṣa-ar-šu* 'we guard it' (line 6)

In these two latter cases, the scribe of this letter felt it necessary to show the full verbal stem in the script (*e-ta-lí* and *e-na-ṣa-ar*, respectively), while adding to them the 1PL person prefix *ni-*, so he did not omit its initial *e* sign. This *e* sign, which shows the basic pronunciation of the stem used in this area, thus becomes superfluous for these specific forms. Of course, the sign NI, used by rote for the 1PL person prefix, can also be read *né*, which would yield pronunciations like *ne:tali* and *ne:naṣṣaršu*. However, at least for the second form, a long vowel is not expected. These forms might be explained as idiosyncrasies of a specific scribe who used this language not speaking but in writing. Still, the constant use of the sign *e* in all other forms, as well as in these two specific forms, may reflect a phonemic or phonetic reality in the substrate dialect. We would think of a timbre [e], which would appear in all these instances when the scribes were trying to *pronounce* these forms on the grounds of their foreign phonological system. Therefore, these two forms would be pronounced *ne:tali* and *nenaṣṣaršu*, respectively.

4.1.2. (Akkadian) *a* → *e*; (Canaano-Akkadian) *e* → *i*

The difference in phonemic status or phonetic distribution of the vowels *e* and *i* between Akkadian and the NWS dialects may explain the introduction of the vowel *i* to the verbal forms of predominating *e* formations of Akkadian in some dialects of Peripheral Akkadian. In another paper (Izre'el 1987a), I suggested a phonological intervention that served as one of the initializing forces for the admission of the Canaanite person prefixes to the Amarna verbal system. Canaano-Akkadian verbal stems can consist of originally 3SGM Akkadian forms[20] thus including their initial *i-* person prefix (Izre'el 2005, pp. 30–31; Izre'el 2007a, §5.2.1; and subsequent analyses). The phonological rule suggested here may have thus become an impetus, or a support, to bring about this structural change. If structural changes of Canaano-Akkadian can be explained by phonological factors, this would support the view that it had a spoken aspect at some point during its history.

In the aforementioned paper, I showed that in some older Amurru letters, verbal forms from roots with *e* as their first radical (usually called "*primae aleph* verbs of the *e*-class")[21] and other verbs with predominant *e* had an initial *i* instead of the expected *e*. The forms affected were 1SG forms of the prefix conjugation and infinitives. The same applies to most of the Byblos letters, for example,

ex. 23. *i-pu-šu-na* 'I should do' (energic; EA 74:63 and passim); *i-pí-iš* '(to) do' (EA 69:17)

Had the change occurred only in forms of the finite verb, one would be tempted to see this change in primae-*e* verbs as part of the overall adoption of the 3SG person prefix into the stem. The fact that this change between Akkadian and Canaano-Akkadian is a feature not only of finite verbal forms but also of infinitives is better explained by phonology than by morphology. Therefore, it may well be that at Byblos and at other Canaanite sites,

[19] The sign *i* is quite clear in Schroeder's copy (1915, no. 103). Knudtzon inserted it between square brackets in his transliteration (1907, p. 690).

[20] The standard Babylonian dialects (Old Babylonian and later) did not have gender distinction in the 3SG person verbal prefix. Old Akkadian, Assyrian, and some Babylonian dialects still distinguish between the two genders also in the third person, which makes gender distinction in the 3SG, attested also in some dialects of Peripheral Akkadian, the linguistic standard upon which the verb structure of Canaano-Akkadian emerged. The reference to 3SGM for the *i-* person marker relates to this structural trait.

[21] For vocalic root radicals in Akkadian, see Izre'el 1991b; Izre'el and Cohen 2004, §2.4.2.5.

we can identify a different phonological structure not only of the NWS substrate dialects, but of Canaano-Akkadian as well. Similar forms occur also in fifteenth-century Ta'anach (Ta'anach Tablet 2:11; Horowitz, Oshima, and Sanders 2006, p. 133) and the recently discovered fragment from Jerusalem (obverse, line 4′; Mazar et al. 2010). This peculiar phonologically feature may further suggest an underlying spoken reality for Canaano-Akkadian.

4.1.3. Vowel Deletion

For vowel deletion, let us look at two examples from Byblos:

ex. 24. *ti-ir-bu* 'you enter' (EA 102:11); ⌈*ir*⌉*-bu-nim* 'they enter' (EA 127:22)

The first form, most probably for *tirbu*, a 2SGM prefix-conjugation verb with an indicative ending, attests to the deletion of the vowel between the second and the third root radicals *r* and *b*. This deletion is not attested in the cognate standard Akkadian form, which is *te:rubu* ('you entered'+subjunctive). Note that vowel deletion in standard Akkadian is inhibited by the long vowel in the first syllable. The second form, to be read *irbu:ni*, attests to the same feature, albeit in a letter that exhibits a different subdialect of Byblos Canaano-Akkadian (for this interpretation, cf. Ebeling 1910, p. 44; for another analysis, see Ebeling in Knudtzon 1915, p. 1406). Whether these forms are the ad hoc result of interference from the phonological structure of the local indigenous dialect or the result of analogical processes within the mixed language (in Izre'el 2005, p. 12, I suggest a hyper-correction), they could not have arisen in any scenario other than one involving an underlying spoken reality. In any circumstances other than actually uttering the forms in question, such written forms simply could not have been generated. The forms that would have been generated would necessarily appear in script as *ti-ri-bu* and *i-ri-bu-nim*, respectively. This is the case with EA 137:42 — [*ti-r*]*i-bu-mi* for the 3PL — or in EA 127 itself, several lines before the above-cited form and in a similar context: *i-ri-bu-nim* (EA 127:19). The spelling of the latter form reflects the correct (Peripheral) Akkadian underlying phonology,[22] which is — for our scribes — a learned conventional spelling.

4.1.4. *n*C → CC

Since Ebeling's presentation of its verbal system (Ebeling 1910, §21), Canaano-Akkadian has been known to have energic forms (see further Moran 1950a, pp. 53–56 = 2003, pp. 50–51; Rainey 1996, vol. 2, pp. 234–44, 263–64; Zewi 1999, pp. 157–73; Izre'el 2005, pp. 42–43; Korchin 2008, §§4.4–6). The energic marker is -(*n*)*na*, but when followed by a suffix or by an enclitic particle, the final vowel is deleted. In such forms the *n* of the energic marker is assimilated to the first consonant of the suffix, for example,

ex. 25. *iš-ti-mu-uš-šu* (←*ištemun+šu*) 'I have indeed heard it' (EA 320:20; Ashkelon)
nu-ub-ba-lu-uš-šu (←*nubbalun+šu*) 'we will indeed bring him' (EA 245:7; Megiddo)
ni-ik-šu-du-um-mi (←*nikšudun+mi*) 'we will indeed capture' (EA 245:5; Megiddo)

In the first two examples, the final *n* of an originally *Canaanite* morpheme is assimilated by the following first consonant of an originally *Akkadian* pronominal suffix, namely, *-šu*. In Canaanite languages this type of assimilation does exist, but only to the initial consonant of the second-person suffixes, for example, (*wa*)***ʔᵃbərkɛkkə*** (<***ʔᵃbərkɛnkə***) 'I will bless you' (Gen 26:3; cf. Joüon-Muraoka 2006, §61f). However, this would not have happened to the initial consonant of the third-person suffixes, which was glottal fricative ("guttural") [h]. In Biblical Hebrew, /*h*/ is usually assimilated to the preceding /*n*/ rather than the /n/ being assimilated by the /h/; for example, (*lo*) ***təbərkɛnnu*** (<***təbərkɛnhu***) 'you will (not) bless him' (2 Kgs 4:29; cf. Joüon-Muraoka 2006, §17g[end]). That the substrate language in our case also had /*h*/ in its third-person pronominal suffix rather than /*š*/ is proved by the gloss *ma-aḫ-ṣú-ú* /*maḫṣu:hu*/, where *-hu* stands for the 3SGM pronominal suffix. This gloss translates Canaano-Akkadian

[22] The second *i* presents a vocalic pattern for this verb which is different from the common standard Akkadian one (with *u*). This *i*-pattern is usually found in Peripheral Akkadian dialects (Hallo and Tadmor 1977, p. 9).

da-ku-šu 'they killed him' in the very same letter as our second example (EA 245:14). This type of assimilation is, therefore, a phonological trait of a spoken language transferred to a written medium. Assimilation of *n* to the following consonant is not only a trait of the substrate language, but also a feature of the mixed language. There is no other way to explain the assimilation of a phone of a *Canaanite* morpheme by the following consonant, which forms part of an originally *Akkadian* morpheme other than realize that Canaano-Akkadian had a spoken reality.

4.1.5. Indication for the Pronunciation of Akkadian Glosses or Akkadian Lexemes

As shown by Gianto (1995, nos. 3–6, 8, 11), Akkadian glosses serve to clarify the reading of a Sumerogram. As I claim above (§2.2), Akkadian glosses serve as support to the hypothesis that the Canaanite scribes thought of their language of correspondence as Akkadian. By implication, this would mean that such lexemes were pronounced in Akkadian, if not in reading aloud before the addressee, definitely so tacitly by the scribe who applied them, intending, as it were, to be read in Akkadian by the receiving scribe.

An interesting case in point that shows the actual pronunciation of a Sumerian logogram is DÙG.GA \ *tu-ka* 'alliance of friendship' (EA 136:28, from Byblos; Gianto 1995, p. 67; already Böhl 1909, p. 85). While we look at this gloss as reflecting a Sumerian lexeme, this was not so for the scribe, who would not make this historical distinction between lexemes according to their original language. This letter exhibits two other Akkadian glosses: SAḪAR \ *e-pé-ri* 'dust' (line 3); LÚ.MEŠ.UN \ *ma-ṣa-ar-ta* 'garrison' (line 18). Note that in a letter from Megiddo, the latter lexeme exhibits a different spelling, suggesting a different pronunciation of this lexeme in the Canaano-Akkadian dialect of Megiddo and its environment: *ma-an-ṣa-ar-ta* (EA 244:35; also EA 238:11 and Ta'anach 6:7; cf. CAD M/1, p. 333b; see also above, §2.2).

Another interesting case is the form of the Akkadian lexeme *eperu* or *epru* 'dust' (CAD E, s.v. *eperu*; see the previous paragraph). In a series of letters from the Bashan and the Damascus area, this lexeme is spelled *up-ri* (e.g., EA 174:5), suggesting the labialization of the first vowel. (In another letter from that area, probably written by a different scribe, this word is spelled as in standard Akkadian, namely, *ep-ri* [EA 185:4].) Interestingly, this word occurs in the opening of these letters, suggesting an actual pronunciation also in this formulaic section. This is also the case with the gloss *e-pe-ru*, discussed above. One should note that the language exhibited in letter-opening formulae is — in the majority of cases — closely related to standard (Peripheral) Akkadian (see above, §2.1).

4.2. Morphological, Morphophonological, and Morphosyntactic Features Representing an Underlying Spoken Reality

Morphological creativity is very difficult to understand within an inherited, fixed, solely written linguistic system. The following examples are instances of creativity that must have occurred in a living, flexible language, representing unconscious processes within an underlying spoken reality. It might not be superfluous to remind my readers that by "underlying spoken reality" I do not necessarily suggest a widespread use of Canaano-Akkadian in the spoken medium but — for our needs here — that the written texts did not serve as a visual code on their own but represent a language that can be decoded phonemically rather than solely graphemically (see §4 above). In paragraph §4.2.1, some paths of morphological development are briefly discussed. In §4.2.2, we see the generation of a new verb out of a borrowed Akkadian unit taken as a stem in the borrowing language, whereas in the donor language it was an adverbial complex. §4.2.3 adduces examples of verb formation in which the morphophonemic routine of person prefix attachment is simplified. In §4.2.4, I illustrate the formation of new, simpler, precative forms that were different from their counterparts in both Babylonian and Assyrian. §4.2.5 deals with the contraction of final vocalic sequences in *tertiae vocalis* verbs.

4.2.1. Lines of Development

As I have shown elsewhere (Izre'el 1984), morphological and morphosyntactic features from various Amarna letters may be cited as evidence for the gradual development of the mixed nature of this language. In that case, it was the perception of the *-ni* (<*-nim*) allomorph of the Akkadian ventive ending as a part of the plural morpheme of the 2PL and 3PL inflection of the verb in letters of Abdi-Ashirta of Amurru, of which the verbal system is halfway between Peripheral Akkadian and Canaano-Akkadian (Izre'el 1991a, vol. 1, pp. 140–41, 260–62). To be sure, this change in function occurs also in Canaano-Akkadian texts southern of Amurru, notably Tyre (e.g., *la-a i-lé-ú-ni*^{m} 'they will not be able,' EA 149:66) and some letters from Byblos (e.g., *i-qa-bu-ni*^{m} 'they say,' EA 127:10). The conflation of the originally ventive allomorph *-ni* with the plural marker *u:* to form a unified plural marker *-u:ni* thus became very similar to the indicative ending of the respective plural marker in NWS *-u:na*. This must have been one of the initial steps in the introduction of the NWS modal system into many of the Canaano-Akkadian lects, which exhibit *-na* for the indicative forms in these two plural forms. It must be emphasized, however, that "gradual" is not necessarily to be understood in chronological terms, as I indicate below (§6.1). In any case, these facts show that a "written-only" understanding of Canaano-Akkadian is not a tenable hypothesis, as here too there is support to the thesis suggesting a spoken reality underlying the development and expansion of this mixed language.

4.2.2. Spontaneous Generation of New Verbal Stems

We now turn to some forms that attest to an actual, contemporary underlying spoken reality. EA 137 from Byblos attests a unique verbal form derived from the Akkadian adverb *arḫiš* 'promptly, quickly, immediately,' namely, *ya-ar-ḫi-ša* 'may he hasten' (EA 137:97). This verbal form is derived in a Canaanite pattern that can be interpreted either as a *qal* form of the *yaqtil* pattern or as a *hifil* form.[23] This must be regarded as a spontaneous production, constructed in accordance with a common procedure in which an Akkadian stem (i.e., root+pattern) is taken as an unanalyzable unit to serve as the lexical morpheme in the verb formation of Canaano-Akkadian (Izre'el 1978, excursus B; Izre'el 2005, pp. 30–32). In this case, the borrowed lexical morpheme is the adverbial form *arḫiš*, which in the source language, namely, Akkadian, consists of the lexical stem *-arḫ-* together with the adverbial ending *-iš*. Such formations are not made deliberately or consciously, as the following parallels from another contact situation show.

Israeli Hebrew, spoken today after two millennia of almost exclusive use as a literary and liturgical language, has borrowed many new verbal lexemes from other languages, notably European. The usual procedure of such borrowings in Israeli Hebrew is according to the common Semitic pattern, that is, extracting the consonants of the foreign word and taking them as a root morpheme in the *piel* pattern, which is the denominative verbal derivation *par excellence* and the default verbal pattern in Israeli Hebrew (Izre'el 2007b, p. 118). Thus we have, for example, *tilfen* 'he telephoned' (<*telephone*), *nitrel* 'he neutralized' (<*neutral*), *fikes* 'he focused' (<*focus*), and many others. There are, however, some borrowed verbal lexemes that have adopted not the *piel* pattern but the *hifil* one. These are verbs like *hišpric* 'he sprayed' (<Yiddish *špric* 'a jet of water'), *hiflik* 'he slapped' (<English *flick*), and *hisnif* 'he sniffed' (<English *sniff*). Such forms are constructed according to their original pattern in the source language or preserve the original consonant clustering structure of the originating language (Bolozky 1999, pp. 76–77). They are used exclusively in informal speech, which supports the view that they are popular, spontaneous formations. I was lucky enough to witness the ad hoc generation of a verb when my son, upon hearing within a Hebrew context the English expression 'let them bleed,' echoed in response its exact translation as *šeyablidu* (lit., nominalizer[24] +they-will-bleed). Obviously, this verb generation in the *hifil* pattern was sensitive to the English consonantal clustering and vocalic pattern of the form 'bleed,' which fits into the Hebrew *hifil* pattern (Izre'el 2007b, pp. 115–16). This is exactly the case with Amarna *yarḫiša*, constructed with this pattern in order to preserve its original form.

[23] If we would assume elision of the *h* already at that early period. For the possibility of such forms in the Amarna tablets, see Sivan 1984, pp. 175–76.

[24] The nominalizer *še* is frequently used for the expression of deontic modality in the environment of prefix-conjugation forms.

4.2.3. Creative Prefixconjugation Verbal Forms

Let us now examine two other instances of verb formation that illuminate another morphological process, very common in Canaano-Akkadian, namely, the adjunction of inflectional prefixes to the stem. The Tyre letters attest the forms *aš-te-mu* 'I hear' and *ta-aš-te-me* 'you have heard' (EA 149:42 and 56, respectively). In these cases, the person prefixes do not exhibit the same change of *a*>*e* as in Babylonian and are therefore examples of a simplification of the system,[25] where no allomorphs are being used in the environment where standard Babylonian would require them. While Assyrian would exhibit a similar form of the stem when vowel harmony would affect the pattern vowel (*GAG*, Verbalparadigma 31), it would not contract the final vowels as is the case with *aš-te-mu* above (cf. below, §4.2.5). Therefore, these forms here seem to be independent innovations of this specific dialect, typical of non-native speech (similar forms are found in other peripheral dialects too, e.g., EA 1:10 from Egypt). In this process, the person prefixes and the modus morphemes (when they exist in the system) are attached to the stem anew, as a dynamic procedure of a living language rather than of linguistic forms taken over by rote from an already existing system. Thus *a+šteme+u* → *aštemu*; *ta+šteme* → *tašteme*. This procedure is, in fact, the norm throughout the entire span of Canaano-Akkadian, yet in this case it plays not with Akkadian stems and Canaanite inflectional morphs, but with the stem and the person prefix taken over both from Akkadian, while the modus morphemes (where they exist) are taken over from Canaanite. Many of the Byblos letters also show this combination of the Akkadian 1SG morpheme and Akkadian stems (Izre'el 2007a, §5).

4.2.4. Innovative Precative Formations

Still in Tyre, note the precative forms *li-ru-ub* 'I may enter' and *li-mu-ur* 'I may see' (EA 148:16, 17; EA 149:19, 20; also EA 151:17, 30). These too are ad hoc formations, sometimes found elsewhere in Peripheral Akkadian (cf. Izre'el 1991a, vol. 1, §2.4.2.3). The consonant *l* is attached to the 1SG verbal form, that is, *l+i:rub* → *li:rub*; *l+i:mur* → *li:mur*. In fact, this is the way Assyrian structures its precative forms (cf. Izre'el 1991b, pp. 47–48). Assyrian, however, would have *le:rub* and *la:mur*, respectively. Babylonian would have *lu:rub* and *lu:mur*. Indeed, the Jerusalem letters, which show Assyrian traits in their language, do attest such borrowings (Moran 1975a, p. 153 = 2003, p. 267; Izre'el 2005, p. 40). Therefore, the Tyre formations are an independent innovation of this dialect. They are made of the linguistic materials of Akkadian, without any triggering from the substrate language. Of course, analogical formations might be postulated rather than restructuring of the system as suggested here (Rainey 1996, vol. 2, p. 212, followed by von Dassow 2004, p. 663). In any case, postulating an underlying spoken reality resulting in the restructuring of forms seems preferable to me in the context of the type of morphological restructuring that results in simplification like the one mentioned in the previous section.

4.2.5. Vowel Contraction at the Boundary between Stem and Modal Morphemes

The last feature I would like to discuss in this section is the usual way in which modal morphemes are attached to the stem of *tertiae vocalis* verbs. These verbs exhibit the tripartite morphosyntactic distinction among the indicative (*yqtlu*), the short volitive (*yqtlø*), and the long volitive (*yqtla*), indicated by the addition of the Canaanite modus morphemes to an adopted Akkadian stem, as is the usual procedure with any other verb (cf. Izre'el 1978, §7.2 with references; further Izre'el 2005, pp. 36–38). However, since the last segment of *tertiae vocalis* verbal stems is a vowel, it contracts with the vowel of the modus morpheme. The resulting forms are as follows:

ex. 26. *yilqu* (←*y+ilqe+u*) for the indicative, as in *yi-ìl-qú* 'he takes' (EA 71:18)
yilqe (←*y+ilqe+ø*) for the short volitive, as in *yi-ìl-qé* 'may he take' (EA 116:36)
yilqa (←*y+ilqe+a*) for the long volitive, as in *yi-ìl-qa* 'may he take' (EA 71:30)

[25] As against pidgins or other drastically reduced languages, reduction or simplification of the system is not a prerequisite of mixed languages (see, briefly, Noonan 2010, p. 61). Still, simplification of the system and reduction of linguistic elements are commonly attested in any contact between languages (for the notions of simplification and reduction, see Trudgill 1983, pp. 109–14), as well as in the linguistic structure of Canaano-Akkadian (Izre'el 2005, §§2.3.1–2, 2.5.3, 2.5.4, 3.8.1).

All three forms are from Byblos, but are widespread throughout the Amarna correspondence from Canaan. At this stage of research, I am unable to reach any conclusion regarding the length of the final vowel (cf. Izre'el 2005, §10). Therefore, what has been referred to here as contraction may have been in fact the deletion of the final stem vowel. (Non-contracted forms occur only in the Jerusalem Amarna letters, where they represent Assyrianisms; Moran 2003, p. 268; Izre'el 2005, §10.)

These contractions also point to an underlying spoken reality. Similar phenomena are attested elsewhere in contact situations in spoken languages. Such is the case, for example, with Israeli Hebrew words borrowed into the Russian speech of new immigrants from the former Soviet Union. For example, the Hebrew loanword *taxana* 'station,' when appearing in the prepositional case, changes its last vowel into *e*. The resulting form is *taxane*, as in the phrase *na taxane* 'in the station.' It is hard to see such contractions occurring in a language that is not spoken at all.

The evidence presented above, both in its individual features and, especially, as a whole, brings ample support to the hypothesis that Canaano-Akkadian had an underlying spoken reality. I suggest above (§2) that the scribes themselves thought of Canaano-Akkadian as (a dialect of) Akkadian. If so, one can further deduce that at least in the course of their studying the language, the scribes-to-be would have vocalized words in that language.

5. On the Nature of Canaano-Akkadian as a Language of Communication: Akkadian, Canaanite, and Canaano-Akkadian

In my first substantive contribution to the study of Canaano-Akkadian (Izre'el 1978), I wondered about its *Sitz im Leben*. As doubts had been raised concerning the underlying spoken reality of Canaano-Akkadian (Rainey 1975, pp. 423–24; see above, §3.1), I could not, at that stage of my research, give a definite answer to this question. Since then, Moran came up with the notion of pidgin for Canaano-Akkadian, with the obvious implication of a spoken background (see above, §1.3). I myself have presented arguments in favor of a spoken reality of Canaano-Akkadian in the centennial celebration of Amarna in 1987 (Izre'el 1987b; see note *, above), and Gianto has presented the idea of an institutionalized interlanguage. Rainey himself has been vacillating between his stand that Canaano-Akkadian was an invented code and the possibility of its being a pidgin, a jargon, or an interlanguage (see §3.1). Only recently he writes,

> So somewhere between the end of the Middle Bronze Age and the beginning of the Late Bronze Age, the scribes of Canaan *came to some kind of agreement* as to the method to be employed whereby "Canaanite" inflection would be applied to the Old Babylonian stems. How we would like to know just where and when that happened! Was it due to some dominant, creative personality in one of the scribal schools? Did this result in, or was it the result of, a spoken "interlanguage" that developed among the local administrators? (Rainey 2002, p. 50; my italics)

Similarly, in her review article on Rainey's *Canaanite in the Amarna Tablets* (Rainey 1996), von Dassow (2003) comes to the conclusion that "one must almost characterize the Canaanite scribes' use of cuneiform as Akkadographic, and the texts they wrote as tablet-length Akkadograms, punctuated by occasional Canaanite words and explanatory glosses" (p. 215). The implication of this hypothesis, according to von Dassow, is "that the true lingua franca shared by Canaanite scribes and their correspondents in the Late Bronze Age was not Akkadian, as is usually assumed, but Canaanite" (p. 216). Von Dassow elaborated her views in a detailed article entitled "Canaanite in Cuneiform" (2004) and then broadened the scope of this outlook to the entire span of Peripheral Akkadian (2010). According to von Dassow, there is need to distinguish between language and text, and

> [t]he idea of a dominant language would be replaced by the idea of a dominant writing system, which was implemented in various ways to encode different languages, in diverse regions: not Sumerian and Akkadian, but cuneiform *litterae francae* (adopting Civil's coinage ...), were the medium of written communication among the multitude of Near Eastern states, with their multiplicity of tongues .... On the theory that Canaano-Akkadian was not a hybrid language but the Akkadographic writing of Canaanite, it emerges that we have numerous extant tablets written in Canaanite, for the scribes of Canaan wrote their own language in cuneiform. (von Dassow 2004, pp. 673–74)

Sanders (2009, ch. 3) discusses the state of the art on this issue, and he too claims that "it is more accurate to say that the Near East was united in this period by a form of writing — the *litterae francae* of Babylonian cuneiform. These *litterae francae* encoded a variety of messages and related to language in a variety of ways" (p. 82). Sanders does not accept, however, the thesis that Canaano-Akkadian always encoded Canaanite rather than the language that seems to be straightforwardly related to these texts, namely Canaano-Akkadian, as there is evidence that Canaano-Akkadian was actually pronounced (see further below). On the other hand, Sanders rightly states that there is ample evidence that Canaano-Akkadian was probably never read aloud before the addressees of the letters. As for the term "litterae francae," suggesting, as it does here, the total disengagement of text from language, or, rather, a polyglot nature of the text, I myself would hesitate to expand its use beyond the lists for which Civil had originally coined this term, namely, Sumerian lexical lists used at Ebla (Civil 1987, p. 140, cited by von Dassow 2004, p. 670). Indeed, the written texts we are dealing with here are related to language in a variety of ways. However, they encode a single linguistic system, a linguistic system abounding with variation, which in itself suggests a living entity. To me it is unimaginable that morphosyntactic variation of the sort manifested in the Amarna letters, involving components from two languages, fine tuned and orchestrated, could have been a feature of mere spelling, or "a rationale for the failure of the data to conform systematically to the rules proposed under that model" (von Dassow 2004, p. 652). That this code could be translated to other linguistic codes does not make it different in essence from any linguistic system encoded in writing or decoded from the written.

Von Dassow's main thesis leans on what she sees as a gap between the written and the spoken systems. For her, "[i]t need not be the case that the signs with which a text is written directly represent the language in which it is written" (2004, p. 641). However, this claim, which obviously (and explicitly) draws its apparent strength from writing systems such as third-millennium Akkadian or Eblaite texts exhibiting mostly Sumerograms, should not be taken further to the extreme of stating that "the language of a text may be dissociated from the language employed to write it" (von Dassow 2010, p. 895).

I definitely endorse the statement that "writing need not (and often does not) straightforwardly represent the language in which a text is read or understood" but not that "writing may not directly encode a specific target language at all" (von Dassow 2010, p. 895). Detachment of text from language as in the case of Aramaic, the Akkadian lingua franca, Canaano-Akkadian, or any other written communication in the ancient world where texts would be read aloud in translation (see also Sanders 2009, pp. 202–03 n. 14) does not mean the detachment of writing from *any* language. Also today, a written language, detached in its linguistic system from the spoken linguistic varieties of the community in which it is used, does not mean that the text must be read in the same linguistic system as its spoken counterpart. When a text is being read (aloud or silently), it usually follows verbatim the language it stands for, even if it differs in its form and structure from the language the readers usually use in their other linguistic performances. Furthermore, there are seemingly aural features to any language when read, even silently, including some intonational features (see. e.g., Fodor 2002).

Writing systems reflect linguistic features remotely or closely. Signs of a newly invented alphabetic system tend to be closely related to the phonemes of that language. However, as a writing system is usually designed for a standard variety of a language, it will never fit exactly all varieties of that language even at the moment of its conception (for the notion of a "standard" variety, see, e.g., Hudson 1996, §2.2.2; McWhorter 1998, pp. 23–31). When time passes, even the phonology of the standard variety will distance itself from the graphemic system of the invented (or adopted) writing system. When such a split occurs, the contemporary phonological structure of a language known only through the written medium may be impossible to retrieve. Anyone who has learned a second language and come to learn its vocabulary from writing knows that similar spellings do not always reflect similar pronunciations. However, despite the distance between the written and the spoken, some notion of the actual phonological structure of the language used by the people using this writing system may nevertheless be retrieved by studying regularities of spellings. For example, we deduce that mimation was lost toward the Middle Babylonian and Middle Assyrian period since we see that spellings with extra *Vm* signs are no longer used. On the other hand, it may happen that some gleanings from the spoken reality of the contemporary language will emerge through irregular spellings or what may *prima facie* seem to be spelling errors. For example, from sporadic spellings without mimation one can deduce that — despite the common knowledge — falling of mimation had started long before the end of the older period (Izre'el 2010, §2.9). It has been noted by many that dialectal features find their way into written texts, including literary ones (e.g., Reiner 1966, p. 21; Huehnergard 1997, p. 595; George 2003, pp. 435–36 and *passim* in his commentaries; Izre'el 2010). Likewise, for the Peripheral dialect of

Emar, Ikeda has recently shown that some features suggest that Akkadian was indeed spoken at that city, at least by the royal scribes (Ikeda 2010).

Indeed, looking for spelling irregularities is the methodology commonly used to get some hold of the spoken reality behind the writing conventions of any language, contemporary or historical, living or dead (cf. Campbell 2004, §14.5.2). Von Dassow seems not to accept this widespread methodology, which for her seems logically flawed or circular argumentation. Obviously, my logic differs radically from hers. I cannot understand the constant objection to any deductions on such bases as being too few or as not having parallels, especially when typological or other comparisons with later Canaanite dialects can be adduced (*pace* von Dassow 2004, p. 650). Therefore, I cannot understand the claim that "these spelling practices are just that, not evidence for phonology" (p. 661). After all, spelling is our main tool for studying a dead language when its attested records allow us to do that, and all we know about ancient languages is due to their having been written.

— Excursus —
A Few Words on von Dassow's Endeavor to Discard the Thesis of an Underlying Spoken Reality for Canaano-Akkadian

Unfortunately, von Dassow tries to base her hypothesis on negative evidence, mainly by trying to refute the hypothesis advanced here on the underlying spoken reality of Canaano-Akkadian. Her main support for her approach is typological, although this too bears little on the case adduced from Canaano-Akkadian (see above). Positive evidence is hardly brought at all apart from an example of a textual sample aiming to show how that allegedly Akkadographic code would actually be reflected upon conception and reading (2004, pp. 665–06). This effort "does not necessarily show anything more than that a scholar skilled in comparative Semitics can fill in the texts' universally acknowledged West Semitic syntax with a reconstructed West Semitic vocabulary and morphology." (Sanders 2009, p. 203 n. 17). Von Dassow seems to have targeted every point I had raised that she deemed to bear even a remote threat to her evolving hypothesis and well beyond.[26] Therefore, it is impossible — and in fact not really necessary — to respond to all the points she raised. I suffice by emphasizing some points of special interest and respond to only some counter-arguments in order to make my methodological requisites stand on a more solid basis.[27]

For the Labanese Baqa forms that constantly exhibit spellings with *e* instead of the expected standard Akkadian *i* (§4.1.1; Izre'el 2007, §2.2.1), von Dassow (2004, p. 662) suggests that such spellings "might have become allographs due to a phonological feature such as Izre'el postulates, but even so, the spellings at issue would be the outcome of orthographic practices influenced by the substrate language's phonology, rather than evidence for the pronunciation of Canaano-Akkadian." We agree, of course, on the origin and nature of the allographs as reflecting differences in phonologies of substrate dialects. However, if Canaano-Akkadian would be used only in writing where words would be representation of different forms of words in another language (viz., Canaanite), why would the phonology of the substrate be reflected in forms that would not be pronounced at all?

Similarly, von Dassow explains the *primae vocalis* 1SG forms with *i* (§4.1.2; Izre'el 2007, §2.2.3) instead of standard Akkadian *e* as reflecting "the orthographic convention of using the Akkadian 3SGM form as the

[26] Is the glass half empty or half full? Unfortunately, for von Dassow it is always half empty. But why is the "half-empty" method, which refuses to see a pattern when there are any exceptions, not productive? This is what von Dassow (2004, pp. 651–52) does in her otherwise unfounded objection to use the data and analyses in Izre'el 2007a, §5.

[27] As it stands now, this paper is of a hybrid nature in itself, being composed in two main layers, that is, the original one to which von Dassow responded, and the one presented here in full, including a response to some of the issues raised by von Dassow. Due to lack of space, I have here omitted the elaborate discussion of the 1SG person verbal prefix variation, dealt with in §5 of the original article. This discussion entailed some further notes in the following sections of the original paper. These discussions and some further notes on the methodological requisites for the study of Canaano-Akkadian omitted from this version can be retrieved in my 2007 version of the paper, which can be downloaded from:
http://www.tau.ac.il/~izreel/publications/CanAkkMethRequisites_2007.pdf
I hope to have an opportunity to publish the discussion of the 1SG person prefix in Byblos letters (§5 in that paper) sometime in the future.

base, to which Canaanite prefixes and suffixes were applied" (2004, p. 662). As already noted, this change between Akkadian and Canaano-Akkadian is a feature not only of finite verbal forms but also of infinitives, ignored by von Dassow, and therefore it is better explained by phonology rather than by morphology, all the more so by a writing convention.

The most striking feature of Canaano-Akkadian, to use Sanders's words (2009, p. 82), is the assimilation of *n* of the originally Canaanite energic morpheme to *š* of the originally Akkadian person marker in forms from Megiddo and Ashkelon (§4.1.4; Izre'el 2007, §2.2.5). This assimilation, which bridges between morphemes of different origins, seems indeed to be the strongest phonological feature (or, rather, morphophonological feature; see below) in favor of the thesis that Canaano-Akkadian had a spoken reality and was not just a conventional written system representing Canaanite as the lingua franca of that region. Von Dassow, alas, has not been convinced even by this feature (2004, p. 662; 2010, pp. 914–15). She wonders about the scantiness of this find. However, as discussed above, this is precisely the type of find we must seek in order to enable ourselves to get some gleanings for the spoken reality of any language through the thick camouflage of its writing system. Still, I should note that this feature is attested in letters from two different Canaanite cities, one northern (Megiddo), one southern (Ashkelon). Von Dassow also wonders why comparable forms not exhibiting this assimilation also occur. As I have shown in my Canaano-Akkadian grammar (2005, §1.3.1), the rule of *n*-assimilation probably did not apply when the consonant following *n* was velar, pharyngeal or the glottal stop (as is the case in Hebrew), or locally, *ṣ*. Lastly, von Dassow suggests that "given that kind of assimilation in both languages, it could have been imported into writing in the absence of speaking of the hypothesized mixed language." However, this is definitely not the case. Besides the improbability, in my mind, that such transfer from linguistic rules to a different system that have existence only in the visual medium would occur, one should note that in both Canaanite (where Hebrew would be a representative) and Akkadian, a rule of *n*-assimilation by a suffix could not possibly happen, since in both Canaanite and Akkadian — and by implication also Canaano-Akkadian — at specific morphemic boundaries, such as between the stem and inflectional morphemes, the original quality of /*n*/ would be retained (with some rare exceptions, notably in forms of the Akkadian root *ndn* and the cognate Canaanite *n/ytn*; *GAG* §33h; Joüon and Muraoka 2006, p. 69).

Von Dassow further explains all morphological transformations of verbal forms as having occurred in writing only. For *yarḫiša* (§4.2.2; Izre'el 2007, §2.3.2), von Dassow raises the possibility that this form is a deliberately introduced Akkadographic stem, very much like the introduction of 3SGM stems from Akkadian to form standard verbal forms in Canaano-Akkadian. First, I wonder whether an Akkadographic representation of a verb would be spelled syllabically as has been done in this case, denoting the final consonant of the borrowed stem and the vocalic morpheme of the borrowing language in one and the same sign. Should we not expect a spelling like **ya-AR-ḪI-IŠ-a*, or perhaps *ya-AR-ḪI-IŠ-ša*? The spelling attested here, *ya-ar-ḫi-ša*, conforms to the general structure of syllabic writing in Canaano-Akkadian, which does not behave as Akkadographic and as a persisting rule visualizes all forms according to their Canaano-Akkadian syllable structure, whether or not they consist of elements from one of the languages involved or both (cf. the spellings of *tertiae vocalis* verbs in §4.2.5 above). But, more importantly, when suggesting a solely written insertion in this outstanding case of a non-verbal stem into this paradigm, one ignores the recurring formation of new hybrid forms in contact languages, as has been demonstrated above and as has been described time and again in the vast secondary literature on the formation of contact languages, of which only a handful has been mentioned above (§§1.4–5).

As for the morphological innovations *aštemu* and *tašteme* (§4.2.3; Izre'el 2007, §2.3.3), von Dassow discards their significance as "insufficient to demonstrate innovation in speech" (2004, p. 663). I, however, believe that using Akkadian morphemes as building blocks — in this case person morphemes and verbal stems — and combining them anew is a feature of a living language rather than of a fossilized structure, and Canaanite in disguise can hardly be the case here. Even in the case of *tertiae vocalis* verbs (§4.2.5; Izre'el 2007, §2.3.5), von Dassow, admitting to the strength of this argument, would not take it at face value, stating that "this, the soundest of Izre'el's arguments, is not sufficient to sustain the case for Canaano-Akkadian having been spoken" (2004, pp. 663–64).

As regards forms reflecting vowel deletion such as *tirbu* and *irbu:ni* (§4.1.3; Izre'el 2007, §2.2.4), von Dassow (2004, p. 662) suggests either scribal errors or an influence of alphabetic or consonantal writing habits. Resorting to explanations such as scribal errors is, of course, totally unwarranted. A possible influence of the scribes' habit to use consonantal script is anachronistic, far-fetched, and remote from the reality of literacy in Canaan at that period. If scribes were so much into consonantal writing, why did they not use it to write their own language, and why were they so desperate as to invent such a cumbersome hybrid as Canaano-Akkadian?

> While not all linguistic features listed above have the same explanatory power, some of them do show even by themselves that a spoken reality must lie at the background of the written texts, notably the assimilation of *n* across morphemes which originate in different languages (§4.1.4; Izre'el 2007, §2.2.5), and the contraction (or deletion) of final stem vowels with the following modus morphemes, again — each originating in a different language (§4.2.5; Izre'el 2007, §2.3.5). Some of the features would prove that at some point in its history, certainly during the time of its formation as a mixed language, this language was spoken. Other features lead to the inevitable conclusion that Canaano-Akkadian was spoken contemporarily with our data, at least to some extent. Of course, looking at the entire picture yields a stronger conviction than any single argument may bring forth. The whole picture is clear and shows — to my mind without any doubt — that a spoken reality for Canaano-Akkadian, at least at some level, must be assumed.
>
> **********

Let us now return to the issue of writing and speech, or rather the issue of written texts and the language they represent. Von Dassow's starting point for her thesis is Gershevitch's notion of alloglottography. This term was coined by Gershevitch (1979) to denote "the use of one writable language for the purpose of writing another language" (p. 138). In his eloquent, witty manner, Gershevitch (p. 117) describes an imaginary scene from Old Persia as follows:

> An ancient Persian, let us call him Miθraδāta, wants to write to his girl-friend, let us call her Hutauθā, fifty miles away. He dictates to a scribe in Persian, the scribe meanwhile inscribing a clay tablet. At the end of dictation, the scribe reads out to him in Persian the text he had dictated. On receipt of the tablet Hutauθā goes to or summons a scribe, who reads to her the message in Persian as often as she asks him or pays him.

The tablet that would remain from that transaction would have not been written in Persian, as one might expect, but in Elamite. Surely this is the kind of setting we can restore for fourteenth-century Canaan. Milkilu, the ruler of Gezer, would probably not dictate his scribe a letter to the pharaoh in Canaano-Akkadian but in the language he would use in his daily life, and when the letter would get to Egypt, surely it was not read aloud in Canaano-Akkadian before the pharaoh. Indeed, there are ample indications that letters written in Canaano-Akkadian, as in other lingua francas of the ancient Near East, would usually be translated upon reading (Izre'el 1995b; Sanders 2009, pp. 84, 99). There are further indications that letters were actually meant to be read by the scribes receiving them rather than by their addressees, as explicitly stated in postscripts addressed to a scribe in Egypt in the Jerusalem Amarna letters (e.g., EA 286:61–64; Izre'el 1995b, p. 107; Sanders 2009, p. 82). As rightly noted by Sanders (n. 14 on pp. 202–03), Canaano-Akkadian and Aramaic differed in this respect, as Aramaic was definitely more widespread in both geographical span and the range of its use than Canaano-Akkadian.

But all of this does not mean that the language was not conceived as such by its scribes. After an analysis that covers two allegedly alloglottographic periods in Iran, that of Elamite and that of Aramaic, Gershevitch concludes as follows:

> And I would urge that the tiresome speculations as to whether an Aramaic text written in the service of Iranians in the third century or second century B.C. is Aramaic or Iranian be henceforward dispensed with. Such texts are all Iranian, despite their being written in Aramaic. The language of each is Iranian, even if it be one of the Iranian languages unknown to us, such as Kambojan, Parnian or Middle Median. They are unknown to us only because the texts speaking to us in them were written alloglottographically. (Gershevitch 1979, p. 143)

While I am definitely not in the position to say whether Gershevitch's conclusions are based on reasonable analysis and solid data, I should point it out to my readers that Gershevitch's setting does not include the role of the scribe except as a carrier of messages, compared by Gershevitch himself to a tape recorder: push button A and the text is recorded, push button B and the text is played back (p. 117).[28] But the poor scribe is not a tape recorder! Even in our technologically sophisticated era, tape recorders, or rather computers, cannot execute the task of translating back and forth a spoken text. Our scribe — very much like any human translator today — had to listen to the context of the letter in Persian, translate it into Elamite, write it down in that language, and, after

[28] Stolper and Tavernier (2007, p. 9 n. 3) speculate that Gershevitch's paper (which stems out of an originally oral presentation) "was meant not only as an amusement in its oral form, but actually as a parody of Iranian philology and epigraphy."

he arrived at his destination, read the letter in Elamite and simultaneously (or not) translate it back into Persian. An old Sumerian proverb, obviously referring to an Akkadian-speaking scribal environment, says, "If the scribe does not know Sumerian, how will the translator succeed?" (Alster 1997, §2.49). But how would a scribe acquire the knowledge to do all this? How would he acquire this sophistication of writing Elamite, Sumerian, Akkadian? Indeed, neither Gershevitch nor von Dassow refers to the system behind the text, which *is* a linguistic system with all its complexities. Both Gershevitch and von Dassow relate only to what happens before the text is written or after it is read aloud rather than taking a look at the text itself, representing a genuine linguistic system on its own, which in the case of Canaano-Akkadian represents also the complexities of a contact language for which parallels are amply attested. "To put it more pointedly," von Dassow (2004, p. 674) concludes, "no longer would we imagine platoons of scribes studying Akkadian in order to write letters to Egypt and elsewhere, then bowdlerizing the language into a host of ultra-localized idiolects whose proper analysis can occupy legions of scholarly careers." How would an ancient Canaanite scholar learn to write Canaano-Akkadian texts, then?

While Gershevitch did not refer at all to scribal education, Rubio (2006), widening the scope of Gershevitch's notion to include other literate societies in the ancient Near East, does refer to scribal learning. While claiming that "(t)he use of a written language different from the language of utterance seems the epitome of textual artificiality and, in many instances, scribal antiquarianism" (pp. 48–49), Rubio endorses the view that Sumerian was spoken in schools long after it had died (p. 50; see also, inter alia, Charpin 2008, pp. 85–87). Rubio states that "a scribe had to deal with two parallel streams of tradition: a written curriculum characterized by an antiquarian ideology and an oral heritage of scholarly interpretation of this written tradition. This situation," Rubio claims, "resembles the linguistic dichotomy of alloglottography, in which the oral component (the language of utterance) is completely divorced from the written anchor (the language in which the text is written)." In a way, it does, as do all diglossic situations, where the language of the written medium is different from the language of everyday life (for diglossia, see above, §3.1). However, in all diglossic societies, even in the extreme cases, at least some spoken variants of the so-called H (high) variant of the diglossia do exist along the written medium. This is the case with Arabic, where spoken varieties of H are quite widespread (Kaye 2001), and this was the case with Hebrew throughout the entire age of Diaspora, where Jews would speak in a variety of the local language and write in Hebrew, but could also converse in this tongue when the need would call for such a means of communication (Izre'el 2003c). In principle, the cases addressed by Rubio are not different, although only a single setting of such speech is described: the school environment. This should imply that Mesopotamian scribes learned not only the Akkadian readings of Sumerograms, but also their respective Sumerian readings. The existence of columns with syllabic spellings of Sumerian signs in lexical lists conforms to this hypothesis (for "pronunciation glosses" in lists and other texts, see Krecher 1969, pp. 433–35).

Scribal education in a spoken environment is also in the heart of analysis of Gianto, who coined the term "institutionalized interlanguage" for the emergence of Canaano-Akkadian (see above, §1.5). It is also in the heart of the interesting analysis by Weeden on logography in Hittite (2007). Weeden's in-depth study of the employment by Hittite scribes of logographic writing in general and of Akkadographic writing in particular is grounded upon a study of scribal education of Hittite scribes:

> Occasional phonetic pronunciations have been uncovered in the course of this investigation. The cases of *BE-LU-uš-ša-an* (p. 145 in Weeden's study; S.I.) and *ANŠE.KUR.RA*$^{ḪI.A}$*-ia* (HKM 15 obv. 8), both from Maşat letters, indicate that at some level at least these were being read phonetically. The fact that these are both in letters may attest to a dictated environment, involving quick writing. ... It is quite possible that a kind of learned pidgin had emerged for dictation purposes, a "scribe-talk" much comparable to the mixture of much Latin, less Greek and various levels of native tongue found in early English or Irish manuscripts. (Weeden 2007, p. 279)

The following remark by Weeden may help us view cuneiform writing in Canaan in a better perspective:

> Hittite cuneiform was at first burdened with a layer of Akkadograms which could not flexibly represent Hittite words. Paradoxically it was the extension of the domain of the Sumerian words that allowed the Hittite language to be expressed more freely but still use logograms. This, in conjunction with the other

items of evidence we have mentioned, indicates that the Akkadian words were most probably pronounced in Akkadian, while the Sumerian ones were really logographic. (Weeden 2007, p. 315)[29]

In sharp contrast with Hittite texts, Canaano-Akkadian is indeed "burdened with a layer of Akkadograms," to use Weeden's wording. If Weeden's thesis is correct, then a text burdened with Akkadograms as the Canaanite extrapolated by von Dassow for the Amarna letters is, in fact, written and pronounced not in Canaanite but in Akkadian.

With a narrow definition of alloglottography, one that sees language learning via speech as inherent to scribal education and scribal life, I could definitely agree. If a process of translation between the oral codes and the written one would be meant by this term, I would also not discard it altogether, as this, of course, is the way things seem to have happened when a Canaano-Akkadian text would be written and read after arriving at its destiny (see above). However, if a total disengagement between text and language is to be meant, as defined by von Dassow, my answer is absolutely not. The language of the Amarna tablets is not Canaanite! In this connection, one should further ask whether Canaano-Akkadian conforms with the general observations of logographic writing to the extent that each written word will have an equivalent in an alleged setting where a scribe would actually conceive of Canaanite structures to be written in syllabically logographic strings.

Logography is known to us from early Semitic writings in Mesopotamia (including Ebla), as well as from genuine systems like the one of early Sumer or the Chinese writing system, to take just the notable examples (for the Chinese writing system, see Sampson 1985, ch. 8). Early Japanese writing, consisting entirely or almost entirely of logographs borrowed from Chinese, has been taken as a supportive evidence for the alloglottographic hypothesis (Rubio 2006, pp. 42–46). One should note at this juncture that Old Japanese writing might not serve as a good example for alloglottography, since "in the 8th and 9th centuries the original Chinese sentences were first and foremost read aloud in Chinese (*ondoku*) .... *Kundoku* was developed in subsequent centuries as a very efficient technique for translating Chinese texts into Japanese rather than as a writing system" (Ikeda 2007, p. 6). In any case, Rubio suggests that "[t]he Semitized forms in Sumerian texts ... can be regarded as the written reflections of an *onduko*-like style of reading Sumerian in Semitic context, and might perhaps point to a *diglossic bilingual* setting within the scribal realm" (2006, p. 44).

As against logographic writing, syllabic writing is a phonetic one (Gelb 1963, pp. 66–68; Sampson 1985, pp. 54–57), and one wonders whether an Akkadographic view of Canaano-Akkadian is sensible at all. After all, syllables are the primary phonological processing units across most of the world's languages (Goswami 2009, pp. 135–36).

Research in the processing of reading, although inconclusive in many respects, has come up with interesting results as regards the differences between processing of reading in logographic scripts and phonetic (mainly alphabetic) ones. While phonology is involved in the reading of both types of script, logographic reading involves different cognitive abilities than those in the process of learning a phonetic-based system such as the English alphabet, because the phonological information is not specified in the script or is specified only indirectly (Wang, Tsai, and Wang 2009, pp. 404–05). The consensus seems to be such that logographic characters are processed differently from phonetic ones because of the greater significance of orthographic information in reading the script (Jahandarie 1999, ch. 9, esp. pp. 155–65).

Still, cases of alleged alloglottography in texts written in phonetic characters are, inter alia, the case of Latin in Romance-speaking environments or the so-called Aramaic heterograms (or, as earlier called, ideograms) used in the writings of Iranian languages. Both cases are different from the case of Canaano-Akkadian. As for Latin, Emilano (1991) suggests that the apparent Latin notarial texts from medieval Spain are to be read in the vernacular, which seems *prima facie* a close case to Gershevitch's alloglottography. However, the majority of changes between the written strings and the allegedly read-aloud ones are shown to be of the type known to us from all languages, where historical changes require readings that are divorced from the spelled word, sometimes quite largely. Still, "[p]honemic and morphophonemic conversion of Latinate spellings seems relatively straightforward when there is a historical link between the written forms of Latin and the spoken forms of Romance vernaculars" (Emiliano 1991, p. 242). Would anyone suggest that French reading today is alloglottohraphic? Or English,

[29] The so-called Hittite Landschenkungsurkunden (Riemschneider 1958) make an exception to the bulk of Hittite texts, as they are indeed abundant in Akkadograms. However, even these texts cannot serve as support to a thesis as advanced by von Dassow for Canaano-Akkadian, since they are formulaic in nature, use fossilized language taken as such from original Akkadian prototypes, and include terminology that was perhaps not readily available in Hittite.

or Israeli Hebrew? There were, to be sure, also lexemic differences in some cases, but these are not many. As for the Aramaic heterograms used for writing Iranian languages, the common impression given by some secondary literature is that the lexical stock of Parthian, Middle Persian, or Pahlavi is written *in toto* in Aramaic or that the majority of words in these texts are written as their Aramaic cognates. However, this is not the case. As explicitly noted by Skjærvø (1995, p. 291) "heterograms are common, but restricted to a relatively limited set of words and forms." Indeed, the Arameograms in Nyberg's *Glossary* (1974, vol. 2, pp. 1–7) are a defined, closed set of words with fewer than 250 entries. The system of heterography in these texts is different from the one we observe in Canaano-Akkadian texts, as the Iranian grammatical elements ("phonetic complements") are not confined to the verbal system (for a discussion with textual samples, see Skjærvø 1995; 1996).

There are Latin words written in English texts that are read in the language in which the majority of words are written, namely, English. Numbers are written logographically in "our" languages. Rubio (2006, pp. 48–49), to be sure, indeed makes a distinction between total and partial alloglottography, as the latter was inherent to the cuneiform culture in Mesopotamia and beyond. Rubio further makes a distinction between "true" alloglottography and partial alloglottography, which he defines not only quantitatively but also qualitatively, that is, whether the text would be read and grammatically understood in the *other* language (p. 44; italics in the original). Rubio goes on to explain the qualitative criterion, which may or may not exist for specific languages, notably ones with a significant number of logographs. As for the quantitative criterion, the following crucial question should be raised: When a text is written in its entirety in a syllabic script, with only occasional or limited insertions of logograms (or other non-syllabic signs like determinatives), would it serve as a pure visual code for a linguistic system that is not directly related to the bulk of its *signifiants*?

Having reviewed some of the issues concerned with phonetic writing and its differences from logographic, it seems useful now to repeat Weeden's conclusion as regards Akkadography in Hittite texts and its implications for Canaano-Akkadian as follows: when a text is "burdened with Akkadograms," it is, in fact, written and pronounced in Akkadian. In addition, I hope to have shown in the previous sections that the evidence as a whole points to the inevitable conclusion that Canaano-Akkadian had indeed been a language rather than a visual code for Canaanite. Furthermore, Canaano-Akkadian had an underlying spoken reality, that is, it was pronounced not as Canaanite but as a language in its own terms. This language was regarded by its users as Akkadian; by us it should be viewed as a mixed language that can be termed Canaano-Akkadian.

Neither Rainey nor von Dassow seems to be convinced of the linguistic evidence, so similar to other language contact phenomena known from all parts of the world. No! There has never been a convention of Canaanite scribes at the Megiddo Hilton[30] that decided upon an artificial written code for correspondence, nor were they writing Canaanite. The evidence points clearly against it. None of the known contact languages, none of the mixed languages mentioned and exemplified above (§§1.4–5), none of the known contact languages, neither Loterā'i, the secret language of Persian Jews, nor any other language into which deliberate changes had been introduced (Thomason 2007), not even one of these languages — with all their complexities — was invented and used solely as a written code. All have emerged in a spoken environment, whatever the reasons for their emergence might have been.

I began this section recalling my views when taking my initial steps into the study of Canaano-Akkadian. Now I would like to reiterate my views regarding the nature of Canaano-Akkadian as they were about thirty-five years ago, when I wrote my conclusions to my master's thesis on the Gezer Amarna letters:

> A language that its writers have never spoken and have never understood in its entirety; a language that had a certain higher status over the language of the scribes who wrote it; an only-written language used for (*logographic only?*) communication between Canaanite scribes and their colleagues in Egypt, who were also speakers of Canaanite. (Izre'el 1976, pp. 98–99; translated from Hebrew; italics added)

I was much more prudent when I rewrote my thesis in English for publication:

> A very interesting question is whether or not the Amarna language was spoken at any time during the history of the land of Canaan by a certain upper social class or by officials or the like, as was the case, for instance, with the Latin spoken by French officials and scholars side by side with French. Otherwise this would

[30] I owe this metaphor to the late Bill Moran, way back in 1988.

> be the only recorded mixed language in the history which was exclusively a written language. This question may never be solved, however we do believe that a thorough investigation of the whole W[est]S[emitic] Akkadian corpus may also lead us to the key for the solution of this problem as well. (Izre'el 1978, p. 83)

As my faithful readers already know, I am glad I have changed my mind between the completion of my master's thesis and the publication of my 1978 article, as I believe I have since found some evidence for the underlying spoken reality, or background, of Canaano-Akkadian as well as support for its classification as a mixed language. As we have seen, von Dassow's hypothesis is founded to a large extent on the refutation of my own hypothesis regarding the underlying spoken reality of Canaano-Akkadian. Therefore, von Dassow's challenges have not convinced me to change my views, which have been forwarded here in enough detail for my readers' own scrutiny and judgment.

It is with this background that we can now step forward and deepen our observations into the linguistic continuum attested in the Amarna letters, in our attempt to gain a better understanding of the linguistic structure of Canaano-Akkadian, of its sociolinguistic background, and of its emergence. A few concluding remarks are now in order.

6. Concluding Remarks

6.1. Synchrony and Diachrony

I hope to have shown that variation is one of the basic characteristics of Canaano-Akkadian, one that actually shapes its system. Moreover, as I have argued more than once, variation of the type exhibited in Canaano-Akkadian texts is a clear manifestation of a living language. Therefore, it must play an important role in our description of its grammar.

I have mentioned above (§§3.0–1) post-creole continua, that is, those linguistic areas in which an emergent creole language has remained in close contact with its model language and has continued to be influenced by it. It has been claimed for such linguistic settings that variation is the synchronic manifestation of the diachronic development of the language. This insight may apply to any other linguistic continuum as well, be it a geographical dialect continuum, a sociolectal continuum, and so on. Cross-variety approach to the study of language change is well established by now. Using data from two or more speech communities, the cross-variety approach seeks or presumes a common historical ancestor for features that are distinct synchronically among varieties. It is through the study of such synchronic variation that we can learn about linguistic change and the diachronic development of linguistic varieties (Weinreich, Labov, and Herzog 1968; Bailey 1973; Bickerton 1973; 1975; Petyt 1980, pp. 185–97; Rickford 1987, pp. 35–38; Fasold 1990, ch. 8; Labov 1994, ch. 1; Montgomery 2007).

> True enough, the end result of many linguistic changes is reported as an invariant outcome, where the original form or rule is said to be entirely extinct. However, this study will turn up more than a few cases where the variation continues over enormous stretches of time, and others where the same process is renewed as if it had never ended. The close examination of the present shows that much of the past is still with us. The study of history benefits from the continuity of the past as well as from analogues with the present. (Labov 1994, p. 27)

A nice metaphor for "the use of the present to explain the past" (taking Labov's title for this study) is looking at a photograph in which — although presented in only two dimensions — the third dimension, that is, the depth, is still reflected in other features of the photographs (size of objects etc.). As much as variation in contemporary speech communities can present us with a different dimension of historical change, so do ancient written documents originating from different places of the same period. As language change occurs in different places in different times, we can learn of changes in a distinct linguistic community by looking at variants not only in contemporary setting, but also from different time settings. Variants may be persistent in some areas for much longer periods than in others and still reflect the historical predecessors of features attested contemporarily in other areas. Semitic languages are abundant with examples for such settings, notably the preservation of case endings in (Classical) Arabic long after their extinction in Hebrew or Aramaic. In order to show the way one can adduce evidence for diachronic change from synchronic variation in Canaano-Akkadian, let me draw briefly one example.

In my study of the ventive morpheme in the Akkadian texts of Amurru (Izre'el 1984; see §4.2.1 above), I discussed a diachronic aspect of the development of Canaano-Akkadian. I have shown that a new plural morpheme, that is, *-u:ni*, has been formed by blending the standard Akkadian plural morpheme *-u:* and the allomorph *-ni*(*m*) of the ventive. This, so I claimed, was a stage in the introduction of the NWS modus morpheme into Canaano-Akkadian. I have also suggested that "the various linguistic systems reflected by the various corpora are in fact those linguistic systems of different phases of linguistic development retained by scribes in diverse peripheral schools" (Izre'el 1984, p. 92).

This insight may now be better understood in the framework of continuum research, where we see variation as an inherent feature of language. In standard Peripheral Akkadian, the ventive ending is operative, very much as in standard Mesopotamian Akkadian. For example, in Ugarit Akkadian the ventive is used throughout in both its allomorphs; still, there are four cases where the morph *-ni*(*m*) is used without the morph *-u:* to indicate the plural (Huehnergard 1989, p. 166).[31] In Amurru Akkadian and in some related lects among the Canaano-Akkadian ones, the morph *-ni*(*m*) has lost its ventive force, as explained above, whereas in "standard" Canaano-Akkadian, with some exceptions, the morph *-na* is used to mark the imperfective (= indicative) (Izre'el 2005, pp. 25, 36). Synchronic variation thus exhibits the various stages on the way to the formation of the basilect extreme of this continuum (i.e., the lect most remote from the model language). In our case it is the mixed language of the Canaanite scribes, which I have termed Canaano-Akkadian.

6.2. Toward Sociolinguistics

The diachronic aspect reflected by linguistic variation raises another very interesting and most important question. That is the sociolinguistic aspect of the formation of Canaano-Akkadian.

We have some evidence for Akkadian writing in Palestine both prior to and contemporary with the Amarna period (Horowitz, Oshima, and Sanders 2006). From the Middle Babylonian period, a Gilgamesh fragment is known from Megiddo (Goetze and Levy 1959; George 2003, pp. 339–47; Horowitz, Oshima, and Sanders 2006, pp. 102–05), suggesting learning at that site,[32] as well as several lexical tablets found at other sites, for example, a trilingual (Sumero-Akkadian-Canaanite) lexical list from Aphek (Horowitz, Oshima, and Sanders 2006, pp. 31–32). These finds and others, roughly contemporary of the Amarna period, add to the finds of older cuneiform materials from that area, that is, Byblos (Edzard 1985, pp. 249 and 256 nn. 9–10; van der Toorn 2000, p. 98). Apart from such finds, Canaanite sites are mentioned in cuneiform tablets from outside Canaan and Mesopotamia itself, as well as from times before the Amarna periods (e.g., Aharoni 1967, p. 87; Rainey and Notely 2006, ch. 5). All these data raise the question of the connections between Palestine and Syria and the Mesopotamian cultures and political powers before the Amarna period (cf. Labat 1962, pp. 26–27; Tadmor 1977, pp. 101–02; Edzard 1985, pp. 252–55).

I believe that a thorough investigation into the formation of the mixed Canaano-Akkadian language of the Canaanite Amarna scribes may help to resolve this enigma. Some clues may be found in searching for the origins of specific linguistic features, for example, in locating various pure Assyrian linguistic traits in a single subcorpus or throughout the whole Amarna corpus (cf. Izre'el 2007a, §5.3). For such an investigation, the study of variation is of extreme importance, since variation, as I have already mentioned, may prove to be but another aspect of diachronic development. Therefore, we must investigate the synchronic aspects of Canaano-Akkadian not just for their own sake, but also for the sake of understanding its line of development — in other words, to search for an answer to the question of how this language evolved. I believe that through the study of variation we shall find an answer to this question, with regard not only to the purely linguistic components, but also to its sociolinguistic ones.

Many years ago, a call for research into the sociolinguistic aspects of Canaano-Akkadian was raised by Oppenheim. With a slight emendation of the timespan mentioned, this call may now be raised again:

---

[31] Out of six plural forms with *-ni*(*m*), the date of only one text is known, which is later than the Amarna period.

[32] Even if this Gilgamesh piece was written elsewhere (cf. George 2003, pp. 339–47; Goren, Finkelstein and Na'aman 2009).

> Although these letters have been known for more than half a century and have been the topic of a number of scholarly investigations, much more is to be learned of their style, the provenience and literacy of the scribes and scribal schools (to teach Akkadian to foreigners) that flourished all over the Near East at that period, and the linguistic features of their several vernaculars. (Oppenheim 1964, pp. 278–79)

Some studies of scribal education in Palestine have been conducted since then (van der Toorn 2000, pp. 105–08 with previous references). It is the integration of purely linguistic investigation and analysis into the study of extralinguistic features done hitherto that I call for here.

To illustrate what kind of questions we may ask when dealing with the linguistic material of the Amarna letters, let me note the following, out of many similar questions that can be asked:

1. Since there is an observable tendency of Canaano-Akkadian to make use of a single borrowed verbal stem into their system, one may ask why was it precisely that stem of a specific verb that had been borrowed and adopted; for example, why for *daga:lu* 'look' it is the *idaggal* stem, while for *šapa:ru* 'write, send' it is mostly *išpur*, the stem used for the preterite in standard Akkadian, and for (*w*)*uššuru* it is the imperative form.
2. Why does the Jerusalem scribe, while adding a special address to his fellow Egyptian scribe (EA 287:64–70), write in a different register that is closer in its linguistic character to the Canaanite substratum than the rest of the letter?
3. What can we learn from a comparison between the language of the Megiddo letters and that of letters from other cities in its vicinity (cf. Rabiner 1981, section VII), in the context of our knowledge of the finding of a Gilgamesh fragment in that site?
4. Why do we find Middle Babylonian forms like *ulte:bila* 'he sent' in the Gezer letters, where we would have expected to find more conservative forms of this verb?
5. Why is there such a form attested in EA 369, a letter from the pharaoh, although other pharaoh's letters use forms with *š* instead?
6. As regards the spoken aspect of Canaano-Akkadian, one may further investigate precisely this point: Who spoke that language? Was it just the scribes themselves,[33] or can we account for a larger circle of speakers, such as messengers, ambassadors, high officials, clerks, and the like? (Cf. Labat 1962; Nougayrol 1962; 1975; Oppenheim 1965; Ikeda 2010 [see above, §5].)

Of course, we have no answers yet for many such questions that may arise, since there is still a long way ahead of us until a thorough and deep understanding of the Amarna linguistic continuum is achieved. Still, I can already point to some starts in this direction.

For example, one may suggest that the use of some features in the language of the Megiddo letters, like the 1SG suffix conjugation marker *-a:ku*, directly taken over from the Akkadian stative paradigm, is preferred over Canaano-Akkadian *-a:ti* precisely because of the alleged existence of a scribal school in that site (see Izre'el 2003b, p. 91, where other features in the Megiddo letters are discussed in this context).

Similarly, the employment of Middle Babylonian forms in letters from Gezer can be ascribed to the existence of a scribal school at Gezer (Goren, Finkelstein, and Na'aman 2009), whereas the use of the "Akkadianized" form *ulte:bila* in EA 369 can serve as yet another support as regards the Gezerite identity of its scribe (cf. Izre'el 1995b, pp. 109–18; cf. above, §2.2).[34]

---

[33] Robert Wilson draws my attention to a general tendency to capitalize on the scribes' special skill by using it as a secret language, as scribes and priests have always done with Latin or Sanskrit.

[34] For the importance of scribal education and the role of scribes in the task of sociolinguistics research of Canaano-Akkadian, see now Vita 2010, a study that was not available to me before the completion of this article.

As for the last question listed, I believe I have done my best to address it in detail in this study, and I would refer my loyal readers again to the final paragraphs in §5 for some retrospective remarks.

We are now only at the beginning of the investigation into the deep and subtle details of lectal variation in Canaano-Akkadian. Still, having at hand the linguistic knowledge accumulated since the discovery of the Amarna corpus, we are now in a better position than ever to study variation and its implications. As for me, I hope to have laid another paving stone in the long and complicated way toward the achievement of this goal, namely, a real understanding of the nature of Canaano-Akkadian.

Abbreviations

AHw	Wolfram von Soden. *Akkadisches Handwörterbuch*. 3 volumes. Wiesbaden: Harrassowitz, 1965–81.
CAD	A. Leo Oppenheim et al., eds. *The Assyrian Dictionary of the Oriental Institute of the University of Chicago*. 21 volumes. Chicago: The Oriental Institute, 1956–2010.
GAG	Wolfram von Soden. *Grundriss der akkadischen Grammatik*. Analecta Orientalia 33/47. Rome: Pontificium Institutum Biblicum, 1969.
NWS	Northwest Semitic

Bibliography

Adler, Hans-Peter

1976 *Das Akkadische des Königs Tušratta von Mitanni*. Alter Orient und Altes Testament 201. Kevelaer: Butzon and Bercker.

Aharoni, Yohanan

1967 *The Land of the Bible: A Historical Geography*. Translated by Anson F. Rainey. London: Burns and Oats.

Ahl, Sally W.

1973 Epistolary Texts from Ugarit: Structural and Lexical Correspondences in Epistles in Akkadian and Ugaritic. Ph.D. dissertation, Brandeis University. University Microfilms, Ann Arbor.

Albright, William F.

1942 "A Case of Lèse-Majesté in Pre-Israelite Lachish, with Some Remarks on the Israelite Conquest." *Bulletin of the Schools of Oriental Research* 87: 32–38.

1943a "Two Little Understood Amarna Letters from the Middle Jordan Valley." *Bulletin of the Schools of Oriental Research* 89: 7–17.

1943b "An Archaic Hebrew Proverb in an Amarna Letter from Central Palestine." *Bulletin of the Schools of Oriental Research* 89: 29–32.

1944 "A Prince of Taanach in the Fifteenth Century B.C." *Bulletin of the Schools of Oriental Research* 94: 12–27.

1966 "The Amarna Letters from Palestine." In *The Cambridge Ancient History*, Volume 2, chapter 20, fascicule 51. Cambridge. [= *The Cambridge Ancient History*, Volume 2, Part 2: *History of the Middle East and the Aegean Region c. 1380–1000 B.C.*, 3rd edition, edited by I. E. S. Edwards, C. J. Gadd, N. G. L. Hammond, and E. Sollberger, pp. 98–116. Cambridge: Cambridge University Press.]

Alster, Bendt

1997 *Proverbs of Ancient Sumer*. Bethesda: CDL Press.

Aquilina, Joseph

1965 *Maltese*. Teach Yourself Books. London: English Universities Press.

Artzi, Pinchas

1963 "The Glosses in the El-Amarna Documents." *Bar Ilan* 1: 57–84. [In Hebrew]

1990 "Studies in the Library of the Amarna Archive." In *Bar-Ilan Studies in Assyriology Dedicated to Pinḥas Artzi*, edited by Jacob Klein and Aaron Skaist, pp. 139–56. Bar-Ilan Studies in Near Eastern Languages and Culture. Publications of the Bar-Ilan University Institute of Assyriology. Ramat-Gan: Bar-Ilan University Press.

Auer, Peter

1999 "From Code-switching via Language Mixing to Fused Lects: Toward a Dynamic Typology of Bilingual Speech." *Journal of Bilingualism* 3: 309–32.

2005 "A Postscript: Code-switching and Social Identity." *Journal of Pragmatics* 37: 403–10.

Bailey, Charles J. N.

1973 *Variation and Linguistic Theory*. Arlington: Center for Applied Linguistics.

Bakker, Peter

1994 "Michif, the Cree-French Mixed Language of the Métis Buffalo Hunters in Canada." In *Mixed Languages: 15 Case Studies in Language Intertwining*, edited by Peter Bakker and Maarten Mous, pp. 13–33. Studies in Language and Language Use 13. Amsterdam: Instituut voor Functioneel Onderzoek naar en Taalgebruik.

Bakker, Peter, and Maarten Mous, editors

1994 *Mixed Languages: 15 Case Studies in Language Intertwining*. Studies in Language and Language Use 13. Amsterdam: Instituut voor Functioneel Onderzoek naar en Taalgebruik.

Bakker, Peter, and Robert A. Papen

1997 "Michif: A Mixed Language Based on Cree and French." In *Contact Languages: A Wider Perspective*, edited by Sarah G. Thomason, pp. 295–363. Amsterdam: Benjamins.

Bickerton, Derek

1973 "The Nature of a Creole Continuum." *Language* 49: 640–69.

1975 *Dynamics of a Creole System*. Cambridge: Cambridge University Press.

Blau, Joshua

1970 *On Pseudo-corrections in Some Semitic Languages*. Jerusalem: Israel Academy of Sciences and Humanities.

Böhl, Franz M. T.

1909 *Die Sprache der Amarnabriefe mit besonderer Berücksichtigung der Kanaanismen*. Leipziger Semitische Studien 5/2. Reprinted, Leipzig: Zentralantiquariat der DDR, 1977.

1914 "Hymnisches und Rhythmisches in den Amarnabriefen aus Kanaan." *Theologisches Literaturblatt* 35/15: 337–40. (= *Opera Minora: Studies en Bijdragen op Assyriologisch en Oudtestamentisch Terrein*, pp. 375–79, 516–17. Groningen: Wolters.)

Bolozky, Shmuel

1999 *Measuring Productivity in Word Formation: The Case of Israeli Hebrew*. Studies in Semitic Languages and Linguistics 27. Leiden: Brill.

Campbell, Lyle

2004 *Historical Linguistics: An Introduction*. 2nd edition. Cambridge: MIT Press.

Chambers, J. K., and Peter Trudgill

1998 *Dialectology*. 2nd edition. Cambridge Textbooks in Linguistics. Cambridge: Cambridge University Press.

Chambers, J. K.; Peter Trudgill; and Natalie Schilling-Estes, editors

2002 *The Handbook of Language Variation and Change*. Blackwell Handbook in Linguistics. Malden: Balckwell.

Charpin, Dominique

2008 *Lire et écrire à Babylone*. Paris: Presses Universitaires de France.

Civil, Miguel

1987 "The Early History of HAR-ra: The Ebla Link." In *Ebla 1975–1985: Dieci anni di studi linguistici e filologici. Atti del convegno internazionale* (Napoli, 9–11 ottobre 1985), edited by Luigi Cagni, pp. 131–58. Istituto Universitare Orientale, Dipartimento di Studi Asiatici, series minor, 27. Naples: Istituto Universitario Orientale.

Cochavi-Rainey, Zippora

1988 The Akkadian Dialect of the Egyptian Scribes in the 14th–13th Centuries B.C.E.: Linguistic Analysis. With Supplement: The Akkadian Texts Written by Egyptian Scribes in the 14th–13th Centuries B.C.E.:

Transliterations and Hebrew Translations. Ph.D. dissertation, Tel Aviv University. [In Hebrew, with English summary]

1989 "Canaanite Influence in the Akkadian Texts Written by Egyptian Scribes in the 14th and 13th Centuries B.C.E." *Ugarit Forschungen* 21: 39–46.

1990a "Tenses and Modes in Cuneiform Texts Written by Egyptian Scribes in the Late Bronze Age." *Ugarit Forschungen* 22: 5–23.

1990b "Egyptian Influences in the Akkadian Texts Written by Egyptian Scribes in the Fourteenth and Thirteenth Centuries B.C.E." *Journal of Ancient Near Eastern Studies* 49: 57–65.

1993 "The Style and Syntax of EA 1." *Ugarit Forschungen* 25: 75–84.

1998 "Some Grammatical Notes on EA 14." In *Past Links: Studies in the Languages and Cultures of the Ancient Near East*, edited by Shlomo Izre'el, Itamar Singer, and Ran Zadok, pp. 207–28. Israel Oriental Studies 18. Winona Lake: Eisenbrauns.

2003 *The Alashia Texts from the 14th and 13th Centuries BCE: A Textual and Linguistic Study*. Alter Orient und Altes Testament 289. Münster: Ugarit-Verlag.

2011 *The Akkadian Dialect of Egyptian Scribes in the 14th and 13th Centuries B.C.E.* Alter Orient und Altes Testament 374. Münster: Ugarit-Verlag.

Cochavi-Rainey, Zipora, and Anson F. Rainey

2007 "Finite Verbal Usage in the Jerusalem Amarna Letters." *Ugarit Forschungen* 39: 37–56.

Crystal, David

2010 *The Cambridge Encyclopedia of Language*. Third edition. Cambridge: Cambridge University Press.

Cunchillos, Jesús-Luis

1999 "The Ugaritic Letters." In *Handbook of Ugaritic Studies*, edited by Wilfred G. E. Watson and Nicolas Wyatt, pp. 359–74. Handbuch der Orientalistik, Erste Abteilung, Der Nahe und Mittlere Osten 39. Leiden: Brill.

DeCamp, David

1971 "Toward a Generative Analysis of a Post-Creole Speech Community." In *Pidginization and Creolization of Languages* (Proceedings of a Conference Held at the University of the West Indies, Mona, Jamaica, April 1968), edited by Dell Hymes, 349–70. Cambridge: Cambridge University Press.

Dhorme, Paul

1913–14 "La langue de Canaan." *Revue Biblique* 10: 369–93; 11: 37–59, 344–72.

Drewes, A. J.

1994 "Borrowing in Maltese." In *Mixed Languages: 15 Case Studies in Language Intertwining*, edited by Peter Bakker and Maarten Mous, pp. 83–111. Studies in Language and Language Use 13. Amsterdam: Instituut voor Functioneel Onderzoek naar en Taalgebruik.

Ebeling, Erich

1910 "Das Verbum der El-Amarna-Briefe." *Beiträge zur Assyriologie und semitischen Sprachwissenschaft* 8: 39–79.

Edel, Elmar

1994 *Die ägyptisch-hethitische Korrespondenz aus Boghazköy in babylonischer und hethitischer Sprache*. 2 volumes. Abhandlungen der Rheinisch-Westfälischen Akademie der Wissenschaften 77. Oplanden: Westdeutscher Verlag.

Edzard, Dietz Otto

1985 "Amarna und die Archive seiner Korrespondenten zwischen Ugarit und Gaza." In *Biblical Archaeology Today* (Proceedings of the International Congress on Biblical Archaeology, Jerusalem, April 1984), pp. 248–59. Jerusalem: Israel Exploration Society.

Emilano, António

1991 "Latin or Romance? Graphemic Variation and Scripto-linguistic Change in Medieval Spain." In *Latin and Romance Languages in the Early Middle Ages*, edited by Roger Wright, pp. 233–47. London: Routledge.

Fasold, Ralph

1984 *Introduction to Sociolinguistics*, Volume 1: *The Sociolinguistics of Society*. Language in Society 5. Oxford: Blackwell.

Fasold, Ralph W.

1990 *Introduction to Sociolinguistics*, Volume 2: *The Sociolinguistics of Language*. Language and Society 6. Oxford: Blackwell.

Ferguson, Charles A.
1959 "Diglossia." *Word* 15: 325–40.

Finkel, Marcie
1977 The Tyre Letters of the El-Amarna Archives: A Study of Selected Linguistic Aspects. M.A. thesis, Tel Aviv University.

Finley, Thomas John
1979 Word Order in the Clause Structure of Syrian Akkadian. Ph.D. dissertation, University of California, Los Angeles. Ann Arbor: University Microfilms International.

Fishman, Joshua A.
1967 "Bilingualism with and without Diglossia: Diglossia with and without Bilingualism." *Journal of Social Issues* 2: 29–38.

Fodor, Janet Dean
2002 "Prosodic Disambiguation in Silent Reading." In *Proceedings of the Northeast Linguistic Society 32*, edited by Masako Hirotani, pp. 113–32. New York: City University of New York and New York University.

Gardner-Chloros, Penelope
2009 *Code-switching*. Cambridge: Cambridge University Press.

Gelb, Ignace J.
1963 *A Study of Writing*. Revised edition. Chicago: University of Chicago Press.

George, Andrew R.
2003 *The Babylonian Gilgamesh Epic: Introduction, Critical Edition and Cuneiform Texts*. Oxford: Oxford University Press.

Gershevitch, Ilya
1979 "Alloglottography of Old Persian." *Transactions of the Phililogical Society* 77: 114–90.

Gevirtz, Stanley
1973 "On Canaanite Rhetoric: The Evidence of the Amarna Letters from Tyre." *Orientalia* 42: 162–77.

Gianto, Agustinus
1990 *Word Order Variation in the Akkadian of Byblos*. Studia Pohl 15. Rome: Pontificio Istituto Biblico.
1995 "Amarna Lexicography: The Glosses in the Byblos Letters." *Studi epigrafi e linguistici sur Vicino Oriente antico* 12 (= *The Lexicography of the Ancient Near Eastern Languages*): 65–73.
2000 "Amarna Akkadian as a Contact Language." In *Languages and Cultures in Contact: At the Crossroads of Civilizations in the Syro-Mesopotamian Realm*, edited by Karel Van Lerberghe and Gabriela Voet, pp. 123–32. Orientalia Lovaniensia Analecta 96. Leuven: Peeters.

Goetze, Albrecht, and Selim Levy
1959 "Fragment of the Gilgamesh Epic from Megiddo." *Atiqot* 2: 121–28.

Golovoko, Evgenij
1994 "Mednyj Aleut or Copper Island Aleut." In *Mixed Languages: 15 Case Studies in Language Intertwining*, edited by Peter Bakker and Maarten Mous, pp. 113–21. Studies in Language and Language Use 13. Amsterdam: Instituut voor Functioneel Onderzoek naar en Taalgebruik.

Goodman, Morris
1971 "The Strange Case of Mbugu." In *Pidginization and Creolization of Languages* (Proceedings of a Conference Held at the University of the West Indies, Mona, Jamaica, April 1968), edited by Dell Hymes, pp. 243–54. Cambridge: Cambridge University Press.

Goren, Yuval; Israel Finkelstein; and Nadav Na'aman
2004 *Inscribed in Clay: Provenance Study of the Amarna Letters and Other Ancient Near Eastern Texts*. Tel Aviv University, Sonia and Marco Nadler Institute of Archaeology, Monograph Series 23. Tel Aviv: Emery and Claire Yass Publications in Archaeology.
2009 "A Provenance Study of the Gilgamesh Fragment from Megiddo." *Archaeometry* 51: 763–73.

Goswami, Usha
2009 "The Basic Processes in Reading: Insights from Neuroscience." In *The Cambridge Handbook of Literacy*, edited by David R. Olson and Nancy Torrance, pp. 134–51. Cambridge: Cambridge University Press.

Hall, Robert A.

1966 *Pidgin and Creole Languages.* Ithaca: Cornell University Press.

Hallo, William W., and Hayim Tadmor

1977 "A Lawsuit from Hazor." *Israel Exploration Journal* 27: 1–11.

Hary, Benjamin

1996 "The Importance of the Language Continuum in Arabic Multiglossia." In *Understanding Arabic: Essays in Honor of El-Said Badawi*, edited by Alaa Elgibali, pp. 69–90. Cairo: American University in Cairo Press.

Hawley, Robert

2003 Studies in Ugaritic Epistolography. Ph.D. dissertation, University of Chicago.

Hayes, John Lewis

1984 Dialectical Variation in the Syntax of Coordination and Subordination in Western Akkadian of the el-Amarna Period. Ph.D. dissertation, University of California–Los Angeles. University Microfilms. UMI no. NBN 84-20184.

Heintz, Jean-Georges

1982 *Index documentaire d'El-Amarna - I.D.E.A., 1 -. Liste/Codage des texts; Index des ouvrages de référence.* Wiesbaden: Harrassowitz.

1995 *Index documentaire d'El-Amarna - I.D.E.A., 2 -. Bibliographie des textsbabyloniens d'El Amarna [1888 à 1993] et Concordances des sigles EA.* With D. Bauer, D. Bodi, L. Millot, and C. B. F. Walker. Wiesbaden: Harrassowitz.

Heintz, Jean-Georges, and Lison Millot

1995 "Bibliographie d'El-Amarna: Supplement I (1994–1995)" (Addenda and Corrigenda - Edition du 31 Déc. 1995). *Ugarit Forschungen* 27: 21–40.

1996 "Bibliographie d'El-Amarna: Supplement II (1995–1996): (Addenda and Corrigenda - Edition du 31 Déc. 1995). *Ugarit Forschungen* 28: 257–74.

2000 "Bibliographie d'El-Amarna: Supplement III (1997-2000)" - [= Supplément à I.D.E.A. 2 (1995): 1–119] - [Addenda and Corrigenda - Edition du 31 Décembre 2000]. *Ugarit Forschungen* 32: 219–36.

Heintz, J.-G.; Lison Millot; and Rijad Mehmedi

2003 "Bibliographie d'El-Amarna: Supplement IV (2000–2003)." *Ugarit Forschungen* 35: 231–38.

Heintz, Jean-Georges; Rijad Mehmedi; and Juan-Pablo Vita

2006 "Bibliographie d'El-Amarna: Supplement V (2003–2006)" - [= Supplément à I.D.E.A. 2 (1995): 1–119] - [Addenda and Corrigenda - Édition du 30 Juin 2007]. *Ugarit Forschungen* 38: 313–39.

Hess, Richard Samuel

1984 Amarna Proper Names. Ph.D. dissertation, Hebrew Union College, Ohio. Ann Arbor: University Microfilms International.

1986 "Divine Names in the Amarna Texts." *Ugarit Forschungen* 18: 149–68.

1989 "Hebrew Psalms and Amarna Correspondence from Jerusalem: Comparisons and Implications." *Zeitschrift für die Alttestamentliche Wissenschaft* 101: 249–65.

1990 "Rhetorical Forms in EA 162." *Ugarit Forschungen* 22: 137–48.

1993a *Amarna Personal Names.* American Schools of Oriental Research Dissertation Series 9. Winona Lake: Eisenbrauns.

1993b "Smitten Ant Bites Back: Rhetorical Forms in the Amarna Correspondence from Shechem." In *Verse in Ancient Near Eastern Prose*, edited by Johannes C. de Moor and Wilfred G. E. Watson, pp. 95–111. Alter Orient und Altes Testament 42. Kevelaer: Butzon and Bercker.

1998 "The Mayarzana Correspondence: Rhetoric and Conquest Accounts." *Ugarit Forschungen* 30: 335–51.

2003 "Preliminary Perspectives on Late Bronze Age Culture from the Personal Names in Palestinian Cuneiform Texts." *Dutch Studies - Society of Near Eastern Languages and Literatures* 5: 35–57.

Holm, John

1988–1989 *Pidgins and Creoles.* 2 volumes. Cambridge Language Surveys. Cambridge: Cambridge University Press.

Horowitz, Wayne

1996 "An Inscribed Beth Shean Clay Cylinder from the Amarna Age." *Israel Exploration Journal* 46: 208–18.

Horowitz, Wayne; Takashi Oshima; and Seth L. Sanders

2006 *Cuneiform in Canaan: Cuneiform Sources from the Land of Israel in Ancient Times.* Jerusalem: Israel Exploration Society and The Hebrew University of Jerusalem.

Hudson, Richard A.

1996 *Sociolinguistics*. 2nd edition. Cambridge Textbooks in Linguistics. Cambridge: Cambridge University Press.

Huehnergard, John

1989 *The Akkadian of Ugarit*. Harvard Semitic Studies 34. Atlanta: Scholars Press.

1997 *A Grammar of Akkadian*. Harvard Semitic Studies 45. Atlanta: Scholars Press.

1998 "A Grammar of Amarna Canaanite." *Bulletin of the American Schools of Oriental Research* 310: 59–77.

1999 "The Akkadian Letters." In *Handbook of Ugaritic Studies*, edited by Wilfred G. E. Watson and Nicolas Wyatt, pp. 375–89. Handbuch der Orientalistik, Erste Abteilung, Der Nahe und Mittlere Osten 39. Leiden: Brill.

Hymes, Dell, editor

1971 *Pidginization and Creolization of Languages* (Proceedings of a Conference Held at the University of the West Indies, Mona, Jamaica, April 1968). Cambridge: Cambridge University Press.

Ikeda, Jun

1992 "Amarnaic: A Pidgin in the Second Millennium B.C.E." *Orient* 35: 1–21. [In Japanese, with English abstract]

2007 "Early Japanese and Early Akkadian Writing Systems: A Contrastive Survey of 'Kunogenesis.'" In *Proceedings of the Conference Origins of Early Writing Systems, October 5 to 7, 2007, Peking University, Beijing*. http://www.caeno.org/origins/papers/Ikeda_Kunogenesis.pdf

2010 "Was Akkadian Spoken in Emar? Diglossia in Emar." In *Language in the Ancient Near East: Proceedings of the 53rd Rencontre Assyriologique Internationale*, Volume 2, edited by L. Cogan, N. Koslova, S. Loesov, and T. Tishchesko, pp. 841–50. Winona Lake: Eisenbrauns.

Israel, Felice

2006 "*Yānu* + accusativo nel semitico siro-palestinese e il sincretismo dei casi nel semitico." In *Loquentes linguis: Studi linguistici e orientali in onore di Fabrizio A. Pennacchietti*, edited by Pier Giorgio Borbone, Allessandro Mengozzi, and Mauro Tosco, pp. 337–53. Wiesbaden: Harrassowitz.

Izre'el, Shlomo

1976 The Gezer Letters of the El-Amarna Archive: Linguistic Analysis. M.A. thesis, Tel Aviv University. [In Hebrew, with English summary]

1978 "The Gezer Letters of the El-Amarna Archive: Linguistic Analysis." *Israel Oriental Studies* 8: 13–90.

1984 "On the Use of the So-called Ventive Morpheme in the Akkadian Texts of Amurru." *Ugarit Forschungen* 16: 83–92. [References in *Ugarit Forschungen* 17 (1985): 403–04.]

1985 The Akkadian Dialect of the Scribes of Amurru in the 14th–13th Centuries B.C. Linguistic Analysis. Ph.D. dissertation, Tel Aviv University. [In Hebrew, with English summary]

1987a "The Complementary Distribution of the Vowels *e* and *i* in the Peripheral Akkadian Dialect of Amurru — A Further Step towards Our Understanding of the Development of the Amarna Jargon." In *Proceedings of the Fourth International Hamito-Semitic Congress* (Marburg, 20–22 September 1983), edited by Herrmann Jungraithmayr and Walter W. Müller, pp. 525–41. Amsterdam Studies in the Theory and History of Linguistic Science Series 4; Current Issues in Linguistic Theory 44. Amsterdam: Benjamins.

1987b "Some Methodological Requisites for the Study of the Amarna Jargon: Notes on the Essence of That Language." http://tau.ac.il/~izreel/publications/amarna-1987.pdf

1991a *Amurru Akkadian: A Linguistic Study*. 2 volumes. Harvard Semitic Studies 40–41. Atlanta: Scholars Press.

1991b "On the Person-prefixes of the Akkadian Verb." *The Journal of the Ancient Near Eastern Society* 20: 35–56.

1995a "The Amarna Letters from Canaan." In *Civilizations of the Ancient Near East*, edited by Jack M. Sasson, pp. 2411–19. 4 volumes. New York: Scribners.

1995b "The Amarna Glosses: Who Wrote What for Whom? Some Sociolinguistic Considerations." In *Language and Culture in the Near East*, edited by Shlomo Izre'el and Rina Drory, pp. 101–22. Israel Oriental Studies 15. Leiden: Brill.

1997 *The Amarna Scholarly Tablets*. Cuneiform Monographs 9. Groningen: Styx.

1998a *Canaano-Akkadian*. Languages of the World/Materials 82. Munich: LINCOM Europa. Second printing, with corrections 2005.

1998b Review of *Dictionary of the North-west Semitic Inscriptions*, Volumes 1–2, by J. Hoftijzer and K. Jongeling. Handbuch der Orientalistik, Erste Abteilung, Der Nahe und Mittlere Osten 21. Leiden: Brill, 1995. In *Past Links: Studies in the Languages and Cultures of the Ancient Near East*, edited by Shlomo Izre'el, Itamar Singer, and Ran Zadok, pp. 421–29. Israel Oriental Studies 18. Winona Lake: Eisenbrauns.

2000 "Linguistics and Poetics in Old Babylonian Literature: Mimation and Meter in Etana." *Journal of the Ancient Near Eastern Society* 20: 57–68.

2003a "Vocalized Canaanite: Cuneiform-Written Canaanite Words in the Amarna Letters: Some Methodological Remarks." *Dutch Studies - Society of Near Eastern Languages and Literatures* 5: 13–34.

2003b "Canaanite Varieties in the Second Millennium BC: Can We Dispense with Anachronism?" *Orient* 38: 66–104.

2003c "The Emergence of Spoken Israeli Hebrew." In Corpus Linguistics and Modern Hebrew: Towards the Compilation of the Corpus of Spoken Israeli Hebrew (CoSIH), edited by Benjamin H. Hary, pp. 85–104. Tel Aviv: Tel Aviv University, The Chaim Rosenberg School of Jewish Studies. http://www.tau.ac.il/~izreel/publications/Emergence_Hary2003(corr).pdf

2005 *Canaano-Akkadian.* Languages of the World/Materials 82. Munich: LINCOM Europa. Second printing, with corrections.

2007a "Canaano-Akkadian: Some Methodological Requisites for the Study of the Amarna Letters from Canaan." http://www.tau.ac.il/~izreel/publications/CanAkkMethRequisites_2007.pdf

2007b "Constructive Constructions: The Semitic Verbal Morphology and Beyond." In *Egyptian, Semitic and General Grammar: Workshop In Memory of H. J. Polotsky* (8–12 July 2001), edited by Gideon Goldenberg and Ariel Shisha-Halevy, pp. 106–31. Jerusalem: Israel Academy of Sciences and Humanities.

2010 "'At Her Speech the Gods of the Land Rejoiced': Some Thoughts on the Language of Old Babylonian Mythologic Narratives." In *Gazing on the Deep: Ancient Near Eastern and Other Studies in Honor of Tzvi Abusch,* edited by Jeffrey Stackert, Barbara Nevling Porter, and David P. Wright, pp. 87–106. Bethesda: CDL Press.

Izre'el, Shlomo, and Eran Cohen

2004 *Literary Old Babylonian.* Languages of the World/Materials 81. Munich: LINCOM Europa.

Jahandarie, Khosrow

1999 *Spoken and Written Discourse: A Multi-disciplinary Perspective.* Contemporary Studies in International Political Communication. Stamford: Abex.

Jirku, Anton

1933 "Kanaanäische Psalmenfragmente in der vorisraelitischen Zeit Palästinas und Syriens." *Journal of Biblical Literature* 52: 108–20.

Joüon SJ, Paul, and Talamitsu Muraoka

2006 *A Grammar of Biblical Hebrew.* Subsidia Biblica 27. Rome: Pontificio Istituto Biblico.

Kaye, Alan S.

2001 "Diglossia: The State of the Art." *International Journal of the Sociology of Language* 152: 117–29.

Kaye, Alan S., and Mauro Tosco

2001 *Pidgin and Creole Languages: A Basic Introduction.* LINCOM Textbooks in Linguistics. Munich: LINCOM Europa.

Knudtzon, J. A.

1907 *Die El-Amarna Tafeln,* Volume 1. Leipzig: J. C. Hinrichs.

1915 *Die El-Amarna Tafeln,* Volume 2. Vorderasiatische Bibliothek 2. Leipzig: J. C. Hinrichs. Reprinted: Aalen, 1964.

Knutson, F. Brent

1982 "Cuneiform Letters and Social Conventions." In *Studies in Ancient Letter Writing,* edited by John L. White, pp. 15–23. Semeia 22. Chico: Society of Biblical Literature.

Korchin, Paul D.

2008 *Markedness in Canaanite and Hebrew Verbs.* Harvard Semitic Series 58. Winona Lake: Eisenbrauns.

Kossmann, Maarten

1987–88 "The Case System of West-Semitized Amarna Akkadian." *Jaarbericht van het Vooraziatisch-Egyptisch Genootschapt "Ex Oriente Lux"* 30: 38–60, 487–88.

1994 "Amarna-Akkadian as a Mixed Language." In *Mixed Languages: 15 Case Studies in Language Intertwining,* edited by Peter Bakker and Maarten Mous, pp. 169–73. Studies in Language and Language Use 13. Amsterdam: Instituut voor Functioneel Onderzoek naar en Taalgebruik.

Krecher, J.

1969 "Glossen." *Reallexikon der Assyriologie* 3: 431–40.

Labat, René

1962 "Le rayonnement de la langue et de l'écriture akkadienne au deuxième millénaire avant notre éra." *Syria* 39: 1–27.

Labov, William

1971 "The Notion of 'System' in Creole Languages." In *Pidginization and Creolization of Languages* (Proceedings of a Conference Held at the University of the West Indies, Mona, Jamaica, April 1968), edited by Dell Hymes, pp. 447–72. Cambridge: Cambridge University Press.

1994 *Principles of Linguistic Change*, Volume 1: *Internal Factors*. Language in Society 20. Oxford: Blackwell.

Lambert, Maurice

1957–60 "Formules de politesse et formules d'introduction dans les langues mésopotamiennes." *Comptes rendus du groupe linguistique d'études chamito-sémitiques* 8: 88–90 (en sumérien), 105–07 (en akkadien).

Lefebvre, Claire

2008 "Relabelling: A Major Process in Language Contact. Persistance et intérêt de la métaphore." *Journal of Language Contact: Evolution of Language, Contact and Discourse*; Thema Series, Language Contact and the Dynamics of Language 2: Language Contact and the Dynamics of Language/Theory and Implications, edited by Robert Nicolaï and Bernard Comrie, 2: 90–111.

Liverani, Mario

1983 "Political Lexicon and Political Ideologies in the Amarna Letters." *Berytus* 3: 41–56.

Mangano, Mark J.

1990 Rhetorical Content in the Amarna Correspondence from the Levant. Ph.D. dissertation, Hebrew Union College, Jewish Institute of Religion, Cincinnati. UMI 9028107.

Matras, Yaron

1996 "Prozedurale Fusion: Grammatische Interferenzschichten im Romances." *Sprachtypologie und Universalien-Forschung* 49: 60–78.

2005 "The Full Extent of 'Fusion': A Test Case for Connectivity and Language Contact." In *Prozesse des Wandels in historischen Spannungfeldern Nordafricas/Westasien* (Akten zum 2. Symposium des SFB 296, Mainz, 15.10.–17.10.2001), edited by Walter Bisang, Thomas Bierschenk, Detlev Krekenbom, and Ursula Verhoeven, pp. 241–55. Kulturelle und Sprachliche Kontakte 2. Würzburg: Ergon.

2009 *Language Contact*. Cambridge Textbooks in Linguistics. Cambridge: Cambridge University Press.

Matthews, Peter H.

2007 *The Concise Oxford Dictionary of Linguistics*. 2nd edition. Oxford Paperback Reference. Oxford: Oxford University Press.

Mazar, Eilat; Wayne Horowitz; Takayoshi Oshima; and Yuval Goren

2010 "A Cuneiform Tablet from the Ophel in Jerusalem." *Israel Exploration Journal* (Miriam Tadmor Volume) 60/1: 4–21.

McWhorter, John

1998 *The Word on the Street: Fact and Fable about American English*. New York: Plenum Trade.

Menovščikov, Georgiy A.

1968 "Aleutskiy Iazyk." In *Iazyki Narodov SSSR*, Volume 5: *Mongol'skie, Tunguso-Manččurskie i Paleoaziatskie Iazyki*, pp. 386–406. Leningrad: Nauka. [In Russian]

Merriam-Webster Collegiate Dictionary

1994–96 Electronic edition, version 1.5.

Mynářová, Jana

2007 *Language of Amarna: Language of Diplomacy: Perspectives on the Amarna Letters*. Prague: Czech Institute of Egyptology, Faculty of Arts, Charles University.

Montgomery, Michael

2007 "Variation and Historical Linguistics." In *Sociolinguistic Variation: Theories, Methods, and Applications*, edited by Robert Bayley and Ceil Lucas, pp. 110–32. Cambridge: Cambridge University Press.

Moran, William L.

1950 A Syntactical Study of the Dialect of Byblos as Reflected in the Amarna Tablets. Ph.D. dissertation, Johns Hopkins University. [= Moran 2003: 1–130, #1.]

1960 "Early Canaanite *yaqtula*." *Orientalia* 29: 1–19. [= Moran 2003, pp. 179–95, #10.]

1971 "Tell el-Amarna." In *Encyclopaedia Judaica*, Volume 15, pp. 933–35. Jerusalem: Keter. [= Moran 2003, pp. 237–41, #15.]

1975 "The Syrian Scribe of the Jerusalem Amarna Letters." In *Unity and Diversity. Essays in History, Literature and Religion of the Ancient Near East*, edited by H. Goedicke and J. J. M. Roberts, pp. 146–66. Baltimore: Johns Hopkins University. [= Moran 2003, pp. 249–74, #17.]

1984 "Additions to the Amarna Lexicon." *Orientalia* 53: 297–302. [= Moran 2003, pp. 301–06, #22.]

1987 *Les lettres d'el-Amarna: Correspondance diplomatique du Pharaon*. Traduction française de Dominique Collon et Henri Cazelles. Littérature anciennes du Proche-Orient 13. Paris: Les Éditions du Cerf.

1992 *The Amarna Letters*. Baltimore: Johns Hopkins University Press.

2003 *Amarna Studies: Collected Writings*, edited by John Huehnergard and Shlomo Izre'el. Harvard Semitic Studies 54. Winona Lake: Eisenbrauns.

Mous, Maarten

1994 "Ma'a or Mbugu." In *Mixed Languages: 15 Case Studies in Language Intertwining*, edited by Peter Bakker and Maarten Mous, pp. 175–200. Studies in Language and Language Use 13. Amsterdam: Instituut voor Functioneel Onderzoek naar en Taalgebruik.

2003 *The Making of a Mixed Language: The Case of Ma'a/Mbugu*. Creole Language Library 26. Amsterdam: John Benjamins.

Mühlhäusler, Peter

1997 *Pidgin and Creole Linguistics*. Expanded and revised edition. Westminster Creolistics Series 3. Westminster: University of Westminster Press.

Muysken, Peter

1994 "Media Lengua." In *Mixed Languages: 15 Case Studies in Language Intertwining*, edited by Peter Bakker and Maarten Mous, pp. 201–05. Studies in Language and Language Use 13. Amsterdam: Instituut voor Functioneel Onderzoek naar en Taalgebruik.

1997 "Media Lengua." In *Contact Languages: A Wider Perspective*, edited by Sarah G. Thomason, pp. 365–426. Creole Language Library 17. Amsterdam: Benjamins.

Nitzán, Shemuél

1973 The Jerusalem Letters from the el-ᶜAmarna Archive: Linguistic Aspects. M.A. thesis, Tel Aviv University. [In Hebrew, with English summary]

Noonan, Michael

2010 "Genetic Classification and Language Contact." In *The Handbook of Language Contact*, edited by Raymond Hickey, pp. 48–65. Blackwell Handbooks in Linguistics. Chichester: Winey-Blackwell.

Nougayrol, Jean

1962 "L'influence babylonienne à l'Ugarit d'après les textes en cunéiformes classiques." *Syria* 39: 28–35.

1975 *La Babylonien, langue internationale de l'antiquité*. Slovenska Akademija Zuanosti in Umetnosti; Academia Scientiarum et Artium Slovenica; Razred za Zgodovinske in Druzğbene vede; Classis 1: Historia et Sociologia. Dissertationes 9/1. Ljubliana: Slovenska akademija znanosti in umetnosti.

Nyberg, Henrik Samuel

1974 *A Manual of Pahlavi*. Wiesbaden: Harrassowitz.

Oppenheim, A. Leo

1964 *Ancient Mesopotamia: Portrait of a Dead Civilization*. Chicago: University of Chicago Press.

1965 "A Note on the Scribes in Mesopotamia." In *Studies in Honor of Benno Landsberger on His Seventy Fifth Birthday, April 21, 1965*, edited by Hans Güterbock and Thorkild Jacobsen, pp. 253–56. Assyriological Studies 16. Chicago: University of Chicago Press.

1977 *Ancient Mesopotamia: Portrait of a Dead Civilization*. Revised edition completed by Erica Reiner. Chicago: University of Chicago Press.

Pearce, Laurie E.

1995 "The Scribes and Scholars of Ancient Mesopotamia." In *Civilizations of the Ancient Near East*, edited by Jack M. Sasson, pp. 2265–78. New York: Scribners.

Petyt, K. M.

1980 *The Study of Dialect: An Introduction to Dialectology*. Language Library. London: André Deutsch.

Rabiner, Sara

1981 Linguistic Features of the El-Amarna Tablets from Akko, Megiddo and Shechem. M.A. thesis, Tel Aviv University. [In Hebrew, with English summary]

Rainey, Anson F.

1970 *El-Amarna Tablets 359–379.* Alter Orient und Altes Testament 8. Kevelaer: Butzon and Bercker.

1971 "Verbal Forms with Infixed -*t*- in the West Semitic El-ʿAmarna Letters." *Israel Oriental Studies* 1: 86–102.

1973 "Reflections on the Suffix Conjugation in West-Semitized Amarna Tablets." *Ugarit Forschungen* 5: 235–62.

1975 "Morphology and the Prefix Tenses of West-Semitized el-ʿAmarna Tablets." *Ugarit Forschungen* 7: 395–426.

1976 "KL 72:600 and the D-Passive in West Semitic." *Ugarit Forschungen* 8: 37–341.

1978a *El-Amarna Tablets 359–379.* 2nd edition, revised. Alter Orient und Altes Testament 8. Kevelaer: Butzon and Bercker.

1978b "The Barth-Ginsberg Law in the Amarna Tablets." *Eretz Israel* 14: 8*–13*.

1991–93 "Is There Really a *yaqtula* Conjugation Pattern in the Canaanite Amarna Tablets?" *Journal of Cuneiform Studies* 43–45: 107–18.

1992 "Topic and Comment in Byblos Akkadian." *Bibliotheca Orientalis* 49: 329–57.

1996 *Canaanite in the Amarna Tablets: A Linguistic Analysis of the Mixed Dialect Used by Scribes from Canaan.* 4 volumes. Handbuch der Orientalistik, Erste Abteilung, Der Nahe und Mittlere Osten 25. Leiden: Brill.

1999 "Taanach Letters." *Eretz-Israel* 26: 153–62.

2002 "The ʿAmârnah Texts a Century after Flinders Petrie." *Ancient Near Eastern Studies* 39: 44–75.

2003 "Syntax, Hermeneutics and History." *Israel Exploration Journal* 48: 239–51.

Rainey, Anson F., and R. Steven Notely

2006 *The Sacred Bridge: Carta's Atlas of the Biblical World.* Jerusalem: Carta.

Reiner, Erica

1966 *A Linguistic Analysis of Akkadian.* Janua Linguarum, Series Practica 21. The Hague: Mouton.

Rickford, John R.

1987 *Dimensions of a Creole Continuum: History, Texts and Linguistics Analysis of Guyanese Creole.* Stanford: Stanford University Press.

2002 "Implicational Scales." In *The Handbook of Language Variation and Change*, edited by J. K. Chambers, Peter Trudgill, and Natalie Schilling-Estes, pp. 142–68. Blackwell Handbook in Linguistics. Oxford: Blackwell.

Riemschneider, K. K.

1958 "Die Hittitische Landschenkungsurkunden." *Mitteilungen des Instituts für Orientforschung* 6: 321–81.

Romaine, Suzanne

1988 *Pidgin and Creole Languages.* Longman Linguistics Library. London: Longman.

Rubio, Gonzalo

2006 "Writing in Another Tongue: Alloglottography in the Ancient Near East." In *Margins of Writing, Origins of Cultures*, edited by Seth L. Sanders, pp. 31–64. Oriental Institute Seminars 2. Chicago: The Oriental Institute.

Salonen, Erkki

1967 *Die Gruss- und Höflichkeitsformeln in babylonisch-assyrischen Briefen.* Studia Orientalia 38. Helsinki: Societas Orientalis fennica.

Sampson, Geoffrey

1980 *Schools of Linguistics. Competition and Evolution.* London: Hutchinson.

1985 *Writing Systems: A Linguistic Introduction.* Stanford: Stanford University Press.

Sanders, Seth L.

2009 *The Invention of Hebrew.* Traditions. Urbana: University of Illinois Press.

de Saussure, Ferdinand

1955 *Cours de linguistique générale.* Publié par Charles Bally et Albert Sechehaye avec la collaboration de Albert Riedlinger. Paris: Payot. First edition 1916.

Schroeder, Otto

1915 *Die Tontafeln von El Amarna.* 2 volumes. Vorderasiatische Schriftdenkmäler der Königliche Museen zu Berlin 11–12. Leipzig: Hinrichs. Reprinted, Osnabrück, 1973.

Scotton, Carol Myers

1988 "Codeswitching as Indexical of Social Negotiations." In *Codeswitching: Anthropological and Sociolinguistic Perspectives*, edited by Monica Heller, pp. 151–86. Berlin: Mouton de Gruyter.

Shehadeh, Lamia A. Rustam

1968 The Sibilants in the West Semitic Languages of the Second Millennium B.C. Ph.D. dissertation, Harvard University.

1987 "Some Observations on the Sibilants in the Second Millennium B.C." In *"Working with No Data": Semitic and Egyptian Studies Presented to Thomas O. Lambdin*, edited by David M. Golomb, pp. 229–46. Winona Lake: Eisenbrauns.

Sivan, Daniel

1984 *Grammatical Analysis and Glossary of the Northwest Semitic Vocables in Akkadian Texts of the 15th–13th c. B.C. from Canaan and Syria.* Alter Orient und Altes Testament 214. Kevelaer: Butzon and Bercker.

Skjærvø, Prods Octor

1995 "Aramaic in Iran." *Aram* 7: 283–318.

1996 "Aramaic Scripts for Iranian Languages." In *The World's Writing Systems*, edited by Peter T. Daniels and William Bright, pp. 515–35. Oxford: Oxford University Press.

Smith, Scobie P.

1998 "The Inflectional Morphology of the *YVQTVL-* Verb in the Šuwardata Amarna Letters (EA 278–284, 366)." In *Past Links: Studies in the Languages and Cultures of the Ancient Near East*, edited by Shlomo Izre'el, Itamar Singer, and Ran Zadok, pp. 125–70. Israel Oriental Studies 18. Winona Lake: Eisenbrauns.

Stolper, Matthew W., and Jan Tavernier

2007 "From the Persepolis Fortification Archive Project, No. 1: An Old Persian Administrative Tablet from the Persepolis Fortification." *ARTA* 2007: 1–27. http://www.achemenet.com/document/2007.001-Stolper-Tavernier.pdf

Tadmor, Hayim

1977 "A Lexicographical Text from Hazor." *Israel Exploration Journal* 27: 98–102.

Tawil, Hayim ben Yosef

2009 *An Akkadian Lexical Companion for Biblical Hebrew: Etymological-semantic and Idiomatic Equivalents with Supplement on Biblical Aramaic.* Jersey City: KTAV.

Thomason, Sarah G.

1997a "Mednyj Aleut." In *Contact languages: A Wider Perspective*, edited by Sarah G. Thomason, pp. 449–68. Amsterdam: Benjamins.

1997b "Ma'a (Mbugu)." In *Contact Languages: A Wider Perspective*, edited by Sarah G. Thomason, pp. 469–87. Amsterdam: Benjamins.

2007 "Language Contact and Deliberate Change." In *Journal of Language Contact: Evolution of Language, Contact and Discourse*; Thema Series 1: *Contact: Framing Its Theories and Descriptions*, edited by Robert Nicolaï, pp. 41–62.

Thomason, Sarah Grey, and Terrence Kaufman

1988 *Language Contact, Creolization, and Genetic Linguistics.* Berkeley: University of California Press.

van der Toorn, Karel

2000 "Cuneiform Documents from Syria-Palestine: Texts, Scribes, and Schools." *Zeitschrift des Deutschen Palästina-Vereins* 116: 97–113.

Tropper, Josef

1997 "Ventiv Oder *yaktula*-Volitiv in den Amarnabriefen aus Syrien-Palestina?" In Ana šadî Labnāni lu allik: *Beiträge zu altorientalischen und mittelmeerischen Kulturen: Festschrift für Wolfgang Röllig*, edited by Beate Pongratz-Leisten, Hartmut Kühne, and Paolo Xella, pp. 397–405. Alter Orient und Altes Testament 247. Kevelaer: Butzon and Bercker.

1997/1998 "Kanaanaischen in den Amarnabriefen." *Archiv für Orientforschung* 44/45: 134–45.

2005 "Der Energikus an Jussiven im Kanaano-Akkadischen der Amarna-Periode." *Orientalia* 74: 57–64.

Trudgill, Peter

1983 "Language Contact in Greece: Reduction and Simplification in the Albanian Dialects of Attica and Biotia." In *On Dialect: Social and Geographical Perspectives*, edited by Peter Trudgill, chapter 6. New York: New York University Press.

Tsuzaki, Stanley

1971 "Coexistent Systems in Language Variation: The Case of Hawaiian English." In *Pidginization and Creolization of Languages* (Proceedings of a Conference Held at the University of the West Indies, Mona, Jamaica, April 1968), edited by Dell Hymes, pp. 327–39. Cambridge: Cambridge University Press.

Versteegh, Kees

1984 *Pidginization and Creolization: The Case of Arabic*. Amsterdam Studies in the Theory and History of Linguistic Science, Series 4: Current Issues in Linguistic Theory 33. Amsterdam: Benjamins.

Vita, Juan-Pablo

2010 "*Scribes and Dialects in Late Bronze Age Canaan.*" In *Language in the Ancient Near East: Proceedings of the 53rd Rencontre Assyriologique Internationale*, Volume 2, edited by L. Cogan, N. Koslova, S. Loesov, and T. Tishchesko, pp. 863–94. Winona Lake: Eisenbrauns.

von Dassow, Eva

2003 "What the Canaanite Cuneiformists Wrote: Review Article." *Israel Exploration Journal* 53: 196–217.

2004 "Canaanite in Cuneiform." *Journal of the American Oriental Society* 124: 641–74.

2010 "Peripheral Akkadian Dialects, or Akkadography of Local Languages?" In *Language in the Ancient Near East: Proceedings of the 53rd Rencontre Assyriologique Internationale*, Volume 2, edited by L. Cogan, N. Koslova, S. Loesov, and T. Tishchesko, pp. 895–924. Winona Lake: Eisenbrauns.

Wang, Feng; Yaching Tsai; and William S.-Y. Wang

2009 "Chinese Literacy." In *The Cambridge Handbook of Literacy*, edited by David R. Olson and Nancy Torrance, pp. 386–417. Cambridge: Cambridge University Press.

Weeden, Mark

2007 Hittite Logograms: Studies in Their Origin and Distribution. Ph.D. dissertation, School of Oriental and African Studies, University of London.

Weinreich, Uriel; William Labov; and Marvin I. Herzog

1968 "Empirical Foundations for a Theory of Language Change." In *Directions for Historical Linguistics*, edited by Winfred P. Lehmann and Yakov Malkiel, pp. 95–195. Austin: University of Texas Press.

Westhuizen, J. P., van der

1991 "Morphology and Morphosyntax of the Verb in the Amqi Amarna Letters." *Journal for Semitics* 3: 54–84.

1993 "Morphology and Morphosyntax of the Noun in the Amqi Amarna Letters." *Journal for Semitics* 5: 18–56.

1994 "Word Order Variation of the Verbal Sentence in Amqi Akkadian." *Journal for Semitics* 6: 117–53.

2005 "Morphology and Morphosyntax of the Adjective as Attributive in the Jerusalem-Amarna Letters." In *An Experienced Scribe Who Neglects Nothing: Ancient Near Eastern Studies in Honor of Jacob Klein*, edited by Yitschak Sefati, Pinhas Artzi, Chaim Cohen, Barry L. Eichler, and Victor A. Hurowitz, pp. 600–23. Publications of the Samuel Noah Kramer Institute of Assyriology and Ancient Near Eastern Studies, The Faculty of Jewish Studies, Bar-Ilan University. Bethesda: CDL Press.

Winford, Donald

1985 "The Concept of 'Diglossia' in Caribbean Creole Situations." *Language in Society* 14: 345–56.

2007 "Some Issues in the Study of Language Contact." In *Journal of Language Contact: Evolution of Language, Contact and Discourse*; Thema Series 1: *Contact: Framing Its Theories and Descriptions*, edited by Robert Nicolaï, pp. 22–40.

2010 "Contact and Borrowing." In *The Handbook of Language Contact*, edited by Raymond Hickey, pp. 170–87. Blackwell Handbooks in Linguistics. Chichester: Winey-Blackwell.

Yarshater, Eshan

1977 "The Hybrid Language of the Jewish Communities of Persia." *Journal of the American Oriental Society* 97: 1–7.

Youngblood, Ronald Fred

1961 The Amarna Correspondence of Rib-Haddi, Prince of Byblos (EA 68–96). Ph.D. dissertation, Dropsie College for Hebrew and Cognate Learnings, Philadelphia. UMI 72-31,957.

Zewi, Tamar

1995 "Subject-predicate Word Order of Nominal Clauses in El-Amarna Letters." *Ugarit Forschungen* 27: 657–93.

1999 *A Syntactic Study of Verbal Forms Affixed by* -n(n) *Endings in Classical Arabic, Biblical Hebrew, El-Amarna Akkadian and Ugaritic.* Alter Orient und Altes Testament 260. Münster: Ugarit-Verlag.

14

The Evidential Function of the Perfect in North-Eastern Neo-Aramaic Dialects

Geoffrey Khan, University of Cambridge

Most North-Eastern Neo-Aramaic (NENA) dialects have a perfect verbal form in addition to the preterite. The basic function of the perfect is to express a state resulting from a preceding event, whereas the function of the preterite is to express an event in the past. When the perfect is used, the event is not expressed directly, but is an implicature. The preterite, by contrast, expresses the event directly. In the majority of NENA dialects, the present perfect, that is, a perfect expressing a resultative state in the present, is formed by combining the resultative participle with the verb "to be," usually in the form of a copula. The resultative participle is derived historically from the passive participle in earlier Aramaic in the determined state (*qṭīlā*). The purpose of this paper is to draw attention to the existence of a secondary function of perfect verbal forms in a number of NENA dialects.

The first dialect to be considered is the Jewish dialect of Sanandaj (western Iran). This dialect has two verbal forms whose basic function is to express the resultative perfect. The present perfect is formed by combining the resultative participle with the present copula. In this dialect the participle has a different pattern for active transitive (e.g., *qəṭla* 'killed') and intransitive/passive verbs (e.g., *smixa* 'stood'):

qəṭla-y 'he has killed'
RESULTATIVE PART TRANS-COP.3MS
qəṭla-yena (contracted to *qəṭlena*) 'I have killed'
RESULTATIVE PART TRANS-COP.1MS

smixa-y 'he has stood up'
RESULTATIVE PART INTRANS-COP.3MS
smixa-yena (contracted to *smixena*) 'I have stood up'
RESULTATIVE PART INTRANS-COP.1MS

The past perfect, on the other hand, is not formed with the resultative participle, but rather by adding an anterior affix *wa* to the preterite. The preterite consists of a past base, which is derived from the historical passive participle in the undetermined form (*qṭīl*). A different pattern of past base is used according to whether the verb is active transitive or intransitive/passive. The transitive form is inflected by an ergative suffix, which is historically a pronominal prepositional phrase containing the preposition *l-*. The intransitive/passive form is inflected by suffixes that derive historically from nominative clitic pronouns:

qṭəl-wa-le 'he had killed'
PAST BASE TRANS-ANTERIOR-ERG.3MS
qṭəl-wa-li 'I had killed'
PAST BASE TRANS-ANTERIOR-ERG.1MS

smix-Ø-wa	'he had stood up'
PAST BASE INTRANS-NOM.3MS-ANTERIOR	
smix-ena-wa	'I had stood up'
PAST BASE INTRANS-NOM.1MS-ANTERIOR	

In the dialect there is a past copula (*yele* 'he was'), for example, *zora-yele* 'he was small,' *gănawa-yele* 'he was a thief,' but this cannot be used with an eventive predicate expressed by a resultative participle (**qəṭla-yele*).

The perfect of the verb 'to be' is formed by using the resultative participle of the verb *xØr* 'to become' (derived historically from *ḥdr*) combined with the present copula, for example, *xira-y* 'he has been/he has become,' *xirena* 'I have been/I have become.'

The present-perfect and past-perfect forms, which for the sake of convenience are henceforth referred to as the *qəṭla-y* and *qṭəlwale* forms, are sometimes used with a secondary function to express a perfective event from which the speaker is in some way distanced. In many cases the distancing arises from the fact that the speaker has not witnessed the event directly and knows about it only indirectly by way of report. One may, therefore, identify this as an expression of evidentiality, that is, the grammatical coding of the source of knowledge in the verbal form. The grammatical coding of evidentiality exists in numerous languages. In the Middle East, this is a well-known feature of Turkish and Iranian languages. In the linguistic literature on these language groups, various terms are used for the phenomenon. Recently a term that has come to be widely used is "indirective," which was introduced originally by Lars Johanson (1996; 2000; 2003). Gilbert Lazard (1985; 1996; 2000) refers to the phenomenon by the French terms "médiatif" and "distancié." Such verbal forms present events that the speaker becomes conscious of from an indirect source of knowledge. I shall use here the term "indirective" to refer to the phenomenon in NENA. As I have remarked, in many cases where indirective forms are used, the speaker is distanced from the event since he or she has learned about the event indirectly by report. In some cases the speaker may have witnessed the event in the past but is distanced from it temporally. In both cases of distancing, one may say that the experience of the described event is not directly accessible to the speaker, but rather the description of the event is based on an abstraction of the experience through the verbal report of somebody else or through an internal mental processing of the experience of the speaker. It is possible that the distancing of the speaker from the event may cause him some degree of uncertainty with regard to it. This phenomenon, therefore, has some association with epistemic modality. Such modality is not, however, grammatically encoded in the verbal forms in question, which are assertive (Lazard 2000; Aikhenvald 2003, p. 25). The existence of modality with regard to the commitment of the speaker to the truth of the utterance should be regarded as an implicature in certain contexts.

In many languages indirective evidential verbal forms developed historically from resultative perfect forms (Aikhenvald 2004, pp. 279–81). This is clearly what happened in Turkish and Iranian languages (Johanson 2000; Lazard 1996). Such a development occurs since the resultative perfect presents events through their results rather than directly (Comrie 1976, p. 110).

The Semitic languages generally express evidentiality by means of adverbials rather than by verbal morphology (Isaksson 2000; Gianto 2005). The identification of grammatical coding of the phenomenon in NENA is, therefore, of particular significance.[1]

In the NENA dialect of the Jews of Sanandaj, the perfect forms may function in an indirective sub-system. This is shown in the following table, in which section I presents the basic function of the forms, and section II presents the indirective sub-system:

[1] Goldenberg (1992, pp. 131–33) has drawn attention to the use of the Ṭuroyo perfect to express mirativity, that is, an unpreparedness of the mind of a speaker for the occurrence of the event. This is a common function of evidential verbal forms (Aikhenvald 2004, pp. 195–215). The phenomenon in Ṭuroyo is likely to have developed under the influence of Turkish evidential verbal forms (containing the affix *miş*). The Ṭuroyo perfect is not used, however, with an indirective function to express events that the speaker learns about by report or from which he or she is distanced temporally. For a discussion of the functions of the Ṭuroyo perfect, see Tomal 2008, pp. 33–49.

I	PRIMARY FUNCTION			
qṭəl-le	*qəṭla-y*		*qăṭəlwa*	*qṭəlwale*
he killed	he has killed		he used to kill	he had killed
II	**SECONDARY FUNCTION (INDIRECTIVE)**			
	qəṭla-y	*qəṭla-y*	*qṭəlwale*	*qəṭla-xira-y*
	he killed	he used to kill	he killed	he had killed

It can be seen that the forms *qəṭla-y* and *qṭəlwale* are used both with the primary function of resultative perfect and also in the indirective sub-system with the function of an indirective perfective or imperfective. They are, therefore, ambiguous with regard to their function. The form *qəṭla-xira-y*, on the other hand, occurs only in the indirective sub-system and so should be identified as an unambiguous indirective verbal form. It consists of the perfect form of the verb 'to be' *xira-y* combined with the resultative participle and is used to express the indirective past perfect ('he had killed').

There is a close parallelism between the indirective sub-system in the NENA dialect and the indirective sub-system of verbs in Persian (Lazard 1985; 1996; 2000), and it is likely that the former imitated the latter:

	I PRIMARY FUNCTION		II INDIRECTIVE	
	NENA	Persian	NENA	Persian
he has killed	*qəṭla-y*	*košte-ast*	—	—
he killed	*qṭəlle*	*košt*	*qəṭla-y* *qṭəlwale*	*košte-ast*
he used to kill	*qăṭəlwa*	*mi-košt*	*qəṭla-y*	*mi-košte-ast*
he had killed	*qṭəlwale*	*košte-bud*	*qəṭla-xira-y*	*košte-bude-ast*

It can be seen that the indirective form *qəṭla-y* in the NENA dialect corresponds not only to the perfective indirective form in Persian *košte-ast* but also to the Persian imperfective indirective form *mi-košte-ast*, which is formed by combining the prefix *mi-* with the perfective form.

In the NENA dialect of the Jews of Sanandaj, one may identify the following functions of the indirective forms.

qəṭla-y II (Indirective)

This form is used to express perfective events that the speaker knows about by way of report. The process of report may be made explicit in the context, for example,

ex. 1. *xaṭrăte nóšef ḥqèle baqán*| ... *ʾó ga-zămán-e Mozăfar-din Šăh*| ***hiyá-y*** *báqa ʾIrăn báqa tasís-e madrăsá ʾaliăns.*|

'He told us his reminiscences. ... *He came* to Iran in the time of Mozafaredin Shah in order to found the school of the Alliance.' (Khan 2009, p. 296)

The form is used in narratives of a legendary nature. In such cases the speaker presents the events as information received indirectly by tradition and not as events that he or she has witnessed directly, for example,

ex. 2. ***zilà-y***| *ṭălăbá málka Šăbà.*| *málka Šăbà* ***gwirté-ya.***|

'**He went** to seek the hand of the Queen of Sheba. **He married** the Queen of Sheba.' (Khan 2009, p. 297)

Another function of the indirective form *qəṭla-y* is to express historical events that occurred in the remote past. The Persian indirective forms sometimes have this function (Lazard 2000, pp. 218–19). In such cases the indirective form expresses temporal distancing between the speaker and the experience of the event, that is, the description of the event is not based directly on the experience of the event. It is possible to use the form with this function in the first person when the speaker has witnessed the event but is separated from it by a considerable temporal distance, for example,

ex. 3. ***zilén*** *baqá Rusìya,*| ***zilén*** *báqa Turkìya.*| *jə̀ns* ***šəqlá-y,***| ***miyá-y*** *ga-Kurdəstā́n* ***zəbnà-y.***|

'**They used to go** to Russia, **they used to go** to Turkey. **They used to buy** goods, **used to bring** them to Kurdistan and **used to sell** them there.' (Khan 2009, p. 297)

ex. 4. *ʾənyexáe paetaxtè*| *Kureš-e Kăbìr* ***xirén.***|

'**These were** the capitals of Cyrus the Great.' (Khan 2009, p. 301)

qṭəlwale II (Indirective)

This form, whose basic function is to express the past perfect ('he had killed'), is used with a secondary indirective function to narrate events in the past that the speaker has not witnessed. In the examples that are found in my corpus of recordings, the form occurs in contexts where there is no explicit reference to the act of reporting. In (ex. 5) the speaker narrates events that occurred in Sanandaj when he himself was in Teheran, and so he was not able to witness them directly:

ex. 5. ^{H}*ʾáz*^{H} ***zìlawa***| ***mírwala*** *baqá ʾăxonàf-u*| *nóšaf là halbắta,*| *xa-năfar-xét* ***šə́rwala*** *baqá ʾăxonàf*| *hămər kè*| *ʾay-bronà*| *həl-d-áy bratá gbè.*| ^{H}*áz*^{H} *ʾoní-č qăbùl* ***wílwalu.***|

'Then **she (my mother) went and said** to her (the girl's) brother — of course not her herself, she **sent** somebody else to her brother to say that the boy loves the girl. Then **they agreed.**' (Khan 2009, p. 287)

In example 6 the speaker uses the *qṭəlwale* form to narrate events that took place inside a house and out of his sight, since he was standing in the street outside. The speaker did witness, however, the event of the man Xănăka looking out of the window and seeing him, and he returns to the normal preterite narrative form:

ex. 6. *ʾay-****zílwala mírwala*** *báqa Mə́rza Xănăkà,*| ***mírwala*** *Mə́rza Xănăká xá-gora gbelòx.*| *la-kắyan mằni-ye.*| *Xănăká-č mən-panjărăké mʿine-ò*| *həl-didí xèle.*|

'**She went and said** to Mərza Xănăka, **she said** "Mərza Xănăka, a man wants you. I do not know who it is." Xănăka looked from the window and saw me.' (Khan 2009, pp. 287–88)

qəṭla-xira-y II (Indirective)

This form has the function of a past perfect in reported discourse. In example 7 the speaker narrates the reminiscences of another man concerning events in the past that the speaker has not witnessed. The past perfective indirective form presents the event in question as anterior to other past events, which are expressed by present historic forms:

ex. 7. *yarxá-u pə́lge ga-Tarán* ***nəṭrà-xira-y***| *ba-wăsáṭ d-éa ʾorxá šŭlùq xirté-ya.*| *là-məhre šắre báqa Kurdəstằn,*| *báqa Hamằn.*| *ta-bəlʾaxərá gezə́l lagèf*| *kmə́r ʾaná là-keli yătunà.*|

'For a month and a half **he had kept him** in Tehran — on account of the fact that there were disturbances on the road, he (the Grand Vizier) did not dare send him to Kurdistan, to Hamadan — until in the end he goes to him and says "I cannot sit (idly)."' (Khan 2009, p. 301)

It is important to note that indirective verbal forms are not obligatory in contexts that may be appropriate for them. In all cases the basic form of the verb with the corresponding tense and aspect may be used. It may be said that the basic forms are unmarked with regard to evidentiality, whereas the set of indirective forms are marked and may be used with their particular tense and aspect only with an indirective function.

Indirective functions of the perfect may be identified also in other NENA dialects. Such forms are used, for example, in the Jewish dialects of Sulemaniyya and Arbel in Iraq, which, like Jewish Sanandaj, belong to the Jewish trans-Zab sub-group of NENA (Mutzafi 2008). These dialects are outside the area of the influence of Persian, the main substrate language being Kurdish in these areas. The most common indirect function of the perfect in these dialects is to express an event in the remote past. Although some indirective functions of the Kurdish perfect have been identified (Bulut 2000), these all appear to be of the inferential type relating to events that have not been witnessed by the speaker. The use of the perfect in the NENA dialects in question to express an event in the remote past, therefore, may be the result of internal development.

In the Jewish dialect of Sulemaniyya, the perfect is formed by combining the resultative participle with the verb 'to be,' usually the copula, as in the Jewish dialect of Sanandaj. In example 8 the indirective perfect form *mila-y* is used to express the temporal remoteness of the death of one of the brothers in contrast to the more recent death of the other brother, which is expressed by the normal narrative perfective form (preterite) *mil*:

ex. 8. *ʾó tre-ʾaxóne ruwwè*| *mìli.*| *xáyu qáme tre-šə́nne mìl,*| *Mòše.*| *Hʾavál*H *ʾó xa-xèt*| *qáme xamšàsar šə́nne bi-zóda* ***milà-y.***|

'The two older brothers of mine died. One of them, Moše, died two years ago, but the other one **died** more than fifteen years ago.' (Khan 2004, p. 317)

As I have remarked, the indirective forms are not obligatory. The unmarked perfective form *qṭəlle* (preterite) can also be used to express the remote past. In some sections of my corpus of recordings of the Jewish Sulemaniyya dialect, the speaker interchanges between the marked indirective forms and the unmarked preterite when narrating events in the remote past. The choice is not random. The speaker uses the marked indirective forms in clauses that have prominence and importance in the discourse. In example 9 the speaker uses the indirective form in the clause that expresses the event of his emigration to Israel, which is the pivotal point in the section of discourse in question and the main concern of the speaker. The event of his getting married is presented as background elaboration, with a lower level of prominence:

ex. 9. *ʾána* ***hiyéna*** *m-Slemaní ba-šatá xamši-u-xà.*| *qáme héna ga-Slemanì*| *ʾána báxta mèli*|

'I **came** from Sulemaniyya in the year fifty-one. Before I came, I married in Sulemaniyya.' (Khan 2004, p. 317)

In the Jewish dialect of Arbel, the perfect is formed by combining the preterite *qṭəlle* with the particle *lā*, which is a fossilized form of the copula without inflection:

I	PRIMARY FUNCTION
qṭəlle	*lā qṭəlle*
he killed	he has killed
II	**SECONDARY FUNCTION (INDIRECTIVE)**
	lā qṭəlle
	he killed

In example 10 the speaker uses the *lā qṭəlle* form in its indirective function to express the remote past. In the same section of discourse, he also uses the preterite form *qṭəlle* to express an event in the remote past. As in the Jewish dialect of Sulemaniyya, the motivation for the use of the marked indirective form is the importance of the clauses in questions in the discourse. They relate to the central point of the section, which concerns the origin of his father from Ruwanduz. The fact that a previous generation came from another town has the status of elaborative background information.

ex. 10. *babí Ruwandəznèle.*| *ʾaṣléu ʾəl-Ruwàndəz* ***lā-ġdíre.***| *sonì-š ʾəl-Ruwándəz* ***lā-ġdíre***| *.... sonə́t babì*| *ʾəl-Bàrzan ġdíre.*|

'My father is from Ruwandiz, he was born in Ruwandiz, also my grandfather was born in Ruwandiz. The grandfather of my father was born in Barzan.' (Khan 1999, p. 269)

In a number of Christian NENA dialects, the perfect verbal form is used in narratives with the function of a preterite to relate a specific punctual event in the past without any assertion of the existence of a resultant state in the present. This may be identified as an indirective usage of the perfect. It is found in various Christian dialects in southeastern Turkey and the adjacent regions of northern Iraq. A detailed study has been made of the phenomenon in the Christian dialect of Barwar, spoken in the Barwar-i-bala region of Iraq, which lies approximately ten miles north of Amedia in Dihok province (Khan 2008), and the following examples are from this dialect.

In the Christian Barwar dialect, the perfect is formed by combining the resultative participle with the verb 'to be.' This is usually some form of copula. The dialect has two forms of present copula and a past copula. The two forms of present copula that are combined with the resultative participle are the enclitic copula, which is attached after the participle, and the deictic copula, which is placed before the participle:

Enclitic copula: *qṭila-ile* (contracted to *qṭilɛle*)

Deictic copula: *hole qṭila*

In non-narrative discourse, the perfect with the present copula is used to express a resultative state. The deictic copula is used with the participle to draw particular attention to a current situation. There is a certain amount of subjectivity in the use of the deictic copula, but it is generally employed in assertive clauses that refer to a resultant state that has some kind of relevance to the immediate present moment in time, for example, *hole ʾəθya* 'He has come.' In interrogative clauses, the enclitic copula is used, for example, *ʾəθyɛle?* 'Has he come?'

When the perfect is used with an indirective function to narrate perfective events, it is normally used with the enclitic copula rather than the deictic copula. This is in contrast to the general use of the deictic copula to express present relevance when the form has a resultative function, for example,

ex. 11. *qìmela*| *b-lɛ̀le*| *ṭrípəlla Zìne*| *ʾu-mùθyəlla,*| *núbləlla kəs-Mămo.*| *núbləlla kəs-Mămo.*| *dmìxela.*| *ṛìštɛla,*| *zìptəllela*| *ṭla-Mămo.*|

'At night they went and seized Zine and brought her, they took her to Mămo. They took her to Mămo. They slept. She woke up and pushed Mămo (out of bed).' (Khan 2008, p. 669)

The copula is sometimes omitted from the participle when it has this narrative indirective function. This typically occurs in a series of clauses that open with a verb with the copula. The clause or clauses without the copula express events that are closely sequential to that of the opening clause. The purpose of the speaker is to present these as components of one overall event rather than as a series of discrete events, for example,

ex. 12. *ʾə́θyela jmìye*| 'They came and gathered together.' (Khan 2008, p. 670)

ex. 13. *ʾə́θyɛle wìra*| 'He came and entered.' (Khan 2008, p. 670)

Normally in such chains of events, the clause with the participle without the copula has the same subject as the preceding clause, as is the case in the examples above. When there is a change in subject, a copula is generally used, for example,

ex. 14. *síqɛle mə́xya l-tăra*| *ʾu-plíṭṭɛla Səttìye.*|

'He went up and knocked on the door and Səttiye came out.' (Khan 2008, p. 670)

In narratives the indirective *qṭilɛle* form is used interchangeably with the perfective past forms *qṭille* and *qəm-qaṭəl*, which are the other main narrative verbal forms. The *qṭille* form consists of a past base, derived historically from the undetermined state of the passive participle (*qṭīl*), and an ergative pronominal suffix containing the preposition *l*. The *qəm-qaṭəl* form, which is used only with pronominal object suffixes, consists of the present base, which is derived historically from the active participle (*qāṭil*), and the prefix *qəm-*, which is probably a contracted fossilized form of the verb *qḏam*. The narrator constantly shifts from the indirective form to the perfective past forms. These shifts often coincide with some kind of reorientation in the narrative, especially where there is a change in subject and the narrator directs attention to another character, for example,

ex. 15. *qímɛle lɛ̀le šə́tya qáwa.*| *tíwɛle l-xáṣə súse dìye*| *ʾu-díṛɛle ṣə́lyɛle rəš-d-ɛ̀-ʾɛna.*| *ʾɛ-ʾɛ́na ṯ̂-ìle ʾə́θya qamáye réša.*| *Qára Téždin dìṛṛe*| *θéle bɛ̀θa*| *ʾámər hà*| *báxta kɛ́le ʾàrxa?*|

'He got up [*qṭilɛle*] and did not drink the coffee [*qṭilɛle*]. He sat on the back of his horse [*qṭilɛle*] and went back down to the spring [*qṭilɛle*], the spring to which he had come previously [*qṭilɛle*]. Qara Teždin returned home [*qṭille*] and said [*qṭille*] "Ah, wife, where is the guest?"' (Khan 2008, p. 671)

On some occasions there is no change in subject across the transition from one verbal form to the other. In such cases some kind of reorientation on another dimension of the discourse can usually be discerned. In example 16, for example, the shift from *qṭilɛle* for *qṭille* coincides with the start of a chain of clauses that narrate a new event, that is, the eating of the third fox cub.

ex. 16. *qímela ʾap-o-tré prìməlle,*| *xìləlle.*| *ʾímət xílla ʾap-o-trè,*| *píšla xà-šabθa,*| *tré šabbàθa,*| *kpìnna.*| *ʾáp-o-ṭlaθa qəm-pɛrmìle.*|

'They slaughtered also the second one [*qṭilɛle*] and ate him [*qṭilɛle*]. After they ate [*qṭille*] the second one, a week, two weeks went by [*qṭille*], they became hungry [*qṭille*] and slaughtered also the third one [*qəm-qaṭəl*].' (Khan 2008, p. 672)

The transition in the narrative between the two verbal forms is also attested where the narrator repeats the mention of an event of particular importance in the story. The shift of verbal form is no doubt exploited in such circumstances to mark off the repeated clause more sharply from what precedes in order to give it prominence, for example,

ex. 17. *ʾó-yomə ṯ̂-íle plíṭa málka m-bɛ̀θa,*| *ʾó-yoma bróne díye mìθɛle.*| *ʾó-yoma mìtle bróne díye.*|

'On the day that the king left home [*qṭilɛle*], on that day his son died [*qṭilɛle*]. On that day his son died [*qṭille*].' (Khan 2008, p. 672)

Occasionally the deictic copula is used with a resultative participle when the construction has the indirective function of expressing a punctual event. This is found when the speaker wishes to give the event particular discourse prominence. In example 18 the motivation for this construction is to give particular attention to the event due to its unexpectedness. It is not usual for a barber to have to bring a ladder to cut a person's hair.

ex. 18. *tíwɛle Zàlo*| *qəm-tắṛət qáṣre dìye*| *ʾo-ḥallàqa*| *hóle múθyəlla xa-semàlta*| *múttəlla baθràt rušáne díye.*|

'Zāl sat before his palace. The barber brought a ladder and placed it behind his shoulders.' (Khan 2008, p. 675)

The indirective perfect form in the Christian Barwar dialect is typically used in narratives of folktales and legends, which are traditions passed down to the speaker that do not consist of events that the speaker has witnessed. It is not used, however, as a general evidential form to convey information that the speaker has acquired by report, but is restricted to the genre of narratives. This differs, for example, from Turkish evidential verbal forms, which are used not only in fictional narratives with no basis in reality, such as myths and folktales (Slobin and Aksu-Koç 1982; Aksu-Koç and Slobin 1986; Aksu-Koç 1988, p. 25), but also outside of this genre of discourse as a general marker of reported information. As in the Jewish Sulemaniyya and Jewish Arbel dialects, the basic function of the indirective perfect in Christian Barwar is to express events that are remote from the speaker. The speaker may have witnessed the events, but they are temporally remote. The construction is attested, for example, in narratives by elderly speakers of events that took place in their childhood. In example 19 a speaker is narrating an experience he had with a refractory ass when he was a young boy. He uses the indirective perfect together with perfective narrative forms:

ex. 19. *ṣríxən hátxa biya-dìya.*| *ʾáyya qəm-patlála gʸān-dìya*| *ʾána xšíwən là maxyáli.*| *qəm-patlála gʸān-dìya*| ... *qəm-maxyála ðà-p̣ena.*|

'I shouted at it like this. It turned itself round. I thought it would not strike me. It turned itself round. It gave me a kick.' (Khan 2008, p. 677)

The indirective evidential function that has been described in this paper is unusual in Semitic. In some dialects, such as Jewish Sanandaj, it is clear that it has developed by imitation of the form and function of verbs in a non-Semitic language with which speakers were in contact. In other dialects, however, the indirective has no or only partial parallels in the non-Semitic languages spoken in the area, and it appears to be largely an internal development of Near-Eastern Neo-Aramaic (NENA).

Abbreviations

COP	Copula	M	masculine
ERG	ergative	NOM	nominative
INTRANS	intransitive	TRANS	transitive

Bibliography

Aikhenvald, Alexandra Y.

2003 "Evidentiality in Typological Perspective." In *Studies in Evidentiality*, edited by Alexandra Y. Aikhenvald and Robert M. W. Dixon, pp. 1–31. Typological Studies in Language 54. Amsterdam: John Benjamins.

2004 *Evidentiality*. Oxford: Oxford University Press.

Aksu-Koç, Ayhan

1988 *The Acquisition of Aspect and Modality: The Case of Past Reference in Turkish*. Cambridge: Cambridge University Press.

Aksu-Koç, Ayhan, and Dan Isaac Slobin

1986 "A Psychological Account of the Development and Use of Evidentials in Turkish." In *Evidentiality: The Linguistic Coding of Epistemology*, edited by Wallace L. Chafe and Johanna Nichols, pp. 159–67. Advances in Discourse Processes 20. Norwood: Ablex Publishing.

Bulut, Christiane

2000 "Indirectivity in Kurmanji." In *Evidentials: Turkic, Iranian and Neighbouring Languages*, edited by Lars Johanson and Bo Utas, pp. 147–84. Empirical Approaches to Language Typology 24. Berlin: Mouton de Gruyter.

Comrie, Bernard

1976 *Aspect: An Introduction to the Study of Verbal Aspect and Related Problems*. Cambridge: Cambridge University Press.

Gianto, Agustinus

2005 "Evidentiality in Biblical Hebrew." In *Biblical and Oriental Essays in Memory of William L. Moran*, edited by Agustinus Gianto, pp. 133–53. Biblica et orientalia 48. Rome: Pontificio Instituto Biblico.

Goldenberg, Gideon

1992 "Aramaic Perfects." *Israel Oriental Studies* 12: 113–33.

Isaksson, Bo

2000 "Expressions of Evidentiality in Two Semitic Languages — Hebrew and Arabic." In *Evidentials: Turkic, Iranian and Neighbouring Languages*, edited by Lars Johanson and Bo Utas, pp. 383–400. Empirical Approaches to Language Typology 24. Berlin: Mouton de Gruyter.

Johanson, Lars

1996 "On Bulgarian and Turkic Indirectives." In *Areale, Kontakte, Dialekte. Sprache und ihre Dynamik in Mehrsprachigen Situationen: Beiträge zum 10. Bochum-Essener Symposium "Areale, Kontakte, Dialekte: Sprache und ihre Dynamik in Mehrsprachigen Situationen*, edited by Norbert Boretzky, Werner Enninger, and Thomas Stolz, pp. 84–94. Bochum-Essener Beiträge zur Sprachwandelforschung 24. Bochum: N. Brockmeyer.

2000 "Turkic Indirectives." In *Evidentials: Turkic, Iranian and Neighboring Languages*, edited by Lars Johanson and Bo Utas, pp. 61–87. Empirical Approaches to Language Typology 24. Berlin: Mouton de Gruyter.

2003 "Evidentiality in Turkic." In *Studies in Evidentiality*, edited by Alexandra Y. Aikhenvald and Robert M. W. Dixon, pp. 273–90. Typological Studies in Language 54. Amsterdam: John Benjamins.

Khan, Geoffrey

1999 *A Grammar of Neo-Aramaic: The Dialect of the Jews of Arbel*. Handbuch der Orientalistik, Erste Abteilung, Nahe und der Mittlere Osten 47. Boston: Brill Academic Publishers.

2004 *The Jewish Neo-Aramaic Dialect of Sulemaniyya and Ḥalabja*. Studies in Semitic Languages and Linguistics 44. Leiden: Brill.

2008 *The Neo-Aramaic Dialect of Barwar*. Handbuch der Orientalistik, Erste Abteilung, Nahe und der Mittlere Osten 96. Leiden: Brill.

2009 *The Jewish Neo-Aramaic Dialect of Sanandaj*. Gorgias Neo-Aramaic Studies 10. Piscataway: Gorgias Press.

Lazard, Gilbert

1985 "L'inférentiel ou passé distancié en persan." *Studia Iranica* 14: 27–42.

1996 "Le médiatif en persan." In *L'énonciation médiatisée*, edited by Zlatka Guentchéva, pp. 21–30. Bibliothèque de l'information gramaticale. Louvain: Peeters.

2000 "Le médiatif: Considérations théoriques et application à l'iranien." In *Evidentials: Turkic, Iranian and Neighbouring Languages*, edited by Lars Johanson and Bo Utas, pp. 209–28. Empirical Approaches to Language Typology 24. Berlin: Mouton de Gruyter.

Mutzafi, Hezy

2008 "Trans-Zab Jewish Neo-Aramaic." *Bulletin of the School of Oriental and African Studies* 71/3: 409–31.

Slobin, Dan Isaac, and Ayhan Aksu-Koç

1982 "Tense, Aspect, and Modality in the Use of the Turkish Evidential." In *Tense-aspect: Between Semantics and Pragmatics; Containing the Contributions to a Symposium on Tense and Aspect* (Held at UCLA, May 1979), edited by Paul J Hopper, pp. 185–200. Typological Studies in Language 1. Amsterdam: John Benjamins.

Tomal, Maciej

2008 *Studies in Neo-Aramaic Tenses*. Austeria: Krakow.

15

Les noms de plantes akkadiens dans leur contexte sémitique

*Leonid Kogan, Russian State University for the Humanities**

En mars de 2008, grâce à l'aimable invitation de Jean-Marie Durand, j'ai pu présenter à l'audience du Collège de France quatre conférences concernant la perspective comparatiste sur la terminologie botanique akkadienne. Il ne s'agissait alors que des premiers prolégomènes pour le futur troisième volume du Dictionnaire étymologique des langues sémitiques (SED III), dédié aux noms de plantes du proto-sémitique. Par conséquent, aucune publication définitive du texte français n'était originellement prévue. Cependant, peu de temps après mon retour à Moscou j'ai commencé à me rendre compte que, pour plusieurs raisons scientifiques autant que personnelles, la publication du SED III était loin d'être imminente. Dans de telles conditions, il m'a paru opportun de présenter au public sémitisant et assyriologue une version renouvelée du texte français. C'est avec un grand plaisir que je dédie ces pages à John Huehnergard, un grand maître de grammaire comparée et d'étymologie sémitiques dont plusieurs études ont joué un rôle prééminent dans ma propre formation scientifique.[1]

I. Terminologie botanique générale

1. Le nom générique pour 'arbre' est ***iṣu***, dont les premiers exemples syllabiques en Mésopotamie proprement dite ne sont pas antérieures aux périodes paléo-assyrienne et paléo-babylonienne (AHw. 390, CAD I 214). Néanmoins, quelques formes comparables sont déjà attestées dans le Vocabulaire d'Ebla: *ì-ṣú ba-ne* = sum. GIŠ. ŠINIG dans VE 395, *ì-ṣú gu*-PI = sum. GIŠ.URUDU.URUDU dans VE 411 (Krebernik 1983, pp. 15–16). Dans la première locution, le second élément est évidemment à identifier avec l'akkadien *bānu* 'tamaris' (voir le numéro 17 ci-dessous). L'identification de *gu*-PI dans la seconde locution reste plus problématique, mais il n'est peut être pas trop osé de mentionner dans ce contexte l'akkadien *ḳû* 'cuivre, bronze' (CAD Q 291; Reiter 1997, pp. 295–99). La comparaison est parfaite du point de vue phonétique (le signe GU étant l'équivalent régulier de la syllabe /ḳu/ à Ebla[2]). Sémantiquement, on pourrait penser à une désignation botanique spécifique comparable a notre *ironwood*, *sidéroxylon*, bien qu'on doive admettre que la correspondance sumérienne de *ḳû* est ZABAR plutôt que URUDU.

Étymologiquement, akk. *iṣu* doit être tracé à proto-sémitique ***ʕiṣ̂-** (Fronzaroli 1969a, pp. 276, 290, 299), très probablement la seule désignation générique d'arbre dans la proto-langue, comme on peut le déduire du fait que cette fonction fondamentale est préservée par ses réflexes dans des domaines géographiquement aussi éloignés

* Je remercie cordialement Hervé Reculeau qui a corrigé le style de cet article, tout en contribuant à plusieurs observations assyriologiques d'une grande utilité. Cet article a été préparé dans le cadre du projet 12-04-00164. Je remercie vivement cette institution pour son support financier.

[1] La présence de plusieurs remarques étymologiques sur la terminologie botanique sémitique dans Huehnergard 2007 — par ailleurs, une étude dédiée à un thème purement morphologique — montre clairement que ce sujet n'est pas trop éloigné de la très vaste sphère d'activité de notre honoré. De même pour la langue française de cette présentation, une langue dont John est un amateur reconnu.

[2] W. von Soden *apud* Krebernik 1982, p. 207.

entre eux que le cananéen (oug. ˁṣ, ph. ˁṣ, héb. ˁēṣ)[3] et l'éthiopien (gez. ˁəŝ).[4] Dans toutes ces langues — tout comme en akkadien — les réflexes de *ˁiŝ- désignent l'arbre comme plante vivante ainsi que le bois comme matériau.

La situation est différente en araméen, où *ˁāˁā* (ou *ˀāˁā* avec dissimilation) ne désigne que le bois comme matériau dès les plus anciens témoignages accessibles.[5] En revanche, l'arbre comme plante est désigné par les réflexes de **ˀīlān-*, un terme étymologiquement intéressant qui sera discuté plus loin en relation avec akk. *allānu* (no. 21 ci-dessous). Une restriction sémantique tout à fait similaire a eu lieu dans la plupart des langues néo-éthiopiennes (par exemple, har. *inči* 'bois,' EDH 28).

En sudarabique épigraphique, ˁŝ est appliqué à un type de matériau de construction dont la nature exacte — bois ou pierre? — nous échappe (pour une discussion détaillée, voir Sima 2000, p. 290). Il est par ailleurs impossible de savoir si ce terme avait aussi été utilisé pour désigner un arbre vivant car la nature des documents n'offre pas de contextes pertinents.

En arabe, le terme proto-sémitique persiste dans *ˁiḍḍ-*, *ˁuḍḍ-*, *ˁiḍāh-* qui désignent différentes variétés d'arbres ou arbrisseaux épineux (Lane 1876, pp. 2070, 2076). En sudarabique moderne, il n'a laissé aucune trace. Dans les deux cas, les mots qui l'ont remplacé (ar. *šaǯar-* et le sudarabique moderne commun **haram-*) sont étymologiquement obscurs.

2. Akk. ***ḳīštu*** 'bois, forêt' n'est pas attesté syllabiquement avant la période paléo-babylonienne (AHw. 923, CAD Q 272), mais, cette fois encore, le mot akkadien a une correspondance transparente à Ebla: *ḳá-sa-tum* = sum. GIŠ.TIR (VE 400; Krebernik 1983, p. 15).

Akk. *ḳīštu* peut être facilement tracé à proto-sémitique ***ḳayŝ**- (Fronzaroli 1969a, pp. 277, 290), une reconstruction qui se base sur les données sudarabiques modernes (soq. *ḳaŝen*, méh. *ḳəŝnīt* 'bois, forêt,'[6] avec un *-n* suffixé) et araméennes (AJP *ḳīs*, syr. *ḳaysā* 'bois [comme matériau]').[7] Contra S. Kaufman (qui, en outre, n'offre aucun support pour son hypothèse [1974, p. 86]), on ne voit pas de raison de traiter les mots araméens comme des emprunts akkadiens. Tout au contraire, il s'agit d'un cas exemplaire — et assez rare — où le caractère autochtone d'un mot sémitique peut être démontré avec toute une série d'arguments.

(1) Consonantisme: au vu de la sifflante latérale en sudarabique moderne, la correspondance Akk. *š* — Aram. *s* est étymologiquement parfaite et ne suggère pas un emprunt.

(2) Vocalisme et structure morphologique: la diphtongue *-ay-* en syriaque est difficile à imaginer dans un emprunt akkadien mais complètement régulière dans un mot autochtone. De même pour le suffixe féminin *-t-*, évident dans la forme akkadienne mais absent de l'araméen.

(3) Distribution dialectale interne: le mot est bien attesté dans la plupart des langues araméennes et pas uniquement dans les langues les plus exposées à l'influence lexicale de l'akkadien (comme le judéo-babylonien ou le mandéen).

(4) Distribution dialectale externe: comme les termes sudarabiques (apparemment inconnus de Kaufman) le montrent, il ne s'agit pas d'une comparaison bilatérale akkadienne-araméenne mais d'une racine sémitique commune d'une considérable ancienneté.

(5) Sémantique: la correspondance sémantique 'bois' — 'forêt,' bien naturelle pour des mots apparentés génétiquement (voir la polysémie de *bois* ou *wood*) serait inattendue dans le cas d'un emprunt.

3. La désignation akkadienne la plus générale pour 'herbe,' plante herbacée en opposition aux arbres, est ***šammu*** (AHw. 1156, CAD Š/1 315). Jusqu'à présent, on n'a pu tracer ce terme à aucune proto-forme sémitique commune car aucun terme génétiquement apparenté n'est connu dans d'autres langues sémitiques: comme cela est reconnu depuis longtemps, les formes du type **samm-* désignant une herbe médicinale ou un poison dans la plupart des langues ouest-sémitiques (l'hébreu *sam*, le syriaque *sammā* ou l'arabe *samm-*)[8] ne sont que des adaptations du terme akkadien dans ses deux sens dérivés bien attestés.[9]

---

[3] DUL 186, DNWSI 879, HALOT 863.

[4] CDG 57.

[5] Off. ˁḳ 'bois' (DNWSI 879), bibl. *ˀāˁā* id. (HALOT 1821), etc.

[6] ML 242, LS 388.

[7] DJPA 491, LSyr. 665.

[8] HALOT 759, LSyr. 479, Lane 1876, p. 1419.

[9] Il est difficile de prendre au sérieux la proposition de S. Kaufman (1974, p. 100) qui a voulu identifier le mot akkadien avec le *masdar* arabe *šamm-* 'action de flairer' (jamais '*smell*' et encore moins '*perfume*').

Il est intéressant d'observer que, bien que le terme akkadien soit complètement isolé en sémitique, P. Fronzaroli (1969a, pp. 274, 289) a pu reconstruire une proto-forme sémitique **šamm-* sur cette seule base — un cas tout à fait extraordinaire dans le cadre de la stricte méthodologie comparatiste caractérisant les travaux du savant italien. Sa décision a été évidemment conditionnée par l'existence d'un parallèle frappant dans une langue afroasiatique non-sémitique, à savoir l'égyptien: le terme égyptien *sm.w*, attesté depuis les textes des Pyramides, est connu pour avoir une sémantique générale exactement similaire à celle du mot akkadien: 'herbe' en opposition à 'arbre' (Wb. IV 119).

4. Akk. ***dīšu*** 'herbe' (AHw. 173, CAD D 163) est bien attesté dans les deux dialectes anciens, bien qu'on doive noter que le paléo-assyrien *dašʔu* est surtout connu avec le sens dérivé de 'printemps.' Le même sens est attesté pour *dīšu* dans le paléo-babylonien de Mari, mais on doit admettre qu'ici la différence entre 'herbe de printemps' et 'printemps comme saison' est souvent élusive.[10]

Le mot akkadien peut être tracé au proto-sémitique ****daṯʔ***- (Fronzaroli 1969a, pp. 275, 289, 299) qui apparaît comme un terme botanique ('herbe') en héb. *däšäʔ* (HALOT 233), aram. bib. *ditʔā* (HALOT 1856) et syr. *tadʔā* (LSyr. 816, avec métathèse). En même temps, il est indubitable qu'une étroite relation entre 'herbe' et 'printemps' était déjà présente en sémitique commun, comme le montrent ar. *daṯaʔiyy-* 'pluie du printemps' (Dozy I 424), sab. *dṯʔ* 'printemps; récolte de printemps' (SD 36),[11] min. *dṯʔ* id. (LM 26), jib. *dóṯɛʔ* 'pluie de printemps' (JL 42) et soq. *dote* 'printemps' (LS 137).

5. Un autre terme proto-sémitique pour 'herbe' ***ʕVŝb**- (Fronzaroli 1969a, pp. 274–75, 289, 299) est connu principalement par ses réflexes dans le sémitique central, tels que héb. *ʕēŝäb* (HALOT 889), syr. *ʕesbā* (LSyr. 536) et ar. *ʕušb-* (Lane 1876, p. 2050).[12] Ce terme commun n'a laissé que de maigres traces en akkadien, étant possiblement préservé dans le verbe (dénominatif?) *ešēbu* 'pousser exubéramment' (AHw. 253, CAD E 352) ainsi que dans *išbabtu*, désignation d'une espèce d'herbe relativement bien attestée dans les listes lexicales du premier millénaire (AHw. 393, CAD I 233).

II. Noms des parties des plantes

6. Akk. ***šuršu*** 'racine' est bien attesté depuis le paléo-babylonien et, dans les noms propres, dès le sargonique (AHw. 1286, CAD Š/3 363). Selon toute vraisemblance, le sumérien a emprunté ce terme comme suḫuš, avec la correspondance *r* — *ḫ* bien connue par ailleurs (Steiner 2003, p. 643; Civil 2007, p. 31) et un léger changement de sens ('racine' > 'fondation'). Selon certains savants, quelques réflexes de ce terme se trouvent aussi dans la liste lexicale éblaite. Pour M. Krebernik, telle est l'interprétation de *si-li-sa-a*, attesté comme l'équivalent du AN.KI sumérien en VE 781, 'terre' et 'ciel' étant ici interprétés mythologiquement comme "deux racines" (Krebernik 1983, p. 30). Au moins du point de vue de l'orthographe, cette comparaison est possible, car l'usage des signes de la série LV avec les valeurs /rV/ est bien connu à Ebla. Pour G. Conti, il faut plutôt prendre en compte *si-su* dans VE 478, équivalent au sumérien GIŠ.ŠE+NÁM (Conti 1990, pp. 138–39). Dans ce cas, on devrait supposer la réduction du *-r-* préconsonantique, un phénomène peu fréquent mais, néanmoins, attesté avec certitude à Ebla (cf. Krebernik 1997, p. 189). Dans les deux cas, on doit admettre que la structure vocalique de la forme éblaïte était similaire à la

---

[10] Cf. *ina ūm dīšim* dans ARM 2, 130:37, traduit 'au moment du printemps' mais commenté "en mot à mot, 'au moment de l'herbe'" dans Durand 1997, p. 525. Il y a, cependant, quelques passages où le sens 'printemps' paraît assez évident, par exemple *ki-ma ša u₄-um di-ši-[im]* ᵈIM *ri-ig-ma-ti-šu [id-di] [š]a-mu-ú-um iz-nu-un* 'comme par un jour de printemps, Adad a tonné; il a plu' (ARM 23, 102:6-8, référence due à Hervé Reculeau).

[11] Cf. *dathiathum* chez Pline (Biella 1982, p. 86). Noter surtout la coïncidence structurelle entre des paires contrastives comme *ištu dašʔē adi ḫarpē* en paléo-assyrien (CAD Ḫ 106) et *dṯʔ w-ḫrf* en sabéen (Jamme 1962, pp. 431, 437).

[12] Sa présence dans les autres langues ouest-sémitiques est beaucoup moins évidente: sab. *ʕs₃bt* 'pâturage' (SD 21) et qat. *ʕs₃b* 'produits agricoles' (LIQ 126) sont difficiles à comparer car *s₃* dans le sudarabique ancien ne correspond pas régulièrement à la sifflante latérale **ŝ* dans les autres langues, tandis que tig. *ʕešbay* 'une plante à cirres' (WTS 466) paraît plutôt un arabisme.

rare variante ouest-sémitique en *-*i*-, limitée à l'araméen et à l'arabe dialectal, et non pas à la variante en -*u*- de l'akkadien standard et de l'hébreu.

Le terme akkadien doit être tracé au proto-sémitique ***ŝVrš**-, désignation d'une partie de plante de loin la plus répandue dans le domaine sémitique (Fronzaroli 1969a, pp. 276, 290, 299). En même temps, il s'agit d'un terme proto-sémitique avec une histoire phonologique très compliquée dont l'évolution (sans parler de la reconstruction même) reste jusqu'à présent extrêmement problématique.

Directement comparables sont oug. *šrš* (DUL 845), héb. *šōräš* (HALOT 1659), AJP *šrš* (DJPA 568), chacun fonctionnant comme le terme de base pour le concept fondamental de 'racine' dans les langues en question.[13] Le sudarabique ancien *s₂rs₁*, préservé avec le sens dérivé 'base, fondation' (SD 134; LM 88; LIQ 172), est d'une grande importance pour la reconstruction phonologique du mot en question car il permet d'établir avec beaucoup de précision la combinaison originelle des sifflantes. Ainsi, on doit admettre que les termes hébreu et araméen sont phonologiquement innovants, avec une assimilation des sifflantes observée dans le cas parallèle de la désignation proto-sémitique du soleil (héb. *šämäš* vs. SAE *s₂ms₁*). L'akkadien et l'ougaritique n'ajoutent rien à la reconstruction phonologique dans ce cas car dans les deux langues les réflexes de proto-sémitique *ŝ et *š ne se distinguent pas dès leur premiers témoins écrits.

La reconstruction phonologique proposée plus haut semble être supportée par les données de l'arabe classique où *šaras*-, *širs*- représentent, du point de vue phonétique, une évolution directe de proto-sémitique *ŝVrš-. La comparaison entre les formes arabes et le terme proto-sémitique en question reste cependant problématique pour des raisons sémantiques: les mots arabes ne désignent pas la racine (qui est *ʔaṣl*-, d'origine peu claire), mais 'les arbres à épines' (Lane 1876, p. 1532), avec un passage sémantique qui n'est guère évident. Quant à l'arabe *širš* 'racine,' noté dans Dozy I 745 pour les sources post-classiques et bien connu dans les dialectes modernes de la région syrienne, il s'agit plus probablement d'un emprunt araméen et non pas d'un mot arabe autochtone.

On ne peut exclure que d'autres mots apparentés à l'akkadien *šuršu* soient attestés dans le domaine sud-sémitique. Plus particulièrement, il s'agirait de gez. *ŝərw* (CDG 535, avec un grand nombre des parallèles dans les langues modernes) ainsi que de jib. *ŝirɔ́ḫ* (JL 256) et soq. *ŝéraḥ* (LS 433). S'ils sont vraiment en relation avec le terme en question, ces mots doivent préserver sa forme la plus originelle — un élément biconsonantique *ŝVr- — augmenté par -*w* ou -*ḫ* comme 'triconsonantisateurs.' Pour une telle reconstruction, avec ses mérites et ses défauts, voir l'article dédié de A. Faber (1984).

7. Akk. ***zēru*** 'graine, semence,' attesté syllabiquement dès le paléo-assyrien et le paléo-babylonien (AHw. 1521; CAD Z 89), a quelques précédents dans le Vocabulaire d'Ebla (Krebernik 1983, p. 26): *ša-la-um* = sum. ŠE.MAR (VE 659), *ša-la-ù* ⌜NI-*dar-tum*⌝, *šar-ù* NI-*dar-tim*, *še₆-ù a-dar-tù* = sum. ŠE.LÚ*šessig* (VE 684).[14] Le mot akkadien dérive du proto-sémitique ***ḏarʕ**- 'grain, semence' (Fronzaroli 1969b, pp. 9–10, 26, 33), dont des réflexes réguliers sont oug. *ḏrʕ*, *drʕ* (DUL 280)[15] et héb. *zäraʕ* (HALOT 282).

Il est difficile de séparer les termes mentionnés ci-dessus des autres formes probablement apparentées qui présentent, néanmoins, quelques changements phonologiques inattendus.

Le premier type de telles formes "mutilées" est représenté par le syriaque *zarʕā* 'grain, semence' (LSyr. 207) et ses parallèles immédiats dans d'autres langues araméennes ainsi que la racine verbale *zrʕ* 'cultiver' en arabe (Lane 1876, p. 1225). La présence de *z*- au lieu de *d*-/*ḏ*- dans ces formes n'est pas régulière et a été quelquefois regardée comme un indice de l'influence cananéenne (Fronzaroli 1969b, p. 10) — une hypothèse assez difficile à prouver. Dans un cadre purement théorique, on pourrait observer que le *z* en akkadien (ainsi qu'en hébreu) est un réflexe légitime de *z autant que *ḏ-. Une reconstruction *zarʕ- (et non pas *ḏarʕ-) pour ces deux langues est donc possible, mais paraît peu probable au vu des données ougaritiques et éblaïtes (dans le syllabaire éblaïte, le syllabogramme ŠA est régulièrement utilisé pour /ḏa/ mais jamais pour /za/, Krebernik 1982, pp. 211–18).

Un autre type d'irrégularité peut être découvert en gez. *zarʔ* (CDG 642), soq. *deri* 'semence, grain' (LS 135) et sab. *mḏrʔt* 'champ cultivé' (SD 40). Dans chacune de ces langues, le *ʕ proto-sémitique devrait être préservé. Par conséquent, son absence complète ou son remplacement par ʔ restent énigmatiques.

[13] Bien qu'on doive reconnaître qu'en araméen, déjà à l'époque ancienne, *ŝVrš- est sérieusement menacé par *ʕiḳḳār-, qui l'évince finalement dans la plupart des dialectes modernes (Kogan 2005, pp. 519–20).

[14] Le sens du second membre de la dernière locution nous échappe malheureusement.

[15] Avec une double réalisation du *ḏ proto-sémitique bien connue par ailleurs dans cette langue (Tropper 2000, pp. 115–19).

8. Akk. ***ašnan*** est une désignation générale (souvent déifiée) de grain ou de céréale (CAD A/2 450; AHw. 82). W. von Soden, vu l'absence d'étymologie sémitique transparente, a qualifié ce mot comme *Lehnwort unbekannter Herkunft*. Toujours conscient du caractère assez osé d'une telle comparaison, on se demande si le mot akkadien pourrait être apparenté à la désignation principale du grain en soqotri (*šáne*, LS 145), à son tour évidemment en relation avec méh. *məhnōy* 'une ferme, un champ cultivé' (ML 159) et jib. *ešné* 'cultiver un jardin, un champ' (JL 263). En outre, bien que la comparaison chamito-sémitique (ou afroasiatique) ne fasse pas l'objet de cette recherche étymologique, il est difficile d'omettre dans ce cas particulier que certains termes pour 'grain, semence' phonétiquement très proches des termes sémitiques en question sont connus depuis longtemps dans le domaine couchitique oriental (Oromo *saňňi*, Somali *šuni*).[16]

9. Akk. ***perʾu*** 'pousse, germe, rejeton, feuille,' bien attesté syllabiquement depuis le paléo-assyrien et le paléo-babylonien (CAD P 416; AHw. 856), a été souvent comparé à proto-sémitique **parḫ*- 'germe, fleur,' représenté par héb. *päraḥ* 'germe' (HALOT 966), syr. *parḥā* 'fleur' (LSyr. 594) et ar. *farḫ*- 'rejeton' (Lane 1876, p. 2362). Une comparaison alternative assez répandue est avec proto-sémitique **piry*- 'fruit': oug. *pr* (DUL 678), héb. *pərī* (HALOT 967), AJP *pyryyh* (DJPA 446), gez. *fəre* (CDG 167), jib. *frét* (JL 59).

Bien qu'on ne puisse pas exclure une relation éventuelle entre ces trois groupes des mots (Fronzaroli 1969a, p. 276), une identification immédiate avec le terme akkadien semble impossible dans les deux cas, car l'akkadien *ʾ* (écrit avec les signes de la série ḪV dans les périodes anciennes) ne correspond jamais ni à **ḫ*, ni à **y* du proto-sémitique. En fait, l'histoire de "l'aleph fort" akkadien reste très peu étudiée, mais une recherche même superficielle montre qu'une des sources principales de "l'aleph fort" est l'uvulaire sonore *ɣ.[17] Effectivement, une recherche dans cette direction permet de découvrir quelques parallèles intéressants dans le sudarabique moderne, à savoir méh. *fátrəɣ* 'fleurir' (ML 98) et jib. *férəɣ* 's'ouvrir (une fleur)' (JL 60). Probablement apparentés sont aussi syr. *perʿā* 'germe, rejeton' (LSyr. 603) et tna. *färrəʿe* 'fleurir' (TED 2667).

10. Le concept de feuille, une notion importante du vocabulaire de base au point de faire partie de la *hundred word list* de Morris Swadesh, n'est que peu développé dans le lexique akkadien, du moins dans les textes qui nous sont accessibles. Le seul candidat qu'on peut reconnaître est ***aru***, attesté aussi comme *eru* et *ḫaru* (la dernière forme dans la lettre paléo-babylonienne YOS 2, 2:20), avec une variante féminine *artu* (CAD A/2 311; AHw. 71), que les auteurs du CAD A/2 traduisent comme *frond*, *leaf*, et *foliage*. Ces termes, dont le premier est d'ordinaire appliqué aux feuilles du palmier et a par conséquent été discuté en détail par B. Landsberger dans son ouvrage sur le palmier-dattier en Mésopotamie (1967, pp. 16, 23–27), sont étymologiquement obscurs. Dans notre étude sur les réflexes akkadiens du *ɣ proto-sémitique (Kogan 2001, p. 282), nous les avons comparés, à titre d'hypothèse, avec l'arabe *ɣār*- 'feuilles de la vigne' (Lane 1876, p. 2308). Cette comparaison, peu assurée du fait de l'attestation assez marginale du mot arabe, est néanmoins attractive phonologiquement, car l'oscillation entre *a*/*e* d'un côté et *ḫ* de l'autre est bien connue dans les mots akkadiens ayant *ɣ dans le proto-type.[18]

11. Akk. ***šubultu*** 'épi,' bien attesté depuis le paléo-babylonien (AHw. 1258, CAD Š/3 187), peut être facilement tracé à proto-sémitique ****šu(n)bul-at***- (Fronzaroli 1969b, pp. 12, 27, 34) représenté par oug. *šblt* (DUL 805), héb. *šibbōlät* (HALOT 1394), syr. *šeblā* (LSyr. 752), ar. *sabalat*-, *sunbulat*- (Lane 1876, p. 1440), sab. s_1*blt* (SD 123), gez. *sabl* (CDG 484), méh. *səbəlēt* (ML 340), soq. *seboleh* (LS 280). La structure vocalique du mot akkadien est très proche de celle des formes arabe et hébraïque.[19] En revanche, l'absence de redoublement du -*b*- est inattendue au vu de la présence constante du redoublement (ou d'un -*n*-) dans le reste du sémitique.

12. Akk. ***tibnu*** 'paille,' connu depuis le paléo-assyrien et le paléo-babylonien (CAD T 380, AHw. 1354), dérive du proto-sémitique ****tibn***- (Fronzaroli 1969b, pp. 12, 27, 34) avec le même sens, dont témoignent héb. *täbän* (HALOT 1685), syr. *tebnā* (LSyr. 814) et ar. *tabn*-, *tibn*- (Lane 1876, p. 297).

---

[16] Pour ce rapprochement, voir Militarev 1999, p. 394.

[17] Telle était la conclusion préliminaire de notre étude portant sur les réflexes akkadiens du *ɣ proto-sémitique (Kogan 2001, pp. 292–93). La même opinion se trouve, plus explicitement formulée, dans le récent article de B. Kouwenberg (2006, p. 152). Il suffit de mentionner quelques exemples évidents comme akk. *buʾʾû* 'chercher, demander, vouloir' vs. ar. *bɣy*, akk. *perʾašu* 'puce' vs. ar. *burɣūṯ*- ou akk. *ruʾtu* 'jus, mucus, résine' vs. ar. *ruɣwat*-.

[18] Pour cette correspondance phonétique voir akk. *āribu*/*ḫāribu*/*ēribu* 'corbeau' vs. ar. *ɣurāb*- ou akk. *apāru*/*ḫapāru*/*epēru* 'couvrir la tête' vs. ar. *ɣfr* (Kogan 2001, pp. 278–82).

[19] Le passage de **u* à *i* dans une syllabe doublement fermée non accentuée est bien connu en hébreu comme en témoignent des exemples tels que héb. *qippod* vs. ar. *qunfuḏ*- 'hérisson' (Huehnergard 1992, p. 222).

III. Plantes sauvages: les herbes

La terminologie proto-sémitique des herbes sauvages est relativement pauvre, et seule une petite partie de ces termes communs est préservée par la langue akkadienne. Les cinq lexèmes suivants sont les plus certains des points de vue philologique et étymologique.

13. Akk. ***daddaru***, interprété comme *an ill-smelling, thorny plant* dans CAD D 17,[20] est possiblement attesté la première fois par le toponyme *Da-da-rí-im* dans le texte sargonique Ancient Kudurrus 38 i 8–9 (1 BUR GÀN *šu pà-la-ag Da-da-rí-im* '18 *iku* du terrain sur "le canal du chardon").[21] La première attestation certaine se trouve dans la composition littéraire paléo-babylonienne du type "juste souffrant." Il s'agit de la tablette AO 4462 (Nougayrol 1952), rééditée avec un commentaire détaillé par W. Lambert (1987). La ligne 29 de ce texte indique:

> *pi-ya-am ma-la*$^{?}$*-am tu-ma-ar-ri-ra-am da-an-ni-iš* x x x x*-tu-šu i-wi da-da-ar-šu*
>
> 'tu m'as rempli la bouche avec des choses amères, gravement, son ... est devenu comme la plante *daddaru*.'

Le sens de ce passage, malheureusement endommagé, peut être facilement compris grâce à quelques évidents parallèles dans les textes du premier millénaire, tels que Ludlul II 88–89:

> *àš-na-an šum-ma da-ad-da-riš a-la-*$^{?}$*-ut*
> ^{d}*siraš nap-šat* UN.MEŠ UGU*-ia im-tar-ṣu*
>
> 'le grain, comme si c'était la plante *daddaru*, j'avale,
> la bière, l'esprit des hommes, est amère pour moi.'

Il s'agit, donc, d'une plante avec un goût (et/ou une odeur) prototypiquement déplaisant.

Une autre catégorie de contexte stéréotypé où *daddaru* est attesté se trouve dans quelques textes du premier millénaire dans lesquels ce mot apparaît, en combinaison avec *giṣṣu*, comme une désignation de plante épineuse:

> GIŠ.TIR.MEŠ *akšiṭ-ma giṣṣu daddaru girriš aḳmu*
>
> 'j'ai abattu les forêts, j'ai brûlé les *giṣṣu* et les *daddaru*.' (*Iraq* 16, 192:69)

Prises ensemble, ces données textuelles permettent une identification étymologique assez certaine avec le terme proto-sémitique ****dardar****- 'chardon' (Fronzaroli 1969a, pp. 276, 289, 299), avec une réduction de la structure quadriconsonantique propre à la langue akkadienne (cf. *ḳaḳḳaru* 'terrain' < proto-sémitique **ḳarḳar-* ou *kakkabu* 'étoile' < proto-sémitique **kabkab-*).

Ce terme est représenté par ailleurs par héb. *dardar* (HALOT 230), syr. *dardrā* (LSyr. 166), gez. *dandar*, *dader* (CDG 123, 136), tna. *dander*, *dandär* (TED 2130), amh. *dändär* (AED 1804).

Dans deux passages de l'Ancien Testament, le terme hébraïque parallèle *dardar* apparaît dans la combinaison stéréotypée *ḳōṣ wə-dardar*[22] qui désigne des mauvaises herbes, des qualités comme mauvaise odeur, amertume ou épines n'étant pas précisées:

> *ḳōṣ wə-dardar taṣmīăḥ lāk* 'elle (la terre) va produire des mauvaises herbes pour toi.' (la fameuse "malédiction agraire" de Genèse 3:18)
>
> *ḳōṣ wə-dardar yaʕălā ʕal-mizbəḥōtām* 'des mauvaises herbes vont croître sur leurs autels.' (Hosée 10:8)

---

[20] Traduit par ailleurs comme (*stinkende*) *Flockenblume* dans AHw. 148.

[21] Proposé avec hésitation par Gelb, Steinkeller, et Whiting 1991, p. 115 (sur l'importance linguistique de cette collocation, voir Sommerfeld 2010, p. 154). Le contexte de *da-da-rí-im* dans la ligne III 11′ du texte littéraire sargonique UmH 342a (Biggs 1989) est malheureusement trop peu certain pour une identification convaincante.

[22] Il est difficile de ne pas rapprocher la locution hébraïque de l'akkadien *giṣṣu daddaru*, bien que l'équivalence entre *giṣṣu* et *ḳōṣ* (observée avec hésitation dans HALOT 1090) ne soit pas parfaite du point de vue de la phonologie historique: la dissimilation **ḳ* > *g* (au lieu de *k*) n'est pas usuelle; la structure vocalique est différente; en hébreu, il ne s'agit pas d'une racine géminée comme le montre clairement le pluriel *ḳōṣīm*.

L'histoire de ce terme en arabe pose d'intéressants problèmes qu'il vaut la peine d'exposer ici. Aucun mot comparable ne semble être enregistré pour la langue classique, car le terme *dardār-* (Lane 1876, p. 864), avec un *a* long et désignant une espèce d'arbre ('orme'), peut difficilement être en relation avec la racine en question. Quelques exemples de *dardar* '*tribulus*' provenant des sources post-classiques ont été notés dans Dozy I 432 mais, comme W. Leslau l'observe justement (CDG 136), il ne s'agit que des transcriptions de *dardar* hébraïque dans les traductions bibliques. En même temps, quelques formes évidemment apparentées ont été notées pour les dialectes arabes modernes de l'Arabie du sud, à savoir *durdurin* dans les parlers du Yémen du Nord (Behnstedt 369). Compte tenu de la présence de notre terme dans le domaine éthiopien, il ne nous paraît pas trop osé de supposer qu'il s'agit ici d'un mot appartenant au substrat sudarabique, dont l'absence dans les sources épigraphiques n'est guère surprenante pour ce type de corpus.

14. Akk. ***ašlu*** 'jonc,' un terme relativement peu utilisé dans les textes mésopotamiens depuis le moyen babylonien (AHw. 81, CAD A/2 449), a un excellent précédent à Ebla (*a-sa-lu* = sum. Ú.NINNI$_5$ dans VE 300), identifié depuis longtemps par M. Krebernik (1983, p. 13) et E. Zurro (1983, p. 265). Il est difficile d'énoncer une opinion cohérente sur la possible identité de ce terme botanique avec *ašlu* comme nom de corde et comme mesure de longueur.[23]

Akk. *ašlu* doit être tracé au proto-sémitique ***ˀašal-*** 'jonc' (Fronzaroli 1969a, pp. 276, 289, 299), qui se base, par ailleurs, sur l'arabe *ˀasal-* (Lane 1876, p. 59) avec le même sens.[24]

15. Beaucoup plus répandu est ***ḳanû*** 'roseau, canne,' bien attesté depuis le paléo-assyrien et le paléo-babylonien (AHw. 898, CAD Q 85). Le terme akkadien dérive sans problème du proto-sémitique **ḳanay-* (Fronzaroli 1969a, pp. 276, 290, 299), bien connu par ses réflexes en oug. *ḳn* (DUL 704), héb. *ḳānā* (HALOT 1113), syr. *ḳanyā* (LSyr. 677) et ar. *qanāt-* (Lane 1876, p. 2994).[25]

Pour l'histoire phonétique du mot akkadien (ainsi que celle de son ancêtre proto-sémitique) ce sont les écritures dites "brisées" en paléo-assyrien (*ḳá-nu-e*, *ḳá-na-im*) qui sont surtout intéressantes. Un bel exemple de ce type se trouve dans la légende sargonique paléo-assyrienne, publiée par C. Günbattı (1997) et récemment rééditée par J. G. Dercksen:

> *ša* NA$_4$.GUG *ù* NA$_4$.ZA.GÌN *ḳà-nu-a-am lu ar-ku-ús* (ll. 44–46),

interprété par Dercksen (2005, p. 109) comme

> 'j'ai pris une canne de mesure décorée de cornaline et de lapis-lazuli.'[26]

---

[23] Pour une réponse affirmative à cette question, voir le traitement de W. von Soden dans AHw.; pour deux lexèmes différents, voir les pages correspondantes du volume A/2 du CAD.

[24] Cette reconstruction n'a aucune relation à proto-sémitique *ˀaṯl- (*ˀiṯl-) 'tamaris,' absent de l'akkadien, mais répandu dans presque tout le domaine ouest-sémitique: héb. *ˀēšäl* (HALOT 95), ar. *ˀaṯl-* (Lane 1876, p. 21), sab. *ˀṯl* (SD 9), méh. *ḥōṯəl* (ML 9), soq. *ʕˀitɔl* (Morris 2002, p. 51). Une élégante explication pour cette lacune a été proposée par P. Fronzaroli (1969a, p. 279), qui observe, à juste titre, que les langues ne faisant pas de distinction entre les réflexes des *ṯ et *š ne préservent qu'une seule des deux désignations botaniques phonétiquement similaires, à savoir *ˀVṯl- 'tamaris' ou *ˀašal- 'jonc.' Ainsi, l'hébreu a choisi la première possibilité, tandis que l'akkadien a opté pour la seconde. En revanche, en arabe, où les deux sifflantes sont préservées, l'opposition entre *ˀasal-* 'jonc' et *ˀaṯl-* 'tamaris' a gardé sa valeur.

[25] Il est curieux d'observer que le sens 'roseau, canne,' toujours enregistré pour le mot arabe dans les dictionnaires comparés des langues sémitiques (e.g., HALOT 1113), est plutôt évité par les lexicographes traditionnels qui préfèrent définir *qanāt-* comme 'quelque chose *semblable* à la canne,' elle-même appelée *qaṣab-* (cf. LA 15 235–36).

[26] "*I did take a measuring rod (decorated with) carnelian and lapis lazuli.*" À la page 113 de son étude, Dercksen présente une riche collection d'exemples provenant des textes littéraires sumériens où l'image de la canne de mesure décorée de pierres précieuses est attestée. Toutefois, l'usage de *rakāsu* 'lier' dans le texte paléo-assyrien offre un redoutable obstacle pour cette interprétation, car ce verbe peut difficilement être compris comme 'prendre' ou 'faire.' La traduction proposée par A. Cavigneaux ("j'avais noué une botte de cornaline et de lapis-lazuli," 2005, p. 599) nous paraît plus attractive: étant parvenu au jardin enchanté, Sargon aurait cueilli une véritable gerbe des précieux roseaux minéraux, qu'il "a distribuée à son pays" après cette formidable aventure. La ressemblance phonétique entre *ḳanuˀum* 'roseau' et *uḳnuˀum* 'lapis-lazuli' aurait pu jouer un certain rôle dans la création de cette image un peu inattendue: bien que la désignation régulière de cette pierre en paléo-assyrien était *ḫusārum* (Michel 2001), le terme babylonien était certainement bien connu de l'auteur de cette remarquable œuvre littéraire.

La présence de la troisième radicale "faible" est aussi évidente dans le précédent éblaïte *ḳá-nu-wu* = sum. GIŠ. GI (VE 416; Krebernik 1983, p. 16). La présence de *-u* dans les formes paléo-assyriennes ainsi que celle du *w* dans la forme éblaïte fait penser à une reconstruction proto-sémitique **ḳanaw-* au lieu du **ḳanay-* énoncé ci-dessus.[27]

16. Akk. ***elpetu*** 'jonc,' bien attesté depuis le paléo-babylonien (AHw. 205; CAD E 108), a été depuis longtemps identifié avec les désignations de l'herbe alfa dans les langues ouest-sémitiques: héb. rabbinique *ḥēläp* (Jastrow 156), syr. *ḥulpā* (LSyr. 237), arb. *ḥalaf-* (Lane 1876, p. 627). Sur cette base, on peut reconstruire un terme botanique proto-sémitique ***ḥVlp(-at)-** (Fronzaroli 1969a, pp. 276, 289, 299), avec une structure vocalique peu claire.

17. Akk. ***peḳû, peḳḳūtu*** 'coloquinte,' peu attesté si ce n'est dans les listes de plantes du premier millénaire (AHw. 854; CAD P 326), peut difficilement être séparé des termes ouest-sémitiques qui désignent la même plante, une espèce de courge sauvage, comme héb. *paḳḳūʕā* (HALOT 960), syr. *paḳḳūʕā* (LSyr. 590), ar. *fuqqāʕ-* (Lane 1876, p. 2428). Le mot hébraïque est attesté dans le contexte remarquable du deuxième livre des Rois (4:39) qui parle des qualités vénéneuses (ou, au moins, de l'extrême amertume) des *paḳḳūʕōt ŝādā*, littéralement "les coloquintes sauvages," dont l'effet a été neutralisé par Elisée à l'aide d'une poignée de farine (Cogan et Tadmor 1988, p. 58).[28]

Tandis qu'on pourrait supposer un araméisme en arabe, la relation entre les termes akkadien et hébraïque peut seulement être celle de mots apparentés génétiquement et non pas d'emprunts grâce à la conduite spécifique de *ʕ proto-sémitique en akkadien (chute accompagnée par une coloration en *e*). Ainsi, postuler un terme botanique proto-sémitique **pVḳVʕ-* nous paraît inévitable.

IV. Plantes sauvages: les arbres

18. Akk. ***buṭnu, buṭumtu*** 'térébinthe' (AHw. 144, CAD B 358–59) a reçu un traitement extrêmement détaillé dans une monographie de M. Stol (1979). Le livre de Stol, dont le niveau de discussion assyriologique ainsi que sémitologique est sans précédent dans l'histoire de la recherche sur la terminologie botanique akkadienne, laisse peu d'espace pour une présentation vraiment originale. Par conséquent, on doit se restreindre à une exposition commentée des résultats obtenus par Stol, tout en mettant en relief quelques aspects moins discutés ou problématiques.

On doit commencer sans doute avec la controverse bien connue sur l'identification botanique de la plante en question: 'térébinthe' (*Pistacia atlantica* ou *Pistacia terebinthus*) ou 'pistache' (*Pistacia vera*)?

D'un côté, Stol attire notre attention sur la théorie selon laquelle l'introduction de la pistache au Proche-orient doit être un phénomène assez récent, probablement pas plus ancien que les conquêtes d'Alexandre le Grand, les lieux d'origine de cette plante étant l'Iran oriental, l'Afghanistan et l'Asie Centrale, une théorie avancée par V. Hehn dès 1902 et qui, selon Stol, reste en accord avec les données paléobotaniques et archéologiques modernes.

D'un autre côté, Stol met en évidence plusieurs témoignages sur l'usage pratique de la noix de térébinthe dans le Proche-Orient moderne, y compris ses qualités comestibles. Ainsi, l'identification de *buṭnu, buṭumtu* avec le térébinthe devient — contrairement à une conception assez répandue — compatible avec leur usage alimentaire illustré par les documents de la pratique.

En somme, Stol s'oppose radicalement au traitement indifférencié de deux concepts par von Soden ('*Terebinthe; Pistazie*') ainsi qu'à la différenciation — pour lui artificielle — *buṭnu* '*terebinth*' et *buṭumtu* '*pistachio tree* (*Pistacia Vera*)' faite par les auteurs du CAD. Pour Stol, toute la variété phonologique et morphologique des termes en question ne s'applique qu'au térébinthe.

En effet, la variation phonologique et morphologique est extrêmement prononcée dans le cas du mot en question, et c'est un grand mérite de Stol que d'en offrir une présentation systématique, organisée par forme et par période d'attestation. Au vu de cette collection, la forme paléo-babylonienne la plus courante est *buṭumtu*, écrite

[27] La situation est donc tout à fait similaire à celle que l'on observe dans le cas bien connu du mot akkadien pour la montagne, *šadû* dans le babylonien classique, mais avec un grand nombre d'écritures "brisées" sargoniques (*śa-dú-e, śa-dú-im*) et paléo-assyriennes (*ša-ad-wi-im, ša-du-im*), voir Kienast 1994, pp. 278–80 et CAD Š/1 51 respectivement. Le **-y* et le **-w* n'étant pas différenciés dans cette position en hébreu, il n'est pas étonnant que la forme hébraïque *ŝādā* 'champ' (HALOT 1307) soit exactement parallèle à *ḳānā* 'canne.'

[28] Curieusement, la plante d'où les fruits ont été cueillis est décrite comme "une vigne sauvage" (*gäpän ŝādā*).

avec le signe TU (*ṭú*) mais, assez souvent, aussi avec DU, dont la lecture *ṭù* n'est pas usuelle dans les régions concernées (par exemple, Mari). D'ici viennent les doutes de Stol sur la prononciation véritable de ce terme ("*buṭumtum* or *budumtum*"). Les formes avec un *-n-* explicite, plutôt rares dans les périodes anciennes (paléo-assyrien *bu*-UD-*ni-ni* dans TCL 4, 42r:4, paléo-babylonien de Mari *bu*-UD-*na-tim* dans ARM 10, 116:28), ne deviennent communes que dans les textes du premier millénaire. Les formes avec un *-t-* double, dû à l'assimilation du *-n-* préconsonantique (connues dès le paléo-babylonien) appartiennent, elles aussi, à cette dernière catégorie.

Pour Stol, la première attestation de ce lexème est le nom propre sargonique *bu*-TU-*um-tum* (Gelb 1957, p. 103). Dès 1979, d'autres exemples plus anciens et surtout plus assurés ont été découverts dans la grande liste lexicale éblaite: bu_{16}(NI)-*ṭù-tù* = sum. GIŠ.IŠ$_{11}$ dans VE 462 et *a-kà-lu bù-ṭa-ma-tim* = sum. NINDA.LAM dans VE 32b. La dernière locution a été interprétée comme '*Terebinthenbrot*' par M. Krebernik, qui ne donne aucune référence sur la nature de la substance en question. P. Fronzaroli (1984a, p. 134) n'est pas beaucoup plus explicite ('*cake (made) with terebinth nuts*'). Dans ce contexte, il est intéressant de noter que M. Stol, qui — en 1979 — ignorait évidemment les données éblaïtes, ne manque pas de mentionner le logogramme NINDA GIŠ.LAM.GAL, attesté dans quelques textes hittites. En s'appuyant sur les données des voyageurs européens du XIX siècle (Grèce et Jebel Sinjar irakien), Stol offre deux explications alternatives: pain à l'huile de térébinthe ou un véritable "pain des pauvres," préparé avec la farine obtenue des noix de térébinthe.

Dans les documents économiques mariotes, *bu*-TU-*um-tum* ou *bu*-DU-*um-tum* est souvent appliqué à une céréale (probablement, un type d'épeautre). Il est difficile de nier une certaine relation étymologique entre ce terme et la désignation de la noix de térébinthe, mais la nature du passage sémantique reste à expliquer. Pour Stol, il s'agirait d'une céréale qui n'est pas complètement mûre, donc "verte" et, par conséquence, comparable à la chair verte de la noix de térébinthe. Comme argument, Stol fait une intéressante comparaison entre le nom allemand d'un type d'épeautre (*Grünkorn*) et la désignation dialectale arabe de la noix de térébinthe *ḥabbat al-ḫaḍrā* 'grain vert.'

Étymologiquement, l'akkadien *buṭnu*, *buṭumtu* est apparenté au terme proto-sémitique reconstruit par P. Fronzaroli comme **buṭm(-at)-* (1969a, pp. 278, 290, 300), représenté par ailleurs par oug. *bṭm* (Pardee 2002, pp. 176–77, Watson 2004, p. 114),[29] héb. *boṭnīm* (HALOT 121), AJP *bwṭnh*, *boṭmā* (DJPA 87, 91), syr. *beṭmtā* (LSyr. 67), arb. *buṭm-* (Lane 1876, p. 219). Les formes *bəṭm*, *buṭm* en éthiopien classique et quelques formes néo-éthiopiennes apparentées sont considérées, probablement à juste titre, comme empruntées à l'arabe (CDG 114).

La seule référence aux *boṭnīm* dans l'Ancien Testament est en Genèse 43:11, où ce terme apparaît dans la liste des cadeaux présentés aux Egyptiens par les fils de Jacob, au côté de *dəbaš* 'miel,' de plusieurs sortes de substances aromatiques (*ṣŏrī*, *nəkāʾōt*, *lōṭ*) et de *šəḳēdīm* 'amandes,' ne paraît pas très informative. Quelques exemples connus des sources rabbiniques ont été soigneusement analysés par I. Löw (1881, pp. 43–44), dont l'identification ('térébinthe' et non pas 'pistache') et les arguments utilisés pour la soutenir sont assez comparables à ceux de Stol.

Il nous reste à traiter l'alternance entre *m* et *n* comme dernière consonne radicale. Pour Stol, la principale raison de cette alternance est l'incompatibilité des deux consonnes labiales dans la racine: ainsi, la forme originelle **buṭm(-at)-* devient *buṭn(-at)-* grâce à la dissimilation des labiales. Dans sa forme générale, cette hypothèse doit être correcte, comme le montrent quelques exemples similaires découverts par Stol à l'intérieur de la langue akkadienne ainsi qu'entre des mots akkadiens et leur parallèles dans les autres langues sémitiques: *baḳāmu*/*baḳānu* 'tondre,' *pasāmu*/*pasānu* 'couvrir,' *pēmu*/*pēnu* 'jambe' (cf. héb. *paʿam* vs. oug. *pʿn*), akk. *bašmu*/ar. *baṯan-*, oug. *bṯn* 'serpent (mythique),' akk. *ubānu*, héb. *bōhän*/ar. *ʾibhām-* 'doigt.' Si le modèle général est assez clair, les détails — comme l'admet Stol lui-même — restent souvent énigmatiques. Par exemple, Stol est enclin à considérer les formes *baḳānu* et *pasānu* comme typiquement assyriennes, en expliquant comme assyrianismes les pluriels en *-n-* (*bu*-UD-*na-tum*, *bu*-UD-*na-tim*) dans les textes paléo-babyloniens de Mari. Il est difficile de nier, cependant, qu'au moins pour *baḳānu* 'tondre' quelques formes en *n* peuvent être trouvées dans les textes où une influence assyrienne serait difficile à imaginer (par exemple, *ib-ḳú-un-šu-m[a]* dans la version paléo-babylonienne du mythe d'Etana, V 6′). Par ailleurs, le même phénomène de l'influence lexicale assyrienne dans le corpus mariote (pour Stol, "*not uncommon*") reste à être soigneusement étudié.[30] En somme, un certain degré de variation au niveau

---

[29] Dans la l. 10′ de l'inédit RS 94.2276:10′.

[30] Cf. Kogan 2006, p. 213.

synchronique peut difficilement être exclu pour la plupart des mots mentionnés ci-dessus. Dans le cas de *buṭnu*, *buṭumtu* cette variation peut être stimulée par le contact entre *-*m*- et les deux dentales (*ṭ* et *t*) qui l'entourent.[31]

19. Akk. ***bīnu*** (CAD B 239; AHw. 127) est le principal terme pour tamaris, attesté syllabiquement dès le sargonique (10 GIŠ *bí-num* dans HSS 10, 38 iii 10) et avec un excellent parallèle dans la liste lexicale éblaïte: *ì-ṣú ba-ne, ba-nu* = sum. GIŠ.ŠINIG (VE 395; Zurro 1983, p. 265).

Ce mot a reçu des traitements étymologiques très divers. Pour quelques savants, la seule forme génétiquement apparentée à *bīnu* est le syriaque *bīnā*, désignant la même espèce botanique, le tamaris.[32] Telle est, par exemple, l'opinion de M. Streck qui a récemment dédié à ce terme une intéressante étude (2004, pp. 251–52). On doit observer, cependant, que l'identité complète entre les deux termes tant dans la forme qu'au niveau du sens signale probablement un emprunt akkadien en syriaque, une opinion énoncée déjà depuis longtemps par C. Brockelmann dans LSyr. 69.

En revanche, les véritables parallèles génétiques pour le mot akkadien peuvent être trouvés en arabe et en sabéen, à savoir, l'arabe *bān*- (Lane 1876, p. 278) et le sabéen *bn* (SD 33). Cette comparaison est loin d'être originale, ayant été proposée par Brockelmann et acceptée dans DRS 62. On trouve surprenant, par conséquent, qu'elle ne soit guère mentionnée dans l'étude encyclopédique sur les noms des plantes sudarabiques anciens par A. Sima (2000, pp. 198–99), tandis que Streck la rejette explicitement dans son article mentionné ci-dessus. La principale raison pour cette décision est évidemment d'ordre sémantique: comme Sima l'a clairement démontré, les termes arabiques ne désignent pas le tamaris mais s'appliquent à un arbre tout à fait différent, à savoir, le *moringa*.[33]

La nature de la controverse est donc méthodologique: la différence biologique entre les espèces est-elle un obstacle pour la comparaison étymologique entre les mots qui les désignent? À notre avis, la réponse est un énergique "non." En effet, il suffit de feuilleter chacun des grands dictionnaires étymologiques des langues indo-européennes pour se convaincre que, dans le domaine de la terminologie biologique, les changements historiques des *signifiés* peuvent être vraiment drastiques, souvent beaucoup plus drastiques que ceux observés pour leur *signifiants*. En ce qui concerne les langues sémitiques, quelques exemples de la terminologie zoologique (d'habitude beaucoup plus concrète pour nous que la terminologie botanique) peuvent être assez frappants. Par exemple: doit-on cesser de comparer l'hébreu *zəʔēb* avec l'akkadien *zību* et l'amharique *ǯəb* (SED II no. 72) sous prétexte que le premier terme désigne le loup, le second, le vautour et le troisième, la hyène? Probablement, non. Un autre exemple: doit-on nier la relation étymologique entre la forme *ṣa-ba-ú* 'ours' dans une liste lexicale émariote (= sum. AZ, akk. *a-su*, Emar 551:37') et les désignations sémitiques de la hyène (ar. *ḍabuʕ*-, héb. *ṣābūaʕ*, SED II no. 220)?

En somme, le fait que les mots phonétiquement comparables peuvent souvent désigner des espèces biologiques plus ou moins différentes ne doit pas être perçu comme un argument contre leur éventuelle parenté étymologique. Tout au contraire, une telle différence peut offrir d'importants arguments *en faveur de* la parenté: c'est précisément l'évolution du sens qui caractérise la parenté génétique, tandis que sa préservation statique est souvent une marque de l'emprunt.

Au vu de ces considérations, postuler une reconstruction proto-sémitique **bay(a)n*- comme un terme désignant une espèce d'arbre (certes, difficile à préciser botaniquement) nous paraît inévitable. En arabe, la combinaison triphtongique *-*aya*- aboutit régulièrement à un *a* long. À Ebla, l'écriture *ba-na* doit probablement être interprétée comme /bayna/, au vu des plusieurs exemples similaires dont le plus connu est *a-na-a* /ʕaynā/, /ʕaynay/ 'les deux yeux' (Fronzaroli 1984b, pp. 155–56). La forme akkadienne standard, avec la contraction *-*ay*- > -*ī*- apparaît ainsi comme la plus évoluée.

20. Une autre désignation akkadienne du tamaris, ***ṭarpaʔu***, est relativement bien attestée depuis le babylonien moyen (AHw. 1382; CAD Ṭ 62). Comme il est connu depuis longtemps, le terme akkadien trouve un parallèle tout à fait frappant en arabe classique où *ṭarfāʔ*- désigne la même espèce d'arbre (Lane 1876, p. 1844). À notre connaissance, aucun intermédiaire araméen n'est connu dans ce cas, ce qui rend peu probable un akkadisme en

[31] Il est intéressant de noter que le même type de variation est observé aussi en dehors de la langue akkadienne, à savoir, dans l'araméen judéo-palestinien: cf. *mšḥ d-bwṭnyn* (fragments targoumiques de la Geniza) et *mšḥ də-boṭmin* (Targoum Neofiti) qui désignent l'huile de térébinthe dans deux versions targoumiques palestiniennes de Genèse 43:11 (on doit admettre que dans le premier cas, une influence hébraïque ne peut pas être exclue).

[32] L'identification de l'ougaritique *bnt* avec ce terme botanique (DUL 233; Watson 2004, p. 114) nous paraît assez osée; voir del Olmo Lete 2004, p. 313.

[33] Tel est aussi le sens du jibbali *yēn* signalé par M. Morris (2002, p. 57).

arabe. Encore plus exotique serait une hypothèse postulant un arabisme dans les textes akkadiens de la période médio-babylonienne. Dans de telles conditions, notre méthodologie nous force à reconstruire une forme proto-sémitique quadriconsonantique ***ṭarpaʔ**- 'tamaris,' à moins que l'on suppose un emprunt indépendant en akkadien et en arabe d'une troisième langue inconnue, une hypothèse attractive mais absolument impossible à vérifier pour le moment.

21. Akk. ***eṭṭettu*** désigne un arbre ou un arbrisseau épineux (selon les auteurs du CAD E 23, *lycium barbarum*, anglais boxthorn). Le mot est surtout attesté dans les textes littéraires et les listes lexicales du premier millénaire, avec un seul précédent plus ancien dans la version d'Amarna du texte épique connu sur le nom de *šar tamḫāri* 'Roi de bataille' (Goodnick Westenholz 1997, p. 120, l. 31). Toutefois, un précédent éblaïte a été correctement identifié par E. Zurro (1983, p. 264) dans VE 436: *a-ṭa-dum* = sum. GIŠ.ÁD.

Traditionnellement, le mot akkadien est comparé à plusieurs désignations d'arbres épineux dans les langues ouest-sémitiques, à savoir, héb. *ʔāṭād* (HALOT 37), syr. *ʔaṭādā* (PS 131, SL 30), ar. *ʔaṭad-* (LA 3 88). C'est sur cette base que la reconstruction proto-sémitique ***ʔaṭad**- a été développée par P. Fronzaroli (1969a, pp. 278, 291, 300). Tandis que l'attestation des mots arabe et syriaque est plutôt problématique, l'hébreu *ʔāṭād* est clairement attesté dans deux passages de l'Ancien Testament.[34] Comme I. Löw l'a souligné depuis longtemps (1881, pp. 44–45, 404), la forme hébraïque trouve un intéressant parallèle punique chez Dioscoride, à savoir αταδιν, expliqué par le grec ῥάμνος.

D'autres parallèles moins assurés ont été proposés pour les mots en question dans l'histoire de la recherche. Il en va ainsi, par exemple, de quelques formes araméennes comme syr. *haṭṭā* (LSyr. 174) et mand. *ʔṭʔṭʔ* (MD 13) avec une assimilation des dentales et un changement sporadique des gutturales. Certaines formes néo-éthiopiennes, à savoir *aṭaṭ* en amharique et gouragué (AED 1340, EDG 110),[35] sont superficiellement similaires, mais une étude phonologique plus approfondie montre que le prototype de ces formes a eu deux *ʕayns* dans la racine (tna. *ʕaṭʕaṭ*, TED 1939). Leur relation éventuelle avec le proto-sémitique **ʔaṭad-* devient, par conséquent, assez problématique.

On doit rappeler que l'identification de *eṭṭettu* avec **ʔaṭad-* proto-sémitique n'est pas la seule interprétation étymologique qui ait été proposée pour le mot akkadien. En effet, les auteurs du CAD ont opté pour une normalisation *eddetu*, en dérivant ce mot du verbe *edēdu* 'être aigu.' Pour eux, une relation étymologique entre *eṭṭettu* et **ʔaṭad-* est douteuse pour des raisons orthographiques, "parce qu'aucun exemple d'orthographe avec *ṭ* n'est connu."

À notre avis, cet argument n'est pas suffisamment convaincant. En effet, le mot en question est toujours écrit avec le signe DI dans les textes du premier millénaire, et il est assez difficile de comprendre pourquoi cette orthographe devrait être tellement incompatible avec la lecture /ṭi/. De même pour *et*-TA-*du* dans *šar tamḫāri*: dans le cadre de l'orthographe périphérique qui caractérise ce texte (à juste titre soulignée dans Goodnick Westenholz 1997, pp. 105–06), TA pour /ṭa/ apparaît tout à fait naturel.

Dans de telles conditions, c'est surtout la structure morphologique du terme akkadien qui paraît importante, à savoir, le fait que les deux dentales sont systématiquement redoublées dans l'écriture (*e**d**-**de**-**et**-tum*). La normalisation *eddettu* que cette écriture implique (AHw. 266) n'est pas facilement compatible avec la proto-forme sémitique **ʔaṭad-*: tandis que le *-tt-* double peut être expliqué par l'addition du suffixe féminin *-t-* (donc, **ʔaṭad-at-*), le *-dd-* (ou plutôt *-ṭṭ-*) reste difficile à comprendre. Le même problème, néanmoins, persiste dans le cas d'une dérivation directe de la racine verbale *edēdu* 'être aigu' préférée par les auteurs du CAD: une identification immédiate avec l'adjectif *eddu* 'aigu' n'est pas possible au vu du redoublement du *t* final.[36] Il est difficile de ne pas penser à quelque type de contamination occasionnée par l'étymologie populaire, l'ancien nom primitif étant déformé par une association secondaire avec le concept de l'acuité. Une telle contamination pourrait aussi expliquer la coloration en *-e-*, naturelle pour la racine verbale *edēdu* (< proto-sémitique **ḥdd*, HALOT 291) mais assez inattendue

[34] Juges 9:14 (la fameuse parabole des plantes qui élisent leur roi) et le Psaume 58:10 (*bə-ṭäräm yābīnū sīrōtēkäm ʔāṭād*). Le dernier passage est difficile à comprendre, la traduction 'avant que vos chaudières sentent les branches sèches (de l'arbre épineux utilisées comme combustible)' n'est qu'une possibilité entre plusieurs autres.

[35] Selon S. Strelcyn, il s'agit d'un arbre 'recouvert sur toute sa surface de petites épines, mais les hommes l'émondent et en font des bâtons' (1973, p. 146).

[36] Comme M. Krebernik me l'indique aimablement, une dérivation de l'adjectif "intensif" **eddedu* 'très aigu' serait toutefois possible: **edded-t-u* > *eddettu*. Il paraît, cependant, qu'un tel adjectif n'est pas présent dans le corpus akkadien disponible (cf. AHw. 185 et CDA 65).

pour un prototype immédiat avec ˀ- (*ˀaṭad-). Cette explication devient encore plus probable au vu de la forme éblaïte *a-ṭa-dum*, dont l'orthographe n'est pas compatible avec *ḥdd dans le prototype.

Un rapport étymologique entre *ˀaṭad-/eddettu* et sa correspondance sumérienne AD$_2$ (ADDA$_4$, ADDU$_3$) (PSD A/3 26) peut difficilement être établi malgré la ressemblance superficielle.

22. Akk. ***ḫilēpu*** 'saule,' connu depuis le paléo-babylonien (AHw. 345, CAD Ḫ 185), se rattache facilement aux syr. *ḥellāpā* (LSyr. 235) et ar. *ḫilāf-* (Lane 1876, p. 797). La reconstruction proto-sémitique ***ḫilāp-*** proposée par P. Fronzaroli (1969a, pp. 278, 291, 300)[37] peut paraître suffisamment assurée grâce à la présence du *ḫ* en arabe qui, *a priori*, devrait exclure la possibilité d'un araméisme.[38]

23. Akk. ***allānu*** 'chêne,' attesté comme un emprunt sémitique al-la-núm dès les documents sumériens de la troisième dynastie d'Ur (PSD A/3 151–52), est relativement bien connu dans les textes d'époques postérieures (AHw. 37, CAD A/1 354). Il faut surtout noter de nombreux exemples paléo-assyriens traités en détail par C. Michel (1997, pp. 106–07), où ce terme est appliqué à une substance comestible.[39]

Néanmoins, c'est à juste titre que les auteurs du CAD observent que les attestations de ce terme sont, en général, assez peu nombreuses. Devrait-on supposer qu'il ne s'agit pas d'un mot akkadien autochtone, mais d'un très ancien emprunt ouest-sémitique? Dans ce cas, *ˀa$_5$-a-la-nu-um* = sum. GIŠ.UD dans l'entrée 496 du vocabulaire bilingue d'Ebla (Krebernik 1983, p. 18; Zurro 1983, p. 265) pourrait être attribué à la couche ouest-sémitique des données lexicales éblaïtes (Lambert 1989, pp. 29–32).[40] Une origine ouest-sémitique d'*allānu* ne serait pas incompatible avec l'usage fréquent de ce terme dans les documents paléo-assyriens: quelques traits particuliers du vocabulaire assyrien sont en effet explicables par une interférence linguistique avec le sémitique de l'ouest, interférence certainement plus prononcée que celle qu'on peut observer pour la Mésopotamie centrale (Kogan 2006, p. 212).

Toutefois, selon la conception traditionnelle le mot akkadien est considéré comme apparenté à des termes ouest-sémitiques comme l'hébreu *ˀayil*, *ˀēlā* et *ˀallōn* (HALOT 40, 51–54), l'araméen commun *ˀīlān- (Kogan 2005, pp. 559–60) et l'ougaritique *ˀaln* (DUL 58). Selon P. Fronzaroli (1969a, pp. 277, 290, 300), ces formes peuvent être réduites à deux proto-formes alternatives, à savoir, ***ˀayl(-ān)-*** et ***ˀall(-ān)-***. Fronzaroli attribue un sens assez général ('*grande albero*') à la première proto-forme, tandis que la seconde est interprétée, d'une manière plus concrète, comme 'chêne.' Il paraît utile d'étudier, dans quelle mesure une telle identification sémantique peut être justifiée par les données disponibles des langues sémitiques où les réflexes de ce terme sont attestés.

(1) Comme on l'a déjà observé ci-dessus, l'araméen commun *ˀīlān- est devenu le terme générique pour l'arbre en araméen, qui a remplacé son précurseur proto-sémitique *ˁiṣ̂-. Par conséquent, le terme araméen n'a aucune pertinence quant au sens exact de sa source proto-sémitique *ˀayl(-ān)-.

(2) La forme ougaritique *ˀaln* n'apparaît, à notre connaissance, que dans KTU 1.12 I 20, dont l'information contextuelle (*ṯˀi b ˀaln tkm* 'part pour *ˀaln tkm*') est minimale. La traduction 'chênaie' est très répandue (voir, par exemple, Watson 2004, p. 113) mais, évidemment, difficile à prouver.

(3) Les deux termes hébraïques — *ˀēlā* et *ˀallōn* — sont traditionnellement interprétés comme 'térébinthe' et 'chêne' respectivement. La tradition, qui s'appuie surtout sur les données des traductions anciennes ainsi que sur les attestations de ces termes dans la littérature post-biblique, peut être correcte, mais on doit admettre que les contextes bibliques, bien que relativement nombreux pour chacun des deux termes, n'offrent jamais d'élément

---

[37] Selon Fronzaroli, cette forme nominale proto-sémitique doit être mise en relation avec la racine verbale reconstruite par lui comme *-ḫlup- 's'entrelacer.' Pour Fronzaroli, le lien sémantique entre le nom et le verbe est dû aux techniques artisanales utilisant les branches du saule comme matériau.

[38] En outre, l'histoire des gutturales sémitiques en araméen telle qu'on la voit maintenant est beaucoup plus complexe qu'on tendait à le penser jadis. Comme le montrent clairement les transcriptions égyptiennes démotiques, la distinction entre *ḥ* et *ḫ*, cachée par l'écriture alphabétique, était tout à fait vivante au moins à l'époque de l'araméen impérial (Steiner 2005, p. 235–37). La même conclusion a été faite depuis longtemps pour l'hébreu biblique — et pour une époque encore plus tardive — sur la base des transcriptions des noms propres hébraïques dans la Septante (Blau 1982). On ne possède pas de données pour les périodes plus récentes, mais il est difficile d'exclure qu'une telle distinction existait encore à l'époque des premiers contacts araméo-arabes (cf. Telegdi 1935, pp. 197–202, Ciancaglini 2008, p. 80).

[39] Donc, une sorte de noix et non pas les glands du chêne?

[40] De même pour *al$_6$-la-nu* comme une désignation d'un bijou en forme de gland à Ebla, identifiée depuis longtemps avec le terme en question et récemment traitée en détail par J. Pasquali (2005b, pp. 98–101).

décisif en faveur de ces identifications. Ainsi, les traductions 'un arbre massif,' 'toute sorte de grand arbre' adoptées par les auteurs du HALOT nous paraissent assez objectives.

On peut conclure, par conséquent, que l'appui sémantique pour l'interprétation de **ˀayl(-ān)-*, **ˀall(-ān)-* comme 'chêne' est extrêmement maigre.

Aucun parallèle assuré pour *allānu* n'est connu en dehors du domaine du sémitique du nord-ouest. Pour Fronzaroli, un terme apparenté en arabe est *ˀallat-* qui désigne un type de javelot (LA 11 27–28), mais l'évolution sémantique assez peu évidente que cette comparaison implique nous paraît un obstacle tout à fait sérieux pour l'accepter.[41]

24. Akk. ***ṣarbatu*** 'peuplier de l'Euphrate,' bien attesté syllabiquement dès le paléo-babylonien (AHw. 1085, CAD Ṣ 108) et avec un net précédent dans la liste lexicale éblaite (VE 397: *ṣàr-ba-tum* = sum. GIŠ.ASAL$_x$) est identifié d'une manière presque unanime avec les désignations de la même espèce en hébreu (*ʕărābā*, HALOT 879), syriaque (*ʕarbtā*, LSyr. 546) et arabe (*ɣarab-*, Lane 1876, p. 2242).

On doit observer que, malgré toute son attractivité sémantique, cette comparaison reste extrêmement difficile du point de vue phonologique.

La référence à "l'alternance *ɣ/*ṣ" faite par les auteurs du CAD ne paraît pas viable pour plusieurs raisons.

(1) L'alternance supposée ne serait attestée, par ailleurs, que dans un seul exemple, à savoir, *emēru* (CAD E 148) et *ṣemēru* (CAD Ṣ 126) 'avoir une indigestion.'

(2) Il est difficile de prouver que, dans ce dernier cas, il s'agisse des variantes d'un seul verbe et non pas de deux verbes différents avec une signification similaire. Au moins du point de vue étymologique, une telle possibilité trouve une confirmation relativement solide, à savoir, l'arabe *ḥmr* 'avoir une indigestion' (Lane 1876, p. 640), opposé au syriaque *ṣmr* 'souffrir de rétention d'urine' (LSyr. 632).[42]

(3) Dans le cas de *ṣarbatu*, il ne s'agit pas d'une variation interne au sein de la langue akkadienne mais de doublets au niveau sémitique commun.

P. Fronzaroli, bien conscient de ces difficultés, a voulu les éviter en séparant les termes akkadien et araméen du reste des données ouest-sémitiques et en postulant sur cette base une reconstruction proto-sémitique ****ṣ̂arb-at-*** (1969a, pp. 278, 291, 300). Effectivement, si la sifflante latérale emphatique *ṣ̂ est postulée dans la proto-forme, la correspondance entre l'akkadien *ṣarbatu* et le syriaque *ʕarbtā* dévient tout à fait régulière: le réflexe pharyngal du *ṣ̂ proto-sémitique est un des traits les plus remarquables de la phonologie historique de la langue araméenne.

Mais que faire des parallèles hébraïque et arabe? Pour Fronzaroli, dans les deux cas il doit s'agir d'emprunts araméens. Théoriquement, on ne peut pas exclure une telle possibilité, et la présence du ɣ en arabe n'y est pas un obstacle trop grave: l'évolution du *ṣ̂ à ʕ en araméen n'a pas été instantanée et c'est précisément un son similaire au ɣ (à savoir, une affriquée glottalisée [x̣]) qui a dû servir d'intermédiaire, exprimée par la lettre ק dans l'écriture araméenne des périodes anciennes (Steiner 1977, pp. 40–41).

Néanmoins, il reste assez difficile de comprendre quels facteurs auraient conduit ce terme botanique araméen à être emprunté d'une manière indépendante en arabe *et* en hébreu. D'un autre côté, on ne devrait pas négliger le fait que d'autres parallèles avec ʕ sont connus pour héb. *ʕărābā*, syr. *ʕarbtā* et ar. *ɣarab-* dans les langues ouest-sémitiques, pour lesquelles une influence lexicale araméenne serait difficile à imaginer: tig. *ʕərəb* 'une plante à cires,' *ʕarob* 'un arbre' (WTS 460)[43] ainsi que soq. *ʕarhieb* 'un arbre' (LS 325).[44]

L'existence d'un terme botanique proto-ouest-sémitique **ɣarab-at-* peut difficilement être niée. Une éventuelle parenté avec l'akkadien *ṣarbatu* reste toujours attractive du fait du parallélisme sémantique, sans qu'il soit possible de la prouver par des stricts moyens de phonologie historique.

---

[41] On doit admettre, cependant, que quelques exemples de désignations de flèches ou javelots dérivées des noms d'arbres (génériques ou concrets) pourraient militer dans ce sens, à savoir l'ougaritique *ʕṣ* 'arbre, bois' (*ḥšk ʕṣk ʕbṣk* 'serre le javelot et la massue' dans KTU 1.3 III 18), l'hébreu *bərōš* 'genièvre' (*bərōšīm horʕālū* 'on brandit les javelots' dans Nahum 2:4) et, en dehors du domaine sémitique, le grec δόρυ 'arbre; javelot,' apparenté à δρῦς 'arbre; chêne' (Buck 1949, p. 1390).

[42] La première comparaison, qui montre un parfait synchronisme sémantique, a été proposée par M. Bulakh (*apud* SED I no. 28); la dernière est universellement reconnue malgré les significations assez différentes.

[43] L'identification botanique reste à préciser.

[44] Selon Miller et Morris 2004, p. 325, c'est le nom du fameux arbre "sang-dragon" (*Dracaena cinnabari*). On remarquera que la forme jibbali *ʕayrób* signalée par M. Morris (2002, p. 52) ne favorise pas l'identification de ce terme avec la reconstruction proto-sémitique avec *ɣ proposée présentement (ce phonème devrait être conservé en jibbali).

25. Akk. ***burāšu*** 'genièvre' (AHw. 139, CAD B 326), bien attesté depuis le paléo-babylonien, est peut-être déjà présent, comme un emprunt akkadien, dans un document sumérien de l'époque de la troisième dynastie d'Ur (Gelb 1957, p. 101). Le terme akkadien est clairement identique aux héb. *bərōš* (HALOT 155)[45] et syr. *brātā* (LSyr. 98).

Sur cette base, la proto-forme **burāṯ-* a été traditionnellement supposée au niveau proto-sémitique (Fronzaroli 1969a, pp. 278, 291, 300). En l'absence d'un parallèle explicite avec l'interdentale sourde *ṯ* (par exemple, en ougaritique ou en arabe), la correspondance de *š* en akkadien et en hébreu à *t* en araméen a été considérée comme une preuve suffisamment solide pour une telle reconstruction.

La reconstruction traditionnelle est devenue plus problématique après la découverte de la grande liste lexicale éblaite, dont l'entrée 374 indique: *ba-ra-su-um* = sum. GIŠ.LI (Krebernik 1983, p. 14). La parenté entre la traduction sémitique du GIŠ.LI dans cette entrée et le terme botanique en question est évidente, mais l'écriture avec SU n'est pas compatible avec cette identification, car c'est la série ŠV qui correspond normalement aux interdentaux proto-sémitiques à Ebla. Aucune explication convaincante pour cette irrégularité n'a été proposée jusqu'à présent. De même pour la vocale *-a-* dans la première syllabe, incompatible avec *-u-* en akkadien et *-ə-* en hébreu.

26. La première attestation syllabique du terme akkadien ***erēnu***, traditionnellement interprété comme 'cèdre' (AHw. 237, CAD E 274), date de la période sargonique et se trouve dans la fameuse incantation MAD 5, 8:29:

śi-ir-gu-a i-da-śu	'ses bras sont beaux,
ì *ù ti-bu-ut-tum śa-ap-tà-śu*	ses lèvres sont huile et *tibbuttum*,[46]
a-sà-am ì *in ḳà-ti-śu*	un vaisseau d'huile est dans sa main,
a-sà-am i-ri-nim in bu-dì-śu	un vaisseau de cèdre[47] est sur son épaule.'

Selon M. Civil (1987, p. 148), une forme apparentée est attestée dans le vocabulaire bilingue éblaïte, à savoir, *ù-ri-núm* comme un équivalent du sumérien GIŠ.Ù.SUH$_4$ dans VE 1362′. Plus spécifiquement, Civil fait référence à la variante *urīnum* attestée comme une désignation du cèdre dans les documents nuziens.

Les dictionnaires akkadiens ne proposent aucune étymologie sémitique pour ce mot, tout en observant son identité avec le terme sumérien eren qui probablement désignait la même espèce d'arbre.

Il n'est pas impossible, néanmoins, qu'une étymologie sémitique pour l'akkadien *erēnu* puisse être trouvée. Plus concrètement, il s'agirait des désignations botaniques ouest-sémitiques qui peuvent être réduites à une proto-forme commune **ʕarʕar-*. Les réflexes de cette proto-forme sont connus pour être appliqués à deux espèces botaniques en principe tout à fait différentes, à savoir, le tamaris et le genièvre. Essayons de suivre la distribution de ces deux significations dans le domaine ouest-sémitique.

(1) En arabe, l'interprétation du *ʕarʕar-* comme **genièvre** est assurée par des définitions détaillées de la lexicographie classique (LA 4 644; Lane 1876, p. 1990), ainsi que par la présence de ce sens dans l'arabe standard moderne (Baranov 509) et dans l'usage dialectal (Behnstedt 819).

(2) Aucun réflexe du proto-sémitique **ʕarʕar-* n'est enregistré dans les dictionnaires "standard" du sudarabique moderne (ML, JL, LS). Néanmoins, une description très détaillée du *ʕarʕeyr* jibbali se trouve dans l'encyclopédie botanique de la région omanaise du Dhofar par A. Miller and M. Morris (1988, p. 282). L'information scientifique recueillie par les auteurs ainsi que les belles images qui l'accompagnent ne laissent pas de doute qu'il s'agisse d'une espèce de **tamaris** (plus concrètement, *Tamarix aphylla*).[48]

---

[45] Un curieux doublet araméisant (*bərōt*) est attesté dans Cantique 1:17.

[46] Une plante?

[47] Ou: 'd'(huile de) cèdre?'

[48] On remarquera toutefois que le terme méhri *ʕarʕōr* enrégistré par A. Sima (2009, p. 200) a été traduit par lui comme *Juniperus*.

(3) Dans la Bible hébraïque, les réflexes de cette racine sont attestés deux fois dans le livre de Jérémie:

wə-hāyā kə-ˁarˁār ba-ˁărābā 'il sera comme un ˁ. dans le désert' (17:6)

tihyānā ka-ˁărōˁēr ba-mmidbār 'vous serez comme des ˁ. dans le désert.' (48:6)[49]

Évidemment, on ne peut pas gagner beaucoup d'information contextuelle pour l'identification de l'arbre de ces passages. Les traductions classiques ont opté pour ***tamaris*** (LXX μυρίκη). Pour quelques commentateurs modernes, la mention de l'habitat désertique a été un sérieux argument en faveur de cette identification. C'est cette opinion qui est codifiée par un des dictionnaires standard de l'hébreu biblique, à savoir, BDB 792. Pour plusieurs autres savants, l'étymologie arabe a été la clé principale pour l'identification botanique du terme hébreu, d'où ***genièvre*** dans HALOT 887 ainsi que dans l'usage actuel de l'hébreu moderne.

(4) En syriaque, la forme avec réduplication *ˁarˁūrā* s'applique à la résine du ***tamaris***, la plante elle-même étant désignée par une forme structuralement plus primitive *ˁarrā* (LSyr. 544, SL 1141, 1133).

(5) Dans le corpus ougaritique, le terme botanique *ˁrˁr* est attesté trois fois (DUL 178). Deux exemples sont concentrés dans l'incantation contre les serpents KTU 1.100 (ll. 64–65) (Pardee 1988, pp. 215–16):

ydy b ˁṣm ˁrˁr	'il rejette le tamaris (de) parmi les arbres,
w b šḥt ˁṣ mt	et la "plante de la mort" (de) parmi les buissons:
ˁrˁrm ynˁrn!h	au moyen du tamaris il l'éloigne
ssnm ysynh	au moyen de la grappe de dattier il le chasse'

La troisième attestation, un peu moins claire, se trouve dans le texte rituel 1.109:29–30 (Pardee 2000, pp. 602–04):

l bˁl ṣpn b ˁrˁr pˀamt ṯlṯm 'pour *bˁl ṣpn*, (l'offrande) dans le(s) tamaris, trente fois'

Pour D. Pardee, l'identification avec le ***tamaris*** est certaine "parce que le tamaris (*bīnu*) joue un grand rôle dans les *namburbi* mésopotamiens, et parce que le *ˁrˁr* est une plante du désert" (1988, p. 216).[50] La mention de *ssnm* 'grappe de dattier' dans la ligne qui suit immédiatement pourrait être prise comme un troisième argument, car l'usage similaire du dattier et du tamaris est bien connu dans les textes rituels mésopotamiens (Streck 2004, pp. 255, 272–73, 282–85). L'identification de *ˁrˁr* avec ***genièvre***, bien qu'elle ne soit complètement absente des études ougaritologiques, est clairement minoritaire.[51]

(6) Le terme botanique *ˁrˁr* a été récemment découvert dans un document sabéen inscrit sur bois (Stein 2010, p. 200, l. 12). Le contexte de ce *Hapax Legomenon* est peu informatif du point de vue botanique, mais ***genièvre*** est la seule interprétation considérée positivement par l'éditeur (Stein 2010, pp. 203, 720).

Malgré la différence sémantique, l'identité étymologique entre les mots ouest-sémitiques est difficile à nier. Quel est donc le sens originel de la proto-forme occidentale **ˁarˁar-*: 'tamaris' ou 'genièvre'? Les deux sens étant solidement attestés dans les langues sémitiques vivantes, le choix risque d'être arbitraire,[52] mais, en tout cas, le passage sémantique du 'tamaris' au 'genièvre' (ou inversement) qu'on doit postuler pour quelques langues

[49] La remarquable différence structurelle entre les deux formes hébraïques en question (*ˁarˁār* vs. *ˁărōˁēr*) doit attirer notre attention. Dans un contexte synchronique, la seconde forme n'est qu'une étrange variante morphologique difficile à expliquer. Cette vision change radicalement dans la perspective comparatiste: l'opposition **ˁarˁar-* vs. **ˁarāˁir-* n'est rien d'autre que l'opposition du singulier au pluriel apophonique (dit "brisé") en arabe, où cette procédure est régulièrement attestée pour tous les noms quadriconsonantiques, y compris *ˁarˁar-* 'genièvre.' Qu'il ne s'agit pas d'une coïncidence fortuite devient clair si on compare les contextes où les deux formes sont attestées: la variante *ˁarˁār* correspond, effectivement, à une forme verbale au singulier (*wə-hāyā*), tandis que la variante *ˁărōˁēr* s'accorde avec *tihyānā* au pluriel. Une explication diachronique pour la présence d'une telle forme de pluriel brisé en hébreu doit encore être proposée.

[50] Mais cf. "un arbre du type des genévriers" dans Pardee 2000, p. 611.

[51] V. Belmonte 1993, où les qualités médicales des "baies du genièvre" sont mises en relief.

[52] Un argument inattendu en faveur de la priorité de 'tamaris' peut être trouvé dans la tradition arabe concernant l'arbre *ˁarˁar-*: "il est réputé ennemi du palmier et tenu à distance de ce dernier" (BK 2 224). Cette allusion est difficile à séparer de la fameuse controverse entre la palme et le tamaris (Streck 2004). La raison d'être de l'antagonisme "palme-tamaris" dans la littérature mésopotamienne reste jusqu'à aujourd'hui mal comprise.

ouest-sémitiques est beaucoup moins compliqué que ce qu'on pourrait penser. Bien sûr, les deux espèces sont complètement différentes du point de vue de la systématique botanique, en commençant par le fait que le premier est un arbre feuillu et le second un conifère. Néanmoins, une convergence morphologique dans la perception visuelle des anciens est tout à fait probable: les "feuilles" du tamaris ont été souvent décrites comme "très petites, alternes et écailleuses, un peu semblables à celles de certains conifères."[53]

En retournant au terme akkadien *erēnu*, on devra admettre que la différence entre 'cèdre' d'un côté et 'tamaris' (ou même 'genièvre') de l'autre est naturellement beaucoup plus sérieuse, mais, probablement, pas insurmontable pour postuler une ancienne parenté étymologique. Il est bien connu que quelques variétés de genièvre (par exemple, *Juniperus polycarpus*, bien répandu dans les régions montagneuses à l'est de la Mésopotamie) peuvent atteindre 20 mètres de hauteur et on n'hésitera pas à rappeler que pour certains assyriologues la location orientale de la "forêt des cèdres" dans les légendes sumériennes de Gilgamesh a été un argument décisif pour l'identification du sumérien eren avec le genièvre et non pas le cèdre (pour une présentation équilibrée de ce complexe problème voir Klein et Abraham 1997).[54]

Du point de vue de la phonologie historique, le rapport étymologique entre l'akkadien *erēnu* et la proto-forme ouest-sémitique **ˁarˁar-* ne pose pas de problèmes majeurs. L'hypothèse la plus probable consiste à envisager une proto-forme **ˁar-ān-*, qui représenterait un ancien élément **ˁar-*, sans réduplication mais augmenté avec le suffixe **-ān-* bien répandu dans la dérivation nominale sémitique et akkadienne. Au vu de la forme syriaque *ˁarrā* mentionnée plus haut, l'existence d'une telle forme primitive n'est guère improbable. D'un autre côté, on ne doit pas exclure une reconstruction **ˁarˁar-* identique à celle postulée pour les formes occidentales, mais avec une dissimilation des sonores (**erēru* > *erēnu*). Dans les deux cas, le passage du **ˁa-* à *e-* est tout à fait régulier et, par conséquent, favorise l'identification proposée.

Si cette approche étymologique est acceptée, le mot sumérien eren doit être considéré comme un ancien emprunt akkadien et non l'inverse comme l'a supposé S. Lieberman dans son livre sur les emprunts sumériens dans le paléo-babylonien (1977, pp. 231–32).[55]

V. Plantes domestiquées: les céréales

Les noms akkadiens des céréales ayant une étymologie sémitique plus ou moins assurée ne sont pas nombreux: on ne connaît guère plus de cinq termes pertinents.

27. Les attestations syllabiques de l'akk. ***buḳlu*** 'malt' (CAD B 323, AHw. 139) sont assez abondantes dans les documents paléo-babyloniens et surtout paléo-assyriens.

M. Streck a consacré à ce problème toute une section dans son article, où il indique plusieurs raisons possibles sans parvenir à aucune solution définitive (2004, pp. 254–55, voir déjà Krebernik 1984, p. 326). Au vu de la tradition arabe qu'on vient de citer (dont les sources devraient évidemment être étudiées d'une façon beaucoup plus détaillée), on se demande si la raison principale de cet antagonisme ne pourrait pas être recherchée dans le domaine des techniques de la culture du dattier — ne serait-il pas en effet incompatible avec le voisinage du tamaris? En ce qui concerne la tradition arabe sur l'incompatibilité du dattier avec le *genièvre*, la seule explication diachronique qu'on puisse envisager est qu'une ancienne tradition concernant le *tamaris* a été transférée au genièvre quand le mot commun ouest-sémitique a changé son sens en arabe.

[53] http://fr.wikipedia.org/wiki/Tamaris. Comme le montrent les images dans Miller et Morris 1988, p. 283, la ressemblance entre les deux espèces est, effectivement, frappante.

[54] On remarquera que le terme proto-ouest-sémitique **ˀarz-* 'cèdre,' représenté par oug. *ˀarz* (DUL 113–14; Watson 2004, p. 113), héb. *ˀäräz* (HALOT 86), syr. *ˀarzā* (LSyr. 47), ar. *ˀarz-* (Lane 1876, p. 47), gez. *ˀarz* (CDG 41) et soq. *ˀárz* (LS 73) est absent de l'akkadien mésopotamien. La présence de *ar-za-tum* = sum. GIŠ.NUN.SAL dans la liste lexicale éblaïte (VE 471) a été expliquée, probablement à juste titre, par une influence ouest-sémitique (Lambert 1989, p. 30).

[55] Une approche plus modérée peut être trouvée dans AHw. qui se borne à constater la parenté entre les deux mots sans préciser les détails diachroniques. Les auteurs du CAD n'énoncent pour leur part aucune opinion sur ce problème.

Pour les auteurs du CAD, le plus ancien exemple syllabique est attesté dans le document sargonique *RA* 55, 94:3 (BU-UK-LU), mais comme l'a montré M. Stol (1989, p. 323), le contexte ne favorise pas une telle identification. Dans son explication de ce passage Stol préfère ne pas rompre complètement avec l'akkadien *buḳlu*, en normalisant BU-UK-LU comme *buqlū* 'légumes.' Une approche différente, récemment proposée dans CAD P 476, nous paraît préférable: la forme sargonique est rendue ici comme *pu-ug-lu* 'radis,' sans aucune relation avec les termes akkadien et sémitique discutés présentement.

À Ebla, notre mot est clairement attesté dans l'entrée VE 856 de la liste lexicale bilingue: *bù-ḳú-lu* = sum. MÙNU. Pour certains savants il existe encore un parallèle pour ce terme dans la liste éblaïte, à savoir, BÙ-GA-LU = sum. ḪI.SAR dans l'entrée VE 1073 (Sjöberg 1999, p. 542). Comme M. Stol l'observe judicieusement (1989, p. 323), l'équivalent sumérien ḪI.SAR ne favorise guère une telle identification, mais milite plutôt en faveur d'une sorte de salade. On se demande, bien sûr, si *puglu* 'radis,' déjà mentionné plus haut, ne serait pas un candidat acceptable.

On sait depuis longtemps qu'une des lectures phonétiques sumériennes pour la combinaison PAP+PAP (= DIM_4) qui désigne le malt et correspond à l'akkadien *buḳlu* est bu-lu-un/bu-lu-ug (Borger 2004, p. 265). Il est bien sûr tentant de supposer une relation étymologique par métathèse entre les mots sumérien et akkadien, et au vu d'une étymologie sémitique tout à fait évidente (voir ci-dessous), il doit s'agir d'un ancien emprunt akkadien en sumérien et non de l'inverse. Une telle hypothèse, implicite déjà dans le traitement classique de ces termes par B. Hrozný (1913, p. 154), paraît assez problématique aujourd'hui, car on sait que dans tous les cas où PAP+PAP correspond à *buḳlu* dans les listes lexicales, c'est la lecture mu-nu et non pas bu-lu-un/bu-lu-ug qui a été choisie par les compilateurs anciens. La lecture qui nous intéresse est réservée, en revanche, pour le sens 'grandir, croître,' appliqué aux enfants et aux plantes (Civil 2007, p. 27). Dans la mesure où ce dernier sens est, lui aussi, très bien attesté pour la racine **bḳl* dans les langues sémitiques (par exemple, l'arabe *bql* 'croître, commencer à avoir des feuilles'), l'hypothèse postulant un ancien emprunt sémitique en sumérien garde son attrait.

L'akkadien *buḳlu* peut être clairement tracé à la racine proto-sémitique ***bVḳl-*** avec un sens assez général de 'plante cultivée, graine, céréale' (Fronzaroli 1969b, pp. 5, 24, 32), qui doit probablement être postulé à la base de syr. *buḳḳālā* 'grain, semence' (LSyr. 87), ar. *baql-* 'plantes qui ne sont ni arbres, ni arbrisseaux; légume, toute plante qu'on recueille après l'avoir semée' (Lane 1876, p. 236), sab. *bḳl* 'plantes cultivées, plantations,' min. s_1-*bḳl* et qat. *bḳl* 'planter' (SD 30, LM 23, LIQ 31, Sima 2000, p. 185), gez. *baḳ*^{w}*l* 'plante, herbe, végétation' (CDG 101), méh. *bēḳəl*, jib. *béḳəl* 'plantes qui croissent après la pluie' (ML 47, JL 25). Mais peut-être doit-on suivre M. Stol, pour qui le composant sémantique 'croître, pousser' est le plus important ici, d'où sa traduction '*grüne (sprießende) Pflanze.*' Et en tout cas, on ne manquera pas d'observer la coïncidence frappante entre l'akkadien et quelques langues néo-éthiopiennes, où les réflexes du **bVḳl-* proto-sémitique s'appliquent non seulement au malt, mais aussi à la bière qu'on prépare avec (par exemple, tigre *bəḳəl*, WTS 284). Et de fait, c'est cette coïncidence qui avait fasciné Hrozný au point de proposer, pour la première fois dans l'histoire de notre discipline, la traduction 'malt' pour l'akkadien *buḳlu*.

Il est difficile de savoir pourquoi un mot si répandu dans les langues sémitiques n'a laissé aucune trace ou presque dans le domaine cananéen. La seule exception est la locution *ḳmḥ bḳl* dans les textes hippiatriques ougaritiques KTU 1.71:25 et 1.85:32: *dblt yṯnt w ṣmḳm yṯn[m] w ḳmḥ bḳl yṣḳ b ʔaph* 'une vieille boulette de figues, des vieux raisins, et de la farine de malt (broyés) ensemble doivent être administrés par ses narines' (traduction adaptée de Pardee 1985, p. 68). Les deux éditions standard de ces textes (Pardee 1985, p. 68; Cohen et Sivan 1983, p. 10) sont unanimes dans leur traduction 'farine de malt' pour cette locution. Pour D. Pardee, il existe un lien immédiat entre cette attestation ougaritique et les données lexicales d'Ebla présentées ci-dessus.[56] Toutefois, la présence de ce terme dans la liste lexicale éblaïte n'offre pas d'argument définitif en faveur de son usage dans les langues ouest-sémitiques de la région. Il serait tentant, au contraire, de supposer que la combinaison *ḳmḥ bḳl* en ougaritique ne représente qu'une adaptation (*loan translation*) de la phrase akkadienne *ḳēm bukli* — une phrase qui (comme Pardee l'observe à juste titre) ne paraît pas être syllabiquement attestée dans les sources.[57]

28. La signification exacte de l'akkadien ***uṭṭetu*** (AHw. 1446) comme désignant une céréale dans les différents couches chronologiques et géographiques de la langue akkadienne n'est pas encore suffisamment bien comprise.

[56] "Nous savons maintenant, d'après les textes d'Ebla, que le mot *buqlu* était connu dans le Levant dès le 3e millénaire."

[57] Dans ce sens voir déjà Fronzaroli 1969b, p. 32.

Les traductions 'blé,' 'orge' et 'céréale en général' peuvent être trouvées dans les dictionnaires ainsi que dans les études dédiées à tels période ou dialecte, et on attend avec beaucoup d'impatience la parution du volume U du CAD pour une opinion commune moderne.[58]

La signification générale ('céréale') paraît convenir avant tout pour la période paléo-assyrienne, comme on peut le déduire de passages comme 21 *naruk uṭṭatam mišlum* ŠE-*am mišlum* GIG '21 sacs de grain, moitié en orge, moitié en blé' (d/k 48b:2, cité d'après CAD Š/2 350), ou 8 *naruk uṭṭatum* ŠÀ.BA 2 *naruk aršātum* 'huit sacs de grain, dont 2 sacs de blé' (d/k 19 enveloppe:5, cité d'après Michel 1997, p. 99). Cependant, comme C. Michel l'observe à juste titre, le problème peut être encore plus compliqué car quelques exemples de formulations dites "tautologiques" sont connues, à savoir 5 *naruk* ŠE-*am mišlum* ŠE-*um mišlum* GIG (d/k 9b:1–4, cité d'après Michel 1997, p. 101). Les exemples paléo-babyloniens restent à étudier en détail, mais une certaine incertitude peut être observée même dans les traductions récentes de K. Veenhof d'AbB 14 (comparer ŠE *uṭṭetīya 'my barley corns'* dans 152:8 et *mimma uṭṭetum ul ibašši 'no grain of barley is available'* dans 168:7). En outre, au vu de la collection d'exemples présentés par W. von Soden dans AHw., on peut remarquer que l'usage de *uṭṭetu, uṭṭatu* comme désignant une céréale est beaucoup plus répandu en assyrien qu'en babylonien.

Du point de vue étymologique, le mot akkadien est inséparable du proto-sémitique **ḥinṭ-at-* (Fronzaroli 1969b, pp. 12, 27, 34), traditionnellement défini comme 'blé.'[59] La traduction généralement acceptée pour la reconstruction proto-sémitique se base évidemment sur les données des langues sémitiques centrales, à savoir oug. *ḥṭt* (DUL 377), héb. *ḥiṭṭā* (HALOT 307), syr. *ḥeṭṭətā* (LSyr. 227), ar. *ḥinṭat-* (Lane 1876, p. 657). Le même sens est propre au soqotri *ḥinṭeh* (LS 182), mais comme un emprunt arabe apparaît très probable dans ce cas, la valeur de la forme soqotri est assez réduite. En revanche, le sens des parallèles sudarabiques modernes continentaux et éthiopiens est différent, à savoir, méh. *ḥəṭāt* 'grain' (ML 192), jib. *ḥíṭét* 'aliments en général, fèves, toute céréale,' *ḥiṭet* 'un épi de riz' (JL 119), gez. *ḥəṭṭat, ḥaṭṭat* 'grain, semence' (CDG 268). La ressemblance sémantique entre ces termes sud-sémitiques et l'akkadien ne doit pas nous échapper, car elle peut avoir des conséquences pour la reconstruction sémantique au niveau proto-sémitique: en effet, le sens 'blé' apparaît plutôt comme une innovation du sémitique central, tandis que les zones latérales, comme souvent, ont possiblement préservé la sémantique originelle plus générale.[60]

Plusieurs savants ont voulu découvrir un réflexe de **ḥinṭ-at-* comme un ouest-sémitisme dans l'akkadien d'Emar, à savoir, dans le nom divin ^{d}KASKAL.KUR.RA.MEŠ *ša ḫi*-ID-DI, supposément "le dieu Balih du froment" (373:158′, 378:43′). Malgré l'opinion commune (Pentiuc 2001, p. 70), cette identification, difficile à prouver contextuellement, reste problématique du point de vue linguistique car (comme Pentiuc lui-même l'observe) virtuellement aucune forme masculine de ce terme n'est connue dans aucune langue sémitique.[61]

29. Les attestations du ***burrum*** pour désigner une céréale sont limités aux textes paléo-babyloniens de Mari, Tuttul, et Chagar-Bazar (AHw. 140; CAD B 330; Bottéro 1957, pp. 251–52; Talon 1997, p. 140; Krebernik 2001, p. 234). Comme l'observe J. Bottéro, le terme doit être apparenté à plusieurs désignations de céréales dans le domaine ouest-sémitique, dont la proto-forme a été reconstruite comme ****burr-*** par P. Fronzaroli (1969b, pp. 12, 27, 34) sur la base de héb. *bar* (HALOT 153), ar. *burr-* (Lane 1876, p. 176), sab. *br* (SD 31), méh. *barr* (ML 51), jib. *bohr* (JL 27), soq. *bor* (LS 98).[62] La traduction 'blé' attribuée à cette reconstruction se base surtout sur les données arabes. Pour le sabéen *br*, A. Sima a pu reconnaître six passages où ce terme, quatre fois suivi par s_2ʿ*r* 'orge,' désigne clairement une espèce concrète de céréale, probablement le blé (Sima 2000, pp. 200–02). En hébreu, la nature des passages relativement peu nombreux où *bar* est attesté est telle que la traduction générale 'grain, céréale,' adaptée par les dictionnaires, paraît raisonnable.[63] Les formes sudarabiques modernes désignent le maïs selon T. M. Johnstone, bien que la traduction 'froment' soit présente dans le *Lexique Soqotri*.

[58] Voir maintenant CAD U/342 ('*edible grain* (*wheat or barley*)'), avec une note détaillée à la p. 357.

[59] La différence vocalique entre *-u-* en akkadien et *-i-* dans les langues occidentales est inattendue mais pas sans précédent; cf. a60[59] La structure phonologique des termes sud-sémitiques est aussi fort intéressante, car le **-n-* proto-sémitique, si vraiment originel, n'aurait pas dû tomber (comme en sudarabique moderne), ni s'assimiler (comme en éthiopien).

[61] Contrairement à ce qu'affirme Pentiuc, les données ougaritiques ne changent en rien la situation: la forme *ḥnṭ* pour le masculin singulier ne paraît pas exister (la référence au DLU 184 est fautive) et serait, de fait, difficile à imaginer avec un *-n-* non assimilé.

[62] Pour Fronzaroli, la forme nominale commune **burr-* doit être dérivée de la racine verbale **brr*, assez répandue dans les langues ouest-sémitiques avec le sens 'être pur, clair,' le lien sémantique entre les deux reposant sur l'idée du grain comme substance pure, débarrassée de la balle.

[63] Par exemple, Jérémie 23:28: *ma-la-ttäbän ˀät-ha-bbār* 'la paille a-t-elle quoi que ce soit à voir avec le grain?'

Selon G. Conti (1990, p. 75), **burr-* est aussi attesté dans la liste lexicale bilingue éblaïte, à savoir, *bù-ur-tum* comme l'équivalent de NINDA.GÉME dans VE 81.[64] La comparaison de Conti doit être sérieusement prise en compte, bien que l'équivalence sémantique ne soit pas parfaite et le *-t-* féminin soit absent dans toutes les formes ouest-sémitiques connues jusqu'à présent.

Quelle est l'origine des termes éblaïte et mariote? S'agit-i-il d'un ancien mot proto-sémitique perdu dans l'akkadien "standard" de l'est mais préservé dans les régions plus occidentales? Ou doit-on, au contraire, considérer ces termes comme des ouest-sémitismes locaux qui n'on pas affecté la Mésopotamie? Il n'y a pas chez les savants de réponse unanime à cette question. Selon Conti, le terme éblaïte est un mot "occidental," et le *burrum* mariote est, lui aussi, explicitement qualifié comme "amorrite" par le même auteur. À notre avis, cette hypothèse est assez probable. D'un autre côté, on remarquera que ce terme est absent de la liste des ouest-sémitismes potentiellement attestés en paléo-babylonien proposée par M. Streck (2000, pp. 82–123), une liste qui, en principe, prend en compte la plupart des hypothèses d'emprunt même lorsqu'elles sont rejetées par Streck lui-même.

30. Akk. ***duḫnu*** désigne le mil dans les textes attestés depuis le médio-babylonien et le médio-assyrien (AHw. 174, CAD D 171). Son absence complète aux périodes plus anciennes ainsi que dans les listes lexicales ne favorise pas une origine akkadienne autochtone. Il s'agit plus probablement d'un emprunt ouest-sémitique relativement ancien ou même d'un emprunt indépendant depuis une troisième langue inconnue, en akkadien comme dans les langues ouest-sémitiques. La présence récurrente de ce terme dans les documents de Nuzi est ainsi tout à fait remarquable.

Dans ce contexte, le proto-sémitique ****duḫn-*** reconstruit par P. Fronzaroli (1969b, pp. 13, 28) sur la base de l'akkadien *duḫnu* et de ses parallèles ouest-sémitiques tels que héb. *dōḥan* (HALOT 218), syr. *duḥnā* (LSyr. 149) et ar. *duḫn-* (Lane 1876, p. 861), devient assez problématique. On ne manquera pas de remarquer que le terme hébraïque, lui aussi, n'est attesté qu'une seule fois, dans un passage tardif d'Ezéchiel 4:9 où l'accumulation la plus grande possible de noms de céréales (froment, orge, fèves, lentilles, mil, épeautre) est évidemment intentionnelle.

31. Akk. ***kunāšu*** 'épeautre' (CAD K 536, AHw. 506), est bien attesté syllabiquement dès la période paléo-babylonienne. Comme il est reconnu au moins depuis Hrozný (1913, p. 55), ce terme est étymologiquement identique à la désignation araméenne commune de cette céréale **kunāt-*, repésentée par off. *knt* (DNWSI 521), AJP *kwnt* (DJPA 254) et syr. *kūnātā* (LSyr. 336).

Dès lors qu'une relation entre les deux mots est évidente, il convient d'en établir la nature. S'agit-t-il d'un terme proto-sémitique qui, accidentellement, a été perdu par toutes les langues sauf l'akkadien et l'araméen? Ou doit-on postuler un ancien emprunt akkadien en araméen? Il n'existe pour le moment pas de consensus sur ce problème.

Pour quelques savants, la correspondance du *š* akkadien au *t* araméen doit sans aucune doute signaler que la parenté entre les deux mots est de nature génétique. Telle est la position de P. Fronzaroli qui n'hésite pas à postuler une reconstruction proto-sémitique ****kunāṯ-*** (1969b, pp. 13, 28).

À notre avis, une comparaison lexicale bilatérale entre un mot akkadien et un mot araméen est toujours suspecte, et on aurait bien voulu suivre Hrozný qui a postulé un emprunt akkadien en araméen. Mais comment pourrait-on prouver cette hypothèse?

L'akkadien *š* ne donnerait pas un *-t-* en araméen, ni dans un mot apparenté génétiquement, ni dans un emprunt. C'est donc une *-ṯ-* interdentale qui, en tous les cas, doit être postulée dans le mot-source akkadien. Mais on sait bien que la distinction entre **š* et **ṯ*, qui en réalité existait en akkadien à l'aube de sa formation comme langue écrite, a commencé à disparaître dès le sargonique tardif (textes de la période de Narām-Sîn et Šar-kali-šarrī) et s'évanouit complètement dès la troisième dynastie d'Ur.[65] Quel type de langue araméenne pourrait-on donc postuler, pour la seconde moitié du troisième millénaire, dans laquelle une certaine forme "proto-akkadienne" de ce mot aurait pu pénétrer?

Il est remarquable que *kunāšu* n'apparaît pas dans le livre sur les emprunts akkadiens en araméen de S. Kaufman, où, néanmoins, deux intéressants parallèles peuvent être trouvés, à savoir, *pātūrā* 'table,' emprunté à l'akkadien *paššūru*, et *ʾātūrā* 'Assyrie,' qui dérive de l'akkadien *Aššur* (1974, pp. 81–82). Dans les deux cas, la présence

[64] Source i. Dans les autres sources pour cette entrée on trouve *a-kà-lu* ᵈNISABA 'pain de la déesse Nisaba' ou ᵈNISABA 'la déesse Nisaba' tout court.

[65] Voir les remarques de W. Sommerfeld dans *GAG* §30. Pour une analyse plus détaillée de ce phénomène, voir Hasselbach 2005, pp. 135–43; Kogan 2011, pp. 179–86.

du *ṯ dans la proto-forme n'est guère évidente mais ne peut pas être exclue non plus. Ainsi, l'akkadien *paššūru* lui-même doit être emprunté au sumérien banšur, mais, à en juger par les valeurs anciennes des signes akkadiens de la série ŠV, il n'est pas impossible que le š sumérien ait été phonétiquement proche de ce qu'on considère comme le réflexe sargonique du *ṯ proto-sémitique. Le second cas est encore plus compliqué, et ce n'est qu'avec une grande précaution que l'on peut supposer que *Aššur* possédait un *ṯ dans la proto-forme: (1) si le nom de la ville (et du pays) d'Assour est vraiment identique au nom divin correspondant et (2) si le nom divin Assour est vraiment apparenté aux théonymes ouest-sémitiques comme l'*ʔaṯrt* ougaritique.

Comme on l'a noté depuis longtemps, la forme akkado-araméenne **kunāṯ-* est à un certain degré similaire aux désignations de l'épeautre en hébreu et en ougaritique, à savoir *ksm*, *kśm* (DUL 462) et *kussämät* (HALOT 490). Ces formes sont d'habitude expliquées comme des dérivés nominaux de la racine verbale **ksm* 'couper, fendre.' Une telle dérivation n'est pas improbable du point de vue de la typologie d'évolution sémantique: comme l'a observé déjà Hrozný (1913, p. 13), le mot latin *spelta* — d'où le français *épeautre* et une bonne partie des autres désignations de cette céréale dans les langues européennes modernes tels que l'anglais *spelt* — est clairement apparenté à la racine indo-européenne **spel-* 'couper, fendre.' Une motivation pour ce développement sémantique a été cherché, non sans raisons, soit dans les techniques spéciales nécessaires au battage de cette céréale (Hrozný 1913, pp. 41, 56; Fronzaroli 1969b, p. 13), soit dans quelques particularités morphologique de sa graine (HALOT 490; I. Löw *apud* Hrozný 1913, p. 41).[66]

VI. Plantes domestiquées: les légumes

32. Akk. ***šūmū*** 'ail,' bien attesté syllabiquement dans la Mésopotamie proprement dite dès la période paléo-babylonienne (AHw. 1275, CAD Š/3 298), montre un clair précédent à Ebla, à savoir *šu-mi* comme le second élément de l'expression li-ma *šu-mi* dans la liste lexicale MEE 3, 61v. iv 6. Cet entrée a été interprétée par M. Civil comme 'un pot pour broyer l'ail,' li-ma étant compris comme une écriture syllabique du logogramme BUR 'pot' (Civil 1987, p. 156).[67]

Le mot akkadien est clairement apparenté à plusieurs termes ouest-sémitiques qui désignent l'ail, à savoir, héb. *šūm* (HALOT 1442), syr. *tūmā* (LSyr. 819), ar. *ṯūm-* (Lane 1876, p. 365), méh. *ṯəmēt* (ML 417), jib. *ṯuhm* (JL 284), gez. *som*, *somat* (CDG 501).[68]

Pour plusieurs savants, il s'agit d'un terme proto-sémitique très ancien qui pourrait être reconstruit comme ****ṯūm-*** (Fronzaroli 1969b, pp. 6, 24). Il est bien connu, néanmoins, qu'une désignation de l'ail (ou d'une autre sorte de bulbe) existe aussi en sumérien, à savoir sum, dont la première attestation certaine se trouve, selon W. Sommerfeld (2006, p. 64), dans le texte UET 2, 163v. i 5 (GÀN sum 'un champ d'ail'), datant de la période d'Ur archaïque.

Comme Sommerfeld l'a observé dans son analyse critique des sémitismes dans les plus anciennes sources sumériennes, la correspondance entre la proto-forme sémitique **ṯūm-* et le sumérien sum est, malgré le désaccord de surface, phonétiquement parfaite. Comme on le sait maintenant, l'akkadien sargonique n'a pas aboli complètement la distinction originelle entre les sifflantes *š et *ś d'un côté et l'interdentale *ṯ de l'autre côté: les phonèmes du premier groupe sont — dans le cas idéal — transcrits par les signes de la série SV, la série ŠV étant réservée à l'ancienne interdentale. Or, cette distinction est valable non seulement pour les syllabogrammes du

---

[66] En outre, on se demande si une dérivation similaire pourrait être responsable de l'émergence de la désignation sumérienne de l'épeautre, à savoir, zíz. Ce terme, sans aucune motivation évidente au sein du sumérien, a été déjà interprété comme un akkadisme par G. Steiner (2003, p. 642), mais son étymologie — **kinšu*, une *Spielform* akkadienne inexistante, avec palatalisation du **k-* et š akkadien correspondant à z en sumérien — peut difficilement nous convaincre (Sommerfeld 2006, p. 66). On ne manquera pas de noter, en revanche, que terme *zīzu*, soit une désignation rare de l'épeautre, existe aussi en akkadien. Depuis Birot 1960, pp. 261–62, on la considère toujours comme un sumérisme, en négligeant qu'une dérivation à partir du verbe akkadien *zâzu* 'diviser, séparer' pourrait offrir un excellent parallèle sémantique aux termes hébraïque et latin discutés ci-dessus. Si la présente hypothèse est correcte, c'est le terme sumérien qui doit être considéré comme un akkadisme et non l'inverse.

[67] Pour Civil, un réflexe akkadien de ce mot est *lummu* 'un petit pot,' bien attesté dans les listes lexicales du premier millénaire (CAD L 246).

[68] Dans le dernier cas, le vocalisme irrégulier pourrait indiquer un arabisme.

type CV, mais aussi pour ceux qui finissent en *-m*, à savoir, ŠUM = /*šum/ et /*šum/ s'oppose à SUM = /*t̠um/ autant qu'à ZUM = /*zum/, /*sum/ et /*ṣum/.[69]

L'identité fondamentale entre le proto-sémitique **t̠ūm-* et le sumérien sum étant assurée sémantiquement autant que phonétiquement, on doit admettre qu'une coïncidence fortuite entre les deux termes, envisagée comme une possibilité par Sommerfeld (2006, p. 65), devient fort difficile à imaginer. Il doit y avoir une certaine relation diachronique entre les deux termes, et il n'existe que trois possibilités concurrentes: un emprunt sémitique en sumérien; un emprunt sumérien en sémitique; un emprunt indépendant fait par les deux langues à une troisième langue inconnue.

La troisième solution, toujours possible théoriquement, ne peut en aucun cas être prouvée et, par conséquent, ne sera pas discutée ici. La première solution est codifiée par les deux traditions assyriologique et sémitologique. Elle repose sur des raisons phonologiques et sémantiques évidentes et ne paraît pas exiger d'argument spécial. C'est la deuxième hypothèse — fort intéressante comme on doit l'admettre dès à présent — qui a besoin d'une sérieuse argumentation. De fait, dans sa vigoureuse défense de cette hypothèse, Sommerfeld (2006, pp. 64–65) a pu énoncer quelques arguments en sa faveur qui méritent d'être soigneusement analysés ici.

(1) Le premier argument concerne la signification exacte du terme sum dans les sources du troisième millénaire. Comme on l'a observé à plusieurs reprises, dans les documents sumériens sum est souvent utilisé comme le premier élément de plusieurs désignations des plantes alliacées. Quant aux contextes où ce terme apparaît comme un mot indépendant, sa haute fréquence à fait penser à plusieurs savants qu'il ne s'agissait pas de la désignation d'une plante concrète mais plutôt d'un terme générique: 'bulbe, plante alliacée.' Telle est, semble-t-il, la situation dans le fameux *Onion Archive* de la période sargonique conservé à Philadelphie (Westenholz 1987, pp. 87–183).

De l'avis de Sommerfeld, l'usage générique si répandu du sumérien sum offre un argument important contre l'origine sémitique de ce terme: pour lui, il serait difficile d'expliquer comment le sumérien a pu donner un sens aussi général à un mot emprunté dont la signification dans la langue-source sémitique (akkadienne) était tout à fait concrète (à savoir, l'ail).

Pour d'autres savants, néanmoins, cet obstacle n'est guère insurmontable. Ainsi, comme l'affirme M. Powell dans sa synthèse récente sur les fruits et légumes en Mésopotamie (2003, p. 21), il y'a rien de surprenant dans le fait qu'un mot qui, en principe, désignait spécifiquement l'ail puisse se transformer en un terme générique pour les bulbes (même ceux qui n'appartiennent pas aux plantes *Allium* proprement dits). Selon Powell, le rôle dominant de l'ail dans la culture alimentaire sumérienne (et, par conséquent, dans la terminologie correspondante) est dû au fait que les bulbes de l'ail sont beaucoup moins périssables que ceux des autres plantes alliacées.[70] En outre, on ne doit pas perdre de vue le fait que sum apparaît au moins dans quelques passages dans des oppositions binaires avec d'autres types de bulbes (par exemple, 5 sila$_3$ s[um] 5 sila$_3$ sum-sikil dans le texte MC 4, 41:7–8). Ici, son interprétation comme la désignation d'une plante concrète devient inévitable, et c'est la traduction 'ail' qui est d'habitude choisie en de tels cas (Steinkeller 1992, p. 76).

---

[69] On doit admettre que la nature du corpus sargonique est telle qu'il serait difficile de trouver un nombre relativement conséquent d'exemples pertinents. Les quelques exemples actuellement connus se limitent à un nombre réduit des noms propres (Gelb 1961, pp. 72–73) tels que *ˀà-ra*-SUM 'cultivateur, fermier' (CAD E 306, cf. ar. *ḥrt̠* 'cultiver') ou *pir*$_5$-*ḫa*-SUM 'puce' (CAD P 411, cf. ar. *burγūt̠*-). En outre, le système des oppositions phonologiques dans le domaine des sifflantes a commencé à s'affaiblir dès le sargonique et, dans de telles conditions, il n'y a rien de surprenant dans le fait que le même nom propre 'cultivateur, fermier' puisse être rendu alternativement comme *ˀà-ra*-ŠUM (Gelb 1957, p. 66). C'est donc à Ebla qu'une preuve définitive de la valeur /t̠um/ pour le signe SUM doit être recherchée, et non sans succès: dans la grande liste lexicale bilingue le système mentionné ci-dessus est bien documenté, comme le montrent des exemples comme *pá-ša*-SUM, *pi*$_5$-SUM = sum. ŠU.Ì 'oindre; oint' (VE 502; Krebernik 1983, p. 18) ou *a-za-ˀa*$_5$-SUM = sum. Ú.LÁ.A.KI 'une plante' (VE 298, Conti 1990, p. 115). Certes, aucune étymologie sémitique avec *t̠* n'est disponible dans les deux cas en question, mais les graphies alternatives avec les syllabogrammes de la série ŠV (*pá-ša-šu-um* et *a-za-šu-um*), une série qui est toujours réservée aux interdentales à Ebla, ne laissent aucune doute sur la nature phonétique du syllabogramme SUM dans les plus anciennes traditions cunéiformes sémitophones. Un exemple étymologiquement plus certain peut être attesté dans VE 1214: *wa-ru*$_{12}$-SUM/*wu-ru*$_{12}$-SUM 1 DAM = sum. Ú.MUNUS.DU$_{11}$ interprété comme '*to give the wife the right to take over the possessions* (*after the death of her husband*)' by Å. Sjöberg (2003, p. 557), qui établit à juste titre un rapport entre les formes éblaïtes et la racine ouest-sémitique commune **wrt̠* 'hériter' (on remarquera, encore une fois dans ce cas, une graphie alternante avec ŠU: *wa-ru*$_{12}$-*šu*). On notera, enfin, *wa-rí*-SUM/*wa-rí-šu* dans VE 608, équivalent au sumérien ZAL.A.ENGUR et mis en rapport avec l'ougaritique *mrt̠* et l'hébreu *tīrōš* 'vin' par Conti (1990, pp. 167–68).

[70] "*That garlic was regarded as the primary bulb vegetable is probably because it is, by far, the least perishable of the Allium crops. The cloves tend to dry out rather than rot like onions, and the loss of a single clove does not mean loss of the whole bulb, as with onions or other juicy Allium species.*"

(2) Le second argument contre l'origine sémitique du sumérien sum concerne la structure morphologique de ce mot. Il est bien connu que les plus anciens sémitismes en sumérien apparaissent typiquement avec la terminaison *-a* (Gelb 1961, pp. 5, 141–42) dont l'origine reste peu claire malgré plusieurs études dédiées a ce problème.[71] Comme on le remarque tout de suite, ce mot se termine en revanche par une consonne.[72] L'importance de cet argument doit néanmoins être relativisée en observant qu'il y a d'autres exemples d'anciens sémitismes en sumérien où la terminaison *-a* fait défaut. Dans les listes de Krebernik, par exemple, on trouve pa-šeš$_4$ 'un prêtre' < akk. *pašīš-um* (Ur archaïque, Fāra) et maš-gag-en '*muškênum*' < akk. *muškênum* (Ebla, Abū Ṣalābīḫ). En somme, bien que dans le cas présent l'absence de terminaison *-a* ne favorise pas un emprunt sémitique, elle peut difficilement être considérée comme un obstacle définitif contre une telle éventualité (cf. Edzard 1961, p. 263).

(3) Le troisième argument met en relief la distribution géographique de l'akkadien *šūmu* pendant les périodes anciennes. Comme cela a été depuis longtemps noté, ce terme manque dans le corpus mariote, où son remplaçant doit être *ḫa-*ZA*-nu*, un terme qui est, en outre, aussi attesté dans les textes paléo-babyloniens provenant de la Mésopotamie proprement dite (CAD A/2 526, AHw. 92). La situation mariote trouve un parallèle frappant dans le corpus éblaïte, récemment discuté dans une étude synthétique (Catagnoti 2007, pp. 221–22). À Ebla, comme on l'a déjà observé ci-dessus, *šūmu* n'est pas complètement méconnu au vu de l'attestation de *šu-mi* dans la liste lexicale MEE 3, 61v. iv 6. Cette liste, cependant, n'appartient pas à la tradition lexicographique locale mais est clairement importée de Mésopotamie. En revanche, dans la grande liste lexicale "autochtone" le terme sumérien SUM.SAR est traduit par *ḫa-*ZA*-núm* (EV 0363, source d) ou laissé sans traduction (VE 1076). L'usage répandu de ce terme à Ebla est confirmé par son utilisation, à plusieurs reprises, comme désignation d'un type de bijou, récemment discutée en détail par J. Pasquali (2005b, pp. 153–55). On remarquera, enfin, que *šūmu* n'est pas attesté dans le corpus paléo-assyrien, tandis que *ḫa-zu-a-*NUM dans OIP 27, 55:33 a correctement été identifié avec l'ail par W. Farber (1981, pp. 135–37).[73]

Pour Sommerfeld, cette distribution géographique est un important argument en faveur de l'origine sumérienne de l'akkadien *šūmu*: ce terme est présent dans le *core Akkadian* (une langue en contact permanent avec le sumérien), mais manque dans les traditions occidentales géographiquement isolées du sumérien.

Pour un argument contraire, on remarquera tout de suite que l'absence de *šūmu* dans l'usage des documents cunéiformes de la zone occidentale est en flagrante opposition avec la présence largement attestée dans ces domaines d'un terme manifestement apparenté à lui, à savoir, *šamaškillu*.

Le mot akkadien *šamaškillu*, traduit généralement comme 'oignon'[74] (CAD Š/1 298, AHw. 1155), est étymologiquement inséparable de son parallèle sumérien sum-sikil, littéralement 'ail clair.'[75] Or, *šamaškillu* est attesté dans la liste bilingue éblaïte: *ša-maš-kí-lu* = sum. SUM.SAR.SIKIL (VE 1080).[76] De même pour Mari, où ce mot est bien attesté, non seulement sous sa forme habituelle *ša-ma-aš-ki-lu* (e.g., ARM 12, 241:5) mais aussi dans un curieux

---

[71] Quelques exemples plus ou moins assurés peuvent être cités d'après la récente synthèse de M. Krebernik sur les rapports linguistiques entre le sumérien et l'akkadien dans les documents de Fāra et Abū Ṣalābīḫ (1998, pp. 265, 269–70): bur-šu-ma 'vieillard(e)' < akk. *puršum-um*, lí-ga 'une mesure' < akk. *litk-um*, dam-gara 'marchand' < akk. *tamkār-um*, na-gada 'berger' < akk. *nāḳid-um*.

[72] Cet argument, malgré son importance, n'est pas explicitement avancé par Sommerfeld.

[73] L'étymologie de *ḫa-*ZA*-nu* reste jusqu'au présent incertaine, il s'agit probablement d'un terme local syro-anatolien que certains savants ont voulu retrouver dans le hittite *ḫazzuwanniš* et l'ougaritique *ḫswn* (Farber 1991, p. 236; HW III 554; DLU 201; Watson 2004, p. 127).

[74] La désignation ouest-sémitique de l'oignon est **baṣal-*: héb. *bāṣāl* (HALOT 147), syr. *beṣlā* (LSyr. 86), ar. *baṣal-* (Lane 1876, p. 212), sab. *bṣl* (SD 33), gez. *baṣal* (CDG 111), méh. *bəṣəlēt* (ML 55), jib. *béṣál* (JL 29), soq. *bíṣle* (LS 93). Ce terme semble être complètement absent de la langue akkadienne, de nombreuses tentatives d'y trouver un réflexe n'ayant jamais abouti (Fronzaroli 1969b, p. 6). Ainsi, le terme *bisru* (*bišru*) qui désigne une sorte d'alliacée dans quelques documents lexicaux et littéraires du premier millénaire (CAD B 268, AHw. 130), est difficilement comparable pour d'évidentes raisons phonologiques, comme l'a déjà observé B. Landsberger dans son édition du *Practical Vocabulary of Assur*, où ce mot explique le sumérien Ú.GARAŠ.TÚL.LA.SAR, donc une sorte de poireau (Landsberger et Gurney 1957–58, p. 337). Akk. *biṣiltu* 'récipient pour l'huile' (CAD B 268, AHw. 130), en revanche, n'est pas une désignation botanique du tout, mais s'applique, dans certaines listes lexicales du premier millénaire, à ce qui paraît être un récipient pour l'huile. Qu'il s'agisse d'un récipient en forme d'oignon (Fronzaroli 1969b, p. 6) est théoriquement possible mais très difficile à prouver.

[75] Une intéressante explication pour le changement vocalique dans la première syllabe a été proposée par P. Steinkeller (1992, p. 76): pour lui, il s'agit d'une association secondaire avec l'akkadien *šammu* 'herbe' par "étymologie populaire."

[76] On remarquera, en outre, que la forme éblaïte est intéressante pour sa graphie: l'usage du syllabogramme ŠA /ṯa/ montre que la relation avec le mot-source **ṯūm-* n'est pas perdue malgré le changement vocalique en *-a-* dû à la contamination avec *šammu* 'herbe' supposée par Steinkeller.

doublet *šu-ma-at-ki-lu* discuté par J.-M. Durand à propos d'ARM 21, 103:5 (une forme qui semble refléter le vocalisme original en *-u-*).

On ne manquera pas d'observer, enfin, l'existence d'un autre mot akkadien évidemment en rapport avec *šūmu*, à savoir, *šumku* (CAD Š/3 274, AHw. 1272). Ce terme, bien attesté dans les documents paléo-assyriens, n'est pas présent dans le dialecte babylonien et semble fonctionner comme un équivalent assyrien du babylonien *šamaškillu*.[77] L'équivalence *šumku* — *šamaškillu* 'oignon' est en outre confirmée par Ú.SUM.SIKIL.LA.SAR = *šu-un-ki* dans l'entrée 82 du *Practical Vocabulary of Assur* (Landsberger et Gurney 1957–58).[78]

Ces facteurs pris en compte, on se demande pourquoi l'absence de contact géographique immédiat entre le domaine sumérophone d'un côté et Ebla, Mari et Assur de l'autre, qui expliquerait l'absence du "sumérisme" *šūmu* dans les textes éblaïtes, mariotes et paléo-assyriens, n'a pas empêché ces dialectes d'emprunter *šamaškillu*, un sumérisme assez évident, ni *šumku* pour lequel un intermédiaire sumérien est fortement probable? À notre avis, dans de telles conditions la logique de l'argument géographique devient beaucoup plus fragile qu'on pourrait le penser.

En résumé, aucun des trois arguments ne paraît suffisamment fort pour nous faire abandonner le concept traditionnel selon lequel *_ṯ_*ūm-* reste un ancien terme proto-sémitique, emprunté comme sum par le sumérien.

33. Akk. ***karašu*** 'poireau' est bien attesté syllabiquement dès le paléo-babyonien (AHw. 448, CAD K 212). Dans la forme standard de ce mot, c'est évidemment la présence du *-r-* qui a protégé de la syncope le *-a-* bref dans la seconde syllabe. Le doublet *karšum* est, cependant, très bien attesté, comme le montre une riche collection d'exemples faite par M. Stol dans son étude synthétique sur les alliacés dans les documents paléo-babyloniens (1987b, pp. 62–63, 71). Pour Stol, c'est précisément la forme syncopée qui apparaît déjà dans quelques noms des champs de l'époque de la troisième dynastie d'Ur (^{giš}SAR GÀR.ŠUM^{ki} dans ITT 5, 6925:8).

En tout cas, c'est à Ebla que l'on trouve les plus anciennes attestations de ce terme au sein d'une tradition sémitophone. Ici, *karašu* apparaît deux fois dans la liste lexicale MEE 3, 61 vi 9 et ibid. vii 8. Dans le premier cas, il s'agit de l'expression NA$_4$ *kà-ra-šè*$^{!}$(TÚG)*-im*, interprétée par M. Civil (1987, p. 153) comme 'une pierre verte, couleur de poireau.' Comme Civil l'observe à juste titre, une telle désignation trouve quelque support dans les sources mésopotamiennes postérieures où certaines pierres sont effectivement comparées au poireau, tandis que dans la lettre ABIM 20:65 le terme *karšum* lui-même paraît désigner une pierre semi-précieuse (*ka-ar-ša-am u šadânam mala tušābilam itbal*). Dans le second cas, le terme se trouve dans l'expression l i-m a *kà-ra-sa*$^{!}$(É) AŠ*tenû*,[79] probablement 'un pot couleur de poireau' ou 'un pot pour préparer le poireau.'

Comme on l'a déjà mentionné dans le cadre de la discussion sur les plus anciennes attestations de *šūmu* 'ail,' la liste MEE 3, 61 n'appartient pas à la tradition éblaïte locale. Par conséquent, les deux formes *kà-ra-šè*$^{!}$*-im* et *kà-ra-sa*$^{!}$ doivent être considérées comme les plus anciens témoins de l'existence de ce mot dans une forme très ancienne de la langue akkadienne. Une possible manifestation locale syrienne sera discutée plus loin.

Étymologiquement, l'akkadien *karašu* 'poireau' est inséparable de l'hébreu post-biblique *kārēšā* (Jastrow 667), syr. *karrātā* (LSyr. 349), arb. *karāṯ-*, *karrāṯ-*, *kurrāṯ-* (Lane 1876, p. 2604). Pour P. Fronzaroli (1969b, p. 6, 24, 32), il s'agit en effet d'un terme proto-sémitique reconstruit par lui comme ***karaṯ**-. On ne manquera pas d'observer, cependant, que la probabilité d'une série d'emprunts est assez haute dans ce cas. Bien sûr, le *ṯ* en arabe peut être un réflexe fidèle de l'interdentale sourde proto-sémitique, mais il est difficile d'exclure qu'il rend plutôt la variante fricative du *t* araméen dans un mot emprunté. Et comme on l'a déjà vu dans le cas de l'akkadien *kunāšu* vs. l'araméen *kūnātā* 'épeautre,' la correspondance du *š* akkadien au *t* araméen, bien que cela ne favorise pas un emprunt, n'est pas suffisante pour l'exclure complètement. La question est donc difficile à résoudre. Elle devient encore plus compliquée au vu de l'orthographe contradictoire des formes "proto-akkadiennes" attestées à Ebla. Comme Civil l'observe à juste titre, le syllabogramme ŠÈ dans *kà-ra-šè*$^{!}$*-im* correspond parfaitement au **-ṯ-* dans la reconstruction proto-sémitique, tandis que l'usage du syllabogramme SA dans *kà-ra-sa*$^{!}$ n'est pas régulier (on attendrait plutôt ŠA).

---

[77] Un rare exemple de nette opposition lexicale "babylonien" vs. "assyrien," dont quelques autres manifestations (telles que *ammium* vs. *ullûm* 'celui-là,' *ḫuzīrum* vs. *šaḫûm* 'cochon,' *adrum* vs. *maškanum* 'aire,' *kēna* vs. *anna/anni* 'oui,' *pūrum* vs. *iskum* 'sort, destin') ont été discutés dans Kogan 2006, pp. 179–80.

[78] L'étymologie de *šumku* reste énigmatique: l'identité de son premier élément (*šum-*) avec *šūmu* 'ail' n'est pas à mettre en doute, mais l'origine de la terminaison *-ku* est obscure. Ne s'agirait-t-il pas d'une adaptation du terme sumérien sum-GUD, bien attesté comme une désignation de plante alliacée dans les sources du troisième millénaire (Waetzoldt 1987, p. 33)?

[79] Sur la lecture difficile de cette cartouche, voir en dernier lieu Civil 2008, p. 72.

Comme on l'a observé depuis longtemps, l'akkadien *karašu* a été emprunté par le sumérien comme ga-raš. Cette graphie, bien connue dans les documents du deuxième millénaire, est en fait attestée dès les sources présargoniques: ga-raš(KASKAL)^{sar} dans la liste lexicale OIP 99, 33 iii 22 (Abū Ṣalābīḫ) ou le document SRU 118 iii 5′ (Lagash présargonique). En outre, d'autres graphies sont attestées pour ce mot dans les sources du troisième millénaire, à savoir, KASKAL.GA^{sar} (e.g., HSS 10, 11:4, Gasur sargonique, transcrit comme GARAŠ$_4$ dans Borger 2004, p. 484) ou KASKAL^{sar} tout court.[80] En tout cas, la lecture /garaš/ pour le mot sumérien paraît être certaine dès le milieu du troisième millénaire, une date fort ancienne pour un emprunt sémitique en sumérien avec une lecture phonétique assurée. L'absence de la terminaison *-a* est donc remarquable au regard de ce qui a été dit sur ce problème dans le cadre de notre discussion du sumérien sum.

Le sumérien ga-raš paraît être re-emprunté en akkadien comme *giršānum*, une désignation d'une plante alliacée bien attestée syllabiquement dès le paléo-babylonien (CAD G 96, AHw. 286). Son équivalent sumérien est ga-raš-sag "poireau à (grande) tête." Ce terme doit être le mot-source de l'akkadien *giršānu*, bien que l'évolution phonologique et structurelle qu'un tel emprunt suppose soit assez singulière (Lieberman 1977, pp. 251–52).

Il nous reste à mentionner, enfin, la forme éblaite GA-BA-*ra-šu* attestée dans la grande liste lexicale (VE 1078) et discutée en détail par A. Catagnoti (2007, p. 226). Il reste toujours tentant de rapprocher cette forme du **karaṯ*- proto-sémitique. Une telle identification pose cependant de redoutables problèmes sur les deux plans sémantique et phonologique. D'un côté, la forme sémitique ne correspond pas au GA.RAŠ^{sar} sumérien, mais plutôt au SUM.KUR, donc une sorte d'ail ou d'oignon et non pas le poireau, une plante qui est "*immer deutlich von den Zwiebeln getrennt*" dans les sources du troisième millénaire (Waetzoldt 1987, pp. 30–31). On doit admettre, cependant, que dans une liste dont l'entrée suivante traduit le sumérien GA.RAŠ^{sar} par *ḫa*-ZA-*nu* 'ail' un tel obstacle est probablement moins grave qu'on ne pourrait le penser. L'aspect phonétique de cette comparaison est, en revanche, beaucoup plus problématique.

Il est vrai que la séquence GA-RA-ŠU pourrait parfaitement correspondre au proto-sémitique **karaṯ*-. Mais que faire du syllabogramme BA? Comme Catagnoti l'observe, une graphie "rapide" (ou plutôt "condensée"), donc "*ga-ra-šu* ou *ba-ra-šu*," est difficilement possible dans ce cas: comme le montre M. Bonechi dans sa note dédiée à ce phénomène orthographique (2008), dans tous les cas assurés il s'agit de variants morphologiques d'un seul mot (ou, au moins, d'une seule racine) et non pas de paronymes.[81] Selon Catagnoti, *ba-ra-šu*, serait théoriquement comparable au *bišru*, une plante alliacée attestée dans les textes du premier millénaire et discutée ci-dessus, mais cette comparaison luit paraît, à juste titre, très peu probable.

Plus attractive, au moins superficiellement, pourrait être une comparaison avec le grec πράσον 'poireau' et le latin *porrus, porrum*. Ces termes, sans aucune étymologie satisfaisante au sein de l'indo-européen, ont été en effet comparés au **karaṯ*- sémitique par W. Vycichl (1963), pour lequel "*der Wechsel* k : p *darf nicht verwundern.*"[82] Cependant, les deux exemples citées par lui comme illustration de ce phénomène — le nom de la ville *Gubla*, rendue en grec comme Βύβλος, et le mot hittite *kurša*- 'peau,' probablement apparenté au grec βύρσα — ne nous aident pas beaucoup, surtout parce que dans le deux cas il s'agit d'un vocalisme stable en *-u-* dans le mot-source, ce qui n'est pas le cas du **karaṯ*- 'poireau.' La coïncidence entre *ba-ra-šu* et πράσον reste toutefois intéressante bien qu'aucune explication convaincante ne puisse être avancée à l'heure actuelle.

34. Akk. ***ḳiššû*** désignait une plante cucurbitacée dont l'identification est assez difficile aujourd'hui. Nos dictionnaires hésitent entre 'concombre,' 'courge,' et 'melon' (AHw. 923, CAD Q 271). La nature des contextes — assez nombreux par ailleurs — est telle qu'une conclusion définitive est difficilement possible. Dans sa synthèse récente M. Powell affirme, tout de même: "*the Akkadian term seems to denote primarily the cucumber*" (2003, p. 20).

Le mot akkadien est clairement apparenté à quelques désignations des cucurbitacées dans d'autres langues sémitiques, à savoir, héb. *ḳiššūʾīm* (HALOT 1151), syr. *ḳaṭṭūtā* (LSyr. 657), ar. *qiṯṯāʾ-*, *quṯṯāʾ-* (Lane 1876, p. 2487), gez. *ḳʷəsyāt* (CDG 447). Une signification botanique plus ou moins exacte est difficile à obtenir. Par exemple, l'hébreu *ḳiššūʾīm* n'est attesté que dans Nombres 11:5, à côté de quatre autres sortes de plantes légumineuses consommées

---

[80] Souvent à Ebla, voir Catagnoti 2007, p. 227 où cette graphie est rendue comme GARAŠ$_x$.SAR, le signe GA qui la précède quelque fois étant interprété comme un complément phonétique (donc ^{ga}GARAŠ$_x$.SAR).

[81] Par exemple, *li-la-šu* = GAR.GÚG.GÚG 'pâte; pétrir la pâte' (VE 127), *si-sa-ša-bù* = Ú.ŠIM.GA 'une plante lacteuse' (VE 286) ou *da-du-du* = ŠÀ.KI.ÀG 'amour' (VE 584).

[82] Pour l'étymologie des mots grec et latin, voir par ailleurs Frisk 1960, p 589; Chantraine 1968, p. 934; Ernout et Meillet 1967, p. 523.

en Égypte dont l'absence a été tellement regrettée par les Israélites dans le désert. De même pour le terme éthiopien classique qui n'est attesté que dans le même passage de la Bible éthiopienne.[83]

La reconstruction proto-sémitique ***ḳVṯ(ṯ)Vˀ**-, proposée sur cette base par P. Fronzaroli (1969b, pp. 6, 25, 32), paraît bien justifiée, bien que les détails de la structure vocalique de la proto-forme restent peu clairs. Toutefois, on remarquera que la graphie *ḳí-iš-šu-e*, attestée dans la lettre paléo-babylonienne VAS 16, 2:18 (5 *ḳí-iš-šu-e šūbilīm* 'envoi-moi cinq *ḳ*.') est structuralement assez proche à la base *ḳiššūˀ*- de la forme hébraïque.

Comme on l'a supposé depuis longtemps, le terme sumérien úkuš(ḪÚL), dont les graphies syllabiques /ukuš/ ou /kuš/ sont attestées dès le paléo-babylonien, doit être mis en rapport avec l'akkadien *ḳiššû*.[84] Bien qu'il reste tentant de penser que les deux formes soient apparentées, on ne doit pas ignorer quelques évidents obstacles structurels, à savoir, le vocalisme -*u*- dans la première syllabe de la forme sumérienne (qui n'est pas attesté pour cette racine en akkadien et, dans les autres langues sémitiques, n'est évident qu'en arabe) autant que la prothèse en *u*-. On doit observer, néanmoins, que la lecture syllabique plus ancienne de ce mot est /ku-uš/ (kuš$_8$), d'où on peut déduire la nature secondaire du *u*- dans l'*Anlaut*.

35. Akk. ***ḫassū*** 'laitue,' bien attesté syllabiquement dès le paléo-babylonien (AHw. 331, CAD Ḫ 128), ne peut pas être séparé du syriaque *ḥastā* (LSyr. 245) et de l'arabe *ḫass*- (Lane 1876, p. 736), qui paraissent désigner la même plante. Pour P. Fronzaroli, il s'agit de réflexes d'une proto-forme commune ***ḫass**- (1969b, pp. 6, 25, 32). Cependant — comme Fronzaroli lui-même l'observe à juste titre — une chaîne d'emprunts n'est pas inenvisageable dans ce cas. Il est vrai que la présence du *ḫ* en arabe ne favorise pas a priori une telle hypothèse, mais comme on a déjà pu le remarquer à propos de l'araméen *ḥellāpā* et de l'arabe *ḫilāf*- 'saule,' elle n'offre pas un obstacle insurmontable non plus, car la perte de l'opposition entre **ḥ* et **ḫ* est un phénomène assez tardif en araméen.

La similitude entre l'akkadien *ḫassu* et son équivalent sumérien ḫi-is^{sar} n'a pas bien sûr échappé à l'attention des assyriologues. Pour les auteurs du CAD, il s'agit d'un emprunt akkadien en sumérien, ou d'un *Kulturwort* (pour la dernière solution voir aussi Farber 1991, p. 236).

Le terme sumérien dans sa graphie "pleine" ne remonte pas au-delà des documents de la troisième dynastie d'Ur mais les sumérologues sont enclins à identifier à ce terme botanique la graphie de la liste lexicale ED Plants 69 et 115. Dans le cas d'un emprunt — soit sumérien > akkadien, soit akkadien > sumérien — une différence vocalique aussi marquante paraît assez difficile à expliquer et on se demande s'il ne s'agirait pas plutôt d'une convergence secondaire entre deux désignations botaniques étymologiquement différentes.

VII. Plantes domestiquées: les arbres

36. L'akkadien ***šiḳdu*** 'amandier,' dont les plus anciennes attestations syllabiques remontent au paléo-babylonien (AHw. 1247, CAD Š/3 94), est présent, comme un emprunt akkadien, dès les documents sumériens de la période sargonique et de la troisième dynastie d'Ur où toute une variété de doublettes ont été enregistrées dans Gelb 1957, pp. 282–83 (ši-ik-dum, si-ik-dum, si-ik-da).

Le mot akkadien trouve des parallèles immédiats dans l'ougaritique *ṯḳd* (DUL 927; Watson 2004, pp. 117–18) et l'hébreu *šāḳēd* (HALOT 1638), ce qui permet de reconstruire une proto-forme sémitique commune ***ṯaḳid**- (Fronzaroli 1969a, pp. 279, 291, 300). Le changement vocalique en akkadien est remarquable mais non sans précédent: comme parallèle exact, on peut mentionner l'hébreu *nāmēr* 'léopard' vs. l'akkadien *nimru* (SED II no. 164).[85] Une structure morphologique plus archaïque du mot akkadien a été signalée au sein de la tradition mariote par J.-M. Durand, à savoir, *ša-ḳí-di* dans les lettres T.135:10 et M.5249:5–6 (Durand 2001, pp. 130–31). Ces graphies pourraient être normalisées comme /šaḳidum/, un prototype idéal pour la forme hébraïque attestée (*šāḳēd*).

[83] Qu'il ne s'agit pas ici d'un *ghost-word* est néanmoins assuré par les parallèles amhariques: *ḳ^{w}asa* 'concombre,' *ḳussəyat* 'sorte de courge' (AED 751, 757).

[84] Pour S. Lieberman (1977, p. 426), il s'agit d'un sumérisme en akkadien, mais la direction inverse de l'emprunt n'est guère inenvisageable.

[85] Voir aussi la variante en -*u*- (*šuḳdu*), attestée dès le médio-assyrien (1 GIŠ *ša šu-uḳ-di mat-ḳi* dans KAJ 310:51) avec un parallèle possible dans les graphies syllabiques de l'ougaritique (^{giš}*šu-uḳ-du*(-)*ma* [...] dans PRU 6, 159:4′, voir Huehnergard 1987, pp. 188–89), la forme alphabétique *ṯḳd* n'étant attestée que dans les textes hippiatriques dans la phrase *ṯḳd mr* 'amandes amères' (Cohen et Sivan 1983, p. 23; Pardee 1985, pp. 55–56).

Selon Zurro 1983, p. 266, la même structure archaïque se trouve dans le précédent éblaïte *ša-ḳì-dum* = sum. GIŠ.DALLA (VE 457).

Les termes akkadiens et cananéens mentionnées ci-dessus sont difficiles à séparer des formes qui ont le même sens et possèdent un *-g-* comme deuxième consonne radicale en araméen et en éthiopien, à savoir, le syriaque *šegdtā* (LSyr. 755) et le guèze *səgd* (CDG 491). Il s'agit manifestement d'une assimilation de sonorité (*-ḳd- > -gd-) qui, apparemment, a affecté les deux langues d'une manière indépendante: on ne manquera pas de remarquer que la racine est absente de l'arabe, tandis qu'un emprunt immédiat de l'éthiopien à l'araméen dans le domaine de la terminologie botanique est improbable.

La vélaire sonore irrégulière dans la forme araméenne ne doit pas nous faire perdre de vue le fait que la même forme présente une autre irrégularité tout à fait remarquable, à savoir, *š* comme réflexe de l'interdentale sourde *ṯ. La nature de cette irrégularité n'est pas difficile à comprendre: il s'agit évidemment d'une incompatibilité de deux dentales dans la racine nominale hypothétique (**tukdu*). Dans un tel contexte, il est très intéressant de remarquer qu'une forme tout à fait proche de la forme araméenne "régulière" nous est probablement parvenue dans la tradition cunéiforme. Il s'agit du lexème normalisé comme *dukdu* ou *duqdu* dans CAD L 238 and CDA 62, qui désigne une sorte de bois et ses fruits comestibles dans quelques textes néo-assyriens. La lecture *dukdu* étant assurée par *du*-UK-*di* dans Cult of Aššur 100 X 21, l'ancienne normalisation **luddu* est donc à abandonner.[86] Comme M. Stol l'a reconnu (1979, p. 14), il est très probable que cette forme soit apparentée à *šuḳdu* akkadien. Mais de quel type de relation s'agirait-il dans ce cas? Dans la mesure où une alternance *š* – *d* au sein de la langue akkadienne paraît peu probable, on est enclin à penser à un araméisme (ou au moins à une forme akkadienne araméisante) **tuḳdu* avec une assimilation de sonorité (*duḳdu*).

Le terme proto-sémitique **ṯaḳid-* ne semble pas être attesté à Ebla. Dans la grande liste lexicale bilingue le sumérogramme ^{giš}IŠ$_{11}$ qui désigne l'amandier dans la tradition lexicographique mésopotamienne correspond à *bu*$_{16}$(NI)-*ṭù-tù* 'térébinthe' (VE 462), une preuve de plus de la relation étroite entre les deux arbres dans les sources cunéiformes déjà observée par Stol. En revanche, la forme *lu-zu-um*, évidemment identique à la désignation de l'amandier dans quelques langues ouest-sémitiques,[87] traduit le sumérien GIŠ.ŠIM.GAM.GAM dans VE 375, dont l'équivalent mésopotamien régulier est *kukru*, une plante aromatique discutée en détail par Stol (1979, pp. 16–18).

37. Akk. ***tittu*** 'figue, figuier,' attesté syllabiquement dès le paléo-assyrien et le paléo-babylonien (CAD T 435, AHw. 1363), montre un clair précédent à Ebla, à savoir, *ti-ì-tum* = sum. GIŠ.PÈŠ dans VE 368a (Catagnoti 2008, p. 181).[88]

Le terme akkadien doit être ramené à la reconstruction proto-sémitique ****taʔin(-at)-*** (Fronzaroli 1969b, pp. 7, 25, 32) ou, comme la forme éblaïte le montre, plutôt **tiʔin(-at)-*, attestée par ailleurs en oug. *ti-*[*n*]*a*$^{?}$-[*t*]*u*$_4$ (Huehnergard 1987, p. 184), héb. *təʔēnā* (HALOT 1675) et syr. *tettā* (LSyr. 813). Le *-n-* préconsonantique, assimilé au suffixe féminin *-t-* en akkadien, devient manifeste dans le pluriel *tīnātum*, attesté plusieurs fois dans les documents paléo-babyloniens ainsi que dans le nom de mois paléo-assyrien *ša tīnātim*.

La forme arabe *tīn-*, connue dès la fameuse sourate coranique qui porte son nom, est considérée d'habitude comme un emprunt araméen (Jeffery 1938, pp. 96–97), probablement à juste titre une fois prise en compte l'absence du -ʔ-.

Dans la liste lexicale Malku II 124, *tittu* dans la colonne de droite a pour équivalent *ti-ʔ-u* (*ti-ʔ-ú*) dans la colonne de gauche, une forme probablement apparentée pour laquelle une explication cohérente nous échappe. Un ouest-sémitisme ne serait bien sûr pas inattendu dans ce cas, mais aucune forme ouest-sémitique n'est même de loin analogue. Serait-il trop osé de penser plutôt à un particularisme néo-assyrien, avec le passage du *-n-* au -ʔ- décrit par W. von Soden dans *GAG* §33c?

38. Akk. ***ḫaḫḫu***, attesté dans quelques documents néo-assyriens autant que dans les listes lexicales du premier millénaire, a été identifié à différentes sortes d'arbres fruitiers: 'prunier' (Powell 2003, pp. 18–19) ou 'pêcher'

[86] La seule attestation sur laquelle cette normalisation aurait pu théoriquement s'appuyer était *lu-ud-di* dans la ligne 83 de la Légende du roi de Cutha, correctement interprétée par J. G. Westenholz comme une forme verbale précative *luddi* 'je vais rejeter' (1997, pp. 316–18).

[87] L'hébreu *lūz* (HALOT 522), le syriaque *lūzā* (LSyr. 361), l'arabe *lawz-* (Lane 1876, p. 2681).

[88] Comme M. Krebernik (1983, p. 14) et E. Zurro (1983, p. 268) l'observent à juste titre, une lecture *ti*-NI-*tum* paraît assez peu probable dans ce cas.

(Postgate 1987, pp. 120–30). Selon W. von Soden (AHw. 308, suivi par CDA 101), le mot akkadien est déjà présent dans le paléo-babylonien, mais la seule référence qu'il a pu citer n'inspire pas beaucoup confiance.[89]

Le mot akkadien a été depuis longtemps identifié aux désignations du prunier dans les langues ouest-sémitiques, à savoir, syr. *ḥaḥḥā*, *ḥōḥā* (PS 1243, 1219), arb. *ḫawḫ-* (Lane 1876, p. 820), gez. *ḫoḫ* (CDG 260). Selon P. Fronzaroli (1969b, pp. 7, 25, 33), il s'agit des réflexes d'un terme proto-sémitique ****ḫāḫ****- 'prunier,' mais on doit admettre que la probabilité d'emprunt est très haute dans ce cas. C'est surtout le terme akkadien — la seule attestation paléo-babylonienne n'étant pas assurée — qui paraît un emprunt (un araméisme?) plutôt qu'un mot autochtone. On remarquera, d'ailleurs, que selon Fronzaroli cette forme est apparentée à quelques désignations d'arbrisseaux épineux sauvages[90] et désignerait donc, à l'origine, le prunier sauvage (*prunus spinosa*), *"che si presenta appunto come un arbusto con rami terminanti in lunghe spine."*

39. Le proto-sémitique ****tam(a)r****- 'palmier dattier' (Fronzaroli 1969a, pp. 291, 279, 300), représenté par héb. *tāmār* (HALOT 1756), AJP *twmrh* (DJPA 577), ar. *tamr-* (Lane 1876, p. 317), sab. et min. *tmr* (Sima 2000, p. 246), gez. *tamr*, *tamart* (CDG 576), méh. *tōmər* (ML 402), jib. *təmrɛ́t* (JL 271), soq. *timreh* (LS 443), n'a laissé aucune trace dans la langue akkadienne, qui désigne le palmier par le sumérisime *gišimmaru*, dont les graphies syllabiques, bien que rares, sont clairement attestées dès le paléo-babylonien (CAD G 102; AHw. 292; Lieberman 1987, p. 297).

Cependant, une certaine ressemblance entre le sumérien gišimmar et le proto-sémitique **tam(a)r-* a mené quelques chercheurs à penser que le terme sumérien lui-même avait été emprunté au sémitique. Plus concrètement, pour G. Pettinato (1981, p. 259) il s'agirait d'une fusion du sumérien giš 'arbre' avec un terme sémitique rendu par lui comme *samar*.

Une telle étymologie — quoi qu'elle soit tentante à première vue (Zurro 1983, p. 268) — se heurte à des obstacles redoutables dans les deux domaines sumérologique et sémitologique.

La présence de l'élément giš dans le mot sumérien est évidemment difficile à nier. Cependant, les plus anciennes graphies syllabiques de la partie restante de ce mot (ni-in-bar, nim-mar, nim-bar) sur lesquelles se base la reconstruction *giš+nimbar récemment proposé par K. Volk (2004, pp. 283–84) ne sont compatibles avec aucune forme sémitique connue. De surcroît, il n y a pas de graphie qui montre un *š* redoublé en sumérien — un redoublement qui serait plutôt nécessaire dans une forme provenant du *giš + *samar* hypothétique.

Quant au sémitique **samar-*, une telle forme n'existe pas. La forme sémitique "standard" est, comme on l'a vu, **tam(a)r-*. La forme **ṯamar-*, souvent perçue comme une sorte de "doublet" du **tamar-*, n'est attesté qu'en arabe et le sudarabique épigraphique, où ces mots, par ailleurs, ne s'appliquent pas au fruit du palmier mais fonctionnent comme termes génériques pour 'fruit' (Lane 1876, p. 353; SD 150). C'est donc la forme éblaïte *sa-ma-lum*, équivalente au sumérien GIŠ.GIŠIMMAR dans VE 399, qui doit attirer notre attention. Comme on le voit clairement, cette forme — correctement normalisée comme **šam(m)arum* par Volk — ne correspond régulièrement ni au **tamar-*, ni même au **ṯamar-*: dans le dernier cas, on attendrait une graphie avec ŠA. La judicieuse remarque de W. Lambert (*"the irregular correspondences with the first consonant suggest a Kulturwort,"* 1989, p. 30) ne change pas grand-chose: la nature de la forme éblaïte reste énigmatique et il ne semble pas qu'une telle forme puisse servir comme base plus au moins solide pour une étymologie sémitique du sumérien gišimmar.

VIII. La vigne

L'importance de la viniculture en Mésopotamie étant assez réduite, on ne s'étonnera pas d'observer que la plupart des termes ouest-sémitiques communs ayant trait à la vigne sont absents ou marginalisés en akkadien. Il nous paraît utile, toutefois, de discuter ici brièvement quatre termes fondamentaux appartenant à ce groupe.

40. Le proto-sémitique ****gapn****- 'vigne' (Fronzaroli 1969b, pp. 8, 25, 33) est bien attesté dans les langues sémitiques centrales, à savoir oug. *gpn* (DUL 304), héb. *gäpän* (HALOT 200), syr. *gpettā* (LSyr. 128), ar. *ǯafn-* (Lane 1876, p. 434). En akkadien, *gapnu* et *gupnu* ne sont attestés que dans les sources tardives (AHw. 281, 298; CAD G 44) et pourraient être considérés, en principe, comme des emprunts ouest-sémitiques. Le vieux problème auquel cette

[89] *ḫa-ṣí-ib* ^giš^*ḫa-ḫe*^!?^*-e*^?^, lu et interprété comme *ḫa-ṣí-ib* ^giš^*ḫa-aḫ-ḫa* '*the cutter of the fruit tree*' dans Leemans 1960, p. 26.

[90] Héb. *ḥōaḥ* (HALOT 296), syr. *ḥōḥā* (LSyr. 226), tig. *ḥaḥot* (WTS 58), tna. *ḥeḥot* (TED 168).

hypothèse se heurte est le sens des termes akkadiens. F. Thureau-Dangin (1912, pp. 29, 42–43) a été le premier à reconnaître qu'au moins *gupnu* fonctionnait comme une désignation générique pour 'arbre' dans les inscriptions royales néo-assyriennes. La même traduction est probable pour les quelques attestations du *gapnu*. Dans les documents néo-babyloniens, ce dernier terme s'applique clairement à différentes sortes d'arbres fruitiers et ce n'est que dans un nombre réduit de passages qu'il désigne spécifiquement la vigne. La différence sémantique entre les termes akkadiens et leur hypothétique source ouest-sémitique paraît suffisamment remarquable pour nous faire douter qu'il s'agisse d'un véritable emprunt. B. Meissner (1931, pp. 27–28) a voulu résoudre ce problème en remarquant que le **gapn-* ouest-sémitique s'applique parfois aux plantes autres que la vigne, mais le seul exemple qu'il a pu citer — le fameux *gäpän śādā̆* désignant les fruits du coloquinte dans le deuxième livre des Rois (4:39) — ne semble guère suffisant, le sens exclusif 'vigne' étant très stable dans tout le domaine ouest-sémitique.

Pourrait-on supposer, en revanche, que *gupnu* et *gapnu* sont en réalité des mots akkadiens autochtones (éventuellement, des dialectismes assyriens, d'où leur absence dans les listes lexicales babyloniennes "classiques"), qui ont peut-être été contaminés par le **gapn-* 'vigne' ouest-sémitique, lequel, effectivement, aurait pu être emprunté aux périodes les plus récentes?[91]

Dans un tel contexte, il est intéressant de suivre l'histoire du terme hittite GA-PA-NU/KA-PA-NU, récemment étudié en détail dans Kassian, Korolëv, et Sidel'tsev 2002, pp. 523–24. Dans la plupart des contextes, ce terme désigne 'arbre,' 'tronc' (dans quelques passages, de façon remarquable, 'tige de la vigne')[92] et il est bien sûr tentant d'y voir un emprunt akkadien qui serait, en même temps, le plus ancien témoignage de l'akkadien (assyrien?) *gapnu* — plusieurs centaines d'années avant les exemples néo-assyriens mentionnés ci-dessus.[93]

On remarquera, enfin, que selon E. Arcari (1984, p. 324) **gapn-* a laissé quelques réflexes à Ebla, à savoir, *ga-pá-na-na-u₉*, *gáp-na-ne-u₉* = sum. Ú.TIR (VE 1431′, EV 0432) et *ga-pá-na-na-ù* = sum. ŠE.NINNI₅ (EV 0392). Cette identification est tentante car il n'y a pas de doute que les équivalents sumériens représentent des termes botaniques, mais la terminaison *-na-ne-u₉*/*-na-na-u₉* (un redoublement suivie par un accroissement guttural ou -*y*-) reste complètement énigmatique.[94]

41. Le proto-sémitique **ʕ**inab**-* 'raisin' est bien attesté dans la plupart des langues ouest-sémitiques: héb. *ʕēnāb* (HALOT 851), syr. *ʕenbtā* (LSyr. 534), ar. *ʕinab-* (Lane 1876, p. 2167), sab. *ʕnb* (SD 17).[95] La racine est aussi attestée en ougaritique, mais sous une forme phonétiquement inattendue *ynb* (DUL 323). Il est bien probable que ce terme soit préservé en akkadien comme *inbu*, attesté syllabiquement dès les noms propres sargoniques. Le sens du mot akkadien est cependant plus général, à savoir, 'fruit' (AHw. 381, CAD I 144).[96]

42. Le proto-sémitique **ʔ**Vṯkāl**-* désignait probablement un racème de fruits, en premier lieu, une grappe de vigne: oug. *ʔuṯkl* (DUL 125; Watson 2004, p. 120), héb. *ʔäškōl* (HALOT 95), AJB *ʔitkālā* (DJBA 178), ar. *ʔiṯkāl-* (Lane 1876, p. 21), gez. *ʔaskāl* (CDG 42). La forme *áš-kà-lum*, *iš₁₁-kà-um* dans VE 660, dont l'équivalent sumérien est ŠE.GEŠTIN, offre un excellent parallèle aux termes ouest-sémitiques sur les deux plans sémantique et phonologique (Zurro 1983, pp. 266; Catagnoti 2008, p. 179).[97]

Il est bien sûr difficile de séparer de ces termes l'akkadien *isḫunnatu*/*išḫunnatu*, un mot relativement peu fréquent qui désigne la même réalité (CAD I 190, AHw. 387), probablement déjà dans le nom propre paléo-babylonien

---

91 Cf. Fronzaroli 1969b, p. 8: "... *un significato non specializzato, che potrebbe essere più antico di quello tecnico della viticoltura.*"

92 *nam-ma* gišGEŠTIN GA-PA-NU *IŠ-TU* t[úgŠÀ.K]A.DÙ *an-da ḫu-u-la-li-an-zi* 'alors ils enveloppent une cein[ture de tiss]us autour de la vigne' (KUB 30, 19+vs. i 10).

93 On doit admettre, cependant, que dans certains contextes le sens du terme hittite reste assez mal compris. Tel est, par exemple, le cas du texte médical StBoT 19, 18 i 11–12 où GA-PA-NU s'applique à l'ail, au poireau et à la plante *šullittini*: SUMsar GA-PA-NU GA.RAŠsar GA-PA-NU ... *šu-ul-li-it-ti-in-ni-iš*sar GA-PA-NU (Burde 1974, p. 19).

94 Dans un tel contexte, l'identification avec *kamūnu* 'cime,' proposée par Steinkeller (1992, p. 77) et développée en détail par Catagnoti (2010, pp. 143–46), devient préférable.

95 Dans le dernier cas, avec un changement du sens en 'vignoble' discuté par A. Sima (Sima 2000, p. 195–96).

96 Au moins en théorie, le mot akkadien pourrait être dérivé d'une autre racine sémitique bien répandue, à savoir **ʔVbb-* 'pousse, germe, fleur, fruit': oug. *ʔib* 'fruit, fleur' (DUL 4), héb. *ʔēb* 'pousse,' *ʔābīb* 'épi' (HALOT 2, 4), syr. *ʔebbā* 'fruit' (LSyr. 1), ar. *ʔabb-* 'végétation' (Lane 1876, p. 3), amh. *abäba* 'fleur' (AED 1197). Le plus grand obstacle pour cette étymologie — qui reste même aujourd'hui assez répandue parmi les sémitisants (HALOT 2; DUL 4; cf. Kaufman 1974, pp. 58–59) — est la nécessité de postuler le développement dissimilatoire **-bb-* > *-mb-* > *-nb-* en akkadien, assez difficile à imaginer pour les phases les plus anciennes de l'histoire de cette langue.

97 Comme on l'a reconnu depuis longtemps, le syllabogramme IŠ₁₁ (LAM×KUR) dans les syllabaires anciens est toujours réservé à rendre l'interdentale sourde (Conti 1990, pp. 12–14; Krebernik 1988, p. 50).

is-ḫu-na-tum (TCL 1, 222:11, 27). Les irrégularités phonologiques très importantes auxquelles cette comparaison se heurte restent inexplicables.

43. Le proto-sémitique ***karm**- 'vignoble' est bien attesté dans les langues centro-sémitiques: oug. *krm* (DUL 455), héb. *käräm* (HALOT 498), syr. *karmā* (LSyr. 347), ar. *karm*- (WKAS K 140). Ce terme a été souvent rapproché du sumérien ka-ra-an, qui s'applique — pour la première fois, dans le document UET 9, 128:4, datant de la troisième dynastie d'Ur — aux racèmes de différentes sortes des fruits (pommes, figues, prunes, vigne). Dans le cadre de cette hypothèse, l'akkadien *karānu* 'vigne,' 'fruit de la vigne' mais surtout 'vin' (CAD K 202, AHw. 446) est expliqué comme un ré-emprunt au sumérien.

La comparaison entre le sumérien ka-ra-an et le sémitique *karm*-, proposée par A. Poebel (1930, p. 149) et acceptée par beaucoup d'auteurs jusqu'à nos jours (Fronzaroli 1969b, p. 7–8, 25, 33; Steiner 2003, p. 633), pose cependant plusieurs problèmes suffisamment graves pour mériter qu'on les prenne en compte: (1) le changement du *-m-* en *-n*, (2) le passage sémantique inattendu (dans aucune langue ouest-sémitique les réflexes de **karm*- ne s'appliquent aux fruits de la vigne, mais désignent plus ou moins strictement l'espace où la vigne est plantée) et, enfin, (3) la nécessité de postuler une source sémitique autre que l'akkadien (où **karm*- n'existe pas avec ce sens).

Dans de telles conditions, il nous paraît préférable de ne pas associer ka-ra-an/*karānu* avec le proto-sémitique **karm*-. Le véritable parallèle akkadien pour ce dernier serait, en revanche, *karmu* 'colline' (CAD K 218, AHw. 449), un rapprochement accepté par von Soden qui trouve une intéressante confirmation dans le sudarabique moderne, à savoir, le méhri *kərmáym*, la désignation principale de la montagne dans cette langue (ML 214). Cette comparaison, proposée par W. W. Müller (1985, p. 272), implique qu'un ancien terme topographique ait préservé son sens originel dans les zones latérales (akkadien et sudarabique moderne), le sens 'vignoble' étant une innovation des langues sémitiques centrales.

IX. Les champignons

44. L'akkadien ***kamʔatu*** est traduit traditionnellement comme 'truffe' (CAD K 120, AHw. 432). Depuis la première identification de ce terme par Ch.-F. Jean (1957), *kamʔatu* a été discuté à plusieurs reprises (voir, par exemple, Stol 1978, p. 220; Charpin 1989; Heimpel 1997). Aujourd'hui, la question de l'identité biologique du champignon en question paraît être définitivement résolue,[98] mais il n y a guère de consensus à propos de la nature diachronique du terme akkadien. Pour A. Salonen (1952, p. 3) et R. Zadok (1993, p. 325) il s'agit d'un emprunt ouest-sémitique. Telle paraît être aussi l'opinion de J.-M. Durand qui qualifie *kamʔatu* comme un terme "occidental" (1997, p. 312). M. Streck, au contraire, ne voit aucune raison pour considérer *kamʔatu* comme un ouest-sémitisme, en l'excluant explicitement de la liste des emprunts ouest-sémitiques dans son ouvrage sur l'anthroponymie amorrite (2000, p. 101).

La question est, effectivement, difficile à résoudre, et il vaut la peine d'évaluer soigneusement les possibles *pros* et *contras* de chacune des deux hypothèses.

Comme J.-M. Durand l'observe à juste titre, les attestations de *kamʔatu* clairement prédominent dans les sources "occidentales." À plusieurs attestations mariotes on peut ajouter maintenant le terme éblaïte *kà-ma-a-tum*/*kam₄-ma-a-tum* qui désigne un objet métallique (une poignée?), probablement en forme de champignon (Pasquali 2005b, pp. 129–32; Pasquali 2005a). En revanche, CAD K 120 ne cite qu'un seul exemple paléo-babylonien non-mariote, à savoir, la lettre ABIM 5:18, où la forme lue comme ḪI-ḪA-TIM[!?] par l'éditeur a été corrigée en **kam*-ḪA-*tim* par B. Landsberger (1964, p. 250). Dans la mesure où la provenance de la lettre est sud-babylonienne (Larsa), on devrait supposer que *kamʔatu* était connu aussi dans les régions fort éloignées de l'espace "occidental" de la civilisation cunéiforme. Toutefois, les données contradictoires sur la lecture de la forme en question doivent nous faire éviter des conclusions prématurées.

Dans de telles conditions, un emprunt ouest-sémitique paraît, en effet, assez probable[99] La forme *ka-ʔ-ma-tú* dans Uruanna III 321 n'offre pas d'obstacle pour une telle interprétation car un emprunt plus au moins exotique

---

[98] Comme le signale J.-M. Durand (1997, p. 312), ce mot désignait probablement une espèce de champignon autre que la truffe. On doit consulter aussi la synthèse récente dans la dissertation d'Hervé Reculeu pour lequel il s'agit d'un représentant de la famille *terfezia*.

[99] Un akkadisme en arabe supposé par H. Zimmern (1917, p. 57) devient, au contraire, presque impossible.

n'est guère inattendu dans cette immense collection des termes botaniques. De même pour le document néo-babylonien Ni. 528:5 où la présence de ce terme a été supposée par R. Zadok (1997).[100]

Un obstacle plus gênant est fourni par les mots akkadiens *kamūnu* (CAD K 133, AHw. 434) et *kammu* (CAD K 125, AHw. 433). Au moins dans le premier cas, la traduction 'une sorte de champignon' est très probable grâce à l'équivalent sumérien UZU.DIR dans les listes lexicales, identifié au champignon par B. Landsberger (1934, p. 111) dans la composition littéraire sumérienne "Le mythe de Martu" (Klein 1997, p. 112, l. 135). Or, les deux mots *kamūnu* et *kammu* sont très bien documentés dans différents types de sources akkadiennes du premier millénaire, ce qui serait assez improbable dans le cas d'un ouest-sémitisme.

Il nous reste, finalement, à étudier les parallèles ouest-sémitiques. Dans la littérature assyriologique, c'est le terme arabe *kamʔat-* qui est le plus souvent mis en rapport avec le mot akkadien, ce qui est bien compréhensible vu la présence massive de ce terme dans les sources arabes classiques (quelques douzaines d'attestations dans WKAS K 346) et sa persistance dans les parlers modernes, y compris ceux de la région syrienne du Moyen Euphrate. On remarquera, cependant, que *kəmēhim*, *kəmēhōt* sont plusieurs fois attestés dans les sources hébraïques rabbiniques.[101] Ces parallèles nous montrent clairement que l'emprunt ouest-sémitique en akkadien envisagé ci-dessus ne doit pas nécessairement être conçu comme un emprunt à une langue du type nord-arabique: il s'agit, selon toute vraisemblance, d'un mot assez répandu dans l'ancien domaine linguistique syro-palestinien,[102] bien que la différence consonantique entre l'arabe (-ʔ-) et l'hébreu (-*h*-) reste mal comprise.

Abréviations

ABIM	A. al-Zeebari. *Altbabylonische Briefe des Iraq-Museums.* Münster, 1964
AED	T. L. Kane. *Amharic-English Dictionary.* Wiesbaden: Harrassowitz, 1990
AHw.	W. von Soden. *Akkadisches Handwörterbuch.* Wiesbaden: Harrassowitz, 1965–1981
ARM	Archives royales de Mari
Baranov	Х. К. Баранов. *Арабско-русский словарь.* Москва
BDB	F. Brown, S. R. Driver, et Ch. A. Briggs. *A Hebrew and English Lexicon of the Old Testament.* Oxford: Clarendon, 1951
Behnstedt	P. Behnstedt. *Die nordjemenitischen Dialekte,* Teil II: *Glossar.* Wiesbaden: Reichert, 1992–2006
BK	A. de Biberstein-Kazimirski. *Dictionnaire arabe-français.* Paris: Maison-neuve et cie, 1860
CAD	A. Leo Oppenheim et al., éds. *The Assyrian Dictionary of the Oriental Institute of the University of Chicago.* Chicago: The Oriental Institute, 1956–2010
CDA	J. Black, A. George, et N. Postgate. *A Concise Dictionary of Akkadian.* Wiesbaden: Harrassowitz, 2000
CDG	W. Leslau. *Comparative Dictionary of Geʕez (Classical Ethiopic).* Wiesbaden: Harrassowitz, 1987
DJPA	M. Sokoloff. *A Dictionary of Jewish Palestinian Aramaic of the Byzantine Period.* Ramat Gan: Bar Ilan University Press, 1990
DLU	G. del Olmo Lete et J. Sanmartín. *Diccionario de la lengua ugarítica.* Aula orientalis. Supplementa 7–8. Barcelona: Editorial AUSA, 1996–2000
DM	E. S. Drower et R. Macuch. *A Mandaic Dictionary.* Oxford: Clarendon, 1963
DNWSI	J. Hoftijzer et K. Jongeling. *Dictionary of the North-West Semitic Inscriptions.* Leyde: Brill, 1995
Dozy	R. Dozy. *Supplément au dictionnaires arabes.* Leyde: Brill, 1927

[100] D'ailleurs, la traduction 'champignon' ne paraît pas évidente dans un contexte qui parle d'un terrain cultivé: *elat* ŠE.NUMUN.MEŠ É *ka-ma-a-tú* ŠE.NUMUN.MEŠ É *as-pa-as-ti* (*'not in arable lands planted with k. (and) the arable lands planted with lucerne?'* dans la traduction de M. Stolper, qui préfère penser à une variante du terme botanique *kamantu* (Donbaz et Stolper 1997, p. 98).

[101] En revanche, *kmhh* en judéo-araméen palestinien n'est attesté qu'une seule fois (DJPA 262). Pour une possible attestation en cunéiforme syllabique à Ougarit, voir Huehnergard 1987, p. 136.

[102] Pour A. Salonen (1952, p. 2; cf. Zimmern 1917, p. 57), il s'agit d'un emprunt araméen en arabe, ce qui est plutôt improbable.

DRS	D. Cohen. *Dictionnaire des racines sémitiques ou attestées dans les langues sémitiques.* Paris: Mouton, 1970–
DUL	G. del Olmo Lete et J. Sanmartín. *A Dictionary of the Ugaritic Language in the Alphabetic Tradition.* Leyde: Brill, 2003
EDG	W. Leslau. *Etymological Dictionary of Gurage* (*Ethiopic*), Vol. 3. Wiesbaden: Harrassowitz, 1979
EDH	W. Leslau. *Etymological Dictionary of Harari.* Berkeley: University of California Press, 1963
EV	Extracts from the Vocabulary of Ebla, dans MEE 4
Frisk	H. Frisk. *Griechisches etymologisches Wörterbuch.* Heidelberg: Winter, 1960
GAG	W. von Soden. *Grundriss der akkadischen Grammatik.* Roma: Pontificium Institutum Biblicum, 1995
HALOT	L. Koehler, W. Baumgartner, et J. J. Stamm. *The Hebrew and Aramaic Lexicon of the Old Testament.* Leyde: Brill, 1994–2000
HSS	Harvard Semitic Studies
HW III	J. Friedrich, A. Kammenhuber, et I. Hoffmann. *Hethitisches Wörterbuch.* III/17. Heidelberg: Winter, 2007
Iraq 16	C. J. Gadd. "Inscribed Prisms of Sargon II from Nimroud." *Iraq* 16/2 (1954): 175–201
ITT	Inventaire des tablettes de Tello
Jastrow	M. Jastrow. *A Dictionary of the Targumim, the Talmud Babli and Yerushalmi, and the Midrashic Literature.* New York: Judaica, 1996
JL	T. M. Johnstone. *Jibbāli Lexicon.* Oxford: Oxford University Press, 1981
KAJ	E. Ebeling. *Keilschrifttexte aus Assur juristischen Inhalts.* Wissenschaftliche Veröffentlichung der Deutschen Orient-Gesellschaft 50. Leipzig: Hinrichs, 1927
KTU	M. Dietrich, O. Loretz, et J. Sanmartín. *Die Keilalphabetischen Texte aus Ugarit.* Alter Orient und Altes Testament 24/1. Kevelaer: Butzon und Bercker, 1976
LA	Ibn Manẓūr. *Lisān al-ʿarab.* Bayrūt: Dār Ṣādir, 1955–1956
LIQ	S. D. Ricks. *Lexicon of Inscriptional Qatabanian.* Roma: Editrice Pontificio Istituto Biblico, 1989
LM	M. Arbach. *Le maḏābien: lexique, onomastique et grammaire d'une langue de l'Arabie méridionale préislamique.* Tome 1. *Lexique maḏābien.* Aix-en-Provence, 1993
LS	W. Leslau. *Lexique Soqoṭri (Sudarabique moderne) avec comparaisons et explications étymologiques.* Paris: Klincksieck, 1938
LSyr.	C. Brockelmann. *Lexicon Syriacum.* Halle: M. Niemeyer, 1928
LXX	Septuagint
MAD	Materials for the Assyrian Dictionary
MC 4	Piotr Steinkeller. *Third-Millennium Legal and Administrative Texts in the Iraq Museum, Baghdad.* Mesopotamian Civilizations 4. Winona Lake: Eisenbrauns, 1992
MD	*Mandaic Dictionary*
MEE 3	Giovanni Pettinato. *Testi lessicali monolingui della Biblioteca L. 2769.* Materiali epigrafici di Ebla 3. Napoli: Istituto universitario orientale di Napoli, 1981
MEE 4	Giovanni Pettinato. *Testi lessicali bilingui della biblioteca L. 2769.* Materiali epigrafici di Ebla 4. Napoli: Istituto universitario orientale di Napoli, 1982
OIP 99	R. D. Biggs. *Inscriptions from Tell Abū Ṣalābīkh.* Oriental Institute Publications 99. Chicago: University of Chicago Press, 1974
ML	T. M. Johnstone. *Mehri Lexicon and English-Mehri word-list.* London: School of Oriental and African Studies, University of London, 1987
PRU	Palais royal d'Ugarit. Mission de Ras Shamra. Paris: Impr. Nationale, 1956–
PS	R. Payne Smith. *Thesaurus Syriacus.* Oxford: Clarendon, 1879–1901
PSD	Å. Sjöberg, éd. *The Sumerian Dictionary of the University Museum of the University of Pennsylvania.* Philadelphia: Babylonian Section of the University Museum, 1984–
Puhvel	J. Puhvel. *Hittite Etymological Dictionary*, Vol. 4: *Words beginning with K.* Berlin: Mouton, 1997
RA	*Revue d'Assyriologie et d'Archéologie Orientale*
RS	Museum siglum of the Louvre and Damascus (Ras Shamra)
SD	A. F. L. Beeston, M. A. Ghul, W. W. Müller, et J. Ryckmans. *Dictionnaire sabéen (anglais-français-arabe).* Louvain-la-Neuve: Peeters, 1982
SED I	A. Militarev et L. Kogan. *Semitic Etymological Dictionary*, Vol. 1: *Anatomy of Man and Animals.* Münster: Ugarit-Verlag, 2000
SED II	A. Militarev et L. Kogan. *Semitic Etymological Dictionary*, Vol. 2: *Animal Names.* Münster: Ugarit-Verlag, 2005
SL	M. Sokoloff. *A Syriac Lexicon.* Winona Lake: Eisenbrauns, 2009

SRU	D. O. Edzard, *Sumerische Rechtsurkunden des III. Jahrtausends.* Abhandlungen der Bayerischen Akademie der Wissenschaften, Philosophisch-historische Klasse, neue Folge, 67. München: Verlag der Bayerischen Akademie der Wissenschaften, 1968
StBoT	Studien zu den Bogazköy-Texten
TCL	Textes cunéiformes, Musées du Louvre
TED	T. L. Kane. *Tigrinya-English Dictionary.* Springfield: Dunwoody, 2000
UET	Ur Excavations, Texts
VE	Vocabulario di Ebla (= MEE 4, 1982)
Wb.	A. Erman et E. Grapow. *Wörterbuch der aegyptischen Sprache.* Berlin: Akademie-Verlag, 1955
WH	A. Walde et J. Hofmann. *Lateinisches etymologisches Wörterbuch.* Heidelberg: Winter, 1938
WKAS	*Wörterbuch der Klassischen Arabischen Sprache.* Wiesbaden: Harrassowitz, 1957–
WTS	E. Littmann et M. Höfner. *Wörterbuch der Tigrē-Sprache. Tigrē-deutsch-englisch.* Wiesbaden: Steiner, 1956
YOS	Yale Oriental Series, Babylonian Texts

Noms des langues

AJP	araméen judéo-paléstinien
akk.	akkadien
amh.	amharique
ar.	arabe
aram.	araméen
gez.	guèze
har.	harari
héb.	hébreu
jib.	jibbali
mand.	mandéen
méh.	méhri
min.	minéen
off.	araméen officiel
oug.	ougaritique
ph.	phénicien
qat.	qatabanien
SAE	sudarabique épigraphique
sab.	sabéen
soq.	soqotri
sum.	sumérien
syr.	syriaque
tig.	tigré
tgn.	tigrinya

Bibliographie

Arcari, E.

1984 "Il bilinguismo nei testi amministrativi di Ebla." Dans *Il bilinguismo a Ebla* (atti del convegno internazionale, Napoli, 19–22 aprile, 1982), édité par L. Cagni, pp. 319–27. Naples: Istituto Universitario Orientale.

Belmonte, J.

1993 "Los productos vegetales de KTU 1.100:64–67." *Aula Orientalis* 11/1: 114–15.

Biella, J. C.

1982 *Dictionary of Old South Arabic (Sabaean Dialect).* Chico: Scholars Press.

Biggs, R. D.

1989 "An Old Akkadian Literary Text from Umm al-Hafriyat." Dans *DUMU-E$_2$-DUB-BA-A: Studies in Honor of Åke W. Sjöberg*, édité par H. Behrens, D. Loding, et M. T. Roth, pp. 33–36. Occasional Publications of the Samuel Noah Kramer Fund 11. Philadelphia: The University Museum.

Birot, M.

1960 *Textes administratifs de la salle 5 du palais*. Archives Royales de Mari 9. Paris: Impr. Nationale.

Blau, J.

1982 *On Polyphony in Biblical Hebrew*. Proceedings of the Israel Academy of Sciences and Humanities 6/2. Jerusalem: Israel Academy of Sciences and Humanities.

Bonechi, M.

2008 "'Synthetic' Writings at Ebla." *NABU: Nouvelles Assyriologiques Brèves et Utilitaires* 2008/2: 26.

Borger, R.

2004 *Mesopotamisches Zeichenlexikon*. Alter Orient und Altes Testament 305. Münster: Ugarit-Verlag.

Bottéro, J.

1957 *Textes économiques et administratifs*. Archives royales de Mari 7. Paris: Impr. Nationale.

Buck, C.

1949 *A Dictionary of Selected Synonyms in the Principal Indo-European Languages*. Chicago: University of Chicago Press.

Burde, C.

1974 *Hethitische medizinische Texte*. Studien zu den Boğazköy-Texten 19. Wiesbaden: Harrassowitz.

Catagnoti, A.

2007 "Il lessico dei vegetali ad Ebla, 1. Aglio, cipolla, porro." *Quaderni del Dipartimento di Linguistica* 17: 215–32.

2008 "Il lessico dei vegetali ad Ebla, 2. La frutta (parte I): Uva, fico, mela." *Quaderni del Dipartimento di Linguistica* 18: 175–87.

2010 "Il lessico dei vegetali ad Ebla, 3. Piante aromatiche (parte I): cumino e timo." *Quaderni del Dipartimento di Linguistica* 20: 143–49.

Cavigneaux, A.

2005 "Les soirées sargoniques des marchands assyriens." Dans *Κορυφαίῳ ἀνδρί: Mélanges offerts à André Hurst*, édité par A. Kolde, A. Lukinovich, et A.-L. Rey, pp. 595–602. Recherches et Rencontres 22. Geneva: Droz.

Chantraine, P.

1968 *Dictionnaire étymologique de la langue grecque*. Paris: Klincksieck.

Charpin, D.

1989 "Cueillette de champignons." *NABU: Nouvelles Assyriologiques Brèves et Utilitaires* 1989/3: 58.

Ciancaglini, C. A.

2008 *Iranian Loanwords in Syriac*. Beiträge zur Iranistik 28. Wiesbaden: Dr. Ludwig Reichert Verlag.

Civil, M.

1987 "The Early History of ḪAR-ra: The Ebla Link." Dans *Ebla 1975–1985: dieci anni di studi linguistici e filologici* (atti del convegno internazionale, Napoli, 9–11 ottobre, 1985), édité par L. Cagni, pp. 131–58. Series minor 27. Naples: Istituto Universitario Orientale.

2007 "Early Semitic Loanwords in Sumerian." Dans *Studies Presented to Robert D. Biggs*, édité par M. T. Roth, W. Farber, M. W. Stolper, et P. von Bechtolsheim, pp. 11–33. Assyriological Studies 27. Chicago: The Oriental Institute.

2008 *The Early Dynastic Practical Vocabulary A (Archaic HAR-ra A)*. Archivi reali di Ebla, Studi 4. Rome: Missione archeologica italiana in Siria.

Cohen, H., et D. Sivan

1983 *The Ugaritic Hippiatric Texts: A Critical Edition*. American Oriental Society Essays 9. New Haven: American Oriental Society.

Conti, G.

1990 *Il sillabario della quarta fonte della lista lessicale bilingue eblaita*. Miscellanea Eblaitica 3. Quaderni di Semitistica 17. Florence: Università di Firenze, Dipartimento di Linguistica.

del Olmo Lete, G.

2004 *Canaanite Religion According to the Liturgical Texts of Ugarit.* Winona Lake: Eisenbrauns.

Dercksen, J. G.

2005 "Adad is King! The Sargon Text from Kültepe." *Jaarbericht van het Vooraziatisch-Egyptisch Genootschap "Ex Oriente Lux"* 39: 107–29.

Donbaz, V., et M. W. Stolper

1997 *Istanbul Murašû Texts.* Uitgaven van het Nederlands Historisch-Archaeologisch Instituut te Istanbul 79. Leyde: Nederlands Instituut voor het Nabije Oosten.

Durand, J.-M.

1983 *Textes administratifs des salles 134 et 160 du palais de Mari.* Archives royales de Mari 21. Paris: Librairie Orientaliste Paul Geuthner.

1997 *Les documents épistolaires du palais de Mari* I. Littératures anciennes du Proche-Orient 16. Paris: Éditions du Cerf.

1998 *Les documents épistolaires du palais de Mari* II. Littératures anciennes du Proche-Orient 17. Paris: Éditions du Cerf.

2001 "Une alliance matrimoniale entre un marchand assyrien de Kanesh et un marchand mariote." Dans *Veenhof Anniversary Volume: Studies Presented to Klaas R. Veenhof on the Occasion of His Sixty-fifth Birthday,* édité par W. H. van Soldt, J. G. Dercksen, N. J. C. Kouwenberg, et Th. J. H. Krispijn, pp. 119–32. Uitgaven van het Nederlands Historisch-Archaeologisch Instituut te Istanbul 89. Leyde: Nederlands Instituut voor het Nabije Oosten.

Edzard, D. O.

1961 "Compte-rendu de Gelb 1957." *Zeitschrift für Assyriologie* 54: 257–64.

Ernout, A., et A. Meillet

1967 *Dictionnaire étymologique de la langue latine.* Paris: Klincksieck.

Faber, A.

1984 "Semitic Sibilants in an Afro-Asiatic Context." *Journal of Semitic Studies* 29/2: 189–224.

Farber, W.

1991 "Altassyrisch *addaḫšū* und *ḫazuannū*, oder von Safran, Fenchel, Zwiebeln und Salat." *Zeitschrift für Assyriologie* 81: 234–42.

Frisk, H.

1960 *Griechisches etymologisches Wörterbuch.* Indogermanische Bibliothek, II. Reihe, Wörterbücher. Heidelberg: Carl Winter.

Fronzaroli, P.

1969a "Studi sul lessico comune semitico. V. La natura domestica." *Accademia Nazionale dei Lincei, Rendiconti* VIII/XXIII/7–12: 267–303.

1969b "Studi sul lessico comune semitico. VI. La natura selvatica." *Accademia Nazionale dei Lincei, Rendiconti* VIII/XXIV/7–12: 1–36.

1984a "The Eblaic Lexicon: Problems and Appraisal." Dans *Studies on the language of Ebla,* édité par Pelio Fronzaroli, pp. 117 57. Quaderni di semitistica 13. Florence: Istituto di linguistica e di lingue orientali, Università di Firenze.

1984b "Materiali per il lessico eblaita." *Studi Eblaiti* 7: 145–90.

Gelb, I. J.

1957 *Glossary of Old Akkadian.* Materials for the Assyrian Dictionary 3. Chicago: University of Chicago Press.

1961 *Old Akkadian Writing and Grammar.* 2ème édition. Materials for the Assyrian Dictionary 2. Chicago: University of Chicago Press.

Gelb, I. J.; P. Steinkeller; et R. M. Whiting

1991 *Earliest Land Tenure Systems in the Near East: Ancient Kudurrus.* Oriental Institute Publications 104. Chicago: The Oriental Institute.

Günbattı, C.

1997 "Kültepe'den akadli Sargon'a âit bir tablet." *Archivum Anatolicum* 3: 131–55.

Hasselbach, R.

2005 *Sargonic Akkadian. A Historical and Comparative Study of the Syllabic Texts.* Wiesbaden: Harrassowitz.

Hehn, V.
1902 *Kulturpflanzen und Hausthiere in ihrem Übergang aus Asien nach Griechenland und Italien sowie in das übrige Europa.* 7ème édition. Berlin: Gebrüder Borntraeger.

Heimpel, W.
1997 "Mushrooms." *NABU: Nouvelles Assyriologiques Brèves et Utilitaires 1997/1:* 3.

Hrozný, F.
1913 *Das Getreide im alten Babylonien.* Vienna: Hölder.

Huehnergard, J.
1987 *Ugaritic Vocabulary in Syllabic Transcription.* Harvard Semitic Studies 32. Atlanta: Scholars Press.
1992 "Historical Phonology and the Hebrew Piel." Dans *Linguistics and Biblical Hebrew*, édité par W. R. Bodine, pp. 209–29. Winona Lake: Eisenbrauns.
2007 "*qātîl* and *qətîl* Nouns in Biblical Hebrew." *Sha'arei Lashon: Studies in Hebrew, Aramaic, and Jewish Languages Presented to Moshe Bar-Asher*, édité par A. Maman, S. E. Fassberg, et Y. Breuer, pp. 3–45. Jerusalem: Mosad Byaliḳ.

Jamme, A.
1962 *Sabaean Inscriptions from Maḥram Bilqîs (Mârib).* Publications of the American Foundation for the Study of Man 3. Baltimore: Johns Hopkins.

Jean, C.-F.
1957 "*Kam-a-tum* 'truffes' (?)." *Revue d'assyriologie et d'archéologie orientale* 43:89–92.

Jeffery, A.
1938 *The Foreign Vocabulary of the Quran.* Gaekwad's Oriental Series 79. Baroda: Oriental Institute.

Kassian, A; A. Korolëv; et A. Sidel'tsev
2002 *Hittite Funerary Ritual* šalliš waštaiš. Alter Orient und Altes Testament 288. Münster: Ugarit-Verlag.

Kaufman, S.
1974 *The Akkadian Influences on Aramaic.* Assyriological Studies 19. Chicago: University of Chicago Press.

Kienast, B.
1994 *Glossar zu den altakkadischen Königsinschriften.* Freiburger Altorientalische Studien 8. Stuttgart: Franz Steiner.

Klein, J.
1997 "The God Martu in Sumerian Literature." Dans *Sumerian Gods and Their Representations*, édité par I. L. Finkel et M. J. Geller, pp. 99–116. Cuneiform Monographs 7. Groningen: STYX Publications.

Klein, J., et K. Abraham
2000 "Problems of Geography in the Gilgameš Epics: The Journey to the 'Cedar Forest.'" Dans *Landscapes: Territories, Frontiers and Horizons in the Ancient Near East* (papers presented to the XLIV Rencontre assyriologique internationale, Venezia, 7–11 July 1997), édité par L. Milano, pp. 63–73. History of the Ancient Near East, Monographs 3/1. Padova: Sargon.

Kogan, L.
2001 "*γ in Akkadian." *Ugarit-Forschungen* 33: 263–98.
2005 "Lexicon of the Old Aramaic Inscriptions and the Historical Unity of Aramaic." *Babel und Bibel* 2: 513–66.
2006 "Old Assyrian vs. Old Babylonian: The Lexical Dimension." Dans *The Akkadian Language in its Semitic Context*, édité par G. Deutscher et N. J. C. Kouwenberg, pp. 177–214. Uitgaven van het Nederlands Instituut voor het Nabije Oosten te Leiden 106. Leyde: Nederlands Instituut voor het Nabije Oosten.
2011 "Old Babylonian Copies of Sargonic Royal Inscriptions as Linguistic Evidence." Dans *Akkade is King: A Collection of Papers by Friends and Colleagues Presented to Aage Westenholz On the Occasion of His 70th Birthday 15th of May 2009*, édité par G. Barjamovic, J. L. Dahl, U. S. Koch, W. Sommerfeld, et J. Goodnick Westenholz, pp. 177–204. Uitgaven van het Nederlands Instituut voor het Nabije Oosten te Leiden 118. Leyde: Nederlands Instituut voor het Nabije Oosten.

Kouwenberg, N. J. C.
2006 "The Reflexes of the Proto-Semitic Gutturals in Old Assyrian." Dans *The Akkadian Language in Its Semitic Context*, édité par G. Deutscher et N. J. C. Kouwenberg, pp. 150–76. Uitgaven van het Nederlands Instituut voor het Nabije Oosten te Leiden 106. Leyde: Nederlands Instituut voor het Nabije Oosten.

Krebernik, M.

1982 "Zu Syllabar und Orthographie der lexikalischen Texte aus Ebla. Teil 1." *Zeitschrift für Assyriologie* 72: 178–236.

1983 "Zu Syllabar und Orthographie der lexikalischen Texte aus Ebla. Teil 2 (Glossar)." *Zeitschrift für Assyriologie* 73: 1–47.

1984 *Die Beschwörungen aus Fara und Ebla.* Texte und Studien zur Orientalistik 2. Hildesheim: Olms.

1988 "Prefixed Verbal Forms in Personal Names from Ebla." Dans *Eblaite Personal Names and Semitic Name-Giving,* édité par A. Archi, pp. 45–69. Rome: Missione archeologica italiana in Siria.

1997 "Zur Interpretation von ARET 5, 24–26." Dans *Ana šadî Labnāni lū allik: Beiträge zu altorientalischen und mittelmeerischen Kulturen. Festschrift für Wolfgang Röllig,* édité par B. Pongratz-Leisten, H. Kühne, et P. Xella, pp. 185–92. Kevelaer: Verlag Butzon & Bercker.

1998 "Die Texte aus Fāra und Tell Abū Ṣalābīḫ." Dans *Mesopotamien: Späturuk-Zeit und Frühdynastische Zeit,* par J. Bauer, R. K. Englund, et M. Krebernik, pp. 235–428. Orbis Biblicus et Orientalis 160/1. Freiburg: Universitätsverlag.

2001 *Tall Bi'a/Tuttul,* II: *Die altorientalischen Schriftfunde.* Ausgrabungen in Tall Bi'a-Tuttul 2. Wissenschaftliche Veröffentlichung der Deutschen Orient-Gesellschaft 100. Saarbrücken: Saarbrücker Druckerei und Verlag.

Lambert, W. G.

1987 "A Further Attempt at the Babylonian 'Man and His God.'" Dans *Language, Literature, and History: Philological and Historical Studies Presented to Erica Reiner,* édité par F. Rochberg-Halton, pp. 187–202. American Oriental Series 67. New Haven: American Oriental Society.

1989 "Notes on a Work of the Most Ancient Semitic Literature." *Journal of Cuneiform Studies* 41/1: 1–33.

Landsberger, B.

1934 *Die fauna des alten Mesopotamien nach der 14. tafel der serie Ḫar-ra = ḫubullu.* Abhandlungen der Sächsischen Akademie der Wissenschaften zu Leipzig, Philologisch-Historische Klasse 42/6. Leipzig: S. Hirzel.

1964 "Einige unerkannt gebliebene oder verkannte Nomina des Akkadischen." *Die Welt des Orients* 3: 246–68.

1967 *The Date-palm and Its By-products according to the Cuneiform Sources.* Archiv für Orientforschung, Beiheft 17. Graz: Weidner.

Landsberger, B., et O. R. Gurney

1957–1958 "Practical Vocabulary of Assur." *Archiv für Orientforschung* 18: 328–41.

Lane, E. W.

1876 *An Arabic-English Lexicon.* London: Williams and Norgate.

Leemans, W. F.

1960 *Legal and Administrative Documents of the Time of Hammurabi and Samsuiluna (mainly from Lagaba).* Studia ad tabulas cuneiformes collectas ab de Liagre Böhl pertinentia 1/3. Leyde: Brill.

Lieberman, S. J.

1977 *The Sumerian Loanwords in Old Babylonian Akkadian.* Harvard Semitic Studies 22. Missoula: Scholars Press.

Löw, I.

1881 *Aramäische Pflanzennamen.* Leipzig: Engelmann.

Meissner, B.

1931 *Beiträge zum assyrischen Wörterbuch,* Volume 1. Assyriological Studies 1. Chicago: University of Chicago Press.

Michel, C.

1997 "A table avec les marchands paléo-assyriens." Dans *Assyrien im Wandel der Zeiten* (XXXIXe Rencontre assyriologique internationale, Heidelberg, 6.–10. Juli 1992), édité par H. Waetzoldt et H. Hauptmann, pp. 95–113. Heidelberger Studien zum alten Orient 6. Heidelberg: Heidelberger Orientverlag.

2001 "Le lapis-lazuli des assyriens au début du IIe millénaire av. J.-C." Dans *Veenhof Anniversary Volume: Studies Presented to Klaas R. Veenhof on the Occasion of His Sixty-fifth Birthday,* édité par W. H. van Soldt, J. G. Dercksen, N. J. C. Kouwenberg, et Th. J. H. Krispijn, pp. 340–59. Uitgaven van het Nederlands Historisch-Archaeologisch Instituut te Istanbul 89. Leyde: Nederlands Instituut voor het Nabije Oosten.

Militarev, A.

1999 "Sumerian-Afrasian Language Contacts." Dans *Landwirtschaft im Alten Orient* (ausgewählte Vorträge der XLI. Rencontre Assyriologique Internationale Berlin, 4.–8. Juli 1994), édité par H. Klengel et J. Renger, pp. 393–402. Berlin: D. Reimer.

Miller, A. G., et M. Morris

2004 *Ethnoflora of the Soqotra Archipelago*. Edinburgh: Royal Botanic Garden Edinburgh.

Morris, M.

2002 "Plant Names in Dhofar and the Soqotra Archipelago." *Proceedings of the Seminar for Arabian Studies* 32: 47–61.

Müller, W. W.

1985 "Beiträge aus dem Mehri zum etymologischen Teil des hebräischen Lexikons." Dans *Mélanges linguistiques offerts à Maxime Rodinson par ses élèves, ses collègues et ses amis*, édité par C. Robin, pp. 267–78. Comptes rendus du Groupe linguistique d'études chamito-sémitiques. Supplément 12. Paris: P. Geuthner.

Nougayrol, J.

1952 "Une version ancienne du 'juste souffrant'." *Revue biblique* 59: 239–50.

Pardee, D.

1985 *Les textes hippiatriques*. Ras Shamra-Ougarit 2. Mémoire, Éditions Recherche sur les civilisations, 53. Paris: Éditions Recherche sur les civilisations.

1988 *Les textes para-mythologiques de la 24e campagne (1961)*. Ras Shamra-Ougarit 4. Mémoire, Éditions Recherche sur les civilisations, 77. Paris: Éditions Recherche sur les civilisations.

2000 *Les textes rituels*. Ras Shamra-Ougarit 12. Paris: Éditions recherche sur les civilisations.

2002 "Un 'nouveau' mot ougaritique." *Aula Orientalis* 20: 163–82.

Pasquali, J.

2005a "Eblaita *kamʔātum* = '(pomelli a forma di) fungo.'" *NABU: Nouvelles Assyriologiques Brèves et Utilitaires* 2005/3: 52.

2005b *Il lessico dell'artigianato nei testi di Ebla*. Quaderni di semitistica 23. Firenze: Dipartimento di linguistica, Università di Firenze.

Pentiuc, E. J.

2001 *West Semitic Vocabulary in the Akkadian Texts from Emar*. Harvard Semitic Museum Publications, Harvard Semitic Studies 49. Winona Lake: Eisenbrauns.

Pettinato, G.

1981 "I vocabolari bilingui di Ebla: Problemi di traduzione e di lessicografia sumerico-eblaita." Dans *La lingua di Ebla* (atti del convegno internazionale, Napoli, 21–23 aprile 1980), édité par L. Cagni, pp. 241–76. Series minor (Istituto universitario orientale, Naples, Italy). Seminario di studi asiatici 14. Naples: Istituto universitario orientale, Seminario di studi asiatici.

Poebel, A.

1930 "Sumerische Untersuchungen IV." *Zeitschrift für Assyriologie* 39: 129–64.

Postgate, J. N.

1987 "Notes on Fruit in the Cuneiform Sources." *Bulletin on Sumerian Agriculture* 3: 115–44.

Powell, M.

1984 "Sumerian Cereal Crops." *Bulletin on Sumerian Agriculture* 1: 48–72.

2003 "Obst und Gemüse." *Reallexikon der Assyriologie* 10: 13–22.

Reiter, K.

1997 *Die Metalle im Alten Orient: Unter besonderer Berücksichtigung altbabylonischer Quellen*. Alter Orient und Altes Testament 249. Münster: Ugarit-Verlag.

Salonen, A.

1952 *Alte Substrat- und Kulturwörter im Arabischen*. Studia Orientalia 17/2. Helsinki: Societas Orientalis Fennica.

Sima, A.

2000 *Tiere, Pflanzen, Steine und Metalle in den altsüdarabischen Inschriften: Eine lexikalische und realienkundliche Untersuchung*. Veröffentlichungen der Orientalischen Kommission 46. Wiesbaden: Harrassowitz.

2009 *Mehri-Texte aus der jemenitischen Šarqīyah*. Semitica Viva 47. Wiesbaden: Harrassowitz.

Sjöberg, Å. W.

1999 "Notes on Selected Entries from the Ebla Vocabulary. eš$_3$-bar-kin$_5$ (II)." Dans *Munuscula Mesopotamica: Festschrift für Johannes Renger*, édité par B. Böck, E. Cancik-Kirschbaum, et T. Richter, pp. 513–52. Alter Orient und Altes Testament 267. Münster: Ugarit-Verlag.

2003 "Notes on Selected Entries from the Ebla Vocabulary. eš$_3$-bar-kin$_5$ (I)." Dans *Festschrift für Burkhart Kienast: zu seinem 70. Geburtstage dargebracht von Freunden, Schülern und Kollegen*, édité par G. J. Selz, pp. 527–68. Alter Orient und Altes Testament 274. Münster: Ugarit-Verlag.

Sommerfeld, W.

2006 "Die ältesten semitischen Sprachzeugnisse — eine kritische Bestandsaufnahme." Dans *The Akkadian Language in Its Semitic Context*, édité par G. Deutscher et N. J. C. Kouwenberg, pp. 30–75. Uitgaven van het Nederlands Instituut voor het Nabije Oosten te Leiden 106. Leyde: Nederlands Instituut voor het Nabije Oosten.

2010 "Prä-Akkadisch: Die Vorläufer der 'Sprache von Akkade' in der frühdynastischen Zeit." Dans *Language in the Ancient Near East. Proceedings of the 53e Rencontre Assyriologique Internationale*,Volume 1, Part 1, édité par L. Kogan, N. Koslova, S. Loesov, et S. Tishchenko, pp. 77–163. Orientalia et Classica 30. Babel und Bibel 4/1. Winona Lake: Eisenbrauns.

Stein, P.

2010 *Die altsüdarabischen Minuskelinschriften auf Holzstäbchen aus der Bayerischen Staatsbibliothek in München*. Epigraphische Forschungen auf der Arabischen Halbinsel 5. Tübingen: Wasmuth.

Steiner, G.

2003 "Akkadische Lexeme im Sumerischen." Dans *Semitic and Assyriological Studies: Presented to Pelio Fronzaroli by Pupils and Colleagues*, édité par P. Marrassini, pp. 630–47. Wiesbaden: Harrassowitz.

Steiner, R. C.

1977 *The Case for the Fricative-Laterals in Proto-Semitic*. American Oriental Series 59. New Haven: American Oriental Society.

2005 "On the Dating of Hebrew Sound Changes (*Ḫ > Ḥ and *Ġ > ʿ) and Greek Translations (2 Esdras and Judith)." *Journal of Biblical Literature* 124/2: 229–67.

Steinkeller, P.

1992 *Third-Millennium Legal and Administrative Texts in the Iraq Museum, Baghdad*. Mesopotamian Civilizations 4. Winona Lake: Eisenbrauns.

Stol, M.

1978 Compte-rendu de *Lettres de Yaqqim-Addu, gouverneur de Sagarātum, transcites, traduites et commentées* et *Lettres de Yaqqim-Addu, gouverneur de Sagarātum*, par M. Birot. *Bibliotheca Orientalis* 35: 217–21.

1979 *On Trees, Mountains and Millstones in the Ancient Near East*. Mededelingen en verhandelingen van het Vooraziatisch-Egyptisch Genootschap "Ex Oriente Lux" 21. Leyde: Ex Oriente Lux.

1985 "Beans, Peas, Lentils and Vetches in Akkadian Texts." *Bulletin on Sumerian Agriculture* 2: 127–39.

1989 "Malz." *Reallexikon der Assyriologie* 7: 322–29.

1987a "The Cucurbitaceae in the Cuneiform Texts." *Bulletin on Sumerian Agriculture* 3: 81–92.

1987b "Garlic, Onion, Leek." *Bulletin on Sumerian Agriculture* 3: 57–80.

Streck, M. P.

2000 *Das amurritische Onomastikon der altbabylonischen Zeit*. Alter Orient und Altes Testament 271. Münster: Ugarit-Verlag.

2004 "Dattelpalme und Tamariske in Mesopotamien nach dem akkadischen Streitgespräch." *Zeitschrift für Assyriologie* 94: 250–90.

Strelcyn, S.

1973 *Médecine et plantes d'Éthiopie, II: Enquête sur les noms et l'emploi des plantes en Éthiopie*. Naples: Istituto Orientale di Napoli.

Cogan, M., et H. Tadmor

1988 *II Kings: A New Translation*. The Anchor Bible 11. Garden City: Doubleday.

Talon, Ph.

1997 *Old Babylonian Texts from Chagar Bazar*. Akkadica, Supplementum 10. Brussels: Fondation assyriologique Georges Dossin.

Telegdi, S.
1935 "Essai sur la phonétique des emprunts iraniens en araméen talmudique." *Journal asiatique* 226: 177–256.

Thureau-Dangin, F.
1912 *Une relation de la huitième campagne de Sargon (714 av. J.-C.).* Textes Cunéiformes 3. Paris: P. Geuthner.

Tropper, J.
2000 *Ugaritische Grammatik.* Alter Orient und Altes Testament 273. Münster: Ugarit-Verlag.

Volk, K.
2004 "Palme." *Reallexikon der Assyriologie* 10: 283–92.

Vycichl, W.
1963 "Der sumerische Ursprung von lateinisch *porrus, porrum* 'Lauch.'" *Die Sprache* 9: 21–22.

Waetzoldt, H.
1987 "Knoblauch und Zwiebeln nach den Texten des 3. Jt." *Bulletin on Sumerian Agriculture* 3: 23–56.

Watson, W.
2004 "A Botanical Snapshot of Ugarit: Trees, Fruit, Plants and Herbs in the Cuneiform Texts." *Aula Orientalis* 22: 107–55.

Westenholz, A.
1987 *Old Sumerian and Old Akkadian Texts in Philadelphia*, Part 2: *The "Akkadian" Texts*, the *Enlilemaba Texts, and the Onion Archive.* Carsten Niebuhr Institute of Ancient Near Eastern Studies 3. Copenhagen: Museum Tusculanum Press.

Westenholz, J. G.
1997 *Legends of the Kings of Akkade: The Texts.* Mesopotamian Civilizations 7. Winona Lake: Eisenbrauns.

Zadok, R.
1993 "On the Amorite Material from Mesopotamia." Dans *The Tablet and the Scroll: Near Eastern Studies in Honor of William W. Hallo*, édité par M. E. Cohen, D. C. Snell, et D. B. Weisberg, pp. 315–33. Bethesda: CDL Press.
1997 "Mushrooms." *NABU: Nouvelles Assyriologiques Brèves et Utilitaires* 1997/3: 88.

Zimmern, H.
1917 *Akkadische Fremdwörter als Beweis für babylonischen Kultureinfluss.* 2ème édition. Leipzig: J. C. Hinrichs.

Zurro, E.
1983 "Notas de lexicografía eblaíta: nombres de árboles y plantas." *Aula Orientalis* 1: 263–69.

16

Grammaticalization and the Biblical Hebrew Pseudo-Cohortative

Paul Korchin, University of Alaska Fairbanks

Scholars of Biblical Hebrew have long been puzzled by more than one hundred ostensible instances of the so-called cohortative (first common singular אֶקְטְלָה *ʾeqṭəlâ* and first common plural נִקְטְלָה *niqṭəlâ*) that do not conform to the normative volitive functions signified by the forms elsewhere in Biblical Hebrew,[1] as well as by the cognate Northwest Semitic paradigm (*yaqtula*) that extends at least as far back as the late second millennium B.C.E.[2] William Moran definitively mapped the core volitional character of Canaanite *yaqtula* more than a half century ago — initially in his groundbreaking dissertation concerning the Byblos (Gubla) dialect within the Amarna Letters (Moran [1950] 2003), and subsequently in an influential *Orientalia* article (Moran 1960). Moran's diligent application of the morphosyntactic method yielded consistent and convincing correlations between the form and the functions of *yaqtula*, thereby confirming its volitive value (occurring, as it does, most frequently in precative, purpose, and asseverative clauses). Similar and often identical form-function connections among most instances of Biblical Hebrew *ʾeqṭəlâ* / *niqṭəlâ* have produced a firm consensus that the Northwest Semitic and the Biblical Hebrew paradigms are genetically related.[3] And yet, in addition to more than 500 genuinely volitive *ʾeqṭəlâ* / *niqṭəlâ* examples, there exist in Biblical Hebrew at least 113 non-volitive instances of the forms.[4] The vague scholarly consensus, inasmuch as there is any agreement, is that these "pseudo-cohortatives" (so called in Waltke and O'Connor 1990, p. 576) constitute a diachronically broad and increasingly frequent — yet essentially optional and random — indicative divergence from the paradigm's volitive core. Indeed, the pseudo-cohortative is often employed in the same past narrative syntagms that are typically filled by the וַיִּקְטֹל *wayyiqṭōl* paradigm, and it frequently occurs in conjunction with this "consecutive preterite" form (so termed by John Huehnergard and Jo Ann Hackett). Waltke and O'Connor (1990, p. 576) observe somewhat plaintively that "the cohortative form is sometimes used where an appropriate sense is lacking [and] the use of a single form to denote both the volitional and indicative moods cannot be readily explained."

Yet a closer inspection of where and how these forms are employed does reveal both a functional and a formal explanation. The pseudo-cohortative is indeed neither cohortative nor even volitive in the broader sense. Instead, the Biblical Hebrew *ʾeqṭəlâ* / *niqṭəlâ* forms in question possess a functional value that consistently signifies verbal action oriented either *away from* or *outside of* the deictic center for each given syntagm. In other words,

---

[1] Driver [1892] 1998, pp. 74–75; Gesenius, Kautzsch, and Cowley 1910, §49e; Joüon and Muraoka 2006, §47d; Polzin 1976, pp. 54–55; McFall 1982, pp. 211–14; Qimron 1986, pp. 44–47; consult Rezetko 2003, p. 227 n. 34 for additional bibliography.

[2] See Korchin 2008, pp. 217–23, for a discussion and an evaluation of the scholarly debate regarding *yaqtula* in Canaano-Akkadian.

[3] Moran ([1950] 2003, pp. 84–87) also delineated a secure functional link between these forms and Classical Arabic *yaqtula*, thereby demonstrating that the paradigm extends at least as far back as Central Semitic (see Huehnergard 2005, p. 165).

[4] Jenni (2002–03, p. 27) tallies 94 non-volitive examples (88 first common singular, 6 first common plural) alongside 527 volitive instances, whereas Rezetko (2003, p. 227) posits 101 examples (95 first common singular, 5 first common plural, 1 third feminine singular). The database for my study comprises an amalgam of Jenni's and Rezetko's respective totals, minus the forms in Ezek 3:3 (containing an unvocalized third feminine singular object suffix) and Zech 11:13 (with a misaligned definite article). This corpus thus consists of 105 first common singular, 7 first common plural, and 1 third feminine singular, all of which are either cited or cross-referenced below.

the activities and movements entailed by verbal lexemes when they appear as non-volitive *ʾeqṭəlâ / niqṭəlâ* are *centrifugal* — proceeding away from, or emanating outside of, their spatial locales of expression. This *andative* or *itive* value (as it also has been termed) is, furthermore, signified explicitly by the ָה- (*qāmeṣ-hê* = *-â*) afformative of the non-volitive, which remains formally equivalent to the affix of the true volitive. In surveying the extant data, however, it becomes evident that the affix on the pseudo-cohortative functions quite differently compared to the affix on the genuine volitive deriving from Canaanite *yaqtula*.

The verbal lexemes to which non-volitive *-â* is appended coagulate around a relatively confined group of functional/semantic categories. All of the examples can be accorded to one of five cognitive domains:[5] verbs of *utterance* (e.g., *speak, call*), verbs of *conveyance* (e.g., *give, carry*), verbs of *perception* (e.g., *look, listen*), verbs of *locomotion* (e.g., *exit, escape*), and verbs of *impact* (e.g., *grab, smash*). Akin to the true cohortative, the Biblical Hebrew pseudo-cohortative occurs almost uniformly in the first person, and mostly in the first common singular (see n. 4). Hence, the expresser of the verb is also the verbal agent, and the speaker-as-agent is directly and paradigmatically associated with the concomitant verbal action. The speaker/agent also regularly functions as the deictic center for his/her communicational matrix, encompassing both the spatial "here" and the temporal "now" (Kuryłowicz 1972, p. 174) to which language defaults, absent explicit deictic indicators to the contrary (known as *shifters*; Jakobson [1957] 1984). It is no surprise, therefore, that verbal lexemes that overtly convey manners of expression occur so frequently with first person (speaker/agent) paradigms.

This is indeed the case with the pseudo-cohortatives, where thirty-one of its occurrences involve *verbs of utterance*. The most commonly used such lexeme is also the most explicit: √*ʾmr* (*say*). The verbal action of pseudo-cohortative √*ʾmr* is always directed from the speaker outward — centrifugally, from an agent as source to a patient as target.[6] Sometimes this is mediated by a locative preposition:

> וָאֹמְרָה לָכֶם אֲנִי יְהוָה אֱלֹהֵיכֶם
>
> 'I said to you, "I am YHWH, your God"' (Judg 6:10)
>
> וָאֹמְרָה אֲלֵהֶם אַתֶּם קֹדֶשׁ לַיהוָה
>
> 'I said to them, "You are holy to YHWH"' (Ezr 8:28)
>
> וָאֹמְרָה לָהֶם אֲנַחְנוּ קָנִינוּ אֶת־אַחֵינוּ הַיְּהוּדִים
>
> 'I said to them, "We have purchased our Jewish brothers"' (Neh 5:8; cf. Neh 13:22, 'I gave order to')

In other instances, the pseudo-cohortative's centrifugal action is not mediated prepositionally:

> וָאֹמְרָה אֱלֹהַי בֹּשְׁתִּי
>
> 'I said (to God), "My God, I am ashamed"' (Ezr 9:6)
>
> וָאֹמְרָה הַאִישׁ כָּמוֹנִי יִבְרָח
>
> 'I said (to Shemaiah), "Should a man such as I flee?"' (Neh 6:11; see also Neh 5:13; cf. Neh 13:9a, 19, 'I commanded')
>
> וָאֹמְרָה יְדַבֵּר אֲדֹנִי
>
> 'I said (to the heavenly messenger), "Let my lord speak"' (Dan 10:19; see also Dan 12:8)

[5] Proceeding heuristically from the *Source-Path-Goal* image schema as envisioned by cognitive linguistics (Johnson 2008, p. 22; Graf 2006, pp. 41–42), wherein a given action (motion event) proceeds from an origin (source), to/toward a target (goal), via a sequence (path) of positions and trajectories.

[6] Contrast this, for example, with the agent-focused *qāṭal* construction אָמַרְתִּי אֲנִי בְּלִבִּי 'I said to myself' (lit. 'in my heart'; Qoh 2:1; 3:17, 18; cf. 2:15).

Affixed √ʾ*mr* and its synonym √*dbr* are attested in a quasi-hendiadys:

> וָאֶפְתַּח־פִּי וָאֲדַבְּרָה וָאֹמְרָה אֶל־הָעֹמֵד לְנֶגְדִּי
>
> 'I opened my mouth and I spoke, saying to the one standing before me' (Dan 10:16)[7]

Affixed √ʾ*mr* is also paired with morphologically congruent lexemes of admonishment (√*rîb*, √ʿ*ûd*) that are trained squarely at the patient from the agent:

> וָאָרִיבָה אֵת חֹרֵי יְהוּדָה וָאֹמְרָה לָהֶם
>
> 'I scolded the nobles of Judah, and I said to them' (Neh 13:17; see also Neh 5:7; 13:11)

> וָאָעִידָה בָהֶם וָאֹמְרָה אֲלֵיהֶם
>
> 'I rebuked them, and I said to them' (Neh 13:21)

In another instance a consecutive string of utterance verbs (√*pll*, √*ydh*, √ʾ*mr*) appended by -*â* underscores the agent-to-patient trajectory of entreaty:

> וָאֶתְפַּלְלָה לַיהוָה אֱלֹהַי וָאֶתְוַדֶּה וָאֹמְרָה
>
> 'I prayed to YHWH my God, and I confessed, and I said' (Dan 9:4)

Conversely, when the desperate king Saul conjures Samuel's ghost, the centrifugal affix is joined only to the petitionary utterance verb √*qr*ʾ, which constitutes the lone speaker/agent-toward-patient trajectory in the syntagm:

> וַיֹּאמֶר שָׁאוּל צַר־לִי מְאֹד וּפְלִשְׁתִּים נִלְחָמִים בִּי
> וֵאלֹהִים סָר מֵעָלַי וְלֹא־עָנָנִי עוֹד גַּם בְּיַד־הַנְּבִיאִם גַּם־בַּחֲלֹמוֹת
> וָאֶקְרָאֶה לְךָ לְהוֹדִיעֵנִי מָה אֶעֱשֶׂה
>
> 'Saul said, "I am very hard pressed; the Philistines are battling against me, and God has turned away from me, for He no longer answers me either by the power of the prophets or in dreams. So *I have called out to you*, to make known to me what I should do"' (1 Sam 28:15)

Verbs of mourning (√*bkh*,[8] √ʾ*bl*) can also be paired with the affix to highlight the outbound trajectories of the entailed actions from their point of origination:

> וָאֶבְכֶּה וָאֶתְאַבְּלָה יָמִים
>
> 'I shed tears and cried out for days' (Neh 1:4)

The centrifugal affix is employed even more frequently (thirty-five times) with first person *verbs of conveyance*, where the incumbent action is borne from the agent to/toward the patient. An apt example involves the transmission of money:

> וָאֶשְׁקֲלָה־לּוֹ אֶת־הַכֶּסֶף
>
> 'I weighed out to him the silver' (√*šql*, Jer 32:9; see also Ezr 8:25, 26)

There is also the transmittal of information:

> וָאֶשְׁלְחָה לְהַגִּיד לַאדֹנִי
>
> 'I have sent to declare to my lord' (√*šlḥ*, Gen 32:6; see also Ezr 8:16; Neh 6:3, 8)

---

[7] Compare the series of *qāṭal* + ʾ*eqṭəlâ* syntagms in Psalm 119: נִשְׁבַּעְתִּי וָאֲקַיֵּמָה 'I have sworn and confirmed' (√*qûm*, v. 106); פִּי־פָעַרְתִּי וָאֶשְׁאָפָה 'I stretched open my mouth and panted' (√*š*ʾ*p*, v. 131); קִדַּמְתִּי בַנֶּשֶׁף וָאֲשַׁוֵּעָה 'I arose at twilight and cried out' (√*šw*ʿ, v. 147).

[8] Regarding the presence of the affix with 3rd-*h* verbs, see n. 18.

Hiphil (C stem) verbs are common in this category, foregrounding the agent's causative role in effecting the action upon the patient, and mediated by a locative preposition:

וָאָשִׂימָה בְּפִיהֶם דְּבָרִים

'I set in their mouths words' (√*śîm*, Ezr 8:17b)[9]

וָאוֹצְרָה עַל־אוֹצָרוֹת

'I delegated as treasurers over the storehouses' (√*ʾṣr*, Neh 13:13)[10]

וָאַעֲמִידָה מִשְׁמָרוֹת לַכֹּהֲנִים וְלַלְוִיִּם

'I set forth regulations before the priests and Levites' (√*ʿmd*, Neh 13:30; see also Neh 12:31)

וָאָבִאָה אֶתְכֶם אֶל־אֶרֶץ הָאֱמֹרִי

'I brought you to the land of the Amorites' (√*bôʾ*, Josh 24:8)

Such centrifugal forms can also convey agent-imposed displacement of a patient from its spatial setting, in concert with an ablative preposition:[11]

וַתִּצְעֲקוּ אֵלַי וָאוֹשִׁיעָה אֶתְכֶם מִיָּדָם

'You cried out to me, and I delivered you from their power' (√*yšʿ*, Judg 10:12)

וָאַבְדִּילָה מִשָּׂרֵי הַכֹּהֲנִים שְׁנֵים עָשָׂר

'I set apart twelve from the leaders of the priests' (√*bdl*, Ezr 8:24)[12]

וָאַשְׁלִיכָה אֶת־כָּל־כְּלֵי בֵית־טוֹבִיָּה הַחוּץ מִן־הַלִּשְׁכָּה

'I tossed all the articles of the household of Tobiah outside from the chamber' (√*šlk*, Neh 13:8)

The conveyance verb attested most frequently with the centrifugal affix is √*ntn* (*give*), used thirteen times in syntagms where a speaker/agent (subject) bestows a patient (direct object) to a recipient (indirect object). Some of these instances are revealing in that they also describe actions that are directed toward or focused upon the deictic center of the syntagm, in which cases the -*â* affix is not employed:

וָאָבוֹא אֶל־פַּחֲווֹת עֵבֶר הַנָּהָר
וָאֶתְּנָה לָהֶם אֵת אִגְּרוֹת הַמֶּלֶךְ

'I came [*without affix*] to the provincial governors Beyond the River, and I gave [*with affix*] to them the letters of the king' (Neh 2:9; see also Neh 2:1, 6)

וָאֶקַּח אֶת־הַלְוִיִּם תַּחַת כָּל־בְּכוֹר בִּבְנֵי יִשְׂרָאֵל
וָאֶתְּנָה אֶת־הַלְוִיִּם נְתֻנִים לְאַהֲרֹן וּלְבָנָיו

'I have taken [*without affix*] the Levites instead of every firstborn among the sons of Israel, and I have given [*with affix*] the Levites as gifts to Aaron and his sons' (Num 8:18–19)

[9] Ezr 8:17a also belongs under this subgroup when its Masoretic vocalization is repointed via the Lucianic recension: וָאוֹצִאָה (√*yṣʾ*) 'I made (them) go out (to Iddo).'

[10] Cf. Qal (G stem, √*qbṣ*) וָאֶקְבְּצָה in Neh 7:5, 'I roused (them to registration).'

[11] Or (once) in combination with a far demonstrative adverb: וָאָשִׁיבָה שָּׁם כְּלֵי בֵּית הָאֱלֹהִים 'I restored there the articles of the house of God' (√*šûb*, Neh 13:9b).

[12] Cf. Qal וָאֶקְבְּצָה in Ezr 7:28, 'I roused (from among Israel).'

אָנֹכִי מְשַׁחְתִּיךָ לְמֶלֶךְ עַל־יִשְׂרָאֵל
וְאָנֹכִי הִצַּלְתִּיךָ מִיַּד שָׁאוּל
וָאֶתְּנָה לְךָ אֶת־בֵּית אֲדֹנֶיךָ וְאֶת־נְשֵׁי אֲדֹנֶיךָ בְּחֵיקֶךָ
וָאֶתְּנָה לְךָ אֶת־בֵּית יִשְׂרָאֵל וִיהוּדָה
וְאִם־מְעָט וְאֹסִפָה לְּךָ כָּהֵנָּה וְכָהֵנָּה

'I myself anointed you king over Israel, and I myself delivered you from the power of Saul. And I gave to you the house of your master, and the wives of your master into your lap. And I gave to you the house of Israel and Judah. And if this were too little, I added for you twice as much!' (2 Sam 12:7–8; see also Judg 6:9; 1 Sam 2:28; Ezek 16:11)

וְאֶתְּנָה לַחֵרֶם יַעֲקֹב וְיִשְׂרָאֵל לְגִדּוּפִים

'I gave over to destruction Jacob, and Israel to revilement' (Isa 43:28)

וָאֶתְּנָה לְבוּשִׁי שָׂק

'I apportioned to my wardrobe sackcloth' (Ps 69:12)

The lexeme √*ntn* is also used with the *-â* affix to convey the speaker/agent's centrifugal orientation toward perspicacity:

וָאֶתְּנָה לִבִּי לָדַעַת חָכְמָה וְדַעַת הוֹלֵלוֹת וְשִׂכְלוּת

'I set my mind toward knowing wisdom, and understanding madness and folly' (Qoh 1:17; see also Dan 9:3)

This last usage shades off into a third semantic domain that is frequently attested (twenty-one times) with the centrifugal affix: *verbs of perception*, whereby the speaker/agent directs sensory attention toward a patient that is either explicitly or implicitly conveyed within the syntagm. Lexemes of understanding and knowing are among the examples:

וָאֵרֶא בַפְּתָאיִם אָבִינָה בַבָּנִים נַעַר חֲסַר־לֵב

'I saw among the simple, I perceived among the youths a boy without sense' (√*bîn*, Prv 7:7)[13]

וַיהוָה הוֹדִיעַנִי וָאֵדָעָה

'YHWH made (it) known to me, and I knew (it)' (√*ydʿ*, Jer 11:18)[14]

מִי־הִגִּיד מֵרֹאשׁ וְנֵדָעָה

'Who has foretold (it) from the beginning, so that we knew (it)?' (√*ydʿ*, Isa 41:26)

There is also an instance of auditory perception:

וָאֶשְׁמְעָה אֶחָד־קָדוֹשׁ מְדַבֵּר

'I heard one of the holy speaking' (√*šmʿ*, Dan 8:13)

Lexemes of inquiry fall under the broader semantic domain of perception verbs and likewise are attested with the centrifugal affix:

כִּי טוֹב קִוִּיתִי וַיָּבֹא רָע
וַאֲיַחֲלָה לְאוֹר וַיָּבֹא אֹפֶל

'For I expected goodness, but evil came; and I longed for light, but darkness arrived' (√*yḥl*, Job 30:26)

[13] This is one of the very few instances of a pseudo-cohortative lacking either a conjunctive or consecutive *waw* (cf. Ezr 8:15 and Neh 13:7, both with *waw*).

[14] Notice here the *qāṭal* form with ventive action, but the pseudo-cohortative with itive action (see also וָאֵדְעָה in Neh 13:10).

וַיְהִי בִּרְאֹתִי אֲנִי דָנִיֵּאל אֶת־הֶחָזוֹן
וָאֲבַקְשָׁה בִינָה

'When I, Daniel, had apprehended the vision, I sought out (its) meaning' (√*bqš*, Dan 8:15)[15]

וָאַכִּירָה וְהִנֵּה לֹא־אֱלֹהִים שְׁלָחוֹ

'I scrutinized, and indeed, it was not God who had sent him' (√*nkr*, Neh 6:12)

וָאֲחַשְּׁבָה לָדַעַת זֹאת

'I resolved to know this thing' (√*ḥšb*, Ps 73:16)

Such a centrifugal orientation can even juxtapose lexemes of perception to more materially grounded actions, yielding hendiadic-like syntagms:

וַנָּצוּמָה וַנְּבַקְשָׁה מֵאֱלֹהֵינוּ עַל־זֹאת

'We fasted and sought after our God concerning this' (√*ṣûm*, √*bqš*, Ezr 8:23)

וָאָנוּשָׁה וָאֲקַוֶּה לָנוּד וָאַיִן

'I have despaired and longed for pity, but there is none' (√*nûš*, √*qwh*, Ps 69:21)

Perception verbs with the centrifugal affix sometimes entail a morally evaluative dimension toward the patient:

וָאֶשְׁמְרָה תּוֹרָתֶךָ

'I have been attentive to your law' (√*šmr*, Ps 119:55)

רָאִיתִי בֹגְדִים וָאֶתְקוֹטָטָה

'I saw treacherous men, and I felt disgust (toward them)' (√*qûṭ*, Ps 119:158)

וַתַּעְגְּבָה עַל פִּלַגְשֵׁיהֶם

'She lusted over their studs' (√*ʿgb*, Ezek 23:20)[16]

Centrifugal verbal orientation is not limited to the waking actions of the speaker/agent(s), either:

וַנַּחַלְמָה חֲלוֹם בְּלַיְלָה אֶחָד אֲנִי וָהוּא

'We dreamed (into) a dream on one night, I and he' (√*ḥlm*, Gen 41:11)

Biblical Hebrew *verbs of locomotion* compose another functional subset employed with the centrifugal affix (twenty times). Movement into the realm of somnolence is again attested:

אֲנִי שָׁכַבְתִּי וָאִישָׁנָה

'I lay myself down and I go (in)to sleep' (√*yšn*, Ps 3:6)

Itive motion can be as close as arm's length:

וַיְהִי כִּי־בָאנוּ אֶל־הַמָּלוֹן וַנִּפְתְּחָה אֶת־אַמְתְּחֹתֵינוּ

'It was when we had come to the lodging place that we accessed our sacks' (√*ptḥ*, Gen 43:21)

[15] Note the morphosyntactic distinction between the *wayyiqṭōl* + infinitive construction conveying speaker/agent-centered action, versus the pseudo-cohortative form signaling deictically itive action.

[16] This is the lone instance of a non-first person pseudo-cohortative form in Biblical Hebrew. Genuine cohortatives in the third person are also rare (Joüon and Muraoka 2006, §45): יָחִישָׁה 'may he hasten' (Isa 5:19); וְתָבוֹאָה 'let it come' (Isa 5:19); תָּעֻפָה 'may it fly away' (Job 11:17).

Or, at the disposal of one's feet:

> וָאֵצְאָה בְשַׁעַר־הַגַּיא לַיְלָה
>
> 'I exited by the Valley Gate at night' (√*yṣ*ʾ, Neh 2:13)

Movement can be oriented toward the ground:

> וַיְהִי כְּהַכּוֹתָם וְנֵאשֲׁאַר אָנִי
> וָאֶפְּלָה עַל־פָּנַי
>
> 'It was while they were smiting, and I alone remained, that I fell upon my face' (√*npl*, Ezek 9:8; see also Dan 8:17)

Or, the trajectory of the verbal action can be more distant:

> כִּי־גָז חִישׁ וַנָּעֻפָה
>
> 'For it (life) passes away quickly, and we fly off' (√*ʿûp*, Ps 90:10)

Even simultaneous and divergent itive motions are possible:

> וָאֶכְרְעָה עַל־בִּרְכַּי וָאֶפְרְשָׂה כַפַּי אֶל־יְהוָה אֱלֹהָי
>
> 'I bent down on my knees, and I stretched out my palms to YHWH my God' (√*kr*ʿ, √*prś*, Ezr 9:5)

The *-â* affix also occurs in circumstances where the speaker/agent has undergone deictic displacement, away from one locale and to another:

> וַנִּסְעָה מִנְּהַר אֲהֲוָא בִּשְׁנֵים עָשָׂר לַחֹדֶשׁ הָרִאשׁוֹן לָלֶכֶת יְרוּשָׁלָ͏ִם
>
> 'We set off from the River Ahava, on the twelfth of the first month, to go to Jerusalem' (√*ns*ʿ, Ezr 8:31)

This deixis-shifting function is invoked repeatedly and with great rhetorical flourish as a refrain to the cascade of catastrophes that befall Job, dutifully recounted by their respective sole survivors:

> וָאִמָּלְטָה רַק־אֲנִי לְבַדִּי לְהַגִּיד לָךְ
>
> 'I escaped (from there) — only I alone! — to report to you' (√*mlṭ*, Job 1:15, 16, 17, 19; see also Job 19:20)

Movement can also entail an ethical (re)orientation of the speaker/agent:

> וָאָשִׁיבָה רַגְלַי אֶל־עֵדֹתֶיךָ
>
> 'I have turned my feet toward your precepts' (√*šûb*, Ps 119:59)

A final and less frequent (six times) lexemic subset occurring with the centrifugal affix involves *verbs of impact*, where the agent impinges directly (and violently) upon the patient via the verbal action. Examples are extant in prosaic texts:

> וָאֹחֲזָה בוֹ וָאֶהְרְגֵהוּ בְּצִקְלָג
>
> 'I grabbed onto him, and I killed him at Ziklag' (√*ʾḥz*, 2 Sam 4:10)

> וָאַכְרִתָה אֶת־כָּל־אֹיְבֶיךָ מִפָּנֶיךָ
>
> 'I cut down all your enemies from before you' (√*krt*, 2 Sam 7:9)

וָאֶמְרְטָה מִשְּׂעַר רֹאשִׁי וּזְקָנִי וָאֵשְׁבָה מְשׁוֹמֵם

‘I tore out hair from my head and my beard, and I sat down in desolation’ (√*mrṭ*, √*yšb*, Ezr 9:3)[17]

As well as in poetic texts:

וָאֲשַׁבְּרָה מְתַלְּעוֹת עַוָּל
וּמִשִּׁנָּיו אַשְׁלִיךְ טָרֶף

‘I smashed (penetrated) the jaws of the wicked, and from his teeth I wrested prey’ (√*šbr*, Job 29:17)

The -*â* affix can even lend a centrifugal nuance to a patient that — whether literally or figuratively — occupies distant space with respect to the agent (like an adversary), versus one that does not (like a friend):

אִם־גָּמַלְתִּי שׁוֹלְמִי רָע
וָאֲחַלְּצָה צוֹרְרִי רֵיקָם

‘If I have repaid my ally with evil, or I have despoiled my enemy without cause’ (√*ḥlṣ*, Ps 7:5)

Via textual doublets, Biblical Hebrew preserves at least three examples[18] of minimal pairs comprising verbs with the centrifugal affix versus verbs without it. One such pair occurs within the poetic account of Sennacherib's unsuccessful siege upon Jerusalem, preserved in both Isaiah and 2 Kings:

וְאָבוֹא מְרוֹם קִצּוֹ יַעַר כַּרְמִלּוֹ

‘I reached its farthest peak, its densest forest’ (Isa 37:24)

וְאָבוֹאָה מְלוֹן קִצֹּה יַעַר כַּרְמִלּוֹ

‘I entered its farthest lodge, its densest forest’ (√*bô*ʾ, 2 Kgs 19:23)

The other minimal pairs are found within David's song of deliverance, preserved in both Psalms and 2 Samuel:

וָאֱהִי תָמִים עִמּוֹ וָאֶשְׁתַּמֵּר מֵעֲוֹנִי

‘I was blameless regarding him, and I kept guard from my sin’ (Ps 18:24)

וָאֶהְיֶה תָמִים לוֹ וָאֶשְׁתַּמְּרָה מֵעֲוֹנִי

‘I went blameless before him, and I was vigilant against my sin’ (√*hyh*, √*šmr*, 2 Sam 22:24)

אֶרְדּוֹף אוֹיְבַי וְאַשִּׂיגֵם

‘I pursued my enemies, and I overtook them’ (Ps 18:38)

אֶרְדְּפָה אֹיְבַי וָאַשְׁמִידֵם

‘I chased after my enemies, and I destroyed them’ (√*rdp*, 2 Sam 22:38)

Despite minor lexical variations, each of these doublets is syntagmatically identical, and there are no obvious temporal and/or modal differences between the verbs in question. Instead, the intended semantic nuance here is spatial, with the -*â* affix functioning as an overt yet optional marker of deictically centrifugal verbal action emanating from the speaker/agent and aimed toward a patient. It is likely that these Isaiah and Psalms excerpts

[17] Notice here a verb of impact paired with a verb of locomotion, both oriented centrifugally.

[18] Counting אֶהְיֶה in 2 Sam 22:24a yields four examples. This relies upon resolving the morphonemic ambiguity of final-*hê* prefixed verbs (see Joüon and Muraoka 2006, §79m, o) in favor of their syntagmatic contiguity with juxtaposed and unambiguous ʾ*eqṭəlâ* / *niqṭəlâ* forms. For every such instance tallied by this study, there also exists no compelling reason why a *yiqṭōl* (< **yaqtulu*, so-called imperfective, future) form should be employed.

antedate their respective parallels in Kings and Samuel, especially since the latter texts overtly reference the characters and traditions associated with the former. Furthermore, the centrifugal affix is most frequently attested in biblical books that are indisputably post-exilic, including Daniel (eleven times), Ezra (seventeen times), and Nehemiah (thirty-three times). Such evidence might suggest that the centrifugal affix is itself a historically late development. Conversely, the affix does not appear at all in Chronicles (another patently late textual tradition), and it *is* sprinkled throughout the ostensibly earlier Pentateuchal, Deuteronomistic, and prophetic books. From a distributional standpoint, therefore, the linguistic origins of the Biblical Hebrew centrifugal affix remain clouded. Yet through a closer investigation of the lexemic, grammatical, and syntactic components that are associated with this affix, a clear diachronic trajectory emerges via the phenomenon of *grammaticalization*.

Grammaticalization is a process of linguistic change that was first explicitly posited a century ago, during the twilight of Neogrammarianism, by Antoine Meillet in his 1912 article entitled "L'évolution des formes grammaticales." The concept was largely eclipsed by the ensuing structuralist and generativist enterprises, which tended to focus upon non-diachronic dimensions of language.[19] But interest in language universals and typology has gradually extended from the synchronic into the diachronic realm, and dynamics of language change have again come to occupy the attentions of linguists. Expanding upon the classic formulation by Jerzy Kuryłowicz ([1965] 1975, p. 52),[20] Paul Hopper and Elizabeth Traugott (2003, p. xv) define grammaticalization as "the change whereby lexical items and constructions come in certain linguistic contexts to serve grammatical functions and, once grammaticalized, continue to develop new grammatical functions." Grammaticalization involves the transformation of a content item into a function item (ibid., p. 4) — or, of an existing function item into a new function item (Bybee, Perkins, and Pagliuca 1994, p. 11) — and it is this dynamic that is responsible for the emergence of the centrifugal affix in Biblical Hebrew.

Both grammaticalization and analogy yield change in language; but whereas analogy entails the extension, often via reanalysis, of an already existing pattern, Meillet and most linguists since have viewed grammaticalization as creating novel forms.[21] A widely acknowledged phenomenon with respect to grammaticalization is the so-called *cline of grammaticality*, by which "crosslinguistically forms tend to undergo the same kinds of changes or have similar sets of relationships, in similar orders" (Hopper and Traugott 2003, pp. 6–7).[22] Numerous instances of grammaticalization in Semitic languages adhere to this typological tendency,[23] and key points along the cline are discernable regarding the development of the Biblical Hebrew centrifugal affix.

Cross-linguistically with regard to verbs, grammaticalization turns out to be especially prevalent among superordinate lexemes known as "hyperonyms" (Hopper and Traugott 2003, p. 101), which convey broad yet core cognitive meanings. These include concepts such as *go*, *come*, *say*, and *give*, to name a few. This typological tendency is highly suggestive concerning Biblical Hebrew, given that the core deictic centrifugal lexeme, √*hlk* (*go*), is attested forty-six times in the volitive *ʾeqṭəlâ / niqṭəlâ* paradigm. This is *more than twice as frequent* as the next most common verbal lexemes so employed with the paradigm (√*šûb* twenty-two times; √*dbr* twenty-one times). Even more pertinent is the cross-linguistic evidence that exists for grammaticalization of the verbal lexeme *go* into a centrifugal verbal affix. Likewise, the verbal lexeme *come* often grammaticalizes into a deictically centripetal (ventive) affix. "For inferences to play a significant role in grammaticalization, they must be frequently occurring, since only standard inferences can plausibly be assumed . . . to function crosslinguistically" (ibid., p.

---

[19] Regarding the development of generative linguistics, see Cook and Newson 2007; on structural linguistics, see Hawkes 2003.

[20] Viz. "Grammaticalization consists in the increase of the range of a morpheme advancing from a lexical to a grammatical or from a less grammatical to a more grammatical status, e.g., from a derivative formant to an inflectional one."

[21] Notable exceptions to this consensus include Paul Kiparsky — one of the founders of Optimality Theory (see McCarthy 2002; Kager 1999) — who argues that grammaticalization is ultimately a subset of analogy motivated by non-exemplar-based categories and constraints grounded within Universal Grammar (Kiparsky 2005, p. 6). Joseph (2004, p. 61) suggests that grammaticalization is really an "epiphenomenon" that is a result or product — rather than a process or mechanism — of language change. On the debated relationship among grammaticalization, reanalysis, analogy, and extension, see Traugott and Trousdale 2010; Campbell 2001; Fischer 1997.

[22] Although instances of "degrammaticalization" have been documented in languages (Harris and Campbell 1995, pp. 337–43; Campbell 2001; cf. Haspelmath 1999; 2004), the consensus among linguists is that grammaticalization most typically proceeds according to uniform directionality constraints, from syntagmatic toward paradigmatic structures (e.g., lexeme > clitic > affix).

[23] See Rubin 2005, pp. 17–64.

82). Indeed, "*come* and *go* are the motion verbs chosen most often for grammaticalization" (Bybee, Perkins, and Pagliuca 1994, p. 9).

Examples of this are found in the Oceanic languages stemming from the Eastern Malayo-Polynesian branch of Austronesian. Toqabaqita (from the Solomon Islands) employs the post-verbal directional particles *mai* for ventive orientation and *kau* for itive orientation (Lichtenberk 2003, p. 152): thus, *lae mai* ('move here') versus *lae kau* ('move away'). Similarly, Tokelauan (from its eponymous atolls northwest of Samoa) uses *mai* for ventive and *atu* for itive (Hooper 2002, pp. 284, 286): thus, *koutou e faitatala mai* ('you-all talk to us') versus *kimātou e faitatala atu* ('we talk to you-all'). Based upon such evidence, linguists can reconstruct for Proto-Oceanic a centripetal enclitic **mai* and a centrifugal enclitic **ua[tu]*, which themselves derive from earlier verbs meaning *come* and *go*, respectively (Lichtenberk 2003, p. 152).

Less far afield genetically to Hebrew are the locative verbal extensions found within the Chadic language subgroup of Afro-Asiatic. In a seminal study of these extensions, Zygmunt Frajzyngier (1987) confirmed, via morphonological patterns, that verbs of movement constitute the lexical sources for the deictic directional extensions: *come* (or, *return*) for the centripetal, *go* (or, *depart*) for the centrifugal. Among the examples (ibid., p. 35), centrifugal *-d* in Hona is traceable to Proto-Chadic **də* (*go*), centrifugal *-li* in Logone derives from verbal *lə* (*go*), and centrifugal *-ba* of Margi stems from the verb *ba* (*go out*). Even more critically, Frajzyngier delineated the syntagmatic origins of these locative affixes, recognizing that "there must once have been a construction consisting of two verbs . . . whereby some verbs become part of a verbal compound, then lose their semantic content and eventually become affixes" (ibid., p. 36). Such deictic directional verbal lexemes, in other words, become grammaticalized. Furthermore, Frajzyngier discovered that a locative extension can develop in Chadic only when the deictic directional verb *follows* the main verb. No such extensions are attested in those languages where the compound order is reversed. This typological path of development is corroborated by Japanese, wherein the deictic directional verbs *kuru* (*come*) and *iku* (*go*) respectively manifest centripetal and centrifugal values as the second elements of verbal compounds linked by the conjunctive particle *te* (Shibatani 2003, pp. 259–61): thus, *Ken-ga heya-ni hait-te ki-ta* 'Ken came into the room' (using compound *enter* + *come*) versus *Ken-ga heya-ni hait-te it-ta* 'Ken went into the room' (using compound *enter* + *go*).

Returning to Biblical Hebrew, conjunctive compounds are attested with volitive *ʾeqṭəlâ* / *niqṭəlâ* forms wherein the deictic directional verb √*hlk* appears in either the first or the second position with respect to the adjoining main verb. The order of the verbal lexemes generally appears to be iconic, reflecting the practical sequence of the actions described. Thus we find examples such as the following:

> נֵלְכָה וְנַעַבְדָה אֱלֹהִים אֲחֵרִים
>
> 'Let us go and serve other gods' (Deut 13:7, 14)
>
> אֵלְכָה וְאָשׁוּבָה אֶל־אִישִׁי הָרִאשׁוֹן
>
> 'I will go and return to my first husband' (Hos 2:9)

But we also find attested the following compounds:

> נִסְעָה וְנֵלֵכָה
>
> 'Let us journey and go' (Gen 33:12)
>
> וְנָקוּמָה וְנֵלֵכָה
>
> 'Let us get up and go' (Gen 43:8)
>
> אָקוּמָה וְאֵלֵכָה
>
> 'I will get up and go' (2 Sam 3:21)

It is precisely this latter construction — supported by the cross-linguistic evidence surveyed above — that provides a conduit for grammaticalization of the itive verb into a centrifugal affix. But exactly how did this happen? What were the mechanisms that permitted the main verb + וְנֵלֵכָה / וְאֵלֵכָה construction in Biblical Hebrew to so grammaticalize? To answer this, we must examine how the typological dynamics composing grammaticalization are manifested within the specific and relevant structures of Biblical Hebrew. Initially, as discussed above, the Biblical Hebrew *ʾeqṭəlâ* / *niqṭəlâ* paradigm conformed formally as well as functionally (albeit largely in the first person) with earlier Canaanite *yaqtula*. This most often entailed syntagms involving precative and/or intentional meanings, including the compound constructions just cited. Thanks to Moran and others, it is recognized that *yaqtula* shares a partial functional overlap with Canaanite *yaqtul*, the prefixed short form that was employed in both volitive and indicative contexts and that persisted into Biblical Hebrew as the jussive and the consecutive preterite. Such formal and functional convergences within a language provide what Bernd Heine (2002, pp. 84–86) refers to as *bridging contexts*. A bridging context is a linguistic environment that can give rise to an inference in favor of a new meaning, and it is a critical prerequisite for grammaticalization. This is because it provides the ground for *reanalysis*, the formal and/or functional reinterpretation of a language unit or sequence.[24] Hopper and Traugott (2003, p. 50) provide a familiar and tasty example of reanalysis with the lexeme *hamburger*, which originally consisted of [*Hamburg* + *er*], 'item (of food) from Hamburg,' but eventually underwent resegmentation and reformulation into [*ham* + *burger*], likely under analogical pressure from the porcine noun. The constituents of *hamburger* are thus redistributed both formally and functionally via processes such as back-formation (now simply *burger*), as well as analogical extension (*cheese-burger*, *tuna-burger*, *veggie-burger*, etc.). But grammaticalization cannot happen without reanalysis, and reanalysis does not occur without a bridging context.

When it comes to Biblical Hebrew, I propose that the functional overlap of volitive *ʾeqṭəlâ* / *niqṭəlâ* and jussive *yiqṭōl* allowed for reanalysis of the former into *ʾeqṭōl* + *â* and *niqṭōl* + *â*. Volitive verbs — including those in compound constructions such as אָקוּמָה וְאֵלֵכָה and נָקוּמָה וְנֵלֵכָה — thus became subject to resegmentation and reinterpretation from *yaqtula cohortatives into *yaqtul jussives + affix. Final *qāmeṣ-hê* was thereby rendered superfluous for explicitly signifying the volitional value of such forms. Instead, this affix — due to its high frequency co-occurrence with the verb √*hlk* — was further reanalyzed and, functionally as well as formally, bracketed with the lexeme *go*. This triggered the transition from an itive lexical construction into a centrifugal morpheme. Indeed, it is not lexemes in isolation that undergo grammaticalization, but rather lexical constructions within particular speech contexts. Hopper and Traugott (2003, pp. 76, 82) assert that "meaning changes are initially pragmatic and associative . . . and for inferences to play a significant role in grammaticalization, they must be frequently occurring." These very circumstances obtain with regard to וְאֵלֵכָה and וְנֵלֵכָה and they allow for *metonymy*, which is definable as "semantic transfer through contiguity" (Anttila 1989, pp. 141–42), that is, meaning change along language's syntagmatic axis, via reanalysis (Hopper and Traugott 2003, p. 93).

Another common corollary of grammaticalization that is evidenced by the emergence of the Biblical Hebrew centrifugal affix involves irregular phonological reduction via *erosion* or *fusion*. Among the more well-known examples of this process is the conversion of the English motion verb construction *be going to* into the imminent future tense *gonna*. Grammaticalization and reduction frequently co-occur because they are both motivated by the metalinguistic principle of *economy*. The economy principle (Kiparsky 2005, p. 6; Hopper and Traugott 2003, pp. 71–73) stipulates that maximal functional output be achieved via minimal formal input — or, more colloquially, that one should speak less and say more. Erosion and fusion aid in the attainment of syntagmatic economy, and grammaticalization systematizes this economy into paradigmatic structures. Clitics and contractions are hallmark instances of grammaticalized economization (e.g., *can not* > *cannot* > *can't*). The volitive "get up and go" compounds of Biblical Hebrew are particularly receptive to similar compression, given that equivalent morphonemic structures (*qāmeṣ-hê*) frame the itive lexeme. This remains congruent with the cross-linguistic cline of grammaticalization, wherein clitics and affixes tend to develop from full verbs that have come to be used as auxiliaries (Hopper and Traugott 2003, pp. 111–12). Furthermore, "phonetic reduction can be manifested in any of the segmental or suprasegmental features of the phonetic string" (Bybee, Perkins, and Pagliuca 1994, p. 107). It is also significant, yet not surprising, that √*hlk* never once occurs as a pseudo-cohortative in Biblical Hebrew, since it would be redundant and thereby violate the principle of economy.[25]

A subtle facet of grammaticalization is that reanalysis is discoverable only in retrospect, once the target form has assumed a new and incongruous function compared to the source form (see Langacker 1977, p. 58; Timberlake 1977, p. 151). This requires what Heine (2002, pp. 85–86) terms a *switch context*. A switch context involves a

---

[24] For seminal studies concerning reanalysis, see Langacker 1977 and Timberlake 1977.

[25] The centrifugal affix is, however, twice attested with √*hyh* (*be*), providing a locomotive nuance to the copular verb that approaches the semantics of √*hlk*: וָאֶהְיֶה עִמְּךָ בְּכֹל אֲשֶׁר הָלַכְתָּ 'I was with you in every (place) which you went' (i.e., *I went where you went*; 2 Sam 7:9a). Also see 2 Sam 22:24a, above (and n. 18).

syntagmatic environment that is incompatible with (or at least in conflict with) some salient property of the source form in its original context, thereby ruling out the original meaning. The new meaning that has arisen via the bridging context becomes applicable within a switch context that favors it over the original meaning. Switch contexts "may be viewed as a filtering device that rules out the source meaning" (Heine 2002, p. 86). I propose that the switch context for the Biblical Hebrew pseudo-cohortative is traceable to the novel use of *ʾeqṭəlâ / niqṭəlâ* with indicative past narrative syntagms, as opposed to the volitive future syntagms that employ the true cohortative.

How and why this new application emerged has to do with what Philippe Bourdin (2002) characterizes as "the grammaticalization of deictic directionals into modulators of temporal distance." Bourdin cites numerous languages that encode what he terms "temporal modulation" via markers that also function as deictic directionals.[26] These markers frequently derive from the verbs *come* and *go* (ibid., p. 182; Nicolle 2007, p. 48). Temporal modulation refers to either the contraction or the expansion of the interval expressed between the event time and the speech time (Bourdin 2002, pp. 181–82). Ventive markers are used to signify interval contraction, whereas itive markers are used to signify interval expansion. For example (ibid., p. 183), Mohawk of the Iroquoian family employs its ventive prefix *t-* in constructions such as *t-ahaté:koʾ* ('he ran away just now'), but its itive prefix *y-* in constructions like *y-ahaté:koʾ* ('he ran away sometime ago'). Also (ibid., p. 184), the Figuig dialect from Morocco — belonging to the Berber group of Afro-Asiatic — can use its ventive morpheme *dd* to signify interval contraction either in the past (*i-syu dd taqeddit-t* — 'he bought the meat just now') or in the future (*sa dd i-seɣ taqeddit-t* — 'he will buy the meat right away'). Returning to the Oceanic languages, Manam from Papua New Guinea (ibid., p. 187) applies its itive affix *laʾo* to a similar range of temporal frames: *zamalu* ('second day after tomorrow') versus *zamalu-laʾo* ('beyond the second day after tomorrow'), and *toira* ('some time ago') versus *toira-laʾo* ('a longer time ago'). There is also the itive marker *aku* of Hawaiian (ibid., p. 188), which signifies a spatio-temporal deictic distance: thus, *nehinei a ia lâ aku* (lit. 'yesterday and day thither' = the day before yesterday), as well as *ʾapôpô a ia lâ aku* (lit. 'tomorrow and day thither' = the day after tomorrow). In all of the foregoing cross-linguistic examples, the deictic directional morphemes signify either a ventive/centripetal nearness to, or an itive/centrifugal remoteness from, the deictic here-and-now of the speaker. The correlative qualities involved with distance in both its spatial and its temporal dimensions thus forge a cognitive conduit through which deictic directionals can be further grammaticalized into temporal modulators. The Biblical Hebrew evidence supports this grammaticalization pathway, whereby the spatially centrifugal affix that emerged within the bridging context of temporally imminent volitive syntagms (e.g., precative and purpose clauses) became conventionalized via the switch context of temporally distal indicative syntagms (i.e., narrative preterite clauses). This development for *ʾeqṭəlâ / niqṭəlâ* was fostered analogically by the core morphonological equivalence of the **yaqtul-Ø* paradigm in both its volitive and its indicative applications.

The diachronically sporadic yet increasing use of the centrifugal affix throughout the Biblical Hebrew corpus attests to what linguists term *layering*, whereby an older form and a newer form can coexist for an extended period of time and produce synchronic variability at particular stages along the grammaticalization cline (Hopper and Traugott 2003, p. 124). Thus, we find the innovative pseudo-cohortative sprinkled into pre-exilic Biblical Hebrew texts where the true cohortative is still normative, as well as vestigial applications of the true cohortative within post-exilic Biblical Hebrew texts where the pseudo-cohortative has become dominant. By the time of Qumranic Hebrew around the turn of the Common Era, *ʾeqṭəlâ / niqṭəlâ* have undergone further *semantic bleaching* — another hallmark feature of grammaticalization — and they are employed universally for the first person conjunctive and consecutive preterites (Qimron 1986, pp. 44–45). Semantic bleaching (Hopper and Traugott 2003, pp. 94–98; Bybee, Perkins, and Pagliuca 1994, pp. 5, 14) involves the gradual functional abstraction and generalization of a grammaticalized element, correlating roughly with its formal erosion.

By way of conclusion, there are two instances among the 113 examples of Biblical Hebrew pseudo-cohortatives that are seemingly resistant to the hypothesis presented herein:

[26] Regarding the cross-linguistic semiotic pathway from spatial markers to temporal markers, see Haspelmath 1997; Bybee, Perkins, and Pagliuca 1994, p. 103.

וָאָעִידָה לִּי עֵדִים נֶאֱמָנִים
'I summoned to myself reliable witnesses' (Isa 8:2)

וָאָשִׂימָה נַפְשִׁי בְכַפִּי
'I placed my life into my hand' (Judg 12:3)

The juxtaposition in Isaiah of the first person reflexive pronoun with the *ʾeqṭəlâ* form starkly contradicts any centrifugal orientation of the verbal action vis-à-vis the speaker/agent. This syntagm also is situated within a consecutive preterite chain that firmly conveys a past narrative context, rendering an explicit cohortative meaning most unlikely. The Judges text too is located within a past narrative sequence (signified by *wayyiqṭōl* and *qāṭal* verbs), and its first person pronominal suffixes linked by a proximal preposition unambiguously convey centripetal deictic orientation. For a potential solution to these anomalies, it is noteworthy that verbs of coming and going are among a small group that have developed into what Indo-Aryan linguists term *vector* verbs (or *light* verbs), which as quasi-auxiliaries modify the meaning of the complex predicate in terms of manner specification, variously signifying values such as deliberateness, volitionality, benefaction, inclusiveness, and transition (Goswami and Tamuli 2007, pp. 469–72; Butt 1995, pp. 90–91; Masica 1991, p. 326).[27] For example, Urdu (Schmidt 2007, pp. 372–73; cf. Hook 1974 for Hindi) employs the vector verb *jānā* (*go*) in combinations such as *kar jānā* (*do* + *go* = 'accomplish'), *khā jānā* (*eat* + *go* = 'gobble'), and *sīkh jānā* (*learn* + *go* = 'master'). Furthermore, Indo-Aryan vectors regularly occur as the second verb in a compound construction, not unlike the Biblical Hebrew "get up and go" conjunctive sequence that triggered the creation of the centrifugal affix.[28] It is possible, therefore, that an intentional dimension of √*hlk* as a light verb got preserved vestigially by the grammaticalized *qāmeṣ-hê*, and that its application in these two instances retains a nuance of speaker/agent benefactive volition with regard to the recounted narrative actions. This would mark a plausible point of intersection along the original volitive spectrum of the *ʾeqṭəlâ* / *niqṭəlâ* paradigm. Indeed, syntagms such as those preserved in Isaiah 8:2 and Judges 12:3 might well have operated as a key functional link in the grammaticalization chain extending from the cohortative verb, via the itive lexeme, to the centrifugal affix of Biblical Hebrew.

Bibliography

Aikhenvald, Alexandra Y.
2006 "Serial Verb Constructions in Typological Perspective." In *Serial Verb Constructions: A Cross-linguistic Typology*, edited by Alexandra Y. Aikhenvald and R. M. W. Dixon, pp. 1–68. Explorations in Linguistic Typology 2. Oxford: Oxford University Press.

Anttila, Raimo
1989 *Historical and Comparative Linguistics*. Second edition. Current Issues in Linguistic Theory 6. Amsterdam: John Benjamins.

Bourdin, Philippe
2002 "The Grammaticalization of Deictic Directionals into Modulators of Temporal Distance." In *New Reflections on Grammaticalization*, edited by Ilse Wisher and Gabriele Diewald, pp. 181–99. Typological Studies in Language 49. Amsterdam: John Benjamins.

[27] Light verbs are therefore distinct from *serial verbs*, which combine to form a single, non-complex predicate (see Aikhenvald 2006, pp. 4–6).

[28] Hopper and Traugott (2003, pp. 108, 111–12) situate light verbs upon the grammaticalization cline as an optional developmental stage in between full verbs and auxiliaries. Butt (2010, pp. 68–69) instead contends that light verbs remain formally associated with full (main) verbs, and that the functional distinctions arise via differing syntactic (predicative) environments.

Butt, Miriam

1995 *The Structure of Complex Predicates in Urdu.* Dissertations in Linguistics. Stanford: Center for the Study of Language and Information.

2010 "The Light Verb Jungle: Still Hacking Away." In *Complex Predicates: Cross-linguistic Perspectives on Event Structure*, edited by Mengistu Amberber, Brett Baker, and Mark Harvey, pp. 48–78. Cambridge: Cambridge University Press.

Bybee, Joan L.; Revere D. Perkins; and William Pagliuca

1994 *The Evolution of Grammar: Tense, Aspect, and Modality in the Languages of the World.* Chicago: University of Chicago Press.

Campbell, Lyle

2001 "What's Wrong with Grammaticalization?" *Language Sciences* 23: 113–61.

Cook, Vivian, and Mark Newson

2007 *Chomsky's Universal Grammar: An Introduction.* Third edition. Malden: Blackwell.

Driver, Samuel R.

[1892] 1998 *A Treatise on the Use of the Tenses in Hebrew and Some Other Syntactical Questions.* Third edition. Biblical Resource Series. Grand Rapids: William B. Eerdmans. Reprint of the 1892 third edition by Oxford University Press.

Fischer, Olga

1997 "On the Status of Grammaticalization and the Diachronic Dimension in Explanation." *Transactions of the Philological Society* 95/2: 149–87.

Frajzyngier, Zygmunt

1987 "Ventive and Centrifugal in Chadic." *Afrika und Übersee* 70: 31–47.

Gesenius, Wilhelm; Emil Kautzsch; and Arthur E. Cowley

1910 *Gesenius' Hebrew Grammar.* Edited by E. Kautzsch, translated by A. E. Cowley. Second English edition. Oxford: Clarendon Press.

Goswami, G. C., and J. Tamuli

2007 "Asamiya." In *The Indo-Aryan Languages*, edited by George Cardona and Dhanesh Jain, pp. 429–84. Routledge Language Family Series. New York: Routledge.

Graf, Eva-Maria

2006 *The Ontogenetic Development of Literal and Metaphorical Space in Language.* Language Development 31. Tübingen: Gunter Narr.

Harris, Alice, and Lyle Campbell

1995 *Historical Syntax in Cross-Linguistic Perspective.* Cambridge Studies in Linguistics 74. Cambridge: Cambridge University Press.

Haspelmath, Martin

1997 *From Space to Time: Temporal Adverbials in the World's Languages.* Lincom Studies in Theoretical Linguistics 3. Munich: Lincom Europa.

1999 "Why Is Grammaticalization Irreversible?" *Linguistics* 37: 1043–68.

2004 "On Directionality in Language Change with Particular Reference to Grammaticalization." In *Up and Down the Cline — The Nature of Grammaticalization*, edited by Olga Fischer, Muriel Norde, and Harry Perridon, pp. 17–44. Typological Studies in Language 59. Amsterdam: John Benjamins.

Hawkes, Terence

2003 *Structuralism and Semiotics.* Second edition. New York: Routledge.

Heine, Bernd

2002 "On the Role of Context in Grammaticalization." In *New Reflections on Grammaticalization*, edited by Ilse Wischer and Gabriele Diewald, pp. 83–101. Typological Studies in Language 49. Amsterdam: John Benjamins.

Hook, Peter Edwin

1974 *The Compound Verb in Hindi.* Ann Arbor: University of Michigan Center for South and Southeast Asian Studies.

Hooper, Robin

2002 "Deixis and Aspect: The Tokelauan Directional Particles *mai* and *atu*." *Studies in Language* 26/2: 283–313.

Hopper, Paul J., and Elizabeth Closs Traugott

2003 *Grammaticalization*. Second edition. Cambridge Textbooks in Linguistics. Cambridge: Cambridge University Press.

Huehnergard, John

2005 "Features of Central Semitic." In *Biblical and Oriental Essays in Memory of William L. Moran*, edited by Agustinus Gianto, pp. 155–203. Biblica et Orientalia 48. Rome: Pontificio Istituto Biblico.

Jakobson, Roman

[1957] 1984 "Shifters, Verbal Categories, and the Russian Verb." Harvard University, Department of Slavic Languages and Literatures Project. Reprinted in *Roman Jakobson: Russian and Slavic Grammar Studies 1931–1981*, edited by Linda R. Waugh and Morris Halle, pp. 41–58. Janua Linguarum Series Maior 106. Berlin: Mouton.

Jenni, Ernst

2002–03 "Untersuchungen zum hebräischen Kohortativ." *Zeitschrift für Althebraistik* 15–16: 19–67.

Johnson, Mark

2008 "The Meaning of the Body." In *Developmental Perspectives on Embodiment and Consciousness*, edited by Willis F. Overton, Ulrich Müller, and Judith L. Newman, pp. 19–43. The Jean Piaget Symposium Series. New York: Lawrence Erlbaum Associates.

Joseph, Brian D.

2004 "Rescuing Traditional (Historical) Linguistics from Grammaticalization Theory." In *Up and Down the Cline — The Nature of Grammaticalization*, edited by Olga Fischer, Muriel Norde, and Harry Perridon, pp. 45–71. Typological Studies in Language 59. Amsterdam: John Benjamins.

Joüon, Paul, and Takamitsu Muraoka

2006 *A Grammar of Biblical Hebrew*. Revised edition. Subsidia Biblica 27. Rome: Pontificio Istituto Biblico.

Kager, René

1999 *Optimality Theory*. Cambridge Textbooks in Linguistics. Cambridge: Cambridge University Press.

Kiparsky, Paul

2005 "Grammaticalization as Optimization." Plenary paper presented at the New Reflections on Grammaticalization 3 conference, Santiago, Chile.

Korchin, Paul

2008 *Markedness in Canaanite and Hebrew Verbs*. Harvard Semitic Studies 58. Winona Lake: Eisenbrauns.

Kuryłowicz, Jerzy

[1965] 1975 "The Evolution of Grammatical Categories." *Diogenes* 13: 55–71. Reprinted in *Esquisses Linguistiques* II, by Jerzy Kuryłowicz, pp. 38–54. International Bibliothek für allgemeine Linguistik 37. Munich: Fink.

1972 "The Role of Deictic Elements in Linguistic Evolution." *Semiotica* 5: 174–83.

Langacker, Ronald

1977 "Syntactic Reanalysis." In *Mechanisms of Syntactic Change*, edited by Charles N. Li, pp. 57–139. Austin: University of Texas Press.

Lichtenberk, Frantisek

2003 "Directionality and Displaced Directionality in Toqabaqita." In *Motion, Direction and Location in Languages: In Honor of Zygmunt Frajzyngier*, edited by Erin Shay and Uwe Seibert, pp. 151–75. Typological Studies in Language 56. Amsterdam: John Benjamins.

Masica, Colin P.

1991 *The Indo-Aryan Languages*. Cambridge Language Surveys. Cambridge: Cambridge University Press.

McCarthy, John J.

2002 *A Thematic Guide to Optimality Theory*. Research Surveys in Linguistics. Cambridge: Cambridge University Press.

McFall, Leslie

1982 *The Enigma of the Hebrew Verbal System: Solutions from Ewald to the Present Day*. Historical Texts and Interpreters in Biblical Scholarship 2. Sheffield: Almond.

Meillet, Antoine

[1912] 1958 "L'évolution des formes grammaticales." Reprinted in *Linguistique historique et linguistique générale*, pp. 130–48. Collection Linguistique publiée par la Société de Linguistique de Paris 8. Paris: Champion.

Moran, William L.

[1950] 2003 "A Syntactical Study of the Dialect of Byblos as Reflected in the Amarna Tablets." In *Amarna Studies: Collected Writings*, edited by John Huehnergard and Shlomo Izre'el, pp. 1–130. Harvard Semitic Studies 54. Winona Lake: Eisenbrauns.

1960 "Early Canaanite *yaqtula*." *Orientalia* 29: 1–19.

Nicolle, Steve

2007 "The Grammaticalization of Tense Markers: A Pragmatic Reanalysis." In *Tense, Mood and Aspect: Theoretical and Descriptive Issues*, edited by Louis de Saussure, Jacques Moeschler, and Genoveva Puskas, pp. 47–65. Cahiers Chronos 17. Amsterdam: Rodopi.

Polzin, Robert

1976 *Late Biblical Hebrew: Toward an Historical Typology of Biblical Hebrew Prose*. Harvard Semitic Monographs 12. Missoula: Scholars Press for the Harvard Semitic Museum.

Qimron, Elisha

1986 *The Hebrew of the Dead Sea Scrolls*. Harvard Semitic Studies 29. Atlanta: Scholars Press.

Rezetko, Robert

2003 "Dating Biblical Hebrew: Evidence from Samuel–Kings and Chronicles." In *Biblical Hebrew: Studies in Chronology and Typology*, edited by Ian Young, pp. 215–50. Journal for the Study of the Old Testament Supplement Series 369. London: T. and T. Clark.

Rubin, Aaron D.

2005 *Studies in Semitic Grammaticalization*. Harvard Semitic Studies 57. Winona Lake: Eisenbrauns.

Schmidt, Ruth Laila

2007 "Urdu." In *The Indo-Aryan Languages*, edited by George Cardona and Dhanesh Jain, pp. 315–85. Paperback edition. Routledge Language Family Series. New York: Routledge.

Shibatani, Masayoshi

2003 "Directional Verbs in Japanese." In *Motion, Direction and Location in Languages: In Honor of Zygmunt Frajzyngier*, edited by Erin Shay and Uwe Seibert, pp. 259–86. Typological Studies in Language 56. Amsterdam: John Benjamins.

Timberlake, Alan

1977 "Reanalysis and Actualization in Syntactic Change." In *Mechanisms of Syntactic Change*, edited by Charles N. Li, pp. 141–77. Austin: University of Texas Press.

Traugott, Elizabeth Closs, and Graeme Trousdale, editors

2010 *Gradience, Gradualness and Grammaticalization*. Typological Studies in Language 90. Amsterdam: John Benjamins.

Waltke, Bruce K., and Michael O'Connor

1990 *An Introduction to Biblical Hebrew Syntax*. Winona Lake: Eisenbrauns.

17

The Biblical Hebrew Verbal System in a Nutshell

Dennis Pardee, University of Chicago

Though I have taught Biblical Hebrew on a regular basis since 1972 and made occasional observations — even proposed some elements of a systematic presentation, in reviews[1] — I have never laid out in a single place the broad explanation of the Biblical Hebrew verbal system as I see it that would enable my various reviewees to take me, reviewee in my turn, to the whipping post. [2]

I lay out here briefly my view of the Biblical Hebrew verbal system as primarily aspectual, only secondarily temporal;[3] I will not touch here on the function of the derived stems (the *binyanim*) as means of expressing various forms of *Aktionsart*.[4] It must further be remarked here that the system is isolatable as a system only in Standard Biblical Hebrew prose: the varieties of usage in Biblical Hebrew poetry, as perhaps in Ugaritic poetry,[5] are such

[1] These minor contributions are cited here not out of rampant immodesty but as proof that I have not been totally uninvolved in the discussions that have taken place on the Biblical Hebrew verbal system over the past three decades: Pardee 1979; 1983a; 1983b; 1985a; 1985b; 1989; 1990; 1993a; 1993b; 1994; 1995; 1999; 2001; 2003–04.

[2] I have only had the courage to put this overview, which has existed in various forms for well over a decade as a class handout, into print because the honorand was kind enough to invite me to present it to his graduate students while he was still at Harvard, and he and Jo Ann Hackett invited me to submit an expanded version for publication as a monograph. Realizing that the burden of other projects coupled with the march of time would almost certainly keep the larger project from ever being realized, I have decided to put the briefer version here. What began as a "nutshell" has been expanded by extensive footnotes and two sample texts to a whole bag of nuts (that many uses may be made of the image is not lost upon me); the title has been maintained, however, because the basic text remains a brief presentation of one person's view of a vast and vastly debated topic of which the footnotes, however extensive, provide an inadequate representation. Finally, lest anyone be deceived by the occasional citation of linguistic literature here below, I should make clear that I do not consider myself to be a general linguist, only to have done some reading in linguistics and perhaps to have picked up a few notions that may have some validity.

[3] On verbal systems as generally expressing both aspect and tense, with one or the other constituting the primary level of expression, see the general works on aspect, e.g., B. Comrie's classic study (1976) — but see below, n. 20. I am well aware of DeCaen's claim that it is theoretically implausible that Biblical Hebrew would have had an aspectual verbal system (e.g., in his 1995 dissertation), but do not presently find it acceptable because of (1) unproven assumptions (ibid., p. 181) regarding the antecedents of Hebrew and possible developments therefrom to an aspectual system, i.e., that the older Semitic languages were tensed (the Ugaritic verbal system is as plausibly aspectual as temporal, though a large body of prose texts by which this could be determined has not yet been discovered; to my knowledge, a thorough study of the Akkadian verbal system in tense-aspect terms remains to be done — note for the present that Huehnergard refers to the principal forms as "tenses," i.e., the word is placed in quotation marks: 1995, p. 205 et passim, and Andrason's recent claim [2010] that the Akkadian *iprus* evolved from originally unmarked for tense/aspect through aspectually marked to significantly tense marked); and (2) DeCaen's failure plausibly to explain the Hebrew system as expressing primarily a form of temporality.

[4] This view was treated in detail by Creason in his 1995 dissertation.

[5] Pardee 1997a, p. 137; 2004, p. 303. Tropper (2000) has made a valiant attempt to explain verbal usage in Ugaritic poetry as a coherent system of which the authors of the poems were fully aware and which they were fully able to manipulate in a systematic way — though he does leave a place for purely stylistic manipulation of the aspectual forms. In our manual of Ugaritic, Bordreuil and I essentially adopted Tropper's view of the Ugaritic verbal system (2004, vol. 1, pp. 60–64); in the English edition, however, convinced by Greenstein's (2006) observation of incongruities between this view and the orthography of YQTL forms of weak roots, particularly III-*alif* roots, we have presented the distribution of *yaqtul* and *yaqtulu* forms in Ugaritic poetry as essentially in free variation (Bordreuil and Pardee 2009, pp. 45–50). If there is anything to this and because the *yaqtul* perfective/preterit was not in use in Ugaritic prose, there is no attested West Semitic verbal system where the *yaqtul* perfective/preterit was fully functional as such alongside the *qatala* perfective.

that the use of the verbal forms must be judged as reflecting remnants of an older system; precisely what the declaimers of Hebrew poetry had in mind in any given case is all too often uncertain — a problem that is exacerbated by doubts regarding the reliability of the Massoretic vocalization tradition.[6]

Finally, it must be noted here that the artificiality that some have ascribed to the Biblical Hebrew verbal system is a figment of their imagination: the growing number of Hebrew inscriptions dating from the last century or so of the kingdom of Judah manifest a verbal system in all essential points identical to that of Standard Biblical Hebrew prose. That they reflect the speech of several strata of society (Parker 1997, pp. 16–18) shows that the verbal system itself, as distinct from various uses thereof,[7] was part of everyday speech, and the view of the system as a post-exilic construct may only be described as absurd.[8]

---

[6] I thus doubt that, even if Tropper is correct about Ugaritic poetry (see preceding note), all the poets represented in the Hebrew Bible — and their redactors and transmitters — were always using the verbal forms according to a linguistically coherent system.

[7] For example, the language attested in the extra-biblical Judaean Hebrew inscriptions makes greater use of non-verb-initial sentences than does Standard Biblical Hebrew prose, and the same may be said of direct speech embedded in narratives in the Hebrew Bible. For this reason, it would be interesting to separate direct speech from reportorial discourse (see below, nn. 16 and 39) in studies of word order in Biblical Hebrew (that is not the case, for example, in Jongeling 1991).

[8] Knauf (1990), though treating the entirety of the Hebrew Bible, recognizes implicitly the essential identity of pre-exilic Judaean Hebrew and Standard Biblical Hebrew prose — the facts that the Judaean Hebrew of the largest body of attested inscriptions patently existed alongside other dialects (much more poorly attested) and that not all strata of the Hebrew Bible represent the dialect spoken in Judah in the two centuries or so preceding the Babylonian exile (viz., the dialect that is attested by inscriptions dating to this period) do not lead to a required negative response to the question in Knauf's title. The verbal system visible in these inscriptions, the point of his paper, is essentially identical to that of Standard Biblical Hebrew prose. Knauf's general treatment is exploited to his own ends by Davies (1992, pp. 104–05): "...'biblical Hebrew' is another scholarly construct; indeed, we might say that it is no more than the imputed language of the scholarly 'ancient Israel,' and thus part of a larger fabrication." One can only express a certain agreement with so general a statement, i.e., when "biblical Hebrew" and "ancient Israel" are viewed as monolithic concepts; but, with the proper limitation of comparable data to Biblical Hebrew prose and pre-exilic Judean Hebrew, the statement loses its force. The differences cited by Knauf between pre-exilic Judaean Hebrew and Biblical Hebrew represent a very small number of morphological features; he has little to say about the essential identity of morphology, syntax, and discourse structure between the Hebrew of the inscriptions from the last two centuries or so before the Babylonian exile and the standard prose of the Hebrew Bible; these are so important, in my estimation, as to preclude attaching a tag of artificiality to the language of the vast majority of the biblical prose texts. Rather, it appears clear that these texts, as we know them today, were for the most part redacted in the literary prose of pre-exilic Judah, which had only undergone minor orthographic and morphological changes; the most likely general date for such a linguistic situation appears to be within or shortly after the Babylonian exile itself, when the pre-exilic language was still a living entity. But in point of fact, the virtual absence of Hebrew inscriptions between the pre-exilic ones and the Dead Sea Scrolls, the latter written by persons whose Hebrew had evolved beyond the language known from the biblical texts, obliges us to leave the question open. This formulation is not meant to imply that even Standard Biblical Hebrew prose does not contain textual and, to a lesser extent, linguistic strata; it says nothing about the possibility of some linguistically aberrant phenomena visible in the Massoretic text representing corruptions within the oral tradition; it says nothing about the pre-history of the redactions actually attested in the Massoretic text (though their existence seems to be proven by the evolution visible within the prose texts themselves, from so-called Standard Biblical Hebrew to Late Biblical Hebrew — it appears difficult to envision circumstances in the post-exilic period that would have created such an evolution, though an explanation by dialectical strata is certainly possible); it explicitly leaves open the possibility that in certain circles pre-exilic Judaean Hebrew may have been maintained as a living entity for several centuries (cf. the prose of the Book of Daniel); it explicitly excludes Biblical Hebrew poetry from the comparison; and it recognizes that the extra-biblical textual data from before the middle of the eighth century B.C.E. are too sparse to allow anything solid to be said about the evolution of Judaean Hebrew (and all the less of Israelian Hebrew) up to that date. But the data do appear sufficient to give a qualified "yes" to Knauf's question: the vast majority of the prose in Genesis–2 Kings does represent a single language and dialect, Judaean Hebrew showing a relatively low level of evolution from that visible in the immediate pre-exilic inscriptions. Only someone unacquainted with the Lachish letters (for example) could entertain the notion that "the consecutive or wayyiqtol ... was actually a strictly literary tense" (Kawashima 2004, p. 39) — there are too many linguistic similarities between the language of the pre-exilic Judaean inscriptions and that of Standard Biblical Hebrew prose (of which one may mention the system constituted by *wayyiqtōl/qātal* in opposition to *wᵊqātal/yiqtōl*) to allow for the hypothesis that the verbal system of Standard Biblical Hebrew prose corresponds to anything but the presence in the literary language of exilic or post-exilic times of the verbal system characteristic of spoken Judaean Hebrew in the pre-exilic period. For a general statement critical of Davies, but one that does not make the requisite distinction between prosaic and poetic texts in the Hebrew Bible, see Hurvitz 1997.

Morphology and Morpho-semantics

The system is binary, expressing perfectivity and imperfectivity,[9] and there are two forms that express each aspect: perfectivity is expressed by *qātal* and *wayyiqtōl*, imperfectivity by *yiqtōl* and *wᵊqātal*.[10] The four forms consist of two that came into use when the proto-West Semitic system began to express perfectivity by QTL ("SC" = suffix conjugation) and imperfectivity by YQTL ("PC" = prefix conjugation) and two that constitute frozen usages retained from a previous stage of the language when the perfective and/or preterit was expressed by *yaqtul* while *qatala* (and its variants) expressed stativity.[11] The view that only *wayyiqtōl* is a true retention, one that I once entertained seriously (Pardee 1983b), seems to be disproved by the fact that both Ugaritic and Phoenician (Pardee 1983a, pp. 66–67) use forms corresponding to *wᵊqātal*,[12] while forms corresponding to *wayyiqtōl* are as yet unattested in Ugaritic prose.

---

[9] Pardee 1990, pp. 202–04; 1993a; 1994, p. 152; 1995. The aspect that is marked in the finite verbal forms is thus the "viewpoint" type: see the summation of the various theories regarding types of aspect in Dobbs-Allsopp 2000, pp. 21–32. The key publications in the history of the debate on aspect in general and on aspect in Biblical Hebrew have been provided recently by Joosten (2002) and in the response by Cook (2006).

[10] The forms cited are to be considered as shorthand for all possible morphological variants of the forms known traditionally as "perfect" and "w-consecutive imperfect" (or whichever of the various terms be preferred), on the one hand, and as "imperfect" and "w-consecutive perfect," on the other. I will below use the forms vocalized as Biblical Hebrew according to the Sephardic tradition to denote Biblical Hebrew forms and the forms with proto-Hebrew vowels (*yaqtul* etc.) to represent proto-Hebrew forms (usually the "proto" stage remains undefined — i.e., the linguistic stages leading up to Biblical Hebrew as we know it were innumerable, and rarely will any attempt be made here to express that history in a properly rule-ordered fashion). I adopt here the term "w-retentive" not because I find it particularly elegant but because it expresses diachronic reality and does not have the obvious weaknesses of such popular terms as "w-conversive" and "w-consecutive" or even "w-conservative" (for a discussion, see Waltke and O'Connor 1990, pp. 466–78, 519–63, whose preferred term, "w-relative," is not, in my estimation, without problems: first, it lends itself to confusion because it introduces clauses that are not "relative" in the traditional sense of the word; second, and fundamentally more important, such verbal forms are not necessarily "relative" to a preceding verb or clause, as we shall see in the course of this study). It is important to note with regard to the traditional use of terms that begin with "w" that (1) it is not the *w* that was an active agent in retaining (or conserving) the archaic forms but that the archaic forms happen to have been retained, for the most part (see below, n. 26), after *w* and (2) that this *w* was in all likelihood simply proto-West Semitic *wa*, not an expanded form of this particle or a totally different one (see below, nn. 12 and 47). Finally, Cook has proposed serious arguments, based on Biblical Hebrew usage rather than on hypothetical proto-Hebrew forms, for *wayyiqtōl* being the only truly tensed form in the system (2001; this conclusion is also assumed in 2006, pp. 33–34), his principal internal argument being that the *w*-retentive + YQTL of stative verbs expresses past state not present state; I remain, however, unconvinced (I see no reason to take *wayyigbah* in Isa 5:16, for example, as past tense and no reason to doubt that more forms with this function would be attested in a larger corpus).

[11] Pardee 1995, pp. 64–66. For the history of the appeal to the Akkadian permansive/stative to explain Biblical Hebrew *qātal* and *wᵊqātal*, see McFall 1982, pp. 182–84 (with more detailed treatments of the theories of J. A. Knudtzon and H. Bauer on pp. 87–115). The view shared by Tropper (1998a, pp. 184–87) and Cook (2001, pp. 134–35) that both *qātal* and *wᵊqātal* function as perfectives in Biblical Hebrew and Tropper's view that Akkadian *paris* was perfective in Akkadian (1998a, p. 182) appear equally untenable to me (on this latter point, contrast Andersen 2000, p. 34). The functional interchangeability of *yiqtōl* and *wᵊqātal* (according to the strictures of morpho-syntax and discourse strategy, of course) in Standard Biblical Hebrew prose as exemplified in the sample passages cited below disallow the description of the former as imperfective the latter as perfective. One must either admit, it appears to me, that *wᵊqātal* arose secondarily in Biblical Hebrew as a counterpart to *wayyiqtōl* (a notion that I no longer accept, as will be indicated below) or that it had a proto-Hebrew origin similar to that of *wayyiqtōl*. That origin can only have been in the proto-West Semitic form corresponding to Akkadian *paris*, which was basically adjectival and hence unmarked for aspect. It appears plausible to explain the origin of the Hebrew *wᵊqātal* form as a frozen form, like *wayyiqtōl*, consisting of *wa-* + this form, which was aspectually neutral but took on the function of expressing non-perfectivity in contrast with *wayyiqtōl* (see Pardee 2003–04, pp. 339–40 n. 1222, 357–58). What might be termed the reigning hypothesis regarding the origin of the *wᵊqātal* imperfective is that it began life in the apodosis of conditional clauses (see the recent statement, with bibliography, by Kawashima 2010, p. 16), an explanation whose origin can only be understood as an attempt to explain the form as part of a tensed system, and a rather desperate one at that.

[12] Insufficient data exist to explain to the satisfaction of all why the *w* appears to derive from a CVC syllable in the case of *wayyiqtōl*, but from a CV syllable in the case of *wᵊqātal* (cf. below, n. 47). It appears in any case likely to me that the proto-Hebrew conjunctival element was identical, i.e., /wa/, and that the doubling of the preformative consonant of the PC is secondary (the plausibility of this hypothesis rests on the observation that the PC presents a small range of consonantal possibilities — /ʾ, t, y, n/ — while the SC, because it has no preformative, presents all such possibilities).

The type of aspect is that which views acts as complete or incomplete;[13] duration versus point in time is subsumed under this heading — that is, either type of act may be expressed perfectively or imperfectively.[14] Time/tense are also subsumed under the aspectual heading — that is, events that have already taken place or that are yet to take place may be expressed perfectively or imperfectively according to whether the speaker wishes to refer to them as complete or incomplete; what some tensed languages express explicitly by a present tense may be expressed in Biblical Hebrew by either of the aspectually marked forms, by non-finite verbal forms, or by nominal phrases.

The details of the historical development from the proto-West Semitic system to Biblical Hebrew are uncertain for paucity of data, but it is clear that Hebrew has retained to some extent the expression of stativity by *Ablaut* within both the perfective and the imperfective systems (fientive is *kātab* - *yiktōb*, stative is *kābēd* - *yikbad*), though the expression is not nearly so systematic as in Arabic.[15]

Because the notions of perfectivity (the viewing of an act in its entirety) and past tense are often related, reportorial discourse[16] is generally expressed by perfective forms. It is nonetheless the case, however, that the verb forms are marked at the surface level for aspect — and the interpreter's role, ancient ("hearer") or modern ("reader"), is thus not to determine the aspect, which is expressed on the surface level of the language and is not ambiguous, but the function of each form.[17] That the opposite is not true — namely, that the hearer automatically registered the tense of an utterance — is clear from the most superficial analysis of both narrative and direct discourse in Biblical Hebrew, perhaps most indubitably in texts such as the ones chosen below as sample texts but in just about any extensive passage that one might choose to examine. The marking of time relationships is not the primary function of the finite verbal forms — and the interpreter must determine from the logic of the situation what these are.[18] Such a description does not deny that Hebrew expresses time/tense; it denies that the Hebrew verbal system is primarily marked for the expression of tense.[19]

---

[13] On the aspects of aspect, see Pardee 1985a, p. 108 (a reference to P. Friedrich's view that verbal aspect includes the expression of completeness vs. incompleteness, duration vs. punctility, and stativity vs. fientiveness). On the distinction between "complete" and "completed," see Waltke and O'Connor 1990, pp. 480–81. The recent refutation of the aspectual theory by Blau (2010, pp. 201–02) is remarkably naive in this regard, depicting the view of those who describe a Semitic verbal system as aspectual in the following way: "According to the prevailing theory of aspect in Semitic languages, the Semitic speaker either looked at the verb as describing its action during its happening (the imperfective aspect) or simply stated that such an action took place (the perfective aspect)" (quotation from p. 201). One would be hard pressed to find a serious proponent of aspect who would so describe the system today.

[14] As shown, for example, by Waltke and O'Connor 1990, p. 480. That duration is one of the features expressed by various aspectual systems is a linguistic given (see preceding note); that it is not the primary feature expressed by the Biblical Hebrew system is proved by the use of both finite forms to express both duration and punctility (for a clear example of a SC durative in the first sample text below, see on v. 5.2; there is another possible example in v. 12.2) as well as by the fact that the expression of duration is one of the important functions of the participle (it is this characteristic of the participle that has led to the various theories criticized below that would see the participle as expressing present tense or progressive acts). This having been said, however, there is no doubt that there is a large gray area between acts that are clearly repeated punctiliar acts and those that clearly constitute duration, e.g., the acts of weeping in 1 Sam 1; another fuzzy case is /wᵊqōʷlāh lōʾ yiššāmēᵃʿ/ in v. 13 (has the use of the Niphal and the negative particle transformed what would normally be a punctiliar act into a durative one? — 'each emission of her voice could not be heard' or 'her voice was unhearable'?).

[15] Stativity thus appears to be the one *Aktionsart* of which the formal expression occurs primarily within the basic verbal system; only secondarily is it expressed by derived stems (see Creason 1995). On stativity as one of the poles of "situation" aspect, see Dobbs-Allsopp 2000.

[16] On this term, see Pardee 1995, p. 65.

[17] Thus, though I agree fully with Long's description of the basic structure of 1 Sam 1:3–5 (1999, pp. 179–80), I must disagree with his explicit classification of the imperfective forms in this passage as expressing "habitual aspect." There is no such thing as "habitual aspect": there is imperfective aspect of which one of the functions is to express habitual acts.

[18] Cf. Pardee 2001. This stance, which appears obvious to me from a passage such as 1 Sam 1 examined below, is in contrast with the view of Endo (1996), who believes that "the time reference and aspect of a verbal form are determined by the context" (quotation from Gianto's review [1997, p. 346]). Even further from plausibility is Nicacci's argument from three brief passages where the perfective and imperfective forms function to express acts that occurred in the past or that will occur in the future that those forms "are tenses and nothing else" (1994, p. 129) — the system is not to be defined by the great number of cases in which the aspects reflect real-world temporal categories but by the many cases in which they do not do so. His claim that "*wayyiqtol* is the only verb form for the mainline...while *waw*-X-*qatal* indicates a unique event and *waw*-X-*yiqtol* repetition or custom" (ibid.) simply does not conform to the structure of 1 Sam 1 (just to cite the example of the first sample text analyzed here below) where *wᵊqātal* appears out of nowhere in v. 3 to express iteritivity. This and many examples like it in 1 Sam 1 and elsewhere show that aspect (admitted by Nicacci only as a form of *Aktionsart*) is not limited to "the subsidiary line of communication" (ibid.), i.e., to sentences that begin with something other than a verb. The distribution of perfective and imperfective forms in conditional sentences, in which the possible forms appear in what in terms

The imperfective forms express acts as incomplete, including any act belonging to the broad category of *irrealis*. The primary sub-categories were expressed in proto-Hebrew by morphemes that were a part of the basic imperfective form, namely, affixed thereunto; certain forms show the system still to be functional in Standard Biblical Hebrew in spite of the modification of final short vowels (loss [e.g., *yaqtulu* > *yiqtōl*] or lengthening [e.g., *ʾaqtula* > *ʾeqtᵊlā*]) in a stage of the language prior to Biblical Hebrew. Acts expressed as future or frequentative[20] were expressed by the **yaqtulu* form (commonly known as "indicative," e.g., *yāqūm* < **yaqūmu*, 'he will arise'), volitivity by **yaqtul* (commonly known as "jussive," e.g., *yāqōm* < **yaqum* < ***yaqūm*, 'may he arise')[21] and *yaqtula* (commonly known as "cohortative," e.g., *ʾāqūmāʰ* < **ʾaqūma*, 'may I arise'). The precise semantics of the "energic" forms (< **yaqtulan* and **yaqtulanna*) is a disputed topic.[22] That the imperative is directly related to the imperfective is shown by the fact that the two forms have identical second vowels (Pardee 1995, p. 65) and that both can be expanded by *-ā* (< **-a*). The multiple forms and nuances within the imperfective system would seem to support Waltke and O'Connor's hypothesis according to which the perfective is the more highly marked of the two forms, that imperfective aspect in Biblical Hebrew is essentially non-perfectivity.[23]

---

of tense may only be termed random distribution (see above, n. 11, and below, n. 72) poses no problem in a system primarily expressive of aspect, in which the speaker's view of the reality of the events expressed in both protasis and apodosis may be ranked by the use of the appropriate forms.

[19] As basic works on the interactions of tense and aspect (and mood), one may consult Bybee, Perkins, and Pagliuca 1994; Bartsch 1995; Chung and Timberlake 1995, pp. 202–58; Hollebrandse and van Hout 2005; as an online resource, Binnick's website, last updated in 2006.

[20] Pardee 1985a, p. 108; 1993a, p. 313. A standard dictionary of the English language defines "frequentative" as "in grammar, denoting the frequent repetition of an action"; "iterative" as "characterized by iteration" (which in turn is defined as "repetition"), "in grammar = frequentative"; "habitual" as "formed or acquired by habit, frequent use, or custom; customary." Thus in standard English usage, the three terms are essentially synonyms; I prefer "frequentative" or "iterative" over "habitual" because they appear to express repetition without the more explicit notion of habit. In the first sample text cited below, 1 Sam 1, some of the acts described by **yaqtulu* forms are presented as being repeated annually (and one may query whether that constitutes an expression of habit), others as constituting repetition or duration within the frame of the present narrative (e.g., v. 8). Though Comrie's distinction between "iterative" and "habitual" is sometimes cited as authoritative, Macaulay (1978) essentially trashed Comrie's linguistic theory in his review of Comrie 1976.

[21] The two asterisks before ***yaqūm* represent the fact that this is the theoretical Ø-ending equivalent to *yaqūmu*, but, because it was a rule in Proto-Semitic that historically long vowels shortened when the syllable in which they appeared became closed, the form could not have existed as such. Since the final syllable of the YQTLØ form was by definition closed, proto-Hebrew *yaqūm* is a strictly theoretical form. I have never expressed and have no strong opinion on the proper explanation for the identity of the jussive and perfective in proto-Semitic. The primary options are Hetzron's (1969), where the distinction is said to have been provided by accent and the view prevailing before Hetzron's article according to which the "jussive" and "perfective/preterit" correspond to two functions of a single form only distinguishable by usage/context. Because Hetzron's theory is not borne out by the data from any functioning Semitic language, perhaps the second view is to be preferred.

[22] Pardee 1999, pp. 313–17. Rainey (2003) has responded to this review, but says nothing new about the questions regarding the semantics and distribution of the energic forms in the various Northwest Semitic languages. See also Tropper 1998b and the longer and more explicit version of his views in Tropper and Vita 2005, where he argues very plausibly that there were only two basic prefix-conjugation forms in early West Semitic, **yaqtulø* and **yaqtulu*; **yaqtula* being an extension of **yaqtul* jussive while **-(a)n(na)* represent a tense/aspect-neutral expanding morpheme that could be added to both **yaqtulø* and **yaqtulu*; the former in both of its functions, as a jussive and as a perfective/preterit. In the singular, both *-an* and *-Vnna* forms are retained in Biblical Hebrew before pronominal suffixes, *yiqtᵊlennū* (< **yaqtul + an + hu*) and *yiqtᵊlenhū* (< **yaqtul + anna + hu*). In the 2 f.s. and the plural, the problem is the origin of the *-n* in forms such as *yiqtᵊlūn*: indicative, energic, or enclitic? Suffixed forms also provide examples of the **yaqtulu* form (*yiqtolḵā*, with aspirated /ḵ/, < **yaqtulu + ka*) and of the **yaqtulø* jussive (inscriptional {ybrk} corresponding to biblical *yᵊbārekḵā* [with "medial" *shewa* between the two tokens of /ḵ/] and hence to be vocalized /yᵊbārekkā/ [in Massoretic terms!] < **yabarrik + ka*). The inscriptional form is attested both in the Ketef Hinnom versions (Barkay et al. 2004) of the Priestly Blessing (the form cited from the Hebrew Bible is in Num 6:24) and in an epistolary graffito from Kuntillet Ajrud (Dobbs-Allsopp et al., p. 293).

[23] Waltke and O'Connor 1990, pp. 347–48; cf. ch. 31, pp. 496–518, entitled "Prefix (Non-perfective) Conjugation." Joosten's claim (2002) that the verbal system is not aspectual because the Hebrew expression of aspect does not conform precisely to other such systems, in particular in not expressing the "real present" by **yaqtulu*, reflects the historical place of **yaqtulu* as part and parcel of the modal system in West Semitic (cf. also the limitation of *-u* forms in Akkadian to subordinate clauses) and contains some intriguing grains of truth. The definition of the YQTL forms as all marked for non-perfectivity, however, handles that problem (cf. Joosten 2002, p. 51 n.15), and the real question, then, boils down to the function of **qatala* and to the functioning together of the primary forms as a *system*. Because the **qatala* form does not have the modal variety of YQTL, it appears better to see the latter as providing the non-perfective counterpart to **qatala* than to see it as having another function altogether. Here Joosten's desire to describe the Biblical Hebrew system purely synchronically leads to implausible results: if what must at some level have characterized the proto-Hebrew verbal system, i.e., what we know empirically as el-Amarna Canaanite or Ugaritic, functioned aspectually (cf. Joosten 2002, p. 52), systems in which **yaqtulu* was no less a part of the modal system than it is in Biblical Hebrew, then is it likely that the morphological and morpho-syntactic developments particular to Biblical Hebrew resulted in a non-aspectual verbal system? As a non-linguist, I have three major questions

The commonly accepted notions that the participle functions as a tense to express contemporaneity, present tense, or progressives (Joosten 1989; 1997a, p. 59; 1997b, p. 76; DeCaen 1995) in Biblical Hebrew is to be rejected. First, it must be recognized that there are three types of participles, not one or two: there is an active participle (*qōtēl* < **qātil*), two stative participles (*qātēl* < **qatil* and *qātōl* < **qatul*), and a passive participle (*qātūl* < **qatūl*). As was clearly demonstrated in Nash's dissertation (1992), the participles are verbal adjectives (i.e., a form productively derivable from any given verb but substantival in form and verbal or substantival in syntax [i.e., the active participle of a transitive verb can take either accusative or genitive complements]) whose function is to express acts non-aspectually by describing the actor adjectivally. As was shown long ago (Kedar-Kopfstein 1977), the range of actual usage in Biblical Hebrew is very broad, from the purely substantival to the purely verbal. The real-world aspect and/or tense reflected by the participle may only be determined from context, which only can indicate whether the act so expressed is past, contemporaneous, or yet to occur; the predicative function of the participial forms is, therefore, essentially that of any other substantive, adjective or noun, functioning as a predicate. The fact that the participle may be marked as a progressive by use with HYH, 'to be' — that is, 'to be in the state of performing such-and-such an act,' a relatively rare usage (not attested in the sample texts below) — is neither, therefore, grounds for seeing that function as a general one nor proof of the tensed nature of the Biblical Hebrew verbal system.[24]

Morpho-syntax[25]

Though two forms exist to express each aspect, use is determined largely, though not exclusively,[26] by the presence or absence of the conjunction *w*, that is, the "frozen" forms exist as composites with this conjunction and only appear where this conjunction can properly be used in a Hebrew sentence. Hence *qātal* can theoretically express perfectivity anywhere in a sentence, while *wayyiqtōl* can do so only at the beginning of a sentence, and the same is true, mutatis mutandis, of *yiqtōl* and *wᵊqātal*.[27]

In spite of the importance of verbal "sequences" (Pardee 1994, pp. 152–53), it must be recognized that the *w*-retentive[28] forms can function independently of the verbal form that appears in the immediately preceding position: a *w*-retentive form not only need not be introduced by its opposite counterpart (*qātal ... wayyiqtōl*, *yiqtōl ... wᵊqātal*), as has long been recognized,[29] but, even more strikingly, it can also express the opposite aspect to that

---

with regard to Joosten's study. (1) Does the fact that the primary expression of the "real present" is not expressed uniquely by what would be the imperfective form really disqualify the Hebrew system as aspectual? This is the real basis for Joosten's attempt to deny the aspectual nature of the system (cf. p. 67), and it deserves assessment by a qualified linguist. My assumption has been that in a primarily aspectual system, the expression of the real-world tenses would vary from language to language and might not be tied to specific forms within a given language. Joosten's assertion that the "real" present (as opposed to the habitual present) is only expressed by the participle in Biblical Hebrew should also be examined in detail (he discounts examples of *yiqtōl* having this function by claiming that they are in fact modal as translatable by English modal forms, e.g., "why might you be weeping" — is this really a plausible approach to a Semitic problem?). But English-translation "presents" (contemporaneity, habit, state) can be expressed by any of the finite and non-finite forms in Biblical Hebrew, i.e., from the aspectual perspective, they are not aspect sensitive, and one wonders if Joosten's strictures on the "real" present are as valid as he believes. (2) Why should the identification of **yaqtulu* as part of a modal system be incompatible with identifying it as an imperfective? (3) Is it plausible to define **qatala* as a past-tense form in Biblical Hebrew, of which **yaqtulu* would be the corresponding future/modal? Since the *qātal* functions in so many ways as the mirror image of *yiqtōl*, but perforce without the attachment of the former to a modal system, it does not appear plausible to limit its function to the expression of tense — diachronically, of course, this cannot be the case considering its origin as an adjective (see above, n. 11).

[24] On the non-finite element of periphrasitic constructions as a "converb," see Haspelmath 1995, pp. 43–45.

[25] The distinction between morphology and morpho-syntax corresponds to what Talstra (1997) refers to as a distinction between clause-level and text-level grammar.

[26] As is well known, the PC appears commonly after the adverb *ʾāz*, 'then.' The semantic conditioning is less clear in this case than in that of (*bᵊ*)*ṭerem*, 'before,' after which the PC is also regularly used. This idiom is sometimes cited as an example of retention of *yaqtul*, but seems rather to express the imperfectivity implied by (*bᵊ*)*ṭerem*.

[27] Nicacci (cf. Pardee 1993a, p. 313) has pointed out actual restrictions on the appearance of the SC and PC forms at the beginning of sentences (see also Joosten 2006).

[28] I have not found this particular term used before; my description of the system is certainly less detailed and comprehensive than was the system created by H. Bauer in which the *wāw* was said to be "conservative" (cf. McFall 1982, pp. 93–115).

[29] Gesenius, Kautzsch, and Cowley 1910, p. 326 (§111a); Joüon 1923, p. 321 (§118c); cf. Longacre 1992, p. 178; Tropper 1996, p. 636.

of the immediately preceding utterances (Pardee 1994, p. 152 n. 3). This is clear in the first sample text examined below ($w^{ə}$ʿ*ālā*^{h}, v. 3, following *wayhî*^{y} in vv. 1, 2), as well as in the second (see v. 13 in particular), and sporadic examples may be found throughout Hebrew prose.[30]

The primary function of the two forms has since the early 1980s been thought by many to express "foregrounding" in the case of *w*-retentive forms and "backgrounding" in the case of the independent forms (e.g., Reinhart 1984; Longacre 1989), and I have in the past accepted this terminology (e.g. 1990; 2001) while wishing that a detailed study of the various functions of backgrounding in Biblical Hebrew would be carried out. Heimerdinger (1999) has, however, shown that this view of Hebrew narrative structure is overly formal and does not properly represent the modern linguistic notion of foregrounding.[31] He provides a convincing critique of Longacre's system, but his own main concern is with defining foregrounding, not with explaining the function of the four principal aspectual forms.[32] He does at one point, however, observe that "all the NP + qatal clauses which indicate markedness for the three types of information structure may be viewed as standing out against the routine development of the narrative provided by vayyiqtol clauses. Such clauses would seem to indicate foregrounded rather than backgrounded material" (p. 219).[33] And in his conclusions, he remarks that foregrounding may be expressed by all types of clauses (pp. 239–40). Taking these observations in conjunction with those of his predecessors, one might conclude that the metaphor for *wayyiqtōl* forms according to which they expressed the "backbone" of the narrative had a grain of truth to it but that it is necessary to lower the frame of the metaphor so that the reference is no longer to the high points or even to the essential points of the story but to its flow. If one accepts Heimerdinger's view that not all *wayyiqtōl* forms express foregrounding, then foregrounding is occurring all around these forms, while backgrounding may be expressed by $w^{ə}$-X *qātal* forms, by non-verbal phrases, and by entire clauses that have this function, particularly circumstantial clauses. One can thus view *wayyiqtōl* forms as expressing the flow of the narrative, including both "routine" events and events essential to the progress of the narrative, while other structures show far more variety of function.[34] It is essential to observe that "flow of the narrative" is not to be understood in strict temporal terms: as the Hebrew verbal system does not primarily express tense, so its contribution to the structure of a narrative cannot be expected to be temporal. The "real-world" flow of the narrative will usually be along a temporal line, but both *qātal* and *wayyiqtōl* forms may (and must) be translated as pluperfects according to the logic of the story (see below on 1 Sam 1:6.2 and 22.2). The conclusion to be drawn from this view of the four finite verbal forms is that their function in discourse is no more predetermined than is their function within a given sentence: the function is not to be defined in terms of information essential ("foregrounding") or

[30] This is always one of the difficult points for students learning Biblical Hebrew from Lambdin's grammar (1971): because he presents the "*wāw*-consecutive" forms as strictly sequential, then, in an exercise (p. 121, c, 8), the sequence consisting of a participle followed by a $w^{ə}$*qātal* form, students are frequently at a loss to know what to do with the "sequence." A more accurate definition of the *w*-retentive forms is required to deal with real biblical texts, such as 1 Sam 1:3 or the striking morpho-syntactic parallel, but where the imperfective expresses a promise to be realized in the future, in 2 Sam 7:9, $w^{ə}$ʿ*āśītî*^{y} drops into a sequence of perfectives that begin in v. 8, two *qātal* and two *wayyiqtōl*, and the hearer/reader must recognize by form alone that the fifth finite verb of the sequence is imperfective.

[31] For a detailed analysis of the various ways of expressing newness, topic, and emphasis within a verbal sentence, but without Heimerdinger's comparison with the attempts to define foregrounding/backgrounding in terms of the use of *w*-retentive forms, see Disse 1998.

[32] Biblical Hebrew does indeed have four forms marked for aspect (cf. Talstra 1997, p. 89), but the four forms represent only the two standard aspects and are distributed according to the syntactic categories of discourse structure, what Talstra calls "text grammar" (cf. Pardee 1993b, p. 314). That the two aspectual forms can express a wide variety of real-world situations is well known to linguists (cf. Comrie 1976), and it should be no surprise that the aspectual parsing of a form is only the first step of analysis and that the determination of the precise function of the form within a particular discourse should require that the rhetorical function of any given form be analyzed within the larger context in which it occurs; indeed, it verges on the incomprehensible that grammarians should have proposed that one or the other of these two levels of analysis be qualified as representing the proper description of the Biblical Hebrew verbal system (some of the major presentations are cited and classified by Talstra). The steps of analysis are, therefore, precisely the opposite of those which Talstra himself proposes (94–101): the decision regarding aspect is a purely formal one and hence extremely easy, but only after it is made can one begin considering what the author intended to convey by the use of one aspect or the other (this formulation is not meant to imply that text-critical decisions may not complicate the task of parsing).

[33] See also Long 1999, pp. 177–81.

[34] For Bailey and Levinsohn 1992 (cf. Andersen 2000, pp. 43–44), $w^{ə}$-X-*qātal* expresses "topic discontinuity." Unfortunately, Heimerdinger disposes of the foregrounding/backgrounding hypothesis without adequately discussing a possible topicalizing function for $w^{ə}$-X-*qātal*. By this hypothesis, the primary function of $w^{ə}$-X-*qātal* formulae would be to topicalize; whether a given one is foregrounding depends on the information it imparts.

non-essential ("backgrounding") for understanding the narrative, but in terms of the author's (speaker's, narrator's ...) desire to stress a given bit of information. Viewed thus, the distribution in discourse of these forms is analogous to their distribution in a clause or sentence: as the author chooses whether to present a given act as complete or incomplete (with certain restrictions imposed by the real-world flow of time), so the author chooses whether to present a given act as occurring in the narrative flow or as narratologically subsumed to another element or to other elements of the clause or sentence.[35]

The explanation for the distribution of forms just outlined is that *wayyiqtōl* and *wᵊqātal* by definition contain a verbal form and must have the conjunction *w* in initial position, while all other structures can mix all the other principal components of a sentence as the speaker/author wishes and place them, theoretically, anywhere in a given phrase. Thus in terms of marking theory, the sentence beginning with something other than a *w*-retentive form is more highly marked than are those beginning with *w*-retentive forms,[36] and it contains by definition much more potential for variety (because any morpho-syntactic element can be fronted); it is hence relatively "emphatic" and serves to set up contrast on many possible levels with the regular flow of *wayyiqtōl* forms.[37] The variety of nuances expressed by the fronting of an element of the sentence other than a *w*-retentive verbal form was probably great and almost certainly varied from one register of speech to another.[38]

The best-known function of *wayyiqtōl*, because so much of the text of the Hebrew Bible is in reportorial discourse (Pardee 1990, p. 203; 1995, p. 65) — the linguistic form, whatever the value of the reporting may be as judged by the historians — is that of expressing a perfective narrative line. The first sample text offered below contains some of the more striking examples of imperfective forms expressing a frequentative narrative line within the larger structure of perfective narrative line.

The use of *wᵊqātal* in volitive sequences is better known and recognized because that usage is more common than is the expression of the frequentative within a perfective narrative line — and because it causes far less difficulty for readers whose own verbal system is primarily tensed rather than aspectual. It may be observed, however, that a purely indicative narrative in the imperfective[39] is easily comprehensible and would be more widely attested if prophetic speech were more commonly given in prose.[40] It will be seen in my second sample text that the nuancing of volitivity, as expressed by both PC and *w*-retentive SC forms, is very complex.[41]

---

[35] Pre-exilic Hebrew prose is famous for its fronting of non-verbal elements. Cf. the striking example of Lachish 3:19–21, where an object phrase consisting of fourteen words precedes the main verb, which bears a resumptive pronominal suffix that gives the entire sentence a cleft structure (for recent treatments, see Pardee 2002, pp. 79–80; Lindenberger 2003, p. 126; Dobbs-Allsopp et al. 2005, pp. 308–14).

[36] Heimerdinger 1999, p. 212; Long 1999, p. 171.

[37] Lambdin's term "disjunctive" (*Introduction* [1971] §132) for phrases that do not begin with a *w*-retentive form, however correct it may be on the discourse level, is pedagogically confusing because many, probably most, *dis*junctive clauses are introduced by a *con*junction (cf. Pardee 1995, p. 64 n. 4).

[38] Compare the relatively high frequency of the use of non-verb fronting in quotations of direct speech in Biblical Hebrew and in epigraphic Hebrew (Pardee 1990, p. 203) with the preference for *casus-pendens* constructions in spoken French: "Jean, je l'ai vu" is almost normative in spoken French, where it is much less highly marked than it would be in the formal register.

[39] On the principal types of discourse as defined by distribution of verbal forms, see Pardee 1990; 1995, p. 65. Niccaci's "basic distinction" in Hebrew and in "practically every language" between "historical narrative and direct speech" (1994, p. 119) corresponds to some extent to what I have called "reportorial discourse" as opposed to the various types of discourse that are expressed imperfectively (1995, p. 65). One must not, of course, forget that direct speech can be embedded in historical narrative while historical narrative can and often is an integral part of direct speech. The most readily visible difference between the two is that the imperfective forms will often express future acts and all sorts of modalities in direct speech while they primarily express iteration in historical narrative; the perfective forms, on the other hand, will often express past acts in historical narrative but primarily acts viewed as complete when embedded in imperfective direct speech (on the example of Num 5:13–14, see Pardee 2001, pp. 310 n. 7 and 311 n. 11). For these reasons, Nicacci's description of the Hebrew *verbal system* in terms of these *discourse types* makes no sense to me. One cannot admit that the verbal system "is built from bottom to top upon a coherent binary basis consisting of two types of sentence" (ibid., p. 130); rather, it is built from bottom to top upon a coherent binary basis consisting of two verbal aspects expressed in four verbal forms. These four forms appear in different distributions to create verbal sentences alongside which various types of nominal sentences occur (Pardee 1993a; for extensive discussion of nominal sentence types, see the various contributions in Miller 1999).

[40] Longacre (1994, p. 51) cites the example of 1 Sam 10:2–6, presented as a speech by Samuel addressed to Saul in which he predicts upcoming events. See the briefer sequence, non-prophetic in nature, below in the first sample text (1 Sam 1:22)

[41] Longacre (1994, pp. 53–55, 91–95) distinguishes five principal types of discourse involving *wᵊqātal* forms: predictive, procedural, instructional, hortatory, and juridical. The last four are *volitive* in the sense that the speaker is imparting his will to the listener, whether or not a marked volitive form appears at the head of the sequence. See the second sample text below, where the only marked volitive in the apodictic first section (vv. 1–13) is a verb of speech. Such commands from YHWH to Moses are, of course, scattered throughout the texts that belong to Longacre's category of "procedural." These four categories are formally dis-

Because of the variety of PC forms, the variety of imperfective structures is particularly daunting. Though improperly defined as "imperative" sequences, Lambdin's classification of the volitive sequences according to the form that follows the first expression of volition covers a vast number of occurrences. The three principal structures as outlined in his §107 are as follow: a volitive form may be followed by (a) another volitive form, whether of the same category or not (and, I would add, whether or not preceded by the conjunction *w*), which expresses a marked continuation of the volitional expression; (b) a *wᵊqātal* form, which expresses the subsequent act as explicitly marked for imperfectivity but for volitivity by the context alone; or (c) a *wᵊyiqtōl* form, that is, a non-*w*-retentive but conjunctive phrase, which expresses purpose, goal, or result more strongly than either of the others.[42] The *wᵊyiqtōl* form also functioned to express purpose or result in non-volitive sequences, though this usage is less frequently attested (no example in the sample texts below).[43]

Because the SC form does not include marking for mood, the *w*-retentive SC functioning as an imperfective does not in and of itself express any of the moods of the PC forms, though, in cases of sequencing with a PC form, the mood of the first form will normally be carried over to the *w*-retentive SC; the precise translation value may only be determined from context, and ambiguities remain, exactly as in the case of the PC itself (see below on 1 Sam 1:17, 18). It appears to me, therefore, that the form, whatever its origin, functions essentially as the equivalent of the *yiqtōl* form, and attempts to bring all uses under a single heading are misguided.[44]

The morpho-syntax of what may broadly be termed "circumstantial" clauses is rendered complex in Biblical Hebrew by the optional use of HYH, 'to be,' to introduce such clauses and by the optional use of so-called *w* of apodosis to introduce the main verb after the circumstantial clause; the complexity produced by these two optional uses is increased by the fact that a circumstantial clause may in fact be followed by one or more similar clauses, and the sequence of these clauses can be expressed in the very same manner as the main clause (hence it is sometimes impossible to determine the cleft between the circumstantial and the main clause by any means other than logic), and by the fact that the circumstantial and the main clause(s) may be expressed in forms other than *wayyiqtōl* (Pardee 1993a, p. 313; 1994, p. 152). Space in the nutshell does not permit a more extensive treatment of these varieties of usage; some examples will be encountered in the texts treated below.

---

tinguished by the incidence and distribution of marked volitive forms, **yaqtulu* imperfectives, and *wᵊqātal* imperfectives; one wonders, however, what the functional difference was among them. It is difficult to believe that YHWH's volition is significantly different in his instructions to Noah on building the ark (Gen 6:13–21; 7:1–4 = "instructional") from the volition expressed in how to present the offering for an inadvertent sin (Lev 4:1–12 = "procedural"). The "juridical" category (only Exod 21 and 22 are cited as examples) as distinct from the other three is defined only by its not showing the same "thematic" connections as are found in the other categories. Here also, then, the literary category has very little to do with morpho-syntactic considerations. My hesitancy regarding Longacre's discourse types was already expressed in my review (1990) of his book on the Joseph narrative (cf. Nicacci 1994, p. 119). His observation expressed in the article under consideration here (Longacre 1994, pp. 55–56: "transformations among discourse types") that the various "discourse types" can melt into one another makes me even more curious about the functional load of each type. The "predictive" category clearly functions differently, however, in that the speaker is describing the future rather than expressing his own volition. It must nevertheless be observed that the distinction between prediction and volition is perceived in a text by pure logic: in 1 Sam 10, for example, instructions (what routes Saul is to take and, especially, the order expressed in v. 8 to the effect that he is to wait seven days in the final place named) are mixed with predictions (various persons whom he will meet, i.e., events over which he has no power). Finally, to me it appears fundamentally misguided to use the same term to designate volitive and narrative imperfective sequences: I refer to the use of "procedural" both for volitional discourse not expressed by explicit volitive forms (just discussed) and for the expression of iteration within perfective discourse (Longacre 1994, pp. 56–66). A procedure that is being dictated for future performance is fundamentally different from acts that happen to have been repeated in the past: repetition is not procedure (though it may become such). Moreover, it appears clear to me, though Longacre appears not to share this view, that the function of the imperfectives in, e.g., Lev 4 is fundamentally different from that in, e.g., 1 Sam 1, viz., volitional vs. descriptive. I, for this reason, hold that volitional procedure will be differentiated from iteration within a narrative by the context in which each is found.

[42] Pardee 1994, pp. 152–53. See Fassberg 2006, who provides statistics on Lambdin's first two categories as restricted to imperative + imperative and imperative + *wᵊqātal* (1150 to 180) but finds no readily definable functional/semantic distinction between them.

[43] E.g., 2 Sam 9:1 *hᵃkīʸ yeš-ʾōʷd ʾᵃšer nōʷtar lᵊbēʸt šāʾūʷl wᵊʾeʿᵉśeʰ ʿimmōʷ ḥesed*, 'Is anyone left of the house of Saul that I might do him well?'

[44] E.g., Joosten 1997b, pp. 81–82.

Some Problematic Morpho-syntactic Types

(1) Perfective *wāʾeqtəlā*^{h}, that is, apparent *w*-retentive + cohortative functioning in a perfective sequence to express a perfective notion. Because (a) this structure is fairly common and appears to have been considered regular in Standard Biblical Hebrew; (b) the **yaqtula* form was historically volitive (Pardee 1993b, pp. 316–17; 1999) only and did not share the perfective/volitive ambiguity of the **yaqtul* form; (c) with very few exceptions, the **yaqtula* form of the second and third persons has disappeared, with only first-person forms remaining; because of these three factors one wonders if already in late proto-Hebrew (i.e., at a stage of the language when the full-blown volitive system no longer existed but before the rise of Biblical Hebrew as we know it) the functional similarity of the cohortative and the first-person jussive did not lead to an extrapolation of usage permitting the cohortative to be used like what was perceived at some level to be the jussive (i.e., the formally identical perfective from an earlier stage of the language) after *w*. The analogy would thus have been as follows: as *ʾaqtul* and *ʾaqtula* both function volitively, so should both be able to appear after *wa-* as expressions of perfectivity.[45]

(2) Perfective "*w*-retentive" + **yaqtulu*, for example, *wayyibne*^{h} instead of *wayyíben*. This appears to be an inner-Biblical Hebrew phenomenon, that is, not to represent the highest form of Standard Biblical Hebrew, and as such probably represents a relatively early stage of confusion between the old "*w*-retentive" perfective and the standard imperfective form. Such a confusion would have arisen because of the formal identity that existed between **yaqtul* and **yaqtulu* forms in most root types (the formal distinction is preserved in Standard Biblical Hebrew only in hollow roots, III-*h* roots, to a lesser extent in geminate roots, and in the Hiphil stem in most root types). It appears that the speaker intuitively broke the *wa* + *yaqtul* unit into its two constitutive elements and considered that if he could say *wayyiqtōl*, he could say *wayyibne*^{h}.

(3) An even harder nut to crack is the use of *w*^{ə}*qātal* as an apparently perfective (or even preterit) form. The basic question is this: was this verbal phrase in Standard Biblical Hebrew symmetrically identical to *w*^{ə}*yiqtōl* (see above) as a mirror image thereof, and did it therefore have a morpho-syntactic functional status that we have yet adequately to describe, or was its aspectual/temporal function the same as *qātal*? Two primary factors lead to the second conclusion: (a) its relative rarity,[46] and (b) the fact that native speakers apparently did not feel the need to devise a means of differentiating this form from the imperfective form, as they did with the *wayyiqtōl* and *w*^{ə}*yiqtōl* forms.[47] If such be the case, it appears necessary to surmise that the perfective **waqatal* fell largely

[45] For a discussion, see Rainey (2003, pp. 401–02), though he refers only to the "relegation of the first person cohortative into the preterite paradigm" (quotation from p. 401). Another solution is to identify the **-a* morpheme as not originally volitive in nature, but etymologically related to the Akkadian ventive (Gentry 1998). To what extent the identification with the morphologically varied ventive morphemes in Akkadian is debatable, but the function of the *yaqtula* form in Arabic as a "subjunctive" (the form appropriate for relative clauses) with no particular volitive function may be taken as an argument for the **-a* morpheme being, like **-an(na)* (see above, n. 22), itself unmarked for volitivity and not necessarily attached to volitive forms. However that may be, *w*-retentive plus a PC form ending in *-ā* occurs in Biblical Hebrew only in the first person, and such forms not preceded by *w*-retentive function as volitives — which allows for the syntagm being a development internal to Biblical Hebrew rather than a retention from proto-Hebrew.

[46] This formulation, which may appear infuriatingly bland to some, is not offered in total unawareness of the ambiguities inherent in a number of passages couched in what is apparently Standard Biblical Hebrew prose. On the example of 2 Kings 23:4–15, see Pietsch 2004–07. The ambiguity arises from the fact that there are several 3 m.s. *w*^{ə}*qātal* forms in this passage whose subject appears to be Hezekiah (though the possibility must be considered that the subject is in fact meant to be indefinite, i.e., the equivalent of "they" in English, "on" in French, or "man" in German) but not a single 3 m.s. *yiqtōl* form appears in the passage, and thus the overall structure of the pericope is very different from that of 1 Sam 1. There is a plural *yiqtōl* form with a specific subject (*lōʾ yaʿ*^{a}*lū*^{w} in v. 9) that fairly clearly has the same function as the *w*^{ə}*qātal* forms — but is that a sufficient indicator of the imperfective function of the latter? If the *w*^{ə}*qātal* forms in this passage are indeed imperfective and not simply indicators of late redaction and expressing the same tense/aspect as the *wayyiqtōl* forms, their function must be that of multiplicatives (the subject performs the act several times within a brief period), not that of frequentatives (the subject repeats the act over an extended period).

[47] This statement assumes (a) that the retention of /a/ and the gemination of the following consonant had already occurred in late proto-Hebrew, i.e., after the disappearance of the final /u/ from the **yaqtulu* form, as a means of distinguishing perfective *wa* + YQTL from imperfective *wa* + YQTL; (b) that the accentual marking of *w*^{ə}*qātal* imperfective (e.g., *w*^{ə}*qātaltā* with final accent) is, on the contrary, late (as is shown by the retention of /ā/ in the open pro-pretonic syllable: cf. Pardee 1985b, p. 69) and hence may perhaps be seen as having arisen as a means of distinguishing imperfective *w*^{ə}*qātal* from perfective *w*^{ə}*qātal* after the latter had begun to be used (Revell [1984, p. 444] dates the secondary form to quite late; on the progressive disappearance of imperfective *w*^{ə}*qātal*, see Joosten 2006).

out of usage at some stage of proto-Hebrew (it remained in usage in Ugaritic and Phoenician, where the usage of "*w*-retentive" forms was never systematized) because of competition from **wayyaqtul*. Note in this respect that *wᵊyiqtōl* survived by taking on a particular function (see above), a development that was easily conceived within the imperfective system but for which **waqatal* found no corresponding place in the more limited perfective system. Perfective *wᵊqātal* was, therefore, to a great extent abandoned by the time that Judaean Hebrew reached the state that we know from the pre-exilic inscriptions and from Standard Biblical Hebrew; it was retained only in morpho-syntactic slots where confusion with imperfective *wᵊqātal* was not a significant problem, particularly as the last of a series of *qātal* forms.[48] Subsequently, as the verbal system that we know from Standard Biblical Hebrew came to be sensed as counter-intuitive because of the formal overlap between categories (cf. the example of *wayyibneʰ* cited in the preceding remark), perfective/temporal *wᵊqātal* appears to have staged a come-back.[49]

Sample Texts: 1 Samuel 1 and Numbers 19

I have decided to append to this brief overview a detailed analysis of two Hebrew texts, one primarily narrative, the other providing an example of prescriptive discourse containing both apodictic (vv. 2–13) and casuisitic (vv. 14–22) forms. In no large part, the decision to include sample texts arose out of frustration with various attempts to define the Biblical Hebrew verbal system that treat the details piecemeal rather than exhaustively.[50] This is even true of studies of which 1 Samuel 1 is the illustrative passage.[51]

1 Samuel 1 was chosen because it incorporates several major types of discourse expressed by a variety of morpho-syntactic structures: narrative discourse, including a relative high incidence of frequentative expression and circumstantial clauses, and various types of imperfective discourse in addition to the frequentatives just mentioned (indicative, volitive, and conditional); Numbers 19 because it illustrates the interplay of *yiqtōl* and *wᵊqātal* in expressing primarily imperfective discourse.

The analysis is arranged as a translation on the left with morpho-syntactic notes to the right. The translations are my own, and in them I attempt to provide a relatively idiomatic English version, with the implications of the Hebrew morpho-syntactic structures indicated in parentheses. To avoid any possible misunderstanding, the purpose of the translation is not to prove my view of the Biblical Hebrew verbal system by appealing to the necessary rendition of this text in English (which would be no more than the translational syntax of which I have doubted the usefulness in the past: Pardee 1979; 1994, p. 151), but to express to the extent possible in English what I believe the Hebrew meant for the speaker/writer-listener/reader of the text in antiquity.

Textual matters are not treated here except to the extent that they impinge directly on the translation or on questions of morpho-syntax.[52] In general, I do not include reconstructed texts as part of my morpho-syntactic analysis in order to avoid the subjectivity of such a procedure. Though such a practice would not be admissible if I were proposing a full-scale commentary, it does not appear to have had any serious effect on the analysis of the text as an illustration of Biblical Hebrew discourse structures.

Each finite verbal and nominal clause is indicated separately (clauses of which the verb is in the infinitival form are not); relative clauses are indicated as dependent on the main clause by a letter of the alphabet (e.g.,

---

48 Several clear examples are cited in Longacre 1994, pp. 68–84.

49 I say "appears to" because of the dearth of post-exilic Hebrew inscriptions — which would allow us to chart the evolution of the language (the literary character of most of the texts known as the Dead Sea Scrolls makes them difficult to exploit as examples of a living language) — and because the links between Biblical Hebrew and Mishnaic Hebrew are uncertain; the latter may go back to an independent dialect (cf. the so-called *marzeaḥ* inscription: Bordreuil and Pardee 1990; 2000) rather than a linear development from the former.

50 DeCaen's dissertation (1995), for example, is said to be based on the Hebrew of Samuel–Kings, but the reader has no way of knowing what the relationship was between the theory and the data in the author's mind. To this reader, it does not appear unlikely that he began with the hypothesis that the Biblical Hebrew verbal system is more plausibly explained as temporal than as aspectual and that he developed this hypothesis, citing passages to illustrate one detail or another of the hypothesis. But, it appears to me, when one sets about a strict parsing of every form and of every paragraph and attempting to determine what the author meant thereby, the temporal hypothesis encounters insurmountable difficulties.

51 Joosten 1997b; van der Merwe 1997.

52 For a textual study of 1 Samuel 1 that takes into account the data from the Dead Sea scrolls, see McCarter 1980.

"17.4a" means verse 17, fourth sentence, relative clause). The expression of a verbal attributive by means of a participle with prefixed definite article is common in Numbers 19; these attributive phrases are not here analyzed as clauses. As regards the stance taken in this study regarding the nature of the participle, namely, that it is neither marked for aspect nor expressive of the present tense, the form in this passage may refer (a) to an event that has already occurred in the time line foreseen by the discourse (e.g., *haśśōrēp*, v. 8, refers back to the person who has burned the cow as prescribed in v. 5, *hāʾōsēp* in v. 10 refers back to the person who has gathered the ashes as prescribed in v. 4, *mazzē^h mê^y hanniddā^h* in v. 21 refers back to the person who has sprinkled the water of purification as prescribed in vv. 18 and 19), (b) to a long-term state (v. 10 *laggēr haggār*), or (c) to an eventuality (e.g., v. 11 *hannōgē^{a}ʿ*, to be contrasted with the usage of the very same form in v. 18, where it refers back to someone who will have touched a corpse). It should be noted that the attributive use of the active participle finds its morphological counterpart in substantivized stative adjectives preceded by the definite article, which, in this text, refer only to persons who occupy a state that is actually or theoretically changeable (e.g., v. 19 *w^{ə}hizzā^h haṭṭāhōr ʿal-haṭṭāmēʾ*).

No attempt is made here to determine the "paragraphs" of the Hebrew text, a concept of dubious value in analyzing ancient narrative.[53] As the concept of "strophe" is generally an invalid one for Hebrew poetry, so the validity of that of the "paragraph" — which in both etymology and actual practice refers to a graphic separation — is debatable for prose narrative. In Ugaritic letters, for example (no prose narrative is yet attested), the horizontal "paragraph" divider is used inconsistently. In both prose and poetry, "sense units,"[54] which vary in length and in distinctiveness one from the other and which may overlap from one level to another, are thus discernable by a combination of formal markers and content. Certain of the biblical texts among the Dead Sea Scrolls indicate "sense units" by horizontal or vertical spacing, but determining the pre-history of this usage would require earlier manuscripts.

	Translation	*Morpho-Syntactic Analysis*
1 SAMUEL 1		
1.1)	*There was a man from Haramataim, a Ṣophite*[55] *from Mount Ephraim,*	*wayhī^y*: w-retentive PC functioning as perfective and expressing the beginning of the narrative as already on the main narrative line[56] and as at least loosely linked with a preceding narrative, though that need not have been the present Book of Judges.
1.2)	*whose name (was) Elqanah ben Yeroham, ben-Elihu, ben-Toḥu, ben-Ṣuph —*	Nominal clause, of which the function is to provide Elqanah's genealogy.[57]
1.1 *cont.*)	*an Ephratite.*	The indefinite form of the gentilic marks this word either as appositional to the indefinite forms in 1.1 or as constituting a predication; the extreme rarity of single-substantive predications makes the former analysis the more likely.

[53] Van der Merwe makes the attempt, while recognizing "how often it is difficult to decide where one paragraph or sub-paragraph ends and the next begins" (1997, p. 157).

[54] Pardee 1981–1982, p. 269; 1983c, p. 300; 1988, pp. 3, 70–71; 1993c, p. 156.

[55] One solution to the problem posed by the phrase *hārāmātayim ṣō^{w}pī^{y}m* is to take the {m} of the second word as dittographic with the following {mhr} (so, e.g., Heimerdinger 1999, p. 136 n. 5).

[56] On the problems of HYH, the most stative of all the stative verbs, within the aspectual system, see Lambdin 1971, pp. 279–82 (§197); Pardee 1985a.

[57] On the identification of referents by their geographical origin in sentences such as these, see Heimerdinger 1999, pp. 136–38.

	Translation	*Morpho-Syntactic Analysis*
1 Samuel 1		
2.1)	*He had two wives;*	Nominal clause; information necessary for the rest of the story.
2.3)	*one (was) named Hannah,*	Asyndetic nominal clause.
2.4)	*the second Peninnah.*	Nominal clause.
2.5)	*Peninnah had children*	*wayhī*^{y}: *w*-retentive PC marking this datum as on the same level of the story line as the first clause of v. 1.[58]
2.6)	*but Hannah did not.*	Nominal clause expressing contrast.
3.1)	*This man used to go*[59] *(on a regular basis) to do obeisance and to offer sacrifices to Yahweh-Ṣebaot at Shiloh*	*w*^{əʿ}*ālā*^{h}: *w*-retentive SC functioning as imperfective and expressing iteration;[60] note use of this form "out of sequence" (see above).
3.2)	*where Ḥophni and Pinḥas were serving as priests of Yahweh.*	Nominal clause; the indefinite form of *khnym* marks this word as predicative.
4.1)	*On each such occasion,*	*wayhī*^{y}: *w* -retentive PC introducing perfective aspect of the following main clause + adverbial phrase.[61]
4.2)	*when Elqanah had offered the sacrifice,*	*wayyizbaḥ*: *w*-retentive PC marking a given occasion within the frequentative structure as belonging to the perfective narrative line.[62]

[58] The relative weakness of *w*-retentive HYH clauses is visible here in the constrastive structure formed by this clause with the following, for the expression of the following clause is markedly nominal (*ʾyn* instead of *lʾ hyh*).

[59] The verb expressing the trip to the sanctuary at Shiloh is consistently ʿLH, 'to ascend,' in this narrative. I have avoided the 'up' part of the lexeme in translation and attempted to represent it where appropriate by reference to the sanctuary.

[60] As stated above, the "*w*-retentive" imperfective may express any of the nuances or moods of the various forms of the imperfective, and reading a notion of *irrealis* into that form (Joosten 1997b, p. 82: "...what is expressed by hl[w (v. 3) is merely that one might expect him to do so") appears to me to be placing too much emphasis on the element of *irrealis* in the imperfective. (This is my perspective — Joosten's view of the Biblical Hebrew verb system is, of course, tense based.) Joosten's analysis, in that he uses the English verb "would" as proof of the *irrealis* character of the expression of iteration in English with no mention of the parallel expression 'used to,' both of which may be used to translate the Hebrew frequentative, is defective. There must be levels of *irrealis*. Here the imperfective expresses the non-boundedness in terms of number of occurrences of the act in question: whenever it was appropriate, he would go.

[61] This appears to be a very brief form of the circumstantial clause structure (Lambdin 1971, pp. 123–24 [§110], 127 [§114]; cf. Pardee 1994, pp. 152–53), and *hayyō*^{w}*m* is thus to be parsed either as a one-word nominal clause, '(there was) a certain day,' or as an unmarked adverbial, 'on a given day.' The rarity of one-noun predicative nominal clauses in Biblical Hebrew makes the latter solution preferable. This structure probably, therefore, corresponds as an unmarked adverbial to structure §III B (preposition + noun), common noun option, in my charting of the circumstantial-clause structures (1994, p. 152 — where I did not point out explicitly that the "embedded clause" may or may not be an independent clause). In any case, the phrase appears to be the structural equivalent of *wayhī*^{y} *bayyāmī*^{y}*m hāhēm*, and it thus is unlikely that *hayyō*^{w}*m* is to be parsed simply as the subject of *wayhī*^{y}. This explanation of *wayhī*^{y} *hayyō*^{w}*m* appears to hold for its occurrences elsewhere (e.g., 1 Sam 14:1; 2 Kings 4:8): in each case the function of the phrase is to mark a break, either from general to specific or from one episode to another, while that of the definite article is to mark the upcoming events as non-general, as occurring on a "certain" day.

[62] Lambdin 1971, pp. 279–82 (§197), terms this structure "anticipatory subordination." Because the structure is not marked as subordinate in Hebrew, that term should be avoided, even though the structure may often be translated felicitously in English as a subordinate clause. Note that the structure does not constitute formally a case of "*wāw* of apodosis," because each clause is formally marked as principal (on the theoretical problem posed by "*wāw* of apodosis" in Biblical Hebrew, see Groß 1987 and Pardee 1989).

	Translation	*Morpho-Syntactic Analysis*
1 Samuel 1		
4.3)	*he would give portions to his wife Peninnah and to all her sons and daughters.*	*w^{ə}nātan*: w-retentive SC expressing return to frequentative discourse; note use of this form "out of sequence" (see above).
5.1)	*But to Hannah he would give a double portion,*[63]	*yittēn*: PC in non-initial position expressing contrast on the imperfective discourse line.
5.2)	*for he loved Hannah*	*ʾāhēb*: SC in explanatory clause (*ky* clauses are formally off the main narrative line); ʾHB is semantically durative[64] and need not be marked for iteration; direct object fronted for emphasis.
5.3)	*but Yahweh had "closed" her womb.*	*sāgar*: SC in *w^{ə}*X-*qāṭal* clause with focus on YHWH; the SC expresses the completeness of the act, viewed as punctual and past, hence translated as a pluperfect.[65]
6.1)	*Her rival-wife would harass her mercilessly in order to upset her,*	*w^{ə}ki^{ʿa}sattā^{h}*: w-retentive SC expressing continuation of frequentative discourse.
6.2)	*on account of the fact*[66] *that Yahweh had closed her womb.*	*sāgar*: SC in explanatory clause expressing the act as complete.
7.1)	*Just as he would act thus every year, as often as she (Hannah) went to the House of Yahweh,*	*ya^{ʿa}śe^{h}*: PC frequentative expressing a summary;[67] correlative with following clause (*kn … kn*).
7.2)	*so she (Peninnah) would harass her*	*takʿisennā^{h}*: PC frequentative correlative with preceding clause.
7.3)	*and (each time that) she wept*	*wattibke^{h}*: w-retentive PC marking a given occasion within the frequentative structure (see 4.2).[68]

[63] Hypothetical translation; on the textual problem, see the commentators.

[64] On semantic iterativity/durativity, see below on 12.2. The verbs ʾHB, 'to love,' and ŚNʾ, 'to hate,' share characteristics of both transitive and intransitive verbs; cf. the somewhat different view of Dobbs-Allsopp (2000, pp. 35–39). In any case, ʾHB clearly carries the aspect of durativity characteristic of stative verbs.

[65] In spite of the English translation as a pluperfect, this is not a "pluperfect" in Biblical Hebrew because Biblical Hebrew is not a tensed language (Pardee 2001).

[66] On the multiple referential functions of *ky*, see Claassen 1983 and, more recently, Meyer 2001 (note that in the putative parallels with English "because" [pp. 50–56], that word never introduces a new rhetorical unit — but that is precisely the problem with Hebrew *ky*; English "so" would have provided a more interesting set of comparisons).

[67] Whether the form *ya^{ʿa}śeh* and the two forms marked for feminine gender simply indicate different subjects (Elqanah and the two wives), or whether the first should be emended to the Niphal, the syntactic analysis remains the same.

[68] This form as marked in the Massoretic text, i.e., as *w*-retentive PC, may be explained along the same lines as 4.2. On the other hand, because the consonantal text here shows the "long" form, i.e., {wtbkh} instead of {wtbk}, one must consider the possibility of an error in the Massoretic vocalization, i.e., *wattibke^{h}*, 'and she wept,' in place of *w^{ə}tibke^{h}*, 'in order that she weep.' Though *w*-retentive PC forms of III-*h* verbs do occur in the "long" form (see above), it nevertheless appears legitimate to take the spelling here with {h} as an indication of a mistake in the Massoretic tradition. The use of non-*w*-retentive PC to mark a purpose clause within a volitive sequence is well known, but it also occurs in indicative sequences (see above). The translation would be '…would harass her so that she would weep and not eat.' In favor of the Massoretic tradition, one could query that Peninnah's specific intention was to incite Hannah not to eat and drink; the interpretation as the narrator's expression of the result of the harassment seems better to reflect the situation. As I have already stated elsewhere, Fokkelman's interpretation (1991) of forms such as this as "unmarked iteratives" makes no linguistic sense to me; cf. my remarks in 2001, p. 311 n. 14.

	Translation	Morpho-Syntactic Analysis
1 Samuel 1		
7.4)	*she would not eat.*	*tōʾkal*: PC in negative imperfective clause expressing frequentatively the result of the weeping.
8.1)	*(On each such occasion,) Elqanah said to her:*	*wayyōʾmer*: w-retentive PC marking a given occasion within the frequentative structure (see 4.2).
8.2)	*"Hannah, why do you weep,*	*tibkī*^{y}: PC expressing iteration in direct speech.
8.3)	*and why do you not eat,*	*toʾk*^{ə}*lī*^{y}: ditto.
8.4)	*and why are you so despondent?*	*yēraʿ*: PC expressing a continuous state in direct speech.
8.5)	*Am I not worth more to you than ten sons?"*	Nominal sentence.
9.1)	*(On the occasion with which this story is dealing particularly,) Hannah arose (and separated from the others) after (everyone else) had eaten in Shiloh and drunk.*	*wattāqom*: w-retentive PC; that we here return to the principal narrative (as distinct from individual moments within the preceding frequentative discourse) is only determinable from context.
9.2)	*Now Eli the priest was (all the while)*[69] *sitting on a chair*[70] *beside the entrance to the temple of Yahweh.*	Nominal clause (participial predicate).
10.1)	*She was feeling very bad*	Nominal clause.
10.2)	*and began to pray to Yahweh,*	*wattitpallēl*: w-retentive PC expressing perfectivity in principal narrative.[71]
10.3)	*weeping all the while.*	*tibke*^{h}: PC in absolute infinitival construction expressing the intensity of the weeping as well as its continuousness during the prayer.
11.1)	*She made*	*wattiddōr*: w-retentive PC.
11.2)	*the following vow:*	*wattōʾmar*: ditto.
11.3)	*"O Yahweh-Ṣebaot, should you deign to look upon my affliction, servant of yours that I am,*	*tirʾeh*: PC + inf. abs. in protasis of conditional sentence in direct speech.[72]
11.4)	*and remember me,*	*ūz*^{ə}*kartanī*^{y}: w-retentive SC as continuation of preceding.

[69] This sentence does not constitute a major change of scene because Eli's position would have been near to where Hannah's family had been banqueting. The function of the clause is to explain how it was that he was able to observe Hannah praying.

[70] The translation of *hakkissēʾ* as indefinite is meant to reflect another standard feature of Hebrew narrative: the first mention of an entity is frequently definite in Hebrew narrative, while it is indefinite in standard English narrative (contrast colloquial English narrative: 'Eli was sitting on this chair…').

[71] The translation as an inchoative only reflects the logic of the story: the verb itself is not marked semantically as inchoative and is here only marked morpho-syntactically for perfectivity. In another narrative where the contents of the prayer itself did not follow, it would be translated as a preterit in English. On "ingressivity" as a pragmatic implicature, see Dobbs-Allsopp 2000, pp. 48–49.

[72] As is well known, the two clauses of a conditional sentence may be expressed either as perfectives or as imperfectives, a situation easily comprehensible in an aspectual system where the speaker/author may choose to phrase either element as complete or as incomplete (see above, n. 11).

	Translation	*Morpho-Syntactic Analysis*
1 Samuel 1		
11.5)	*and not forget me your servant,*	*tiškaḥ*: PC in negative continuation of preceding.
11.6)	*and grant to me your servant male offspring,*	*w^{ə}nātattā^{h}*: w-retentive SC as continuation of preceding.
11.7)	*I would give him*[73] *to Yahweh for his entire life,*	*ūn^{ə}tattī^{y}w*: w-retentive SC in apodosis of conditional sentence; note the absence of a specific marking for the junction of protasis and apodosis (the junction is only determinable by the logic of a given statement).
11.8)	*and a razor would never touch his head."*	*ya$^{c a}$le^{h}*: PC in continuation of apodosis with fronted subject noun (the function of the fronting may have been to emphasize the somewhat elliptically expressed promise to vow the child as a Nazirite).
12.1)		*w^{ə}hāyā^{h}*: w-retentive SC introducing the long series of nominal and frequentative (13.3) clauses that lead up to the perfective expression (13.4) that functions narratologically as the main clause.[74]

[73] The direct object (and other pronominal indicators further along in the utterance) agree in gender and number with the head noun of the construct chain *zera^{c} ^{xa}nāšī^{y}m*, lit. 'offspring of men,' but in context refer to the male child for which Hannah hopes and which she will in fact receive.

[74] This circumstantial-clause sequence is one of the most complex in the corpus: the HYH introducer, instead of agreeing in aspect with the logical main clause, *wayyaḥš^{ə}behā* (13.4), assumes the structure of an imperfective circumstantial-clause sequence, as though the nominal clauses 12.3–13.3 were the main clauses. Because the function of everything up to *wayyaḥš^{ə}behā* appears to be to explain why Eli accounted Hannah a drunk (three nominal clauses and a subject-fronted verbal clause), it appears best to see this as a truly mixed structure, i.e., as one in which *w^{ə}hāyā^{h}* introduces, as is normal, an imperfective clause or series of clauses (it is not, therefore, so-called conjunctive *w*, *contra* Fokkelman 1991, p. 55), with this sequence of clauses serving as explanation for a perfective main clause. Verses 12 and 13 constitute, therefore, a combination of the imperfective and perfective circumstantial-clause sequences. This sequence incorporates a further anomaly, viz., the presence of a SC verb within the imperfective sequence (see 12.2). Fokkelman and van der Merwe (1997, p. 164) cite 1 Sam 17:48 as a parallel to this verse without noting the complexity of this passage as compared with the other, where *w^{ə}hāyā^{h}* follows an imperfective sequence in direct speech and precedes a perfective one of reportorial narrative — and appears, therefore, to constitute a textual error (McCarter 1980, pp. 285, 289). Fokkelman also cites 1 Sam 10:9, an example similar to 1 Sam 17:48, and 1 Sam 25:20 and 2 Sam 6:16, two examples where *w^{ə}hāyā^{h}* introduces participial duratives followed by perfective main clauses — it appears valid to see in those cases mixed structures similar to the present text. The value of the present text is that, by its inclusion of a lexical frequentative/durative, three participles, and a PC (12.2–13.3), the function of *w^{ə}hāyā^{h}* as introducing these various expressions of iteration is relatively clear. Longacre (1994, pp. 84–91) cites a number of examples, including those to which reference has just been made and 1 Sam 1:12, in support of his claim that *w^{ə}hāyā^{h}* was used to mark "significant background or important events to follow," and this example would not, according to that classification, have functioned to introduce the imperfectivity of the embedded clauses. I wonder, however, if it is not the case, in the examples cited by Longacre, that *w^{ə}hāyā^{h}* expresses the overlap of the action in the embedded clause with that of the main clause and the ongoing nature of the two acts and this to an extent that is significantly different from what *wayhī^{y}* expresses in similar clauses (the temporal overlap is clear in 1 Sam 25:20 and 2 Sam 6:16: "while X was going on Y occurred"). The function of the structure would be to express the imperfectivity inherent in the concurrency of the two acts and the resultant durativity whereas the function of the structure with *wayhī^{y}* is to introduce the perfectivity of the main clause. Also, though Longacre is loath to accept emendation, *w^{ə}hāyā^{h}* might in some of his examples be simply erroneous for *wayhī^{y}* and owing to the presence in the immediately preceding passage of *w^{ə}qātal* forms expressing iteration (emendation is the common approach among grammarians and text critics to several of these texts, including 1 Sam 1:12, where I judge that solution to be unnecessary).

	Translation	*Morpho-Syntactic Analysis*
1 Samuel 1		
12.2)	*Now, as she was a long time praying,*	*hirb*^{ə}*tā*^{h}: SC in embedded clause, formally the first of five clauses of the circumstantial sequence introduced by 12.1[75]; lexically frequentative or durative (RBH Hiphil + inf., 'do something repeatedly or lengthily').[76]
12.3)	*and Eli was watching her mouth,*	Nominal (participial) clause.
13.1)	*but Hannah was speaking inwardly,*	Nominal (participial) clause continuing the circumstantial sequence.
13.2)	*only her lips were moving*	Asyndetic nominal (participial) clause expanding on previous.
13.3)	*and her voice could not be heard;*	*yiššāmē*^{a}*ʿ*: PC in a strongly marked circumstantial clause (the structure is verbal — in contrast with the preceding nominal clauses — , imperfective and frequentative, and the subject is fronted).
13.4)	*(for these reasons) Eli took her to be a drunk.*[77]	*wayyaḥš*^{ə}*behā*: w-retentive PC expressing return to main narrative line.
14.1)	*Eli said to her:*	*wayyōʾmer*: w-retentive PC expressing continuation of main narrative line.
14.2)	*"How long will you keep getting drunk?*	*tištakkārī*^{y}*n*: PC (with "paragogic" *nun*) reflecting Eli's perception of Hannah as capable of getting drunk on a regular basis.
14.3)	*Get rid of that wine!"*[78]	*hāsī*^{y}*rī*^{y}: Impv.
15.1)	*Hanna replied:*	*wattaʿan*: w-retentive PC expressing return to main narrative line.
15.2)		*wattōʾmer*: w-retentive PC expressing continuation of main narrative line.
15.3)	*"You're wrong, my lord!*	One-word adverbial clause, functioning as assertion to the contrary of what the interlocutor had just said, followed by vocative.

[75] See two preceding footnotes and Pardee 1994, p. 152, §III E. As regards the function of the participle here and in the next two clauses, it expresses an ongoing act, a nuance deducible from the surrounding context, in particular the preceding *w*^{ə}*hāyā*^{h} and the following *yiššāmē*^{a}*ʿ*.

[76] The structure of this clause is rare: normally a finite verb in an embedded clause is marked for the same aspect as the introducing form of HYH (*yiššāmē*^{a}*ʿ* [13.3] is so marked) and as the main verb (see two preceding notes and Pardee 1994, p. 152). The presence of the perfective form may be explained by two factors: (1) the verb is semantically frequentative or durative, or (2) the "mainest" of the "main" clauses, *wayyaḥš*^{ə}*behā* (13.4) — see preceding note — is perfective. Because the prayer as quoted is very brief, it is not possible to determine whether the author wished to say by the use of *hirb*^{ə}*tā*^{h} that Hannah kept repeating the words quoted (in which case the verb is lexically frequentative) or that these words were to be considered a summary of a much longer prayer (in which case the verb is lexically durative, as was ʾHB in v. 5); the meaning of the root does not help us here, for the Hiphil of RBB 'to be many' + HTPLL could here mean either 'to produce many repetitions of a short prayer' or 'to produce many words in a long prayer.' I thus agree with Fokkelman (1991, p. 53) as regards the semantics of *hirb*^{ə}*tā*^{h}, but cannot agree with his "exegetical" method for determining such matters in general.

[77] Nominal forms from the *qattāl* base, whether *qittōl* or *qattāl* in Biblical Hebrew, correspond to the traditional category of the *nomen professionis* and thus carry semantically a notion of long-term state (see 14.2).

[78] The *ʿl* here is *incommodus*.

	Translation	*Morpho-Syntactic Analysis*
1 Samuel 1		
15.4)	*I'm a very troubled woman,*	Nominal sentence functioning as self-description.
15.5)	*but I haven't had a drop of anything with alcohol in it.*	*šātī^{y}tī^y*: SC in strongly marked clause (verb at end of sentence) expressing contrast to what the interlocutor has just stated and hence a refutation of that assertion.
15.6)	*I have only poured out my soul to Yahweh.*	*wāʾešpōk*: *w*-retentive PC continuing perfective expression within direct speech.[79]
16.1)	*Don't consider me, your servant, as a corrupt women.*	*tittēn*: PC (jussive) after *ʾal* in negative impv.
16.2)	*For it is on account of my being so downcast and so vexed that I have spoken the whole time."*	*dibbartī^y*: SC in motivation clause (i.e., the reason Hannah presents for not being accounted a corrupt woman).
17:1)	*Eli replied:*	*wayyaʿan*: *w*-retentive PC expressing return to main narrative line.
17.2)		*wayyōʾmer*: *w*-retentive PC expressing continuation of main narrative line.
17.3)	*"Go in peace.*	*l^{ə}kī^y*: impv.
17.4)	*The god of Israel will grant the request*	*yittēn*: PC functioning either as indicative or as jussive.[80]
17.4a)	*that you have made to him."*[81]	*šāʾalt*: SC in relative clause.
18.1)	*She said:*	*wattōʾmer*: *w*-retentive PC expressing return to main narrative line.
18.2)	*"May your servant-woman* (i.e., *I*) *find favor with you."*	*timṣāʾ*: PC functioning as jussive (cf. note 80).
18.3)	*So the woman went her way,*	*wattēlek*: *w*-retentive PC expressing return to main narrative line.
18.4)	*ate,*	*wattōʾkal*: *w*-retentive PC expressing continuation of main narrative line.
18.5)	*and was no longer despondent.*	*hāyū^w*: SC in negative contrastive clause.[82]

[79] Note that the fact that the act was, as previously described, frequentative or durative is not expressed here or in the following sentence (16.2). The author presents Hannah's act as complete in her mind — as indeed it was, at this point of the encounter, when Eli had interrupted her and she had stopped praying. Note also that, in both cases, the act may be coherently expressed in English either as durative ('I was pouring out' ... 'I have been speaking') or as perfective, i.e., by the present perfect ('I have poured out' ... 'I have spoken').

[80] The absence of markedly distinct (indicative) imperfective and jussive forms in most root forms requires the interpreter working in English to make a choice based on the surrounding context.

[81] The double marking of the initiator of the request characteristic of Hebrew (lit. 'your request which you made to him') need not be expressed in English.

[82] Whatever the textual solution be to the problematic last clause of this verse, it appears likely that its form was negative and hence by definition not expressive of progress on the main narrative line. It is to be noted that negative clauses, because the negative adverb normally intervenes between a possible *w* and the verb, are by definition non-*w*-retentive in nature.

	Translation	*Morpho-Syntactic Analysis*
1 Samuel 1		
19.1)	*Early next morning*	*wayyaškīmū^{w}*: w-retentive PC expressing continuation of main narrative line.[83]
19.2)	*they did obeisance to Yahweh,*	*wayyištaḥ^{a}wū^{w}*: ditto.
19.3)	*and returned*	*wayyāšūbū^{w}*: ditto.
19.4)	*home to Haramatah.*	*wayyābōʾū^{w}*: ditto.[84]
19.5)	*Elqanah and Hannah had conjugal relations*	*wayyēdaʿ*: ditto.
19.6)	*and Yahweh remembered her.*	*wayyizk^{ə}rehā*: ditto.
20.1)	*As time went by,*	*wayhī^{y}*: w-retentive PC introducing a circumstantial clause embedded in the main narrative line + adverbial phrase.[85]
20.2)	*Hannah became pregnant*	*wattahar*: w-retentive PC marking main verb of circumstantial structure.
20.3)	*and bore a son.*	*wattēled*: w-retentive PC expressing continuation of main narrative line.
20.4)	*She called his name Samuel,*	*wattiqrāʾ*: ditto.
20.5)	"*For,*" (*said she,*) "(*it is*) *from Yahweh* (*that*) *I requested him.*"	*š^{ə}ʾiltī^{y}w*: SC in direct speech.
21.1)	*Elqanah and his entire household went to offer to Yahweh the periodic sacrifice and ... .*[86]	*wayyaʿal*: w-retentive PC expressing return to main narrative line.
22.1)	*But Hannah did not go along,*	*ʿālātā^{h}*: SC in negative contrastive clause.
22.2)	*for she had said to her husband*	*ʾām^{ə}rā^{h}*: SC in motivation clause.[87]
22.3)	"(*I will not go*) *until the child is weaned.*	*yiggāmēl*: PC expressing imperfective (here the future) in direct speech.
22.4)	*Then I will take him*	*wah^{a}bīʾōtī^{y}w*: w-retentive SC expressing continuation of previous structure.

[83] This and the following verbal clauses illustrate a feature of Hebrew morpho-syntax not discussed above, i.e., what Lambdin (1971, pp. 238–40 [§173]) calls "hendiadys," in this case a structure in which the verb is translated as an adverb in English. As Lambdin indicates, the coordinate structure (attested here) is only one of three possible sequences (the others being asyndetic and finite + infinitive).

[84] This and the preceding verb do not reflect the structure discussed in the preceding note because ŠB does not here express repetition but literal return. On the other hand, two verbs are used because verbs of movement are not in Biblical Hebrew marked for direction in terms of the speaker, as in English, but in terms of the spaces to which reference is made. Thus ŠB is to be translated either 'go back' or 'come back' (i.e., 'return') and Bʾ either 'go in' or 'come in' (i.e., 'enter' or 'arrive') according to the position of the speaker. This has long been observed (e.g., by Rosén 1969, pp. 98–101), but is still not always correctly registered in the introductory grammars (e.g., in Lambdin 1971, p. 28 [§36], YṢʾ is glossed as 'going forth, leaving,' but not as 'coming forth' and 'exiting'; p. 32 [§39] YRD is glossed as 'descending, going down,' but not as 'coming down').

[85] On the structure, see above on 4.1. The plural *t^{ə}qūpō^{w}t* either expresses the stages of childbearing or refers to the return of the time to go to Shiloh to sacrifice (cf. McCarter 1980, p. 55). If the former solution is correct, the reference may be to the appearance of a visible bulge in the fifth month, accounted as the halfway point of pregnancy in the ancient Semitic world (cf. Pardee 1997b, p. 282 with n. 60).

[86] MT appears corrupt here (cf. McCarter 1980, p. 55).

[87] The motivation clause, which logically includes Elqanah's reply recorded in the next verse, describes what had occurred before Elqanah left and Hannah did not leave and hence is to be translated with the pluperfect in English. Note that this structure does not correspond to what has been called the "anterior construction" (*ʿālātā^{h}* is not logically "anterior," whereas *ʾām^{ə}rā^{h}* and *wayyōʾmer* are — cf. Pardee 2001).

	Translation	Morpho-Syntactic Analysis
1 Samuel 1		
22.5)	*and he will make his appearance in the presence of Yahweh*	*w*^{ə}*nirʾā*^{h}: ditto.
22.6)	*and stay there permanently.*"	*w*^{ə}*yāšab*: ditto.
23.1)	*Elqanah her husband had said to her:*	*wayyōʾmer*: w-retentive PC sequential to 22.2 (i.e., part of motivation structure, not of main narrative line) and hence to be translated as a pluperfect.
23.2)	"*Do as you see fit.*	^{ʿa}*śī*^{y}: impv.
23.3)	*Stay (here) until you wean the child.*	*š*^{ə}*bī*^{y}: impv. in asyndetic continuation of the volitive sequence.
23.4)	*Moreover, may Yahweh carry out his promise.*"[88]	*yāqēm*: jussive (new subject preceded by asseverative adverb) in asyndetic continuation of the volitive sequence.
23.5)	*So the woman stayed (at home)*	*wattēšeb*: w-retentive PC expressing return to main narrative line.
23.6)	*and nursed the child until she weaned him.*	*wattê*^{y}*neq*: w-retentive PC expressing continuation of main narrative line.
24.1)	*She took him with her (to the sanctuary)*	*watta*^{ʿa}*lēhū*^{w}: ditto.
24.2)	*when she had weaned him,*	*g*^{ə}*mālattū*^{w}: SC in temporal clause.
24.1 cont.)	*along with a three-year-old bull*[89] *and an ephah of flour and a skin of wine.*	
24.3)	*So she brought him to the House of Yahweh*	*watt*^{ə}*bīʾēhū*^{w}: w-retentive PC expressing return to main narrative line.
24.4)	*where the boy was to serve.*	Nominal clause; MT usually taken as corrupt but cf. Exod 33:11.
25.1)	*They slaughtered the bull*	*wayyišḥ*^{a}*ṭū*^{w}: -retentive PC expressing return to main narrative line.
25.2)	*and brought the boy to Eli.*	*wayyābī*^{y}*ʾū*^{w}: w-retentive PC expressing continuation of main narrative line.
26.1)	*She said:*	*wattōʾmer*: ditto.
26.2)	"*If you please, my lord, may your life prosper, my lord.*	Nominal clause(s) expressing greeting.
26.3)	*I am the woman who (once) stood near you here praying to Yahweh.*	Nominal self-identification clause (participle marked as attributive adjective).

88 MT translated literally; Qumran and other witnesses show a different text (see McCarter 1980, p. 56).

89 The correction of MT *pārī*^{y}*m š*^{ə}*lōšā*^{h} appears clear, though doubt remains regarding other segments of the text (cf. McCarter 1980, pp. 56–57).

	Translation	*Morpho-Syntactic Analysis*
1 Samuel 1		
27.1)	*For this boy did I pray*	*hitpallāltī*^{y}: SC in asyndetic clause (in MT) which places the object of the prayer in focus: the prepositional phrase is fronted for purposes of emphasis and contrast (between the humble human request and YHWH's gracious granting thereof).[90]
27.2)	*and Yahweh has granted the request*	*wayyittēn:* w-retentive PC sequential to SC in preceding clause.
27.2a)	*that I asked of him.*	*šāʾaltī*^{y}: SC in relative clause.
28.1)	*Now I, for my part, hereby return the requested boy to Yahweh:*	*hišʾiltīhū*^{w}: SC functioning as performative.[91]
28.1a)	*as long as he lives,*	The form of predication in the relative clause is uncertain for textual reasons (*hāyā*^{h} SC is present in the text as it stands).[92]
28.2)	*he is (to be considered as) one requested of Yahweh."*	Nominal clause.
28.3)	*Then he did obeisance to Yahweh there.*	*wayyištaḥū*^{w}: w-retentive PC expressing return to main narrative line.[93]

	Translation	*Morpho-Syntactic Analysis*
Numbers 19		
1)	*Yahweh said to Moses and to Aaron:*	*waydabbēr:* w-retentive PC expressing the narrative context of the following legal section and linking it, in the expression of the author/redactor, to the preceding section, which was also introduced narratively.
2.1)	"'*This is a statute regarding legal procedure*	Nominal sentence.

[90] Direct speech, both in the Hebrew Bible and in the extra-biblical inscriptions, shows a higher incidence of fronting of non-verbal elements than does perfective narrative, even when, as here, the discourse is perfective.

[91] To my knowledge, a comprehensive study of SC performatives in Biblical Hebrew remains to be done, though it is clear that performativity is expressed perfectively (cf. Pardee and Whiting 1987; more recently and with broader perspectives, Sanders 2004; Dobbs-Allsopp 2004–2007).

[92] The LXX reflects the root ḤYH here; the text is not extant in the witnesses from the Dead Sea Scrolls (see McCarter 1980, p. 57).

[93] In MT, Hanna's prayer in ch. 2 appears to be marked as a continuation of this clause, in spite of the fact that the verb in this clause in MT is 3 m.s. The text here appears corrupt (cf. McCarter 1980, pp. 57–58).

	Translation	*Morpho-Syntactic Analysis*
Numbers 19		
2.1a)	*that Yahweh has ordained:'*	With attributive relative clause (ṣiwwā^{h}: SC expressing perfectivity of the act within the context of the ordained speech).
2.2)	*Tell the Israelites*	*dabbēr:* impv. beginning a volitive sequence that continues without a marked break through verse 13 (i.e., after this imperative, the volition is expressed only by forms not explicitly marked for volitivity: there are no cohortatives, imperatives, or marked jussives).[94]
2.3)	*that they should bring to you* (sing., point of reference Moses) *a red cow in perfect condition*	*w^{ə}yiqḥū^{w}*: w-conjunctive PC expressing the volition in the form of indirect discourse and as formally sequential to Moses' speech (this first verb in the sequence following the imperative represents Lambdin's type §107c, expressive of a purpose);
2.3a)	*without a blemish,*	this sentence contains two attributive relative clauses, one nominal,
2.3b)	*one that has never borne the yoke.*	the other verbal: *ʿālā^{h}*, SC expressing perfectivity of the negatively stated act.
3.1)	*You* (pl., the point of reference, if the form is correct, is Moses and Aaron) *are to turn it over to Eliezer the priest.*	*ūn^{ə}tattem*: w-retentive SC continuing the volitive sequence as part of YHWH's address to Moses and Aaron (this and all following forms introduced by *w* belong formally to Lambdin's type §107b, which expresses the simplest form of continuity in a volitive sequence, simple imperfectivity with the volitive expressed only by the preceding form, in this case the impv. in 2.2).
3.2)	*He is to have it taken outside the camp*	*w^{ə}hô^{w}ṣī^{yʾ}*: w-retentive SC, 3 m.s., marking the shift from Moses and Aaron as indirect objects of the address to third-person forms designating the actors in the rite being prescribed.[95]

[94] The absence of marked volitive forms is characteristic of casuistic juridical expression (which takes two principal forms: "if X happens, Y occurs" or "a man who does X, then Y occurs" – the macro-structure of the second part of this chapter is based on the latter form); but, by definition, apodictic law giving allows for explicitly volitive expression in addition to the use of the **yaqtulu* and *w^{ə}qātal* imperfectives. Here, the only explicit volitive is in this introduction to the law, which presents YHWH as ordaining the following directives, a common paradigm for both casuistic and apodictic formulations. The tying together of the narrative and the law is here more extensive than in many cases (i.e., second-person forms continue into v. 3) and morphosyntactically more intricate (with both **yaqtulu* and *w^{ə}qātal* forms used in vv. 2 and 3).

[95] According to the *Codex Leningradensis*, this is the last second-person form in the chapter (there is, however, manuscript and versional evidence for reading *lākem* in 21.1).

	Translation	*Morpho-Syntactic Analysis*
Numbers 19		
3.3)	*and see that it is slaughtered there.*	*wᵊšāḥaṭ*: w-retentive SC, 3 m.s. indefinite subject, lit. 'and (someone) is to slaughter it in his presence.'
4.1)	*Then Eliezer the priest is to take some of its blood on his finger*	*wᵊlāqaḥ*: w-retentive SC expressing continuation of the volitive sequence.
4.2)	*and sprinkle it seven times in the direction of the front of the Tent of Meeting.*	*wᵊhizzāʰ*: ditto.
5.1)	*The cow is to be burned in his sight:*	*wᵊśārap*: w-retentive SC active with 3 m.s. indefinite subject; as in the previous verse, the literal translation would be 'and (someone) is to (perform the act in question)' — this interpretation is made certain here by the fact that the actor is mentioned explicitly in v. 8.
5.2)	*its skin, its flesh, its blood, even its offal are to be burned.*	*yiśrōp*: PC, 3 m.s. indefinite subject, expressing the continuation of the volitive sequence with fronted objects; the function of the fronting here appears to be to make explicit that the person responsible is to burn the cow in its entirety.
6.1)	*Then the priest himself is to take some cedar-wood, hyssop, and a piece of scarlet cloth*	*wᵊlāqaḥ*: w-retentive SC expressing continuation of the volitive sequence.
6.2)	*and throw them into the fire in which the cow is burning.*	*wᵊhišlîʸk*: ditto.
7.1)	*Next the priest will wash his clothes*	*wᵊkibbes*: ditto.
7.2)	*and bathe his body in water.*	*wᵊrāḥaṣ*: ditto.
7.3)	*Thereafter he may re-enter the camp,*	*yābōʷʾ*: PC expressing the continuation of the volitive sequence with fronted adverb.
7.4)	*but the priest will remain ritually unclean until sun-set.*	*wᵊṭāmēʾ*: w-retentive SC expressing continuation of the volitive sequence (here translated indicatively as a state, but there can be no doubt that the state is being ordained within the volitive sequence).
8.1)	*The person who burned it must also wash his clothes in water,*	*yᵊkabbēs*: PC expressing the continuation of the volitive sequence with fronted (participial) subject (the fronting is rendered in the translation by 'also').
8.2)	*bathe his body in water,*	*wᵊrāḥaṣ*: w-retentive SC expressing continuation of the volitive sequence.

	Translation	Morpho-Syntactic Analysis
Numbers 19		
8.3)	*and (he also) will remain ritually unclean until sun-set.*	*wᵊṭāmēʾ*: ditto.
9.1)	*Someone who is ritually pure is to collect the ashes of the cow*	*wᵊʾāsap*: ditto.
9.2)	*and deposit them in a pure place outside the camp.*	*wᵊhinnīʸᵃḥ*: ditto.
9.3)	*The congregation of the Israelites are to preserve (the ashes of the cow) for the water of purification:*	*wᵊhāyᵊtāʰ*: w-retentive SC, 3 f.s., apparently with 'cow' as the grammatical subject,[96] expressing the continuation of the volitive sequence.
9.4)	*it ([the sacrifice of] the cow) is (classified as) a sin-offering.*[97]	Nominal sentence.
10.1)	*The one who collected the ashes of the cow must wash his clothes*	*wᵊkibbes*: w-retentive SC expressing continuation of the volitive sequence.
10.2)	*and will (also) remain ritually unclean until sun-set.*	*wᵊṭāmēʾ*: ditto.
10.3)	*This will be a perpetual statute for Israelites and for persons of other ethnicities dwelling among them.*	*wᵊhāyᵊtāʰ*: ditto.
11)	*As for anyone who touches a human corpse, he remains ritually unclean for seven days.*	*wᵊṭāmēʾ*: w-retentive SC expressing the continuation of the volitive sequence with fronted (participial) subject and pleonastic *w* (the equivalent of the '*wāw* of apodosis' in a marked conditional sentence).
12.1)	*Such a person will undergo the rite of purification from sin on the third day*	*yitḥaṭṭāʾ*: PC expressing the continuation of the volitive sequence with fronted pronominal subject in what is formally a *casus pendens* (lit., 'As for him, the rite of purification from sin will be performed for him').
12.2)	*but only on the seventh day will he legally become pure.*	*yiṭhār*: PC expressing the continuation of the volitive sequence with fronted adverbial phrase.
12.3)	*If the sin-offering is not performed on the third day,*	*yitḥaṭṭāʾ*: PC in protasis of conditional sentence.
12.4)	*then he will not be pure on the seventh.*	*yiṭhār*: PC in apodosis of conditional sentence with fronted adverbial phrase.

[96] According to the traditional interpretation of this verse (e.g., Levine 1993, pp. 459, 463), the subject of the verb is *ʾēper happārāʰ*, with grammatical attraction to the second word of the construct chain. The literal translation is 'It [3 f.s.] is to be for the congregation of the Israelites for a preservation for water of purification.'

[97] 'Sin offering' reflects the traditional etymological translation, the functional inadequacy of which has been demonstrated by J. Milgrom (see Pardee 1996, which follows Milgrom's arguments but finds 'decontamination offering/sacrifice' preferable as a technical term to Milgrom's choice of 'purification offering/sacrifice' because it avoids confusion with Hebrew expressions for 'purification'). See also below, n. to 19.2.

	Translation	*Morpho-Syntactic Analysis*
NUMBERS 19		
13.1)	*Anyone who touches a dead person, (that is) the body of a human being*	First element of complex subject: *kol* + substantivized participle.[98]
13.1a)	*who should die,*	Relative clause: *yāmū*^{w}*t*, PC expressing the eventuality of the case.
13.1b)	*but refuses to undergo the rite of purification from sin*	*yitḥaṭṭāʾ*: PC in coordinate clause with negative verb continuing the presentation of the case.
13.1 *cont.*)	*will (thereby) have rendered unclean Yahweh's dwelling.*	*ṭimmēʾ*: SC in main clause with fronted object expressing the act of defilement as complete (note absence here of pleonastic *w*, in contrast with 20.1).
13.2)	*Such a person is to be cut off from Israel*	*w*^{ə}*nikr*^{ə}*tā*^{h}: *w*-retentive SC expressing the conclusion of the casuistic sequence.
13.3)	*because the purifying water will not have been cast over him.*	*zōraq*: SC in explanatory clause expressing the act as never having been carried out.
13.4)	*(Therefore) he remains impure:*	*yihye*^{h}: PC in periphrastic verbal phrase, *yaqtulu* expressing the inevitability and the permanency of the state, the stative verbal adjective the state itself.
13.5)	*his impurity (is still) upon him.*	Nominal sentence expressing the final legal situation.
14.1)	*This is the law:*	Nominal sentence functioning to introduce the stipulations for the preparation and use of the water of purification.
14.2)	*When a man dies in a tent,*	*yāmū*^{w}*t*: PC in a marked subordinate clause introducing a case.
14.3)	*anyone who enters the tent, as well as anyone in the tent (when the death occurs), remains ritually impure for seven days.*	*yiṭmāʾ*: PC, stressing continuity of the state, in main clause (complex subject expressed by two tokens of the noun *kol*, the first followed by a substantivized participle, the second by a relative nominal clause).
15)	*As for (the contents of) any vessel without a tight cover, it is ritually impure.*	Nominal sentence (complex subject containing relative nominal clause).
16)	*Anyone*	First element of complex subject (*kol* alone).
16a)	*who, in the open countryside, happens to touch someone who has died by the sword or of natural causes, or a bone, or a grave,*	Relative clause: *yiggaʿ*, PC expressing the eventuality of the case.

[98] This verse is divided as follows because of the two finite verbal clauses, the first functioning as attributive to the substantivized participle, the second as sequential to this participle. Each of the subject phrases of the casuistic formulae in vv. 13–16, 20, and 22 is different, some containing explicit relative clauses with a finite verb, others containing only nominal/participial formulae, others containing both. Only the clauses with finite verbs are analyzed independently here.

	Translation	*Morpho-Syntactic Analysis*
NUMBERS 19		
16 *cont.*)	*shall be unclean for seven days.*	*yiṭmāʾ*: PC, stressing continuity of the state, in (asyndetic) main clause.
17.1)	*They shall take for the person who has become impure some of the 'dust' of the cow that was burned as a sin-offering,*	*w^{ə}lāq^{ə}ḥū^w*: w-retentive SC, 3 m.pl., indefinite subject with stress on the plurality of the actors (contrast following sentence), expressing the legal/ritual remedy for the case.
17.2)	*and then (one of them) shall pour fresh water over it into a container.*	*w^{ə}nātan*: ditto but 3 m.s.
18.1)	*(The actual rite of purification takes place as follows:) A pure person is to take some hyssop*	*w^{ə}lāqaḥ*: ditto but with expressed subject (after next verb).
18.2)	*and dip (it) into the water*	*w^{ə}ṭābal*: ditto.
18.3)	*then sprinkle (it) over the tent, over the vessels, over the persons*	*w^{ə}hizzā^h*: ditto.
18.3a)	*who were there,*	Relative clause: *hāyū^w*, SC expressing complete state.
18.3 *cont.*)	*and over the person who has touched a bone or the body of someone killed by the sword or the body of someone who has died of natural causes or a grave.*	Here it is the prepositional phrase that is expanded (the four categories of items touched are expressed definitely in Hebrew in explicit reference to v. 16).
19.1)	*The pure person is to sprinkle (the water) on the unclean person on the third day then (again) on the seventh day.*	*w^{ə}hizzā^h*: w-retentive SC expressing the continuation of the remedy sequence.
19.2)	*The actual purification from sin will take place on the seventh day*	*w^{ə}ḥiṭṭ^{ə}ʾô^w*: ditto (lit. 'he will unsin him' — the so-called 'privative Piel').[99]
19.3)	*(at which time) (the previously unclean one) shall wash his clothes*	*w^{ə}kibbes*: ditto.
19.4)	*and bathe (his body) in water.*	*w^{ə}rāḥaṣ*: ditto.
19.5)	*He will legally become pure at sun-set.*	*w^{ə}ṭāhēr*: ditto.
20.1)	*(As for) a man*	First element of complex subject (ʾī^{y}š alone).
20.1a)	*who is impure*	Relative clause: *yiṭmāʾ*, PC expressing a sub-case.
20.1b)	*and does not undergo the rite of purification from sin,*	*yitḥaṭṭāʾ*: PC in negative coordinate clause continuing the presentation of the case.
20.1 *cont.*)	*such a person shall be cut off from the congregation,*	*w^{ə}nikr^{ə}tā^h*: w-retentive SC (pleonastic *w*) in main clause.

[99] The semantics of the verb and of the related noun are discussed briefly and with reference to the problems of translation into English in Pardee 1996.

	Translation	Morpho-Syntactic Analysis
NUMBERS 19		
20.2)	*for he will (thereby) have rendered unclean the sanctuary of Yahweh.*	*ṭimmēʾ*: SC in marked explanatory clause expressing the defilement as complete (as in 13.3).[100]
20.3)	*The water of purification will not have been cast over him.*	*zōraq*: SC in (unmarked) explanatory clause expressing the act as never having been carried out (as in 13.3).
20.4)	*He remains an unclean person.*	Asyndetic nominal sentence (contrast PC in 13.6) expressing the final legal situation.
21.1)	*This shall be for them an eternal statute.*	*wᵊhāyᵊtāʰ*: w-retentive SC expressing the continuation of the primary sequence.
21.2)	*The person who has sprinkled the water of purification must wash his clothes.*	*yᵊkabbēs*: PC after fronted (participial) subject expressing a further stipulation regarding the use of the purifying water.
21.3)	*Moreover, anyone who touches the water of purification remains legally impure until sun-set.*	*yiṭmāʾ*: ditto.
22.1)	*Anything*	First element of complex subject (*kol* alone).
22.1a)	*that such an impure person touches*	Relative clause: *yiggaʿ*, PC expressing an act constituting a sub-case.
22.1 *cont.*)	*shall be impure,*	*yiṭmāʾ*: PC in main clause after fronted subject phrase, expressing result of sub-case.
22.2)	*and any person who touches (such an object) remains legally impure until sun-set."*	*tiṭmāʾ*: ditto in coordinate clause wherein the characterization of the subject is by means of a participle rather than by a relative clause with PC.

Abbreviations

C	consonant
f.	feminine
impv.	imperative
m.	masculine
MT	Massoretic text
PC	prefix conjugation
pl.	plural
s.	singular

[100] The two final clauses of this sequence are here in reversed order as compared with v. 13. The two verb forms are nevertheless identical (*ṭimmēʾ* and *wᵊnikrᵊtāʰ*), and the *w*- of *wᵊnikrᵊtāʰ* is thus formally "pleonastic" here. Also, *ṭimmēʾ* is introduced by *kīʸ*, making it a marked explanatory clause, while the *zōraq* clause, which was markedly explanatory in v. 13, is here asyndetic.

SC	suffix conjugation
V	vowel
v(v).	verse(s)

Bibliography

Andersen, T. David

2000 "The Evolution of the Hebrew Verbal System." *Zeitschrift für Althebraistik* 13: 1–66.

Andrason, Alexander

2010 "The Akkadian *iprus* from the Unidirectional Perspective." *Journal of Semitic Studies* 55: 325–45.

Bailey, Nicholas A., and Stephen H. Levinsohn

1992 "The Function of Preverbal Elements in Independent Clauses in the Hebrew Narrative of Genesis." *Journal of Translation and Textlinguistics* 5: 179–207.

Barkay, Gabriel; Marilyn J. Lundberg; Andrew G. Vaughn; and Bruce Zuckerman

2004 "The Amulets from Ketef Hinnom: A New Edition and Evaluation." *Bulletin of the American Schools of Oriental* Research 334: 41–71.

Bartsch, Renate

1995 *Situations, Tense, and Aspect: Dynamic Discourse Ontology and the Semantic Flexibility of Temporal System in German and English.* Groningen-Amsterdam Studies in Semantics 13. Berlin: Mouton de Gruyter.

Binnick, Robert I.

2002–2006 "The Project on Annotated Bibliography of Contemporary Research in Tense, Grammatical Aspect, Aktionsart, and Related Areas." http://www.scar.utoronto.ca/~binnick/TENSE/

Blau, Joshua

2010 *Phonology and Morphology of Biblical Hebrew.* Linguistic Studies in Ancient West Semitic 2. Winona Lake: Eisenbrauns.

Bordreuil, Pierre, and Dennis Pardee

1990 "Le papyrus du marzeah." *Semitica* 38: 49–68.

2000 "Nouvel examen du 'Papyrus du Marzeaḥ.'" *Semitica* 50: 224–26.

2004 *Manuel d'ougaritique.* 2 volumes. Geuthner manuels. Paris: Geuthner.

2009 *A Manual of Ugaritic.* Linguistic Studies in Ancient West Semitic 3. Winona Lake: Eisenbrauns.

Bybee, Joan L.; Revere D. Perkins; and William Pagliuca

1994 *The Evolution of Grammar: Tense, Aspect, and Modality in the Languages of the World.* Chicago: University of Chicago Press.

Chung, Sandra, and Alan Timberlake

1995 "Tense, Aspect, and Mood." In *Language Typology and Syntactic Description*, Volume 3: *Grammatical Categories and the Lexicon*, edited by Timothy Shopen, pp. 202–58. Cambridge: Cambridge University Press.

Claassen, Walther T.

1983 "Speaker-Oriented Functions of *kî* in Biblical Hebrew." *Journal of Northwest Semitic Languages* 11: 29–46.

Comrie, Bernard

1976 *Aspect: An Introduction to the Study of Verbal Aspect and Related Problems.* Cambridge Textbooks in Linguistics. Cambridge: Cambridge University Press.

Cook, John A.

2001 "The Hebrew Verb — A Grammaticalization Approach." *Zeitschrift für Althebraistik* 14: 117–43.

2006 "The Finite Verbal Forms in Biblical Hebrew Do Express Aspect." *Journal of the Ancient Near Eastern Society* 30: 21–35.

Creason, Stuart

1995 Semantic Classes of Hebrew Verbs: A Study of *Aktionsart* in the Hebrew Verbal System. Ph.D. dissertation, University of Chicago.

Davies, Philip R.

1992 *In Search of "Ancient Israel."* Journal for the Study of the Old Testament Supplement Series 148. Sheffield: Journal for the Study of the Old Testament Press.

DeCaen, Vincent J. J.

1995 On the Placement and Interpretation of the Verb in Standard Biblical Hebrew Prose. Ph.D. dissertation, University of Toronto.

Disse, Andreas

1998 *Informationsstruktur im Biblischen Hebräisch. Sprachwissenschaftliche Grundlagen und exegetische Konsequenzen einer Korpusuntersuchung zu den Büchern Deuteronomium, Richer und 2 Könige.* Arbeiten zu Text und Sprache im Alten Testament 56/1. St. Ottilien: EOS Verlag.

Dobbs-Allsopp, F. W.

2000 "Biblical Hebrew Statives and Situation Aspect." *Journal of Semitic Studies* 45: 21–53.

2004–07 "(More) on Performatives in Semitic." *Zeitschrift für Althebraistik* 17–20: 36–81.

Dobbs-Allsopp, F. W.; J. J. M. Roberts; C. L. Seow; and Richard E. Whitaker

2005 *Hebrew Inscriptions: Texts from the Biblical Period of the Monarchy with Concordance.* New Haven: Yale University Press.

Endo, Yoshinobu

1996 *The Verbal System of Classical Hebrew in the Joseph Story: An Approach from Discourse Analysis.* Studia Semitica Neerlandica 32. Assen: Van Gorcum.

Fassberg, Steven E.

2006 "Sequences of Positive Commands in Biblical Hebrew: לֵךְ אֱמֹר, לֵךְ וְאָמַרְתָּ, הָלוֹךְ וְאָמַרְתָּ " In *Biblical Hebrew in Its Northwest Semitic Setting: Typological and Historical Perspectives*, edited by Steven E. Fassberg and Avi Hurvitz, pp. 51–64. Jerusalem: Magnes; Winona Lake: Eisenbrauns.

Fokkelman, Jan P.

1991 "Iterative Forms of the Classical Hebrew Verb: Exploring the Triangle of Style, Syntax, and Text Grammar." In *Studies in Hebrew and Aramaic Syntax: Presented to Professor J. Hoftijzer on the Occasion of His Sixty-Fifth Birthday*, edited by K. Jongeling, Hendrika L. Murre-Van den Berg, and Lucas van Rompay, pp. 38–55. Leiden: Brill.

Gentry, Peter J.

1998 "The System of the Finite Verb in Classical Biblical Hebrew." *Hebrew Studies* 39: 7–39.

Gesenius, Wilhelm; Emil Kautzsch; and Arthur E. Cowley

1910 *Gesenius' Hebrew Grammar.* Edited by E. Kautzsch, translated by A. E. Cowley. 2nd English edition. Oxford: Clarendon Press.

Gianto, Agustinus

1997 Review of *The Verbal System of Classical Hebrew in the Joseph Story: An Approach from Discourse Analysis*, by Yoshinobu Endo. *Catholic Biblical Quarterly* 59/2: 346–47.

Greenstein, Edward L.

2006 "Forms and Functions of the Finite Verb in Ugaritic Narrative Verse." In *Biblical Hebrew in Its Northwest Semitic Setting: Typological and Historical Perspectives*, edited by Steven E. Fassberg and Avi Hurvitz, pp. 75–102. Jerusalem: Magnes Press; Winona Lake: Eisenbrauns.

Groß, Walter

1987 *Die Pendenskonstrucktion im Biblischen Hebräisch: Studien zum althebräischen Satz I.* Arbeiten zu Text und Sprache im Alten Testment 27. St. Ottilien: EOS Verlag.

Haspelmath, Martin

1995 "The Converb as a Cross-linguistically Valid Category." In *Converbs in Cross-linguistic Perspective: Structure and Meaning of Adverbial Verb Forms — Adverbial Participles, Gerunds*, edited by Martin Haspelmath and Ekkehard König, pp. 1–55. Empirical Approaches to Language Typology 13. Berlin: Mouton de Gruyter.

Heimerdinger, Jean-Marc
1999 *Topic, Focus and Foreground in Ancient Hebrew Narratives*. Journal for the Study of the Old Testament Supplement Series 295. Sheffield: Sheffield Academic Press.

Hetzron, Robert
1969 "The Evidence for Perfect **yáqtul* and Jussive **yaqtúl* in Proto-Semitic." *Journal of Semitic Studies* 14: 1–21.

Hollebrandse, Bart; Angeliek van Hout; and Co Vet
2005 *Crosslinguistic Views on Tense, Aspect and Modality*. Cahiers Chronos 13. Amsterdam: Rodopi.

Huehnergard, John
1995 *A Grammar of Akkadian*. Harvard Semitic Museum Studies 45. Atlanta: Scholars Press.

Hurvitz, Avi
1997 "The Historical Quest for 'Ancient Israel' and the Linguistic Evidence of the Hebrew Bible and Some Methodological Observations." *Vetus Testamentum* 47: 301–15.

Jongeling, Karel
1991 "On the VSO Character of Hebrew." In *Studies in Hebrew and Aramaic Syntax Presented to Professor J. Hoftijzer on the Occasion of His Sixty-fifth Birthday*, edited by K. Jongeling, Hendrika L. Murre-Van den Berg, and Lucas van Rompay, pp. 103–11. Leiden: Brill.

Joosten, Jan
1989 "The Predicative Participle in Biblical Hebrew." *Zeitschrift für Althebraistik* 2: 128–59.
1997a "The Indicative System of the Biblical Hebrew Verb and Its Literary Exploitation." In *Narrative Syntax and the Hebrew Bible: Papers of the Tilburg Conference 1996*, edited by Ellen van Wolde, pp. 51–71. Biblical Interpretation Series 29. Leiden: Brill.
1997b "Workshop: Meaning and Use of the Tenses in 1 Samuel 1." In *Narrative Syntax and the Hebrew Bible: Papers of the Tilburg Conference 1996*, edited by Ellen van Wolde, pp. 72–83. Biblical Interpretation Series 29. Leiden: Brill.
2002 "Do the Finite Verbal Forms in Biblical Hebrew Express Aspect?" *Journal of the Ancient Near Eastern Society* 29: 49–70.
2006 "The Disappearance of Iterative WEQATAL in the Biblical Hebrew Verbal System." In *Biblical Hebrew in Its Northwest Semitic Setting: Typological and Historical Perspectives*, edited by Steven E. Fassberg and Avi Hurvitz, pp. 135–47. Jerusalem: Magnes Press; Winona Lake: Eisenbrauns.

Joüon, Paul
1923 *Grammaire de l'hébreu biblique*. Rome: Institut Biblique Pontifical.

Kawashima, Robert S.
2004 *Biblical Narrative and the Death of the Rhapsode*. Bloomington: Indiana University Press.
2010 "'Orphaned' Converted Tense Forms in Classical Biblical Hebrew Prose." *Journal of Semitic Studies* 55: 11–35.

Kedar-Kopfstein, Benjamin
1977 "Semantic Aspects of the Pattern Qôtel." *Hebrew Annual Review* 1: 155–76.

Knauf, Ernst A.
1990 "War 'Biblisch-Hebräisch' eine Sprache?" *Zeitschrift für Althebraistik* 3: 11–23.

Lambdin, Thomas O.
1971 *Introduction to Biblical Hebrew*. New York: Scribners.

Levine, Baruch A.
1993 *Numbers 1–20: A New Translation with Introduction and Commentary*. Anchor Bible 4A. New York: Doubleday.

Lindenberger, James M.
2003 *Ancient Aramaic and Hebrew Letters*. 2nd edition. Writings from the Ancient World 14. Atlanta: Society of Biblical Literature.

Long, Gary A.
1999 "The Written Story: Toward Understanding Text as Representation and Function." *Vetus Testamentum* 49: 165–85.

Longacre, Robert E.

1989 *Joseph: A Story of Divine Providence. A Text Theoretical and Textlinguistic Analysis of Genesis 37 and 39–40*. Winona Lake: Eisenbrauns.

1992 "Discourse Perspective on the Hebrew Verb: Affirmation and Restatement." In *Linguistics and Biblical Hebrew*, edited by Walter R. Bodine, pp. 177–89. Winona Lake: Eisenbrauns.

1994 "*Weqatal* Forms in Biblical Hebrew Prose. A Discourse-Modular Approach." In *Biblical Hebrew and Discourse Linguistics*, edited by Robert D. Bergen, pp. 50–98. Winona Lake: Summer Institute of Linguistics/ Eisenbrauns.

Macaulay, R. K. S.

1978 Review of *Aspect: An Introduction to the Study of Verbal Aspect and Related Problems*, by Bernard Comrie. *Language* 54: 416–20.

McCarter, P. Kyle, Jr.

1980 *I Samuel: A New Translation with Introduction, Notes and Commentary*. Anchor Bible 8. New York: Doubleday.

McFall, Leslie

1982 *The Enigma of the Hebrew Verbal System: Solutions from Ewald to the Present Day*. Historic Texts and Interpreters in Biblical Scholarship 2. Sheffield: Almond Press.

Meyer, Esias E.

2001 "The Particle כִּי, a Mere Conjunction or Something More?" *Journal of Northwest Semitic Languages* 27/1: 39–62.

Miller, Cynthia L., editor

1999 *The Verbless Clause in Biblical Hebrew, Linguistic Approaches*. Linguistic Studies in Ancient West Semitic 1. Winona Lake: Eisenbrauns.

Nash, Peter Theodore

1992 The Hebrew Qal Active Participle: A Non-aspectual Narrative Backgrounding Element. Ph.D. dissertation University of Chicago.

Nicacci, Alviero

1994 "On the Hebrew Verbal System." In *Biblical Hebrew and Discourse Linguistics*, edited by Robert D. Bergen, pp. 117–37. Winona Lake: Summer Institute of Linguistics/Eisenbrauns.

Pardee, Dennis

1979 Review of *Hebrew Syntax: An Outline* (2d edition), by Ronald J. Williams. *Journal of Near Eastern Studies* 38: 148.

1981–82 Review of *A Matter of "Life" and "Death": A Study of the Baal-Mot Epic (CTA 4-5-6)*, by Baruch Margalit. *Archiv für Orientforschung* 28: 267–70.

1983a Review of *Recherches sur les inscriptions phéniciennes de Karatepe*, by François Bron. *Journal of Near Eastern Studies* 42: 63–67.

1983b Review of *Hebräisches Perfekt und Imperfekt mit voangehendem* w[e], by Bo Johnson. *Journal of Near Eastern Studies* 42: 161–63.

1983c Review of *Hebrew Verse Structure*, by Michael Patrick O'Connor. *Journal of Near Eastern Studies* 42: 298–301.

1985a Review of *HYH: Bedeutung und Funktion eines hebräischen "Allerweltwortes"; Zugleich ein Beitrag zur Frage des hebräischen Tempussystems*, by Rüdiger Bartelmus. *Catholic Biblical Quarterly* 47: 107–10.

1985b Review of *Arad Inscriptions*, by Yohanan Aharoni, English translation by J. Ben-Or. *Journal of Near Eastern Studies* 44: 67–71.

1988 *Ugaritic and Hebrew Poetic Parallelism: A Trial Cut (ʿnt I and Proverbs 2)*. Supplements to Vetus Testamentum 39. Leiden: Brill.

1989 Review of *Die Pendenskonstruktion im biblischen Hebräisch*, by Walter Groß. *Catholic Biblical Quarterly* 51: 326–29.

1990 Review of *Joseph: A Story of Divine Providence: A Text Theoretical and Textlinguistic Analysis of Genesis 37 and 39–48*, by Robert E. Longacre. *Hebrew Studies* 31: 200–04.

1993a Review of *The Syntax of the Verb in Classical Hebrew Prose*, by Alviero Nicacci. *Journal of Near Eastern Studies* 52: 313–14.

1993b Review of *Modi Ugaritici: Eine morpho-syntaktische Abhandlung über das Modalsystem im Ugaritischen*, by E. Verreet. *Journal of Near Eastern Studies* 52: 314–17.

1993c Review of *Directions in Biblical Hebrew*, edited by Elaine R. Follis. *Journal of Near Eastern Studies* 52: 155–56.

1994 Review of *An Introduction to Biblical Hebrew Syntax*, by Bruce K. Waltke and M. O'Connor. *Journal of Near Eastern Studies* 53: 150–53.

1995 Review of *Studies in Verbal Aspect and Narrative Technique in Biblical Hebrew Prose*, by Mats Eskhult. *Journal of Near Eastern Studies* 54: 64–66.

1996 Review of *Leviticus 1-16: A New Translation with Introduction and Commentary*, by Jacob Milgrom. *Journal of Near Eastern Studies* 55: 300–01.

1997a "Ugaritic." In *The Semitic Languages*, edited by Robert Hetzron, pp. 131–44. London: Routledge.

1997b "Dawn and Dusk: The Birth of the Gracious and Beautiful Gods." In *The Context of Scripture*, Volume 1: *Canonical Compositions from the Biblical World*, edited by William W. Hallo and K. Lawson Younger, pp. 274–83. Leiden: Brill.

1999 Review of *Canaanite in the Amarna Tablets: A Linguistic Analysis of the Mixed Dialect Used by the Scribes from Canaan*, by Anson F. Rainey. *Journal of Near Eastern Studies* 58: 313–17.

2001 Review of *The Anterior Construction in Classical Hebrew*, by Ziony Zevit. *Journal of Near Eastern Studies* 60: 308–12.

2002 "Hebrew Letters." In *The Context of Scripture*, Volume 3: *Archival Documents from the Biblical World*, edited by William W. Hallo and K. Lawson Younger, pp. 77–87. Leiden: Brill.

2003–2004 Review of *Ugaritische Grammatik*, by Joseph Tropper. *Archiv für Orientforschung* online version 50: 1–404.

2004 "Ugaritic." In *Encyclopedia of the World's Ancient Languages*, edited by Roger D. Woodard, pp. 288–318. Cambridge: Cambridge University Press.

Pardee, Dennis, and Robert M. Whiting

1987 "Aspects of Epistolary Verbal Usage in Ugaritic and Akkadian." *Bulletin of the School of Oriental and African Studies* 50: 1–31.

Parker, Simon B.

1997 *Stories in Scripture and Inscriptions: Comparative Studies on Narratives in Northwest Semitic Inscriptions and the Hebrew Bible*. Oxford: Oxford University Press.

Pietsch, Michael

2004–2007 "Einige Überlegungen zur syntaktischen Funktion der *w^{e}qāṭal*-Formen in 2 Kön 23,4–15." *Zeitschrift für Althebraistik* 17–20: 159–77.

Rainey, Anson F.

2003 "The *yaqtul* Preterite in Northwest Semitic." In *Hamlet on a Hill: Semitic and Greek Studies Presented to Professor T. Muraoka on the Occasion of his Sixty-fifth Birthday*, edited by Martin F. J. Baasten and W. T. Van Peursen, pp. 395–407. Orientalia Lovaniensia Analecta 118. Louvain: Peeters.

Reinhart, Tanya

1984 "Principles of Gestalt Perception in the Temporal Organization of Narrative Texts." *Linguistics* 22: 779–809.

Revell, Ernest J.

1984 "Stress and the WAW 'Consecutive' in Biblical Hebrew." *Journal of the American Oriental Society* 104: 437–44.

Rosén, Haiim B.

1969 "Israel Language Policy, Language Teaching and Linguistics." *Ariel* 25: 92–111.

Sanders, Seth L.

2004 "Performative Utterances and Divine Language in Ugaritic." *Journal of Near Eastern Studies* 63: 161–81.

Talstra, Eep

1997 "Tense, Mood, Aspect and Clause Connections in Biblical Hebrew." *Journal of Northwest Semitic Languages* 23/2: 81–103.

Tropper, Josef

1996 "Aramäisches *wyqtl* und hebräisches *wayyiqtol*." *Ugarit-Forschungen* 28: 633–45.

1998a "Althebräisches und semitisches Aspektsystem." *Zeitschrift für Althebraistik* 11: 153–90.

1998b Review of *A Syntactical Study of Verbal Forms Affixed by -n(n) Endings in Classical Arabic, Biblical Hebrew, el-Amarna Akkadian and Ugaritic*, by Tamar Zewi. *Ugarit-Forschungen* 30: 947–48.

2000 *Ugaritische Grammatik*. Alter Orient und Altes Testament 273. Münster: Ugarit-Verlag.

Tropper, Josef, and J.-P. Vita

2005 "Der Energikus an Jussiven im Kanaano-Akkadischen der Amarna-Periode." *Orientalia* 74: 57–64.

van der Merwe, C. H. J.

1997 "Workshop: Text Linguistics and the Strucutre of 1 Samuel 1." In *Narrative Syntax and the Hebrew Bible: Papers of the Tilburg Conference 1996*, edited by Ellen van Wolde, pp. 157–65. Biblical Interpretation Series 29. Leiden: Brill.

Waltke, Bruce; K. Waltke; and M. O'Connor

1990 *An Introduction to Biblical Hebrew Syntax*. Winona Lake: Eisenbrauns.

18

The Syntax of *ʾăšer* and *šeC* — Yet Again

*Naʿama Pat-El, University of Texas at Austin**

1. *Status Quaestionis*

Biblical Hebrew has three attested relative particles: the reflex of the common Semitic relative pronoun, which is mostly found in relics, *ze*; a new form, *ʾăšer*, which is written as an independent form, but shows distinct vocalization as a construct (i.e., dependent) form;[1] and finally another form, *šeC*, which is systematically written as proclitic to a following word and causes gemination. This latter particle appears infrequently in the Bible, but spreads thereafter. While it is widely agreed that *ʾăšer* replaced *ze*, the relationship between *ʾăšer* and *šeC* is less obvious. This relationship will be the subject of the current paper.

There are two major theories regarding the relationship between *ʾăšer* and *šeC*: (a) *šeC* is a reduced form of *ʾăšer*, or (b) *ʾăšer* and *šeC* are unrelated, the latter possibly a borrowing from Akkadian.[2] The nature of *ʾăšer* and *šeC*, and the historical relationship between them, is still hotly debated (Holmstedt 2007). In the last several years, this relationship, as well as the syntax of these particles, has been addressed by a number of scholars from a variety of approaches (e.g., Givón 1991; Holmstedt 2001; 2006; 2007; Huehnergard 2006; Huehnergard and Pat-El 2006; Pat-El 2010).

In a 2006 paper, John Huehnergard suggested that *šeC* is a result of aphaeresis of the glottal stop in *ʾăšer*, and a metanalysis succeeding an assimilation of the final *-r* to a following consonant. This is not a novel idea, but Huehnergard explained the change as a result of known, though sporadic, phonological changes (Boyarin 1976; Huehnergard 2006, pp. 121–22). The process is essentially the following: *ʾăšer#* > **ʾăšer*-C- > **ʾăšeC*-C- > *šeC*-C-. The phonological changes suggested as the basis for this change are not widespread changes, nor are they regular changes in Biblical Hebrew. Therefore, Huehnergard used grammaticalization as a theoretical framework for his reconstruction, pointing to similar processes in other languages, where irregular sound changes caused localized changes (Engish one > an). In other words, the changes involved in the process *ʾăšer* > *šeC* are not assumed to be part of the set of sound changes that underlie Hebrew and are expressed in the Tiberian vocalization of the MT.

In a 2007 paper, which is largely a response to Huehnergard (2006), Robert Holmstedt rejects the proposed connection *ʾăšer* > *šeC*, primarily because the sound changes are ad hoc and would therefore complicate the phonology of the Canaanite languages (2007, p. 190). He is also skeptical about the etymology of *ʾăšer*, because "the evidence does not allow us to trace a sure diachronic path of reanalysis, semantic bleaching, and phonetic reduction for **ʾaṯar* in Hebrew or other Semitic languages; we simply lack the appropriate pieces of the puzzle" (ibid., p. 188). In addition, Holmstedt argues that the grammaticalization of *ʾăšer* to *šeC* did not occur in all the languages where *ʾăšer* is attested (Akkadian, Aramaic, and Ugaritic), a fact that he considers to be a weakness (ibid., p. 190).

* I wish to thank John Huehnergard for helpful comments on an earlier draft. All remaining errors are my own.

[1] The origin of this particle has been connected to a spatial noun, **ʾaṯar*, 'place.'

[2] A comprehensive bibliography and history of research is found in Huehnergard 2006, and partially in Holmstedt 2007.

After rejecting Huehnergard's proposal and any connection between *ʾăšer* and *šeC*, Holmstedt suggests that *šeC* could be a borrowing of the Akkadian relative pronoun *ša*. In order to explain the gemination caused by *šeC* in Hebrew, but not in Akkadian, he postulates that the Akkadian masculine form was similar to the feminine singular relative pronoun *šātu*, that is, it had a long vowel /ā/, which was the result of a compensatory lengthening after a sonorant (ʾ/*n*) had dropped: **šaʾtu/*šaltu/šantu* > *šātu* (ibid., p. 183). The masculine form would therefore have had a consonant to account for the gemination in Hebrew, and the process should be reconstructed as this: **šaʾ/*šal/*šan* > *šā*. According to Holmstedt, "in the absence of any other apparent cognate, it seems not only feasible but likely that Akkadian *ša* is the source for Hebrew *šeC-*" (ibid., p. 183). Holmstedt advocates a solution that is based on regular sound changes (ibid., p. 191) and, when regular sound changes cannot be applied, prefers the solution of language contact.

Holmstedt's objections are, of course, legitimate and need to be addressed before moving on to my own arguments. First and foremost, it is important to understand the role and limitations of historical comparative linguistics. Holmstedt's complaint that we "lack the appropriate pieces of the puzzle" (Holmstedt 2007, p. 188) is exactly where historical linguistics operates through reconstruction. If we had all the pieces of the puzzle, the method to use would be descriptive linguistics. Historical linguistics is a hypothesis very often based on incomplete sets of evidence.[3] Meillet rightly observes that "[t]outefois ce sont des observations isolées, precieuses en ceci qu'elles permettent de se former une idée de la façon dont les langues evoluent, mais dont on n'a jamais l'équivalent pour les périods plus anciennes, et dont one a même très peu d'example encore à l'époque actuelle" (1965, p. 45).[4] Historical linguists are no longer content with merely pointing to a change, but seek to explain *how* and, if at all possible, *why* a certain change occurred (Campbell 1998, p. 5). Thus, sparse or partial attestation is a natural hurdle to deal with in reconstruction, and not a deterrent.

Holmstedt's rejection of the etymology of *ʾăšer* — because not all languages show the changes *ʾaṯar* > *ʾăšer* and *ʾăšer* > *šeC* — should also be dismissed. Not all related languages share every change; if they had, we would not have a language *family*, but rather *a* language.[5] First, innovative features are what set one language family apart from its sister (Hetzron 1976). But even within closely related languages, selective changes, which take part only in some sister languages and even outside the dialect group, may occur. This type of change is referred to as "parallel development." A well-known parallel development in Semitic is the loss of final feminine *-t*, which in Hebrew happened in both the verbal and nominal systems, in Phoenician only in the verbal, and in Aramaic only in the nominal (Blau 1980).[6] In short, a change does not have to be sweeping to constitute a change, and there is no necessity for a language to change in a certain direction, even if its sister language had. Thus, this counter-argument does not hold.

Holmstedt further rejects Huehnergard's suggested *-r* assimilation because it complicates the phonology of Hebrew, while admitting that sporadic changes do occur in Semitic (Holmstedt 2007, p. 190). For example, Holmstedt's own etymology of the Akkadian relative pronoun, outlined above, is ad hoc: *n, l* do not cause compensatory lengthening in Akkadian, and the glottal stop does not cause gemination in Hebrew.[7] Moreover, beyond invoking it as support for Homstedt's language-contact hypothesis, there is no reason to assume that a glottal stop closed an initial syllable in the Akkadian relative pronoun. No other language provides evidence to support such

[3] See Forston regarding the development of the different branches of proto-Indo-European: "The evidence that can confidently be used to evaluate these claims is unfortunately sparse" (2004, p. 11).

[4] This was said in the context of internal reconstruction of French, but the same principles apply to comparative reconstruction (Hock 1986, p. 581).

[5] Holmstedt's doubts regarding the etymology *ʾaṯar* > *ʾăšer* is based on the syntax of *ʾăšer* in Hebrew, which is only attested as a relative particle and never as a noun. Homstedt notes that "[w]e simply lack the necessary data to complete the reconstruction" (2007, p. 181). But this argument is not relevant. The comparative method allows us to reconstruct forms whose history is known only from data gathered in related languages (external reconstruction). Most languages have grammatical forms whose lexical origin has been lost; e.g., the post-positive negation particle in many Neo-Arabic dialects, *-š*, originated from the noun *šayʾ* 'thing' — however, this noun is no longer extant in these dialects. Yet, the etymology of *-š* is certain, thanks to comparative data. Similarly, the Hebrew preposition *ʿēqeb* 'because' is not found as an isolated noun in Hebrew, but the Arabic equivalent *ʿaqibun* 'consequence' is an indication of its previous meaning and function. In short, Holmstedt's objection quoted above is perhaps adequate for isolated languages, like Sumerian, but not for Hebrew, which has multiple well-attested relatives.

[6] See also Rendsburg 1991 for other types of parallel development in Semitic.

[7] An alternative explanation for the gemination in Hebrew is Lambdin's junctural doubling (1971), which he originally postulated to explain the gemination caused by the definite article; as far as I know, junctural doubling has never been suggested as an explanation in this context.

a reconstruction, including Akkadian itself. Since there is very little doubt regarding the origins of the Akkadian relative pronoun,[8] such an alternative unsubstantiated etymology is less than convincing.

Finally, Holmstedt suggests that Hebrew had synchronically three particles of different origin, zV, *ʾăšer*, and *šeC*, but offers no distinction among them (2007, p. 191). Following his own insistence on Occam's Razor (Holmstedt 2001; 2007), one may note that this is hardly the most economical solution.

Although, as was shown above, some of Holmstedt's arguments are not persuasive, the fact that Huehnergard's phonological reconstruction is ad hoc still stands. Holmstedt advocates a strict "no exceptions" rule,[9] while admitting exceptions do occur, whereas Huehnergard relies on grammaticalization to account for the phonological irregularities. So can there be a solution, or will this issue continue to plague Hebrew historical grammar? I suggest that we should look at other aspects of this problem as complementary evidence to tilt the scale.

While the phonological aspects of this problem have by now been thoroughly exhausted, the syntax of the relevant particles has not been sufficiently studied. An investigation of the syntax of these particles, specifically *ʾăšer* and *šeC*, in comparison to one another and to other Semitic languages, may point to the difference among them and subsequently may point to their origin. If indeed their syntax is identical, then Holmstedt's assertion that Hebrew had three relative particles with the same function synchronically stands, along with the difficulties he raised regarding the phonology of Huehnergard's reconstruction. However, if *ʾăšer* and *šeC* differ in their syntax from each other and from other languages, primarily Akkadian, then Holmstedt's proposal should seriously be questioned, along with his language contact solution for *šeC*.

2. Introduction: Marking Nominal Dependency in Semitic

The relative pronoun in Semitic is traced to two proto-forms: *ðV in proto-West Semitic and *θV in proto-East Semitic (Huehnergard 2006; Hasselbach 2007, pp. 22–24). In terms of syntax, both branches of proto-Semitic are in complete agreement; in all the Semitic languages, the so-called relative pronoun may be followed by a sentence, a prepositional phrase or an adverb, or a noun. These elements are thus marked as attributes of a head noun (Pat-El and Treiger 2008). Note the following examples from Akkadian, where the attribute in (1a) is a sentence, (1b) a prepositional phrase, and (1c) a noun:

(1a) Sentence:

Šarru-kīn	*šar*	*māt-im*	***šu***	***Enlil***	***māḫir-a***	***lā***	***iddin-u-šum ...***
Sargon	king.ms.cnst	land-gen	REL.ms.nom	Enlil	rival-acc	Neg.	he.gave-SUB-to him

'Sargon, king of the land, to whom Enlil has given no rival' (RIME 2.1.1.6.)

(1b) Adverb/Preposition:

kaspu	*u-šīpāti*	*gabbi*	***ša***	***itti-ya***	*ana*	*agrūti*	*attadin*
silver	and-wool	all	REL.ms.acc	with-me	to	wages	I.gave

'All the silver and wool with me I gave as wages' (VOS III 19, 12–13, apud Aro 1963, p. 403)

(1c) Noun:

ŠE	***ša***	***Naṣirʾilī***
barley	REL.ms	PN

'The barley of Naṣirʾilī' (OAIC 6:9 Di, apud Hasselbach 2005, p. 163)

[8] Huehnergard 2006, pp. 114–16, and see the extensive bibliography quoted there, starting from the late nineteenth century.

[9] "I suggest following a variation of Occam's razor for historical and comparative linguistics: 'If the apparent connection between two words contains phonetic difficulties, the linguist should look elsewhere for a more economic solution'" (Holmstedt 2007, p. 191).

Several languages have lost some of these patterns during their attested history, and some differentiate among the different patterns. Classical Arabic, for example, has a different form of the relative pronoun for sentential attributes (*lladī*) and nominal attributes (*dū*);[10] both, however, share the same etymon, West Semitic *ðV. Several languages severely restricted or slightly changed the distribution of these patterns. In most Neo-Arabic dialects, for example, it is no longer possible to use the relative pronoun to mark a relationship between two nouns.[11]

3. Hebrew: Three Relative Particles

The Canaanite languages are the only branch that replaced its inherited relative particle in antiquity.[12] The exact etymology and process of change to account for the form *ʾăšer* are irrelevant for the current discussion. Suffice it to note that the new relative particle did not develop from, and is not related to, the original West Semitic relative pronoun *ðV. What is of interest to us is the relationship between this particle and *šeC*.

A question, which is hardly ever addressed, is whether the change of the relative particle zV > *ʾăšer* was followed by, or caused, a change in syntax, or whether the syntax remained unchanged and the change of relative particles was a mere lexical replacement. It is implied in Holmstedt's discussion, as well as in earlier studies, that at least *ʾăšer* and zV have the same syntax. Holmstedt seems to assume that this is also true for *šeC*. If Holmstedt is correct, we would expect all three particles to have the same syntax as well as show a distribution similar to what other Semitic languages have, that is, to introduce attributive sentences, nouns, and prepositions. Let us review the distribution of these particles to make sure this is indeed the case:

(a) Sentence:

ZE:	*hinne*	*ʾĕlōhê-nû*	***ze***	*qiwwînû*	*l-ô*
	here	god.mp-our	REL	hope.pf.1cp	to-him

'Here is our god whom we trust.' (Isa 25:9)

ʾĂŠER:	*hinnə-kā*	*mēt*	*ʿal*	*hā-ʾiššā*	***ʾăšer***	*lāqaḥtā*
	here-you.ms	dead	because	DEF-woman	REL	take.pf.2ms

'You will die on account of the woman you have taken.' (Gen 20:3)

ŠE:	*ʾak*	*ze*	*hay-yôm*	***šeq**-qiwwînū-hû*
	but	DEM.ms	DEF-day	REL-hope.pf.1cp-him

'This is the day we have waited for.' (Lam 2:16)

(b) Adverb/Preposition

ZE:	*tiṣṣəren-nû*	*min*	*had-dôr*	***zû***	*lə ʿôlām*
	protect.impf.2ms-us	from	DEF-generation	REL	for-ever

'You shall protect us from these eternal people.' (Ps 12:8)

ʾĂŠER:	*û-mip-pərî*	*hā-ʿēṣ*	***ʾăšer***	*bə-tôk*	*hag-gān...*	*lōʾ*	*tōʾkəlû*	*mimmen-nû*
	and-from-fruit	DEF-tree	REL	in-inside	DEF-garden	NEG	eat.impf.2mp	from-him

'Do not eat any of the fruit of the tree in the garden.' (Gen 3:3)

[10] Both particles were inflected for gender-number-case in Classical Arabic.

[11] Such dependency is marked either by annexation, or by a genitive exponent, normally based on a noun. Only Moroccan *dyāl* possibly goes back to a relative pronoun, though it is no longer an independent relative (see Brustad 2000, pp. 85–87 for syntax).

[12] The origin of Neo-Arabic *illi* is still debated.

ŠE:	*wə-li-gəmallê-hem*	*ʾên*	*mispār*	*ka-ḥôl*	***še**-ʿal*	*śəpat*	*hay-yām*	*la-rōb*
	and-to-camels-their	NEG	number	as-sand	REL-on	bank.cnst	DEF-sea	to-many

'Their camels are innumerable as the sand on the sea-shore.' (Judg 7:12)

(c) Noun:

ZE:	*hārîm*	*nāzəlû*	*mip-pənê*	*YHWH*	***ze***	*Sinay*
	mountains	melt.pf.3mp	from-face	PN	REL	PN

'Mountains melted before YHWH of Sinai.' (Judg 5:5)

ʾĂŠER:	*lam-môʿēd*	***ʾăšer***	*Šəmûʾēl*
	to.DEF-time	REL	PN

'Samuel's appointed time.' (1 Sam 13:8)

ŠE: NONE

While *ʾăšer*, *ze*, and *šeC* share most of their syntax, the genitive marker is not a function of the particle *šeC*, although it is of *ʾăšer* and zV. The function of *ʾăšer* in 1 Sam 13:8 is not a unique example; the genitival function of *ʾăšer* is attested a number of times. Note the following, where an *ʾăšer* genitival pattern is compared with the more common construct pattern:[13]

5) ʾĂŠER as a Genitive Marker:

hā-rāʿā	*ʾăšer*	*Hădād*		*rāʿat*	*Nābāl*
DEF-evil	REL	PN	Cf.	evil.CNST	PN
'Hadad's mischief' (1 Kgs 11:25)				'Nabal's mischief' (1 Sam 25:39)	
ham-mizrāqôt	*ʾăšer*	*zāhāb*		*mizrəqê*	*zāhāb*
DEF-basins	REL	gold	Cf.	basins.CNST	gold
'The golden basins' (2 Kgs 25:15)				'The golden basins' (2 Chr 4:8)	

It is important to note that the number of genitive clauses with *ʾăšer* far exceeds those with *z-, and thus the absence of the pattern with *šeC* cannot be dismissed as a mere coincidence. Moreover, even after *šeC* pushed *ʾăšer* and *ze* out and became the sole relative particle in post-Biblical Hebrew,[14] it is never attested as a genitive marker. It rather developed a genitive exponent on the basis of the attributive prepositional phrase *šel-l-* > *šel-*.[15]

6) Mishnaic Hebrew:	*hab-bəśāmîm*	*šel*	*nokrîm*
	DEF-perfumes	GEN	foreigners
	'The perfumes of foreigners' (Ber 8:6)		
Qumran Hebrew:[16]	*h-gnwt*	*šl-ʿyn Gdy*	
	DEF-gardens	GEN-En Gedi	
	'The Gardens of En Gedi' (apud Mor §5.27)		

---

[13] For a full discussion of this pattern, see Pat-El 2010. This piece of readily available information is not mentioned in any of the regular Biblical Hebrew grammars, nor in Holmstedt 2002.

[14] Qumran Hebrew normally uses *ʾăšer*, and *šeC* appears there only sporadically. Morag (1988, pp. 160–61) believes that this is an intrinsic feature of Qumran Hebrew, possibly evidence of dialectical differentiation, while Qimron (1986, p. 82) claims that *šeC* was deemed inappropriate for literary style, but was in fact a part of the language.

[15] Mor (2009, pp. 247–48) notes that in Qumran, the second noun is always definite (either a definite noun or a pronoun). Mor emphasizes that although *š-l* is similar in some aspects to Aramaic *dīl-*, there are some substantial syntactic differences between them. He concludes that the syntax of *š-l* is a typical Qumran development and not an Aramaism (ibid., p. 285).

[16] The genitive marker *šl* is not necessarily attached to a following noun.

So it seems that *ʾăšer* shares its syntax with the old relative particle *ze*; this indicates lexical replacement, as has been assumed by many linguists. Since many Semitic languages use their relative particle for the three patterns discussed above, the existence of *ʾăšer* and *ze* in similar patterns is hardly surprising. It should be expected. The particle *šeC*, however, shows fewer patterns than both of them. The absence of any attestation of *šeC* as a marker of possession is significant. If *šeC* cannot mark possession, it cannot possibly be a borrowing from Akkadian, where *ša-* is regularly used for this function (see example 1c above). There is no scenario that might explain why *šeC* was borrowed into Hebrew without a prominent part of its syntax.

Other languages in the vicinity of Hebrew, most prominently Aramaic,[17] also regularly use their bare relative particle to mark possession, yet Late Biblical Hebrew and post-Biblical Hebrew, which show many syntactic Aramaisms, have not been influenced by this feature (Mor 2009, p. 285). Moreover, two etymologies have been offered for *šeC* (Huehnergard's *ʾăšer* > *šeC*; Holmstedt's Akk. *ša* > *šeC*), under both of which we would expect *šeC* to have a genitive function. But this function is not attested. So how can this distribution of *šeC* be explained? And what can it possibly tell us about the history and origin of *šeC*?

4. Syntactic Reduction

I suggest that the situation observed above is a likely consequence of phonological and syntactic reduction of a function word. This phenomenon is well known cross-linguistically. One of the most famous examples is the phonological and syntactic reduction of verbal negation in English.

As Zwicky and Pullum noted in their 1983 paper, the loss of independent status has distributional consequences. They had observed that while the English verbal negation NOT can negate non-finite verbs or clitic forms of verbs, the reduced form -N'T is highly selective: it can be attached only to full-form finite auxiliary verbs. Semantically NOT and -N'T are equivalent, and they obviously share the same etymon; but syntactically -N'T covers only a part of the functions of NOT:

7) Syntactic Erosion: English *not* and *-n't*

(a) negating non-finite verbs:

i. *Would the police have not been informed?*

ii. ***Would the police haven't been informed?*

(b) negating clitic verbal forms:

i. *I'd not be doing this unless I had to.*

ii. ***I'dn't be doing this unless I had to.*

BUT: *I wouldn't be doing this unless I had to.*

Similarly, I argue, *šeC* is a reduced form of *ʾăšer*, both phonologically and syntactically, and thus shares only a part of its syntax. This scenario is far more reasonable and better documented than the borrowing of a function word without a significant part of its syntax.

One may justifiably wonder, however, why a reduced form *šeC* should be excluded from marking genitive relations? After all, in Syriac *də-*, a phonologically reduced form of *dī*, is perfectly capable of marking genitive relation; in fact nothing in the distribution of the Aramaic relative particle had changed due to this development:

[17] Several linguists have claimed that the function of Akkadian *ša* as a genitive exponent influenced Aramaic *dī* (Kutscher 1971; Kaufman 1974). I strongly disagree (Pat-El 2008), but this is an indication of how prominent and widespread this function of *ša-* is.

8) Aramaic: phonological reduction without syntactic reduction.

(a) Qumran Aramaic (Middle A): *ḥzwʾ* **dy** *lylyʾ*
vision REL night
'dream' (1Q20: 21.8)

(b) Syriac (Late A):[18] *ləbūšē* *ṭābē* ***də**-gabrē*
clothes good REL-men
'fine male attire' (Bar Daiṣan 46:2)

A possible reason for the difference between Hebrew and Aramaic is the nature of their relative pronouns. The Semitic *ðV pronoun is a bound form, i.e., it is the head in a construct pattern.[19] When the Canaanite languages replaced their original pronoun with a nominal form, it too had a bound form (Huehnergard 2006, p. 121). *ŠeC* appears very early after this innovation. Unlike *ʾăšer*, which has a clear construct form, *šeC* is not formally a construct, but rather a clitic, and so perhaps was not capable of functioning as a head in a construct pattern. But, as was already mentioned above, there is no necessity for a change to occur. The fact that one language shows phonological reduction alongside syntactic reduction does not necessitate such a change in every case of phonological reduction.

A similar syntactic reduction, though without a phonological reduction, as is argued for Hebrew, is also attested in Classical Arabic. The original relative pronoun *ḏū* is attested as a genitive marker, but the innovative one *llāḏī*, although it is genetically derived from *ḏū*, is never used to mark genitive, because it is not a bound form:

(9) Arabic: Innovation and Syntactic Reduction

(a) Sentence:

ṯumma *ʾinna* *waladay-hi* ***llaḏayni*** *qatalā-hu* *fī Ninwā* *harabā*
then Adv child.m.du.obl-his REL.m.du.obl. kill.pf.3md-him in Ninwe flee.pf.3md
'Then, his children, who killed him in Nineveh, fled.'

(b) Adverb/Preposition:

ʾal-kaʾsu ***llatī*** *fī* *yadi-ka*
DEF-cup.fs.nom REL.fs in hand-your.ms
'The cup in your hand'

(c) Noun:

ḏū *māl-in*
REL.ms.nom wealth-gen.
'Wealthy' (= of wealth)

Again, the forms of the relative pronouns in Arabic, unlike the genitive marker *dū*, are not bound forms. Note the plural *llādīna* and dual *llādāni*; had these forms been bound, their form should have been ***llādī* and ***llādā*.[20] The current form of these pronouns is an independent form, not a construct, which means that their syntax is different from that of *ḏū*, which is a construct form.

[18] The vowel of the relative particle in Syriac is conditioned on the following syllabic structure: *a* before #CC, and *ə* before #CV.

[19] Semitic is typologically a head-marked language (Nichols 1986).

[20] Furthermore, the Arabic relative pronouns contain a definite article that excludes a construct morphology.

5. Conclusions

This paper points to a significant syntactic difference between *ʾăšer* and *šeC*-, which proves that it is highly unlikely that *šeC* was borrowed from Akkadian. It is further suggested that this difference is well known from cases of a dependent, phonologically reduced form, which developed from a full independent form. English supplied a classic example, but the phenomenon is attested in other Semitic languages as well.

The paper did not address the issue of grammaticalization and the possibility of the phonological changes suggested by Huehnergard (2006), but rather suggested that the syntactic evidence supports a connection between *ʾăšer* and *šeC*- and rejects language contact as an explanation.

Bibliography

Allegro, J. M.

1955 "Uses of the Semitic Demonstrative Element z in Hebrew." *Vetus Testamentum* 5/3: 309–12.

Aro, Jussi

1963 "Präpositionale Verbindungen als Bestimmungen des Nomens im Akkadischen." *Orientalia* 32: 395–406.

Blau, Joshua

1980 "The Parallel Development of the Feminine Ending *-at* in Semitic Languages." *Hebrew Union College Annual* 51: 17–28.

Boyarin, Daniel

1976 "The Loss of Final Consonants in Babylonian Jewish Aramaic (BJA)." *Afroasiatic Linguistics* 3/5: 103–07.

Brustad, Kristen E.

2000 *The Syntax of Spoken Arabic: A Comparative Study of Moroccan, Egyptian, Syrian, and Kuwaiti Dialects.* Washington, D.C.: Georgetown University Press.

Campbell, Lyle

1998 *Historical Linguistics: An Introduction.* Cambridge: MIT Press.

Forston, Benjamin W.

2004 *Indo-European Language and Culture.* Blackwell Textbooks in Linguistics 19. Malden: Blackwell.

Givón, T.

1991 "The Evolution of Dependent Clause Morpho-syntax in Biblical Hebrew." In *Approaches to Grammaticalization*, edited by Elizabeth C. Traugott and Bernd Heine, vol. 2, pp. 257–310. Typological Studies in Language 19. Amsterdam: John Benjamins.

Goldenberg, Gideon

1995 "Attribution in the Semitic Languages." *Langues orientales anciennes: philologie et linguistique* 5/6: 1–20.

Hasselbach, Rebecca

2005 *Sargonic Akkadian: A Historical and Comparative Study of the Syllabic Texts.* Wiesbaden: Harrassowitz.

2007 "Demonstratives in Semitic." *Journal of the American Oriental Society* 127/1: 1–27.

Hetzron, Robert

1976 "Two Principles of Genetic Reconstruction." *Lingua* 38: 89–198.

Hock, Hans Henrich

1986 *Principles of Historical Linguistics.* Berlin: Mouton de Gruyter.

Holmstedt, Robert D.

2001 "Headless and Extraposition: Another Look at the Syntax of אשׁר." *Journal of Northwest Semitic Linguistics* 27/1: 1–16.

2002 The Relative Clause in Biblical Hebrew: A Linguistic Analysis. PhD. dissertation submitted to the University of Wisconsin.

2006 "The Story of Ancient Hebrew *ʾăšer*." *Journal of the Ancient Near Eastern Society* 43: 7–26.

2007 "The Etymologies of Hebrew *ʾăšer* and *šeC-*." *Journal of Near Eastern Studies* 66/3: 177–92.

Huehnergard, John

2006 "On the Etymology of the Hebrew Relative *šɛ-*." In *Biblical Hebrew in Its Northwest Semitic Setting: Typological and Historical Perspectives*, edited by Avi Hurvitz and Steven E. Fassberg, pp. 103–25. Winona Lake: Eisenbrauns.

Huehnergard, John, and Naʿama Pat-El

2006 "Some Aspects of the Cleft in Semitic Languages." In *Studies in Semitic and General Linguistics in Honor of Gideon Goldenberg*, edited by Tali Bar and Eran Cohen, pp. 325–42. Alter Orient und Altes Testament 334. Münster: Ugarit-Verlag.

Kaufman, Stephen A.

1974 *The Akkadian Influences on Aramaic*. Assyriological Studies 19. Chicago: University of Chicago Press.

Kutscher, Edward Y.

1971 *A History of Aramaic*. Jerusalem: Akademon. [In Hebrew]

Lambdin, Thomas O.

1971 "The Junctural Origin of the West Semitic Definite Article." In *Near Eastern Studies in Honor of William Foxwell Albright*, edited by H. Goedicke, pp. 315–33. Baltimore: Johns Hopkins Press.

Meillet, Antoine

1965 *Linguistique historique et linguistique générale*, Volume 1. Collection Linguistique publiée par la Société de Linguistique de Paris 8. Paris: Champion.

Mor, Uri

2009 The Grammar of the Epigraphic Hebrew Documents from Judaea between the First and the Second Revolts. Ph.D. dissertation submitted to Ben Gurion University, Beer-Sheva. [In Hebrew]

Morag, Shelomo

1988 "Qumran Hebrew: Some Typological Observations." *Vetus Testamentum* 38: 148–64.

Nichols, Johanna

1986 "Head-Marking and Dependent-Marking Grammar." *Language* 62/1: 56–119.

Pat-El, Naʿama

2008 "The Proleptic Genitive in Aramaic: A Re-evaluation." A talk delivered at the American Oriental Society annual meeting in Chicago, IL, March 2008.

2010 "On Periphrastic Genitive Constructions in Biblical Hebrew." *Hebrew Studies* 51: 43–48.

Pat-El, Naʿama, and Alexander Treiger

2008 "On Adnominalization of Prepositional Phrases and Adverbs in Semitic." *Zeitschrift der Deutschen Morgenländischen Gesellschaft* 158/2: 265–352.

Qimron, Elisha

1986 *The Hebrew of the Dead Sea Scrolls*. Harvard Semitic Studies 29. Atlanta: Scholars Press.

Rendsburg, Gary A.

1991 "Parallel Developments in Mishnaic Hebrew, Colloquial Arabic, and Other Varieties of Spoken Semitic." In *Semitic Studies: In Honor of Wolf Leslau on the Occasion of His Eighty-Fifth Birthday*, edited by Alan S. Kaye, vol. 2, pp. 1265–77. Wiesbaden: Harrassowitz.

Zwicky, Arnold M., and Geoffrey K. Pullum

1983 "Cliticization vs. Inflection: English *N'T*." *Language* 59/3: 502–13.

19

Late Biblical Hebrew in the Book of Haggai

*Gary A. Rendsburg, Rutgers University**

Among the venerable and time-honored methodologies in the field of biblical studies specifically, ancient Near Eastern studies generally, and philology more broadly is the application of diachronic linguistic analysis to the texts at hand. Thus, already in the nineteenth century, or the early twentieth century at the latest, scholars had distinguished among Old Akkadian, Old Babylonian, and Late Babylonian (in addition to the Assyrian dialects); Old Egyptian, Middle Egyptian, and Late Egyptian; Old Latin and Classical Latin (in addition to Vulgar Latin); Old Chinese and Middle Chinese; and so on.

As intimated in the opening sentence above, the world of biblical studies participated in this trend, with the major finding differentiating between Standard Biblical Hebrew (SBH) and Late Biblical Hebrew (LBH). In the words of one classical reference work, "Even in the language of the Old Testament, notwithstanding its general uniformity, there is noticeable a certain progress from an earlier to a later stage. Two periods, though with some reservations, may be distinguished: the *first*, down to the end of the Babylonian exile; and the *second*, after the exile" (GKC, 12). This judgment in the field of Hebrew studies has been more recently ensconced in the two standard histories of the Hebrew language, by E. Y. Kutscher (1982, pp. 12, 45, 81–84) and by Angel Sáenz-Badillos (1993, pp. 112–29).

A challenge to this approach has been introduced of late through the work of Ian Young, Robert Rezetko, and Martin Ehrensvärd. These scholars argue that seeing SBH and LBH "as two successive chronological phases of BH is incompatible with the evidence." Rather, they aver, "a better model sees LBH as merely one style of Hebrew in the Second Temple period and quite possibly First Temple period also. 'Early' BH [= SBH] and 'Late' BH, therefore, do not represent different chronological periods in the history of BH, but instead represent co-existing styles of literary Hebrew throughout the biblical period." Which is to say, "these two general language styles, EBH and LBH, are best taken as representing two tendencies among scribes of the biblical period: conservative and non-conservative" — which is to say, not as successive chronological stages of the language, as per the dominant approach.[1]

---

* It is my great pleasure to dedicate this article to my friend, colleague, and (on one occasion) co-author, John Huehnergard, who has done so much to place the field of Semitic studies at the center of the humanities and whose own humanity and good cheer are among his most enduring traits. I take the opportunity to thank Shalom Holtz (himself a student of our jubilarian during his undergraduate career; see Holtz 2001, p. 241 n. *) for his very insightful comments on an earlier version of this article. We had the good fortune of presenting our somewhat interrelated studies at the same panel during the fifteenth World Congress of Jewish Studies, Jerusalem, August 2009, with Holtz's research already in print (see below, n. 21) and with mine now included herein. Finally, it is my pleasant duty to thank the Oxford Centre for Hebrew and Jewish Studies at Yarnton Manor for granting me visiting scholar status and for providing the perfect environment in which to conduct research. It was during my residency at Yarnton Manor during Michaelmas Term 2010 that the present study was completed.

[1] For the direct quotations, see Young, Rezetko, and Ehrensvärd 2008, vol. 1, p. 361. For the most recent statements, see Young 2009b and Rezetko 2009, with the former essay representing a fine summary of the findings of the co-authored 2008 book. As an aside, note that Young, Rezetko, and Ehrensvärd use the term EBH (Early Biblical Hebrew) as the equivalent of SBH (Standard Biblical Hebrew) employed by most scholars, myself included (see also Ben Zvi 2009, p. 269 n. 1). For the periodization of ancient Hebrew, see Kutscher 1982, p. 12, and Sáenz-Badillos 1993, p. 52.

This assertion thereby allows Young, Rezetko, and Ehrensvärd to claim that certain books of the Persian period are written in "Early" BH (see below for sample statements), and by extension to claim that books written in SBH and hence traditionally dated to the First Temple period (for example, virtually all of Genesis through Kings) may be dated to the Persian period as well.[2] I have already voiced my opinion on the subject (Rendsburg 2003; 2006), siding with those scholars who adhere to the traditional scholarly methodology, embodied most of all in the work of Avi Hurvitz.[3] There is much more work to be done, however, in order to demonstrate that the conclusions drawn by Young, Rezetko, and Ehrensvärd are incorrect, based on a misinterpretation of the data.

The present essay will expound the point vis-à-vis the book of Haggai, dated by all responsible scholars to the early part of the Persian period, around 520–500 B.C. Haggai is a parade example for the Young-Rezetko-Ehrensvärd thesis, since they contend that this short book of two chapters is devoid of LBH features, even though it is written during the (early) post-exilic period. The following statements are illustrative:[4] "undisputed postexilic texts, including Haggai, Zechariah, and Malachi, and probably also Isaiah 40–66 and Joel, *lack* characteristic LBH features, and instead, when the opportunities arise, they *use* linguistic features that are characteristic of EBH texts" (1.56; see also 1.87); "We certainly have undisputed postexilic texts written in EBH (e.g., Haggai-Malachi)" (1.56); "EBH continued in the postexilic period, as demonstrated by the EBH language of Haggai, Zechariah and Malachi, but also II–III Isaiah and Joel" (1.141); and "However, there are very few good LBH candidates in Haggai and Malachi" (2.68).[5] As the evidence below will make clear, there are ample lexical and grammatical LBH traits present in the book of Haggai; these features collectively constitute sufficient evidence to refute the aforecited comments by Young, Rezetko, and Ehrensvärd.[6] I anticipate my conclusion: no writer of the Persian period could write in pre-exilic Hebrew any longer; it was simply beyond his/her ability to do so.

Before proceeding to the specific LBH characteristics, it is apposite to mention the recent dissertation of Seoung-Yun Shin (2007), written under Hurvitz's guidance, to be cited freely below.[7] Note, however, that this work was devoted to Haggai, Zechariah, and Malachi as a collective unit, representing the three prophets of the early Persian period, plus it dealt with lexical features only. Since Haggai is the smallest of these three books, only a very few traits were recognized in its two chapters. Not only do I identify several more LBH lexemes in what follows, but I also deal with grammatical features and further expand the discussion in the direction of phraseology, syntax, and poetic elements.

I begin with a few basic grammatical points, to set the stage.

I. The coordinating particle הֵ֣ן 'if' appears in Hag 2:12:

הֵ֣ן ׀ יִשָּׂא־אִ֨ישׁ בְּשַׂר־קֹ֜דֶשׁ בִּכְנַ֣ף בִּגְד֗וֹ וְנָגַ֣ע בִּ֠כְנָפוֹ אֶל־הַלֶּ֨חֶם וְאֶל־הַנָּזִ֜יד וְאֶל־הַיַּ֧יִן
וְאֶל־שֶׁ֛מֶן וְאֶל־כָּל־מַאֲכָ֖ל הֲיִקְדָּ֑שׁ וַיַּעֲנ֧וּ הַכֹּהֲנִ֛ים וַיֹּאמְר֖וּ לֹֽא׃

> 'If a man carries sacrificial flesh in the fold of his garment, and with his fold touches the bread or the stew or the wine or oil or any food, will it [sc. any of the foodstuffs] become holy? And the priests answered and said, "No."'

The particle הֵ֣ן 'if' is well known from Aramaic (e.g., it appears sixteen times in Biblical Aramaic and throughout Egyptian Aramaic [BDB: 1090; Muraoka and Porten 1998, p. 94]); it is attested elsewhere in BH in Lev 25:20, Jer 2:10, 3:1, Prov 11:31, 2 Chr 7:13 (two times). Lev 25:20 appears in an Israelian pericope (see Rendsburg 2008), while Prov 11:31 occurs in a book replete with Israelian Hebrew features (Ginsberg 1982, pp. 35–36; Chen 2000).

---

[2] The latter contention, in turn, serves to bolster the allegations of other scholars (most prominently, N.-P. Lemche, T. L. Thompson, and P. R. Davies) who have dated virtually the entire biblical corpus to the Persian if not Hellenistic period. Note, however, that these scholars completely ignore the linguistic evidence, which remains the most objective criterion for the dating of biblical texts. See the perceptive comment of Joosten (2005, p. 328): "Linguistic data are no longer expected, it seems, to play a part within the historical-critical approach."

[3] The most important works are the two books: Hurvitz 1972a and Hurvitz 1982. Among the more recent articles, see Hurvitz 2006.

[4] Quotations from Young, Rezetko, and Ehrensvärd 2008 — page numbers are indicated in the body of the article.

[5] See also Ehrensvärd 2003, p. 185: "It seems fair, then, to regard Isaiah 40–66, Joel, Haggai, Zechariah, and Malachi as EBH texts; they have their (expected) share of features that *may* belong to LBH, and no clear LBH features."

[6] In addition, note that Young, Rezetko, and Ehrensvärd also err regarding Isaiah 40–66, which is replete with LBH features, for which see the convenient list compiled in Paul 2008, vol. 1, pp. 31–33.

[7] I am grateful to Dr. Shin for providing me with a copy of his dissertation.

The twofold use of הֵן 'if' in Jeremiah may reflect the Benjaminite dialect that characterizes this book, or it may be due to Aramaic influence already in late First Temple times (see Smith 2003). The presence of this form in Judean texts of the Persian period, namely, Hag 2:12 and 2 Chr 7:13 (alongside אִם later in the verse), is plainly due to Aramaic influence.

II. SBH retains the distinction between עַד 'until' and עוֹד 'still, while,' whereas Aramaic uses only עַד for the range of meanings 'until, still, while, during' (note, for example, Dan 6:8, 13 עַד יוֹמִין תְּלָתִין 'during [the next] thirty days'; the Targumic use of עַד to render עוֹד; etc.). The employment of עַד 'still, while' for expected עוֹד occurs in the Hebrew portions of the Bible in 2 Kgs 9:22 and Ps 141:10, as an Israelian Hebrew trait in these northern compositions (Rendsburg 2002, pp. 116–17); in Judg 3:26 and 1 Sam 14:19, in passages concerning Benjaminite heroes (Ehud and Saul, respectively) and thus reflecting the Benjaminite dialect; and in the LBH texts Jon 4:2, Job 1:18, and Neh 7:3,[8] under Aramaic influence, in addition to our relevant text, Hag 2:19:[9]

הַעְוֹד הַזֶּרַע בַּמְּגוּרָה וְעַד־הַגֶּפֶן וְהַתְּאֵנָה וְהָרִמּוֹן וְעֵץ הַזַּיִת לֹא נָשָׂא

> 'Indeed the seed is still in the granary, and the vine and the fig and the pomegranate and the olive tree still has not borne fruit.'[10]

III. Twice in Haggai (1:5, 7) we encounter the idiom שִׂים לֵב 'place (one's) heart' > 'consider, pay heed, pay mind' followed by the preposition עַל, in the following verbatim expression:

'pay mind to your ways' שִׂימוּ לְבַבְכֶם עַל־דַּרְכֵיכֶם

Normally in BH this idiom governs the preposition -לְ, (as in Deut 32:46; 1 Sam 9:20; and Ezek 40:4; 44:5), or the preposition אֶל (as in Exod 9:21; 1 Sam 25:25; 2 Sam 18:3; Job 2:3, 34:14). Also germane is the semantically equivalent idiom שִׁית לֵב, which governs the preposition -לְ (in Exod 7:23; 2 Sam 13:20; Jer 31:21; Ps 48:14; Prov 22:17; 27:23), and the preposition אֶל (in Job 7:17). Against all these cases stand the two aforecited Haggai passages and only one other instance with the preposition עַל, namely, Job 1:8, within the LBH prose prologue.[11] This shift from SBH שִׂים (שִׁית) לֵב לְ-/אֶל to LBH שִׂים לֵב עַל, with no apparent change in meaning, is part of the larger picture of the increased use of the preposition עַל during the Persian period in a wide variety of contexts (most likely due to Aramaic influence) — as illustrated by several idioms studied by Hurvitz (1974, pp. 23, 25–26). In fact, the Aramaic nature of this idiom is detectable via the translation technique reflected in Targum Yonatan, which uses עַל to render the SBH idiom with -לְ (in 1 Sam 9:20; 25:25; 2 Sam 18:3), and in the Targum to Job, which does likewise when it translates Job 2:3.

IV. The form הַרְבֵּה 'much, greatly,' which originates as a Hiphʿil infinitival form from the root רבה, serves as an adverb throughout the history of the Hebrew language. Two developments transpire in LBH: (a) the word itself is used much more frequently (thirty times [Jonah once, Haggai twice, Qohelet fifteen times,[12] Ezra–Nehemiah six times, Chronicles six times], out of a total of forty-nine occurrences in the Bible), and (b) the word undergoes substantivization.[13]

---

[8] On the Job and Nehemiah passages, with the specific usage of עַד + participle, see Hurvitz 1974, pp. 26–28. Since I deduce another LBH feature in the prose framework of Job (see immediately below, no. III), it is appropriate to mention the recent challenge to Hurvitz's position by Young (2009a) — even if I side with Hurvitz against Young on the matter.

[9] Another factor is at play in two of these passages, namely, the employment of morphological variation, as described by Ratner (1992). Note how עַד in Job 1:18 parallels עוֹד in Job 1:16, 17; and observe the presence of both forms in Hag 2:19 — though such variation is possible in these late texts only because of the neologistic usage of עַד 'still, while' as part of the Aramaic impact on LBH. See further n. 11 below.

[10] For the use of the interrogative marker -הֲ (in this case -הַ before the *ʿayin* in עוֹד) with an exclamatory nuance, see Joüon and Muraoka 1991, pp. 609–10.

[11] Note that the SBH idiom can continue in late texts, such as Job 2:3, but that the LBH idiom occurs *only* in late texts, such as Job 1:8. This allows the author of the prose prologue in Job to employ morphological variation (see above, n. 9), with the two expressions in Job 1:8, 2:3, using different prepositions — though once more this specific application of this technique is feasible only because the new usage is now available.

[12] For discussion, see Schoors 2004, pp. 263–66.

[13] I am grateful to Jan Joosten for drawing this feature to my attention.

The two occurrences in Haggai (see the passages below) represent both of these developments, though it is the process of substantivization that attracts our attention here.

1:6 זְרַעְתֶּם הַרְבֵּה וְהָבֵא מְעָט
'you have sown much and harvested little'

1:9 פָּנֹה אֶל־הַרְבֵּה וְהִנֵּה לִמְעָט
'you have expected much, and behold a little'

In both of these passages,[14] the word הַרְבֵּה no longer functions as an adverb, but now appears as a noun, with the connotation 'great quantity,' especially in contrast to its opposite member מְעַט (pausal מְעָט) 'little, small amount.' In SBH, the polar opposite to מְעַט is either רַב or רֹב (but never הַרְבֵּה — as illustrated by Gen 30:30; Lev 25:16; Num 13:18; 26:54, 56; 33:54; 35:8; Deut 28:62; 1 Sam 14:6; Prov 16:8). The LBH usage, as reflected in the two Haggai passages, occurs elsewhere in the Bible only in Jer 42:2 (on the way to LBH) and Qoh 5:11 (a decidedly late text).[15]

Other LBH texts that reflect substantivized הַרְבֵּה 'much, large quantity, abundance' include Jon 4:11; Qoh 5:16; Neh 5:18; and 2 Chr 25:9.[16] The only SBH text that includes this usage is 2 Sam 1:4 וְגַם־הַרְבֵּה נָפַל מִן־הָעָם 'and there fell many from among the people.'[17] Given the placement of these words in the mouth of the Amalekite, who reports the death of Saul and Jonathan to David, one wonders whether a colloquial, non-standard, or sub-standard phrase is not represented here, which only in later times surfaced in literary usage.[18] Regardless, the evidence demonstrates quite clearly that substantivized הַרְבֵּה 'much, large quantity, abundance' is an LBH feature, with seven of the nine attestations occuring in post-exilic compositions, along with one attestation in Jeremiah.

One also should note that the two aforementioned developments concerning הַרְבֵּה continue into post-biblical Hebrew as well. The figures for the total number of usages are Ben Sira four, Dead Sea Scrolls three, Tannaitic texts 185 (with the latter demonstrating the continuation of this trend most dramatically). Among these (especially, though not only, in the Tannaitic corpus) one finds more instances of substantivized הַרְבֵּה, including cases of the word standing as the antithesis of מְעַט, for example, Ben Sira 5:15 מעט והרבה אל תשחת 'small and large, do not ruin,'[19] M. ʾAvot 1:15 אמור מעט ועשה הרבה 'say little and do much' (the famous dictum of Shammai), and so on.

I now turn to some basic lexical items found in the book of Haggai.

V. The noun פֶּחָה 'governor' occurs in pre-exilic and exilic texts to refer to foreign rulers only: 1 Kgs 10:15 (even if the exact country is unclear); 1 Kgs 20:24 (Aram, in the mouth of the king's advisors to their king); 2 Kgs 18:24 // Isa 36:9 (used by Rabshaqeh); Jer 51 (three times, with reference to Babylonian governors); and Ezek 23 (three times, with reference to [mainly] Assyrian governors). This usage continues in post-exilic texts as well, for example, three times in Esther and five times in Ezra–Nehemiah, all with reference to Persian governors, along with 2 Chr 9:14 (// 1 Kgs 10:15). At the same time, however, the word פֶּחָה 'governor' now comes to be used for Jewish governors serving at the pleasure of the Persian emperor. Thus we find the term applied to Zerubavel (Hag 1:1, 14; 2:2, 21) and to Nehemiah (5:14 [twice], 18; 12:26), in addition to one generic usage in Mal 1:8. Obviously, this new application of the term arises from the new political structure within the Persian empire (with Jews serving as governors of Judea), but the new linguistic usage remains such nonetheless. Also relevant here are the Persian-period epigraphic attestations (bullae, seals, jar impressions — from Ramat Raḥel and other sites) of the word פחה and פחוא, including those with Yahwistic names.[20]

---

[14] By coincidence, these two passages are treated below, item no. XIII, concerning the infinitive absolute.

[15] In 2 Kgs 10:18, the two words מְעָט and הַרְבֵּה also stand in contrast, though both serve as adverbs here.

[16] See the examples presented in König 1897, p. 339; BDB: 915; *DCH*: 7.401 — though without attention to the lateness of this feature.

[17] Note the comment of Driver (1913, p. 232): "Almost = רַבִּים. Strictly, of course, הרבה is an inf. abs. in the accus., qualifying נפל, lit. 'with a much-making there fell.'"

[18] For general orientation, see Rendsburg 1990.

[19] See also Ben Sira 35:8 כל לאמר ומעט הרבה, difficult as the text may be.

[20] For a listing, see Davies 1991, p. 470; for discussion, see Meyers and Meyers 1987, p. 14.

VI. Among the findings of E. Y. Kutscher (1962–1963, p. 124; 1982, p. 84) relevant to this subject is the greatly expanded semantic range of the verb עמד (lit.) 'stand' in LBH, especially in the direction of the semantic field typically occupied by the root קום (lit.) 'arise' (again, most likely due to Aramaic influence).[21] This drift is nicely exemplified by comparing two biblical passages, in which the same idiom occurs, with the two aforecited verbs bearing the special nuance 'abide, endure':

Josh 2:11 וְלֹא־קָמָה עוֹד רוּחַ בְּאִישׁ מִפְּנֵיכֶם
'and the spirit no longer abides in anyone on account of you'

Hag 2:5 וְרוּחִי עֹמֶדֶת בְּתוֹכְכֶם
'and my spirit abides in your midst'

The former passage employs the SBH idiom (with קום), while the latter presents the LBH idiom (with עמד).

To complete this picture, I submit the data compiled by Francis Andersen and Dean Forbes, regarding the general increase in the use of the verb עמד in LBH. I utilize here sizable chunks of text (since a book such as Haggai is too short for this kind of analysis), presenting both (a) the raw number of attestations, and (b) the ratio based on number of attestations per 10,000 words, as per the method employed by these two scholars (Andersen and Forbes 1989, p. 32):[22]

	a	*b*
Torah	69x	9:10,000
Samuel	32x	13:10,000
Kings	54x	21:10,000
Zechariah	12x	38:10,000
Psalms V	13x	26:10,000
Esther	11x	36:10,000
Daniel	39x	66:10,000
2 Chronicles	31x	23:10,000

VII. The word מַלְאֲכוּת 'message (of God)' is a *hapax legomenon* appearing in Hag 1:13, with no parallel usage elsewhere in Northwest Semitic. Normally under such circumstances, a lone usage serves little or no diagnostic purpose. In the present instance, however, we note the abstract suffix -וּת, a common feature of both LBH and post-Biblical Hebrew, including Mishnaic Hebrew (MH). Compare, for example, BH זִקְנָה / MH זִקְנוּת 'old age,' BH אֵבֶל / MH אֲבֵלוּת 'mourning,' BH תֹּם / MH תְּמִימוּת 'integrity,' and so on. We can conclude, therefore, that מַלְאֲכוּת 'message (of God)' was formed during the early Persian period, based on the common noun מַלְאָךְ 'messenger (of God)' (see Shin 2007, pp. 72–73, with additional discussion).

Several phrases appear in Haggai, which also reflect new developments of the sixth century and following.

VIII. The idiom הֵעִיר רוּחַ 'rouse one's spirit' occurs eight times in the Bible: Jer 51:1, 11; Hag 1:14; Ezra 1:1, 5; 1 Chr 5:26; 2 Chr 21:16, 36:22. There is no SBH expression to serve as a contrast, though one observes the following. In 2 Kgs 15:19, 29; 17:6; and 18:11, the Assyrian king (Pul/Tiglat-Pileser in the first two verses; the unnamed Sargon in the second two) simply arrives and deports Israelites, whereas in 1 Chr 5:26 we read,

וַ֠יָּעַר אֱלֹהֵ֨י יִשְׂרָאֵ֜ל אֶת־ר֣וּחַ ׀ פּ֣וּל מֶֽלֶךְ־אַשּׁ֗וּר וְאֶת־ר֙וּחַ֙ תִּלְּגַ֤ת פִּלְנֶ֙סֶר֙ מֶ֣לֶךְ אַשּׁ֔וּר
וַיַּגְלֵם֙ לָרֽאוּבֵנִ֣י וְלַגָּדִ֔י וְלַחֲצִ֖י שֵׁ֣בֶט מְנַשֶּׁ֑ה

'And the God of Israel roused the spirit of Pul king of Assyria and the spirit of Tilgat-Pileser king of Assyria; and he exiled the Reubenites, the Gadites, and half the tribe of Manasseh'

[21] See now also Holtz 2009/2010.

[22] Note that I do not include 1 Chronicles here, since the long lists of personal names at the beginning of the book skew the data considerably.

The verse in Hag 1:14 fits well into this overall picture:

וַיָּעַר יְהוָה אֶת־רוּחַ זְרֻבָּבֶל בֶּן־שַׁלְתִּיאֵל פַּחַת יְהוּדָה וְאֶת־רוּחַ יְהוֹשֻׁעַ בֶּן־יְהוֹצָדָק הַכֹּהֵן
הַגָּדוֹל וְאֶת־רוּחַ כֹּל שְׁאֵרִית הָעָם וַיָּבֹאוּ וַיַּעֲשׂוּ מְלָאכָה בְּבֵית־יְהוָה צְבָאוֹת אֱלֹהֵיהֶם׃

> 'And YHWH roused the spirit of Zerubavel ben Shaltiel, governor of Judah, and the spirit of Joshua ben Jehozadaq, the high priest, and the spirit of the all the rest of the people; and they came and they did the work in the house of YHWH of Hosts, their God.'

In earlier accounts of the building of the Tabernacle and the construction of the First Temple, no such statements occur (in general see Hurowitz 1992).

IX. The phrase הֵיכַל יהוה 'temple of YHWH' occurs twice in Haggai (2:15, 18a), as another lexical feature of the times. The expression is rare in SBH, occuring only three times (1 Sam 1:9; 3:3; 2 Kgs 18:16). During the texts emanating from the sixth century B.C. (the transitional period between SBH and LBH), the phrase is more common (eight times: 2 Kgs 23:4; 24:13; Jer 7:4 [three times]; 24:1; Ezek 8:16 [twice]). And then during the LBH stage of the language, one encounters הֵיכַל יהוה a 'temple of YHWH' relatively frequently (eleven times: Hag 2:15, 18; Zech 6:12, 13, 14, 15; Ezra 3:6, 10; 2 Chr 26:16; 27:2; 29:16).

X. The expression (כֹּה) אָמַר יְהוָה צְבָאוֹת '(thus) says YHWH of Hosts' occurs only twice in SBH (1 Sam 15:2; 2 Sam 7:8 // 1 Chr 17:7). It becomes a pet phrase of Jeremiah, with fifty-one occurrences in the book (fifty times with introductory כֹּה, once without); while a half century later, Second Isaiah employs the expression once (45:13, without כֹּה). The three prophets of the Persian period then make (כֹּה) אָמַר יְהוָה צְבָאוֹת '(thus) says YHWH of Hosts' a regular part of their phraseology:

Haggai seven times (five times with כֹּה, twice without)

Zechariah twenty-one times (seventeen times with כֹּה, four without)

Malachi twenty-one times (once with כֹּה, twenty without)

The attestations in Haggai are 1:2, 5, 7; 2:6, 7, 9, 11 (with 2:7 and 9 lacking כֹּה 'thus'). Clearly, this phrase achieved great currency during the sixth and fifth centuries B.C. (presumably popularized by Jeremiah himself), becoming a hallmark of prophetic speech in the century and a half following.[23] The SBH usage is the simpler (כֹּה) אָמַר יְהוָה '(thus) says YHWH,' attested throughout prose books such as Exodus, Samuel, and Kings and in eighth-century prophets such as Amos, Isaiah, and Micah, but hardly used by the Persian-period trio (see only Hag 1:8; Zech 8:3; 11:4; Mal 1:2; 3:13 — and of these only the two Zechariah passages with כֹּה).

XI. An important and well-recognized diagnostic in the diachronic study of BH is the shift from SBH 'X הַמֶּלֶךְ' to LBH 'הַמֶּלֶךְ X,' that is, whether the word הַמֶּלֶךְ 'the king' either precedes (as in SBH) or follows (as in LBH) the personal name of the monarch (Kropat 1909, pp. 48, 74; Hurvitz 1972a, p. 45).[24] The SBH phrase may continue into later texts, as it does in Esther twenty-five times, perhaps as an intentional archaism by the author. The LBH phrase is exceedingly limited in earlier texts (1 Sam 18:6; 2 Sam 13:39; 1 Kgs 2:17; 2 Kgs 8:29; 9:15);[25] it is used twice by Jeremiah (3:6; 29:2) and then becomes the characteristic mark of Persian-period compositions: Haggai twice (1:1, 15), Zechariah once (7:1), Daniel twice (1:21; 8:1), and Chronicles twenty-once times (again, Esther excepted). The two Haggai attestations are the same phrase:

'of Darius the king'	לְדָרְיָוֶשׁ הַמֶּלֶךְ

[23] For the larger picture concerning this divine name, see Rofé 1991 (with special attention to Haggai-Zechariah-Malachi on p. 315 n. 31). My thanks to Dr. Holtz for calling this essay to my attention.

[24] For a different interpretation of the data, see Rezetko 2003, p. 229; Young, Rezetko, and Ehrensvärd 2007, vol. 2, p. 103.

[25] 2 Sam 24:23 אֲרַוְנָה הַמֶּלֶךְ is not a relevant example, since the first word is not a personal name, but rather the Hurrian title *erwi-ne* 'the lord,' which then is glossed with the Hebrew term 'the king.'

This ordering, with royal name preceding הַמֶּלֶךְ, reflects Aramaic influence over Hebrew during the Persian period, since in the former language 'מלכא X' is preferred over 'X מלכא.' In Biblical Aramaic, for example, the phrase 'מלכא X' occurs thirteen times in Daniel and fourteen times in Ezra; whereas the phrase 'X מלכא' occurs six times in Daniel and not at all in Ezra. In the Aramaic papyri from Egypt, published by Cowley (1923), the 'מלכא X' formula is the only one attested (Darius: letters 1, 20, 21, 25, 27, 28, 29, 30, 31, 32; Behustan, line 37; Artaxerxes: letters 6, 7, 8, 9, 10, 13, 14; Sennacherib: Ahiqar 27, 50, 51, 55; Esarhaddon: Ahiqar 53, 70–71, 76–77, 78).[26]

XII. The Bible attests to a number of different calendar formulas, though three are most dominant. Moreover, these options may be plotted on a diachronic development, as follows (Wright 2005, pp. 56–59; Shin 2007, pp. 134–37):

A. SBH — ב-X יום לחדש (e.g., Gen 7:11; Num 28:17; 1 Kgs 12:32)

B. Transitional — ב-X לחדש (e.g., Lev 23:5; 2 Kgs 25:27 // Jer 52:31; Hag 2:1, 20; Ezek 29:21; Esth 8:12)

C. LBH — ביום X לחדש (e.g., Hag 1:1, 15; Esth 9:17; Dan 10:4; Neh 9:1; 2 Chr 7:10); see also BA Ezra 6:15 עַד יוֹם תְּלָתָה לִירַח אֲדָר

Note the overlap of Type B, which spans both a Torah text such as Lev 23:5 and a late text such as Esth 8:12, but which concentrates most of all in works emanating from the late monarchic period, the exile, and early Persian period. On either side of Type B, then, we have the earlier Type A and the later Type C (with the latter paralleled by the Aramaic usage). In light of this scheme, one is not surprised to learn (as indicated in the above listings of illustrative passages) that Haggai attests to two instances of Type B and two instances of type C:

Hag 2:1 בַּשְּׁבִיעִי בְּעֶשְׂרִים וְאֶחָד לַחֹדֶשׁ (type B)
Hag 2:20 בְּעֶשְׂרִים וְאַרְבָּעָה לַחֹדֶשׁ (type B)
Hag 1:1 בְּיוֹם אֶחָד לַחֹדֶשׁ (type C)
Hag 1:15 בְּיוֹם עֶשְׂרִים וְאַרְבָּעָה לַחֹדֶשׁ בַּשִּׁשִּׁי (type C)

Which is to say, the linguistic profile of Haggai on this particular usage sits right at the cusp of the transitional formula and the LBH formula (and with no instances of the SBH formula), exactly as one would expect from a composition dated to circa 520 B.C.

We turn now to a set of three (somewhat) interrelated grammatical issues relevant to our study, all concerning the infinitive absolute.

XIII. As is well known, the employment of the infinitive absolute in place of the finite verb is common in Ugaritic, Phoenician, Byblos Amarna, and Israelian Hebrew.[27] Somewhat surprisingly, especially since instances of this syntagma are rare in SBH (that is, Judahite Hebrew of the First Temple period), this usage appears relatively frequently in LBH:[28] Isa 42:20; 59:4; Ezek 23:30, 36, 47; Hag 1:6, 9; Zech 3:4; 7:5; 12:10; Job 15:35; Qoh 4:2; 8:9; 9:11; Esther fourteen times (e.g., 9:16–18 [seven times]); Dan 9:5, 11; Neh 7:3; 8:8; 9:8, 13; 1 Chr 5:20; 16:36; 2 Chr 28:19; 31:10. The two Haggai examples are the following:

1:6 'you have sown much and harvested little' זְרַעְתֶּם הַרְבֵּה וְהָבֵא מְעָט
1:9 'you have expected much' פָּנֹה אֶל־הַרְבֵּה

[26] As far as I know, no systematic study of the 'מלכא X' formula in Aramaic (along with its counterpart 'X מלכא') has been undertaken, but the dozens of instances of the former (to the exclusion of the latter) in the Cowley corpus of documents clearly represents the norm during the heyday of Imperial Aramaic. As an aside, in light of the Aramaic evidence, I would note that two instances of the 'הַמֶּלֶךְ X' formula in early texts reflect Israelian Hebrew, with an isogloss to Aramaic. I refer to 2 Kgs 8:29 and 9:15, parallel passages dealing with Joram of Israel (in fact, just wounded by the Arameans).

[27] For a survey of the evidence, see Rendsburg 2002, pp. 77–79.

[28] For general orientation, see Gordon 1955 and Gevirtz 1986.

The presence of these two infinitive absolute forms in place of the finite verb in Haggai[29] is yet another example of how the language of this book reflects the developments of the Persian period (see further Cohen 2008, pp. 215–22).[30]

XIV. In contrast to the above point, that the infinitive absolute in place of the finite verb appears more frequently in LBH, the employment of this grammatical form for the imperative appears far less frequently in late texts. The following chart demonstrates the point clearly. The first column of numbers presents the number of infintive absolutes serving as the imperative (IA.Impv.), the second column presents the number of morphological imperatives (Impv.), and the third column furnishes the ratio of the former per hundred instances of the latter.[31] The corpora are, respectively, (a) all books in the great narrative that spans Genesis through Kings, plus Ruth; (b) the prophets who can confidently be dated 750–550 B.C., namely, Amos, Hosea, Isaiah, Micah, Nahum, Habakkuk, Zephaniah, Jeremiah, Obadiah, and Ezekiel;[32] (c) the late prose books Qohelet, Esther, Daniel, Ezra-Nehemiah, and Chronicles; and (d) the prophets of the period 550–450 B.C., that is, Second Isaiah, Haggai, Zechariah, and Malachi.[33]

		IA.Impv.	Impv.	IA.Impv. per Impvs.
	Entire Bible:	*61*	*4,253*	*1.43*
a)	Genesis–Kings + Ruth	27	1,744	1.55
b)	Amos–Ezekiel	31	938	3.30
c)	Late Prose Books	2	265	0.75
d)	SecIsa–Hag–Zech–Mal	1	230	0.43

As can be seen, a comparison between (a) and (c) reveals that later prose books use the infinitive absolute for the imperative less than half as frequently as earlier prose books (see also Cohen 2008, pp. 227–30), while a comparison between (b) and (d) reveals even more strikingly the precipitous drop in this usage in the later prophetic books, with Zech 6:10 the sole attestation in the four works included in group (d).[34] The total absence of the infinitive absolute with imperative force in Haggai (alongside fourteen instances of the regular imperative in this book) is yet another LBH element in this book.

XV. Yet a third discernible trend concerning the infinitive absolute in LBH is the great decrease in the usage of this form to add emphasis to the finite verb, what scholars call the paronomastic infinitive absolute or the tautological infinitive absolute, that is, *qāṭōl yiqṭōl* (with the prefix conjugation) and *qāṭōl qāṭal* (with the suffix

[29] Hag 1:6 includes three other instances of the infinitive absolute – אָכוֹל 'eat,' שָׁתוֹ 'drink,' and לָבוֹשׁ 'dress' – which some have taken as additional examples of this form with predicative use, but which I would prefer to render as true verbal nouns, akin to the English gerund. Thus I would translate the middle section of this verse: '(like) eating though without being satiated, (like) drinking though without being inebriated, (like) dressing though without his being warm.'

[30] My thanks to Naʿama Pat-El for bringing Ohad Cohen's dissertation to my attention.

[31] I adopt here the statistical methodology of (and utilize the data provided by) Young, Rezetko, and Ehrensvärd (2008, vol. 2, pp. 130–31). The number of attestations of the imperative registered in Andersen and Forbes 1989, pp. 23–29, is ever-so-slightly different from time to time, but none of these extremely minor deviations affects the overall statistical analysis presented here.

[32] I omit here Joel, since its date remains questionable, and Jonah, since the book is mainly prose.

[33] The chart does not include the data from works for which a diachronic comparison cannot be made, such as Psalms, Proverbs, Job, and Song of Songs. Though it is worth noting that Psalms uses the imperative more frequently (354 times per 10,000 words) than any other biblical book (save Joel, whose 45 imperatives or 470 times per 10,000 words is a statistical outlier in a short composition), no doubt because of the psalmists' constant petitions and entreaties to God. For the data, see Andersen and Forbes 1989, pp. 23–29.

[34] As one might expect, Young, Rezetko, and Ehrensvärd (2008, vol. 2, pp. 128–32) arrive at a different conclusion, based on the same data. They make much of the fact, for example, that Judges also has no instances of the infinitive absolute with imperative force. For that reason, I have arranged the data as above, to show the larger picture and to allow comparison between sizeable chunks of material of the same genre (early prose vs. late prose; early prophets vs. late prophets). In such a picture, the absence of the grammatical usage under consideration here in Judges remains a curiousity, but it is less critical to the larger issue.

conjugation)[35] (see Eskhult 2000a; 2000b, p. 90; Cohen 2008, pp. 215–17, 230; Kim 2009, pp. 99, 106–07). This major shift is especially demonstrable via the following data for the narrative books.[36] There are 324 examples of this usage in SBH prose (that is, Genesis–Kings + Ruth), but only thirteen occurrences in LBH prose (that is, Esther, Daniel, Ezra–Nehemiah, Chronicles [and of these note that four examples in the latter book appear in passages parallelling Samuel–Kings]). One hardly needs to present the ratios (as presented in the preceding section, for example) to realize the point for the prose texts of the Bible. The decrease in this usage is less marked in prophetic books, but a decrease is present nonetheless. I count 137 examples among the 57,878 words in the group (b) prophets listed above, that is, 2.36 per 1,000 words; and only fifteen examples (nine in Second Isaiah, six in Zechariah) among the 11,636 words in the group (d) prophets noted, that is, 1.29 per 1,000 words. In Haggai specifically, however, there are no examples of this usage, so once more we observe how the language of this book fits into the LBH stratum.

The final set of items presented in this essay derives from the methodology introduced into the field of Hebrew studies by Frank Polak.[37]

XVI. Polak has determined that (a) the ratio of nouns to verbs (NV ratio) in BH prose greatly increases with the passage of time, from the classical period (= SBH) to the Persian era (= LBH); and (b) within the verbal group, the ratio of nominal verbs (participle, infinitive) to finite verbs (suffix conjugation, prefix conjugation, imperative) (NF ratio) also increases during the same span of time.[38] In the book of Haggai, most scholars would agree that the following verses are written in prose: 1:1, 12–15; 2:1, 10–14, 20. Within this material, one encounters 140 nouns and 33 verbs, yielding an exceedingly high NV ratio of .809, exactly as one would expect from a Persian-era composition.[39] On the other hand, these 33 verbs divide as 5 nominal verbs and 28 finite verbs, yielding a low NF ratio of .152, more befitting the classical stratum. According to Polak's methodology, however, it is the NV ratio that is more consistent and thus serves as a better diagnostic to situate a particular composition within a particular stratum. The prose verses of Haggai would not be the only instance of a text with a high (or relatively high) NV ratio with a concomitant low (or relatively low) NF ratio.[40]

The database for the above figures is naturally very small, since the prose portion of Haggai amounts to only twelve verses. Accordingly, even though the NV and NF ratios are relevant for prose texts mainly (or perhaps only), according to the method developed by Polak, it may be worth expanding the database, if for no other reason than the data are so readily available. The full two chapters of Haggai present the following figures: 323 nouns and 120 verbs, yielding an NV ratio of .729, with a division of the latter figure into 27 nominal verbs and 93 finite verbs, yielding an NF ratio of .225. The former places Haggai on the cusp of the Late Monarchic/Exilic- and Persian-era strata, while the latter places the book in the Late Monarchic/Exilic period.

XVII. Polak also has demonstrated that Persian-period prose compositions reflect a much more complex syntax, with greater use of hypotaxis (subordinate clauses) and with more explicit syntactic constituents (arguments) per clause. Again we limit the data to the prose sections of the book (with the number in the second column indicating the percentage of clauses):

0–1 arg	43.91
2+ arg	29.26
Hypotaxis	26.83
Complex Hypotaxis	9.76
3+ arg	12.20

[35] Thus the most common patterns, since the infinitive absolute also may follow the finite verb, plus there are several arrangements to express the negative. For a thorough treatment, see now Kim 2009.

[36] See the data furnished by Young, Rezetko, and Ehrensvärd 2008, vol. 2, pp. 132–41.

[37] I issue here a blanket expression of gratitude to Professor Polak for graciously providing me with the various data sets presented below.

[38] The basic work remains Polak 1998.

[39] In fact, this NV ratio is higher than other (slightly later) texts, for example, Ezra: .772; Esther: .714; Nehemiah 8–10: .731; Daniel 1:1–2:3: .749 — for which see Polak 1998, p. 70.

[40] Again, see the summary chart at Polak 1998, p. 70.

These figures comport with a later (not earlier) style of prose writing.[41] For a sample passage, reflecting the complex syntax of Haggai, consider the following, Hag 1:12, with the subordination in the last four words:

וַיִּשְׁמַע זְרֻבָּבֶל ׀ בֶּן־שַׁלְתִּיאֵל וִיהוֹשֻׁעַ בֶּן־יְהוֹצָדָק הַכֹּהֵן הַגָּדוֹל וְכֹל ׀ שְׁאֵרִית הָעָם בְּקוֹל
יְהוָה אֱלֹהֵיהֶם וְעַל־דִּבְרֵי חַגַּי הַנָּבִיא כַּאֲשֶׁר שְׁלָחוֹ יְהוָה אֱלֹהֵיהֶם

'And Zerubavel son of Shaltiel, and Joshua son of Jehozadaq the high priest, and all the rest of the people obeyed the voice of YHWH their God and the words of Haggai the prophet, as YHWH their God had sent him'

And then the following verse, Hag 1:13, with four arguments serving the single verb:

וַיֹּאמֶר חַגַּי מַלְאַךְ יְהוָה בְּמַלְאֲכוּת יְהוָה לָעָם לֵאמֹר

'And Haggai the messenger of YHWH said, in the message of YHWH to the people, saying'

In an earlier style of Hebrew prose, one could imagine a far simpler wording, something like this perhaps:

*'and Haggai said to the people, saying' *וַיֹּאמֶר חַגַּי לָעָם לֵאמֹר

Or even simpler yet:

*'and Haggai said to the people' *וַיֹּאמֶר חַגַּי לָעָם

And even though our treatment here concerns prose, I also take the opportunity to present the following verse from the poetic material, Hag 2:3, with double subordination, the first introduced by the definite article -הַ (as expected before the participle) and the second introduced by the standard relative marker אֲשֶׁר before the finite verb (both rendered as 'who' below):

מִי בָכֶם הַנִּשְׁאָר אֲשֶׁר רָאָה אֶת־הַבַּיִת הַזֶּה בִּכְבוֹדוֹ הָרִאשׁוֹן

'who among you who remains, who saw this house in its first glory'

XVIII. Polak also has observed the manner in which extended noun groups characterize LBH texts. According to his calculations, the percentage of such noun groups in the prose sections of Haggai is 145 percent, which is to say, almost every noun clause has a noun group consisting of three nouns, as the mean.[42] The following passages are illustrative:

Hag 1:11

וָאֶקְרָא חֹרֶב עַל־הָאָרֶץ וְעַל־הֶהָרִים וְעַל־הַדָּגָן וְעַל־הַתִּירוֹשׁ וְעַל־הַיִּצְהָר וְעַל אֲשֶׁר
תּוֹצִיא הָאֲדָמָה וְעַל־הָאָדָם וְעַל־הַבְּהֵמָה וְעַל כָּל־יְגִיעַ כַּפָּיִם׃

'And I summoned a drought upon the land and upon the mountains and upon the grain and upon the wine and upon the oil and upon that which the soil brings forth, and upon humankind and upon the animals and upon all the toil of your palms'

Hag 2:6

וַאֲנִי מַרְעִישׁ אֶת־הַשָּׁמַיִם וְאֶת־הָאָרֶץ וְאֶת־הַיָּם וְאֶת־הֶחָרָבָה׃

'And I will shake the heavens and the earth and the sea and the dry-land'

---

[41] Again, see Polak 1998 for a sampling of passages by way of comparison.

[42] The figure of 145 percent represents an exceedingly high number, as can be determined by perusing the key study Polak 2006 (see also Polak 2009a).

Hag 2:12

וְנָגַע בִּכְנָפוֹ אֶל־הַלֶּחֶם וְאֶל־הַנָּזִיד וְאֶל־הַיַּיִן וְאֶל־שֶׁמֶן וְאֶל־כָּל־מַאֲכָל

'and with his fold touches the bread or the stew or the wine or oil or any food'

Anyone with a sense of the workings of earlier biblical writings (prose or poetry) will realize that such strings of nouns are well nigh never encountered in the classical stage of the language and its literature.

XIX. Yet another diagnostic tool developed by Polak is the distribution of key verbs in the biblical corpus, based on their association within the same semantic field. Polak noticed that (a) within the "conveyance" field, לקח 'take' is more common in earlier texts, and הביא 'bring' is more common in later texts (with נשׂא 'bear, carry' serving as the control verb); (b) within the 'motion' field, הלך 'go' is more common in earlier texts, and בוא 'come' is more common in later texts (with יצא 'go out' serving as the control verb); and (c) within the 'cognition' field, ראה 'see' is more common in earlier texts, and שמע 'hear' is more common in later texts (with ידע 'know' serving as the control verb).[43] The data for the book of Haggai are as follows:

a) Conveyance

לקח 'take'	1x
הביא 'bring'	3x
נשׂא 'bear, carry'	2x

b) Motion

הלך 'go'	0x
בוא 'come'	5x
יצא 'go out'	1x

c) Cognition

ראה 'see'	2x
שׁמע 'hear'	1x
ידע 'know'	0x

When we total these verbs, we note that (a) those more characteristic of the classical stratum (the first in each list) occur three times, representing 20 percent of the attestations; (b) those more characteristic of the late stratum (the second in each list) occur nine times, representing 60 percent of the attestations; and (c) the control verbs (the third in each list) occur three times, representing 20 percent of the attestations.

If we now chart these figures against Polak's aggregate data of the relevant verbs for the Persian period, we note a remarkable correspondence between the two:

	Classical	*Late*	*Control*
Conveyance	23.9%	48.9%	27.3%
Motion	24.5%	64.1%	11.4%
Cognition	21.8%	50.0%	28.2%
Aggregate	23.4%	54.3%	22.3%
Haggai	20.0%	60.0%	20.0%

Once more, the linguistic profile of the book of Haggai, even when the data are relatively limited (that is, fifteen verbs altogether, due to the brevity of the book), is exactly what one would expect from a Persian-period composition.

---

[43] The basic studies are Polak 1997/1998 and Polak 2009b.

XX. The final point raised by Polak, relevant to the current study, is the change in poetic parallelism in the later biblical books. The richness of word pairs evident in classical poetry is frequently not encountered in poetic texts dated to the Persian era (Polak 2009a). In Haggai, for example, one finds the collocations of lexemes known chiefly from prose texts — indeed, in Polak's words, "collocations with trivial, prosaic lexemes" (Polak 2009a, p. 205):

1:6 — זרע // הביא 'sow : bring'

1:6 — הרבה // מעט 'much : little'

1:8 — עלה // הביא 'go up : bring'

Plus one instance of two stichs containing words "that are rarely associated and do not reveal semantic correspondence" (Polak 2009a, p. 205):

1:10 — טל // יבול 'dew : yield'

Even more common are the many instances of repetitive parallelism, with parallel stichs employing the same lexeme:

1:2 — עת 'time'

1:4 — בית 'house'

1:10 — כלא 'withhold'

2:4 — חזק 'be strong'

2:6-7 — רעשׁ 'shake'

2:7 — גוים 'nations'

2:16 — בוא 'come'

2:16 — היה 'be'

2:22 — ממלכות 'kingdoms'

2:22 — רכב 'rider'

In addition, as Polak further notes, compositions of the Persian era reveal a conspicuous decline in the use of gapping (typically with compensation or "ballast variant"), a distinctive trait of both Ugaritic and classical Hebrew poetry (Polak 2009a, p. 210). Consider, for example, Hag 1:10:

'the heavens withhold the dew — כָּלְאוּ שָׁמַיִם מִטָּל

and the earth withholds its produce' — וְהָאָרֶץ כָּלְאָה יְבוּלָהּ׃

In classical Hebrew poetry, one could imagine any number of two-word phrases that would serve in the b-line, without repetition of the verbal root כלא 'withhold,' expressions such as פְּרִי תְבוּאָתָהּ 'the fruit of its yield' (cf. Ps 107:37) and תְּבוּאַת הָאֲדָמָה 'the yield of the soil' (cf. Isa 30:23). In short, the poetry of Haggai represents a major departure (deterioration, to be subjective) from the richly imaginative poetry of the pre-monarchic and monarchic periods — such as many of the psalms, poems embedded into narrative texts (e.g., the song of Deborah and the song of Hannah), and the oracles of Amos and Isaiah.

The twenty items canvassed here make it abundantly clear that the judgment expressed by Young, Rezetko, and Ehrensvärd (see above) is incorrect. Far from being generally devoid of LBH features, the book of Haggai reflects LBH developments at every turn, in grammar, lexicon, phraseology, prose syntax, and poetic style.[44] This is not to say that certain SBH features do not appear in Haggai (see below), but the author of Haggai clearly was no longer writing in SBH (= EBH, to use the term preferred by Young, Rezetko, and Ehrensvärd).

---

[44] Conveniently, the book of Haggai has 600 words, which allows us to compare the accumulation of LBH features in the book to that of other compositions, using the method of Young, Rezetko, and Ehrensvärd (2008, vol. 1, pp. 129–36), which counts LBH traits in 500-word samples. Twenty features have been identified in the present study (= 16.6 features per 500 words), which places Haggai on a par with Esther 5:1–6:13a, as analyzed by the co-authors. If the five traits derived from Polak's studies are removed (since

Of the various discriminants between SBH and LBH recognized by scholars (Avi Hurvitz *super omnes alios*), I have identified only three of the former in Haggai. The first is the word order כֶּסֶף > זָהָב 'silver : gold' in 2:8 לִי הַכֶּסֶף וְלִי הַזָּהָב (as opposed to LBH where the typical word order is כֶּסֶף > זָהָב 'gold : silver') (Hurvitz 1972b; Rooker 1990, pp. 174–75; Shin 2007, pp. 126–29). The second is the phrase מִ- ... וָמַעְלָה used to express direction (either in space or in time), found in identical phrases in 2:15, 18: מִן־הַיּוֹם הַזֶּה וָמָעְלָה 'from this day onward' (as opposed to LBH מִ- ... וּלְמַעְלָה) (Hurvitz 1982, pp. 107–09; Shin 2007, pp. 145–47).[45] And the third is the personal name יְהוֹשֻׁעַ 'Joshua' found throughout the book (1:1, 12, 14; 2:2, 4) (in contrast to LBH יֵשׁוּעַ [Ezra ten times, Nehemiah seventeen times, Chronicles twice]; see also BA יֵשׁוּעַ [Ezra 5:2]) (Shin 2007, pp. 141–44). To this list one could add the absence of Persian loanwords in the book, though one must recall that the Jewish experience within the Achaemenid empire was only two decades old at the time of the floruit of the prophet Haggai. Which is to say, the author of this short book, at the beginning of the Persian period, still utilizes several SBH elements, but both his prose and his poetry are infused with LBH traits, so much so that this latter stratum of the language clearly dominates.

In sum, no writer during the Persian period — certainly not the author of the book of Haggai, still at the onset of Achaemenid rule over the land of Israel — could compose in SBH. By the year 520 B.C., such an achievement no longer was possible.

Abbreviations

BA	Biblical Aramaic
BDB	Brown, Driver, and Briggs 1906
BH	Biblical Hebrew
DCH	Clines 1993–2010
EBH	Early Biblical Hebrew
GKC	Gesenius, Kautzsch, and Cowley 1910
IA	infinitive absolute
impv.	imperative
LBH	Late Biblical Hebrew
MH	Mishnaic Hebrew
N	noun
SBH	Standard Biblical Hebrew
V	verb

typically Young, Rezetko, and Ehrensvärd do not contend with these), then one still counts fifteen LBH features in Haggai (= 12.5 features per 500 words), which would place the book on a par with portions of Chronicles, as analyzed by the co-authors. True, the individual features treated herein are not necessarily the ones treated by Young, Rezetko, and Ehrensvärd (thus, for example, the trio [2008, vol. 1, p. 135] specifically omit עַד 'still, while' from consideration [see also Young 2009a, pp. 616–17], while I have included this feature [item no. II above]) — and thus to some extent the aforecited figures derive from a comparison of apples and oranges. Nonetheless, the overall analysis presented herein, demonstrating an accumulation of LBH features in Haggai, should dispel any notion that the book of Haggai represents an "undisputed postexilic text," which lacks LBH features and is written in EBH (paraphrasing Young, Rezetko, and Ehrensvärd 2008, vol. 1, p. 56 [cited above]).

[45] One should note, though, that the specific phrase with יוֹם occurs only in 1 Sam 16:13; 30:25 מֵהַיּוֹם הַהוּא וָמָעְלָה 'from that day onward'; the more standard usage is with the word וָהָלְאָה, attested in Lev 22:27; Num 15:23; 1 Sam 18:9; Ezek 39:22; 43:27. The general point remains, nonetheless.

Bibliography

Andersen, Francis I., and A. Dean Forbes

1989 *The Vocabulary of the Old Testament.* Rome: Pontifical Biblical Institute.

Ben Zvi, Ehud

2009 "The Communicative Message of Some Linguistic Choices." In *A Palimpsest: Rhetoric, Ideology, Stylistics, and Language Relating to Persian Israel*, edited by Ehud Ben Zvi, Diana V. Edelman, and Frank Polak, pp. 269–90. Perspectives on Hebrew Scriptures and Contexts 5. Piscataway: Gorgias Press.

Brown, Francis; S. R. Driver; and Charles A. Briggs

1906 *A Hebrew and English Lexicon of the Old Testament.* Oxford: Clarendon Press.

Chen, Yiyi

2000 Israelian Hebrew in the Book of Proverbs. Ph.D. dissertation, Cornell University.

Clines, David J. A., editor

1993–2011 *The Dictionary of Classical Hebrew.* 8 volumes. Sheffield: Sheffield Academic Press.

Cohen, Ohad

2008 Maʿareket ha-Zemanim šel ha-Poʿal ba-ʿIvrit ha-Miqraʾit ha-Meʾuḥeret. Ph.D. dissertation, Hebrew University.

Cowley, A. E.

1923 *Aramaic Papyri of the Fifth Century B.C.* Oxford: Clarendon.

Davies, Graham I.

1991 *Ancient Hebrew Inscriptions: Corpus and Concordance.* Cambridge: Cambridge University Press.

Driver, S. R.

1913 *Notes on the Hebrew Text and the Topography of the Books of Samuel.* Second edition. Oxford: Clarendon Press.

Ehrensvärd, Martin

2003 "Linguistic Dating of Biblical Texts." In *Biblical Hebrew: Studies in Chronology and Typology*, edited by Ian Young, pp. 164–88. Journal for the Study of the Old Testament, Supplement Series 369. London: T. & T. Clark.

Eskhult, Mats

2000a "Hebrew Infinitival Paronomasia." *Orientalia Suecana* 49: 27–32.

2000b "Verbal Syntax in Late Biblical Hebrew." In *Diggers at the Well* (Proceedings of a Third International Symposium on the Hebrew of the Dead Sea Scrolls and Ben Sira), edited by T. Muraoka and John F. Elwolde, pp. 84–93. Studies on the Texts of the Desert of Judah 36. Leiden: Brill.

Gesenius, Wilhelm

1910 *Gesenius' Hebrew Grammar.* 2nd English edition. Edited by E. Kautzsch, translated by A. E. Cowley. Oxford: Clarendon Press.

Gevirtz, Stanley

1986 "Of Syntax and Style in the 'Late Biblical Hebrew'–'Old Canaanite' Connection." *Journal of the Ancient Near Eastern Society* 18: 25–29.

Ginsberg, H. L.

1982 *The Israelian Heritage of Judaism.* Texts and Studies of the Jewish Theological Seminary of America 24. New York: Jewish Theological Seminary.

Gordon, Cyrus H.

1955 "North Israelite Influence on Post-Exilic Hebrew." *Israel Exploration Journal* 5: 85–88.

Holtz, Shalom E.

2001 "'To Go and Marry Any Man That You Please': A Study of the Formulaic Antecedents of the Rabbinic Writ of Divorce." *Journal of Near Eastern Studies* 60/4: 241–58.

2009/10 (5770) "Hitpatḥuyot Semanṭiyot ba-Ṣeruf *ʿamad ʿal* ba-ʿIvrit ha-Miqraʾit ha-Meʾuḥeret." *Lešonenu* 72: 7–18.

Hurowitz, Victor

1992 — *"I Have Built You an Exalted House": Temple Building in the Bible in Light of Mesopotamian and Northwest Semitic Writings.* Journal for the Study of the Old Testament, Supplement Series 115. Sheffield: Journal for the Study of the Old Testament Press.

Hurvitz, Avi

1972a — *Ben Lašon le-Lašon.* Jerusalem: Bialik.

1972b — "'Kiʾazmus Diʾakroni' ba-ʿIvrit ha-Miqraʾit." In *Ha-Miqraʾ we-Toldot Yiśraʾel: Meḥqarim ba-Miqraʾ u-we-Sifrut Yeme Bayit Šeni le-Zikro šel Yaʿaqov Liver*, edited by B. Uffenheimer, pp. 248–55. Tel-Aviv: Tel-Aviv University.

1974 — "The Date of the Prose-Tale of Job Linguistically Reconsidered." *Harvard Theological Review* 67: 17–34.

1982 — *A Linguistic Study of the Relationship between the Priestly Source and the Book of Ezekiel.* Paris: J. Gabalda.

2006 — "The Recent Debate on Late Biblical Hebrew: Solid Data, Experts' Opinions, and Inconclusive Arguments." *Hebrew Studies* 47: 191–210.

Joosten, Jan

2005 — "The Distinction between Classical and Late Biblical Hebrew as Reflected in Syntax." *Hebrew Studies* 46: 327–39.

Joüon, Paul, and T. Muraoka

1991 — *A Grammar of Biblical Hebrew.* 2 volumes. Rome: Pontificio Istituto Biblico.

Kim, Yoo-ki

2009 — *The Function of the Tautological Infinitive in Classical Biblical Hebrew.* Winona Lake: Eisenbrauns.

König, Eduard

1897 — *Historisch-comparative Syntax der hebräischen Sprache.* Leipzig: J. C. Hinrichs.

Kropat, Arno

1909 — *Die Syntax des Autors der Chronik verglichen mit der seiner Quellen.* Beihefte zur Zeitschrift für die alttestamentliche Wissenschaft 16. Giessen: A. Töpelmann.

Kutscher, E. Y.

1962–63 (5723) — "Bavuʾa (calque) šel ha-ʾAramit be-ʿIvrit." *Tarbiz* 33: 118–30. Reprinted in Kutscher 1977, pp. 374–406 (Hebrew section).

1977 — *Meḥqarim be-ʿIvrit u-ve-ʾAramit.* Edited by Zeʾev Ben-Ḥayyim, et al. Jerusalem: Magnes.

1982 — *A History of the Hebrew Language.* Jerusalem: Magnes; Leiden: E. J. Brill.

Meyers, Carol L., and Eric M. Meyers

1987 — *Haggai, Zechariah 1-8.* Anchor Bible. Garden City: Doubleday.

Muraoka, T., and Bezalel Porten

1998 — *A Grammar of Egyptian Aramaic.* Leiden: Brill.

Paul, Shalom M.

2008 — *Yešaʿyahu 40-66.* 2 volumes. Miqraʾ le-Yisraʾel. Tel-Aviv: ʿAm ʿOved.

Polak, Frank

1997/98 — "Temurot u-Tequfot bi-Lšon ha-Siporet ba-Miqraʾ." *Bet Miqraʾ* 43: 30–52, 142–60.

1998 — "The Oral and the Written: Syntax, Stylistics and the Development of Biblical Prose Narrative." *Journal of the Ancient Near Eastern Society* 26: 59–105.

2006 — "Sociolinguistics: A Key to the Typology and the Social Background of Biblical Hebrew." *Hebrew Studies* 47: 115–62.

2009a — "Parallelism and Noun Groups in Prophetic Poetry from the Persian Era." In *A Palimpsest: Rhetoric, Ideology, Stylistics, and Language Relating to Persian Israel*, edited by Ehud Ben Zvi, Diana Edelman, and Frank Polak, pp. 199–235. Perspectives on Hebrew Scriptures and Contexts 5. Piscataway: Gorgias Press.

2009b — "Verbs of Motion in Biblical Hebrew: Lexical Shifts and Syntactic Structure." In *A Palimpsest: Rhetoric, Ideology, Stylistics, and Language Relating to Persian Israel*, edited by Ehud Ben Zvi, Diana Edelman, and Frank Polak, pp. 161–97. Perspectives on Hebrew Scriptures and Contexts 5. Piscataway: Gorgias Press.

Ratner, Robert J.

1992 — "Morphological Variation in Biblical Hebrew Rhetoric." In "Let Your Colleagues Praise You: Studies in Memory of Stanley Gevirtz," volume 2, edited by Robert J. Ratner, et al., special issue *Maarav* 8: 143–59.

Rendsburg, Gary A.

1990 *Diglossia in Ancient Hebrew*. American Oriental Series 72. New Haven: American Oriental Society.

2002 *Israelian Hebrew in the Book of Kings*. Occasional Publications of the Department of Near Eastern Studies and the Program of Jewish Studies, Cornell University 5. Bethesda: CDL Press.

2003 "Hurvitz Redux: On the Continued Scholarly Inattention to a Simple Principle of Hebrew Philology." In *Biblical Hebrew: Studies in Chronology and Typology*, edited by Ian Young, pp. 104–28. Journal for the Study of the Old Testament, Supplement Series 369. London: T. & T. Clark.

2006 "Aramaic-Like Features in the Pentateuch." *Hebrew Studies* 47: 163–76.

2008 "Qeṭaᶜ Šenat ha-Yovel (Vayyiqraᵓ 25:8–24) ke-Ḥibbur Ṣefoni." *Meḥqarim be-Lashon* 11–12 (= *Sefer ha-Yovel le-Avi Hurvitz*): 297–308.

Rezetko, Robert

2003 "Dating Biblical Hebrew: Evidence from Samuel-Kings and Chronicles." In *Biblical Hebrew: Studies in Chronology and Typology*, edited by Ian Young, pp. 215–50. Journal for the Study of the Old Testament, Supplement Series 369. London: T. & T. Clark.

2009 "What Happened to the Book of Samuel in the Persian Period and Beyond?" In *A Palimpsest: Rhetoric, Ideology, Stylistics, and Language Relating to Persian Israel*, edited by Ehud Ben Zvi, Diana V. Edelman, and Frank Polak, pp. 237–52. Perspectives on Hebrew Scriptures and Contexts 5. Piscataway: Gorgias Press.

Rofé, Alexander

1991 "The Name YHWH SĔBĀ'ÔT and the Shorter Rescension of Jeremiah." In *Prophetie und geschichtliche Wirklichkeit im alten Israel: Festschrift für Siegried Herrmann zum 65. Geburtstag*, edited by Rüdiger Liwak and Siegried Wagner, pp. 307–16. Stuttgart: W. Kohlhammer.

Rooker, Mark F.

1990 *Biblical Hebrew in Transition: The Language of the Book of Ezekiel*. Journal for the Study of the Old Testament, Supplement Series 90. Sheffield: Journal for the Study of the Old Testament Press.

Sáenz-Badillos, Angel

1993 *A History of the Hebrew Language*. Cambridge: Cambridge Univerisity Press.

Schoors, Anton

2004 *The Preacher Sought to Find Pleasing Words: A Study of the Language of Qoheleth*, Part 2: *Vocabulary*. Leuven: Peeters.

Shin, Seoung-Yun

2007 A Lexical Study on the Language of Haggai-Zechariah-Malachi and Its Place in the History of Biblical Hebrew. Ph.D. dissertation, Hebrew University.

Smith, Colin

2003 "With an Iron Pen and a Diamond Tip": Linguistic Peculiarities in the Book of Jeremiah. Ph.D. dissertation, Cornell University.

Wright, Richard M.

2005 *Linguistic Evidence for the Pre-Exilic Date of the Yahwistic Source*. Library of Hebrew Bible/Old Testament Studies 419. London: T. & T. Clark.

Young, Ian

2009a "Is the Prose Tale of Job in Late Biblical Hebrew?" *Vetus Testamentum* 59: 606–29

2009b What is 'Late Biblical Hebrew'? In *A Palimpsest: Rhetoric, Ideology, Stylistics, and Language Relating to Persian Israel*, edited by Ehud Ben Zvi, Diana V. Edelman, and Frank Polak, pp. 253–68. Perspectives on Hebrew Scriptures and Contexts 5. Piscataway: Gorgias Press.

Young, Ian; Robert Rezetko; and Martin Ehrensvärd

2008 *Linguistic Dating of Biblical Texts*. 2 volumes. London: Equinox.

20

Two Modern South Arabian Etymologies

*Aaron D. Rubin, Penn State University**

Modern South Arabian *lxm* 'shark'

It is well known that the Hebrew noun *lεḥεm* 'bread; food' and the very rare verb *laḥam* 'eat' (e.g., Prov 4:17) have a number of cognates in Central Semitic that fall within the same semantic field. These include Ugaritic *lḥm* (noun) 'food, bread, meat?,'[1] *lḥm* (G-Stem verb) 'eat,' *lḥm* (D-Stem verb) 'feed,' *šlḥm* (C-Stem verb) 'feed, fatten'; Syriac *laḥmā* 'bread, food'; and Arabic *laḥm* 'meat, flesh,' *laḥḥām* 'butcher.' Despite the differences as to which food the above substantives can signify, the semantic differences pose no problem to relating these words to a common root.[2] Let us, for the moment, assume a Central Semitic noun **laḥm* 'food,' and a verb **laḥama* 'eat.' There are clear cognates to this root in Akkadian, on which more below.

Scholars have long debated the connection of this Central Semitic root with Geʻez *lahm* 'cow' and its cognates in the modern Ethiopian tongues (Amharic *lām* etc.). Isenberg (1841, p. 6), Armbruster (1920, p. 29), and Ullendorff (1956, p. 192; 1967, p. 126) have all maintained that the Ethiopic term is cognate with the Central Semitic terms, while Leslau (1958, p. 29; 1991, p. 309) and others have argued that they are not. Leslau's reasonable rejection of this idea is based simply on the fact that Semitic *ḥ* does not normally appear as *h* in Geʻez, though he recognizes that such a change is simple enough. We will not concern ourselves here with whether either of these camps can be proven correct, but rather with a related topic. Ullendorff makes an interesting argument, which is that a noun from the root *lḥm* is not simply 'food,' but refers to the dietary staple, which necessarily differs from region to region. A similar idea was devised by Swiggers (1981), who suggests that the basic meaning of the noun from the root *lḥm* is 'common food,' which is bread among sedentary groups (e.g., Hebrews) and meat among nomads (e.g., Arabs). This neatly explains the semantic differences noted above.

Both Ullendorff and Swiggers consider another set of words to be cognate with this root, namely, the Modern South Arabian words for "shark." These are Soqoṭri *léḥem*, pl. *lḥom*;[3] Eastern Jibbali *əlxím* (Central Jibbali *lxum*, pl. *lxihm*);[4] Yemeni Mehri *laxaym* or *ləxaym* (< **laxīm*), pl. *laxawmət*;[5] Omani Mehri *əwxaym* (< **ləxaym* < **ləxīm*), pl. *əwxawmət* (< **ləxawmət*);[6] and Ḥarsusi *léxem*.[7] It is possible that this word can also mean "big fish" in Soqoṭri, though

* I am delighted to be able to write this article in honor of John Huehnergard, my teacher and my friend. My thanks to Rebecca Hasselbach and Naʿama Pat-El for organizing this well-deserved volume, and for their helpful comments on this piece. Thanks also to Leonid Kogan and Gary Rendsburg for fruitful discussions related to the first section of this article.

[1] The evidence for *lḥm* meaning 'meat' in Ugaritic is slim. The most convincing, but still uncertain, context is KTU 1.114:7; see del Olmo Lete and Sanmartín 2004, pp. 495–97.

[2] A few general studies of this root can be found in Krotkoff 1969; Fronzaroli 1971, pp. 615–16; and Dolgopolsky 1999.

[3] Leslau 1938, p. 232; Naumkin 1981, p. 53. Four versions (Mehri, Jibbali, Soqoṭri, and Arabic) of a story containing this word can be found in D. H. Müller 1907, p. 23. Note that, in the context of that story, the word "shark" is not used independently, but rather all four languages use a word for "fish" before the word for "shark."

[4] Johnstone 1981, p. 167; 1987, p. 259.

[5] Jahn 1902, pp. 209, 252. See also Sima 2009, text 16, for numerous occurrences of this word.

[6] Johnstone 1987, p. 259.

[7] Johnstone 1977, p. 86.

this is very uncertain.[8] A related word for "shark" occurs also in South Arabian Arabic dialects, in the forms *luxam*, *laxam*, or *laxm*,[9] and it is reasonable to suspect that this is a borrowing from Modern South Arabian.[10] The phonological correspondence of the Modern South Arabian words with the Central Semitic ones is problematic, since we must reconstruct a root **lxm* for Modern South Arabian.[11] The problem, recognized by others before me,[12] is that Central Semitic **lḥm* and Modern South Arabian **lxm* do not exhibit a regular sound correspondence. That is, Central Semitic **lḥm* should derive from Proto-Semitic **lḥm*, while Modern South Arabian **lxm* should derive from Proto-Semitic **lxm*. The irregular correspondence of the middle gutturals is precisely the issue that renders Ge'ez *lahm* problematic. But Ullendorff's and Swiggers' idea that a single word meaning "staple food" has come to refer to either bread, meat, or a kind of fish in communities of different types is quite tempting. So, can it be possible that Central Semitic **lḥm* and Modern South Arabian **lxm* are somehow related?

We might suggest a simple irregular shift of *ḥ* to *x* within Modern South Arabian. Such a change is not unknown in this language group. For example, the verb "want" in Mehri is normally *ḥōm*, but in the dialect of the village of Redan, in the southeastern corner of Yemen, it is *xōm*, as it is also in Ḥarsusi, which I consider to be a dialect of Mehri.[13] Still, such examples are very rare. We can also point to irregular correspondences between *ḥ* and *x* elsewhere in West Semitic. Huehnergard (2003, p. 111 n. 17) gives several examples, including Ugaritic *ḥdr* 'room' versus Arabic, Ge'ez, and Sabaic *xdr* 'reside'; Ge'ez *ʾalḥosasa* 'whisper' versus Ugaritic *lxšt* 'whispering'; and Ge'ez *ṭabḥa* 'slaughter' versus Arabic *ṭabaxa* 'cook' and Ugaritic *ṭbx* 'sacrifice, slaughter.' So perhaps to this list we could add Central Semitic **lḥm* and Modern South Arabian **lxm*.

At this point let us introduce the Akkadian evidence. Old Akkadian *laʾāmum*, Old Babylonian *lêmum*,[14] and Neo-Assyrian *liʾāmu* or *leʾāmu* 'eat; taste; drink' reflect a Proto-Semitic root **lḥm*.[15] Middle, Neo-, and Standard Babylonian *laxāmu* or *lexēmu* 'eat; taste,'[16] and Neo-Assyrian *lexmu* 'food' seem to reflect a Proto-Semitic root **lxm*. So, both **lḥm* and **lxm* are attested in Akkadian with a meaning connected to eating. There are two ways to account for this fact. The first possibility is that biforms existed in Proto-Semitic. If this were the case, then Central Semitic **lḥm* and Modern South Arabian **lxm* could also reflect these biforms. A second possibility, noted by Huehnergard (2003, p. 110 n. 16), is that the Akkadian forms with *x* do not reflect a Proto-Semitic **x*, but rather are the result of inter-dialectal mixing. Huehnergard (2003, p. 110) suggests, "Perhaps some early dialects of Akkadian preserved Proto-Semitic **ḥ* (as some dialects of Old Akkadian almost certainly did). Some dialectal words with Proto-Semitic **ḥ* could well have been borrowed into the later mainstream or literary (written) dialects, in which Proto-Semitic **ḥ* was otherwise lost, and in which [ḥ] would probably have been assimilated to /ḫ/, or at least written as such."

A third possibility, which Huehnergard (2003, p. 110 n. 16) believes to be more likely, is that the Akkadian forms with *x*, all of which are in later dialects, are borrowings from West Semitic. This is essentially the same idea as the second possibility, namely, that the Akkadian forms with *x* are borrowed and not inherited from Proto-Semitic, only in this case the borrowing is inter-Semitic, rather than intra-Akkadian.

---

[8] Leslau's (1938, p. 232) definition of "requin" is based on the passage cited in note 4. His secondary definition of "grand poisson" is based on D. H. Müller 1905, p. 68, in which *léḥem* is translated into German as "einen großen Fisch." In this folktale, the main character is supposed to climb into the mouth (*Rachen*) of this large fish, which will then take him to his homeland. It is certainly possible that this refers to some unspecified sea creature large enough to hold a man in its jaws, but equally possible that it refers to a shark. It is believed on some Pacific islands that sharks can help man in a time of need. Naumkin's secondary definition of "*bol'šaja ryba*" ('big fish') is presumably taken from Leslau.

[9] Arabic forms can be found in Stace 1893, p. 154; Jahn 1902, p. 274; Jayakar 1904, p. 268; and Landberg 1909, p. 396; 1942, p. 2625; cf. also Dozy 1881, vol. 2, p. 531. This word can also mean "stingray" or other poisonous fish in some Eastern (Gulf) Arabian dialects; see Holes 2000, p. 476.

[10] Militarev and Kogan (2005, p. 198) have raised the possibility that Modern South Arabian has borrowed from Arabic, but given that the word occurs in all of the Modern South Arabian languages, including the relatively isolated Soqoṭri, but only in South Arabian dialects of Arabic, a borrowing into Arabic seems more likely.

[11] In the dialect of Soqoṭri on which Leslau based his lexicon, the fricative *x* has merged with *ḥ*, hence Soqoṭri *léḥem*. It has been reported that some dialects of Soqoṭri do preserve *x* (Simeone-Senelle 1998), though, as far as I am aware, the word for "shark" has not been documented for such dialects.

[12] Fronzaroli (1971, p. 615), Dolgopolsky (1999, pp. 157–58).

[13] For Ḥarsusi, see Johnstone 1977, p. 145. For the dialect of Rehan, see Sima 2009; an example of *xōm* can be found on p. 474, text 83/2.

[14] Old Babylonian also has *lemûm*, which reflects metathesized root **lmḥ*.

[15] On the Old Akkadian writing of *ḥ*, see Hasselbach 2005, pp. 80–82.

[16] The only Middle Babylonian attestation of which I am aware is in an Amarna letter from Mitanni, EA 29:57. In this context, the word could easily be viewed as a West Semitic lexeme.

In short, we can make a case that Central Semitic *lḥm and Modern South Arabian *lxm are related, by suggesting either Proto-Semitic biforms — though the Akkadian evidence for this is extremely shaky — or by suggesting an irregular, but not unknown, correspondence of *ḥ and *x. Both scenarios have weak supporting evidence, but are not impossible. However, I think that the relationship of Central Semitic *lḥm and Modern South Arabian *lxm can be conclusively disproven on other grounds.

First, let us re-examine the semantic connection of Central Semitic *lḥm and Modern South Arabian *lxm. Following the argument of Ullendorff and Swiggers that *lḥm refers to the staple food item, it does not seem to be a stretch to suggest that this root could have come to refer to fish on an island like Soqoṭra, which still today depends largely on fishing, at least in the coastal regions. However, the root *lxm refers not to fish in general (as Central Semitic *lḥm refers to 'bread' or 'meat' in general), but rather to 'shark.' As noted above, the Soqoṭri word can possibly refer to 'a big fish,' but even if this is correct (which I doubt), it is still not the general word for fish, but rather is just one of many different words for types of fish.[17] The general words for fish are *ṣodəh* and *ḥot*; the latter term may refer to larger fish, as it does in Mehri and Jibbali. Moreover, while shark is an important export of Soqoṭra, and while dried shark is a common food item in the coastal areas of Soqoṭra, it is not commonly eaten in the pastoral areas of the island (Naumkin 1993, pp. 162–63). Fish is also not an important part of the diet of modern Mehri or Jibbali speakers. We can perhaps overlook the fact that the word refers not to fish in general, but to a specific kind of fish; such a semantic shift is well attested cross-linguistically (cf. English *deer* < Old English *dēor* 'animal'). However, when we consider the fact that fish is simply not the staple food item of most Modern South Arabian speakers, we have to seriously question the semantic link between Central Semitic *lḥm and Modern South Arabian *lxm.

An even more damaging argument against the relationship of Central Semitic *lḥm and Modern South Arabian *lxm is the simple fact that Modern South Arabian *lxm has a far more likely cognate. As noted briefly by Fronzaroli (1971, p. 615), and outlined in convincing detail by Militarev and Kogan (2005, pp. 197–98), Modern South Arabian *lxm should be connected to the Akkadian word *lax(a)mu*, attested in several dialects, including Old Akkadian. This Akkadian word is most often used to refer to some kind of mythological sea monster, and the fact that it refers to a sea creature, coupled with the regular correspondence of Modern South Arabian and Akkadian consonants, makes it highly probable that the Akkadian word is cognate with the Modern South Arabian words. Therefore, Modern South Arabian *lxm is not cognate with Central Semitic *lḥm.

In the end, though we have only disproven an etymology that many did not believe in the first place, and ultimately presented a known etymology, we have at least adduced a further example of a word attested only in East Semitic and "South" Semitic (i.e., Modern South Arabian and Ethiopian Semitic), which can be added to the lists compiled by Leslau (1962; 1964; 1969) and Huehnergard (1991).

Mehri *nəxāli* 'under'

There are many examples of prepositions in Semitic that stem from the grammaticalization of nouns with a spatial connotation.[18] A few examples are Palestinian Arabic *ḥadd* 'next to' (< Classical Arabic *ḥadd* 'border'), Modern Standard Arabic *janba* 'next to' (< *janb* 'side'), Maltese *flok* 'instead of' (< Arabic *fī* 'in'+ Sicilian *locu* 'place'), Aramaic *bātar* 'after' (< *b-* 'in' + *ʾatar* 'place'), and Amharic *bä-...bet* 'according to' (< *bä* 'in' + *bet* 'house'). However, in none of these examples does the original noun refer to a particular feature of topography.[19] At least one example is possibly to be found in Modern South Arabian.

---

[17] See Naumkin 1981, pp. 52–54, for a long list of fish names in Soqoṭri.

[18] Numerous Arabic examples can be found in Procházka 1993. For some discussion of the grammaticalization aspect, see Rubin 2005, pp. 46–48; Esseesy 2010.

[19] The preposition *yamm* 'beside, next to, near; toward' found in a wide variety of Arabic dialects is probably not connected with the word *yamm* 'sea' (Procházka 1993, pp. 247–49).

It has been suggested that the Mehri preposition *nəxāli* 'under'[20] is cognate with Akkadian *naxallu* (also *naxlu*), Hebrew *naḥal*, Aramaic *naḥlā*, and Ugaritic *nxl*,[21] all having the meaning "wadi, stream, (river-)valley."[22] We can imagine a source phrase "(in) the valley of X" becoming grammaticalized as "under X." Can this idea be supported?

In fact, this idea is supported most strongly by Omani Mehri *xōṭər* 'down(ward), downstairs (directional)' and *b-xōṭər* 'down there, downstairs (locational),' which have as their source the noun *xōṭər* 'valley.'[23] Though we are dealing in this case with adverbs rather than a preposition, the connection between a locational function word and a topographical noun is clear. This example has a nice parallel in Polish *na górę* 'upstairs (directional),' *na górze* 'upstairs (locational),' *do góry* 'up, upward,' and several other similar constructions, all of which are based on the noun *góra* 'mountain.'

We can also turn to Jibbali for another possible parallel to the derivation of Mehri *nəxāli*. In Jibbali, the preposition *ʿaḳ* 'in, inside; at' (before suffixes, *ʿamḳ-*) clearly derives from the word *ʿamḳ* 'middle; place.' The basic meaning of *ʿamḳ* in Modern South Arabian is 'middle,' as attested by Soqoṭri, Mehri, and Ḥarsusi, in which it has only this meaning; only in some dialects of Jibbali does it have the secondary meaning 'place.' That the preposition and the noun are distinct (i.e., that the noun has been fully grammaticalized as *ʿaḳ*) is proven by a phrase like *ʿaḳ ʿamḳ aġág* 'among [lit. in the middle of] the men,'[24] in which we see both the source lexeme and the grammaticalized form used side by side. The irregular loss of the *m* in the form *ʿaḳ* is simply a by-product of the grammaticalization. Still, the grammaticalization of a noun meaning "middle" or "place" into a locative preposition is unremarkable. More interesting is that some cognates of the word *ʿamḳ* have a topographical sense, namely, Hebrew *ʿemεq*, Ugaritic *ʿmq*,[25] and Phoenician *ʿmq*, all meaning 'valley.'[26] However, in each of these languages, as in Aramaic, Arabic, and Ethiopic, the basic meaning of the root *ʿmq* is 'be deep,' as attested by a wide variety of verbal, nominal, and adjectival forms.[27] So the use of this root to indicate a feature of topography would seem to be secondary. However, this example highlights once again the close connection between topographical words and words describing physical/spatial relations. In sum, there is a very plausible semantic connection between Mehri *nəxāli* 'under' and the Akkadian and Northwest Semitic words for "wadi, (river-)valley."

But let us now consider another possible etymology of Mehri *nəxāli*, for which we must turn to Soqoṭri. The Soqoṭri word for 'under' is *nəḥaṭ* (or *nəḥat*).[28] Bittner (1918, p. 62) suggested a possible connection between this word and Mehri *nəxāli*, despite the obvious phonetic differences. Soqoṭri *ḥ* can correspond to Mehri *x* or *ḥ*, as noted in the previous section (note 11), but the correspondence of Mehri *l* and Soqoṭri *ṭ* (or *t*) is totally irregular. The Soqoṭri word is possibly to be connected with the root *nḥt* 'descend, go down,' attested in Hebrew, Aramaic, and Ugaritic, as suggested by Leslau (1938, p. 263). This connection still leaves the final glottalic *ṭ* unexplained, but the Soqoṭri word is attested with non-glottalic *t* (see note 28), and a shift *t* > *ṭ* is not overly problematic.[29]

We have suggested a plausible etymology for Soqoṭri *nəḥaṭ* (Semitic root *nḥt*) and a plausible etymology for Mehri *nəxāli* (Semitic root *nxl*), but the fact that two of the three consonants of the Mehri and Soqoṭri prepositions correspond must give us pause. There is no obvious way to derive *nəḥaṭ* from *nəxāli*, but what if we assume that these two words are cognate, deriving from a form **nəxaṭ* (or **nəxat*)? This is explainable if this **nəxaṭ* were used in conjunction with the common preposition **li-*; compare Hebrew *mit-taḥat lə-*.[30] We might suggest the following chain of events: *(*mən*) *nəxaṭ li-* → *(*mən*) *nəxal li-* → *nəxāli*. The assimilation of the preposition *li-* to a preceding word is known elsewhere in Semitic; compare Syriac *netel* 'he will give,' back-formed from phrase such as *netel li* <

[20] This Mehri preposition can also be pronounced (and transcribed) as *ənxāli* or *nxāli*. This minor phonetic variation is irrelevant to the present discussion.

[21] The Ugaritic form is possibly attested syllabically as *naxal(l)u*; see Huehnergard 2008, p. 152.

[22] The same suggestion was also made by Bittner (1918, p. 62) and W. W. Müller (1985, p. 272), though they provide no discussion. I have also mentioned this idea previously (Rubin 2011).

[23] The noun is not found in Johnstone's lexicon (1987), but appears in the lexicons of Jahn (1902) and Nakano (1986). This etymology was also recognized by Bittner (1918, p. 62).

[24] Johnstone 1981, p. 193.

[25] This is attested syllabically as *ʿamuqu* (Huehnergard 2008, p. 160).

[26] Corresponding forms in Samaritan Aramaic and in some of the Targumim are perhaps Hebraisms.

[27] Cf. Leslau 1991, p. 63.

[28] The form appears as *nəḥaṭ* or *nəḥat* in the texts collected by the South Arabian Expedition, on which Leslau based his lexicon (1938). Johnstone, in various publications, only gives *n(ə)ḥaṭ* or *náḥaṭ* (1975, p. 118; 1977, p. 99; 1981, p. 167; 1987, p. 308). Nakano (1986, p. 134), on the other hand, gives only *nḥāt*.

[29] It is not clear what to make of Soqoṭri (*di-*)*ḥale* 'under' Leslau (1938, p. 175), attested only twice, in poetic contexts (D. H. Müller 1902, p. 162; 1905, p. 193). Clearly, having more reliable data for Soqoṭri remains a desideratum.

[30] In fact, Mehri *nəxāli* sometimes appears in the compound *mən nəxāli* with the simple meaning 'under'; see Rubin 2010, p. 199, for examples.

neten li 'he will give me.'[31] The loss of gemination (i.e., *nəxalli > nəxāli) is regular in Modern South Arabian; compare Mehri D/L-Stem *ḥōməl* versus Arabic D-Stem *ḥammala* 'he loaded.'[32] It is noteworthy that in Müller's Mehri texts, the preposition is sometimes transcribed *inxálli*, with a geminate consonant.[33]

We are thus presented with two options:

1. Mehri *nəxāli* is connected with the Akkadian and Northwest Semitic words for 'wadi, (river-) valley.' Soqoṭri *nəḥaṭ* is not cognate and may be connected with the Northwest Semitic root *nḥt* 'descend, go down.'
2. Mehri *nəxāli* is cognate with Soqoṭri *nəḥaṭ*, and the final *l* is the result of a misanalysis of an earlier compound *nəxaṭ li-*. Both forms may still then be connected with the Northwest Semitic root *nḥt* 'descend, go down' — however, we would have an irregular correspondence of Modern South Arabian *x* and Northwest Semitic *ḥ*.[34] See the previous section for discussion of such a correspondence, which is not unknown.

Both of these etymologies for Mehri *nəxāli* are quite acceptable. But there remain a handful of other details to consider. Regardless of which etymology is correct, we could argue that the final *-i* of *nəxāli* is unexpected, as inherited final short vowels are normally lost in Mehri. If *nəxāli* comes from an earlier noun meaning something like 'valley,' we could explain the *-i* as a genitive case ending; this should have dropped, but could have been frozen along with the grammaticalization. Frozen case endings are found in various Semitic languages that have otherwise lost the case system. If Mehri *nəxāli* derives from an earlier compound **nəxaṭ li-*, then the final *-i* would be the original vowel of the preposition *li-*. This clitic preposition has normally lost the vowel (cf. Mehri *l(ə)-* 'to, for'), but its survival can be attributed to the re-analysis of the original compound in general, or, specifically, to the re-analysis of the *i* as part of the pronominal suffixes in the suffixed forms (see below).

Whatever the source of the final *-i* of *nəxāli*, its presence has had consequences for the declension of this preposition. When *nəxāli* takes pronominal suffixes, it takes those suffixes used with plural nouns (cf. Hebrew *taḥat* and others).[35] The dual and plural pronominal suffixes used with plural nouns are identical to those that attach to singular nouns, except that they are preceded by the vowel *i*, for example, *ḥayb-həm* 'their father' (< *ḥayb* 'father'), but *ḥə́b-ihəm* 'their fathers' (< *ḥawb* 'fathers, parents').[36] So, an original *nəxāli-həm* 'under them,' for example, was re-interpreted as *nəxāl-ihəm*, with the suffix *-ihəm* that is found attached to plural nouns, and subsequently the entire paradigm shifted to the pattern used for plural nouns. We might then expect the non-suffixed form to be *nəxāl*, since the final *-i* was re-interpreted as part of the pronominal suffixes. In fact, a shorter form without the final *-i* is indeed found in some Mehri dialects and in Jibbali (see below). This leads us to the next remaining issue, which is the form of this lexeme in the other Modern South Arabian languages.

In Ḥarsusi, the form of 'under' is essentially the same as in Mehri: *ənxāli* or *ənxə́li*. In Jibbali, however, this preposition is attested in a variety of forms. Johnstone records *nxín* for the Eastern dialect, and *lxín* for the Central dialect;[37] Nakano records *lxī*;[38] the texts of Müller, recorded seventy or eighty years before Johnstone and Nakano collected their data, have *nxal*.[39] In addition to the difference in vowel quality found in the more modern Jibbali forms (and here we can cite the vowel correspondence of Mehri *əlhān* 'all that which' and Jibbali *əlhín* 'idem'), the Jibbali forms show either an assimilation of the initial and final consonants (*nxín*) or a metathesis (*lxín*). A metathesized form *lxān* is also attested in some Mehri dialects, for example in the Mehri of the Yemeni Šarqiyah.[40]

[31] For similar cases of the assimilation of the preposition *l-* in Aramaic, though with a different result, see Boyarin 1976.

[32] See Rubin 2010, pp. 94–97, for more examples. Also note that if this derivation of *nəxāli* < **nəxalli* is correct, and if it proceeded by regular sound change, it must have taken place *after* the shift of *ā > ō that we see in the D/L-Stem and elsewhere.

[33] An example can be found in D. H. Müller 1905, p. 43. Note that Bittner (1914) adjusted this transcription to *(i)nxáli*, without the gemination, in his edition of Müller's text. It is also worth noting that the preposition is transcribed once as just *xāli* in a text collected by Hein (1909, p. 115).

[34] If the root *nḥt* 'descend, go down' is connected with the common West Semitic **taḥt* 'under' (see Leslau 1991, pp. 572–73), then the *ḥ* can be reconstructed for all of West Semitic.

[35] See Rubin 2010, p. 207, or Johnstone 1987, p. xviii, for a complete set of forms.

[36] Rubin 2010, p. 36.

[37] Johnstone 1977, p. 99; 1981, p. 167; 1987, p. 308.

[38] Nakano 1986, p. 134.

[39] An example can be found in D. H. Müller 1907, p. 43.

[40] Numerous examples can be found in Sima 2009; one example is on p. 200, text 36/6. The form *nxāl* is found only about six or seven times in this large collection (e.g., p. 518, text 91/2), all of which are from the dialect of Redan.

In the Jibbali dialects, as well as in Šarqiyah Mehri, the preposition still takes the pronominal suffixes attached to a plural noun, even though they have lost the final *-i* in the base. The loss of the final *-i* is presumably the next step in the analogy that caused this preposition to take the plural suffixes in the first place, as described above.

In the end, we can explain the forms of the preposition "under" in the Modern South Arabian languages, though we are left with a choice with regard to their etymology (or etymologies).

Bibliography

Armbruster, Charles H.

1920 *Initia Amharica: An Introduction to Spoken Amharic*, Part 3: *Amharic-English Vocabulary with Phrases*. Cambridge: Cambridge University Press.

Bittner, Maximilian

1914 *Studien zur Laut- und Formenlehre der Mehri-Sprache in Südarabien*, Volume 5: *Zu ausgewählten Texten*, Part 1: *Nach den Aufnahmen von D. H. v. Müller*. Sitzungsberichte der Kaiserlichen Akademie der Wissenschaften in Wien, Philosophisch-Historische Klasse 176/1. Vienna: Hölder.

1918 *Vorstudien zur Grammatik und zum Wörterbuche der Soqoṭri-Sprache*, Volume 2: *Das Märchen vom Aschenputtel in den drei Mahra-Sprachen (Soqoṭri, Mehri und Šḫauri): Eine sprachvergleichende Studie*. Sitzungsberichte der Kaiserlichen Akademie der Wissenschaften in Wien, Philosophisch-Historische Klasse 186/4. Vienna: Hölder.

Boyarin, Daniel

1976 "The Loss of Final Consonants in Babylonian Jewish Aramaic (BJA)." *Afroasiastic Linguistics* 3/5: 103–07 [19–23].

del Olmo Lete, Gregorio, and Joaquín Sanmartín

2004 *A Dictionary of the Ugaritic Language in the Alphabetic Tradition*. Translated by Wilfred G. E. Watson. Second edition. 2 volumes. Leiden: Brill.

Dolgopolsky, Aharon

1999 "On the Etymology of Hebrew לֶחֶם." In *Michael: Historical, Epigraphical, and Biblical Studies in Honor of Prof. Michael Heltzer*, edited by Yitzhak Avishur and Robert Deutsch, pp. 157–60. Tel Aviv: Archaeological Center Publications.

Dozy, R.

1881 *Supplément aux dictionnaires arabes*. 2 volumes. Leiden: Brill.

Esseesy, Mohssen

2010 *Grammaticalization of Arabic Prepositions and Subordinators: A Corpus-Based Study*. Leiden: Brill.

Fronzaroli, Pelio

1971 "Studi sul lessico comune semitico, VII: L'alimentazione." *Accademia Nazionale dei Lincei, Rendiconti* 26: 603–42.

Hasselbach, Rebecca

2005 *Sargonic Akkadian: A Historical and Comparative Study of the Syllabic Texts*. Wiesbaden: Harrassowitz.

Hein, Wilhelm

1909 *Mehri- und Ḥaḍrami-Texte Gesammelt im Jahre 1902 in Gischin*. Compiled and edited by David Heinrich Müller. Südarabische Expedition 9. Vienna: Alfred Hölder.

Holes, Clive

2000 *Dialect, Culture, and Society in Eastern Arabia*, Volume 1: *Glossary*. Handbuch der Orientalistik. Erste Abteilung, Nahe und der Mittlere Osten 51. Leiden: Brill.

Huehnergard, John

1991 "Further South Semitic Cognates to the Akkadian Lexicon." In *Semitic Studies: In Honor of Wolf Leslau on the Occasion of his Eighty-fifth Birthday*, edited by Alan S. Kaye, volume 1, pp. 690–713. Wiesbaden: Harrassowitz.

2003 "Akkadian ḫ and West Semitic ḥ." In *Orientalia: Papers of the Oriental Institute 3* (*Studia Semitica*), edited by Leonid Kogan, pp. 102–19. Moscow: Russian State University for the Humanities.

2008 *Ugaritic Vocabulary in Syllabic Transcription*. Revised edition. Winona Lake: Eisenbrauns.

Isenberg, Charles William

1841 *Dictionary of the Amharic Language*. London: The Church Missionary Society.

Jahn, Alfred

1902 *Die Mehri-Sprache in Südarabien: Texte und Wörterbuch*. Südarabische Expedition 3. Vienna: Alfred Hölder.

Jayakar, A. S. G.

1904 "The Shahee Dialect of Arabic." *Journal of the Bombay Branch of the Royal Asiatic Society* 21: 246–77.

Johnstone, T. M.

1975 "The Modern South Arabian Languages." *Afroasiatic Linguistics* 1/5: 93–121 [1–29].

1977 *Ḥarsūsi Lexicon and English-Ḥarsūsi Word-List*. London: Oxford University Press.

1981 *Jibbāli Lexicon*. London: Oxford University Press.

1987 *Mehri Lexicon and English-Mehri Word-List*. London: School of Oriental and African Studies.

Krotkoff, Georg

1969 *Laḥm* "Fleisch" und *leḥem* "Brot." *Wiener Zeitschrift für die Kunde des Morgenlandes* 62: 76–82.

Landberg, Carlo

1909 *Études sur les dialectes de l'Arabie méridionale*, Volume 2: *Daṯînah*, Part 2: *Commentaire des textes prosaïques*. Leiden: Brill.

1942 *Glossaire daṯînois*, Volume 3. Published by K. V. Zetterstéen. Leiden: Brill.

Leslau, Wolf

1938 *Lexique Soqoṭri (sudarabique moderne)*. Paris: C. Klincksieck.

1958 *Ethiopic and South Arabic Contributions to the Hebrew Lexicon*. Berkeley and Los Angeles: University of California Press.

1962 "Southeast Semitic Cognates to the Akkadian Vocabulary 1." *Journal of the American Oriental Society* 82: 1–4.

1964 "Southeast Semitic Cognates to the Akkadian Vocabulary 2." *Journal of the American Oriental Society* 84: 115–18.

1969 "Southeast Semitic Cognates to the Akkadian Vocabulary 3." *Journal of the American Oriental Society* 89: 18–22.

1991 *Comparative Dictionary of Geʿez (Classical Ethiopic)*. Wiesbaden: Harrassowitz.

Militarev, Alexander, and Leonid Kogan

2005 *Semitic Etymological Dictionary*, Volume 2: *Animal Names*. Münster: Ugarit-Verlag.

Müller, David Heinrich

1902 *Die Mehri- und Soqoṭri-Sprache*, Volume 1: *Mehri-Texte*. Südarabische Expedition 4. Vienna: Alfred Hölder

1905 *Die Mehri- und Soqoṭri-Sprache*, Volume 2: *Soqoṭri-Texte*. Südarabische Expedition 6. Vienna: Alfred Hölder.

1907 *Die Mehri- und Soqoṭri-Sprache*, Volume 3: *Šḫauri-Texte*. Südarabische Expedition 7. Vienna: Alfred Hölder.

Müller, Walter W.

1985 Beiträge aus dem Mehri zum etymologischen Teil des hebräischen Lexicons. In *Mélanges linguistiques offerts à Maxime Rodinson par ses élèves, ses collègues et ses amis*, edited by Christian Robin, pp. 267–78. Paris: P. Geuthner.

Nakano, Aki'o

1986 *Comparative Vocabulary of Southern Arabic: Mahri, Gibbali, and Soqotri*. Tokyo: Institute for the Study of Languages and Cultures of Asia and Africa.

Naumkin, Vitaly V.

1981 *Очерки по этнолингвистике Сокотры* (Essays in the Ethnolinguistics of Soqotra). Moscow: Nauka.

1993 *Island of the Phoenix: An Ethnographic Study of the People of Socotra*. Translated by Valery A. Epstein. Reading, UK: Ithaca.

Procházka, Stephan

1993 *Die Präpositionen in den neuarabischen Dialekten*. Vienna: VWGÖ-Verlag.

Rubin, Aaron D.

2005 *Studies in Semitic Grammaticalization.* Winona Lake: Eisenbrauns.

2010 *The Mehri Language of Oman.* Leiden: Brill.

2011 "Mehri Dialect Studies: Omani and Šarqīyah Mehri." *Zeitschrift für Arabische Linguistik* 54: 67–83.

Sima, Alexander

2009 *Mehri-Texte aus der jemenitischen Šarqīyah.* Annotated and edited by Janet C. E. Watson and Werner Arnold, and in collaboration with 'Askari Ḥugayrān Sa'd. Wiesbaden: Harrassowitz.

Simeone-Senelle, Marie-Claude

1998 "The Soqotri Language." In *Proceedings of the First International Symposium on Soqotra Island: Present and Future,* Volume 1, edited by H. J. Dumont. New York: United Nations.

Stace, E. V.

1893 *An English-Arabic Vocabulary for the Use of Students of the Colloquial.* London: Bernard Quaritch.

Swiggers, Pierre

1981 "The Meaning of the Root *lḥm* 'food' in the Semitic Languages." *Ugarit-Forschungen* 13: 307–08.

Ullendorff, Edward

1956 "The Contribution of South Semitics to Hebrew Lexicography." *Vetus Testamentum* 6: 190–98.

1967 *Ethiopia and the Bible.* The Schweich Lectures 1967. Oxford: Oxford University Press.

21

"If Water Had Not Been Made to Dry Up, This Earth Would Have Been Drowned": Pahlavi *āwās- 'to dry'

Prods Oktor Skjærvø, Harvard University

Old Iranian literature contains a number of statements phrased as irrealis conditions that justify common practices: if something were (not) so, the order of the cosmos would be hopelessly corrupted. One of the most famous occurs in chapter five of the Avestan *Videvdad*, a book dealing with the pollution of this world caused by the forces of evil in the Zoroastrian dualist cosmology. The setting is that of a bird, which, having nibbled on a corpse, flies from the deepest valley up to the highest mountain and onto a tree, on which it vomits, defecates, and ...-s. A man comes up from the deepest valley up to the highest mountain seeking firewood. He chops down the tree and uses the wood as firewood. The question Zarathustra asks god (Ahura Mazdā) is whether the pollution caused by the bird also pollutes the fire, Ahura Mazdā's son. Ahura Mazdā sensibly answers no. For if (non-obvious) polluting matter brought by birds, wolves, wind, or flies were polluting, then the entire world of the living would have been hopelessly polluted by all the dead things (of which we are not aware) that lie all over the earth, and salvation would have been beyond everybody's reach.[1]

The Zoroastrian priests of the Sasanian period (A.D. 224–650) had serious problems with the passage, with the nature of the pollution (whether *hixr* or *nasāy*, see below), in what way the dead matter was affected by digestion, whether there were aggravating circumstances (the wood had been used for hanging, had been touched by a menstruating woman, etc.), and so on.

I am happy to offer to John Huehnergaard, who introduced me to Harvard in 1991 (and advised me on how to negotiate with the dean!), in acknowledgment of a long friendship, these notes, which also highlight the fate of the Aramaic script among the Sasanian Iranians.

The statement quoted in the title is from the so-called *Pahlavi Rivāyat*, a miscellany of texts on a large variety of issues of Zoroastrian theology.[2] In chapter 13 Zarathustra asks Ahura Mazdā about a number of things caused by Ahrimen (the creator of evil) that might seem only evil, but Ahura Mazdā explains what their functions are in the great scheme of things. Our passage is edited by Alan V. Williams as follows (text in brackets added):[3]

---

[1] Another such statement is in the first book of the *Videvdad*, in which the two "creators" create the lands and the things that are good and bad for the lands, respectively. Ahura Mazdā tells Zarathustra that, first of all, he made a very nice land, where all is pleasure, and explains that if he had not done so, then the whole world would have flocked into the Aryan Expanse, the mythical homeland of the Iranians, which he then goes on to make. This type of statement may be part of the Indo-European poetic language as it is also found in other Indo-European literatures. There is, for instance, a quite similar statement in Snorri Sturluson's *Edda*, where Gangleri asks the High One why there is fire on the Bifrost bridge (which leads from earth to heaven). The answer is that the red in the rainbow is fire. If it were not, then any and all evil beings would have been able to cross over and up to heaven.

[2] *The Pahlavi Rivāyat Accompanying the Dādestān ī Dēnīg* (Williams 1990). It "accompanies" the *Dādestān ī Dēnīg* because they are associated in the manuscripts.

[3] The text is not metrical, but I have divided the text so as to make it easier to orient oneself in the text and translation.

Pahlavi Rivāyat 13a9

> *ēk ān ka-š āb bē (hōšēnīd*
> *čē agar āb) hōšēnišn nē hē*
> *hamāg ēn zamīg (āb) bē estād hē*
> *u-š aziš garān anāgīh hē*
>
> One (i.e., yet another) is when he made the water dry up,
> for, if the water had not been made to dry up,
> water would have stood all (over) this earth,
> and there would be severe evil from it.

The restorations in (...) are justified by the parallel next sentence:

Pahlavi Rivāyat 13a10

> *ēk ān ka-š ātaxš bē afsārd*
> *čē agar ātaxš ōh sōxt hē bē nē afsārd hē*
> *hamāg en gēhan ātaxš bē estād hē*
>
> One (i.e., yet another) is when he cooled the fire,
> for, if the fire had burnt (on) in the usual way (and) had not been cooled down,
> fire would have stood all (over) this world of the living.

The reading *hōšēn-išn*, <hwšyn-šn'> , however, is an emendation for <'w'yšn-šn'> , which is, most probably, for 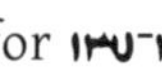 <'w'syn-šn'> **āwāsēn-išn*.[4]

This verb is found in three basic spellings:

1.  <'w's->, past tense in *-īd*, and causative in *-ēn-* (most common);[5] the spelling is very ambiguous: **awās-*, **āwās-*, **hawās-*, **xwās-*, *anās-*, *ānās-*; **awāh-*, **āwāh-*, etc.; **awāy-*, *āwāy-*, etc. are the most obvious alternatives.

2. 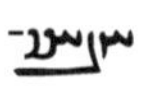 <'wb's->; this spelling rules out forms in *xw-* and *an-/ān-*, while the spelling <'w's-> rules out a reading of <'wb's-> as <hnb's-> with initial *hanb-* (*hamb-*).

3.  <'wp's->; taken together with 1 and 2, this spelling fairly guarantees the readings with *awā-* or *āwā-* (with <-wp-> = -w-).

As the reading of the verb is still conjectural, it has been given an asterisk **āwās-* here, which does not mean that the identity of the letters is in doubt, only their interpretation.

The Pahlavi verb was discussed by Jehangir C. Tavadia in his edition of the *Šāyest nē šāyest*,[6] where he pointed out several passages in which it occurs. His discussion, unfortunately, has been overlooked.

Williams also edited *hōšēn-* in the following passage:

Pahlavi Rivāyat 35c2

> *ēn-iz stārag ī be widerēd cē*
> *ēn āhōgēnisn ī az ahrimen*
> *ka ō mardōmān ōftēd wars spēd kunēd*
> *ud ka ō urwarān ōftēd bē hōšēnēd*
> *ud ka bē (ō) gospandān ōftēd mīrēd*

---

[4] Recall that the Pahlavi script descended ultimately from Imperial Aramaic and, still fairly unambiguous in the third to fourth centuries, had become much less so by the time the Zoroastrian texts were written down in the ninth century. In the manuscripts (13th to 19th centuries), we have <ʾ> = <h> (for <ḥ> or <ẖ>); <w> = <n> = <r> = <ʿayn>; <y> = <d> = <g> = <b>; <s> = <yy>; <š> ≈ or = <yʾ, yh>; etc. In arameograms, <ʾ> and <'> are interchangeable.

[5] Further derivatives from both the intransitive stem **āwās-* and the transitive **āwās-ēn-* include those in *-išn*, active verbal action noun and participle of necessity and those in *-īh* and *-išn-īh*, verbal action nouns.

[6] Tavadia (1930) suggested the readings *hawās-* or *hanbās-*, which he pointed out look like inchoatives in *-s-*.

And what is this star that passes by! (falling star)
This is a pollution from Ahrimen.
When it falls on humans, it makes the hair white;
and when it falls on plants, it makes them dry out;
and when (it falls on) animals, they die (lit.: 'it dies').

Here, the analysis of the manuscripts is slightly more complex.[7] Apparently, the passage is only found in late manuscripts: BKa (a later replacement of a number of folios in BK [1572]) has <'wptyt'>, that is, *ōftēd* 'falls.' MR1a (copied from BKa in 1867) and Jb (unrelated to BKa, copied between 1841 and 1847) have *hōšēnēd*. As the late manuscripts MR1a and Jb, despite not being directly related, may have interdependent readings, it is possible that BKa contains an older form. Perhaps unfamiliar with the form <'wp'syt'> *āwāsēd* in the original he was copying, the scribe may have "corrected" it to <'wptyt'> *ōftēd* 'falls,' which was already used three times in this passage.[8]

The first time, however, I noticed the verb *āwās-* was in the Pahlavi translation of a repeated Avestan phrase in chapter five of the *Videvdad* (5.12–13),[9] which I have been studying for years at the instigation of my Talmudist friend and colleague Yaakov Elman at the Yeshiva University in New York. Later on, I remembered my former acquaintance with the verb when I came across it again in the *Zand ī fragard ī Jud-dēw-dād* ('commentary on chapters of the *Videvdad*') in a passage dealing with the pollution of water, which I also read with Yaakov.[10] Having begun looking for other occurrences, I came across two in the *Šāyest nē šāyest* ('what should or should not be done'), which I originally studied with Yaakov and his student Shai Secunda during their sojourns at Harvard and which led me to Tavadia's discussion. In all three texts, the same kind of problems encountered by both the rabbis and the Zoroastrian priests are discussed and are of great importance for understanding the intellectual development of these two groups, who shared living spaces in Sasanian Ctesiphon, older Babylon, in the fourth to seventh centuries. Lastly, after having begun to suspect all instances of the verb *hōš-ēn-*, I came across the verb in the *Pahlavi Rivāyat* and the *Nērangistān*.

The two passages from *Šāyest nē šāyest* (both <ʾwbʾs->) are the following:

Šāyest nē šāyest 3.10

*dast ī pad pādyābīh *āwāsīdag*
ka zan ī daštān wēnēd
pad wēnišn apādyāb bē bawēd

A hand that has been dried in the ritual cleansing,[11]
if a menstruant woman sees it,
by being seen (by her) it becomes unclean.

Šāyest nē šāyest 10.5

ēk ēn kū hēnd az-iz hāwištān ī
ka ō yazišn ī yazdān kerdan hamē šawēnd
*mēwag hamē *āwāsēnēnd*
*ud agar ān *āwāsišn namb-ēw aziš bē burdan rāy kunēd*
nišīnān kunišn

One thing is this: there are even some of the students who,
when they go to perform a sacrifice for the gods,
keep drying off the fruits.

[7] See Williams 1990, part 1, pp. 20–25.

[8] But cf. also the unexplained readings , <'wc(y)yyyt> in the *Nērangestān* 10.15 (below).

[9] The standard edition of the Pahlavi *Videvdad* is that of Hoshang Jamasp (1907). The Pahlavi text here is heavily edited, however, and it is crucial to consult available manuscripts, many of which are now accessible at the website of the Avestan Digital Archive (http://www.avesta-archive.com/). The Avestan text is cited after Karl Friedrich Geldner (1886–95).

[10] The text is in the manuscript TD2, published by Kaikhusroo M. JamaspAsa and Y. Mahyar Nawabi (1978–79). It was brought to the attention of my Talmudist friends and me by Dr. Götz König at the Freie Universität, Berlin.

[11] On this term, see Boyce 1991.

> And if one does the drying in order to remove (even?) a single (drop) of moisture from it, one should do it sitting down.

The passage from *Videvdad* chapter five is the following:[12]

Videvdad 5.12 (Avestan)[13]

> *aētaδa hē uzbaoδąm tanūm nidaiθiiąn*
> *bixšaparəm vā θrixšaparəm vā māzdrājahīm vā*
> *vīspəm ā ahmāt̰ yat̰ frā vaiiō patąn frā uruuara uzuxšiiąn*[14]
> *niiåṇcō apa tacin us vātō ząm haēcaiiāt̰*
>
> Here they should lay down the body whose consciousness has left it
> for two nights or three nights or a whole month,
> until the (scavenging?) birds fly away (from it) and plants grow forth (over it),
> the waters flow down (over it), and the wind *dries out the earth.

Videvdad 5.13

> *āat̰ yat̰ hīš frā vaiiō patąn frā uruuara uzuxšiiąn*
> *niiåṇcō apa tacin us vātō ząm haēcaiiāt̰*
> *aētaδa hē aēte mazdaiiasna*
> *aētəm kəhrpəm huuarə.darəsīm kərənaot̰*
>
> Then, when the birds fly away (from it) and plants grow forth (over it),
> the waters flow down, and the wind *dries out the earth,
> here these Mazdayasniansv
> should expose this his body to the sun.

The Avestan phrases *vīspəm ā ahmāt̰ yat̰ ... us vātō ząm haēcaiiāt̰* and *āat̰ yat̰ hīš ... us vātō ząm haēcaiiāt̰* are rendered in Pahlavi as follows, according to Jamasp's edition:

> *hamē az ān tā ka ... ul wād zamīg *āwāsēnād*
> *ka ... ul wād zamīg *āwāsēnīd hād*
>
> until the wind dries the earth;
> when the wind has dried the earth.

Here, the two oldest manuscripts with Pahlavi translation, K1 (1324; Royal Library, Copenhagen) and L4 (1323; British Library), copied by the same scribe, are missing, and only some of their descendants are available. The passage is present in another old manuscript, however, Jamasp's IM (1575), which is from an independent branch from K1 and L4, but whose whereabouts are unknown.

In the first occurrence, Jamasp edits <'wsyn't'> and gives the following manuscript reading from IM <'w'syn't'>. Online mss.: B1 <'w'st't>; E10 (derived from L4) <'wsyn't'>.

In the second occurrence Jamasp edits <'wsynyt'>, but gives IM <'ww'st't'> (with <-st-> a common error for <-syn->). Online mss.: B1 <'ww'synyt' >; E10 <'synyt'>.

The meaning of the Avestan verb *us ... haēcaiia-* is also disputed, although, from the context, it should mean something like 'dry out.' Bartholomae connected the Avestan verb etymologically with Avestan *hiku-* 'dry' and rendered it as 'dry up,'[15] and this seems to me to be the most likely derivation, although Kellens has objected,

[12] Jamasp 1907, pp. 155–56. See also Skjærvø 2009, especially pp. 291–93.

[13] There are three branches of manuscripts of the *Videvdad*: Persian manuscripts with Pahlavi translation (PPV: K1, L4; B1, M3; IM), Persian manuscripts without Pahlavi translation (PVS: Mf2, Jp1), and Indian manuscripts without Pahlavi translation (IVS: the rest).

[14] The manuscripts Mf2 and Jp1 have *uzuxšiiąn* 'will grow *up*' (here and next).

[15] Bartholomae (1904, col. 1728) has ²*haēk* only with *us* 'exarescere' ('dry out' intrans.), causative 'arefacere' ('dry out' trans.).

arguing that the root *HIC* has two primary meanings, 'to sprinkle (water)' and 'to draw (water).'[16] Drawing water (out of a well), however, is not quite like drawing water out of wet matter, making it dry.[17] See more below.

The passages I have noted so far in the *Zand ī fragard ī J̌ud-dēw-dād* are the following.[18] The first deals with the same issue as *Videvdad* 5.12–13:

Zand ī fragard ī J̌ud-dēw-dād (TD2, 443)

čand zamān andar ān xānag pādixšāy dāštan.
mard-ēw rōz- ud māh-drahnāy
*ud ka wafr bē nē šawēd zamīg bē nē *āwāsēd* <'wb's->
wēš-iz pādixšāy.

For how long is it allowed to keep them in that house?[19]
One man: for the length of a day and a month.
And if the snow does not go away (and) the earth does not dry out,
even more is allowed.

Zand ī fragard ī J̌ud-dēw-dād (TD2, 559–60)

*ēn-iš tōzišn kē hamāg tan bē *ō āb barēd*
ayāb srišk-ēw āb pad tan ī daštān abāz paššinǰēd
ēg-iš bē abāyēd kerdan ayāb ǰuttar.
*ka hamāg tan bē *āwāsēnēd* <'w's-> *ēg-iš* 15 *tanābuhl.*
ud ka-iz [560] *handām-ēw guft*
ēg-iš grihagān ī angust handām ī guft

Should he atone for this too, who immerses his/her whole body in water
or splatters a drop of water back onto the body of a menstruous woman?
Should he do it (in the same manner) then too or differently?
If he dries the whole body, then (a sin accrues) to him of 15 *tanābuhl*
(or: [a merit accrues] to him [worth] 15 *tanābuhl*).
And also if he said "(it was just) a limb,"
then the smallest joints of the finger (would count for?) the "limb" mentioned.

ka dast andar āb frōd kunēd
ud pad daštān abāz paššinǰēd
pad harw srišk-ēw tanābuhl ōh bawēd.

If he/she puts a hand down into the water
and splatters some back onto the body of a menstruous woman,
for every drop he will incur, as usual, a *tanābuhl* sin.

ka 15-sālag ēg-iš čē paššixt
ēg-iš wināh ī hamāg tan ō xōn burdan
pad ān ēwēnag hangōšīdag ō bun

If it is a fifteen-year-old, then whatever he splattered,
then the sin of bringing the entire body into (contact with) blood (accrues) to him.
In this way and manner (these things?) accrue to him.

---

[16] Kellens 1984, p. 151.

[17] Grassmann (1976, col. 1515) suggested the meaning 'to dry' was from 'pour empty.'

[18] One of them was noticed by Tavadia (1930, viii, p. 75) as well, who referred to "MF. 438.8 *havāsēnīt*," a manuscript in the Mulla Firoze Library (MS D 51), which contains another copy of the *Zand ī fragard ī J̌ud-dēw-dād.*

[19] The house to store dead bodies in winter; see Skjærvø 2009.

*ān tōzišn ī čiyōn pad hamāg tan bē *āwāsēnīdan* <'w's->
wizārišn abāyēd kerdan ayāb nē.
āsrō sprixtīg ēwkardag bē-š wizārišn
az ān ī ka hamāg tan andǰuttar kū
hamē ka pad ēk tis-ēw gōnag wizārēd
ā-š pad wizārd dārišn.

How is that atonement in the case he dries the whole body?
Must it be resolved (expiated) or not?
If it is in contact with a "sprouting fire,"[20] he must resolve it.
It is so much different from when it is the whole body that,
as long as he resolves it in the manner of "one thing,"
then it is to be regarded as having been resolved by him.

Tavadia also referred to four further examples found in the *Pahlavi Rivāyat* and the *Nērangestān*, all concerned with the presentation of the *drōn* (the ritual cake). In all four instances, the manuscripts have <'w's->, but the editors *hōš-*:

Pahlavi Rivāyat 58.9

drōn sāzag ud padišxwar ēdōn pad-pādyāb bē kunišn
ka-š barsom abar rasē
*ā-iz šāyē ud bē *āwāsēnišn*
*ka *āwāsēnīdan nē šāyēd nē šōyišn*
čē hušk ī apādyāb weh kū xwēd ī pad-pādyāb

The tray and bowl for the *drōn* should be ritually cleansed in this manner
— if some barsom were to get onto it
it would, then too, be permissible — and should be dried.[21]
If it is not possible to dry it, it should not be washed.
For dry and not ritually cleansed is better than wet and ritually cleansed.

The same passage is in the *Nērangestān* with minor differences:[22]

Nērangestān 10.15 (HJ, p. 82, TD, fol. 29r)[23]

drōn sāzag ud padišxwar ēdōn pad-pādyāb bē kunišn
*ka-š barsom abar rasēd ā-iz šāyēd ud bē *āwāsēnišn*
*(ka) *āwāsēnīdan nē šāyēd ā nē šōyišn*
čē hušk ī apādyāb weh kū xwēd ī pad-pādyāb

The tray and bowl for the *drōn* should be ritually cleansed in this manner
— if some *barsom* gets onto it, then too it is permissible — and should be dried.
(If) it is not possible to dry it, then it should not be washed.
For dry and not ritually cleansed is better than wet and ritually cleansed.

Nērangistān 10.26 (HJ, p. 86, TD, fol. 30v)

ka tābīhēd[24] *ayāb bē sōzēd ayāb bē *hōšēd*
pādyābīh wehīh
pas dīdan ud pas xwārom

[20] With the common *āsrō* for *āθrō* and *sprixt-* 'sprout, blossom,' Manichean Middle Persian *wisprixt*, idem, cf. *ispixt ispēz-* 'sprout, blossom,' said of fires and luminaries. Cf. also Pahlavi *spīg/spēg* 'brilliance, sprout,' New Persian *saprīg*.

[21] See Boyce 1991, p. 283.

[22] Most recent edition: Kotwal and Kreyenbroek 1992–2009. Manuscripts: HJ; TD.

[23] Discussed in Tavadia 1930, p. 76. Kotwal and Kreyenbroek 1992–2009, vol. 2 (Cahiers de Studia Iranica 16), pp. 66–67.

[24] Spelled HJ <ŠAKWN-šyt'>, TD <ŠYKWN-yhyt'> (identical with the common <ŠBKWN-> hil- 'let'). The verb

When it is heated or burns or dries up.
(First) ritual purity (is to be considered), (then) goodness,
then appearance, and then taste.

Here, the manuscripts read as follows (\ ... / = superscript interlinear):

HJ (p. 86): *ayāb bē* <'wcyyyyt>

TD (30v): *ayāb bē* <'wcyyyt> \ <'w'yyt'> *: drōn tis* /

For the moment, I do not know what to do about the word spelled HJ <'wcyyyyt'>, TD <'wcyyyt'>, but the scribe of TD obviously added the more familiar verb <'w'yyt'> **āwāsēd*, commenting: *drōn tis* 'a *drōn* thing.' It could be a scribal misunderstanding of <'wp'syt'> as <'wyc'syt'>, "corrected" to , but that is quite uncertain.

Our verb occurs once more in the *Nērangistān* in a passage containing instructions for how to cut the meat of a sacrificial animal and the *barsom*, presumably, the grass on which the meat was laid out:[25]

Nērangistān 47.15 (HJ, pp. 254–55; TD, fols. 86v–87r)[26]

barsom abāz ō war brīnišn
ka bē brīnišn ā-š band[27] *bē brīnišn*
u-š pādyāb andak-ēw abar frōd hilišn
*u-š bē-*āwāsišnīh pad esm ēw-tāg*
pādyāb abāg[28] *kunišn.*
az kust ī dašn bē nihišn
ast kē ēdōn gōwēd az ān ī hōy bē-hilišnīh [ī] xōb[29]
*bē-*āwāsišnīh pad* yåŋhąmcā

The *barsom* should be cut back to(ward) the chest.
If it must be cut, then the string should be cut (first).
And a little ritual water should be let down upon it.
And its drying should be done with a single piece of firewood.
The ablution should be done together with (it).
It should be left on the right side.
There is one who says thus: "Leaving it on the left is (also) fine.[30]
The drying should be done at *yåŋhąmcā*."[31]

Here, both manuscripts have <'wp'ssnyh> the first time, the second time <'w's->, both of which Kotwal and Kreyenbroek emended, to **xūb *hōšēnišn* and **xūb bē *hōšēnišn* 'let it be dried well,' respectively.

A final remark. The meaning of **āwās-* would clearly seem to be 'dry off, dry up, dry out,' but it is remarkable that the drying could be done with firewood: *u-š bē-āwāsišnīh pad esm ēw-tāg* 'and its drying should be done with a single piece of firewood.' Thus firewood could be used to dry an object that had been wetted in the ritual cleansing process. Is it possible that the piece of firewood might still be lit and that it was the heat of the fire that dried the object? If so, that may provide a clue to the correct reading of the verb. Although the burning firewood cannot be expected, literally, to cook the meat, the Avestan word for "cooked" meat is, in fact, *x^{v}āsta*, which is close to

is included as <YHKHWN-> in some manuscripts of the *Frahang ī Pahlawīg*; see Nyberg 1988, pp. 24–25, 99, according to whom the expected form would be <YHKDHWN-> (√qdḥ) corrupted to <YHKHWN->.

[25] Discussed in part by Tavadia (1930, p. 76).

[26] Kotwal and Kreyenbroek 1992–2009, vol. 3 (Cahiers de Studia Iranica 30), pp. 204–05.

[27] Manuscripts <bwny> for <bnd>? Tavadia read *bun* and rendered it as 'root end.' Unfortunately, he did not comment on the preceding text.

[28] Kotwal and Kreyenbroek omit.

[29] In HJ, *ēdōn gōwēd* 'he says thus' follows *hōy*; in TD it is omitted.

[30] This is a common usage of *xōb* 'good, well,' for instance, in the *Šāyest nē šāyest*.

[31] Part of the *Yeŋ́hē hātąm* formula, which is recited during this ritual.

one of the possible readings of our verb: *xwās-*. Thus, the Pahlavi verb might be *xwās-* and signify 'heat up,' which was further restricted to the drying process.

Clearly, there are other possible explanations. The more obvious one would be to derive the verb from the root *wā-* 'blow,' with intransitive-inchoative **wā-sa-* 'be blown' and **ā-wāsa-*, Pahlavi *āwās-* 'be blown upon,' causative *āwās-ēn-* 'cause to be blown upon.'

The technical meaning might also be 'to wipe' rather than 'to dry,' but for the moment I do not see how to decide.

Additional Note

After this had been submitted, I noticed the term *āsišn* '...-ing' in a fragmentary Manichean Middle Persian text describing the effect on the earth of the various months and seasons.[32] The term is found in the description of the month of Ābān and the sign of Taurus and corresponds to *garmāg* 'heat' in the description of the following month of Ādur and the sign of Gemini.[33] Both months are the opponents of the demons that dry out (*hōšāgēn*) and burn (*sōzāgēn*) the land. If the term *āsišn* is related, then the Pahlavi verb would have to be read as *awās-* and be from a form of the same basic verb *ās-* with the preverb *awa-*.

Note on *haik/hik*

Derived from this root are *hiku* 'dry' (Bartholomae 1904, col. 1812) and *hixra*, Pahlavi *hixr*, which appear to refer to dry dead matter, as opposed to Pahlavi *nasāy* (*nasā*) which is non-dry dead matter, although the distinction may actually be more sophisticated than this.[34] The contrast between *hixr* and *nasā* is seen, for instance, in *Videvdad*, chapter 5, the passage about the bird cited at the beginning of this article and the second regarding the spread of pollution among several men sleeping on the same bed:

Pahlavi *Videvdad* 5.1[35]

abar ān wāmēd
abarg hixr guft
mēdōmāh nasā
abar ān riyēd hixr ud abar ān paššinǰēd hixr

(The bird) 'vomits on that (tree)'
Abarg said: (then it is) *hixr* 'dry dead matter,'
Mēdōmāh said: (then it is) *nasā* 'wet dead matter.'
'it defecates on it': *hixr*, 'and it *sprinkles on it': *hixr*.

This passage involves another verb of uncertain meaning: *paššinǰ-*, which here renders Avestan *paitita*. The common meaning of the verb *paššinǰ-* (past stem *paššixt*) is 'to sprinkle,' but here it obviously has a technical meaning. The Avestan verb ought to mean "come onto," which may be a euphemism (sexual?). The verb *riyēd* apparently means 'to defecate,' so the third verb might mean 'to urinate,' but that is usually *mistan* (present *mēz-*).[36]

---

[32] Manuscript M506 recto, p. 68 (Berliner Turfantexte 4).

[33] Manuscript M7981/II/R/ii (*Šābuhragān*); Andreas and Henning 1932.

[34] Bartholomae 1904, col. 1812: *hixra'* 'fluid excrement' from [1]*haēk* is wrong.

[35] In the translation, the passages that render the Avestan are in single quotes. The rest are glosses.

[36] A passage in the *Zand ī fragard ī Jud-dēw-dād* shows that sprinkling may be connected with urinating, however (JamaspAsa and Nawabi 1978–79, vol. 1, pp. 613–14): *dūr bē mēzēd dūr bē kanēd was srišk bē paššinjēd ēg-iš wināh čand* 'Someone who urinates far, throws it far, sprinkles many drops, how great then is his sin?'

The verb paššinǰ- is found in several other places, as well; notably, it renders another problematic Avestan verb, also one of a series of three, the precise meanings of which are all unclear:

Videvdad 5.27

āaṯ aēšąm narąm aēuuō iriθiiāṯ
cuuaṯ aṇtarə narə̄š aēša druxš yā nasuš
axtica piuuatica āhitica frāšnaoiti

Then one of these men passes away.
How much among (between) the men does this corpse demon
reach with *axti*, *piuuatī*, and *āhitī*?

Videvdad 5.27

az awēšān mardān ēk be widerēd
čand andarg awēšān mardān ā-šān ān druz ī nasuš
pad xīndagīh waštagīh
paššinǰišn rēmanīh
ud āhōgēnišn akārīh frāz rasēd

'of those men, one passes away;
how much among those men does that corpse demon
reach with illness,' (i.e.) sickness,
'*sprinkling,' (i.e.) filth, 'and *contagion,' (i.e.) *impotence?

The same phrases are found in *Videvdad* 6.30, where the demon pollutes standing water. The word that concerns us here is *piuuatī*, which is rendered as *paššinǰišn* '*sprinkling' (or 'splattering') and glossed with the common term *rēmanīh* 'filth,' which is the most common term for things that cause pollution.[37]

Two of the terms are also found in *Videvdad* 20.3, in a list of evil things produced by the Evil Spirit to plague humanity that must be withstood.
The manuscript readings vary considerably, however:

V.5.27 (instrumental): *pauuiti°* K1; *pauuaiti°* B1, M3; *piuuati°* Pt2 (< L4), Mf2, Jp1, L2, Br1, K10, L1, B2.

V.6.30 (instrumental): *pauuiti°* K1; *pauuaiti°* B1, M3; *piuuati°* Pt2, Jp1, L2, K10, B2; *piuuate°* Mf2; *piuuiti°* Br1, Dh1, L1.

V.20.3 (genitive): *puitiiå* L4; *pūitiiå* K1, L2, Br1, M2, L1, B2; *pūitaiiå* Mf2, Jp1.

The oldest readings are those of manuscripts L4 and K1, which point to early forms in *pauui-*, but the consensus of two other branches of the tradition points to old forms in *piuua-*. The forms in *Videvdad* 20.3 are easier to analyze: *pūitiiå* is the correct genitive of *pūitī-*, presumably the demoness of rot (root *pū-*, Pahlavi *pūdag* 'rotten'). The other forms could then conceivably be explained as developments of **pūiti* > **puuiti* (with the insertion of a glide: **puu̯iti*) > **puuaiti*, **pauuaiti* (with the common insertion of epenthetic *-a-*), which was then variously "corrected" by the scribes. That this is the correct analysis of the word is suggested by the fact that the passage in V.6.30 is the answer to a question involving the two verbs *friθiieti-ca puiieti-ca* 'decays and rots' describing corpses.[38]

[37] Note that Avestan *paiti-šiṇca-* (from which *paššinǰ-* is descended) is rendered by Pahlavi *āšinǰ-*, not *paššinǰ-*.

[38] Bartholomae (1904, col. 849) simply assumes that *pauuiti-* is the correct form, derived directly from *pauu-*, but the correct form is obviously *pūiti-*. See Kellens 1984, pp. 120–21. Note also the description of the evil *dēn* in the *Ardā Wirāz-namag* (17.9) *zan ī ǰeh rūdag ī pūdag ī paššixtag ī frāz-šnūg ī abāz-kūn* 'an evil woman, plucked(?), rotted, *sprinkled (with filth?), knob-kneed, flat-assed' (see Gignoux 1984, pp. 70–71).

The only problem, of course, is that "rot" does not really fit the contexts, unless it means something like "leprosy," but, in that case, the Pahlavi translation must continue a tradition in which the original meaning had been lost. Thus the meaning of *paššinǰ-* has not been clarified and we are left with a *non liquet*.

With these sprinklings I hope I have given some idea of the problems of the Zoroastrian priests and how similar they are to those of the rabbis who composed the Babylonian Talmud. I also hope that they have shown how problematic the Pahlavi (and Avestan) texts can be, on account of both the language and script they are written in and our deficient knowledge of the issues involved. Most of all, I hope that our dedicatee may have been, at times, amused.

Abbreviations

HJ	Sanjana 1894
Šāyast-nē šāyast	Tavadia 1930
TD	Kotwal and Boyd 1980

Bibliography

Andreas, Friedrich Carl, and Walter B. Henning

1932 "Manuscript M7981/II/R/ii (*Šābuhragān*)." In *Mitteliranische Manichaica aus Chinesisch-Turkistan*, by Friedrich Carl Andreas and Walter B. Henning, volume 1, p. 17 [189]. Sitzungsberichte der Preussischen Akademie der Wissenschaften 10. Berlin: Verlag der Akademie der Wissenschaften.

Bartholomae, Christian

1904 *Altiranisches Wörterbuch*. Strassburg: Trübner.

Boyce, Mary

1991 "'Pādyāb' and 'Nērang.' Two Pahlavi Terms Further Considered." *Bulletin of the School of Oriental and African Studies* 54: 281–91.

Geldner, Karl Friedrich

1886–95 *Avesta, the Sacred Book of the Parsis*. 3 volumes. Stuttgart: Kohlhammer.

Gignoux, Philippe

1984 *Le livre d'Ardā Vīrāz*, Paris: Éditions Recherche sur les civilisations.

Grassmann, Hermann

1976 *Wörterbuch zum Rig-Veda*. 5th edition. Wiesbaden: Harrassowitz.

Jamasp, Asa Hoshang

1907 *Vendidâd: Avesta Text with Pahlavi Translation and Commentary, and Glossarial Index*, Volume 1: *The Texts*. Bombay: Government Central Book Depot.

JamaspAsa, Kaikhusroo M., and Y. Mahyar Nawabi

1978–1979 *MS. TD 2: Iranian Bundahišn and Rivāyat-i Ēmēt-i Ašavahištān, etc.* 2 volumes. The Pahlavi Codices and Iranian Researches 54–55. Shiraz: Asia Institute of the Pahlavi University.

Kellens, Jean

1984 *Le verbe avestique*. Wiesbaden: Ludwig Reichert.

Kotwal, Firoze M., and James W. Boyd

1980 *Ērbadistān ud Nīrangistān: Facsimile Edition of the Manuscript TD*. Harvard Iranian Series 3. Cambridge: Harvard University Press.

Kotwal, Firoze M., and Philip G. Kreyenbroek, editors

1992–2009 *The Hērbedestān and Nērangestān*, Volumes 1–4. Cahiers de Studia Iranica 10, 16, 30, 38. Paris: Association pour l'avancement des études iraniennes.

Nyberg, Henrik S.

1988 *Frahang i Pahlavīk*. Edited with transliteration, transcription, and commentary from the postumous papers of H. S. Nyberg by Bo Utas and Christopher Toll. Wiesbaden: Harrassowitz.

Sanjana, Darab Dastur Peshotan

1894 *Nirangistan: A Photozincographed Facsimile of a MS Belonging to Shams-ul-Ulama Dastur Dr. Hoshangjee Jamaspjee of Poona; Edited with an Introduction and Collation with an Older Iranian MS in the Possession of Ervad Tahmuras D. Anklesaria*. The Pahlavi Text Series 1. Bombay: Trustees of the Parsee Punchayet.

Skjærvø, Prods Oktor

2009 "On Videvdad 5.11 and Its Pahlavi Commentaries." In *Zarathushtra entre l'Inde et l'Iran: études indo-iraniennes et indo-européennes offertes à Jean Kellens à l'occasion de son 65e anniversaire*, edited by Éric Pirart and Xavier Tremblay, pp. 289–304. Beiträge zur Iranistik 30. Wiesbaden: Ludwig Reichert.

Sundermann, Werner

1973 "Manuscript M506 recto." In *Mittelpersische und parthische kosmogonische und Parabeltexte der Manichäer*. Schriften zur Geschichte und Kultur des alten Orients 8; Berliner Turfantexte 4. Berlin: Akademie-Verlag.

Tavadia, Jehangir C.

1930 Šāyast-nē šāyast: *A Pahlavi Text on Religious Customs*. Alt- und Neu-Indische Studien 3. Hamburg: Friederichsen, de Gruyter.

Williams, Alan V.

1990 *The Pahlavi Rivāyat Accompanying the Dādestān ī Dēnīg*. 2 parts. Det Kongelige Danske Videnskabernes Selskab, Historisk-filosofiske meddelelser 60/1–2; Copenhagen: Munksgard.

22

Vowel Syncope and Syllable Repair Processes in Proto-Semitic Construct Forms: A New Reconstruction Based on the Law of Diminishing Conditioning

*Richard C. Steiner, Yeshiva University**

1. Introduction

The idea of a Proto-Semitic syncope rule has its roots in the nineteenth century. Ewald (1863, p. 443, §173) conjectured that **-at* is the original feminine ending but that, even so, the vowel syncope that abbreviated the ending to **-t* took place already in Proto-Semitic.[1] Lagarde (1889–1891, p. 72), generalizing from a dozen segolate (**CvCC-*) construct forms of bisyllabic (**CvCvC-*) nouns and adjectives in Hebrew (e.g., *kắṯäᵽ*, the construct of *kåṯeᵽ* 'shoulder'), theorized that *all* segolate nouns originated as Proto-Semitic construct forms of bisyllabic nouns, and that their use as absolute forms was a late and erroneous development.

At the beginning of the twentieth century, Brockelmann (1903, p. 6) attempted to make Ewald's insight more precise by formulating a rule:

> Short vowels drop out in open unstressed medial syllables immediately after an open syllable with a short vowel and a ... primary or secondary accent.

Later in the article (p. 11), Brockelmann amends the rule:

> So too after an open syllable with a long vowel and a two-peak accent.

This addendum is meant to account for forms such as Akkadian *tali(:)mtum* 'sister' (Brockelmann 1903, p. 11), Geez *nəgəšt* 'queen' < **nvguštu* (vs. masc. *nəguš* 'king' < **nvgu:šu*); Hebrew *ʾašmóräṯ* < **ʾašmurtu* (vs. *ʾašmu*^{w}*rå*^{h}), and *gǝ̆ḇắräṯ* < **gvbirtu* (vs. *gǝ̆ḇi*^{y}*rå*^{h}) (Brockelmann 1903, p. 12).

Brockelmann's Proto-Semitic syncope rule has been accepted by some Semitists, with or without modification. Bauer and Leander (1922, p. 176) formulate the rule in diachronic terms: "Short free vowels fell out immediately after a free stressed vowel." Bravmann (1977, p. 134) writes, "Though some of [Barth's] objections[2] may be justified,

* Parts of this article are based on a paper entitled "A Proto-Semitic Alternation and Its Flip-flopped Akkadian Reflex," read at the Third North American Conference on Semitic Linguistics, on April 22, 1975. I alluded to the paper in my two earliest published articles, and then I put it aside. The invitation to honor an outstanding Semitist has inspired me to dust it off and rethink the issue. I have added many new proposals, deliberately erring on the side of incaution in an attempt to provoke debate. Professors J. Blau and L. Kogan have read the article and, like the editors of this volume, have done their best to save me from error, but that task is a daunting one, even for them.

[1] That seems to be the meaning of the phrase *im Semitischen* in line 17. Cf. the assertion in n. 3 that **-t* is *uralt*.

[2] See below.

I adhere on the whole to Brockelmann's opinion." He believes that Proto-Semitic **t* was "particularly frequent in biliteral monosyllabic nouns and in triliteral nouns with a long vowel in the second syllable" (ibid., p. 133).

Blau (2010, p. 264) appears to be in this camp as well, although he is pessimistic about the possibility of reconstructing the original structural description of the rule:

> It stands to reason that these two feminine suffixes are genetically related, *-at* being the original ending from which, under certain phonetic conditions (caused by stress), the *a* was elided. The original conditioning of this elision has been blurred by widespread analogy, so that the original constraints can no longer be reconstructed.[3] In Biblical Hebrew, there is a certain tendency to use *-at* (< *-ā*) in the absolute, *-t* in the construct and preceding pronominal suffixes (such as **mamlakat* > מַמְלָכָה 'kingdom' in the absolute, מַמְלֶ֫כֶת < **mamlakt* in the construct, and מַמְלַכְתִּי).

Other scholars have rejected Brockelmann's Proto-Semitic syncope rule. Barth (Barth 1903, p. 628) admits that **-at* and **-t* are etymologically related and that they split apart from each other already in the Proto-Semitic period. Nevertheless, he argues (ibid., pp. 628–36) that Proto-Semitic could not have had such a syncope rule because it is possible to reconstruct many counterexamples to it — verbs and nouns that seemingly did not undergo syncope in Proto-Semitic. In addition, he sharply criticizes Brockelmann's methodology. In his view, a Proto-Semitic *Lautgesetz* must be based solely on reconstructed Proto-Semitic forms.

Janssens (1975/1976, p. 278) believes that "in many of these cases *-t* has developed from *-at* in the separate languages, not in Proto-Semitic." For example, he argues that "in a prehistoric stage of Accadian the ending *-at* occurred more often than in the historic stage" (ibid., p. 279). He concludes that "no wordstructure (*sic*) had with certitude the ending *-t* in Proto-Semitic, except nouns ending in *-īt*, *-ūt* and the word **bintum* 'daughter'" (ibid., p. 284).

Greenstein (1984, p. 40) eliminates the possibility of a Proto-Semitic syncope rule by assigning a late date to vowel syncope in West Semitic: "It is a bit startling to a Semitist ... to find that a rule of VOWEL DELETION had developed in Akkadian by the middle of the third millennium B.C.E. when the syncopation of short internal open vowels did not occur in the West Semitic languages before the first millennium B.C.E."

Dolgopolsky (1999, p. 102) believes that vowel syncope occurred in some of the West Semitic protolanguages, after the Proto-Semitic stage:

> ... any short vowel in the posttonic open syllable that follows another open short syllable is syncopated:
> pS * *ˈkalab-um*[4] > pCan., pArab. * *ˈkalb-Vm* (> Hb. *ˈkɛlɛḇ*, Ar. *kalbun*).
> pS * *ˈŝamalat-um* > prae-Can., pArab. * *ˈŝaml-at-Vm* (> Hb. * *ŝimˈlā*, Ar. * *šamlatun*).
> pS * *ḳāˈbir-at-Vm* > pCan., pArab. * *ḳāˈbirt-Vm* 'burrying' [*sic*] (> Hb. *ḳōˈḇɛrɛṯ*, but in Ar. the form has reintroduced *a* in the feminine ending due to morphological generalization of the fem. ending *at-*: *qābir-at-un*).
> pS * *ˈbin-at-um* > pCan., pArab. * *ˈbint-um* 'daughter' (> Hb. *ˈbaṯ*, Ar. *bintun*).

Dolgopolsky's theory resembles Lagarde's in deriving segolate nouns in the Semitic languages from Proto-Semitic bisyllabic nouns.

Huehnergard (2004, p. 144) accepts the existence of a Proto-Semitic syncope rule, but he restricts it drastically: "Internal reconstruction indicates the existence of a Proto-Semitic rule of vowel syncope: $a > \phi\ /\ aC_1\_\_C_1V$, as in *k'alalum* > *k'allum* 'light, small.'"[5] Concerning syncope in the feminine ending and noun stems, he writes (2006, p. 8),

> Another characteristic of Akkadian is the syncope of unstressed short vowels. Internal reconstruction of course shows that this is not a feature of Proto-Semitic: most West Semitic languages do not exhibit such syncope,[6] and in Akkadian allomorphs such as *damqum* ~ *damiqtum* and *damiq* ~ *damqat* show that we must

[3] Cf. Huehnergard (2004, p. 147): "The original distribution of **-t* versus **-at* is difficult to recover with certainty."

[4] The sign ˈ indicates that the following syllable is stressed.

[5] Huehnergard 2004, p. 231.

[6] This assertion needs clarification; it seems to contradict Huehnergard's own detailed description of Ugaritic vowel syncope (1987, pp. 280–83), which includes a comparison with vowel syncope in Aramaic, Hebrew, and Akkadian (ibid., p. 282 n. 66). The syncope of unstressed short vowels is also attested in Old Arabic (see below).

reconstruct earlier forms such as **damiqum* and **damiqatum*. The evidence of Eblaite is mixed here, but some forms, such as *wa-ri/rí-gúm/gú-um* = *warikum* 'side, flank' (cf. Akkadian *warkatum*) do not exhibit syncope where Akkadian would. Since the process is attested in all forms of Akkadian, however, we may safely assign it to Proto-Akkadian.

In Steiner 1975, I restricted Proto-Semitic syncope to the construct state, based on internal reconstruction from Hebrew. I never published that paper, but I briefly mentioned the idea in a footnote a few years later (Steiner 1979, p. 166 n. 20):

> ... the alternation between absolute *CVCVC and construct *CVCC in a few Hebrew nouns (צֵלָע/צֶלַע ['rib'], כָּתֵף/כֶּתֶף ['shoulder'], יָרֵךְ/יֶרֶךְ ['thigh'], שֵׂעָר/שַׂעַר ['hair'], גָּדֵר/גֶּדֶר ['wall'], אָשֵׁד/אֶשֶׁד ['slope'], עָשָׁן/עֶשֶׁן ['smoke'], שָׂכָר/שֶׂכֶר ['wages']) and adjectives (כָּבֵד/כֶּבֶד ['heavy'], עָרֵל/עֶרֶל ['uncircumcised'], אָרֹךְ/אֶרֶךְ ['long']) and the existence of feminine construct forms ending in *-CVC*t* (e.g. מַמְלֶכֶת ['kingdom of'], מִרְכֶּבֶת ['chariot of'], מִשְׁפַּחַת ['family of'], עֲטֶרֶת ['crown of']) are surely products of a very early syncope rule affecting construct forms.[7]

This theory, too, bears some resemblance to Lagarde's theory, although I did not know of the latter until shortly before finishing the present article.

In the remainder of this essay, I present arguments for this theory, but one of them can be stated already at this point. In my view, most of the arguments that have been adduced against Proto-Semitic syncope do not apply to the version of the rule presented here. Thus, Barth's counter-examples are not nouns in the construct state but rather nouns in the absolute state and verbs. Similarly, Greenstein's dating of syncope in West Semitic (1984, pp. 40–41) is based on two verbal forms, one from Amarna Canaanite and the other from Ugaritic. Such evidence is, of course, perfectly compatible with a thesis that deals with construct forms. The same goes for Janssens' claim that "in a prehistoric stage of Accadian the ending *-at* occurred more often than in the historic stage," as well as Huehnergard's claim that unsyncopated forms such as **damiḳum* and **damiḳatum* existed in Proto-Akkadian. I would only add that the attested, syncopated Akkadian forms, *damḳum* and *damiḳtum*, also existed in Proto-Akkadian, as conditioned variants and/or doublets of the fuller forms.

Finally, a word about Barth's methodological strictures. Brockelmann's methodology is indeed rather loose; his article presents an interesting idea without much in the way of rigorous proof. In rebutting that idea, however, Barth may have gone too far in the opposite direction, imposing an overly rigorous methodological requirement that would inevitably hinder progress in the field if strictly observed.[8] I attempt to steer a middle course, basing my Proto-Semitic phonological rule not only on reconstructed Proto-Semitic forms (as demanded by Barth) but also on what I take to be vestiges of the rule that have survived in only one or two of the daughter languages. I present my methodology more fully in §3 below.

2. Proto-Semitic Syllable Constraints and Syllable Repair Processes

The thesis of this article is that at least one short open-syllabic vowel[9] was deleted in Proto-Semitic construct forms of nouns and adjectives, as long as the deletion did not violate Proto-Semitic syllable constraints — but what were those constraints? It is generally agreed that Proto-Semitic did not permit syllables to begin or end with any of the following clusters: *CC*, *C:*, and *:C*.[10]

---

[7] See also Steiner 2010, p. 227.

[8] Barth himself based most of the "Proto-Semitic" reconstructions in his rebuttal on West Semitic data alone. Just as Brockelmann preferred to ignore Arabic in reconstructing his syncope rule, Barth preferred to ignore Akkadian in refuting it!

[9] For nouns with more than one vowel of this type, see §10 below.

[10] In this article, the symbol *:* represents any kind of length, be it consonant length (*C:*) or vowel length (*v:*). Thus, *v:* represents any long vowel, and *v* represents any short one.

I argue below that these syllable constraints did not interfere with the syncope rule as much as one might imagine, thanks to four Proto-Semitic syllable repair processes:

(1) prothesis;

(2) loss of length in/after consonants (degemination);

(3) loss of length in/after vowels (vowel shortening);

(4) syllabicization of semivowels and nasals.[11]

These repair processes allowed syncope to operate at times in initial syllables, in syllables following syllables of the form *CvC* and *Cv:*, and in two consecutive syllables.

I attempt to show that both the syncope rule and the syllable repair processes have left traces in the Semitic languages and that among these traces are phonological enigmas such as Hebrew *šte^y^* 'two of (fem.),' *mǝlāḵāṯ* 'queen of,' *lǝḇān* 'white of,' Aramaic *tarte^y^* 'two of (fem.),' Arabic *(i)smu* 'name of,' Mehri *bǝrt* 'daughter of,' and Akkadian *ašti* 'wife of (gen.).'

It should be stressed that I am not claiming that the construct state was the only environment for Proto-Semitic syncope; the conditioning may well have been broader than that (including perhaps imperatives[12] and nouns with some[13] or all of the suffixed pronouns), but I shall leave that possibility to others.

3. Methodology

During the past half century, historical linguists have turned their attention to linguistic universals, including universals that govern the evolution of phonological rules. When my (soon-to-be) teacher asked "Are There Universals of Linguistic Change?" he answered in the affirmative (Hoenigswald 1966, pp. 41–42):

> Greenberg and others feel that sound change has a typical mechanism of successively widening scope. Sound change, they say, may begin as "sporadic," then become phonologically conditioned, and finally unconditional .... There is no doubt that here we have an important principle.

Not long afterward, Wang (1969, pp. 22–23) found that "the phonetic condition that originally stimulated the change may create a 'snowball' effect across the lexicon, so that the condition itself eventually becomes irrelevant." More recently, Janda and Joseph (2003, p. 214) have asserted that "sound-change rapidly yields to generalization along non-phonetic (phonological or morphological) and social lines that may contribute further regularity via extension to broader contexts."

In this article, I take it as a given that change in the conditioning of phonological rules is largely unidirectional. When phonological rules change, they normally do so in the direction of diminished phonetic conditioning, with one or more of the original phonetic conditions being eliminated through analogical change.

Analogical change can affect phonological rules in various ways; the elimination of original phonetic conditions is only one of the possible outcomes. Another possible outcome is elimination of the rules themselves. This occurs when analogical leveling turns most of the conditioned allomorphs generated by the rule into doublets,[14]

---

[11] It is remarkable that this list does not include epenthesis, the best-known syllable repair process in the daughter languages (e.g., mobile *shewa* and segolation in Hebrew). Epenthesis in Akkadian feminine segolates (**CiCCatu* > *CiCiCtu*) has been discussed since the nineteenth century; e.g., Zimmern 1890, p. 379; Janssens 1975/76, pp. 278–79, 283–84; Greenstein 1984, p. 44; Testen 2003.

[12] See note 74 below.

[13] Possibly just the "heavy" suffixes (plural second and third persons), which always attract the stress.

[14] Hoenigswald (1960, p. 39) explains how conditioned allomorphs become differentiated into doublets: "The Latin noun stem for 'god, divine' once had, owing to an earlier conditioned sound change ..., two alternants, *de-* and *deiv-* (nominative singular *deus*; genitive singular *deivī*). Each was extended into the former domain of the other so that later there are two paradigms: **deos* (later *deus*), genitive *deī*; and *deivos* (later *dīvus*), genitive *deivī* (*dīvī*)." My sense is that analogical leveling works especially quickly in the Semitic languages because the root-and-pattern system tends to promote it. Although one occasionally finds the opposite process, in which two paradigms merge into one paradigm, the result is a syncretistic paradigm, in which the conditioning is clearly non-phonetic; for a Hebrew example, see Steiner 1996, pp. 255, 259 n. 5.

leaving at best a few relics of the original phonetic conditioning (or of the later, diminished phonetic conditioning). This too can be viewed as a kind of unidirectional reduction of phonetic conditioning.

In short, phonetic conditioning tends to be diminished by analogy, through either the loss of conditions or the loss of conditioned allomorphs. I refer to this as "the law of diminishing conditioning."[15] In my view, this law can be very useful in reconstructing the original conditioning of phonological rules in proto-languages. That is one of the reasons that I do not share the pessimism implicit in Blau's assertion that "the original conditioning of this elision has been blurred by widespread analogy, so that the original constraints can no longer be reconstructed."

Another reason for optimism is what I shall call "the principle of cognate anomalies." This principle, explained below, is another tool that can be used to reconstruct the structural description of the Proto-Semitic syncope rule.

4. Syncope in Non-initial Syllables of the Stem

In Akkadian, "the last of two or more non-final short vowels in open syllables was syncopated" (Huehnergard and Woods 2004, p. 240; cf. Hasselbach 2005, p. 105). Greenstein's formulation (1984, pp. 13–14) of the rule is similar: "Delete a short vowel in the environment *VC_CV*." Greenstein (ibid., pp. 40–42) argued that the Akkadian syncope rule had a Sumerian origin, but Edzard (1986, p. 360) was not convinced. To my mind, the fact that the Sumerian loanwords in Akkadian were exceptions to the Akkadian syncope rule (Greenstein 1984, pp. 31–32) is evidence against Greenstein's thesis. It may well be true, as Greenstein believes, that borrowings from Sumerian retained their foreign phonological structure (at least for a while), but if the Akkadian syncope rule was really borrowed from Sumerian, a word like *nuḫatimmum* should have lost its second vowel *before* being borrowed. My own view is that Akkadian inherited the rule from Proto-Semitic but eliminated one of the original phonetic conditions. Fortunately, the lost condition can be recovered with the help of Hebrew.

In the Hebrew vocalization of the Masoretes (Tiberian more than Babylonian), there are adjectives of the form **CvCvC* that have two construct forms. The adjectives *kåḇeḏ* 'heavy' and *ʿårel* 'uncircumcised,' in addition to the expected construct forms *kǝḇaḏ* and *ʿăral* found in biblical prose, have segolate (**CvCC*) construct forms, *kắḇäḏ* < **kabdu* and *ʿắräl* < **ġarlu*, in poetry (Steiner 2010, pp. 226–27). No synchronic rule can explain the shift of these adjectives to the segolate class in the construct state. These are clearly very archaic forms — relics preserved in poetry. Other segolate construct forms of adjectives are *ʾắräḵ* (the construct of *ʾåroḵ*)[16] and, in my opinion (ibid., pp. 209–13), *yắṯär* (the construct of *yåṯer* in Gen 49:3).[17] Segolate construct forms of nouns are slightly more common; as noted above, they include words for body parts ("rib," "shoulder," "thigh," "hair") and others ("slope," "smoke," "wages,"[18] "fence").[19]

Most of these examples have the form **CaCiCu(m)* in the absolute state, syncopated to **CaCCu* in the construct state; however, some of them have the form **CaCaCu(m)* > **CaCCu*, or **CiCaCu(m)* > **CiCCu*, or **CaCuCu(m)* > **CaCCu*. I have argued elsewhere (Steiner 1979, pp. 166–67 n. 20) that the vowel syncope in these forms must have preceded the loss of case endings in the construct state. Since the Hebrew case endings were lost earlier in the construct

---

15 This should be understood as an abbreviation of "the law of diminishing phonetic conditioning." It applies only to *phonetic* conditioning.

16 Thus we have *ʾắräḵ ʾap:ayim* 'long of patience' (Prov 14:29, etc.) contrasting with *ʾóräḵ ʾap:ayim* 'length of patience' (Prov 25:15) and with *ḳǝṣar ʾap:ayim* 'short of patience' (Prov 14:17).

17 Another form that probably belongs here is the obscure **lǝben*, attested only in its proclitic form *lǝḇän-* 'white of (teeth)' (Gen 49:12). I suggest that its obscurity derives from the fact that it combines the peculiarities of both *kắḇäḏ* 'heavy of' and the noun *hăḇel* 'vanity of.' Thus, the original construct form of **lábanum* was the syncopated **lábnu*. Unlike most segolates, it did not keep its *CvCC* pattern very long after the loss of case endings in the construct state. Instead, thanks to its final resonant, it underwent epenthesis early enough to be affected by the general stress shift, much like the noun **háblu* > **hábl* > **hábel* > **habél* > *hăḇel* (cf. Steiner 1976). The complete sequence of changes affecting the construct of **lábanum* was thus: **lábanu* > **lábnu* > **lábn* > **láben* > **labén* > **lǝben* > *lǝḇän-*. The enigmatic construct form *ḥăleḇ* 'milk of' must have a similar origin even though it does not end in a resonant.

18 The context of *śắḵär* in Prov 11:18 suggests that it is the construct form of *śåḵår*.

19 The construct form of *gåzel* 'robbery,' attested in Ezek 18:18 and Eccl 5:7, may belong here as well. Although the Tiberian reading tradition has *gézäl* < **gizlu*, the Babylonian reading tradition has the equivalent of *gắzäl* < **gazlu* (Yeivin 1985, p. 923) — the expected outcome of the syncope rule applied to **gazilu*.

state than in the absolute,[20] the vowel syncope that produced the construct forms discussed in this paragraph must be very early indeed.

These reconstructed examples of syncope look very much like the Akkadian examples, except for the fact that the Akkadian examples are not restricted to the construct state. Indeed, when we examine the state of the Akkadian examples, they seem, at first glance, to exhibit precisely the *opposite* conditioning, with syncopated *kabtum* 'heavy' in the reflex of the Proto-Semitic absolute state versus unsyncopated *kabit* 'heavy of' in the construct state. However, this is just an illusion created by the loss of case endings in the construct state, which turns the open penultimate syllable into a closed final one; the Akkadian syncope rule is, of course, not really conditioned by state.

In the Hebrew dual and plural too, there are a few alternations that seem to point to an old syncope rule conditioned by state. The most interesting is the word for 'rear/remote parts': *yarḵåṯayim* (absolute) ~ *yarkǝṯe*ʸ (construct). The absolute form occurs always (3x) with a spirantized *ḵ*, while the construct form occurs always (15x) with an unspirantized *k* (pointing to early elision of the preceding vowel). This could very well be the reflex of a Proto-Semitic alternation: **warikataym/nv* (absolute) ~ **warkatay* (construct). Note the perfect match between this alternation and the one involving its masculine singular counterpart:

yarḵåṯayim < **warikataym/nv* ~ *yarkǝṯe*ʸ < **warkatay*

yåreḵ < **warikum* ~ *yắräḵ* < **warku*[21]

The Masoretes cannot possibly have manufactured this match or even been aware of it, for it is visible only through the lens of comparative and internal reconstruction. A similar match can be seen in the word for "slope(s)." In the plural, we find *ʾăšeḏo*ʷ*ṯ* (absolute) ~ *ʾašdo*ʷ*ṯ* (construct). The relationship between the singular construct form *ʾắšäḏ* < **ʾašdu* and the plural construct *ʾašdo*ʷ*ṯ* (with unspirantized *d* in the construct form pointing to early elision of the preceding vowel) is comparable to the relationship between *yắräḵ* and *yarkǝṯe*ʸ.

Also worth mentioning here is example 5 below, the word for 'pairs/teams (of yoked/harnessed draft animals)': *ṣǝmåḏi*ʸ*m* (absolute) ~ *ṣimde*ʸ (construct). Here again we find unspirantized *d* in the construct form pointing to early elision of the preceding vowel. Most such construct forms underwent analogical leveling; in the case of the word for 'flames,' *rǝšap̄i*ʸ*m* ~ *rišpey/rišp̄e*ʸ,[22] both the old construct form and the new one are attested.

In short, the pre-Hebrew syncope rule was more restricted than the Akkadian syncope rule, because it was conditioned by syntax in addition to syllable structure. We may assume that the syntactic conditioning reflects an original phonetic conditioning, with nouns in the construct state losing their stress (morphosyntactic proclisis).[23] Accordingly, the "law of diminishing conditioning" leads us to conclude that the pre-Hebrew version of the rule is more archaic than the Akkadian version.

In syllabic transcriptions of Ugaritic, we find doublets differing in the presence/absence of one short vowel, sometimes in the very same text, e.g., *ma-sa-wa-tu* = /masawa:tu/ alongside *ma-ás-wa-tu* = /maswa:tu/ 'cypress(?) logs'; and *na-bá-ki-ma* = /nabaki:ma/ alongside *na-AB/NAB-ki-ma* = /nabki:ma/ 'springs' (Huehnergard 1987, p. 281).[24] Based on such pairs, Huehnergard (ibid., pp. 281–83) reconstructs two optional rules of vowel syncope, one pretonic in the environment *vC_Cv́* and the other posttonic. The pretonic rule looks very much like our Proto-Semitic rule, except of course that it is (1) optional, (2) restricted to pretonic vowels, and (3) not restricted to the construct state. At least two of these differences are attributable to analogical leveling.

In the Aramaic vocalization of the Tiberians and the Syrians, the syncope/reduction[25] rule is even more general than the one in Akkadian. However, Beyer (1984, pp. 128–36) has claimed that this is a late development, and he has amassed an impressive body of evidence in support of this claim.[26] None of this evidence contradicts

---

[20] For bibliography and discussion, see Steiner 1976, p. 92.

[21] For this alternation, see below.

[22] Song 8:6, Ps 76:4. The variation between *rišpey* and *rišp̄e*ʸ, is pointed out already by David Ḳimḥi (1847, p. 361, col. b s.v. *ršp*).

[23] In the Masoretic vocalization, construct forms have normal stress, but they exhibit vowel changes that are associated with destressing elsewhere in the language: vowel reduction (e.g., *dǝḇar* 'word of' ~ *dåḇår*), vowel shortening (e.g., *bän* 'son of' ~ *ben*), and monophthongization (e.g., *be*ʸ*ṯ* 'house of' ~ *bayiṯ*). All of these suggest that in pre-Masoretic Hebrew, construct forms were proclitic.

[24] Cf. the fluctuation in the Uruk incantation between *ga-[a]b-re-e* (line 12) and *ga-ba-re-e* (line 37) (Geller 2006, pp. 82, 86, 88). There too we are dealing with the segolate plural infix (see below).

[25] By reduction I mean the replacement of vowels with mobile *shewa* instead of zero (quiescent *shewa*).

[26] For discussion of this and other evidence, see Kaufman 1983.

our thesis (since it includes no construct forms), and some of it may actually support it. Take, for example, the infix *-a-* inserted between the second and third consonants of at least some segolate plurals in virtually all of the pre-modern West Semitic languages.[27] In addition to citing transcriptions of the infix with cuneiform *a*,[28] Beyer (ibid., pp. 129, 453) points to Official Aramaic plurals such as *ʿmmyn* 'peoples,' *kddn* 'pitchers,' *śḳkn* 'sack-cloths,' *dššn* 'doors,' and so on. In these segolate plurals in the absolute state, the double letters (not found in the singular)[29] seem to indicate that the infix was still pronounced. If so, the variation in TAD A4.7 Cowley 30 between *dššyʾ* 'the doors' in line 11 and *dšyhm* 'their doors' in line 10[30] may indicate that Official Aramaic segolate plurals had the infix in the determined state but not in the bound state — or, at least, not with the suffix *-hm*.[31] The analogy of Biblical Aramaic (not to mention Biblical Hebrew) suggests that segolate plurals had the same vocalization with the suffix *-hm* that they had in the construct state.[32] In short, this variation may hint at a connection between syncope and the construct state.

In Arabic, bisyllabic nouns frequently have segolate variants that seem to exhibit syncope, but their relevance for the reconstruction of Proto-Semitic is uncertain. Sībawaihi (1885–1889, vol. 2, p. 277, lines 21–23) asserts that some Arabic nouns and verbs may be pronounced without one of their underlying vowels for ease of articulation.[33] His examples are all of the form *faʿl-* < *faʿil-/faʿul-*, e.g., *kabdun* < *kabidun* 'liver.' He tells us that such syncopated variants occur in the speech of some tribes (Banū Bakr b. Wāʾil and many of the Banū Tamīm), but unfortunately he does not mention if these tribes have the unsyncopated variants alongside the syncopated ones. This dialectal variation is, of course, reminiscent of the variation in some Semitic words for 'heavy': Hebrew *kåḇeḏ* < **kabidum* ~ *kắḇäḏ* < **kabdu* and Akkadian *kabtum* ~ *kabit*. However, it is far from clear that the Arabic form *kabdun* is inherited from Proto-Semitic. The fact that Sībawaihi's examples include verbs as well as nouns and exhibit the elision of high vowels only (as in the later so-called "differential dialects") suggests that this may be an independent development within Arabic. In his initial remarks, Rabin (1951, p. 97) seems to be a firm proponent of this view:

> The most outstanding difference between the phonetics of the Eastern dialects and West-Arabian is that in the former vowels are changed under the influence of surrounding phonemes and of stress, while such influences are almost wholly absent from West-Arabian. The latter preserves the fuller forms found in cognate languages, such as Canaanite and Ethiopic. Classical Arabic on the whole sides more with West-Arabian in this respect than with the Eastern dialects. Since it exhibits this character in the oldest poetry, where Hijazi influence is quite unthinkable, we can only attribute the preservation of the full vowels to the archaic character of Classical Arabic, and assign to the vowel elision of the Eastern dialects a comparatively late date.

A few lines later, however, he backtracks a bit:

> It cannot always be said that the Hijazi form is older and the Eastern form produced by elision. As the instance of Arabic *malik* and Hebrew *malk-* proves, there was a good deal of wavering between segolate and bisyllabic noun forms in Semitic.

This statement leaves the door open a crack for the possibility that the Eastern form *kabdun* 'liver' and the Hebrew construct form *kắḇäḏ* 'heavy of' are both reflexes of the Proto-Semitic construct form **kabdu* 'liver of; heavy of,' just as *kabidun* 'liver' in West-Arabian and Classical Arabic and *kåḇeḏ* 'liver; heavy' in Hebrew are both reflexes of the Proto-Semitic absolute form **kabidum* 'liver; heavy.'

---

[27] According to Huehnergard (2006, p. 9), there may also be an Old Assyrian example.

[28] For example, *ga-ba-re-e* 'men' and *ru-ga-ze-e* '(eruptions of) anger' in the Uruk incantation. However, as noted in note 24 above, the syncopated form *ga-[a]b-re-e* 'men' occurs there as well. Was the spread of syncope just beginning at the time? Was it a variable rule outside of the construct state?

[29] Muraoka and Porten (1998, p. 39) muddy the waters by raising the possibility that singular forms like *lbby* and *bṭllh* show "that the phenomenon is not confined to plural nouns, unless one should postulate two distinct variants." Since these non-segolate biforms are well established on independent grounds (see, e.g., ibid., n. 187), they should not be cited as counterexamples.

[30] This variation is noted but not explained by Muraoka and Porten (1998, p. 38).

[31] It is possible that the alternation between [dašašay:aʾ] and [daš:ayhum] was an innovation on the analogy of the alternation between [kalabay:aʾ] and [kalbayhum]. If that is the case, then, strictly speaking, only [kalbayhum] can be described as a product of syncope.

[32] See note 13 above.

[33] For discussion, see Rabin 1951, p. 97; and Fleisch 1961, p. 157.

We can now turn to some Proto-Semitic examples. Many of them are drawn from the groundbreaking dictionary of Militarev and Kogan (2000–), which the reader should consult for a full presentation and evaluation of the data. One of the many important contributions of this work is the decision to "postulate two or even three alternative protoforms, especially in cases in which deviations from traditional reconstructions are identical in more than one language" (ibid., vol. 1, p. cxxxvi). Among the examples given of this approach are reconstructed forms with vowels in parentheses (ibid., vol. 1, p. cxxxvii). This is quite legitimate, even by the strict standard I have called for elsewhere (Steiner 1987), because it is not uncommon for individual Semitic languages to have two variants of a single noun, one with vowel syncope and one without it.

(1) '(back of) shoulder, shoulder blade': **katipum* (absolute) ~ **katpu* (construct); cf. Militarev and Kogan (2000–, vol. 1, pp. 138–39, no. 154): **kat*(*i*)*p*-, that is, **katip*- and **katp*-. The alternation survives in Hebrew: *kåṯep̄* (absolute) ~ *kə́ṯäp̄* (construct). It is possible, but not certain, that Arabic *katfun* (alongside *katifun* and *kitfun*)[34] is a direct descendant of Proto-Semitic **katpu* rather than an inner-Arabic parallel development from Proto-Semitic **katipum*.

(2) 'rib, (side of) chest': **ṣ́ilaʿum* (absolute) ~ **ṣ́ilʿum* (construct); cf. Militarev and Kogan (2000–, vol. 1, pp. 243–44, no. 272): **ṣ̂il*(*a*)*ʿ*-, that is, **ṣ̂ilaʿ*- and **ṣ̂ilʿ*-. Here, too, the alternation survives in Hebrew: *ṣelā́ʿ* (absolute) ~ *ṣə́laʿ* (construct). And here, too, it is possible, but not certain, that Arabic *ḍilʿun* (alongside *ḍilaʿun*)[35] is a direct descendant of Proto-Semitic **ṣ́ilʿu* rather than an inner-Arabic parallel development from Proto-Semitic **ṣ́ilaʿum*.

(3) 'hip(-bone)': **warikum* (absolute) ~ **warku* (construct); cf. Militarev and Kogan (2000–, vol. 1, pp. 258–59, no. 288): **warik*(*-at*)-. As noted above, the alternation survives in Hebrew: *yårek̲* (absolute) ~ *yə́räk̲* (construct). And once again, it is possible, but not certain, that Arabic *warkun* (alongside *warikun*)[36] is a direct descendant of Proto-Semitic **warku* rather than an inner-Arabic parallel development from Proto-Semitic **warikum*.

(4) 'moon, month': **wariḫum* (absolute) ~ **warḫu* (construct); cf. Kogan (2011, p. 193 §2.3.3): **war*(*i*)*ḫ*-. In Hebrew, *yåréaḥ* 'moon' is normally in the absolute state,[37] while singular *yə́raḥ* 'month' is normally in the construct state.[38] In Standard Biblical Hebrew, the word for 'month' in the absolute state is *ḥṓḏäš*, as a result of the following semantic development:

	month	month of	moon	new moon
Pre-Hebrew	**yariḫu*	**yarḫ*	**yariḫu*	**ḫudṯ yariḫi*[39]
Hebrew	*ḥṓḏäš*[40]	*yə́raḥ/ḥṓḏäš*	*yåréaḥ*	*ḥṓḏäš*[41]
(cf. Akkadian	*warḫum*	*warḫu*	*warḫum*	*warḫum*)

[34] See Zimmern 1890, p. 369; Ullmann 1970–, vol. 1, p. 48 s.v. *katifun*.

[35] See Rabin 1951, p. 97.

[36] See Zimmern 1890, p. 369.

[37] Twenty-six examples plus one example with suffixed pronoun.

[38] Five examples plus one Late Biblical Hebrew example in the absolute state.

[39] The original meaning of this phrase must have been "renewal of the moon"; cf. the phrase *ḥid:uwš hay:åréaḥ* used by David Ḳimḥi (1847, p. 97, col. a, l. 7 s.v. *ḥdš*) in explaining the etymology of *ḥoḏäš*. Cf. Ugaritic *b ḥdṯ yrḫ* 'on the new moon' (Olmo Lete and Sanmartín 2003, p. 356 s.v. *ḥdṯ* II). Cf. also Phoenician *bḥdš yrḥ ʾtnm* and *bḥdš yrḥ pʿlt*, but these are usually taken to mean 'at/with the new moon of the month of E./P.' (Donner and Röllig 1973–79, vol. 2, p. 54 [37A 2; 37B 2]; Amadasi and Karageorghis 1977, pp. 104–05, 118–19; Hoftijzer and Jongeling 1995, p. 351 s.v. $ḥdš_2$). If this interpretation is precise, the phrase has undergone semantic reanalysis in Phoenician.

[40] The shift from 'new moon' to 'month' is of course a case of synecdoche, as pointed already by David Ḳimḥi in his commentary to Ps 81:4. The shift seems to be exhibited in Ugaritic dates such as *b šbʿ ḥdš*, even though Olmo Lete and Sanmartín (2003, p. 356 s.v. *ḥdṯ* II) render this as 'on the seventh (day) of the new moon.'

[41] Already in Ugaritic the phrase *ḥdṯ yrḫ* is abridged to *ḥdṯ* in the phrase *ym ḥdṯ* 'day of the new moon' (Olmo Lete and Sanmartín 2003, p. 356 s.v. *ḥdṯ* II).

Alternation between the two Hebrew words for "month" can be seen in 1 Kgs 6:38 (*bəyắraḥ buʷl huʷʾ haḥóḏäš haš:əmiʸniʸ*) and 8:2 (*bəyắraḥ hâʾeṯâniʸm … huʷʾ haḥóḏäš haš:əḇiʸʿiʸ*). This alternation supports the claim that *yắraḥ* could not be used in the absolute state in Standard Biblical Hebrew.

(5) 'pairs/teams (of yoked/harnessed draft animals)': *ṣimadu:ma* (absolute) ~ *ṣimdu:* (construct). Note the reconstruction of the absolute plural form with the vocalic infix *-a-*, despite the fact that it is absent in Akkadian *ṣindu:*. As noted above, the vocalic infix is attested for at least some segolate plurals in virtually all of the pre-modern West Semitic languages; our reconstruction assumes that it goes back to Proto-Semitic (not merely Proto-West-Semitic)[42] and that it was lost in Akkadian when the syncope rule was extended to the absolute state[43] and other non-proclitic forms. As noted further above, the alternation survives in Hebrew: *ṣəmâḏiʸm* (absolute) ~ *ṣimdeʸ* (construct).

5. Syncope in the Feminine Ending

Reflexes of both *-*at* and *-*t* survive in virtually all of the ancient descendants of Proto-Semitic, but none of those languages has a (productive) phonological rule that governs the relationship between the two feminine endings. That is the case even in Akkadian, where the similarity between *šanat* ~ *šantum* and *rapaš* ~ *rapšum* led Delitzsch (1906, p. 97, §45b) to view these alternations as products of the same vowel syncope rule.[44] This view is no longer accepted. There appears to be a consensus today that, from a synchronic point of view, the absence of a second *a* in *rapšum* is the result of a vowel syncope rule, while the absence of *a* in the feminine ending of *šantum* is not. From a diachronic point of view, however, I believe that Delitzsch was right. In other words, Proto-Semitic *-*t* was derived from underlying *-*at* by a vowel syncope rule.

The relationship between *-*at* and *-*t* is less obvious in Hebrew, but it is arguably more revealing there. As noted above, in some nouns the two proto-variants are in complementary distribution, conditioned by the syntax (absolute state vs. construct state), e.g., *mamlâḵâʰ* < **mamlakatum* ~ *mamlắḵäṯ* < **mamlaktu* 'kingdom'; *märkâḇâʰ* < **markabatum*[45] ~ *mirkắḇäṯ* < **markabtu* 'chariot'; *məlʾâḵâʰ* ~ *məlʾắḵäṯ* 'work';[46] *map:âlâʰ* ~ *map:ắläṯ* 'ruin'; *mišpâḥâʰ* ~ *mišpáḥaṯ* 'clan'; *ʿăṭârâʰ* ~ *ʿăṭắräṯ* 'crown'; *dəḇelâʰ* ~ *dəḇắläṯ* 'cake of pressed figs'; *šəlošâʰ* ~ *šəlóšäṯ* 'three'; *ʾarbâʿâʰ* ~ *ʾarbáʿaṯ* 'four'; *ḥămiš:âʰ* ~ *ḥăméšäṯ* 'five'; *šiš:âʰ* ~ *šéšäṯ* 'six'; *ʿăśârâʰ* ~ *ʿăśắräṯ* 'ten.' In my view, this alternation cannot be separated from the alternation discussed in the preceding section; both derive from a Proto-Semitic vowel syncope rule. It is true that a number of these lexical items seem to postdate Proto-Semitic. For example, there is no evidence for chariots or other wheeled vehicles in Mesopotamia before the third millennium B.C. (Dalley 1995, p. 414).[47] We must assume, therefore, that the Proto-Semitic syncope rule continued to operate in Northwest Semitic down to historical times.

In other Hebrew nouns, the two proto-variants are in free variation in the absolute state, e.g., *moʾăḇiy:âʰ* ~ *moʾăḇiʸṯ* 'Moabitess'; *šiḇyâʰ* ~ *šəḇiʸṯ* 'female captives (collective)'; *ḥaṭ:âʾâʰ* ~ *ḥaṭ:âʾṯ* 'sin'; *mat:ânâʰ* ~ *mat:aṯ* < **mantantu* 'gift'; *tip̄ʾârâʰ* ~ *tip̄ʾắräṯ* 'glory'; *buʷšâʰ* ~ *bóšäṯ* 'shame'; *nəḥuʷšâʰ* ~ *nəḥóšäṯ* 'copper'; *yab:âšâʰ* ~ *yab:ắšäṯ* 'dry land' (together in Exod 4:9!). The same free variation is found in G-stem participles, e.g., *ʾoḵəlâʰ* ~ *ʾoḵắläṯ* (pausal *ʾoḵelâʰ* ~ *ʾoḵắläṯ*) 'consuming' (three verses apart in Isa 30 in the expression "consuming fire"!); and in Iy/w G-stem verbal

[42] For a possible trace in Old Assyrian, see Huehnergard 2006, p. 9.

[43] Once the infix was lost in the overwhelming majority of segolate plurals, there would be no reason for speakers to preserve it in the few segolate plurals where syncope may have been blocked.

[44] For a survey of the scholarly literature, see Greenstein 1984, pp. 45–46.

[45] Cf. Coptic *brčoout* 'chariot' < New Kingdom *mrkbt* (Hoch 1994, pp. 145–47). According to Hoch (ibid., p. 146) the Coptic vowel points to *markábatu* rather than *markabtu*.

[46] So in the Tiberian reading tradition; the Babylonian reading tradition has *malʾâḵâʰ* ~ *malʾáḵaṯ* (Yeivin 1985, p. 1015).

[47] Of course, we cannot rule out the possibility that **markabatum* originally had a different meaning.

nouns, e.g., *deʿå*[h] ~ *dáʿaṯ* 'knowledge.'[48] Free variation between *-*at* and *-*t* is found only rarely in the construct state, e.g., *maṣ:ǝḇaṯ* ~ *maṣ:ắḇäṯ* 'pillar of'; *malkaṯ* ~ *mǝläḵäṯ* 'queen of';[49] and *mat:ǝnaṯ yådoʷ* ~ *mat:aṯ yådoʷ* 'his donation (lit., the gift of his hand).' According to the "law of diminishing conditioning," all of this free variation must be a later development, a product of analogical leveling.

In Ugaritic, only -*at* is found after bases ending in *CC* (Huehnergard 1987, p. 295). This "phonologically necessary" distribution appears in all of the Semitic languages (Huehnergard 2004, p. 147). In other environments, no regularity is apparent in the data collected by Gordon (1965, pp. 52–53 §8.3) and Huehnergard (1987, pp. 295–96).[50]

We may now consider three Proto-Semitic examples:

(6) 'childbirth, giving birth': **lidatum* (absolute) ~ **lidtu*/**lit:u*[51] (construct). Most of the Semitic languages preserve only one of these three forms. The absolute form survives in Arabic *lidatun*, Geez *lǝdat*, and Ugaritic *ldt*.[52] Two of the forms survive in the Akkadian word for 'offspring': *lit:um* (absolute) ~ *lidat* (construct). All three forms survive in Hebrew: *leḏåh*, *lắḏäṯ*, and *laṯ* (1 Sam 4:19).[53] Of these, only *lắḏäṯ* is attested as a construct form.

(7) 'ten': *ʿ*aśaratum* (absolute) ~ *ʿ*aśartu* (construct). The alternation survives in Hebrew: ʿ*ăśårå*[h] ~ ʿ*ăśắräṯ* 'ten.'

In the third example, the Semitic conditioned variants ended up as Canaanite dialectal variants:

(8) 'year': **šanatum* (absolute) ~ **šantu*/**šat:u*[54] (construct). In Northern Hebrew, Moabite, and Phoenician, we find *šat* < **šat:u* even in the absolute state (Garr 1985, pp. 93–94). In Biblical Hebrew, we have *šånå*[h] < **šanatum* in the absolute state and *šǝnaṯ* in the construct state. The simplest explanation is that Proto-Semitic **šanatum* and **šat:u* became doublets in Proto-Canaanite and that the daughter languages selected one or the other. This is a good example of dialectal differentiation following analogical leveling. Something similar may have happened with the word for 'widow,' appearing as ʾ*almånå*[h] in Hebrew but ʾ*almat* in Phoenician.

Another example of dialectal differentiation has been suggested by Blau (2010, p. 264). According to him, the Hebrew absolute form *bårǝḳaṯ* 'emerald,' a doublet of *bårắḳäṯ* 'id.,' is "presumably borrowed from another dialect that preserved -*at*." Blau compares the Phoenician toponym *Ṣårǝp̄aṯ* 'Sarepta,'[55] a comparison that is of interest for two reasons. First, it suggests that *bårǝḳaṯ*, attested in a prophecy addressed to the king of Tyre (Ezek 28:12–13), is a Phoenician form.[56] Second, the ending of the toponym in question reflects *-*at* in some sources and *-*t* in others: Hebrew *Ṣårǝp̄aṯ*, Egyptian *Ḏa-ar-pá-ta* (so according to Albright 1934, p. 42), Arabic *Ṣarafand* vs. *Ṣariptu*, Greek Σαρεπτα, Σαριφθα, and so on (Murtonen 1986–1990, vol. 1, p. 319).

Hebrew is the only Semitic language in which we find a significant number of examples of *-*t* in the construct state alternating with *-*at* (> -*å*[h]) in the absolute. In Akkadian, the situation looks very different; indeed, at first glance it appears to be the polar opposite, with **šat:um* in the reflex of the Proto-Semitic absolute state versus **šanat* in the construct state. Here too, however, the reversal is just an illusion created by the loss of case endings in the construct state.[57]

There is, in fact, one indication in Akkadian that -*t* was once associated with the construct state. Alongside of *aš:at* 'wife of,' there is a second, irregular construct form *ašti* occurring only in the genitive case. This form bears a remarkable resemblance to the Hebrew construct form ʾ*éšäṯ* < *ʾ*išt*- 'wife of' (abs. ʾ*iš:å*[h]) in that both exhibit an

[48] The forms *toḵeḥå*[h] and *toḵắḥaṯ* appear to have diverged to the point where they have distinct plural forms and perhaps different nuances as well.

[49] See example 29 below.

[50] Huehnergard (1987, p. 295) refers to the distribution in these other environments as "free variation," but given the dearth/absence of actual doublets in Ugaritic (comparable to the Hebrew doublets immediately above), it may be preferable to use the term "lexical conditioning."

[51] For assimilation in Proto-Semitic, see §8 below.

[52] For -*at* as the feminine ending of the last form, cf. Ugaritic *ṣat* 'coming out of.'

[53] For the vowel of the last form, cf. *baṯ* 'daughter' and *mǝšåraṯ* 'serving' (1 Kgs 1:15).

[54] For assimilation in Proto-Semitic, see §8 below.

[55] For personal names in the Bible with an -*at* ending, see Driver 1913, p. 139 (although the Semitic origin of the name *Goliath* has been contested).

[56] If so, the vowel of the ending (*a* rather than *o*) hints that this borrowing predates the transcription *Ab-di-mil-ku-ut-ti* from the time of Esarhaddon; see Friedrich and Röllig 1999, p. 40, §78.

[57] See the discussion of Akkadian *kabtum* ~ *kabit* in §4 above.

unexpected absence of gemination. The importance of this similarity cannot be overstated, because these forms are anomalous in both Akkadian[58] and Hebrew.

Here we may invoke what I shall call "the principle of cognate anomalies": corresponding forms in two cognate languages that are anomalous in both are very reliable witnesses to the proto-language (or even the pre-proto-language), since they are highly unlikely to have resulted from parallel (independent) development. To my mind, the correspondence between these aberrant construct forms, *ašti* in Akkadian and *ʾéšät̲* in Hebrew, is the closest thing that students of Proto-Semitic have to the holy grail.[59] I shall return to these forms and similar ones in §8 below.

Another very significant vestige of what must now be considered the original conditioning is found in Mehri. In that language, the feminine singular ending is virtually always derived from **-at*, with the vowel usually lengthened and often raised to [e:] or [i:], as in *kəwbe:t* 'bitch' and *ba:li:t* 'mistress' (Rubin 2010, pp. 59–60). Although "the construct state ... has all but disappeared ..., remnants of the older construction survive with a handful of words" (ibid., p. 74). Among these words is one that is relevant to our topic, namely, the word for "daughter." This appears as *bri:t* (definite *ḥəbri:t*) in the absolute state, but *bərt* in the construct (ibid., pp. 60, 74). Thus, the interrogative phrase "whose daughter? (lit., the daughter of whom?)" can be expressed in Mehri either as *bərt mo:n* or as *ḥəbri:t d̲-mo:n* (Watson 2009, p. 232). Here we have a clear case of **-at* in the absolute alternating with **-t* in the construct. I return to this form in §10 below.

In Arabic, too, **-t* survives in only a handful of forms, including *bintun* (alongside *(i)bnatun*) 'daughter' and *uḫtun* 'sister.' I agree with the view of Dolgopolsky (1999, p. 160 n. 53) that "in Arabic the syncopated *a* in *-at-* was reintroduced everywhere, except for some archaisms like *bint-un* 'daughter' (< pS **ʹbin-at-um*), due to grammatical analogy." The survival of **-t* in Arabic *bintun* and *uḫtun* must be attributed to the common use of "daughter of X" and "sister of X" — both in the construct state — to identify women. This usage is well attested in Arabic,[60] not to mention Biblical Hebrew[61] and so on. Here we see another correlation, albeit a weak one, between **-t* and the construct state.

6. Syncope in Initial Syllables of the Stem and "Prothetic Aleph"

The use of prothetic vowels (the so-called prothetic *aleph*) in the Semitic languages has been discussed for at least a millennium,[62] and yet its origin is still poorly understood. Militarev and Kogan (2000–, vol. 1, cxliii) state that "the strict phonetic conditions under which the prothesis must take place have never, to our knowledge,

---

[58] So I was assured by Walter Farber and the late Erica Reiner in 1981; cf. Soden 1995, p. 17, §12f: "ganz ungewöhnlich." Most of the parallels I know of have *-artum* for *-ar:atum*, viz., *martum* 'gall bladder' < **mar:atum* (contrast *mar:atum* 'bitter [fem.]') and *sartum* 'falsehood' < **sar:atu* (contrast *sar:a:tum* 'lies'). Greenstein (1984, pp. 52–53) views the degemination that produced *ašti* as a later development, an example of "weak" phonological change within Akkadian, comparable to the "weak" diachronic phonological change in *be:la/etum* > *beltum* 'lady' and *ma:ratum* > *martum* 'daughter.' He argues (ibid., p. 53) that "the stem was ... restructured as /ʾaš+t/ ... and the construct was formed by the phonological rule of *i*-ADDITION." In Greenstein's analysis, the ending of the construct form *ašti* is quite different from the ending of the construct forms *belti* (for *belet*) and *marti* (for *marat*): "These words ... are not simple constructs but archaic formations in which the genitive case ending *i* is preserved word-finally" (ibid., p. 52). Since *ašti*, too, is a construct form in the genitive case according to the editors of the CAD, the reason for this difference is not completely clear to me. Why not include *ašti* among the "archaic formations in which the genitive case ending *i* is preserved word-finally"?

[59] Brockelmann (1903, p. 15) believes that the correspondence between *ašti* and *ʾéšät̲* is the product of parallel development, but this belief forces him to posit various contaminations and folk-etymologies to account for the exceptions on an ad-hoc basis. Janssens (1975/76, p. 281) mentions the Hebrew alternation but not the Akkadian parallel.

[60] Cf. "O sister of Aaron!" addressed to Mary (not Miriam) in Quran 19:28 and the many examples of "sister of" found in the searchable databases of the Hadith online.

[61] Cf. the commentary of R. Joseph Bekhor Shor to Exod 15:20: "'Then Miriam the prophetess, Aaron's sister took' — the way of Scripture is that when it mentions a woman, it mentions her oldest brother, as in 'Basemath, [daughter of Ishmael and] sister of Nebaioth' (Gen 36:3) and 'Elisheba, [daughter of Amminadab and] sister of Nahshon' (Exod 6:23)."

[62] The literature on this subject is vast, stretching back to the tenth century (Dunash 1866, p. 49, §141), if not further. In addition to the well-known classics (e.g., Barth 1889, pp. 218–26; Brockelmann 1908–13, vol. 1, pp. 209–17, 371–74; Blake 1911, pp. 217–19), I mention a few recent studies: Talshir 1992; Militarev and Kogan 2000–, vol. 1, cxlii–cxliii, vol. 2, lxxiii–lxxiv; Steiner 2001a; and Lipiński 2001, pp. 186–87, 200–01, 221–22. Brockelmann and Lipiński cite much evidence from modern Semitic languages for the use of prothetic vowels to break up initial con-

been adduced," adding that "it is not impossible that future research in the historical morphology of the bases in question will reveal such conditions."

An important contribution of Militarev and Kogan (2000–, vol. 1, p. cxlii) to the solution of this problem is their recognition that, "in a considerable number of roots, *ʾV- can obviously be traced to the proto-level, so that bases with and without prefixed *ʾV- are to be reconstructed as alternative Proto-Semitic variants." As we shall see below, it is not uncommon for individual Semitic languages to have two variants of a single noun, one with vowel prothesis and one without it.

I would argue that, although the two variants are doublets in some of the Semitic languages, they were not doublets in Proto-Semitic but rather conditioned allomorphs. More precisely, vowel prothesis originally functioned as a syllable-repair process[63] necessitated by syncope in the initial syllable of a construct form — except when the resulting cluster could be repaired by a vowel at the end of the preceding word.

The original conditioning of vowel prothesis has not survived unchanged in any of the Semitic languages; however, various traces of it can be occasionally be discerned, as we shall see in the following Proto-Semitic examples:

(9) 'finger': **ṣibaʿum* (absolute) ~ **(i)ṣbaʿu* (construct); cf. Militarev and Kogan (2000–, vol. 1, pp. 227–28, no. 256): **ṣVbʿ(-at)-* and **ʾV-ṣbaʿ-*. Reflexes of both forms are widely attested in West Semitic. It is true that only forms with a prothetic vowel are known from East Semitic (Eblaite *iš-ba-um* etc.), but adding Egyptian *ḏbʿ* 'finger' (Coptic *tēēbe*) to the picture would seem to compensate for this deficiency by pushing **ṣibaʿ-* back to Proto-Egypto-Semitic. I disagree with the claim of Militarev and Kogan (2000–, vol. 1, p. 228) that "the underlying protoforms are presumably **ṣibʿ(at)-*, **ʾa-ṣibʿ-*." It is true that one occasionally finds prothetic vowels in the Semitic languages even where there is no initial consonant cluster that needs resolving, but, in my opinion, the assumption that such examples are to be reconstructed for Proto-Semitic (Militarev and Kogan 2000–, vol. 1, p. cxlii–cxliii) needs to be reexamined.

(10) 'posterior, buttocks': **šitum* (absolute) ~ **(i)štu* (construct); cf. Militarev and Kogan (2000–, vol. 1, p. 225–27, no. 255): **šVt-* and **ʾi-šVt-*. The prothetic vowel of Arabic *(i)stu(n)* exhibits *sandhi* conditioning (see below). The same is true of the Arabic prothetic vowel in the following three examples:

(11) 'son': **binum* (absolute) ~ **(i)bnu* (construct);[64] cf. Phoenician *ʾbn* alongside *bn*; Arabic *(i)bnu(n)*; Mandaic *ʿbra* (pronounced [ebra]), *abra*, *bra* (determined) ~ *br*, *bar* (construct).[65]

(12) 'name': **šimum* (absolute) ~ **(i)šmu* (construct); cf. Old Aramaic *ʾšm* alongside *šm*; Mandaic *ʿušma*, *ʿšuma* (pronounced [ošma], [ešma]) alongside *šuma*;[66] Tur Abdin *išm-*; Arabic *(i)smu(n)* alongside *si/u/amu(n)*.

(13) 'two (masc.)': **ṯina:m/nv* (absolute) ~ **(i)ṯna:* (construct); cf. Phoenician *ʾšnm*; Arabic *(i)ṯna:(ni)*.[67]

The last four examples are important because they enable us to recover another piece of the puzzle, another detail of the conditioning for vowel prothesis in Proto-Semitic. All of them exhibit prothetic vowels in Arabic in addition to at least one other Semitic language; we even find doublets in examples 11 (Phoenician and Mandaic) and 12 (Old Aramaic). However, it is only in Arabic that the prothetic vowel (*ʾalifu l-waṣl*) is known to have a *sandhi* condition, occurring at the beginning of a sentence but not after a word ending in a vowel unless there is an intervening pause.[68] It seems very likely that something like this Arabic *sandhi* restriction operated in Proto-Semitic — hence the parentheses that I place around the Proto-Semitic prothetic vowel. The Arabic word for "name" (example 12) is of particular importance since it exhibits three major variants, reflecting all three of

sonant clusters resulting from syncope. An intriguing example worth adding here is the Palestinian Arabic toponym *Jebel Usdum* "Mt. Sodom." The form *Usdum* < *Sḏom* presumably goes back to a time when Palestinian Aramaic allowed words to begin with a consonant cluster but Palestinian Arabic did not.

63 Cf. the much later use of vowel prothesis as a syllable repair process in Semitic loanwords from Greek.

64 See also examples 33a and 33b below.

65 See Macuch 1965, pp. 14, 227.

66 See Drower and Macuch 1963, pp. 454–55; Macuch 1965, p. 21.

67 See also examples 34a and 34b below.

68 After words ending in a consonant, a linking vowel is inserted. For the details, see Wright 1967, vol. 1, pp. 19–24.

the reconstructed Proto-Semitic variants (albeit with some distributional changes): *simu*(*n*) < **šimum* (absolute); *ismu*(*n*) < **išmu* (construct, post-pausal/consonantal); and *smu*(*n*) < **šmu* (construct, post-vocalic). If prothetic vowels did not exhibit this *sandhi* condition in most of the daughter languages,[69] we must attribute that fact to the law of diminishing conditioning.

Evidence for this reconstruction can be adduced from the history of prothesis in Late Latin (Sampson 2010, pp. 72–73):

> [W]e can see I-prosthesis as a development which arose in Latin for syllabic reasons .... [I]t seems likely that I-prosthesis was carried through in a two stage process; first, these sequences were modified in contexts where they were anomalously tautosyllabic, i.e. post-consonantally and post-pausally, and subsequently the restructuring could be generalized to post-vocalic contexts (where the sequences were already heterosyllabic).

Vestiges of the original conditioning (or something close to it) survive in modern Romance. In the Gascon dialect of Bagnères-de-Luchon, the word for 'thorn,' derived from Latin *spina*, is *espyó* after a pause or a word ending in a consonant but *spyó* after a word ending in a vowel (Sampson 2010, p. 66). In addition, "other Romance varieties have continued to operate with a sandhi-style prosthesis which typically inserts the prosthetic vowel in just post-consonantal contexts only, e.g. in Piedmontese varieties and, in a more marginal way, standard Italian" (ibid., p. 66).

In most Romance varieties, as in most of the Semitic languages, prothetic vowels do not exhibit this *sandhi* condition. Janda and Joseph (2003, p. 209) have cited this fact as evidence for non-phonetic generalization (= the law of diminishing conditioning):

> ... in origin, this development was not a word-boundary phenomenon; rather, it was sensitive to sentence-level sandhi conditioning, referred to in German under the rubric of *Satzphonetik*. That is, originally the prothesis was just for initial *s*C- after a consonant — /...C#_*s*C... — but not after a vowel. This distribution is still preserved in (prescriptive) standard Italian, where one finds *in iscuola* 'in school,' with prothesis, but *la scuola* 'the school,' with no prothesis. Thus, it seems that this innovation was, at the outset, a syllable-structure-based development repairing the *per se* unsyllabifiable sequence ...C#*s*C... (but not ...V#*s*C..., which required no adjustment). The extension of prothesis to any word-initial *s*C- cluster, regardless of the preceding sound, must be a later (non-phonetic, non-syllable-structure-driven) generalization.

Three additional Proto-Semitic examples are worthy of consideration:

(14) 'arm': **ḏira:ʕum* (absolute) ~ *(*i*)*ḏra:ʕu* (construct); cf. Militarev and Kogan (2000–, vol. 1, p. 62, no. 65): **ḏVra:ʕ-*. Doublets are attested in two Northwest Semitic languages: *zərόaʕ*/*ʾäzrόaʕ* in Biblical Hebrew and *dəråʕ*/*ʾädråʕ* in Biblical Aramaic. Indeed, one could argue that Hebrew has a reflex of **ḏra:ʕu* as well, in *u-zrόaʕ* 'and the arm of' (Isa 53:1).[70] The examples of vowel prothesis considered above go back to Proto-Semitic, and there is no reason to assume that this example is any different.

(15) 'armpit': **šaḫa:tum* (absolute) ~ *(*i*)*šḫa:tu* (construct); cf. Militarev and Kogan (2000–, vol 1, p. 212, no. 240): **šaḫw/y-at-* and Kogan (2011, p. 217, §6.1.11): **šaḫ*(*a*)*y*(*-at*)*-*. The form with prothesis is attested only in Eblaite: *iš-ḫa-tum* 'flank' (Conti 1990, p. 159, no. 569). Thus, there is no certainty that it existed in Proto-Semitic. Nevertheless, it is worth citing because Eblaite *iš-ḫa-tum* interchanges with *sa-ḫa-tum* 'flank' in copies of the bilingual lexical list (loc. cit.). Unless this variation is purely orthographic, it shows the correlation between prothesis and syncope.

---

69 I say "if" because there is no way of being certain that this is the case. The Arabic *sandhi* condition is, to a large extent, disguised by morphophonemic spelling in unvocalized texts; the prothetic vowel is usually represented by *ʾalif* even when elided. Hence, we cannot totally rule out the possibility that Old Aramaic *ʾšm* (alongside *šm*) and Hebrew *ʾäzrόaʕ* (alongside *zərόaʕ*) exhibited a similar *sandhi* condition.

70 See the discussion of example 36 below.

(16) 'thumb, big toe': **baha:num* (absolute) ~ **(i)bha:nu* (construct); cf. Militarev and Kogan (2000–, vol. 1, p. 33, no. 34): **bVhā/īn-*, **ʾV-bhān-*. Both forms are attested in East Semitic and West Semitic. The form without prothesis survives in Eblaite and Hebrew (plur. *bǝhonoʷṯ*), while the form with prothesis survives in Arabic *ʾibha:mun* and probably in Akkadian *uba:nu* 'finger, toe.' Arabic *ʾibha:mun* has several biforms. In addition to *bahi:mun*, there was a form *biha:mun*, which al-Azharī (895–981 C.E.) considered unacceptable (Lane 1863–1877, p. 269, col. b s.v. *ʾibha:mun*). It is possible, although far from certain, that this substandard form goes back to **baha:num*. If so, Arabic once again preserves variants with and without a prothetic vowel,[71] although in this case we are not dealing with *ʾalifu l-waṣl*.

In short, prothetic vowels were used in Proto-Semitic to break up initial consonant clusters resulting from syncope in the construct state. Their connection with the construct state, which has not previously been recognized, may help to explain the fact that "animal names with prefixed *ʾV-* which is clearly detectable as early as in PS are less in number in comparison to the anatomic terms, among which this element was certainly rather widespread already in the proto-language" (Militarev and Kogan 2000–, vol. 2, p. lxxiii). This distribution follows naturally from the fact that names of body parts occur far more often in the construct state than do names of animals.

Another form worth mentioning in this connection, even though it is not a noun, is the negator *ʾal*, widely attested in West Semitic. A century ago, Blake (1911, pp. 217–18) suggested that it too exhibits prothesis.[72] Blake noted that Biblical Hebrew/Aramaic, *loʾ/låʾ* "is regularly authotonic," whereas *ʾal* "is proclitic, as is indicated by the Maqqeph which joins it to the following word" (ibid., p. 217). Similarly, in Ethiopic "we find it only in the quasi-adverb *ʾalbô* 'there is not, has not' and in the negative *ʾakkô*, in both cases without accent" (ibid., p. 218). Blake concludes that proclitic *ʾal* "may have been developed from the authotonic *lâ* as follows. With loss of accent the vowel *â* was shortened and finally disappeared, leaving only *l*, probably pronounced as *l̥*; this vocalic *l* developed a prothetic vowel ..." (ibid., p. 218).

Blake's characterization of the Tiberian Masorah is reasonably accurate. A search with the *Haketer* program turns up 733 occurrences of (*wǝ̆-*)*ʾal* of which 726 are followed by *maq:ep*; 4,834 occurrences of (*wǝ̆-*)*loʾ* of which 2,061 are followed by *maq:ep*; and 78 occurrences of (*wǝ̆-*)*låʾ* of which 25 are followed by *maq:ep*. The difference between *ʾal* (99 percent proclitic) and *loʾ/låʾ* (43 percent/32 percent proclitic) is striking. It is therefore reasonable to assume that the stress contrast between *loʾ ṯas:iʸg gǝ̆ḇuʷl* (Deut 19:14) and *ʾal-tas:eg gǝ̆ḇuʷl* (Prov 22:28) is original. But how did it arise? I suggest that prothesis may have arisen in cases where the negator *la:/laʾ* had a proclitic allomorph *la-* (with a short vowel)[73] that underwent syncope when attached to a word that was itself proclitic.[74]

Is *ʾal* comparable to *ʾb-* 'in' in Phoenician-Punic and Postbiblical Hebrew, to *ʾǝb-* 'in' in Tigre and *ʾab-* 'in' in Tigrinya, and to *ab* 'in' and *al* 'to' in the modern Samaritan Hebrew reading tradition (Lipiński 2001, p. 470; Steiner 2001a, p. 102)? Blake's discussion of prothesis is limited to cases involving resonants that became syllabic. However, examples 9 and 10 above seem to show that the presence of an initial resonant was not a necessary condition for prothesis.

7. Syncope Following Syllable-initial Semivowels

Another syllable-repair process, syllabicization of semivowels, is illustrated by the following examples:

(17) 'hand': **yadum* (absolute) ~ **idu* (construct); cf. Militarev and Kogan (2000–, vol. 1, pp. 262–63 no. 291): **yad-* and **ʾid-*. Forms that could reflect **i* or **i:* instead of **ya* are attested in Geez

[71] Cf. *si/u/amun* alongside (*i*)*smun* in example 12 above.

[72] I am indebted to the editors for reminding me of this article; I had internalized the suggestion when I read this article as a graduate student and subsequently forgotten the source. They also called my attention to Lipiński 2001, p. 464.

[73] Cf. CAD *la* versus *AHw lā*.

[74] Since *ʾal* normally precedes the jussive in Hebrew (e.g., *ʾal-tas:eg* in the preceding example), one might suggest that transitive jussives were originally proclitic (e.g., **ʾal-tas:eg-gǝ̆ḇuʷl*). And since the jussive stands in for the imperative following *ʾal*, one could support this suggestion by pointing to the prothetic vowel of the Arabic G-stem imperative, which hints that (transitive) imperatives were proclitic.

(ʾəd), Modern South Arabian (Jibbali éd, Soqotri ʾed) and Aramaic.[75] To the copious evidence that Militarev and Kogan cite from Late and Modern Aramaic, I would add the form *eytyh.*[m] = *ʾydyh* 'her hands' in pAmherst 63 (IX/18), alongside many examples without the initial *e* = *ʾ* (Steiner and Mosak Moshavi 1995, p. 1257).[76] The construct form *idu* makes excellent phonetic sense: when the initial consonant was a semivowel, no prothetic vowel would have been needed to repair an impermissible cluster resulting from syncope. When semivowels are neither preceded nor followed by a vowel, they undergo syllabicization and function as vowels themselves.

(18) 'kidney': **kvlyatum* (absolute) ~ **kvlitu* (construct); cf. Militarev and Kogan (2000–, vol. 1, p. 141, no. 156): **kʷaly-at-*. Forms that could reflect **i* or **i:* instead of **ya* are attested in Akkadian (*kali:tu*), Syriac (*ko(:)li:ta:*), and Geez (*kʷəlit*). Moreover, in Syriac we find an alternation between **i* and **y* in this word: *ko(:)li:ta:* (singular) ~ *kolya:ta:* (plural).

(19) 'afterbirth, fetal membrane': **švlyatum* (absolute) ~ **švlitu* (construct); cf. Militarev and Kogan (2000–, vol. 1, pp. 216–17, no. 246): **ša/ily-at-*. Forms that could reflect **i* or **i:* instead of **ya* are attested in Akkadian (*sili:tu, šeli:tu, šali:tu*) and Syriac (*šli:ta:*). Syriac has an alternation between **i* and **y* in this word: *šli:ta:* (singular) ~ *šelya:ta:* (plural).

(20) 'gazelle': **ṭabyatum* (absolute) ~ **ṭabitu* (construct); cf. Militarev and Kogan (2000–, vol. 2, pp. 310–12, no. 242): **ṭaby(-at)-*. Forms that could reflect **i* or **i:* instead of **ya* are attested in Akkadian (*ṣabi:tu*) and Aramaic (Syriac *ṭbi:ta:* and the New Testament name Ταβ(ε)ιθα). Syriac has an alternation between **i* and **y* in this word, as well: *ṭbi:ta:* (singular) ~ *ṭabya:ta:* (plural).

(21) 'female captives (collective)': **švbyatum* (absolute) ~ **švbitu* (construct). Reflexes of this word (and/or its masculine counterpart) are widely distributed in West Semitic (Hebrew, Aramaic, Arabic, Epigraphic South Arabian) but are not attested in East Semitic. Thus, there is no certainty that it existed in Proto-Semitic. Nevertheless, it is worth citing because Hebrew preserves both forms as doublets, both with the meaning 'female captives': *šiḇyå*[h] and *šəḇi*[y]*ṯ*. They interchange in virtually identical contexts in Num 21:29 and Jer 48:46.

(22) 'town': **ḳaryatum* (absolute) ~ **ḳaritu* (construct). Reflexes of these forms are attested in West Semitic (Ugaritic, Hebrew, Aramaic, Arabic)[77] but not in East Semitic. Thus, there is no certainty that it existed in Proto-Semitic. Nevertheless, it is worth citing because forms that could reflect **i* or **i:* instead of **ya* are attested not only in Syriac (*ḳri:ta:*) but also in Ugaritic (**ḳa-ri-t*[u$_4$]).[78] Syriac has an alternation between **i* and **y* in this word too: *ḳurya:* (singular absolute) ~ *ḳri:ta:* (singular determined).[79]

The last five examples belong to the class of feminine segolates (e.g., **kalbatum* 'bitch'). Nouns of this class normally did not permit the vowel of the feminine ending to undergo syncope (in the construct state), since that would have yielded a form that could not be divided into acceptable syllables (e.g., ***kalbtu*). In these five

[75] One is tempted to add Akkadian *idu*; however, Sargonic Akkadian forms like *i-dam* 'hand' and *i-da-su* 'his hands' are now understood to represent /yidam/ and /yidāsu/ (Hasselbach 2005, pp. 86–87, 271; Militarev and Kogan 2000–, vol. 2, p. 344). (For Eblaite *i-da*, understood to represent /yiday(n)/, see Conti 1990, p. 172 no. 626). Even so, the fact that *i-ti* 'from' represents /it:i/ (Hasselbach 2005, p. 272) seems to show that we cannot completely rule out /idam/ and /idāsu/.

[76] That Demotic *ey* can represent word-initial [ʾi] in this text is clear from its use in the words *eymr*[m] = *ʾymr* 'a lamb' (VII/8) and *eynt*⌜*.*/*y*⌝ = *ʾynt(y)*/⌜*y*⌝ 'my wife' (XVI/7), where it represents word-initial [ʾi] or [ʾe].

[77] It has often been noted that this noun has a variant *ḳart* in West Semitic. Huehnergard (1987, p. 286 n. 86) describes this variant (attested in Targumic Aramaic, poetic Biblical Hebrew, and Phoenician) as a biform "based on a biradical root." It is also possible that the triradical root *ḳ-r-y* (meaning 'cover with a roof' in Hebrew) had a metathesized biform *ḳ-y-r*, which survives in Moabite *ḳr* 'city' and perhaps also in Hebrew *ḳi*[y]*r* 'wall.' The Moabite meaning of *ḳi*[y]*r-Mo*[wʾ]*åb* (Isa 15:1) is recognized by Targum Jonathan ("city of Moab"). For the connection between the meanings 'city' and 'wall,' cf. Greek τεῖχος, which has the meaning 'walled city' in addition to the meaning 'wall.' The feminine of *ḳi:r* 'city' would be *ḳirt*, with shortening of the long vowel.

[78] Huehnergard (1987, p. 286 n. 86) derives the latter from a **ḳariy-tu*, but, as he himself notes, this form "deviates from all of these [other Semitic forms of the word for 'town']."

[79] See Sokoloff 2009, p. 1410, col. a bottom.

examples, however, it appears that syncope was allowed thanks to a syllable repair process that made *y* syllabic: **CvCyatu* > **CvCytu* > *CvCitu*.

For another example of a semivowel becoming syllabic in Proto-Semitic, see example 36 in §10.

8. Syncope Following Long Consonants

Proto-Semitic **ʾanṯatum* 'woman, wife' and **šidṯatum* 'six' also belonged to the class of feminine segolates; hence, they did not have syncopated construct forms. However, it appears that these absolute forms had assimilated variants already in Proto-Semitic, variants that *did* have syncopated construct forms:

(23) 'woman, wife': **ʾanṯatum* / **ʾaṯ:atum* (absolute) ~ ***ʾaṯ:tu* > **ʾaṯṯu* (construct). The alternation survives in Hebrew and Akkadian: *ʾiš:å*[h] (absolute) ~ *ʾéšäṯ* (construct); *aš:atum* (reflex of absolute) ~ *ašti* (construct). Note also *ʾənšət:a* 'women' in some of the Gurage languages (Masqan, Gogot, and Soddo) versus *ʾəšta* 'women' in others (Čaha, Eža, and Gyeto) (Leslau 1979, vol. 2, pp. 684–85, vol. 3, p. 102).[80] Should the distribution of these Gurage forms be viewed as another case of dialectal differentiation following analogical leveling, as in example 8 above?

(24) 'six': **šidṯatum* / **šiṯ:atum* (absolute) ~ ***šiṯ:tu* > **šiṯṯu* (construct). The alternation survives in Hebrew: *šiš:å*[h] (absolute) ~ *šéšäṯ* (construct).

In each of these forms, assimilation replaced a sequence of two consonants with one long consonant. This made syncope possible in the feminine ending because Proto-Semitic had a syllable repair process for this case: degemination (loss of consonant length).

The assumption of an assimilated form **ʾaṯ:atum*, alongside **ʾanṯatum*, in Proto-Semitic may go against the grain of some Semitists, who are used to attributing such "secondary" forms to the daughter languages. However, as noted above, the principle of cognate anomalies requires that we reconstruct something like **ʾaṯṯu* for the construct state, which, in turn, implies the existence of **ʾaṯ:atum* in the absolute state. In other words, the agreement between Hebrew *ʾiš:å*[h] (absolute) ~ *ʾéšäṯ* (construct) and Akkadian *aš:atum* (reflex of absolute) ~ *ašti* (construct) cannot be plausibly explained without positing such protoforms. Moreover, if Proto-Semitic was a natural language, rather than some sort of artificial construct, there is no reason to assume that it did not have such forms, at least in rapid speech.[81] Last but not least, many of the daughter languages have an *n*-less form of this word: Akkadian *aš:atum*, Ugaritic *aṯt*, Hebrew *ʾiš:å*[h], Phoenician-Punic *ʾšt*, Lihyanite *ʾṯt*, Qatabanian *ʾṯt*, Sabaic *ʾṯt* (alongside *ʾnṯt*), Tigre *ʾəssit*. In my view, we have more than enough evidence to reconstruct **ʾaṯ:atum* as a biform or sociolinguistic variant of **ʾanṯatum* in Proto-Semitic. More generally, I would suggest that *n*-assimilation was a variable rule in Proto-Semitic.

This approach is not all that different from that of Sanmartín 1995.[82] Sanmartín stresses the extreme antiquity of *n*-assimilation: "The first orthographic witnesses to Semitic testify to a total assimilation of syllable-final preconsonantal /n/; this goes for the Fara and late Presargonic documentation through Ur III down to Old Assyrian and Old Babylonian scribal practice .... Moreover, in the 'West' (Ugarit) too, /n/ was regularly assimilated; possible, apparent exceptions can be explained on purely *orthographic* grounds (avoidance of homography in vowelless orthography)" (ibid., p. 458).[83] Sanmartín suggests that the *n*-assimilation rule is conditioned by sociolinguistic factors: "The ubiquitous alternation between /n/-assimilating and /n/-preserving spellings is only one of the signs of a permanently diglossic society in the ancient Orient, which used both a relatively standardized written

[80] These are cognates of *ʾanəst* 'woman, wife, female' in Geez (Leslau 1987, p. 32). For a chart showing the genealogy of the Ethiopian Semitic languages, including the six Gurage languages cited here, see Hetzron 1977, p. 17.

[81] Cf. Bolozky (1977, p. 220): "Since in fast speech a given string must be articulated in a shorter time-span than in normal speech, assimilation of segments to neighboring elements is to be expected; it makes articulatory transitions easier and smoother, and possibly also requires less time to articulate."

[82] I read this article after writing the preceding paragraph.

[83] We may now add that the oldest connected Semitic texts, the Northwest Semitic serpent spells in the Pyramid Texts, have a rather clear example of the assimilation of the final *n* of *min* 'from' in PT 286 (Steiner 2011, pp. 52, 54–55).

language as well as a spontaneous, informal, 'vulgar' variant" (ibid., p. 459). I would add only that, in my view, *n*-assimilation was a variable rule even before the invention of writing.

Degemination following assimilation of *n* seems to be attested as a syllable repair process in Akkadian. According to Soden (1995, p. 43, §33j): "Before a two-consonant cluster in certain *-tan-* forms of the verb, *n* is completely elided, as, e.g., *ittapras* < **ittanpras* ..., since a sequence of three consonants was not permitted." There is no need to assume that the *n* was immediately elided; it seems more likely that this was a two-step process: assimilation followed by degemination.

Degemination is also found as a repair process for long consonants that are *not* the product of assimilation:

(25) 'daughter-in-law, bride': **kallatum* (absolute) ~ **kaltu* (construct); cf. Kogan (2011, p. 236, §8.4.3): **kall-at-*. The degeminated form is attested only in Eblaite: *gal-tum* 'daughter-in-law' (Conti 1990, p. 118, no. 322). Thus, there is no certainty that it existed in Proto-Semitic. Nevertheless, it is worth citing because Eblaite *gal-tum* interchanges with *gal-la-du* and *gal-la-tum* in copies of the bilingual lexical list (loc. cit.). Unless this variation is purely orthographic, it shows the correlation between degemination and syncope. Is *gal-tum* a construct form, comparable Akkadian *ašti*? There is no evidence that it is, but the possibility cannot excluded.[84]

(26) ending for feminine singular relational adjectives: **-iy:atum* (absolute) ~ ***-iy:tu* > **-iytu* > **-i:tu* (construct); cf. the Hebrew doublets *moʾăḇiy:å*^{h} ~ *moʾăḇí*^{y}*ṯ* 'Moabitess.'

This syllable-repair process can perhaps also be seen in a more common Hebrew alternation between the absolute and construct states: *zik:åro*^{w}*n* ~ *zik̠ro*^{w}*n*, *šib:åro*^{w}*n* ~ *šiḇro*^{w}*n*, *ḥiz:åyo*^{w}*n* ~ *ḥäzyo*^{w}*n*, *hig:åyo*^{w}*n* ~ *hägyo*^{w}*n*, *kil:åyo*^{w}*n* ~ *kilyo*^{w}*n*, *nik̠:åyo*^{w}*n* ~ *nik̠yo*^{w}*n*, and so on. Now, the Hebrew pattern *CiC:åCo*^{w}*n* < **CaC:aCo:n*[85] is generally believed to postdate Proto-Semitic (Barth 1889, pp. 324–26; Bauer and Leander 1922, p. 498).Be that as it may, this alternation is important because it clearly demonstrates the connection between the construct state and degemination as a repair process for syncope.[86] My claim is that the use of this repair process for syncope in the construct state is inherited from Proto-Semitic, even if these specific examples of it are not.

9. Syncope Following Long Vowels

Vowel shortening is a syllable-repair process that has much in common with degemination. It can be seen in the following example:

(27) 'shame': **bu:ṯatum* (absolute) ~ ***bu:ṯtu* > **buṯtu* (construct); cf. the Hebrew doublets *bu*^{w}*šå*^{h}/ *bóšäṯ*.

Unfortunately, this example does not provide conclusive proof that vowel shortening took place already in Proto-Semitic, since the length of the stem vowel in Akkadian *bu(:)štum* 'shame' is uncertain,[87] part of a larger, unresolved controversy (Edzard 1986, p. 361; Knudsen 1986, cols. 728–31). In theory, then, vowel shortening as a syllable-repair process in closed syllables could be a Proto-West-Semitic innovation. However, vowel shortening is a special case of loss of length, which can be reconstructed as a syllable repair process in at least one Proto-Semitic construct form (***ʾaṯ:tu* > **ʾaṯtu* 'wife of').[88] It seems likely, therefore, that Huehnergard (2006, p. 10) is right in claiming that vowel shortening in closed syllables goes back to Proto-Semitic.[89]

---

[84] The mimation is no obstacle, since construct forms are sometimes written with (apparently purely orthographic) mimation in the Eblaite bilingual lexical list; see the examples given by Krebernik (1996, p. 235 n. 1) and add /kaṣri buʿdim/ 'the articulation of the shoulder,' which appears as both *ga-za-rúm bù-tum* and *gi-zi-rí bù-tim* (Conti 1990, p. 153 no. 544). According to Krebernik (1996, p. 235), this is "logographic spelling," possibly characteristic of "dictionary style."

[85] For this pattern, its appearance in transcriptions (ἀρραβών 'deposit, pledge'; ακκαρων, *Am-qar-ru-na*, *Am-qar-u-na*, Egyptian *ʿngrn* 'Ekron'), and its alternation with *CiCCo*^{w}*n*, see Hurvitz 1968–69, supplemented by Koehler, Baumgartner, et al. 1994–2000 s.v. *ʿäk̠ro*^{w}*n*, and by Masson 1967, pp. 30–31.

[86] Cf. the use of degemination as a (diachronic) repair process for apocope (loss of case endings) in Hebrew and other Semitic languages.

[87] It is normalized with a short vowel in CAD and a long one in *AHw*.

[88] See §§4 and 8.

[89] Cf. the literature cited in Greenstein 1984, pp. 42–43, and add now Steiner 1996, p. 259 n. 10.

In any event, it is clear that Proto-Semitic allowed syncope in the feminine ending following a long vowel. Was the same true in the stem? According to Fox (2003, p. 237), **ḳa:tilum*, the active participle of the G-stem, is "the only reconstructible pattern with the syllabic structure *CV̄CvC." If so, our question reduces to the question of whether **ḳa:tilum* had a construct form **ḳatlu* (with vowel shortening), identical to the construct form of **ḳatilum*. We should not be overly optimistic about the possibility of reconstructing such a form, even if it existed, since it would have been highly vulnerable to analogy. I can think of only one or two segolate nouns in Hebrew that could possibly be viewed as relics of such a form. One of them is *héläḵ* 'traveler' in 2 Sam 12:4, although this form would seem to be derived from **hilk*.[90] Another is *rǻḵäḇ* 'upper millstone,' attested in Deut 24:6, Jud 9:53, 2 Sam 11:21, and in a Northwest Semitic text in Egyptian hieratic script from around the early eleventh century B.C.E. (Shisha-Halevy 1978, pp. 146, 157–58).[91] The etymological meaning of this is "rider," referring to one stone mounted on another. This is a meaning for which the participle would be appropriate, and, indeed, Onḳelos uses the Aramaic participle *ra:ḵăḇa:* to render *rǻḵäḇ* at Deut 24:6.[92] Other possible relics of a Proto-Semitic **rakbu* 'rider' may be cited from Akkadian,[93] Arabic,[94] and Hebrew.[95] Thus, a Proto-Semitic alternation **rākibum* (absolute) ~ **rakbu* (construct) is not out of the question.

10. Syncope in Nouns with Two Elidable Vowels

How did the Proto-Semitic syncope rule treat nouns with more than one short open-syllabic vowel? In example 7 above (**ʿaśaratum* ~ **ʿaśartu* 'ten'), the last non-final short open-syllabic vowel is deleted, but is that always the case? It is obvious that no definitive answer can be given, but the daughter languages do provide some tantalizing hints. For such nouns, one occasionally finds several different construct forms or several different syncopated forms surviving in a single language as doublets or dialectal variants. In such cases, I would tentatively reconstruct several Proto-Semitic construct forms:

(28) 'holy' (fem.): **ḳadišatum* (absolute) ~ **ḳadištu*/**ḳadšatu* (construct); cf. Akkadian *ḳadištum*/*ḳaš:atum*.[96]

(29) 'queen': **malikatum* (absolute) ~ **malkatu*/**maliktu* (construct); cf. Hebrew *malkaṯ*/*məläḵäṯ*.[97]

(30) 'man (of high status)'?: **marvʾum* (absolute) ~ **marʾu*/*(i)mrvʾu* (construct); cf. Arabic *marʾu(n)*/*(i)mra/uʾu(n)*.[98]

(31) 'heavy': **kabidum* (absolute) ~ **kabdu*/*(i)kbidu* (construct); cf. Hebrew *kåḇeḏ* (absolute) ~ *kåḇäḏ*/*kəḇaḏ* (construct poetry/prose).

---

[90] The expected form is **halk*, but cf. *gézäl* (the construct of *gåzel*) and Arabic forms like *kibdu* < *kabidu* as discussed by Rabin (1951, p. 97).

[91] In this text, we find the phrase *škbu-rkbu*. Although the context of the latter is obscure, *škb* and *rkb* also occur together in mBaba Batra 2:1 as the words for the lower and upper millstones. The Bible's failure to mention the *škb* together with the *rkb* is easily explained on the assumption that the former was fixed to the ground; unlike the *rkb*, it could not be taken in pawn (Deut 24:6) or dropped on a besieger's head (Jud 9:53; 2 Sam 11:21).

[92] As for the Peshiṭta, there are two traditions: *rakba:* and *ra:kba:* (Sokoloff 2009, p. 1467, col. b).

[93] See Soden 1965–81, p. 947, col. b s.v. *rakbu(m)*: "'Meldereiter'? (auch Fahrer?? ...)."

[94] See the discussion of the mass noun *rakbun* 'riders (on horses and/or camels)' in Lane 1863–1877, p. 1144, cols. b–c s.v. *ra:kibun*.

[95] See Brown, Driver, and Briggs 1907, p. 939 s.v. *rǻḵäḇ* mng. 4.

[96] The latter form is a dialectal variant, known only from Mari (Greenstein 1984, p. 53).

[97] Hebrew *məläḵäṯ* 'queen' occurs only in the phrase meaning "Queen of Heaven" (five times in Jeremiah), where it is ordinarily emended to *malkaṯ* (McKane 1986–1996, vol. 1, p. 170; Holladay 1986, p. 251; Lundbom 1999, p. 476). The emendation is shown to be unnecessary by comparative Semitic evidence. Hebrew *məläḵäṯ* corresponds perfectly to the form *maliktum* 'queen' in Eblaite and the pre-Sargonic native language of Mari (Gelb 1992, p. 148). It is also close to Arabic *malikatun* and to Akkadian *malikatu*, attested as a variant of Ishtar's title *malkatu* (CAD s.v. *malkatu* B). The Akkadian title of Ishtar is particularly important here because the "Queen of Heaven" in Jeremiah is believed to be Ishtar and because two verses (7:18 and 44:19) refer to cakes made for her using an appropriate Akkadian loanword (*kaw:åniʸm* < Akkadian *kamānu*) that is unattested elsewhere in Hebrew (Holladay 1986, pp. 254–55; Lundbom 1999, pp. 476–77). It is therefore possible that the non-standard form *məläḵäṯ* < **maliktu* is used deliberately, together with the Akkadian loanword, to evoke the foreign goddess.

[98] For the various vocalizations of the Arabic, see Lane 1863–1877, pp. 2702–03.

(32) ‘uncircumcised’: *ġarilum (absolute) ~ *ġarlu/*(i)ġrilu (construct); cf. Hebrew ʿårel (absolute) ~ ʿåräl/ʿăral (construct poetry/prose).[99]

(33a) ‘daughter’: *binatum (absolute) ~ *bintu/*(i)bnatu (construct); cf. Arabic *bintu(n)/(i)bnatu(n)*, not to mention Phoenician *bn/ʾbn*, cited in example 11 above.

(34a) ‘two (fem.)’: *ṯinata:m/nv (absolute) ~ *ṯinta:/*(i)ṯnata: (construct); cf. Arabic *ṯinta:(ni)/(i)ṯnata:(ni)* not to mention Phoenician *ʾšnm*, cited in example 13 above.

In most of these cases, the deletion of one vowel would have sufficed to block the rule from deleting the other, since deletion of both would have created a sequence of three consonants. However, in the last two examples, there seems to have been a third construct form with both vowels deleted. I would conjecture that, in these cases, syllabicization made it possible for both elidable vowels to undergo syncope in the same construct form:

(33b) ‘daughter’: *binatum (absolute) ~ *(i)bn̥tu (construct). In one dialect (or immediate descendant) of Proto-Semitic, the alternation turns into *binatum (absolute) ~ *(i)br̥tu (construct). This later alternation is partially preserved in Mehri: *bri:t* (absolute) ~ *bǝrt* (construct).[100]

(34b) ‘two (fem.)’: *ṯinata:m/nv (absolute) ~ *(i)ṯn̥ta: (construct). In one dialect (or immediate descendant) of Proto-Semitic, *(i)ṯn̥ta: > *(i)ṯr̥ta:, perhaps as a means of blocking assimilation to **(i)ṯt:a:; in another dialect (or immediate descendant) of Proto-Semitic, *(i)ṯn̥ta: > **(i)ṯt:a: > *(i)ṯta:.

The reconstruction given in examples 33b and 34b corrects the conjecture I made in Steiner 1982, p. 195:

> It is striking that MSA and Aramaic, against all of the other Semitic languages, have an *r* in the words for ‘son,’ ‘daughter,’ and ‘two,’ and when the alternation with *n*[101] is taken into account, the similarity becomes astounding. No wonder Christian (1944) was convinced that MSA and Aramaic are closely related! Scholars who reject this view, and that includes just about everyone, must project this alternation back into Proto-(West-)Semitic.
>
> It is worth noting that the two morphemes involved here have something else in common: their Arabic forms, *ibn(at)un* and *iṯn(at)āni*, have a base consisting of two consonants WITH NO VOWEL IN BETWEEN. A similar form must be reconstructed as the ancestor of the much-discussed Hebrew *štayim* ‘two (f.).’ The latter can hardly be the reflex of *ṯintaym since vowels in closed syllables are immune to deletion in Hebrew. It is more reasonable to posit an original *ṯn̥taym or *iṯn̥taym, with a syllabic *n̥*, which yielded *(i)šttayim and then *(i)štayim. If so, it is conceivable that *r* alternated with *n* in Proto-(West-)Semitic in positions where a syllabic consonant was called for, e.g., *ṯn̥taym* ~ *ṯr̥taym*, *bn̥tum* ~ *br̥tum* ....[102]

When I made this conjecture, it did not occur to me to restrict it to the construct state, let alone to suggest that all of the processes posited in my presentation of it — syllabicization, degemination, and prothesis — were employed regularly in Proto-Semitic construct forms as syllable repair processes. The relevance of prothesis here is clear; in addition to the Arabic and Phoenician evidence, we have more than ample testimony from Masoretic treatises and medieval grammars (as well as hints from the Masoretic accents) that the word for ‘two (fem.)’ was read with a prothetic vowel: *i/äštayim* ~ *i/äšte*^{y} (Neuman 2009, pp. 290–93).

In short, I now suggest that *i/äštayim* ~ *i/äšte*^{y} be derived as follows: Pre-Proto-Semitic *ṯinatay (accusative-genitive construct) > Proto-Semitic *(i)ṯn̥tay > **(i)ṯt:ay > *(i)ṯtay > Hebrew *i/äšte*^{y} ‘two of.’ The *n* must have become syllabic as the result of a syllable-repair process when the two vowels that flanked it were elided in the construct

[99] The absence of prothetic vowels for *kǝḇaḏ* and *ʿăral* does not preclude a derivation from *(i)kbidu and *(i)ġrilu. Hebrew developed a new syllable repair process, *shewa*-epenthesis, that superseded prothesis except with consonant clusters that resisted epenthesis, e.g., *št*.

[100] See the end of §5 above.

[101] Both languages have an *n* in the words for “sons,” “daughters,” and “second.”

[102] For a subsequent discussion of this alternation with a somewhat similar conclusion, see Testen 1985, p. 145: “Proto-Semitic *n becomes r when it is the second element of an initial consonant cluster - #Cn->#Cr-.” (Coincidentally, Dr. Testen took my course, Introduction to Comparative Semitics, at the University of Chicago in the spring of 1981, when I was working on the problem; I am sure that neither of us can recall whether I discussed it in class.)

state. When syllabic *n̥* assimilated to the *t* of the feminine ending in a dialect (or immediate descendant) of Proto-Semitic, an additional syllable-repair process would have been triggered: degemination. That explains why the *t* of *i/äštey* is not geminated in Hebrew. This suggestion also explains why the ungeminated *t* is not spirantized; Hebrew spirantization is a partial assimilation to an immediately preceding vowel, but, according to my reconstruction, there was no vowel immediately preceding *t* in this form at any point in its development after Pre-Proto-Semitic. It also explains the contrast between *ma*^{h}*-š:ə̆ne*^{y} 'what are the two (masc.)' (Zech 4:11) and *ma*^{h}*-šte*^{y} 'what are the two (fem.)' (Zech 4:12). Only the feminine form blocks the secondary gemination normally found in the consonant following *ma*^{h}*-* (in this case, *š*), because only the feminine form never had a vowel following that consonant. The same goes for the even more striking absence of gemination in *mište*^{y}*m-ʿäśre*^{h} 'more than twelve (fem.)' (Jon 4:11; contrast Jud 16:28, where analogy eliminated the anomaly).

As for the replacement of *n* by *r*, I now believe that it was originally restricted to two feminine construct forms ("two of," "daughter of"), spreading by analogy to masculine and absolute forms only later, in Aramaic[103] and Modern South Arabian. It was only in the feminine construct that these two biconsonantal lexemes were in danger of losing their second consonant to assimilation. The replacement of *n* by *r*, a consonant that does not undergo total assimilation, eliminated this danger.

In the preceding two examples, I conjectured that two vowels that flanked a nasal were deleted in the same construct form. There may be a third Proto-Semitic example of this very specific scenario:

(35) 'tear(drop)s': **dimaʿa:tum* (absolute) ~ **(i)dm̥ʿa:tu* (construct). Militarev and Kogan (2000–, vol. 1, p. 49 no. 51) correctly reconstruct the singular as **dimʿ(-at)-*, with no prothetic vowel.

As explained above, segolate nouns have a syllable structure that blocks syncope in the construct state of the singular (in both the stem and the feminine ending). Segolate plurals, however, are a different story; as already noted, they have a vocalic infix, *-a-*, inserted between the second and third consonants of the stem. This (short) vowel is open-syllabic, and it makes the preceding (short) vowel open-syllabic, as well; it appears that both vowels were elided in our construct form. The plural form with prothesis survives in both East Semitic (Eblaite *ì-ti-ma-a-tum*) and West Semitic (Ugaritic *udmʿt*). In Soqotri *ʾedmíʿa* 'tear(drop)' (Leslau 1938, p. 130), the prothesis has spread to the singular.[104] The Eblaite spelling may reflect syllabicization as well as prothesis; *ì-ti-ma-a-tum* (Conti 1990, p. 183 no. 716) seems to make better sense as a spelling of [idm̥ʿa:tu] than as a spelling of [idmaʿa:tu]. The plural form without prothesis survives in both East Semitic (Akkadian *di:ma:tum*) and West Semitic (Syriac *demʿe:*). The Ugaritic alternation *dmʿ* [dimʿu] 'tear' ~ *udmʿt* [udmaʿa:tu] 'tears' is very significant; it appears to be another vestige of the link between Proto-Semitic vowel prothesis and syncope.[105]

I conclude with another possible case of double syncope made possible by syllabicization:

(36) 'and two': **wa-ṯina:m/nv/*wa-ṯinaym/nv* (absolute nominative/oblique) ~ **u-ṯna:/*u-ṯnay* (construct nominative/oblique); cf. Akkadian *u-še/ina* and Hebrew *u-šne*^{y}.

The syllabicization of *w-* allows the Proto-Semitic construct form of the word for "two" to dispense with its prothetic vowel.[106] This reconstruction explains one of the anomalies of Hebrew morphophonemics, namely, the form adopted by the conjunction **wa-* when it is attached to a word whose first vowel has been reduced to *shewa*. Analogy would predict that the reflex of **wa-* in that environment would be *wi-* (like *li-* for **la-* and *ki-* for **ka-*), and that is indeed what we find in the Babylonian reading tradition (Yeivin 1985, p. 1152). In the Tiberian tradition, however, we find *u-* (with a short vowel) for **wa-*.[107] This reflex of **wa-* is anomalous in another way as

[103] For a full presentation of the Aramaic data, see Fassberg 2008.

[104] Do the Ethiopian Semitic nouns meaning 'tear' (Geez *ʾanbəʿ*, Tigre *ʾəmbəʿ*, *ʾənbəʿ*, Tigrinya *nəbʿat*, Amharic, Gurage and Argobba *əmba*, Gafat *əmb*^{w}*ä*, and Harari *əbiʾ*) belong here as well? Leslau (1987, p. 382) connects them with Arabic *nabaʿa* 'gush forth, flow,' etc., but their similarity to the Soqotri form makes one wonder whether *ʾ-nb-ʿ* could be derived from **ʾ-dm-ʿ* by metathesis of nasalization. In that case, the related verbs in Geez, Tigre, and Tigrinya meaning 'shed tears, weep' would have to be taken as denominatives, comparable to Arabic *damaʿa* 'shed tears, flow,' Mehri *ado:ma* 'to weep, (of tears) to drip from the eyes' (Johnstone 1987, pp. 71 [misprinted], 618), etc. If Leslau's list of nouns and verbs is complete, the verb forms are geographically restricted, suggesting that they are younger than the noun forms.

[105] For other examples of vowel prothesis connected with syncope in Ugaritic, see Huehnergard 1987, p. 285.

[106] See example 13 above.

[107] For syllabic *w* in Hebrew, see Steiner 1997, p. 148. The spelling of the conjunction *u-* with *waw* is morphophonemic; there is no *mater lectionis*, and no reason to consider this ו long (except secondarily, in cases like וְזָהָב). Malone (1993, pp. 142–44) has demonstrated that in medieval Sephardic poetry, the conjunc-

well: it is the only example of a word-initial vowel that is clearly reflected in the biblical vocalization. Like many synchronic anomalies, this one has a simple diachronic explanation. We need only assume that we are dealing with a fossil, another relic of the Proto-Semitic syncope rule. Note that the phonetic conditioning governing the use of the *u*- allomorph of the conjunction has remained more or less unchanged in Hebrew.[108] Nevertheless the allomorph is far more common in Hebrew than it was in Proto-Semitic. In Hebrew, it is common not only with singular construct forms (e.g., *u-ḵbod* 'and the glory of' and *u-ḵbad* 'and heavy of'), but also with singular absolute forms derived from Proto-Semitic construct forms (e.g., *u-zróaᶜ* 'and an arm,' also attested with the meaning 'and the arm of') and with plural absolute forms (e.g., *u-nhåroʷṯ* 'and rivers'). The increased frequency of the *u*- allomorph is the product of a change in the conditioning of the syncope/reduction rule. In Akkadian *u*-, by contrast, the *u*- allomorph is no longer phonetically conditioned, being used in all environments. This may well be another example of the law of diminishing conditioning.

11. Conclusions

Phonetic conditioning tends to be diminished over time by analogy, through the loss of conditions or the loss of conditioned allomorphs. This "law of diminishing conditioning" makes it possible to reconstruct details of Proto-Semitic phonology from faint traces that have survived in the daughter languages. It enables us to recover a Proto-Semitic vowel syncope rule, together with the syllable-repair processes that allowed it to operate unhindered in unexpected environments.

The syncope rule of Proto-Semitic affected construct forms of nouns and adjectives, because they were unstressed (morphosyntactically proclitic). It deleted at least one short open-syllabic vowel in each construct form as long as the deletion did not create syllables containing an impermissible cluster, namely, two consonants (CC) or a long consonant (C:) or a consonant preceded by length (:C). These syllable constraints did not interfere with the syncope rule as much as one might imagine, thanks to four Proto-Semitic syllable repair processes: (1) prothesis, (2) loss of length in/after consonants (degemination), (3) loss of length in/after vowels (vowel shortening), and (4) syllabicization of semivowels and nasals.

The alternations produced by the syncope rule and the syllable-repair processes were subjected to massive analogical leveling in the daughter languages. In Classical Arabic, the construct forms were replaced by absolute forms, the few exceptions being nouns that were typically used in the construct state (e.g., *ibn* and *bint*). As a result, the rule was obliterated, with only a few vestiges surviving. Akkadian and Aramaic preserved the rule but changed its conditioning. Hebrew is the only Semitic language that has preserved a fair number of syncope alternations with their original conditioning, both in the stem (e.g., *kåḇeḏ* ~ *kǻḇäḏ*) and in the feminine ending (e.g., *mamlåḵåʰ* ~ *mamlǻḵäṯ*).

Traces of the repair processes are even harder to find. Repair process (1) is best preserved in Arabic (e.g., *ismu(n)* ~ *smu(n)* / *si/u/amu(n)*); (4) is best preserved in Syriac (e.g., *ṭbi:ta:* ~ *ṭabya:ta:*); and (2) can be glimpsed in Hebrew (e.g., *buʷšåʰ* / *bóšäṯ*). In some of the daughter languages, new repair processes have replaced the old ones. Thus, in Hebrew examples of prothesis as a repair process are very rare. Instead, we usually find epenthesis of mobile *shewa* (e.g., *zǝróaᶜ* rather than the rare *ʾäzróaᶜ*).

---

tion *u*- scans as a short vowel. The only exception, he says (ibid., p. 145), is immediately preceding a sequence of two consonants (e.g., *ulšon*), where it scans as long. In my view, this exception is illusory. It is based on the assumption that meter in Sephardic poety is based on vowel length, whereas, in fact, it is based on syllable weight, with all closed syllables (and most open ones as well!) being heavy. Thus, the form *ulšon* consists of two heavy syllables. It must have had a short vowel in the first syllable, because long vowels were not permitted in closed unstressed syllables in any period of Hebrew, including the medieval period. For a discussion of the history of vowel length in Hebrew, see Steiner 1997, p. 149; and Steiner 2001b. For the quiescent *shewa* following *u*-, see Yalon 1963.

[108] I am not referring to the use of this allomorph before bilabials, whose dating is unclear.

Abbreviations

AHw Wolfram von Soden. *Akkadisches Handwörterbuch.* 3 volumes. Wiesbaden: Harrassowitz, 1965–1981.

CAD A. Leo Oppenheim et al., eds. *The Assyrian Dictionary of the Oriental Institute of Chicago.* Chicago: The Oriental Institute, 1956–2010.

Bibliography

Albright, William Foxwell

1934 *The Vocalization of the Egyptian Syllabic Orthography.* New Haven: American Oriental Society.

Amadasi, Maria Giulia G., and Vassos Karageorghis

1977 *Inscriptions phéniciennes.* Fouilles de Kition 3. Nicosia: Department of Antiquities, Cyprus.

Barth, J.

1903 "C. Brockelmann, Die Femininendung *t* im Semitischen." *Zeitschrift der Deutschen Morgenländischen Gesellschaft* 57: 628–36.

1889 *Die Nominalbildung in den semitischen Sprachen.* Leipzig: J. C. Hinrichs.

Bauer, Hans, and Pontus Leander

1922 *Historische Grammatik der hebräischen Sprache des Alten Testamentes.* 2 volumes. Halle: M. Niemeyer.

Beyer, Klaus

1984 *Die aramäischen Texte vom Toten Meer.* Göttingen: Vandenhoeck & Ruprecht.

Blake, Frank R.

1911 "Vocalic *r, l, m, n* in Semitic." *Journal of the American Oriental Society* 31: 217–22.

Blau, Joshua

2010 *Phonology and Morphology of Biblical Hebrew.* Linguistic Studies in Ancient West Semitic 2. Winona Lake: Eisenbrauns.

Bolozky, Shmuel

1977 "Fast Speech as a Function of Tempo in Natural Generative Phonology." *Journal of Linguistics* 13: 217–38.

Bravmann, M. M.

1977 *Studies in Semitic Philology.* Studies in Semitic Languages and Linguistics 6. Leiden: Brill.

Brockelmann, Carl

1903 "Die Femininendung T im Semitischen." *Sitzung der orientalisch-sprachwissenschaftlichen Sektion der schlesischen Gesellschaft für vaterländische Kultur* 81: 3–23.

1908–1913 *Grundriß der vergleichenden Grammatik der semitischen Sprachen.* 2 volumes. Berlin: Reuther & Reichard.

Brown, Francis; S. R. Driver; and Charles A. Briggs

1907 *A Hebrew and English Lexicon of the Old Testament.* Oxford: Clarendon Press.

Conti, Giovanni

1990 *Il sillabario della quarta fonte della lista lessicale bilingue eblaita.* Miscellanea eblaitica 3, Quaderni di semitistica 17. Florence: Università di Firenze.

Dalley, Stephanie

1995 "Ancient Mesopotamian Military Organization." In *Civilizations of the Ancient Near East*, edited by J. M. Sasson, vol. 1, pp. 413–22. New York: Scribner.

Delitzsch, Friedrich

1906 *Assyrische Grammatik.* 2nd edition. Berlin: Reuther & Reichard.

Dolgopolsky, A.

1999 *From Proto-Semitic to Hebrew: Phonology; Etymological Approach in a Hamito-Semitic Perspective.* Studi Camito-Semitici 2. Milan: Centro Studi Camito-Semitici.

Donner, Herbert, and Wolfgang Röllig

1973–79 *Kanaanäische und aramäische Inschriften.* 3 volumes. Wiesbaden: Harrassowitz.

Driver, S. R.

1913 *Notes on the Hebrew Text and the Topography of the Books of Samuel.* 2nd edition. Oxford: Clarendon Press.

Drower, E. S., and Rudolf Macuch

1963 *A Mandaic Dictionary.* Oxford: Clarendon Press.

Dunash b. Labrat

1866 ספר תשובות דונש הלוי בן לברט על רבי סעדיה גאון. Edited by R. Schröter. Breslau: Schletter.

Edzard, Dietz Otto

1986 "Edward Greenstein, The Phonology of Akkadian Syllable Structure." *Journal of the American Oriental Society* 106: 359–62.

Ewald, Heinrich

1863 *Ausführliches Lehrbuch der hebräischen Sprache des Alten Bundes.* 7th edition. Göttingen: Dieterich.

Fassberg, Steven E.

2008 "The Forms of 'Son' and 'Daughter' in Aramaic." In *Aramaic in Its Historical and Linguistic Setting*, edited by Holger Gzella and Margaretha L. Folmer, pp. 41–53. Veröffentlichungen der Orientalischen Kommission 50. Wiesbaden: Harrassowitz.

Fleisch, Henri

1961 *Traité de philologie arabe.* Recherches publiées sous la direction de l'Institut de lettres orientales de Beyrouth 16. Beirut: Imprimerie catholique.

Fox, Joshua

2003 *Semitic Noun Patterns.* Harvard Semitic Studies 52. Winona Lake: Eisenbrauns.

Friedrich, Johannes, and Wolfgang Röllig

1999 *Phönizisch-Punische Grammatik.* 3rd edition, by M. G. Amadasi Guzzo with W. R. Mayer. Rome: Editrice Pontificio Istituto Biblico.

Garr, W. Randall

1985 *Dialect Geography of Syria-Palestine, 1000–586 B.C.E.* Philadelphia: University of Pennsylvania Press.

Gelb, Ignace J.

1992 "Mari and the Kish Civilization." In *Mari in Retrospect: Fifty Years of Mari and Mari Studies*, edited by Gordon D. Young, pp. 121–202. Winona Lake: Eisenbrauns.

Geller, M. J.

2006 "Philology versus Linguistics and Aramaic Phonology." *Bulletin of the School of Oriental and African Studies* 69: 79–90.

Gordon, Cyrus H.

1965 *Ugaritic Textbook.* 3 volumes. Analecta Orientalia 38. Rome: Pontificium Institutum Biblicum.

Greenstein, Edward L.

1984 "The Phonology of Akkadian Syllable Structure." *Afroasiatic Linguistics* 9: 1–71.

Hasselbach, Rebecca

2005 *Sargonic Akkadian: A Historical and Comparative Study of the Syllabic Texts.* Wiesbaden: Harrassowitz.

Hetzron, Robert

1977 *The Gunnän-Gurage Languages.* Naples: Istituto orientale di Napoli.

Hoch, James E.

1994 *Semitic Words in Egyptian Texts of the New Kingdom and Third Intermediate Period.* Princeton: Princeton University Press.

Hoenigswald, Henry M.

1960 *Language Change and Linguistic Reconstruction.* Chicago: University of Chicago Press.

1966 "Are There Universals of Linguistic Change?" In *Universals of Language*, edited by Joseph H. Greenberg, pp. 30–52. 2nd edition. Cambridge: M.I.T. Press.

Hoftijzer, J., and K. Jongeling

1995 — *Dictionary of the North-west Semitic Inscriptions.* 2 volumes. Handbuch der Orientalistik, Erste Abteilung, Der Nahe und Mittlere Osten 21. Leiden: Brill.

Holladay, William Lee

1986 — *Jeremiah* 1: *A Commentary on the Book of the Prophet Jeremiah, Chapters 1–25.* Philadelphia: Fortress Press.

Huehnergard, John

1987 — *Ugaritic Vocabulary in Syllabic Transcription.* Atlanta: Scholars Press.

2004 — "Afro-Asiatic." In *Cambridge Encyclopedia of the World's Ancient Languages*, edited by Roger D. Woodard, pp. 138–59. Cambridge: Cambridge University Press.

2006 — "Proto-Semitic and Proto-Akkadian." In *The Akkadian Language in Its Semitic Context: Studies in the Akkadian of the Third and Second Millennium B.C.*, edited by G. Deutscher and N. J. C. Kouwenberg, pp. 1–18. Leiden: Nederlands Instituut voor het Nabije Oosten.

Huehnergard, John, and Christopher Woods

2004 — "Akkadian and Eblaite." In *Cambridge Encyclopedia of the World's Ancient Languages*, edited by Roger D. Woodard, pp. 218–87. Cambridge: Cambridge University Press.

Hurvitz, A.

1968–1969 — פרק בדקדוק היסטורי : Ακκαρων = Amqar(r)una = עֶקְרוֹן. *Lešonenu* 33: 18–24.

Janda, Richard D., and Brian D. Joseph

2003 — "Reconsidering the Canons of Sound-change: Towards a 'Big Bang' Theory." In *Historical Linguistics 2001* (Selected Papers from the 15th International Conference on Historical Linguistics, Melbourne, 13–17 August 2001), edited by Barry J. Blake and Kate Burridge, pp. 205–19. Amsterdam: John Benjamins.

Janssens, G.

1975/1976 — "The Feminine Ending -*(a)t* in Semitic." *Orientalia Lovaniensia Periodica* 6/7: 277–84.

Johnstone, T. M.

1987 — *Mehri Lexicon and English-Mehri Word-list.* London: School of Oriental and African Studies, University of London.

Kaufman, S. A.

1983 — "The History of Aramaic Vowel Reduction." In *Arameans, Aramaic and the Aramaic Literary Tradition*, edited by Michael Sokoloff, pp. 47–55. Ramat-Gan: Bar-Ilan University Press.

Ḳimḥi, David

1847 — ספר השרשים. Berlin: G. Bethge.

Knudsen, E. E.

1986 — "Edward L. Greenstein, The Phonology of Akkadian Syllable Structure." *Bibliotheca Orientalis* 43: 723–32.

Koehler, Ludwig; Walter Baumgartner; et al.

1994–2000 — *The Hebrew and Aramaic Lexicon of the Old Testament.* 5 volumes. Leiden: Brill.

Kogan, Leonid

2011 — "Proto-Semitic Lexicon." In *The Semitic Languages: An International Handbook*, edited by Stephan Weninger, Geoffrey Khan, Michael P. Streck, and Janet C. E. Watson. Berlin: de Gruyter Mouton.

Krebernik, Manfred

1996 — "The Linguistic Classification of Eblaite: Methods, Problems, and Results." In *The Study of the Ancient Near East in the Twenty-first Century: The William Foxwell Albright Centennial Conference*, edited by Jerrold S. Cooper and Glenn M. Schwartz, pp. 233–49. Winona Lake: Eisenbrauns.

Lagarde, Paul de

1889–91 — *Übersicht über die im Aramäischen, Arabischen und Hebräischen übliche Bildung der Nomina.* Göttingen: Dieterich.

Lane, E. W.

1863–77 — *Arabic-English Lexicon.* London: Williams and Norgate.

Leslau, Wolf

1938 — *Lexique Soqoṭri.* Paris: C. Klincksieck.

1979 — *Etymological Dictionary of Gurage (Ethiopic).* 3 volumes. Wiesbaden: Harrassowitz.

1987 — *Comparative Dictionary of Geʿez (Classical Ethiopic).* Wiesbaden: Harrassowitz.

Lipiński, Edward
2001 *Semitic Languages: Outline of a Comparative Grammar*. 2nd edition. Orientalia Lovaniensia analecta 80. Leuven: Peeters.

Lundbom, Jack R.
1999 *Jeremiah 1-20: A New Translation with Introduction and Commentary*. New York: Doubleday.

Macuch, Rudolf
1965 *Handbook of Classical and Modern Mandaic*. Berlin: Walter de Gruyter.

Malone, Joseph L.
1993 *Tiberian Hebrew Phonology*. Winona Lake: Eisenbrauns.

Masson, Émilia
1967 *Recherches sur les plus anciens emprunts sémitiques en grec*. Paris: C. Klincksieck.

McKane, William
1986–1996 *A Critical and Exegetical Commentary on Jeremiah*. 2 volumes. Edinburgh: T. and T. Clark.

Militarev, Alexander, and Leonid Kogan
2000– *Semitic Etymological Dictionary*. Alter Orient und Altes Testament 278. Münster: Ugarit-Verlag.

Muraoka, Takamitsu, and Bezalel Porten
1998 *A Grammar of Egyptian Aramaic*. Handbuch der Orientalistik. Erste Abteilung, Nahe und Mittlere Osten 32. Leiden: Brill.

Murtonen, A.
1986–1990 *Hebrew in Its West Semitic Setting: A Comparative Survey of Non-Masoretic Hebrew Dialects and Traditions*. 4 volumes. Studies in Semitic Languages and Linguistics 13, 16. Leiden: Brill.

Neuman, Yishai
2009 הצורה שְׁתַּיִם בעברית המקראית. In צָפְנַת פַּעְנֵחַ: מחקרי לשון מוגשים לאלישע קימרון במלאות לו שישים וחמש שנה, edited by D. Sivan, D. Talshir and C. Cohen, pp. 289–318. Beer Sheva: Ben-Gurion University of the Negev Press.

Olmo Lete, Gregorio del, and Joaquín Sanmartín
2003 *A Dictionary of the Ugaritic Language in the Alphabetic Tradition*. Handbuch der Orientalistik, Erste Abteilung, Nahe und der Mittlere Osten 67. Leiden: Brill.

Rabin, Chaim
1951 *Ancient West-Arabian*. London: Taylor's Foreign Press.

Rubin, Aaron D.
2010 *The Mehri Language of Oman*. Leiden: Brill.

Sampson, Rodney
2010 *Vowel Prosthesis in Romance: A Diachronic Study*. Oxford: Oxford University Press.

Sanmartín, Joaquín
1995 "Über Regeln und Ausnahmen: Verhalten des vorkonsonantischen /n/ im 'Altsemitischen.'" In *Vom Alten Orient zum Alten Testament: Festschrift für Wolfram Freiherrn von Soden*, edited Manfried Dietrich and Oswald Loretz, pp. 433–66. Alter Orient und Altes Testament 240. Kevelaer: Butzon and Bercker; Neukirchen-Vluyn: Neukirchener Verlag.

Shisha-Halevy, A.
1978 "An Early North-west Semitic Text in the Egyptian Hieratic Script." *Orientalia* 47: 145–62.

Sībawaihi
1885–89 *Le livre de Sîbawaihi: traité de grammaire arabe*. Edited by Hartwig Derenbourg. 2 volumes. Paris: Imprimerie Nationale.

Soden, Wolfram von
1965–1981 *Akkadisches Handwörterbuch*. Wiesbaden: Harrassowitz.
1995 *Grundriß der akkadischen Grammatik*. 3rd edition. Rome: Pontifium Institutum Biblicum.

Sokoloff, Michael
2009 *A Syriac Lexicon: A Translation from the Latin; Expansion and Update of C. Brockelmann's Lexicon Syriacum*. Winona Lake: Eisenbrauns.

Steiner, Richard C.

1975 "A Proto-Semitic Alternation and its Flip-flopped Akkadian Reflex." Unpublished paper read at the North American Conference on Semitic Linguistics, April 22, 1975.

1976 "On the Origin of the ḥéðɛr ~ ḥăðár Alternation in Hebrew." *Afroasiatic Linguistics* 3: 85–102.

1979 "From Proto-Hebrew to Mishnaic Hebrew: The History of ךָ- and הָ-." *Hebrew Annual Review* 3: 157–74.

1982 "T. M. Johnstone, *Ḥarsūsi Lexicon and English-Ḥarsūsi Word-List*." *Afroasiatic Linguistics* 8: 189–200.

1987 "*Lulav* versus **lu/law*: A Note on the Conditioning of **aw* > ū in Hebrew and Aramaic." *Journal of the American Oriental Society* 107: 121–22.

1996 "The History of the Ancient Hebrew Modal System and Labov's Rule of Compensatory Structural Change." In *Towards a Social Science of Language: Papers in Honor of William Labov*, edited by G. R. Guy, C. Feagin, D. Schiffrin, and J. Baugh, vol. 1, pp. 253–61. Amsterdam: John Benjamins.

1997 "Ancient Hebrew." In *The Semitic Languages*, edited by R. Hetzron, pp. 145–73. London: Routledge.

2001a "*Albounout* 'Frankincense' and *Alsounalph* 'Oxtongue': Phoenician-Punic Botanical Terms with Prothetic Vowels from an Egyptian Papyrus and a Byzantine Codex." *Orientalia* 70: 97–103.

2001b משך התנועות בעברית: תאורים ותאוריות מהיירונימוס עד ריה"ל לאור הפולמוס הדתי. *Meḥqarim Belašon* 8: 203–28.

2010 "Poetic Forms in the Masoretic Vocalization and Three Difficult Phrases in Jacob's Blessing: יֶתֶר שְׂאֵת (Gen 49:3), יְצוּעִי עָלָה (Gen 49:4) and יָבֹא שִׁילֹה (Gen 49:10)." *Journal of Biblical Literature* 129: 209–35.

2011 *Early Northwest Semitic Serpent Spells in the Pyramid Texts*. Winona Lake: Eisenbrauns.

Steiner, Richard C., and A. Mosak Moshavi

1995 "A Selective Glossary of Northwest Semitic Texts in Egyptian Script." In *Dictionary of the North-west Semitic Inscriptions*, edited by J. Hoftijzer and K. Jongeling, pp. 1249–66. Leiden: Brill.

Talshir, D.

1992 אלף קלה. *Lešonenu* 56: 285.

Testen, David

1985 "The Significance of Aramaic *r* < **n*." *Journal of Near Eastern Studies* 44: 143–46.

2003 "Evidence of an Early Metathesis among Akkadian *piristum*-stem Nouns." *Journal of the American Oriental Society* 123: 577–94.

Ullmann, Manfred

1970– *Wörterbuch der klassischen arabischen Sprache*. Wiesbaden: Harrassowitz.

Wang, William S-Y.

1969 "Competing Changes as a Cause of Residue." *Language* 45: 9–25.

Watson, Janet C. E.

2009 "Annexion, Attribution and Genitives in Mahriyyōt." In *Relative Clauses and Genitive Constructions in Semitic*, edited by Janet C. E. Watson and Jan Retsö, pp. 229–44. Journal of Semitic Studies Supplement 25. Oxford: Oxford University Press.

Wright, William

1967 *A Grammar of the Arabic Language*. 3rd edition. 2 volumes. Cambridge: Cambridge University Press.

Yalon, Henoch

1963 שוא שאחרי שורק בראש המלה. In קונטרסים לעניני הלשון העברית, edited by H. Yalon, section 1, pp. 16–19. Jerusalem: Wahrmann.

Yeivin, Israel

1985 מסורת הלשון העברית המשתקפת בניקוד הבבלי. 2 volumes. Jerusalem: Academy of the Hebrew Language.

Zimmern, H.

1890 "Zur assyrischen und vergleichenden semitischen Lautlehre." *Zeitschrift für Assyriologie und Vorderasiatische Archäologie* 5: 367–98.

23

Reconciling Some Morphological Eccentricities of the Semitic Genitive Case Marker

David Testen

For the most part, reconstructing the case markers of the ancestral Semitic substantival system has been treated as a comparatively simple task. It is possible to arrive at what appears to be a quite tidy constellation of endings by juxtaposing paradigms such as the following from early Akkadian and Literary Arabic, the two languages which show us the most extensive and, it may be presumed, best-preserved case systems in Semitic.

Inflection of reflexes of the participles 'eating' (*'ākil-) and 'building' (*bāniy-) in early Akkadian and Arabic: singular m. (f.)

Case	*Old Babylonian*	*Literary Arabic*
Nominative	ākil(-t)-um	'ākil(-at)-u-n
	bānûm (bānī-t-u-m)	bāni-n (bāniy-at-u-n)
Accusative	ākil(-t)-am	'ākil(-at)-a-n
	bānâm (bānī-t-a-m)	bāniy-(at-)a-n
Genitive	ākil(-t)-im	'ākil(-at)-i-n
	bānîm (bānī-t-i-m)	bāni-n (bāniy-at-i-n)

This three-case (triptotic) pattern characterizes the inflection of the Akkadian singular and is the prevailing system for Arabic singular stems, as well as for a good number of Arabic's broken-plural stems — compare, for example, *kutub-u-n, -a-n, -i-n* 'books (nom., acc., gen.),' the plural of *kitāb-*; *'awlād-u-n, -a-n, -i-n* 'children (nom., acc., gen.),' the plural of *walad-*.[1]

The triptotic paradigm contrasts with several paradigms reflecting diptotic patterns, which distinguish between a nominative shape and a common oblique (accusative-genitive) shape and which are most familiar through the declensions of dual and sound plural substantives.[2]

[1] In certain circumstances, the surface paradigm does not display the full three-way opposition but it may be presumed that the endings **-u-n, *-a-n, *i-n* are to be understood at an underlying level. When the final consonant of the stem is a semivowel, the vowel of the stem's final syllable often melds with the case ending. The stem *bāniy-* 'building' in the table above thus shows only two surface-level distinctions, viz., nominative/genitive *bāni-n* (definite *al-bānī*) (< **bāniy-u-n* or **bāniy-i-n*) versus accusative *bāniy-a-n* (definite *al-bāniy-a*). When the stem-final semivowel is preceded by an underlying short **-a-*, there is no case distinction at the surface level whatsoever; cf. *musammä-n* (definite *al-musammä*) 'named (passive participle)' < underlying **musammay-u-n, *-a-n, *i-n.*

[2] The diptotic declension of singular (and broken-plural) stems is addressed below.

Inflection of reflexes of the participles 'eating' (*'*ākil*-) and 'building' (**bāniy*-) in early Akkadian and Arabic: plural and dual

	Case	*Old Babylonian*	*Literary Arabic*
M. Plural	*Nominative*	ākil-ū	'ākil-ū-na
		bānû	bān-ū-na
	Oblique	ākil-ī	'ākil-ī-na
		bānî	bān-īna
F. Plural	*Nominative*	ākil-āt-um	'ākil-āt-u-n
		bānât-um	bāniy-āt-u-n
	Oblique	ākil-āt-im	'ākil-āt-i-n
		bānât-im	bāniy-āt-in
Dual m. (f.)[3]	*Nominative*	[(-t)-ān]	'ākil(-at)-ā-ni
			bāniy(-at)-ā-ni
	Oblique	[(-t)-īn]	'ākil(-at)-ay-ni
			bāniy(-at)-ay-ni

Starting from paradigms like those above, historians of Semitic have reconstructed an early Semitic case-marking system that juxtaposed a triptotic singular distinguishing three cases and a set of non-singular paradigms that formally distinguished only two. The triptotic type was expressed through a tripartite paradigm of short vowels (**-u-*, **-a-*, **-i-*), while in the diptotic patterns of the other numbers, the principal marker of number took the shape of a long vowel or a diphthong, located either after the stem (*ākil-ū, 'ākil-ū-na*, Hebrew *'ôḵəl-îm,* Syriac *'āḵəl-în*, etc.) or, in the feminine plural, as part of the stem-suffix (*ākil-ā-t-um, 'ākil-āt-un*, Hebrew *'ôḵəl-ô-ṯ*, Syriac *'āḵəl-ā-ṯ-ā*).[4]

	"Singular"	*Dual*	*M. Sound Plural*	*F. Sound Plural*	
Nominative	*-u-m	*-ā-n-	*-ū-(m)	*-āt-	-u-m
Accusative	*-a-m	*-ay-n-	*-ī-(m)		-i-m
Genitive	*-i-m				

This general picture is supported by the other, somewhat less transparent, case-marking systems employed or residually attested elsewhere among the documented Semitic languages.

(1) On those occasions in which the alphabetic writing system of Ugaritic provides information on that language's vocalization, the case markers that we find are consistent with the Arabic and Akkadian case systems, with the proviso that Ugaritic has lost the final nasal after short vowels (cf. nominative *ksu* 'chair' [to be read **kVssV'-u*] vs. accusative *ksa* vs. genitive *ksi*). Deviations from the triptotic pattern prevailing in Ugaritic are discussed below.

[3] In Old Babylonian, the dual "is generally confined to natural pairs of objects," in addition to surviving in "a small number of nouns with the same meaning as the singular" such as *išdān* (= *išd-um* 'foundation'), *qablān* (= *qabl-um* 'middle, waist, hips') (Huehnergard 1997, p. 8).

[4] The details of the reconstruction of the endings of the dual (Arabic *-āni/-ayni*, Babylonian *-ān/-īn*, etc.) and of the masculine sound plural (Arabic *-ūna/-īna*, Babylonian *–ū/-ī*, Hebrew *-îm*, Syriac *-în*, etc.) are not relevant to the present discussion. It is likely that the historical forerunner of these shapes contained one or more final nasals, and it is quite possible that the final vowels seen in Arabic are secondary. The conventional labeling of the triptotic type as "singular" is inaccurate, since it is likely that early Semitic had broken plural stems — like those which have survived most robustly in Arabic and Southwest Semitic — that were declined using the "singular" inflectional endings (cf. *'awlād-u-n, -a-n, -i-n* 'children (nom., acc, gen.)' and many other "singularly" declined stems such as those exemplified below).

(2) Phoenician provides even less evidence about its voweling, but early Phoenician nouns seem to have possessed genitive-case shapes distinct from non-genitive forms, at least in the environment of a following possessive suffix — compare *bt aby* (Kilamuwa 3) 'the house of my father' (presumably to be read **'abī-ya*) with *wkn ab* (Kilamuwa 5) 'and my father (presumably **'ab-ī*) was,' *'d mb'y* (Karatepe A i 5) 'until its setting' (= **mabō'-iy-u?*) versus *šm* (Karatepe A iii 14) 'his name' (= **šVm-ô?*) as a direct object (Garr 2004, pp. 100f.).

(3) Certain of the Semitic languages seem to have preserved the nominative/oblique distinction in their masculine sound plural endings but offer no evidence — in their written shape, at least — of further case distinctions. Compare Sam'ali (nominative *'lhw* 'gods' vs. *qdm.'lhy* 'before the gods [gen.],' [Garr 2004, p. 62]) and apparently Sabaean — compare nominative *bnw* 'the sons of' versus genitive *bny* (Kogan and Korotayev, p. 230).

(4) The accusative marker *-a* of Ge'ez seems to be a survival of the original Semitic **-a-*. The early Semitic case-markers **-u-* and **-i-* apparently underwent the regular shift to **ə* and were ultimately lost in word-final position — hence pre-Ethiopic **kalb-u, *kalb-i, *kalb-a* > **kalb-ə* vs. **kalb-a* > Ge'ez *kalb* vs. *kalb-a*.

Even in those Semitic languages whose grammars preserve no productive case-marking distinctions, it is possible to explicate many details of the substantival morphology of these languages by positing that their grammars and lexica preserve frozen remnants of a prehistorical case-marking stage like the one outlined above. Thus, for example, resolving the discrepancy between the second syllables of Hebrew *'āḇî-ḵā* 'your (m.sg.) father' and its Syriac cognate *'aḇû-ḵ* becomes simple if we assume that these languages shared a common ancestor that featured case-governed vowel-quality distinctions (cf. Arabic *'abū-ka, 'abā-ka, 'abī-ka*), and that the documented shapes have preserved one or another shape drawn from the original paradigm.[5] Similarly, the distinction between the forms of the third-person masculine singular possessive suffixes of Hebrew (*malk-ô* 'his king') and Aramaic (e.g., Syriac *malk-eh* id.) is routinely ascribed to a contrast in the case forms underlying each — thus *malk-ô* < pre-Hebrew **malk-a-(h)u* (accusative) versus *malk-eh* < pre-Aramaic **malk-i-hu* (genitive).

Diptosis in Arabic and Ugaritic

In addition to the diptotic inflectional systems associated with the masculine and feminine sound plural and the dual, a further diptotic pattern is extensively attested in literary Arabic. While the diptotic types of the plural and the dual outlined above were characterized by an oblique-case vowel that mirrors in its quality the triptotic system's genitive **-i-* (sound m.pl. **-ī-*, sound f.pl. **-āt-i-*, dual **-ay-*), this additional diptotic pattern of Arabic features a genitive case marker that looks superficially like the triptotic pattern's accusative *-a-*. In addition to showing this curious *-a* in the genitive, substantives following this diptotic pattern are distinguished from the triptotic type by the absence of the indefinite-marking final nasal *-n*. Contrast the declension of the literary Arabic noun phrase '(a) white dog,' the noun of which (*kalb-*) belongs to the triptotic type while its accompanying adjective (*'abyaḍ-*) is of the diptotic type.

<table>
<tr><td>Nominative</td><td>'ilä janbi-hi</td><td>kalb-u-n</td><td>'abyaḍ-u</td><td>'Next to him (there is) a white dog.'</td></tr>
<tr><td>Accusative</td><td>ra'aytu</td><td>kalb-a-n</td><td rowspan="2">'abyaḍ-a</td><td>'(I) saw a white dog.'</td></tr>
<tr><td>Genitive</td><td>marar-tu bi-</td><td>kalb-i-n</td><td>'(I) passed by a white dog.'</td></tr>
</table>

[5] The long vowels of **'abū-*, **'abā-*, **'abī-* and comparable stems presumably represent a fusing of the ending of the stem with the following case marker (i.e., **'abū-ka* < **'abX-u-ka*).

Literary Arabic nominal and adjectival stems are thus divided into two classes, distinguished by the endings that they show in their indefinite form. Lexical items in literary Arabic showing the *-u/-a* diptotic paradigm are not rare, but they are largely restricted to specific subsets of the substantival lexicon — certain singular and broken-plural nominal and adjectival classes — and, even among these, only to the non-determined manifestations of these substantives. If the definite article or a possessive suffix is added to a substantive of the diptotic type, the case marking shifts to the triptotic pattern.

<table>
<tr><th colspan="2">'(a) desert, (some) keys, (an)other (m.)'</th><th>'the...'</th><th>'his...'</th></tr>
<tr><td>Nominative</td><td>ṣaḥrā'-u
mafātīḥ-u
'āxar-u</td><td>('a)l- ṣaḥrā'-u
('a)l- mafātīḥ-u
('a)l-'āxar-u</td><td>ṣaḥrā'-u-hu
mafātīḥ-u-hu
'āxar-u-hu</td></tr>
<tr><td>Accusative</td><td rowspan="2">ṣaḥrā'-a
mafātīḥ-a
'āxar-a</td><td>('a)l- ṣaḥrā'-a
('a)l- mafātīḥ-a
('a)l-'āxar-a</td><td>ṣaḥrā'-a-hu
mafātīḥ-a-hu
'āxar-a-hu</td></tr>
<tr><td>Genitive</td><td>('a)l- ṣaḥrā'-i
('a)l- mafātīḥ-i
('a)l-'āxar-i</td><td>ṣaḥrā'-i-hi
mafātīḥ-i-hi
'āxar-i-hi</td></tr>
</table>

Evidence from the cuneiform rendering of Ugaritic indicates that this diptotic pattern was not restricted to Arabic. A small number of Ugaritic substantives, many of which have stems ending in the stem-formant *-ān-*, are documented with genitive-case shapes ending either in the vowel *-a* or in *-a* apparently alternating with *-i*.[6] See, for example, *i-na* A.ŠÀ : *ra-aḫ-ba!-na* (PRU 3 91f.:6) 'in the field, the wide (place)' (Huehnergard 1987, pp. 178f.).

In short, Arabic and Ugaritic provide evidence suggesting that early West Semitic possessed two contrasting case-marking regimens, distinguished from each other by (1) the quality of the vowel by which the genitive case is marked, and (2) the absence of the final nasal from the diptotic type.

Alternations in Quantity in the Akkadian Genitive

The ending *-a* of the Arabic and Ugaritic diptotic pattern is an interesting deviation from the simple paradigm that has been drawn up for the Semitic case system. Another deviation is to be found in the shape assumed by the Akkadian genitive marker when the latter is followed by a possessive pronominal suffix. In such situations, we encounter evidence that also runs counter to the simple case paradigm as it is conventionally reconstructed.

When a singular noun in the genitive is followed by a pronominal suffix, Akkadian consistently shows the noun's case vowel, despite the fact that the corresponding nominative and accusative forms typically show no sign of their case markers.

<table>
<tr><th></th><th>'his lord'</th><th>'her god'</th><th>'her daughter'</th><th>'your (m.sg.) donkey'</th><th>'their (m.) dog'[7]</th></tr>
<tr><td>Nominative</td><td rowspan="2">bēl-šu</td><td rowspan="2">il-ša</td><td rowspan="2">māras-sa
(< * mārat-ša)</td><td rowspan="2">imēr-ka</td><td rowspan="2">kalab-šunu</td></tr>
<tr><td>Accusative</td></tr>
<tr><td>Genitive</td><td>bēl-i-šu</td><td>il-i-ša</td><td>mārt-i-ša</td><td>imēr-i-ka</td><td>kalb-i-šunu</td></tr>
</table>

[6] The diptotic Ugaritic stems in *-ān-* are reminiscent of the Arabic adjective class of *sakrān-u* 'drunken' and its ilk, which are likewise diptotic.

[7] The stem is **kalb-*, with a stem-final cluster — cf. Arabic *kalb-un*, Hebrew *kéleḇ* (suffixed form *kalb-î* 'my dog') — into which an epenthetic vowel is inserted when a following consonant-initial suffix is added. For Akkadian nominal stems ending in a geminate rather than a cluster, the addition of a consonant-initial suffix leads to the insertion of an epenthetic vowel between the geminate and the suffix (e.g., *ṭupp-a-šunu* 'their (m.) tablet' (nominate/accusative; the genitive counterpart *ṭupp-i-šunu* displays the case vowel.

When such genitive forms are masculine, their syllabic rendering is often superficially indistinguishable from the plural, but the context on many occasions renders it clear that they are singular.

Genitive (*with -i-*)	*Nominative, Accusative* (*without case vowel*)
... *ana Adad i-li-šu* ana NU.GIG iqīš (Grant Smith College 260:3) '[the father] presented [his daughter] *to his god Adad* to become a *qadištum*'	... *il-ka Adad* lidammi[qqum] (PBS 7 61:4) 'may your god Adad show you favor'
ina amat ì-lí-šu Nergal šumšu lidmiq (Corpus of Ancient Near Eastern Seals 1 No. 571:4) 'may his reputation become good *by the command of his god Nergal*'	Aššur u *il$_5$-kà* qātī iṣṣabtuma (CCT 4 14b:8) 'Aššur and *your god* have helped me'
	... *il-šú* ana idišu šukun (4R 17:55f.) 'place *his god* at his side!'

Note that forms such as *il-i-ša* — in which the case-marker *-i-* is found following a short open syllable — demonstrate that the genitive marker *-i-* is not subject to Akkadian's overarching syncope rule, which typically deletes the second of two vowels in consecutive short, open syllables.[8] The syncope rule similarly fails to delete the genitive marker following longer stems containing a short vowel in their final syllable — hence *ākil-i-šu* 'the one (masc. gen.) eating it' rather than **ākil-šu*, the anticipated outcome of **'ākĭl-ĭ-šu*. The fact that we find the genitive marker preserved between a stem-final short syllable and a following suffix is a good indication that the syllable containing the genitive *-i-* counted as phonologically long. While Assyriologists differ on this point, it seems appropriate to read genitive forms such as those above as containing a long vowel *-ī-* (hence *bēl-ī-šu, id-ī-ša, imēr-ī-ka, kalb-ī-šunu,* etc.). The alternative would amount to positing an unmotivated and otherwise unparalleled blocking of Akkadian's pervasive and productive syncope rule.

We thus find ourselves obliged to reconstruct what appears to be an odd fluctuation in the quantity of the Akkadian case markers: the genitive marker seems to have been long before a following possessor suffix, whereas there is no reason to reconstruct length in the corresponding nominative and accusative forms. The apparent length of the presuffixal genitive marker notwithstanding, the genitive of the status rectus with its final *-m* (*-i-m*) is conventionally — and in all likelihood correctly — read as a short vowel (*il-ĭ-m*). It is unclear whether we can presume that the shortness of the vowel of *-im* is original — either we are to follow the model of the nominative and accusative markers (and of Arabic) and reconstruct a short **-i-* here, or we can posit that in the casus rectus a long **-ī-* like that of the presuffixal case marker has been shortened in the syllable closed by the *-m*. Before a following noun in the genitive, finally, the overall absence of the case marker in standard Akkadian suggests that the marker of the genitive here was, like those of the the other cases, short. However, the genitive singular of the Old Akkadian status constructus was *-i* contrasting with the zero of the nominative and accusative (*GAG* §64.a), suggesting that the genitive originally was quantitatively different from the other cases and that the restructuring of the genitive had not been completed by the time of early documented Akkadian.

	Presuffixal	*Status Rectus*	*Status Constructus*
Akkadian[9]	šum-ī-šu	šum-i-m	šum(i) abī-šu
	< *š(u)m-ī-šu	< *š(u)m-i/ī?-m	< *š(u)m-ī 'abī-šu
vs. Arabic	('i)sm-i-hi	('i)sm-in	('i)sm-i 'abī-hi

[8] Cf., e.g., *paris* '(he) has been divided' vs. *pars-āku, pars-at* (< **paris-āku, *paris-at*) 'I have, she has been divided.'

[9] On the reconstruction of the Proto-Semitic stem meaning "name" as vowelless **šm-*, see Testen 1985.

Synthesis: Two Genitive Markers Rather Than Three

The two languages that provide the clearest evidence of the Semitic case-marking system — Arabic and Akkadian — thus show genitive-case evidence that deviates from the familiar **-i-* both in vowel quality (e.g., Arabic *li-'abyaḍ-a* 'to a white one' vs. *li-bayt-i-n* 'to a house') and in vowel quantity (e.g., Akkadian *ana ilī-šu* 'to god-his' rather than the expected **ana il-su* < **ana ilĭ-šu*). We thus seem to be obliged to reconstruct multiple allomorphs of the ancestral Semitic genitive case marker.

To be sure, the student of the prehistory of these languages might opt simply to note that each of these "deviant" shapes is restricted to a single corner of the Semitic family and therefore posit that the familiar **-ĭ-* alone merits being traced back to the ancestral language. This approach amounts to the tacit assumption that any shape other than **-ĭ-* reflects a historically secondary innovation, leaving Akkadian *-ī-* and Arabic/Ugaritic *-a* to be explained as local and — in the absence of any non-arbitrary explanation for how they could have arisen — more or less spontaneous deviations from the original **-ĭ-*. Such an approach is predicated on the assumption that it is mere coincidence that it is specifically the genitive that is the locus of these putative secondary perturbations. Until such time as coherent, independently justifiable theories can be advanced to explain how each of these shapes could have arisen secondarily, treating the indeterminacy in the shapes of the genitive marker(s) as anything other than a Common Semitic issue will remain more convenient than it is convincing.

A more specific objection to ignoring these alternative genitive markers draws upon Ockham's admonition to minimize wherever possible the number of theoretical entities that a given theory posits. In other words, are we truly justified in concluding that each of the three of the shapes noted above — *-ĭ-*, *-ī-*, and *-a* — is sufficiently supported to be regarded as a discrete entity, or might there be some avenue by which this hypothetical inventory of synonymous elements can be reduced?

In assessing the diptotic genitive *-a* of Arabic, it should be borne in mind that observing an Arabic *-a* is not the same thing as reconstructing a Pre-Arabic **-a*. It is abundantly clear that a word-final Arabic *-a* may potentially originate with a historically underlying diphthong **-ay*. This may be seen clearly from the internal reconstruction of the jussive forms of verbs containing **-a-* as the vowel of their final stem-syllable and **-y* as their final radical.[10]

Jussive	y-a-bqa 'may (he) remain'	< *y-a-bqa(y)	y-u-bna 'may (it) be built'	< *y-u-bna(y)
Contrast ...				
Non-past indicative	y-a-bqä '(he) remains'	< *y-a-bqay-u	y-u-bnä '(it) is built'	< *y-u-bnay-u
Subjunctive	y-a-bqä '(that he) remain'	< *y-a-bqay-a	y-u-bnä '(that it) be built'	< *y-u-bnay-a

Since the imperative endings mirror the endings of the jussive, the same picture emerges from an inspection of the endingless (= masculine singular) form of the imperative of stems ending in **-ay*. Compare, for example, *ta'āla*, the masculine singular form of the stem *ta'ālay-* 'come!'

[10] The character *ä* is used here and in what follows to represent the Arabic character *'alif maqṣūrah*, a variant of the character *yā'*. In standard literary Arabic, this character serves as an alternate means of graphically rendering the vowel *ā*, but in early Arabic it most probably represented a long vowel differing in one manner or another from the typical *ā*. Whatever the details of its articulation in early Arabic might have been, the vowel represented by *-ä* is historically the outcome of the loss of an intervocalic semivowel **-y-* and the subsequent contraction of **a* and a following short vowel — hence, e.g., *banä* (read today as if it were **banā*) '(he) built' < **banay-a*; *ya-bqä* (read as if it were **yabqā*) '(he) remains' < **ya-bqay-u*; contrast *da'ā* '(he) called' (with *-ā* rather than **-ä*) < **da'aw-a*. Reconstructing an underlying **-y-* in a form such as *banä* or *ya-bqä* is justified by those portions of the paradigm in which the syllabic structure allows the underlying **-y-* to escape deletion (cf. *banay-na*, *ya-bqay-na* '(they fem.) built, remain,' *banay-ā*, *ya-bqay-ā-ni* '(the two of them) built, remain.'

	Masculine	*Feminine*
Singular	taʻāla (< *taʻāla(y))	taʻāla-y (< *taʻālay-ī)
Plural	taʻāla-w (< *taʻālay-ū)	taʻālay-na
Dual	taʻālay-ā	

I suspect that a further instance of the development of *-ay > -a is to be seen in the equative particle *ka-* 'like, as.' This is transparently akin to Akkadian *kīma* 'like,' the -ī- of which can easily have arisen from an earlier Semitic *-ay-. It is therefore possible to trace both *ka-* and *kī-ma* back to a historically underlying *kay- (i.e., Akkadian *kīma* < *kay- + mā [retaining a reflex of the original diphthong] but Arabic *ka-* < *kay through the regular loss of word-final *-y).[11]

A pair of Arabic particles suggests that an analogous simplification occurred in words that originally contained a word-final diphthong *-aw. This assumption provides the simplest way to account for the existence of the synonym pair *sawfa* and *sa-*, both of which serve as future-tense markers in literary Arabic. I suggest that we reconstruct the prehistorical precursor to the Arabic future construction as a syntagm composed of an element reconstructable as *saw — a form that early lexicographers documented as an alternate shape of the future particle (*saw yakūnu* = *sawfa yakūnu*, *sa- yakūnu* '[he] will be'), according to Stewart (1998, p. 122) — followed by an indicative clause. This *saw evidently served as a full clause in its own right, followed by a second full clause — [[*saw] [*yajī'-u*]] '*[[saw] [(he) comes]].' The particle *sa-* seems to reflect a simplification of word-final *-aw > *-a — comparable to the *-ay > -a that we saw above in jussive *ya-bqa* and imperative *taʻāla* — with the resulting *sa subsequently cliticized at the head of the clause in the course of its grammaticalization as a preverbal particle. *Sawfa*, in contrast, apparently arose from the same pre-Arabic syntagm, albeit with the following clause introduced by the familiar conjunction *fa-* 'for, then' ([*saw [*fa-yajī'-u*]] '*[[saw] for-[(he) comes]].' In this case, the *saw evidently melded with the conjunction, which acted as a buffer and kept the diphthong from being reduced.[12]

In short, the evidence provided by Arabic allows for the possibility of reconstructing the diptotic genitive marker of Arabic as a diphthong *-ay rather than as *-a.[13] It is entirely possible that the Ugaritic diptotic genitive -a might have arisen from the same source, although, given the empirical indeterminacies surrounding the historical phonology of Ugaritic word-final vowels, the discussion must of necessity be conducted at a much lower degree of certainty.[14] In the absence of good evidence elsewhere in Ugaritic indicating how an original Semitic word-final *-ay would have emerged in Ugaritic, we cannot rule out that the genitive -a seen in Ugaritic reflects

---

[11] If this interpretation of *ka-* is valid, it is possible that the shift of *-ay > *-a took place quite early, since we find reflexes of this particle that are compatible with the reconstruction *ka- elsewhere in West Semitic (cf. Ge'ez *ka-ma* 'like'; Hebrew *kå-mô-nî* 'like me,' *kå-'éllê* 'like these,' but generally with -ə- reduced from *-a—*kə-'ōyeḇ* 'like an enemy,' etc.).

Positing that word-final *-ay systematically gave rise to Arabic -a leads to the conclusion that the few cases in which -ay appears at the end of an Arabic word are likely to have other sources — cf., e.g., the feminine singular imperative *taʻāla-y* above. It is unlikely, for example, that the Arabic subordinating conjunction *kay* 'so that' represents a simple pre-form *kay. I would like to posit provisionally that *kay* arose through the contraction of two syllables — thus Arabic *kay* < *ka(w/y)i/ī (?) vel sim., a preform that, in any case, seems to provide a likelier source for the vowel of the Hebrew subordinating conjunction *kî* than a simple reconstruction *kay would.

[12] See Stewart 1998 for previous discussion of the topic, as well as for an alternative approach to their etymology. The lexical value of the reconstructed element *saw remains to be determined. Given the semantic function of *sa-/sawfa*, and given the historically underlying syntax reconstructed above, we may speculate that the proto-construction originally served to alert the addressee to the future event that would be identified in the following clause ("*be aware! take note! (for) he is coming ..." vel sim.). For other Arabic particles that presumably originated as small clauses introduced by *fa-*, cf. the adverbials *faqaṭ* and *fa-ḥasb* 'only,' which evidently originated as small postposed clauses (presumably on the order of "*... and that's all!").

[13] The outcome of the word-final diphthong *-ay as historical Arabic -a mirrors what we see resulting from the word-final sequences *-iy and *-uw. Here too the semivowel has been lost, yielding a short word-final vowel; cf., e.g., the masculine singular imperatives (*'i)bni* 'build!' (< *bni(y) < *bniy) and (*'u)dʻu* 'call!' (< *dʻu(w) < *dʻuw).

[14] Please note that, for Ugaritic as for the remaining West Semitic languages in question, we are addressing the outcome of a word-final *-ay (or *-aw) at the Proto-Semitic level, not at the level of the historical languages or their immediate prehistorical forerunners. Thus, of the III-y verbs, only the outcome of the endingless jussive/imperative shapes (*yi-CCay, *CCay) is of relevance, since we may presume that, at the deepest historical level, the shapes of the other moods were marked by a final vowel (cf. indicative *yi-CCay-u). Similarly, the shapes assumed by semivowel-final nominal stems (e.g., Hebrew *mirʻê* 'pasture,' *sətåw* 'winter,' etc.) will not be of relevance to the issue unless it can be demonstrated that they are to be traced back specifically to morphosyntactic environments in which there was no case vowel.

the same underlying diphthong. As we saw above in the discussion of Arabic *ka-*, there is a good chance that the shift of word-final **-ay* > *-a* took place rather early in West Semitic.[15]

Such a reconstructed **-ay-*, in turn, is entirely consistent with the -ī- that we find representing the Akkadian genitive case before the possessive suffixes — that is, the presuffixal *-ī-* in *bīt-ī-šu* 'house-genitive-his' could have arisen entirely regularly from a diphthong (i.e., *bīt-ī-šu* < Pre-Akkadian **bēt-ē-šu* ultimately < **bayt-ay-šu*).

To be sure, the distribution of the Arabic/Ugaritic *-a* does not match that of Akkadian *-ī-*. Judging by what is found in Arabic and (apparently) Ugaritic, the posited West Semitic **-ay* seems to have been restricted to a certain subsection of the lexicon and moreover was quite possibly limited to certain morphosyntactic circumstances (i.e., in predicate position and similar non-determined situations). The Akkadian *-ī-*, in contrast, shows no sign of having been restricted within the lexicon, and the morphosyntactic position in which it occurs differs from the environment defined for Arabic *-a*. The discrepancies in the details of distribution do not necessarily gainsay drawing a connection between **-ay* and *-ī-*, however. It is likely that neither West Semitic nor Akkadian has preserved the full details surrounding the original distribution of this element, but rather each has developed its own system to manage the remnants that it inherited from the original proto-system. The chief point is that — regardless of whether the **-ay-* was employed with all substantives or only with a subset, and regardless of what its originally morphosyntactic conditioning might have been — the two reconstructable shapes of the Semitic genitive (**-ĭ-* and **-ay-*) seem to have been in systematic alternation with each other.[16]

We can thus imagine that the familiar asymmetrical paradigm of a suffixed Akkadian noun (nominative/accusative *il-šu* but genitive *il-ī-šu*) preserves a fundamental asymmetry in the historically underlying shapes of the case markers (nominative **-u-*, accusative **-a-*, but genitive **-ay-*). In the Arabic case system, in contrast, this asymmetry has evidently been abandoned under the analogical pressure of the more general genitive allomorph **-i-*.

	Akkadian	**Pre-Akkadian*	*Contrast Arabic*
Nominative	*il-šu*	< **'il-(u-)šu*	*bayt-u-hu*
Accusative	*il-šu*	< **'il-(a-)šu*	*bayt-a-hu*
Genitive	*il-ī-šu*	< **'il-ay-šu*	*bayt-i-hi*

Speculation: One Genitive Marker Rather Than Two?

By reconstructing both Arabic *-a* and Akkadian -ī- as **-ay(-)*, it becomes possible to reconcile two of the three allomorphs identified above for the Semitic genitive case marker and thereby reduce the three shapes that we find representing the genitive (*-ĭ-*, *-ī-*, and *-a-*) down to a bipartite alternation (**-i-* vs. **-ay-*).

[15] Conversely, it might be useful to reflect on the apparent indeterminacy shown by the Ugaritic diptotic genitive. As was noted above, such forms are marked either with *-i* or *-a*, with the two endings alternating within the same lexeme in some cases (cf., e.g., PRU 3 72f., where both spellings occur in a single text; Huehnergard 1987, p. 299). While this indeterminacy may quite plausibly be taken as an indication of wavering between the triptotic and diptotic inflections, if we reconstruct the diptotic ending as word-final **-ay* it behooves us to wonder whether the graphic *-i/-a* alternation might reflect differing ways of rendering a vowel whose quality the cuneiform syllabary was not equipped to handle adequately. Let us call this hypothetical vowel *"e_x." To be sure, word-internal Semitic **-ay-* fairly clearly yielded Ugaritic *-ē-* (Huehnergard 1987, pp. 258f.), but there is no a priori reason that in word-final position **ay* could not have had its own peculiar outcome in Ugaritic just as it did in Arabic. We might in theory speculate that this *e_x arose early in West Semitic — hence an early West Semitic (diptotic) genitive **raḥbān-*e_x, an equative particle *ke_x, a III-infirmae jussive (a-vowel type) **(y)i-bq*e_x—but the distinction between *e_x and **a* was subsequently lost everywhere but in Ugaritic.

[16] It will be recalled that the suffixed forms of Phoenician showed a comparable disjunction between genitive and non-genitive shapes, reflected in the suffix *-y* for 'my, his' attached to genitive nouns vs. zero for non-genitive nouns. This has been conventionally ascribed to the effects of the quality of the case marker **-i-* (*'d mb'y* (Karatepe A i 5) 'until its setting' < **'ad(ē) mabō'-i-hu*). At the same time, the discrepancy is equally consistent with what we have posited here, viz. an asymmetry between nominative **-u-* and accusative **-a-* on the one hand and a diphthongal genitive **-ay-* on the other. In other words, the *-y* of *'d mb'y* could thus just as easily be traced back to a diphthongal case marker such as the one envisioned above (**mabō'-ē-hu*?).

Of the two shapes *-i- and *-ay-, *-i- is consistently found before Semitic mimation (Akkadian *bīt-i-m*, Arabic *bayt-i-n*), whereas our reconstructed *-ay- seems never to have been found in this situation.[17] At this point, Ockham's dictum obliges us to assess the strength of the evidence supporting the notion that these two shapes of the genitive reconstructed above — *-i- versus *-ay — were truly distinct at the deepest historical level.

To a considerable degree, the pattern outlined above is marked by complementary distribution — that is, whenever we reconstruct mimation, we reconstruct the case marker as *-i- (*ākil-i-m, 'ākil-i-n*), while whenever we reconstruct the case marker as *-ay-, we reconstruct a syllable that is not closed through the presence of mimation. This distribution renders it likely that the original distinction between the triptotic and diptotic declensions resided at least as much in the presence versus absence of the final nasal as it did in the nature of the case-marking vowel. In other words, the distribution noted above licenses us to consider the possibility of reconstructing a unified Pre-Semitic genitive marker *-ay-, positional variants of which have given rise to the various parallel allomorphs (*-i-, -a, -ī-*) documented in the descendant languages. Given the fact that, on the whole, the Semitic languages avoid surface-level diphthongs in closed syllables, it is entirely conceivable that the *-i- that we conventionally reconstruct as the default manifestation of the genitive marker might ultimately reflect the shape that *-ay- assumed when it occured in a syllable closed by a following nasal — that is, that *bayt-i-m arose from an earlier **bayt-ay-m.

There is independent evidence indicating that an original *-ay- might have developed into *-ī- under comparable circumstances in at least certain branches of Semitic. The high vowel that we find in the Ethiopic negative particle *'i* and its Arabic counterpart *'in* (pointing to a common "South Semitic" *'īn) corresponds to an original Semitic diphthong *-ay-, judging by Hebrew *'áyin, 'ên-* and the Akkadian vetitive particle *ayy-*. If we reconstruct this negative particle as *'ayn, it becomes possible to speculate that — in the common ancestor of Arabic and Ethiopic, at least — *-ay- developed into *-ī- in a syllable closed by a word-final nasal (Testen 2007). The development of *'ayn > *'īn entitles us to speculate that — in pre-South-Semitic, if not earlier — there was an intermediate stage in which the genitive marker featured a long vowel *-ī- before mimation, that is, mimated *'ākil-ī-m (< *'ākil-ay-m) versus mimation-less *ākil-ay, from which the attested short vowel (*ākil-i-m, 'ākil-i-n*) would have subsequently arisen naturally in a closed syllable.[18]

From this perspective, we should rephrase the question of the Semitic diptotic declension from "Why is the diptotic genitive marker *-a*?" to "Why do the diptotes lack a final nasal?" If the speculations above are justified, the relation between the diptotic *-ay and the triptotic *-i- ultimately hinges on whether the case marker was followed by mimation. Whatever factors might ultimately have governed the presence or absence of the Proto-Semitic nasal remain to be determined, but this question, I suggest, should be handled independently from the question of the nature of the vowel by which the genitive was expressed in Proto-Semitic.

---

[17] It is presumed here that the *-n* of Arabic nunation results from a general shift of pre-Arabic *-m in word-final position to *-n*, comparable to what took place in pre-Greek and other Indo-European branches (cf. Greek *e-lip-on* '(I) left (aorist),' *agr-o-n* 'field (accusative) < Indo-European *(-)likʷ-o-m, *Hagr-o-m vs. Sanskrit *a-ric-am, ajram*).

I see good evidence that a shift of *-m > -n took place in pre-Arabic in the stem *'alin-* (reflected in the adjective *'alin-un* 'publicly known,' whence the verbs *'alin-a* '(it) was/became known' and its causative derivative *'a'lan-a* '(he) announced') alongside *'alim-a* '(he) learned, knew.' I take *'alin-* to have originated as a predicate participle *'alim '(it is) known' built from of the ancestor of the verb *alim-a in a structure corresponding to the Akkadian "stative" (the type of Akkadian *paris* '(it) is divided,' which is equivalent to the adjective *pars-um* 'divided' in predicate position). In other words, the Pre-Arabic verb *'alim-a '(he) knew' seems to have originally had a corresponding "resultative" adjective *'alim-um '*known' (subsequently replaced by what has emerged as the productive passive participle, *ma'lūm-*) which in its endingless predicate form underwent the regular shift of *-m > -n — thus *'alim '*(it is) known' > *'alin. Once the *-m > *-n shift was no longer an active factor in the language's phonology, the new shape *'alin came to be treated as an independent stem and served as the starting for the creation of a new constellation of derivatives (*'alin-a, 'a'lan-a*, etc.).

[18] The fact that Hebrew *'ên* shows the reflex of an earlier diphthong rather than a long vowel does not necessarily gainsay the possibility that *-ay- became a long high vowel in early West Semitic before a word-final nasal. Unlike Ethiopic *'i* and Arabic *'in*, Pre-Hebrew *'ayn retained or acquired a capacity for taking clitic pronouns, which means that, in many cases, it did not meet the conditions for the hypothetical raising of *-ay-. In other words, while simple *'ayn might have yielded something like *'în in Pre-Hebrew, that form would have coexisted with alternate manifestations in which the diphthong survived. It would have been a simple matter for this diphthong to spread by analogy to yield what would appear to be a survival of *-ay in unprefixed *'ayn.

Hypothetical reconstruction of the posited Proto-Semitic genitive case marker *-*ay*-[19]

<table>
<tr><th></th><th>*'*In (the) house*'</th><th colspan="2">*'*In the king's house*'</th><th>*'*In his house*'</th></tr>
<tr><td>*Mimated</td><td>*bV-bayt-ay-m</td><td rowspan="2">*bV-
bayt-ay</td><td>malk-ay-m</td><td rowspan="2">*bV-
bayt-ay-š/hu</td></tr>
<tr><td>*Non-mimated</td><td>*bV-bayt-ay-Ø</td><td>malk-ay-Ø</td></tr>
</table>

Regardless of the ultimate nature of the relation between the final *-*m* and its zero-marker counterpart, once the shape *-*i-m* had arisen from **-*ay-m*, analogical pressure — capitalizing on the metrical similarity between the new genitive *-*i*- and the original nominative and accusative *-*u*- and *-*a*- — could have easily expanded it beyond the pre-mimation position so that it emerged as the default shape of the case-marker. Consequently, the tidy tripartite pattern *-*u*-/*-*a*-/*-*i*- that we conventionally reconstruct would be — like many tidy patterns — historically secondary, and the historically original aspects of the paradigm as preserved in the descendant languages (Arabic -*a*, Ugaritic -*a*, Akkadian -*ī*-) would have survived as synchronic eccentricities.

The Sound Feminine Plural *-*āt-ay*-: A Trace of the Original Genitive?

I suspect that we may find indirect evidence for our reconstructed genitive marker *-*ay*- if we examine the sound plural endings associated with feminine substantives. As is noted above, the sound feminine plural throughout Semitic is marked by *-*āt*-. In the casus rectus, the languages preserving case markers indicate that the resulting stem was followed by a special paradigm of case markers — a paradigm that was diptotic like the sound masculine plural but had the vowel quantity and final nasal of the singular.

Case	*Old Babylonian*	*Literary Arabic*
Nominative	ākil-āt-um bānât-um	' ākil-āt-u-n bāniy-āt-u-n
Oblique	ākil-āt-im bānât-im	' ākil-āt-i-n bāniy-āt-in

The various descendant languages differ, however, in the shape assumed by feminine-plural-ending substantives when they are followed by a possessive suffix. While some languages (e.g., Arabic and Aramaic) handle the addition of a possessive pronoun to sound feminine plural nouns in much the same way that they deal with singular nouns, in other languages we find an extra, heavy syllable interposed before the suffix. This syllable is homophonous with the presuffixal case-number ending of the masculine-sound plural noun.

"Your (m. sg.) queens" exemplifying the intrusive syllable following the feminine plural stem ending

<table>
<tr><th></th><th colspan="2">Feminine pl. *-āt-</th><th colspan="2">Feminine pl. *-āt- + X -</th></tr>
<tr><th></th><th>Arabic</th><th>Syriac</th><th>Hebrew</th><th>Akkadian</th></tr>
<tr><td>Nominative</td><td>malik-āt-u-ka</td><td rowspan="2">malḵ-āṯ-āḵ</td><td rowspan="2">malḵ-ôṯ-ê-ḵā</td><td>šarr-āt-ū-ka</td></tr>
<tr><td>Oblique</td><td>malik-āt-i-ka</td><td>šarr-āt-ī-ka</td></tr>
<tr><td></td><td></td><td>Compare:</td><td>malḵ-ê-ḵā
'your kings'</td><td>šarr-ū-ka
'your kings'
(obl. šarr-ī-ka)</td></tr>
</table>

[19] Purely for illustrative purposes, the same noun **bayt*- is used to examplify both the mimated and non-mimated morphology. As noted above, it remains to be determined whether the non-mimated shape was an option in Proto-Semitic for any given substantive or, as in historical Arabic, this shape was limited to specific subset of the lexicon.

How is it that the Semitic languages have come to differ from one another in the formation of the presuffixal feminine plural ending? I suggest that we can reconcile these varying shapes if we assume that, in the original ancestral language, the possessive suffixes were added to a diptotic paradigm composed of elements drawn from the triptotic paradigm, just as we find in historical Arabic — compare *malikāt-u*-ka 'your (m.sg.) queens' (nom.), *malikāt-i-ka* (obl.), in which we see the genitive marker *-i-* pressed into service as the marker of the accusative/genitive oblique. If in early Semitic, however, the genitive marker was originally **-ay-* rather than **-i-*, we can reconstruct a diptotic paradigm like the following, in which the genitive marker **-ay-* of the possessed shape is juxtaposed to the more prosaic paradigm of the casus rectus:

	Presuffixal	*Casus Rectus*
Nominative	*malakāt-u-ka	*malakāt-u-m
Oblique	*malakāt-ay-ka	*malakāt-i-m (ult. < *-āt-ay-m?)

Once the new, contracted genitive marker **-i-* of the casus rectus had replaced the original **-ay-*, the various language branches seem to have differed on how to deal with the "singular" genitive ending in the context of a plural noun like **malakāt-*. Pre-Arabic and Pre-Aramaic simply extended the new, generalized genitive *-i-* into this position as well, yielding the structure *malak-āt-i-ka*. Early Canaanite, by contrast, evidently preserved the now-stranded genitive marker **-ay*, but reassigned it a new role within the new inflectional pattern that it was developing for the marking of plurality.

	*'*kings, your (m.sg.) kings'*	*'*queens, your (m.sg.) queens'*
Nominative	*malak -ū-m *malak-ū-ka	*malak-āt-u-m *malak-āt-u-ka
Oblique	*malak-ī-m *malak-ī-ka	*malak-āt-i-m *malak-āt-ay-ka

In languages like Hebrew, the loss of the case system led to what were originally the oblique forms assuming the role of the default shape of the plural noun — hence, for example, the Hebrew (now caseless) *məlāḵ-îm* was expanded at the expense of the original nominative **malak-ūm*. In the course of this generalization, the presuffixal shape **-āt-ay-* would have come to yield the (now caseless) shape **malakātay-ka*. This in turn seems to have served as the starting point for a restructuring of the masculine plural, with the presuffixal **-ay-* of the feminine plural expanding to replace the masculine plural **-ī-* before suffixes (hence **malak-ī-ka* '*your kings' was replaced by **malak-ay-ka* [whence ultimately Hebrew *malḵê-ḵā*], on the model of **malakāt-ay-ka*). In other words, the **-ay-*, which originated as a case marker, was regrammaticalized first as a redundant component in the presuffixal manifestation of the gender/number marker — hence **malak-āt-ay-ka*, where **-āt-ay-* had become the presuffixal counterpart to the feminine plural **-āt-* — and later as the general presuffixal shape for the marking of plurality, hence the general presuffixal plural **-ay-*, added to either the feminine plural stem (**malakāt-ay- ka*) or to the masculine plural stem (**malak-ay-ka*).[20]

[20] Traditionally the **-ay-* of the Hebrew presuffixal plural, feminine as well as masculine (see below) — *malḵ-ôṯ-ê-ḵå, malḵ-ê-ḵå* — has been ascribed to an analogical spread of the obsolescent dual ending, but it remains unclear what could have motivated such a spread.

Regrammaticalization of *-ay- in the evolution of the pre-Hebrew presuffixal declension ('your [m. sg.] kings, queens')

		**āt+ay- = fem. pl.*		**-ay- (> -ê-) = plural*				
*malak-ū-ka	>	*malak-ī-ka	>	*malak-	[ø]	ay-	-ka	= malk̲-ê-k̲ā
*malak-ī-ka								
*malakāt-u-ka	>	*malakāt-ay-ka	>	*malak-	āt-		-ka	= malk̲ôt̲-ê-k̲ā
*malak-āt-ay-ka								

Pre-Akkadian evidently preserved the genitive marker **-ay-* in the presuffixal feminine plural oblique (*šarrāt-ī-ka* 'your [m.sg.] queens') just as it seems to have done, we have seen, in the presuffixal singular (*šarrat-ī-ka* vs. nominative/accusative *šarrat-ka*). Just as in early Canaanite, Pre-Akkadian identified the reflex of the **-ay-* of **-āt-ay-* with the oblique ending of the masculine. As a result of this identification, Pre-Akkadian reshaped the original nominative counterpart to this form (originally **šarrāt-u-ka,* cf. Arabic *malikāt-u-ka*) by creating a new presuffixal nominative form *šarrāt-ū-ka,* where -*ū*- has drawn upon the nominative plural marker of the masculine (*šarr-ū-ka* 'your [m.sg.] kings').[21] The outcome of all this is historical Akkadian's systematic but rather asymmetrical number-marking system, which opposes the more archaic shapes used in the casus rectus to the refashioned shapes that appear before the possessive suffixes.

Morphological decompositon of Akkadian 'kings, queens' and 'your (m.sg.) kings, queens'

	Casus Rectus			*Presuffixal Position*			
M	šarr-	-ū/-ī		šarr-	(ø)	-ū/ī-	ka
		Gender/Number/Case					
F	šarr-	-āt-	-um/-im	šarr-	-āt-	-ū/ī-	ka
		Gender/Number	Case				
					Gender	Number/Case	

Conclusion

The aim of the preceding pages was to raise the possibility that the simple, symmetrical case-marking paradigm that is conventionally assumed for early Semitic reflects a secondary development. Once we are willing to ascribe significance to the deviations from this pattern that we find in Akkadian and Arabic — the languages providing us with our best evidence of the case system — we must be ready to entertain the possibility that the morphology of the early Semitic case system was more complex than the conventional reconstruction allows. We have a choice as to where we ultimately envision the morphological complexity that the data seem to demand — either in a fundamental coexistence of parallel by-forms (**-i-* vs. **-a-* vs. **-ī-*) or in a fundamental asymmetry in the paradigm (viz. genitive (**-i-*)/**-ay-* vs. nominative **-u-*, accusative **-a-*). The latter approach, it is suggested, has more to commend it. Its chief cost resides in our acknowledging that — like so much that has become familiar to students of the history of the Semitic languages — the case system will benefit from a careful reexamination of some of our fundamental assumptions.

[21] It remains possible, of course, that Pre-Canaanite shared this restructuring to create a new feminine plural nominative (**malak-āt-ū-ka*) but subsequently lost this when it abandoned its case-marking mechanisms. Since the Northwest Semitic languages that provide details on their voweling have not retained their case systems, we cannot know by what steps the philologically familiar Semitic languages may have reached their attested shapes.

Appendix: What Has Become of the Arabic Diptotic Stems in *-*iy*-?

A considerable number of the Arabic stems displaying the characteristic features of the diptotic declension — namely, the appearance of *-a* rather than *-*i* as the genitive marker and the absence of the final nasal — are to be traced back to stems ending in a semivowel preceded either by *-a-* or *-ā-*. However, given the various general processes by which Arabic eliminates semivowels in many enviroments — through either syllable contraction or a shift to the glottal stop — many such forms will overtly reveal neither the underlying semivowel nor the case marker. For example, on the basis of the absence of the indefinite nasal, we may infer that *kubrä*, the feminine counterpart to the elative adjective *'akbar-* 'greater, greatest,' is just as much a diptote as its masculine analogue, but this fact is not evident from the form itself.

<table>
<tr><td></td><td>"Great" m./ (f.)</td><td>"Greater" m.</td><td colspan="2">"Greater" f.</td></tr>
<tr><td></td><td>Triptotic</td><td>Diptotic</td><td colspan="2">"Monoptotic"</td></tr>
<tr><td>Nominative</td><td>kabīr(-at)-u-n</td><td>'akbar-u</td><td rowspan="3">kubrä</td><td>< *kubray-u</td></tr>
<tr><td>Accusative</td><td>kabīr(-at)-a-n</td><td rowspan="2">'akbar-a</td><td rowspan="2">< *kubray-a</td></tr>
<tr><td>Genitive</td><td>kabīr(-at)-i-n</td></tr>
</table>

Stems ending in an underlying short *-a- + a semivowel — whether those stems be diptotic or triptotic — thus appear to be "monoptotic," showing a neutralization of the surface-level case distinctions.

<table>
<tr><td></td><td colspan="2">"Triptotic" Declension</td><td colspan="4">"Diptotic" Declension</td></tr>
<tr><td>Nominative</td><td rowspan="3">‘aṣa-n
'a staff'</td><td>< *‘aṣaw-u-n</td><td rowspan="3">'ūlä
'first' (f.)</td><td>< *'ūlay-u</td><td rowspan="3">'asrä
'captives'</td><td>< *'asray-u</td></tr>
<tr><td>Accusative</td><td>< *‘aṣaw-a-n</td><td rowspan="2">< *'ūlay-a</td><td rowspan="2">< *'asray-a</td></tr>
<tr><td>Genitive</td><td>< *‘aṣaw-i-n</td></tr>
</table>

Stems in which the underlying semivowel is preceded by a vowel other than *-*a*-, in contrast, preserve a fragment of the underlying case paradigm in the form of the accusative *-*a*-, which remains uncontracted — compare the nominative/genitive shape *bāni-n* 'one who builds' (< **bāniy-u-n*, **bāniy-i-n*) versus the accusative *bāniy-a-n*. While in principle we can readily envision how diptotic stems corresponding to this shape might show a comparable lack of contraction, such diptotic stems seem not to be attested in historical Arabic.

<table>
<tr><td></td><td>"Triptotic" Declension</td><td>"Diptotic" Declension</td></tr>
<tr><td>Stems ending in *-ay-</td><td>-ä-n</td><td>-ä</td></tr>
<tr><td>Stems ending in *-iy-</td><td>Nom./gen. -i-n
vs. acc. -iy-a-n</td><td>Unattested *Nom. *-ī
vs. acc./gen. *-iy-a</td></tr>
</table>

It is in this light that we should consider the eccentricities of the various shapes assumed by quadriconsontal broken plurals built from semivowel-final stems. As a general rule, the quadriconsonantal broken plurals belong to the diptotic declension type.[22]

[22] Arabic morphology subsumes under its quadriconsonantal broken plurals many forms built from triconsonantal singular stems containing a long vowel — cf. *‘awāmil-* (sg. *‘āmil-*), *jazā'ir-* (sg. *jazīr-at-*) —where -'- < *-*w*- or *-*y*-, cf. Ge‘ez *qäsawəs-t*, *wəḥayəz-t*, the plurals of *qäsis* 'priest,' *wəḥiz* 'river,' etc. — *hadāyā* 'gifts' (< **hadāyay-*) (singular *hadiyy-at-* < **hadīy-at-*), etc. The plural-formation morphology treats such singular stems as if their long vowels reflected an underlying semivowel.

makātib-u (acc./gen. *-a*), plural of *maktab-u-n* '(an) office'

mafātīḥ-u (acc./gen. *-a*), plural of *miftāḥ-u-n* '(a) key'

'awāmil-u (acc./gen. *-a*), plural of *'āmil-u-n* '(a) factor'

jazā'ir-u (acc./gen. *-a*), plural of *jazīr-at-u-n* '(an) island'

The quadriconsonantal plural stems ending in a semivowel, however, deviate from the typical quadriconsonantal in two noteworthy respects:

(1) As may be seen from the examples cited above (*makātib-*, *mafātīḥ-*, *'awāmil-*, *jazā'ir-*, etc.), the quadriconsonantal broken plurals systematically show an *-i*-quality vowel in their final stem syllable. Stems ending in a semivowel, however, routinely display a final *-ä*, an ending associated with stems ending in an underlying **-ay-* rather than in **-iy-*.

(2) Unlike other types of quadriconsonantal broken plurals, many semivowel-final quadriconsonantal broken plurals show what appear to be alternants displaying triptotic-style morphology, including the final nasal. These alternants show the *-i*-quality expected in the final stem syllable of a quadriconsonantal broken plural — thus *CaCāCiy- (cf. *makātib-*, etc.), whence indefinite CaCāCi-n, definite *al*-CaCāCī. For some plural stems of this structure, only the diptotic or the triptotic type is documented.

	Quadriconsonantal Broken Plural Stems (IV-infirmae)	
	"Diptotic" Type	*"Triptotic" Type*
fatwä 'legal opinion'	fatāwä (< *fatāway-u)	fatāwi-n (def. al-fatāwī)
ṣaḥrā'-u 'desert'	ṣaḥārä (< *ṣaḥāray-u)	ṣaḥāri-n (def. al-ṣaḥārī)
laylä 'night'	layālä (< *layālay-u)	layāli-n (def. al-layālī)
[*'asīr- 'prisoner'*[23]]	'asārä (< *'asāray-u)	—
jāriy-at-u-n 'girl'	—	jawāri-n (def. al-jawārī)

An additional eccentricity of the "triptotic" variant of the semivowel-final quadriconsontantal plural type is the absence in the accusative of the indefinite final *-n* which characterizes the remaining shapes in the paradigm.

Nominative	fatāwi-n	layāli-n
Accusative	fatāwiy-a	layāliy-a [rather than *-iy-a-n like bāniy-a-n, etc.]
Genitive	fatāwi-n	layāli-n

This odd accusative ending in *-iy-a* is in fact the very shape that I posited above as the expected form for the oblique case of a semivowel-final diptote. I would like to suggest that the various morphological eccentricities of the semivowel-final quadriconsonantal broken plurals are ultimately to be traced back to an inflectional pattern that no longer exists in documented Arabic — namely, diptotically declined stems ending in **-iy-*. Apparently Pre-Arabic abandoned the morphological mechanism for producing such forms, but in the quadriconsonantal plurals — a subsection of the lexicon where such forms would presumably have originally been quite routine — it

[23] Most probably *'asārä* (root *'-s-r*) originated not as a plural built anomalously from *'asīr-* but as a secondary plural built regularly from *'asrä* (< **'asr-ay-*). The latter is documented as an alternate plural of *'asīr-* constructed in accordance with the pattern shown by *qatlä* (pl. of *qatīl-* 'slain'), *jarḥä* (pl. of *jarīḥ-* 'wounded'), *'aylä* (pl. of *'ā'il-* (< **'āyil-*) 'poor,' etc.

compensated for the resulting gap by splicing together a new paradigm from the endings of the semivowel-final stems which it still possessed — viz. the contracted diptotes in **-ay-* and the triptotes in **-iy-*. The odd indefinite accusative shape *-iy-a*, which has no counterpart in either of the familiar surviving paradigms, seems to be a fossil, the sole fragmentary remnant of the now-lost diptotic **-iy-*stem type.

The inflection of semivowel-final quadriconsonantal plurals in Arabic, featuring forms drawn from the paradigms of the diptotic stems in **-ay-*, the triptotic stems in **-iy-*, and a trace of the now-lost diptotic paradigm in **-iy-*

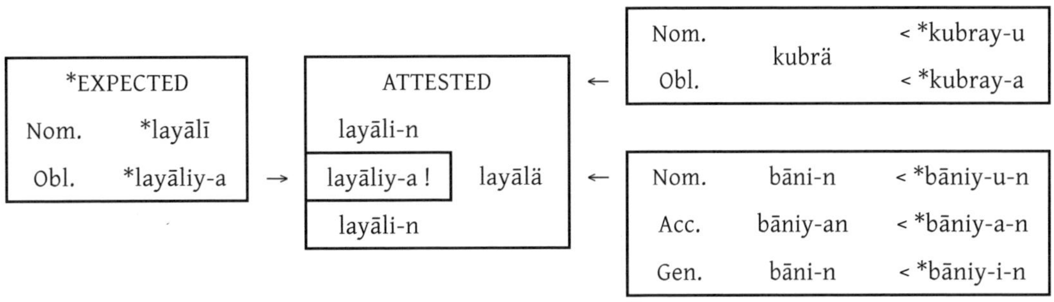

Abbreviations

acc.	accusative
def.	definite
f.	feminine
gen.	genitive
m.	masculine
nom.	nominative
obl.	oblique
pl.	plural
sg.	singular

BIBLIOGRAPHY

Garr, W. Randall

2004 *Dialect Geography of Syria-Palestine, 1000–586 B.C.E.* Winona Lake: Eisenbrauns. Reprint of 1985 University of Pennsylvania Press edition.

Huehnergard, John

1987 *Ugaritic Vocabulary in Syllabic Transcription.* Atlanta: Scholars Press.

1997 *A Grammar of Akkadian.* Atlanta: Scholars Press.

Kogan, Leonid E., and Andrey V. Korotayev

1997 "Sayhadic (Epigraphic South Arabian)." In *The Semitic Languages*, edited by Robert Hetzron, pp. 220–41. London and New York: Routledge.

Stewart, Devin J.

1998 "Clitic Reduction in the Formation of the Modal Prefixes in the Post-Classical Arabic Dialects and Classical Arabic sa-/sawfa." *Arabica* 45: 104–28.

Testen, David

1985 "The Significance of Aramaic *r* < **n*." *Journal of Near Eastern Studies* 44: 143–46.

2007 "West Semitic Perspectives on the Akkadian Vetitive." In *Studies in Semitic and Afroasiatic Linguistics Presented to Gene B. Gragg*, edited by Cynthia L. Miller, pp. 201–13. Studies in Ancient Oriental Civilizations 60. Chicago: The Oriental Institute.

24

Mixed Linguistic Features in a Judeo-Arabic Text from Algeria: The *šarḥ* to the *hafṭarot* from Constantine

*Ofra Tirosh-Becker, The Hebrew University of Jerusalem**

It is my pleasure to dedicate this paper, which focuses on the Judeo-Arabic language of a Bible translation (*šarḥ*) from eastern Algeria, to my colleague and friend John Huehnergard. On this festive occasion I would like to congratulate him by quoting from the *šarḥ* to Proverbs 3:13–14:[1]

אסקל בן אדם וג'ד כייאסא ובן אדם יכ'ררג' (ילחק) פ'האמא.

אין מליח סבבהא מן סבב פ'צ'א ומן דהאב גלתהא.

אַשְׁרֵי אָדָם מָצָא חָכְמָה וְאָדָם יָפִיק תְּבוּנָה.

כִּי טוֹב סַחְרָהּ מִסְּחַר־כָּסֶף וּמֵחָרוּץ תְּבוּאָתָהּ.

Happy is the man who finds wisdom, the man who attains understanding.
Her value in trade is better than silver, her yield, greater than gold.

1. Introduction

Selections from the biblical books of Prophets, known in Hebrew as *hafṭarot* (singular *hafṭara*), are publicly read in Jewish synagogues as part of the religious practice. A *hafṭara* is read on each Sabbath, and on Jewish festivals and fast days, after reading the Torah portion (*paraša*), and is usually thematically linked to it. The specific sections from the books of Prophets that are read as the *hafṭarot* vary to a certain extent among different Jewish communities. Since in these communities Hebrew did not serve as a spoken language, but rather primarily as a language of prayer, the biblical text has become largely unintelligible to all but the most scholarly members of the community. The elevated language in the books of Prophets, compared to that of the Torah stories, made the *hafṭara* even less widely comprehensible. Consequently the Torah, the *hafṭarot*, and a few other biblical books, such as the biblical Scrolls, were translated into various Jewish languages, among them Judeo-Arabic.

Early Judeo-Arabic translations of the Bible precede even the famous Bible translation of Rabbi Saʿadya Gaʾon (882–942), known as the *Tafsīr*.[2] Modern Judeo-Arabic translations of the Bible, which have evolved mainly

* This paper is based on a lecture presented at the third international symposium of the International Association for the Study of Middle Arabic and Mixed Arabic (AIMA 3), Florence, Italy, October 13, 2010. This research was supported by grant no. 814/03 from the Israel Science Foundation.

[1] Renassia 1916a. The English translation is according to Jewish Publication Society 1985.

[2] See, for example, Blau 1992; Blau and Hopkins 2007, pp. 235–38, pp. 281–82; Tobi 1993, pp. 87–127; Tobi 1996.

since the fifteenth century in many Jewish communities in the Muslim world, known as *Šurūḥ* (singular, *Šarḥ*), were orally transmitted through the generations from teacher to disciple, and from father to son. Only in recent centuries were some of these translation traditions recorded in manuscripts or in printed books, ensuring their preservation for future generations.[3]

In this paper I discuss the language of an Algerian Judeo-Arabic translation of the *hafṭarot*. This *šarḥ* tradition was printed circa 1935 by Rabbi Yosef Renassia (1879–1962), one of the pillars of the Jewish community of Constantine, which is the largest city in eastern Algeria. This book, entitled *Pəṭirat Moše,* comprises six parts encompassing all eighty-five *hafṭarot*. Seventy-four of the *hafṭarot* were accompanied by a Judeo-Arabic translation and a Judeo-Arabic commentary, written as customary in Hebrew characters. In addition, the book also includes a French translation of the *hafṭarot*.[4]

Such a complete Judeo-Arabic translation to almost all of the *hafṭarot* is quite rare. Rabbi Raphael Berdugo of Miknes, Morocco (eighteenth to nineteenth centuries), compiled in his *Ləšon Limmudim* a partial *šarḥ* to the *hafṭarot*, focusing on difficult verses, phrases, and words.[5] This compilation survived in several manuscripts.[6] A *šarḥ* to the *hafṭarot* from Aleppo, Syria, was preserved both in manuscripts and in recordings of its oral tradition.[7] One also finds printed editions for a limited number of specific *hafṭarot* from Algeria and Tunisia. For example, translations of a few *hafṭarot* were printed in the widely disseminated book *Four Grails* (*Arbaʿa Gəḇiʿim*), which was first published in 1839,[8] and a handful of others were printed in short booklets.[9]

The Judeo-Arabic translation of the *hafṭarot* was used primarily for didactic purposes. In the different maghrebian Jewish communities there were varied customs with regard to reading out loud the translation of specific *hafṭarot* in the synagogue.[10] Only on selected holidays was the translation of the *hafṭara* read out loud in some Moroccan synagogues alongside the Hebrew original and the Aramaic translation.[11] In some synagogues in the Jewish communities of Constantine and its vicinity, there was a custom to read out loud the Judeo-Arabic translation of the *hafṭarot* for the three Sabbaths between seventeenth of Tammuz and ninth of ʾAḇ, known as *telata de-purʿanuta* (the three [Sabbaths] of tribulation).[12]

In the book *Pəṭirat Moše* Rabbi Yosef Renassia had put down in writing the translation tradition of the majority of the *hafṭarot* for the benefit of his young students in the *talmud torah* and in the *ʿEṣ Ḥayyim yeshivah*, to help them understand the original Hebrew text. The publication of this *šarḥ* to the *hafṭarot* is part of an extraordinary endeavor undertaken by this prominent leader of the Constantinian Jewish community. Rabbi Yosef Renassia took upon himself the preservation of the Judeo-Arabic culture of his community, publishing scores of books, among them translation traditions (*šurūḥ*), dictionaries, history books, and commentaries.[13] It should be noted that since Algeria's French colonization in 1830, and especially after Algerian Jews were granted French citizenship in 1870, they gradually adopted the French language as their main means of communication at the expense of their Judeo-Arabic dialect. Nonetheless, one can study the Constantinian Judeo-Arabic in the first half of the

---

[3] Bar-Asher 1988; Bar-Asher 2001; Maman 2000, pp. 48–53; Avishur 2001, pp. 106–11. The *šarḥ* often includes a variety of post-biblical texts, such as the Passover Haggadah, tractate *ʾAḇot* of the Mishnah, and the liturgical poem Mi ḵamoḵa. See Maman 1999; Hary 2009; Bar-Asher 2010c; Tirosh-Becker 2006; Tirosh-Becker 2011.

[4] The book comprises six parts that were printed in several printing houses in different cities in Algeria and Tunisia. The different parts were bound into several volumes in various combinations, e.g., Volume 1: Genesis, Exodus, Leviticus – Hebrew, Judeo-Arabic, and French; Volume 2: Numbers, Deutronomy, Moʿadim – Hebrew, Judeo-Arabic, and French. For details see Fraenkel 1982, vol. 2, pp. 243–44; also see the bibliography at the end of this paper. In another binding combination, we have found only the *hafṭarot* to Exodus and Leviticus bound in a single volume, with a French translation that was printed in a different printing house: Imprimerie Assoun, Philippeville.

[5] *Ləšon Limmudim* is a short commentary on the Bible written by Rabbi Raphael Berdugo of Miknes, Morocco (1747–1821), which aimed to replace the oral *šarḥ* tradition of this community and correct inaccuracies that were introduced into it throughout the generations; see Bar-Asher 2001, part 1, pp. 5–7.

[6] An annotated scientific edition of the entire *Ləšon Limmudim* was published in Bar-Asher 2001. Part 4 includes the *šarḥ* to the *hafṭarot.* On the transmission of this partial *šarḥ* to the *hafṭarot* and its characteristics, see Bar-Asher 2001, part 4, pp. 3–35.

[7] Avishur 2006, pp. xvii*–xix*; Avishur 2009, p. 137.

[8] *Arbaʿa Geḇiʿim, Livorno* 1839. Due to its popularity, this book was reprinted in many editions; see Ilan and Dahan 2002, pp. 1–4.

[9] E.g., *Sep̄er Qeren Mešiḥo ʾo Hafṭarat Šəmini šel Pesaḥ*. Tunis 1910; *Hafṭarat Tišʿa Bə-ʾAḇ*. Tunis: Wazan imprimerie (n.d.). For more details, see Attal 2007, pp. 32–33, 38, 40–41; Tobi and Tobi 2000, p. 26. A *hafṭara* for the first day of *Rosh Ha-Shanah* was published in Tedghi 2006, pp. 301–04, 307–10. For a *šarḥ* to *hafṭarat Tišʿa Bə-ʾAḇ* in Egyptian Judeo-Arabic, see Hary 2009, p. 64. *Šurūḥ* to *hafṭarat Tišʿa Bə-ʾAḇ* were also printed in Baghdad, Calcutta, Bombay, and Livorno.

[10] Bar-Asher 2001, part 4, pp. 10, 14–16; Tedghi 2008, pp. 143–44.

[11] Chetrit 1994, pp. 38, 183–84; Maman 2003, p. 147.

[12] Tedghi 2008, p. 144; Bar-Asher 2001, part 4, p. 19 n. 57.

[13] Charvit 2010; Tirosh-Becker 1988, pp. 4–6.

twentieth century from compositions that were penned in this dialect, from the Judeo-Arabic newspaper *əl-Ḥikma*, which was published in this city (1912–13, 1922–23), and from recordings of elderly informants who emigrated from Constantine to Israel and France, both in free speech and in reading selections from the *šarḥ*.[14]

2. The Language of the *šarḥ*

By its nature the language of the *šarḥ* was forged under the influence of two opposing forces. On the one hand, the goal of the translation is to make the text comprehensible to the local community, leading to the use of vernacular features. On the other hand, the sanctity of the text that is being translated imposes an elevated style and conservative traits. As a consequence the language of *šarḥ* traditions is characterized by a mixture of layers.[15] It includes conservative Arabic elements, features from Medieval Judeo-Arabic, dialectal features that are not used in the daily spoken dialect, and local vernacular traits. Naturally, different *šurūḥ* vary in the relative prevalence of conservative components versus vernacular features, reflecting the sanctity of the text and the period in which its translation tradition was formulated.[16] Furthermore, despite the presence of some colloquial features in the language of the *šarḥ*, this language remains significantly elevated even with respect to the language used by the rabbinic elite in their original exegetical compositions and other writings.[17] In this paper I examine the Mixed Judeo-Arabic of the Constantinian *šarḥ* to the *hafṭarot*, mainly in the realm of morphology and lexicon.

It should be noted that the *šurūḥ* adopt a word-for-word translation method, due to the traditional influence of the famous ancient Aramaic translation of the Torah, *Targum Onqelos*.[18] Hence, the syntax of the *šarḥ* reflects the syntax of the original biblical Hebrew text, and not Arabic syntax. Moreover, even the Hebrew direct-object particle *ʾeṯ* (אֶת), which does not have an exact counterpart particle in Arabic syntax, is translated in this *šarḥ* by an artificial equivalent *ila* (אילא).[19] For example:[20]

1 Kings 3:20 (*hafṭarat Miqqēṣ*):

וקאמת פ׳י וסט אליל וכ׳דאת **אילא** ולדי מן חדאייא

וַתָּקָם בְּתוֹךְ הַלַּיְלָה וַתִּקַּח **אֶת**־בְּנִי מֵאֶצְלִי

'She arose in the night and took my son from my side.'

In this respect the *šarḥ* to the *hafṭarot* aligns with the Constantinian *šarḥ* to other books of the Bible (except for the *šarḥ* to Ecclesiastes) and with the Constantinian *šarḥ* to *Mishnah* tractate *ʾAḇot*.[21]

---

[14] E.g., Tirosh-Becker 2010a; 2010b; 2011.

[15] Bar-Asher 1991; Bar-Asher 1988, pp. 30–32; Tedghi 1993; Tirosh-Becker 1990a.

[16] For example, the language of the Moroccan *šarḥ* to the Passover Haggadah is not as elevated as the language of the Moroccan *šarḥ* to the Bible; see Bar-Asher 1985, pp. 242–44. On the classification of the *šurūḥ* from Constantine to different Bible books according to their linguistic characteristics, see Tirosh-Becker 1990a.

[17] For a detailed comparison between the language of the Constantinian *šarḥ* to tractate *ʾAḇot* and the language of Rabbi Renassia's commentary on this tractate, see Tirosh-Becker 2011.

[18] Bar-Asher 1988, p. 27.

[19] The Arabic particle *ʾilā* (إِلَى) usually carries the meaning 'to'; see Wright 1981, vol. 1, p. 280, §358a. The direct object is expressed in Arabic by the accusative case, although in some instances it can be expressed by *li-*, *bi-* or *ʾiyya-*. See Wright 1981, vol. 1, pp. 103–04, §188–89; vol. 2, pp. 159–60, §56b). On the use of *li-*, *bi-*, and *ʾiyya-* in Medieval Judeo-Arabic, see Blau 1980a, pp. 172, §254e; 177–80, §§265c, 266d, 269a; 325, §252. For a detailed discussion on *ila* as a translation to **את**, see Tirosh-Becker 1988, pp. 294–97; Hary 1991.

[20] I adopt the following conventions for all the examples in this paper: The Judeo-Arabic text appears exactly as it is printed in the book *Pəṭirat Moše*. The biblical verses are quoted from M. Breuer's addition of the Tanakh (Jerusalem, Ḥorev publishing), which is based on *Keter Aram Ṣoḇa*. The English translation is according to Jewish Publication Society 1985.

[21] Tirosh-Becker 2006, pp. 326–28. Tirosh-Becker 2011. *Ila* for **את** is also found in a Judeo-Arabic translation of the Passover Haggadah from Algiers; see Attal 1975. It is also present in *šurūḥ* from Baghdad; see Blanc 1964b, p. 28. Artificial translations for **את** are found already in Pre-Saʿadianic Bible translations; see, for example, Blau 1992, pp. 32–33; Tobi 1993, pp. 89–90; Tobi 1996, p. 486.

3. Mixed Features in the Pronominal System

The mixture of linguistic elements in the *šarḥ* to the *hafṭarot* from Constantine (SHC) is observed even in the same paradigm. I demonstrate it here in the paradigm of the independent personal pronouns, and in the paradigm of the demonstrative pronouns used in this *šarḥ*.

3.1. Independent Personal Pronouns

In the spoken dialect of this community, Judeo-Arabic of Constantine (JAC), there is no distinction between the masculine and feminine forms of the second-person singular independent pronouns, and both are denoted by *ənti*.[22] In contrast, SHC preserves the distinction between the masculine and feminine forms: the masculine pronoun is *ənta* (אנתא), while the feminine pronoun is **אנת** (*ənt / ant*).[23] Examples in SHC:

Jon 4:2 (*hafṭarat Minḥa le-Yom Kippur*):

אן ערפ'ת אן **אנתא** טאייק חנין ורחים

כִּי יָדַעְתִּי כִּי **אַתָּה** אֵל־חַנּוּן וְרַחוּם

'For I know that **You** are a compassionate and gracious God.'

Isa 51:12 (*hafṭarat Šōp̄əṭīm*):

מן **אנת** וכ'ופ'תי מן אנסאן ימות

מִי־**אַתְּ** וַתִּירְאִי מֵאֱנוֹשׁ יָמוּת

'What ails **you** that you fear.'

The preservation of the distinction between masculine and feminine forms, as well as the use of the archaic pronoun *ənta* (cf. CA أَنْتَ), are among the conservative features in SHC. These two forms are also used in the Constantinian *šarḥ* to the book of Proverbs.[24] Interestingly, unlike the loss of the distinction between 2mSg and 2fSg pronouns in JAC, this distinction is preserved in the Muslim dialect of Constantine (MAC), where *nta* or *ntāya* are used for 2mSg and *nti* or *ntiyya* for 2fSg.[25]

The 2mPl independent personal pronoun, *əntum* (אנתום, אנתם), is another conservative feature in SHC. Example:

1 Sam 12:20 (*hafṭarat Qōraḥ*):

אנתום עמלתיו אילא ג'מיע אדונייה האדי

אַתֶּם עֲשִׂיתֶם אֵת כָּל־הָרָעָה הַזֹּאת

'**You** have, indeed, done all those wicked things.'

---

[22] Tirosh-Becker 1988, pp. 256–58; P. Marçais 1977, p. 189.

[23] It is noteworthy that the occurrence of 2fSg pronoun is rare in the original Hebrew text of the *hafṭarot*. The 2mSg form *ənta* (אנתא) occurs numerous times in this text. Only once did we find in SHC, in one of the *hafṭarot* for Leviticus, the dialectal form *ənti* (אנתי) for 2mSg (Ezek 22:2: *hafṭarat ʾAḥărê Môṯ*), although even in the *šarḥ* to the *hafṭarot* for Leviticus, *ənta* is usually used. On the uniqueness of the *hafṭarot* to Leviticus, see §4.1 below.

[24] Renassia 1916a; Prov 7:4: קול ללכ'ייאסא כ'תי **אנת** (אֱמֹר לַחָכְמָה אֲחֹתִי **אָתְּ** 'Say to Wisdom, "**You** are my sister"'). In the books of Psalms, Job, Ecclesiastes, and Lamentations, for which we also have printed editions of the *šarḥ* from Constantine, there were no occurrences of the 2fSg pronoun in Hebrew. The form *ant* (אנת) appears twice in the *šarḥ* to the book of Daniel denoting 2mSg pronoun; see Renassia 1917b. However, since the typical 2mSg pronoun in the *šarḥ* to Daniel is *ənta* (אנתא), and in these two specific occurrences the original Qre Aramaic form is אַנְתְּ (Dan 6:17, 21), the occurrence of **אנת** in the *šarḥ* to these two verses in Daniel is most likely influenced by the original Aramaic form.

[25] According to Laraba, the short or long forms are variants conditioned by phrase stress; see Laraba 1981, p. 103.

This pronoun is similar to its CA form *ʾantum* (أَنْتُمْ), while in the local dialect, it is replaced by the vernacular forms *ᵊntūma* or *ᵊntūman*, usually with an initial ultra-short vowel.[26]

Nonetheless, alongside these conservative features, we also find in SHC several dialectal independent personal pronouns. For example, in CA the 1Pl independent personal pronoun is *naḥnu* (نَحْنُ). However, in SHC we find the vernacular forms *əḥna* (אחנא) or *ḥna* (חנא) for the 1Pl independent personal pronoun.[27] The dialectal JAC form for this pronoun is *ḥna*. Examples:

Josh 2:17 (*hafṭarat Šəlaḥ Ləḵā*):

באריין **אחנא** מן ימינך האדא אלדי חללפ'תינא

נְקִיִּם **אֲנַחְנוּ** מִשְּׁבֻעָתֵךְ הַזֶּה אֲשֶׁר הִשְׁבַּעְתָּנוּ

'**We** will be released from this oath which you have made us take.'

Josh 2:18 (*hafṭarat Šəlaḥ Ləḵā*):

האודא **חנא** ג'איין פ'לארץ'

הִנֵּה **אֲנַחְנוּ** בָאִים בָּאָרֶץ

'When **we** invade the country.'

Likewise, the 3Pl independent personal pronoun in SHC is *hum(m)ān* (הומאן), similar to the dialectal JAC form for this pronoun, *hum(m)ān* or *hum(m)a*,[28] and in contrast to CA *hum* (هُمْ). For example:

Jer 2:11 (*hafṭarat Masʿê*):

אש בדדל קום מעבוד **והומאן** ליש מעאבד

הַהֵימִיר גּוֹי אֱלֹהִים **וְהֵמָּה** לֹא אֱלֹהִים

'Has any nation changed its gods, Even though **they** are no-gods?'

2 Kings 4:5 (*hafṭarat Wayyērā*):

הומאן מקררבין אילהא

הֵם מַגִּשִׁים אֵלֶיהָ

'**They** kept bringing [vessels].'

To conclude, the paradigm of the independent personal pronouns used in SHC exhibits a mixture of conservative and colloquial forms, as is clearly seen in comparison to this paradigm in JAC:

[26] No 2fPl independent pronoun appeared in the *hafṭarot*. In JAC there is no distinction between 2mPl and 2fPl pronouns. In MAC *ntūma* for both 2mPl and 2fPl pronouns, see Laraba 1981, p. 103. See the variants of this personal pronoun form in other maghrebian dialects: M. Cohen 1912, pp. 336–37; D. Cohen 1975, p. 210; Grand'Henry 1972, pp. 129, 131; P. Marçais 1977, p. 189.

[27] The pronoun אחנא is sometimes pronounced *aḥna*, due to the proximity of the initial vowel to the pharyngeal consonant *ḥ*. The form אחנא (*əḥna*) is more frequent than חנא (*ḥna*) in SHC, and no conditioning for their use could be determined, at least according to the written text (i.e., it was not dependent on the last phoneme of the preceding word). There was only one occurrence in SHC for the conservative 1Pl independent personal pronoun נחן; cf. CA نَحْنُ. Interestingly, in the first occurrence of this pronoun in the same verse, the dialectal form *əḥna* was used: 2 Kings 7:9 (*hafṭarat Məṣōrāʿ*): וקאלו ראג'ל אילא צאחבהו. ליס הכדאך **אחנא** עאמלין אלנהאר האדא נהאר בשארה הווא **ונחן** סאכתין (וַיֹּאמְרוּ אִישׁ אֶל־רֵעֵהוּ לֹא־כֵן **אֲנַחְנוּ** עֹשִׂים הַיּוֹם הַזֶּה יוֹם־בְּשֹׂרָה הוּא **וַאֲנַחְנוּ** מַחְשִׁים 'Then they said to one another: "**We** are not doing right. This is a day of good news, and **we** are keeping silent!"'). Note that this sole occurrence appeared in one of the *hafṭarot* for Leviticus; on the linguistic features in the *šarḥ* to the *hafṭarot* for Leviticus, see §4.1 below.

[28] When reading the *šarḥ* to Psalms, the rabbi informants usually pronounced this pronoun with a doubled *m*; see Tirosh-Becker 1988, p. 260. This pronoun was usually pronounced with doubled *m* also in the recordings of linguistic questionnaires. A form with doubled *m*, *hŭmma*, is documented in south Tunisia and Libya; see P. Marçais 1977, p. 190. See also *əmma* in the Arabic dialect of the Jews of Tripoli, Libya, in Yoda 2005, p. 115.

SHC:	1Sg	(ʾ)*ana* (אנא)		
	2mSg	*ənta* (אנתא)	2fSg	*ənt* / *ant* (אנת)
	3mSg	*huwa* / *huwwa* (הווא)	3fSg	*hiyya* (הייא)
	1Pl	*əḥna* (אחנא) / *ḥna* (חנא)		
	2mPl	*əntum* (אנתום, אנתם)	2fPl	[no examples]
	3Pl	*hum(m)ān* (הומאן)		
JAC:	1Sg	(ʾ)*ana*		
	2Sg	*ənti*		
	3mSg	*huwa* / *huwwa*	3fSg	*hiyya*
	1Pl	*ḥna*		
	2Pl	*ᵊntūma* / *ᵊntūman*		
	3Pl	*hum(m)a* / *hum(m)ān*		
MAC:[29]	1Sg	*ʾāna*		
	2mSg	*nta* / *ntāya*	2fSg	*nti* / *ntiyya*
	3mSg	*huwwa*	3fSg	*hiyya*
	1Pl	*ḥna*		
	2Pl	*ntūma*		
	3Pl	*hūma*		

3.2. Plural Demonstrative Pronouns

Another example for the blend of conservative and dialectal properties in SHC is the plural demonstrative pronouns. The plural demonstrative for near deixis is *hāwlay* (האולאי),[30] which is similar to the CA form *hāʾulāʾi* (هؤلاء) and differs from the local dialectal form *hādu*. In contrast to the near deixis by *hāwlay*, the plural demonstrative for distant deixis is *hādūk* (האדוך), which is part of the common maghrebian dialectal paradigm of demonstratives for distant deixis *hādāk, hādīk, hādūk,*[31] and differs from the CA demonstrative *ʾūlāʾika* (أولئك). For example:

Isa 44:21 (*hafṭarat Wayyiqrā*):

אתפ'ככר **האולאי** יעקב וישראל אן כ'דימי אנתא

זְכָר־**אֵלֶּה** יַעֲקֹב וְיִשְׂרָאֵל כִּי עַבְדִּי־אָתָּה

'Remember **these** things, O Jacob. For you, O Israel, are My servant.'

Zech 14:3 (*hafṭara* for the first day of *Sukkot*):

ויכ'רג' אללאה ויתטארד פ'לאומום **האדוך** כיף נהאר טראדו פ'י נהאר לבראז (אטראד)

וְיָצָא יְהוָה וְנִלְחַם בַּגּוֹיִם **הָהֵם** כְּיוֹם הִלָּחֲמוֹ בְּיוֹם קְרָב

'Then the Lord will come forth and make war on **those** nations as He is wont to make war on a day of battle.'

---

[29] Laraba 1981, p. 103.

[30] On similar variants in Spanish-Arabic, see Corriente 1977, p. 98, §5.12.3. See also the other variants in Fischer and Jastrow 1980, p. 256, §12.2.2.1.

[31] P. Marçais 1977, pp. 197–98; Laraba 1981, p. 108. In many maghrebian Jewish dialects, the fricative interdentals shift to their plosive counterparts (e.g., *ḏ > d); see Fischer and Jastrow 1980, p. 256, §12.2.2.1.

We found the colloquial demonstrative pronoun *hādu* (האדו) in SHC only once in parenthesis, as an alternative translation to the conservative pronoun *hāwlay*.[32]

Ezek 37:18 (*hafṭarat Wayyiggaš*):

האודא תכ'בבר לינא אש **האולאי (האדו)** ליך

הֲלוֹא־תַגִּיד לָנוּ מָה־**אֵלֶּה** לָּךְ

'Won't you tell us what **these** actions of yours mean?'

As in many other maghrebian dialects, when *hādu* appears in JAC before a definite noun, it shortens to *hād* regardless of gender or number, for example, *hād əl-bnāt* ('these girls').[33] In SHC we found only one occurrence for *hād* as a plural demonstrative pronoun before a definite noun.[34] The plural demonstrative האוולאי (*hawlay*) also appears in R. Berdugo's *Lǝšon Limmudim*,[35] while it is not used in the spoken dialect of Miknesian Jews. Nonetheless, there are other maghrebian *šarḥ* traditions in which the colloquial form *hādu* is employed.[36]

The following table summarizes the common plural (cPl) demonstratives of near and distant deixis discussed herein:

	Near deixis (cPl)	Distant deixis (cPl)
SHC	*hāwlay* (האולאי)	*hādūk* (האדוך)
JAC	*hādu*	*hādūk*
MAC[37]	*hādu*	*hādūk*
CA	*hāʾulāʾi* (هَؤُلاءِ)	*ʾūlāʾika* (أُولَئِكَ)

4. Conservative Features in SHC

The conservative components in the language of SHC are not limited to pronouns, but rather they are observed in all parts of speech. Their occurrence in SHC reflects the elevated and venerable language of the *šarḥ*. Following are some of the conservative elements in SHC.

4.1. The Negation Particle

The negation particle that is used in SHC to translate the various Hebrew negation words *ʾên* (אַיִן), *bal* (בַּל), *ʾal* (אַל), and *lō* (לֹא) is *layš* (ליש), which reflects the CA *laysa* (لَيْسَ). The negation particle *laysa* has become invariable in Medieval Arabic, that is, in Jewish and Christian Middle Arabic and in early Muslim Middle Arabic.[38] It is sometimes accompanied by suffixed pronouns,[39] a phenomenon that is also observed in SHC, where we find the forms *layši*, *layšu*, and *layškum* as translations for *ʾênennī* (אֵינֶנִּי), *ʾênennû* (אֵינֶנּוּ), *ʾênḵem* (אֵינְכֶם). The particle *layš* is not used in the Constantinian local Jewish dialect (JAC), where negation is expressed mainly by the pattern *mā -š*, for example, *mā ktǝbš* ('he did not write'), like in many other maghrebian dialects.[40] It is noteworthy, however, that

[32] The alternative translation in parenthesis often offers explanations or synonyms of a vernacular nature, and rarely even the French equivalent of the Judeo-Arabic word, especially when the word refers to a term for realia (in the entire SHC, there were approximately thirty occurrences of French words in parenthesis). Hebrew words are seldom used in these parentheses. On the various applications of parenthesis in the Constantinian *šarḥ*, see Tirosh-Becker 2006, pp. 329–38. Cf. Tedghi 2006, pp. 297–99.

[33] A similar shortening to *hād* occurs also when *hāda* or *hādi* appear before a definite noun. See, for example, P. Marçais 1977, p. 197.

[34] Isa 42:16 (*hafṭarat Bǝrēšīṯ*): **האד** לכלאיים עמלתהם וליש תרכתהם (**אֵלֶּה** הַדְּבָרִים עֲשִׂיתִם וְלֹא עֲזַבְתִּים 'These are the promises — I will keep them without fail').

[35] Bar-Asher 2001, part 3, pp. 94, 485, and n. 4.

[36] Bar-Asher 2010a, p. 184.

[37] Laraba 1981, p. 108.

[38] Blau 2002, p. 47, §89; Blau 1980a, pp. 143–44, 317, §206; Blau 1999, pp. 87, 132; Blau 1966–67, 2, p. 305, §204.

[39] Blau 1980a, p. 144, §206c; Blau 1966–67, vol. 2, p. 310, §204.5.1.

the negation particle that serves in some Algerian Bedouin dialects is *leys*.[41] The voiceless post-alveolar fricative /š/ in the SHC word *layš*, instead of the voiceless alveolar fricative /s/, is notable as these two consonants are distinct phonemes in this dialect.[42] Examples:

Mic 7:18 (*hafṭarat Wayyēleḵ*):

ליש מסך לדואם חרג'ו

לֹא־הֶחֱזִיק לָעַד אַפּוֹ

'Who has **not** maintained His wrath for ever.'[43]

2 Kings 12:8 (*hafṭarat Shabbat Shəqalim*):

עלאש **לישכם** מצחחין אילא תכציר אלבית

מַדּוּעַ **אֵינְכֶם** מְחַזְּקִים אֶת־בֶּדֶק הַבָּיִת

'Why have you **not** kept the House in repair?'

Isa 1:15 (*hafṭarat Dəḇārīm*):

חתא אן תכתרו אצלה **ליישי** סאמאע

גַּם כִּי־תַרְבּוּ תְפִלָּה **אֵינֶנִּי** שֹׁמֵעַ

'Though you pray at length, I will **not** listen.'[44]

In SHC we found only two occurrences of the colloquial negation pattern *mā -š*. Both examples appeared in parenthesis, which often present explanations, different interpretations, parallel traditions, or synonyms of vernacular nature, for example:[45]

1 Kings 1:4 (*hafṭarat Ḥayyê Sārâ*):

ואלצולטאן **ליש** ערפ'הא (**מא** זווג'האש)

וְהַמֶּלֶךְ **לֹא** יְדָעָהּ

'But the king was **not** intimate with her.'[46]

In this respect, the *šarḥ* to the *hafṭarot* for Leviticus differs from the Constantinian *šarḥ* to all the other *hafṭarot*. In contrast to the spelling ליש used in the other sections of SHC, in the *šarḥ* to the *hafṭarot* for Leviticus the negation particle is spelled ליס, for example:

2 Sam 6:10 (*hafṭarat Šəmīnī*):

וליס חב דוד ליזוול אילהו אילא צנדוק אללה עלא בלאד דוד

וְלֹא־אָבָה דָוִד לְהָסִיר אֵלָיו אֶת־אֲרוֹן יְהוָה עַל־עִיר דָּוִד

'So David would **not** bring the Ark of the Lord to his place in the City of David.'

---

[40] On negation particles in maghrebian dialects, see P. Marçais 1977, pp. 275–80.

[41] Grand'Henry 1995, p. 52.

[42] Tirosh-Becker 1988, pp. 34–39. Both spellings לאייס and לאייש are attested in the *šarḥ Ləšon Limmudim* from Miknes, Morocco; see Bar-Asher 2001, part 4, pp. 94, 116, 153, 168, 203 (even side by side, see n. 2).

[43] The word מסך' was printed with ך' although it should be read מסך. This was the method that this specific printing house used to denote a final ך (ك). In other printing houses it was denoted by ךּ.

[44] The spelling with two *yods* is found only in a few examples of this negation particle, which had a pronominal suffix (ליישי, ליישו).

[45] The other example: Jer 31:14 (*hafṭarah* for the second day of *Rosh Ha-Shanah*): רחל תבכי עלא ולאדהא. מא אבאת (**מא חבבתש**) ליצבר עלא ולאדהא. אן **ליישו**
רָחֵל מְבַכָּה עַל־בָּנֶיהָ **מֵאֲנָה** לְהִנָּחֵם עַל־בָּנֶיהָ כִּי **אֵינֶנּוּ** 'Rachel weeping for her children. She **refuses** to be comforted. For her children who **are gone**').

[46] While the main translation of the biblical phrase לֹא יְדָעָהּ is literal ליש ערפ'הא ('did not know her'), the alternative translation in parenthesis, מא זווג'האש, conveys the meaning of 'mating.' Note however, that in some maghrebian dictionaries, عرف also means 'to have relations with a woman'; see Beaussier 1958, p. 645; Marçais and Guîga 1958–61, 5:2529.

This is not the only feature in which the *šarḥ* to the *hafṭarot* for Leviticus differs from the rest of SHC. Among its distinctive characteristics are the use of the perfect inflectional morpheme *-tu* for 2cPl (§6.4 below), and the plural form *umam* (§6.5 below).[47] A possible explanation for the somewhat different character of this section of *Pəṭirat Moše* is that it was printed in Makhluf Najjār's printing house in Sousse, Tunisia, while the other volumes were printed in other printing houses in Djerba and Constantine.[48] Alternatively, it is possible that Rabbi Renassia incorporated in his edition of SHC a version of the *šarḥ* to the *hafṭarot* for Leviticus that was put down in writing by someone else and was available to him.

4.2. The Relative Pronoun

The main relative pronoun in SHC is *əldi* (אלדי), which translates the Hebrew relative pronoun *ʾăšer* (אֲשֶׁר).[49] The pronoun *əldi* reflects the CA form *ʾallaḏī* (ٱلَّذِي). However, in contrast to the inflection of *ʾallaḏī* in CA, the pronoun אלדי was mostly invariable already in Medieval Judeo-Arabic,[50] and *əldi* is invariable in the Constantinian *šarḥ*. The relative pronoun *əldi* (אלדי) is also characteristic of the literary language of the Jews of Tunis and of the Jews of Baghdad (where it is pronounced *əllaḏi*).[51] The following examples demonstrate the invariability of this pronoun in SHC:

Isa 1:1 (*hafṭarat Dəḇārīm*):

נבואת ישעיהו ולד אמוץ **אלדי** תנבבא עלא יאודה וירושלים

חֲזוֹן יְשַׁעְיָהוּ בֶן־אָמוֹץ **אֲשֶׁר** חָזָה עַל־יְהוּדָה וִירוּשָׁלָ͏ִם

'The prophecies of Isaiah son of Amoz **who** prophesized concerning Judah and Jerusalem.'

Ezek 44:22 (*hafṭarat ʾĔmōr*):

ואלהג'ג'אלה **אלדי** תכון הג'ג'אלה מן אימאם יאכ'דו

וְהָאַלְמָנָה **אֲשֶׁר** תִּהְיֶה אַלְמָנָה מִכֹּהֵן יִקָּחוּ

'Or widows **who** are widows of priests.'

The dialectal relative pronoun *əlli* occurs in SHC only in 15 percent of the occurrences of the Hebrew relative pronouns in the original biblical text, reflecting a limited penetration from the spoken dialect.[52] The pronoun *əlli* follows one of the two directions in which the relative pronoun has evolved in North African Arabic dialects, each preserving a different element of the CA pronoun *ʾallaḏī* (ٱلَّذِي). The dialectal forms *əlli* and *lli* preserve the alveolar liquid element *ll*, while the dialectal forms *ddi* and *əddi* reflect the original interdental element *ḏi*.[53]

In most of the occurrences of *əlli* in SHC, it stands for the Hebrew definite article *ha* (ה) when it is used as a relative before attributive participles,[54] a use that is also found in the Constantinian *šarḥ* to Psalms.[55] Albeit not

---

[47] See also the marginal examples in notes 23 (אנתי) and 27 (נחן) above, and note 81 (דאלוקת) below.

[48] On the distinctive character of the language of the *šarḥ* to the Scroll of Ruth, which was also printed in Sousse and bound with another work by Rabbi Renassia, see Tirosh-Becker 1990a, pp. 198, 204.

[49] The pronoun *əldi* (אלדי) is also one of the two alternative translation options for the Hebrew pronoun *zû* (זוּ), the other option being *hāda/hādi* (האדא/האדי). Both translation options are given side by side in the following example: Isa 43:21 (*hafṭarat Wayyiqrā*): עַם־זוּ יָצַרְתִּי לִי (אלקום האדא (**אלדי**) כ'לקת לייא 'The people I formed for Myself'). See also Tirosh-Becker 1988, pp. 274–75.

[50] Blau 2002, p. 55, §139; Blau 1980a, pp. 235–37, §361.

[51] D. Cohen 1975, p. 221; Blanc 1964b, p. 28.

[52] In JAC both *əlli* and *lli* are used. In MAC the typical form is *lli*; see Laraba 1981, p. 109. The form אלי is documented, albeit rarely, in medieval Judeo-Arabic manuscripts. See Blau 1980a, pp. 237, 338, §362.

[53] Fischer and Jastrow 1980, pp. 84–85, §6.3.1; 258, §12.2.4; Huehnergard 2006, p. 120. Note, however, that the origin of the form *əlli* is still debated; see, for example, the discussion in Grand'Henry 1972, pp. 141–42; D. Cohen 1975, p. 221.

[54] Joüon and Muraoka 1991, vol. 2, pp. 537–38, §145d.

[55] Tirosh-Becker 1988, pp. 251, 273.

every such use of Hebrew *ha* is translated by *əlli*, and we also find examples of *əlli* translating the Hebrew relative pronoun *ʾăšer*. Examples:

Jer 34:18 (*hafṭarat Mišpāṭīm*):

ונג'על אילא ארג'אל **אלי** ג'אייזין אילא העדי. **אלדי** ליש תבתו אילא כלאם אלהאעד

וְנָתַתִּי אֶת־הָאֲנָשִׁים **הָעֹבְרִים** אֶת־בְּרִתִי **אֲשֶׁר** לֹא־הֵקִימוּ אֶת־דִּבְרֵי הַבְּרִית

'I will make the men **who** violated My covenant, **who** did not fulfill the terms of the covenant.'[56]

1 Kings 6:2 (*hafṭarat Tərûmâ*):

ואלבית **אלי** בנא אצולטאן שלמה לאללאה

וְהַבַּיִת **אֲשֶׁר** בָּנָה הַמֶּלֶךְ שְׁלֹמֹה לַיהוָה

'The House **which** King Solomon built for the Lord.'

This pronoun also serves as the first component in the pattern אלי יפעל that translates some of the occurrences of an infinitive construct in the original Hebrew text,[57] for example:

Mal 3:14 (*hafṭarat Shabbat Ha-Gadol*):

קולתיו באטל **אלי יעבד** אללאה

אֲמַרְתֶּם שָׁוְא **עֲבֹד** אֱלֹהִים

'You have said, "It is useless **to serve** God." '

4.3. The Eighth Verbal Stem

The conservative traits of SHC are observed also in verb morphology. Such is the presence of the verbal stem with the infix *t* (eighth stem) in SHC, **iCtaCaCa > iCtəCəC* (**iftaʿala > iftəʿəl*). It should be noted that the use of this verbal stem has diminished in maghrebian dialects and is on the verge of disappearing.[58] Eighth verbal stem forms are documented also in the Constantinian *šarḥ* to other biblical and post-biblical books as well as in Moroccan *šarḥ* traditions.[59] Examples:

Isa 41:5 (*hafṭarat Lēḵ Ləḵā*):

נצ'רו לג'זיראת ויכ'אפ'ו. טראף לארץ' **ירתעדו**

רָאוּ אִיִּים וְיִרָאוּ קְצוֹת הָאָרֶץ **יֶחֱרָדוּ**

'The coastlands look on in fear. The ends of earth tremble.'

1 Sam 20:30 (*hafṭarat Maḥar Ḥodeš*):

האודא ערפ'ת אן **תכ'תאר** אנתא לולד ישי

הֲלוֹא יָדַעְתִּי כִּי־**בֹחֵר** אַתָּה לְבֶן־יִשַׁי

'I know that you side with the son of Jesse.'

---

[56] On the metathesis in the word האעד, see Tirosh-Becker 2010a, pp. 513–15.

[57] See also in the *šarḥ* to Psalms: Tirosh-Becker 1988, p. 252. For other options for translating Hebrew infinitive constructs in Constantinian Judeo-Arabic, see Tirosh-Becker 2006, pp. 350–52.

[58] M. Cohen 1912, pp. 222–27; P. Marçais 1956, p. 196; Grand'Henry 1972, pp. 63–64; D. Cohen 1975, p. 126; P. Marçais 1977, pp. 63–64; Yoda 2005, pp. 179–81.

[59] Tirosh-Becker 2006, pp. 356–57; Tirosh-Becker 1990a, p. 199; Tirosh-Becker 2011, pp. 194–95; Bar-Asher 1988, p. 17; Bar-Asher 1991, p. 21; Bar-Asher 2010a, p. 184.

4.4. The Seventh Verbal Stem

Another conservative phenomenon in SHC's verbal system is the favoring of the seventh verbal stem **inCaCaCa* > *nəCCəC* (**infaʿala* > *nəfʿəl*) for denoting the passive voice, over the colloquial reflexive/passive verbal stem with a prefix *t/tt*, *ttəCCəC* (*ttəfʿəl*).[60] Examples:

Isa 41:16 (*hafṭarat Lēḵ Ləḵā*):

ואנתא תזהא באללאה. במקדדס ישראל **תנשכר**

וְאַתָּה תָּגִיל בַּיהוָה בִּקְדוֹשׁ יִשְׂרָאֵל **תִּתְהַלָּל**

'But you shall rejoice in the Lord, and glory in the Holy One of Israel.'

Hos 12:2 (*hafṭarat Wayyēṣē*):

והאעד מעא אשור יקטעו. ואלזית למאצר **ינג'אב**

וּבְרִית עִם־אַשּׁוּר יִכְרֹתוּ וְשֶׁמֶן לְמִצְרַיִם **יוּבָל**

'Now they make a covenant with Assyria, now oil is carried to Egypt.'

4.5. Remnants of the Fourth Verbal Stem

As in other maghrebian dialects, the fourth verbal stem has ceased to function as a productive category in JAC, with only a few relic participle forms in the language of the Constantinian *šarḥ*.[61] The word *muxīf* (מוכ'יף), which translates the Hebrew word *nôrā* (נוֹרָא 'awe-inspiring, revered'), is an active participle of the fourth verbal stem of the root √*xwf*[62] and is an example of this conservative trait in SHC. Another such example in SHC is the form *muġīt* (מוגית 'savior') from the root √*ġwṯ*.[63] The Hebrew letter *vav* in both מוכ'יף and מוגית denotes the quality of the vowel *u* and not its length. For example:

Mal 3:23 (*hafṭarat Shabbat Ha-Gadol*):

קבל מג'י נהאר אללאה אלכביר **ולמוכ'יף**

לִפְנֵי בּוֹא יוֹם יְהוָה הַגָּדוֹל **וְהַנּוֹרָא**

'Before the coming of the awesome, **fearful** day of the Lord.'

2 Sam 22:42 (*hafṭarat Haʾăzīnû*):

יעייטו וליש **מוגית**

יִשְׁעוּ וְאֵין **מֹשִׁיעַ**

'They looked, and there was none to deliver.'

The Hebrew word *nôrā* (נוֹרָא) is sometimes translated in SHC by the word *mawxūf* (מוכ'וף). This word is also limited to the language of the *šarḥ*,[64] for example:

---

[60] I do not elaborate on this phenomenon herein, as I have discussed it at length elsewhere; see Tirosh-Becker 1989, pp. 305–09; Tirosh-Becker 2006, pp. 355–56. On the seventh verbal stem in maghrebian dialects, see P. Marçais 1977, pp. 62–63; D. Cohen 1975, p. 125; M. Cohen 1912, pp. 218–22; Grand'Henry 1972, pp. 62–63. On the verbal stem with a prefix *t/tt*, see P. Marçais 1977, pp. 66–67; D. Cohen 1975, pp. 123–24; M. Cohen 1912, pp. 227–31; Fischer and Jastrow 1980, p. 264, §12.4.6.2. For a comprehensive study on the passive voice in Arabic dialects, see Retsö 1983.

[61] On this phenomenon in maghrebian dialects, see Fischer and Jastrow 1980, p. 46, §3.8.1. A few participle forms of the fourth verbal stem are documented also in the JA dialect of Algiers; see M. Cohen 1912, p. 212. Cf. in Baghdad Blanc 1964b, p. 26.

[62] Ben Sedira 1995, p. 95.

[63] On the shift of the fricative interdental consonants, see n. 31 above. The participle form *muġīt* occurs also in the Constantinian *šarḥ* to Psalms (e.g., Psalm 7:11, מוֹשִׁיעַ); see Tirosh-Becker 1988, pp. 227–28.

[64] This passive participle of the hollow triliteral stem √*xwf* follows the pattern of verbs with a weak first radical; see §5.4 below.

Mal 1:14 (*hafṭarat Tôlədōṯ*):

וסמי **מוכ'וף** פ'לאומום

וּשְׁמִי **נוֹרָא** בַגּוֹיִם

'My name in **revered** among the nations.'

Both translation alternants for *nôrā* (נוֹרָא), *mawxūf* and *muxīf*, appear also in the Constantinian *šarḥ* to Psalms.[65] *Muxīf* as a translation of *nôrā* appears in Moroccan *šarḥ* traditions as well.[66]

The two aforementioned alternants, *mawxūf* and *muxīf*, also translate the Hebrew word *môrā* (מוֹרָא 'fear, reverence'), although due to the rareness of this biblical Hebrew word, we did not find both alternants in the same text. Namely, in the sole occurrence in which *môrā* was translated by a participle form in SHC, it was translated as *mawxūf* (מוכ'וף).[67] While in the only occurrence of *môrā* in Psalms, it was translated *muxīf* (מוכ'יף).[68] The example in SHC is:

Jer 32:21 (*hafṭarat Bəhar Sīnay*):

וביד קוייה ובדראע ממדודה **ובמוכ'וף** כביר

וּבְיָד חֲזָקָה וּבְאֶזְרוֹעַ נְטוּיָה **וּבְמוֹרָא** גָּדוֹל

'With a strong hand and an outstretched arm, and with great terror.'

In a Passover Haggadah from Algiers, we also find the word *môrā* translated *muxīf* (מוכ'יף).[69]

4.6. Plural Feminine Participle Forms

Unlike the spoken Judeo-Arabic dialect of Constantine (JAC), and many other maghrebian dialects,[70] in which the distinct feminine plural participle forms ceased to exist, these forms were preserved in SHC. Hence, while in JAC the masculine plural form with the suffix *-īn* denotes the participle of both genders, in SHC the feminine plural form with the suffix *-āt* is still in use, reflecting the Hebrew feminine plural participle forms. For example:

1 Kings 3:17 (*hafṭarat Miqqēṣ*):

אנא ולמרה האדי. **סאכנאת** פ'י בית וחדה

אֲנִי וְהָאִשָּׁה הַזֹּאת **יֹשְׁבֹת** בְּבַיִת אֶחָד

'This woman and I live in the same house.'[71]

Ezek 29:12 (*hafṭarat Vāʾērā*):

ובלדאנהא פ'י וסט בלדאן **מכ'רובאת** יכונו כ'אלייה

וְעָרֶיהָ בְּתוֹךְ עָרִים **מָחֳרָבוֹת** תִּהְיֶיןָ שְׁמָמָה

'And its cities shall be the most desolate of ruined cities.'

---

[65] E.g., Renassia 1954; Psalm 47:3 אין אללאה עאלי **מוכ'וף** (כִּי־יְהוָֹה עֶלְיוֹן **נוֹרָא** 'For the Lord Most High is **awesome**'); Psalm 76:8 אנתא **מוכ'יף** אנתא ומן יוקף קודאמך (אַתָּה **נוֹרָא** אַתָּה וּמִי־יַעֲמֹד לְפָנֶיךָ 'O You! You are **awesome**! Who can withstand You').

[66] Bar-Asher 2001, part 2, pp. 54, 399, 518; Tedghi 2006, p. 305.

[67] Other occurrences of מורא in the *hafṭarot* were translated by the noun *xawf* ('fear'), e.g., Mal 1:6 (*hafṭarat Tôlədōṯ*): ואידא סייד אנא. ואיין **כ'אופ'י** (וְאִם־אֲדוֹנִים אָנִי אַיֵּה **מוֹרָאִי** 'and if I am a master, where is the **reverence** due Me?').

[68] Renassia 1954; Psalm 76:12 ואעדו ואכ'לצו לאללאה אילאהכום ג'מיע דואיירו ידדיו יג'יבו הדייא ללכ'וף (**ללמוכ'יף**) (נִדְרוּ וְשַׁלְּמוּ לַיהוָה אֱלֹהֵיכֶם כָּל־סְבִיבָיו יֹבִילוּ שַׁי **לַמּוֹרָא** 'Make vows and pay them to the Lord your God; all who are around Him shall bring tribute to the **Awesome** One'). Note here the use of the alternant *xawf.*

[69] Attal 1975, p. 21 — a translation of Deuteronomy 21:8. According to Ratzabi, the Hebrew word *môrā* was translated in different sources of Saʿadya Gaʾon's *Tafsīr* as מכ'וף or מכ'יף; Ratzabi 1985, p. 63. See also the translation variants of נוראות therein.

[70] D. Cohen 1975, p. 94; W. Marçais 1908, p. 76.

[71] Note that the dual form of the participle is not used in the JA translation to this verse in SHC. The dual participle form is not used in JAC. On the limited presence of dual forms in Arabic dialects, see Blanc 1970, pp. 42–57. In SHC we do find dual forms denoting quantities, for example: 2 Kings 7:18 (*hafṭarat Məṣōrāʿ*): **כילתין** שעיר במתקאל וכילה סמיד במתקאל (**סָאתַיִם** שְׂעֹרִים בְּשֶׁקֶל וּסְאָה־סֹלֶת בְּשֶׁקֶל '**Two** ***seahs*** of barley ... and a *seah* of choice flour').

The conservative trait of preserving feminine plural participle form is found also in the Constantinian *šarḥ* to Psalms, and in the *šarḥ* tradition from Tafilalt, Morocco.[72]

5. Non-classical Features Unique to the *šarḥ*

In addition to phenomena that are clearly conservative in nature, the language of the *šarḥ* also includes non-classical features that are not used in the spoken dialect. These are identified by the speakers of the dialect as characteristic of the elevated language of the *šarḥ*. Some of these features may have been introduced into the *šarḥ* during the period when they were employed in the spoken dialect, as part of the effort to make the biblical text more comprehensible to the community. However, with time the *šarḥ* itself gained a special status and has become more resistant to change, while the spoken dialect continued to evolve. As a result these dialectal features are found only, or mainly, in the language of the *šarḥ*. It should be noted that *šarḥ* traditions were also influenced by relocation, from one community to another, of rabbis who taught the *šarḥ*, adding further complexity to its language by introducing features from other dialects.[73]

5.1. The Adverb "Now"

It is well known that the adverb "now," which is frequently conveyed in CA by the word *alʾān* (أَلْآنَ), is expressed in Arabic dialects by a variety of lexemes.[74] Even among maghrebian dialects, one finds several dialectal words to denote 'now':[75] *tawwa* in Tunisian dialects[76] and *tˁuwa* in the dialect of the Jews of Tripoli, Libya (both from CA *tawwan*, تَوًّا),[77] *dāba* in Moroccan dialects and in the Jewish dialects of Tlemcen and Algiers,[78] and *dəlwaqt* in Algerian dialects (with numerous variants such as *dəlwaq*, *dərwaq*, *ḏərwaq*, *dlūk*, and *drūk*).[79] Many of the dialectal words for 'now' are constructed from a demonstrative pronoun accompanied with a definite noun that denotes time; for example, هٰذِهِ ٱلسَّاعَة leads to the Baghdadi variant *hassa*, هٰذَا ٱلْحِين leads to *halḥīn* in some Palestinian dialects, and ذَا ٱلْوَقْت leads to *dəlwaqt* and its variants.[80]

The adverb denoting 'now' in the spoken JAC dialect is *dūqa*, also pronounced *dawqa* and *ḍūqa*. In SHC, on the other hand, the dialectal variants that are used to denote 'now' are *dəlwaq* (דלווק) and less frequently *dəlwaqt* (דלווקת).[81] This form, which is not used in daily spoken JAC, is common to various Constantinian *šurūḥ* and is also used in the language register of the Constantinian rabbanite elite.[82] In this register this aforementioned word is sometimes pronounced *dərwaq*, with an interchange of the liquid consonants *l* and *r*.

---

[72] Tirosh-Becker 1989, pp. 304–05, and n. 100; Bar-Asher 1991, p. 22.

[73] An example is the use of the Tunisian adverb *yāsər* as an alternative translation in the Constantinian *šarḥ*; see §5.3 below.

[74] Fischer 1959, pp. 143–56; Levin 1994, p. 259.

[75] I mention here only representative examples of the main dialectal forms; needless to say, each has many local variants. For a more detailed review of the various variants, see P. Marçais 1977, pp. 254–55.

[76] The Jews of Tunis also use, albeit less frequently, the form *ḥīna*, and rarely the older form *delḥīn*; see D. Cohen 1975, p. 243. Also see Talmoudi 1980, p. 160 [tɛw:ɛ]; Cheraifi 2005, p. 480; Attal 1999, pp. 46*, 48.

[77] Yoda 2005, pp. 265, 267.

[78] Heath 2002, pp. 118–19, 452; Colin 1993–96, vol. 3, p. 495; according to Collin, *drūk* is used in Marakesh; see ibid., p. 524; Cheraifi 2005, p. 480; M. Cohen 1912, pp. 373–74, 478; Ben Sedira 1995, p. 98; W. Marçais 1911, pp. 289–90.

[79] M. Cohen 1912, pp. 373–74, 478; Tirosh-Becker 1988, pp. 301–02; Laraba 1981, p. 112 [*ḍurk*]); Grand'Henry 1972, pp. 160–61; P. Marçais 1977, pp. 254–55.

[80] Fischer 1959, pp. 143–49; Blanc 1964a, pp. 138–39; Levin 1994, p. 259.

[81] These variants are sometimes spelled with a single *vav*: דלוקת ,דלוק. There were two occurrences in SHC of the spelling דאלוקת in the *šarḥ* to the *hafṭarot* for Leviticus (Jer 32:8, *hafṭarat Bəhar Sīnay*; Isa 44:1, *hafṭarat Wayyiqrā*), although it is usually spelled in this section of the *šarḥ* דלווק as in the rest of SHC.

[82] This register was used in conversations among rabbis and scholars, and in the original literature composed by them, such as commentaries.

The adverb *dəlwaq* / *dəlwaqt* that translates the biblical Hebrew *ʿattâ* (עַתָּה 'now') also frequently renders the Hebrew modal interjection (or vocative) *nā* (נָא), which indicates a request or a plea.[83] Interpreting *nā* (נָא) as denoting "now" is an age-old tradition that goes back to the Second Temple period and is attested in numerous Judeo-Arabic Bible translations.[84] Examples in SHC:

Jud 13:4 (*hafṭarat Nāśō*):

ודלווק אשחרזי **דלווק**. וליש תשרבי אשראב ואסכר

וְעַתָּה הִשָּׁמְרִי **נָא** וְאַל־תִּשְׁתִּי יַיִן וְשֵׁכָר

'Now be careful not to drink wine or other intoxicant.'

1 Sam 20:29 (*hafṭarat Maḥar Ḥodeš*):

ודלווקת אידא וג'דת מחננה פ'י עייניך. נתמנע **דלווק** וננצ'ר אילא כ'ואני

וְעַתָּה אִם־מָצָאתִי חֵן בְּעֵינֶיךָ אִמָּלְטָה **נָּא** וְאֶרְאֶה אֶת־אֶחָי

'Do me a favor, let me slip away to see my kinsmen.'

5.2. The Presentative *hawda*

The presentative *hawda* (האודא) is unique to the language of SHC and is not used in JAC.[85] It translates the Hebrew presentatives *hinnē* (הִנֵּה) and *halô* (הֲלוֹא), which occur in the biblical text of the *hafṭarot*. *Hawda* is an invariable form, possibly originating from *hā-huwa-ḏā* (هَا هُوَ ذَا) in CA.[86] Note that already the Medieval Judeo-Arabic הוד'א and Medieval Christian Arabic هوذا were invariable in the 3mSg form.[87] It is found, spelled הוד'א, also in Saʿadya Gaʾon's *Tafsīr* as a translation of the Hebrew *hinnē* (הִנֵּה). In addition to SHC, *hawda* also serves in *šarḥ* traditions of other Jewish communities in North Africa and Egypt, and likewise *hōḏa* in Iraq.[88] Examples:

Ezek 37:19 (*hafṭarat Wayyiggaš*):

האודא אנא נאכ'ד אילא עוד יוסף

הִנֵּה אֲנִי לֹקֵחַ אֶת־עֵץ יוֹסֵף

'I am going to take the stick of Joseph.'

1 Kings 1:11 (*hafṭarat Ḥayyê Sārâ*):

האודא סמעתי אן צלטן אדוניה ולד חגית

הֲלוֹא שָׁמַעַתְּ כִּי מָלַךְ אֲדֹנִיָּהוּ בֶן־חַגִּית

'You must have heard that Adonijah son of Ḥaggit has assumed the kingship.'

---

[83] The Hebrew word *nā* (נָא) is sometimes translated as *b-ġərba* (בגרבה). For example, in the first occurrence of נָא in the verse 1 Sam 20:29 (*hafṭarat Maḥar Ḥodeš*), a part of which is cited in the main text, it was translated as *b-ġərba*: וקאל אטלקני **ברגבה** (וַיֹּאמֶר שַׁלְּחֵנִי **נָא** 'He said, "**please** let me go"'). Another example: Jud 4:19 (*hafṭarat Bəšallaḥ*): אסקיני **ברגבה** שואי מא אן עטשת (הַשְׁקִינִי־**נָא** מְעַט־מַיִם כִּי צָמֵאתִי '**Please** let me have some water, I am thirsty'). On *b-ġərba* in other *šarḥ* traditions, see Bar-Asher 2001, part 2, pp. 496–97; part 4, p. 85; Doron 1979, pp. 338–39.

[84] Blau 1980b, pp. 187–91. For examples, see Bar-Asher 1988, p. 28; Bar-Asher 2001, part 4, p. 97; Tedghi 1994, p. 110; Hary 2009, pp. 195–96; Doron 1979, pp. 335–38.

[85] In SHC this presentative is almost always spelled האודא. There were only two occurrences of the spelling האודה, and two occurrences of the spelling הודא. A detailed discussion on the various presentatives used in the different genres of the Judeo-Arabic literature of Constantine, based on a lecture that I presented at a Conference "On Hebrew and Jewish Languages" in honor of Professor Moshe Bar-Asher, held in Jerusalem November 2007, will be published elsewhere.

[86] For a discussion on the derivation of هوذا, see Blau 1966–67, vol. 2, p. 466 n. 15; Fischer 1959, pp. 161–62, 180. Cf. Blanc 1964b, p. 30 and n. 32.

[87] Blau 1980a, pp. 174, 325–26, §260; Blau 2002, pp. 51, §119; Blau 2006, pp. 737–38; Blau 1966–67, pp. 465–67, §§364–65.

[88] Bar-Asher 1988, p. 18; Bar-Asher 2001, 3, pp. 168, 350, 355, 514–15, 535; Tedghi 1993, pp. 538–39; Tedghi 1994, p. 110; Hary 2009, pp. 197–98; Blanc 1964b, pp. 29–30. The word הודא is used also in *əš-Šarḥ əS-Sūsānī* from the sixteenth century, see Doron 1979, pp. 328–31.

5.3. The Adverb "Very"

The Hebrew adverb *mə'ōḏ* (מְאֹד), which means 'exceedingly, greatly, very,' is translated in SHC by the Arabic word *mawǧūd* (מוג'וד), sometimes pronounced by informants who are rabbis as *mowǧūd*.[89] The use of *mawǧūd* as an adverb to denote 'very' by the Jews of Constantine is restricted to the language of the *šarḥ*.[90] This probably results from a semantic extension of the regular meaning of this word in spoken JAC and other Algerian Arabic dialects, which is "exists."[91] In contrast, in spoken JAC the word *bəzzāf* is used to denote 'very' and 'much.'[92] The word *bəzzāf* is frequent also in the Jewish dialect of Algiers, in the Muslim dialect of Cherchell (near Algiers), and in Moroccan dialects.[93] Evidently, the use of the word *mawǧūd* to denote the adverb 'very' was unfamiliar to speakers of JAC, hence an alternative translation was added in parenthesis for most of the occurrences of this word in SHC. The alternative translation that was offered in parenthesis was *yāsər* (יאסר), which is typical to Tunisian dialects,[94] and not the local colloquial word *bəzzāf*. This is not that surprising since Constantine is relatively close to the Tunisian border.[95] In a few occurrences in SHC, *ǧidda* (ג'דדא, from CA جدًّا) was favored over *mawǧūd*, suggesting an influence of the famous Medieval Judeo-Arabic Bible translation of Saʿadya Gaʾon, which is known to have influenced many later *šurūḥ*.[96] Like *mawǧūd*, the word *ǧidda* is also accompanied in SHC by the colloquial word *yāsər* in parenthesis. Examples:

1 Sam 11:15 (*hafṭarat Qōraḥ*):

> ופ'רח תממא שאול וג'מיע נאס ישראל חתא **מוג'וד (יאסר)**
>
> וַיִּשְׂמַח שָׁם שָׁאוּל וְכָל־אַנְשֵׁי יִשְׂרָאֵל עַד־**מְאֹד**
>
> 'and Saul and all the men of Israel had a great celebration there.'

Ezek 37:10 (*hafṭarat Sabbath Ḥol Ha-Moʿed Pesaḥ*):

> ג'יש כביר **מוג'וד מוג'וד (יאסר יאסר)**
>
> חַיִל גָּדוֹל **מְאֹד־מְאֹד**
>
> 'a vast multitude.'

1 Kings 2:12 (*hafṭarat Wayəḥī*):

> ותצאוובת צלטנתו **ג'דדא (יאסר)**
>
> וַתִּכֹּן מַלְכֻתוֹ **מְאֹד**
>
> 'and his rule was firmly established.'

---

[89] This adverb is in the form of the passive participle of √wǧd. In Constantine the diphthong in this form is preserved; see Tirosh-Becker 1988, pp. 189, 192, 301. It is also preserved in the Arabic dialect of Tlemcen; see W. Marçais 1902, pp. 66–67. In the Judeo-Arabic dialects of Algiers and Tunis, the diphthong in this word is contracted; see M. Cohen 1912, pp. 188–89; D. Cohen 1975, p. 101.

[90] *Mawǧūd* is not listed among the maghrebian words that denote "beaucoup," see P. Marçais 1977, pp. 267–68.

[91] Ben Sedira 1995, p. 266. In Takroûna (Tunisia) the word *mužûd* also has the meaning of "exists in abundance"; see Marçais and Guîga 1958–61, p. 4251. The active participle of the same root, *wāǧəd*, is used to denote "abundant, many, much" in post-classical Yemeni Arabic; see Piamenta 1991, vol. 2, p. 518. In Gulf Arabic, the word *wājid*, and its variant *wāyid*, denotes "much, many" and is also used as an adverb meaning "very"; see Holes 2001, vol. 1, p. 552. I would like to thank Professor Antoine Lonnet for referring me to this use of *wāǧəd*.

[92] See already in Dozy 1881, vol. 1, p. 614.

[93] M. Cohen 1912, p. 375; P. Marçais 1977, p. 267; Caubet 1993, p. 197; Colin 1993–96, vol. 3, p. 692; Bar-Asher 2001, part 4, p. 215; Grand'Henry 1972, p. 138.

[94] D. Cohen 1975, p. 238; Attal 1999, pp. 31*, 77.

[95] The word *yāsər* was also known to Jews from southeast Morocco as characteristic of Tunisian Judeo-Arabic. They encountered it in the speech of Tunisian Jews who immigrated to their Moroccan towns, and in Judeo-Arabic books printed in Tunisia. See Bar-Asher 2010b, pp. 285–86.

[96] On the influence of Saʿadya Gaʾon's *Tafsīr* on the translation of Hebrew *mə'ōḏ* by *zədda* (זדא) in Moroccan *šarḥ* traditions, see Bar-Asher 1991, p. 23. Cf. Tedghi 1993, pp. 540–41 n. 1. The word *giddan* (גדן) as a translation of the Hebrew *mə'ōḏ* occurs also in a Judeo-Arabic *šarḥ* of the Scroll of Esther from Egypt (while in the Egyptian *šarḥ* to Genesis and to the Passover Haggadah the word קווי is used); see Hary 2009, p. 197.

5.4. Passive Participles of Some Hollow Triliteral Roots

Another dialectal feature that is limited to the language of SHC is the passive participle forms of hollow triliteral roots, which follow the pattern of roots with a weak first radical. In SHC we found two roots that exhibit this phenomenon. These are the participle *mawxūf* (מוכ'וף) of the hollow triliteral root √*xwf*, and the participle *mawǧūb* of the hollow triliteral root √*ǧyb*. While their perfect forms are *xāf* ('was afraid') and *ǧāb* ('brought') as expected of hollow triliteral roots, their dialectal passive participle in SHC *mawxūf* and *mawǧūb* follow the pattern of roots with a weak first radical, such as *mawǧūd*, whose root is √*wǧd*.[97] In CA we would have expected the passive participle *maxūf* (مَخُوف) for the root √*xwf*. Note that the verbal form *ǧāb* in itself is non-classical, as it originated from *ǧāʾa bi* (جَاءَ ب), and its record in Judeo-Arabic dates back at least to the ninth century.[98] Examples:

Mal 1:14 (*hafṭarat Tôlədōṯ*):

וסמי **מוכ'וף** פ'לאומום

וּשְׁמִי **נוֹרָא** בַגּוֹיִם

'My name is **revered** among the nations.'[99]

2 Kings 12:10 (*hafṭarat Shabbat Shəqalim*):

אילא ג'מיע לפ'צ'צ'ה **אלמוג'וב** לבית אללאה

אֶת־כָּל־הַכֶּסֶף **הַמּוּבָא** בֵית־יְהוָה

'All the money that **was brought** into the House of the Lord.'[100]

Another example of a dialectal passive participle of a hollow triliteral stem √*qwl*, which follows the pattern of stems with a weak first radical, is *mawqūl* ('was told'). This form is found in the Constantinian *šarḥ* to Mishnah tractate *ʾAḇot*, in R. Renassia's commentary on tractate *ʾAḇot*, and in his commentary on Psalms.[101] Likewise, the passive participle *muqul* is documented in the JA dialect of Tripoli, Libya.[102] A similar form *mūṣūb*, from the root √*ṣwb*, is used in the JA dialect of Algiers.[103]

6. Dialectal Features in SHC

The language of SHC also includes some dialectal features that are prevalent in spoken JAC. Some of these colloquial attributes are pan-maghrebian, while others are of a local character. Furthermore, a few of these vernacular features are frequent in the *šarḥ*, while others reflect only a sporadic penetration of the spoken dialect into this text. I demonstrate a few of these traits herein.

6.1. Imperfect Forms of the First Person

The most prominent characteristic of maghrebian dialects is *nafʿal* for 1cSg imperfect and *nafʿalu* for 1cPl imperfect.[104] These forms are prevalent in SHC. For example:

---

[97] The root √*wxf* (probably through a methatesis of √*xwf*) appears in Dozy's dictionary, which reports the form *waxfān* (وَخْفَان) denoting a fearful person; see Dozy 1881, vol. 2, p. 798. As to *mawǧūb*, cf. the JA dialect of Tripoli, Libya, in which the passive participle form of √*žyb* is *məžyúb*; see Yoda 2005, p. 162.

[98] Blau 2006, p. 106; Blau 1980a, pp. 67, §54a; 69, §60a.

[99] See also §4.5 above.

[100] Note that in this example there is an attraction in gender. The word *mawǧūb* has a masculine form, although the grammatical gender of *fəḍḍa* is feminine, reflecting the grammatical masculine gender of the Hebrew word *kesef* (כֶּסֶף). The plural feminine form *mawǧūbāt* (מוג'ובאת) appears in the *šarḥ* to Psalm 45:15 as a translation for *mûḇāʾôṯ* (מוּבָאוֹת); see Renassia 1954[?].

[101] E.g., Renassia 1916b; *ʾAḇot* 5:8; *ʾAḇot* 1:1 (commentary); Renassia 1954[?]; Tirosh-Becker 2011, p. 198.

[102] Yoda 2005, p. 162.

[103] M. Cohen 1912, p. 191.

[104] Fischer and Jastrow 1980, p. 261, §12.4.2; P. Marçais 1977, p. 37.

1 Kings 1:14 (*hafṭarat Ḥayyê Sārâ*):

ואנא **נג'י** מן וראךּ. **ונכממל** אילא כלאמךּ

וַאֲנִי **אָבוֹא** אַחֲרַיִךְ **וּמִלֵּאתִי** אֶת־דְּבָרָיִךְ

'and I will come in after you and confirm your words.'

2 Kings 4:10 (*hafṭarat Wayyērā*):

נעמלו דלווקת עלי חייט סגיר. **ונג'עלו** ליה תממא סריר וטאבלה וכרסי ומנארה

נַעֲשֶׂה־נָּא עֲלִיַּת־קִיר קְטַנָּה **וְנָשִׂים** לוֹ שָׁם מִטָּה וְשֻׁלְחָן וְכִסֵּא וּמְנוֹרָה

'Let us make a small enclosed upper chamber and place a bed, a table, a chair, and a lamp stand there for him.'

6.2. The Verbal Stem *CCāC*

Another well-documented North African phenomenon is the use of the verbal stem *CCāC* (*fʿāl*) for indicating a process of change in the properties of an object or a person, for example, *smān* 'to gain weight' and *ḍyāq* 'to become narrow.' This verbal stem originated probably from the CA eleventh stem اِفْعَالّ, or possibly from the CA ninth verbal stem اِفْعَلّ.[105] However, the use of the *CCāC* stem in the Maghreb[106] is much broader than the respective use of the eleventh and ninth verbal stems in CA, where it had been limited to colors and defects.[107] The dialectal verbal stem *CCāC* is also attested in SHC, for example:[108]

Isa 1:18 (*hafṭarat Dəḇārīm*):

אידא יכונו כ'טייאתכם כיף לקרמז. כיף אתלג' **יבייאצ'ו**. אידא **יחמארו** כיף אלפ'ווה. כיף אצוף יכונו

אִם־יִהְיוּ חֲטָאֵיכֶם כַּשָּׁנִים כַּשֶּׁלֶג **יַלְבִּינוּ** אִם־**יַאְדִּימוּ** כַתּוֹלָע כַּצֶּמֶר יִהְיוּ

'Be your sins like crimson they can turn snow-white. Be they red as dyed wool they can become like fleece.'

6.3. The Verbs "Eat" and "Take"

The CA verbs *ʾakala* (أَكَلَ 'ate') and *ʾaxaḏa* (أَخَذَ 'took') have undergone a variety of changes in Arabic dialects once the initial glottal stop was lost.[109] Among the Jewish dialects of the Maghreb, there are three distinct paths of change in these verbs.[110] In most of the Jewish Moroccan dialects, the perfect form of these verbs is *kəl* and *xəd*, reflecting a strong biliteral stem.[111] In contrast, in the Jewish dialects of eastern Morocco, Algiers, Constantine, and Tunis, the perfect form of these verbs reflects a weak triliteral stem, *kla* and *xda*.[112] A third option, reflecting a hollow triliteral stem, *kal* and *xad*, is used in Tafilalt in southeastern Morocco.[113] In SHC we find the dialectal forms *kla* and *xda* that are common in JAC. Interestingly, the imperative forms of these verbs in JAC, *kūl* and *xūd*,[114]

[105] Fischer and Jastrow 1980, p. 264, §12.4.6.1; Grand'Henry 1972, p. 66; P. Marçais 1977, pp. 55, 64–65; P. Marçais 1956, p. 200; D. Cohen 1975, p. 122.

[106] Brunot 1950. On the inflection patterns of this stem in various maghrebian dialects, see M. Cohen 1912, p. 236–37; W. Marçais 1902, p. 85.

[107] Wright 1981, vol. 1, pp. 43–44, §§58–59.

[108] A possible example for such a verb is found already in an incunabula of *Maqre Dardeqe* (Naples 1488) – *mlāḥ* ('became pretty'), although it may alternatively be the plural form of *mlīḥ* ('pretty'); see Tirosh-Becker 1990b, p. 66.

[109] Fischer and Jastrow 1980, pp. 67, §5.1.3.1; 183–84, §10.2.3.1; 226, §11.2.5.9.

[110] Heath 2002, pp. 379–86, 571. A fourth possibility, *kəll*, with a geminate triliteral stem, occurs in a few Muslim Moroccan dialects, but is not documented in Jewish Moroccan dialects; see ibid., p. 381.

[111] Heath 2002, pp. 380–81, 571.

[112] M. Cohen 1912, pp. 198–99; D. Cohen 1975, pp. 108–10; Tirosh-Becker 1988, pp. 203–04. These forms are also common in Muslim dialects, e.g., Talmoudi 1980, pp. 92–93; P. Marçais 1956, p. 173; W. Marçais 1902, p. 71; Laraba 1981, p. 77.

[113] The Jews of Tafilalt pronounce it *tal*, due to the *k > t shift in their dialect; see Heath and Bar-Asher 1982, p. 67.

[114] On the long vowel in the imperative form of hollow triliteral stems in maghrebian dialects, see M. Cohen 1912, pp. 189–90; D. Cohen 1975, pp. 102–03; P. Marçais 1956, pp. 162, 164; Talmoudi 1980, pp. 85–86; W. Marçais 1902, p. 68.

reflect a hollow triliteral stem, and not a weak triliteral stem as in the perfect forms.[115] These imperative forms appear in SHC as well. Finally, the imperfect forms in JAC *nākul*, *tākul*, and so on exhibit a long vowel compensating for the loss of the original glottal stop (CA *taʾkulu*).[116] Examples:

1 Kings 3:20 (*hafṭarat Miqqēṣ*):

וכ'דאת אילא ולדי מן חדאייא

וַתִּקַּח אֶת־בְּנִי מֵאֶצְלִי

'and **took** my son from my side.'

1 Kings 19:21 (*hafṭarat Pīnḥās*):

ופ'י מואען לבקר טבכ'להם אלחם. ועטא ללקום **וכלאו**

וּבִכְלִי הַבָּקָר בִּשְּׁלָם הַבָּשָׂר וַיִּתֵּן לָעָם **וַיֹּאכֵלוּ**

'He boiled their meat with the gear of the oxen and gave it to the people, and they **ate.**'

1 Sam 20:31 (*hafṭarat Maḥar Ḥodeš*):

ודלווק אבעת **וכ'וד** אילו אילי

וְעַתָּה שְׁלַח **וְקַח** אֹתוֹ אֵלַי

'Now then, have him brought to me.'

Jer 7:21 (*hafṭarat Ṣav*):

צעידאתכם זידו עלא דבאיחכם **וכולו** לחם

עֹלוֹתֵיכֶם סְפוּ עַל־זִבְחֵיכֶם **וְאִכְלוּ** בָשָׂר

'Add your burnt offerings to your other sacrifices and **eat** the meat!'

6.4. Perfect Inflectional Morpheme of 2cPl

An example for a dialectal phenomenon in SHC, which is characteristic of the local spoken JAC, is the 2cPl perfect suffix *-tīw*. As in many other sedentary Arabic dialects, the distinction between 2mPl and 2fPl forms in the perfect conjugation has ceased to exist in JAC.[117] The common form in many North African dialects ends with the suffix *-tu*, for example *ktəbtu* ('you [pl.] wrote'). However, in JAC and SHC, we find the 2cPl perfect suffix *-tīw* (e.g., *ktəbtīw*) in which the plural inflectional morpheme *-u* is realized as a semi-vowel *w* when added to the 2cSg morpheme *-ti*. It should be noted that in JAC, like in many other maghrebian sedentary dialects, the distinction between 2mSg and 2fSg perfect was also lost.[118] However, unlike other dialects, in JAC there is a free alternation between two 2cSg perfect forms: *ktəbt* and *ktəbti*.[119] This phenomenon reflects the location of the city of Constantine on a dialectal junction,[120] between a region in which the form *ktəbt* is used for both 2mSg and 2fSg perfect (e.g., in Jijel [formerly Djidjelli]), and a region in which the form *ktəbti* is used for both 2mSg and 2fSg perfect (e.g., in Skikda [formerly Phillipeville] and Edough).[121] Nonetheless, in JAC when a pronominal object suffix is added to a 2cSg perfect form, the alternant *ktəbti* is always selected, for example, *trəktīh* ('you left him'). Similarly, when the plural morpheme *-u* is added to the 2cSg form, the *-ti* alternant is always used resulting in the suffix *-tīw*.[122] This form is also documented in Skikda and in the dialect of one of the tribes in the Edough

[115] This is attested in other maghrebian dialects as well; see for example D. Cohen 1975, p. 109.

[116] Tirosh-Becker 1988, p. 204. Cf. Fischer and Jastrow 1980, p. 67, §5.1.3.1.

[117] Fischer and Jastrow 1980, pp. 61–64, §5.1.1.

[118] For details regarding dialects in which this distinction was lost or preserved, see Tirosh-Becker 1989, p. 301 and n. 83.

[119] Tirosh-Becker 1989, pp. 301–03.

[120] Another phenomenon that reflects the "junctionalism" in JAC is the two free alternative realizations [ž] and [ǧ] of the phoneme /ǧ/; see Tirosh-Becker 1989, pp. 296–97.

[121] Cantineau 1938, pp. 853–54, 864; Ostoya-Delmas 1938, p. 64.

[122] Tirosh-Becker 1989, pp. 303–04.

region (where *ktəbti* is used),[123] although it is not used by the Muslims of Constantine (MAC), who use the more customary form *ktəbtu*.[124] Examples:

Mal 1:2 (*hafṭarat Tôlədōṯ*):

חבבית אילכם קאל אללאה. **וקולתיו** באש חבביתינא

אָהַבְתִּי אֶתְכֶם אָמַר יְהוָה **וַאֲמַרְתֶּם** בַּמָּה אֲהַבְתָּנוּ

'I have shown you love, said the Lord. But **you ask**, "How have You shown us love?"'

Amos 2:12 (*hafṭarat Wayyēšeḇ*):

וסקיתיו אילא לפ'ראייז שראב. ועלא לאנבייא **וציתיו** ליקול. ליש תתנבבאו

וַתַּשְׁקוּ אֶת־הַנְּזִרִים יָיִן וְעַל־הַנְּבִיאִים **צִוִּיתֶם** לֵאמֹר לֹא תִּנָּבְאוּ

'But you made the nazirites drink wine and **ordered** the prophets not to prophecy.'

The only occurrence of a 2cPl perfect form in the *šarḥ* to the *hafṭarot* for Leviticus was *šʿaltu* (שאעלתו), which is of the *ktəbtu* type and not the *ktəbtīw* type:[125]

Jer 17:4 (*hafṭarat Bəḥuqqōtay*):

אן אלנאר **שאעלתו** פ'י אנפ'י חתא ללדואם תוקד (תשעל)

כִּי־אֵשׁ **קְדַחְתֶּם** בְּאַפִּי עַד־עוֹלָם תּוּקָד

'For you **have kindled** the flame of My wrath, which shall burn for all time.'

Note, however, that elsewhere in SHC the same word was written in the regular JAC form *šʿaltīw*:

Isa 50:11 (*hafṭarat ʿĒqeḇ*):

אמשיו פ'י צ'או נארכם. ופ'תשאשאת (אלדי) **שעלתיו**

לְכוּ בְּאוּר אֶשְׁכֶם וּבְזִיקוֹת **בִּעַרְתֶּם**

'Walk by the blaze of your fire. By the brands that you have lit!'

6.5. The Plural Form for "Nations"

Another dialectal phenomenon in SHC is the plural form of the word *ʾumma* (أُمَّة 'a nation'). In CA the plural form of this noun is *ʾumam* (أُمَم). This plural form (often pronounced without the initial glottal stop) is documented in many Arabic dictionaries.[126] On the other hand, in SHC as well as in other JA texts from Constantine, the plural form of this noun is *umūm* (אומום). *Umūm* most likely resulted from the phonetic process of vowel harmonization, assisted by the nasal-bilabial phoneme /m/ that occurs twice in this word. Examples:

Isa 49:22 (*hafṭarat ʿĒqeḇ*):

האודא נרפ'ד אילא **לאומום** ידדי. ואילא **לאומום** נרפ'פ'ע עלאמי

הִנֵּה אֶשָּׂא אֶל־**גּוֹיִם** יָדִי וְאֶל־**עַמִּים** אָרִים נִסִּי

'I will raise My hand to Nations and lift up My ensign to peoples.'

---

[123] Ostoya-Delmas 1938, p. 64; Mangion 1937, p. 374.

[124] Laraba 1981, p. 71.

[125] On the uniqueness of the *hafṭarot* to Leviticus, see §4.1 above.

[126] E.g., Cherbonneau 1973, vol. 1, p. 14; Beaussier 1958, p. 17; Biberstein-Kazimirski 1860, vol. 1, p. 52; Ben Sedira 1995, p. 6; Colin 1993–96, vol. 1, p. 28; Cheraifi 2005, p. 526; Blau 2001, p. 19; Avishur 2008, vol. 1, p. 90.

We find this plural form in the Constantinian *šarḥ* to other Books of the Bible (e.g., Psalms[127] and Job[128]), in the *šarḥ* to the liturgical poems known as the *Hošaʿnot,*[129] and even in the local Constantinian Judeo-Arabic newspaper *əl-Ḥikma.*[130] This plural form is also documented in a few other Algerian and Tunisian JA texts, including a *šarḥ* to a Passover Haggadah from Djerba[131] and a *šarḥ* to a Passover Haggadah from Algiers.[132]

Interestingly, in the *šarḥ* to the *hafṭratot* for Leviticus, the plural form *umam* (אמם) is used in all the occurrences, for example:[133]

Ezek 22:4 (*hafṭarat ʾAḥărê Môṯ*):

עלא האדך ג'עלתך מעאירה **ללאמם** ומסכ'רה לג'מיע אלאראצ'י

עַל־כֵּן נְתַתִּיךְ חֶרְפָּה **לַגּוֹיִם** וְקַלָּסָה לְכָל־הָאֲרָצוֹת

'Therefore I will make you the mockery of the nations and the scorn of all the lands.'

7. Summary

To conclude, in this discussion we demonstrated that the language of the Constantinian Judeo-Arabic translation of portions of the books of prophets, known as *hafṭarot,* is characterized by a mixture of linguistic elements. Conservative linguistic features are interwoven with colloquial phenomena creating an intricate combination, unique to this type of text. Nonetheless, despite the penetration of vernacular features, the numerous conservative traits as well as certain dialectal features that were perceived as characteristic of the *šarḥ* indicate that the language of the *šarḥ* was significantly elevated compared to the spoken dialect of this community, reflecting the revered status of this text.

[127] E.g., Renassia 1954[?]; Psalm 102:23: פ'י תג'מיע **אומום** אג'מיע ותצלטנאת ליעבד אילא אללאה (בְּהִקָּבֵץ **עַמִּים** יַחְדָּו וּמַמְלָכוֹת לַעֲבֹד אֶת־יְהוָה) 'When the nations gather together, the kingdoms, to serve the Lord').

[128] E.g., Renassia 1917a; Job 36:31: אין ביהום ישראע **אומום** יעטי מאכול ליכתתר (כִּי־בָם יָדִין **עַמִּים** יִתֶּן־אֹכֶל לְמַכְבִּיר) 'By these things He controls peoples; He gives food in abundance').

[129] E.g., Renassia 1930, p. 40b: תככלתיה ליורת אראצ'י **אומום** סבעא (הבטחתו לרשת ארצות **עממים** שבעה).

[130] For more details about this newspaper, see Tirosh-Becker 2010b, pp. 118, 132.

[131] B.-Z. Cohen 1931, e.g., in a translation to Psalm 117:1, which appears in the *Hallel* section of the Haggadah: שכרו אללה ג'מיע **לאומום** (הַלְלוּ אֶת־יְהוָה כָּל־**גּוֹיִם**) 'Praise the Lord, all you nations'); see B.-Z. Cohen 1931, p. 49.

[132] Attal 1975, e.g., the translation to Psalm 117:1 (אשכרו אילא אללה ג'מיע **להומום**); see ibid., p. 52. On the occasional realization of the Arabic *hamza* as a glottal fricative /h/ in the JA dialect of Algiers, see M. Cohen 1912, p. 39. The form אומום is also documented in an incunabula of *Maqre Dardeqe* (Naples 1488); see Tirosh-Becker 1990b, p. 66.

[133] On some special features in the *šarḥ* to the *hafṭarot* for Leviticus, see §4.1 above.

Abbreviations

CA	Classical Arabic
JA	Judeo-Arabic
JAC	Judeo-Arabic of Constantine
MAC	Muslim Arabic of Constantine
SHC	*šarḥ* to the *hafṭarot* from Constantine

Judeo-Arabic Sources

Main Source

Renassia, Y. circa 1935, *Sep̄er Pəṭirat Moše*: [= *šarḥ* to *hafṭarot*]
Volume 1:
Genesis, David Idan and Raḥamim Sofer Imprimerie, Djerba
Exodus [no details]
Leviticus, Makhluf Najjār Imprimerie, Sousse
French translation, Attali Imprimerie, Constantine
Volume 2:
Numbers, Yaʿaqov Ḥaddād Imprimerie, Djerba
Deutronomy, Yaʿaqov Ḥaddād Imprimerie, Djerba
Moʿadim [no details]
French translation, Audrino Imprimerie, Constantine

Additional Sources

Attal, R.
1975 *Haggadat Algiers: A Facsimile Edition of the First Haggadah that Was Printed in North Africa, Alger 1855*. Jerusalem.

Cohen, B.-Z.
1931 *LeSapper be-Ṣiyyon*, Djerba.

Renassia, Y.
1916a *ʾAzharot ben David: Sep̄er Mišle bə-Šarḥ ʿArab̠i*, Tunis [= *šarḥ* to Proverbs]
1916b *Sep̄er Milḥama be-Šalom: Pirqe ʾAb̠ot bə-Sap̄a ʿArab̠it*, Tunis [= *šarḥ* to Mishnah *ʾAb̠ot*]
1917a *Bne Šiməʿon, wə-hu Sep̄er ʾIyob̠ bə-Šarḥ ʿArab̠i*, Tunis [= *šarḥ* to Job]
1917b *Maʿase Nissim*, Tunis [= *šarḥ* to Daniel]
1930 *Sep̄er Kibbud ʾAb̠ Wa-ʾEm: Livre des Hochaânoths traduits et commentés en judéo-arabe*, Djerba [Rep. Jerusalem, 1987] [= *šarḥ* to *Hošʿanot*]
1954[?] *Zik̠ron Yaʿaqob̠: Tafsir Təhillim Pəšaṭ u-Dəraš*, Djerba [= *šarḥ* to Psalms]

Bibliography

Attal, Robert

1999 *Lexique judéo-arabe tunisien.* Jerusalem. [In Hebrew]

2007 *Un siècle de littérature judéo-arabe tunisienne (1861–1961): Notices bibliographiques.* Jerusalem. [In Hebrew]

Avishur, Yitsḥaḳ

2001 "Modern Judaeo-Arabic Translations of the Bible in the East: A Cultural-Linguistic Presentation." In *Studies in Judaeo-Arabic Translations of the Bible*, by Yitsḥaḳ Avishur, pp. 106–21. Tel-Aviv. [In Hebrew]

2006 *The Aleppo Sharḥ of the Torah.* Tel-Aviv. [In Hebrew]

2008 *A Dictionary of the New Judeo-Arabic Written and Spoken in Iraq (1600–2000).* Tel Aviv. [In Hebrew]

2009 "Literature in Judeo-Arabic." In *Jewish Communities in the East in the Nineteenth and Twentieth Centuries: Syria*, edited by Y. Harel, pp. 135–46. Jerusalem. [In Hebrew]

Bar-Asher, Moshe

1985 "The Hebrew Elements in the Šarḥ of Morocco (According to the Traditions of Tafilalt)." *Ləshonenu* 48–49: 227–52. Reprinted in *Traditions linguistiques des juifs d'Afrique du nord*, by Moshe Bar-Asher, pp. 173–97. Jerusalem, 1999.

1988 "The Sharḥ of the Maghreb: Judeo-Arabic Exegesis of the Bible and Other Jewish Literature – Its Nature and Formulation." In *Studies in Jewish Languages: Bible Translations and Spoken Dialects*, edited by Moshe Bar-Asher, pp. 3–34. Jerusalem. Reprinted in *Traditions linguistiques des juifs d'Afrique du nord*, by Moshe Bar-Asher, pp. 3–34. Jerusalem, 1999. [In Hebrew]

1991 "Les couches linguistiques dans le šerḥ marocain." In *Recherches sur la culture des juifs d'Afrique du Nord*, edited by I. Ben-Ami, pp. 19–24. Jerusalem. Reprinted in *Traditions linguistiques des juifs d'Afrique du nord*, by Moshe Bar-Asher, pp. 45–56. [In Hebrew]

1999 *Traditions linguistiques des juifs d'Afrique du nord.* 2nd edition. Jerusalem. [In Hebrew]

2001 *Le commentaire biblique Leshon Limmudim de Rabbi Raphaël Berdugo.* 4 parts in 3 volumes. Jerusalem. [In Hebrew]

2010a "Bible Study in North African Jewish Communities." In *Leshonot, Massorot u-Minhagot: Linguistics, Traditions and Customs of Maghrebi Jews and Studies in Jewish Languages*, by Moshe Bar-Asher, pp. 176–87. Jerusalem. [In Hebrew]

2010b "A New Sharḥ to Ecclesiastes." In *Leshonot, Massorot u-Minhagot: Linguistics, Traditions and Customs of Maghrebi Jews and Studies in Jewish Languages*, by Moshe Bar-Asher, pp. 281–304. Jerusalem.

2010c "On the Šarḥ to Tractate Avot." In *Leshonot, Massorot u-Minhagot: Linguistics, Traditions and Customs of Maghrebi Jews and Studies in Jewish Languages*, by Moshe Bar-Asher, pp. 329–39. Jerusalem. [In Hebrew]

Beaussier, Marcelin

1958 *Dictionnaire pratique arabe-français: contenant tous les mots employés dans l'arabe parlé en Algérie et en Tunisie.* Nouvelle édition, revue, corrigée et augmentée par M. Mohamed ben Cheneb. Algiers.

Ben Sedira, Bel Kassem

1995 *Dictionnaire arabe-français (langue, letters, conversation).* Beirut.

Biberstein-Kazimirski, Albert de

1860 *Dictionnaire Arabe-Français.* 2 volumes. Paris.

Blanc, Haim

1964a *Communal Dialects in Baghdad.* Harvard Middle Eastern Monographs 10. Cambridge.

1964b "Notes on the Literary Idiom of the Baghdadi Jews." In *For Max Weinreich on his Seventieth Birthday: Studies in Jewish Languages, Literature and Society*, edited by Lucy S. Dawidowicz et al., pp. 18–30. Mouton: The Hague.

1970 "Dual and Pseudo-Dual in the Arabic Dialects." *Language* 46: 42–57.

Blau, Joshua

1966–67 *A Grammar of Christian Arabic, Based Mainly on South-Palestinian Texts from the First Millennium.* Corpus Scriptorum Christianorum orientalium 267. Louvain.

1980a *A Grammar of Mediaeval Judaeo-Arabic.* 2nd, enlarged edition. Jerusalem. [In Hebrew]

1980b "On General and Specific Features in Judeo-Arabic." In *Cairo Geniza Studies*, edited by Mordechai A. Friedman, pp. 185–92. Teʿuda: The Chaim Rosenberg School of Jewish Studies Research Series 1. Tel Aviv. [In Hebrew]

1992 "On a Fragment of the Oldest Judaeo-Arabic Bible Translation Extant." In *Genizah Research after Ninety Years: The Case of Judaeo-Arabic*, edited by Joshua Blau and Stefan C. Reif, pp. 31–39. University of Cambridge Oriental Publications Series 47. Cambridge.

1999 *The Emergence and Linguistic Background of Judaeo-Arabic*. 3rd, revised edition. Jerusalem: Ben-Zvi Institute for the Study of Jewish Communities in the East.

2002 *A Handbook of Early Middle Arabic*. Max Schloessinger Memorial Series, Monographs 6. Jerusalem.

2006 *A Dictionary of Mediaeval Judaeo-Arabic Texts*. Jerusalem. [In Hebrew]

Blau, Joshua, and Simon Hopkins

2007 "The Beginnings of Judaeo-Arabic Bible Exegesis According to an Old Glossary to the Book of Psalms." In *A Word Fitly Spoken: Studies in Mediaeval Exegesis of the Hebrew Bible and the Qurʾān Presented to Haggai Ben-Shammai*, edited by Meir M. Bar-Asher et al., pp. 235–84. Jerusalem. [In Hebrew]

Brunot, Louis

1950 "Sur le theme verbal *fʿāl* en dialectal marocain." In *Mélanges offerts à William Marçais par l'Institut d'études islamiques de l'Université de Paris*, pp. 55–62. Paris.

Cantineau, Jean

1938 "Les parlers arabes du département de Constantine." In *IVe congrès de la Fédération des sociétés savantes de l'Afrique du Nord*, vol. 2, pp. 849–63. Rabat.

Caubet, Dominique

1993 *L'Arabe marocain*, Volume 1: *Phonologie et morphosyntaxe*. Paris.

Charvit, Yossef

2010 "Renassia, Joseph." In *Encyclopedia of Jews in the Islamic World*, edited by N. A. Stillman, vol. 4, pp. 157–59. Leiden.

Cheraifi, Claudie

2005 *L'arabe maghrébin: petit dictionnaire français-arabe*. Geneva.

Cherbonneau, Auguste

1973 *Dictionnaire arabe-français: langue écrite*. Beirut.

Chetrit, Joseph

1994 *The Written Judeo-Arabic Poetry in North-Africa: Poetic, Linguistic and Cultural Studies*. Jerusalem. [In Hebrew]

Cohen, David

1975 *Le parler arabe des juifs de Tunis*, Volume 2: *Étude linguistique*. Paris-The Hague.

Cohen, Marcel

1912 *Le parler arabe des juifs d'Alger*. Paris.

Colin

1993–96 *Le dictionnaire Colin d'arabe dialectal marocain*. Edited by Zakia Iraqui Sinaceur. Rabat.

Corriente, Federico

1977 *A Grammatical Sketch of the Spanish Arabic Dialect Bundle*. Madrid.

Doron, David

1979 The Arabic Translation of the Torah by Issachar ben Susan Hammaʿravi. Ph.D. thesis, Bar-Ilan University, Ramat-Gan. [In Hebrew]

Dozy, Reinhart

1881 *Supplément aux dictionnaires arabes*. 2 volumes. Leiden. Reproduction of the original edition, Beirut, 1991.

Fischer, Wolfdietrich

1959 *Die Demonstrativen Bildungen der Neuarabischen Dialekte*. Gravenhage.

Fischer, Wolfdietrich, and Otto Jastrow

1980 *Handbuch der Arabischen Dialekte*. Wiesbaden.

Fraenkel, Jacqueline

1982 L'imprimerie hébraïque à Djerba (étude bibliographique). 2 volumes. Ph.D. dissertation, Université de Paris III (Sorbonne Nouvelle).

Grand'Henry, Jacques

1972 *Le parler arabe de Cherchell, Algérie*. Louvain-la-Neuve: Université catholique de Louvain.

1995 "Conservation and Change in Algerian Bedouin Arabic." *Proceedings of the 2nd International Conference of L'Association internationale pour la dialectologie arabe* (held at Trinity Hall in the University of Cambridge, 10–14 September 1995), pp. 51–57. Cambridge.

Hary, Benjamin H.

1991 "On the Use of *ʾilā* and *li* in Judeo-Arabic Texts." In *Semitic Studies: In Honor of Wolf Leslau on the Occasion of His Eighty-Fifth Birthday*, edited by Alan S. Kaye, vol. 1, pp. 595–608. Wiesbaden: Harrassowitz.

2009 *Translating Religion: Linguistic Analysis of Judeo-Arabic Sacred Texts from Egypt.* Leiden-Boston.

Heath, Jeffrey

2002 *Jewish and Muslim Dialects of Moroccan Arabic.* London.

Heath, Jeffrey, and Moshe Bar-Asher

1982 "A Judeo-Arabic Dialect of Tafilalt (Southeast Morocco)." *Zeitschrift für arabische Linguistik* 9: 32–78.

Holes, Clive

2001 *Dialect, Culture, and Society in Eastern Arabia.* Handbuch der Orientalistik, Erste Abteilung: Nahe und der Mittlere Osten 51. Leiden.

Huehnergard, John

2006 "On the Etymology of the Hebrew Relative *šε-*." In *Biblical Hebrew in Its Northwest Semitic Setting: Typological and Historical Perspectives*, edited by Steven E. Fassberg and Avi Hurvitz, pp. 103–25. Jerusalem-Winona Lake.

Ilan, Nahem, and Na'im Dahan

2002 "'Ten Things were Created at Twilight on the Eve of the First Sabbath': From Partial Midrashim to an Oral Maghrebian Folktale." *Massorot* 12: 1–32. [In Hebrew]

Jewish Publication Society

1985 *Tanakh: The Holy Scriptures - The New JPS Translation According to the Traditional Hebrew Text*, Philadelphia-Jerusalem.

Joüon, Paul, and Takamitsu Muraoka

1991 *A Grammar of Biblical Hebrew.* 2 volumes. Rome.

Laraba, Ahmed

1981 A Linguistic Description of the Algerian Arabic Dialect of Constantine. Ph.D. dissertation, University of Manchester.

Levin, Aryeh

1994 *A Grammar of the Arabic Dialect of Jerusalem.* Jerusalem. [In Hebrew]

Mangion, M.

1937 "Le dialecte arabe de l'Edough." *Revue Africaine* 81: 373–80.

Maman, Aharon

1999 "The Šarḥ of the Haggadah from Sefrou (Morocco): Provenance, Linguistic Features, Hebrew and Hebraisms." In *Vena Hebraica in Judaeorum Linguis: Proceedings of the 2nd International Conference on the Hebrew and Aramaic Elements in Jewish Languages*, edited by Shelomo Morag, Moshe Bar-Asher, and Maria Mayer-Modena, pp. 289–320. Studi camito-semitici 5. Milan-Jerusalem.

2000 "The Maghrebi Šarḥ of the Bible." *Peʿamim* 83: 48–56. [In Hebrew]

2003 "Language." In *Jewish Communities in the East in the Nineteenth and Twentieth Centuries: Morocco*, edited by Haim Saadoun, pp. 143–54. Jerusalem. [In Hebrew]

Marçais, Philippe

1956 *Le parler arabe de Djidjelli, Nord constantinois, Algerie.* Paris: Librairie d'Amérique et d'Orient.

1977 *Esquisse grammaticale de l'Arabe Maghrébin.* Paris.

Marçais, William

1902 *Le dialecte arabe parlé à Tlemcen.* Paris.

1908 *Le dialecte arabe des Ūlād Brāhîm de Saïda.* Paris.

1911 *Textes arabes de Tanger.* Paris.

Marçais, William, and Abderrahmân Guîga

1958–1961 *Textes arabes de Takroûna*, Volume 2: *Glossaire.* Paris.

Ostoya-Delmas, S.
1938 "Notes préliminaires à l'étude des parlers de l'arrondissement de Philippeville." *Revue Africaine* 82: 60–83.

Piamenta, Moshe
1991 *Dictionary of Post-Classical Yemeni Arabic.* Leiden.

Ratzabi, Yehudah
1985 *A Dictionary of Judaeo-Arabic in R. Saadya's Tafsir.* Ramat-Gan.

Retsö, Jan
1983 *The Finite Passive Voice in Modern Arabic Dialects.* Orientalia Gothoburgensia 7. Göteborg.

Talmoudi, Fathi
1980 *The Arabic Dialect of Sūsa (Tunisia).* Orientalia Gothoburgensia 4. Göteborg.

Tedghi, Joseph
1993 "Lange élevée et langue parlée dans une version du *maḥzor* – rituel juif – en judéo-arabe marocain." In *Actes des premières Journées internationales de dialectologie arabe de Paris*, edited by Dominique Caubet and Martine Vanhove, pp. 533–45. Paris.
1994 "A Moroccan *Maḥzor* in Judeo-Arabic." *Massorot* 8: 91–160. [In Hebrew]
2006 "Translation of Hebrew Prayers into Judeo-Arabic by Shmuel Malka." *Massorot* 13–14: 279–314. [In Hebrew]
2008 "Yehudah Ibn ʿAbbās' Judeo-Arabic ʿEṯ Shaʿare Raṣon" In *Ben ʿEver la-ʿArav* 4: *Prof. Amnon Shiloaḥ Jubilee Volume*, edited by Yosef Tobi, pp. 142–58. Haifa. [In Hebrew]

Tirosh-Becker, Ofra
1988 The Phonology and Topics in the Morphology of a Judeo-Arabic Translation of the Book of Psalms from Constantine (Algeria). Master's thesis, Hebrew University of Jerusalem. [In Hebrew]
1989 "A Characterization of the Judeo-Arabic Language of Constantine." *Massorot* 3–4: 285–312. [In Hebrew]
1990a "On the Linguistic Uniformity of the 'Sharḥ' of the Jews of Constantine." In *Proceedings of the Tenth World Congress of Jewish Studies*, section D:1, pp. 197–204. Jerusalem: World Union of Jewish Studies. [In Hebrew]
1990b "On the Arabic Glosses in the Italian Version of the 'Maqre Dardeqe.'" *Italia - Studi e ricerche sulla storia, la cultura e la letteratura degli ebrei d'Italia* 9, pp. 37–77. [In Hebrew]
2006 "An Algerian Judeo-Arabic Translation of Piyyuṭ 'Mi Khamokha' by Rabbi Yehuda Ha-Levi." *Massorot* 13–14: 315–69. [In Hebrew]
2010a "On Dialectal Roots in Judeo-Arabic Texts from Constantine (East Algeria)." *Revue des études juives* 169: 497–523.
2010b "The Languages of Algerian Jewry." In *Jewish Communities in the East in the Nineteenth and Twentieth Centuries: Algeria*, edited by Haim Saadoun, pp. 117–32. Jerusalem. [In Hebrew]
2011 "Archaic and Dialectal Features in an Algerian Judeo-Arabic Translation and Commentary of Tractate Avot." In *Ḥikrei Maʿarav u-Mizraḥ: Studies in Language, Literature and History, Presented to Joseph Chetrit*, edited by Yosef Tobi and Dennis Kurzon, pp. 181–207. Jerusalem. [In Hebrew]

Tobi, Yosef
1993 "Pre-Saʿadianic Arabic Translation of the Pentateuch." *Massorot* 7: 87–127. [In Hebrew]
1996 "Another Popular Judeo-Arabic Translation of the Pentateuch." In *Studies in Hebrew and Jewish Languages Presented to Shelomo Morag*, edited by Moshe Bar-Asher, pp. 481–501. Jerusalem. [In Hebrew]

Tobi, Yosef, and Zivia Tobi
2000 *La littérature judéo-arabe en Tunisie (1850–1950).* Tel Aviv. [In Hebrew]

Wright, William
1981 *A Grammar of the Arabic Language.* 3rd, revised edition. 2 volumes in 1. Cambridge.

Yoda, Sumikazu
2005 *The Arabic Dialect of the Jews of Tripoli (Libya): Grammar, Text and Glossary.* Semitica viva 35. Wiesbaden.

25

Alternierende Metrik in der akkadischen Poesie

Josef Tropper, Freie Universität Berlin

The present contribution presents the hypothesis that Akkadian poetry as a whole was composed according to the principle of alternating-accentual metrics as known from classical Syriac poetry and, in the author's opinion, from the whole corpus of early Northwest Semitic poetry (for example Biblical Hebrew and Ugaritic). The basic principle of alternating metrics is simple: every second (metrically counted) syllable in a verse is stressed, so that we have an evenly spread pattern of stressed and unstressed syllables (or: beats and offbeats; in German: *Hebungen und Senkungen*). Every verse — or stichos — ends in a stressed syllable (beat). At the beginning of a verse, both stressed and unstressed syllables can occur. The majority of verses in Akkadian narrative literature (epic poetry) have ten or nine syllables. Verses with ten syllables begin with an unstressed syllable (offbeat), while verses with nine begin with a stressed syllable (beat). Both types have five stressed syllables. The present contribution should be considered a pioneering enterprise and is, as such, for certain not free of errors. Even if the basic thesis should prove to be correct, it is well possible that many of the conclusions drawn regarding meter might turn out to be incorrect in detail. The current contribution introduces text samples of various periods and genres, epic poetry, and hymns, and it provides both a translation and commentary.

Einleitung

Nachfolgend wird die These vertreten, dass die akkadische Poesie insgesamt nach dem Prinzip der alternierend-akzentuierenden Metrik komponiert wurde, wie wir sie aus der klassisch-syrischen Poesie[1] und meines Erachtens ebenso aus der gesamten frühen nordwestsemitischen Poesie (z.B. Althebräisch und Ugaritisch) kennen.[2] Und im Gegensatz zu den nordwestsemitischen Quellen ist der akkadische Befund insofern klarer, weil es sich hier um vokalisierte Originaltexte handelt. Ein weiterer Vorteil besteht darin, dass die Zeilen auf einer Tontafel poetischen Inhalts in der Regel den Verszeilen (Stichoi) entsprechen.[3]

Das Grundprinzip der alternierenden Metrik ist einfach: Betont wird im Vers jede zweite (metrisch gezählte) Silbe, so dass ein gleichmäßiger Wechsel von betonter und unbetonter Silbe entsteht. Jede Verszeile (= Stichos) endet mit einer betonten Silbe (= Hebung). Am Beginn der Verszeile kann aber entweder eine unbetonte Silbe (= Senkung) oder eine betonte Silbe (= Hebung) stehen.

[1] Siehe dazu vor allem Hölscher 1932.

[2] Der vorliegende Beitrag ist Teil einer längeren Studie des Verfassers, die auch poetische Texte des Biblisch-Hebräischen, Aramäischen und Ugaritischen erfasst. Sie wird als Monographie im Verlag Hartmut Spenner, Kamen, unter dem Titel *Altsemitische Metrik. Alternierende Metrik im Biblisch-Hebräischen, Aramäischen, Ugaritischen und Akkadischen* erscheinen (voraussichtlich 2011). Die Grundprinzipien der hier vertretenen Metrik wurden ausgehend von klassisch-syrischen Texten einerseits und biblisch-hebräischen Texten andererseits entworfen.

[3] Für Sekundärliteratur zur akkadischen Metrik siehe vor allem von Soden 1981 und West 1997, bes. S. 175, Anm. 1.

Die Mehrzahl der Verszeilen der akkadischen narrativen Poesie (Epik) hat zehn oder neun Silben. Zehnsilbler setzen mit einer Senkung ein, Neunsilbler mit einer Hebung. Beide Typen haben fünf Hebungen. Ich bezeichne deshalb — weil es vor allem auf die Zahl der Hebungen ankommt — ersteren als Typ 5, letzteren als Typ 5′. Graphisch lässt sich dies wie folgt darstellen (x = Senkung; X = Hebung):

Typ 5: x X x X x X x X x X

Typ 5′ X x X x X x X x X

Als illustratives Textbeispiel für Verstyp 5 mag *Enūma eliš*, Tafel IV, Z. 4 = 6 dienen:

šīmatka lā šanān siqirka An^{um}

Dein Schicksal ist ohne gleichen, dein Name ist An^{um}.

Ein illustratives Textbeispiel für Verstyp 5′ begegnet etwa im Gilgamesch-Epos (jB.), Tafel XI, Z. 140:

appalis kibrāti pattu (oder: pāṭu) tâmt^{i}

Ich betrachtete die Himmelsufer, die Begrenzung des Ozeans.

Die zu betonenden Silben sind hier unterstrichen dargestellt. In der Umschrift hochgestellte Vokale oder Silben werden metrisch nicht gezählt (sie wurden in der Rezitation entweder flüchtig artikuliert oder ganz elidiert).

Da Verse entweder mit einer Senkung oder mit einer Hebung einsetzen können, gibt es in der akkadischen Poesie keinen einheitlichen Versfuß (= Metrum) im Sinne eines metrischen Grundbausteins wie etwa Jambus oder Trochäus. Zwar besteht der Verstyp 5 aus einer Abfolge von genau fünf Jamben. Bei Typ 5′ kann man jedoch nicht von einem jambischen Grundcharakter sprechen, da er zwar jambisch endet, aber trochäisch einsetzt.

Rein theoretisch ist die alternierende Metrik somit ein sehr einfaches System. Die Problematik für uns besteht jedoch darin, dass ganz offensichtlich nicht jede geschriebene Silbe metrisch gezählt wurde. Auch der umgekehrte Fall ist denkbar, nämlich, dass scheinbar plene geschriebene Silben in Wirklichkeit metrisch für zwei Silben stehen können. Metrisch unberücksichtigt bleiben m.E. auf jeden Fall nicht betonte Silben am Versende als Folge der sogenannten Pausalaussprache. Somit gibt es in der akkadischen Poesie entgegen älteren Lehrmeinungen gerade keinen „trochäischen Versschluss" (Landsberger 1926, S. 371).[4] Vielmehr steht am Versende — metrisch betrachtet — immer eine Hebung. Auch im Versinnern werden m.E. gewisse Silben metrisch nicht gezählt, da beispielsweise unbetonte Auslautvokale vor vokalisch anlautenden Folgewörtern relativ regelmäßig elidiert. Schließlich ist auch nicht auszuschließen, dass die Akkader sporadisch das Stilmittel der metrischen Synkope eingesetzt haben. Man versteht darunter die Auslassung einer Senkung, so dass zwei Hebungen direkt aufeinander folgen, mit dem Effekt, das die erstere Hebung stark betont (weil gedehnt skandiert) wird.

Es sei mir an dieser Stelle ein Wort zur Tragweite dieses Forschungsansatzes gestattet: Wenn die hier vertretene metrische Analyse auch nur in groben Zügen korrekt ist, dann handelt es sich um eine Entdeckung mit weitreichenden Folgen. Denn mit einem Mal wäre es forthin möglich, die Jahrtausende alte akkadische Poesie im ursprünglichen Rhythmus zu skandieren, was beispielsweise die dramaturgische Aufführung eines ganzes Epos im Original-„Ton" ermöglichen würde. Zum anderen hat der Ansatz aber ganz konkret auch wesentliche phonologische und grammatische Implikationen (Wortbetonung; Definition von Vokalquantitäten bei diversen Morphemen). Er könnte so zu einem erheblich besseren Verständnis der akkadischen Schriftsprache(n) beitragen.

Was spricht dafür, dass der hier präsentierte metrische Ansatz in seinen wesentlichen Punkten korrekt ist? Die Analyse liefert alles in allem ein durchaus kohärentes System. Die Betonung der Wortformen im Vers ist im Großen und Ganzen phonologisch plausibel, zumindest, wenn man davon ausgeht, dass die Versakzentuierung

[4] Für eine Kritik an diesem Konzept siehe bereits Hecker 1974, S. 102–08.

— wie etwa im Altgriechischen — in etwa 70–80% der Fälle dem natürlichen Wortakzent entsprechen sollte. Und identische Wortformen bleiben in unterschiedlichen Kontexten und Texten weitgehend gleich betont.

Auf der anderen Seite ist aber auch zu betonen, dass sich der vorliegende Beitrag als Pionierarbeit versteht und als solche gewiss nicht frei von Fehlern ist. Selbst wenn sich die Grundidee als korrekt herausstellen sollte, könnten im Detail viele hier getroffenen metrischen Festlegungen falsch sein. Fehler sind auch deshalb vorprogrammiert, weil über die tatsächlichen Betonungsverhältnisse akkadischer Wortformen nur sehr wenig Sicheres bekannt ist. Da dieser Beitrag auf einem völlig neuen Forschungsansatz beruht, fehlt im Übrigen auch die Auseinandersetzung mit Sekundärliteratur zum Thema der akkadischen Metrik fast vollständig.

Im Folgenden werden Textbeispiele unterschiedlicher Epochen und Gattungen (Epik und Hymnus) mit Übersetzung und Kommentierung vorgestellt. Sie sollen die Prinzipien und Raffinessen, aber auch die Probleme des hier postulierten Metrik-Systems illustrieren.

1. *Enūma eliš*, Tafel IV, Z. 3–6:

3 attām^{a} kabtāta in^{a} ilī rabût^{um}
4 šīmatka lā šanān siqirka An^{um}
5 Marduk(?) kabtāta in^{a} ilī rabût^{um}
6 šīmatka lā šanān siqirka An^{um}

Du bist der Wichtigste unter den großen Göttern,
dein Schicksal ist ohne gleichen, dein Name ist An^{um};
Marduk, du bist der Wichtigste unter den großen Göttern,
dein Schicksal ist ohne gleichen, dein Name ist An^{um}.

Es handelt sich um vier Stichoi mit je 10 Silben, die jeweils mit einer unbetonten Silbe (= Senkung) beginnen und mit einer betonten Silbe (= Hebung) enden. Jeder Stichos hat somit fünf Hebungen. Diesen Verstyp bezeichne ich als „Verstyp 5." Dieser Befund ist charakteristisch für die akkadische Poesie: Die Verszeilen des Akkadischen sind durchschnittlich länger als die in nordwestsemitischen Sprachen. Verse haben hier eine durchschnittliche Länge von zehn Silben (gegenüber häufigen Achtsilblern im Nordwestsemitischen).

Die Zeilen 4 // 6 sind darüberhinaus geprägt durch die Stilmittel „Stabreim" (*šī/ša/si*) und Endreim (*šanān* || *An*).

Aus dem Textbeispiel ist zu ersehen, dass die Versakzente in der Regel zusammenfallen mit den als „lang" geltenden Silbentypen, nämlich a) den geschlossenen (bzw. geschärften) Silben oder b) den (offenen) Silben, die einen Langvokal aufweisen. Wir dürfen annehmen, dass diese Versakzente weitgehend die natürlichen Wortakzente widerspiegeln, z.B. *šīmatka*, *kabtāta*, *šanān*. Das Beispiel *šīmatka* zeigt ferner, dass der Wortakzent nicht auf die drittletzte (= erste) Silbe zurückgeht, wenn die vorletzte (= Pänultima) „lang" ist. Am Namen *Marduk* lässt sich ablesen, dass bei zwei langen Silben die letztere den Wortton erhält (entgegen der Schulaussprache im anglophonen und deutschsprachigen Raum [„Márduk"]). Ganz häufig wird die Silbe vor einem „leichten" Pronominalsuffix betont, z.B. *šīmatka* und *siqirka* (sonst z.B. regelmäßig *bītīšu* „seines Hauses").

Die am Versende stehenden Wortformen *rabût^{um}* und *An^{um}* zeugen von der sogenannten Pausalaussprache. Dabei werden unbetonte Auslautsilben (bzw. in anderen Fällen unbetonte Auslautvokale) metrisch nicht berücksichtigt. Die Wortformen zeigen zugleich, dass die Kasusendungen, sofern sie sich aus einem kurzen Kasusvokal und der Mimation zusammensetzen, nicht betont wurden (obwohl es sich um eine geschlossene Silbe handelt).

Aus dem Beispiel *in^{a} ilī* ist zu ersehen, dass Auslautvokale häufig — aber nicht immer — elidiert werden, wenn die folgende Wortform vokalisch anlautet (vgl. die „Elisionsregel 1" der lateinischen Metrik).

Die Wortform *attām*^{a} zeigt, dass der Auslautvokal der enklitischen Partikel *-ma*, nach Vokal metrisch unberücksichtigt bleiben kann (nach einer geschlossenen Silbe wird *-ma* dagegen metrisch regelmäßig als Silbe gezählt).

2. *Enūma eliš*, Tafel IV, Z. 22 und 28

22 abātum u banû qibi liktūn^{i}

Befiel Zerstörung oder Erschaffung — es soll geschehen!

28 iḫdû (oder dreisilbig: iḫdūʾū) ikrubū Mardukma šarr^{u}

Sie freuten sich und erteilten den Segen (mit den Worten): *„Marduk ist König!“*

Die Zeile 22 hat zehn Silben bei fünf Hebungen (= Verstyp 5); die Zeile 28 hat neun Silben, aber ebenfalls fünf Hebungen (= Verstyp 5′).

Die Wortformen *liktūn*^{i} und *šarr*^{u} zeugen wiederum von der Pausalaussprache am Versende (dabei werden unbetonte Auslautvokale metrisch nicht berücksichtigt). An *abātum* lässt sich wiederum ablesen, dass die Kasusendung (bei Kurzvokal) unbetont bleibt. Die Konjunktion *u* „und“ kann (wie hier) im Vers betont sein. In der Imperativform *qibi* (von *qabû*) ist die zweite Silbe betont. Daraus könnte zu entnehmen sein, dass der Auslautvokal hier in Wirklichkeit — entgegen *GAG* — doch als Langvokal zu normalisieren ist: *qibī*. Das Beispiel *ikrubū* zeigt, dass längere Wortformen auch mehr als einen Akzent haben können. In diesem Fall dürfte der Hauptakzent auf der langen Endsilbe und ein Nebenakzent auf der ersten Silbe ruhen (d.h. *ìkrubú*). Die Betonung von *iḫdû* scheint den bisher genannten Regeln zu widersprechen (man erwartet eher *iḫdû*). Es könnte tatsächlich einer der (nach meiner Einschätzung insgesamt nicht besonders häufigen) Fälle vorliegen, wo die Versakzentuierung nicht mit den natürlichen Wortakzenten kongruiert. Andererseits ist aber auch sonst mehrfach zu beobachten, dass gerade Kontraktionsvokale im Auslaut, die traditionell als „überlang“ gelten, in der Metrik nicht betont werden. Denkbar ist aber auch, dass die Wortform metrisch dreisilbig behandelt und als *iḫdūʾū* (Grundform *iḫdū-* [Verb III *w*] + Pluralendung *-ū*) skandiert wurde.

3. Gilgamesch-Epos (jB.), Tafel VIII, Z. 131

131 [alpī kabrū]tu immerī marût^{i} (|) uṭṭabbiḫ ittabak ana (oder: itt^{a}bak an^{a}) ibrīš^{u}

Fette Rinder (und) gemästete Schafe — schlachtete (und) opferte er für seinen Gefährten.

Es handelt sich — metrisch betrachtet — um einen überlangen Stichos, eventuell mit einer Mittelzäsur (wofür ich das Symbol „|“ verwende), mit insgesamt 20 Silben (alternativ 18 Silben) und zehn bzw. neun Hebungen (= Verstyp 10 [alternativ: Typ 9]). Oder es handelt sich überhaupt um zwei Stichoi à zehn Silben mit je fünf Hebungen bzw. fünf + vier Hebungen (5 + 5 [bzw. 4]).

Wiederum sind die Versakzente überzeugend, weil sie — abgesehen von *ana* — immer auf langen Silben liegen, die wahrscheinlich „natürlich“ betont wurden. Nur die Akzentuierung der Präposition *ana* auf der zweiten Silbe entspricht nicht dem natürlichen Akzentbefund (ist aber meinen Untersuchungen zufolge häufig so bezeugt). Möglicherweise ist der Befund aber metrisch ohnehin anders zu analysieren: Statt *ittabak ana* könnte einfach *itt*^{a}*bak an*^{a} (*ibrīš*^{u}) zu skandieren sein, mit einer Silbenellipse (bzw. einer nur flüchtigen, metrisch nicht gezählten Artikulation der zweiten Silbe) im Zusammenhang mit einer (möglichen Aufgabe einer)

Konsonantengemination und der Elision des Auslautvokals von *ana* vor der vokalisch anlautenden Wortform *ibrīšu*.

Die Wortform *ibrīš*^{u} zeigt ferner, dass am Versende in Pausalposition auch der Auslautvokal eines Pronominalsuffixes metrisch unberücksichtigt bleibt. Der Genitiv-Kasusvokal /i/ vor dem Suffix scheint der Metrik zufolge tatsächlich (sekundär) gelängt gesprochen worden zu sein, da betreffende Silben durchgehend akzentuiert sind (siehe *GAG* §38h und §65a).

4. Gilgamesch-Epos (jB.), Tafel XI, Z. 138–40

138 uktammisma attašab abakk^{i}
139 eli dūr appīja illakā dimāj^{a}
140 appalis kibrāti pattu (oder: pāṭu) tâmt^{i}

Ich warf mich auf die Knie und hockte dann weinend da,
dabei liefen mir Tränen über meine beiden Wangen.
Ich betrachtete die Himmelsufer, die Begrenzung des Ozeans.

Die Stichoi haben neun, elf und wieder neun Silben (Verstypen: 5′ + 6′ + 5′). Jeder Stichos beginnt mit einer Hebung. Alle Versbetonungen (Hebungen) — außer im Falle von *eli* (Z. 139) — liegen auf langen Silben und gehen mit den mutmaßlich natürlichen Wortbetonungen konform. Bei Wortformen wie *appalis* (Z. 140), die zwei Hebungen aufweisen, ist in der Regel davon auszugehen, dass sie den Hauptton auf der Ultima und einen Nebenton auf der drittletzten Silbe haben, d.h. *àppalís*. Am Versende werden kurze unbetonte Vokale, wie etwa die Auslautvokale von Pronominalsuffixen oder kurze Kasusvokale, metrisch nicht berücksichtigt (= Pausalaussprache).

5. *Enūma eliš*, Tafel I, Z. 1 und Z. 7

1 enūma eliš lā nabû šamām^{ū}
7 enūma ilū lā šūpû manâm^{a}

Als oben die Himmel (noch) nicht benannt worden waren.
Als die Götter überhaupt (noch) nicht hervorgebracht worden waren.

Die vorgestellten Stichoi bestehen aus je zehn Silben (Verstyp: 5). Betont werden wiederum weitgehend die als „lang" und deshalb „betont" geltenden Silben. Scheinbare oder echte Ausnahmen bilden *eliš* „oben" und *ilū* „Götter". Die Wortform *eliš* könnte aber durchaus die natürliche Akzentuierung widerspiegeln (die Kasusendung *-iš* trug — wie die Endungen *-um*, *-im* und *-am* — an sich wohl nicht den Hauptton im Wort). *ilū* „Götter" wird auch sonst — in anderen von mir metrisch untersuchten Texten — überwiegend auf der ersten Silbe betont (auch bei anderen Nomina wird die Pluralendung *-ū* bzw. *-ī* durchaus nicht immer betont).

6. Nergal und Ereškigal (mB.), Z. 1–5

1 inūma ilū iškunū qerēt^{a}
2 an^{a} aḫātišun^{u} Ereškigal
3 išpurū mār šipr^{i}
4 nīnu ulu nurradakk^{i}
5 u attī (oder: u att^{ī}) ul tillinnâš^{i}

Als die Götter ein Gastmahl veranstalteten,
schickten sie zu ihrer Schwester Ereškigal
einen Boten:
„Wir können nicht zu dir hinabsteigen,
und du kannst nicht zu uns herausfsteigen ..."

Die fünf Verszeilen (Tristichon + Distichon) sind unterschiedlich lang: zehn, neun, fünf, sieben und sieben (bzw. sechs) Silben: Verstypen 5 + 5′ + 3′ + 4′ + 4′ (bzw. 3). Trotz der unterschiedlichen Verslängen ist der Textabschnitt als Ganzes rhythmisch und metrisch beeindruckend durchkomponiert. Vers- und natürliche Wortakzente fallen weitestgehend oder gar vollständig zusammen. — Es folgen Einzelbemerkungen:

ilū (Z. 1) ist wiederum auf der ersten Silbe betont (vgl. *Enuma eliš* I 1 und 7).

iškunū (Z. 1) und *išpurū* (Z. 3) sind als Formen des Prät. 3.c.pl. charakteristisch betont: Hauptton auf der langen Endsilbe, Nebenton auf der (geschlossenen und deshalb ebenfalls langen) Präfixsilbe (d.h. *ìškunú*).

an^{a} (*aḫātišun^{u}*, Z. 2) zeugt von der Elision des Auslautvokals vor einem vokalisch anlautendem Folgewort (Elisionsregel 1).

aḫātišun^{u} (Z. 2): Der Auslautvokal des Suffixes *-šunu* wird meinen Untersuchungen zufolge sehr häufig elidiert. Man beachte in diesem Zusammenhang, dass in der akkadischen Poesie bekanntlich auch Schreibungen ohne Auslaut-„u" bezeugt sind.

mār šipr^{i} (Z. 3): Die Wortform *mār* wird als einsilbige Form des St.cs. erwartungsgemäß nicht betont; betont wird dagegen das folgende Nomen rectum.

attī (Z. 5): Es ist nicht klar, ob dieses Pronomen auf der ersten oder der zweiten Silbe betont wurde. Das mask. Pendant, *attā*, wird metrisch nicht einheitlich behandelt (überwiegend *attā*, teilweise aber auch *attā*, z.B. AH VI 27: [*aša*]*r attā tallikum^{a}*).

Nebenbei sei bemerkt, dass analog zu Enuma eliš I Z. 1 und 7 sowie Nergal und Ereškigal, Z. 1, auch Atramḫasis I 1 wohl wie folgt metrisch analysiert werden kann: *inūma il$^{ū/u}$ awīl^{um}* (mit Elision des Auslautvokals bei *ilū/u* [Pl. oder Sg.]; alternativ: *inūm^{a} ilū awīl^{um}*).

7. Gilgamesch (jB.), Tafel XI, Z. 161–63 (ähnlicher Text: Atramḫasīs III v 34–35)

161 ilū īṣinū irīš^{a}
162 ilū īṣinū irīša ṭāb[^{a}]
163 ilū kīma zumbē eli bēl niqî iptaḫr^{ū}

Die Götter rochen den Duft;
die Götter rochen den guten Duft;
da sammelten sich die Götter wie die Fliegen über dem Opferspender.

Die Verszeilen haben sieben, neun und dreizehn Silben (Verstypen: 4′ + 5′ + 7′). Es folgen Einzelbemerkungen:

ilū: Diese Wortform ist wiederum durchgehend auf der ersten Silbe betont.

zumbē: Auch hier ist der auslautende Langvokal sehr wahrscheinlich nicht betont.

iptaḫr^{ū}: Die Form zeigt, dass auch lange Auslautvokale — wenn sie unbetont sind — am Versende metrisch unberücksicht bleiben.

8. Nanâ-Hymnus (18. Jh.)

Wurden bisher hauptsächlich epische Texte aus dem 1. Jt. vorgestellt, so zeigen die folgenden Texte, dass das gleiche Metrik-System auch schon im 2. Jt. und auch außerhalb der Gattung Epik anzuwenden ist.

Als erstes möchte ich alle relativ gut erhaltenen und verständlichen Verszeilen des Nanâ-Hymnus des Samsu-iluna vorstellen (2. Hälfte des 18. Jhs.).

9 [itt]allakū idušš^{a} kināt^{um}
10 [šu]lmum bāštum simt^{um}
11 [mal]û ša šulmi u balāṭ^{im}
12 [al]kass^{a} addār damiqtum itt^{um}
[....]

17 ikkullatu ilātim lābum An^{um}
18 āliduš ulli rēšuš
19 ettum muštarḫat u kanât
20 išīmši našmaḫī kadāša ulṣ^{am}

9 *[Es] gehen ihr zur Seite Stetigkeit,*
[He]il, Würde, gute Erscheinung,
[(und) Fü]lle an Heil und Leben.
Ihr [Wa]ndel ist auf ewig ein gutes Zeichen.
[.....]

17 *Unter allen Göttinnen hat der Löwe Anu,*
ihr Erzeuger, ihr Haupt erhöht.
Sie ist als einzige voller Pracht und gehegt.
Er bestimmte für sie Üppigkeit, festliche Freude (und) Jubel.

Die Verszeilen dieses Hymnus schwanken in ihrer Länge zwischen fünf Silben (Z. 33) und zwölf Silben (Z. 7). Die Mehrzahl hat entweder acht Silben (Z. 11, 12, 19 u.a. = Verstyp 4) oder zehn Silben (Z. 17, 20 u.a. = Verstyp 5). Die Akzentuierungen im Vers (d.h. die Hebungen) gehen wohl weitgehend konform mit den natürlichen Wortbetonungen.

Eine Besonderheit dieses Hymnus und wohl auch anderer früher Hymnen des sogenannten hymnisch-epischen Dialekts (HED) besteht darin, dass die genitivischen (= possessivischen) Pronominalsuffixe an Nomina allgemein metrisch nicht als eigene Silben gezählt und damit wohl ohne Auslautvokal rezitiert werden, z.B.

[al]kass^{a} (< **alkat-ša*) „ihr Wandel“ (Z. 12) oder *iduššš*^{a} (< **idum-ša*) „an ihrer Seite“ (Z. 9). Mehrfach werden die betreffenden Auslautvokale auch orthographisch nicht berücksichtigt, z.B. *a-li-du-uš* „ihr Erzeuger“ und *[r]e-e-šu-uš* „ihr Haupt“ (jeweils Z. 15).

Einzelbeobachtungen:

Z. 9–12: ein Musterbeispiel für die „Gültigkeit“ des hier zugrunde gelegten metrischen Systems. Alle Versbetonungen (Hebungen) liegen auf langen und mutmaßlich natürlich betonten Silben; vgl. besonders Z. 10-11: *šulmum bāštum simt*^{um} / *malû ša šulmi u balāṭ*^{im}. Eine andere Betonung der betreffenden Wortformen ist hier gar nicht möglich. So ergibt sich gleichsam von selbst der beeindruckende alternierende Grundrhythmus, der charakteristisch ist für die altsemitische Poesie als Ganze.

ikkullatu bzw. *ikkullatū* (Z. 17): Die Endung des Lokativ-Adverbial ist möglicherweise langvokalisch anzusetzen.
ulli (Z. 18): auffallende Ultima-Betonung.

9. Etana-Epos (aB.): BRM 4, Nr. 2, I 1–5

1 rabûtum Anunna šā'imū(?) šimt^{im}
2 ušbū imlikū milikša māt^{am}
3 bānû kibrātim šākinū šikitt^{im}

4 ṣīrū ana nīš^{ī} ilū Igig^{ū}
5 isinnam ana nīš^{ī} išīm^{ū}

Die großen Anunna, die Bestimmer der Geschicke,
setzten sich (und) hielten Rat über das Land,
die Bildner der Weltufer, die Schöpfer der Schöpfung,
die erhaben sind über den Menschen, die Igigu-Götter;
sie setzten für die Menschen ein Fest ein.

Die fünf Verse haben meiner metrischen Analyse zufolge zehn, neun, zehn, neun und acht Silben (Verstypen 5 + 5′ + 5 + 5′ + 4). Einzelbeobachtungen:

Anunna (Z. 1): zu dieser Betonung vgl. etwa AH II vi 23 (ergänzt nach Parallelen): *rabûtum Anunna kalun*^{i} „Wir, die großen Anunna allesamt“; vgl. ferner AH III iii 30: *Anunna ilū rabût*^{um}.

šā'imū (Z. 1): Partizip (G-Stamm, m.pl.), hier wohl mit nicht-charakteristischer Betonung (dieses Phänomen ist im St.cs. häufiger zu beobachten als im St.rectus).

ušbū (Z. 2): Man achte auf die Betonung der ersten Silbe (< **ūšibū*).

bānû und *šākinū* (Z. 3): Partizipien (m.pl.) mit charakteristischer Betonung.

nīš^{ī} (Z. 4 und 5): Man beachte die Betonung der ersten Silbe (und nicht der langvokalischen Endung); vgl. hierzu etwa Gilgāmeš (aB.) OB III (iv) 165 und 167: *pāšī* / *patrī išpukū rabût*^{im} „Sie gossen (zwei) große Äxte / Schwerter“ (*pāšī* und *patrī* jeweils mit Betonung der Stammsilbe). In anderen Texten findet sich sowohl diese Betoung (*nīšī*) als auch die Betonung der Ultima (*nīšī*).

išīm^{ū}: Man beachte, dass hier — bei einer Verbalform *mediae infirmae* — der Akzent auf der Stammsilbe und nicht auf der Endung liegt (vgl. etwa hebr. *yaśīmū* „sie setzen/stellen“).

10. Gilgamesch-Epos (aB.), OB II (vi), Z. 212–17

212 itbēma Enkīdu 213 ana pānīš^{u}
214 ittamḫarū ina ribītu māt^{i}
215 Enkīdu bābam iptarik 216 ina šīpīš^{u}
217 Gilgāmeš erēbam ul iddin

Enkīdu wandte sich ihm entgegen.
Sie trafen in der Hauptstraße des Landes aufeinander.
Enkīdu blockierte den Eingang mit seinem Bein;
er ließ Gilgāmeš nicht eintreten.

Bemerkungen:

ana, *ina* (Z. 213 / 214): Bei den betreffenden Präpositionen wird nicht selten die zweite Silbe betont (häufiger trägt jedoch die erste Silbe den Ton).

11. Gilgamesch-Epos (aB.) OB VA+BM: Kol. III, Z. 1–14

1 Gilgāmeš êš tadâl (oder: Gilgāmeš e?eš ...)
2 balāṭam ša tasaḫḫuru lā tutt^{a}
(oder: balāṭam ša tasaḫḫ^{u}ru lā tutta)
3 inūma ilū ibnû awīlūt^{am}
4 mūtam iškunū an^{a} awīlūt^{im}
5 balāṭam ina qātišun^{u} iṣṣabt^{ū}
(oder: ... in^{a} qātišun^{u} iṣṣabtū)
6 attā Gilgāmeš lū mali karašk^{a}
7 urrī u mūšī ḫitaddu att^{ā} (oder: ... ḫitadd^{u} attā)
8 ūmišam šukun ḫidūt^{am}
9 urrī u mūšī sūr u mēlil (?)
[.....]
12 ṣubbi ṣeḫram ṣābitu qātīk^{a}
13 marḫītum liḫtaddâm ina sūnīk^{a}
14 annāma šī[mti awīlūt^{im} (?)]

„Gilgāmeš, wohin willst du denn gehen?
Das (ewige) Leben, das du suchst, wirst du nicht finden!
Als die Götter die Menschheit erschufen,
legten sie den Tod auf die Menschheit,
das Leben aber behielten sie in ihren Händen zurück.

6 *Du aber, Gilgāmeš, — dein Bauch sei voll;*
Du sollst du dich ständig erfreuen, Tag und Nacht!
Veranstalte täglich ein Freudenfest;
tanze und spiele Tag und Nacht!
[.....]

12 *Starre (lustvoll) auf den jungen Mann, der deine Hand hält;*
eine Frau soll sich ständig deines Schoßes erfreuen!
Von dieser Art ist die Bestim[mung des Menschen“. (?)]

Bemerkungen:

Z. 1: sehr kurzer Stichos, eventuell nur sechs Silben (Typ 3).

tutt^{a} bzw. *tutta* (Z. 2): *watû*, Präs. 2.m.sg., mit Pänultima- oder Ultima-Betonung.

urrī u mūšī vs. *urrī u mūšī* (Z. 7 / Z. 9): gegenläufige Betonung als bewusstes Stilmittel (sogenannte metrische Variation).

šukun (Z. 8): Imp. m.sg. mit charakteristischer Ultima-Betonung.

mēl^{i}*l* bzw. *mēl*^{il} (Z. 9): (unregelmäßiges Verb) *mēlulu*, G-Imp.; eventuell in der Pausa so zu rezitieren (Pänultima-Betonung).

Abkürzung

GAG Wolfram von Soden. *Grundriss der akkadischen Grammatik*. Analecta Orientalia 33. Roma: Pontificium Institutum Biblicum, 1995.

Bibliographie

Hecker, Karl

1974 *Untersuchungen zur akkadischen Epik*. Alter Orient und Altes Testament 8. Neukirchen Vluyn: Neukirchener Verlag.

Hölscher, Gustav

1932 *Syrische Verskunst*. Leipziger semitistische Studien, n.F., Band 5. Leipzig: J. C. Hinrichs.

Landsberger, Benno

1926 „Die Eigenbegrifflichkeit der babylonischen Welt". *Islamica* 2: 355–72. Translated as *The Conceptual Autonomy of the Babylonian World*, by Thorkild Jacobsen, Benjamin R. Foster, and Heinrich von Siebenthal. Sources and Monographs, Monographs on the Ancient Near East 1/4. Malibu: Undena, 1976.

von Soden, Wolfram

1981 „Untersuchungen zur babylonischen Metrik, Teil I". *Zeitschrift für Assyriologie und Vorderasiatische Archäologie* 71: 161–204.

Tropper, Josef

2011 *Altsemitische Metrik. Alternierende Metrik im Biblisch-Hebräischen, Aramäischen, Ugaritischen und Akkadischen*. Kamen: Spenner.

West, M. L.

1997 „Akkadian Poetry: Metre and Performance". *Iraq* 59: 175–87.

26

On Personal Names Ending in *-āyu* in the Amarna Letters and in Texts from Canaan

*Wilfred van Soldt, Leiden University**

In two recent articles,[1] I have discussed abbreviated personal names attested in texts from Ugarit and the suffixes that were added to these names. My main conclusion was that the suffixes that were used most frequently were *-ān-*, *-āy-*, *-n-*, and *-y-*. To these the case vowels were added, so that the suffixes appear in the nominative as *-ānu*, *āyu*, *-nu*, and *-yu*. I also concluded that the suffixes *-ānu* and *-āyu* were normally used in abbreviated names ending in a consonant (Baᶜlānu), whereas in names ending in a vowel, the suffix was usually preceded by *-y-* (Nuᶜmeyānu). Both suffixes could be shortened to *-ā* (Yaᶜḏirā[nu], Eliyā[yu]). The suffixes *-n-* and *-y-* were normally used after an abbreviated name ending in a vowel (Nuᶜmeyu, Nuᶜmenu). Names ending in *-āyu* and *-yu* were triptotically declined, while those ending in *-ānu* and *-nu* had a diptotic declension.[2]

Among the many names mentioned in the Amarna letters,[3] there are several that appear to have the same suffixes as the ones identified in names from Ugarit. However, since the Amarna corpus is very limited in comparison with the material from Ugarit, the number of names is much smaller, and their spelling is often ambiguous. As in Ugarit, the suffixes *-āyu* and *-ānu* can also be added to place names.[4] I first discuss the names that I have collected from Hess's study. The names are discussed in the order of their frequency in the corpus.

Names with the Suffix *-āyu* in the Amarna Letters

Lab'āyu

This name is certainly the best-documented one in our corpus. It refers to the ruler of Shechem and occurs in letters written at Jerusalem, Megiddo, Ginti-Padalla, Shechem, Beth-Shean, and possibly Rehob.[5] There are two different spellings for this name, *la-ab-a-*PI and *la-ab-a-*IA, and according to Hess[6] the name should be normalized Lab'aya. First I discuss the attestations from Lab'āyu's own town Shechem, then the ones from the other towns.

In letters from Shechem, *la-ab-a-*PI occurs in EA 252:3, 253:2, and 254:3 and in all three in the formula *umma* PN, 'Thus (says) PN.' In Mesopotamia *umma* is followed by a nominative, but in western peripheral texts, *umma* was often interpreted as a word for 'message.' Because of this, the following name often appears in the genitive,[7] but this is certainly not always the case.[8] Thus the name that appears after *umma* can have either the nominative

* It is a pleasure for me to contribute to John Huehnergard's Festschrift. I wish to express my admiration for his scholarship and to thank him for his friendship.

[1] Van Soldt 2010 and forthcoming.

[2] Van Soldt 2005, pp. 165f., and 2010, pp. 318f.

[3] The Amarna personal names have been discussed in detail in Hess 1993.

[4] Van Soldt 2005, pp. 162ff.

[5] For the political situation, see Finkelstein and Na'aman 2005.

[6] Hess 1993, p. 103.

[7] See the discussion in Rainey 1996, vol. 3, pp. 174–80.

[8] Compare, for example, *umma* ^{m}èr-*aš-ra-tu*$_4$ in EA 60:2.

or the genitive case, and instead of *-ya* (Hess) the sign PI can also be read *yu* or *yi*. As can be seen from the verbal forms, the latter interpretation is consistent with the use of PI in these two letters.[9] Whenever /*ya*/ has to be expressed, the sign IA is written.[10] On the basis of the use of the sign PI, it seems likely that this sign should not be interpreted as /*ya*/, but either as /*yu*/ or /*yi*/, as in Ugaritic.[11]

As for the texts sent from other towns, the letters sent by Biridiyu of Megiddo (EA 244–46) are most instructive. The form *la-ab-a-*PI appears where the context requires a nominative (244:11, 29, 38) or a genitive (244:17, 41; 246 rev. 6), but where an accusative is required, the spelling *la-ab-a-*IA is used (245:6, 43). The sign PI is attested in several verbal forms and nouns as a spelling for /*yi*/ or /*yu*/.[12] As in the Shechem letters, the sign IA is only used for /*ya*/.[13] However, in EA 245, PI can sometimes also be used for /*ya*/, as in ^{m}*ya-aš-da-ta* (245:12, 15[14]) and *ya-qí-ìl-li-ni* (245:38).

In two letters from Baˁlu-UR.SAG of Ginti-padalla (EA 249 and 250), we find a similar distribution, PI for /*yi*/ and /*yu*/[15] and IA for /*ya*/.[16] *La-ab-a-*PI serves again as nominative (249:17?; 250:14, 39) or genitive (2 DUMU *la-ab-a-*PI, 250:6 and passim).

In a letter from Mut-Baˁlu of Pella,[17] we possibly find another attestation of Lab'āyu, this time spelled ^{m}*[la-a]b-a-ia* (EA 255:15). Since the name is preceded by *amur*, it is possible that it was understood here as an object.[18] Note that the spelling of PI and IA follows that of the previously discussed texts.[19]

In EA 263[20] the last line has *i-na* ^{m}*la-ab-a-*P[I], which requires a genitive. There are no other examples of PI to write *y*+vowel in this text.

In a letter from Šuwardata of Gath (EA 280), *la-ab-a-*PI occurs twice, both times in the nominative (30, 33). In this text, too, the signs PI and IA are used in the way that has been observed for the previous texts.[21]

A number of references to Lab'āyu can also be found in two letters of Abdi-Ḫeba of Jerusalem. In EA 287 he is attested in line 30 in a context that requires the genitive (dumu.meš *la-ab-a-*PI). In this letter the sign PI is not used in verbal forms, but only in names, where it stands for /*yu*/ or /*yi*/.[22] The sign IA is always used for /*ya*/.[23] In letter EA 289, there are two attestations, one in the genitive (6, dumu.meš *la-ab-a-yi*) and one in the nominative (22, ^{m}*la-ab-a-yu*). With one exception, the sign PI is only used for /*yu*/ or /*yi*/ in this text,[24] and the sign IA is only used for /*ya*/.[25]

Finally, Lab'āyu is attested in a letter from Tagi found in Beth-Shean.[26] He occurs as addressee in the first line, *la-ab-a-*P[I], where the context requires a genitive. This is the only occurrence of PI in this letter. Note, however, that IA is consistently used for /*ya*/.[27]

---

[9] Compare *yi-ma-ḫa-aš-ši* (252:19); *ye-en-ni-nu-nu-mi* (253:24); *yi-iq-ta-bu* (253:30); *yi-iḫ-li-qú* (254:9); *yi-ka-lu* (16); *yu-sà-an-ni-qú* (18); *yi-il-te-qú* (25).

[10] Compare the first person suffix *-ia* (252:1, 4, 11, and passim), *ia-(a-)*ši (252:6, 254:41), *ia-nu* (253:26); *mi-ia-ti* (254:8); *a-ia-ka-am* (27); ^{m}*ad-da-[i]a* (37). For the last example, see below, Addāyu.

[11] See van Soldt 2010 and forthcoming.

[12] ^{m}*bi-ri-di-yu/i* (244:3, 246:3); *yi-iṣ-bat-ši* (244:28,37); *yu-ba-aḫ-ú* (244:43); *yi-pu-šu-mi* (245:3); *yi-ru-ub-mi* (245:17); *ye-el-qé-me* (245:25); *yi-iq-bi* (245:27); *a-na-yi* (245:28); *yi-íl-qé-šu* (245:30); *yu-ta-šar* (245:31, 42, 44); *yu-ka-bi-id* (245:39); *yi-de-mi* (245:46).

[13] Apart from the many occurrences of *-ia* (1st p. sg.), cf. *i-ia-nu* (244:39); *ḫa-ia-ma* (245:6, see Rainey 1996, vol. 1, p. 167); *ia-a-*[ši] (245:27).

[14] The name is also attested in EA 248:3.

[15] *yi-ḫa-ba-lu* (249:7); *yi-[i]p-[pu-šu]* (249:18); *yi-de* (250:4, 9); *yi-(ik)-ki-im-ni-mi* (20, 48); *yi-it-r[u-u]ṣ* (22); *ye-e[n]-na-bi-il* (33); *yi-iz-zi-iz* (42); *yi-is-sú-uḫ-ši-ni* (45); *yi-iṣ-bat-mi* (46); *yu-pa-at-ti* (47); *yi-nam-mu-šu* (53); *yu-ba-aḫ-ú* (56); *yi-qa-bu* (59).

[16] Cf. *i[a]-aš-p[ur-m]e* (250:23); *ia-a[š]-p[u-r]a* (28); ^{m}*bir*$_{5}$*-ia-wa-za* (250:24); *ia-a[n*$^{?}$*-š]u*$^{?}$ (45, see Moran 1992, p. 304); *i-ia-nu-um* (57); *ia-ši* (58).

[17] According to Goren, Finkelstein, and Na'aman (2004, p. 261) the tablet was written at Beth Shean.

[18] The translation should then be 'See my father Lab'āyu, he used to serve the king, his lord.' This use of *amur* is also attested in other letters, see Rainey 1996, vol. 3, pp. 169f., but the phrasing is usually different (*amur* X *ša* ...).

[19] PI: *yu-wa-še-ru* (255:17). IA: *-ia* (1st p. sg.); ^{m}*ḫa-a-ia* (255:8); *mi-ia-ti* (12); KUR *ka-ra-du-ni-ia-aš* (21).

[20] The names of the sender and the addressee are broken. According to Goren, Finkelstein, and Na'aman 2004, p. 250, the letter was possibly sent from Rehob or Beth-Shean.

[21] PI: *yu-uš-ši-ir-ni* (280:9); *yi-de* (21, 36); *yi-iš-ta-al* (25); *ye-el-te-qú* (31, 35); *yu-šu-te-ru* (39; Moran 1992, p. 322: *yu-na-ki-ru*?). IA: *-ia* (1st p. sg.); *ia-ti-ia* (13, 15).

[22] *ka-ši-yi* (287:33); ^{m}*ad-da-yu* (47); ^{m}*a-da-yu* (49). Moran (1975, p. 151) discusses the use of the sign PI in the Jerusalem letters, but only the values *pi* and *à*.

[23] *-ia* (1st p. sg.); *ia-a-ši* (287:12, 28, 32, 49, 78?); *ia-(a)-nu* (23); ^{uru}*ia-lu-na*^{ki} (57).

[24] *ar-za-yi* (289:7, see below); *an-ni-yu* (12); *ad-da-yu* (32); ^{m}*yi-in-ḫa-m[u]* (45). The exception is *an-ni-ya* in line 9. The reading of the personal name *ḫa-*PI (31) is unclear, but the name is usually spelled with IA, see Moran 1992, p. 382, and Hess 1993, pp. 75f.

[25] *-ia* (1st p. sg.); *mi-ia-re-e* (31); *ia-a-nu-mi* (36).

[26] Horowitz and Oshima 2006, pp. 48f.

[27] Cf. *-ia* (1st p. sg., 2, 6) and *[i]a-ši* (9).

In view of the prevalent distribution of PI and IA for writing the sound combinations /yu/ and /yi/ (PI) and /ya/ (IA), it seems likely that the name *la-ab-a*-PI/IA should be read Lab'āyu in the nominative, Lab'āya in the accusative, and Lab'āyi in the genitive. These spellings, in particular those in the accusative written with IA, show that the name was triptotically declined. I return to the length of the vowel *a* at the end of this article.

The name Lab'āyu should be interpreted as a hypocoristicon of a name starting with the element *lab'u* 'lion'[28] and ending with the suffix *-āyu*. A similar name is attested in Ugarit, but instead of *-āyu*, the suffix appears to be *-iyu* (or *-i-yu*); compare [m]*la-ab-ʾi-yu* in 19.42:3 (PRU 6, no. 79) and *lbiy* in KTU 4.376:2.

Addāyu

This name is attested only in a letter from Lab'āyu and in three letters sent by Abdi-Ḫeba of Jerusalem. The name is spelled in three different ways: *ad-da*-PI, *a-da*-PI, and *ad-da*-IA. According to Hess[29] the name should be read Addaya, and he includes the name *an-da-a*-PI mentioned in EA 175:3.[30] However, the identification of these two persons is far from certain. Addāyu was a commissioner who, according to EA 289:33, had a house in Gaza.

In the letter sent by Lab'āyu of Shechem, the name is written *ad-da-ia* (254:37). The sign IA is broken, but according to Knudtzon's collation, the reading is certain.[31] The context requires a genitive: *i-na* šu [m]*ad-da-*[*i*]*a*, 'in the hand of Addaya.' Since the texts from Shechem generally distinguish between PI (for /yu/ and /yi/) and IA (for /ya/),[32] it seems certain that the scribe interpreted the name as Addaya.

In the three letters from Jerusalem, the spelling varies. In EA 285:24, only part of the sign IA remains, and the rest of the name has disappeared. The restoration proposed by Campbell[33] is based on a parallel passage in EA 287:47. In the reconstruction the context would require a genitive ([*a-na* [m]*ad-da-i*]*a*. In 287:47 the name is written [[m]*a*]*d-da*-PI, and it is the subject of the infinitive *pa-ṭa-a*[!]*-ri*[!] in line 46.[34] As we have seen above, the signs PI and IA are clearly separated according to the vowels they represent in EA 287, and the name should probably be read 'Addāyu. In line 49 the name is spelled *a-da*-PI, and here, too, a nominative is required. In EA 289:32 we find again *ad-da*-PI, and also here a nominative must be assumed. With one exception, text 289 is as consistent as EA 287 in its use of the signs PI and IA (see above, Lab'āyu).

Although the evidence for Addāyu is ambivalent, one may conclude that the scribe of the Schechem letter EA 254 possibly understood the name as Addaya, while the Jerusalem scribe probably declined it triptotically as Addāyu/a/i.

For the interpretation of this name, there are several possibilities. First, the name can be a hypocoristicon in *-āyu* of a name beginning with the divine name (H)addu. A parallel from Ugarit would be dumu [d]u-TA-*yi* (15.09:4[35]), which probably has to be read [d]u-*dá-yi*, that is, (H)addāyu.[36] However, there is also the frequently attested Ugaritic name *ʿdy* and the longer *ʿdyn*, of which the vocalizations are uncertain.[37]

*Arzāyu

Only two attestations of this name are known, and its interpretation is not clear. Izre'el and Moran read it Arsawa,[38] while Hess interpreted it as a variant of the name Arsa(w)uya, the mayor of Ruḫizzi.[39] Since the spellings of these two names are different in the sense that Arsa(w)uya is always written with an extra sign PI or Ú, I prefer to treat the name Arzāyu separately. Note also that the two forms do not occur in one text. The two attestations discussed here probably refer to different persons.

---

[28] See the literature in Hess 1993, p. 103; and cf. *DULAT* 490.

[29] Hess 1993, pp. 19f.

[30] For the reading of this name, see Hess ibid.; Na'aman 1988, p. 188, n. 41; Moran (1992, p. 261} reads 'Ildayyi.

[31] Knudtzon 1915, p. 812.

[32] See the discussion of EA 254 under Lab'āyu.

[33] Campbell 1964, p. 103 n. 75. See Moran 1992, p. 325 n. 8.

[34] Rainey 1996, vol. 2, p. 384.

[35] See PRU 3, p. 195.

[36] One could compare this name with [du]mu *a-da-ta-yi* in 17.430 IV:11 (PRU 6, no. 83), a name that occurs in alphabetic script as *adty*; see Gröndahl 1967, p. 90, and *DULAT* 23, but this name is probably derived from *adt* 'lady' and not from Haddu.

[37] See Gröndahl 1967, pp. 196f., and *DULAT* 152. For *ʿdyn* there is one possible syllabic match, [m]*a-da-ia-nu* in 15.09:20 (PRU 3, p. 195).

[38] Izre'el 1991, vol. 1, pp. 42, 141; vol. 2, p. 11. Moran 1992, p. 380.

[39] Hess 1993, pp. 40f.

In EA 62:27, a letter from ʿAbdi-Aširta of Amurru to Paḫanate, a certain ᵐ*ar-za*-PI is said to have stayed behind with three others in the palace of Ṣumur. The context requires a nominative. In this text the sign PI is attested only in this name, and the sign IA is used only for /*ya*/.[40]

In EA 289:7, *ar-za*-PI is mentioned in the same context as Lab'āyu. The text says that Milkilu does not break away from the sons of Lab'āyu and *ar-za*-PI. In both names a genitive is required.[41] For the use of PI and IA in this text, see under Lab'āyu and Addāyu.

In an adoption contract from Ugarit, a *ḫazannu* called ᵐ*ar-za*-PI acts as a supervisor.[42] Since the context requires a genitive,[43] we have to read the name Arzāyi.[44]

An explanation of this name is difficult. Hess suggested Indo-Aryan, West Semitic, and Egyptian origins, but one could also think of an Anatolian origin, as for Ugaritian Arsuwā(nu).[45] However, if the ending -*āyu* is indeed part of this name, one would expect the first element to be of West Semitic origin, and the first word that comes to mind is *'arzu* 'cedar.' The same word is probably attested in the personal name *arz* attested in an Ugaritic text.[46]

Bayāyu

The name is attested in two letters in which this person acts as the sender. It is usually read *ba-ia-wa*.[47] The interpretation of the name is uncertain, but most scholars tend to see in it a writing for Indo-Aryan *pāyúḥ*, 'protector.'[48]

In EA 215 the name appears as *ba-ia*-PI in line 3 after *umma*, which probably points to a genitive in -*i*. This short text contains no other examples of PI, but it is clear that IA is only used for /*ya*/.[49]

In EA 216 the name appears in the same spelling and context, but here we have more evidence for the spelling with PI. The attestations show that PI is used for /*yu*/ and /*yi*/,[50] whereas IA represents /*ya*/.[51]

Although a reading *ba-ia-wa* is acceptable, I would prefer to interpret the sequence IA-PI in the light of a few other attestations in texts from Ugarit where this spelling indicates the suffix -*āy* preceded by /*y*/ and followed by the case vowel.[52] The reading of the name would then be Bayāyu, to be understood as Ba-y-āy-u. In the context of these two letters, the case vowel should be either the nominative in -*u* or the genitive in -*i*.

In Ugarit similar names are attested. There are the alphabetic spellings *by* and *byy*,[53] and there is the syllabic spelling *be*-PI.[54] The spelling *byy* probably stands for a name with the suffix -*āyu*, which, like Bayāyu, is separated from the name element by an inserted /*y*/. If the vowel in *byy* were the same as that in *be*-PI, the name would be reconstructed as Beyāyu, that is, Be-y-āy-u. Since the vowel differs from the one in the Amarna name, the first element may have to be explained differently. I can offer no explanation for either Bayāyu or Beyāyu.

*Andāyu

The interpretation of this name is too uncertain; see footnote 29.

---

[40] IA: *i-na* (62:12, 23); *ia-ši* (29); cf. the name *ia-ma-a-ia* in lines 42 and 45.

[41] See also above, Lab'āyu.

[42] 25.134:2; see Lackenbacher 1991.

[43] *a-na pa-ni* ᵐ*ar-za*-PI.

[44] Since IA is used consistently in this text to spell /*ya*/ the sign PI was most probably employed to write either /*yu*/ or /*yi*/. Spellings with IA are *a-ia i-din* (25.134:20); ᵐ*i-ḫi-ia-nu* (27); ᵐ*ia-ap-lu-tu*₄ (29).

[45] Gröndahl 1967, p. 272.

[46] *bn.arz.š*ʿ*rty*, 5.248:25 (KTU 4.33).

[47] Moran 1992, pp. 283f., and Hess 1993, p. 48.

[48] Hess 1993, p. 48, no. 40.

[49] Cf. -*ia* (1st p. sg., 215:1, 2, 7, 8), ᵐ*ia-an-ḫa-ma* (10); *i-ia-a-nu* (11).

[50] Cf. *yu-ši-ra* (216:15), *yi-im-lu-ku* (20). PI is used for /*wa*/ in *a-wa-ti* (13).

[51] Cf. -*ia* (1st p. sg., passim); ᵐ*ma-ia* (216:13).

[52] van Soldt 2010 and forthcoming.

[53] For attestations, see *DULAT* 253.

[54] Compare also the names *byn* (11.788:30′; KTU 4.86) and ᵐ*be-ia-nu* (15.37:15; PRU 3, p. 35). The name ᵐ*be-e-ia* in RS 86.2230:1 (RSO 14, no. 18) is borne by an Egyptian and is irrelevant for the name discussed here.

Names with the Suffix -*āyu* in Texts from Canaan

Several names ending in -(*C*)*a*-PI are attested in the documents found in Canaan. Most of these are found in the texts discovered at Taanach,[55] which are about a century older than the texts of the Amarna archive.

I discuss the names in alphabetical order.

ʿAbdāyu

ᵐèr-*da*-PI (Taanach 14:7).[56] The text contains a list of personal names that are probably all in the nominative case. The only proof for this comes from ᵐ*zi-bi-lu* in line 4, but note that all names ending in /*y*/ use the sign PI, which should probably be read /*yu*/. Although this makes a reconstruction of this name as ʿAbdāyu likely, it cannot be shown that PI is used only for /*yu*/ and /*yi*/ in this text. In line 12 we find the name ᵐ*bi-ir*-PI-*ma-aš-da*, in which the vowel /*a*/ seems certain.[57] The sign IA is not attested in the text. The full name probably consisted of the element ʿ*abdu*, 'servant, slave,' and the name of a god.

Purdāyu

ᵐ*pur-da*-PI (Taanach 2:12).[58] According to the context, the name should have the genitive case. This is the only occurrence of PI in this text, but note that IA is used consistently for /*ya*/.[59] The meaning of this name, that is to say of the first element, is unclear.[60]

Rabbāyu

ᵐdumu-*ra-ba*-PI (Taanach 3: obv. 9′)[61] and ᵐ*ra-ba-ia* (Taanach 8: obv. 4′).[62] In Taanach 3 the word for 'son' is written after the determinative preceding personal names. The first element of the name could be the word *rabbu* 'big,' the suffix is probably āyu (in the first text the genitive -*āyi*, in the second the accusative -*āya*). Taanach 3 is a list of personal names in the nominative, for example, [ᵐ]*e-li-tu* (obv. 7′), ᵐ*ta-a-gu* (rev. 5′), [ᵐ*ka-m*]*a-ru* (8′), [ᵐ*ia-d*]*i-in-nu* (12′), and [ᵐx]-x-*lu* (15′), which makes the reading of PI as /*yu*/ at the end of the names in this text rather likely. Note that the sign IA is used for /*ya*/ in [ᵐ*a-i*]*a-ri* (rev. 11′). Taanach 8 is a fragment of a letter in which the name ᵐ*ra-ba-ia* seems to be an object to a lost verb in obv. 4′. The only other occurrence of IA is the pronoun *ia-ši* in rev. 3′. Since in both attestations the spellings of the suffix -*āyu* appear to be consistent with the required case endings, the name should probably be explained as Rabbāyu, that is, Rabb-āy-u.

Ṯābāyu

ᵐša-ba-PI (Taanach 14:2).[63] For the orthography of this text, see above, ʿAbdāyu. I have assumed that the first element is derived from the verb *ṯwb*, 'to return.' Names beginning with Ṯāb(a)- are attested, for example, in the Amarna letters[64] and in Ugarit. Parallels for the name Ṯābāyu can be found in Ugarit, ᵐ*šá-be*-PI[65] and *ṯby*.[66] Note,

---

[55] Horowitz and Oshima 2006, pp. 127ff.

[56] Ibid., pp. 150f.

[57] Ibid., p. 151.

[58] Ibid., pp. 133f.

[59] For IA, see -*ia* (1st p. sg., 2, 15, 23); ᵗᵘᵍ*up-pa-aš-ia-ni-ma* (9).

[60] Compare the names *brdd, brdn, prd,* and *prdny* in Ugaritic; see Gröndahl 1967, pp. 120 and 174; *DULAT* 236 and 679f.; Watson 1990, p. 247.

[61] Gröndahl 1967, p. 135. For the high percentage of names with *bin*-, see van Soldt 2010, p. 155.

[62] Ibid., p. 145.

[63] Horowitz and Oshima 2006, p. 150.

[64] Cf. ᵐ*ša-bi*-dingir in EA 62:26 (Hess 1993, pp. 138f.) and in RS 11.787:7 (PRU 3, p. 194). Compare also the alphabetic spelling *ṯbil* (*DULAT* 896). For the Ugaritic toponym Ṯāba'il, see van Soldt 2005, p. 186. For other personal names from Ugarit containing forms of this verb, see Gröndahl 1967, p. 200.

[65] 19.65:7′, PRU 6, no. 72.

[66] 16.193:11′, KTU 4.222.

however, that the syllabic spelling suggests a form Ṯābe-y-u, and a similar reconstruction could be applied to the Taanach attestation, Ṯāba-y-u, in which the second *-a-* would be part of the verbal form.

ZIrāyu[67]

ᵐZI-*ra*-PI (Taanach 3: rev. 4′).[68] For the orthography of this text, see above, Rabbāyu. Since the reading of the first sign is unclear, the etymology of the first element of the name remains uncertain. Possible parallels from Ugarit are *zry*[69] and *ṣry*.[70] The name is certainly a hypocoristicon, but the nature of the suffix cannot be determined with any precision.

Three names are too uncertain to be included here:

> *ya-ṣur-rù-zi-ir-ta*-PI (Taanach 3: rev. 9′[71]). The meaning of this name is obscure. It is probably not a hypocoristicon.[72]
>
> *za*-PI-*ia* (Taanach 7: rev. 1:2′).[73] Since the names in this text tend to be written in the nominative[74] and since at least one name ending in *-yi* is written with PI,[75] I have assumed that the suffix that was intended in *za*-PI-*ia* is /ya/. How the sign PI should be read in this name is not clear.
>
> x-*da*-PI (Taanach 4: rev. 6′).[76] The name could be a hypocoristicon ending in *-āyu*.

Conclusion

On the basis of the orthography of the texts studied in this contribution, it seems inevitable to concede that names written with PI as their last sign and attested in contexts that require either a nominative or a genitive ending in *-yu* and *-yi*, respectively. Since the sound combinations *-ayu/a/i* would have resulted in the contracted vowels *-û/â/î*, respectively, the suffix *-a-yu* must be reconstructed as /āy/ plus the case vowel, the same suffix that was used in texts written in Ugarit.[77]

Only nine cases of hypocoristicons with the suffix *-āyu* have been found in the Amarna letters and the texts from Canaan. Hess (1993) lists 217 names in the Amarna texts, but if we exclude the broken names, we are left with 194. In their edition of the texts from Canaan, Horowitz and Oshima (2006) list about 75 names in the texts from Taanach. Texts from other Canaanite Late Bronze Age towns provide about 25. All in all we have almost 300 names from these two text groups. The names in *-āyu* form 3 percent of the total.

If we compare this figure with the number of names in the texts from Ugarit, we have 52 certain cases of hypocoristicons with the suffix *-āyu*, but more cases can be expected among alphabetic names ending in *-y*. How many there are remains unknown. The 52 attestations amount to less than 1 percent of the total number of 6,000 names in texts from Ugarit, but in view of the large number of alphabetic names ending in *-y*, the total could be as high as 2 or 3 percent. The difference in percentages is almost negligeable.

In the texts from Ugarit, the suffix *-āyu* was often used in names of women.[78] The number of cases was no less than 40 percent of the total, and my conclusion was that women are overrepresented in this group. In the texts studied here, no women are mentioned, and all nine instances refer to names borne by men. The limited number of documents of the corpus used in this article is certainly partially to be blamed for this outcome.

---

[67] Horowitz and Oshima 2006, p. 135, read ᵐ*Ze-ra-ya* without further commentary. In the text this person is referred to as a Sutean (ˡᵘ́SU).

[68] The same name could be attested in Taanach 7: rev. 1:5′ ᵐZI-*ra*-[...].

[69] Gröndahl 1967, p. 313; *zry* is also attested in 19.60:1, KTU 4.628.

[70] Gröndahl 1967, p. 190.

[71] Horowitz and Oshima 2006, p. 136.

[72] See the remarks of Horowitz and Oshima 2006, p. 137.

[73] Horowitz and Oshima 2006, p. 143, read ᵐ*Za-wa-ia*.

[74] Cf. obv. 5 and rev. 9′–11′.

[75] Cf. obv. 6.

[76] Horowitz and Oshima (2006, p. 138) read ᵐ*Dup-da-ya*.

[77] For examples from the Amarna texts, see Sivan 1984, p. 18; for Ugarit, see van Soldt 2005, p. 165 with previous literature.

[78] See van Soldt 2010, p. 316.

Abbreviations

DULAT	Gregorio del Olmo Lete and Joaquín Sanmartín *A Dictionary of the Ugaritic Language in the Alphabetic Tradition.* 2nd edition. 2 volumes. Handbuch der Orientalistik, Erste Abteilung, Nahe und der Mittlere Osten 67. Leiden: Brill, 2004
EA	siglum of the Amarna tablets
KTU	Manfried Dietrich, Oswald Loretz, and Joaquín Sanmartín. *The Cuneiform Alphabetic Texts from Ugarit, Ras Ibn Hani and Other Places (KTU).* 2nd edition. Abhandlungen zur Literatur Alt-Syrien-Palästinas und Mesopotamiens 8. Münster: Ugarit-Verlag, 1995
PRU 3	Jean Nougayrol. *Textes accadiens et hourrites des archives est, ouest et centrales.* Mission de Ras Shamra 6, Palace Royal d'Ugarit 3. Paris: Imprimerie Nationale, 1957
PRU 6	Jean Nougayrol. *Textes en cunéiformes babyloniens des archives du grand palais et du palais sud d'Ugarit.* Mission de Ras Shamra 12, Palace Royal d'Ugarit 6. Paris: Imprimerie Nationale, 1970
RS	siglum of texts from Ras Shamra
RSO 14	Marguerite Yon and Daniel Arnaud. *Études ougaritiques 1: travaux 1985–1995.* Ras Shamra-Ougarit 14. Paris: Éditions Recherche sur les Civilisations, 2001

Bibliography

Campbell, Edward F., Jr.

1964 *The Chronology of the Amarna Letters with Special Reference to the Hypothetical Coregency of Amenophis III and Akhenaten.* Baltimore: Johns Hopkins Press.

Finkelstein, Israel, and Nadav Na'aman

2005 "Shechem of the Amarna Period and the Rise of the Northern Kingdom of Israel." *Israel Exploration Journal* 55/2: 172–93.

Goren, Yuval; Israel Finkelstein; and Nadav Na'aman

2004 *Inscribed in Clay: Provenance Study of the Amarna Letters and Other Ancient Near Eastern Texts.* Monograph Series 23. Tel Aviv: Emery and Claire Yass Publications in Archaeology.

Gröndahl, Frauke

1967 *Die Personennamen der Texte aus Ugarit.* Studia Pohl 1. Rome: Päpstliches Bibelinstitut.

Hess, Richard S.

1993 *Amarna Personal Names.* American Schools of Oriental Research Dissertation Series 9. Winona Lake: Eisenbrauns.

Horowitz, Wayne, and Takayoshi Oshima

2006 *Cuneiform in Canaan: Cuneiform Sources from the Land of Israel in Ancient Times.* Jerusalem: Israel Exploration Society and The Hebrew University of Jerusalem.

Izre'el, Shlomo

1991 *Amurru Akkadian: A Linguistic Study.* 2 volumes. Harvard Semitic Studies 41. Atlanta: Scholars Press.

Knudtzon, Jørgen A.

1915 *Die El-Amarna-Tafeln.* 2 volumes. Vorderasiatische Bibliothek 2. Leipzig: J. C. Hinrichs.

Lackenbacher, S.

1991 "Un contrat d'adoption en fraternité." In *Marchands, diplomates et empereurs: études sur la civilisation mésopotamienne offertes à Paul Garelli,* edited by Dominique Charpin and Francis Joannès, pp. 341–43. Paris: Éditions Recherche sur les civilisations.

Moran, William L.

1975 "The Syrian Scribe of the Jerusalem Amarna Letters." In *Unity and Diversity: Essays in the History, Literature, and Religion of the Ancient Near East,* edited by Hans Goedicke and Jimmy J. M. Roberts, pp. 146–66. Baltimore: Johns Hopkins University Press.

1992 *The Amarna Letters.* Baltimore: Johns Hopkins University Press.

Na'aman, Nadav
1988 "Biryawaza of Damascus and the Date of the Kāmid el-Lōz ʿApiru Letters." *Ugarit-Forschungen* 20: 179–93.

Rainey, Anson F.
1996 *Canaanite in the Amarna Tablets. A Linguistic Analysis of the Mixed Dialect Used by Scribes from Canaan.* 4 volumes. Handbuch der Orientalistik, Erste Abteilung, Nahe und der Mittlere Osten 21–25. Leiden: E. J. Brill.

Sivan, Daniel
1984 *Grammatical Analysis and Glossary of the Northwest Semitic Vocables in Akkadian Texts of the 15th–13th Centuries B.C. from Canaan and Syria.* Alter Orient und Altes Testament 214. Kevelaer: Butzon & Bercker.

van Soldt, Wilfred H.
2005 *The Topography of the City-State of Ugarit.* Alter Orient und Altes Testament 324. Münster: Ugarit-Verlag.
2010 "The Ugaritic Suffixes *-āyu* and *-ānu*." In *Von Göttern und Menschen. Beiträge zu Literatur und Geschichte des Alten Orients. Festschrift für Brigitte Groneberg*, edited by Dahlia Shehata, Frauke Weiershäuser, and Kamran V. Zand, pp. 307–27. Leiden: Brill.
Forthcoming "On Abbreviated Personal Names in Texts from Ugarit." To be published in the Proceedings of the Rencontre Assyriologique Internationale, Paris 2009.

Watson, Wilfred G. E.
1990 "Ugaritic Onomastics (2)." *Aula Orientalis* 8: 243–50.

27

Jumping Spiders (Araneae: Salticidae) of the Concord Area, Middlesex County, Massachusetts

Preliminary List, Annotations, and Video Footage Based on the Observations of John Huehnergard and Dick Walton

Richard K. Walton

Concord, Massachusetts, the Commonwealth's first inland settlement, was founded by men seeking land they could call their own. While religious persecution motivated some of the earliest immigrants, most Europeans were drawn to the New World by the economic possibilities. Potential colonists facing bleak prospects at home were also motivated by speculators and promoters in England and on the Continent touting America's natural resources in their glowing accounts of a land of milk and honey.

The realities of eastern North America in the seventeenth century presented a stark contrast to the romanticized descriptions of the promotional literature. The lessons of Jamestown and Plymouth included starvation, death, and failure along with opportunity. One mirror on the undaunted colonists, freshly arrived in the New World, is their attitude toward the natural world. While this untamed wilderness offered untold promise, it was at the same time a very real threat to their dreams. This duality is also reflected by contemporary religious and philosophical tenants (Walton 1984, pp. 1–11).

The Judeo-Christian concept of land is, in essence, utilitarian. As Aldo Leopold points out, "Abraham knew exactly what the land was for: It was to drip milk and honey into Abraham's mouth" (Leopold 1949, pp. 205–06). That the natural world might be seen in any other way was moot.

John Locke, whose concepts informed Jefferson's work on America's founding documents, states, "land that is left wholly to nature, that hath no improvement of pasturage, tillage, or planting, is called, as indeed it is, 'waste,' and we shall find the benefit of it amount to little more than nothing" (Locke 1689, p. 42). The colonists' focus was to "improve" their piece of the natural world and in so doing to make their acreage profitable.

Wilderness was the enemy, cultivated acres the ally. And for the most part, the lives of Concord's founding fathers and their immediate descendants were defined by their struggle to establish and maintain crops in rock-filled fields. Woodlands and woodchucks, meadow grasses and meadow larks, raccoons and river otters, cardinal flowers and crows were either a nuisance to be eliminated or, in a few cases, were deemed suitable for the pot.

In the early 1800s, nearly two centuries after its founding, most Concordians were still engaged in a perennial struggle to turn a profit on their land. At this same time a small group of citizens established Concord's reputation as a center of intellectual activity. Often referred to as "transcendentalists," this learned group included among their number Henry David Thoreau. The transcendentalists' metaphor for nature was also a utilitarian one, but one that envisioned nature as a source of inspiration on the path to philosophical, even divine, truths. And much of Thoreau's writing is characterized by philosophical musings inspired by Concord's woodlands and wildlife. During the last decade of his life, Thoreau devoted most of his time to local nature studies (Walton 1984, pp. 12–19). At this point, however, both his motivation and his focus were transformed. Thoreau was studying the natural world as an end in itself. "Are we to be put off or amused in this life, as it were with a mere allegory? Is not nature, rightly read, that which she is commonly taken to be the symbol merely" (Thoreau 1849, p. 250). To his twenty-first-century admirers, Thoreau's attention to the intrinsic value of the natural world, his preoccupation with learning the specific details of bird identification or the exact day on which each local wildflower bloomed, and even his investigations of the ecological complexities of the effects of wood cutting on species composition in a particular woodlot, seems anything but surprising. This is Thoreau the naturalist and field biologist. And yet, measured against the prevailing attitudes of his fellow townsfolk Thoreau's perspective was revolutionary.

For present-day naturalists, Thoreau is the originator of a unique tradition of nature studies in and around Concord, Massachusetts. No other place in North America has a longer written record of its natural history and Thoreau penned the first significant chapters. Scattered throughout his journals and manuscripts are references to the intellectual seeds of Thoreau's transformation. His conversion to naturalist is also reflected in his library. While his focus is local and devotedly on Concord, Thoreau is influenced by his cosmopolitan embrace of ideas from the ancient Far East to contemporary western Europe. From the Bhagavad Gita (Mitchell 2000, p. 13) to Darwin's revolutionary *On the Origin of Species* (Darwin 1859) and from the parochial perspective of Gilbert White of Selborne (White 1887) to the cosmos of von Humbolt (von Humbolt 1806), Thoreau draws on numerous sources and then concocts a unique brew to inspire his work.

Nearly two centuries after Thoreau's birth, the naturalist with an interest in Concord has access to a comprehensive record of the areas' birdlife and botany. In addition to these subjects, whose foundations are the direct legacy of Thoreau, subsequent fieldwork and research have defined the region's butterflies and dragonflies, its reptiles and amphibians, and even several rather more obscure groups including freshwater bivalves and solitary wasps. A search of Thoreau's forty-seven manuscript journal volumes will return observations and comments, in some cases voluminous, on each of these subjects.

In 2004 John Huehnergard and I began work on a project focusing on the specific plants and animals observed by Thoreau. Ultimately we combined narrative from his journals (Thoreau 1671–) with video of the same flora and fauna occurring in Concord today (Walton and Huehnergard 2006). In 2007 John and I were spending much of our field time looking for solitary wasps. This project, however, was nearing completion and I was gradually paying more attention to spiders, in particular a group called jumping spiders. While arachnids were not a subject of particular interest to Thoreau, spiders and especially their webs do receive some attention in his writings. As far as we could determine, however, Thoreau never mentioned jumping spiders in his field notes. His legacy, however, invites and encourages new discoveries. And new discoveries on familiar ground constitute one of the delights of naturalizing no matter where you make your home. In the spring of 2008, John and I made a beginning to what was and is the initial study of the jumping spiders in the Concord area. In August 2009, John moved to Texas, where he and his wife and colleague, Professor Jo Ann Hackett, joined the faculty of the Department of Middle Eastern Studies at the University of Texas at Austin. I have continued to search for and record local jumping spiders. The list that follows and the accompanying video footage are the results of John's and my collaborative efforts as well as my ongoing studies.

Jumping Spiders (Araneae: Salticidac) Observed

Spiders belong to the class arachnida. They have two main body parts (cephalothorax and abdomen), as distinct from insects, which have three body parts. The salticids or jumping spiders is the largest family of spiders. Members of this family are easily recognized by their two large, prominent eyes located centrally on the front of the face (six smaller eyes are located on the sides and the top of the head). These large eyes provide jumping spiders with unusually acute vision. Unlike many spiders, salticids do not build a fixed web but rather are free-roaming predators. Their keen vision and powerful legs enable jumping spiders to locate and pounce on their prey from a relatively long distance. Salticids are also known for their elaborate mating behavior and, in the case of the males, ornate and colorful anatomical embellishments. Although common in almost all habitats, salticids are easily overlooked due to their small size.

This list comprises jumping spiders seen in the towns of Acton, Carlisle, Concord, and Sudbury during the period of June 2008 through July 2012. In all cases identifications and/or confirmations have been made by professional arachnologists. Names follow the currently accepted nomenclature (Platnick 2000–2012). Specific data for each record are referenced with the online video footage on my website: www.rkwalton.com. This is a preliminary list for the Concord area as there are likely a number of species present here but not observed by the author. The annotations are included to note points of interest about the biology of salticids and the historical context of jumping spider studies in Massachusetts rather than to elucidate in any systematic way the details of the species listed.

Burgess 1875, pl. 8, fig. 21

Admestina wheeleri (Peckham & Peckham) — Video Length: 00:53

http://oi.uchicago.edu/research/pubs/catalog/saoc/saoc67/saoc67_admestina_wheeleri.mp4

Eris militaris (Hentz) — Video Length: 02:37

http://oi.uchicago.edu/research/pubs/catalog/saoc/saoc67/saoc67_eris_militaris.mp4

Evarcha hoyi (Peckhams) — Video Length: 02:01

http://oi.uchicago.edu/research/pubs/catalog/saoc/saoc67/saoc67_evarcha_hoyi.mp4

Habronattus calcaratus maddisoni (Banks) — Video Length: 02:39

http://oi.uchicago.edu/research/pubs/catalog/saoc/saoc67/saoc67_habronattus_calcaratus_maddisoni.mp4

The genus *Habronattus* includes some of North America's most colorful and behaviorally interesting jumping spiders. The etymology of the generic name is derived from *habron*, the Greek adjective for 'graceful, delicate, pretty,' and *attus*, the old genus name for jumping spiders (Ubick et al. 2005): thus, the pretty jumping spider. And indeed, many of *Habronattus* males are strikingly adorned with bright green leg parts with showy fringes as well as bold red facial markings. These adaptations all play their role in attracting females.

Habronattus coecatus (Hentz) — Video Length: 02:13

http://oi.uchicago.edu/research/pubs/catalog/saoc/saoc67/saoc67_habronattus_coecatus.mp4

Previously the northern limit of *H. coecatus* was thought to be Long Island, New York. In October 2011, I found a worn male of this species in Middlesex County, Massachusetts (Harvard University's Museum of Comparative Zoology archive). In the spring of 2012 I located several *H. coecatus* subadult males as well as adult females. Although this species has likely expanded its range northward it may also have been overlooked in part because of its furtive behavior. *H. coecatus* spends a good deal of time hidden in grasses and thatch and is, in my experience, quicker to head for cover as compared with other *Habronattus* spiders.

Habronattus decorus (Blackwall) — Video Length: 02:08

http://oi.uchicago.edu/research/pubs/catalog/saoc/saoc67/saoc67_habronattus_decorus.mp4

While spiders are a "hard sell" even to naturalists, anyone willing to take the time to look for jumping spiders will be richly rewarded. Perhaps the most significant hurdle is size. Most jumping spiders are small and an appreciation of their Lilliputian world may be best achieved through a macro lens. The present species is a medium-sized jumper and a thing of beauty. The adult male combines soft, rose-colored and pearly-gray hues with black-striped legs.

Habronattus viridipes (Hentz) — Video Length: 02:59

http://oi.uchicago.edu/research/pubs/catalog/saoc/saoc67/saoc67_habronattus_viridipes.mp4

The video of this species includes a segment showing male–female interactions. Much of the male's short adult life is spent searching for receptive females. Ultimately the female makes her selection(s) influenced at least in part by the males' bright colors and striking patterns.

Hentzia mitrata (Hentz) — Video Length: 01:34

http://oi.uchicago.edu/research/pubs/catalog/saoc/saoc67/saoc67_hentzia_mitrata.mp4

Nicholas Marcellus Hentz, considered the father of American arachnology, was born in France and came to America in 1816 at the age of nineteen. While he made his living as a teacher and briefly attended medical lectures at Harvard, his passion was the study of insects and spiders. A short biographical sketch based on his son's recollections relates that, "[a]lthough of a genial, affectionate, and generous nature, his peculiarly nervous organization made him often morbidly sensitive and suspicious, and a prey to groundless fears, which not a little marred his enjoyment of life." Hentz habitually and without regard to circumstance would "drop on his knees, press his hands to his forehead, and raising his eyes heavenward, remain in more or less protracted prayer." Despite these apparent burdens, Hentz published the first important works on American spiders. A brief look at the nomenclature of the present list indicates the significance of his contribution. And his fieldwork and notes on Massachusetts' spiders are considerable. Hentz lived and worked in Northampton, Massachusetts, in the 1820s. While he and Thoreau shared acquaintances at Harvard and in the larger natural history community, it is unlikely they ever met. The last quarter century of his life was spent in the southern states. Much of Hentz's work on spiders was published by the Boston Society of Natural History (BSNH); twenty years after Hentz died the BSNH produced a volume of his collected works (Burgess 1875, pp. x–xi).

Hentzia palmarum (Hentz) — Video Length: 01:27

http://oi.uchicago.edu/research/pubs/catalog/saoc/saoc67/saoc67_hentzia_palmarum.mp4

Maevia inclemens (Walckenaer) — Dimorphic Jumper — Video Length: 02:17

http://oi.uchicago.edu/research/pubs/catalog/saoc/saoc67/saoc67_maevia_inclemens.mp4

While variation in physical appearance is typical of jumping spiders as they mature from immature to adult, mature adults typically have a single characteristic form for the female and for the male. The dimorphic jumper is an exception to the rule as there are two adult male forms. One is overall gray in appearance, the other is black.

Marpissa lineata (C. L. Koch) — Video Length: 01:15

http://oi.uchicago.edu/research/pubs/catalog/saoc/saoc67/saoc67_marpissa_lineata.mp4

Naphrys pulex (Hentz) — Video Length: 01:33

http://oi.uchicago.edu/research/pubs/catalog/saoc/saoc67/saoc67_naphrys_pulex.mp4

Pelegrina galathea (Walckenaer) — Peppered Jumper — Video Length: 02:16

http://oi.uchicago.edu/research/pubs/catalog/saoc/saoc67/saoc67_pelegrina_galathea.mp4

Pelegrina *sp.* **(*proterva*)** (Walckenaer) — Video Length: 02:17

http://oi.uchicago.edu/research/pubs/catalog/saoc/saoc67/saoc67_pelegrina_sp.mp4

Most arachnologists work with collected and preserved spiders. And traditionally, spider identification relies on microscopic examination. The naturalist is more interested in the living animal in the field. Identification to species level, therefore, may at times be difficult if not impossible. Such is the case with *Pelegrina proterva* and its congeners *P. peckhamorum*, *P. montana*, and *P. insignis*. While *P. proterva* is the most likely species in our area the similarity of external characteristics precludes accurate field identification to species (Maddison 1996, pp. 270–73).

Phidippus audax (Hentz) — Bold Jumper — Video Length: 02:14

http://oi.uchicago.edu/research/pubs/catalog/saoc/saoc67/saoc67_phidippus_audax.mp4

This large jumping spider is widespread and abundant and may be the most commonly observed salticid in our area. Like many *Phidippus* jumpers, the adult male had large, iridescent green chelicerae (jaws with fangs). First described by Hentz, this species' varied forms have caused a good deal of confusion, much of which is reflected in the literature subsequent to Hentz's original description (Hentz 1845). G. B. Edwards' "Revision" of this genus details the synonomy for each species and the spider we now call *Phidippus audax* has over fifty entries for its various synonyms (Edwards 2004, pp. 72–74).

Phidippus cardinalis (Hentz) — Video Length: 03:07

http://oi.uchicago.edu/research/pubs/catalog/saoc/saoc67/saoc67_phidippus_cardinalis.mp4

Phidippus clarus Keyserling– Video Length: 02:18

http://oi.uchicago.edu/research/pubs/catalog/saoc/saoc67/saoc67_phidippus_clarus.mp4

Phidippus princeps (Peckhams) — Video Length: 02:19

http://oi.uchicago.edu/research/pubs/catalog/saoc/saoc67/saoc67_phidippus_princeps.mp4

Phidippus whitmani (Peckhams) — Video Length: 02:57

http://oi.uchicago.edu/research/pubs/catalog/saoc/saoc67/saoc67_phidippus_whitmani.mp4

The Brister's Hill site, preserved and maintained by the Walden Woods Project, includes part of the route Thoreau walked from Concord center to his cabin at Walden. Short quotes from Thoreau, engraved in granite, are placed along the trail. John and I visited here several times to enjoy the natural delights as well as Thoreau's inspirational words. On May 15, 2010, I was at Brister's Hill where just off the path among the oak leaves scattered under lowbush blueberries I noticed movement. It wasn't long before I was admiring the first *P. whitmani* I had ever seen — a bright red male jumping spider with dark legs heavily fringed with gray. Initially it seemed a puzzle that although Thoreau walked here many times he apparently never saw this spider. But *P. whimani* is restricted to woodland edges and in Thoreau's day this was an area of fields and meadows.

Phlegra hentzi (Marx) — Video Length: 01:42

http://oi.uchicago.edu/research/pubs/catalog/saoc/saoc67/saoc67_phlegra_hentzi.mp4

Platycryptus undatus (De Geer) — Familiar Jumper — Video Length: 02:09

http://oi.uchicago.edu/research/pubs/catalog/saoc/saoc67/saoc67_platycryptus_undatus.mp4

Jumping spiders do not build fixed web snares as do many spiders but do produce silk for a variety of uses including as material to build protective enclosures during molt, to fashion a container for their eggs, or for constructing an over-wintering shelter. When jumping to catch prey they also use a silken strand much like a rock climber uses a rope. Hentz's description includes the following: "Before leaping, this Attus always fixes a thread on the point from which it departs; by this it is suspended in the air if it miss its aim, and it is secure against falling far from its hunting ground" (Burgess 1875, p. 57).

Salticus scenicus (Clerck) — Zebra Jumper — Video Length: 02:26

http://oi.uchicago.edu/research/pubs/catalog/saoc/saoc67/saoc67_salticus_scenicus.mp4

Sitticus concolor (Banks) — Video Length: 01:33

http://oi.uchicago.edu/research/pubs/catalog/saoc/saoc67/saoc67_sitticus_concolor.mp4

Sitticus fasciger (Simon) — Video Length: 00:56

http://oi.uchicago.edu/research/pubs/catalog/saoc/saoc67/saoc67_sitticus_fasciger.mp4

Sitticus floricola palustris (Peckhams) — Video Length: 00:57

http://oi.uchicago.edu/research/pubs/catalog/saoc/saoc67/saoc67_sitticus_floricola_palustris.mp4

Sitticus pubescens (Fabricius) — Video Length: 02:05

http://oi.uchicago.edu/research/pubs/catalog/saoc/saoc67/saoc67_sitticus_pubescens.mp4

Synemosyna formica (Hentz) — Video Length: 01:24

http://oi.uchicago.edu/research/pubs/catalog/saoc/saoc67/saoc67_synemosyna_formica.mp4

Mimicry is a common adaptation in a variety of organisms and is especially prevalent in the insect world. Some arachnids are also mimics and mimetic adaptations may function in different ways. Many red salticids living in xeric habitats are thought to mimic velvet "ants" (wasps). The mutillids are actually kleptoparisitic wasps whose wingless females are known for their powerful sting. A jumping-spider mimic of this wasp may deter predators by its look-alike form (Edwards 1984). The present species is an ant mimic. Their rather astonishing similarity to ants may function as a protective adaptation against potential predators that find ants distasteful, but it may also provide "cover" as the spider hunts the ants themselves by facilitating a close approach without alarming its prey.

Talavera minuta (Banks) — Video Length: 00:44

http://oi.uchicago.edu/research/pubs/catalog/saoc/saoc67/saoc67_talavera_minuta.mp4

Tutelina elegans (Hentz) — Video Length: 03:02

http://oi.uchicago.edu/research/pubs/catalog/saoc/saoc67/saoc67_tutelina_elegans.mp4

Tutelina harti (Peckham in Emerton) — Video Length: 01:09

http://oi.uchicago.edu/research/pubs/catalog/saoc/saoc67/saoc67_tutelina_harti.mp4

Zygoballus nervosus (Peckham & Peckham) — Video Length: 01:35

http://oi.uchicago.edu/research/pubs/catalog/saoc/saoc67/saoc67_zygoballus_nervosus.mp4

Zygoballus rufipes (Peckhams) — Hammerjawed Jumper — Video Length: 01:54

http://oi.uchicago.edu/research/pubs/catalog/saoc/saoc67/saoc67_zygoballus_rufipes.mp4

Acknowledgments

Jay Barnes, Contributing Editor, *BugGuide*; G. B. Edwards, Curator: Arachnida (except Acari), Myriapoda, Terrestrial Crustacea, Thysanoptera Florida State Collection of Arthropods; Patsy Eickelberg; Jo Ann Hackett; John Heuhnergard; and Wayne Maddison, Professor and Canada Research Chair, Departments of Zoology and Botany University of British Columbia.

Bibliography

Burgess, Edward, editor

1875 *The Spiders of the United States: A Collection of the Arachnological Writings of Nicholas Marcellus Hentz M.D.* Boston: Boston Society of Natural History.

Cameron, H. D.

2005 "An Etymological Dictionary of North American Spider Genus Names." In *Spiders of North America: An Identification Manual*, edited by D. Ubick, P. Paquin, P. E. Cushing, and V. Roth, chapter 73. 2005. Poughkeepsie: American Arachnology Society.

Darwin, Charles

1859 *On the Origin of Species by Means of Natural Selection, or the Preservation of Favoured Races in the Struggle for Life.* London: John Murray.

Edwards, G. B.

1984 "Mimicry of Velvet Ants (Hymenoptera: Mutillidae) by Jumping Spiders (Araneae: Salticidae)." *Peckhamia* 2/4: 46–49. *Peckhamia* 2/4: 46–49. Available online; search for Peckhamia 59.1: http://peckhamia.com/pubs.html

2004 *Revision of the Jumping Spiders of the Genus Phidippus (Araneae: Salticidae).* Occasional Papers of the Florida State Collection of Arthropods 11. Gainesville: Florida Department of Agriculture and Consumer Services.

Emerson, Ralph Waldo

1862 "Thoreau." *The Atlantic Monthly* 10/58: 124–36.

Hentz, Nicholas Marcellus

1845 "Descriptions and Figures of the Araneides of the United States." *Boston Journal of Natural History* 5: 189–202.

Leopold, Aldo

1949 *A Sand County Almanac, and Sketches Here and There.* New York: Oxford University Press.

Locke, John

1689 *An Essay Concerning the True Original, Extent and End of Civil Government.* Published Anonymously. Printed for Awnsham and John Churchill, at the Black Swan in Pater-Noster-Row.

Maddison, Wayne P.

1996 "*Pelegrina Franganillo* and Other Jumping Spiders Formerly Placed in the Genus *Metaphidippus* (Araneae: Salticidae)." *Bulletin of the Museum of Comparative Zoology.* 154/4: 215–368.

Mitchell, Stephen, translator

2000 *Bhagavad Gita: A New Translation.* New York: Three Rivers Press.

Platnick, Norman I.

2000–2012 *The World Spider Catalog*, Version 13.0. New York: American Museum of Natural History. Available online: http://research.amnh.org/iz/spiders/catalog/

Thoreau, Henry David

1849 *A Week on the Concord and Merrimack Rivers.* Boston and Cambridge: James Munroe.

1971– *Writings.* 13 volumes to date. Princeton: Princeton University Press.

Ubick, D.; P. Paquin; P. E. Cushing; and V. Roth, editors

2005 *Spiders of North America: An Identification Manual.* Poughkeepsie: American Arachnology Society.

von Humboldt, Alexander

1806 *Personal Narrative of a Journey to the Equinoctial Regions of the New Continent.* Abridged edition. New York: Penguin Books, 1696.

Walton, Richard K.

1984 *Birds of the Sudbury River Valley: An Historical Perspective.* Lincoln: Massachusetts Audubon Society.

Walton, Richard K., and John Huehnergard

2006 *Henry David Thoreau — Speaking for Nature.* Concord: Three Rivers Productions. DVD, 50 minutes.

White, Gilbert

1887 *The Natural History of Selborne.* London: Walter Scott.

28

Verbal Endings in the Afroasiatic Prefix Conjugations

Andrzej Zaborski, Jagiellonian University

Contemporary — that is, the living — Afroasiatic/Hamitosemitic languages represent different stages: some of them have preserved many important archaisms going back to the oldest historical periods and even to prehistorical Proto-Afroasiatic dialect cluster, while others have introduced radical changes that make them very innovative even in comparison with languages that had undergone substantial evolution from Old Afroasiatic much earlier. Just like in the case of the living Indo-European languages, there are very archaic and very innovating living Afroasiatic languages today. There are very few true Hamitosemitists since one cannot study Hamitosemitic/Afroasiatic linguistics at a university, although one can study Indo-European linguistics, and, therefore, among Semitists, not to mention Egyptologists, there is still a strong tendency to ignore the evidence of the languages from other branches, which, except Egyptian and Berber (the latter unnecessarily misnamed "Libyan" as far as the oldest deciphered ancient records are concerned) are known almost exclusively from the sources going back to the nineteenth or the twentieth century. There are two answers that can be given to the hypercritical questions about a possibility of comparison of ancient and modern languages. (1) The relative chronology of language history and change is different from the chronology of written records so that there are cases of very early recording of not very archaic languages (e.g., early recorded Hittite shows a number of morphological innovations; in case of Afroasiatic, Egyptian has lost the prefix conjugation and has developed a new verbal system based on nominalizations that have typological parallels, e.g., in much later Aramaic and Ethiosemitic), and there are cases of rather late records of languages that have preserved many archaic features — Lithuanian is a classical example within Indo-European, while Modern Semitic of Southern Arabia (usually called Modern South Arabian) represents Semitic in this case. Archaic and innovating languages coexist — for example, today within the Germanic branch archaic, and typically inflectional Icelandic coexists with Afrikaans, which is the most analytic or "inflectionless" Indo-European language; within contemporary Semitic (apart from Modern South Arabian), relatively many conservative Arabic dialects (not to mention Modern Literary Arabic!) coexist with very innovative Neoaramaic. (2) The result is that even if we had known only the living Semitic languages since the nineteenth century ignoring earlier records of Semitic, nevertheless it would be possible (using the evidence of such conservative languages like Modern South Arabian, Tigre, and many archaic Arabic dialects even without Modern Literary Arabic) to write a comparative-historical grammar of the Semitic languages that would not be radically different (although it would certainly be more controversial and less detailed) from the grammar that is based on Akkadian, Classical Arabic, Ugaritic, and so on. There is no doubt that longer-range comparison, that is, the comparison of Semitic with other branches (first of all Berber and Old Cushitic, which have preserved the prefix conjugation), can be sometimes rather risky, but there is also no doubt that there is no scientific excuse for ignoring these and other archaic contemporary languages that may elucidate some problems of the internal reconstruction of Proto-Semitic. A long time ago, Marcel Cohen maintained that allegedly Proto-Hamitosemitic was tantamount to Proto-Semitic, but in my opinion the nearest relatives, Berber and Old Cushitic (Beja, ʿAfar-Saho, and Rendille), have preserved some archaic features that had been either lost or marginalized in the oldest (both in relative and in absolute terms) Semitic languages — for example, the system of stem and prefix vowels in Berber and in Old Cushitic is in many respects more archaic than in Semitic (probably with the exception of Modern South Arabian; see Zaborski 2007), despite the fact that, quite naturally, even in the most conservative Berber and Cushitic dialects, archaisms coexist with innovations like everywhere.

The vocalic endings of the verbal categories (tense/aspect and mood, i.e., TAM) conjugated with prefixes (traditionally called "prefix conjugation") started disappearing very early in Proto-Afroasiatic, but at least in Semitic and in Old Cushitic represented by ʿAfar[1] and Saho, the following morphemes have been preserved: (1) *-u* of the Imperfect Indicative (shifted to future and conjunctive in ʿAfar and Saho), (2) *-a* of the subjunctive (in ʿAfar preserved in the negative present), (3) zero ending of the past (any connection with **-i/e* of the Cushitic past?) with a secondary function of jussive, and (4) *-an(na)/-am* of the *modi energici* (in Akkadian surviving as "ventive" mainly, but not exclusively, with the verbs of motion). As is well known, in Semitic these morphemes have partially survived almost exclusively in Modern Literary Arabic[2] as a result of the traditional school teaching of this language, which is not a real mother tongue of any Arab today. The question is whether these endings have survived elsewhere and what can be hypothetically reconstructed for Proto-Afroasiatic.

Let me introduce some elementary data on the Beja verbs conjugated with prefixes that represent both archaisms and innovations. I was the first after Reinisch (1893, §202) to remind years ago (Zaborski 1997a and 1997b; cf. Fleisch 1944, who missed the fact, although he did check the grammars of Beja) that the third derivational class of Semitic verbs — that is, *qātala* (misnamed "conative") being a variant of the second or D "intensive" or rather "multiple action" class — has a cognate in Beja (e.g., *o-tak i-dír-na* 'they killed the man' but *ēn-da i-dār-na* 'they killed the men'; cf. verbal nouns, i.e., *nomina actionis* with *-ā-*, in this case *dār*) in which the plural forms of the present of the first class go back to the intensive with *-ē-* (< **ā*) in the prefix vowel.[3] In biconsonantal verbs, this long *-ē-* of the prefix occurs together with the *-i* ending in "intensive" forms of the present, for example, *ē-dir-i* 'I kill often/many' and *nē-dir-i* 'we kill often/many,' but the *-i* ending in at least some verbs may go back rather to root final *-y* (or *-ʾ* as Reinisch [1895, p. 69] connected Beja *d-r* tentatively with Arabic *d-r-ʾ*) — since there is, for example, *tē-diri-y-i* 'you (fem.) kill often/many,' *tē-diri-a* 'you (masc.) kill often/many,' *tē-diri-na* 'you (pl.) kill often/many,' and so on (Roper 1928, pp. 68–69) — although *-i* does not appear in other "tenses," for example, *a-dir* 'I killed,' *tí-dir-a* 'you (masc.) killed,' *tí-dir-i* 'you (fem.) killed.' There is another problem — Reinisch (1895, p. 69) provides an intensive pluperfect (old past used also in conditional clauses) form *ī-der-a* with *-a*, which needs verification since it is not mentioned in other sources!

Apart from the doubtful -i of the intensive present of biconsonantal verbs discussed above, there are some other alleged remnants of the TAM endings in Beja — for example, the past of *hay* has *-i*, such as *ī-h-í* and *ī-f-i* 'he was,' *nī-h-í* 'we were,' but in the present it has *-é* (< *a ?) in the dialect described by Roper (1928, p. 78) , such as *i-h-é* and *ē-f-e* 'he is,' *ne-h-é* and *nē-f-e* 'we are,' but *-i* and *-a* in the dialect described by Wedekind, Wedekind, and Abuzeinab (2007, pp. 123–24), that is, *ē-f-i* and *ih-a* 'he is.' Negative present has a zero ending, such as *k-í-hay* 'he is not' and *kí-n-hay* 'we are not,' and optative has *-a*, for example, *bā-y-hi-a* 'let him be' and *bā-n-hi-a* 'let us be.' Perhaps the optative *-a* could be identified with the Semitic *-a* of the subjunctive, but there are big questions concerning these final vowels since there are also verbs that have *-i* in the present, such as *i-bār-i* 'he has,' and in the past, such as *ī-bir-i* 'he had'; compare *ē-yīm-i* 'it is raining' (Roper 1928, p. 69). There are also past forms with *-e*, such as *ī-yih-é* 'he took,' *ē-n-e* or *í-d-e* 'he said' (Morin 2001, p. 121, has only forms with *-i*, e.g., *ídi* in the dialect of Gash) and with *-a* (see above). Since these endings occur with "defective," that is, monoconsonantal or biconsonantal verbs, a lot of further research is needed to elucidate the problem.

A similar problem exists in Berber, where vocalic endings occur also with "defective" verbs, although there are also triconsonantal verbs that have such endings, such as Tuareg present *yu-rd-u*, past *yu-rd-a*, negative past *yu-rd-e* 'to think,' then (in the same order) *yu-qq-u*, *yu-qq-a*, *yu-qq-e* 'to vomit'; Kabyle past *i-wal-i*, present *i-wal-a*, 'to think,' then (in the same order) *i-li*, *i-l-a* 'to have,' *yi-n-i* and *ye-nn-a* 'to say,' *ye-sfuhr-i* and *ye-sfuhr-a* 'to make insolent.' There are different endings in the intensive past, such as Ahaggar Tuareg past *ils-a*: intensive past *ils-â*, Irjen dialect *yelsa*: *yels-i* 'to dress oneself'; Kabyle dialect: *yefk-a* : *yefk-i* 'to give.' There is *-i* in some negative paradigms, and Brugnatelli (2002) has repeated his earlier hypothesis that the appearance of *-i* instead of *-a* in negative paradigms may be due to a postposed negative particle — this is possible but not quite clear, since *-i* with some verbs occurs also in the imperfect/"aorist" (see examples in Naït-Zerrad 1994, pp. 191–92 and elsewhere; cf. Kossmann 1989, pp. 21–22). Berber *-u* of the present seems to correspond to the *-u* of the Semitic imperfect, whose cognate has been shifted in ʿAfar to a conjunctive (usually called subjunctive) function. By the way: the Semitic imperfect *yaqtul-u* does not go back to the

[1] The spelling "Qafar" with <q> for *ʿayn* should be avoided in foreign languages.

[2] Another, somewhat controversial, case is Gurage, e.g., Goggot and Muxer; see Hetzron 1977, pp. 90–92, and 1972, pp. 37–38.

[3] Original auxiliary 'to be' < 'to live' allegedly surviving with a secondary meaning 'to say, to speak'; there is a chance that it might be either the well-known *h-w-y* as suggested by Hetzron (1975 and 1980) at least for passive forms or *H-y-y* reduced to a vowel.

Akkadian subordinative allegedly shifted to main clauses, but *iprus-u* = *yaqtul-u* survived, ousted by *iparras* from the main clauses, in subordinate clauses, namely, not before a pause as subordinative *iprus-u* (Kuryłowicz 1972, pp. 53–54). This was explained already by Sarauw (1912, p. 68) and was accepted by, among others, Hetzron (1974, pp. 187–89), but ignored by Assyriologists so much that I rediscovered it in my paper of 2010, where Sarauw should have been quoted. In general the *-u* of the indicative survived in Akkadian in non-pausal forms, that is, not only in the old imperfect shifted to subordinative as *iprus-u* but also in non-pausal, that is, in subordinate clause forms of *iparras-u*.

Prasse — the great master of Tuareg and general Berber linguistics — has ascribed every survival of final vowels in "weak" verbs to the alleged original *-h*. It is clear, however, that Berber had and still has *ultimae w* and *ultimae y* verbs like Semitic and Cushitic (not to mention Egyptian and Chadic) in which final /w/ and /y/ conditioned the vocalic *Auslaut* (see Basset 1929, pp. 58–66, 197–213). It is rather improbable that only final *-h* ("original" or secondary?) could be responsible for that. Actually, Prasse (1972–2009, §1:114–16) discusses the alternation of Tuareg /w/, /y/, and */h/ (the last one with asterisk!). When we have in Tuareg imperfect *yurd-u*, perfect positive *yurd-a*, perfect negative *yurd-e*, intensive perfect *yurd-â*, positive intensive imperfect *itûrd-u*, and negative intensive imperfect *iturd-u* of 'to think' reconstructed respectively as **yārduh, *yūrdah, *yūrdīh, *yūrdâh, *yitûrdūh, *yitūrdūh,*[4] and *iruh-u, yaruh-a* = *yaruh-a, yarūh-u* and *itirūh-u* of '(French) dégringoler' (Prasse 1972–2009, §§3:245, 4:371), it is not quite certain that all the verbs of this kind must be reconstructed only in this way. Compare also (in the same order) *ilk-u, ilk-a, ilk-e, ilûkk-u,* and *ilukk-u* 'to hate, to despise'; *yar, yur-a, yur-e, itâr,* and *itir* 'to open'; *ilw-i, yälw-a, yälw-e, itîlw-i,* and *itilw-i* 'to be large'; and *ilkensi, ilkän-sa=ilkäns-a, yälîkäns-a, itîlkens-i,* and *itelkens-i* 'to lie dead.' Compare Arabic imperfect *yarmī* and subjunctive *yarmiy-a*, passive imperfect *yurm-ā* of 'to throw.' It is highly probable that the Tuareg forms like imperfect *yämmät* and perfect *yämmut* of 'to die' (cf. Rendille *yamūt* 'he is dying') originally not only differed in the stem apophony but also had different endings, probably *-u* and zero. The problem of the Berber short vocalic endings in verbs requires a lot of further research — phonological, morphological, and etymological reconstruction.

Is it possible to find traces of the original Proto-Berber vocalic endings in verbal forms elsewhere? Vocalic endings could have survived in front of the suffixed personal pronouns and other possible suffixes. Actually, the Berber prefix conjugation uses both personal prefixes and personal suffixes going back to personal pronouns with the exception of the future in the dialect of Ghadames, which is an archaism as pointed out by Kossmann (2000, p. 250, and 2001, p. 35). Prasse (1963 and 1972–2009, §§2:9–11, 4:95) speaks about a mixed "prefix and suffix conjugation," for example, 1st sing. *e-kres-äG*, 2nd sing. *te-kres-äd* 'to make a knot' where *-äG* (< (*n*)-*ak* 'I') and *-äd* (<*-*at* 'you (sing.)') are used with quality verbs in the paradigm cognate to the Akkadian stative, for example, Tuareg (Prasse 1972–2009, §§2:11, 4:356) *waššar-äG* 'I am old,' (*te*)*waššar-äd* 'you are old' (with facultative prefix!), Kabyle *meqqr-eG* 'I am big,' *meqqr-ed* 'you are big' (Naït-Zerrad 1994, pp. 214–34; 2001, pp. 88–89), but see Galand-Pernet 1991 and Galand 2010, pp. 108–09, for alternative hypothetical etymologies. The question is whether in Berber and in the Cushitic languages personal pronouns in their elsewhere-independent forms are simply suffixed to verbs conjugated with prefixes. Is it possible that it was rather a postposed suffix-conjugated auxiliary whose stem had been reduced to a vowel that was later elided? This would be the model of the Neoethiosemitic (there probably due to the contact with Cushitic) periphrastic conjugation used for example in Amharic, that is *ye-säbr-allä-h, EnnE-säbr-allä-n* but in more innovative Harari *yi-säbr-āx, ni-säbr-āna*, Selti *tE-sabr-a* (Hetzron 1972, pp. 39–40). In this way forms like Tuareg *e-lmed-aG* 'I learn' and *te-lmed-ad* 'you learn' could go back to something like **e-lmad-Vk(u), *telmed-Vat*, where -V- stands for an original suffix-conjugated auxiliary reduced to a vowel. I emphasize that this is only an *Arbeitshypothese*. Compare also Somali *ti-râh-da/ti-râh-a/ti-râh* 'you say,' *ni-râhan-na/ni-râh-na/ni-râh* 'we say,' and so on, and *ti-râh-did* 'that/let you say,' which suggest a relationship with Berber (Zaborski 1975, pp. 48–49). In this case one of the difficulties consists in the fact that in Berber these personal suffixes occur in all the "tenses"[5] of the prefix conjugation. Analogy could work in this direction. A more complicated and therefore less probable assumption would be that there were several suffix-conjugated auxiliaries in postposition, but the whole explanation must be much more sophisticated and requires further research. In any case, Galand's reservation (Galand 2010, p. 108) is that Prasse's hypothesis about the mixed prefix and suffix conjugation in Berber is too vague — actually Galand says only that this hypothesis may be too much influenced by the data of West Semitic.

---

[4] Prasse 1972–2009, §§2:134, 1:73; cf. 4:ix, where he quotes intensive imperfect forms of the *ultimae y* verbs with *-iy*, and see paradigms on pp. 354–55.

[5] Except the Ghadamsi future mentioned above; see also Galand 2010, pp. 106–07, for forms without these suffixes.

Original verbal endings might have survived also before suffixed pronouns. While suffixed indirect-object personal pronouns have initial -â-, [6] suffixed object personal pronouns with vocalic *Anlaut* — that is, *i, î-k, î-m, ê, ê-t, â-nä-G, î-wän, î-k-mä-t, î-n, î-nä-t* — replace the vocalic endings of the "weak" verbs, namely, of the imperfect and, less frequently, **-a* of the intensive imperfect, while in Kabyle final vowels of the "weak verbs" remain, and the hiatus is eliminated by *-y-*, for example, *inna-y-as* 'he told him' (Naït-Zerrad 1994, p. 28). The same happens in Beja, for example, *áne deyā-y-ó-ki* 'I told you' (Roper 1928, pp. 31–32), although this may be due to phonological universals. It is remarkable that the vowels of the personal possessive pronouns suffixed to nouns in Tuareg have also variants (Prasse 2009, p. 1012) with *-e-* and *-i-*, such as *-ek* and *-ik*, *-ak* 'your (masc.),' and *-em* and *im*, *-am* 'your' (fem.). Thus the evidence of the initial vowels of the suffixed personal pronouns is not clear, and it is possible that the original verbal endings have not survived before them, but this problem also requires further research. The same concerns the forms in front of other suffixes (demonstratives and particles).

By the way: there is an *-h-* before personal suffixed direct and indirect object personal pronouns in Beja 1st sing. *-h-e-b* 'me,' *-h-o-k* 'you,' *-h-o-s* 'him/her,' *-h-o-n* 'us,' *-h-o-k-na* 'you (pl.),' *-h-o-s-na* 'them,' for example, *áne irhán-hokna* 'I saw you (pl.).'[7] In Tuareg the indirect-object personal pronouns are (Prasse 1972–2009: 1:176–77): 1st sing. *h-i*, 2nd masc. sing. *hâ-k*, 2nd fem. sing. *hâ-m*, 3rd *hâ-s*, 1st pl. *hâ-na-G*, 2nd masc. pl. *hâ-wan*, 2nd fem. pl. *hâ-k-mä-t*, 3rd masc. pl. *hâ-s-än*, 3rd fem. pl. *hâ-s-nä-t*. The forms of 1st sing. *hi* and 1st pl. hâ-näG are used also for the direct object. These pronouns are usually preverbal, but with a few verbs they are suffixed, for example, *aba-hâs* 'there is no ... for him,' *inna-hâs* = *inn-âs* 'he told him.' The origin of this *-h* (originally deictic, a preposition, or a particle?) remains obscure (Prasse 1972–2009, §1:177–78, 173), but a connection with the Arabic (also Ugaritic, Middle Aramaic, etc.) prefix in *hā-ka* 'here, take it' is probable (cf. Prasse 1972–2009, §1:179).

Mainly in Old Assyrian, but with remnants in Old Akkadian and in Old Babylonian (von Soden 1995, p. 135; Huehnergard 2005, p. 602), the ending of subordinative forms has additional *-ni* suffixed to the preserved vocalic ending *-u*, such as *iprus-ū-ni*. In Awngi[8] there is a paradigm called "conditional protasis imperfect" by Hetzron (1969, pp. 24–25) with the *-ú-ni* ending, that is, the ending of the Old Cushitic Subjunctive *-u* (< Proto-Afroasiatic imperfect/present; subjunctive *-u* survives also in Chadic) and the following *-ni*, such as *án des-ú-ni EncGe yégcé* 'if I study, I shall find work.' This occurs also in the "temporal" (Hetzron 1969, pp. 21–22) after the ending *-á* (going back to the Old Cushitic Present *-a*), and it expresses the idea of "when" and indicates that the main action was performed at the same time as the subordinate one, for example, *án des-á-ni kówa antáta kantGwà* 'when I studied, I saw you coming.' The "temporal" is also used in narrative texts as a connective element, that is, the last verb of the preceding sentence is repeated in the temporal form to continue the narration. It is a big question of whether Cushitic Awngi has preserved a morpheme that was used in Assyrian since the relative chronology gap (real time difference is not so important at all!) is very considerable. Perhaps this similarity is too nice to be a case of relationship. Nevertheless it should be taken into consideration even if Hetzron, who admitted the existence of very old archaisms in otherwise "late" or innovating languages (e.g., in Gurage), says (1969, p. 74) that "[t]he element *-ni* can be related etymologically to the second part of the interrogative pronoun *wóni* 'when.'" It is rather improbable that two semantically related suffixes meaning "if" and "when" could have a different origin. Theoretically the interrogative *wó-ni* could be a secondary formation using the postverbal *-ni*, but this weak hypothesis would need a lot of additional support.

General conclusion: as expected, TAM endings must be reconstructed for Proto-Afroasiatic prefix conjugation, or rather, conjugations. They have largely disappeared in Berber and in Beja and Somali (including Rendille) but have survived in Old Semitic (Akkadian, Classical Arabic, and Ugaritic) and in ʿAfar-Saho.

---

[6] Except 1st sing. *-i*; see Prasse 1972–2009, §1:176 and 173; Prasse 2009, pp. 1012–15 and 1972–2010, §4:342–43; Galand 2010, pp. 110–22.

[7] Wedekind et al. 2007, p. 133; Roper 1928, p. 29; with the old past/conditional and when the meaning of intention is dubious forms without *-h* are used — Roper 1928, para. 100 and 102.

[8] Pronounced [awNi], sometimes misspelled "Awnji," also called "Southern Agaw."

Abbreviations

A	aspect
fem.	feminine
M	mood
masc.	masculine
pl.	plural
sing.	singular
T	tense

Bibliography

Basset, André

1929 *La langue berbère — Morphologie — Le verbe — Étude de thèmes.* Paris: E. Leroux.

Brugnatelli, Vermondo

2002 "Les thèmes verbaux négatifs du berbère." In *Articles de linguistique berbère: mémorial Werner Vycichl,* edited by Kamal Naït-Zerrad, pp. 165–80. Paris: L'Harmattan.

Fleisch, Henri

1944 *Les verbes à allongement vocalique interne en sémitique.* Travaux et mémoires de l'Institut d'ethnologie 43. Paris: Institut d'ethnologie.

Galand, Lionel

2010 *Regards sur le berbère.* Studi camito-semitici 8. Milan: Centro studi camito-semitici.

Galand-Pernet, P.

1991 "Sur l'origine des désinences verbales en berbère." *Comptes rendus du Groupe linguistique d'études chamito-sémitiques* 29–30: 7–38.

Hetzron, Robert

1969 *The Verbal System of Southern Agaw.* Near Eastern Studies 12. Berkeley: University of California Press.

1972 *Ethiopian Semitic: Studies in Classification.* Journal of Semitic studies. Monograph 2. Manchester: Manchester University Press.

1974 "La division des langues sémitiques." In *Actes du premier Congrès international de linguistique sémitique et chamito-sémitique,* edited by André Caquot and David Cohen, pp. 181–94. Janua linguarum. Series practica 159. The Hague: Mouton.

1975 "La vocalisation de préfixes verbaux en sémitique." In *Etudes sémitiques,* edited by André Caquot, pp. 23–24. Actes du 29e Congrès international des orientalistes. Paris: L'Asiathèque.

1977 *The Gunnän-Gurage Languages.* Naples: Istituto orientale di Napoli.

1980 "The Vocalization of Prefixes in Semitic Active and Passive Verbs." *Mélanges de l'Université St. Joseph* 48: 35–48.

Huehnergard, John

2005 *A Grammar of Akkadian.* 2nd edition. Winona Lake: Eisenbrauns.

Kossmann, Marteen

1989 "L'inaccompli négatif en berbère." *Etudes et documents Berbères* 6: 19–29.

2000 "Le futur à Ghadamès et l'origine de la conjugaison verbale en berbère." In *Études berbères et chamito-sémitiques: mélanges offerts à Karl-G. Prasse,* edited by Salem Chaker, pp. 337–56. M.S. — Ussun amazigh 15. Louvain: Peeters.

2001 "Les désinences modales en berbère." *Rivista degli Studi Orientali* 74: 25–39.

Kuryłowicz, Jerzy

1972 *Studies in Semitic Grammar and Metrics.* Krakow: Ossolineum.

Morin, D.

2001 "Bridging the Gap between Northern and Eastern Cushitic." In *New Data and New Methods in Afroasiatic Linguistics: Robert Hetzron in memoriam*, edited by Andrzej Zaborski, pp. 117–24. Wiesbaden: Harrassowitz.

Naït-Zerrad, Kamal

1994 *Manuel de conjugaison kabyle.* Paris: L'Harmattan.

2001 *Grammaire modern du kabyle.* Paris: Karthala.

Prasse, Karl-G.

1957 "Le problème berbère des radicales faibles." In *Mémorial André Basset, 1895-1956*, edited by G.-S. Colin et al., pp. 121–30. Paris: A. Maisonneuve.

1963 "Les affixes personnels du verbe berbère." *Acta Orientalia* 27: 11–21.

1972–2009 *Manuel de grammaire touarègue.* Copenhagen: Akademisk Forlag.

2009 "Grammatik und Verbalsystem." In *Wörterbuch zur Sprache und Kultur der Twareg*, by Hans Ritter and Karl-G. Prasse, vol. 2, pp. 1003–89. Wiesbaden: Harrassowitz.

Reinisch, Leo

1893 *Die Bedauye-Sprache in Nordost-Afrika.* Vienna: A. Hölder.

1895 *Wörterbuch der Bedauye-Sprache.* Vienna: A. Hölder.

Roper, E. M.

1928 *Tu Beḍauye: An Elementary Handbook.* Hertford: S. Austin.

Sarauw, Ch.

1912 "Das altsemitische Tempussystem." In *Festschrift: Vilhelm Thomsen zur Vollendung des siebzigsten Lebensjahres am 25. Januar 1912*, edited by friends and colleagues, pp. 59–69. Leipzig. Harrassowitz.

von Soden, W

1995 *Grundriß der akkadischen Grammatik.* 3rd edition. Rome: Pontifium Institutum Biblicum

Wedekind, Klaus; Charlotte Wedekind; and Musa Abuzeinab

2007 *A Learner's Grammar of Beja (East Sudan).* Cologne: Rüdiger Köppe.

Zaborski, Andrzej

1975 *The Verb in Cushitic.* Krakow: PWN.

1997a "Qātala and Qattala in Semitic and Hamitosemitic." *Rocznik Orientalistyczny* 50: 257–62.

1997b "Problems of the Beja Present Seven Years Later." *Lingua Posnaniensis* 39: 145–53.

1997c "The Position of Cushitic and Berber within Hamitosemitic Dialects." In *Afroasiatic Neapolitana: contributi presentati all'8° Incontro di linguistica afroasiatic (camito-semitica)*, edited by Alessandro Bausi and Mauro Tosco, pp. 49–59. Naples: Istituto universitario orientale.

2005 "Tense, Aspect and Mood Categories in Proto-Semitic." In *Current Issues in the Analysis of Semitic Grammar and Lexicon*, edited by Lutz Edzard and Jan Retsö, vol. 1, pp. 11–30. Wiesbaden: Harrassowitz.

2007 "Notes on the Reconstruction of the 'Prefix-Conjugations' in Modern South Arabian Languages." *Lingua Posnaniensis* 49: 195–206.

2009 "Akkadian 'Subjunctive' *iprus-a*, Old Imperfective *iprus-u* and Energici *-am, -anni*." In *Language. Science and Culture: Essays in Honor of Professor Jerzy Bańczerowski*, edited by Piotra Łobacz, Piotr Nowak, and Wladyslaw Zabrocki, pp. 379–86. Poznan: Adam Mickiewicz University.

2010 "ʿAfar-Saho and the Position of of Cushitic within Hamitosemitic/Afroasiatic." In *Camsemud 2007: Proceedings of the 13th Italian Meeting of Afro-Asiatic Linguistics*, edited by Frederick Mario Fales and Giulia Francesca Grassi, pp. 139–47. History of the Ancient Near East, Monographs 10. Padua: S.A.R.G.O.N.

29

Prepositional Phrases as Subjects in Several Semitic Languages

Tamar Zewi, Haifa University

1. Prepositional Phrases as Subjects

Prepositional phrases might regularly play the role of logical/psychological subjects, namely topics or themes, as do all main word categories in many languages. But can they also serve as grammatical subjects?[1] Logical and grammatical subjects generally differ in their degree of grammaticalization, the latter being more formally marked as subject than the former. As Li and Thompson put it, "Subjects are essentially grammaticalized topics" (Li and Thompson 1976, p. 484; see also Hopper and Traugott 2003, pp. 28–29). Grammaticalization might be reflected in various language properties, a prominent one being verbal agreement between a subject and a verb (Hopper and Traugott 2003, p. 28). Although prepositional phrases cannot carry agreement markers, some prepositional phrases serving as grammatical subjects in English are indeed recognized and presented in English grammars, albeit as no more than a marginal feature: "prepositional phrases taking a nominal function." Some examples are "*Between six and seven* will suit me" (Quirk et al. 1972, p. 305), "*On Tuesday* will be fine," "*In March* suits me," "*During the vacation* is what we decided," and "*Between 6 and 7* may be convenient" (Quirk et al. 1985, p. 658).

Jaworska (1986) tackled this question yet again in English and Polish, principally to offer solutions for the proper presentation of prepositional phrases as subjects and objects in the government-binding framework. As she comments, various scholars writing in the frame of generative grammar have claimed that prepositional phrases serve as subjects in English only in copular constructions (Jaworska 1986, pp. 356–57, and other references there). Disputing these scholars, Jaworska presents other examples of prepositional phrases as subjects in English and Polish in non-copular constructions, suggesting that this feature is somewhat less marginal than previously assumed (Jaworska 1986, pp. 357–60). To the English examples already discussed in the linguistic literature, she adds passive and non-passive sentences, such as "*Until Christmas* was planned in detail," "*Behind the garage* is being reclaimed by the new tenants,"[2] and "*By air* seems to be quite cheap." She indicates that the prepositional phrases in these cases are temporal, are locative, or express manner, and must be "referential."[3]

[1] Logical/psychological subjects usually refer to the components conveying the given information or the information talked about in a clause, while another component serves in it as a grammatical subject, prevalently displaying grammatical agreement with the predicate and playing a role of an agent or a patient (Crystal 2003, pp. 441–42, 468). For parallel terms to "logical/psychological subjects," also see Goldenberg 1971, p. 37 n. 3. For discussion of various definitions of subject and predicate in Biblical Hebrew nominal clauses, see Zewi and van der Merwe 2001.

[2] This statement refers to prepositional phrases as both subjects and objects. The locative prepositional phrases presented in Jaworska 1986, p. 359, are in the role of object, and the example presented here in the role of subject is from ibid., p. 356.

[3] Prepositional phrases may also function as subjects in other languages. See, e.g., Frajzyngier 2008 on prepositional phrases in the role of subjects in Wandala (Central Chadic), their conditioning and limitations, in comparison to some other cases of dative subjects in other languages. I thank Professor Zygmunt Frajzyngier for this reference.

2. Prepositional Phrases as Subjects in Semitic Languages

Now, what do we see in Semitic languages? The languages examined in this paper are Hebrew, Arabic, Geʿez, and Biblical Aramaic. Their syntax is generally considered typical of Semitic languages in their classical phases, though Hebrew, Arabic, and Geʿez have been subject to change through the years, and they have adopted, adapted, and absorbed foreign syntactic patterns through contact with other Semitic and non-Semitic languages. The syntactic patterns discussed in this paper are mostly original in these four Semitic languages and have not evolved from such language contact. Though some of the constructions in question are not shared by all Semitic languages, not necessarily even by the four discussed here, and a few constructions appear only in one language, they should not be regarded as marginal developments but as genuine representative Semitic syntactic patterns.

Nominal clauses and verbal clauses are best treated separately here, as each clause type shows independent properties and might display different syntactic patterns of prepositional phrases as subjects.

2.1. Prepositional Phrases as Subjects in Semitic Nominal Clauses

Nominal clauses are profuse and central in Semitic languages, far more than in English and other Indo-European languages. They include (1) simple nominal-clause patterns consisting of just two main members, subject and predicate, without any additional member to express the predicative relation, and (2) extended nominal-clause patterns that include a pronominal element. This element is sometimes interpreted as a resumptive pronoun, or alternatively as a copula representing the predicative relation (e.g., Zewi 1996; Khan 2006, and more references there). With either interpretation, prepositional phrases are mostly found functioning as subjects in simple nominal clauses lacking additional pronominal elements.

Determining which of the two main components of a nominal clause plays the role of subject and which that of predicate is difficult, and often controversial. The main point to consider in this respect is that, except for nominal clauses with adjective or participle predicates, nominal clauses are in fact indifferent to the distinction between logical and grammatical subjects and predicates, as grammatical agreement between subject and predicate is regularly not required or marked in them. So many logical subjects and predicates in a nominal clause can also be interpreted and presented as grammatical subject and predicate. Prepositional phrases are well recognized as capable of serving as predicates in Semitic nominal clauses, and it remains to be seen whether they can also play a parallel role as subjects. The following discussion aims to prove that a subject role can regularly be played by prepositional phrases in Semitic nominal clauses, and it is clearly revealed in those expressing possession, location, time, manner, comparison, and partitive. As indicated above, Jaworska (1986, p. 359) recognized referential prepositional phrases expressing time, location, or manner as typical of prepositional phrases in the role of subjects in English verbal clauses. As the examples below suggest, there is a partial overlap in the patterns and contexts where prepositional phrases in the role of subject are found in Semitic and non-Semitic languages.

As to the syntactic analysis of the two main components of a Semitic simple nominal clause, where grammatical agreement is nowhere to be found, the predicative status should be attributed to the clause component that conveys the new information in the clause, or to the indefinite noun phrase, should there be one.[4] In such cases, if the other clause component is a prepositional phrase, it remains to serve as the subject. Even though this is a logical, not a grammatical, definition, it is the only one available or possible in such constructions. That is, the predicate status of one main clause component in this pattern and the subject status of the other component, the prepositional phrase, are established by the indefiniteness of the former, when available, and by context. From a standpoint expecting a subject role to be fulfilled by a nominal phrase, certain prepositional phrases replacing nouns, and involving ellipsis of a nominal head to which they are implicitly attributed, are defined as "nominalized," and the entire feature belongs to the domain of nominalization. This explanation is certainly apt when omission of a certain head is involved (ellipsis), and consequently the prepositional phrase becomes the predicate, for example, Modern Hebrew **בכתב** [זה] יותר טוב מאשר בעל פה 'A written [agreement/contract/etc.]

[4] On the contribution of "definiteness" to the identification of subject and predicate in Biblical Hebrew nominal clauses, see Zewi 1994, pp. 151–53; Lowery 1999; and Zewi and van der Merwe 2001. However, note that this feature is not available for us in all Semitic languages.

(literally: in writing) is better than an oral [one] (or: by heart),' where בכתב 'in writing' presumably stands for הסכם בכתב 'written agreement,' חוזה בכתב 'written contract,' and so on. In such cases the prepositional phrase is originally an attribute to a nominal head, which is absent but implicit in the clause. However, not all examples demonstrate ellipsis. Nominal clauses expressing possession, for example, contain prepositional phrases indicating possession in the role of subject without any ellipsis, and similarly certain prepositional phrases expressing location and manner. These are illustrated below.

Classification according to types is as follows.

2.1.1. Nominal Clauses Expressing Possession

Possession is mainly expressed in Biblical Hebrew[5] by the preposition לְ *lə*, for example, וַיְהִי-**לוֹ** צֹאן-וּבָקָר וַחֲמֹרִים וַעֲבָדִים וּשְׁפָחֹת וַאֲתֹנֹת וּגְמַלִּים 'And he had sheep, oxen, he-asses, menservants, maidservants, she-asses, and camels' (Gen 12:16) and הִנֵּה-נָא **לִי** שְׁתֵּי בָנוֹת אֲשֶׁר לֹא-יָדְעוּ אִישׁ 'Behold, I have two daughters who have not known man' (Gen 19:8). Possession is also revealed in a structurally similar construction expressing defiance, for example, מַה-**לִּי** וָלָךְ אִישׁ הָאֱלֹהִים 'What have you against me, O man of God' (1 Kgs 17:18), מַה-**לִּי** וָלָךְ 'What have I to do with you?' (2 Kgs 3:13), מַה-**לִּי** וָלָךְ מֶלֶךְ יְהוּדָה 'What have we to do with each other, king of Judah?' (2 Ch 35:21). In all these examples, the possessive pronouns attached to the Biblical Hebrew preposition לְ *lə* are incarnated in the English translation by subject pronouns, as obliged by the English rules for possessives.

Logically, the Biblical Hebrew possessive suffixes and the English subject pronouns play in these examples a similar role. This similitude appears yet again in the interchange of prepositional phrases with subject pronouns in clauses like וַיֹּאמֶר לָהֶם הֲשָׁלוֹם **לוֹ** וַיֹּאמְרוּ שָׁלוֹם 'He said to them, 'Is it well with him?' They said, "It is well"' (Gen 29:6), and שלום הוא* *'He is well,' as in וְאַתָּה שָׁלוֹם 'Peace be to you' (1 Sam 25:6), according to the *RSV*, or alternatively 'be well' (Kogut 1993, p. 102; Zewi 2002, p. 112). Such an interchange also occurs in Bible translations, for example, Saadya Gaon's translation of Genesis 29:6 by אסאלם הו (Derenbourg edition) or אהו סאלם (Ḥasīd edition), in which an independent personal pronoun in a subject role replaces the Biblical Hebrew prepositional phrase לו (Zewi 2002, p. 112). Similar replacement appears in the translation of this verse in the Geʿez Octateuch: **ዳኅን ፡ ውእቱ ፡** *dāḫn-ə-nu wəʾətu?* 'Is he well?' where *wəʾətu* is a 3rd personal pronoun and not a possessive prepositional phrase. Also notable is the reply to the question הֲשָׁלוֹם **לוֹ** in Gen 29:6 only by שָׁלוֹם: the elliptical reply maintains only the predicate, leaving the role of the subject to the prepositional phrase.[6] In all these examples, the prepositional phrases serve as logical as well as grammatical subjects. The construction itself is made up of an indefinite noun phrase, provided that indefiniteness is possible and marked, along with a preceding or following prepositional phrase indicating possession. It is a regular pattern in Biblical Hebrew, which does not involve any special linguistic operations like ellipsis or nominalization.

In later stages of Hebrew, the relative particle שֶׁ gradually merged with the following preposition לְ *lə* to create a new preposition of possession: *šel* שֶׁל. Originating as a relative clause expressing possession, this preposition came to play a role of a subject in a nominal clause, as in, for example, אַרְבַּע מִדּוֹת בָּאָדָם. הָאוֹמֵר **שֶׁלִּי** שֶׁלִּי **וְשֶׁלְּךָ** שֶׁלָּךְ, זוֹ מִדָּה בֵינוֹנִית. וְיֵשׁ אוֹמְרִים, זוֹ מִדַּת סְדוֹם. **שֶׁלִּי** שֶׁלָּךְ **וְשֶׁלְּךָ** שֶׁלִּי, עַם הָאָרֶץ. **שֶׁלִּי** שֶׁלָּךְ **וְשֶׁלְּךָ** שֶׁלָּךְ, חָסִיד. **שֶׁלִּי** שֶׁלִּי **וְשֶׁלְּךָ** שֶׁלִּי, רָשָׁע 'There are four sorts of people: He who says, "What's mine is mine and what's yours is yours" — this is the average sort. (And some say, "This is the sort of Sodom."). "What's mine is yours and what's yours is mine" — this is a boor. "What's mine is yours and what's yours is yours" — this is a truly pious man. "What's mine is mine and what's yours is mine" — this is a truly wicked man' (*Mishnah*, *Avot* 5,10).[7] Eight nominal clauses in this example consist of nothing but two prepositional phrases, composed of the prepositional particle שֶׁל plus possessive suffixes in the role of subject and predicate next to each other: **שֶׁלִּי** שֶׁלִּי, **וְשֶׁלְּךָ** שֶׁלָּךְ, **שֶׁלִּי** שֶׁלָּךְ, **וְשֶׁלְּךָ** שֶׁלִּי, **שֶׁלִּי** שֶׁלָּךְ, **וְשֶׁלְּךָ** שֶׁלָּךְ, **שֶׁלִּי** שֶׁלִּי, **וְשֶׁלְּךָ** שֶׁלִּי. These are justly translated into English as equative nominal clauses in the pattern 'What's mine/yours is mine/yours.' Since both the subject and the predicate in these clauses are prepositional phrases, there is no way but to analyze one of them as filling the role of a logical as well as a grammatical subject, while the other is the predicate. Since the prepositional phrases

---

[5] All Bible translations into English in this paper are according to the *RSV* unless indicated otherwise.

[6] See a brief discussion of this example in Zewi 1994, pp. 154–55 n. 29, where it is stated that prepositional phrases can function as subjects in Biblical Hebrew nominal clauses. For another brief discussion of prepositional phrases as subjects, see Zewi 2002, pp. 111–12.

[7] Translation is according to Neusner 1988.

שֶׁלִּי and שֶׁלְּךָ stand in these examples as replacements for relative clauses, they should be analyzed as nominalized, or more specifically as adjectivized, and as equivalent to independent relative clauses lacking a head. That is, שֶׁלִּי is equivalent to אשר לי without a head and הדבר/מה אשר/ש- לי with a head (Goldenberg 1995; Pat-El and Treiger 2008, p. 277). This parallelism is also reflected in the English translation employing the word "what" in "what's mine/yours."

Constructions similar to the Biblical Hebrew pattern of a prepositional phrase composed of *lə* plus a personal suffix, which marks possession, and an indefinite noun phrase indicating the item in possession, also exist in Arabic. Examples in Classical Arabic are, for example, وَلَهُمْ عَذَابٌ عَظِيمٌ 'Theirs is great deprivation (literally: for them is great deprivation)' (Koran 2:7),[8] in which the noun عَذَابٌ is indefinite and therefore should be understood as a predicate. Similarly وَلَهُمْ عَذَابٌ أَلِيمٌ 'Theirs is suffering/painful punishment (literally: for them is suffering// painful punishment)' (Koran 2:10). Another pattern in which the prepositional phrase should be regarded as a subject is demonstrated in the negative clause with a prepositional phrase composed of *ʿalā* plus a personal suffix and a negated indefinite noun phrase وَلَا خَوْفٌ عَلَيْهِمْ '[They] will have no fear' (Koran 2:62). Especially notable is the following example in which two prepositional phrases serve as the two main parts of the clause, the former as a predicate and the latter as a subject: وَمَا لِلظَّالِمِينَ مِنْ أَنصَارٍ 'But the wicked will have none to help them (lit.: No[ne] to the wicked out of/as to helpers)' (Koran 2:270). The subject, مِنْ أَنصَارٍ, is initiated by the Arabic preposition *min* as a partitive particle.[9] A closely similar example is وَمَا لَهُمْ مِّن نَّاصِرِينَ 'And none will they have to help them' (Koran 3:22). More examples with this *min lil-bayān* are further discussed below. Another type expressing possession by a prepositional phrase introduced by *lə*, in which both subject and predicate are prepositional phrases, is, for example, هل لكم بسيّد أهل الشأم 'Do you have/Can you get the chieftain of the people of aš-Šaʾm?' (Nöldeke 1895, p. 50). In such examples, again, only prepositional phrases can serve as subject and predicate, since there are no other main components in the clause to play this role.

A similar pattern, consisting of a prepositional phrase composed of *lə* plus a personal suffix, which marks possession, next to an indefinite noun phrase indicating the item in possession, also exists in Biblical Aramaic, for example, וְאַרְבְּעָה רֵאשִׁין **לְחֵיוְתָא** 'And the beast had four heads' (Dan 7:6), וְשִׁנַּיִן דִּי-פַרְזֶל **לַהּ** 'And it had great iron teeth' (Dan 7:7), וְקַרְנַיִן עֲשַׂר **לַהּ** 'And it had ten horns' (Dan 7:7).

In Geʿez the preposition **በ** *ba* with suffixed personal pronouns assumes a similar role to express possession (Dillmann 1907, p. 407–08, §167, 437–38, §176h; Tropper 2002, pp. 218–20) and in the same way can also serve in such cases as a subject, for example, the translation of Gen 19:8 mentioned above הִנֵּה-נָא **לִי** שְׁתֵּי בָנוֹת 'Behold, I have two daughters' **ናሁ ፡ ብየ ፡ ክልኤ ፡ አዋልደ ፡** *nāhu **bəya** kəlʾe ʾawāləda*. Interestingly, the noun in possession might occasionally take the nominative in Geʿez but usually takes the accusative, consequently leaving the nominative slot to the prepositional phrase (Dillmann 1907, p. 438, §176h).

2.1.2. Nominal Clauses Expressing Location

Location, frequently expressed by the preposition בְּ *bə* in Biblical Hebrew, is found in, for example, אֲשֶׁר-**בּוֹ** רוּחַ חַיִּים '... in which is the breath of life' (Gen 6:17, 7:15). The indefinite status of the noun phrase רוּחַ חַיִּים indicates that it is the predicate and the new information in this clause. This leaves the prepositional phrase בּוֹ in the status of a subject. Likewise in **וּבוֹ** שֵׂעָר צָהֹב דָּק '...and the hair in it is yellow and thin' (*RSV*) / '... and there is thin yellow hair in it' (*JPS*) (Lev 13:30). The *JPS* translation in this case seems to reflect better the original Biblical Hebrew syntactic construction. Prepositional phrases in the subject role also exist in interrogative nominal clauses, for example, מִי **בֶחָצֵר** 'Who is in the court?' (Esth 6:4). In such clauses the interrogative pronoun is the logical predicate, because the reply to it is the new information, and once a logical predicate is acknowledged as identical to the grammatical predicate in every nominal clause lacking grammatical agreement, the prepositional phrase is left to play the role of a subject.

Modern Hebrew displays equative explicative nominal clauses that include a locative prepositional phrase in the role of subject in, for example, **בבית** זה בתוך הבית, לא בחצר 'In the house is inside the house, not in the

[8] Translations of the Koran are according to Ali 1988 with minor changes, mostly syntactic, where necessary.

[9] The Arabic grammatical term for this is *min lil-bayān* (Nöldeke 1895, p. 52; Wright 1896–1898, vol. 2, pp. 135–38; Reckendorf 1921, p. 254; Fischer 2002, p. 160). Note that Fischer (ibid., p. 185) acknowledges the subject role of a prepositional phrase introduced by this preposition.

backyard.' Modern Hebrew also displays examples like **בבית** מתאים לי 'At home suits me,' **בבית** זה מה שהחלטנו 'At home is what we decided,' and so on, which are counterparts of English (and Hebrew) examples similar to the temporal English ones presented above, such as "*In March* suits me" and "*During the vacation* is what we decided." All these Modern Hebrew examples can be explained as nominalizations, in which infinitives are omitted before noun phrases like 'to be at home'/'to do it at home' and so on.

Clauses consisting of locative prepositional phrases in the role of subject alongside an indefinite noun phrase are very common in Classical Arabic, for example, **فِي قُلُوبِهِم** مَّرَضٌ 'Sickness is in their hearts' (Koran 2:10), in which the noun مَّرَضٌ is indefinite and consequently should be interpreted as a predicate. Likewise **وَفِي ذَٰلِكُم** بَلَاءٌ مِّن رَّبِّكُمْ عَظِيمٌ 'In this was a great trial from your Lord' (Koran 2:49) and **فِيهِ** آيَاتٌ بَيِّنَاتٌ مَّقَامُ إِبْرَاهِيمَ 'It contains (literally, in it) clear signs, and the spot where Abraham had stood' (Koran 3:97).[10] Another example of a prepositional phrase as subject in Arabic is **وعلى رأسه** كالقلنسُوَة 'And on the top of it (the pillar) is (something) like a pointed cap' (Wright 1896–1898, vol. 2, p. 176d). This example includes two prepositional phrases as the main components of the clause, so necessarily one, probably the former is the subject, and the other, probably the latter, is the predicate.[11]

Such a pattern comprising locative prepositional phrases in the role of subjects also exists in Biblical Aramaic. A similar example in Biblical Aramaic is **וּתְלָת עִלְעִין בְּפֻמַּהּ בֵּין [כתיב: שִׁנַּיִהּ] שִׁנַּהּ**: 'It had three ribs in its mouth between its teeth' (Dan 7:5). **וּתְלָת עִלְעִין** is the predicate in this example.

Examples of equivalent locative prepositional phrases as subjects in Ge'ez appear in, for example, the translation of קוֹל מִלְחָמָה בַּמַּחֲנֶה 'There is a noise of war in the camp' (Exod 32:17) **[ድ]ምፀ ፡ ፀባኢት ፡ ውስተ ፡ ትዕይንት ።** *[d]əmḍa ṣ(!)abāʾīt* ***wəsta təʿəyyənt***, and in the negative in כִּי לֹא-נַחַשׁ **בְּיַעֲקֹב** וְלֹא-קֶסֶם **בְּיִשְׂרָאֵל** 'For there is no enchantment in Jacob, no divination in Israel' (Num 23:23) **እስመ ፡ አልቦቱ ፡ ሰገለ ፡ ውስተ ፡ ያዕቆብ ፡ ወአልቦቱ ፡ መቅሰመ ፡ ውስተ ፡ እስራኤል ፡** *ʾəsma ʾalbotu sagala* ***wəsta Yāʿqob*** *wa-ʾalbotu maqsama* ***wəsta ʾəsrāʾel.***

2.1.3. Nominal Clauses Expressing Time

Prepositional phrases expressing time might also play the subject role in Biblical Hebrew, when an adjacent indefinite noun clause functions as a predicate. An example of this pattern, which is very similar to the nominal clauses expressing possession and location presented above, appears in the second part of the verse שִׁבְעַת יָמִים תֹּאכַל מַצֹּת **וּבַיּוֹם הַשְּׁבִיעִי** חַג לַה׳ 'Seven days you shall eat unleavened bread, and on the seventh day there shall be a feast to the LORD' (Exod 13:6). In the second half of this sentence, בַּיּוֹם הַשְּׁבִיעִי is the subject, and חַג לַה׳ the predicate. This can be learned from the contrast between וּבַיּוֹם הַשְּׁבִיעִי חַג לַה׳ and שִׁבְעַת יָמִים תֹּאכַל מַצֹּת of the first half of the sentence, which tells us that the new contrasting information is חַג לַה׳. Since this nominal clause shows no grammatical agreement, the new contrasting information is not just the logical but the grammatical predicate as well, so the temporal prepositional phrase בַּיּוֹם הַשְּׁבִיעִי is the logical and grammatical subject.

Constructions in which temporal prepositional phrases serve as subjects are typical of Modern Hebrew, in equative explicative nominal clauses involving some kind of ellipsis, like **בשש** זה בעצם בשמונה. כולם מאחרים. — '[Coming/being/starting] on six is in fact on eight. Everybody is late.' Parallels of clauses involving temporal expressions like the English examples cited above — "*Between six and seven* will suit me," "*On Tuesday* will be fine," "*In March* suits me," "*During the vacation* is what we decided," "*Between 6 and 7* may be convenient" — are also possible in Modern Hebrew, with their verbal translations: **במהלך החופשה** זה מה שהחלטנו; **במרץ** מתאים לי; **ביום שלישי** יהיה בסדר; **בין שש לשבע** יתאים לי [**בין שש לשבע** יכול להיות נוח]. The prepositional phrases in the role of subjects in all these Modern Hebrew examples should be regarded as nominalized and as involving the omission of possible nominal heads to which the prepositional phrases are implicitly attributed.

---

[10] Several colloquial Arabic prepositional phrases might play a similar role (e.g., Fischer and Jastrow 1980, p. 186, §10.2.5). Beeston (1970, p. 68) defines the role of the indefinite locative prepositional phrases preceding indefinite nouns in such nominal clauses as "theme," while he defines the indefinite nouns themselves as "predicates." Beeston indicates (ibid.) that his analysis "runs counter to that of the Arab grammarians, who identify the prepositional phrase as predicate and the substantive as theme, and are hence obliged to say that a theme *can* be undefined *if* it follows a prepositional predicate."

[11] Wright indicates that the preposition *ka* is in fact not a preposition but a substantive "formally developed ... but may stand in any case ... [as] a governing word, to a following noun in the genitive" (Wright 1896–1898, vol. 2, p. 176d). These words actually suit most prepositions in Semitic languages, which are indeed grammaticalized nouns.

Similar constructions also appear in Arabic, for example, the translation of Saadya Gaon to וּבַיּוֹם הַשְּׁבִיעִי חַג לַה׳ '... and on the seventh day there shall be a feast to the LORD' (Exod 13:6) mentioned above, which is **ופי אליום אלסאבע** חג׳ ללה (Derenbourg and Ḥasīd editions), maintaining a structure similar to the Hebrew.

2.1.4. Nominal Clauses Expressing Manner

Nominal clauses expressing manner may also occasionally consist of prepositional phrases in the role of subject. A Biblical Hebrew example is כִּי **בְּאֵימָה עֲלֵיהֶם** מֵעַמֵּי הָאֲרָצוֹת 'for fear was upon them because of the peoples of the lands,' literally, 'for in fear was upon them...' (Ezra 3:3), which means 'they were in fear.' This is indeed rare in Biblical Hebrew.

Another possible Modern Hebrew example involving ellipsis and nominalization has already been mentioned above: **בכתב** [זה] יותר טוב מאשר בעל פה 'A written [agreement/contract/etc.] (lit.: in writing) is better than an oral [one] (or: by heart).'

2.1.5 Comparative Nominal Clauses

Biblical Hebrew examples consisting of prepositional phrases as subjects regularly appear in comparative nominal clauses in which two parts are compared to each other, both introduced by the comparative preposition כְּ *kə*. Examples of such comparative clauses in Biblical Hebrew are, for example, וְהָיָה **כַצַּדִּיק** כָּרָשָׁע '...so that the righteous fare as the wicked' (Gen 18:25), **כַּגֵּר** כָּאֶזְרָח יִהְיֶה 'As the sojourner, so will the native' (Lev 24:22),[12] **כָּכֶם** כַּגֵּר יִהְיֶה לִפְנֵי ה׳ 'As you are, so shall the sojourner be before the LORD' (Num 15:15), **כָּמוֹנִי** כָמוֹךָ **כְּעַמִּי** כְעַמֶּךָ **כְּסוּסַי** כְּסוּסֶיךָ 'I am as you are, my people as your people, my horses as your horses' (1 Kgs 22:4), וְהָיָה **כָעָם** כַּכֹּהֵן **כַּעֶבֶד** כַּאדֹנָיו **כַּשִּׁפְחָה** כַּגְּבִרְתָּהּ **כַּקּוֹנֶה** כַּמּוֹכֵר **כַּמַּלְוֶה** כַּלֹּוֶה **כַּנֹּשֶׁה** כַּאֲשֶׁר נֹשֶׁא בוֹ 'And it shall be, as with the people, so with the priest; as with the slave, so with his master; as with the maid, so with her mistress; as with the buyer, so with the seller; as with the lender, so with the borrower; as with the creditor, so with the debtor' (Isa 24:2). Since the particle כְּ *kə* is regarded as a preposition, each phrase it introduces is prepositional. In all the above examples, prepositional phrases introduced by the particle כְּ *kə* form both the subject and the predicate.

Other examples of similar prepositional phrases expressing comparison in the role of subject are found in Modern Hebrew equative nominal clauses, for example, **כמו/כפי שאמרת לי** זה בסדר 'It is OK as you said (literally, As you said is OK),' **כמו/כפי שהחליטו** זה טוב – 'It is good as decided.' The particles כמו and כפי are considered prepositions in Hebrew, and they evidently introduce the phrases serving as subject in these clauses.

The Arabic translation by Saadya Gaon for **כָּכֶם** כַּגֵּר יִהְיֶה לִפְנֵי ה׳ 'As you are, so shall the sojourner be before the LORD' (Num 15:15), mentioned above, presents a similar structure, in which a prepositional phrase serves as a subject: **כמא אן אלגריב** מת׳לכם בין ידי אללה (Derenbourg and Ḥasīd editions). Yet at the same time, it is different, because it employs not only the preposition *ka* but also a nominalizing complex כמא אן. Another Arabic example is فِي كَبِدِي كالنَّفْطِ 'There is something (burning) like oil in my liver' (cited in Fischer 2002, p. 185).

A similar pattern with prepositional phrases as subject and predicate is also attested in the Geʿez Bible translation of this verse: **በከመ ፡ አንትሙ** ፡ ከማሁ ፡ ግዩራን ፡ ቅድመ ፡ እግዚአብሔር ። ***bakama ʾantəmu*** *kamāhu gəyyurān qədma ʾƏgziʾabəher*. Here the comparative prepositions *bakama* and *kamāhu* introduce the two main components of the clauses.

2.1.6. Nominal Clauses Whose Subject Is a Prepositional Phrase Introduced by a Partitive Preposition *min*

Examples of the partitive *min* in Biblical Hebrew are, for example, **וּמִבְּנֵי הַכֹּהֲנִים** בְּנֵי חֳבַיָּה בְּנֵי הַקּוֹץ בְּנֵי בַרְזִלַּי 'Also, of the sons of the priests: the sons of Habaiah, the sons of Hakkoz, and the sons of Barzillai' (Ezra 2:61), and **וּמִן-הַנְּתִינִים** שֶׁנָּתַן דָּוִיד וְהַשָּׂרִים לַעֲבֹדַת הַלְוִיִּם נְתִינִים מָאתַיִם וְעֶשְׂרִים 'Besides two hundred and twenty of the temple

[12] I have used for Lev 24:22 my own translation to better reflect the special comparative pattern. The *RSV* has here 'You shall have one law for the sojourner and for the native.'

servants, whom David and his officials had set apart to attend the Levites,' according to the *RSV*, or 'And of the temple servants whom David and the officers had appointed for the service of the Levites — 220 temple servants,' according to the *JPS* (Ezra 8:20). The latter translation better reflects the use of the partitive prepositional phrase in the role of subject in this verse. The partitive *min* is more common in Late than in Classical Biblical Hebrew, and "it refers to persons and not to objects," as Qimron and Strugnell point out (1994, p. 93).[13]

A prepositional phrase containing the partitive *min* (*min lil-bayān*) is especially common in the role of subject in Arabic, for example, in Classical Arabic **وَمِنَ النَّاس** مَن يَقُولُ 'And there are some who say' (Koran 2:8), **وَمِنَ النَّاس** مَن يَشْرِي نَفسَهُ ابْتِغَاءَ مَرْضَاتِ اللَّهِ 'And there is a man who is willing to sell even his soul to win the favour of God' (Koran 2:207), **مِنكُم** مَّن يُرِيدُ الدُّنْيَا وَمِنكُم مَّن يُرِيدُ الْآخِرَةَ 'Some of you desired this world, and some of you the next' (Koran 3:152); وَإِنَّ **مِنْ أَهْلِ الْكِتَابِ** لَمَن يُؤْمِنُ بِاللَّهِ 'Certainly among the people of the Book are some who believe in God' (Koran 3:199). In all these clauses, the subject is the prepositional phrase introduced by the partitive *min* (*min lil-bayān*), and the predicate is a following phrase introduced by the nominalizing particle *man*.

More examples with the partitive *min* in verbal clauses in Arabic, Biblical Hebrew, and more are presented below.

Following the discussion and demonstration of the most common patterns in which prepositional phrases play a subject role in nominal clauses in Hebrew, Arabic, Biblical Aramaic, and Geʻez, it is time to see how this feature is used in verbal clauses in these languages.

2.2. Prepositional Phrases as Subjects in Semitic Verbal Clauses

Can a prepositional phrase serve as a grammatical subject in a clause whose grammatical predicate is a verb? It can in English and Polish, according to Jaworska (1986), as mentioned above. The situation in Semitic languages seems generally similar, and all the earlier English examples might retain a similar pattern in Modern Hebrew translation. In addition, verbal clauses in which prepositional phrases play a subject role seem generally to correspond to nominal clauses with prepositional subjects. Thus, in Modern Hebrew prepositional phrases expressing possession might be manifested in verbal clauses, such as **שלך** גדל **ושלי** לא 'Yours has grown and mine hasn't'; prepositional phrases expressing location can be found in verbal clauses, such as **בבית** התאים לנו 'At home suited us'; temporal prepositional phrases can be found in verbal clauses, such as **בשלוש** יתאים לנו 'At three will suit us'; and prepositional phrases expressing manner can be found in verbal clauses, such as **ברגל** נראה לנו יותר טוב מאוטובוס 'On foot seemed to us better than by bus.' All these clauses involve omission of an implicit nominal head (ellipsis) and should be defined in terms of nominalization.

In addition, certain constructions regularly employ prepositional phrases in the role of subject in verbal clauses, only in one Semitic language or more. The following are such patterns.

2.2.1. Verbal Clauses Whose Subject Is a Comparative Prepositional Phrase

Verbal clauses whose subject is a prepositional phrase introduced by the comparative preposition *kə* in Biblical Hebrew are, for example, וְהִנֵּה עֹמֵד לְנֶגְדִּי **כְּמַרְאֵה-גָבֶר** 'and behold, there stood before me [one] having the appearance of a man' (Dan 8:15), וְהִנֵּה **כִּדְמוּת בְּנֵי אָדָם** נֹגֵעַ עַל-שְׂפָתָי 'And behold, [one] in the likeness of the sons of men touched my lips' (Dan 10:16), and וַיֹּסֶף וַיִּגַּע-בִּי **כְּמַרְאֵה אָדָם** וַיְחַזְּקֵנִי 'Again [one] having the appearance of a man touched me and strengthened me' (Dan. 10:18). The comparative prepositional phrases of these examples כְּמַרְאֵה-גָבֶר, כִּדְמוּת בְּנֵי אָדָם, and כְּמַרְאֵה אָדָם are all grammatical subjects of adjacent participles and verbs, עֹמֵד, נֹגֵעַ, and וַיֹּסֶף וַיִּגַּע-בִּי, וַיְחַזְּקֵנִי, and they are also marked as such by grammatical agreement between the nouns following the prepositions and the verbs.

A similar example in Biblical Aramaic is **כְּבַר אֱנָשׁ** אָתֵה הֲוָה 'There came [one] like a son of man' (Dan 7:13), in which כְּבַר אֱנָשׁ is a comparative prepositional phrase serving as grammatical subject, the noun of which shows grammatical agreement with the following verbal phrase אָתֵה הֲוָה.

---

[13] I thank Dr. Matthew Morgenstern for mentioning this reference to me. On this use see also *BDB* 580b–581a and Ewald 1881, p. 41, mentioned in Qimron and Strugnell 1994, p. 93.

In all the examples in this section, a head "one/someone" is omitted and should be regarded as implicit. Consequently, the comparative prepositional phrases can be regarded as nominalized.

2.2.2. Verbal Clauses Whose Subject Is a Prepositional Phrase Introduced by the Partitive Preposition *min*

A prepositional phrase introduced by the partitive *min* is attested in Biblical Hebrew as a subject in nominal clauses as presented above, but also in verbal clauses. Examples of this construction are וַיְהִי בַּיּוֹם הַשְּׁבִיעִי יָצְאוּ **מִן-הָעָם** לִלְקֹט וְלֹא מָצָאוּ 'On the seventh day some of the people went out to gather, and they found none' (Exod. 16:27), in which the prepositional phrase מִן-הָעָם is the subject of the verb יָצְאוּ; אוֹ-דֹדוֹ אוֹ בֶן-דֹּדוֹ יִגְאָלֶנּוּ אוֹ-**מִשְּׁאֵר בְּשָׂרוֹ מִמִּשְׁפַּחְתּוֹ** יִגְאָלֶנּוּ 'Or his uncle, or his cousin may redeem him, or a near kinsman belonging to his family may redeem him' (Lev 25:49), in which the prepositional phrase מִשְּׁאֵר בְּשָׂרוֹ is the subject of the verb יִגְאָלֶנּוּ of a status equivalent to the noun phrases דֹּדוֹ and בֶן-דֹּדוֹ; וַיִּפֹּל **מִן-הָעָם מֵעַבְדֵי דָוִד** 'And some of the servants of David among the people fell' (2 Sam 11:17), in which the prepositional phrase מִן-הָעָם מֵעַבְדֵי דָוִד is the subject of the verb וַיִּפֹּל; וַיָּמוּתוּ **מֵעַבְדֵי הַמֶּלֶךְ** 'Some of the king's servants are dead' (2 Sam 11:24), in which the prepositional phrase מֵעַבְדֵי הַמֶּלֶךְ is the subject of the verb וַיָּמוּתוּ; **וּמִן-הַמַּשְׂכִּילִים** יִכָּשְׁלוּ לִצְרוֹף בָּהֶם וּלְבָרֵר וְלַלְבֵּן 'And some of those who are wise shall fall, to refine and to cleanse them and to make them white' (Dan. 11:35), in which the prepositional phrase וּמִן-הַמַּשְׂכִּילִים is the subject of the verb יִכָּשְׁלוּ; **וּמֵרָאשֵׁי הָאָבוֹת** בְּבוֹאָם לְבֵית ה' אֲשֶׁר בִּירוּשָׁלִָם הִתְנַדְּבוּ לְבֵית הָאֱלֹהִים לְהַעֲמִידוֹ עַל-מְכוֹנוֹ 'Some of the heads of families, when they came to the house of the LORD which is in Jerusalem, made freewill offerings for the house of God, to erect it on its site' (Ezra 2:68), in which the prepositional phrase וּמֵרָאשֵׁי הָאָבוֹת is the subject of the verb הִתְנַדְּבוּ; and **וּמֵרָאשֵׁי הָאָבוֹת** נָתְנוּ לְאוֹצַר הַמְּלָאכָה 'And some of the heads of fathers' houses gave into the treasury of the work' (Neh. 7:70), in which וּמֵרָאשֵׁי הָאָבוֹת is the subject of the verb נָתְנוּ. Compare the last example with its preceding verse **וּמִקְצָת רָאשֵׁי הָאָבוֹת** נָתְנוּ לַמְּלָאכָה 'Now some of the heads of fathers' houses gave to the work' (Neh 7:69), in which the prepositional phrase וּמִקְצָת introduces a noun, and together they constitute a prepositional phrase serving as subject. The word מִקְצָת is probably originally an Aramaic loanword and is demonstrated in a Biblical Aramaic example below.[14] As stated by Qimron and Strugnell (1994, p. 93) and mentioned above, the partitive *min* is found in Classical and Late Biblical Hebrew, but is more common in the latter.

An example in which the partitive *min* introduces prepositional phrases in the subject role is attested in Biblical Aramaic: וְאֶצְבְּעָת רַגְלַיָּא [כתיב: מִנְּהוֹן] מִנְּהֵין פַּרְזֶל [כתיב: וּמִנְּהוֹן] וּמִנְּהֵין חֲסַף **מִן-קְצָת מַלְכוּתָא** תֶּהֱוֵה תַקִּיפָה **וּמִנַּהּ** תֶּהֱוֵה תְבִירָה 'And as the toes of the feet were partly iron and partly clay, so the kingdom shall be partly strong and partly brittle' (Dan. 2:42). In the Biblical Aramaic construction, the prepositional phrases מִן-קְצָת מַלְכוּתָא and וּמִנַּהּ serve as grammatical subjects of the verbal phrases תֶּהֱוֵה תַקִּיפָה and תֶּהֱוֵה תְבִירָה. A literal translation would be 'part of the kingdom shall be strong and part of it brittle.'[15]

The Arabic partitive *min* (*min lil-bayān*) introducing a prepositional phrase in a subject role in a verbal clause is revealed in, for example, the negative expression لا يَأْتِنِي **مِنْ أحدٍ** 'let no one come to me' (Wright 1896–1898, vol. 2, p. 136), in which مِنْ أحدٍ is the grammatical subject of the negated verb يَأْتِنِي, and the noun following the preposition shows grammatical agreement with it.

The translation into Ge'ez in the Ethiopic Bible of the verse presented above, וַיְהִי בַּיּוֹם הַשְּׁבִיעִי יָצְאוּ **מִן-הָעָם** לִלְקֹט וְלֹא מָצָאוּ 'On the seventh day some of the people went out to gather, and they found none' (Exod 16:27), is especially interesting. It does not employ the prepositional phrase introduced by the Ethiopic partitive preposition *ʾəmwəsta* 'out of,' parallel to *min,* as a subject by itself but inserts the word *boza* before the verb. This word means "someone" or "something," and the combination of *boza* with the following verb and prepositional phrase means in this example "some went out, out of the people": **ወአመ ፡ ሳብዕት ፡ ዕለት ፡ ቦዘወፅአ ፡ እምውስተ ፡ ሕዝብ ፡ ከመ ፡ ያስተጋብእ ፡ ወኢረከበ ።** *wa-ʾama sābəʿt ʿəlat* ***boza****-waḍʾa* ***ʾəmwəsta ḥəzb*** *kama yāstagābəʾ wa-ʾi-rakaba.* Nonetheless, the Ethiopic word *boza* is also a prepositional phrase in itself.

[14] On the use of מִקְצָת in various Hebrew stages, its origin, and its connection with the partitive *min*, see Qimron and Strugnell 1994, p. 93.

[15] For more on this example and this use, see Qimron and Strugnell 1994, p. 93.

2.2.3. Arabic Verbal Clauses Whose Subject Follows the Phrase *'iḏā bi*

Special phrases that include prepositions as part of one lexical unit can also make prepositional phrases serve as subjects. One such Arabic lexical unit is *'iḏā bi*. In the following examples, a prepositional phrase serves as a grammatical subject in a verbal clause introduced by *'iḏā bi* 'behold': إذا **برجلٍ** يُقال له السيّدُ بركةُ قد أقبل 'Behold, a man called Sayyid Baraka came forward' (Wright 1896–1898, vol. 2, p. 158a), in which برجلٍ is the grammatical subject of the verb أقبل; فإذا **به** قد دخل المسجد 'And behold, he has entered the mosque' (Nöldeke 1895, p. 50), in which به is the grammatical subject of the verb دخل .

2.2.4. Biblical Hebrew Verbal Clauses Whose Subject Follows the Preposition *ᵓεṯ*

Contrary to all other syntactic patterns discussed above, the one presented in this section is not a typical pattern of prepositions introducing prepositional phrases in a subject role. The occurrence of the preposition *ᵓεṯ* before subjects in Biblical Hebrew is well known and has been explained in various ways, namely, as an emphatic particle preceding and highlighting subjects, as part of impersonal passive constructions, and even as related to ergative or semi-ergative patterns (e.g., Blau 1954; 1956; 1978; Joüon and Muraoka 2006, p. 431–32; Khan 1984; Muraoka 1985, pp. 152–58; Zewi 1997, and more references there). Examples of this construction are וַיֻּגַּד לְרִבְקָה **אֶת-דִּבְרֵי עֵשָׂו בְּנָהּ הַגָּדֹל** 'But the words of Esau her older son were told to Rebekah' (Gen 27:42), **אֶת-אַרְבַּעַת אֵלֶּה** יֻלְּדוּ לְהָרָפָה בְּגַת 'These four were descended from the giants in Gath' (2 Sam 21:22), **וְאֶת-הָאָח** לְפָנָיו מְבֹעָרֶת 'And there was a fire burning in the brazier before him' (Jer 36:22), and **אֶת-עַמּוּד הֶעָנָן** לֹא-סָר מֵעֲלֵיהֶם 'The pillar of cloud which led them in the way did not depart from them' (Neh 9:19). Here I stay with my earlier suggestion (Zewi 1997) that the preposition *ᵓεṯ* in such cases should not be regarded as anything but an accusative particle in Biblical Hebrew. It is primarily a particle preceding an object; it precedes a subject mostly in hybrid cases, in which the subjects introduced by *ᵓεṯ* were originally objects (Zewi 1997, p. 181).

Similar cases are certain extrapositions in Biblical Hebrew, in which one sentence component is transferred to the beginning of a clause to serve as a logical subject, and a resumptive pronoun refers to it in the following clause. In some cases a leftover in the form of a preposition is maintained both in its original place in the clause and at its beginning, for example, כִּי **אֶת**-אֲשֶׁר יֹאמַר ה' אֵלַי **אֹתוֹ** אֲדַבֵּר 'What the LORD says to me, that I will speak' (1 Kgs 22:14). Such examples occur with *ᵓεṯ*, but with other prepositions as well, for example, **וּמֵ**עֵץ הַדַּעַת טוֹב וָרָע לֹא תֹאכַל **מִמֶּנּוּ** 'But of the tree of the knowledge of good and evil you shall not eat [lit.: from it]' (Gen 2:17) (Zewi 1997, pp. 176–77).

According to some interpretations, these are cases of prepositions introducing subjects in Biblical Hebrew; still, they are not consistent and regular patterns of prepositional phrases serving in a subject role in Biblical Hebrew and should be regarded as marginal non-representative constructions of hybrid nature.

3. Final Words

In this paper I first suggested that prepositional phrases regularly serve as subjects in nominal clauses in Semitic languages. Prepositional phrases occurring in nominal clauses along with indefinite noun phrases should be analyzed as logical as well as grammatical subjects. The interpretation of nominal clauses in which the two main components of a clause, the subject and the predicate, are both prepositional phrases is obvious, since only prepositional phrases are available to serve as subjects in such constructions. Also, the syntactic status of prepositional clauses involving omission of nominal heads (ellipsis) is conclusive: these prepositional phrases are considered nominalized, playing the role of an implicit noun phrase and functioning as subjects in its place. Next, I showed that prepositional phrases can also serve in a subject role in verbal clauses just as in nominal clauses, when involving ellipsis of a nominal head and nominalization. Furthermore, certain prepositional phrases, like comparative prepositional phrases and the phrases introduced by the partitive *min*, regularly occur in a subject role in nominal and verbal clauses alike.

On the basis of the data and discussion presented in this paper, my main assertion is that prepositional phrases regularly serve as subjects in nominal and verbal clauses in Semitic languages.

Abbreviations

BDB	F. Brown, S. R. Driver, and C. A. Briggs. *A Hebrew and English Lexicon of the Old Testament.* Oxford: Clarendon Press, 1906
Derenbourg edition	J. Derenbourg et al., eds. *Oeuvres complètes de R. Saadia ben Iosef al-Fayyoûmî,* Volume 1:*Version arabe du Pentateuque.* Paris: E. Leroux. Hildesheim: Georg Olms. 1893. Reprint 1979
Ge'ez Bible translation	August Dillman. *Octateuchus Aethiopicus.* Lipsiae: Guil. Vogelii, 1853–1855. Available online: http://www.ranhacohen.info/Biblia.html
Ḥasīd edition	A. Ḥasīd. ספר כתר תורה הנקרא בלשון קדמונינו תאג. Jerusalem: יוסף בן אהרון חסיד, 1968. Revised reprint of A. Nadaf and S. Katz. תאג. Jerusalem, 1899
JPS	*Tanakh, A New Translation of the Holy Scriptures according to the Traditional Hebrew Text.* Philadelphia, New York, and Jerusalem: The Jewish Publication Society, 1985
RSV	H. G. May and B. M. Metzger, eds. *The New Oxford Annotated Bible with the Apocrypha, Revised Standard Version.* New York and Oxford: Oxford University Press, 1977

Bibliography

Ali, Ahmed

1988 *Al-Qur'ān: A Contemporary Translation.* Revised definitive edition. Princeton: Princeton University Press.

Beeston, A. F. L.

1970 *The Arabic Language Today.* London: Hutchinson University Library.

Blau, Joshua

1954 "Zum angeblichen Gebrauch von את vor dem Nominativ." *Vetus Testamentum* 4: 7–19.

1956 "Gibt es ein emphatisches *ʾeṯ* im Bibelhebräisch?" *Vetus Testamentum* 6: 211–12.

1978 "On Invariable Passive Forms in Biblical Hebrew and Classical Arabic." In *Studies in Bible and the Ancient Near East,* edited by Y. Avishur and Joshua Blau, pp. 85–94. Jerusalem. E. Rubinstein. [In Hebrew]

Crystal, David

2003 *A Dictionary of Linguistics and Phonetics.* 5th edition. Oxford: Blackwell.

Dillmann, August

1907 *Ethiopic Grammar.* 2nd edition, by Carl Bezold, translated by James A. Crichton. Amsterdam: Philo Press. Reprint 1974

Ewald, Heinrich

1881 *Syntax of the Hebrew Language of the Old Testament.* Translated by J. Kennedy. Edinburgh: T. and T. Clark.

Fischer, Wolfdietrich

2002 *A Grammar of Classical Arabic.* 3rd, revised edition, translated from the German by Jonathan H. Rodgers. New Haven: Yale University Press.

Fischer, Wolfdietrich, and Otto Jastrow

1980 *Handbuch der arabischen Dialekte.* Porta linguarum orientalium, neue Serie, 16. Wiesbaden: Otto Harrassowitz.

Frajzyngier, Zygmunt

2008 "One Way of Becoming a Dative Subject." In *Interaction of Morphology and Syntax: Case Studies in Afroasiatic,* edited by Zygmunt Frajzyngier and Erin Shay, pp. 61–83. Typological Studies in Language 75. Amsterdam: John Benjamins.

Goldenberg, Gideon

1971 "Tautological Infinitive." *Israel Oriental Studies* 1: 36–85. Reprinted in *Studies in Semitic Linguistics: Selected Writings,* by Gideon Goldenberg, pp. 66–115. Jerusalem: Magnes Press, 1998.

1995 "Attribution in Semitic Languages." *Langues orientales anciennes: philologie et linguistique* 5–6: 1–20. Reprinted in *Studies in Semitic Linguistics: Selected Writings,* by Gideon Goldenberg, pp. 46–65. Jerusalem: Magnes Press, 1998.

1998 *Studies in Semitic Linguistics: Selected Writings.* Jerusalem: Magnes Press.

Hopper, Paul J., and Elizabeth Closs Traugott
2003 *Grammaticalization.* 2nd edition. Cambridge: Cambridge University Press.

Jaworska, Ewa
1986 "Prepositional Phrases as Subjects and Objects." *Journal of Linguistics* 22: 355–74.

Joüon, Paul, and T. Muraoka
2006 *A Grammar of Biblical Hebrew.* Revised English edition. Subsidia Biblica 27. Rome: Pontificio Istituto Biblico.

Khan, Geoffrey
1984 "Object Markers and Agreement Pronouns in Semitic Languages." *Bulletin of the School of Oriental and African Studies* 47: 468–500.
2006 "Some Aspects of the Copula in North West Semitic." In *Biblical Hebrew in Its Northwest Semitic Setting: Typological and Historical Perspectives,* edited by Steven E. Fassberg and Avi Hurvitz, pp. 155–76. Jerusalem: Magnes Press; Winona Lake: Eisenbrauns.

Kogut, Simha
1993 "Alternative Usages of Independent and Suffixed Personal Pronouns to Express Possession in Biblical Hebrew." In *Studies in Bible and Exegesis,* Vol. 3: *Moshe Goshen-Gottstein — In Memoriam,* edited by Moshe Bar-Asher et al., pp. 401–11. Ramat Gan: Bar-Ilan University Press. [In Hebrew]

Li, Charles N., and S. A. Thompson
1976 "Subject and Topic: A New Typology of Language." In *Subject and Topic,* edited by Charles N. Li, pp. 457–89. New York: Academic Press.

Lowery, K. E.
1999 "Relative Definiteness and the Verbless Clause." In *The Verbless Clause in Biblical Hebrew: Linguistic Approaches,* edited by Cynthia L. Miller, pp. 251–72. Winona Lake: Eisenbrauns.

Muraoka, T.
1985 *Emphatic Words and Structures in Biblical Hebrew.* Jerusalem: Magnes; Leiden: E. J. Brill.

Neusner, Jacob
1988 *The Mishnah: A New Translation.* New Haven: Yale University Press.

Nöldeke, Theodor
1895 *Zur Grammatik des classischen Arabisch.* Vienna: Correspondierendem Mitgliede der Kais. Akademie der Wissenschaften.

Pat-El, Naʿama, and Alexander Treiger
2008 "On Adnominalization of Prepositional Phrases and Adverbs in Semitic." *Zeitschrift der deutschen morgenländischen Gesellschaft* 158: 265–83.

Qimron, Elisha, and John Strugnell
1994 *Qumrân Cave 4.* V: *Miqṣat Maʿaśe ha-Torah.* Discoveries in the Judaean Desert 10. Oxford: Clarendon Press.

Quirk, Randolph; Sidney Greenbaum; Geoffrey Leech; and Jan Svartvik
1972 *A Grammar of Contemporary English.* London: Longman.
1985 *A Comprehensive Grammar of the English Language.* London: Longman.

Reckendorf, H.
1921 *Arabische Syntax.* Heidelberg: C. Winter.

Tropper, Joseph
2002 *Altäthiopisch: Grammatik des Geʿez mit Übungstexten und Glossar.* Elementa linguarum orientis 2. Münster: Ugarit-Verlag.

Wright, William
1896–1898 *A Grammar of the Arabic Language.* 2 volumes. 3rd, revised edition. Cambridge: Cambridge University Press.

Zewi, Tamar
1994 "The Nominal Sentence in Biblical Hebrew." In *Semitic and Cushitic Studies,* edited by Gideon Goldenberg and Shlomo Raz, pp. 145–67. Wiesbaden: Harrassowitz.

1996 "The Definition of the Copula and the Role of 3rd Independent Personal Pronouns in Nominal Sentences of Semitic Languages." *Folia Linguistica Historica* 17: 41–55.

1997 "Subjects Preceded by the Preposition *ʾet* in Biblical Hebrew." In *Studien zur hebräischen Grammatik*, edited by Andreas Wagner, pp. 171–83. Orbis Biblicus et Orientalis 156. Freiburg: Universitätsverlag; Göttingen: Vandenhoeck & Ruprecht.

2002 "Syntactic Questions in Saadya Gaon's Translation of the Pentateuch." *Massorot* 12: 103–15. [In Hebrew]

Zewi, Tamar, and Christo H. J. van der Merwe

2001 "Biblical Hebrew Nominal Clause: Definitions of Subject and Predicate." *Journal of Northwest Semitic Languages* 27: 81–99.